FIFTH CANADIAN EDITION

ESSENTIALS OF UNDERSTANDING
PSYCHOLOGY

Robert S. Feldman
University of Massachusetts at Amherst

Karen Catney
Seneca College

Laura Cavanagh
Seneca College

Andrea Dinardo
St. Clair College

Mc
Graw
Hill
Education

Essentials of Understanding Psychology
Fifth Canadian Edition

The Internet addresses listed in the text were accurate at the time of publication. The inclusion of a Web site does not indicate an endorsement by the authors or McGraw-Hill Ryerson, and McGraw-Hill Ryerson does not guarantee the accuracy of the information presented at these sites.

ISBN-13: 978-1-25-902464-1
ISBN-10: 1-25-902464-4

2 3 4 5 6 7 8 9   WEB   22 21 20 19 18 17

Printed and bound in Canada.

Care has been taken to trace ownership of copyright material contained in this text; however, the publisher will welcome any information that enables them to rectify any reference or credit for subsequent editions.

Director of Product Management: Rhondda McNabb
Product Manager: Scott Hardie
Senior Marketing Manager: Margaret Greenfield
Senior Product Developer: Katherine Goodes
Senior Product Team Associate: Marina Seguin
Supervising Editor: Jessica Barnoski
Photo/Permissions Editor: Photo Affairs, Inc.
Copy Editor: Erin Moore
Plant Production Coordinator: Sarah Strynatka
Manufacturing Production Coordinator: Sheryl MacAdam
Cover Design: Dianne Reynolds
Cover Image: Kay/Getty Images Royalty Free
Interior Design: Jodie Bernard
Page Layout: SPi Global
Printer: Webcom, Ltd.

To Jon, Leigh, Alex, Josh, Julie, Sarah, and Kathy

–Robert S. Feldman

To my husband Steve, for kindness and patience, and for his endless love and support.

–Karen Catney

To Bernie, my love
To Chloé and Jacob, my greatest blessings and greatest joys
To Emma, always in our hearts

–Laura Cavanagh

To My Students and Fellow Professors, a constant source of inspiration

–Andrea Dinardo

About the Authors

Robert S. Feldman is Professor of Psychology and Dean of the College of Social and Behavioral Sciences at the University of Massachusetts, Amherst. A recipient of the College Distinguished Teacher Award, he teaches psychology classes ranging in size from 15 to nearly 500 students. During the course of more than two decades as a college instructor, he has taught undergraduate and graduate courses at Mount Holyoke College, Wesleyan University, and Virginia Commonwealth University in addition to the University of Massachusetts.

Professor Feldman, who initiated the Minority Mentoring Program at the University of Massachusetts, also has served as a Hewlett Teaching Fellow and Senior Online Teaching Fellow. He initiated distance learning courses in psychology at the University of Massachusetts.

A Fellow of both the American Psychological Association and the Association for Psychological Science, Professor Feldman received a BA with High Honors from Wesleyan University and an MS and PhD from the University of Wisconsin-Madison. He is a winner of a Fulbright Senior Research Scholar and Lecturer Award and the Distinguished Alumnus Award from Wesleyan. He is on the boards of the Federation of Associations in Behavioral and Brain Sciences (FABBS) and the FABBS Foundation, which advocate for the field of psychology.

He has written and edited more than 150 books, book chapters, and scientific articles. He has edited *Development of Nonverbal Behavior in Children, Applications of Nonverbal Behavioral Theory and Research, Improving the First Year of College: Research and Practice,* and co-edited *Fundamentals of Nonverbal Behavior.* He is also author of *Development Across the Life Span, Child Development,* and *P.O.W.E.R. Learning: Strategies for Success in College and Life.* His books have been translated into many languages, including Spanish, French, Portuguese, Dutch, Chinese, Korean, and Japanese. His research interests include deception and honesty in everyday life, work that he described in *The Liar in Your Life,* a trade book published in 2009. His research has been supported by grants from the National Institute of Mental Health and the National Institute on Disabilities and Rehabilitation Research.

Professor Feldman loves music, is an enthusiastic pianist, and enjoys cooking and travelling. He has three children and a young grandson. He and his wife, a psychologist, live in western Massachusetts in a home overlooking the Holyoke mountain range.

Karen Catney is an Adjunct Professor at Seneca College in Toronto, as well as King City, Ontario. Professor Catney is also the Clinical Director at Alliance Youth Services Inc. and specializes in working with children, adults, and families affected by Fetal Alcohol Spectrum Disorder (FASD), Autism Spectrum Disorder (ASD), developmental disabilities, and challenging behaviour.

Professor Catney has been working in Child Welfare and with Children's Aid Societies for over 15 years. She oversees all of Alliance Youth Services Inc.'s residential and foster care programs for individuals with special needs, ASD, and FASD, as well as conducts cognitive, psychological, and educational assessments as an associate with Mills Psychology Prof. Corp. Professor Catney provides FASD training workshops for professionals and caregivers across Canada and internationally, as well as consults to schools, child welfare agencies, and the justice system. She advocates for individuals with special needs, has a passion for teaching, and has been influential in best practice and policy development as it relates to FASD.

Professor Catney holds a Bachelor of Arts degree in Psychology, a Master's degree in Educational Psychology, and is the only Certified Clinical Examiner in Ontario offering the OBD (Organic Brain Dysfunction) Triage Instrument: A Screening Instrument for the Use in the Evaluation of Teratogenic Effects on Embryonic Development (OBD Triage Institute).

Professor Catney enjoys travelling, riding horses, beekeeping, and spending time with her family, friends, and two dogs. She lives in beautiful Prince Edward County, Ontario, with her husband Steve.

Laura Cavanagh is a mother, clinician, and Professor of Psychology & Behavioural Sciences at Seneca College in King City, Ontario. She has a Master of Arts degree in Clinical/Developmental Psychology from York University. Professor Cavanagh is the lead faculty in the Behavioural Sciences diploma program, which was launched at Seneca College in 2013. Professor Cavanagh was the project leader for the development, research, and implementation of this program, and is now its full-time program coordinator.

Professor Cavanagh has extensive experience in clinical practice with various exceptional populations, including individuals who have experienced trauma, children with ADHD, and teens in foster care. Her primary area of clinical focus has been with individuals on the autism spectrum. She has provided direct therapy to individuals with autism, and has consulted to therapy programs, schools, and families.

Professor Cavanagh has been teaching Psychology at the college level since 2005 and has taught at San José City College, Humber College, and now Seneca College. She is deeply committed to student success. An Ontario College of Teachers certified teacher, she consistently models best practice in the classroom. In 2015, she was nominated for the Colleges and Institutes of Canada's Teaching Excellence award.

Professor Cavanagh is a mom with two wonderful children. She loves animals and has two cats and a membership to the Toronto Zoo. She enjoys reading, baking, and—most of all—spending time with her husband and kids. She lives in Toronto, Ontario.

Andrea Dinardo is a Professor of Psychology at St. Clair College of Applied Arts in Windsor, Ontario. Professor Dinardo also teaches psychology at the Faculty of Education at the University of Windsor, Ontario. She is a member of the Canadian Psychological Association and the Ontario College of Psychologists. Her work as a registered psychologist complements her passion for teaching. Professor Dinardo advocates for students with disabilities as a consulting psychologist for community groups such as the Learning Disabilities Association of Ontario.

Professor Dinardo received an Honours BA from Huron College University and an MA and PhD from the University of Western Ontario. She is the recipient of the Robert J. Menges New Researcher Award from the AERA Special Interest Group on Faculty Teaching, Evaluation, and Development for her doctoral research: An experimental analysis of the effects of teacher enthusiasm on student attention, motivation, and learning.

Professor Dinardo's spare time is divided equally between family, friends, running, and movies. She lives in Tecumseh, Ontario, with her husband John.

Brief Contents

Contents

Contents

Contents

CHAPTER 12
Psychological Disorders *390*

CHAPTER 13
Treatment of Psychological Disorders *426*

Contents

Preface

Using *Essentials of Understanding Psychology,* Fifth Canadian Edition

If you're reading this page, you're probably taking an introductory psychology course. Maybe you're studying psychology because you've always been interested in what makes people tick. Or perhaps you've had a friend or family member who has sought assistance for a psychological disorder. Or maybe you're taking this course because it's required for your program.

Whatever your motivation for taking the course and reading this book, here's our commitment to you: By the time you finish this text, you will have a better understanding of why people—including you—behave the way they do. You will know how, and why, psychologists conduct research, and will have an understanding of the theories that guide their research. You will become acquainted with the breadth of the field and will obtain practical, useful information, as well as a wealth of knowledge that hopefully will excite your curiosity and increase your understanding of people's behaviour.

To meet this commitment, *Essentials of Understanding Psychology,* Fifth Canadian Edition, has been written and revised with you, the reader, in mind. While covering 14 chapters of material providing an extensive introduction into psychology, it is a briefer text than its predecessor, the fourth edition. At every step in the development of the book, students and instructors have been consulted in an effort to identify the combination of learning tools that would maximize readers' ability to learn and retain the subject matter of psychology. The result is a book that contains features that will not only help you to understand psychology, but also make it a discipline that is part of your life. An additional result is that this text looks like you want it to—because you told us what you want it to look like, and we listened.

Now it's your turn. You will need to take several steps to maximize the effectiveness of the learning tools in the book. These steps include familiarizing yourself with the scope and structure of the book, using the built-in learning aids, and employing a systematic study strategy using the text and *Connect.* Oh, and take a look at those assigned course readings too! Your textbook plays a key part in supporting your learning. Reading the chapter BEFORE you go to class will help provide context to the material covered in the lecture.

Familiarize Yourself with the Scope and Organization of *Essentials of Understanding Psychology*

Begin by reading the list of modules and skimming the detailed table of contents at the front of the book. From this exercise, you will get a sense of the topics covered and the logic behind the sequence of modules. Then take some time to flip through the book. Choose a section that looks particularly interesting to you, skim it, and see for yourself how the modules are laid out.

Each module provides logical starting and stopping points for reading and studying. You can plan your studying around the modules that cover a particular topic. For instance, if your instructor assigns a group of modules to read over the course of a week, you might plan to read and study one module each day, using later days in the week to review the material. Your course may not cover the chapters in order, or may only cover some of the chapters. Reading the content before it is covered in class will make it easier to process the information presented by your instructor during class time. Your textbook will play a critical role in supporting your learning.

Finally, as you work through Chapter 1, you will notice "pop-up boxes" that describe how each of the elements in the text will inform and engage you, and provide you with the tools you need to succeed.

Students first.

If we were to use only a few words to summarize our goal for this book, as well as our teaching philosophy, we would say "students first." We believe that an effective textbook must be oriented to our students—informing them, engaging them, exciting them about the field, and expanding their intellectual capabilities. When students are engaged and challenged, they understand psychology at a deep and meaningful level. Only then are they able to learn and retain the material.

Luckily, psychology is a science that is inherently interesting to students. It is a discipline that speaks with many voices, offering a personal message to each student. To some, psychology provides a better understanding of others' behaviour. Some view psychology as a pathway to self-understanding. Others see the potential for a future career, and some are drawn to psychology by the opportunity for intellectual discovery that its study provides.

No matter what brings each student into the introductory course, and regardless of their initial motivation, *Essentials of Understanding Psychology*, Fifth Canadian Edition, is designed to draw students into the field, stimulate their thinking, and integrate a variety of elements that foster their understanding of psychology and its impact on their everyday lives. This textbook will be an effective and important support for your student learning.

A Framework for Learning and Assessment

Essentials of Understanding Psychology, Fifth Canadian Edition, is the core of a learning-centred multimedia package that comprises a complete framework for learning and assessment. Every component of the package is tied to specific psychological concepts and their application to everyday life. Though the book forms the core of this framework, its power to enrich and empirically demonstrate learning is expanded through *Connect* Psychology, a unique library of electronic resources, activities and quizzes, all developed to accompany this text. Instructors can opt for a traditional, text-based approach, or create a seamless, custom set of assignments from the available resources. Instructors and students alike have choices depending on their specific needs.

Chapter and Modular Format

The text contains 14 numbered chapters covering the major areas of psychology. Each chapter is divided into three or more short modules, a format that has proven highly popular. Rather than facing a long and potentially daunting chapter, students can study material in smaller chunks, which psychological research long ago found to be the optimal way to learn. Moreover, instructors can customize assignments for their students by asking them to read only those modules that fit their course outline and in the sequence that matches their syllabus. Alternatively, instructors who prefer to assign whole chapters can do so. The modular format allows the instructor to go for depth or breadth in their course.

Many instructors find it a challenge to teach psychology to non-psychology majors in a wide variety of disciplines. The modular format of this book facilitates changeover between programs and semesters. Instructors can customize each class to the background and interests of each discipline. You choose which sections of each chapter work best for each course. You choose what to focus on. You are the expert in your own classroom.

Psychology and Everyday Life

Putting students first and teaching them the science of psychology by helping them make the connection between psychology and everyday life has been a goal of this text from its first edition. The prologues that open each chapter, together with *Becoming an Informed Consumer of Psychology, Applying Psychology in the Real World, PsychWork,* and *Exploring Diversity* boxes, and examples presented throughout the text, help students see the real, everyday benefits of psychological research. For example, the *Applying Psychology in the Real World* boxes help students make connections between new information (in this textbook and in the classroom), and what is happening in the real world (e.g., social networking, the dangers of texting while driving). Students are often surprised by what they already know about psychology. Throughout the book, examples were updated and references to popular culture were included to make the material more relevant to the life of the college or university student. In the Rethink section, program-specific questions were added to target critical thinking in students from a variety of disciplines. Our job as instructors is to put the framework on their knowledge and to give them the tools to apply this information every day. Each type of box can be used very effectively as written assignments.

Ways of Connecting with Today's Students

Today's students are as different from the learners of the last generation as today's discipline of psychology is different from the field 30 years ago. Students now learn in multiple modalities; rather than sitting down and reading traditional printed chapters in linear fashion from beginning to end, their work preferences tend to be more visual and more interactive, and their reading and study often occur in short bursts. For many students, a traditionally formatted printed textbook is no longer enough when they have instant, 24/7 access to news and information from around the globe.

Connect Psychology is our response to today's student. The groundbreaking adaptive diagnostic tool helps students "know what they know" while helping them learn what they don't know through engaging interactivities, exercises, videos, and readings. Instructors using *Connect* are reporting their students' performance is improving by a letter grade or more.

Through this unique tool, *Essentials of Understanding Psychology* gives instructors the ability to identify struggling students quickly and easily before the first exam. *Connect* Psychology's adaptive diagnostic tool develops an individualized learning plan for every student. Confidence levels tailor the next question to each individual, helping students to know what they don't know. If your student is doing well, the adaptive diagnostic tool will challenge the student with more applied and conceptual questions. If your student is struggling, the system identifies problem areas and directs the student to the topic they need to study. In doing so, it works like a GPS, helping students to master key concepts efficiently and effectively. Regardless of individual study habits, preparation, and approaches to the course, students will find the modular format of *Essentials of Understanding Psychology*, coupled with *Connect* Psychology, adapts to them individually and provides a road map for success.

Students First: The Bottom Line

Based on extensive student feedback, systematic research involving a wide range of instructors, and endorsements received from reviewers at a variety of schools, we are confident that this fifth Canadian edition reflects what students want and need: a book that motivates them to understand and apply psychology to their own lives. *Essentials of Understanding Psychology*, Fifth Canadian Edition, exposes students to the content—and promise—of psychology, and does so in a way that feels modern and relevant, and will nurture their excitement about psychology.

Engaging Students

Prologue Each chapter starts with an account of a real-life situation that demonstrates the relevance of basic principles and concepts of psychology to pertinent issues and problems. These prologues depict well-known people and events and many were updated for this edition.

Prologue

Why Psychology?

How many times have you asked yourself: *Why am I taking this course? What does this course have to do with my job? My life? My livelihood?* These are all great critical questions you should ask at the beginning of every course. Knowing "*why we do what we do*" is the foundation of inner drive and intrinsic motivation.

Source: © Pot of Grass Productions, Shutterstock.

Epilogue Found at the end of every set of modules, *the Epilogue* relates to the *Prologue* at the opening of the set of modules and illustrates how the concepts addressed in each module apply to the real-world situation described in the *Prologue*.

Epilogue

The field of psychology is broad and diverse. It encompasses many different subfields and specialties practised in a variety of settings, with new subfields continually arising. We have also seen that even within the various subfields of the field, it is possible to adopt several different approaches, including the neuroscience, psychodynamic, behavioural, cognitive, and humanistic perspectives. For all its diversity, though, psychology focuses on certain key issues that serve to unify the field along common lines and shared findings.

Source: © Blend Images/Ariel Skelley/Getty Images RF.

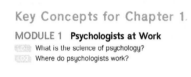

Key Concepts for Chapter 1

MODULE 1 **Psychologists at Work**

What is the science of psychology?
Where do psychologists work?

Key Concepts Each major section of a module begins with questions about the key concepts addressed in that section. These questions provide a framework for understanding and organizing the material that follows, as well as providing assessment benchmarks.

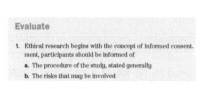

Evaluate

1. Ethical research begins with the concept of informed consent. ment, participants should be informed of
   a. The procedure of the study, stated generally
   b. The risks that may be involved

Evaluate Each module concludes with an Evaluate section. These *Evaluate* sections test recall of the material, assessing the degree of initial learning.

Recap/Rethink The end of every chapter concludes with Recap and Rethink sections that are organized according to modules. The *Recap* sections review the concept questions found at the beginning of each module. The *Rethink* sections provide thought-provoking questions designed to provoke critical thinking about the material.

Recap/Rethink

Module 1: Psychologists at Work
Recap

What is the science of psychology?
• Psychology is the scientific study of behaviour and mental processes, encompassing not just what people do but their biological activities, feelings, perceptions, memory, reasoning, and thoughts.
Where do psychologists work?

Study Alerts *Study Alerts* are notes found throughout the modules, which point out especially important and difficult concepts and topics. These *Study Alerts* offer suggestions for learning the material effectively and highlight important study topics. In Module 12, for example, a Study Alert emphasizes the importance of differentiating the five stages of sleep; and in Module 14 a Study Alert highlights the importance of Figure 2 for learning the different ways that drugs produce their effects at a neurological level.

STUDY ALERT!

Knowing the basic outlines of the history of the field will help you understand how today's major perspectives have evolved.

Running Glossary Key terms are highlighted in boldface type within the text where they are introduced, and definitions are given at the bottom of the page, along with pronunciation guides for difficult words. To facilitate study, at the end of each module there is a list of the key terms and concepts introduced in that module. There is also a glossary of all key terms and concepts at the end of the book.

Neuroscience perspective
The approach that views behaviour from the perspective of the brain, the nervous system, and other biological functions.
Psychodynamic perspective
The approach based on the view that behaviour is motivated by unconscious inner forces over which the individual has little control.

PsychWork *PsychWork* introduces students to different career paths to which the study of psychology can lead. Each *PsychWork* profile illustrates people in a variety of occupations whose knowledge of psychology informs and

PsychWork

Licensed Social Worker

Name: Christin Poirier, Hon BA, MSW, RSW
Position: Social Worker
Education: Honours BA in Psychology, York University; MA in Social Work, University of Windsor

For Christin Poirier, psychology is central to her occupation as a social worker, a field dedicated to enhancing the well-being of individuals, families, groups, and communities. As a social worker, Poirier works at a community mental health centre where she helps children and adolescents who are experiencing emotional or behavioural difficulties or both. Says Poirier, "The strategies I employ in counselling sessions are derived from basic psychological concepts and theories. In addition, in

enhances their work. Among the individuals profiled are a social worker, a rehabilitation counsellor, a sleep technologist, and a child protection caseworker, showing that psychology is all around us and important to many occupations.

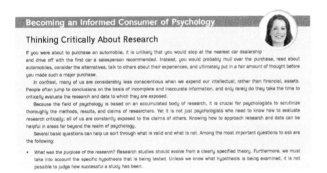

Exploring DIVERSITY

Choosing Participants Who Represent the Scope of Human Behaviour

When Latané and Darley, both university professors, decided who would participate in their experiment, they turned to the most available people: college and university students. In fact, college and university students are used so frequently in experiments that psychology has been called—somewhat contemptuously—the "science of the behaviour of the college sophomore" (Rubenstein, 1982).

Using college and university students as participants has both advantages and drawbacks. The big benefit is that because most research occurs in university settings, students are readily available. Typically, they cost the researcher very little: They participate for either extra course credit or a relatively small payment.

The problem is that college and university students may not represent the general population adequately. They tend to be younger and better educated than a significant percentage of the rest of the North American population. Compared with older adults, their attitudes are likely to be less well formed, and they are more apt to be influenced by authority figures and peers (Sears, 1986). College and university students are also disproportionately white and middle class (Graham, 1992).

Applying Psychology in the Real World These boxes highlight the relevance of psychology by presenting current and potential applications of psychological theory and research findings to real-world problems. For example, one box discusses the psychological principles that explain the dangers of texting while driving, while another highlights how Facebook and other social media are changing social connections and interactions.

Exploring Diversity In addition to substantial coverage of material relevant to diversity throughout, there are special sections devoted to an aspect of racial, ethnic, gender, or cultural diversity. Examples of topics highlighted in these boxes include cultural influences on learning and sex differences in the brain. These sections highlight the way in which psychology informs (and is informed by) issues relating to the increasing multiculturalism of our global society.

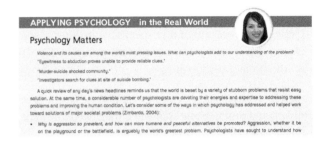

APPLYING PSYCHOLOGY in the Real World

Psychology Matters

Violence and its causes are among the world's most pressing issues. What can psychologists add to our understanding of the problem?

"Eyewitness to abduction proves unable to provide reliable clues."

"Murder-suicide shocked community."

"Investigators search for clues at site of suicide bombing."

A quick review of any day's news headlines reminds us that the world is beset by a variety of stubborn problems that resist easy solution. At the same time, a considerable number of psychologists are devoting their energies and expertise to addressing these problems and improving the human condition. Let's consider some of the ways in which psychology has addressed and helped work toward solutions of major societal problems (Zimbardo, 2004):

• Why is aggression so prevalent, and how can more humane and peaceful alternatives be promoted? Aggression, whether it be on the playground or the battlefield, is arguably the world's greatest problem. Psychologists have sought to understand how

Becoming an Informed Consumer of Psychology

Thinking Critically About Research

If you were about to purchase an automobile, it is unlikely that you would stop at the nearest car dealership and drive off with the first car a salesperson recommended. Instead, you would probably mull over the purchase, read about automobiles, consider the alternatives, talk to others about their experiences, and ultimately put in a fair amount of thought before you made such a major purchase.

In contrast, many of us are considerably less conscientious when we expend our intellectual, rather than financial, assets. People often jump to conclusions on the basis of incomplete and inaccurate information, and only rarely do they take the time to critically evaluate the research and data to which they are exposed.

Because the field of psychology is based on an accumulated body of research, it is crucial for psychologists to scrutinize thoroughly the methods, results, and claims of researchers. Yet it is not just psychologists who need to know how to evaluate research critically; all of us are constantly exposed to the claims of others. Knowing how to approach research and data can be helpful in areas far beyond the realm of psychology.

Several basic questions can help us sort through what is valid and what is not. Among the most important questions to ask are the following:

• What was the purpose of the research? Research studies should evolve from a clearly specified theory. Furthermore, we must take into account the specific hypothesis that is being tested. Unless we know what hypothesis is being examined, it is not possible to judge how successful a study has been.

Becoming an Informed Consumer of Psychology *Becoming an Informed Consumer of Psychology* includes material designed to make readers more informed consumers of psychological information by giving them the ability to evaluate critically what the field of psychology offers. These discussions also provide sound, useful guidance concerning common problems. For example, one box explains how you can apply findings in psychological research on sleep/wake cycles to improve your own sleep, while another discusses how to identify if you or a loved one is struggling with alcohol or other substance abuse issues.

Market Leading Technology

Mc Graw Hill Education **connect®**

Learn without Limits

McGraw-Hill Connect® is an award-winning digital teaching and learning platform that gives students the means to better connect with their coursework, with their instructors, and with the important concepts that they will need to know for success now and in the future. With Connect, instructors can take advantage of McGraw-Hill's trusted content to seamlessly deliver assignments, quizzes and tests online. McGraw-Hill Connect is a learning platform that continually adapts to each student, delivering precisely what they need, when they need it, so class time is more engaging and effective. Connect makes teaching and learning personal, easy, and proven.

Connect Key Features:

SmartBook® As the first and only adaptive reading experience, SmartBook is changing the way students read and learn. SmartBook creates a personalized reading experience by highlighting the most important concepts a student needs to learn at that moment in time. As a student engages with SmartBook, the reading experience continuously adapts by highlighting content based on what each student knows and doesn't know. This ensures that he or she is focused on the content needed to close specific knowledge gaps, while it simultaneously promotes long-term learning.

Connect Insight® Connect Insight is Connect's new one-of-a-kind visual analytics dashboard—now available for both instructors and students—that provides at-a-glance information regarding student performance, which is immediately actionable. By presenting assignment, assessment, and topical performance results together with a time metric that is easily visible for aggregate or individual results, Connect Insight gives the user the ability to take a just-in-time approach to teaching and learning, which was never before available. Connect Insight presents data that empowers students and helps instructors improve class performance in a way that is efficient and effective.

Simple Assignment Management With Connect, creating assignments is easier than ever, so instructors can spend more time teaching and less time managing.

- Assign SmartBook learning modules.
- Instructors can edit existing questions and create their own questions.
- Draw from a variety of text specific questions, resources, and test bank material to assign online.
- Streamline lesson planning, student progress reporting, and assignment grading to make classroom management more efficient than ever.

Smart Grading When it comes to studying, time is precious. Connect helps students learn more efficiently by providing feedback and practice material when they need it, where they need it.

- Automatically score assignments, giving students immediate feedback on their work and comparisons with correct answers.
- Access and review each response; manually change grades or leave comments for students to review.
- Track individual student performance—by question, assignment or in relation to the class overall—with detailed grade reports.
- Reinforce classroom concepts with practice tests and instant quizzes.
- Integrate grade reports easily with Learning Management Systems including Blackboard, D2L, and Moodle.

Instructor Library The Connect Instructor Library is a repository for additional resources to improve student engagement in and out of the class. It provides all the critical resources instructors need to build their course.

- Access Instructor resources.
- View assignments and resources created for past sections.
- Post your own resources for students to use.

Instructor Resources

Feldman/Catney/Cavanagh/Dinardo Connect is a one-stop shop for instructor resources, including:

Instructor's Manual. This comprehensive guide provides all the tools and resources instructors need to present and enhance their introductory psychology course. The Instructor's Manual contains detailed lecture launchers, learning objectives, interesting lecture and media presentation ideas, student assignments and handouts. The many tips and activities in this manual can be used with any class, regardless of size or teaching approach.

Computerized Test Bank. The computerized test bank has been analyzed to ensure complete accuracy and correlation to the fifth Canadian edition text. Each multiple-choice item is classified by type (factual, conceptual, or applied) and difficulty level, and is keyed to the appropriate page number in the textbook. Available for Macintosh or Windows users, the computerized test bank using EZ Test—a flexible and easy-to-use electronic testing program—allows instructors to create tests from book-specific items. EZ Test accommodates a wide range of question types and allows instructors to add their own questions. Test items are also available in Word format (rich-text format). For secure online testing, exams created in EZ Test can be exported to WebCT, Blackboard, and EZ Test Online. EZ Test comes with a Quick Start Guide, and once the program is installed, users have access to a User's Manual and Flash tutorials. Additional help is available online at www.mhhe.com/eztest.

Microsoft® PowerPoint® Slides. Microsoft PowerPoint slides accompany each chapter. In addition, **Dynamic PowerPoints** cover more than 80 core concepts in psychology. They are designed to be incorporated into lectures to help you present concepts more visually and engagingly.

Image Gallery. The complete set of figures from the text can be downloaded from the Image Gallery in the Instructor Resource area of Connect and easily imbedded into instructors' PowerPoint slides.

Superior Learning Solutions and Support

The McGraw-Hill Education team is ready to help you assess and integrate any of our products, technology, and services into your course for optimal teaching and learning performance. Whether it's helping your students improve their grades, or putting your entire course online, the McGraw-Hill Education team is here to help you do it. Contact your Learning Solutions Consultant today to learn how to maximize all of McGraw-Hill Education's resources!

For more information on the latest technology and Learning Solutions offered by McGraw-Hill Education and its partners, please visit us online: http://www.mheducation.ca/highereducation/educators/digital-solutions.

Chapter Changes

The chapter-by-chapter changes listed below represent only a small number of the literally hundreds of changes made to the fifth Canadian edition of the text. Research has been updated in every chapter. For this edition over 1,000 new and updated references have been added.

Chapter 1: Introduction to Psychology
- Updated Canadian data on where psychologists work
- Discussion of perspectives and subfields of psychology integrated into one cohesive section
- Continuous example threaded throughout discussion of theory and hypothesis in section on Research methods
- Section on the History of Psychology expanded to be more comprehensive
- Viktor Frankl included in History of Psychology to provide more context to humanistic psychology movement
- Tightened focus of Diversity box to look at issues involved in using student participants
- More recent Canadian example used in Applying Psychology special topic
- Program-specific critical thinking questions added to Recap/Rethink section

Chapter 2: Neuroscience and Behaviour
- New topic added for Applying Psychology in the Real World on Mirror Neurons
- Reference to new Canadian research on the therapeutic application of oxytocin in Autism Spectrum Disorders was added in the discussion of hormones in the endocrine system
- Section on neural plasticity revised to emphasize the universal implications of plasticity, including brain fitness and aging
- New research on neural plasticity integrated with a focus on synaptogenesis
- Section on the forebrain was divided into two separate subsections on Subcortical Structures and the Neocortex to enhance clarity and readability

Chapter 3: Sensation and Perception
- Updated hearing loss and deaf culture reference
- Expanded on hearing loss in teenagers and dangerous noise levels

Chapter 4: States of Consciousness
- New information added on the serious consequences of sleep deprivation
- Canadian statistics added to section on Alcohol Use
- Section on marijuana use and its risks heavily revised to reflect new understandings and research findings
- Canadian data on use and abuse of prescription drugs added
- Benzodiazepines added to section on frequently used and abused substances
- Term addict replaced with person-first language

Chapter 5: Learning
- Section on biological constraints on learning was updated to reflect current understandings in research
- New section on biological preparedness theory added to section on classical conditioning
- More examples added to section on negative reinforcement to make this concept clearer

- References to corporal punishment and the use of electrical shocks as a teaching method were removed to reflect current reinforcement-based directions in behavioural intervention
- Link between schedules of reinforcement and gambling addiction added to section on operant conditioning
- Information on sports aggression added to section on Observational Learning

Chapter 6: Memory
- Updated Applying Psychology in the Real World "Enhancing Memory: Are We on the Road to 'Cosmetic Neurology'?" section
- Updated content on Alzheimer's Syndrome

Chapter 7: Thinking, Language, and Intelligence
- Updated references
- Updated content on *DSM-IV* to reflect *DSM-5*
- Updated IQ tests to most current version (WISC-V and WAIS-IV)

Chapter 8: Motivation and Emotion
- Updated content on Sexual Motivation
- Applying the different approaches to motivation section condensed
- Eating disorders section condensed

Chapter 9: Development
- Added information on methadone treatment with pregnant women
- Updated and improved section on prenatal environmental influences
- Nature versus Nurture section condensed

Chapter 10: Personality
- Biological and Evolutionary Approaches condensed
- New example added in "Freud's Defence Mechanisms"

Chapter 11: Health Psychology, Stress, Coping, and Well-Being
- Included Canadian content on soldier suicide
- New Applying Psychology in the Real World "Does Money Buy Happiness?"
- Updated references
- Smoking content condensed
- Changed module title to Health and Wellness

Chapter 12: Psychological Disorders
- Updated references
- Updated content to reflect *DSM-5*
- New Applying Psychology in the Real World "Internet Addiction"
- New Becoming an Informed Consumer of Psychology "When You Need Help"
- Updated figures

Chapter 13: Treatment of Psychological Disorders
- Updated "Getting Help from the Right Person"
- Added content on mindfulness therapy

Chapter 14: Social Psychology
- Section added on Zimbardo's classic study, the Stanford Prison Experiment
- Issue of domestic violence integrated into the section on Aggression
- Evolutionary psychology theory introduced into section on Physical Attractiveness, with reference to new Canadian research
- New Prologue: A Heroic Escape—referencing the Ariel Castro Cleveland Kidnapping Case and Charles Ramsey, the hero who assisted the victims in escaping
- Canadian research on prejudice and discrimination integrated into this section of the text
- New research information added on the effect of observation and social influence on helping behaviour

Acknowledgments

One of the central features of *Essentials of Understanding Psychology* is the involvement of both professionals and students in the review process. The fifth Canadian edition of *Essentials of Understanding Psychology* has relied heavily—and benefited substantially—from the advice of instructors and students from a wide range of backgrounds.

We are extraordinarily grateful to the following instructors who provided their time and expertise to help ensure that *Essentials of Understanding Psychology*, Fifth Canadian Edition, reflects the best that psychology has to offer.

Anastasia Bake, *St. Clair College*
Alice Barron, *St. Clair College*
Wendy Bourque, *University of New Brunswick, Fredericton*
Kristen Buscaglia, *Niagara College*
Maria Iannuzziello, *Durham College*
Manuela Keeler, *Niagara College*
Todd Leader, *St. Mary's University*
Karen Mcdonald, *Mount St. Vincent University*
Jennifer Potton-Roberts, *Mohawk College*
Kimberly J. Robinson, *St. Mary's University*
Joel St. Pierre, *Mohawk College*
Lisa Sinclair, *University of Winnipeg*
Selina Tombs, *Sheridan Davis*

CHAPTER 1
Introduction to Psychology

Source: © Blend Images/Ariel Skelley/Getty Images RF.

Each module begins with the key concepts discussed in that section. The key concepts, phrased as questions, provide a framework for understanding and organizing the material that follows. They will also help you to understand what the important content is.

Key Concepts for Chapter 1

MODULE 1 Psychologists at Work

LO1 What is the science of psychology?

LO2 Where do psychologists work?

The Science of Psychology

Working at Psychology

> PsychWork: *Licensed Social Worker*

MODULE 2 A Science Evolves: The Past, the Present, and the Future

LO3 What are the origins of psychology?

LO4 How did the history of psychology shape the major approaches in contemporary psychology?

LO5 What are the important subfields in the field of psychology?

The Roots of Psychology

Historical Perspectives: What Has Stood the Test of Time?

The Subfields of Psychology: Psychology's Family Tree

> Applying Psychology in the Real World: *Psychology Matters*

Psychology's Future: Expanding Psychology's Frontiers

MODULE 3 Research in Psychology

LO6 What is the scientific method?

LO7 What role do theories and hypotheses play in psychological research?

LO8 What research methods do psychologists use?

LO9 How do psychologists establish cause-and-effect relationships using experiments?

The Scientific Method

Psychological Research

Descriptive Research

Experimental Research

MODULE 4 Research Challenges: Exploring the Process

What major issues confront psychologists conducting research?

The Ethics of Research

Exploring Diversity: *Choosing Participants Who Represent the Scope of Human Behaviour*

Should Animals be Used in Research?

Threats to Experiment Validity: Experimenter and Participant Expectations

Becoming an Informed Consumer of Psychology: *Thinking Critically About Research*

> Each chapter begins with an introduction (the Prologue) and ends with a summary (the Epilogue). The Prologue sets the stage for the chapter, providing a brief account of a real-life event that is relevant to the content of the modules, and demonstrating why the material in the chapter is important.

Prologue

Why Psychology?

Source: © Pot of Grass Productions. Shutterstock.

How many times have you asked yourself: *Why am I taking this course? What does this course have to do with my job? My life? My livelihood?* These are all great critical questions you should ask at the beginning of every course. Knowing *"why we do what we do"* is the foundation of inner drive and intrinsic motivation.

Why Study Psychology?

The field of psychology gives students insight into the inner workings of the brain, vulnerability to conformity, how personality traits influence occupational success, beneficial effects of meditation at work, to name just a few.

In addition to increased self-awareness and self-knowledge, psychology also benefits students in their chosen field. For example, health science students discover how connecting with patients promotes healing (Chapter 11). Business students learn how right vs. left brain hemispheric dominance determines which aspect of their career they will be most successful in (Chapter 2). Manufacturing students recognize the critical link between an automobile driver's unique personality and sound automotive design (Chapter 10). Computer students learn how cognitive psychology predicts the attention span of computer users (Chapter 3). Marketing students discover how addressing the needs and motivations of consumers results in higher sales and profits (Chapter 8).

Using this textbook as their guide, students learn to approach their job, life, and livelihood from a deeper, broader, more meaningful perspective. Psychology gives students an "edge" over their counterparts, thereby increasing their chances of success in a fast-paced, ever-changing world. Psychology students learn everything they need to know about themselves, and the people around them. PSYCHOLOGY IS ALL ABOUT YOU!

Psychologists at Work

LEARNING OBJECTIVES

LO1 **What is** the science of psychology?

LO2 **Where do** psychologists work?

The Science of Psychology

Psychology is the scientific study of behaviour and mental processes.

The phrase *behaviour and mental processes* in the definition of **psychology** must be understood to mean many things: It encompasses not just what people do but also their thoughts, emotions, perceptions, reasoning processes, memories, and even the biological activities that maintain bodily functioning.

Psychologists try to describe, predict, and explain human behaviour and mental processes, and to help change and improve the lives of people and the world in which they live. They use scientific methods to find answers that are far more valid and legitimate than those resulting from intuition and speculation, which are often inaccurate (see Figure 1).

FIGURE 1

The scientific method is the basis of all psychological research and is used to find valid answers. Test your knowledge of psychology by answering these questions.

Psychological Truths?

To test your knowledge of psychology, try answering the following questions:

1. Infants love their mothers primarily because their mothers fulfill their basic biological needs, such as providing food. True or false? _____
2. Geniuses generally have poor social adjustment. True or false? _____
3. The best way to ensure that a desired behaviour will continue after training is completed is to reward that behaviour every single time it occurs during training rather than rewarding it only periodically. True or false? _____
4. People with schizophrenia have at least two distinct personalities. True or false? _____
5. If you are having trouble sleeping, the best way to get to sleep is to take a sleeping pill. True or false? _____
6. Children's IQ scores have little to do with how well they do in school. True or false? _____
7. Frequent masturbation can lead to mental illness. True or false? _____
8. Once people reach old age, their leisure activities change radically. True or false? _____
9. Most people would refuse to give painful electric shocks to other people. True or false? _____
10. One of the least important factors affecting how much we like another person is that person's physical attractiveness. True or false? _____

Scoring: The truth about each of these items: They are all false. Psychological research suggests that each of these "facts" is untrue. You will learn the reasons why as we explore what psychologists have discovered about human behaviour.

Source: From Lamal, P. A. Students common beliefs about psychology. *Teaching of Psychology, 6,* Copyright © 1979 Lawrence Erlbaum Associates.

> **Psychology**
> The scientific study of behaviour and mental processes.

The questions in Figure 1 provide just a hint of the topics that we will encounter in the study of psychology. Our discussions will take us through the range of what is known about behaviour and mental processes.

STUDY ALERT!

When a key term or concept appears in the text, it appears either in **boldface** or *italics*. Boldfaced words are of primary importance; italicized words are of secondary importance. Terms and concepts in bold are defined in the text where they are introduced and at the bottom of the pages, as well as in the glossary at the back of the book. In addition, boldfaced terms are included in the list of Key Terms at the end of every module. You might want to highlight these terms.

Material in tables and figures can be just as important as the text. Be sure you read these sections.

Working at Psychology

Apply Today: Psychology professor needed to teach in Liberal Arts & Science Department at a City College. Teach courses in introductory psychology and electives to a wide range of programs across the college, including interior design, ECE, dental hygiene, business, and engineering. Strong commitment to quality teaching is critical.

* * *

Apply Today: Management firm looking to hire industrial-organizational consulting psychologist. International firm seeks psychologists for full-time career positions as consultants to management. Candidates must have the ability to establish a rapport with senior business executives and help them find innovative, practical, and psychologically sound solutions to problems concerning people and organizations.

* * *

Apply Today: Clinical psychologist sought for multi-disciplinary team. Ph.D., internship experience, and licence required. Comprehensive clinic seeks psychologist to work with children and adults providing individual and group therapy, psychological evaluations, crisis intervention, and development of behaviour treatment plans. Broad experience with substance abuse problems is desirable.

As these job postings suggest, psychologists are employed in a variety of settings. Many doctoral-level psychologists are employed by institutions of higher learning (universities and colleges) or are self-employed, usually working as private practitioners treating clients (see Figure 2). Other work sites include hospitals, clinics, mental health centres, counselling centres, government human-services organizations, and schools (APA, 2007; CPA, 2008).

Where do psychologists work in Canada? As in the U.S., psychologists work in many different employment settings, including post-secondary institutions, schools, hospitals, and community-based agencies. Although no national data exist, a 2006 Quebec census showed that approximately 75 percent of psychologists worked in the health care and social assistance sectors. Psychologists also worked in hospitals (14 percent) and local community service centres (8 percent). About 18 percent of psychologists worked in education services (18 percent) (Statistics Canada, 2013). One of the biggest challenges for Canadians is finding access to health services in rural areas (Government of Canada, 2002). A survey of the geographic locations of psychologists by the Canadian Psychological Association (1999) indicates that Canadians living in urban areas such as Toronto have access to almost five times as many psychologists as Canadians living in rural settings. More specifically, the ratio of psychologists to individuals in urban centres of Canada is 1:2195, while the ratio is 1:9619 in rural populations such as Northern Ontario and Eastern Canada (CPA, 1999).

Careers for Psychology Majors

Although some psychology majors head for graduate school in psychology or a related field, the majority join the workforce immediately after graduation. Most report that the jobs they take after graduation are related to their psychology background.

FIGURE 2

The breakdown of where U.S. psychologists (who have a Ph.D. or Psy.D. degree) work (American Psychological Association, 2007). Why do you think so many psychologists work in college and university settings?

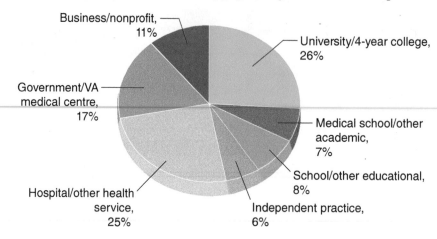

Business/nonprofit, 11%

University/4-year college, 26%

Government/VA medical centre, 17%

Medical school/other academic, 7%

School/other educational, 8%

Hospital/other health service, 25%

Independent practice, 6%

Source: Adapted from Michaels, 2011.

An undergraduate major in psychology provides excellent preparation for a variety of occupations. Because undergraduates who specialize in psychology develop good analytical skills, are trained to think critically, and are able to synthesize and evaluate information well, employers in business, industry, and the government value their preparation (Kuther, 2003).

Psychology departments at Canadian universities do a great job of highlighting the vast array of career options available to psychology undergraduates. For example, University of Windsor's psychology website lists 30 career options for psychology majors, ranging from police work to teaching to advertising. Canadian Psychological Association's (2008) Quick Facts publication on "What is Psychology?" also includes several career options for psychology majors.

The most common areas of employment for psychology majors are in the social services, including working as an administrator, serving as a counsellor, and providing direct care. Some 20 percent of recipients of bachelor's degrees in psychology work in the social services or in some other form of public affairs. In addition, psychology majors often enter the fields of education or business or work for federal, provincial, and local governments (APA, 2000; Murray, 2002; see Figure 3). In summary, think of it this way—if a job that you are interested in includes people—then a degree in psychology will be beneficial!

FIGURE 3

Although many psychology majors pursue employment in social services, a background in psychology can prepare one for many professions outside the social services field, such as occupational therapy and teaching (which both require schooling beyond a degree in psychology). What is it about the science of psychology that makes it such a versatile field?

Positions Obtained by Psychology Majors		
Business Field	**Education/Academic**	**Social Fields**
Administrative assistant	Administration	Activities coordinator
Advertising trainee	Childcare provider	Behavioural specialist
Benefits manager	Childcare worker/supervisor	Career counsellor
Claims specialist	Data management	Case worker
Community relations officer	Laboratory assistant	Child protection worker
Customer relations	Parent/family education	Clinical coordinator
		(continued)

Business Field	Education/Academic	Social Fields
Data management	Preschool teacher	Community outreach worker
Employee recruitment	Public opinion surveyor	Corrections officer
Employee counsellor	Research assistant	Counsellor assistant
Employment equity officer	Teaching assistant	Crisis intervention counsellor
Labour relations manager/specialist		Employment counsellor
Loan officer		Group home attendant
Management trainee		Occupational therapist
Marketing		Probation officer
Personnel manager/officer		Program manager
Product and services research		Rehabilitation counsellor
Programs/events coordination		Residence counsellor
Public relations		Mental health assistant
Retail sales management		Social service assistant
Sales representative		Social worker
Special features writing/reporting		Substance abuse counsellor
Staff training and development		Youth counsellor
Trainer/training officer		

Source: From *The Psychology Major's Handbook*, 1st Edition by Kuther. © 2003 with permission of Wadsworth, a division of Thomson Learning: www.thomsonrights.com. Fax 800-730-2215.

Many chapters include a box that focuses on how a non-psychologist uses psychology.

PsychWork

Licensed Social Worker

Name: Christin Poirier, Hon BA, MSW, RSW
Position: Social Worker
Education: Honours BA in Psychology, York University;
MA in Social Work, University of Windsor

For Christin Poirier, psychology is central to her occupation as a social worker, a field dedicated to enhancing the well-being of individuals, families, groups, and communities. As a social worker, Poirier works at a community mental health centre where she helps children and adolescents who are experiencing emotional or behavioural difficulties or both. Says Poirier, "The strategies I employ in counselling sessions are derived from basic psychological concepts and theories. In addition, in order to know what strategies are age-appropriate for a particular client, I need to consider their stage of psychological development. Finally, it is necessary to consider how culture and ethnicity affect clients, so I incorporate these aspects into my clients' treatment plans."

> Every module ends with an *Evaluate* segment. Evaluate segments provide a series of questions on the module content that ask for concrete information, in a matching, multiple choice, fill-in, or true-false format.

Evaluate

Answer the *Evaluate* questions! Your responses will indicate both your degree of mastery of the material and the depth of your knowledge. If you have no trouble with the questions, you can be confident that you are studying effectively. Use questions with which you have difficulty as a basis for further study.

Evaluate

1. Psychology is defined as the scientific study of _____ and _____.
2. True or False: There are many interesting careers in the field of psychology that do not require a Ph.D. in psychology.

Answers to Evaluate Questions

1. behaviour and mental processes; 2. True

Key Terms

psychology

A Science Evolves: The Past, the Present, and the Future

LEARNING OBJECTIVES

What are the origins of psychology?

How did the history of psychology shape the major approaches in contemporary psychology?

What are the important subfields in the field of psychology?

Seven thousand years ago, people assumed that psychological problems were caused by evil spirits. To allow those spirits to escape from a person's body, ancient healers performed an operation called *trephining*. Trephining consisted of chipping a hole in a patient's skull with crude stone instruments. Because archaeologists have found skulls with signs of healing around the opening, it's a fair guess that some patients survived the "cure."

* * *

Franz Josef Gall, an eighteenth-century physician, argued that a trained observer could discern intelligence, moral character, and other basic personality characteristics from the shape and number of bumps on a person's skull. His theory gave rise to the "science" of phrenology, employed by hundreds of devoted practitioners in the nineteenth century.

Although these explanations might sound far-fetched, in their own times they represented the most advanced thinking about what might be called the psychology of the era. Our understanding of behaviour has progressed tremendously since the eighteenth century, but most of the advances have been recent. As sciences go, psychology is one of the "new kids on the block." (For highlights in the development of the field, see Figure 1.)

The Roots of Psychology

Although psychology is a relatively new scientific discipline, the subjects that psychologists study have captivated humankind for all of recorded history. These subjects fell under the discipline of philosophy in the time before psychology emerged as a scientific discipline. Psychology's roots can be traced back to the ancient Greeks, who considered the mind to be a suitable topic for scholarly contemplation. Later philosophers argued for centuries about some of the questions psychologists grapple with today. For example, the seventeenth-century British philosopher John Locke (1632–1704) believed that children were born into the world with minds like "blank slates" (*tabula rasa* in Latin) and that their experiences determined what kind of adults they would become. His views contrasted with those of philosophers such as Plato (427–347 BCE) and French philosopher and mathematician Renée Descartes (1596–1650), who believed that some knowledge was inborn in humans.

However, the formal beginning of psychology as a scientific discipline is generally considered to be in the late nineteenth century, when, in Leipzig, Germany, Wilhelm Wundt established the first experimental laboratory devoted to psychological phenomena. At about the same time, William James was setting up his laboratory in Cambridge, Massachusetts.

When Wundt set up his laboratory in 1879, his aim was to study the building blocks of the mind. He considered psychology to be the study of conscious experience. His perspective, which came to be known as **structuralism**, focused

Structuralism
Wundt's approach, which focuses on uncovering the fundamental mental components of consciousness, thinking, and other kinds of mental states and activities.

This timeline illustrates the major milestones in the development of psychology.

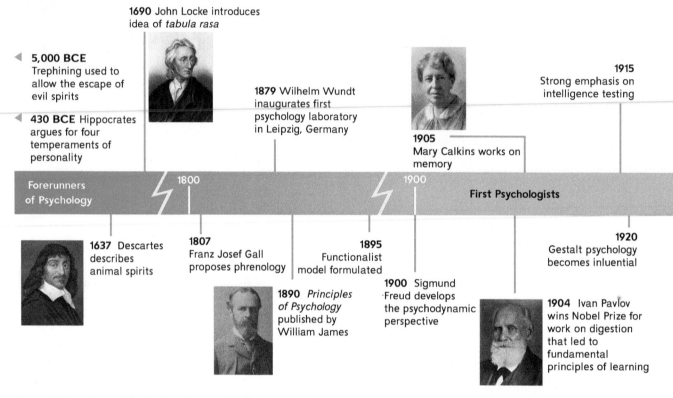

1690 John Locke introduces idea of *tabula rasa*

5,000 BCE Trephining used to allow the escape of evil spirits

430 BCE Hippocrates argues for four temperaments of personality

1879 Wilhelm Wundt inaugurates first psychology laboratory in Leipzig, Germany

1915 Strong emphasis on intelligence testing

1905 Mary Calkins works on memory

Forerunners of Psychology

1800

1900

First Psychologists

1637 Descartes describes animal spirits

1807 Franz Josef Gall proposes phrenology

1895 Functionalist model formulated

1890 *Principles of Psychology* published by William James

1900 Sigmund Freud develops the psychodynamic perspective

1920 Gestalt psychology becomes inluential

1904 Ivan Pavlov wins Nobel Prize for work on digestion that led to fundamental principles of learning

Sources: © Science Source; © Corbis; © Paul Thompson/FPG/Getty Images; © Bettmann/Corbis; Courtesy, Wellesley College Archives. Photographed by Notman; © Underwood & Underwood/Corbis; © The Granger Collection, New York; © The Granger Collection, New York; Courtesy, Elizabeth Loftus.

on uncovering the fundamental mental components of perception, consciousness, thinking, emotions, and other kinds of mental states and activities. He likened psychology to the chemistry, with the fundamental mental components being like the fundamental periodic table of elements.

To determine how basic sensory processes shape our understanding of the world, Wundt and other structuralists used a procedure called **introspection**, in which they presented people with a trigger or stimulus—such as a bright green object or a sentence printed on a card—and asked them to describe, in their own words and in as much detail as they could, what they were experiencing. Wundt argued that by analyzing their reports, psychologists could come to a better understanding of the structure of the mind.

STUDY ALERT!

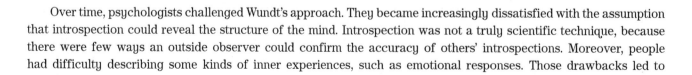

Knowing the basic outlines of the history of the field will help you understand how today's major perspectives have evolved.

Over time, psychologists challenged Wundt's approach. They became increasingly dissatisfied with the assumption that introspection could reveal the structure of the mind. Introspection was not a truly scientific technique, because there were few ways an outside observer could confirm the accuracy of others' introspections. Moreover, people had difficulty describing some kinds of inner experiences, such as emotional responses. Those drawbacks led to

Introspection
A procedure used to study the structure of the mind in which subjects are asked to describe in detail what they are experiencing when they are exposed to a stimulus.

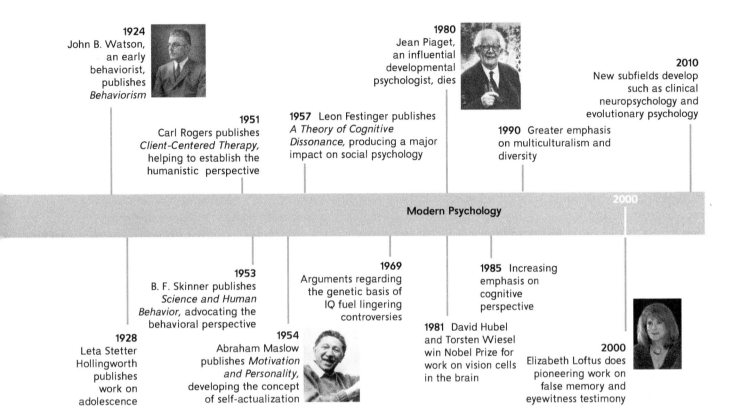

1924
John B. Watson, an early behaviorist, publishes *Behaviorism*

1951 Carl Rogers publishes *Client-Centered Therapy*, helping to establish the humanistic perspective

1957 Leon Festinger publishes *A Theory of Cognitive Dissonance*, producing a major impact on social psychology

1980 Jean Piaget, an influential developmental psychologist, dies

1990 Greater emphasis on multiculturalism and diversity

2010 New subfields develop such as clinical neuropsychology and evolutionary psychology

Modern Psychology

2000

1928 Leta Stetter Hollingworth publishes work on adolescence

1953 B. F. Skinner publishes *Science and Human Behavior*, advocating the behavioral perspective

1954 Abraham Maslow publishes *Motivation and Personality*, developing the concept of self-actualization

1969 Arguments regarding the genetic basis of IQ fuel lingering controversies

1981 David Hubel and Torsten Wiesel win Nobel Prize for work on vision cells in the brain

1985 Increasing emphasis on cognitive perspective

2000 Elizabeth Loftus does pioneering work on false memory and eyewitness testimony

the development of new approaches, which largely supplanted structuralism. However, Wundt can be credited with establishing the first formal research studies in psychology, and being the first to conceptualize psychology as an academic discipline.

The perspective that replaced structuralism is known as functionalism. Rather than focusing on the mind's structure, **functionalism** concentrated on what the mind *does* and how behaviour functions. Functionalists, whose perspective became prominent in the early 1900s, asked what role behaviour plays in allowing people to adapt to their environments. For example, a functionalist might examine the function of the emotion of fear in preparing us to deal with an emergency situation. This perspective in understanding human behaviour is still highly influential in contemporary psychology.

Led by the American psychologist William James, the functionalists examined how behaviour allows people to satisfy their needs and how our "stream of consciousness" permits us to adapt to our environment. The American educator John Dewey drew on functionalism to develop the field of school psychology, proposing ways to best meet students' educational needs. James was the first to conceptualize psychology as an applied discipline, with practical applications in diverse fields like education, parenting, and more. William James was heavily influenced by the work of Charles Darwin, and functionalism can be thought of as an early precursor of the contemporary field of evolutionary psychology.

Women in Psychology: Founding Mothers

As in many scientific fields, social prejudices hindered women's participation in the early development of psychology. For example, many universities would not even admit women to their graduate psychology programs in the early 1900s.

Functionalism
An early approach to psychology that concentrated on what the mind does—the functions of mental activity—and the role of behaviour in allowing people to adapt to their environments.

Still, despite the hurdles they faced, several women made major contributions to psychology, although their impact on the field was largely overlooked until recently. For example, Margaret Floy Washburn (1871–1939) was the first woman to receive a doctorate in psychology, and she did important work on animal behaviour. Leta Stetter Hollingworth (1886–1939) was one of the first psychologists to focus on child development and on women's issues. She collected data to refute the view—popular in the early 1900s—that women's abilities periodically declined during parts of the menstrual cycle (Hollingworth, 1943/1990; Denmark & Fernandez, 1993; Furumoto & Scarborough, 2002).

Mary J. Wright became the first female president of the Canadian Psychological Association in 1969. In 2001, Dr. Wright, a pioneer in the field of developmental psychology, was awarded the Gold Medal Award for Distinguished Lifetime Contributions to Canadian Psychology (Wright, 2002). In addition to breaking through the glass ceiling for female psychologists, Dr. Wright defied ageism stereotypes by working until the age of 85 at the University of Western Ontario (Rumleski, 2007).

Mary Calkins (1863–1930), who studied memory in the early part of the twentieth century, became the first female president of the American Psychological Association. Karen Horney (pronounced "HORN-eye") (1885–1952) focused on the social and cultural factors behind personality, and June Etta Downey (1875–1932) spearheaded the study of personality traits and became the first woman to head a psychology department at an American state university. Anna Freud (1895–1982), the daughter of Sigmund Freud, also made notable contributions to the treatment of abnormal behaviour, and Mamie Phipps Clark (1917–1983) carried out pioneering work on how children of colour grew to recognize racial differences (Horney, 1937; Stevens & Gardner, 1982; Lal, 2002).

Brenda Milner is recognized by fellow academics as one of Canada's "great Canadian psychologists." A former graduate student of Donald Hebb at McGill University, Milner first received recognition for her work in 1955 with a brain surgery patient without short-term memory known only as "HM." Since then, students and scholars in neuropsychology have come from all parts of the world to collaborate with and be trained by her at the Montreal Neurological Institute (The Great Canadian Psychology website, 2008).

Historical Perspectives: What Has Stood the Test of Time?

The women and the men who laid the foundations of psychology shared a common goal: to explain and understand behaviour using scientific methods. Seeking to achieve the same goal, the tens of thousands of psychologists who followed those early pioneers embraced—and often rejected—a variety of broad perspectives.

The perspectives of psychology offer distinct outlooks and emphasize different factors. Just as we can use more than one map to find our way around a particular region—for instance, a map that shows roads and highways and another map that shows major landmarks—psychologists developed a variety of approaches to understanding behaviour. When considered jointly, the different perspectives provide the means to explain behaviour in its amazing variety.

Today, the history of psychology has left a legacy of five major perspectives that have stood the test of time (summarized in Figure 2). These broad perspectives emphasize different aspects of behaviour and mental processes, and each takes our understanding of behaviour in a somewhat different direction.

FIGURE 2

The major perspectives of psychology.

Neuroscience	Psychodynamic	Behavioural	Cognitive	Humanistic
Views behaviour from the perspective of biological functioning	Believes behaviour is motivated by inner, unconscious forces over which a person has little control	Focuses on observable behaviour	Examines how people understand and think about the world	Contends that people can control their behaviour and that they naturally try to reach their full potential

The Neuroscience Perspective: Biopsychology and Behavioural Neuroscience

In the most fundamental sense, people are biological organisms. *Behavioural neuroscience* is the perspective of psychology that mainly examines how the brain and the nervous system—as well as other biological processes—determine behaviour. Thus, neuroscientists consider how our bodies influence our behaviour. For example, they may examine the link between specific sites in the brain and the muscular tremors of people affected by Parkinson's disease or attempt to determine how our emotions are related to physical sensations. Behavioural neuroscientists might want to know what physiological changes occurred in people who survived the 7.0 magnitude earthquake in Haiti.

Nova Scotia, Canada-born Donald Hebb (1904–1985) is known as the father of neuropsychology. Because every behaviour can be broken down to some extent into its biological components, the neuroscience perspective has broad appeal. Psychologists who subscribe to this perspective have made major contributions to the understanding and betterment of human life, ranging from cures for certain types of deafness to drug treatments for people with severe mental disorders.

When we get down to the basics, humans are animals made of skin and bones. The **neuroscience perspective** considers how people and nonhumans function biologically: how individual nerve cells are joined together, how the inheritance of certain characteristics from parents and other ancestors influences behaviour, how the functioning of the body affects hopes and fears, which behaviours are instinctual, and so forth. Even more complex kinds of behaviours, such as a baby's response to strangers, are viewed as having critical biological components by psychologists who embrace the neuroscience perspective. This perspective includes the study of heredity and evolution, considering how heredity may influence behaviour, and behavioural neuroscience, which examines how the brain and the nervous system affect behaviour.

The Psychodynamic Perspective: Understanding the Inner Person

Proponents of the **psychodynamic perspective** argue that behaviour is motivated by inner forces and conflicts about which we have little awareness or control. Dreams and slips of the tongue are viewed as indications of what a person is truly feeling within a seething cauldron of unconscious psychic activity.

The origins of the psychodynamic view are intimately linked with the man who is arguably the most famous psychologist, living or dead: Sigmund Freud. Freud was a Viennese physician in the early 1900s whose ideas about unconscious determinants of behaviour had a revolutionary effect on twentieth-century thinking, not just in psychology but in related fields as well. Although some of the original Freudian principles have been roundly criticized, the contemporary psychodynamic perspective has provided a means not only to understand and treat some kinds of psychological disorders but also to understand everyday phenomena such as prejudice and aggression. Additionally, Freud made three major contributions that have had an incalculable influence on the field of psychology and even on popular culture. First, he was the first to propose the notion that we have a subconscious—that parts of our mind are not always accessible to us and that our behaviour may be shaped by forces outside of our conscious awareness. Second, he was the first to propose one of the most widely accepted notions not just in psychology but in our popular culture: that our experiences in early childhood shape us as adults. Finally, Freud was the first to propose that psychological difficulties can be treated with psychological (rather than biomedical) means. Although there are few therapists that practice using a strict Freudian approach today, all forms of talk therapy owe a debt to Freud and his theories.

Neuroscience perspective
The approach that views behaviour from the perspective of the brain, the nervous system, and other biological functions.

Psychodynamic perspective
The approach based on the view that behaviour is motivated by unconscious inner forces over which the individual has little control.

The Behavioural Perspective: Observing the Outer Person

For a long time, the psychodynamic perspective was the dominant theory in the field of psychology. The **behavioural perspective** grew out of a rejection of psychology's early emphasis on the inner workings of the mind. Instead, behaviourists suggested that the field should focus on observable behaviour that can be measured objectively. One of the behaviourists' main criticisms of Freud was that his theories lacked scientific rigour and were difficult to study objectively. They felt that if psychology were to stand as an academic discipline, it should focus only on the study of that which could be measured: observable behaviour. In this sense, although their view of the scope of psychology would now be seen as far too narrow, the behaviourists can be credited with turning psychology into a truly rigorous academic discipline.

John B. Watson was the first major American psychologist to advocate a behavioural approach. Working in the 1920s, Watson was adamant in his view that one could gain a complete understanding of behaviour by studying and modifying the environment in which people operate.

In fact, Watson believed rather optimistically that it was possible to elicit any desired type of behaviour by controlling a person's environment. This philosophy is clear in his own words: "Give me a dozen healthy infants, well-formed, and my own specified world to bring them up in and I'll guarantee to take any one at random and train him to become any type of specialist I might select—doctor, lawyer, artist, merchant-chief, and yes, even beggar-man and thief, regardless of his talents, penchants, tendencies, abilities, vocations and race of his ancestors" (Watson, 1924).

The behavioural perspective was championed by B. F. Skinner, a pioneer in the field. A great deal of our understanding about how people learn new behaviours is based on the behavioural perspective. In 1977, Canadian-born Albert Bandura proposed a ground-breaking theory in behavioural psychology. Bandura's social learning theory focuses on learning which takes place within social contexts (Bandura, 1977). Bandura continues to have a significant influence in the twenty-first century. A survey published in the *Review of General Psychology* deemed Bandura as the most-cited living psychologist today (Haggbloom, 2002).

As we will see, the behavioural perspective crops up along every byway of psychology. Along with its influence in the area of learning processes, one of the most important contributions of the behavioural theory is in its clinical applications. Behavioural therapy has been shown to be effective in such diverse areas as treating mental disorders, curbing aggression, resolving sexual problems, and ending drug addiction (Silverman, Roll, & Higgins, 2008).

The Cognitive Perspective: Identifying the Roots of Understanding

Evolving in part from structuralism and in part as a reaction to behaviourism, which focused so heavily on observable behaviour and the environment, the **cognitive perspective** focuses on how people think, understand, and know about the world. The cognitive revolution in psychology arose in the 1950 and 1960s when psychologists began to find rigorous and scientific ways to study mental processes, which the behaviourists had deemed to be unmeasurable and therefore unfit for scientific inquiry.

Cognitive psychology focuses on higher mental processes, including thinking, memory, reasoning, problem solving, judging, decision making, and language.

Many psychologists who adhere to the cognitive perspective compare human thinking to the workings of a computer, which takes in information and transforms, stores, and retrieves it. In their view, thinking is *information processing*.

Psychologists who rely on the cognitive perspective ask questions ranging from how people make decisions to whether a person can watch television and study at the same time. The common elements that link cognitive approaches are an emphasis on how people understand and think about the world and an interest in describing the patterns and irregularities in the operation of our minds. This continues to be a very active perspective in psychology today.

Behavioural perspective
The approach that suggests that observable, measurable behaviour should be the focus of study.

Cognitive perspective
The approach that focuses on how people think, understand, and know about the world.

The Humanistic Perspective: The Unique Qualities of the Human Species

Rejecting the view that behaviour is determined largely by automatically unfolding biological forces, unconscious processes, or the environment, the **humanistic perspective** instead suggests that all individuals naturally strive to grow, develop, and be in control of their lives and behaviour. Humanistic psychologists maintain that each of us has the capacity to seek and reach fulfillment. The humanistic movement arose as a reaction to the pessimistic nature of Freud's theories—that we were held hostage by our early childhood experiences, and that we were only barely managing to keep a lid on the darker urges of our subconscious. The field of humanistic psychology was influenced by the work of Austrian psychiatrist and Holocaust survivor Viktor Frankl, whose book *Man's Search for Meaning* (1963) argues that one can find an experience meaningful even under the most brutal of circumstances.

According to Carl Rogers and Abraham Maslow, who were central figures in the development of the humanistic perspective, people will strive to reach their full potential if they are given the opportunity. The emphasis of the humanistic perspective is on *free will*, the ability to freely make decisions about one's own behaviour and life. The notion of free will stands in contrast to *determinism*, which sees behaviour as caused, or determined, by things beyond a person's control.

The humanistic perspective assumes that people have the ability to make their own choices about their behaviour rather than relying on societal standards. Although the humanistic approach has been criticized as being overly optimistic in terms of its views of human nature, it has had a profound impact on the field of psychology, including the subfield of positive psychology, which looks at how to apply the principles of psychology to allow people to lead more satisfying and fulfilling lives. More than any other approach, it stresses the role of psychology in enriching people's lives and helping them achieve self-fulfillment. By reminding psychologists of their commitment to the individual person in society, the humanistic perspective has been an important influence (Robbins, 2008).

It is important not to let the abstract qualities of the broad approaches we have discussed lull you into thinking that they are purely theoretical: These perspectives underlie ongoing work of a practical nature, as we will discuss throughout this book. To start seeing how psychology can improve everyday life, read the nearby *Applying Psychology in the Real World* box.

The Subfields of Psychology: Psychology's Family Tree

As the study of psychology has grown, it has given rise to a number of subfields (described in Figure 3). The subfields of psychology can be likened to an extended family, with assorted nieces and nephews, aunts and uncles, and cousins who, although they may not interact on a day-to-day basis, are related to one another because they share a common goal: understanding behaviour. One way to identify the key subfields is to look at some of the basic questions about behaviour that they address.

Experimental Psychology: Sensation and Perception and More

If you have ever wondered why you are susceptible to optical illusions, how your body registers pain, or how to make the most of your study time, an experimental psychologist can answer your questions. *Experimental psychology* is the branch of psychology that studies the processes of sensing, perceiving, learning, and thinking about the world. (The term *experimental psychologist* is somewhat misleading: Psychologists in every specialty area use experimental techniques.)

STUDY ALERT!

Use Figure 3 to learn the key issues that underlie every subfield of psychology.

Humanistic perspective
The approach that suggests that all individuals naturally strive to grow, develop, and be in control of their lives and behaviour.

FIGURE 3

The major subfields of psychology.

Subfield	Description
Behavioral genetics	*Behavioral genetics* studies the inheritance of traits related to behaviour.
Behavioral neuroscience	*Behavioral neuroscience* examines the biological basis of behaviour.
Clinical psychology	*Clinical psychology* deals with the study, diagnosis, and treatment of psychological disorders.
Clinical neuropsychology	*Clinical neuropsychology* unites the areas of biopsychology and clinical psychology, focusing on the relationship between biological factors and psychological disorders.
Cognitive psychology	*Cognitive psychology* focuses on the study of higher mental processes.
Counselling psychology	*Counseling psychology* focuses primarily on educational, social, and career adjustment problems.
Cross-cultural psychology	*Cross-cultural psychology* investigates the similarities and differences in psychological functioning in and across various cultures and ethnic groups.
Developmental psychology	*Developmental psychology* examines how people grow and change from the moment of conception through death.
Educational psychology	*Educational psychology* is concerned with teaching and learning processes, such as the relationship between motivation and school performance.
Environmental psychology	*Environmental psychology* considers the relationship between people and their physical environment.
Evolutionary psychology	*Evolutionary psychology* considers how behaviour is influenced by our genetic inheritance from our ancestors.
Experimental psychology	*Experimental psychology* studies the processes of sensing, perceiving, learning, and thinking about the world.
Forensic psychology	*Forensic psychology* focuses on legal issues, such as determining the accuracy of eyewitness memories.
Health psychology	*Health psychology* explores the relationship between psychological factors and physical ailments or disease.
Industrial/organizational psychology	*Industrial/organizational psychology* is concerned with psychological factors in the workplace, such as job satisfaction, performance, and work-family balance.
Personality psychology	*Personality psychology* focuses on the consistency in people's behavior over time and the traits that differentiate one person from another.
Positive psychology	*Positive psychology* builds upon people's strengths in order to optimize their happiness, well-being, and overall functioning.
Program evaluation	*Program evaluation* focuses on assessing large-scale programs, such as preschool programs, to determine whether they are effective in meeting their goals.
Psychology of women	*Psychology of women* focuses on issues such as discrimination against women and the causes of violence against women.
School psychology	*School psychology* is devoted to counselling children in elementary and secondary schools who have academic or emotional problems.
Social psychology	*Social psychology* is the study of how people's thoughts, feelings, and actions are affected by others.
Sport psychology	*Sport psychology* applies psychology to athletic activity and exercise.

Sources: © Spencer Grant/Science Source; © Chris Ryan/agefotostock RF; © Don Hammond/DesignPics RF.

Many chapters will include a box describing psychological research that is being applied to everyday problems. Read these boxes to understand how psychology promises to improve the human condition, in ways ranging from the development of ways to reduce violence to explaining the behaviour of suicide bombers.

APPLYING PSYCHOLOGY in the Real World

Psychology Matters

Violence and its causes are among the world's most pressing issues. What can psychologists add to our understanding of the problem?

"Eyewitness to abduction proves unable to provide reliable clues."

"Murder-suicide shocked community."

"Investigators search for clues at site of suicide bombing."

A quick review of any day's news headlines reminds us that the world is beset by a variety of stubborn problems that resist easy solution. At the same time, a considerable number of psychologists are devoting their energies and expertise to addressing these problems and improving the human condition. Let's consider some of the ways in which psychology has addressed and helped work toward solutions of major societal problems (Zimbardo, 2004):

- *Why is aggression so prevalent, and how can more humane and peaceful alternatives be promoted?* Aggression, whether it be on the playground or the battlefield, is arguably the world's greatest problem. Psychologists have sought to understand how aggression begins in children and how it may be prevented. For example, psychologists Brad Bushman and Craig Anderson have been looking at the ways in which violent video games may result in heightened violence on the part of those who play them. They have found that people who play such games have an altered view of the world, seeing it as a more violent place. In addition, they are more apt to respond to aggression even when provoked only minimally. Other psychologists are working to limit the prevalence of violent behaviour, and some have designed programs to teach people how to cope with exposure to violence (Bushman & Anderson, 2001, 2002; Crawford, 2002).

- *Why do eyewitnesses to crimes often remember the events inaccurately, and how can we increase the precision of eyewitness accounts?* Psychologists' research has come to an important conclusion: Eyewitness testimony in criminal cases is often inaccurate and biased. Memories of crimes are often clouded by emotion, and the questions asked by police investigators often elicit inaccurate responses. Work by psychologists has been used to provide national guidelines for obtaining more accurate memories during criminal investigations (Kassin, 2005; Loftus & Bernstein, 2005).

- *Who studies acts of terrorism?* What are the practice areas of psychologists who study terrorism? Psychologists that do research on terrorism often work in a variety of criminal justice and forensic settings. For example, the Criminal Justice Psychology Section (CJPS) of the Canadian Psychological Association published several articles on terrorism in *Crime Scene*, a journal which covers a wide range of issues in criminal justice psychology (CPA, 2007)

- *What are the causes of terrorism?* What motivates suicide bombers? Are they psychologically disordered, or can their behaviour be seen as a rational response to a particular system of beliefs? As we'll see in Chapter 12 when we discuss abnormal

On May 6, 2013, Tim Bosma was abducted from his Ancaster, Ontario home when he went on a test-drive with two men who had responded to his ad on Kijiji, selling his truck. On May 14, Bosma's body was recovered on a rural property in Ayr, Ontario belonging to Dellen Millard. Millard and his accomplice, Mark Smich, were arrested shortly after the discovery (The Globe and Mail, 2013). Psychologists study criminal behaviour to try to understand it—and hopefully prevent tragedies such as the Tim Bosma case.

Source: © Nathan Denette/CP Images.

(continued)

(continued)

behaviour, psychologists are gaining an understanding of the factors that lead people to embrace suicide and to engage in terrorism to further a cause in which they deeply believe.

These four topics represent just a few of the issues that psychologists interested in violence and criminal behaviour address on a daily basis. To further explore the many ways that psychology has an impact on everyday life in Canada, check out the Your Health: Psychology Quick Facts website of the Canadian Psychological Association at www.cpa.ca/public/your healthpsychologyworksfactsheets/.

Developmental Psychology and Personality Psychology: Stability and Change Over Time

A baby producing her first smile . . . taking her first step . . . saying her first word. These universal milestones in development are also singularly special and unique for each person. *Developmental psychology* studies how people grow and change from the moment of conception through death. *Personality psychology* focuses on the consistency in people's behaviour over time and the traits that differentiate one person from another.

Developmental and personality psychologists are particularly interested in the issue of nature (genes or heredity) versus nurture (environment or experience). The nature–nurture issue asks how much of people's behaviour is due to their genetically determined nature (heredity), and how much is due to nurture, the influences of the physical and social environment in which a child is raised. Furthermore, what is the interplay between heredity and environment? These questions have deep philosophical and historical roots, and are a factor in many topics in psychology.

However, every psychologist would agree that neither nature nor nurture alone is the sole determinant of behaviour; rather, it is a combination of the two. In a sense, then, the real controversy involves how much of our behaviour is caused by heredity and how much is caused by environmental influences.

Health Psychology, Clinical Psychology, and Counselling Psychology: Psychological Factors and Mental Health

Frequent depression, stress, and fears that prevent people from carrying out their normal activities are topics that would interest a health psychologist, clinical psychologist, and a counselling psychologist. *Health psychology* explores the relationship between psychological factors and physical ailments or disease. For example, health psychologists are interested in how long-term stress (a psychological factor) can affect physical health and in identifying ways to promote behaviour that brings about good health (Belar, 2008; Yardley & Moss-Morris, 2009). The beneficial effects of exercise and healthy eating habits during stressful times at college or university, especially final exams, would be of concern to a health psychologist.

Clinical psychology deals with the study, diagnosis, and treatment of psychological disorders. Clinical psychologists are trained to diagnose and treat problems that range from the crises of everyday life, such as unhappiness over the breakup of a relationship, to more extreme conditions, such as profound, lingering depression. Some clinical psychologists also research and investigate issues that range from identifying the early signs of psychological disturbance to studying the relationship between family communication patterns and psychological disorders. A clinical psychologist might be called on to help a Haiti earthquake survivor cope with the loss of a loved one.

Like clinical psychologists, counselling psychologists deal with people's psychological problems, but the problems they deal with are more specific. *Counselling psychology* is the branch of psychology that focuses primarily on educational, social, and career adjustment problems. Almost every college and university has a centre staffed with counselling psychologists. This is where students can get advice on the kinds of jobs they might be best suited for, methods of studying effectively, and strategies for resolving everyday difficulties, such as problems with roommates and concerns about a specific professor's grading practices. Many large business organizations also employ counselling psychologists to help employees with work-related problems.

Social Psychology and Cross-Cultural Psychology: Behaviour in Context

Our complex networks of social interrelationships are the focus of study for a number of subfields of psychology. For example, *social psychology* is the study of how people's thoughts, feelings, and actions are affected by others. Social psychologists focus on such diverse topics as human aggression, liking and loving, persuasion, and conformity. For a social psychologist, the 2010 Haiti earthquake raises questions about why so many people volunteered to help in the search and rescue operation and so few took advantage of the situation for their own personal gain.

Cross-cultural psychology investigates the similarities and differences in psychological functioning in and across various cultures and ethnic groups. For example, cross-cultural psychologists examine how cultures differ in their use of punishment during child rearing or why certain cultures view academic success as being determined mostly by hard work while others see it as being determined mostly by innate ability (Schoenpflug, 2003; Shweder, 2003).

Psychology's Future: Expanding Psychology's Frontiers

We have examined psychology's foundations, but what does the future hold for the discipline? The boundaries of the science of psychology are constantly growing. Three newer members of the field's family tree—evolutionary psychology, behavioural genetics, and clinical neuropsychology—have sparked particular excitement, and debate, within psychology.

EVOLUTIONARY PSYCHOLOGY

Evolutionary psychology considers how behaviour is influenced by our genetic inheritance from our ancestors. The evolutionary approach suggests that the chemical coding of information in our cells not only determines traits such as hair colour and race but also holds the key to understanding a broad variety of behaviours that helped our ancestors survive and reproduce.

Evolutionary psychology is not strictly a new approach, in fact it stems from Charles Darwin's arguments in his groundbreaking 1859 book, *On the Origin of Species*. Darwin suggested that a process of natural selection leads to the survival of the fittest and the development of traits that enable a species to adapt to its environment.

Darwin wrote about how the environment shapes our physical traits over evolutionary times (white polar bears will be found in the snowy Arctic, brown bears further south in the forests, because those colours will help them to be better camouflaged in their respective environments). Evolutionary psychologists argue that evolutionary pressures will similarly shape psychological traits, in the same way that as physical traits. For example, evolutionary psychologists suggest that behaviour such as shyness, jealousy, and cross-cultural similarities in qualities desired in potential mates are at least partially determined by genetics, presumably because such behaviour helped increase the survival rate of humans' ancient relatives (Buss, 2003; Sefcek, Brumbach, & Vasquez, 2007).

The evolutionary approach has stimulated a significant amount of new research on how our biological inheritance influences our traits and behaviours (Buss, 2004; Begley, 2005a; Neher, 2006).

BEHAVIOURAL GENETICS

Another rapidly growing area in psychology focuses on the biological mechanisms, such as genes and chromosomes, which enable inherited behaviour to unfold. *Behavioural genetics* seeks to understand how we might inherit certain behavioural traits and how the environment influences whether we actually display such traits (Bjorklund & Ellis, 2005; Moffitt & Caspi, 2007; Rende, 2007).

CLINICAL NEUROPSYCHOLOGY

Clinical neuropsychology unites the areas of neuroscience and clinical psychology: It focuses on the origin of psychological disorders in biological factors. Building on advances in our understanding of the structure and chemistry of the brain, this specialty has already led to promising new treatments for psychological disorders as well as debates over the use of medication to control behaviour.

Evaluate

1. Wundt and his followers used a research procedure known as _____ in which they asked people to describe what they were experiencing when exposed to various stimuli.

2. Jeanne's therapist asks her to recount a violent dream she recently experienced in order to gain insight into the unconscious forces affecting her behaviour. Jeanne's therapist is working from a _____ perspective.

3. "It is behaviour that can be observed that should be studied, not the suspected inner workings of the mind." This statement was most likely made by someone with which perspective?

   a. Cognitive perspective

   b. Neuroscience perspective

   c. Humanistic perspective

   d. Behavioural perspective

4. In the nature–nurture issue, nature refers to heredity, and nurture refers to the _____.

5. Match each subfield of psychology with the issues or questions posed below.

   a. Behavioural neuroscience

   b. Cognitive psychology

   c. Clinical psychology

   d. Counselling psychology

   (i) Joan, a university freshman, is worried about her grades. She needs to learn better organizational skills and study habits to cope with the demands of university.

   (ii) What chemicals are released in the human body as a result of a stressful event? What are their effects on behaviour?

   (iii) A strong fear of crowds and a history of panic attacks leads a young woman to seek treatment for her problem.

   (iv) What mental strategies are involved in solving complex word problems?

Answers to Evaluate Questions

1. introspection; 2. psychodynamic; 3. d; 4. environment; 5. a. (ii) b. (iv) c. (iii) d. (i)

Key Terms

behavioural perspective	humanistic perspective	psychodynamic
cognitive perspective	introspection	perspective
functionalism	neuroscience perspective	structuralism

Research in Psychology

LEARNING OBJECTIVES

What is the scientific method?

What role do theories and hypotheses play in psychological research?

What research methods do psychologists use?

How do psychologists establish cause-and-effect relationships using experiments?

Do "birds of a feather flock together" . . . or do "opposites attract"?

Are "two heads are better than one" . . . or is it that "if you want a thing done well, do it yourself"?

Is it true that "the more the merrier" . . . or is it that "two's company, three's a crowd"?

If we were to rely on common sense to understand behaviour, we'd have considerable difficulty—especially because commonsense views are often contradictory. In fact, one of the major undertakings for the field of psychology is to develop suppositions about behaviour and to determine which of those suppositions are accurate.

The Scientific Method

Psychologists—as well as scientists in other disciplines—meet the challenge of posing appropriate questions and properly answering them by relying on the scientific method. The **scientific method** is the approach used by psychologists to systematically acquire knowledge and understanding about behaviour and other phenomena of interest. As illustrated in Figure 1, it consists of three main steps: (1) identifying questions of interest, (2) formulating an explanation, and (3) carrying out research designed to support or refute the explanation.

Theories: Specifying Broad Explanations

In using the scientific method, psychologists start by identifying questions of interest. We have all been curious at some time about our observations of everyday behaviour. If you have ever asked yourself why some couples stay together when others divorce, or why some people love roller-coasters when for others they are torturous, you have been formulating questions about behaviour.

Psychologists, too, ask questions about the nature and causes of behaviour. Once a question has been identified, the next step in the scientific method is to develop a theory to explain the observed phenomenon. **Theories** are plausible explanations for existing and true facts. For example, the existing and true *fact* that some couples divorce while others stay together may be explained by the *theory* that the more you have in common with your spouse before you are married, the less likely you are to divorce. Psychologists base their theories on previous findings and observations related to their field of inquiry (Sternberg & Beall, 1991; McGuire, 1997).

Kitty Genovese was living in New York City in 1964. When she returned to her apartment one night, she was attacked just outside her building. Thirty-eight neighbours watched her being attacked, and did nothing. Her attacker left when

Scientific method
The approach through which psychologists systematically acquire knowledge and understanding about behaviour and other phenomena of interest.

Theories
Plausible explanations for existing and true facts.

FIGURE 1

The scientific method, which encompasses the process of identifying, asking, and answering questions, is used by psychologists, and by researchers from every other scientific discipline, to come to an understanding about the world. What do you think are the advantages of this method?

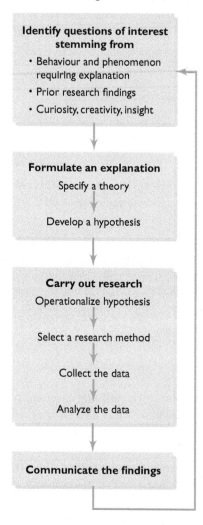

Kitty was desperately injured but still alive. Despite the fact that she was screaming and begging for help, no one so much as called the police. Her murderer came back, then left again, then came back a third time, fleeing after Kitty was finally dead (Rosenthal, 1964). How could so many people have watched these horrific, violent acts and done nothing—not even called the police? Psychologists Bibb Latané and John Darley, eager to explain why this could have happened, developed what they called a theory of *diffusion of responsibility* (Latané & Darley, 1970). According to their theory, the greater the number of bystanders or witnesses to an event that calls for helping behaviour, the more the responsibility for helping is perceived to be shared by all the bystanders (see Chapter 14 for more on this phenomenon). Thus, the greater the number of bystanders in an emergency situation, the smaller the share of the responsibility each person feels—and the less likely it is that any single person will come forward to help. In other words, their theory was that if a lot of people are watching, everyone assumes someone else will help. This *theory* provided a plausible explanation for the *fact* that no one helped Kitty Genovese.

Bystander apathy occurs when individuals witness someone in distress and do nothing to alleviate their suffering.

Source: © Ingram Publishing/agefotostock RF.

Hypotheses: Crafting Testable Predictions

Although the diffusion of responsibility theory seems to make sense, it represented only the beginning phase of Latané and Darley's investigative process. Their next step was to devise a way to test their theory. To do this, they needed to create a hypothesis. A **hypothesis** is a prediction stated in a way that allows it to be tested. Hypotheses stem from theories; they help test the underlying validity of theories.

Latané and Darley's hypothesis was a straightforward prediction from their more general theory of diffusion of responsibility: The more people who witness an emergency situation, the less likely it is that help will be given to a victim. According to this hypothesis, *if* you are the victim of a violent crime, *then* you are better off—in terms of the likelihood of receiving help—with only one or two witnesses than with many. Hypotheses can be stated in an *if/then* statement as above: if this theory is correct, then this should happen. Latané and Darley's theory of diffusion of responsibility (the presence of more bystanders leads each witness to feel less responsibility to respond with help) led them directly to their hypothesis statement (*if* there are more witnesses present, *then* witnesses are less likely to call for help).

The if/then hypothesis statement provides a reasoned guide to the direction that future investigation ought to take (Howitt & Cramer, 2000; Cohen, 2003; Gurin, 2006). Once the hypothesis is properly stated, psychologists then can choose from a variety of research methods to find answers. For example, to test Latané and Darley's hypothesis, a researcher could analyze crime data and see whether victims with fewer witnesses were more likely to receive help.

If Latané and Darley did do their study by analyzing crime data from the past few years, this would be called doing *archival research.* This is because they would be using already existing, archived data rather than collecting new data. This is a strategy that psychologists sometimes use.

> ## STUDY ALERT!
>
> Remember that a theory is a broad explanation for observable and true facts, while a hypothesis is an if/then prediction statement.

◌ Psychological Research

Research—systematic inquiry aimed at the discovery of new knowledge—is a central ingredient of the scientific method in psychology. It provides the key to understanding the degree to which hypotheses (and the theories behind them) are accurate. Just as we can apply different theories and hypotheses to explain the same phenomena, we can use a number of alternative methods to conduct research (Ray, 2000). First, though, the hypothesis must be restated

Hypothesis
A prediction, stemming from a theory, stated in a way that allows it to be tested.

in a way that will allow it to be tested, which involves creating an operational definition. An **operational definition** is the translation of a hypothesis into specific, testable procedures that can be measured and observed. For instance, in the example provided above, where Latané and Darley were studying bystander apathy, "feeling apathy" could be defined as "failing to call the police." Feelings of apathy cannot be measured, but calls to the police can.

In our discussion of research methods, we will consider several major tools in the psychologist's research kit. Knowledge of the research methods used by psychologists permits us to better evaluate the research that others conduct. The media constantly bombard us with claims about research studies and findings. Knowledge of research methods allows us to sort out what is credible from what should be ignored. Understanding the methods by which psychologists conduct research can enhance our ability to analyze and evaluate the situations we encounter in our everyday lives (Shaughnessy, Zechmeister, & Zechmeister, 2000; Shadish, Cook, & Campbell, 2002; Tryon & Bernstein, 2003).

Descriptive Research

Let's begin by considering several types of **descriptive research** designed to systematically investigate a person, group, or patterns of behaviour. These methods include naturalistic observation, survey research, and case studies.

Naturalistic Observation

In **naturalistic observation**, the investigator observes some naturally occurring behaviour and does not make a change in the situation. For example, a researcher investigating helping behaviour might observe the kind of help given to victims in a high-crime area of a city. The important point to remember about naturalistic observation is that the researcher simply records what occurs, making no modification in the situation that is being observed (Schutt, 2001; Moore, 2002; Rustin, 2006).

Debra Pepler, a psychology professor at York University [and your author's (LC's) former thesis advisor], uses naturalistic observation to study bullying behaviour from a distance. In doing so, her observational research captures hidden nuances that occur in the interactions and relationships between bullies, bystanders, and victims that often disappear when adults are present (Craig & Pepler, 2007). Some phenomenon, like bullying, lend themselves well to studying in this way. It would be difficult, not to mention unethical, to create an authentic bullying situation in a lab.

Although the advantage of naturalistic observation is obvious—we get a sample of what people do in their "natural habitat"—there is also an important drawback: the inability to control any of the factors of interest. For example, we might find so few naturally occurring instances of helping behaviour that we would be unable to draw any conclusions. Because naturalistic observation prevents researchers from making changes in a situation, they must wait until the appropriate conditions occur (your lab assistant could possibly sit in a high-risk area for days and not see any instances of criminal activity—and this could get expensive if he or she charges you by the hour). Furthermore, if people know they are being watched, they may alter their reactions, producing behaviour that is not truly representative.

Survey Research

There is no more straightforward way of finding out what people think, feel, and do than asking them directly. For this reason, surveys are an important research method. In **survey research**, a *sample* of people chosen to represent a larger group of interest (a *population*) are asked a series of questions about their behaviour, thoughts, or attitudes.

Operational definition
The translation of a hypothesis into specific, testable procedures that can be measured and observed.

Descriptive research
An approach to research designed to systematically investigate a person, group, or patterns of behaviour.

Naturalistic observation
Research in which an investigator simply observes some naturally occurring behaviour and does not make a change in the situation.

Survey research
Research in which people chosen to represent a larger population are asked a series of questions about their behaviour, thoughts, or attitudes.

Survey methods have become so sophisticated that even with a very small sample researchers are able to infer with great accuracy how a larger group would respond. For instance, a sample of just a few thousand voters is sufficient to predict within one or two percentage points which party will win a federal election—if the representative sample is chosen with care (Sommer & Sommer, 2001; Groves et al., 2004; Igo, 2006).

Surveys allow researchers to collect a huge amount of data quickly and cheaply. It also allows people to study phenomenon that might not easily be studied in a lab situation, like sexual behaviour. However, survey research has several potential pitfalls. For one thing, if the sample of people who are surveyed is not representative of the broader population of interest, the results of the survey will have little meaning. For instance, if a sample of voters in a city only included conservatives, it would hardly be useful for predicting the results of an election in which both conservatives and liberals were voting (Daley et al., 2003; Dale 2006).

People may also respond inaccurately if the survey itself is biased, or worded in such a way as to lead participants to respond in a particular manner. For example, suppose a marketing team wants to get dentists to recommend sugarfree gum. If dentists are asked: "should a patient chew sugarfree gum or chew on a piece of taffy?" it is likely that the dentist will choose the gum. This allows the marketers to make the statement that 9 out of 10 dentists recommend sugarfree gum. However, if the dentists were asked whether patients should chew sugarfree gum or brush their teeth, the responses would likely be quite different—and no longer in line with the marketers' goals. In psychological research, surveys are tested and validated to ensure that they are not biased—in other words, to ensure that they are measuring what they are supposed to measure.

Finally, survey respondents may not want to admit to holding socially undesirable attitudes. Put more bluntly, survey respondents often lie—sometimes with a deliberate purpose and sometimes for no particular reason at all. Survey respondents will sometimes lie on purpose, to make themselves look better, or just because they do not take the survey particularly seriously. Good surveys contain "lie items" which, if scored positively, are indicators that the respondent is not being completely honest.

The Case Study

Russell Williams was a standout officer, a Colonel in the Canadian Forces Base in Trenton Ontario, commanding Canada's largest air base. The army and the entire nation were shocked when Williams was arrested in 2010 for the sexual torture and murder of two women (Ruocco, 2010). The case of Russell Williams is of interest to researchers who want to understand the psychology of serial killers. Williams's particular pathology would be studied using a research method called the case study. In contrast to a survey, in which many people are studied, a **case study** is an in-depth, intensive investigation of an individual or small group of people.

Case studies allow us to study phenomenon that are rare or unusual. They give rich and detailed information. They also allow psychologists to study phenomenon that would not be possible to study in other ways, like the psychology of serial killers like Russell Williams.

The drawback to case studies? If the individuals examined are too unique, it is impossible to make valid generalizations to a larger population. Still, they sometimes lead the way to new theories and treatments.

Correlational Research

In using the descriptive research methods we have discussed, researchers often wish to determine the relationship between two variables. **Variables** are behaviours, events, or other characteristics that can change, or vary, in some way. For example, in a study to determine whether the amount of studying makes a difference in test scores, the variables would be study time and test scores.

In **correlational research**, two sets of variables are examined to determine whether they are associated, or "correlated." The strength and direction of the relationship between the two variables are represented by a mathematical statistic known as a *correlation* (or, more formally, a *correlation coefficient*), which can range from +1.0 to −1.0.

Case study
An in-depth, intensive investigation of an individual or small group of people.

Variables
Behaviours, events, or other characteristics that can change, or vary, in some way.

Correlational research
Research in which the relationship between two sets of variables is examined to determine whether they are associated, or "correlated."

Correlation coefficients provide information regarding the strength and direction of a relationship. A *positive correlation* indicates that as the value of one variable increases, the value of the other variable will also increase. For example, if we predict that the more time students spend studying for a test, the higher their grades on the test will be, and that the less they study, the lower their test scores will be, we are expecting to find a positive correlation. (Higher values of the variable "amount of study time" would be associated with higher values of the variable "test score," and lower values of "amount of study time" would be associated with lower values of "test score.") The correlation, then, would be indicated by a positive number, and the stronger the association was between studying and test scores, the closer the number would be to +1.0. For example, we might find a correlation of +.85 between test scores and amount of study time, indicating a strong positive association.

In contrast, a *negative correlation* tells us that as the value of one variable increases, the value of the other decreases. For instance, we might predict that as the number of hours spent studying increases, the number of hours spent partying decreases. Here we are expecting a negative correlation, ranging between 0 and −1.0. More studying is associated with less partying, and less studying is associated with more partying. The stronger the association between studying and partying is, the closer the correlation will be to −1.0. For instance, a correlation of −.85 would indicate a strong negative association between partying and studying. In this context, negative does not indicate good or bad, but just describes the nature of the relationship. The more you smoke, the shorter your life expectancy would describe a negative correlation, because as one factor increases, the other decreases. However, the statement: the more friends you have, the less stress you experience *also* describes a negative correlation, because as one variable (number of friends) goes up, the other (amount of stress) goes down. Similarly, the more you exercise the lower your risk of heart disease is also a negative correlation. This is because as one variable (exercise) increases, the other (risk of heart disease) decreases.

This same point is true for positive correlation. A positive correlation does not imply a "good" outcome; it just indicates that an increase in one variable predicts an increase in another. The more hours you study, the higher your grades represents a *positive* correlation, because as one variable (hours spent studying) increases, so does the other (grade on the test). However, "the more you smoke, the higher your risk of heart disease" is also a positive correlation. This is because as one factor (smoking) increases, so does the other (risk of heart disease).

Of course, it's quite possible that little or no relationship exists between two variables. For instance, we would probably not expect to find a relationship between number of study hours and height. Lack of a relationship would be indicated by a correlation close to 0. For example, if we found a correlation of −.02 or +.03, it would indicate that there is virtually no association between the two variables; knowing how much someone studies does not tell us anything about how tall he or she is. Sometimes finding no correlation between variables is an important research result. Canadian scientist Eric Fombonne and his research team at the Montréal Children's Hospital published an important study showing that there was no correlation between rates of autism and the measles-mumps-rubella (MMR) vaccine immunization schedule. This finding helps to refute the theory that there is a link between vaccines and autism.

When two variables are strongly correlated with each other, it is tempting to assume that one variable causes the other. For example, if we find that more study time is associated with higher grades, we might guess that more studying *causes* higher grades. Although this is not a bad guess, it remains just a guess—because finding that two variables are correlated does not mean that there is a causal relationship between them. The strong correlation suggests that knowing how much a person studies can help us predict how that person will do on a test, but it does not mean that the studying causes the test performance. It might be, for instance, that people who are more intelligent tend to study more than do those who are less intelligent, but that one's grades are actually determined by one's intelligence, not by amount of studying.

Another example illustrates the critical point that correlations tell us nothing about cause and effect but merely provide a measure of the strength of a relationship between two variables. For example, suppose that the students that sit in the front row tend to do better than students that sit in the back row. There is nothing magical about the front row that causes students to out-perform their back row peers. Just moving to the front row will not miraculously cause your grades to increase if you continue to sleep through class. The reality is that sitting in the front row is associated with other variables that do predict class performance: attendance, motivation, and so on.

Jenny McCarthy has said that autism is a "vaccine injury." Medical researchers beg to disagree.

Another example of the difficulty involved in separating correlation from causation is in the study of the association between violent television viewing and aggression. We might find that children who watch a lot of television programs featuring high levels of aggression are likely to demonstrate a relatively high degree of aggressive behaviour and that those who watch fewer violent television shows less likely to exhibit aggressive behaviour (see Figure 2). But we cannot say that the aggression is *caused* by the TV viewing, because several other explanations are possible: children who are already aggressive may prefer violent TV shows, or children with aggressive parents may be raised to be aggressive and be allowed to watch as much violent TV as they want.

FIGURE 2

If we find that frequent viewing of television programs with aggressive content is associated with high levels of aggressive behaviour, we might cite several plausible causes, as suggested in this figure. For example, choosing to watch shows with aggressive content could produce aggression (a); or being a highly aggressive person might cause one to choose to watch televised aggression (b); or having a poor or harsh parenting style might cause a person to both choose to watch aggressive shows and act aggressively (c). Correlational findings, then, do not permit us to determine causality. Can you think of a way to study the effects of televised aggression on aggressive behaviour that is not correlational?

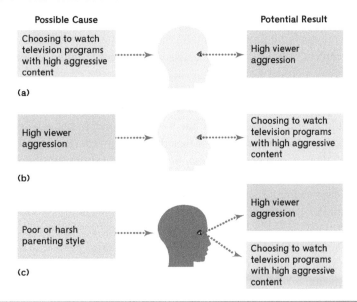

STUDY ALERT!

The concept that "correlation does not imply causation" is a key principle.

The inability of correlational research to demonstrate cause-and-effect relationships is a crucial drawback to its use. There is, however, an alternative technique that does establish causality: the experiment.

Experimental Research

The only way psychologists can establish cause-and-effect relationships through research is by carrying out an experiment. In a formal **experiment**, the relationship between two (or more) variables is investigated by deliberately changing one variable in a controlled situation and observing the effects of that change on other aspects of the situation. In an experiment, then, the conditions are created and controlled by the researcher, who deliberately makes a change in those conditions in order to observe the effects of that change.

Experiment
The investigation of the relationship between two (or more) variables by deliberately producing a change in one variable in a situation and observing the effects of that change on other aspects of the situation.

The change that the researcher deliberately makes in an experiment is called the **experimental manipulation**. Experimental manipulations are used to detect relationships between different variables.

Several steps are involved in carrying out an experiment, but the process typically begins with the development of one or more hypotheses for the experiment to test. For example, Latané and Darley (1970), in testing their theory of the diffusion of responsibility in bystander behaviour, developed this hypothesis: If a higher number of people witness an emergency situation, then the less likely it is that any of them will help the victim. They then designed an experiment to test this hypothesis.

Their first step was to formulate an operational definition of the hypothesis by conceptualizing it in a way that could be tested. Latané and Darley had to take into account the fundamental principle of experimental research mentioned earlier: Experimenters must manipulate at least one variable in order to observe the effects of the manipulation on another variable while keeping other factors in the situation constant. However, the manipulation cannot be viewed by itself, in isolation; if a cause-and-effect relationship is to be established, the effects of the manipulation must be compared with the effects of no manipulation. This gives you a baseline with which to compare your results and determine whether or not the independent variable had an effect.

Experimental Groups and Control Groups

Experimental research requires, then, that the responses of at least two groups be compared. One group will receive some special **treatment**—the manipulation implemented by the experimenter—and another group will receive either no treatment or a different treatment. Any group that receives a treatment is called an **experimental group**; a group that receives no treatment is called a **control group**.

By employing both experimental and control groups in an experiment, researchers are able to rule out the possibility that something other than the experimental manipulation produced the results observed in the experiment. For example, suppose we have a theory that hunger increases motivation, and we wanted to know whether being hungry made rats run a maze faster to find a food reward. We cannot say that the hungry rats (the experimental group) ran the maze quickly unless we can compare them with a control group. In this case, the control group would be rats that were not food-deprived. We would expect, if our hypothesis is correct, that the hungry rats (the experimental group) will run the maze faster than their non-hungry counterparts (the control group rats). Only if there is a significant difference between experimental and control groups can the effect of hunger assessed. Through the use of control groups, then, researchers can isolate specific causes for their findings—and draw cause-and-effect inferences.

Returning to Latané and Darley's experiment, we see that the researchers needed to translate their hypothesis into something testable. To do this, they decided to create a false emergency situation that would appear to require the aid of a bystander. As their experimental manipulation, they decided to vary the number of bystanders present. They could have had just one experimental group with, say, two people present, and a control group for comparison purposes with just one person present. Instead, they settled on a more complex procedure involving the creation of groups of three sizes—consisting of two, three, and six people—that could be compared with one another.

STUDY ALERT!

To remember the difference between dependent and independent variables, recall that a hypothesis predicts how a dependent variable depends on the manipulation of the independent variable.

Experimental manipulation
The change that an experimenter deliberately produces in a situation.

Treatment
The manipulation implemented by the experimenter.

Experimental group
Any group participating in an experiment that receives a treatment.

Control group
A group participating in an experiment that receives no treatment.

Independent and Dependent Variables

Latané and Darley's experimental design now included an operational definition of what is called the **independent variable**. The independent variable is the condition that is manipulated by an experimenter. (You can think of the independent variable as being independent of the actions of those taking part in an experiment; it is controlled by the experimenter.) In the case of the Latané and Darley experiment, the independent variable was the number of people present, which was manipulated by the experimenters.

The next step was to decide how they were going to determine the effect that varying the number of bystanders had on behaviour of those in the experiment. Crucial to every experiment is the **dependent variable**, the variable that is measured and is expected to change as a result of changes caused by the experimenter's manipulation of the independent variable. The dependent variable is dependent on the actions of the *participants or subjects*—the people taking part in the experiment.

Latané and Darley had several possible choices for their dependent measure. One might have been a simple yes/no measure of the participants' helping behaviour. But the investigators also wanted a more precise analysis of helping behaviour. Consequently, they also measured the amount of time it took for a participant to provide help.

Latané and Darley now had all the necessary components of an experiment. The independent variable, manipulated by them, was the number of bystanders present in an emergency situation. The dependent variable was the measure of whether bystanders in each of the groups provided help and the amount of time it took them to do so. Consequently, like all experiments, this one had both an independent variable and a dependent variable. (To remember the difference, recall that a hypothesis predicts how a dependent variable depends on the manipulation of the independent variable.) All true experiments in psychology fit this straightforward model.

Random Assignment of Participants

To make the experiment a valid test of the hypothesis, Latané and Darley needed to add a final step to the design: properly assigning participants to a particular experimental group.

The significance of this step becomes clear when we examine various alternative procedures. For example, the experimenters might have assigned just males to the group with two bystanders, just females to the group with three bystanders, and both males and females to the group with six bystanders. If they had done this, however, any differences they found in helping behaviour could not be attributed with any certainty solely to group size, because gender has now been introduced as a **confound**. A confound is any extraneous variable that could affect the dependent variable and therefore the validity of the experiment.

Participants in each of the experimental groups ought to be comparable, and it is easy enough to create groups that are similar in terms of gender. The problem becomes a bit trickier, though, when we consider other participant characteristics. How can we ensure that participants in each experimental group will be equally intelligent, extroverted, cooperative, and so forth, when the list of characteristics—any one of which could be important—is potentially endless?

The solution is a simple but elegant procedure called **random assignment to condition**: Participants are assigned to different experimental groups or "conditions" on the basis of chance and chance alone. The experimenter might, for instance, flip a coin for each participant and assign a participant to one group when "heads" came up, and to the other group when "tails" came up. The advantage of this technique is that participant characteristics have an equal chance of being distributed across the various groups. When a researcher uses random assignment it controls for

---

Independent variable
The variable that is manipulated by an experimenter.

Dependent variable
The variable that is measured and is expected to change as a result of changes caused by the experimenter's manipulation of the independent variable.

Confound
Any extraneous variable that could affect the dependent variable and therefore the validity of the experiment.

Random assignment to condition
A procedure in which participants are assigned to different experimental groups or "conditions" on the basis of chance and chance alone.

confounds because chances are that each of the groups will have approximately the same proportion of intelligent people, cooperative people, extroverted people, males and females, and so on.

Besides random assignment, experimenters must control for confounds by treating the experimental group and the control group in the same way in all respects other than the independent variable. So if a researcher is testing whether a vitamin improves memory, her experimental group will receive the vitamin, but her control group must receive a placebo or sugar pill that looks just like the vitamin.

Figure 3 provides another example of an experiment. Like all experiments, it includes the following set of key elements, which are important to keep in mind as you consider whether a research study is truly an experiment:

- An independent variable, the variable that is manipulated by the experimenter. In this case it is the drug propranolol (compared to a placebo).

- A dependent variable, the variable that is measured by the experimenter and that is expected to change as a result of the manipulation of the independent variable. In this example, the variables that the experimenters are measuring are heart rate and other indicators of heart disease.

- An experimental group (the monkeys receiving propranolol), which will be compared to a control group (the monkeys receiving the placebo).

- A procedure that randomly assigns participants to different experimental groups or "conditions" of the independent variable. The monkeys were randomly selected to be part of one group or another using a computer-generated random assignment protocol.

- A hypothesis that predicts the effect the independent variable will have on the dependent variable. The hypothesis in this experiment is that if propranolol is effective in preventing heart disease, then the monkeys taking propranolol should have lower heart rates and other indicators of heart disease than the monkeys taking the placebo. The results of this study showed this hypothesis to be correct.

FIGURE 3

In this depiction of a study investigating the effects of the drug propranolol on stress, we can see the basic elements of all true experiments. The participants in the experiment were monkeys, who were randomly assigned to one of two groups. Monkeys assigned to the treatment group were given a drug, propranolol, hypothesized to prevent heart disease, whereas those in the control group were not given the drug. Administration of the drugs, then, was the independent variable. All the monkeys were given a high-fat diet that was the human equivalent of two eggs with bacon every morning, and they occasionally were reassigned to different cages to provide a source of stress. To determine the effects of the drug, the monkeys' heart rates and other measures of heart disease were assessed after twenty-six months. These measures constituted the dependent variable. (The results? As hypothesized, monkeys that received the drug showed lower heart rates and fewer symptoms of heart disease than those who did not.)

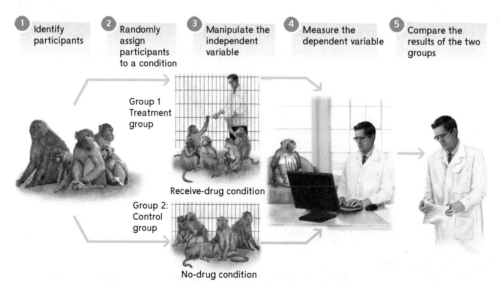

Source: Based on a study by Kaplan & Manuck, 1989.

Only if each of these elements is present can a research study be considered a true experiment in which cause-and-effect relationships can be determined. (For a summary of the different types of research that we've discussed, see Figure 4.)

FIGURE 4

Research strategies.

Research Method	Description	Advantages	Shortcomings
Descriptive and correlational research	Researcher observes a previously existing situation but does not make a change in the situation	Offers insight into relationships between variables	Cannot determine causality
Naturalistic observation	Observation of naturally occurring behaviour, without making a change in the situation	Provides a sample of people in their natural environment	Cannot control the "natural habitat" being observed
Survey research	A sample is chosen to represent a larger population and asked a series of questions	A small sample can be used to infer attitudes and behaviour of a larger population	Sample may not be representative of the larger population; participants may not provide accurate responses to survey questions
Case study	Intensive investigation of an individual or small group	Provides a thorough, in-depth understanding of participants	Results may not be generalizable beyond the sample
Experimental research	Investigator produces a change in one variable to observe the effects of that change on other variables	Experiments offer the only way to determine cause-and-effect relationships	To be valid, experiments require random assignment of participants to conditions, well-conceptualized independent and dependent variables, and other careful controls

Were Latané and Darley Right?

To test their hypothesis that increasing the number of bystanders in an emergency situation would lower the degree of helping behaviour, Latané and Darley placed the participants in a room and told them that the purpose of the experiment was to talk about personal problems associated with university. The discussion was to be held over an intercom, supposedly to avoid the potential embarrassment of face-to-face contact. Chatting about personal problems was not, of course, the true purpose of the experiment, but telling the participants that it was kept their expectations from biasing their behaviour. (Consider how they would have been affected if they had been told that their helping behaviour in emergencies was being tested. The experimenters could never have gotten an accurate assessment of what the participants would actually do in an emergency. By definition, emergencies are rarely announced in advance.)

The sizes of the discussion groups were two, three, and six people, which constituted the manipulation of the independent variable of group size. Participants were randomly assigned to these groups upon their arrival at the laboratory. Each group included a trained *confederate*, or employee, of the experimenters. In each two-person group, then, there was only one real "bystander"—the participant in the experiment.

As the participants in each group were holding their discussion, they suddenly heard through the intercom one of the other participants—the confederate—having what sounded like an epileptic seizure and calling for help.

The participant's behaviour was now what counted. The dependent variable was the time that elapsed from the start of the "seizure" to the time a participant began trying to help the "victim." If six minutes went by without a participant's offering help, the experiment was ended.

As predicted by the hypothesis, the size of the group had a significant effect on whether a participant provided help. The more people who were present, the less likely it was that someone would supply help, as you can see in Figure 5 (Latané & Darley, 1970).

Because these results are so straightforward, it seems clear that the experiment confirmed the original hypothesis. However, Latané and Darley could not be sure that the results were truly meaningful until they determined whether the

FIGURE 5

The Latané and Darley experiment showed that as the size of the group witnessing an emergency increased, helping behaviour decreased.

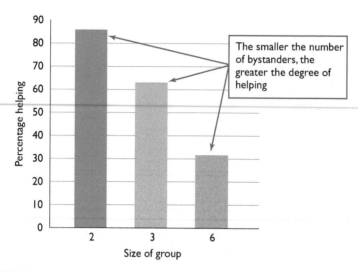

Source: Darley, J. M., & Latané, B. (1968). Bystanders intervention in emergencies: Diffusion of responsibility. *Journal of Personality and Social Psychology*, 8, 377–383. Copyright © 1968 American Psychological Association. Adapted with permission.

results represented a **significant outcome**. Using statistical analysis, researchers can determine whether a numeric difference is a real difference or is due merely to chance. Only when differences between groups are large enough that statistical tests show them to be significant is it possible for researchers to confirm a hypothesis (Cwikel, Behar, & Rabson-Hare, 2000; Cohen, 2002).

Moving Beyond the Study

The Latané and Darley study contains all the elements of an experiment: an independent variable, a dependent variable, random assignment to conditions, and multiple experimental groups. Consequently, we can say with some confidence that group size caused changes in the degree of helping behaviour.

Of course, one experiment alone does not forever resolve the question of bystander intervention in emergencies. Psychologists require that findings be replicated **(replicated research)**, or repeated, sometimes using other procedures, in other settings, with other groups of participants, before full confidence can be placed in the validity of any single experiment. A procedure called *meta-analysis* permits psychologists to combine the results of many separate studies into one overall conclusion (Tenenbaum & Ruck, 2007; Cooper & Patall, 2009).

Before leaving the Latané and Darley study, it's important to note that it represents a good illustration of the basic principles of the scientific method that we considered earlier (as outlined in Figure 1). The two psychologists began with a *question of interest,* in this case stemming from a real-world incident in which bystanders in an emergency did not offer help. They then *formulated an explanation* by specifying a theory of diffusion of responsibility, and from that formulated the specific hypothesis that increasing the number of bystanders in an emergency situation would lower the degree of helping behaviour. Finally, they *carried out research* to test their hypothesis. This three-step process embodied in the scientific method underlies all scientific inquiry, allowing us to develop a valid understanding of others'—and our own—behaviour.

Significant outcome
Meaningful results that make it possible for researchers to feel confident that they have confirmed their hypotheses.

Replicated research
Research that is repeated, sometimes using other procedures, settings, and groups of participants, to increase confidence in prior findings.

Evaluate

1. A reasonable explanation for existing and true facts is known as a _____.

2. To test this explanation, it must be stated in terms of a testable question in an if/then format. This if/then statement is known as a _____.

3. Match the following forms of research to their definition:

   (i) Naturalistic observation

   (ii) Survey research

   (iii) Case study

   a. Directly asking a sample of people questions about their behaviour

   b. Looking at behaviour in its true setting without intervening in the setting

   c. Doing an in-depth investigation of a person or small group

4. A psychologist wants to study the effect of caffeine on memory. He gives half his class caffeinated coffee, and the other half decaffeinated coffee. He then compares the two groups' results on their math test. Caffeine (versus decaf) would be the _____ variable, and the score on the test would be the _____ variable.

5. In the example in question 4 above, the students that receive the decaffeinated coffee are the _____ group.

Answers to Evaluate Questions

1. theory; 2. hypothesis; 3. (i)-b, (ii)-a, (iii)-c; 4. independent, dependent; 5. control

Key Terms

case study	experimental manipulation	scientific method
confound	hypothesis	significant outcome
control group	independent variable	survey research
correlational research	naturalistic observation	theories
dependent variable	operational definition	treatment
descriptive research	random assignment to	variables
experiment	condition	
experimental group	replicated research	

Research Challenges: Exploring the Process

LEARNING OBJECTIVES

LO10 **What** major issues confront psychologists conducting research?

You probably realize by now that there are few simple formulas for psychological research. Psychologists must make choices about the type of study to conduct, the measures to take, and the most effective way to analyze the results. Even after they have made these essential decisions, they must still consider several critical issues. We turn first to the most fundamental of these issues: ethics.

The Ethics of Research

Put yourself in the place of one of the participants in the experiment conducted by Latané and Darley to examine the helping behaviour of bystanders, in which another "bystander" simulating a seizure turned out to be a confederate of the experimenters (Latané & Darley, 1970). How would you feel when you learned that the supposed victim was in reality a paid accomplice?

Although you might at first experience relief that there had been no real emergency, you might also feel some resentment that you had been deceived by the experimenter. You might also experience concern that you had been placed in an embarrassing or compromising situation—one that might have dealt a blow to your self-esteem, depending on how you had behaved.

Most psychologists argue that deception is sometimes necessary to prevent participants from being influenced by what they think a study's true purpose is. (If you knew that Latané and Darley were actually studying your helping behaviour, wouldn't you automatically have been tempted to intervene in the emergency?) To avoid such outcomes, a small proportion of research involves deception.

STUDY ALERT!

Because protecting participants is so essential, it is important to understand the key ethical guideline of informed consent.

Nonetheless, because research has the potential to violate the rights of participants, psychologists are expected to adhere to a strict set of ethical guidelines aimed at protecting participants (CPA, 2000; APA, 2002). These guidelines involve the following safeguards:

- Protection of participants from physical and mental harm
- The right of participants to privacy regarding their behaviour
- The assurance that participation in research is completely voluntary
- The necessity of informing participants about the nature of procedures before their participation in the experiment

All experiments that use humans as participants must be reviewed by an independent panel before being conducted, including the minority of studies that involve deception (Fisher et al., 2002, 2003; Smith, 2003).

Most chapters include at least one section devoted to an aspect of racial, ethnic, gender, or cultural diversity. These features focus on the contributions of psychology to a better understanding of multicultural issues that are so central to our global society.

Exploring DIVERSITY

Choosing Participants Who Represent the Scope of Human Behaviour

When Latané and Darley, both university professors, decided who would participate in their experiment, they turned to the most available people: college and university students. In fact, college and university students are used so frequently in experiments that psychology has been called—somewhat contemptuously—the "science of the behaviour of the college sophomore" (Rubenstein, 1982).

Using college and university students as participants has both advantages and drawbacks. The big benefit is that because most research occurs in university settings, students are readily available. Typically, they cost the researcher very little: They participate for either extra course credit or a relatively small payment.

The problem is that college and university students may not represent the general population adequately. They tend to be younger and better educated than a significant percentage of the rest of the North American population. Compared with older adults, their attitudes are likely to be less well formed, and they are more apt to be influenced by authority figures and peers (Sears, 1986). College and university students are also disproportionately white and middle class (Graham, 1992).

Although similar, the Canadian Psychological Association (CPA) and the American Psychological Association (APA) codes of ethics remain as unique as the two countries. Sinclair (1998; CPA, 2000), an award-winning expert in the field of ethics, identified nine distinct features of the Canadian code of ethics. For example, one unique feature of the Canadian code is its assignment of different weights to each of the four ethical principles.

One of psychologists' key ethical principles is **informed consent**. Before participating in an experiment, the participants must sign a document affirming that they have been told the basic outlines of the study and are aware of what their participation will involve, what risks the experiment may hold, and the fact that their participation is purely voluntary and they may terminate it at any time. Furthermore, after participation in a study, they must be given a debriefing in which they receive an explanation of the study and the procedures involved. The only time informed consent and a debriefing can be eliminated is in experiments in which the risks are minimal, as in a purely observational study in a public place (Koocher, Norcross, & Hill, 2005; Fallon, 2006; Barnett et al., 2007).

Should Animals be Used in Research?

Like those who work with humans, researchers who use nonhuman animals in experiments have their own set of exacting guidelines to ensure that the animals do not suffer. Specifically, researchers must make every effort to minimize discomfort, illness, and pain. Procedures that subject animals to distress are permitted only when an alternative procedure is unavailable and when the research is justified by its prospective value. Moreover, there are federal regulations specifying how animals are to be housed, fed, and maintained. In the early 1980s, the Canadian Psychological Association published the first set of guidelines for care and research of animals. In 1982, Canadian Council on Animal Care (CCAC) was established to oversee all research involving animals in Canada. Not only must researchers strive to avoid causing physical discomfort, but they are also required to promote the *psychological well-being* of some species of research animals, such as primates (Novak & Petto, 1991; APA, 1993; Rusche, 2003; Lutz & Novak, 2005; Auer et al., 2007).

But why should animals be used for research in the first place? Is it really possible to learn about human behaviour from the results of research employing rats, gerbils, and pigeons?

Informed consent
A document signed by participants affirming that they have been told the basic outlines of the study and are aware of what their participation will involve.

Research involving animals is controversial but, when conducted within ethical guidelines, yields significant benefits for humans.

Source: © Douglas Faulner/Science Source.

The answer is that psychological research that employs nonhumans is designed to answer questions that are different from those posed in research with humans. For example, the shorter life span of animals (rats live an average of two years) allows researchers to learn about the effects of aging in a relatively short time frame. It is also possible to provide greater experimental control over nonhumans and to carry out procedures that might not be possible with people. For example, some studies require large numbers of participants that share similar backgrounds or have been exposed to particular environments—conditions that could not practically be met with human beings.

Research with animals has provided psychologists with information that has profoundly benefited humans. For instance, it furnished the keys to detecting eye disorders in children early enough to prevent permanent damage; to communicating more effectively with severely cognitively-impaired children; and to reducing chronic pain in humans. Still, the use of research using nonhumans is controversial, involving complex moral and philosophical concerns. Consequently, all research involving nonhumans must be carefully reviewed beforehand to ensure that it is conducted ethically (Saucier & Cain, 2006; Hackam, 2007; Shankar & Simmons, 2009).

Threats to Experiment Validity: Experimenter and Participant Expectations

Even the best-laid experimental plans are susceptible to **experimental bias**—factors that distort the way the independent variable affects the dependent variable in an experiment. One of the most common forms of experimental bias is *experimenter expectations:* An experimenter unintentionally transmits cues to participants about the way they are expected to behave in a given experimental condition. The danger is that those expectations will bring about an "appropriate" behaviour—one that otherwise might not have occurred (Rosenthal, 2002, 2003).

A related problem is *participant expectations* about appropriate behaviour. If you have ever been a participant in an experiment, you know that you quickly develop guesses about what is expected of you. In fact, it is typical for people to develop their own hypotheses about what the experimenter hopes to learn from the study. If participants form their own hypotheses, it may be the participant's expectations, rather than the experimental manipulation, that produce an effect.

STUDY ALERT!

It's important to know the main types of potential bias in experiments: experimenter expectations, participant expectations, and placebo effects.

To guard against participant expectations biasing the results of an experiment, the experimenter may try to disguise the true purpose of the experiment. Participants who do not know that helping behaviour is being studied, for example, are more apt to act in a "natural" way than they would if they knew.

Sometimes it is impossible to hide the actual purpose of research; when that is the case, other techniques are available to prevent bias. Suppose you were interested in testing the ability of a new drug to alleviate the symptoms of severe depression. If you simply gave the drug to half your participants and not to the other half, the participants who were given the drug might report feeling less depressed merely because they knew they were getting a drug. Similarly,

Experimental bias
Factors that distort how the independent variable affects the dependent variable in an experiment.

the participants who got nothing might report feeling no better because they knew that they were in a no-treatment control group.

To solve this problem, psychologists typically use a procedure in which all the participants receive a treatment, but those in the control group receive only a **placebo**, a false treatment, such as a pill, "drug," or other substance, that has no significant chemical properties or active ingredient. Because members of both groups are kept in the dark about whether they are getting a real or a false treatment, any differences in outcome can be attributed to the quality of the drug and not to the possible psychological effects of being administered a pill or other substance (Rajagopal, 2006; Crum & Langer, 2007).

However, there is one more safeguard that a careful researcher must apply in an experiment such as this. To overcome the possibility that *experimenter* expectations will affect the participant, the person who administers the drug shouldn't know whether it is actually the true drug or the placebo. By keeping both the participant and the experimenter who interacts with the participant "blind" to the nature of the drug that is being administered, researchers can more accurately assess the effects of the drug. This method is known as the *double-blind procedure*. The double-blind procedure represents the highest-standard of good experimental design.

One of the major goals of *Essentials of Understanding Psychology* is to make readers more informed, critical consumers of information relating to psychological issues. These discussions give you the tools to evaluate information concerning human behaviour that you may hear or read about in the media or on the Web.

Becoming an Informed Consumer of Psychology

Thinking Critically About Research

If you were about to purchase an automobile, it is unlikely that you would stop at the nearest car dealership and drive off with the first car a salesperson recommended. Instead, you would probably mull over the purchase, read about automobiles, consider the alternatives, talk to others about their experiences, and ultimately put in a fair amount of thought before you made such a major purchase.

In contrast, many of us are considerably less conscientious when we expend our intellectual, rather than financial, assets. People often jump to conclusions on the basis of incomplete and inaccurate information, and only rarely do they take the time to critically evaluate the research and data to which they are exposed.

Because the field of psychology is based on an accumulated body of research, it is crucial for psychologists to scrutinize thoroughly the methods, results, and claims of researchers. Yet it is not just psychologists who need to know how to evaluate research critically; all of us are constantly exposed to the claims of others. Knowing how to approach research and data can be helpful in areas far beyond the realm of psychology.

Several basic questions can help us sort through what is valid and what is not. Among the most important questions to ask are the following:

- *What was the purpose of the research?* Research studies should evolve from a clearly specified theory. Furthermore, we must take into account the specific hypothesis that is being tested. Unless we know what hypothesis is being examined, it is not possible to judge how successful a study has been.

- *How well was the study conducted?* Consider who the participants were, how many were involved, what methods were employed, and what problems the researcher encountered in collecting the data. There are important differences, for example, between a case study that reports the anecdotes of a handful of respondents and a survey that collects data from several thousand people.

- *Are the results presented fairly?* It is necessary to assess statements on the basis of the actual data they reflect and their logic. For instance, when the manufacturer of car X boasts that "no other car has a better safety record than car X," this does not mean that car X is safer than every other car. It just means that no other car has been proved safer, though many other cars could be just as safe as car X. Expressed in the latter fashion, the finding doesn't seem worth bragging about.

These three basic questions can help you assess the validity of research findings you come across—both within and outside the field of psychology. The more you know how to evaluate research in general, the better you will be able to assess what the field of psychology has to offer.

Placebo

A false treatment, such as a pill, "drug," or other substance, without any significant chemical properties or active ingredient.

Evaluate

1. Ethical research begins with the concept of informed consent. Before signing up to participate in an experiment, participants should be informed of

   a. The procedure of the study, stated generally

   b. The risks that may be involved

   c. Their right to withdraw at any time

   d. All of the above

2. A false treatment, such as a pill, that has no significant chemical properties or active ingredient, is known as a _____

3. According to a report, a study has shown that men differ from women in their preference for ice cream flavours. This study was based on a sample of two men and three women. What might be wrong with this study?

Answers to Evaluate Questions

1. d; 2. Placebo; 3. There are far too few participants. Without a larger sample, no valid conclusions can be drawn about ice cream preferences based on gender.

Key Terms

experimental bias	informed consent	placebo

Epilogue

Source: © Blend Images/Ariel Skelley/Getty Images RF.

The field of psychology is broad and diverse. It encompasses many different subfields and specialties practised in a variety of settings, with new subfields continually arising. We have also seen that even within the various subfields of the field, it is possible to adopt several different approaches, including the neuroscience, psychodynamic, behavioural, cognitive, and humanistic perspectives. For all its diversity, though, psychology focuses on certain key issues that serve to unify the field along common lines and shared findings.

Every chapter ends with *Recap/Rethink* segments—one for each module in the chapter. *Recap* sections review the key concepts found at the beginning of each module. The questions in the *Rethink* sections are designed to encourage you to think critically about a topic or issue, and they often have more than one correct answer.

Recap/Rethink

Module 1: Psychologists at Work

Recap

What is the science of psychology?

- Psychology is the scientific study of behaviour and mental processes, encompassing not just what people do but their biological activities, feelings, perceptions, memory, reasoning, and thoughts.

Where do psychologists work?

- Psychologists are employed in a variety of settings. Although the primary sites of employment are private practice and colleges and universities, many psychologists are found in hospitals, clinics, community mental health centres, and counselling centres.

Rethink

1. In many colleges, psychology is a required course in programs as diverse as Nursing, Police Foundations, Early Childhood Education, Behavioural Sciences, and Social Service Worker. Why do you think psychology is required in so many different programs? In what ways does the study of psychology make us better citizens, regardless of our occupational interests?

2. Do you think intuition and common sense are sufficient for understanding why people act the way they do? In what ways is a scientific approach appropriate for studying human behaviour?

Module 2: A Science Evolves: The Past, The Present, and The Future

Recap

What are the origins of psychology?

- Wilhelm Wundt laid the foundation of psychology in 1879, when he opened his laboratory in Germany.
- Early perspectives that guided the work of psychologists were structuralism and functionalism theory.

How did the history of psychology shape the major approaches in contemporary psychology?

- The neuroscience approach focuses on the biological components of the behaviour of people and animals.
- The psychodynamic perspective suggests that powerful, unconscious inner forces and conflicts about which people have little or no awareness are the primary determinants of behaviour.
- The behavioural perspective de-emphasizes internal processes and concentrates instead on observable, measurable behaviour, suggesting that understanding and control of a person's environment are sufficient to fully explain and modify behaviour.
- Cognitive approaches to behaviour consider how people know, understand, and think about the world.
- The humanistic perspective emphasizes that people are uniquely inclined toward psychological growth and higher levels of functioning and that they will strive to reach their full potential.

What are the important subfields in the field of psychology?

- Developmental psychologists study how people grow and change throughout the life span.
- Personality psychologists consider the consistency and change in an individual's behaviour, as well as the individual differences that distinguish one person's behaviour from another's.
- Health psychologists study psychological factors that affect physical disease, while clinical psychologists consider the study, diagnosis, and treatment of abnormal behaviour. Counselling psychologists focus on educational, social, and career adjustment problems.
- Social psychology is the study of how people's thoughts, feelings, and actions are affected by others.
- Cross-cultural psychology examines the similarities and differences in psychological functioning among various cultures.
- Other increasingly important fields are evolutionary psychology, behavioural genetics, and clinical neuropsychology.

Rethink

1. *From a journalist's perspective:* Choose a current major political controversy. What psychological approaches or perspectives can be applied to that issue?

2. *Especially for Early Childhood Education (ECE) students:* Suppose you are working with a 7-year-old child who is having unusual difficulty learning to read. Imagine that you could consult as many psychologists with different specialities that you wanted. What are the different types of psychologists that you might approach to address the problem?

3. What do *you* think are the major problems affecting society today? What are the psychological issues involved in these problems, and how might psychologists help find solutions to them?

Module 3: Research in Psychology

Recap

LO6 What is the scientific method?

- The scientific method is the approach psychologists use to understand behaviour. It consists of three steps: identifying questions of interest, formulating an explanation, and carrying out research that is designed to support or refute the explanation.

LO7 What role do theories and hypotheses play in psychological research?

- Research in psychology is guided by theories (plausible explanations for observable and existing facts) and hypotheses (predictions stated in a way that allows them to be tested).

LO8 What research methods do psychologists use?

- In naturalistic observation, the investigator acts mainly as an observer, making no change in a naturally occurring situation. In survey research, people are asked a series of questions about their behaviour, thoughts, or attitudes. The case study is an in-depth interview and examination of one person or group.
- These descriptive research methods rely on correlational techniques, which describe associations between variables but cannot determine cause-and-effect relationships.

LO9 How do psychologists establish cause-and-effect relationships using experiments?

- In a formal experiment, the relationship between variables is investigated by deliberately producing a change—called the experimental manipulation—in one variable and observing changes in the other variable.
- In an experiment, at least two groups must be compared to assess cause-and-effect relationships. The group receiving the treatment is the experimental group; the second group (which receives no treatment) is the control group.
- The variable that experimenters manipulate is the independent variable. The variable that they measure and expect to change as a result of manipulation of the independent variable is called the dependent variable.
- In an experiment, participants must be randomly assigned to either the experimental or control groups.
- Psychologists use statistical tests to determine whether research findings are significant.

Rethink

1. Can you describe how a researcher might use naturalistic observation, case studies, and survey research to investigate gender differences in aggressive behaviour at the workplace? First state a hypothesis and then describe your research approaches. What positive and negative features does each method have?

2. *Especially for Nursing students:* Tobacco companies have asserted that no experiment has ever proved that tobacco use causes cancer. Can you explain this claim in terms of the research procedures and designs discussed in this module? What sort of research would establish a cause-and-effect relationship between tobacco use and cancer? Is such a research study possible?

Module 4: Research Challenges: Exploring the Process

Recap

LO10 What major issues confront psychologists conducting research?

- One of the key ethical principles followed by psychologists is that of informed consent. Participants must be informed, before participation, about the basic outline of the experiment and the risks and potential benefits of their participation.

- Although the use of college and university students as participants has the advantage of easy availability, there are drawbacks too. For instance, students do not necessarily represent the population as a whole. The use of animals as participants may also have costs in terms of generalizability.
- Experiments are subject to a number of threats, or biases. Experimenter expectations can produce bias when an experimenter unintentionally transmits cues to participants about her or his expectations regarding their behaviour in a given experimental condition. Participant expectations can also bias an experiment. Among the tools experimenters use to help eliminate bias are placebos and double-blind procedures.

Rethink

1. A researcher strongly believes that university professors tend to show male students less attention and respect in the classroom than they show female students. She sets up an experimental study involving observations of classrooms in different conditions. In explaining the study to the professors and students who will participate, what steps should the researcher take to eliminate experimental bias based on both experimenter expectations and participant expectations?

CHAPTER 2
Neuroscience and Behaviour

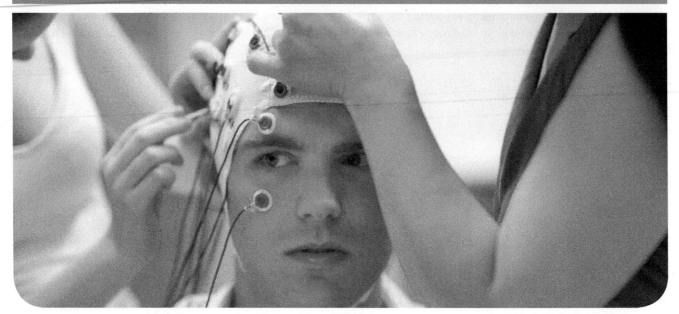

Source: © annedde/Getty Images RF.

Key Concepts for Chapter 2

MODULE 5   Neurons: The Basic Elements of Behaviour

LO1   Why do psychologists study the brain and the nervous system?

LO2   What are the basic elements of the nervous system?

LO3   How does the nervous system communicate electrical and chemical messages from one part to another?

The Structure of the Neuron

How Neurons Fire

> Applying Psychology in the Real World: *Mirror Mirror on the Wall: Mirror Neurons in the Brain*

Where Neurons Meet: Bridging the Gap

Neurotransmitters: Multitalented Chemical Couriers

MODULE 6   The Brain

LO4   How do researchers identify the major parts and functions of the brain?

LO5   What are the major parts of the brain, and for what behaviours is each part responsible?

LO6   How do the halves of the brain operate interdependently?

Studying the Brain's Structure and Functions: Spying on the Brain

The Hindbrain: Our "Reptilian Brain"

The Midbrain

The Forebrain

Neuroplasticity and the Brain

The Specialization of the Hemispheres: Two Brains or One?

The Split Brain: Exploring the Two Hemispheres

> Exploring Diversity: *Sex and the Brain*

MODULE 7   The Nervous System and the Endocrine System: Communicating Within the Body

LO7   How are the structures of the nervous system linked?

LO8   How does the endocrine system affect behaviour?

The Nervous System

The Endocrine System: Of Chemicals and Glands

Prologue

Canadian Crusader for Parkinson's Research

Source: © Theo Wargo/ Getty Images.

Canadian Michael J. Fox, was diagnosed with Parkinson's disease (PD) at the young age of 30. PD is a neurodegenerative disease that affects movement through the loss of dopamine-producing neurons (brain cells). Fox fought PD privately for seven years; this was a secret that was relatively easy to keep given that most people mistake Parkinson's for a "senior citizen's" disease. In actuality, as many as 1 in 10 individuals diagnosed with the disease are under the age of 40. Young-onset PD is the unique diagnosis made to this age group (Nussbaum & Ellis, 2003; Davis, 2007).

In 1998, Fox began his very public crusade to find a cure for the disease. The Michael J. Fox Foundation has raised more than $115 million for research and treatment of Parkinson's disease. In 2007, Fox received international recognition when nominated by *Time Magazine* as one of the world's Top 100 Heroes and Pioneers (Davis, 2007). On May 22, 2008, Michael J. Fox received an honorary degree from the University of British Columbia; an honour that "deeply moved and humbled" the BC born actor and Parkinson's advocate (Sinoski, 2008).

What does Parkinson's disease look like? What are the initial symptoms? How visible are they? Preliminary symptoms of PD include: tremors, rigidity, and slow movement that progressively deteriorate over time (Jung, 2004). As the disease progresses individuals with PD typically lose the ability to walk and eventually the ability to control all voluntary muscle movements.

What treatment options are available? Current treatments range from conservative, non-pharmacological treatments (e.g., speech therapy) to non-surgical options such as dopamine replacement medications (e.g., Levodopa) to surgical interventions (e.g., deep brain stimulation (DBS)). In DBS, surgeons implant a battery-operated neurostimulator that delivers tiny electric pulses to specific areas of the brain that control movement. The electrical stimulation blocks abnormal nerve signals that produce the symptoms of Parkinson's. Because DBS requires patients to be awake during the operation, patients are well aware of the procedure as it happens (Farkas, 2004; The Michael J. Fox Foundation, 2008). Stem cell research also is beginning to show some promising directions in the treatment of PD (Lunn et. al., 2011)).

Our brain's abilities are astounding. An organ roughly half the size of a loaf of bread, the brain controls our behaviour through every waking and sleeping moment. Our movements, thoughts, hopes, aspirations, dreams—our very awareness that we are human—all depend on the brain and the nerves that extend throughout the body, constituting the nervous system.

Because of the importance of the nervous system in controlling behaviour, and because humans at their most basic level are biological beings, many researchers in psychology and other fields as diverse as computer science, zoology, and medicine have made the biological underpinnings of behaviour their specialty. These experts collectively are called *neuroscientists* (Beatty, 2000; Posner & DiGiorlamo, 2000; Gazzaniga, Ivry, & Mangun, 2002).

Psychologists who specialize in considering the ways in which the biological structures and functions of the body affect behaviour are known as **behavioural neuroscientists (or biopsychologists).** They seek to answer several key questions: How does the brain control the voluntary and involuntary functioning of the body? How does the brain communicate with other parts of the body? What is the physical structure of the brain, and how does this structure affect behaviour? Are psychological disorders caused by biological factors, and how can such disorders be treated?

As you consider the biological processes that we'll discuss in this chapter, it is important to keep in mind why behavioural neuroscience is an essential part of psychology: our understanding of human behaviour requires knowledge of the brain and other parts of the nervous system. Biological factors are central to our sensory experiences, states of consciousness, motivation and emotion, development throughout the life span, and physical and psychological health. Furthermore, advances in behavioural neuroscience have led to the creation of drugs and other treatments for psychological and physical disorders, including PD. In short, we cannot understand behaviour without understanding our biological makeup (Kosslyn et al., 2002; Plomin, 2003; Compagni & Manderscheid, 2006).

Behavioural neuroscientists (or biopsychologists)
Psychologists who specialize in considering the ways in which the biological structures and functions of the body affect behaviour.

Neurons: The Basic Elements of Behaviour

LEARNING OBJECTIVES

LO1 **Why do** psychologists study the brain and the nervous system?

LO2 **What are** the basic elements of the nervous system?

LO3 **How does** the nervous system communicate electrical and chemical messages from one part to another?

Watching Mike Weir hit a golf ball, Serena Williams hit a stinging backhand, DeMar DeRozan make an impossible shot, or Carey Price stop a flying puck, you may have marvelled at the complexity—and wondrous abilities—of the human body. But even the most everyday tasks, such as picking up a pencil, writing, and speaking, depend on a sophisticated sequence of events in the body that is itself truly impressive. For instance, the difference between saying the words *dime* and *time* rests primarily on whether the vocal cords are relaxed or tense during a period lasting no more than one one-hundredth of a second, yet it is a distinction that most of us can make with ease.

The nervous system is the pathway for the instructions that permit our bodies to carry out such precise activities. Here we will look at the structure and function of neurons, the cells that make up the nervous system, including the brain.

The Structure of the Neuron

Playing the piano, driving a car, or hitting a tennis ball depends, at one level, on exact muscle coordination. But if we consider *how* the muscles can be activated so precisely, we see that there are more fundamental processes involved. For the muscles to produce the complex movements that make up any meaningful physical activity, the brain has to provide the right messages to them and coordinate those messages.

Such messages—as well as those which enable us to think, remember, and experience emotion—are passed through specialized cells called neurons. **Neurons**, or nerve cells, are the basic elements of the nervous system. Their quantity is staggering—perhaps as many as 100 billion neurons in the human brain and 1 *trillion* neurons throughout the body are involved in the control of behaviour (Boahen, 2005).

STUDY ALERT!

Remember that dendrites detect messages from other neurons; axons carry signals away from the cell body.

Although there are several types of neurons, they all have a similar structure, as illustrated in Figure 1. Like most cells in the body, neurons have a cell body that contains a nucleus. The nucleus incorporates the hereditary material that determines how a cell will function. Neurons are physically held in place by *glial cells*. Glial cells provide nourishment to neurons, insulate them, help repair damage, and generally support neural functioning (Kettenmann & Ransom, 2005; Fields, 2004).

In contrast to most other cells, however, neurons have a distinctive feature: the ability to communicate with other cells and transmit information across relatively long distances. Many of the body's neurons receive signals from the

Neurons
Nerve cells, the basic elements of the nervous system.

FIGURE 1

The primary components of the specialized cell called the neuron, the basic element of the nervous system (Van De Graaff, 2000). A neuron, like most types of cells in the body, has a cell body and a nucleus, but it also contains structures that carry messages: the dendrites, which receive messages from other neurons, and the axon, which carries messages to other neurons or body cells. In this neuron, as in most neurons, the axon is protected by the sausage-like myelin sheath. What advantages does the tree-like structure of the neuron provide?

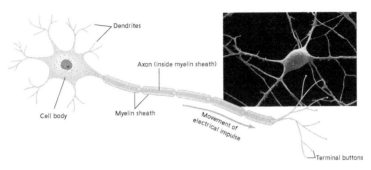

Source: From *Human Anatomy*, 5th edition, by K. Van DeGraaff, p. 339. Copyright © 2000 by McGraw-Hill Education. Photo: © David McCarthy/Science Source.

environment or relay the nervous system's messages to muscles and other target cells, but the vast majority of neurons communicate only with other neurons in the elaborate information system that regulates behaviour.

As you can see in Figure 1, a neuron has a cell body with a cluster of fibres called **dendrites** at one end. Those fibres, which look like the twisted branches of a tree, receive messages from other neurons. On the opposite end of the cell body is a long, slim, tube-like extension called an **axon**. The axon carries messages received by the dendrites to other neurons. The axon is considerably longer than the rest of the neuron. Although most axons are several millimetres in length, some are as long as a metre. Axons end in small bulges called **terminal buttons**, which send messages to other neurons.

The messages that travel within a neuron are electrical in nature. Although there are exceptions, those electrical messages, or *impulses*, generally move across neurons in one direction only, as if they were travelling on a one-way street. Impulses follow a route that begins with the dendrites, continues into the cell body, and leads ultimately along the tube-like extension, the axon, to adjacent neurons. *D*endrites, then, *d*etect messages from other neurons; *a*xons carry signals *a*way from the cell body.

Most axons are insulated by a **myelin sheath**, a protective coat of fat and protein that wraps around the axon like links of sausage. This protective coat literally speeds up our thinking by allowing the electrical impulses to move more quickly down the neuron.

Since the myelin sheath also serves to increase the velocity with which electrical impulses travel through axons, it is those axons that carry the most important and most urgently required information that have the greatest concentrations of myelin. If your hand touches a hot stove, for example, the information regarding the pain is passed through axons in the hand and arm that have a relatively thick coating of myelin, speeding the message of pain to the brain so that you can react instantly. In certain diseases, such as multiple sclerosis, the myelin sheath surrounding the axon deteriorates, exposing parts of the axon that are normally covered. This short-circuits messages between the brain and muscles and results in symptoms such as the inability to walk, difficulties with vision, and general muscle impairment.

Dendrites
A cluster of fibres at one end of a neuron that receives messages from other neurons.

Axon
The part of the neuron that carries messages destined for other neurons.

Terminal buttons
Small bulges at the end of axons that send messages to other neurons.

Myelin sheath
A protective coat of fat and protein that wraps around the axon.

How Neurons Fire

Like a gun, neurons either fire—that is, transmit an electrical impulse along the axon—or don't fire. There is no in-between stage, just as pulling harder on a gun trigger doesn't make the bullet travel faster. Similarly, neurons follow an **all-or-none law**: They are either on or off, with nothing in between the on state and the off state. Once there is enough force to pull the trigger, a neuron fires.

Before a neuron is triggered—that is, when it is in a **resting state**—it has a negative electrical charge of about 70 millivolts (a millivolt is one one-thousandth of a volt). This charge is caused by the presence of more negatively charged ions within the neuron than outside it. (An ion is an atom that is electrically charged.) You might think of the neuron as a miniature battery in which the inside of the neuron represents the negative pole and the outside represents the positive pole.

When a message arrives at a neuron, its cell membrane opens briefly to allow positively charged ions to rush in at rates as high as 100 million ions per second. The sudden arrival of these positive ions causes the charge within the nearby part of the cell to change momentarily from negative to positive. When the positive charge reaches a critical level, the "trigger" is pulled, and an electrical impulse, known as an action potential, travels along the axon of the neuron (see Figure 2).

FIGURE 2

Movement of an action potential across an axon. Just before Time 1, positively charged ions enter the cell membrane, changing the charge in the nearby part of the neuron from negative to positive and triggering an action potential. The action potential travels along the axon, as illustrated in the changes occurring from Time 1 to Time 3 (from top to bottom in this drawing). Immediately after the action potential has passed through a section of the axon, positive ions are pumped out, restoring the charge in that section to negative. The change in voltage illustrated at the top of the axon can be seen in greater detail in Figure 3. (Source: Stevens, 1979.)

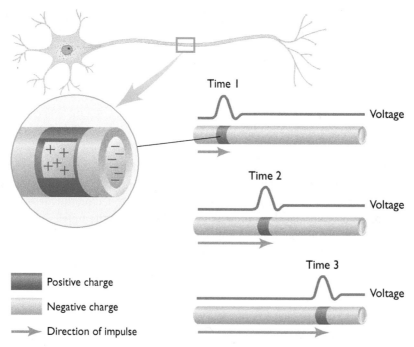

Source: From C. F. Stevens, "The Neuron" *Scientific American*, September 1979, page 56. Reprinted with permission of Carol Donner.

All-or-none law
The rule that neurons are either on or off.

Resting state
The state in which there is a negative electrical charge of about −70 millivolts within a neuron.

The **action potential** moves from one end of the axon to the other like a flame moving along a fuse. As the impulse travels along the axon, the movement of ions causes a change in charge from negative to positive in successive sections of the axon (see Figure 3). After the impulse has passed through a particular section of the axon, positive ions are pumped out of that section, and its charge returns to negative while the action potential continues to move along the axon.

FIGURE 3

Changes in the electrical charge in a neuron during the passage of an action potential. In its normal resting state, a neuron has a negative charge. When an action potential is triggered, however, the charge becomes positive, increasing from around −70 millivolts to about +40 millivolts. Following the passage of the action potential, the charge becomes even more negative than it is in its typical state. It is not until the charge returns to its resting state that the neuron will be fully ready to be triggered once again. (Source: Mader, 2000.)

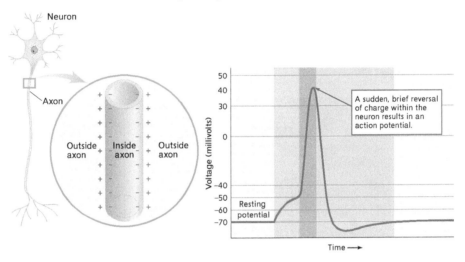

Source: From *Human Biology*, 6th edition, by S. Mader, page 250. Copyright © 2000 by McGraw-Hill Education.

Just after an action potential has passed through a section of the axon, the cell membrane in that region cannot admit positive ions again for a few milliseconds, and so a neuron cannot fire again immediately no matter how much stimulation it receives. It is as if the gun has to be reloaded after each shot. There then follows a period in which, though it is possible for the neuron to fire, a stronger stimulus is needed than would be needed if the neuron had reached its normal resting state. Eventually, though, the neuron is ready to fire once again.

These complex events can occur at dizzying speeds, although there is great variation among different neurons. The particular speed at which an action potential travels along an axon is determined by the axon's size and the thickness of its myelin sheath. Axons with small diameters carry impulses at about 3 km per hour; longer and thicker ones can average speeds of more than 360 km per hour.

Neurons differ not only in terms of how quickly an impulse moves along the axon but also in their potential rate of firing. Some neurons are capable of firing as many as a thousand times per second; others fire at much slower rates. The intensity of a stimulus determines how much of a neuron's potential firing rate is reached. A strong stimulus, such as a bright light or a loud sound, leads to a higher rate of firing than a less intense stimulus does. Thus, even though all impulses move at the same strength or speed through a particular axon—because of the all-or-none law—there is variation in the frequency of impulses, providing a mechanism by which we can distinguish the tickle of a feather from the weight of someone standing on our toes.

The structure, operation, and functions of the neuron are fundamental biological aspects of the body that underlie several primary psychological processes. Our understanding of the way we sense, perceive, and learn about the world would be greatly restricted without the knowledge about the neuron that behavioural neuroscientists and other researchers have acquired.

Action potential
An electric nerve impulse that travels through a neuron's axon when it is set off by a "trigger," changing the neuron's charge from negative to positive.

APPLYING PSYCHOLOGY   in the Real World

Mirror Mirror on the Wall: Mirror Neurons in the Brain

Although all neurons operate through the firing of action potentials, there is significant specialization among different types of neurons. For example, in the last decade, neuroscientists have discovered the existence of **mirror neurons**, neurons that fire not only when a person enacts a particular behaviour but also when a person simply observes *another* individual carrying out the same behaviour (Falck-Ytter & Gredebäck, 2006; Lepage & Theoret, 2007; Schulte-Ruther et al., 2007).

Mirror neurons may help explain how (and why) humans have the capacity to understand others' intentions. Specifically, mirror neurons may fire when we view someone doing something, helping us to predict what their goals are and what they may do next.

The discovery of mirror neurons suggests that the capacity of even young children to imitate others may be an inborn behaviour. Furthermore, mirror neurons may be at the root of empathy—those feelings of concern, compassion, and sympathy for others—and even the development of language in humans (Triesch, Jasso, & Deák, 2007; Iacoboni, 2009; Ramachandran, 2009).

Autism is a developmental disability most distinctively characterized by deficits in social skills and social understanding. Some studies have shown disruption of the mirror neuron system in individuals with autism (Perkins et al., 2010). This new evidence may lead to a deeper understanding of the development and even treatment of autism (Rizzolatti, Fabbri-Destro, & Cattaneo, 2009).

Mirror neurons become active when an animal observes another. This may account for how social behaviour is learned.

Source: © L Turay/iStockphoto.com.

Where Neurons Meet: Bridging the Gap

If you have ever looked inside a computer, you've seen that each part is physically connected to another part. In contrast, evolution has produced a neural transmission system that at some points has no need for a structural connection between its components. Instead, a chemical connection bridges the gap, known as a synapse, between two neurons (see Figure 4). The **synapse** is the space between two neurons where the axon of a sending neuron communicates with the dendrites of a receiving neuron by using chemical messages (Fanselow & Poulos, 2005; Dean & Dresbach, 2006).

Mirror neurons
Neurons that fire when a person enacts a particular behaviour and when a person observes *another* individual carrying out the same behaviour.

Synapse
The space between two neurons where the axon of a sending neuron communicates with the dendrites of a receiving neuron by using chemical messages.

(a) A synapse is the junction between an axon and a dendrite. The gap between the axon and the dendrite is bridged by chemicals called neurotransmitters (Mader, 2000). (b) Just as the pieces of a jigsaw puzzle can fit in only one specific location in a puzzle, each kind of neurotransmitter has a distinctive configuration that allows it to fit into a specific type of receptor cell (Johnson, 2000). Why is it advantageous for axons and dendrites to be linked by temporary chemical bridges rather than by the hard wiring typical of a radio connection or telephone hookup?

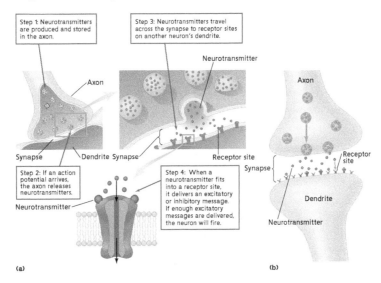

Step 1: Neurotransmitters are produced and stored in the axon.

Step 3: Neurotransmitters travel across the synapse to receptor sites on another neuron's dendrite.

Neurotransmitter

Axon

Synapse   Dendrite Synapse   Receptor site

Step 2: If an action potential arrives, the axon releases neurotransmitters.

Neurotransmitter

Step 4: When a neurotransmitter fits into a receptor site, it delivers an excitatory or inhibitory message. If enough excitatory messages are delivered, the neuron will fire.

Axon

Receptor site

Synapse

Dendrite

Neurotransmitter

(a)   (b)

Sources: Figure 4a: From *Human Biology*, 6th edition, by S. Mader, page 250. Copyright ©2000 by McGraw-Hill Education. Figure 4b: From *The Living World*, 2nd edition, by G. B. Johnson, page 600. Copyright © 2000 by McGraw-Hill Education.

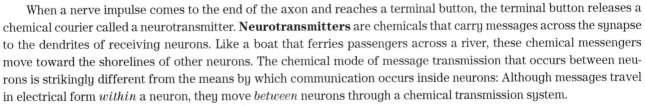

STUDY ALERT!

Remember this key fact: Messages travelling within neurons are transmitted in electrical form, whereas messages travelling between neurons travel via chemical means.

When a nerve impulse comes to the end of the axon and reaches a terminal button, the terminal button releases a chemical courier called a neurotransmitter. **Neurotransmitters** are chemicals that carry messages across the synapse to the dendrites of receiving neurons. Like a boat that ferries passengers across a river, these chemical messengers move toward the shorelines of other neurons. The chemical mode of message transmission that occurs between neurons is strikingly different from the means by which communication occurs inside neurons: Although messages travel in electrical form *within* a neuron, they move *between* neurons through a chemical transmission system.

There are several types of neurotransmitters, and not all neurons are capable of receiving the chemical message carried by a particular neurotransmitter. In the same way that a jigsaw puzzle piece can fit in only one specific location in a puzzle, each kind of neurotransmitter has a distinctive configuration that allows it to fit into a specific type of receptor site on the receiving neuron (see Figure 4b). It is only when a neurotransmitter fits precisely into a receptor site that successful chemical communication is possible.

If a neurotransmitter does fit into a site on the receiving neuron, the chemical message it delivers is basically one of two types: excitatory or inhibitory. **Excitatory messages** make it *more* likely that a receiving neuron will fire and

Neurotransmitters
Chemicals that carry messages across the synapse to the dendrite (and sometimes the cell body) of a receiver neuron.

Excitatory messages
A chemical message that makes it more likely that a receiving neuron will fire and an action potential will travel down its axon.

an action potential will travel down its axon. **Inhibitory messages**, in contrast, do just the opposite; they provide chemical information that make it *less* likely that the receiving neuron will fire (Mel, 2002).

If neurotransmitters remained at the site of the synapse, receiving neurons would be awash in a continual chemical bath, producing constant stimulation of the receiving neurons—and effective communication across the synapse would no longer be possible. To solve this problem, once neurotransmitters have passed along their chemical message they are either deactivated by enzymes or—more commonly—reabsorbed by the terminal button in an example of chemical recycling called **reuptake**. Like a vacuum cleaner sucking up dust, neurons reabsorb the neurotransmitters that are now clogging the synapse. All this activity occurs at lightning speed, with the process taking just several milliseconds (Helmuth, 2000; Holt & Jahn, 2004).

Our understanding of the process of reuptake has permitted the development of a number of drugs used in the treatment of psychological disorders. As we'll discuss later in the book, some antidepressant drugs, called *SSRIs* or *selective serotonin reuptake inhibitors*, permit certain neurotransmitters to remain active for a longer period at certain synapses in the brain, thereby reducing the symptoms of depression. Prozac, Zoloft, Lexapro, Celexa and many other antidepressants are examples of SSRIs.

Neurotransmitters: Multitalented Chemical Couriers

Neurotransmitters are a particularly important link between the nervous system and behaviour. Not only are they important for maintaining vital brain and body functions, a deficiency or an excess of a neurotransmitter can produce severe behaviour disorders. More than a hundred chemicals have been found to act as neurotransmitters, and neuroscientists believe that more may ultimately be identified (Penney, 2000; Schmidt, 2006).

Neurotransmitters vary significantly in terms of how strong their concentration must be to trigger a neuron to fire. Furthermore, the effects of a particular neurotransmitter vary, depending on the area of the nervous system in which it is produced. The same neurotransmitter, then, can act as an excitatory message to a neuron located in one part of the brain and can inhibit firing in neurons located in another part. (The major neurotransmitters and their effects are described in Figure 5.)

FIGURE 5

Major neurotransmitters.

Neurotransmitter Name	Location	Effect	Function
Acetylcholine (ACh)	Brain, spinal cord, peripheral nervous system, especially some organs of the parasympathetic nervous system	Excitatory in brain and autonomic nervous system; inhibitory elsewhere	Muscle movement, cognitive functioning
Glutamate	Brain, spinal cord	Excitatory	Memory
Gamma-amino butyric acid (GABA)	Brain, spinal cord	Main inhibitory neurotransmitter	Eating, aggression, sleeping
Dopamine (DA)	Brain	Inhibitory or excitatory	Movement control, pleasure and reward, attention
Serotonin	Brain, spinal cord	Inhibitory	Sleeping, eating, mood, pain, depression
Endorphins	Brain, spinal cord	Primarily inhibitory, except in hippocampus	Pain suppression, pleasurable feelings, appetites, placebos

Dopamine pathways

Serotonin pathways

Inhibitory messages
A chemical message that prevents or decreases the likelihood that a receiving neuron will fire.

Reuptake
The reabsorption of neurotransmitters by a terminal button.

One of the most common neurotransmitters is *acetylcholine* (or ACh, its chemical symbol), which is found throughout the nervous system. ACh is involved in our every move, because—among other things—it transmits messages relating to our skeletal muscles. ACh is also involved in memory capabilities, and diminished production of ACh may be related to Alzheimer's disease (Mohapel et al., 2005; Bazalakova et al., 2007).

Another common excitatory neurotransmitter, *glutamate*, plays a role in memory. Memories appear to be produced by specific biochemical changes at particular synapses, and glutamate, along with other neurotransmitters, plays an important role in this process (Riedel, Platt, & Micheau, 2003; Winters & Bussey, 2005; Carvalho et al., 2006).

Gamma-amino butyric acid (GABA), which is found in both the brain and the spinal cord, appears to be the nervous system's primary inhibitory neurotransmitter. It moderates a variety of behaviours, ranging from eating to aggression. Several common substances, such as the tranquilizer Valium and alcohol, are effective because they permit GABA to operate more efficiently (Ball, 2004; Criswell et al., 2008; Lobo & Harris, 2008).

Another major neurotransmitter is *dopamine (DA),* which is involved in movement, attention, and learning. The discovery that certain drugs can have a significant effect on dopamine release has led to the development of effective treatments for a wide variety of physical and mental ailments. For instance, Parkinson's disease, from which actor Michael J. Fox suffers, is caused by a deficiency of dopamine in the brain. Techniques for increasing the production of dopamine in Parkinson's patients are proving effective (Willis, 2005; Antonini & Barone, 2008).

In other instances, *over*production of dopamine produces negative consequences. For example, researchers have hypothesized that schizophrenia and some other severe mental disturbances are affected or perhaps even caused by the presence of unusually high levels of dopamine. Drugs that block the reception of dopamine reduce the symptoms displayed by some people diagnosed with schizophrenia (Di Forti, Lappin, & Murray, 2007; Murray, Lappin, & Di Forti, 2008; Howes & Kapur, 2009). Anti-psychotic drugs like Seroquel, Risperdal, and Zyprexa work in this way.

Another neurotransmitter, *serotonin,* is associated with the regulation of sleep, eating, mood, and pain. A growing body of research points toward a broader role for serotonin, suggesting its involvement in such diverse behaviours as alcoholism, depression, suicide, impulsivity, aggression, and coping with stress (Murray, Lappin, & Di Forti, 2008; Popa et al., 2008; Carrillo et al., 2009).

Endorphins, another class of neurotransmitters, are a family of chemicals produced by the brain that are similar in structure to painkilling drugs such as morphine. The production of endorphins seems to reflect the brain's effort to deal with pain as well as to elevate mood (Pert, 2002).

Evaluate

1. The _____ is the fundamental element of the nervous system.
2. Neurons receive information through their _____ and send messages through their _____.
3. Just as electrical wires have an outer coating, axons are insulated by a coating called the _____.
4. The chemical "messengers" that allow for communication between neurons are called _____.

Answers to Evaluate Questions

1. neuron; 2. dendrites, axons; 3. myelin sheath; 4. neurotransmitters.

Key Terms

action potential	excitatory messages	resting state
all-or-none law	inhibitory messages	reuptake
axon	mirror neurons	synapse
behavioural neuroscientists (or biopsychologists)	myelin sheath	terminal buttons
	neurons	
dendrites	neurotransmitters	

The Brain

LEARNING OBJECTIVES

LO4 **How do** researchers identify the major parts and functions of the brain?

LO5 **What are** the major parts of the brain, and for what behaviours is each part responsible?

LO6 **How do** the halves of the brain operate interdependently?

Our brain is not much to look at. Soft, spongy, mottled, and pinkish-grey in colour, it hardly can be said to possess much in the way of physical beauty. Despite its physical appearance, however, it ranks as the greatest natural marvel that we know and has a beauty and sophistication all its own.

The brain is responsible for our loftiest thoughts—and our most primitive urges. It is the overseer of the intricate workings of the human body. If one were to attempt to design a computer to mimic the range of capabilities of the brain, the task would be impossible; in fact, it has proved difficult even to come close. The sheer quantity of nerve cells in the brain is enough to daunt even the most ambitious computer engineer. Many billions of neurons make up a structure weighing just 1.3 kg in the average adult. However, it is not the number of cells that is the most astounding thing about the brain but its ability to allow the human intellect to flourish by guiding our behaviour and thoughts.

We turn now to a consideration of the particular structures of the brain and the primary functions to which they are related. However, a caution is in order. Although we'll discuss specific areas of the brain in relation to specific behaviours, this approach is an oversimplification. No simple one-to-one correspondence exists between a distinct part of the brain and a particular behaviour. Instead, behaviour is produced by complex interconnections among sets of neurons in many areas of the brain: Our behaviour, emotions, thoughts, hopes, and dreams are produced by a variety of neurons throughout the nervous system working in concert.

Studying the Brain's Structure and Functions: Spying on the Brain

The brain has posed a continual challenge to those who would study it. For most of history, its examination was possible only after an individual had died. Only then could the skull be opened and the brain cut into without serious injury. Although informative, this procedure could hardly tell us much about the functioning of the healthy brain.

Today, however, brain-scanning techniques provide a window into the living brain. Using these techniques, investigators can obtain an image of the internal workings of the brain without having to cut open a person's skull. The most important scanning techniques, illustrated in Figure 1, are the electroencephalogram (EEG), positron emission tomography (PET), functional magnetic resonance imaging (fMRI), and transcranial magnetic stimulation imaging (TMS).

The *electroencephalogram (EEG)* records electrical activity in the brain through electrodes placed on the outside of the skull. Although traditionally the EEG could produce only a graph of electrical wave patterns, new techniques are now used to transform the brain's electrical activity into a pictorial representation of the brain that, as a result of

STUDY ALERT!

Remember that EEG, fMRI, PET, and TMS differ in terms of whether they examine brain *structures* or brain *functioning*.

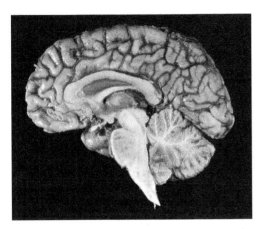

The brain (shown here in cross section) may not be much to look at, but it represents one of the great marvels of human development. Why do most scientists believe that it will be difficult, if not impossible, to duplicate the brain's abilities?

Source: © Martin Rotker/Science Source.

their greater detail, allows more precise diagnosis of disorders such as epilepsy and learning disabilities.

Positron emission tomography (PET) scans show biochemical activity within the brain at a given moment. PET scans begin with the injection of a radioactive (but safe) liquid into the bloodstream, which makes its way to the brain. By locating radiation within the brain, a computer can determine which are the more active regions, providing a striking picture of the brain at work. For example, PET scans may be used in cases of memory problems, seeking to identify the presence of brain tumours (Gronholm et al., 2005; McMurtray et al., 2007).

Functional magnetic resonance imaging (fMRI) scans provide a detailed, three-dimensional computer-generated image of brain structures and activity by aiming a powerful magnetic field at the body. With fMRI scanning, it is possible to produce vivid, detailed images of the functioning of the brain.

Using fMRI scans, researchers are able to view features of less than a millimetre in size and view changes occurring in intervals of one-tenth of a second. For example, fMRI scans can show the operation of individual bundles of nerves by tracing the flow of blood, opening the way for improved diagnosis of ailments ranging from chronic back pain to nervous system disorders such as strokes, multiple sclerosis, and Alzheimer's. Scans using fMRI are routinely used in planning brain surgery, because they can help surgeons distinguish areas of the brain involved in normal and disturbed functioning. In addition, fMRI scans have become a valuable research tool in a variety of areas of psychology, ranging from better understanding thinking, and memory to learning about the development of language (Knops et al., 2005; Mazard et al., 2005; Quenot et al., 2005).

Transcranial magnetic stimulation (TMS) is one of the newest types of scans. By exposing a tiny region of the brain to a strong magnetic field, TMS causes a momentary interruption of electrical activity. Researchers then are able to note the effects of this interruption on normal brain functioning. The procedure is sometimes called a "virtual lesion" because it produces effects analogous to what would occur if areas of the brain were physically cut. The enormous advantage of TMS, of course, is that the virtual cut is only temporary.

In addition to identifying areas of the brain that are responsible for particular functions, TMS has the potential to treat certain kinds of psychological disorders, such as depression and schizophrenia, by shooting brief magnetic pulses through the brain. Also, TMS might be used on patients who have suffered brain damage due to a stroke. TMS has the potential to activate undamaged areas of the brain to take over the functions of the damaged areas (Fitzgerald & Daskalakis, 2008; Rado, Dowd, & Janicak, 2008; Pallanti & Bernardi, 2009).

FIGURE 1

Brain scanning techniques. (a) A computer-produced EEG image. (b) The fMRI scan uses a magnetic field to provide a detailed view of brain activity on a moment-by-moment basis. (c) Transcranial magnetic stimulation (TMS), the newest type of scan, produces a momentary disruption in an area of the brain, allowing researchers to see what activities are controlled by that area. TMS also has the potential to treat some psychological disorders. (d) The PET scan displays the functioning of the brain at a given moment.

(a) EEG

(b) fMRI scan

(c) TMS apparatus

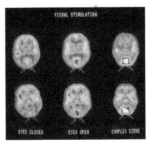

(d) PET scan

Sources: (a): © SPL/Science Source; (b): © Volker Steger/Peter Arnold; (c): © Garo/Phanie/Science Source; (d): © Bryan Christie Design.

The Hindbrain: Our "Reptilian Brain"

Although the capabilities of the human brain may exceed those of the brain of any other species, humans share some basic functions, such as breathing, eating, and sleeping, with all other animals. Not surprisingly, those activities are directed by a relatively primitive part of the brain. A portion of the brain known as the **hindbrain** coordinates signals coming into and out of the spinal cord. This part of the brain is not that different than in any other vertebrates (species with backbones), which is why it is sometimes referred to as the *reptilian brain*. The hindbrain is made up of the cerebellum, the medulla, and the pons (see Figure 2).

The medulla controls a number of critical body functions, the most important of which are breathing and heartbeat. The *pons* comes next, joining the halves of the cerebellum, which lies adjacent to it. Containing large bundles of nerves, the pons acts as a transmitter of motor information, coordinating muscles and integrating movement between the right and left halves of the body. It is also involved in regulating sleep.

The **cerebellum** is found just above the medulla and behind the pons. Without the help of the cerebellum we would be unable to walk a straight line without staggering and lurching forward, for it is the job of the cerebellum to control bodily balance. It constantly monitors feedback from the muscles to coordinate their placement, movement, and tension. In fact, drinking too much alcohol seems to depress the activity of the cerebellum, leading to the unsteady gait and movement characteristic of drunkenness. The cerebellum is also involved in several intellectual functions, ranging from the analysis and coordination of sensory information to problem solving (Bower & Parson, 2003; Paquier & Mariën, 2005; Vandervert, Schimpf, & Liu, 2007).

The Midbrain

The midbrain is a relatively small part of the human brain. As its name suggests, it connects the hindbrain and the forebrain. The **reticular formation** extends from the medulla through the pons, passing through the middle section of the brain—or *midbrain*—and into the front-most part of the brain, called the *forebrain*. Like an ever-vigilant guard, the reticular formation is made up of groups of nerve cells that can activate other parts of the brain immediately to produce general bodily arousal. If, for example, we are startled by a loud noise, the reticular formation can prompt a heightened state of awareness to determine whether a response is necessary. The reticular formation serves a different function when we are sleeping, seeming to filter out background stimuli to allow us to sleep undisturbed.

FIGURE 2

The major structures in the brain.

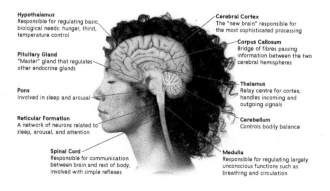

Source: Adapted from Bloom, 1975.

Hindbrain
The part of the brain that controls basic functions such as eating and sleeping and is common to all vertebrates.

Cerebellum (ser uh BELL um)
The part of the brain that controls bodily balance.

Reticular formation
The part of the brain extending from the medulla through the pons and made up of groups of nerve cells that can immediately activate other parts of the brain to produce general bodily arousal.

The Forebrain

The forebrain is the foremost part of our brain, and it is responsible for all our higher cognitive functions—emotions, memory, thinking, language, and complex sensory and motor function. The forebrain consists of two sections: the subcortical structures and the cerebral cortex. These will be discussed in turn below.

The Subcortical Structures: The Thalamus, Hypothalamus, and Limbic Systems

Hidden within the forebrain, the **thalamus** acts primarily as a relay station for information about the senses. Messages from the eyes, ears, and skin travel to the thalamus to be communicated upward to higher parts of the brain. The thalamus also integrates information from higher parts of the brain, sorting it out so that it can be sent to the cerebellum and medulla.

The **hypothalamus** is located just below the thalamus. Although tiny—about the size of a fingertip—the hypothalamus plays an extremely important role. One of its major functions is to maintain *homeostasis*, a steady internal environment for the body. The hypothalamus helps provide a constant body temperature and monitors the amount of nutrients stored in the cells. A second major function is equally important: The hypothalamus produces and regulates behaviour that is critical to the basic survival of the species, such as eating, self-protection, and sex.

The **limbic system** is a group of structures deep within the forebrain that controls emotional expression, aggression, eating, and reproduction. The limbic system also plays a role in learning and memory. Consisting of a series of doughnut-shaped structures that include the *amygdale* and *hippocampus*, the limbic system borders the top of the central core and has connections with the cerebral cortex (see Figure 3).

FIGURE 3

The limbic system consists of a series of doughnut-shaped structures that are involved in self-preservation, learning, memory, and the experience of pleasure.

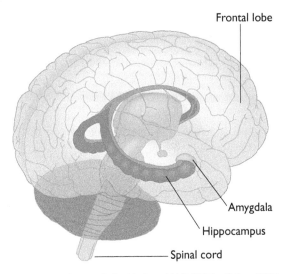

Source: From *Elements of Physiological Psychology*, by A.M. Schneider and B. Tarshis. Copyright © 1995 by McGraw-Hill Education.

Thalamus
The part of the brain located in the middle of the central core that acts primarily to relay information about the senses.

Hypothalamus
A tiny part of the brain, located below the thalamus, that maintains homeostasis and produces and regulates vital behaviour, such as eating, drinking, and sexual behaviour.

Limbic system
The part of the brain that controls eating, aggression, and reproduction.

Injury to the limbic system can produce striking changes in behaviour. Such injuries can turn animals that are usually docile and tame into aggressive wild beasts. Conversely, animals that are usually wild and uncontrollable may become meek and obedient following injury to the limbic system (Bedard & Parsinger, 1995; Gontkovsky, 2005).

Research examining the effects of mild electric shocks to parts of the limbic system and other parts of the brain has produced some thought-provoking findings (Olds & Milner, 1954; Olds & Fobes, 1981). In one experiment, rats that pressed a bar received mild electric stimulation through an electrode implanted in their brains, which produced pleasurable feelings. Even starving rats on their way to food would stop to press the bar as many times as they could. Some rats would actually stimulate themselves literally thousands of times an hour—until they collapsed with fatigue (Routtenberg & Lindy, 1965; Fountas & Smith, 2007).

The limbic system also plays an important role in learning and memory, a finding demonstrated in patients with epilepsy. In an attempt to stop their seizures, such patients have had portions of the limbic system removed. One unintended consequence of the surgery is that individuals sometimes have difficulty learning and remembering new information. In one case, a patient who had undergone surgery was unable to remember where he lived, although he had resided at the same address for eight years. Further, even though the patient was able to carry on animated conversations, he was unable, a few minutes later, to recall what had been discussed (Milner, 1966; Rich & Shapiro, 2007).

The limbic system, then, is involved in several important functions, including self-preservation, learning, memory, and the experience of pleasure. These functions are hardly unique to humans; in fact, the limbic system is sometimes referred to as the "animal brain" because its structures and functions are so similar to those of other mammals. To identify the part of the brain that provides the complex and subtle capabilities that are uniquely human, we need to turn to another structure—the cerebral cortex.

The Cerebral Cortex: Our "New Brain"

As we have proceeded up the spinal cord and into the brain, our discussion has centred on areas of the brain that control functions similar to those found in less sophisticated organisms. But where, you may be asking, are the portions of the brain that enable humans to do what they do best and that distinguish humans from all other animals? Those unique features of the human brain—indeed, the very capabilities that allow you to come up with such a question in the first place—are embodied in the ability to think, evaluate, and make complex judgments. The principal location of these abilities, along with many others, is the **cerebral cortex**.

The cerebral cortex is referred to as the "new brain" because of its relatively recent evolution. It consists of a mass of deeply folded, rippled, convoluted tissue. Although only about 2 mm thick, it would, if flattened out, cover an area more than 0.69 m². This configuration allows the surface area of the cortex to be considerably greater than it would be if it were smoother and more uniformly packed into the skull. The uneven shape also permits a high level of integration of neurons, allowing sophisticated information processing.

The cortex has four major sections called **lobes**. If we take a side view of the brain, the *frontal lobes* lie at the front centre of the cortex and the *parietal lobes* lie behind them. The *temporal lobes* are found in the lower centre portion of the cortex, with the *occipital lobes* lying behind them. These four sets of lobes are physically separated by deep grooves called sulci. Figure 4 shows the four areas.

Another way to describe the brain is in terms of the functions associated with a particular area. Figure 4 also shows the specialized regions within the lobes related to specific functions and areas of the body. Three major areas are known: the motor areas, the sensory areas, and the association areas. Although we will discuss these areas as though they were separate and independent, keep in mind that this is an oversimplification. In most instances, behaviour is influenced simultaneously by several structures and areas within the brain, operating interdependently. To give one example, people use different areas of the brain when they create sentences (a verbal task) compared with when they improvise musical tunes. Furthermore, when people suffer brain injury, uninjured portions of the brain can sometimes take over the functions that were previously handled by the damaged area. In short, the brain is extraordinarily adaptable (Sacks, 2003; Boller, 2004; Brown, Martinez, & Parson, 2006).

Cerebral cortex
The "new brain," responsible for the most sophisticated information processing in the brain; contains four lobes.

Lobes
The four major sections of the cerebral cortex: frontal, parietal, temporal, and occipital.

FIGURE 4

The cerebral cortex of the brain. The major physical structures of the cerebral cortex are called lobes. This figure also illustrates the functions associated with particular areas of the cerebral cortex. Are any areas of the cerebral cortex present in nonhuman animals?

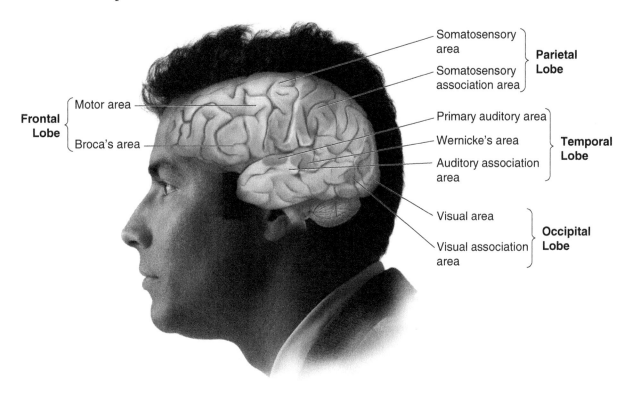

The Motor Area of the Cortex

If you look at the frontal lobe in Figure 4, you will see a shaded portion labelled **motor area**. This part of the cortex is largely responsible for the body's voluntary movement. Every portion of the motor area corresponds to a specific locale within the body. If we were to insert an electrode into a particular part of the motor area of the cortex and apply mild electrical stimulation, there would be involuntary movement in the corresponding part of the body. If we moved to another part of the motor area and stimulated it, a different part of the body would move.

The motor area is so well mapped that researchers have identified the amount and relative location of cortical tissue used to produce movement in specific parts of the human body. For example, the control of movements that are relatively large scale and require little precision, such as the movement of a knee or a hip, is centred in a very small space in the motor area. In contrast, movements that must be precise and delicate, such as facial expressions and finger movements, are controlled by a considerably larger portion of the motor area. In short, the motor area of the cortex provides a guide to the degree of complexity and the importance of the motor capabilities of specific parts of the body.

The Sensory Area of the Cortex

Given the one-to-one correspondence between the motor area and body location, it is not surprising to find a similar relationship between specific portions of the cortex and the senses. The **sensory area** of the cortex includes three regions: one that corresponds primarily to body sensations (including touch and pressure), one relating to sight, and

Motor area
The part of the cortex that is largely responsible for the body's voluntary movement.

Sensory area
The site in the brain of the tissue that corresponds to each of the senses, with the degree of sensitivity related to the amount of tissue.

a third relating to sound. For instance, the *somatosensory area* encompasses specific locations associated with the ability to perceive touch and pressure in a particular area of the body. As with the motor area, the amount of brain tissue related to a particular location on the body determines the degree of sensitivity of that location: the greater the area devoted to a specific area of the body within the cortex, the more sensitive that area of the body. As you can see from the weird-looking individual in Figure 5, parts such as the fingers are related to proportionally more area in the somatosensory area and are the most sensitive.

The senses of sound and sight are also represented in specific areas of the cerebral cortex. An *auditory area* located in the temporal lobe is responsible for the sense of hearing. If the auditory area is stimulated electrically, a person will hear sounds such as clicks or hums. It also appears that particular locations within the auditory area respond to specific pitches (Hudspeth, 2000; Brown & Martinez, 2007; Hyde, Peretz, & Zatorre, 2008; Bizley et al., 2009).

The visual area in the cortex, located in the occipital lobe, responds in the same way to electrical stimulation. Stimulation by electrodes produces the experience of flashes of light or colours, suggesting that the raw sensory input of images from the eyes is received in this area of the brain and transformed into meaningful stimuli. The visual area provides another example of how areas of the brain are intimately related to specific areas of the body: Specific structures in the eye are related to a particular part of the cortex—with, as you might guess, more area of the brain given to the most sensitive portions of the retina (Wurtz & Kandel, 2000; Stenbacka & Vanni, 2007).

Association Areas of the Cortex

Twenty-five-year-old Phineas Gage, a railroad employee, was blasting rock one day in 1848 when an accidental explosion punched a 3-foot-long [1-m-long] spike, about an inch [almost 3 cm] in diameter, completely through his skull. The spike entered just under his left cheek, came out the top of his head, and flew into the air. Gage immediately suffered a series of convulsions, yet a few minutes later was talking with rescuers. In fact, he was able to walk up a long flight of stairs before receiving any medical attention. Amazingly, after a few weeks his wound healed, and he was physically close to his old self again. Mentally, however, there was a difference: Once a careful and hardworking person, Phineas now became enamored with wild schemes and was flighty and often irresponsible. As one of his physicians put it, "Previous to his injury, though untrained in the schools, he possessed a well-balanced mind, and was looked upon by those who knew him as a shrewd, smart businessman, very energetic and persistent in executing all his plans of operation. In this regard his mind was radically changed, so decidedly that his friends and acquaintances said he was 'no longer Gage'." (Harlow, 1869, p. 14)

What had happened to the old Gage? Although there is no way of knowing for sure—science being what it was in the 1800s—we can speculate that the accident may have injured the region of Gage's cerebral cortex known as the

---

FIGURE 5

The greater the amount of tissue in the somatosensory area of the brain that is related to a specific body part, the more sensitive is that body part. If the size of our body parts reflected the corresponding amount of brain tissue, we would look like this strange creature.

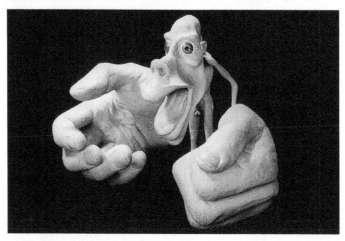

association areas, which generally are considered to be the site of higher mental processes such as thinking, language, memory, and speech (Rowe et al., 2000).

The association areas make up a large portion of the cerebral cortex and consist of the sections that are not directly involved in either sensory processing or directing movement. Most of our understanding of the association areas comes from patients who, like Phineas Gage, have suffered some type of brain injury. In some cases, the injury stemmed from natural causes, such as a tumour or a stroke, either of which would block certain blood vessels in the cerebral cortex. In other cases, accidental causes were the culprits, as was true of Gage. In any event, damage to these areas can result in unusual behavioural changes, indicating the importance of the association areas to normal functioning (Gannon et al., 1998; Macmillan, 2000).

Gage's case provides evidence that there are specialized areas for making rational decisions. When those areas are damaged, people undergo personality changes that affect their ability to make moral judgments and process emotions. At the same time, people with damage in those areas can still be capable of reasoning logically, performing calculations, and recalling information (Damasio, 1999).

Injuries to other parts of the association areas can produce a condition known as *apraxia*. Apraxia occurs when an individual is unable to integrate activities in a rational or logical manner. The disorder is most evident when people are asked to carry out a sequence of behaviours requiring a degree of planning and foresight, suggesting that the association areas act as "master planners," that is, organizers of actions.

Injuries to the association areas of the brain can also produce aphasia, problems with language. In *Broca's aphasia* (caused by damage to the part of the brain first identified by a French physician, Paul Broca, in 1861), speech becomes halting, laborious, and often ungrammatical. The speaker is unable to find the right words in a kind of tip-of-the-tongue phenomenon that we all experience from time to time. People with aphasia, though, grope for words almost constantly, eventually blurting out a kind of "verbal telegram." A phrase like "I put the book on the table" comes out as "I . . . put . . . book . . . table" (Kearns, 2005).

Wernicke's aphasia is a disorder named for Carl Wernicke, who identified it in the 1870s. Wernicke's aphasia produces difficulties both in understanding others' speech and in the production of language. The disorder is characterized by speech that sounds fluent but makes no sense. For instance, one patient, asked what brought him to a hospital, gave this rambling reply: "Boy, I'm sweating, I'm awful nervous, you know, once in a while I get caught up, I can't mention the tarripoi, a month ago, quite a little, I've done a lot well, I impose a lot, while, on the other hand, you know what I mean, I have to run around, look it over, trebbin and all that sort of stuff" (Gardner, 1975, p. 68).

Foreign accent syndrome is another unusual disorder that originates from injuries to association areas of the brain. Karin Humphreys, a cognitive psychologist specializing in psycholinguistics at McMaster University in Hamilton, Ontario, studies this rare syndrome. Foreign accent syndrome is an acquired brain injury resulting in articulation errors that sound like a "foreign accent." A recent case involved an extraordinary transformation of a speaker's accent from Southern Ontario to a distinctive Atlantic Canadian accent (Naidoo, Warriner, Oczkowski, Sévigny, & Humphreys, 2008).

Neuroplasticity and the Brain

Shortly after he was born, Jacob Stark's arms and legs started jerking every 20 minutes. Weeks later he could not focus his eyes on his mother's face. The diagnosis: uncontrollable epileptic seizures involving his entire brain.

His mother, Sally Stark, recalled: "When Jacob was 2½ months old, they said he would never learn to sit up, would never be able to feed himself. . . . They told us to take him home, love him, and find an institution. (Blakeslee, 1992: C3)

Instead, Jacob had brain surgery when he was five months old in which physicians removed 20 percent of his brain. The operation was a complete success. Three years later Jacob seemed normal in every way, with no sign of seizures.

The surgery that helped Jacob was based on the premise that the diseased part of his brain was producing seizures throughout the brain. Surgeons reasoned that if they removed the misfiring portion, the remaining parts of the brain, which appeared intact in PET scans, would take over. They correctly bet that Jacob could still lead a normal life after surgery, particularly because the surgery was being done at so young an age.

Association areas
One of the major regions of the cerebral cortex; the site of the higher mental processes, such as thought, language, memory, and speech.

The success of Jacob's surgery illustrates that the brain has the ability to shift functions to different locations after injury to a specific area or in cases of surgery. But equally encouraging are some new findings about the *regenerative* powers of the brain and nervous system.

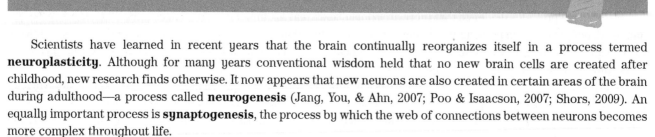

STUDY ALERT!

Remember that *neuroplasticity* is the reorganization of existing neuronal connections, whereas *neurogenesis* is the creation of new neurons.

Scientists have learned in recent years that the brain continually reorganizes itself in a process termed **neuroplasticity**. Although for many years conventional wisdom held that no new brain cells are created after childhood, new research finds otherwise. It now appears that new neurons are also created in certain areas of the brain during adulthood—a process called **neurogenesis** (Jang, You, & Ahn, 2007; Poo & Isaacson, 2007; Shors, 2009). An equally important process is **synaptogenesis**, the process by which the web of connections between neurons becomes more complex throughout life.

The plasticity of our brain throughout our lifetime has significant implications for the potential treatment of disorders of the nervous system. For example, drugs that trigger the development of new neurons might be used to counter such diseases as Alzheimer's, which are produced when neurons die (Tsai, Tsai, & Shen, 2007; Eisch et al., 2008; Waddell & Shors, 2008).

Furthermore, specific experiences can modify the way in which information is processed. For example, if you learn to read Braille, the amount of tissue in your cortex related to sensation in the fingertips will expand. Similarly, if you take up the violin, the area of the brain that receives messages from your fingers will grow—but only relating to the fingers that actually move across the violin's strings (Schwartz & Begley, 2002; Kolb, Gibb, & Robinson, 2003).

At a certain point in life, losses begin to outweigh gains, in terms of neuro- and synaptogenesis. It is at this point that brain activity becomes even more important as a richer web of neuronal interconnections can help to offset the normal cell death associated with aging (Snowdon, 2002). Taking up the violin and learning to read Braille are great activities for encouraging synaptogenesis, but so are any activities that keep the brain active: reading, writing, listening to music, meditating, and more. Physical exercise is also a key contributor to neuroplasticity. Research shows that being physically active fosters synaptogenesis and even neurogenesis throughout the lifespan (Hillman, Erickson, & Kramer, 2008). Canadian psychiatrist Norman Doidge's pioneering work indicates that taking advantage of our brain's plasticity by stimulating neural connections is an effective treatment for individuals with pathological cell death more dramatic than that seen in normal aging, such as stroke patients or patients with multiple sclerosis (Doidge, 2015).

The Specialization of the Hemispheres: Two Brains or One?

The most recent development, at least in evolutionary terms, in the organization and operation of the human brain probably occurred in the last million years: a specialization of the functions controlled by the left and right sides of the brain (Hopkins & Cantalupo, 2008; MacNeilage, Rogers, & Vallortigara, 2009; Tommasi, 2009).

The brain is divided into roughly mirror-image halves. Just as we have two arms, two legs, and two lungs, we have a left brain and a right brain. Because of the way nerves in the brain are connected to the rest of the body, these symmetrical

Neuroplasticity
Changes in the brain that occur throughout the life span relating to the addition of new neurons, new interconnections between neurons, and the reorganization of information-processing areas.

Neurogenesis
The creation of new neurons.

Synaptogenesis
The process by which the web of connections between neurons becomes more complex throughout life.

left and right halves, called **hemispheres**, control motion in—and receive sensation from—the side of the body opposite their location. The left hemisphere of the brain, then, generally controls the right side of the body, and the right hemisphere controls the left side of the body. Thus, damage to the right side of the brain is typically indicated by functional difficulties in the left side of the body.

Despite the appearance of similarity between the two hemispheres of the brain, they are somewhat different in the functions they control and in the ways they control them. Certain behaviours are more likely to reflect activity in one hemisphere than in the other. Early evidence for the functional differences between the halves of the brain came from studies of people with aphasia. Researchers found that people with the speech difficulties characteristic of aphasia tended to have physical damage to the left hemisphere of the brain. In contrast, physical abnormalities in the right hemisphere tended to produce far fewer problems with language. This finding led researchers to conclude that for most people, language is lateralized (**lateralization**), or located more in one hemisphere than in the other—in this case, in the left side of the brain (Grossi et al., 1996; Ansaldo, Arguin, & Roch-Locours, 2002).

It now seems clear that the two hemispheres of the brain are somewhat specialized in the functions they carry out. The left hemisphere concentrates more on tasks that require verbal competence, such as speaking, reading, thinking, and reasoning. The right hemisphere has its own strengths, particularly in nonverbal areas such as the understanding of spatial relationships, recognition of patterns and drawings, music, and emotional expression. Cerebral specialization starts at a very early age. For example, even before infants under the age of one year have developed real language skills, their babbling involves left hemisphere specialization (Holowka & Petitto, 2002).

In addition, information is processed somewhat differently in each hemisphere. The left hemisphere tends to consider information sequentially, one bit at a time, whereas the right hemisphere tends to process information globally, considering it as a whole (Turkewitz, 1993; Banich & Heller, 1998; Hines, 2004).

However, it is important to keep in mind that the differences in specialization between the hemispheres are not great and that the degree and nature of lateralization vary from one person to another. If, like most people, you are right-handed, the control of language is probably concentrated more in your left hemisphere. By contrast, if you are among the 10 percent of people who are left-handed or are ambidextrous (you use both hands interchangeably), it is much more likely that the language centres of your brain are located more in the right hemisphere or are divided equally between the left and right hemispheres.

Researchers have also unearthed evidence that there may be subtle differences in brain lateralization patterns between males and females. In fact, some scientists have suggested that there are slight differences in the structure of the brain according to sex and culture. As we see next, such findings have led to a lively debate in the scientific community.

The Split Brain: Exploring the Two Hemispheres

The patient, V.J., had suffered severe seizures. By cutting her corpus callosum, the fibrous portion of the brain that carries messages between the hemispheres, surgeons hoped to create a firebreak to prevent the seizures from spreading. The operation did decrease the frequency and severity of V.J.'s attacks. But V.J. developed an unexpected side effect: She lost the ability to write at will, although she could read and spell words aloud. (Strauss, 1998, p. 287)

Hemispheres
Symmetrical left and right halves of the brain that each control the *opposite* side of the body.

Lateralization
The dominance of one hemisphere of the brain in specific functions, such as language.

Exploring DIVERSITY

Sex and the Brain

The interplay of biology and environment in behaviour is particularly clear when we consider evidence suggesting that even in brain structure and function there are sex differences. Accumulating evidence seems to show intriguing differences in males' and females' brain lateralization and weight, although the nature of those differences—and even their existence—is the source of considerable controversy (Hugdahl & Davidson, 2002; Boles, 2005; Clements, Rimrodt, & Abel, 2006).

Canadian neuroscientist and behavioural psychologist Doreen Kimura adds to the controversy by using her research on sex differences in the brain to condemn preferential treatment for women in male-dominated fields such as engineering and mathematics. Kimura argues that it is natural for men and women to choose different fields based on their unique brain functioning and associated inborn strengths. Kimura believes that social policy that goes against natural gender-based differences, like affirmative action hiring practices, is the most horrible kind of discrimination and actually demeans women. Accordingly, she became the founding president of the Society of Academic Freedom and Scholarship in 1992.

Some statements can be made with reasonable confidence. For instance, most males tend to show greater lateralization of language in the left hemisphere. For them, language is clearly relegated largely to the left side of the brain. In contrast, women display less lateralization, with language abilities apt to be more evenly divided between the two hemispheres (Gur et al., 1982; Kulynych et al., 1994; Shaywitz et al., 1995). Such differences in brain lateralization may account, in part, for the superiority often displayed by females on certain measures of verbal skills, such as the onset and fluency of speech, and the fact that far more boys than girls have reading problems in elementary school (Kitterle, 1991).

Other research suggests that men's brains are somewhat bigger than women's brains even after taking differences in body size into account. In contrast, part of the *corpus callosum,* a bundle of fibres that connects the hemispheres of the brain, is proportionally larger in women than in men. Furthermore, some research suggests that in women, a higher proportion of brain neurons are actually involved in thinking compared with men (Falk et al., 1999; Gur et al., 1999; Cahill, 2005).

The meaning of such sex differences is far from clear. Consider one possibility related to differences in the proportional size of the corpus callosum. Its greater size in women may permit stronger connections to develop between the parts of the brain that control speech. In turn, this would explain why speech tends to emerge slightly earlier in girls than in boys.

Before we rush to such a conclusion, though, it is important to consider an alternative hypothesis: The reason verbal abilities emerge earlier in girls may be that infant girls receive greater encouragement to talk than do infant boys. In turn, this greater early experience may foster the growth of certain parts of the brain. Hence, physical brain differences may be a *reflection* of social and environmental influences rather than a *cause* of the differences in men's and women's behaviour. At this point, it is impossible to confirm which of these two alternative hypotheses is correct.

People like V.J., whose corpus callosum has been surgically cut to stop seizures and who are called *split-brain patients,* offer a rare opportunity for researchers investigating the independent functioning of the two hemispheres of the brain. For example, psychologist Roger Sperry—who won the Nobel Prize for his work—developed a number of ingenious techniques for studying how each hemisphere operates (Sperry, 1982; Baynes et al., 1998; Gazzaniga, 1998).

In one experimental procedure, blindfolded patients touched an object with their right hand and were asked to name it. Because the right side of the body corresponds to the language-oriented left side of the brain, split-brain patients were able to name it. However, if blindfolded patients touched the object with their left hand, which connects to the nonverbally oriented right hemisphere, they were unable to name it aloud, even though the information had registered in their brains: When the blindfold was removed, patients could identify the object they had touched. Information can be learned and remembered, then, using only the right side of the brain. (By the way, unless you've had a split-brain operation, this experiment won't work with you, because the bundle of fibres called the corpus callosum connecting the two hemispheres of a normal brain immediately transfers the information from one hemisphere to the other.)

Evaluate

1. Match the name of each brain scan with the appropriate description:

   a. EEG

   b. fMRI

   c. PET

   1. By locating radiation within the brain, a computer can provide a striking picture of brain activity.

   2. Electrodes placed around the skull record the electrical signals transmitted through the brain.

   3. Provides a three-dimensional view of the brain by aiming a magnetic field at the body.

2. Match the portion of the brain with its function:

   a. medulla

   b. pons

   c. cerebellum

   d. reticular formation

   1. Maintains breathing and heartbeat

   2. Controls bodily balance

   3. Coordinates and integrates muscle movements

   4. Activates other parts of the brain to produce general bodily arousal

3. A surgeon places an electrode on a portion of your brain and stimulates it. Immediately, your right wrist involuntarily twitches. The doctor has most likely stimulated a portion of the _____ area of your brain.

4. Each hemisphere controls the _____ side of the body.

5. Nonverbal realms, such as emotions and music, are controlled primarily by the _____ hemisphere of the brain, whereas the _____ hemisphere is more responsible for speaking and reading.

Answers to Evaluate Questions

1. a-2, b-3, c-1; 2. a-1, b-3, c-2, d-4; 3. motor; 4. opposite; 5. right, left.

Key Terms

association areas	lateralization	reticular formation
cerebellum (ser uh BELL um)	limbic system	sensory area
cerebral cortex	lobes	synaptogenesis
hemispheres	motor area	thalamus
hindbrain	neurogenesis	
hypothalamus	neuroplasticity	

The Nervous System and the Endocrine System: Communicating Within the Body

LEARNING OBJECTIVES

LO7 **How are** the structures of the nervous system linked?

LO8 **How does** the endocrine system affect behaviour?

In light of the complexity of individual neurons and the neurotransmission process, it should come as no surprise that the connections and structures formed by the neurons are complicated. Because each neuron can be connected to 80,000 other neurons, the total number of possible connections is astonishing. For instance, estimates of the number of neural connections within the brain fall in the neighbourhood of 10 quadrillion—a 1 followed by 16 zeros—and some experts put the number even higher. However, connections among neurons are not the only means of communication within the body; as we'll see, the endocrine system, which secretes chemical messages that circulate through the blood, also communicates messages that influence behaviour and many aspects of biological functioning (Kandel, Schwartz, & Jessell, 2000; Forlenza & Baum, 2004; Boahen, 2005).

STUDY ALERT!

Use Figures 1 and 2 to learn the components of the central and peripheral nervous systems.

The Nervous System

Whatever the actual number of neural connections, the human nervous system has both logic and elegance. We turn now to a discussion of its basic structures.

The Central and Peripheral Nervous Systems

As you can see from the schematic representation in Figure 1, the nervous system is divided into two main parts: the central nervous system and the peripheral nervous system. The **central nervous system (CNS)** is composed of the brain and spinal cord. The **spinal cord**, which is about the thickness of a pencil, contains a bundle of neurons that leaves the

> **Central nervous system (CNS)**
> The part of the nervous system that includes the brain and spinal cord.
>
> **Spinal cord**
> A bundle of neurons that leaves the brain and runs down the length of the back and is the main means for transmitting messages between the brain and the body.

FIGURE 1

A schematic diagram of the structure and functions of the parts of the nervous system.

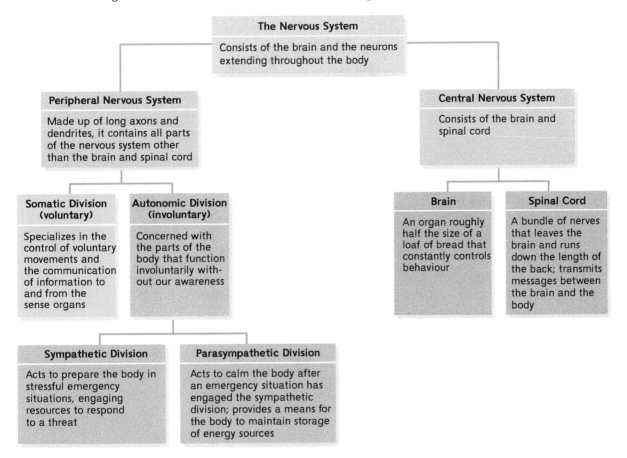

brain and runs down the length of the back (see Figure 2). As you can see in Figure 1, the spinal cord is the primary means for transmitting messages between the brain and the rest of the body.

However, the spinal cord is not just a communication channel. It also controls some simple behaviours on its own, without any help from the brain. An example is the way the knee jerks forward when it is tapped with a rubber hammer. This behaviour is a type of **reflex**, an automatic, involuntary response to an incoming stimulus. A reflex is also at work when you touch a hot stove and immediately withdraw your hand. Although the brain eventually analyzes and reacts to the situation ("Ouch—hot stove—pull away!"), the initial withdrawal is controlled only by neurons in the spinal cord.

Three kinds of neurons are involved in reflexes. **Sensory (afferent) neurons** transmit information from the perimeter of the body to the central nervous system. **Motor (efferent) neurons** communicate information from the nervous system to muscles and glands. **Interneurons** connect sensory and motor neurons, carrying messages between the two.

The importance of the spinal cord and reflexes is illustrated by the outcome of accidents in which the cord is injured or severed. In some cases, injury results in *quadriplegia*, a condition in which voluntary muscle movement

Reflex
An automatic, involuntary response to an incoming stimulus.

Sensory (afferent) neurons
Neurons that transmit information from the perimeter of the body to the central nervous system.

Motor (efferent) neurons
Neurons that communicate information from the nervous system to muscles and glands.

Interneurons
Neurons that connect sensory and motor neurons, carrying messages between the two.

FIGURE 2

The central nervous system, consisting of the brain and spinal cord, and the peripheral nervous system encompasses the network of nerves connecting the brain and spinal cord to other parts of the body.

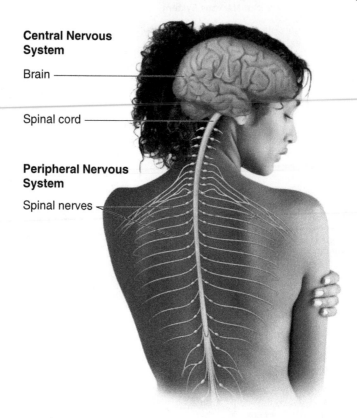

Central Nervous System

Brain

Spinal cord

Peripheral Nervous System

Spinal nerves

below the neck is lost. In a less severe but still debilitating condition, *paraplegia*, people are unable to voluntarily move any muscles in the lower half of the body.

As suggested by its name, the **peripheral nervous system** branches out from the spinal cord and brain and reaches the extremities of the body. Made up of neurons with long axons and dendrites, the peripheral nervous system encompasses all the parts of the nervous system other than the brain and spinal cord. There are two major divisions—the **somatic division** and the autonomic division—both of which connect the central nervous system with the sense organs, muscles, glands, and other organs. The somatic division specializes in the control of voluntary movements—such as the motion of the eyes to read this sentence or those of the hand to turn this page—and the communication of information to and from the sense organs. On the other hand, the **autonomic division** controls the parts of the body that keep us alive—the heart, blood vessels, glands, lungs, and other organs that function involuntarily without our awareness. As you are reading at this moment, the autonomic division of the peripheral nervous system is pumping blood through your body, pushing your lungs in and out, overseeing the digestion of the meal you had a few hours ago, and so on—all without a thought or effort on your part.

Peripheral nervous system
The part of the nervous system that includes the autonomic and somatic subdivisions; made up of neurons with long axons and dendrites, it branches out from the spinal cord and brain and reaches the extremities of the body.

Somatic division
The part of the peripheral nervous system that specializes in the control of voluntary movements and the communication of information to and from the sense organs.

Autonomic division
The part of the peripheral nervous system that controls involuntary movement of the heart, glands, lungs, and other organs.

The autonomic division plays a particularly crucial role during emergencies. Suppose that as you are reading you suddenly sense that a stranger is watching you through the window. As you look up, you see the glint of something that might be a knife. As confusion clouds your mind and fear overcomes your attempts to think rationally, what happens to your body? If you are like most people, you react immediately on a physiological level. Your heart rate increases, you begin to sweat, and you develop goose bumps all over your body.

The physiological changes that occur during a crisis result from the activation of one of the two parts of the autonomic nervous system: the **sympathetic division**. The sympathetic division acts to prepare the body for action in stressful situations by engaging all of the organism's resources to run away or confront the threat. This response is often called the "fight or flight" response. Unexpectedly seeing a stranger at your bedroom window would activate your sympathetic nervous system. In contrast, the **parasympathetic division** acts to calm the body after the emergency has ended. When you find, for instance, that the stranger at the window is actually your roommate, who has lost his keys and is climbing in the window to avoid waking you, your parasympathetic division begins to predominate, lowering your heart rate, stopping your sweating, and returning your body to the state it was in before you became alarmed. The parasympathetic division also directs the body to store energy for use in emergencies. The sympathetic and parasympathetic divisions work together to regulate many functions of the body (see Figure 3).

The Evolutionary Foundations of the Nervous System

The complexities of the nervous system can be better understood if we take the course of evolution into consideration. The forerunner of the human nervous system is found in the earliest simple organisms to have a spinal cord. Basically, those organisms were simple input-output devices: When the upper side of the spinal cord was stimulated by, for instance, being touched, the organism reacted with a simple response, such as jerking away. Such responses were completely a consequence of the organism's genetic makeup.

Over millions of years, the front end of the spinal cord became more specialized, and organisms became capable of distinguishing between different kinds of stimuli and responding appropriately to them. Ultimately, the front end of the spinal cord evolved into what we would consider a primitive brain. At first, it had just three parts, devoted to close stimuli (such as smell), more distant stimuli (such as sights and sounds), and the ability to maintain balance and bodily coordination. In fact, many animals, such as fish, still have a nervous system that is structured in roughly similar fashion today. In contrast, the human brain evolved from this three-part configuration into an organ that is far more complex and differentiated (Merlin, 1993).

Furthermore, the nervous system is *hierarchically organized,* meaning that relatively newer (from an evolutionary point of view) and more sophisticated regions of the brain regulate the older, and more primitive, parts of the nervous system. As we move up along the spinal cord and continue upward into the brain, then, the functions controlled by the various regions become progressively more advanced.

Why should we care about the evolutionary background of the human nervous system? The answer comes from researchers working in the area of **evolutionary psychology**, the branch of psychology that seeks to identify how behaviour is influenced and produced by our genetic inheritance from our ancestors.

Evolutionary psychologists argue that the course of evolution is reflected in the structure and functioning of the nervous system and that evolutionary factors consequently have a significant influence on our everyday behaviour. Their work, in conjunction with the research of scientists studying genetics, biochemistry, and medicine, has led to an understanding of how our behaviour is affected by heredity, our genetically determined heritage. In fact, evolutionary psychologists have spawned a new and increasingly influential field: behavioural genetics.

Sympathetic division
The part of the autonomic division of the nervous system that acts to prepare the body for action in stressful situations, engaging all the organism's resources to respond to a threat.

Parasympathetic division
The part of the autonomic division of the nervous system that acts to calm the body after an emergency has ended.

Evolutionary psychology
The branch of psychology that seeks to identify behaviour patterns that are a result of our genetic inheritance from our ancestors.

FIGURE 3

The major functions of the autonomic nervous system. The sympathetic division acts to prepare certain organs of the body for stressful situations, and the parasympathetic division acts to calm the body after the emergency has been passed. Can you explain why each response of the sympathetic division might be useful in an emergency?

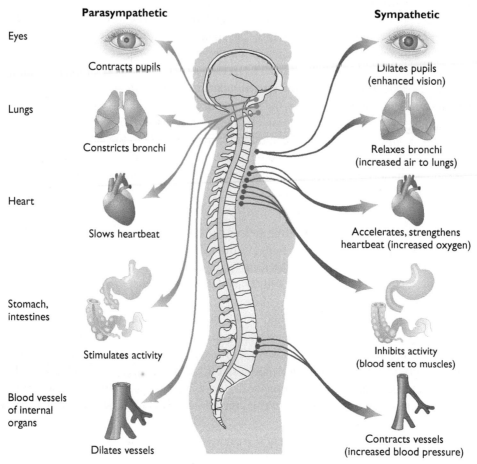

Source: From Michael W. Passer and Ronald E. Smith, *Psychology*, p. 91. Copyright ©2001 by McGraw-Hill Education. Reprinted with permission of McGraw-Hill Education.

Behavioural Genetics

Our evolutionary heritage manifests itself not only through the structure and functioning of the nervous system but through our behaviour as well. In the view of a growing area of study, people's personality and behavioural habits are affected in part by their genetic heritage. **Behavioural genetics** studies the effects of heredity on behaviour. Behavioural genetics researchers are finding increasing evidence that cognitive abilities, personality traits, sexual orientation, and psychological disorders are determined to some extent by genetic factors (Ilies, Arvey, & Bouchard, 2006; Livesley & Jang, 2008; Vernon et al., 2008).

Behavioural genetics lies at the heart of the nature–nurture question, one of the key issues in the study of psychology. Although no one would argue that our behaviour is determined *solely* by inherited factors, evidence collected by behavioural geneticists does suggest that our genetic inheritance predisposes us to respond in particular ways to our environment, and even to seek out particular kinds of environments. For instance, research indicates that genetic factors may be related to such diverse behaviours as level of family conflict, schizophrenia, learning disabilities, and general sociability (Ball et al., 2008; Davis, Haworth, & Plomin, 2009; Lakhan & Vieira, 2009).

Behavioural genetics
The study of the effects of heredity on behaviour.

Furthermore, important human characteristics and behaviours are related to the presence (or absence) of particular *genes*, the inherited material that controls the transmission of traits. For example, researchers have found evidence that novelty-seeking behaviour is determined, at least in part, by a certain gene.

Despite its relative infancy, the field of behavioural genetics has already made substantial contributions to our understanding of behaviour. By finding *genetic markers*—genes with a known location—that are linked to a disorder, scientists are beginning to learn how disorders such as schizophrenia and depression develop and can potentially be treated. Geneticists have already found that the risk of developing autism (a disorder that influences the development of language and effective social functioning) is increased in the presence of a gene related to early brain development (Hyman, 2003; Gregg et al., 2007).

Advances in research on behavioural genetics have allowed scientists to begin treating brain diseases with gene therapy. Dr. Max Cynader, director of the Brain Research Centre at University of British Columbia (UBC), researches the use of biotechnology to treat neurological conditions (e.g., Parkinson's disease) and psychological disorders (e.g., clinical depression). The Canadian government demonstrated their commitment to these new technologies and treatments with a $25-million contribution to brain health research on March 11, 2008 by the BC government (Skelton, 2008).

Advances in behavioural genetics also have led to the development of a profession that did not exist several decades ago: genetic counselling. Genetic counsellors help people deal with issues related to inherited disorders. For example, genetic counsellors provide advice to prospective parents about the potential risks in a future pregnancy, based on their family history of birth defects and hereditary illnesses. In addition, the counsellor will consider the parents' age and problems with children they already have. They also can take blood, skin, and urine samples to examine specific chromosomes.

Scientists have already developed genetic tests to determine whether someone is susceptible to certain types of cancer or heart disease, and it may not be long before analysis of a drop of blood can indicate whether a child—or potentially an unborn fetus—is susceptible to certain psychological disorders. How such knowledge will be used is a source of considerable speculation and controversy, controversy that is certain to grow as genetic testing becomes more common (Etchegary, 2004; Malpas, 2008).

The Endocrine System: Of Chemicals and Glands

Another of the body's communication systems, the **endocrine system** is a chemical communication network that sends messages throughout the body via the bloodstream. Its job is to secrete **hormones**, chemicals that circulate through the blood and regulate the functioning or growth of the body. It also influences—and is influenced by—the functioning of the nervous system. Although the endocrine system is not part of the brain, it is closely linked to the hypothalamus.

STUDY ALERT!

The endocrine system produces hormones, chemicals that circulate through the body via the bloodstream.

As chemical messengers, hormones are like neurotransmitters, although their speed and mode of transmission are quite different. Whereas neural messages are measured in thousandths of a second, hormonal communications may take minutes to reach their destination. Furthermore, neural messages move through neurons in specific lines (like a signal carried by wires strung along telephone poles), whereas hormones travel throughout the body, similar to the way radio waves are transmitted across the entire landscape. Just as radio waves evoke a response only when a radio is tuned to the correct station, hormones flowing through the bloodstream activate only those cells which are receptive and "tuned" to the appropriate hormonal message.

Endocrine system
A chemical communication network that sends messages throughout the body via the bloodstream.

Hormones
Chemicals that circulate through the blood and regulate the functioning or growth of the body.

A key component of the endocrine system is the tiny **pituitary gland**, which is found near—and regulated by—the hypothalamus. The pituitary gland has sometimes been called the "master gland" because it controls the functioning of the rest of the endocrine system. But the pituitary gland is more than just the taskmaster of other glands; it has important functions in its own right. For instance, hormones secreted by the pituitary gland control growth. Extremely short people and unusually tall ones usually have pituitary gland abnormalities. Other endocrine glands, shown in Figure 4, affect emotional reactions, sexual urges, and energy levels.

FIGURE 4

Location and function of the major endocrine glands. The pituitary gland controls the functioning of the other endocrine glands and in turn is regulated by the hypothalamus.

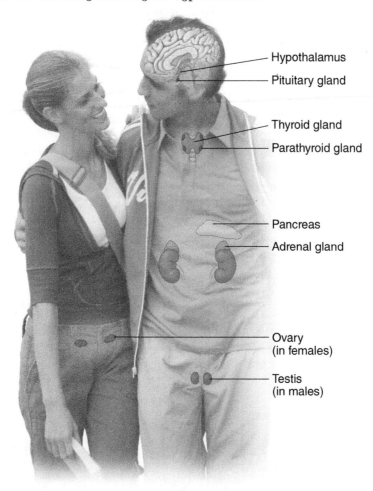

- Hypothalamus
- Pituitary gland
- Thyroid gland
- Parathyroid gland
- Pancreas
- Adrenal gland
- Ovary (in females)
- Testis (in males)

Despite its designation as the "master gland," the pituitary is actually a servant of the brain, because the brain is ultimately responsible for the endocrine system's functioning. The brain regulates the internal balance of the body, ensuring that homeostasis is maintained through the hypothalamus.

Individual hormones can wear many hats, depending on circumstances. For example, the hormone oxytocin is at the root of many of life's satisfactions and pleasures. In new mothers, oxytocin produces an urge to nurse newborn offspring. The same hormone also seems to stimulate cuddling between species members. And—at least in rats—it encourages sexually active males to seek out females more passionately, and females to be more receptive to males' sexual advances. There's even evidence that oxytocin is related to the development of trust in others, helping to grease the wheels of effective social interaction (Kosfeld et al., 2005; Meinlschmidt & Heim, 2007; Guastella, Mitchell, & Dadds,

> **Pituitary gland**
> The major component of the endocrine system, or "master gland," which secretes hormones that control growth and other parts of the endocrine system.

2008). Dr. Evdokia Anagnostou of Sunnybrook Hospital in Toronto and her research team are studying the use of oxytocin therapy to address the social deficits in autism (Anagnostou et al., 2012).

Although hormones are produced naturally by the endocrine system, the ingestion of artificial hormones has proved to be both beneficial and potentially dangerous. For example, research has shown the dangers of the use of testosterone, a male hormone, and drugs known as *steroids*, which act like testosterone. For athletes and others who want to bulk up their appearance, steroids provide a way to add muscle weight and increase strength. However, these drugs can lead to heart attacks, strokes, cancer, and even violent behaviour, making them extremely dangerous (Kolata, 2002). For example, in one infamous case, professional wrestler Chris Benoit strangled his wife, suffocated his son, and later hanged himself—acts that were attributed to his use of steroids (Klötz et al., 2006; Pagonis, Angelopoulos, & Koukoulis, 2006; Sandomir, 2007).

Evaluate

1. The central nervous system is composed of the _____ and _____.
2. In the peripheral nervous system, the _____ division controls voluntary movements, whereas the _____ division controls organs that keep us alive and functioning without our awareness.
3. Maria saw a young boy run into the street and get hit by a car. When she got to the fallen child, she was in a state of panic. She was sweating, and her heart was racing. Her biological state resulted from the activation of the _____ division of the peripheral nervous system.
4. The emerging field of _____ studies ways in which our genetic inheritance predisposes us to behave in certain ways.

Answers to Evaluate Questions

1. brain, spinal cord; 2. somatic, autonomic; 3. sympathetic; 4. behavioural genetics

Key Terms

autonomic division	interneurons	sensory (afferent) neurons
behavioural genetics	motor (efferent) neurons	somatic division
central nervous system (CNS)	parasympathetic division	spinal cord
endocrine system	peripheral nervous system	sympathetic division
evolutionary psychology	pituitary gland	
hormones	reflex	

Epilogue

In our examination of neuroscience, we've traced the ways in which biological structures and functions of the body affect behaviour. Starting with neurons, we considered each of the components of the nervous system, culminating in an examination of how the brain permits us to think, reason, speak, recall, and experience emotions—the hallmarks of being human.

Source: © annedde/Getty Images RF.

Recap/Rethink

Module 5: Neurons: The Basic Elements of Behaviour

Recap

LO1 Why do psychologists study the brain and the nervous system?

- A full understanding of human behaviour requires knowledge of the biological influences underlying that behaviour, especially those originating in the nervous system.

LO2 What are the basic elements of the nervous system?

- Neurons, the most basic elements of the nervous system, carry nerve impulses from one part of the body to another. Information in a neuron generally follows a route that begins with the dendrites, continues into the cell body, and leads ultimately down the tube-like extension, the axon.

LO3 How does the nervous system communicate electrical and chemical messages from one part to another?

- When a neuron receives a message to fire, it releases an action potential, an electric charge that travels through the axon. Neurons operate according to an all-or-none law: Either they are at rest, or an action potential is moving through them. There is no in-between state.
- Once a neuron fires, nerve impulses are carried to other neurons through the production of chemical substances, neurotransmitters, that actually bridge the gaps—known as synapses—between neurons. Neurotransmitters may be either excitatory, telling other neurons to fire, or inhibitory, preventing or decreasing the likelihood of other neurons firing.

Rethink

1. How might psychologists use drugs that mimic the effects of neurotransmitters to treat psychological disorders?
2. What is the process by which one neuron sends a message to another neuron? How is that process both chemical and electrical?
3. Exercise produces natural endorphins in the brain. Based on your understanding of the role of endorphins, what benefits would this incur for those with a regular fitness regimen?

Module 6: The Brain

Recap

LO4 How do researchers identify the major parts and functions of the brain?

- Brain scans take a "snapshot" of the internal workings of the brain without having to cut surgically into a person's skull. Major brain-scanning techniques include the electroencephalogram (EEG), positron emission tomography (PET), functional magnetic resonance imaging (fMRI), and transcranial magnetic stimulation imaging (TMS).

LO5 What are the major parts of the brain, and for what behaviours is each part responsible?

- The hindbrain is made up of the medulla (which controls functions such as breathing and the heartbeat), the pons (which coordinates the muscles and the two sides of the body), and the cerebellum (which controls balance).
- The reticular formation (which acts to heighten awareness in emergencies) passes through the midbrain and connects the hindbrain and forebrain.
- The forebrain consists of subcortical structures and the cerebral cortex. The subcortical structures include the thalamus and the hypothalamus.
- The cerebral cortex—the "new brain"—has areas that control voluntary movement (the motor area); the senses (the sensory area); and thinking, reasoning, speech, and memory (the association areas). The limbic system, found on the border of the "old" and "new" brains, is associated with eating, aggression, reproduction, and the experiences of pleasure and pain.

LO6 How do the halves of the brain operate interdependently?

- The brain is divided into left and right halves, or hemispheres, each of which generally controls the opposite side of the body. Each hemisphere can be thought of as being specialized in the functions it carries out: The left is best at verbal tasks, such as logical reasoning, speaking, and reading; the right is best at nonverbal tasks, such as spatial perception, pattern recognition, and emotional expression.

Rethink

1. Before sophisticated brain-scanning techniques were developed, behavioural neuroscientists' understanding of the brain was based largely on the brains of people who had died. What limitations would this pose, and in what areas would you expect the most significant advances once brain-scanning techniques became possible?

2. Could personal differences in people's specialization of right and left hemispheres be related to occupational success? For example, might an architect who relies on spatial skills have a different pattern of hemispheric specialization than a writer?

3. *Especially for students getting ready to write exams:* It is very difficult to simultaneously complete two tasks that primarily rely on the same hemisphere. This is why it is easy to talk (left hemisphere) while you are doodling a picture (right hemisphere) but much more difficult to talk when you are trying to count something (left hemisphere). Given this information, how many activities should you do or NOT do during studying to allow you to concentrate on your reading, a left hemisphere task?

Module 7: The Nervous System and the Endocrine System: Communicating Within the Body

Recap

How are the structures of the nervous system linked?

- The nervous system is made up of the central nervous system (the brain and spinal cord) and the peripheral nervous system. The peripheral nervous system is made up of the somatic division, which controls voluntary movements and the communication of information to and from the sense organs, and the autonomic division, which controls involuntary functions such as those of the heart, blood vessels, and lungs.
- The autonomic division of the peripheral nervous system is further subdivided into the sympathetic and parasympathetic divisions. The sympathetic division prepares the body in emergency situations, and the parasympathetic division helps the body return to its typical resting state.
- Evolutionary psychology, the branch of psychology that seeks to identify behaviour patterns that are a result of our genetic inheritance, has led to increased understanding of the evolutionary basis of the structure and organization of the human nervous system. Behavioural genetics extends this study to include the evolutionary and hereditary basis of human personality traits and behaviour.

How does the endocrine system affect behaviour?

- The endocrine system secretes hormones, chemicals that regulate the functioning of the body, via the bloodstream. The pituitary gland secretes growth hormones and influences the release of hormones by other endocrine glands, and in turn is regulated by the hypothalamus.

Rethink

1. *Especially for Police Foundations and EMS students:* In what ways is the fight-or-flight response helpful to humans in emergency situations?

2. Arbor was once chased by an angry pitbull. He ran faster than he had every run before and scaled a high fence in seconds, something he would never have thought he would be able to do. What cascade of events in his central and peripheral nervous system would have allowed him to be able to perform these feats in this situation of sudden danger?

CHAPTER 3
Sensation and Perception

Source: © Darryl Leniuk/Taxi/Getty Images.

Key Concepts For Chapter 3

Prologue

Never Forgetting a Face

She never forgets a face. Literally.

For a woman known as C. S., remembering people is not a problem. In fact, she—like a very few other individuals—can remember faces of people she met years ago, sometimes only in passing. These "super-recognizers," as they are called, excel at recalling faces.

One super-recognizer said she had identified another woman on the street who served her as a waitress five years earlier in a different city. Critically, she was able to confirm that the other woman had, in fact, been a waitress in the different city. Often, super-recognizers are able to recognize another person despite significant changes in appearance, such as aging or a different hair colour.

But being a super-recognizer is a mixed blessing. As one woman with this ability says, "It doesn't matter how many years pass, if I've seen your face before I will be able to recall it." In fact, she sometimes pretends she doesn't remember a person, "because it seems like I stalk them, or that they mean more to me than they do when I recall that we saw each other once walking on campus four years ago in front of the quad!" (Munger, 2009; Russell, Duchaine, & Nakayma, 2009).

Most of us are reasonably good at recognizing people's faces of people we know, thanks in part to regions of the brain that specialize in detecting facial patterns. Super-recognizers represent a small minority of people who happen to be exceptionally good at facial recognition. At the other extreme are people with "faceblindness," a rare disorder that makes it extremely difficult for them to recognize faces at all—even those of friends and family.

Disorders such as super-recognition and faceblindness illustrate how much we depend on our senses to function normally. Our senses offer a window to the world, not only providing us with an awareness, understanding, and appreciation of the world's beauty, but alerting us to its dangers. Our senses enable us to feel the gentlest of breezes, see flickering lights kilometres away, and hear the soft murmuring of distant songbirds.

To a psychologist interested in understanding the causes of behaviour, sensation and perception are fundamental topics, because so much of our behaviour is a reflection of how we react to and interpret stimuli from the world around us. The areas of sensation and perception deal with a wide range of questions—among them, how we respond to the characteristics of physical stimuli; what processes enable us to see, hear, and experience pain; why visual illusions fool us; and how we distinguish one person from another. As we explore these issues, we'll see how the senses work together to provide us with an integrated view and understanding of the world.

In the next four modules, we focus on the field of psychology that is concerned with the ways our bodies take in information through the senses and the ways we interpret that information. We explore both sensation and perception. *Sensation* encompasses the processes by which our sense organs receive information from the environment. *Perception* is the brain's and the sense organs' sorting out, interpretation, analysis, and integration of stimuli.

Sensing the World Around Us

LEARNING OBJECTIVES

LO1 **What is** sensation, and how do psychologists study it?

LO2 **What is** the relationship between a physical stimulus and the kinds of sensory responses that result from it?

It is a sunny autumn day in October when Isabel sits down to Thanksgiving dinner. Her father carries the turkey into the dining room on a tray and places it squarely in the centre of the table. The noise level, already high from the talking and laughter of family members, grows louder still. As Isabel picks up her fork, the smell of the turkey reaches her and she feels her stomach growl hungrily. The sight and sound of her family around the table, along with the smells and tastes of the holiday meal, make Isabel feel more relaxed than she had since starting classes in the fall.

STUDY ALERT!

Remember that *sensation* refers to the activation of the sense organs (a physical response), whereas *perception* refers to how stimuli are interpreted (a psychological response).

Put yourself in this setting and consider how different it might be if any one of your senses was not functioning. What if you were blind and unable to see the faces of your family members or the welcome shape of the golden-brown turkey? What if you had no sense of hearing and could not listen to the conversations of family members or were unable to feel your stomach growl, smell the dinner, or taste the food? Clearly, you would experience the dinner very differently than would someone whose sensory apparatus was intact.

Moreover, the sensations mentioned above barely scratch the surface of sensory experience. Although perhaps you were taught, as we were, that there are just five senses—sight, sound, taste, smell, and touch—that enumeration is too modest. Human sensory capabilities go well beyond the basic five senses. For example, we are sensitive not merely to touch but to a considerably wider set of stimuli—pain, pressure, temperature, and vibration, to name a few. In addition, vision has two subsystems—relating to day and night vision—and the ear is responsive to information that allows us not only to hear but also to keep our balance.

To consider how psychologists understand the senses and, more broadly, sensation and perception, we first need a basic working vocabulary. **Sensation** is the activation of the sense organs by a source of physical energy. Sensation includes our five senses—vision, hearing, smell, taste, and touch. **Perception** is the sorting out, interpretation, analysis, and integration of stimuli carried out by the sense organs and brain. Perception is how our brain interprets information (i.e., stimuli) coming in through our five senses. A **stimulus** (e.g., light) is any passing source of physical energy that produces a response in a sense organ (e.g., vision).

Sensation
The activation of the sense organs by a source of physical energy.

Perception
The sorting out, interpretation, analysis, and integration of stimuli by the sense organs and brain.

Stimulus
Energy that produces a response in a sense organ.

Stimuli vary in both type and intensity. Different types of stimuli activate different sense organs. For instance, we can differentiate light stimuli (which activate the sense of sight and allow us to see the colours of a tree in autumn) from sound stimuli (which, through the sense of hearing, permit us to hear the sounds of an orchestra).

How intense a light stimulus needs to be before it can be detected and how much perfume a person must wear before it is noticed by others are questions related to stimulus intensity.

The issue of how the intensity of a stimulus influences our sensory responses is considered in a branch of psychology known as psychophysics. Psychophysics is the study of the relationship between the physical aspects of stimuli and our psychological experience of them. **Psychophysics** played a central role in the development of the field of psychology, and many of the first psychologists studied issues related to psychophysics (Chechile, 2003; Gardner, 2005; Hock & Ploeger, 2006).

Absolute Thresholds: Detecting What's Out There

Just when does a stimulus become strong enough to be detected by our sense organs? The answer to this question requires an understanding of the concept of **absolute threshold**. An absolute threshold is the smallest intensity of a stimulus that must be present for it to be detected (Aazh & Moore, 2007).

Our senses are extremely responsive to stimuli. For example, the sense of touch is so sensitive that we can feel a bee's wing falling on our cheeks when it is dropped from a distance of one centimetre. Test your knowledge of the absolute thresholds of other senses by completing the questionnaire in Figure 1.

FIGURE 1

This test can shed some light on how sensitive the human senses are.

How Sensitive Are You?

To test your awareness of the capabilities of your senses, answer the following questions:

1. How far can a candle flame be seen on a clear, dark night:
   a. From a distance of 10 miles (16 km) _____
   b. From a distance of 30 miles (48 km) _____

2. How far can the ticking of a watch be heard under quiet conditions?
   a. From 5 feet (1.5 m) away _____
   b. From 20 feet (6 m) away _____

3. How much sugar is needed to allow it to be detected when dissolved in 2 gallons (7.5 l) of water?
   a. 2 tablespoons (30 g) _____
   b. 1 teaspoon (5 g) _____

4. Over what area can a drop of perfume be detected?
   a. A 5-foot by 5-foot (1.5 m2) area _____
   b. A 3-room apartment _____

Scoring: In each case, the answer is b, illustrating the tremendous sensitivity of our senses.
Source: Galanter, 1962.

Psychophysics
The study of the relationship between the physical aspects of stimuli and our psychological experience of them.

Absolute threshold
The smallest intensity of a stimulus that must be present for the stimulus to be detected.

In fact, our senses are so fine-tuned that we might have problems if they were any more sensitive. For instance, if our ears were slightly more acute, we would be able to hear the sound of air molecules in our ears knocking into the eardrum—a phenomenon that would surely prove distracting and might even prevent us from hearing sounds outside our bodies.

Of course, the absolute thresholds we have been discussing are measured under ideal conditions. Normally our senses cannot detect stimulation quite as well because of the presence of noise. *Noise*, as defined by psychophysicists, is background stimulation that interferes with the perception of other stimuli. Hence, noise refers not just to auditory stimuli, as the word suggests, but also to unwanted stimuli that interfere with other senses. Picture a talkative group of people crammed into a small, crowded, smoke-filled room at a party. The din of the crowd makes it hard to hear individual voices, and the smoke makes it difficult to see, or even taste, the food. In this case, the smoke and the crowded conditions would both be considered "noise" because they are preventing sensation at more discriminating levels. To learn more about the detrimental impact of distracting conditions, including the sights and sounds of texting and cell phones that can all be considered as noise that interferes with sensation, see the *Applying Psychology in the Real World* box.

APPLYING PSYCHOLOGY   in the Real World

Driven to Distraction

Twenty-four year old Aiden Quinn couldn't believe his good fortune. At his young age, he had beaten the competition to land his dream job of conducting trolleys through the streets of Vancouver. But in just one moment his world came crashing down around him: It was the moment when he took his eyes off the tracks to send a text message to his girlfriend and the trolley he was driving crashed into the one ahead of it.

A recent survey conducted by the AAA Foundation for Traffic Safety shows that nearly half of drivers aged 18 to 24 admit to texting while driving, even though the majority of them were aware that they were increasing their risk of having an accident. In fact, nearly 90 percent of survey respondents rated texting while driving as a very serious threat to safety (AAA Foundation for Traffic Safety, 2008, 2009).

Researchers are now confirming what intuition suggests is true: The distraction caused by texting while driving is extremely dangerous. One study used video cameras to monitor truckers on long hauls and found that they were 23 times more likely to be in a collision while texting than while not texting (Virginia Tech Transportation Institute, 2009). Another study using university students and a driving simulator showed that texting produced approximately 5 seconds of distraction and that the students were 8 times more likely to have a collision while texting (Cooper & Strayer, 2008).

If you, like many of the respondents to the AAA Foundation for Traffic Safety survey, believe that you're the exception to the rule, just keep one thing in mind: that's what Aiden Quinn thought, too. He lost his job and is facing civil lawsuits and criminal prosecution.

Increasing research shows that texting while driving is extremely dangerous.

Source: © Michael Krinke/Getty Images RF.

Difference Thresholds: Noticing Distinctions Between Stimuli

Suppose you wanted to choose the six best apples from a supermarket display—the biggest, reddest, and sweetest apples. One approach would be to compare one apple with another systematically until you were left with a few so similar that you could not tell the difference between them. At that point, it wouldn't matter which ones you chose.

Psychologists have discussed this comparison problem in terms of the **difference threshold (just noticeable difference)**, the smallest level of added (or reduced) stimulation required to sense that a *change* in stimulation has occurred. Thus, the difference threshold is the minimum change in stimulation required to detect the difference between two stimuli, and so it also is called a *just noticeable difference* (Nittrouer & Lowenstein, 2007).

The stimulus value that constitutes a just noticeable difference depends on the initial intensity of the stimulus. The relationship between changes in the original value of a stimulus and the degree to which a change will be noticed forms one of the basic laws of psychophysics: Weber's law. **Weber's law** (with *Weber* pronounced "vay-ber") states that a just noticeable difference is a *constant proportion* of the intensity of an initial stimulus.

For example, Weber found that the just noticeable difference for weight is 1:50. Consequently, it takes a 1-gram increase in a 50-gram weight to produce a noticeable difference, and it would take a 10-gram increase to produce a noticeable difference if the initial weight were 500 grams. In both cases, the same proportional increase is necessary to produce a just noticeable difference—1:5 = 10:500. Similarly, the just noticeable difference distinguishing changes in loudness between sounds is larger for sounds that are initially loud than it is for sounds that are initially soft, but the *proportional* increase remains the same.

Weber's law helps explain why a person in a quiet room is more apt to be startled by the ringing of a telephone than is a person in an already noisy room. To produce the same amount of reaction in a noisy room, a telephone ring might have to approximate the loudness of cathedral bells. Similarly, when the moon is visible during the late afternoon, it appears relatively dim—yet against a dark night sky, it seems quite bright.

STUDY ALERT!

Remember that Weber's law holds for every type of sensory stimuli: vision, sound, taste, and so on.

Sensory Adaptation: Turning Down Our Responses

You arrive at a cottage in Grand Bend in the dead heat of August. You jump out of the car, kick off your sandals, and begin running as fast as you can towards the cold, refreshing lake. But the hot sand on your bare feet almost stops you in your tracks. You shuffle along, jumping from side to side, attempting to lessen the pain. A few minutes later, though, you barely notice the hot sand. Did we turn down the temperature of the sand? No, it is sensory adaptation! **Sensory adaptation** is an adjustment in sensory capacity after prolonged exposure to unchanging stimuli. Adaptation occurs as people become accustomed to a stimulus and change their frame of reference. In a sense, our brain mentally turns down the volume of the stimulation it is experiencing.

Difference threshold (just noticeable difference)
The smallest level of added or reduced stimulation required to sense that a change in stimulation has occurred.

Weber's law
A basic law of psychophysics stating that a just noticeable difference is a constant proportion to the intensity of an initial stimulus (rather than a constant amount).

Sensory adaptation
An adjustment in sensory capacity after prolonged exposure to unchanging stimuli.

One example of adaptation is the decrease in sensitivity that occurs after repeated exposure to a strong stimulus. If you were to hear a loud tone over and over again, eventually it would begin to sound softer. Similarly, although jumping into a cold lake may be temporarily unpleasant, eventually we probably will get used to the temperature—just as we get used to the temperature of hot sand at the beach!

This apparent decline in sensitivity to sensory stimuli is due to the inability of the sensory nerve receptors to fire off messages to the brain indefinitely. Because these receptor cells are most responsive to *changes* in stimulation, constant stimulation is not effective in producing a sustained reaction (Wark, Lundstrom, & Fairhall, 2007).

Judgments of sensory stimuli are also affected by the context in which the judgments are made. This is the case because judgments are made not in isolation from other stimuli but in terms of preceding sensory experience. You can demonstrate this for yourself by trying a simple experiment:

Take two envelopes, one large and one small, and put fifteen nickels in each one. Now lift the large envelope, put it down, and lift the small one. Which seems to weigh more? Most people report that the small one is heavier, although, as you know, the weights are nearly identical. The reason for this misconception is that the visual context of the envelope interferes with the sensory experience of weight. Adaptation to the context of one stimulus (the size of the envelope) alters responses to another stimulus (the weight of the envelope) (Coren, 2004).

Evaluate

1. _____ is the stimulation of the sense organs; _____ is the sorting out, interpretation, analysis, and integration of stimuli by the sense organs and the brain.

2. The term *absolute threshold* refers to the _____ intensity of a stimulus that must be present for the stimulus to be detected.

3. Weber discovered that for a difference between two stimuli to be perceptible, the stimuli must differ by at least _____ a proportion.

4. After completing a very difficult rock climb in the morning, Carmella found the afternoon climb unexpectedly easy. This case illustrates the phenomenon of _____.

Answers to Evaluate Questions

1. sensation, perception; 2. smallest; 3. constant; 4. adaptation

Key Terms

absolute threshold	perception	sensory adaptation
difference threshold (just noticeable difference)	psychophysics	stimulus
	sensation	Weber's law

Vision: Shedding Light on the Eye

LEARNING OBJECTIVES

What basic processes underlie the sense of vision?

How do we see colours?

If, as poets say, the eyes provide a window to the soul, they also provide us with a window to the world. Our visual capabilities permit us to admire and react to scenes ranging from the beauty of a sunset, to the configuration of a lover's face, to the words written on the pages of a book.

Vision starts with light, the physical energy that stimulates the eye. Light is a form of electromagnetic radiation waves, which, as shown in Figure 1, are measured in wavelengths. The sizes of wavelengths correspond to different types of energy. The range of wavelengths that humans are sensitive to—called the *visual spectrum*—is relatively small. Many nonhuman species have different capabilities. For instance, some reptiles and fish sense energies of longer wavelengths than humans do, and certain insects sense energies of shorter wavelengths than humans do.

Light waves coming from some object outside the body (such as the tree in Figure 2) are sensed by the only organ that is capable of responding to the visible spectrum: the eye. Our eyes convert light to a form that can be used by the neurons that serve as messengers to the brain. The neurons themselves take up a relatively small percentage of the total eye. Most of the eye is a mechanical device that is similar in many respects to a camera without film, as you can see in Figure 2.

Despite the similarities between the eye and a camera, vision involves processes that are far more complex and sophisticated than those of any camera. Furthermore, once an image reaches the neuronal receptors of the eye, the eye/camera analogy ends, for the processing of the visual image in the brain is more reflective of a computer than it is of a camera.

FIGURE 1

The visible spectrum—the range of wavelengths to which people are sensitive—is only a small part of the kinds of wavelengths present in our environment. Is it a benefit or disadvantage to our everyday lives that we aren't more sensitive to a broader range of visual stimuli? Why?

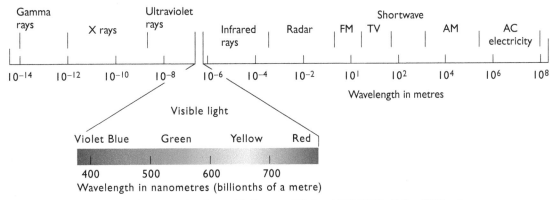

Source: From *Psychology*, 5th edition, by C. Wortman, E. Loftus, and C. Weaver, p. 113. Copyright © 1999 by McGraw-Hill Education.

FIGURE 2

Although human vision is far more complicated than the most sophisticated camera, in some ways basic visual processes are analogous to those used in photography.

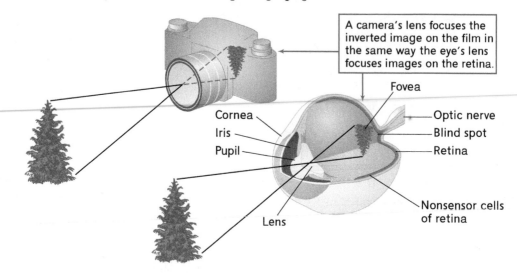

A camera's lens focuses the inverted image on the film in the same way the eye's lens focuses images on the retina.

Cornea
Iris
Pupil
Lens
Fovea
Optic nerve
Blind spot
Retina
Nonsensor cells of retina

Illuminating the Structure of the Eye

The ray of light being reflected off the tree in Figure 2 first travels through the *cornea*, a transparent, protective window. The cornea, because of its curvature, bends (or *refracts*) light as it passes through to focus it more sharply. After moving through the cornea, the light traverses the pupil. The *pupil* is a dark hole in the centre of the *iris*, the coloured part of the eye, which in humans ranges from a light blue to a dark brown. The size of the pupil opening depends on the amount of light in the environment. The dimmer the surroundings are, the more the pupil opens to allow more light to enter. In dim light the pupil expands to enable us to view the situation better—but at the expense of visual detail. (Perhaps one reason candlelight dinners are thought of as romantic is that the dim light prevents one from seeing a partner's physical flaws.).

Once light passes through the pupil, it enters the lens, which is directly behind the pupil. The lens acts to bend the rays of light so that they are properly focused on the rear of the eye. The lens focuses light through a process called *accommodation:* It becomes flatter when viewing distant objects and rounder when looking at closer objects. How does this happen? The muscles in the iris pull on the thick lens to make it thinner and when the muscles relax, the lens returns to its original state.

Reaching the Retina

Having travelled through the pupil and lens, our image of the tree finally reaches its ultimate destination in the eye—the **retina**. Here the electromagnetic energy of light is converted to electrical impulses for transmission to the brain. It

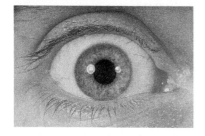 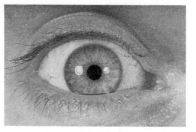

Like the automatic lighting system on a camera, the pupil in the human eye expands to let in more light (left) and contracts to block out light (right). Can humans adjust their ears to let in more or less sound in a similar manner?

Retina
The part of the eye that converts the electromagnetic energy of light to electrical impulses for transmission to the brain.

is important to note that because of the physical properties of light, the image has reversed itself in travelling through the lens, and it reaches the retina upside down (relative to its original position). Although it might seem that this reversal would cause difficulties in understanding and moving about the world, this is not the case. The brain interprets the image in terms of its original position.

The retina consists of a thin layer of nerve cells at the back of the eyeball (see Figure 3). There are two kinds of light-sensitive receptor cells in the retina. The names they have been given describe their shapes: rods and cones. **Rods** are thin, cylindrical receptor cells that are highly sensitive to light. **Cones** are cone-shaped, light-sensitive receptor cells that are responsible for sharp focus and colour perception, particularly in bright light. The rods and cones are distributed unevenly throughout the retina. Cones are concentrated on the part of the retina called the *fovea*. The fovea is a particularly sensitive region of the retina. If you want to focus on something of particular interest, you will automatically try to centre the image on the fovea to see it more sharply.

The density of cones declines just outside the fovea, although cones are found throughout the retina in lower concentrations. In contrast, there are no rods in the fovea. The density of rods is greatest just outside the fovea and then gradually declines toward the edges of the retina. Because the fovea covers only a small portion of the eye, we have fewer cones (between 5 million and 7 million) than rods (between 100 million and 125 million).

FIGURE 3

The basic cells of the eye. Light entering the eye travels through the ganglion and bipolar cells and strikes the light-sensitive rods and cones located at the back of the eye. The rods and cones then transmit nerve impulses to the brain via the bipolar and ganglion cells.

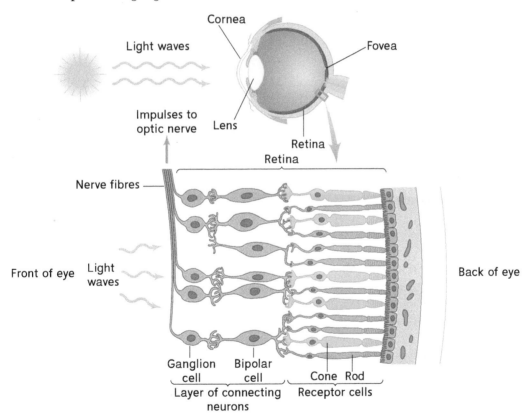

Source: From *Hole's Essentials of Human Anatomy and Physiology*, 7th edition, by D. Sheir, J. Butler, and R. Lewis, p. 283. Copyright © 2000 by McGraw-Hill Education.

Rods
Thin, cylindrical receptor cells in the retina that are highly sensitive to light.

Cones
Cone-shaped, light-sensitive receptor cells in the retina that are responsible for sharp focus and colour perception, particularly in bright light.

The rods and cones are not only structurally dissimilar but they also play distinctly different roles in vision. Cones are primarily responsible for the sharply focused perception of colour, particularly in brightly lit situations; rods are related to vision in dimly lit situations and are largely insensitive to colour and to details as sharp as those the cones are capable of recognizing. The rods play a key role in *peripheral vision*—seeing objects that are outside the main centre of focus—and in night vision.

STUDY ALERT!

Remember that cones relate to colour vision.

Rods and cones also are involved in *dark adaptation*, the phenomenon of adjusting to dim light after being in brighter light. (Think of the experience of walking into a dark movie theatre and groping your way to a seat but a few minutes later seeing the seats quite clearly.) The speed at which dark adaptation occurs is a result of the rate of change in the chemical composition of the rods and cones. Although the cones reach their greatest level of adaptation in just a few minutes, the rods take 20 to 30 minutes to reach the maximum level. The opposite phenomenon—*light adaptation*, or the process of adjusting to bright light after exposure to dim light—occurs much faster, taking only a minute or so.

The distinctive abilities of rods and cones make the eye analogous to a camera that is loaded with two kinds of film. One type is a highly sensitive black-and-white film (the rods). The other type is a somewhat less sensitive colour film (the cones).

Sending the Message from the Eye to the Brain

When light energy strikes the rods and cones, it starts a chain of events that transforms light into neural impulses that can be communicated to the brain. Even before the neural message reaches the brain, however, some initial coding of the visual information takes place.

What happens when light energy strikes the retina depends in part on whether it encounters a rod or a cone. Rods contain *rhodopsin*, a complex reddish-purple substance whose composition changes chemically when energized by light. The substance in cone receptors is different, but the principles are similar. Stimulation of the nerve cells in the eye triggers a neural response that is transmitted to other nerve cells in the retina called *bipolar cells* and *ganglion cells*.

Bipolar cells receive information directly from the rods and cones and communicate that information to the ganglion cells. The ganglion cells collect and summarize visual information, which is then moved out of the back of the eyeball and sent to the brain through a bundle of ganglion axons called the **optic nerve**.

Because the opening for the optic nerve passes through the retina, there are no rods or cones in the area, and that creates a blind spot. Normally, however, this absence of nerve cells does not interfere with vision because you automatically compensate for the missing part of your field of vision (Ramachandran, 1995). To find your blind spot, see Figure 4.

Once beyond the eye itself, the neural impulses relating to the image move through the optic nerve. As the optic nerve leaves the eyeball, its path does not take the most direct route to the part of the brain right behind the eye. Instead, the optic nerves from each eye meet at a point roughly between the two eyes—called the optic chiasm (pronounced "ki-asm")—where each optic nerve then splits.

When the optic nerves split, the nerve impulses coming from the right half of each retina are sent to the right side of the brain, and the impulses arriving from the left half of each retina are sent to the left side of the brain. Because the image on the retinas is reversed and upside down, however, those images coming from the right half of each retina actually originated in the field of vision to the person's left, and the images coming from the left half of each retina originated in the field of vision to the person's right (see Figure 5).

Optic nerve
A bundle of ganglion axons that carry visual information to the brain.

FIGURE 4

To find your blind spot, close your right eye and look at the haunted house with your left eye. You will see the ghost on the periphery of your vision. Now, while staring at the house, move the page toward you. When the page is about 30 cm from your eye, the ghost will disappear. At this moment, the image of the ghost is falling on your blind spot.

But also notice how, when the page is at that distance, not only does the ghost seem to disappear, but the line seems to run continuously through the area where the ghost used to be. This shows how we automatically compensate for missing information by using nearby material to complete what is unseen. That's the reason you never notice the blind spot. What is missing is replaced by what is seen next to the blind spot. Can you think of any advantages that this tendency to provide missing information gives humans as a species?

Processing the Visual Message

By the time a visual message reaches the brain, it has passed through several stages of processing. One of the initial sites is the ganglion cells. Each ganglion cell gathers information from a group of rods and cones in a particular area of the eye and compares the amount of light entering the centre of that area with the amount of light in the area around it. Some ganglion cells are activated by light in the centre (and darkness in the surrounding area). Other ganglion cells are activated when there is darkness in the centre and light in the surrounding areas. The ultimate effect of this

FIGURE 5

Because the optic nerve coming from each eye splits at the optic chiasm, the image to a person's right is sent to the left side of the brain and the image to the person's left is transmitted to the right side of the brain.

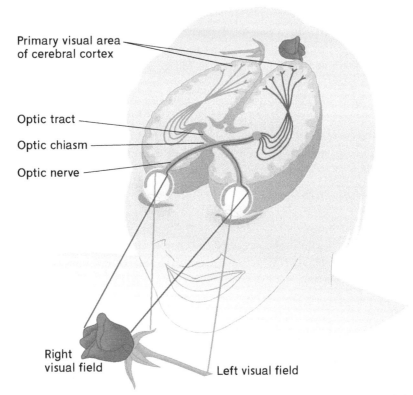

Primary visual area of cerebral cortex

Optic tract

Optic chiasm

Optic nerve

Right visual field

Left visual field

Source: From Sylvia S. Mader, *Human Biology*, 6th edition, page 250. Copyright © 2000 by McGraw-Hill Education. Reprinted with permission of McGraw-Hill Education.

process is to maximize the detection of variations in light and darkness. The image that is passed on to the brain, then, is an enhanced version of the actual visual stimulus outside the body (Kubovy, Epstein, & Gepshtein, 2003; Pearson & Clifford, 2005; Lascaratos, Ji, & Wood, 2007).

The ultimate processing of visual images takes place in the visual cortex of the brain, and it is here that the most complex kinds of processing occur. Psychologists David Hubel and Torsten Wiesel won the Nobel Prize in 1981 for their discovery that many neurons in the cortex are extraordinarily specialized, being activated only by visual stimuli of a particular shape or pattern—a process known as **feature detection**. They found that some cells are activated only by lines of a particular width, shape, or orientation. Other cells are activated only by moving, as opposed to stationary, stimuli (Hubel & Wiesel, 2004; Pelli, Burns, & Farell, 2006).

More recent work has added to our knowledge of the complex ways in which visual information coming from individual neurons is combined and processed. Different parts of the brain process nerve impulses in several individual systems simultaneously. For instance, one system relates to shapes, one to colours, and others to movement, location, and depth. Furthermore, different parts of the brain appear to be involved in the perception of specific *kinds* of stimuli, showing distinctions between the perception of faces, cats, and inanimate stimuli (Winston, O'Doherty, & Kilner, 2006; Werblin & Roska, 2007; Bindemann et al., 2008; Platek & Kemp, 2009).

If separate neural systems exist for processing information about specific aspects of the visual world, how are all these data integrated by the brain? Although the exact process is not well understood, it seems likely that the brain makes use of information regarding the frequency, rhythm, and timing of the firing of particular sets of neural cells. Furthermore, it appears that the brain's integration of visual information does not occur in any single step or location in the brain but instead is a process that occurs on several levels simultaneously. The ultimate outcome, though, is indisputable: a vision of the world around us (de Gelder, 2000; Macaluso, Frith, & Driver, 2000; Werner, Pinna, & Spillmann, 2007).

Colour Vision and Colour Blindness: The Seven-Million-Colour Spectrum

Although the range of wavelengths to which humans are sensitive is relatively narrow, at least in comparison with the entire electromagnetic spectrum, the portion to which we are capable of responding allows us great flexibility in sensing the world. Nowhere is this clearer than in terms of the number of colours we can discern. A person with normal colour vision is capable of distinguishing no less than 7 million different colours (Bruce, Green, & Georgeson, 1997; Rabin, 2004).

Although the variety of colours that people are generally able to distinguish is vast, there are certain individuals whose ability to perceive colour is quite limited—the colour-blind. Interestingly, the condition of these individuals has provided some of the most important clues to understanding how colour vision operates (Neitz, Neitz, & Kainz, 1996; Bonnardel, 2006).

Before continuing, though, look at the photos shown in Figure 6. If you have difficulty seeing the differences between the two photos, you may well be one of the 1 in 50 men or 1 in 5,000 women who are colour-blind.

For most people with colour-blindness, the world looks quite dull. Red fire engines appear yellow, green grass seems yellow, and the three colours of a traffic light all look yellow. In fact, in the most common form of colour-blindness, all red and green objects are seen as yellow. There are other forms of colour-blindness as well, but they are quite rare. In yellow-blue blindness, people are unable to tell the difference between yellow and blue, and in the most extreme case an individual perceives no colour at all. To such a person the world looks something like the picture on a black-and-white television set.

Explaining Colour Vision

To understand why some people are colour-blind, we need to consider the basics of colour vision. There are two processes involved. The first process is explained by the **trichromatic theory of colour vision**. This theory suggests that there are three kinds of cones in the retina, each of which responds primarily to a specific range of wavelengths. One

---

Feature detection
The activation of neurons in the cortex by visual stimuli of specific shapes or patterns.

Trichromatic theory of colour vision
The theory that there are three kinds of cones in the retina, each of which responds primarily to a specific range of wavelengths.

FIGURE 6

(a) Those with colour blindness see a very different view of the world (left) compared to those who have normal vision (right).

Source: © Ralph C. Eagle Jr./Science Source.

is most responsive to blue-violet colours, one to green, and the third to yellow-red (Brown & Wald, 1964). According to trichromatic theory, perception of colour is influenced by the relative strength with which each of the three kinds of cones is activated. If we see a blue sky, the blue-violet cones are primarily triggered, and the others show less activity. The trichromatic theory provides a straightforward explanation of colour-blindness. It suggests that one of the three cone systems malfunctions, and thus colours covered by that range are perceived improperly (Nathans et al., 1989).

However, there are aspects of colour vision that the trichromatic theory is less successful at explaining. For example, the theory does not explain what happens after you stare at something like the Canadian flag shown in Figure 7 for about a minute. Try this yourself and then look at a blank white page: You'll see an image of the traditional red and white Canadian flag. Where there was green, you'll see red, and where there was black, you'll see white.

The phenomenon you have just experienced is called an *afterimage*. It occurs because activity in the retina continues even when you are no longer staring at the original picture. However, it also demonstrates that the trichromatic theory does not explain colour vision completely. Why should the colours in the afterimage be different from those in the original?

Because trichromatic processes do not provide a full explanation of colour vision, alternative explanations have been proposed. According to the **opponent-process theory of colour vision**, receptor cells are linked in pairs, working in opposition to each other. Specifically, there is a blue-yellow pairing, a red-green pairing, and a black-white

FIGURE 7

Stare at the dot in this flag for about a minute and then look at a piece of plain white paper. What do you see? Most people see an afterimage that converts the colours in the figure into the traditional red and white Canadian flag. If you have trouble seeing it the first time, blink once and try again.

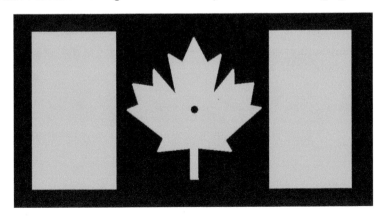

Opponent-process theory of colour vision
The theory that receptor cells for colour are linked in pairs, working in opposition to each other.

pairing. If an object reflects light that contains more red than green, it will stimulate the firing of the cells sensitive to red, simultaneously discouraging or inhibiting the firing of receptor cells sensitive to green—and the object will appear red. If, in contrast, a light contains more green than red, the cells that respond to green will be stimulated to fire while the red ones are inhibited, and the object will appear green.

The opponent-process theory provides a good explanation for afterimages. When we stare at the green in the figure, for instance, our receptor cells for the green component of the green-red pairing become fatigued and are less able to respond to green stimuli. In contrast, the receptor cells for the red part of the pair are not tired, because they are not being stimulated. When we look at a white surface, the light reflected off it would normally stimulate both the green and the red receptors equally. But the fatigue of the green receptors prevents this from happening. They temporarily do not respond to the green, which makes the white light appear to be red. Because the other colours in the figure do the same thing relative to their specific opponents, the afterimage produces the opponent colours—for a while. The afterimage lasts only a short time, because the fatigue of the green receptors is soon overcome, and the white light begins to be perceived more accurately.

Both opponent processes and trichromatic mechanisms are at work in allowing us to see colour. However, they operate in different parts of the visual sensing system. Trichromatic processes work within the retina itself, whereas opponent mechanisms operate both in the retina and at later stages of neuronal processing (Gegenfurtner, 2003; Chen, Zhou, & Gong, 2004; Baraas, Foster, & Amano, 2006).

STUDY ALERT!

Keep in mind that there are two explanations for colour vision: trichromatic and opponent-process theories.

Evaluate

1. Light entering the eye first passes through the _____, a protective window.

2. The structure that converts light into usable neural messages is called the _____.

3. A woman with blue eyes could be described as having blue pigment in her _____.

4. What is the process by which the thickness of the lens is changed in order to focus light properly?

5. The proper sequence of structures that light passes through in the eye is the _____, _____, _____, and _____.

6. Match each type of visual receptor with its function.

   a. Rods

   b. Cones

   1. Used for dim light, largely insensitive to colour

   2. Detect colour, good in bright light

7. _____ theory states that there are three types of cones in the retina, each of which responds primarily to a different colour.

Answers to Evaluate Questions

1. cornea; 2. retina; 3. iris; 4. accommodation; 5. cornea, pupil, lens, retina; 6. a-1, b-2; 7. trichromatic

Key Terms

cones	optic nerve	trichromatic theory of colour
feature detection	retina	vision
opponent-process theory of colour vision	rods	

Hearing and the Other Senses

MODULE 10

LEARNING OBJECTIVES

What role does the ear play in the senses of sound, motion, and balance?

How do smell and taste function?

What are the skin senses, and how do they relate to the experience of pain?

The blast-off was easy compared with what the astronaut was experiencing now: space sickness. The constant nausea and vomiting were enough to make him wonder why he had worked so hard to become an astronaut. Even though he had been warned that there was a two-thirds chance that his first experience in space would cause these symptoms, he wasn't prepared for how terribly sick he really felt.

Whether or not the astronaut wishes he could head right back to earth, his experience, a major problem for space travellers, is related to a basic sensory process: the sense of motion and balance. This sense allows people to navigate their bodies through the world and keep themselves upright without falling. Along with hearing—the process by which sound waves are translated into understandable and meaningful forms—the sense of motion and balance resides in the ear.

Sensing Sound

Although many of us think primarily of the outer ear when we speak of the ear, that structure is only one simple part of the whole. The outer ear acts as a reverse megaphone, designed to collect and bring sounds into the internal portions of the ear (see Figure 1). The location of the outer ears on different sides of the head helps with *sound localization*, the process by which we identify the direction from which a sound is coming. Wave patterns in the air enter each ear at a slightly different time, and the brain uses the discrepancy as a clue to the sound's point of origin. In addition, the two outer ears delay or amplify sounds of particular frequencies to different degrees (Yost, 2000).

Sound is the movement of air molecules brought about by a source of vibration. Sounds travel through the air in wave patterns similar in shape to those made in water when a stone is thrown into a still pond. Sounds, arriving at the outer ear in the form of wave-like vibrations, are funnelled into the *auditory canal*, a tube-like passage that leads to the eardrum. The **eardrum** is aptly named because it operates like a miniature drum, vibrating when sound waves hit it. The more intense the sound, the more the eardrum vibrates. These vibrations are then transferred into the middle ear, a tiny chamber containing three bones (the *hammer*, the *anvil*, and the *stirrup*) that transmit vibrations to the oval window, a thin membrane leading to the inner ear. Because the hammer, anvil, and stirrup act as a set of levers, they not only transmit vibrations but increase their strength. Moreover, because the opening into the middle ear (the eardrum) is considerably larger than the opening out of it (the *oval window*), the force of sound waves on the oval window becomes amplified. The middle ear, then, acts as a tiny mechanical amplifier.

The *inner ear* is the portion of the ear that changes the sound vibrations into a form in which they can be transmitted to the brain. (As you will see, it also contains the organs that allow us to locate our position and determine how

Sound
The movement of air molecules brought about by a source of vibration.

Eardrum
The part of the ear that vibrates when sound waves hit it.

FIGURE 1

The major regions and parts of the ear (Seeley, Stephens, & Tate, 2000). (b) The eardrum. This structure is aptly named because it operates like a miniature drum, vibrating when sound waves hit it.

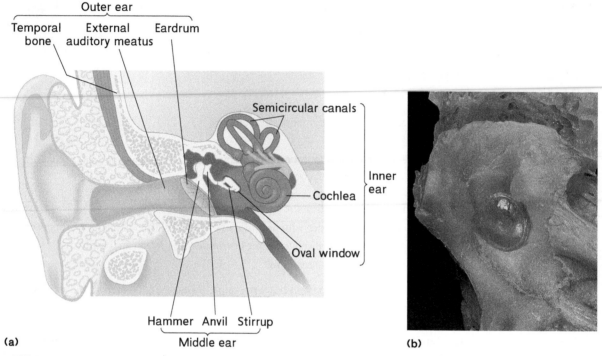

(a)

(b)

we are moving through space.) When sound enters the inner ear through the oval window, it moves into the **cochlea**, a coiled tube that looks something like a snail and is filled with fluid that vibrates in response to sound. Inside the cochlea is the **basilar membrane**, a structure that runs through the centre of the cochlea, dividing it into an upper chamber and a lower chamber. The basilar membrane is covered with hair cells. When the **hair cells** are bent by the vibrations entering the cochlea, the cells send a neural message to the brain (Cho, 2000; Zhou, Liu, & Davis, 2005).

The Physical Aspects of Sound

As we mentioned earlier, what we refer to as sound is actually the physical movement of air molecules in regular, wave-like patterns caused by a vibrating source. Sometimes it is even possible to see these vibrations: If you have ever seen an audio speaker that has no enclosure, you know that, at least when the lowest notes are playing, you can see the speaker moving in and out. What is less obvious is what happens next: The speaker pushes air molecules into waves with the same pattern as its movement. Those wave patterns soon reach your ear, although their strength has been weakened considerably during their travels. All other sources that produce sound work in essentially the same fashion, setting off wave patterns that move through the air to the ear. Air—or some other medium, such as water—is necessary to make the vibrations of objects reach us. This explains why there can be no sound in a vacuum.

Cochlea (KOKE lee uh)
A coiled tube in the ear filled with fluid that vibrates in response to sound.

Basilar membrane
A vibrating structure that runs through the centre of the cochlea, dividing it into an upper chamber and a lower chamber and containing sense receptors for sound.

Hair cells
Tiny cells covering the basilar membrane that, when bent by vibrations entering the cochlea, transmit neural messages to the brain.

We are able to see the audio speaker moving when low notes are played because of a primary characteristic of sound called frequency. *Frequency* is the number of wave cycles that occur in a second. At very low frequencies there are relatively few wave cycles per second (see Figure 2). These cycles are visible to the naked eye as vibrations in the speaker. Low frequencies are translated into a sound that is very low in pitch. (*Pitch* is the characteristic that makes sound seem "high" or "low.") For example, the lowest frequency that humans are capable of hearing is 20 cycles per second. Higher frequencies are heard as sounds of higher pitch. At the upper end of the sound spectrum, people can detect sounds with frequencies as high as 20,000 cycles per second.

Amplitude is a feature of wave patterns that allows us to distinguish between loud and soft sounds. Amplitude is the spread between the up-and-down peaks and valleys of air pressure in a sound wave as it travels through the air. Waves with small peaks and valleys produce soft sounds; those with relatively large peaks and valleys produce loud sounds (see Figure 2).

We are sensitive to broad variations in sound amplitudes. The strongest sounds we are capable of hearing are over a trillion times as intense as the very weakest sound we can hear. This range is measured in decibels. When sounds get higher than 120 decibels, they become painful to the human ear.

Hearing Loss and Deaf Culture

Most young people dismiss hearing loss as their grandparents' problem; however, hearing loss in adolescents has increased by approximately 30 percent between 1998 and 2006 (Shargodsky et al., 2010). A recent poll by the American Speech-Language-Hearing Association found quite the opposite. In reality, more than half of all high school students suffer at least one symptom of hearing loss. A realistic finding given an iPOD's maximum volume of 120 dB is louder than the average live rock concert (115 dB) (American Speech-Language-Hearing Association, 2006; Perusse, 2008).

The delicacy of the organs involved in hearing makes the ear vulnerable to damage. While listening to music or in a noisy area, the noise level is dangerous if you need to raise your voice to be heard, if you can't hear someone 1 metre (3 feet) away from you, if things sound muffled or dull, or if you have pain or ringing in your ears after being in a noisy area (American Speech-Language-Hearing Association, 2015). Exposure to intense levels of sound—coming from events ranging from rock concerts to overly loud earphones—eventually can result in hearing loss, as the hair cells of the basilar membrane lose their elasticity (see Figure 3). Such hearing loss is often permanent.

According to the Canadian Association of the Deaf (CAD) (2008a), approximately 1 in 10 Canadians have some degree of hearing loss. Some Canadians may be unaware that their country's two official languages also extends to the hearing impaired community. There are two official sign language systems in Canada: (1) American Sign Language (ASL) and (2) la Langue des Sourds du Quebec (LSQ) (Canadian Association of the Deaf (CAD), 2008b).

Although minor hearing impairment can be treated with hearing aids that increase the volume of sounds reaching the ear, in some cases they are ineffective. In such situations, technological advances have provided some amazing innovations.

While the restoration of hearing to a deaf person may seem like an unquestionably positive achievement, some advocates for the deaf suggest otherwise, especially when it comes to deaf children who are not old enough to provide informed consent. These critics suggest that deafness represents a legitimate culture—no better or worse than the

---

FIGURE 2

The waves produced by different stimuli are transmitted—usually through the air—in different patterns, with lower frequencies indicated by fewer peaks and valleys per second.

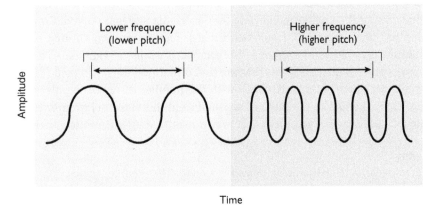

Time

Source: From Rod R. Seeley, Trent D. Stephens, and Philip Tate, *Anatomy & Physiology*, 5th edition, p. 384. Copyright © 2000 by McGraw-Hill Education. Reprinted with permission of McGraw-Hill Education.

FIGURE 3

Various sounds, their decibel levels, and the amount of exposure that results in hearing damage.

Sound	Decibel Level	Exposure Time Leading to Damage	
Whispering	25 dB		
Library	30 dB		
Average home	50 dB		
Normal conversation	60 dB		
Washing machine	65 dB		
Car	70 dB		
Vacuum cleaner	70 dB		
Busy traffic	75 dB		
Alarm clock	80 dB		
Noisy restaurant	80 dB		
Average factory	85 dB	16	hours
Live rock music (moderately loud)	90 dB	8	hours
Screaming child	90 dB	8	hours
Subway train	100 dB	2	hours
Jackhammer	100 dB	2	hours
Loud song played through earphones	100 dB	30	minutes
Helicopter	105 dB	1	hour
Sandblasting	110 dB	30	minutes
Auto horn	120 dB	7.5	minutes
Live rock music (loud)	130 dB	3.75	minutes
Air raid siren	130 dB	3.75	minutes
THRESHOLD OF PAIN	140 dB	Immediate damage	
Jet engine	140 dB	Immediate damage	
Rocket launching	180 dB	Immediate damage	

Source: © 1998 Better Hearing Institute, Washington, DC. All rights reserved.

Photo Source: NASA.

hearing culture—and that providing even limited hearing to deaf children robs them of their natural cultural heritage. It is, without doubt, a controversial position clearly outlined by the Canadian Association of the Deaf on their website.

Sorting Out Theories of Sound

How are our brains able to sort out wavelengths of different frequencies and intensities? One clue comes from studies of the basilar membrane, the area in the cochlea that translates physical vibrations into neural impulses. It turns out that sounds affect different areas of the basilar membrane, depending on the frequency of the sound wave. The part of the basilar membrane nearest to the oval window is most sensitive to high-frequency sounds, and the part nearest to the cochlea's inner end is most sensitive to low-frequency sounds. This finding has led to the **place theory of hearing**, which states that different areas of the basilar membrane respond to different frequencies.

However, place theory does not tell the full story of hearing, because very low frequency sounds trigger neurons across such a wide area of the basilar membrane that no single site is involved. Consequently, an additional explanation for hearing has been proposed: frequency theory. The **frequency theory of hearing** suggests that the entire basilar membrane acts like a microphone, vibrating as a whole in response to a sound. According to this explanation, the nerve receptors send out signals that are tied directly to the frequency (the number of wave crests per second) of the sounds to which we are exposed, with the number of nerve impulses being a direct function of a sound's frequency. Thus, the higher the pitch of a sound (and therefore the greater the frequency of its wave crests), the greater the number of nerve impulses that are transmitted up the auditory nerve to the brain.

Place theory of hearing
The theory that different areas of the basilar membrane respond to different frequencies.

Frequency theory of hearing
The theory that the entire basilar membrane acts like a microphone, vibrating as a whole in response to a sound.

Neither place theory nor frequency theory provides the full explanation for hearing (Hirsh & Watson, 1996; Hudspeth, 2000). Place theory provides a better explanation for the sensing of high-frequency sounds, whereas frequency theory explains what happens when low-frequency sounds are encountered. Medium-frequency sounds incorporate both processes.

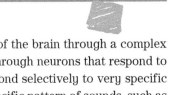

STUDY ALERT!

Be sure to understand the differences between the place and frequency theories of hearing.

After an auditory message leaves the ear, it is transmitted to the auditory cortex of the brain through a complex series of neural interconnections. As the message is transmitted, it is communicated through neurons that respond to specific types of sounds. Within the auditory cortex itself, there are neurons that respond selectively to very specific sorts of sound features, such as clicks and whistles. Some neurons respond only to a specific pattern of sounds, such as a steady tone but not an intermittent one. Furthermore, specific neurons transfer information about a sound's location through their particular pattern of firing (Middlebrooks et al., 2005; Wang et al., 2005; Alho et al., 2006).

Speech perception requires that we make fine discriminations among sounds that are quite similar in terms of their physical properties. Furthermore, not only are we able to understand what is being said from speech, we can use vocal cues to determine who is speaking, if they have an accent and where they may be from, and even their emotional state. Such capabilities illustrate the sophistication of our sense of hearing (Fowler & Galantucci, 2008; Massaro & Chen, 2008; Pell et al., 2009).

Balance: The Ups and Downs of Life

Several structures of the ear are related more to our sense of balance than to our hearing. The **semicircular canals** of the inner ear (refer to Figure 1) consist of three tubes containing fluid that sloshes through them when the head moves, signalling rotational or angular movement to the brain. The pull on our bodies caused by the acceleration of forward, backward, or up-and-down motion, as well as the constant pull of gravity, is sensed by the **otoliths**, tiny, motion-sensitive crystals in the semicircular canals. When we move, these crystals shift like sands on a windy beach. The brain's inexperience in interpreting messages from the weightless otoliths is the cause of the space sickness commonly experienced by two-thirds of all space travellers (Flam, 1991; Stern & Koch, 1996).

Smell and Taste

Until he bit into a piece of raw cabbage on that February evening . . . Raymond Fowler had not thought much about the sense of taste.

The cabbage, part of a pasta dish he was preparing for his family's dinner, had an odd, burning taste, but he did not pay it much attention. Then a few minutes later, his daughter handed him a glass of cola, and he took a swallow. "It was like sulfuric acid," he said. "It was like the hottest thing you could imagine boring into your mouth" (Goode, 1999, pp. D1–D2).

It was evident that something was very wrong with Fowler's sense of taste. After extensive testing, it became clear that he had damaged the nerves involved in his sense of taste, probably because of a viral infection or a medicine he was taking. (Luckily for him, a few months later his sense of taste returned to normal.)

Even without disruptions in our ability to perceive the world such as those experienced by Fowler, we all know the important roles that taste and smell play. We'll consider these two senses next.

Semicircular canals
Three tube-like structures of the inner ear containing fluid that sloshes through them when the head moves, signalling rotational or angular movement to the brain.

Otoliths
Tiny, motion-sensitive crystals within the semicircular canals that sense body acceleration.

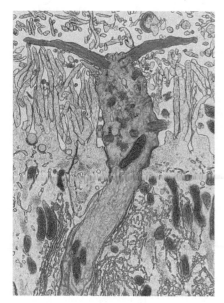

More than 1,000 receptor cells, known as olfactory cells, are spread across the nasal cavity. The cells are specialized to react to particular odours. Do you think it is possible to "train" the nose to pick up a greater number of odours?

Source: © Prof. P. Motta/Dept. of Anatomy/University "La Sapienza," Rome/SPL/Science Source.

Smell

Although many animals have keener abilities to detect odours than we do, the human sense of smell (*olfaction*) permits us to detect more than 10,000 separate smells. We also have a good memory for smells, and long-forgotten events and memories can be brought back with the mere whiff of an odour associated with a memory (Stevenson & Case, 2005; Schroers, Prigot, & Fagen, 2007).

Results of "sniff tests" have shown that women generally have a better sense of smell than men do (Engen, 1987). People also seem to have the ability to distinguish males from females on the basis of smell alone. In one experiment, blindfolded students who were asked to sniff the breath of a female or male volunteer who was hidden from view were able to distinguish the sex of the donor at better than chance levels. People can also distinguish happy from sad emotions by sniffing underarm smells, and women are able to identify their babies solely on the basis of smell just a few hours after birth (Doty et al., 1982; Haviland-Jones & Chen, 1999; Fusari & Ballesteros, 2008).

The sense of smell is sparked when the molecules of a substance enter the nasal passages and meet *olfactory cells*, the receptor neurons of the nose, which are spread across the nasal cavity. More than 1,000 separate types of receptors have been identified on those cells so far. Each of these receptors is so specialized that it responds only to a small band of different odours. The responses of the separate olfactory cells are then transmitted to the brain, where they are combined into recognition of a particular smell (Murphy et al., 2004; Marshall, Laing, & Jinks, 2006; Zhou & Buck, 2006).

Smell may also act as a hidden means of communication for humans. It has long been known that nonhumans release *pheromones*, chemicals they secrete into the environment that produce a reaction in other members of the same species, permitting the transmission of messages such as sexual availability. For instance, the vaginal secretions of female monkeys contain pheromones that stimulate the sexual interest of male monkeys (Holy, Dulac, & Meister, 2000; Touhara, 2007; Hawkes & Doty, 2009).

The degree to which pheromones are part of the human experience remains an open question. Some psychologists believe that human pheromones affect emotional responses, although the evidence is inconclusive. For one thing, it is not clear what specific sense organ is receptive to pheromones. In non-humans, it is the *vomeronasal* organ in the nose, but in humans the organ appears to recede during fetal development (Haviland-Jones & Wilson, 2008; Hummer & McClintock, 2009).

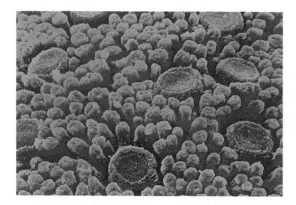

There are 10,000 taste buds on the tongue and other parts of the mouth. Taste buds wear out and are replaced every ten days. What would happen if taste buds were not regenerated?

Source: © Omikron/Science Source.

Taste

The sense of taste (*gustation*) involves receptor cells that respond to four basic stimulus qualities: sweet, sour, salty, and bitter. A fifth category also exists, a flavour called *umami*, although there is controversy about whether it qualifies as a fundamental taste. Umami is a hard-to-translate Japanese word, although the English "meaty" or "savory" comes close. Chemically, umami involves food stimuli that contain amino acids (the substances that make up proteins) (McCabe & Rolls, 2007; Erickson, 2008).

Although the specialization of the receptor cells leads them to respond most strongly to a particular type of taste, they also seem capable of responding to other tastes as well. Ultimately, every taste is simply a combination of the basic flavour qualities, in the same way that the primary colours blend into a vast variety of shades and hues (DiLorenzo & Yougentob, 2003; Yeomans, Tepper, & Ritezschel, 2007).

The receptor cells for taste are located in roughly 10,000 *taste buds*, which are distributed across the tongue and other parts of the mouth and throat. The taste buds wear out and are replaced every ten days or so. That's a good thing, because if our taste buds weren't constantly reproducing, we'd lose the ability to taste after we'd accidentally burned our tongues.

The sense of taste differs significantly from one person to another, largely as a result of genetic factors. Some people, dubbed "supertasters," are highly sensitive to taste; they have twice as many taste receptors as "nontasters," who are relatively insensitive to taste. Supertasters (who, for unknown reasons, are more likely to be female than male) find sweets sweeter, cream creamier, and spicy dishes spicier, and weaker concentrations of flavour are enough to satisfy any cravings they may have. In contrast, because they aren't so sensitive to taste, nontasters may seek out relatively sweeter and fattier foods in order to maximize the taste. As a consequence, they may be prone to obesity (Bartoshuk, 2000; Snyder, Fast, & Bartoshuk, 2004; Pickering & Gordon, 2006).

Are you a supertaster? To find out, complete the questionnaire in Figure 4.

FIGURE 4

All tongues are not created equal, according to taste researchers Linda Bartoshuk and Laurie Lucchina. Instead, they suggest that the intensity of a flavour experienced by a given person is determined by that person's genetic background. This taste test can help determine if you are a nontaster, average taster, or supertaster.

Take a Taste Test

1. **Taste Bud Count**
   Punch a hole with a standard hole punch in a square of wax paper. Paint the front of your tongue with a cotton swab dipped in blue food colouring. Put wax paper on the tip of your tongue, just to the right of centre. With a flashlight and magnifying glass, count the number of pink, unstained circles. They contain taste buds.

2. **Sweet Taste**
   Rinse your mouth with water before tasting each sample. Put 1/2 cup (113 ml) sugar in a measuring cup, and then add enough water to make 1 cup (227 ml). Mix. Coat front half of your tongue, including the tip, with a cotton swab dipped in the solution. Wait a few moments. Rate the sweetness according to the scale shown below.

3. **Salt Taste**
   Put 2 teaspoons (10 g) of salt in a measuring cup and add enough water to make 1 cup (227 ml). Repeat the steps listed above, rating how salty the solution is.

4. **Spicy Taste**
   Add I teaspoon (5 g) of Tabasco sauce to I cup (227 ml) of water. Apply with a cotton swab to first half inch (1.25 cm) of the tongue, including the tip. Keep your tongue out of your mouth until the burn reaches a peak, then rate the burn according to the scale.

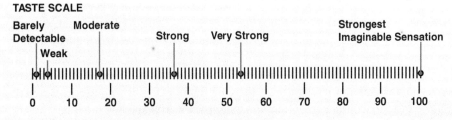

	SUPERTASTERS	NONTASTERS
Number of taste buds	25 on Average	10
Sweet rating	56 on Average	32
Tabasco	64 on Average	31

Average tasters lie in between supertasters and nontasters. Bartoshuk and Lucchina lack the data at this time to rate salt reliably, but you can compare your results with others taking the test.

Source: Adapted from S. Brownlee and T. Watson, "The Senses," *US News & World Report*, January 13, 1997, pp. 51–59. Reprinted with permission of Linda M. Bartoshuk.

The Skin Senses: Touch, Pressure, Temperature, and Pain

It started innocently when Jennifer Darling hurt her right wrist during gym class. At first it seemed like a simple sprain. But even though the initial injury healed, the excruciating, burning pain accompanying it did not go away. Instead, it spread to her other arm and then to her legs. The pain, which Jennifer described as similar to "a hot iron on your arm," was unbearable—and never stopped.

The source of Darling's pain turned out to be a rare condition known as "reflex sympathetic dystrophy syndrome," or RSDS for short. For a victim of RSDS, a stimulus as mild as a gentle breeze or the touch of a feather can produce agony. Even bright sunlight or a loud noise can trigger intense pain.

STUDY ALERT!

Remember that there are multiple skin senses, including touch, pressure, temperature, and pain.

Pain like Darling's can be devastating, yet a lack of pain can be equally bad. If you never experienced pain, for instance, you might not notice that your arm had brushed against a hot pan, and you would suffer a severe burn. Similarly, without the warning sign of abdominal pain that typically accompanies an inflamed appendix, your appendix might eventually rupture, spreading a fatal infection throughout your body.

In fact, all our **skin senses**—touch, pressure, temperature, and pain—play a critical role in survival, making us aware of potential danger to our bodies. Most of these senses operate through nerve receptor cells located at various depths throughout the skin, distributed unevenly throughout the body. For example, some areas, such as the fingertips, have many more receptor cells sensitive to touch and as a consequence are notably more sensitive than other areas of the body (Gardner & Kandel, 2000; see Figure 5).

Probably the most extensively researched skin sense is pain, and with good reason: People consult physicians and take medication for pain more than for any other symptom or condition. Pain costs $100 billion a year in the United States alone (Kalb, 2003; Pesmen, 2006).

Pain is a response to a great variety of different kinds of stimuli. A light that is too bright can produce pain, and sound that is too loud can be painful. One explanation is that pain is an outcome of cell injury; when a cell is damaged, regardless of the source of damage, it releases a chemical called *substance P* that transmits pain messages to the brain.

Some people are more susceptible to pain than others. For example, women experience painful stimuli more intensely than men. These gender differences are associated with the production of hormones related to menstrual cycles. In addition, certain genes are linked to the experience of pain, so that we may inherit our sensitivity to pain (Edwards & Fillingim, 2007; Nielsen et al., 2008; Kim, Clark, & Dionne, 2009; Nielsen, Staud, & Price, 2009).

But the experience of pain is not determined by biological factors alone. For example, women report that the pain experienced in childbirth is moderated to some degree by the joyful nature of the situation. Research at University of Toronto also found mother's satisfaction with the childbirth experience (e.g., physical birth environment, involvement in decision making) to be a significant moderator of the pain experienced in childbirth (Hodnett, 2002). In contrast, even a minor stimulus can produce the perception of strong pain if it is accompanied by anxiety (like a visit to the dentist). Clearly, then, pain is a perceptual response that depends heavily on our emotions and thoughts (Hadjistavropoulos, Craig, & Fuchs-Lacelle, 2004; Rollman, 2004; Lang, Sorrell, & Rodgers, 2006).

In some situations, it is possible to quantify an individual's level of pain using a method developed by Ronald Melzack at McGill University (Melzack & Katz, 2004). Melzack developed the McGill Pain Questionnaire to measure pain level, changes in pain over time, and assess treatment results. Melzack's questionnaire includes three sections on pain: (1) What Does Your Pain Feel Like? (2) How Does Your Pain Change with Time? (3) How Strong is Your Pain? In section one, the individual circles words that best describe his or her pain—ranging from "flickering" to "throbbing"

Skin senses
The senses of touch, pressure, temperature, and pain.

FIGURE 5

Skin sensitivity in various areas of the body. The lower the mean threshold is, the more sensitive a body part is. The fingers and thumb, lips, nose, cheeks, and big toe are the most sensitive. Why do you think certain areas are more sensitive than others?

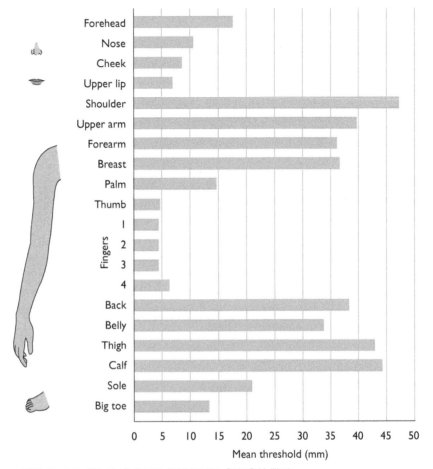

Source: From Kenshalo, *The Skin Senses*, 1968. Courtesy of Charles C. Thomas, Publisher, Ltd., Springfield, Illinois.

to "pounding." In section two, the individual circles words that best describe his or her pain over time—ranging from "flickering" to "brief momentary transient" to "continuous steady constant." In section three, the individual circles words that best describe his or her pain intensity—ranging from "mild" to "discomforting" to "excruciating."

According to the **gate-control theory of pain**, particular nerve receptors in the spinal cord lead to specific areas of the brain related to pain. When these receptors are activated because of an injury or problem with a part of the body, a "gate" to the brain is opened, allowing us to experience the sensation of pain (Melzack & Katz, 2004).

However, another set of neural receptors can, when stimulated, close the "gate" to the brain, thereby reducing the experience of pain. The gate can be shut in two different ways. First, other impulses can overwhelm the nerve pathways relating to pain, which are spread throughout the brain. In this case, non-painful stimuli compete with and sometimes displace the neural message of pain, thereby shutting off the painful stimulus. This explains why rubbing the skin around an injury (or even listening to distracting music) helps reduce pain. The competing stimuli can overpower the painful ones (Villemure, Slotnick, & Bushnell, 2003).

Psychological factors account for the second way a gate can be shut. Depending on an individual's current emotions, interpretation of events, and previous experience, the brain can close a gate by sending a message down the spinal cord to an injured area, producing a reduction in or relief from pain. Thus, soldiers who are injured in battle may

Gate-control theory of pain
When particular nerve receptors are activated because of an injury or problem with part of the body, a "gate" to the brain is opened allowing us to experience the sensation of pain. When stimulated, another set of neural receptors can close the "gate" and reduce the experience of pain.

experience no pain—the surprising situation in more than half of all combat injuries. The lack of pain probably occurs because a soldier experiences such relief at still being alive that the brain sends a signal to the injury site to shut down the pain gate (Turk, 1994; Gatchel & Weisberg, 2000; Pincus & Morley, 2001).

Gate-control theory also may explain cultural differences in the experience of pain. Some of these variations are astounding. For example, in India people who participate in the "hook-swinging" ritual to celebrate the power of the gods have steel hooks embedded under the skin and muscles of their backs. During the ritual, they swing from a pole, suspended by the hooks. What would seem likely to induce excruciating pain instead produces a state of celebration and near euphoria. In fact, when the hooks are later removed, the wounds heal quickly, and after two weeks almost no visible marks remain (Kosambi, 1967; Melzack & Katz, 2001).

Gate-control theory suggests that the lack of pain is due to a message from the participant's brain, which shuts down the pain pathways. Gate-control theory also may explain the effectiveness of *acupuncture,* an ancient Chinese technique in which sharp needles are inserted into various parts of the body. The sensation from the needles may close the gateway to the brain, reducing the experience of pain. It is also possible that the body's own painkillers—called endorphins—as well as positive and negative emotions, play a role in opening and closing the gate (Fee et al., 2002; Witt, Jena, & Brinkhaus, 2006).

Although the basic ideas behind gate-control theory have been supported by research, other processes are involved in the perception of pain. For instance, it appears that there are multiple neural pathways involved in the experience of pain. Furthermore, it is clear that the suppression of pain can occur through the natural release of endorphins and other compounds that produce a reduction of discomfort and a sense of well-being (Grahek, 2007).

For some people, pain is an everyday part of life, sometimes so much so that it interferes with the simplist tasks. Chronic, lingering pain may start when someone experiences an injury that damages neurons involved in the transmission of pain. These injured neurons send out endless false alarms to the brain and cause the brain to experience pain (Clay, 2002; Marx, 2004). For many people, pain is unceasing: According to the Canadian Psychological Association (2008), 1 in 10 Canadians suffer from chronic pain.

Evaluate

1. The tube-like passage leading from the outer ear to the eardrum is known as the _____.
2. The purpose of the eardrum is to protect the sensitive nerves underneath it. It serves no purpose in actual hearing. True or false?
3. The three middle ear bones transmit their sound to the _____.
4. The _____ theory of hearing states that the entire basilar membrane responds to a sound, vibrating more or less, depending on the nature of the sound.
5. The three fluid-filled tubes in the inner ear that are responsible for our sense of balance are known as the _____ _____.
6. The _____ – _____ theory states that when certain skin receptors are activated as a result of an injury, a "pathway" to the brain is opened, allowing pain to be experienced.

Answers to Evaluate Questions

1. auditory canal; 2. false: it vibrates when sound waves hit it, and transmits the sound; 3. oval window; 4. frequency; 5. semicircular canals; 6. gate-control

Key Terms

basilar membrane	gate-control theory of	semicircular canals
cochlea (KOKE lee uh)	pain	skin senses
eardrum	hair cells	sound
frequency theory of	otoliths	
hearing	place theory of hearing	

Perceptual Organization: Constructing Our View of the World

LEARNING OBJECTIVES

What principles underlie our organization of the visual world and allow us to make sense of our environment?

How are we able to perceive the world in three dimensions when our retinas are capable of sensing only two-dimensional images?

What clues do visual illusions give us about our understanding of general perceptual mechanisms?

Consider the vase shown in Figure 1a for a moment. Or is it a vase? Take another look, and instead you may see the profiles of two people.

Now that an alternative interpretation has been pointed out, you will probably shift back and forth between the two interpretations. Similarly, if you examine the shapes in Figures 1b and 1c long enough, you will probably experience a shift in what you're seeing. The reason for these reversals is this: Because each figure is two-dimensional, the usual means we employ for distinguishing the figure (the object being perceived) from the ground (the background or spaces within the object) do not work.

The fact that we can look at the same figure in more than one way illustrates an important point. We do not just passively respond to visual stimuli that happen to fall on our retinas. Instead, we actively try to organize and make sense of what we see.

We turn now from a focus on the initial response to a stimulus (sensation) to what our minds make of that stimulus—perception. Perception is a constructive process by which we go beyond the stimuli that are presented to us and attempt to construct a meaningful situation.

FIGURE 1

When the usual cues we use to distinguish figure from ground are absent, we may shift back and forth between different views of the same figure. If you look at each of these objects long enough, you'll probably experience a shift in what you're seeing. In (a), you can see either a vase or the profiles of two people. In (b), the shaded portion of the figure, called a Necker cube, can appear to be either the front or the back of the cube. Finally, in (c), you'll be able to see a face of a woman if you look at the drawing long enough.

(a)

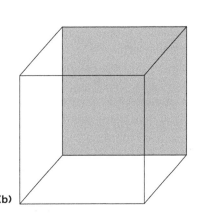

(b)

(c)

The Gestalt Laws of Organization

Some of the most basic perceptual processes can be described by a series of principles that focus on the ways we organize bits and pieces of information into meaningful wholes. Known as **gestalt laws of organization**, these principles were set forth in the early 1900s by a group of German psychologists who studied patterns, or gestalts (Wertheimer, 1923). Those psychologists discovered a number of important principles that are valid for visual (as well as auditory) stimuli, illustrated in Figure 2: closure, proximity, similarity, and simplicity.

Figure 2a illustrates *closure*. We usually group elements to form enclosed or complete figures rather than open ones. We tend to ignore the breaks in Figure 2a and concentrate on the overall form. Figure 2b demonstrates the principle of *proximity*. We perceive elements that are closer together as grouped together. As a result, we tend to see pairs of dots rather than a row of single dots in Figure 2b.

Elements that are *similar* in appearance we perceive as grouped together. We see, then, horizontal rows of circles and squares in Figure 2c instead of vertical mixed columns. Finally, in a general sense, the overriding gestalt principle is *simplicity:* When we observe a pattern, we perceive it in the most basic, straightforward manner that we can. For example, most of us see Figure 2d as a square with lines on two sides, rather than as the block letter *W* on top of the letter *M*. If we have a choice of interpretations, we generally opt for the simpler one.

STUDY ALERT!

The gestalt laws of organization are classic principles in the field of psychology. Figure 2 can help you remember them.

FIGURE 2

Organizing these various bits and pieces of information into meaningful wholes constitutes some of the most basic processes of perception, which are summed up in the gestalt laws of organization. Do you think any other species share this organizational tendency? How might we find out?

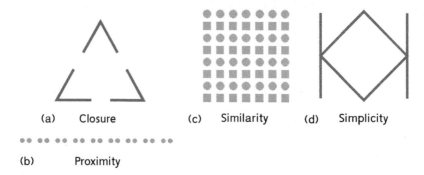

(a)   Closure   (c)   Similarity   (d)   Simplicity

(b)   Proximity

Although gestalt psychology no longer plays a prominent role in contemporary psychology, its legacy endures. One fundamental gestalt principle that remains influential is that two objects considered together form a whole that is different from the simple combination of the objects. Gestalt psychologists argued, quite convincingly, that the perception of stimuli in our environment goes well beyond the individual elements that we sense. Instead, it represents an active, constructive process carried out within the brain. There, bits and pieces of sensations are put together to make something more meaningful than the separate elements (Humphreys & Müller, 2000; Lehar, 2003; van der Helm, 2006; see Figure 3).

Gestalt laws of organization
A series of principles that describe how we organize bits and pieces of information into meaningful wholes.

FIGURE 3

Although at first it is difficult to distinguish anything in this drawing, keep looking, and eventually you'll probably be able to see the figure of a dog. The dog represents a gestalt, or perceptual whole, which is something greater than the sum of the individual elements.

Top-Down and Bottom-Up Processing

Ca- yo- re-d t-is -en-en-e, w-ic- ha- ev-ry -hi-d l-tt-r m-ss-ng? It probably won't take you too long to figure out that it says, "Can you read this sentence, which has every third letter missing?"

If perception were based primarily on breaking down a stimulus into its most basic elements, understanding the sentence, as well as other ambiguous stimuli, would not be possible. The fact that you were probably able to recognize such an imprecise stimulus illustrates that perception proceeds along two different avenues, called top-down processing and bottom-up processing.

In **top-down processing**, perception is guided by higher-level knowledge, experience, expectations, and motivations. You were able to figure out the meaning of the sentence with the missing letters because of your prior reading experience, and because written English contains redundancies. Not every letter of each word is necessary to decode its meaning. Moreover, your expectations played a role in your being able to read the sentence. You were probably expecting a statement that had *something* to do with psychology, not the lyrics to an Eminem song.

Top-down processing is illustrated by the importance of context in determining how we perceive objects. Look, for example, at Figure 4. Most of us perceive that the first row consists of the letters A through F, while the second contains the numbers 10 through 14. But take a more careful look and you'll see that the "B" and the "13" are identical. Clearly, our perception is affected by our expectations about the two sequences—even though the two stimuli are exactly the same.

However, top-down processing cannot occur on its own. Even though top-down processing allows us to fill in the gaps in ambiguous and out-of-context stimuli, we would be unable to perceive the meaning of such stimuli without bottom-up processing. **Bottom-up processing** consists of the progression of recognizing and processing information

Top-down processing
Perception that is guided by higher-level knowledge, experience, expectations, and motivations.

Bottom-up processing
Perception that consists of the progression of recognizing and processing information from individual components of a stimuli and moving to the perception of the whole.

FIGURE 4

The power of context is shown in this figure. Note how the B and the 13 are identical.

A B C D E F

10 11 12 13 14

from individual components of a stimuli and moving to the perception of the whole. We would make no headway in our recognition of the sentence without being able to perceive the individual shapes that make up the letters. Some perception, then, occurs at the level of the patterns and features of each of the separate letters.

It should be apparent that top-down and bottom-up processing occur simultaneously, and interact with each other, in our perception of the world around us. Bottom-up processing permits us to process the fundamental characteristics of stimuli, whereas top-down processing allows us to bring our experience to bear on perception. As we learn more about the complex processes involved in perception, we are developing a better understanding of how the brain continually interprets information from the senses and permits us to make responses appropriate to the environment (Sobel et al., 2007; Folk & Remington, 2008; Westerhausen et al., 2009).

An example of both top-down and bottom-up processing is Ontario's consideration of a law to have medical prescriptions prepared on a computer rather than being handwritten by the doctor. This new practice, known as *e-prescribing*, demonstrates top-down processing for the pharmacist who fills prescriptions based on higher-level knowledge and experience in pharmaceuticals and bottom-up processing for the patient who recognizes prescription contents based on individual letters and patterns produced by the computer (Eggertson, 2009).

Perceptual Constancy

Consider what happens as you finish a conversation with a friend and she begins to walk away from you. As you watch her walk down the street, the image on your retina becomes smaller and smaller. Do you wonder why she is shrinking?

Of course not. Despite the very real change in the size of the retinal image, you factor into your thinking the knowledge that your friend is moving farther away from you because of perceptual constancy. **Perceptual constancy** is a phenomenon in which physical objects are perceived as unvarying and consistent despite changes in their appearance or in the physical environment.

In some cases, though, our application of perceptual constancy can mislead us. One good example of this involves the rising moon. When the moon first appears at night, close to the horizon, it seems to be huge—much larger than when it is high in the sky later in the evening. You may have thought that the apparent change in the size of the moon was caused by the moon's being physically closer to the earth when it first appears. In fact, though, this is not the case at all: the actual image of the moon on our retina is the same, whether it is low or high in the sky.

Instead, the moon appears to be larger when it is close to the horizon primarily because of the phenomenon of perceptual constancy. When the moon is near the horizon, the perceptual cues of intervening terrain and objects such as trees on the horizon produce a misleading sense of distance. The phenomenon of

When the moon is near the horizon, we do not see it by itself and perceptual constancy leads us to take into account a misleading sense of distance.

Source: © Paul Souders/The Image Bank/Getty Images RF.

Perceptual constancy
The phenomenon in which physical objects are perceived as unvarying and consistent despite changes in their appearance or in the physical environment.

perceptual constancy leads us to take that assumed distance into account when we view the moon, and it leads us to misperceive the moon as relatively large.

In contrast, when the moon is high in the sky, we see it by itself, and we don't try to compensate for its distance from us. In this case, then, perceptual constancy leads us to perceive it as relatively small. To demonstrate perceptual constancy for yourself, try looking at the moon when it is relatively low on the horizon through a paper-towel tube; the moon suddenly will appear to "shrink" back to normal size (Coren, 1992; Ross & Plug, 2002; Kaufman, Johnson, & Liu, 2008).

In addition to the phenomenon of perceptual constancy, other factors may contribute to the moon illusion. In fact, scientists have put forward a variety of possibilities over the years and have yet to agree on the best explanation (Kim, 2008; Gregory, 2008).

Depth Perception: Translating 2-D to 3-D

As sophisticated as the retina is, the images projected onto it are flat and two-dimensional. Yet the world around us is three-dimensional, and we perceive it that way. How do we make the transformation from 2-D to 3-D?

The ability to view the world in three dimensions and to perceive distance—a skill known as **depth perception**—is due largely to the fact that we have two eyes. Because there is a certain distance between the eyes, a slightly different image reaches each retina. The brain integrates the two images into one composite view, but it also recognizes the difference in images and uses it to estimate the distance of an object from us. The difference in the images seen by the left eye and the right eye is known as *binocular disparity* (Hibbard, 2007; Kara & Boyd, 2009).

To get a sense of binocular disparity for yourself, hold a pencil at arm's length and look at it first with one eye and then with the other. There is little difference between the two views relative to the background. Now bring the pencil just 15 cm away from your face, and try the same thing. This time you will perceive a greater difference between the two views.

The fact that the discrepancy between the images in the two eyes varies according to the distance of objects that we view provides us with a means of determining distance. If we view two objects and one is considerably closer to us than the other is, the retinal disparity will be relatively large and we will have a greater sense of depth between the two. However, if the two objects are a similar distance from us, the retinal disparity will be minor, and we will perceive them as being a similar distance from us.

In some cases, certain cues permit us to obtain a sense of depth and distance with just one eye. These cues are known as *monocular cues*. One monocular cue—*motion parallax*—is the change in position of an object on the retina caused by movement of your body relative to the object. For example, suppose you are a passenger in a moving car, and you focus your eye on a stable object such as a tree. Objects that are closer than the tree will appear to move backward, and the nearer the object is, the more quickly it will appear to move. In contrast, objects beyond the tree will seem to move at a slower speed, but in the same direction as you are. Your brain is able to use these cues to calculate the relative distances of the tree and other objects.

Railroad tracks that seem to join together in the distance are an example of linear perspective.

Similarly, experience has taught us that if two objects are the same size, the one that makes a smaller image on the retina is farther away than is the one that provides a larger image—an example of the monocular cue of *relative size*. But it's not just size of an object that provides information about distance; the quality of the image on the retina helps us judge distance. The monocular cue of *texture gradient* provides information about distance because the details of things that are far away are less distinct (Proffitt, 2006).

Finally, anyone who has ever seen railroad tracks that seem to join together in the distance knows that distant objects appear to be closer together than are nearer ones, a phenomenon called linear perspective. People use *linear perspective* as a monocular cue in estimating distance, allowing the two-dimensional image

Depth perception
The ability to view the world in three dimensions and to perceive distance.

on the retina to record the three-dimensional world (Bruce, Green, & Georgeson, 1997; Dobbins et al., 1998; Shimono & Wade, 2002; Bruggeman, Yonas, & Konczak, 2007).

Motion Perception: As the World Turns

When a batter tries to hit a pitched ball, the most important factor is the motion of the ball. How is a batter able to judge the speed and location of a target that is moving at some 145 km per hour?

The answer rests in part on several cues that provide us with relevant information about the perception of motion. For one thing, the movement of an object across the retina is typically perceived relative to some stable, unmoving background. Moreover, if the stimulus is heading toward us, the image on the retina will expand in size, filling more and more of the visual field. In such cases, we assume that the stimulus is approaching—not that it is an expanding stimulus viewed at a constant distance.

It is not, however, just the movement of images across the retina that brings about the perception of motion. If it were, we would perceive the world as moving every time we moved our heads. Instead, one of the critical things we learn about perception is to factor information about our own head and eye movements along with information about changes in the retinal image.

Sometimes we perceive motion when it doesn't occur. Have you ever been on a stationary train that feels as if it is moving, because a train on an adjacent track begins to slowly move past? Or have you been in an IMAX movie theatre, in which you feel as if you were falling as the huge image of a plane moves across the screen? In both cases, the experience of motion is convincing. *Apparent movement* is the perception that a stationary object is moving. It occurs when different areas of the retina are quickly stimulated, leading us to interpret motion (Ekroll & Scherzer, 2009; Lindemann & Bekkering, 2009).

Perceptual Illusions: The Deceptions of Perceptions

If you look carefully at the Parthenon, one of the most famous buildings of ancient Greece, still standing at the top of an Athens hill, you'll see that it was built with a bulge on one side. If it didn't have that bulge—and quite a few other "tricks" like it, such as columns that incline inward—it would look as if it were crooked and about to fall down. Instead, it appears to stand completely straight, at right angles to the ground.

The fact that the Parthenon appears to be completely upright is the result of a series of visual illusions. **Visual illusions** are physical stimuli that consistently produce errors in perception. In the case of the Parthenon, the building appears to be completely square, as illustrated in Figure 5a. However, if it had been built that way, it would look to us as it does in Figure 5b. The reason for this is an illusion that makes right angles placed above a line appear as if they were bent. To offset the illusion, the Parthenon was constructed as in Figure 5c, with a slight upward curvature.

Such perceptual insights did not stop with the Greeks. Modern-day architects and designers also take visual distortions into account in their planning. For example, the New Orleans Superdome makes use of several visual tricks. Its seats vary in colour throughout the stadium to give the appearance, from a distance, that there is always a full house. The carpeting in some of the sloping halls has stripes that make people slow their pace by producing the perception that they are moving faster than they actually are. The same illusion is used at toll booths on superhighways. Stripes painted on the pavement in front of the toll booths make drivers feel that they are moving more rapidly than they actually are and cause them to decelerate quickly.

The implications of visual illusions go beyond design features. For instance, suppose you were an air traffic controller watching a radar screen like the one shown in Figure 6a. You might be tempted to sit back and relax as the two planes, whose flight paths are indicated in the figure, drew closer and closer together. If you did, however, the result might be an air disaster. Although it looks as if the two planes will miss each other, they are headed for a collision. Investigation has suggested that some 70 to 80 percent of all airplane accidents are caused by pilot errors of one sort or another (Krause, 2003; Shappell & Wiegmann, 2003).

Visual illusions
Physical stimuli that consistently produce errors in perception.

FIGURE 5

In building the Parthenon, the Greeks constructed an architectural wonder that looks perfectly straight, with right angles at every corner, as in (a). However, if it had been built with completely true right angles, it would have looked as it does in (b). To compensate for this illusion, the Parthenon was designed to have a slight upward curvature, as shown in (c).

(a) (b) (c)

Source: (b) and (c): Figure from *Sensation and Perception*, 3rd edition, by Stanley Coren and Lawrence M. Ward, copyright © 1989 by John Wiley & Sons reproduced by permission of the publisher.

Photo Source: © John G. Ross/Science Source.

The flight-path illustration provides an example of a well-known visual illusion called the *Poggendorf illusion*. As you can see in Figure 6b, the Poggendorf illusion, when stripped down to its basics, gives the impression that line X would pass below line Y if it were extended through the pipelike figure, instead of heading directly toward line Y as it actually does.

The Poggendorf illusion is just one of many that consistently fool the eye (Perkins, 1983; Greist-Bousquet & Schiffman, 1986). Another, illustrated in Figure 7, is called the *Müller-Lyer illusion*. Although the two lines are the same length, the one

FIGURE 6

Put yourself in the shoes of a flight controller and look at the flight paths of the two planes on this radar screen. A first glance suggests that they are headed on different courses and will not hit each other. But now take a ruler and lay it along the two paths. Your career as a flight controller might well be over if you were guiding the two planes and allowed them to continue without a change in course (Coren, Porac, & Ward, 1984, p. 7). (b) The Poggendorf illusion, in which the two diagonal lines appear (incorrectly) as if they would not meet if extended toward each other.

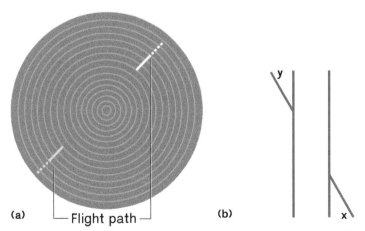

(a) └ Flight path ┘ (b)

Source: From Coren, *Sensation and Perception*, 1st edition. © 1989 Global Rights & Permissions, a part of Cengage Learning, Inc. Reproduced by permission. www.cengage .com/permissions.

FIGURE 7

In the Müller-Lyer illusion (a), the upper horizontal line appears longer than the lower one. One explanation for the Müller-Lyer illusion suggests that the line with arrow points directed inward is to be interpreted as the inside corner of a rectangular room extending away from us (b), and the line with arrow points directed outward is viewed as the relatively close corner of a rectangular object, such as the building corner in (c). Our previous experience with distance cues leads us to assume that the outside corner is closer than the inside corner and that the inside corner must therefore be longer.

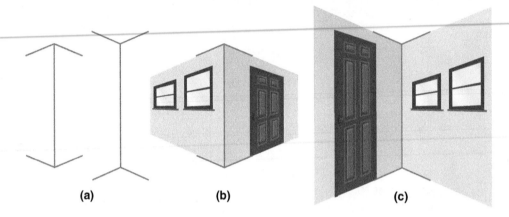

(a)   (b)   (c)

with the arrow tips pointing inward (Figure 7a, top) appears to be longer than the one with the arrow tips pointing outward (Figure 7a, bottom).

Although all kinds of explanations for visual illusions have been suggested, most concentrate either on the physical operation of the eye or on our misinterpretation of the visual stimulus. For example, one explanation for the Müller-Lyer illusion is that eye movements are greater when the arrow points inward, making us perceive the line as longer than it is when the arrow faces outward. In contrast, a different explanation for the illusion suggests that we unconsciously attribute particular significance to each of the lines (Gregory, 1978; Redding & Hawley, 1993). When we see the top line in Figure 7a, we tend to perceive it as if it were the inside corner of a room extending away from us, as illustrated in Figure 7b. In contrast, when we view the bottom line in Figure 7a, we perceive it as the relatively close outside corner of a rectangular object such as the building corner in Figure 7c. Because previous experience leads us to assume that the outside corner is closer than the inside corner, we make the further assumption that the inside corner must therefore be larger.

Despite the complexity of the latter explanation, a good deal of evidence supports it. For instance, cross-cultural studies show that people raised in areas where there are few right angles—such as the Zulu in Africa—are much less susceptible to the illusion than are people who grow up where most structures are built using right angles and rectangles (Segall, Campbell, & Herskovits, 1966).

STUDY ALERT!

The explanation for the Müller-Lyer illusion is complicated. Figure 7 will help you master it.

Subliminal Perception

Can stimuli that we're not even aware we've been exposed to change our behaviour in a significant way? Probably not.

Subliminal perception refers to the perception of messages about which we have no awareness. The stimulus could be a word, a sound, or even a smell that activates the sensory system but that is not intense enough for a person to report having experienced it. For example, in some studies people are exposed to a descriptive label—called a *prime*—about a person (such as the word *smart* or *happy*) so briefly that they cannot report seeing the label. Later, however, they form impressions that are influenced by the content of the prime. Somehow, they have been influenced by the prime that they say they couldn't see, providing some evidence for subliminal perception (Greenwald, Draine, & Abrams, 1996; Key, 2003).

Although subliminal messages (which social psychologists refer to as *priming*) can influence behaviour in subtle ways, there's little evidence that it can lead to major changes in attitudes or behaviour. Most research suggests that they cannot. For example, people who are subliminally exposed to an image of a Coke can and the word "thirst" do later rate themselves as thirstier, and they actually do drink more when given the opportunity. However, they don't particularly care if they drink Coke or some other liquid to quench their thirst (Dijksterhuis, Chartrand, & Aarts, 2007).

In short, although we are able to perceive at least some kinds of information of which we are unaware, there's little evidence that subliminal messages can change our attitudes or behaviour in substantial ways. At the same time, subliminal perception does have at least some consequences. If our motivation to carry out a behavior is already high and the appropriate stimuli are presented subliminally, subliminal perception may have at least some effect on our behaviour (Abrams, Klinger, & Greenwald, 2002; Pratkanis, Epley, & Savitsky, 2007; Randolph-Seng & Nielsen, 2009).

Exploring DIVERSITY

Culture and Perception

As the example of the Zulu indicates, the culture in which we are raised has clear consequences for how we perceive the world. Consider the drawing in Figure 8. Sometimes called the "devil's tuning fork," it is likely to produce a mind-boggling effect, as the centre tine of the fork alternates between appearing and disappearing.

Now try to reproduce the drawing on a piece of paper. Chances are that the task is nearly impossible for you—unless you are a member of an African tribe with little exposure to Western cultures. For such individuals, the task is simple; they have

---

FIGURE 8

The "devil's tuning fork" has three prongs . . . or does it have two?

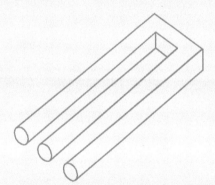

---

no trouble reproducing the figure. The reason seems to be that Westerners automatically interpret the drawing as something that cannot exist in three dimensions, and they therefore are inhibited from reproducing it. The African tribal members, in contrast, do not make the assumption that the figure is "impossible" and instead view it in two dimensions, a perception that enables them to copy the figure with ease (Deregowski, 1973).

Cultural differences are also reflected in depth perception. A Western viewer of Figure 9 would interpret the hunter in the drawing as aiming for the antelope in the foreground, while an elephant stands under the tree in the background. A member of an isolated African tribe, however, interprets the scene very differently by assuming that the hunter is aiming at the elephant. Westerners use the difference in sizes between the two animals as a cue that the elephant is farther away than the antelope (Hudson, 1960).

The misinterpretations created by visual illusions are ultimately due, then, to errors in both fundamental visual processing and the way the brain interprets the information it receives. But visual illusions, by illustrating something fundamental about perception, become more than mere psychological curiosities. There is a basic connection between our prior knowledge, needs, motivations, and expectations about how the world is put together and the way we perceive it. Our view of the world is very much a function, then, of fundamental psychological factors. Furthermore, each person perceives the environment in a way that is unique and special—a fact that allows each of us to make our own special contribution to the world.

(continued)

FIGURE 9

Is the man aiming for the elephant or the antelope? Westerners assume that the difference in size between the two animals indicates that the elephant is farther away, and therefore the man is aiming for the antelope. In contrast, members of some African tribes, not used to depth cues in two-dimensional drawings, assume that the man is aiming for the elephant. (The drawing is based on Deregowski, 1973.) Do you think Westerners, who view the picture in three dimensions, could explain what they see to someone who views the scene in two dimensions and eventually get that person to view it in three dimensions?

Evaluate

1. Match each of the following organizational laws with its meaning:

   a. Closure

   b. Proximity

   c. Similarity

   d. Simplicity

   1. Elements close together are grouped together.

   2. Patterns are perceived in the most basic, direct manner possible.

   3. Groupings are made in terms of complete figures.

   4. Elements similar in appearance are grouped together.

2. Processing that involves higher functions such as expectations and motivations is known as _____, whereas processing that recognizes the individual components of a stimulus is known as _____.

3. When a car passes you on the road and appears to shrink as it gets farther away, the phenomenon of _____ permits you to realize that the car is not in fact getting smaller.

4. _____ is the ability to view the world in three dimensions instead of two.

5. The brain makes use of a phenomenon known as _____, or the difference in the images the two eyes see, to give three dimensions to sight.

Answers to Evaluate Questions

1. a-3, b-1, c-4, d-2; 2. top-down, bottom-up; 3. perceptual constancy; 4. depth perception; 5. binocular disparity

Key Terms

bottom-up processing

depth perception

gestalt laws of organization

perceptual constancy

top-down processing

visual illusions

Epilogue

Source: © Darryl Leniuk/Taxi/Getty Images.

We have noted the important distinction between sensation and perception, and we have examined the processes that underlie both of them. We've seen how external stimuli evoke sensory responses and how our different senses process the information contained in those responses. We have also focused on the physical structure and internal workings of the individual senses, including vision, hearing, balance, smell, taste, and the skin senses, and we've explored how our brains organize and process sensory information to construct a consistent, integrated picture of the world around us.

Recap/Rethink

Module 8: Sensing the World Around Us

Recap

LO1 What is sensation, and how do psychologists study it?

- Sensation is the activation of the sense organs by any source of physical energy. In contrast, perception is the process by which we sort out, interpret, analyze, and integrate stimuli to which our senses are exposed.

LO2 What is the relationship between a physical stimulus and the kinds of sensory responses that result from it?

- Psychophysics studies the relationship between the physical nature of stimuli and the sensory responses they evoke.
- The absolute threshold is the smallest amount of physical intensity at which a stimulus can be detected. Under ideal conditions absolute thresholds are extraordinarily sensitive, but the presence of noise (background stimuli that interfere with other stimuli) reduces detection capabilities.
- The difference threshold, or just noticeable difference, is the smallest change in the level of stimulation required to sense that a change has occurred. According to Weber's law, a just noticeable difference is a constant proportion of the intensity of an initial stimulus.
- Sensory adaptation occurs when we become accustomed to a constant stimulus and change our evaluation of it. Repeated exposure to a stimulus results in an apparent decline in sensitivity to it.

Rethink

1. Do you think it is possible to have sensation without perception? Is it possible to have perception without sensation?

2. *From the perspective of a manufacturer:* How might you need to take psychophysics into account when developing new products or modifying existing ones?

3. Most people assume that they are able to text and drive at the same time without declines in their driving ability. Why do you think that is the case, and how accurate is their assumption? Why would frequent multitaskers be more distractible than those who multitask less frequently?

4. Why might some people be extremely capable at recognizing faces? Is having extremely sensitive perception always a good thing? What might be some drawbacks to being a super-recognizer?

Module 9: Vision: Shedding Light on the Eye

Recap

LO3 What basic processes underlie the sense of vision?

- Vision depends on sensitivity to light, electromagnetic waves in the visible part of the spectrum (wavelengths of roughly 390 to 770 nm) that are either reflected off objects or produced by an energy source. The eye shapes the light into an image that is transformed into nerve impulses and interpreted by the brain.
- As light enters the eye, it passes through the cornea, pupil, and lens and ultimately reaches the retina, where the electromagnetic energy of light is converted to nerve impulses for transmission to the brain. These impulses leave the eye via the optic nerve.
- The visual information gathered by the rods and cones is transferred via bipolar and ganglion cells through the optic nerve, which leads to the optic chiasm—the point where the optic nerve splits.

LO4 How do we see colours?

- Colour vision seems to be based on two processes described by the trichromatic theory and the opponent-process theory.
- The trichromatic theory suggests that there are three kinds of cones in the retina, each of which is responsive to a certain range of colours. The opponent-process theory presumes pairs of different types of cells in the eye that work in opposition to each other.

Rethink

1. If the eye had a second lens that "unreversed" the image hitting the retina, do you think there would be changes in the way people perceive the world?

2. *From the perspective of an advertising specialist:* How might you market your products similarly or differently to those who are colour-blind versus those who have normal colour vision?

Module 10: Hearing and the Other Senses

Recap

LO5 What role does the ear play in the senses of sound, motion, and balance?

- Sound, motion, and balance are centred in the ear. Sounds, in the form of vibrating air waves, enter through the outer ear and travel through the auditory canal until they reach the eardrum.
- The vibrations of the eardrum are transmitted into the middle ear, which consists of three bones: the hammer, the anvil, and the stirrup. These bones transmit vibrations to the oval window.
- In the inner ear, vibrations move into the cochlea, which encloses the basilar membrane. Hair cells on the basilar membrane change the mechanical energy of sound waves into nerve impulses that are transmitted to the brain. The ear is also involved in the sense of balance and motion.
- Sound has a number of physical characteristics, including frequency and amplitude. The place theory of hearing and the frequency theory of hearing explain the processes by which we distinguish sounds of varying frequency and intensity.

LO6 How do smell and taste function?

- Smell depends on olfactory cells (the receptor cells of the nose), and taste is centred in the tongue's taste buds.

LO7 What are the skin senses, and how do they relate to the experience of pain?

- The skin senses are responsible for the experiences of touch, pressure, temperature, and pain. Gate-control theory suggests that particular nerve receptors, when activated, open a "gate" to specific areas of the brain related to pain, and that another set of receptors closes the gate when stimulated.

Rethink

1. Much research is being conducted on repairing faulty sensory organs through devices such as personal guidance systems and eyeglasses, among others. Do you think that researchers should attempt to improve normal sensory capabilities beyond their "natural" range (for example, make human visual or audio capabilities more sensitive than normal)? What benefits might this ability bring? What problems might it cause?

2. *From the perspective of a social worker:* How would you handle the case of a deaf child whose hearing could be restored with a cochlear implant, but different family members had conflicting views on whether the procedure should be done?

Module 11: Perceptual Organization: Constructing Our View of the World

Recap

What principles underlie our organization of the visual world and allow us to make sense of our environment?

- Perception is a constructive process in which people go beyond the stimuli that are physically present and try to construct a meaningful interpretation.
- The gestalt laws of organization are used to describe the way in which we organize bits and pieces of information into meaningful wholes, known as gestalts, through closure, proximity, similarity, and simplicity.
- In top-down processing, perception is guided by higher-level knowledge, experience, expectations, and motivations. In bottom-up processing, perception consists of the progression of recognizing and processing information from individual components of a stimuli and moving to the perception of the whole.
- Perceptual constancy permits us to perceive stimuli as unvarying in size, shape, and colour despite changes in the environment or the appearance of the objects being perceived.

How are we able to perceive the world in three dimensions when our retinas are capable of sensing only two-dimensional images?

- Depth perception is the ability to perceive distance and view the world in three dimensions even though the images projected on our retinas are two-dimensional. We are able to judge depth and distance as a result of binocular disparity and monocular cues, such as motion parallax, the relative size of images on the retina, and linear perspective.
- Motion perception depends on cues such as the perceived movement of an object across the retina and information about how the head and eyes are moving.

What clues do visual illusions give us about our understanding of general perceptual mechanisms?

- Visual illusions are physical stimuli that consistently produce errors in perception, causing judgments that do not reflect the physical reality of a stimulus accurately. Two of the best-known illusions are the Poggendorf illusion and the Müller-Lyer illusion.
- Visual illusions are usually the result of errors in the brain's interpretation of visual stimuli. Furthermore, culture clearly affects how we perceive the world.

Rethink

1. In what ways do painters represent three-dimensional scenes in two dimensions on a canvas? Do you think artists in non-Western cultures use the same or different principles to represent three-dimensionality? Why?

2. *From the perspective of a corporate executive:* What arguments might you make if a member of your staff proposed a subliminal advertising campaign? Do you think your explanation would be enough to convince them? Why?

CHAPTER 4
States of Consciousness

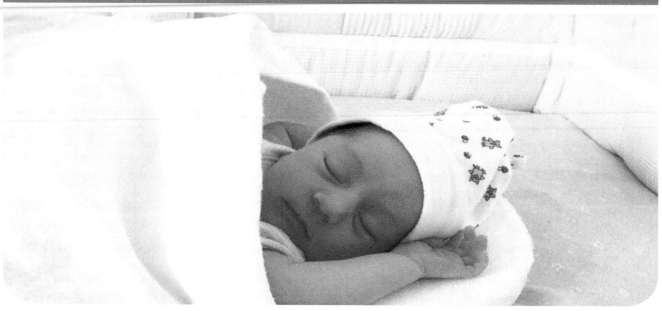

Source: © Laura Cavanagh.

Key Concepts for Chapter 4

MODULE 12 Sleep and Dreams

LO1 What are the different states of consciousness?

LO2 What happens when we sleep, and what are the meaning and function of dreams?

LO3 What are the major sleep disorders, and how can they be treated?

The Stages of Sleep

Rem Sleep: The Paradox of Sleep

Why Do We Sleep, and How Much Sleep Is Necessary?

The Function and Meaning of Dreaming

Sleep Disturbances: Slumbering Problems

> **PsychWork:** *Sleep Technologist*

Circadian Rhythms: Life Cycles

> Becoming an Informed Consumer of Psychology: *Sleep Better*

MODULE 13 Hypnosis and Meditation

LO4 What is hypnosis, and are hypnotized people in a different state of consciousness?

LO5 What are the effects of meditation?

Hypnosis: A Trance-Forming Experience?

Meditation: Regulating Our Own State of Consciousness

> **Exploring Diversity:** *Cross-Cultural Routes to Altered States of Consciousness*

MODULE 14 Drug Use: The Highs and Lows of Consciousness

LO6 What are the major classifications of drugs, and what are their effects?

Stimulants: Drug Highs

Depressants: Drug Lows

Narcotics: Relieving Pain and Anxiety

> Becoming an Informed Consumer of Psychology: *Identifying Drug and Alcohol Problems*

Prologue

Sleepwalker

Kenneth Parks, a Toronto man in his twenties, was acquitted by the Supreme Court of Canada in 1992 of killing his mother-in-law and brutally assaulting his father-in-law during the spring of 1987.

What happened?

Kenneth Parks fell asleep in front of the television and awoke hours later 23 kilometres from his home covered in blood from head to toe. Parks immediately drove to a nearby police station, and declared "I think I have just killed some people with my bare hands" (Pentland, 2009).

A defence team of sleep experts, psychiatrists, psychologists, neurologists, and lawyers argued that Parks was not responsible for his actions because he was asleep and thus unconscious when he bludgeoned his mother-in-law to death with a tire iron, and nearly choked his father-in-law to death.

A history of severe insomnia compounded by unemployment, gambling debt, and the growing needs of a young family further substantiated his "*sleepwalking defence*" (Hildebrant, 2009).

We know relatively little about sleepwalking, a sleep disturbance that is usually harmless, except in rare cases such as the case of Kenneth Parks discussed above. Sleepwalking occurs during stage 4 sleep and is more common in children than in adults. Sleepwalkers usually have a vague consciousness of the world around them, and may be able to walk with agility around obstructions in a crowded room. This may explain how a sleepwalking Kenneth Parks managed to drive 23 kilometres without incident to his in-laws' house on that fateful day in 1987 (Hobson & Silvestri, 1999; Baruss, 2003; Guilleminault et al., 2005; Hildebrant, 2009; Pentland, 2009).

In the following modules we'll consider a range of topics about sleep and, more broadly, states of consciousness. What is sleep? Why do we dream, and do dreams have meaning? Can people enter into altered states of consciousness through hypnosis or meditation? What leads people to use consciousness-altering drugs? In the following modules we will address these questions by considering the nature of both normal and altered states of consciousness.

Consciousness is the awareness of the sensations, thoughts, and feelings being experienced at a given moment. Consciousness is our subjective understanding of both the environment around us and our private internal world, unobservable to outsiders.

In waking consciousness, we are awake and aware of our thoughts, emotions, and perceptions. All other states of consciousness are considered altered states of consciousness. Among these, sleeping and dreaming occur naturally; drug use and hypnosis, in contrast, are methods of deliberately altering one's state of consciousness.

Psychologists have been reluctant to study consciousness because it is unique to each individual. After all, who can say that your consciousness is similar to or, for that matter, different from anyone else's? Although the earliest psychologists, including William James (1890), saw the study of consciousness as central to the field, later psychologists suggested that it was out of bounds for the discipline. They argued that consciousness could be understood only by relying "unscientifically" on what experimental participants said they were experiencing.

Contemporary psychologists reject the view that the study of consciousness is unsuitable for the field of psychology. Instead, they argue that several approaches permit the scientific study of consciousness. For example, behavioural neuroscientists can measure brain-wave patterns under conditions of consciousness ranging from sleep to waking to hypnotic trances. And a new understanding of the chemistry of drugs such as marijuana and alcohol has provided insights into the way they produce their pleasurable—as well as adverse—effects (Damasio, 1999; Sommerhof, 2000).

Whatever state of consciousness we are in—be it waking, sleeping, hypnotic, or drug-induced—the complexities of consciousness are profound.

Consciousness
The awareness of the sensations, thoughts, and feelings being experienced at a given moment.

Sleep and Dreams

LEARNING OBJECTIVES

LO1 **What are** the different states of consciousness?

LO2 **What happens** when we sleep, and what are the meaning and function of dreams?

LO3 **What are** the major sleep disorders, and how can they be treated?

Mike Trevino, 29, slept nine hours in nine days in his quest to win a 3,000-mile [4,800 km] cross-country bike race. For the first 38 hours and 646 miles [1,033 km], he skipped sleep entirely. Later he napped—with no dreams he can remember—for no more than 90 minutes a night. Soon he began to imagine that his support crew was part of a bomb plot. "It was almost like riding in a movie. I thought it was a complex dream, even though I was conscious," says Trevino, who finished second (Springen, 2004, p. 47).

Sometimes we learn more about sleep from people who have difficulty sleeping. Although, Trevino's case is unusual—the sad reality is that more and more Canadians are experiencing sleep deprivation. A recent survey by the Better Sleep Council Canada found 1 in 4 Canadians to be sleep deprived (Harris, 2007). Mike Trevino's case and the Sleep Council's survey of 1,003 Canadians raise a host of questions about sleep and dreams. Can we live without sleep? What is the meaning of dreams? More generally, what is sleep?

Although sleeping is a state that we all experience, sleep largely remains a mystery, psychologically-speaking. Many myths exist around sleep, dreams, and altered consciousness. Test your knowledge of sleep and dreams by answering the questionnaire in Figure 1.

The Stages of Sleep

Most of us consider sleep a time of tranquility when we set aside the tensions of the day and spend the night in uneventful slumber. However, a closer look at sleep shows that a good deal of activity occurs throughout the night, and that what at first appears to be a unitary state is, in fact, quite diverse.

Much of our knowledge of what happens during sleep comes from the *electroencephalogram*, or EEG, a measurement of electrical activity in the brain. When probes from an EEG machine are attached to the surface of a sleeping person's scalp and face, it becomes clear that the brain is active throughout the night. It produces electrical discharges with systematic, wave-like patterns that change in height (or amplitude) and speed (or frequency) in regular sequences. Instruments that measure muscle and eye movements also reveal a good deal of physical activity.

People progress through five distinct stages of sleep during a night's rest—known as *stage 1* through *stage 4* and *REM sleep*—moving through the stages in cycles lasting about ninety minutes. Each of these sleep stages is associated with a unique pattern of brain waves, which you can see in Figure 2.

STUDY ALERT!

Differentiate the five stages of sleep (stage 1, stage 2, stage 3, stage 4, and REM sleep), which produce different brain-wave patterns.

FIGURE 1

There are many unanswered questions about sleep. Taking this quiz can help you clear up some of the myths.

Sleep Quiz

Although sleeping is something we all do for a significant part of our lives, myths and misconceptions about the topic abound. To test your own knowledge of sleep and dreams, try answering the following questions before reading further.

_____ 1. Some people never dream. *True or false?*

_____ 2. Most dreams are caused by bodily sensations such as an upset stomach. *True or false?*

_____ 3. It has been proved that people need eight hours of sleep to maintain mental health. *True or false?*

_____ 4. When people do not recall their dreams, it is probably because they are secretly trying to forget them. *True or false?*

_____ 5. Depriving someone of sleep will invariably cause the individual to become mentally imbalanced. *True or false?*

_____ 6. If we lose some sleep we will eventually make up all the lost sleep the next night or another night. *True or false?*

_____ 7. No one has been able to go for more than 48 hours without sleep. *True or false?*

_____ 8. Everyone is able to sleep and breathe at the same time. *True or false?*

_____ 9. Sleep enables the brain to rest because little brain activity takes place during sleep. *True or false?*

_____ 10. Drugs have been proved to provide a long term cure for sleeplessness. *True or false?*

Scoring: This is an easy set of questions to score for every item is false. But don't lose any sleep if you missed them; they were chosen to represent the most common myths regarding sleep.

Source: From Palladino, J. J. & Carducci, B. J. Students' knowledge of sleep and dreams. *Teaching of Psychology, 11,* 189–191. Reprinted by permission of the publisher (Taylor & Francis, http://www.informaworld.com).

To enter the first stage of sleep, we must first get to sleep. We call it falling asleep, but psychologists refer to this phase of pre-sleep consciousness as the hypnagogic state. Some people experience vivid images called hypnagogic images during this period (McCarthy-Jones et al., 2011). Many people may also experience a "hypnic jerk," which is a feeling of falling or uncontrolled muscle spasms (Oswald, 1959).

FIGURE 2

Brain-wave patterns (measured by an EEG apparatus) vary significantly during the different stages of sleep (Hobson, 1989). As sleep moves from stage 1 through stage 4, brain waves become slower.

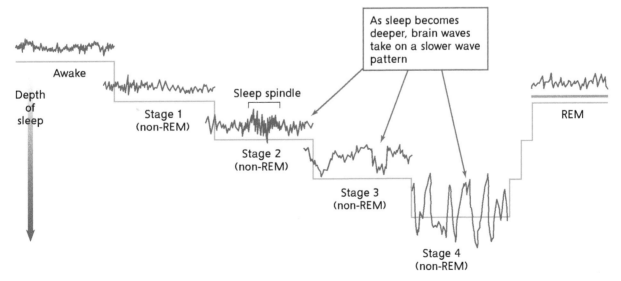

Source: Figure on p. 16 from the book *Sleep* by J. Allan Hobson. Copyright © 1989 by J. Allan Hobson. Reprinted by permission of Henry Holt and Company, LLC.

When people fall asleep, they move from a waking state in which they are relaxed with their eyes closed into **stage 1 sleep,** which is characterized by relatively rapid, low-amplitude brain waves. This is actually a stage of transition between wakefulness and sleep and lasts only a few minutes. During stage 1, images sometimes appear, as if we were viewing still photos, although this is not true dreaming, which occurs later in the night.

As sleep becomes deeper, people enter **stage 2 sleep,** which makes up about half of the total sleep of those in their early twenties and is characterized by a slower, more regular wave pattern. However, there are also momentary interruptions of sharply pointed, spiky waves that are called, because of their configuration, *sleep spindles.* It becomes increasingly difficult to awaken a person from sleep as stage 2 progresses.

As people drift into **stage 3 sleep,** the brain waves become slower, with higher peaks and lower valleys in the wave pattern. By the time sleepers arrive at stage 4 sleep, the pattern is even slower and more regular, and people are least responsive to outside stimulation.

As you can see in Figure 3, **stage 4 sleep,** which is the deepest stage of sleep, is most likely to occur during the early part of the night. In the first half of the night, sleep is dominated by stages 3 and 4. The second half is characterized by stages 1 and 2—as well as a fifth stage during which dreams occur.

FIGURE 3

During the night, the typical sleeper passes through all four stages of sleep and several REM periods.

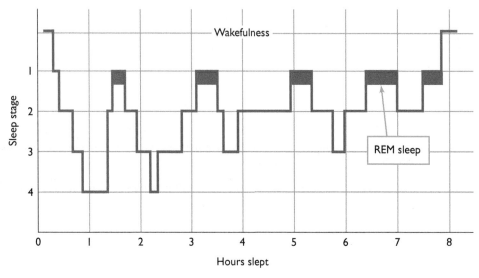

Source: From Ernest Hartmann, *The Biology of Dreaming* (1967), p. 6. Courtesy of Charles C Thomas Publisher, Ltd., Springfield, Illinois.

REM Sleep: The Paradox of Sleep

Several times a night, when sleepers have cycled back to a shallower state of sleep, something curious happens. Their heart rate increases and becomes irregular, their blood pressure rises, their breathing rate increases, and males—even male infants—have erections. Most characteristic of this period is the back-and-forth movement of their eyes, as if they

Stage 1 sleep
The state of transition between wakefulness and sleep, characterized by relatively rapid, low-amplitude brain waves.

Stage 2 sleep
A sleep deeper than that of stage 1, characterized by a slower, more regular wave pattern, along with momentary interruptions of "sleep spindles."

Stage 3 sleep
A sleep characterized by slow brain waves, with greater peaks and valleys in the wave pattern than in stage 2 sleep.

Stage 4 sleep
The deepest stage of sleep, during which we are least responsive to outside stimulation.

were watching an action-filled movie. This period of sleep is called **rapid eye movement (REM) sleep** and contrasts with stages 1 through 4, which are collectively labelled *non-REM* (or *NREM*) sleep. REM sleep occupies a little over 20 percent of adults' total sleeping time.

Paradoxically, while all this activity is occurring, the major muscles of the body appear to be paralyzed—except in rare cases of REM sleep behaviour disorder. In addition, and most important, REM sleep is usually accompanied by dreams, which—whether or not people remember them—are experienced by *everyone* during some part of the night. Although some dreaming occurs in non-REM stages of sleep, dreams are most likely to occur in the REM period, where they are the most vivid and easily remembered (Titone, 2002; Conduit, Crewther, & Coleman, 2004; Lu et al., 2006).

There is good reason to believe that REM sleep plays a critical role in everyday human functioning. People deprived of REM sleep—by being awakened every time they begin to display the physiological signs of that stage—show a *rebound effect* when allowed to rest undisturbed. With this rebound effect, REM-deprived sleepers spend significantly more time in REM sleep than they normally would. In addition, REM sleep may play a role in learning and memory, allowing us to rethink and process information and emotional experiences that we've had during the day (Nishida et al., 2009; Walker & van der Helm, 2009).

Why Do We Sleep, and How Much Sleep Is Necessary?

Sleep is a requirement for normal human functioning, although, surprisingly, we don't know exactly why. It is reasonable to expect that our bodies would require a tranquil "rest and relaxation" period to revitalize themselves, and experiments with rats show that total sleep deprivation results in death. But why?

One explanation, based on an evolutionary perspective, suggests that sleep protected our ancestors from nighttime predators and allowed them to conserve energy at night, a time when food was relatively hard to come by. Consequently, they were better able to forage for food when the sun was up.

A second explanation for why we sleep is that sleep restores and replenishes our brains and bodies. For instance, the reduced activity of the brain during non-REM sleep may give neurons in the brain a chance to repair themselves. Furthermore, the onset of REM sleep stops the release of neurotransmitters called *monoamines* and so permits receptor cells to get some necessary rest and to increase their sensitivity during periods of wakefulness (Siegel, 2003; McNamara,

People progress through four distinct stages of sleep during a night's rest spread over cycles lasting about ninety minutes. REM sleep, which occupies only 20 percent of adults' sleeping time, occurs in stage 1 sleep. These photos, taken at different times of night, show the synchronized patterns of a couple accustomed to sleeping in the same bed.

Source: © Ted Spagna/Science Source.

Rapid eye movement (REM) sleep
Sleep occupying 20 percent of an adult's sleeping time, characterized by increased heart rate, blood pressure, and breathing rate; erections; eye movements; and the experience of dreaming.

2004; Steiger, 2007). Sleep certainly seems to play a crucial role in memory consolidation and learning (Rasch & Born, 2008)—so think twice before pulling an all-nighter before a big exam.

Finally, sleep may be essential, because it assists physical growth and brain development in children. For example, the release of growth hormones is associated with deep sleep (Peterfi et al., 2010).

Still, these explanations remain speculative, and there is no definitive answer as to why sleep is essential. Furthermore, scientists have been unable to establish just how much sleep is absolutely required. Most people today sleep between seven and eight hours each night, which is three hours a night *less* than people slept a hundred years ago. In addition, there is wide variability among individuals, with some people needing as little as three hours of sleep (see Figure 4). Sleep requirements also vary over the course of a lifetime: As they age, people generally need less and less sleep.

People who participate in sleep-deprivation experiments, in which they are kept awake for stretches as long as 200 hours, show no permanent effects. It's no fun—they feel weary and irritable, can't concentrate, and show a loss of creativity, even after only minor deprivation. They also show a decline in logical reasoning ability. However, after being allowed to sleep normally, they bounce back quickly and are able to perform at predeprivation levels after just a few days (Babson et al., 2009; Mograss et al., 2009). But many people stay in a chronic state of sleep deprivation. Given the evidence we have of the immediate effects of minor sleep deprivation, being chronically sleep-deprived may affect every aspect of your social, academic, vocational, and adaptive functioning.

As far as we know, most people suffer no permanent consequences of such temporary sleep deprivation. But—and this is an important but—sleep deprivation is still dangerous. A lack of sleep can make us feel edgy, slow our reaction time, and lower our performance on academic and physical tasks. In addition, we put ourselves and others at risk when we carry out routine activities, such as driving, when we're very sleepy (Philip et al., 2005; Anderson & Horne, 2006; Morad et al., 2009). And animal studies show us that total sleep deprivation is no laughing matter: animals completely deprived of sleep will simply die—with no clear anatomical cause of death (Everson, Bergmann, & Rechtschaffen, 1989).

In summary, the importance of sleep should not be taken lightly. Chronic sleep deprivation can have a profound effect on our health. Even more so, when sleep deprivation takes place at a young age—children who experience sleep deprivation night after night are twice as likely to be obese when compared to children who regularly receive a full night's rest (CBC, 2008).

For strategies on helping you and your family sleep better, read *Becoming an Informed Consumer of Psychology* at the end of Module 12.

FIGURE 4

Although most people report sleeping between eight and nine hours per night, the amount varies a great deal (Borbely, 1988). Where would you place yourself on this graph, and why do you think you need more or less sleep than others?

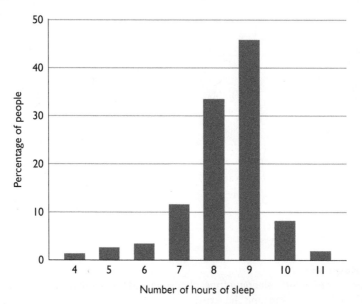

Source: From *Secrets of Sleep* by Alexander Borbély, p. 43. Copyright © 1988 Alexander Borbléy. Reprinted by permission of Basic Books, a member of the Perseus Books Group.

The Function and Meaning of Dreaming

I was sitting at my desk when I remembered that this was the day of my chemistry final! I was terrified, because I hadn't studied a bit for it. In fact, I had missed every lecture all semester. In a panic, I began running across campus desperately searching for the classroom, to which I'd never been. It was hopeless; I knew I was going to fail and flunk out of school.

If you have had a similar dream—a surprisingly common dream among people involved in academic pursuits—you know how utterly convincing are the panic and fear that the events in the dream can bring about. *Nightmares,* unusually frightening dreams, occur fairly often. In one survey, almost half of a group of university students who kept records of their dreams over a two-week period reported having at least one nightmare. This works out to some twenty-four nightmares per person each year, on average (Nielson, Stenstrom, & Levin, 2006; Levin & Nielsen, 2009; Schredl et al., 2009).

However, most of the 150,000 dreams the average person experiences by the age of 70 are much less dramatic. They typically encompass everyday events such as going to the supermarket, working at the office, and preparing a meal. Students dream about going to class; professors dream about lecturing. Dental patients dream of getting their teeth drilled; dentists dream of drilling the wrong tooth. The English take tea with the queen in their dreams; in Canada, people go to a bar with the prime minister (Webb, 1992; Potheraju & Soper, 1995; Domhoff, 1996; Schredl & Piel, 2005; Taylor & Bryant, 2007).

But what, if anything, do all these dreams mean? Whether dreams have a specific significance and function is a question that scientists have considered for many years, and they have developed several alternative theories.

Psychoanalytic Explanations of Dreams: Do Dreams Represent Unconscious Wish Fulfillment?

Sigmund Freud viewed dreams as a guide to the unconscious (Freud, 1900). In his **unconscious wish fulfillment theory,** he proposed that dreams represent unconscious wishes that dreamers desire to see fulfilled. However, because these wishes are threatening to the dreamer's conscious awareness, the actual wishes—called the **latent content of dreams**—are disguised. The true subject and meaning of a dream, then, may have little to do with its apparent story line, which Freud called the **manifest content of dreams** (see Figure 5).

Many psychologists reject Freud's view that dreams typically represent unconscious wishes and that particular objects and events in a dream are symbolic. Instead, they believe that the direct, overt action of a dream is the focal point of its meaning. For example, a dream in which we are walking down a long hallway to take an exam for which we haven't studied does not relate to unconscious, unacceptable wishes. Instead, it simply may mean that we are concerned about an impending test. Even more complex dreams can often be interpreted in terms of everyday concerns and stress (Picchioni et al., 2002; Cartwright, Agargum, & Kirkby, 2006).

Evolutionary Explanations of Dreams: Dreams-for-Survival Theory

According to the **dreams-for-survival theory,** dreams permit information that is critical for our daily survival to be reconsidered and reprocessed during sleep. Dreaming is seen as an inheritance from our animal ancestors, whose

Unconscious wish fulfillment theory
Sigmund Freud's theory that dreams represent unconscious wishes that dreamers desire to see fulfilled.

Latent content of dreams
According to Freud, the "disguised" meanings of dreams, hidden by more obvious subjects.

Manifest content of dreams
According to Freud, the apparent story line of dreams.

Dreams-for-survival theory
The theory suggesting that dreams permit information that is critical for our daily survival to be reconsidered and reprocessed during sleep.

FIGURE 5

According to Freud, objects in dreams represent the "disguised" meanings of dreams. For example, peaches in dreams symbolize breasts.

Symbol (Manifest Content of Dream)	Interpretation (Latent Content)
Climbing up a stairway, crossing a bridge, riding an elevator, flying in an airplane, walking down a long hallway, entering a room, train travelling through a tunnel	Sexual intercourse
Apples, peaches, grapefruits	Breasts
Bullets, fire, snakes, sticks, umbrellas, guns, hoses, knives	Male sex organs
Ovens, boxes, tunnels, closets, caves, bottles, ships	Female sex organs

Source: © TheCrimsonMonkey/iStockphoto.com.

smaller brains were unable to sift through sufficient information during waking hours. Consequently, dreaming provided a mechanism that permitted the processing of information twenty-four hours a day.

According to this theory, dreams represent concerns about our daily lives, illustrating our uncertainties, indecisions, ideas, and desires. Dreams are seen, then, as consistent with everyday living. Rather than being disguised wishes, as Freud suggested, they represent key concerns growing out of our daily experiences (Winson, 1990; Ross, 2006).

Research supports the dreams-for-survival theory, suggesting that certain dreams permit people to focus on and consolidate memories, particularly dreams that pertain to "how-to-do-it" memories related to motor skills. For example, rats seem to dream about mazes that they learned to run through during the day, at least according to the patterns of brain activity that appear while they are sleeping (Kenway & Wilson, 2001; Stickgold et al., 2001; Kuriyama, Stickgold, & Walker, 2004; Smith, 2006).

A similar phenomenon appears to work in humans. For instance, in one experiment, participants learned a visual memory task late in the day. They were then sent to bed, but awakened at certain times during the night. When they were awakened at times that did not interrupt dreaming, their performance on the memory task typically improved the next day. But when they were awakened during rapid eye movement (REM) sleep—the stage of sleep when people dream—their performance declined. The implication is that dreaming, at least when it is uninterrupted, can play a role in helping us remember material to which we have been previously exposed (Karni et al., 1994; Marshall & Born, 2007; Nishida et al., 2009). Again, think carefully before deciding to cram all night before a final exam!

Neuroscience Explanations of Dreams: Activation-Synthesis Theory

According to psychiatrist J. Allan Hobson, who proposed the **activation-synthesis theory,** the brain produces random electrical energy during REM sleep, possibly as a result of changes in the production of particular neurotransmitters. This electrical energy randomly stimulates memories lodged in various portions of the brain. Because we have a need to make sense of our world even while asleep, the brain takes these chaotic memories and weaves them into a logical story line, filling in the gaps to produce a rational scenario (Porte & Hobson, 1996; Hobson, 2005).

Activation-synthesis theory
Hobson's theory that the brain produces random electrical energy during REM sleep that stimulates memories stored in the brain.

However, Hobson does not entirely reject the view that dreams reflect unconscious wishes. He suggests that the particular scenario a dreamer produces is not random but instead is a clue to the dreamer's fears, emotions, and concerns. Hence, what starts out as a random process culminates in something meaningful.

STUDY ALERT!

Use Figure 6 to learn the differences between the three main explanations for dreams.

Dream Theories in Perspective

The range of theories about dreaming clearly illustrates that researchers have yet to agree on the fundamental purpose of dreams. Figure 6 summarizes the three major theories. In fact, there are quite a few additional theories of dreaming, probably reflecting the fact that dream research ultimately must rely on self-reports of hidden phenomena that are not directly observable. For now, the true meaning of dreams remains a mystery (Domhoff, 2001, 2003; Stern, 2001).

FIGURE 6

Three theories of dreams. Researchers have yet to agree on the fundamental meaning of dreams, and so several theories about dreaming have emerged.

Theory	Basic Explanation	Meaning of Dreams	Is Meaning of Dreams Disguised?
Unconscious wish fulfillment theory (Freud)	Dreams represent unconscious wishes the dreamer wants to fulfill	Latent content reveals unconscious wishes	Yes, by manifest content of dreams
Dreams-for-survival theory	Information relevant to daily survival is reconsidered and reprocessed	Clues to everyday concerns about survival	Not necessarily
Activation-synthesis theory	Dreams are the result of random activation of various memories, which are tied together in a logical story line	Dream scenario that is constructed is related to dreamer's concerns	Not necessarily

Source: Used with permission of Rockefeller University.

Sleep Disturbances: Slumbering Problems

At one time or another, almost all of us have difficulty sleeping—a condition known as insomnia. It could be due to a particular situation, such as the breakup of a relationship, concern about a test score, or the loss of a job. Some cases of insomnia, however, have no obvious cause. Some people are simply unable to fall asleep easily, or they go to sleep readily but wake up frequently during the night. Insomnia is a problem that afflicts as many as one-third of all people. Women and older adults are more likely to suffer from insomnia, as well as people who are unusually thin or are depressed (Bains, 2006; Cooke & Ancoli-Israel, 2006; Henry et al., 2008).

Interestingly, some people who *think* they have sleeping problems are mistaken. For example, researchers in sleep laboratories have found that some people who report being up all night actually fall asleep in thirty minutes and stay asleep all night. Furthermore, some people with insomnia accurately recall sounds that they heard while they were asleep, which gives them the impression that they were awake during the night. In fact, some researchers suggest that future drugs for insomnia could function by changing people's *perceptions* of how much they have slept, rather than by making them sleep more (Semler & Harvey, 2005; Yapko, 2006).

Other sleep problems are less common than insomnia, although they are still widespread. For instance, as many as 20 percent of Canadians suffer from *sleep apnea*, a condition in which a person has difficulty breathing while sleeping (Canadian Lung Association, 2008). The result is disturbed, fitful sleep, as the person is constantly reawakened when the lack of oxygen becomes great enough to trigger a waking response. Some people with apnea wake as many as 500 times during the course of a night, although they may not even be aware that they have wakened. Not surprisingly, such disturbed sleep—which may be related to a loss of neurons in the brain stem—results in complaints of fatigue the next day. Sleep apnea also may play a role in *sudden infant death syndrome (SIDS)*, a mysterious killer of seemingly normal infants who die while sleeping (Gami et al., 2005; Aloia, Smith, & Arnedt, 2007; Tippin, Sparks, & Rizzo, 2009).

Night terrors are sudden awakenings from non-REM sleep that are accompanied by extreme fear, panic, and strong physiological arousal. Usually occurring in stage 4 sleep, night terrors may be so frightening that a sleeper awakens with a shriek. Although night terrors initially produce great agitation, victims usually can get back to sleep fairly quickly. They occur most frequently in children between the ages of 3 and 8, although adults may suffer from them as well. Their cause is not known, but they are unrelated to emotional disturbance.

Tore Nielsen at the University of Montreal, Department of Psychiatry, is revolutionizing our understanding of nightmares and night terrors. According to Nielson, in order to know why we dream, we must first understand the *"dreamscape of nightmares."* Nielson theorizes that nightmares allow individuals to recycle and dispose of old fears and bad memories (Angier, 2007; Levin & Nielson, 2007).

Narcolepsy is uncontrollable sleeping that occurs for short periods while a person is awake. No matter what the activity—holding a heated conversation, exercising, or driving—a narcoleptic will suddenly fall asleep. People with narcolepsy go directly from wakefulness to REM sleep, skipping the other stages. The causes of narcolepsy are not known, although there could be a genetic component because narcolepsy runs in families (Lockrane, Bhatia, & Gore, 2005; Mahmood & Black 2005).

We know relatively little about sleeptalking and sleepwalking, two sleep disturbances that are usually harmless. Both occur during stage 4 sleep and are more common in children than in adults. Sleeptalkers and sleepwalkers usually have a vague consciousness of the world around them, and a sleepwalker may be able to walk with agility around obstructions in a crowded room. Unless a sleepwalker wanders into a dangerous environment, sleepwalking typically poses little risk (Hobson & Silvestri, 1999; Baruss, 2003; Guilleminault et al., 2005).

PsychWork

Sleep Technologist

Name: Brandon Liebig
Position: Sleep Technologist, Central Sleep Diagnostics
Education: Bachelor of Science in Nursing (BScN), Fanshawe College in association with the University of Western Ontario; graduate of Accredited Sleep Technologist Education Program, London Health Sciences Centre; certified by the Board of Registered Polysomnographic Technologists (BRPT)

Sleep—or rather a lack of it—is a state that is problematic for many people. For those seeking treatment for sleep disorders, sleep technologist Brandon Liebig is on the front lines, assisting in clinical assessments, helping to monitor and test patients, and participating in the development of treatment procedures.

As Liebig notes, "Patients seen in the sleep lab often have complicated medical backgrounds and health needs, and some may have cognitive limitations/disabilities or coexisting psychological conditions in addition to their sleep symptoms."

"Sleep technologists must recognize the particular needs of a patient and adjust their style of providing care to best suit the patient and promote the best possible outcomes, both for the patient's experience in the sleep lab and the data collected in research studies," he added.

"Often, patients may find it stressful, unfamiliar, and sometimes uncomfortable to sleep in a lab setting with the sensors and other equipment attached to their bodies. Sleep technologists use their knowledge of psychology to provide the patient with understanding, reassurance, respect, and patience," said Liebig.

Circadian Rhythms: Life Cycles

The fact that we cycle back and forth between wakefulness and sleep is one example of the body's circadian rhythms. **Circadian rhythms** (from the Latin *circa diem*, or "around the day") are biological processes that occur regularly on approximately a twenty-four-hour cycle. Sleeping and waking, for instance, occur naturally to the beat of an internal pacemaker that works on a cycle of about twenty-four hours. Several other bodily functions, such as body temperature, hormone production, and blood pressure, also follow circadian rhythms (Oren & Terman, 1998; Czeisler et al., 1999; Young, 2000; Saper et al., 2005).

Circadian cycles are complex, and they involve a variety of behaviours. For instance, sleepiness occurs not just in the evening but throughout the day in regular patterns, with most of us getting drowsy in midafternoon—regardless of whether we have eaten a heavy lunch. By making an afternoon siesta part of their everyday habit, people in several cultures take advantage of the body's natural inclination to sleep at this time (Wright, 2002; Takahashi et al., 2004; Reilly & Waterhouse, 2007).

The brain's *suprachiasmatic nucleus* (SCN) controls circadian rhythms. However, the relative amount of light and darkness, which varies with the seasons of the year, also plays a role in regulating circadian rhythms. In fact, some people experience *seasonal affective disorder,* a form of severe depression in which the characteristic cognitive, physical, emotional and behavioural symptoms of depression, including feelings of despair and hopelessness, increase during the winter and lift during the rest of the year. The disorder appears to be a result of the brevity and gloom of winter days. Daily exposure to bright lights is sometimes sufficient to improve the mood of those with this disorder (Golden et al., 2005; Kasof, 2009).

Becoming an Informed Consumer of Psychology

Sleep Better

» Do you have trouble sleeping? You're not alone—1 in 7 Canadians over the age of 15 have sleep problems. Participants in a Canadian Community Health Survey (CCHS) identified life stress as the number one cause of sleep disturbance (Statistics Canada, 2002; CTV.ca/Canadian Press 2005). For those of us who spend hours tossing and turning in bed, psychologists studying sleep disturbances have a number of suggestions for overcoming insomnia (Edinger et al., 2001; Benca, 2005; Finley & Cowley, 2005). Here are some ideas.

- *Exercise during the day (at least six hours before bedtime) and avoid naps.* Not surprisingly, it helps to be tired before going to sleep! Moreover, learning systematic relaxation techniques and biofeedback can help you unwind from the day's stresses and tensions.

- *Choose a regular bedtime and stick to it.* Adhering to a habitual schedule helps your internal timing mechanisms regulate your body more effectively.

- *Don't use your bed as an all-purpose area.* Leave studying, reading, eating, watching TV, and other recreational activities to some other part of your living quarters. If you follow this advice, your bed will become a cue for sleeping.

- *Avoid drinks with caffeine after lunch.* The effects of beverages such as coffee, tea, and some soft drinks can linger for as long as eight to twelve hours after they are consumed.

- *Drink a glass of warm milk at bedtime.* Your grandparents were right when they dispensed this advice. Although we're really sure why, warm milk seems to make people sleepy, most likely because drinking a warm, creamy beverage is a pretty relaxing thing to do!.

- *Avoid sleeping pills.* Health Canada's drug survey found sleeping pill usage nearly doubled with age (4.5 percent under the age of 55 versus 7.7 percent over the age of 55). A disturbing finding given that sleep medications can do more harm than good in the long run because they disrupt the normal sleep cycle.

- *Try not to sleep.* This approach works because people often have difficulty falling asleep because they are trying so hard. A better strategy is to go to bed only when you feel tired. If you don't get to sleep within ten minutes, leave the bedroom and do something else, returning to bed only when you feel sleepy. Continue this process all night if necessary. But get up at your usual hour in the morning, and don't take any naps during the day. After three or four weeks, most people become conditioned to associate their beds with sleep—and fall asleep rapidly at night (Sloan et al., 1993; Ubell, 1993; Smith, 2001).

For long-term problems with sleep, you might consider visiting a sleep disorders centre. For sleep brochures and information on accredited clinics, consult the Canadian Sleep Society at www.css.to/.

Circadian rhythms
Biological processes that occur regularly on approximately a twenty-four-hour cycle.

Evaluate

1. _____ is the term used to describe our understanding of the world external to us, as well as our own internal world.

2. A great deal of neural activity goes on during sleep. True or false?

3. Dreams occur in _____ sleep.

4. _____ are internal bodily processes that occur on a daily cycle.

5. Freud's theory of unconscious _____ states that the actual wishes an individual expresses in dreams are disguised because they are threatening to the person's conscious awareness.

Answers to Evaluate Questions

1. consciousness; 2. true; 3. REM; 4. circadian rhythms; 5. wish fulfillment

Key Terms

activation-synthesis theory	latent content of dreams	stage 2 sleep
circadian rhythms	manifest content of dreams	stage 3 sleep
consciousness	rapid eye movement (REM) sleep	stage 4 sleep
dreams-for-survival theory	stage 1 sleep	unconscious wish fulfillment theory

Hypnosis and Meditation

MODULE

13

LEARNING OBJECTIVES

What is hypnosis, and are hypnotized people in a different state of consciousness?

What are the effects of meditation?

You are feeling relaxed and drowsy. You are getting sleepier and sleepier. Your body is becoming limp. Now you are starting to become warm, at ease, more comfortable. Your eyelids are feeling heavier and heavier. Your eyes are closing; you can't keep them open anymore. You are totally relaxed.

Now, as you listen to my voice, do exactly as I say. Place your hands above your head. You will find they are getting heavier and heavier—so heavy you can barely keep them up. In fact, although you are straining as hard as you can, you will be unable to hold them up any longer.

An observer watching the above scene would notice a curious phenomenon occurring. Many of the people listening to the voice would, one by one, drop their arms to their sides, as if they were holding heavy lead weights. The reason for this strange behaviour? Those people have been hypnotized.

It is only recently that hypnotism has become an area considered worthy of scientific investigation. In part, the initial rejection of hypnosis relates to its bizarre eighteenth-century origins, in which Franz Mesmer argued that a form of "animal magnetism" could be used to influence people and cure their illnesses. After a commission headed by Benjamin Franklin discredited the phenomenon, it fell into disrepute, only to rise again to respectability in the nineteenth century. But even today, as we will see, the nature of hypnosis is controversial.

Hypnosis: A Trance-Forming Experience?

People under **hypnosis** are in a trance-like state of heightened susceptibility to the suggestions of others. In some respects, it appears that they are asleep. Yet other aspects of their behaviour contradict this notion, for people are attentive to the hypnotist's suggestions and may carry out bizarre or silly suggestions.

Despite their compliance when hypnotized, people do not lose all will of their own. They will not perform antisocial behaviours, and they will not carry out self-destructive acts. People will not reveal hidden truths about themselves, and they are capable of lying. Moreover, people cannot be hypnotized against their will—despite popular misconceptions (Gwynn & Spanos, 1996; Raz, 2007).

There are wide variations in people's susceptibility to hypnosis. About 5 to 20 percent of the world's population cannot be hypnotized at all, and some 15 percent of the world's population are very easily hypnotized. Most people fall somewhere in between. Moreover, the ease with which a person is hypnotized is related to a number of other characteristics. People who are hypnotized readily are also easily absorbed while reading books or listening to music, becoming unaware of what is happening around them, and they often spend an unusual amount of time daydreaming. In sum, then, they show a high ability to concentrate and to become completely absorbed in what they are doing (Rubichi et al., 2005; Benham, Woody, & Wilson, 2006).

Hypnosis
A trance-like state of heightened susceptibility to the suggestions of others.

Despite common misconceptions, people cannot be hypnotized against their will, nor do they lose all will of their own. Why, then, do people sometimes behave so unusually when asked to by a hypnotist?

Source: From *The Relaxation Response* by Herbert Benson, M.D., with Miriam Z. Klipper. Copyright © 1975 by William Morrow & Company, Inc. Reprinted by permission of Harper-Collins Publishers.

A Different State of Consciousness?

The question of whether hypnosis is a state of consciousness that is qualitatively different from normal waking consciousness is controversial. Psychologist Ernest Hilgard presented one side of the argument when he argued convincingly that hypnosis represents a state of consciousness that differs significantly from other states. He contended that particular behaviours clearly differentiate hypnosis from other states, including higher suggestibility, increased ability to recall and construct images, and acceptance of suggestions that clearly contradict reality. Moreover, changes in electrical activity in the brain are associated with hypnosis, supporting the position that hypnosis is a state of consciousness different from normal waking (Hilgard, 1992; Kallio & Revonsuo, 2003; Fingelkurts, Fingelkurts, & Kallio, 2007).

On the other side of the controversy were theorists who rejected the notion that hypnosis is a state significantly different from normal waking consciousness. They argued that altered brain wave patterns are not sufficient to demonstrate a qualitative difference in light of the fact that no other specific physiological changes occur when a person is in a trance. Furthermore, little support exists for the contention that adults can recall memories of childhood events accurately while hypnotized. That lack of evidence suggests that there is nothing qualitatively special about the hypnotic trance (Lynn et al., 2003; Lynn, Fassler, & Knox, 2005; Hongchun & Ming, 2006; Wagstaff, 2009).

There is increasing agreement that the controversy over the nature of hypnosis has led to extreme positions on both sides of the issue. More recent approaches suggest that the hypnotic state may best be viewed as lying along a continuum in which hypnosis is neither a totally different state of consciousness nor totally similar to normal waking consciousness (Kihlstrom, 2005b; Jamieson, 2007).

As arguments about the true nature of hypnosis continue, though, one thing is clear: Hypnosis has been used successfully to solve practical human problems. In fact, psychologists working in many different areas have found hypnosis to be a reliable, effective tool. It has been applied to a number of areas, including the following:

- *Controlling pain.* Patients suffering from chronic pain may be given the suggestion, while hypnotized, that their pain is gone or reduced. They also may be taught to hypnotize themselves to relieve pain or gain a sense of control over their symptoms. Hypnosis has proved to be particularly useful during childbirth and dental procedures (Mehl-Madrona, 2004; Hammond, 2007; Accardi & Milling, 2009).

- *Reducing smoking.* Although it hasn't been successful in stopping drug and alcohol abuse, hypnosis sometimes helps people stop smoking through hypnotic suggestions that the taste and smell of cigarettes are unpleasant (Elkins et al., 2006; Fuller, 2006; Green, Lynn, & Montgomery, 2008).

- *Treating psychological disorders.* Hypnosis sometimes is used during treatment for psychological disorders. For example, it may be employed to heighten relaxation, reduce anxiety, increase expectations of success, or modify self-defeating thoughts (Zarren & Eimer, 2002; Iglesias, 2005; Golden 2006).

- *Assisting in law enforcement.* Witnesses and victims are sometimes better able to recall the details of a crime when hypnotized. In one often-cited case, a witness to the kidnapping of a group of California schoolchildren was placed under hypnosis and was able to recall all but one digit of the licence number on the kidnapper's vehicle. However, hypnotic recollections may also be inaccurate, just as other recollections are often inaccurate. Consequently, the legal status of hypnosis is unresolved in the United States, with some jurisdictions accepting information obtained through hypnosis, while others reject it (Drogin, 2005; Whitehouse et al., 2005; Knight & Meyer, 2007).

Canada, on the other hand, is very clear about the admissibility of information recalled through hypnosis. On February 1, 1997, the Supreme Court of Canada ruled in *R v. Trochym* that testimony from hypnosis is no longer admissible in Canadian courts. Prior to that decision, information acquired through hypnosis was permissible in court on condition that a judge established that the "memories refreshed through hypnosis" were reliable (Soh, 2007; Supreme Court of Canada, 2007).

- *Improving athletic performance.* Athletes sometimes turn to hypnosis to improve their performance. For example, some baseball players have used hypnotism to increase their concentration when batting, with considerable success (Lindsay, Maynard, & Thomas, 2005; Barker & Jones, 2008).

Meditation: Regulating Our Own State of Consciousness

When traditional practitioners of the ancient Eastern religion of Zen Buddhism want to achieve greater spiritual insight, they turn to a technique that has been used for centuries to alter their state of consciousness. This technique is called meditation.

Meditation is a learned technique for refocusing attention that brings about an altered state of consciousness. Meditation is a technique that has been used as part of different religious traditions, but can also be used as a secular practice without a spiritual element to the activity. Meditation typically consists of the repetition of a mantra—a sound, word, or syllable—over and over. In other forms of meditation, the focus is on a picture, flame, or specific part of the body. Regardless of the nature of the particular initial stimulus, the key to the procedure is concentrating on it so thoroughly that the meditater becomes unaware of any outside stimulation and reaches a different state of consciousness.

After meditation, people report feeling thoroughly relaxed. They sometimes relate that they have gained new insights into themselves and the problems they are facing. The long-term practice of meditation may even improve health because of the biological changes it produces. For example, during meditation, oxygen usage decreases, heart rate and blood pressure decline, and brain-wave patterns may change (Barnes et al., 2004; Travis et al., 2009; see Figure 1).

Anyone can meditate by following a few simple procedures. The fundamentals include sitting in a quiet room with the eyes closed, breathing deeply and rhythmically, and repeating a word or sound—such as the word one—over and over. Practised regularly, the technique is effective in bringing about relaxation (Benson et al., 1994; Aftanas &

FIGURE 1

The body's use of oxygen declines significantly during meditation.

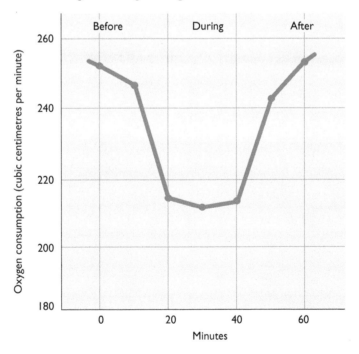

Source: Benson et al.

Meditation
A learned technique for refocusing attention that brings about an altered state of consciousness.

Golosheykin, 2005). For more information on meditation, contact the Benson-Henry Institute for Mind Body Medicine at www.bensonhenryinstitute.org.

As you may have gathered from this discussion, meditation is a means of altering consciousness that is practised in many different cultures, though it can take different forms and serve different purposes across cultures. In fact, one impetus for the study of consciousness is the realization that people in many different cultures routinely seek ways to alter their states of consciousness.

Exploring DIVERSITY

Cross-Cultural Routes to Altered States of Consciousness

A group of Ojibway First Nation men sit naked in a steaming sweat lodge as a medicine man throws water on sizzling rocks to send billows of scalding steam into the air.

Aztec priests smear themselves with a mixture of crushed poisonous herbs, hairy black worms, scorpions, and lizards. Sometimes they drink the potion.

During the sixteenth century, a devout Hasidic Jew lies across the tombstone of a celebrated scholar. As he murmurs the name of God repeatedly, he seeks to be possessed by the soul of the dead wise man's spirit. If successful, he will attain a mystical state, and the deceased's words will flow out of his mouth.

Each of these rituals has a common goal: suspension from the bonds of everyday awareness and access to an altered state of consciousness. Although they may seem exotic from the vantage point of many Western cultures, these rituals represent an apparently universal effort to alter consciousness (Bartocci, 2004; Irwin, 2006).

Some scholars suggest that the quest to alter consciousness represents a basic human desire (Siegel, 1989). Whether or not one accepts such an extreme view, it is clear that variations in states of consciousness share some basic characteristics across a variety of cultures. One is an alteration in thinking, which may become shallow, illogical, or otherwise different from normal. In addition, people's sense of time can become disturbed, and their perceptions of the world and of themselves may be changed. They may experience a loss of self-control, doing things that they would never otherwise do. Finally, they may feel a sense of *ineffability*—the inability to understand an experience rationally or describe it in words (Martindale, 1981; Finkler, 2004; Travis, 2006).

Evaluate

1. _____ is a state of heightened susceptibility to the suggestions of others.
2. A friend tells you, "I once heard of a person who was murdered by being hypnotized and then told to jump from the Confederation Bridge!" Could such a thing have happened? Why or why not?
3. _____ is a learned technique for refocusing attention to bring about an altered state of consciousness.

Answers to Evaluate Questions

1. hypnosis; 2. no; people who are hypnotized cannot be made to perform self-destructive acts; 3. meditation;

Key Terms

hypnosis   meditation

Drug Use: The Highs and Lows of Consciousness

LEARNING OBJECTIVE

What are the major classifications of drugs, and what are their effects?

Jessica Weihrich was once a healthy, happy, straight-A student from a middle class family in Smith Falls, Ontario. That was until she began drinking, hanging out with the wrong crowd, experimenting with drugs, which developed into an addiction to morphine, heroin, and crack. At rock bottom, Jessica weighed only 79 pounds (36 kilograms), had rotting, crumbling teeth, and a body covered in black and blue bruises.

What makes Jessica's story different from those of others who struggle with addictions? Just one thing: her descent into hell began well before the age of 16 (CAMH, 2006).

Jessica Weihrich was lucky. Now 18 and in recovery, Jessica decided to use her addiction to help others. She shares her story in a seminar called "Not My Kids" everywhere and anywhere she can—from police stations, to churches, to schools. Unfortunately, Jessica is not alone in her young story of addiction. A 2004 survey found that major alcohol and drug use of young Canadians has doubled in the past decade (Canadian Addiction Survey, 2004; Health Canada, 2004).

Drugs of one sort or another are a part of almost everyone's life. Consistent with Canadian addiction surveys, drug surveys in the United States found that 80 percent of adults have taken an over-the-counter pain reliever in the last six months (Dortch, 1996; Canadian Addiction Survey, 2004).

Some substances, known as psychoactive drugs, lead to an altered state of consciousness. **Psychoactive drugs** influence a person's emotions, perceptions, and behaviour. Yet even this category of drugs is common in most of our lives. If you have ever had a cup of coffee or sipped a beer, you have taken a psychoactive drug. A large number of individuals have used more potent—and dangerous—psychoactive drugs than coffee and beer (see Figure 1); for instance, surveys find that 41 percent of high school seniors across the United States have used an illegal drug in the last year. In addition, 30 percent report having been drunk on alcohol. The figures for the U.S. adult population are even higher (Johnston et al., 2009).

Of course, drugs vary widely in the effects they have on users, in part because they affect the nervous system in very different ways. Some drugs alter the limbic system, and others affect the operation of specific neurotransmitters across the synapses of neurons. For example, some drugs block or enhance the release of neurotransmitters, others block the receipt or the removal of a neurotransmitter, and still others mimic the effects of a particular neurotransmitter (see Figure 2).

The most dangerous drugs are addictive. **Addictive drugs** produce a biological or psychological dependence (or both) in the user, and withdrawal from them leads to a craving for the drug that, in some cases, may be nearly irresistible. In *biologically based* addictions, the body becomes so accustomed to functioning in the presence of a drug that it cannot function without it. *Psychologically based* addictions are those in which people believe that they need the drug to respond to the stresses of daily living. Although we generally associate addiction with drugs such as heroin, everyday sorts of drugs, such as caffeine (found in coffee) and nicotine (found in cigarettes), have addictive aspects as well.

Psychoactive drugs
Legal or illegal drugs that influence a person's emotions, perceptions, and behaviour.

Addictive drugs
Drugs that produce a biological or psychological dependence (or both) in the user so that withdrawal from them leads to a craving for the drug that, in some cases, may be nearly irresistible.

FIGURE 1

How many teenagers use drugs? The results of the most recent comprehensive survey of 14,000 high school seniors across the United States show the percentage of respondents who have used various substances for nonmedical purposes at least once. Can you think of any reasons why teenagers—as opposed to older people—might be particularly likely to use drugs?

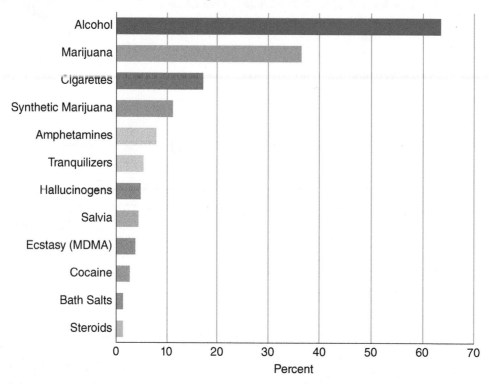

Source: Adapted from Johnston et al., 2012.

FIGURE 2

Different drugs affect different parts of the nervous system and brain and each drug functions in one of these specific ways.

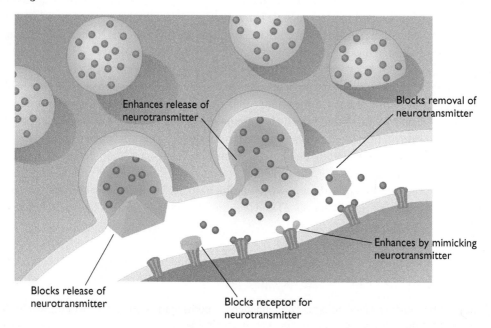

Source: From Sylvia S. Mader, *Human Biology*, 6th ed., p. 250. Copyright © 2000 by McGraw-Hill Education. Reprinted with permission of McGraw-Hill Education.

We know surprisingly little about the underlying causes of addiction. One of the problems in identifying those causes is that different drugs (such as alcohol and cocaine) affect the brain in very different ways—yet may be equally addicting. Furthermore, it takes longer to become addicted to some drugs than to others, even though the ultimate consequences of addiction may be equally grave (Crombag & Robinson, 2004; Nestler & Malenka, 2004; Smart, 2007).

Why do people take drugs in the first place? There are many reasons, ranging from the perceived pleasure of the experience itself, to the escape that a drug-induced high affords from the everyday pressures of life, to an attempt to achieve a religious or spiritual state. However, other factors having little to do with the nature of the experience itself, also lead people to try drugs (McDowell & Spitz, 1999).

STUDY ALERT!

Use Figure 2 to learn the different ways that drugs produce their effects on a neurological level.

For instance, the alleged drug use of well-known role models, the easy availability of some illegal drugs, and peer pressure all play a role in the decision to use drugs. In some cases, the motive is simply the thrill of trying something new. Finally, the sense of helplessness experienced by unemployed individuals trapped in lives of poverty may lead them to try drugs as a way of escaping from the bleakness of their lives. Regardless of the forces that lead a person to begin using drugs, drug addiction is among the most difficult of all behaviours to modify, even with extensive treatment (Lemonick, 2000; Mosher & Akins, 2007; Ray & Hutchison, 2007).

Because of the difficulty in treating drug problems, there is little disagreement that the best hope for dealing with the overall societal problem of substance abuse is to prevent people from becoming involved with drugs in the first place. However, there is little accord on how to accomplish this goal.

The Centre for Addiction and Mental Health (CAMH) is Canada's leading institution for researching and treating addiction and mental health. CAMH offers a number of services and resources including: comprehensive assessment, differential diagnosis, early intervention, residential programs, continuing care, and family support. For further information, visit CAMH's website at www.camh.net/.

Stimulants: Drug Highs

It's one o'clock in the morning, and you still haven't finished reading the last chapter of the text on which you will be tested later that morning. Feeling exhausted, you turn to the one thing that may help you stay awake for the next two hours: a cup of strong black coffee.

If you have ever found yourself in such a position, you have resorted to a major *stimulant*, caffeine, to stay awake. *Caffeine* is one of a number of **stimulants,** drugs whose effect on the central nervous system causes a rise in heart rate, blood pressure, and muscular tension. Caffeine is present not only in coffee; it is an important ingredient in tea, soft drinks, and chocolate as well (see Figure 3).

Caffeine produces several reactions. The major behavioural effects are an increase in attentiveness and a decrease in reaction time. Caffeine can also bring about an improvement in mood, most likely by mimicking the effects of a natural brain chemical, adenosine. Too much caffeine, however, can result in nervousness and insomnia. People can build up a biological dependence on the drug. Regular users who suddenly stop drinking coffee may experience headaches or depression. Many people who drink large amounts of coffee on weekdays have headaches on weekends because of the sudden drop in the amount of caffeine they are consuming (Kendler, Gatz, & Gardner, 2006; Hammond & Gold, 2008; Clayton & Lundberg-Love, 2009).

Nicotine, found in cigarettes, is another common stimulant. The soothing effects of nicotine help explain why cigarette smoking is addictive. Smokers develop a dependence on nicotine, and those who suddenly stop smoking develop

Stimulants
Drugs that have an arousal effect on the central nervous system, causing a rise in heart rate, blood pressure, and muscular tension.

The Faces of Meth informational campaign (www.facesofmeth.us) graphically illustrates the toll taken by regular meth use, even over a short period of time.

strong cravings for the drug. This is not surprising: Nicotine activates neural mechanisms similar to those activated by cocaine, which, as we see later in this section, is also highly addictive (Haberstick et al., 2007; Ray et al., 2008).

The long-term risks of tobacco use are more lethal than all other forms of drug use combined. Tobacco use contributes to more than 45,000 deaths a year in Canada. Three times the number of Canadians die each year from cigarette smoking than are killed by car accidents, other forms of drug use, homicide, suicide, and AIDS combined (Health Canada, 1999, 2009).

Amphetamines

Amphetamines are strong stimulants, such as Dexedrine and Benzedrine, popularly known as speed. In small quantities, amphetamines—which stimulate the central nervous system—bring about a sense of energy and alertness, talkativeness, heightened confidence, and a mood "high." They increase concentration and reduce fatigue. Amphetamines also cause a loss of appetite, increased anxiety, and irritability. When taken over long periods of time, amphetamines can cause feelings of being persecuted by others, as well as a general sense of suspiciousness. People taking amphetamines may lose interest in sex. If taken in too large a quantity, amphetamines overstimulate the central nervous system to such an extent that convulsions and death can occur (Carhart-Harris, 2007).

Methamphetamine is a white, crystalline drug that police now say is the most dangerous street drug. "Meth" is highly addictive and relatively cheap, and it produces a strong, lingering high. It has made addicts of people across the social spectrum, ranging from soccer moms to urban professionals to poverty-stricken inner-city residents. After

---

FIGURE 3

How much caffeine do you consume? This chart shows the range of caffeine found in common foods and drinks. The average coffee drinker in the United States consumes about 200 milligrams of caffeine each day, or around three cups of coffee

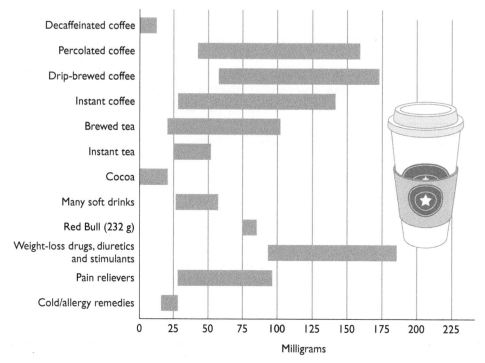

This composite MRI brain scan illustrates that deficits in grey matter (indicated in red) in long-term methamphetamine abusers are particularly pronounced in an area around the corpus callosum. The volume of grey matter is more than 10 percent lower in users than non-users.

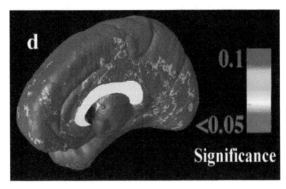

Source: Thompson, P.M., et al., "Structural abnormalities in the brains of human subjects who use methamphetamine," *J. Neurosci.* 2004 Jun 30, 24(26): 6028–6036. Fig. 1d, p. 6031. Photo courtesy Dr. Paul Thompson, UCLA Laboratory of Neuroimaging.

becoming addicted, users take it more and more frequently and in increasing doses. Long-term use of the drug can lead to brain damage (see Figure 4 above).

Canadian Addiction Survey (2004) indicated that 6.4 percent of Canadians reported using methamphetamine in their lifetime and less than 1 percent using the drug in the past twelve months. Because it can be made from nonprescription cold pills, retailers such as Walmart have removed these medications from their shelves. Illicit meth labs devoted to the manufacture (or "cooking") of methamphetamines have sprung up in many locations around North America (Jefferson, 2005).

Cocaine

Although its use has declined over the last decade, the addictive stimulant cocaine and its highly addictive derivative, crack, still represent a serious concern. Cocaine is inhaled or "snorted" through the nose, smoked, or injected directly into the bloodstream. It is rapidly absorbed into the body and takes effect almost immediately.

When used in relatively small quantities, cocaine produces feelings of profound psychological well-being, increased confidence, and alertness. Cocaine produces this "high" through the neurotransmitter dopamine. Dopamine is one of the chemicals that transmit between neurons messages that are related to ordinary feelings of pleasure. Normally when dopamine is released, excess amounts of the neurotransmitter are reabsorbed by the releasing neuron. However, when cocaine enters the brain, it blocks reabsorption of leftover dopamine. As a result, the brain is flooded with dopamine-produced pleasurable sensations (Redish, 2004; Jarlai, Arasteh, & Perlis, 2007). Figure 5 provides a summary of the effects of cocaine and other illegal drugs.

However, there is a steep price to be paid for the pleasurable effects of cocaine. The brain may become permanently rewired, triggering a psychological and physical addiction in which users grow obsessed with obtaining the

Drugs and their effects. A comprehensive breakdown of effects of the most commonly used drugs.

Drugs	Street Name	Effects	Withdrawal Symptoms	Adverse/ Overdose Reactions
Stimulants				
Cocaine	Coke, blow, snow, lady, crack	Increased confidence, mood elevation, sense of energy and alertness, decreased appetite, anxiety, irritability, insomnia, transient drowsiness, delayed orgasm	Apathy, general fatigue, prolonged sleep, depression, disorientation, suicidal thoughts, agitated motor activity, irritability, bizarre dreams	Elevated blood pressure, increase in body temperature, face picking, suspiciousness, bizarre and repetitious behaviour, vivid hallucinations, convulsions, possible death
Amphetamines	Speed			
Benzedrine	Speed			
Dexedrine	Meth, crystal meth			
Methamphetamine				

(continued)

Drugs	Street Name	Effects	Withdrawal Symptoms	Adverse/ Overdose Reactions
Depressants				
Alcohol	Booze	Anxiety reduction, impulsiveness, dramatic mood swings, bizarre thoughts, suicidal behaviour, slurred speech, disorientation, slowed mental and physical functioning, limited attention span	Weakness, restlessness, nausea and vomiting, headaches, nightmares, irritability, depression, acute anxiety, hallucinations, seizures, possible death	Confusion, decreased response to pain, shallow respiration, dilated pupils, weak and rapid pulse, coma, possible death
Barbiturates Nembutal Seconal Phenobarbital	Yellowjackets, yellows Reds			
Benzodiazepines	Valium, Librium, Xanax, Ativan	Muscle relaxation, amnesia, sleep	Anxiety, sleeplessness, irritability, memory impairment	Coma, incapacitation, inability, heart failure (especially when combined with alcohol)
Narcotics				
Heroin	H, hombre, junk, smack, dope, crap, horse	Anxiety and pain reduction, apathy, difficulty in concentration, slowed speech, decreased physical activity, drooling, itching, euphoria, nausea	Anxiety, vomiting, sneezing, diarrhea, lower back pain, watery eyes, runny nose, yawning, irritability, tremors, panic, chills and sweating, cramps	Depressed levels of consciousness, low blood pressure, rapid heart rate, shallow breathing, convulsions, coma, possible death
Morphine	Drugstore dope, cube, first line, mud			
Hallucinogens				
Cannabis Marijuana Hashish Hash oil	Bhang, kif, ganja, dope, grass, pot, hemp, joint, weed, bone, Mary Jane, reefer	Euphoria, relaxed inhibitions, increased appetite, disoriented behaviour	Hyperactivity, insomnia, decreased appetite, anxiety	Severe reactions rare but include panic, paranoia, fatigue, bizarre and dangerous behaviour, decreased testosterone over long-term; immune-system effects
MDMA	Ecstasy, Molly	Heightened sense of oneself and insight, feelings of peace, empathy, energy	Depression, anxiety, sleeplessness	Increase in body temperature, memory difficulties, brain damage
LSD	Acid, quasey, microdot, white lightning	Heightened aesthetic responses; vision and depth distortion; heightened sensitivity to faces and gestures; magnified feelings; paranoia, panic, euphoria	Not reported	Nausea and chills; increased pulse, temperature, and blood pressure; slow, deep breathing; loss of appetite; insomnia; bizarre, dangerous behaviour

drug. Over time, users deteriorate mentally and physically. In extreme cases, cocaine can cause hallucinations—a common one is of insects crawling over one's body. Ultimately, an overdose of cocaine can lead to death (George & Moselhy, 2005; Little et al., 2009).

Canadian Addiction Survey (2004) indicated that 10.6 percent of Canadians reported using cocaine in their lifetime with 1.9 percent using cocaine in the past twelve months. Given the strength of cocaine, withdrawal from the drug is difficult. Although the use of cocaine among high school students has declined in recent years, the drug still represents a major problem (Johnston et al., 2004).

STUDY ALERT!

Figure 5, which summarizes the different categories of drugs (stimulants, depressants, narcotics, and hallucinogens), will help you learn the effects of particular drugs.

Depressants: Drug Lows

In contrast to the initial effect of stimulants, which is an increase in arousal of the central nervous system, the effect of **depressants** is to impede the nervous system by causing neurons to fire more slowly. Small doses result in at least temporary feelings of *intoxication*—drunkenness—along with a sense of euphoria and joy. When large amounts are taken, however, speech becomes slurred and muscle control becomes disjointed, making motion difficult. Ultimately, heavy users may lose consciousness entirely.

Alcohol

The most common depressant is alcohol, which is used by more people than is any other drug. Based on liquor sales, the average person over the age of 14 drinks nine litres of pure alcohol over the course of a year. This works out to more than 200 drinks per person. Although alcohol consumption has declined steadily over the last decade, surveys show that more than three-fourths of college and university students indicate that they have had a drink within the last thirty days (CAMH College Campus Survey, 2004; Midanik, Tam, & Weisner, 2007).

Although most people fall into the category of casual users, 17.1 percent of Canadians—almost 1 in every 5 adults in Canada are considered high-risk drinkers according to World Health Organization's Alcohol Use Disorders Identification Test (AUDIT). The effects of alcohol vary significantly, depending on who is drinking and the setting in which people drink. If alcohol were a newly discovered drug, do you think it would be legal?

Sources: © Exactostock/Superstock RF; © Jim Abrogast/Getty Images RF.

One of the more disturbing trends is the high frequency of binge drinking among college and university students. For men, *binge drinking* is defined as having five or more drinks in one sitting; for women, who generally weigh less than men and whose bodies absorb alcohol less efficiently, binge drinking is defined as having four or more drinks at one sitting.

As shown in Figure 6, some 37.6 percent of male college students and 27.5 percent of female college students in Canada responding to the College Campus Survey (2004) said they had engaged in binge drinking within the prior thirty days. In addition to gender, the drinking patterns of Canadian students also vary according to living arrangements and geography. Rates of hazardous drinking were highest among students living on campus (42.7 percent), and students attending university in the Atlantic region (46.5 percent). Some 43.9 percent of Canadian students reported at least one indicator of harmful drinking such as feeling guilty, experiencing memory loss, or having others worried about their drinking behaviour. Furthermore, 31.6 percent of undergraduates admitted dependent behaviours such as feeling unable to stop and drinking first thing in the morning. Students were also affected by other students' high rate of alcohol use: one-third of lighter drinkers said that they had had their studying or sleep disturbed by drunk students, and around one-fifth had been insulted or humiliated by a drunk student. Ten percent of women said they had been the target of an unwanted sexual advance by a drunk classmate (CAMH College Campus Survey, 2004).

Women are typically somewhat lighter drinkers than men—although the gap between the sexes is narrowing for older women and has closed completely for teenagers. Women are more susceptible to the effects of alcohol, and alcohol abuse may harm the brains of women more than men (Wuethrich, 2001; Mann et al., 2005; Mancinelli, Binetti, & Ceccanti, 2007).

Although alcohol is a depressant, most people claim that it increases their sense of sociability and well-being. The discrepancy between the actual and the perceived effects of alcohol lies in the initial effects it produces in the majority

Depressants
Drugs that slow down the nervous system.

FIGURE 6

Drinking habits of college and university students (Wechsler et al., 2000). For men, binge drinking was defined as consuming five or more drinks in one sitting; for women, the total was four or more.

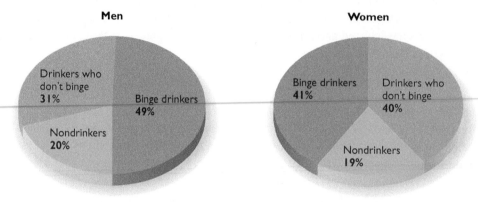

Men

Drinkers who don't binge 31%

Binge drinkers 49%

Nondrinkers 20%

Women

Binge drinkers 41%

Drinkers who don't binge 40%

Nondrinkers 19%

Source: Wechsler et al, 2000.

of individuals who use it: release of tension and stress, feelings of happiness, and loss of inhibitions (Steele & Josephs, 1990; Sayette, 1993).

As the dose of alcohol increases, however, the depressive effects become more pronounced (see Figure 7). People may feel emotionally and physically unstable. They also show poor judgment and may act aggressively. Moreover, memory is impaired, brain processing of spatial information is diminished, and speech becomes slurred and incoherent. Eventually they may fall into a stupor and pass out. If they drink enough alcohol in a short time, they may die of alcohol poisoning (Zeigler et al., 2005; Thatcher & Clark, 2006).

Although most people fall into the category of casual users, 17.1 percent of Canadians—almost 1 in every 5 adults in Canada—are considered high-risk drinkers according to World Health Organization's Alcohol Use Disorders Identification Test (AUDIT), and a much higher percentage than that—up to 62 percent of Canadians according to a 2014 Globe and Mail survey—binge drink on occasion. The largest proportion of high-risk drinkers were males under the age of 25—not surprising considering the results of the campus survey discussed earlier (Canadian Addiction Survey, 2004; CAMH College Campus Survey, 2004).

Alcoholics, people with alcohol-abuse problems, come to rely on alcohol and continue to drink even though it causes serious difficulties. In addition, they become increasingly immune to the effects of alcohol. Consequently, alcoholics must drink progressively more to experience the initial positive feelings that alcohol produces (Galanter & Kleber, 1999; Jung, 2002).

In some cases of alcoholism, people must drink constantly in order to feel well enough to function in their daily lives. In other cases, though, people drink inconsistently, but occasionally go on binges in which they consume large quantities of alcohol.

It is not clear why certain people become alcoholics and develop a tolerance for alcohol, whereas others do not. Some evidence suggests a genetic cause, although the question whether there is a specific inherited gene that produces alcoholism is controversial. What is clear is that the chances of becoming an alcoholic are considerably higher if alcoholics are present in earlier generations of a person's family. However, not all alcoholics have close relatives who are alcoholics. In these cases, environmental stressors are suspected of playing a larger role (Whitfield et al., 2004; Zimmermann, Blomeyer, & Laucht, 2007).

Barbiturates

Barbiturates, which include drugs such as Nembutal, Seconal, and phenobarbital, are another form of depressant. Frequently prescribed by physicians to induce sleep or reduce stress, barbiturates produce a sense of relaxation. Yet they too are psychologically and physically addictive and, when combined with alcohol, can be deadly, since such a combination relaxes the muscles of the diaphragm to such an extent that the user stops breathing.

Benzodiazepines

Benzodiazepines are anti-anxiety drugs that include Valium, Xanax, and Atavan. Highly addictive, these drugs are prescribed to treat anxiety and panic (Licata & Rowlett, 2008). Excessive use of benzodiazepines can quickly build tolerance, and is associated with serious memory impairment (Paraherakis, Charney, & Gill, 2001). Benzodiazepines can be fatal in large doses, especially when combined with alcohol.

FIGURE 7

The effects of alcohol. The quantities represent only rough benchmarks; the effects vary significantly depending on an individual's weight, height, recent food intake, genetic factors, and even psychological state.

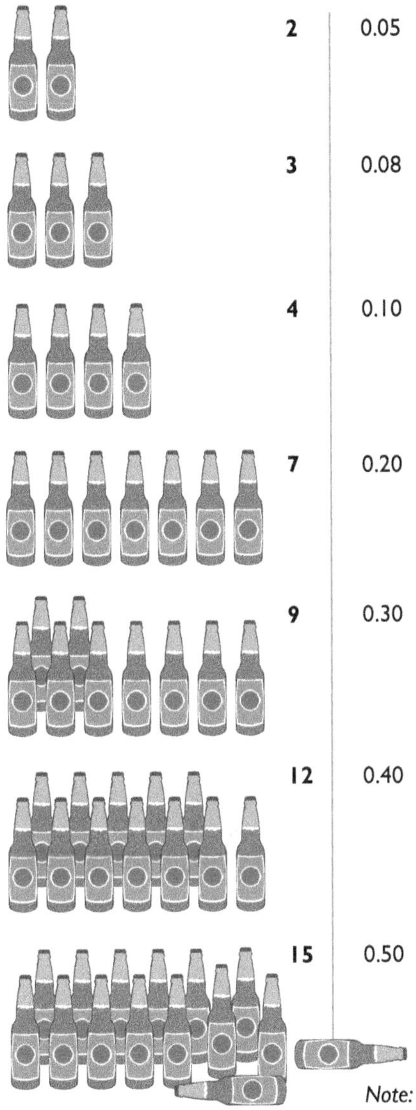

Number of drinks consumed in two hours		Alcohol in blood (percentage)	Typical effects
	2	0.05	Judgment, thought, and restraint weakened; tension released, giving carefree sensation
	3	0.08	Tensions and inhibitions of everyday life lessened; cheerfulness
	4	0.10	Voluntary motor action affected, making hand and arm movements, walk, and speech clumsy
	7	0.20	Severe impairment—staggering, loud, incoherent, emotionally unstable, 100 times greater traffic risk; exuberance and aggressive inclinations magnified
	9	0.30	Deeper areas of brain affected, with stimulus-response and understanding confused; stuporous; blurred vision
	12	0.40	Incapable of voluntary action; sleepy, difficult to arouse; equivalent of surgical anesthesia
	15	0.50	Comatose; centres controlling breathing and heartbeat anesthetized; death increasingly probable

Note: A drink refers to a typical 12-ounce bottle of beer, a 1.5-ounce shot of hard liquor, or a 5-ounce glass of wine.

Narcotics: Relieving Pain and Anxiety

Narcotics are drugs that increase relaxation and relieve pain and anxiety. Two of the most powerful narcotics, *morphine* and *heroin*, are derived from the poppy seed pod. Although morphine is used medically to control severe pain, heroin is illegal in Canada and the United States. This has not prevented its widespread use.

Heroin users usually inject the drug directly into their veins with a hypodermic needle. The immediate effect has been described as a "rush" of positive feeling, similar in some respects to a sexual orgasm—and just as difficult to describe. After the rush, a heroin user experiences a sense of well-being and peacefulness that lasts three to five hours. When the effects of the drug wear off, however, the user feels extreme anxiety and a desperate desire to repeat the

Narcotics
Drugs that increase relaxation and relieve pain and anxiety.

experience. Moreover, users quickly build up **tolerance,** meaning that larger amounts of heroin are needed each time to produce the same pleasurable effect. These last two properties are all the ingredients necessary for biological and psychological addiction: The user is constantly either shooting up or attempting to obtain ever-increasing amounts of the drug. Eventually, the life of the user revolves around heroin. Because of the powerful positive feelings the drug produces, heroin addiction is particularly difficult to overcome.

Oxycodone (sold as the prescription drug *OxyContin and known by the street name of Oxy*) is a type of pain reliever that has led to a significant amount of abuse. Many well-known people (including Courtney Love and Rush Limbaugh) have become dependent on it.

Hallucinogens: Psychedelic Drugs

What do mushrooms, jimsonweed, and morning glories have in common? Besides being fairly common plants, each can be a source of a powerful **hallucinogen,** a drug that is capable of producing *hallucinations,* or changes in the perceptual process.

There is debate over what category of drug marijuana belongs to, but it is most often classified as a hallucinogen. Certainly the most common illicit drug in in widespread use on Canadian campuses today is *marijuana,* whose active ingredient—tetrahydrocannabinol (THC)—is found in a common weed, cannabis. Marijuana is typically smoked in cigarettes or pipes, although it can be cooked and eaten. Just over half of Canadian university students reported using pot during their lifetime, one-third during the past twelve months, and one-sixth of students during the past month (CAMH College Campus Survey, 2004).

The effects of marijuana vary from person to person, but they typically consist of feelings of euphoria and general well-being. Sensory experiences seem more vivid and intense, and a person's sense of self-importance seems to grow. Memory may be impaired, causing the user to feel pleasantly "spaced out." However, the effects are not universally positive. Individuals who use marijuana when they feel depressed can end up even more depressed, because the drug tends to magnify both good and bad feelings. Many users report unpleasant feelings of intense paranoia.

There are clear risks associated with long-term, heavy marijuana use. Heavy use at least temporarily decreases the production of the male sex hormone testosterone, potentially affecting sexual activity and sperm count (Iverson, 2000; Lane, Cherek, & Tcheremissine, 2007; Rossato, Pagano, & Vettor, 2008). Marijuana use impairs short-term and long-term memory, attention, working memory, and executive functioning (Fletcher et al., 1996; Solowji et al., 2002). Chronic use is also associated with a decline in school performance and achievement (Sanders, Field, & Diego, 2001). Heavy use also affects the ability of the immune system to fight off germs and infection. Marijuana use increases stress on the heart, although it is unclear how strong these effects are.

In addition, marijuana smoked during pregnancy may have lasting effects on children who are exposed prenatally, although the results are inconsistent.

There is evidence that marijuana may have several medical uses; it can be used to prevent nausea from chemotherapy, treat some AIDS symptoms, and relieve muscle spasms for people with spinal cord injuries. In a controversial move, several U.S. states have made the use of the drug legal if it is prescribed by a physician—although it remains illegal under U.S. and Canadian federal laws (Iverson, 2000; Seamon et al., 2007; Chapkis & Webb, 2008; Cohen, 2009).

MDMA (Ecstasy) and LSD

MDMA ("Ecstasy" or "Molly") and *lysergic acid diethylamide (LSD, or "acid")* fall into the category of hallucinogens. Both drugs affect the operation of the neurotransmitter serotonin in the brain, causing an alteration in brain-cell activity and perception (Cloud, 2000; Buchert et al., 2004).

Ecstasy users report a sense of peacefulness and calm. People on the drug report experiencing increased empathy and connection with others, as well as feeling more

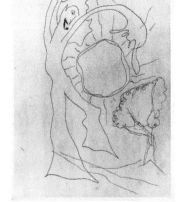

This drawing, made by someone taking LSD, suggests the effects of hallucinogens on thinking.

Source: © Omikron/Getty Images.

Tolerance
An insensitivity to the effects of a drug caused by repeated use of the drug, such that larger amounts of the drug are needed to produce the same effect.

Hallucinogen
A class of drug that is capable of producing hallucinations or changes in the perceptual process.

relaxed, yet energetic. Although the data are not conclusive, some researchers have found permanent declines in memory and performance on intellectual tasks, and such findings suggest that there may be long-term changes in serotonin receptors in the brain (Montgomery et al., 2005; El-Mallakh & Abraham, 2007; Jones et al., 2008).

LSD, which is structurally similar to serotonin, produces vivid hallucinations. Perceptions of colours, sounds, and shapes are altered so much that even the most mundane experience—such as looking at the knots in a wooden table—can seem moving and exciting. Time perception is distorted, and objects and people may be viewed in a new way, with some users reporting that LSD increases their understanding of the world. For others, however, the experience brought on by LSD can be terrifying, particularly if users have had emotional difficulties in the past. Furthermore, people occasionally experience flashbacks, in which they hallucinate long after they initially used the drug (Baruss, 2003; Wu, Schlenger, & Galvin, 2006).

Becoming an Informed Consumer of Psychology

Identifying Drug and Alcohol Problems

In a society bombarded with commercials for drugs that are guaranteed to do everything from curing the common cold to giving new life to "tired blood," it is no wonder that drug-related problems are a major social issue. Yet many people with drug and alcohol problems deny they have them, and even close friends and family members may fail to realize when occasional social use of drugs or alcohol has turned into abuse.

Certain signs, however, indicate when use becomes abuse (National Institute on Drug Abuse, 2000; Health Canada, 2008c). Among them are the following:

- Always getting high to have a good time
- Being high more often than not
- Getting high to get oneself going
- Going to work or class while high
- Missing or being unprepared for class or work because you were high
- Feeling bad later about something you said or did while high
- Driving a car while high
- Coming in conflict with the law because of drugs
- Doing something while high that you wouldn't do otherwise
- Being high in nonsocial, solitary situations
- Being unable to stop getting high
- Feeling a need for a drink or a drug to get through the day
- Becoming physically unhealthy
- Failing at school or on the job
- Thinking about liquor or drugs all the time
- Avoiding family or friends while using liquor or drugs

Any combination of these symptoms should be sufficient to alert you to the potential of a serious drug problem. Because drug and alcohol dependence are almost impossible to cure on one's own, people who suspect that they have a problem should seek immediate attention from a psychologist, physician, or counsellor.

You can also get help from national hotlines. For alcohol and drug difficulties, call the Drug and Alcohol Registry of Treatment (DART) at (800) 565-8603. DART provides information and referral to alcohol and drug treatment services. You can also check your telephone book for a local listing of Alcoholics Anonymous or Narcotics Anonymous. Finally, check out the website of the Centre for Addiction and Mental Health at www.camh.net/.

Evaluate

1. Drugs that affect a person's consciousness are referred to as _____.

2. Classify each drug listed as a stimulant (S), depressant (D), hallucinogen (H), or narcotic (N).

   1. Nicotine   **3.** Alcohol   **5.** Marijuana

   2. Cocaine   **4.** Morphine

3. The effects of LSD can recur long after the drug has been taken. True or false?

Answers to Evaluate Questions

1. psychoactive; 2. 1-S, 2-S, 3-D, 4-N, 5-H; 3. true

Key Terms

addictive drugs

depressants

hallucinogen

narcotics

psychoactive drugs

stimulants

tolerance

Epilogue

Our examination of states of consciousness has ranged widely. It focuses both on natural factors such as sleep, dreaming, and daydreaming and on more intentional modes of altering consciousness, including hypnosis, meditation, and drugs. As we consider why people seek to alter their consciousness, we need to reflect on the uses and abuses of the various consciousness-altering strategies in which people engage.

Source: © Laura Cavanagh.

Recap/Rethink

Module 12: Sleep and Dreams

Recap

LO1 What are the different states of consciousness?

- Consciousness is a person's awareness of the sensations, thoughts, and feelings at a given moment. Waking consciousness can vary from more active to more passive states.
- Altered states of consciousness include naturally occurring sleep and dreaming, as well as hypnotic and drug-induced states.

LO2 What happens when we sleep, and what are the meaning and function of dreams?

- Using the electroencephalogram, or EEG, to study sleep, scientists have found that the brain is active throughout the night, and that sleep proceeds through a series of stages identified by unique patterns of brain waves.
- REM (rapid eye movement) sleep is characterized by an increase in heart rate, a rise in blood pressure, an increase in the rate of breathing, erections, and eye movements. Dreams occur during this stage.
- According to Freud, dreams have both a manifest content (an apparent story line) and a latent content (a true meaning). He suggested that the latent content provides a guide to a dreamer's unconscious, revealing unfulfilled wishes or desires.
- The dreams-for-survival theory suggests that information relevant to daily survival is reconsidered and reprocessed in dreams. The activation-synthesis theory proposes that dreams are a result of random electrical energy that stimulates different memories, which then are woven into a coherent story line.

What are the major sleep disorders, and how can they be treated?

- Insomnia is a sleep disorder characterized by difficulty sleeping. Sleep apnea is a condition in which people have difficulty sleeping and breathing at the same time. People with narcolepsy have an uncontrollable urge to sleep. Sleepwalking and sleeptalking are relatively harmless.
- Psychologists and sleep researchers advise people with insomnia to increase exercise during the day, avoid caffeine and sleeping pills, drink a glass of warm milk before bedtime, and try not to sleep.

Rethink

1. *Especially for ECE students:* How might you utilize the findings in sleep research to maximize student learning?

2. What advice would you give to a fellow classmate struggling with insomnia?

3. Suppose that a new "miracle pill" will allow a person to function with only one hour of sleep per night without feeling tired. However, because the night's sleep is so short, a person who takes the pill will never dream again. Knowing what you do about the functions of sleep and dreaming, what would be some advantages and drawbacks of such a pill from a personal standpoint? Would you take such a pill?

Module 13: Hypnosis and Meditation

Recap

What is hypnosis, and are hypnotized people in a different state of consciousness?

- Hypnosis produces a state of heightened susceptibility to the suggestions of the hypnotist. Under hypnosis, significant behavioural changes occur, including increased concentration and suggestibility, heightened ability to recall and construct images, lack of initiative, and acceptance of suggestions that clearly contradict reality.

What are the effects of meditation?

- Meditation is a learned technique for refocusing attention that brings about an altered state of consciousness.
- Different cultures have developed their own unique ways to alter states of consciousness.

Rethink

1. *From the perspective of a human resources specialist:* Would you allow (or even encourage) employees to engage in meditation during the work day? Why or why not?

2. Your cousin is pregnant with her first baby and asks you what you think about using hypnosis rather than conventional pain medications. What information would you give her, based on what you have learned in this chapter?

3. Why do you think that in almost every culture, people use psychoactive drugs or other methods to search for altered states of consciousness?

Module 14: Drug Use: The Highs and Lows of Consciousness

Recap

What are the major classifications of drugs, and what are their effects?

- Drugs can produce an altered state of consciousness. However, they vary in how dangerous and how addictive they are.
- Stimulants cause arousal in the central nervous system. Two common stimulants are caffeine and nicotine. More dangerous are cocaine and amphetamines, which in large quantities can lead to convulsions and death.
- Depressants decrease arousal in the central nervous system. They can cause intoxication along with feelings of euphoria. The most common depressants are alcohol, barbiturates, and benzodiazepines.
- Morphine and heroin are narcotics, drugs that produce relaxation and relieve pain and anxiety. Because of their addictive qualities, morphine and heroin are particularly dangerous.
- Hallucinogens are drugs that produce hallucinations or other changes in perception. The most frequently used hallucinogen is marijuana, which has several long-term risks. Two other hallucinogens are LSD and Molly or Ecstasy.
- A number of signals indicate when drug use becomes drug abuse. A person who suspects that he or she has a drug problem should get professional help. People are almost never capable of solving drug problems on their own.

Rethink

1. *Especially for Social Service Worker students:* How would you explain why people start using drugs to the family members of someone who was addicted? What types of drug prevention programs would you advocate?

2. Your friend is worried about her brother's substance use. What advice would you give her in terms of warning signs to look for that might signal a serious substance abuse issue?

Source: © Blend Images/Getty Images RF.

Prologue

Disabled Teen Wins Dog Fight

Source: © Calgary Sun/Jack Cusano/ Sun Media.

Disabled Alberta teenager wins the fight to have his guide dog Kodak accompany him to school. The Calgary Board of Education initially banned Kodak from Dr. E. P. Scarlett High School. School board officials quoted board policy prohibiting dogs of any kind from being on school property. The James family fought back with a doctor's note from Alberta Children's Hospital indicating that Cooper requires his guide dog at his side at all times.

Cooper James, a grade 11 student, has spinal muscular dystrophy—and as a result is confined to a wheelchair. Cooper's guide dog Kodak helps him in countless ways, such as picking up dropped books and binders, helping Cooper when he falls, and opening doors around the school.

Where do these specially trained guide dogs come from? Kodak was trained and provided by the Lions Foundation of Canada Dog Guides, a charitable group that has transformed the lives of more than 1,200 disabled Canadians since 1983. Dog guides are a true blessing to physically challenged Canadians—bringing independence, safety, and increased mobility (CTV.ca/Canadian Press, 2006; Reynolds, 2006).

Kodak's expertise did not just happen, of course. It is the result of painstaking training procedures—the same ones that are at work in each of our lives, illustrated by our ability to read a book, drive a car, play poker, study for a test, or perform any of the numerous activities that make up our daily routine. Like Kodak, each of us must acquire and then refine our skills and abilities through learning. Learning is a fundamental topic for psychologists and plays a central role in almost every specialty area of psychology.

Psychologists have approached the study of learning from several angles. Among the most fundamental are studies of the type of learning that is illustrated in responses ranging from a dog salivating when it hears its owner opening a can of dog food to the emotions we feel when our national anthem is played. Other theories consider how learning is a consequence of rewarding circumstances. Finally, several other approaches focus on the cognitive aspects of learning, or the thought processes that underlie learning.

Classical Conditioning

LEARNING OBJECTIVES

LO1 **What is** learning?
LO2 **How do** we learn to form associations between stimuli and responses?

Does the mere sight of the Starbucks logo make you crave caffeine and think about coffee? If it does, you are displaying an elementary form of learning called classical conditioning. Classical conditioning helps explain such diverse phenomena as crying at the sight of a bride walking down the aisle, fearing the dark, and falling in love.

Classical conditioning is one of a number of different types of learning that psychologists have identified, but a general definition encompasses all types of learning: **Learning** is a relatively permanent change in behaviour that is brought about by experience.

How do we know when a behaviour has been influenced by learning—or even is a result of learning? Part of the answer relates to the nature–nurture question, one of the fundamental issues underlying the field of psychology. Nature is the part of our behaviour that does not require learning; it is inborn or innate. For example, a baby "grows bigger" without being taught to do so. Nurture, on the other hand, is the part of our behaviour that is acquired through learning and interacting with the environment around us. For example, learning to read comes about with practise, teaching, experience, and associations. It is not always easy to identify whether a change in behaviour is due to nature or nurture. For example, some changes in behaviour or performance come about through maturation alone, and don't involve experience. For instance, children become better tennis players as they grow older partly because their strength increases with their size—a maturational phenomenon. In order to understand when learning has occurred, we must differentiate maturational changes from improvements resulting from practise, which indicate that learning actually has occurred.

Similarly, short-term changes in behaviour that are due to factors other than learning, such as declines in performance resulting from fatigue or lack of effort, are different from performance changes that are due to actual learning. If you are being chased by a pitbull and run faster than you have ever run before, this does not mean that you have learned a new, faster way to run. Under ordinary, non-stressful conditions you would likely be unable to replicate your speed. Because performance does not always reflect learning, determining when true learning has occurred is difficult.

It is clear that we are primed for learning from the beginning of life. Infants exhibit a primitive type of learning called habituation. *Habituation* is the decrease in response to a stimulus that occurs after repeated presentations of the same stimulus. For example, young infants may initially show interest in a novel stimulus, such as a brightly coloured toy, but they will soon lose interest if they see the same toy over and over. (Adults exhibit habituation, too: newlyweds soon stop noticing that they are wearing a wedding ring.) Habituation permits us to ignore things that have stopped providing new information.

Most learning is considerably more complex than habituation, and the study of learning has been at the core of the field of psychology. Although philosophers since the time of Aristotle have speculated on the foundations of learning, the first systematic research on learning was done at the beginning of the twentieth century, when Ivan Pavlov (does the name ring a bell?) developed the framework for learning called classical conditioning.

Learning
A relatively permanent change in behaviour brought about by experience.

The Basics of Classical Conditioning

Ivan Pavlov, a Russian physiologist, never intended to do psychological research. In 1904 he won the Nobel Prize for his work on digestion, testimony to his contribution to that field. Yet Pavlov is remembered not for his physiological research, but for his experiments on basic learning processes—work that he began quite accidentally (Marks, 2004; Samoilov & Zayas, 2007).

Pavlov had been studying the production of stomach acids and saliva in dogs after they ate different amounts and kinds of food. While doing that, he observed a curious phenomenon: Sometimes stomach secretions and salivation (drooling) would begin in the dogs when they had not yet eaten any food. The mere sight of the experimenter who normally brought the food, or even the sound of the experimenter's footsteps, was enough to produce salivation in the dogs. At first, Pavlov believed his dogs had become psychic! However, he soon recognized that the dogs had learned an association between the stimuli that surrounded food (the experimenter's footsteps and the sight of the experimenter) and the food itself. We might say that the dogs saw the experimenter and knew they were about to get food. Pavlov would say we cannot ever know for sure what is happening inside a dog's mind but we can look at the dog's behaviour and say that the dog is now responding to the experimenter's footsteps in the same way that he responds to food, i.e., by drooling. Pavlov saw that the dogs were responding not only on the basis of a biological need (hunger), but also as a result of learning—or, as it came to be called, classical conditioning. **Classical conditioning** is a type of learning in which a neutral stimulus (such as the experimenter's footsteps) comes to bring about a response after being paired with a stimulus (such as food) that naturally brings about that response.

To demonstrate and analyze classical conditioning, Pavlov conducted a series of experiments (Pavlov, 1927). In one, he attached a tube to the salivary gland of a dog; that would allow him to measure precisely the dog's salivation. He then rang a bell and, just a few seconds later, presented the dog with meat. This pairing occurred repeatedly and was carefully planned so that each time exactly the same amount of time elapsed between the presentation of the bell and the meat. At first the dog would salivate only when the meat was presented, but soon it began to salivate at the sound of the bell. In fact, even when Pavlov stopped presenting the meat, the dog still salivated after hearing the sound. The dog had been classically conditioned to salivate to the bell.

As you can see in Figure 1, the basic processes of classical conditioning that underlie Pavlov's discovery are straightforward, although the terminology he chose is not simple. Consider first the diagram in Figure 1a. Before conditioning, there are two unrelated stimuli: the ringing of a bell and meat. We know that normally the ringing of a bell does not lead to salivation but to some irrelevant response, such as pricking up the ears or perhaps a startle reaction. The bell is therefore called the **neutral stimulus** because it is a stimulus that, before conditioning, does not naturally bring about the response in which we are interested. We also have meat, which naturally causes a dog to salivate—the response we are interested in conditioning. The meat is considered an **unconditioned stimulus (UCS),** because food placed in a dog's mouth automatically causes salivation to occur. The response that the meat elicits (salivation) is called an **unconditioned response (UCR)**—a natural, innate, reflexive response that is not associated with previous learning. Unconditioned responses are always brought about by the presence of unconditioned stimuli.

Figure 1b illustrates what happens during conditioning. The bell is rung just before each presentation of the meat. The goal of conditioning is for the dog to associate the bell with the unconditioned stimulus (meat) and therefore to bring about the same sort of response as the unconditioned stimulus. After a number of pairings of the bell and meat, the bell alone causes the dog to salivate.

Classical conditioning

A type of learning in which a neutral stimulus comes to bring about a response after it is paired with a stimulus that naturally brings about that response.

Neutral stimulus

A stimulus that, before conditioning, does not naturally bring about the response of interest.

Unconditioned stimulus (UCS)

A stimulus that naturally brings about a particular response without having been learned.

Unconditioned response (UCR)

A response that is natural and needs no training (e.g., salivation at the smell of food).

FIGURE 1

The basic process of classical conditioning. (a) Before conditioning, the ringing of a bell does not bring about salivation—making the bell a neutral stimulus. In contrast, meat naturally brings about salivation, making the meat an unconditioned stimulus and salivation an unconditioned response. (b) During conditioning, the bell is rung just before the presentation of the meat. (c) Eventually, the ringing of the bell alone brings about salivation. We now can say that conditioning has been accomplished: The previously neutral stimulus of the bell is now considered a conditioned stimulus that brings about the conditioned response of salivation.

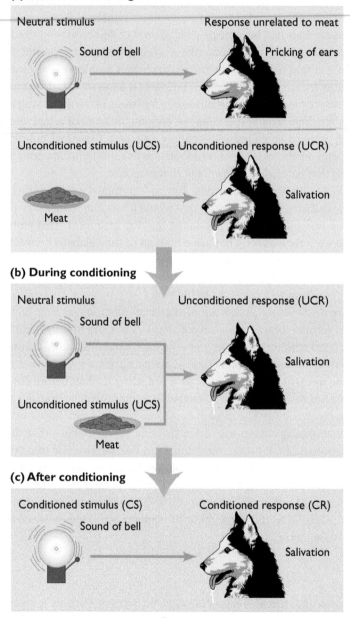

(a) Before conditioning

Neutral stimulus — Sound of bell → Response unrelated to meat — Pricking of ears

Unconditioned stimulus (UCS) — Meat → Unconditioned response (UCR) — Salivation

(b) During conditioning

Neutral stimulus — Sound of bell

Unconditioned stimulus (UCS) — Meat → Unconditioned response (UCR) — Salivation

(c) After conditioning

Conditioned stimulus (CS) — Sound of bell → Conditioned response (CR) — Salivation

When conditioning is complete, the bell has evolved from a neutral stimulus to what is now called a **conditioned stimulus (CS).** At this time, salivation that occurs as a response to the conditioned stimulus (bell) is considered a

Conditioned stimulus (CS)
A once-neutral stimulus that has been paired with an unconditioned stimulus to bring about a response formerly caused only by the unconditioned stimulus.

conditioned response (CR). This situation is depicted in Figure 1c. After conditioning, then, the conditioned stimulus evokes the conditioned response.

STUDY ALERT!

Figure 1 can help you to learn and understand the process (and terminology) of classical conditioning, which can be confusing.

The sequence and timing of the presentation of the unconditioned stimulus and the conditioned stimulus are particularly important. A neutral stimulus that is presented *just before* the unconditioned stimulus is most apt to result in successful conditioning. A neutral stimulus that is presented *after* the unconditioned stimulus is much less likely to condition a response. This is why your cat may become excited when you pull out the can opener (which precedes opening a can of catfood), but not when you put it away (which comes afterward). Research has shown that conditioning is most effective if the neutral stimulus (which will become a conditioned stimulus) precedes the unconditioned stimulus by between a half second and several seconds, depending on what kind of response is being conditioned (Wasserman & Miller, 1997; Bitterman, 2006).

Although the terminology Pavlov used to describe classical conditioning may seem confusing at first, the following summary can help make the relationships between stimuli and responses easier to understand and remember:

- Conditioned = learned; unconditioned = not learned.
- An *un*conditioned stimulus leads to an *un*conditioned response.
- An *un*conditioned stimulus triggers the *un*conditioned response innately (it is unlearned and untrained)
- During conditioning, a previously neutral stimulus is transformed into the conditioned stimulus because it is being repeatedly paired with the unconditioned stimulus.
- The neutral stimulus and the conditioned stimulus are the same thing. Once the neutral stimulus triggers a response we can no longer call it neutral, so after conditioning has occurred we refer to the (previously) neutral stimulus as the conditioned stimulus.
- A conditioned stimulus triggers the conditioned response, as a consequence of conditioning.
- The unconditioned response and a conditioned response are the same behaviour (such as salivation in Pavlov's experiment). The difference between them is what triggers the response: the unconditioned response is triggered by the unconditioned stimulus while the conditioned response is triggered by the conditioned stimulus.

Applying Conditioning Principles to Human Behaviour

Although the initial conditioning experiments were carried out with animals, classical conditioning principles were soon found to explain many aspects of everyday human behaviour. Recall, for instance, the earlier example of how people crave a coffee when they see the Starbucks logo. The cause of this reaction is classical conditioning: The previously neutral logo has become associated with the coffee inside the restaurant (the unconditioned stimulus), causing the logo to become a conditioned stimulus that brings about the conditioned response of the craving. Marketers put the principles of classical conditioning to work for their brands all the time.

Pavlov studied salivation, which is a physiological reaction. However, emotional responses are also likely to be learned through classical conditioning processes. In a now-infamous case study, psychologist John B. Watson and colleague Rosalie Rayner (1920) showed that classical conditioning was at the root of such fears by conditioning an 11-month-old infant named Albert to be afraid of rats. "Little Albert," like most infants, initially was frightened by loud noises but had no fear of rats.

In the study, the experimenters sounded a loud noise just as they showed Little Albert a rat. The noise (the unconditioned stimulus) evoked fear (the unconditioned response). However, after just a few pairings of noise and rat, Albert began to show fear of the rat by itself, bursting into tears when he saw it. The rat, then, had become a CS that brought

Conditioned response (CR)
A response that, after conditioning, follows a previously neutral stimulus (e.g., salivation at the ringing of a bell).

about the CR, fear. Furthermore, the effects of the conditioning lingered: Five days later, Albert reacted with fear not only when shown a rat, but when shown objects that looked similar to the white, furry rat, including a white rabbit, a white sealskin coat, and even a white Santa Claus mask. It is clear that Watson, the experimenter, has been condemned for using ethically questionable procedures and that such studies would never be conducted today.

Until recently, we did not know what happened to the unfortunate Little Albert after Watson and Rayner's experiment ended. A team of researchers spent almost seven years investigating the course of events following the notorious 1920 experiment. Dr. Hall Beck and his research team discovered that Little Albert's real name was Douglas Merritte, that he suffered no post-experiment effects, and that he died at only six years of age of hydrocephalus on May 10, 1925 (Beck, Levinson, & Irons, 2009).

Learning by means of classical conditioning also occurs during adulthood. For example, you may not go to a dentist as often as you should because of prior associations of dentists with pain. A case of food poisoning may lead to lifelong avoidance of the food that caused the sickness. In more extreme cases, classical conditioning can lead to the development of *phobias,* which are intense, irrational fears that we will consider later when we discuss psychological disorders. For example, an individual might develop a lifelong phobia of dogs after being bitten by a dog as a child. Similarly, an insect phobia might develop in someone who is stung by a bee. The insect phobia might be so severe that the person refrains from leaving home. *Posttraumatic stress disorder (PTSD),* suffered by some war veterans and others who have had traumatic experiences, can also be explained by classical conditioning. Even years after their battlefield experiences, a stimulus such as a loud noise may trigger an emotional response of fear or panic. In some cases, they may have a full-blown *panic attack,* characterized by intense fear (Kozaric-Kovacic & Borovecki, 2005; Roberts, Moore, & Beckham, 2007).

On the other hand, classical conditioning also accounts for pleasant experiences. For instance, you may have a particular fondness for the smell of a certain perfume or aftershave lotion because the feelings and thoughts of an early love come rushing back whenever you smell it.

In summary, classical conditioning, explains many of the emotional and physiological reactions we have to stimuli in the world around us.

Extinction

What do you think would happen if a dog that had become classically conditioned to salivate at the ringing of a bell never again received food when the bell was rung? The answer lies in one of the basic phenomena of learning: extinction. **Extinction** occurs when a previously conditioned response decreases in frequency and eventually disappears.

To produce extinction, one needs to end the association between conditioned stimuli and unconditioned stimuli. For instance, if we had trained a dog to salivate (the conditioned response) at the ringing of a bell (the conditioned stimulus), we could produce extinction by repeatedly ringing the bell but *not* providing meat. At first the dog would continue to salivate when it heard the bell, but after a few such instances, the amount of salivation would probably decline, and the dog would eventually stop responding to the bell altogether. At that point, we could say that the response had been extinguished. In sum, extinction occurs when the conditioned stimulus is presented repeatedly without the unconditioned stimulus (see Figure 2).

Extinction can be a helpful phenomenon. If you had a painful root canal, you might experience fear when you visit the dentist's office. After a few uneventful cleanings, however, that fear may well dissipate.

Once a conditioned response has been extinguished, has it vanished forever? Not necessarily. Pavlov discovered this when he returned to his dog a few days after the conditioned behaviour had seemingly been extinguished. If he rang a bell, the dog once again salivated—an effect known as **spontaneous recovery,** or the re-emergence of an extinguished conditioned response after a period of rest and with no further conditioning.

Spontaneous recovery helps explain why it is so hard to overcome drug addictions. For example, cocaine addicts who are thought to be "cured" can experience an irresistible impulse to use the drug again if they are subsequently confronted by a stimulus with strong connections to the drug, such as a white powder (DiCano & Everitt, 2002; Plowright, Simonds, & Butler, 2006).

Extinction
A basic phenomenon of learning that occurs when a previously conditioned response decreases in frequency and eventually disappears.

Spontaneous recovery
The re-emergence of an extinguished conditioned response after a period of rest and with no further conditioning.

FIGURE 2

Acquisition, extinction, and spontaneous recovery of a classically conditioned response. A conditioned response (CR) gradually increases in strength during training (a). However, if the conditioned stimulus is presented by itself enough times, the conditioned response gradually fades, and extinction occurs (b). After a pause (c) in which the conditioned stimulus is not presented, spontaneous recovery can occur (d). However, extinction typically reoccurs soon after.

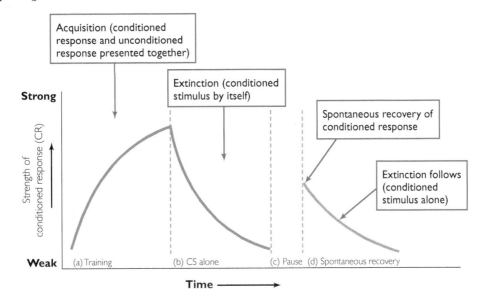

Generalization and Discrimination

Despite differences in colour and shape, to most of us a rose is a rose is a rose. The pleasure we experience at the beauty, smell, and grace of the flower is similar for different types of roses. Pavlov noticed a similar phenomenon. His dogs often salivated not only at the ringing of the bell that was used during their original conditioning but at the sound of a buzzer as well.

> ### STUDY ALERT!
> Remember that stimulus generalization relates to stimuli that are similar to one another, while stimulus discrimination relates to stimuli that are different from one another.

Such behaviour is the result of stimulus generalization. **Stimulus generalization** is a process in which, after a stimulus has been conditioned to produce a particular response, stimuli that are similar to the original stimulus produce the same response. The greater the similarity between two stimuli, the greater the likelihood of stimulus generalization. Little Albert, who, as we mentioned earlier, was conditioned to be fearful of rats, grew afraid of other furry white things as well. However, according to the principle of stimulus generalization, it is unlikely that he would have been afraid of a black dog, because its colour and size would have differentiated it sufficiently from the original fear-evoking stimulus (the small white rat).

Stimulus generalization is an important phenomenon as it allows us to adapt our learning in different situations. Stimulus generalization permits us to know, for example, that we ought to brake at all red lights, even if there are minor variations in size, shape, and shade.

Stimulus generalization
A process in which, after a stimulus has been conditioned to produce a particular response, stimuli that are similar to the original stimulus produce the same response.

On the other hand, **stimulus discrimination** occurs if two stimuli are sufficiently distinct from one another that one triggers a conditioned response but the other does not. Stimulus discrimination provides the ability to differentiate between stimuli. For example, our friend's dog Cleo comes running into the kitchen when she hears the sound of the electric can opener, which she has learned is used to open her dog food when her dinner is about to be served. She does not bound into the kitchen at the sound of the food processor, although it sounds similar. In other words, she discriminates between the stimuli of can opener and food processor. Similarly, our ability to discriminate between the behaviour of a growling dog and that of one whose tail is wagging can lead to adaptive behaviour—avoiding the growling dog and petting the friendly one.

Beyond Traditional Classical Conditioning: Challenging Basic Assumptions

Although Pavlov hypothesized that all learning is nothing more than long strings of conditioned responses, this notion has not been supported by subsequent research. It turns out that classical conditioning provides us with only a partial explanation of how people and animals learn and that Pavlov was wrong in some of his basic assumptions (Hollis, 1997).

For example, according to Pavlov, the process of linking stimuli and responses occurs in a mechanistic, unthinking way. In contrast to this perspective, learning theorists influenced by cognitive psychology have argued that learners actively develop an understanding and expectancy about which particular unconditioned stimuli are matched with specific conditioned stimuli. A ringing bell, for instance, gives a dog something to think about: the impending arrival of food (Kirsch et al., 2004).

Traditional explanations of how classical conditioning operates have also been challenged by John Garcia, a learning psychologist whose research was initially concerned with the effects of exposure to nuclear radiation on laboratory animals. In the course of his experiments, he realized that rats placed in a radiation chamber drank almost no water, even though in their home cage they drank eagerly. The most obvious explanation—that it had something to do with the radiation—was soon ruled out. Garcia found that even when the radiation was not turned on, the rats still drank little or no water in the radiation chamber (Garcia, 1990, 2003).

Initially puzzled by the rats' behaviour, Garcia eventually figured out that the drinking cups in the radiation chamber were made of plastic, giving the water an unusual, plastic-like taste. In contrast, the drinking cups in the home cage were made of glass and left no abnormal taste.

As a result, the plastic-tasting water had become repeatedly paired with illness brought on by exposure to radiation, and that had led the rats to form a classically conditioned association. The process began with the radiation acting as an unconditioned stimulus evoking the unconditioned response of sickness. With repeated pairings, the plastic-tasting water had become a conditioned stimulus that evoked the conditioned response of sickness.

The same phenomenon operates when humans learn that they are allergic to certain foods. If every time you ate peanuts you had an upset stomach several hours later, eventually you would learn to avoid peanuts, despite the time lapse between the stimulus of peanuts and response of getting ill. In fact, you might develop a *learned taste aversion*, so that peanuts no longer even tasted good to you.

Garcia's finding violated one of the basic rules of classical conditioning—that an unconditioned stimulus should *immediately* follow a conditioned stimulus for optimal conditioning to occur. Instead, Garcia showed that conditioning could occur even when the interval between exposure to the conditioned stimulus and the response of sickness was as long as eight hours. Furthermore, the conditioning persisted over very long periods and sometimes occurred after just one exposure to water that was followed later on by illness.

Psychologist Martin Seligman refined our understanding of classical conditioning with his **biological preparedness** theory, which says that we are primed to learn certain kinds of associations over others. We are most

---

Stimulus discrimination
The process that occurs if two stimuli are sufficiently distinct from one another that one evokes a conditioned response but the other does not; the ability to differentiate between stimuli.

Biological preparedness
A theory that explains our propensity to learn certain classically conditioned associations over others that is linked to our evolutionary history.

likely to become classically conditioned to fear stimuli that were dangerous to our ancestors over evolutionary time, such as lightning, snakes, or rats. The ease with which animals can be conditioned to avoid certain kinds of dangerous stimuli, such as tainted food, supports this evolutionary theory. As Darwin suggested, organisms that have traits and characteristics that aid survival are more likely to thrive and have descendants. Our evolutionary ancestors would not have survived if they went back time and again to sample a food that made them sick. Consequently, organisms that ingest unpalatable foods (whether rats drinking water during the radiation sickness experiment described above or humans who suffer food poisoning after eating spoiled sushi) are likely to avoid similar foods in the future, making their survival more likely (Steinmetz, Kim, & Thompson, 2003). This explains why if you overindulge on tequila margaritas with your friends at the bar you are likely to develop an aversion so powerful that just the smell of a margarita makes you feel a bit nauseous. You will not, however, develop an aversion to the song that was playing in the background while you were pounding those margaritas. You are biologically prepared to make associations between feeling sick with what you were eating or drinking, not with what you were hearing.

Overindulging in a particular alcoholic beverage may result in a powerful aversion to that beverage in the future. Fortunately, biological preparedness tells us you are unlikely to develop an aversion to the song that was playing in the background or to the friends who were our drinking buddies that night.

Source: © Photolyric/iStockphoto.com.

Evaluate

1. _____ is a relatively permanent change in behaviour brought about by experience.

2. _____ is the name of the scientist responsible for discovering the learning phenomenon known as _____ conditioning, in which an organism learns a response to a stimulus to which it normally would not respond.

Refer to the passage below to answer questions 3 and 4:

The last three times little Theresa visited Dr. Lopez for checkups, he administered a painful preventive immunization shot that left her in tears. Today, when her mother takes her for another checkup, Theresa begins to sob as soon as she comes face to face with Dr. Lopez, even before he has had a chance to say hello.

3. The painful shot that Theresa received during each visit was a(n) _____ that elicited the _____, her tears.

4. Dr. Lopez's presence has become a _____ for Theresa's crying.

Answers to Evaluate Questions

1. learning 2. Pavlov, classical; 3. unconditioned stimulus, unconditioned response 4. conditioned stimulus

Key Terms

biological preparedness	learning	unconditioned response
classical conditioning	neutral stimulus	(UCR)
conditioned response (CR)	spontaneous recovery	unconditioned stimulus
conditioned stimulus (CS)	stimulus discrimination	(UCS)
extinction	stimulus generalization	

Operant Conditioning

LEARNING OBJECTIVES

LO3 **What is** the role of reward and punishment in learning?
LO4 **What are** some practical methods for bringing about behaviour change, both in ourselves and in others?

Very good . . . What a clever idea . . . Fantastic . . . I agree . . . Thank you . . . Excellent . . . Super . . . Right on . . . This is the best paper you've ever written; you get an A . . . You are really getting the hang of it . . . I'm impressed . . . You're getting a raise . . . Have a cookie . . . You look great . . . I love you . . .

Few of us mind being the recipient of any of the above comments. But what is especially noteworthy about them is that each of these simple statements can be used, through a process known as operant conditioning, to bring about powerful changes in behaviour and to teach the most complex tasks. Operant conditioning is the basis for many of the most important kinds of human, and animal, learning.

Operant conditioning is learning in which a voluntary response is strengthened or weakened, depending on its favourable or unfavourable consequences. When we say that a response has been strengthened or weakened, we mean that it has been made more or less likely to recur regularly.

Unlike classical conditioning, in which the original behaviours are the natural, biological responses to the presence of a stimulus such as food, water, or pain, operant conditioning applies to voluntary responses, which an organism performs deliberately to produce a desirable outcome. The term *operant* emphasizes this point: The organism *operates* on its environment to produce a desirable result. Operant conditioning is at work when we learn that toiling industriously can bring about a raise or that studying hard results in good grades.

As with classical conditioning, the basis for understanding operant conditioning was laid by work with animals. We turn now to some of that early research, which began with a simple inquiry into the behaviour of cats.

Thorndike's Law of Effect

If you placed a hungry cat in a cage and then put a small piece of food outside the cage, just beyond the cat's reach, chances are that the cat would eagerly search for a way out of the cage. The cat might first meow, scratch at the sides of the cage or push against an opening. Suppose, though, you had rigged things so that the cat could escape by stepping on a small paddle that released the latch to the door of the cage (see Figure 1). Eventually, as it moved around the cage, the cat would happen to step on the paddle, the door would open, and the cat would eat the food.

What would happen if you then returned the cat to the box? The next time, it would probably take a little less time for the cat to step on the paddle and escape. After a few trials, the cat would deliberately step on the paddle as soon as it was placed in the cage. What would have occurred, according to Edward L. Thorndike (1932), who studied this situation extensively, was that the cat would have learned that pressing the paddle was associated with the desirable consequence of getting food. Thorndike summarized that relationship by formulating the *law of effect:* Responses that lead to satisfying consequences are more likely to be repeated.

Operant conditioning
Learning in which a voluntary response is strengthened or weakened, depending on its favourable or unfavourable consequences.

FIGURE 1

Edward L. Thorndike devised this puzzle box to study the process by which a cat learns to press a paddle to escape from the box and receive food. Do you think Thorndike's work has relevance to the question of why humans voluntarily solve puzzles, such as crossword puzzles and jigsaw puzzles? Do they receive any rewards?

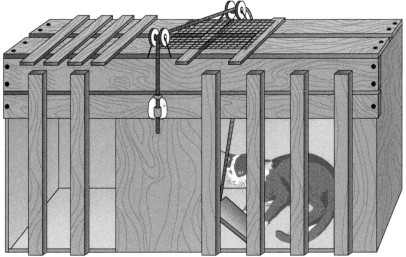

Thorndike believed that the law of effect operates as automatically as leaves fall off a tree in autumn. It was not necessary for an organism to understand that there was a link between a response and a reward. Instead, Thorndike believed, over time and through experience the organism would make a direct connection between the stimulus and the response without any awareness that the connection existed.

The Basics of Operant Conditioning

Thorndike's early research served as the foundation for the work of one of the twentieth century's most influential psychologists, B. F. Skinner, who died in 1990. You may have heard of the Skinner box (shown in Figure 2), a chamber with a highly controlled environment that was used to study operant conditioning processes with laboratory animals. Whereas Thorndike's goal was to get his cats to learn to obtain food by leaving the box, animals in a Skinner box learn to obtain food by operating on their environment within the box. Skinner became interested in specifying how behaviour varies as a result of alterations in the environment.

Skinner, whose work went far beyond perfecting Thorndike's earlier apparatus, is considered the inspiration for a whole generation of psychologists studying operant conditioning (Keehn, 1996; Pascual & Rodríguez, 2006). To illustrate Skinner's contribution, let's consider what happens to a rat in the typical Skinner box.

Suppose you want to teach a hungry rat to press a lever that is in its box. At first the rat will wander around the box, exploring the environment in a relatively random fashion. At some point, however, it will probably press the lever by chance, and when it does, it will receive a food pellet. The first time this happens, the rat will not learn the connection between pressing a lever and receiving food and will continue to explore the box. Sooner or later the rat will press the lever again and receive a pellet, and in time the frequency of the pressing response will increase. Eventually, the rat will press the lever continually until it satisfies its hunger, thereby demonstrating that it has learned that the receipt of food is contingent on pressing the lever.

Reinforcement: The Central Concept of Operant Conditioning

Skinner called the process that leads the rat to continue pressing the key "reinforcement." Although reinforcement is similar to getting a reward, **reinforcement** is technically defined as the process by which a stimulus increases the

Reinforcement
The process by which a stimulus increases the probability that a preceding behaviour will be repeated.

FIGURE 2

(a) Laboratory rats learn to press the lever in order to obtain food, which is delivered in the tray.
(b) B. F. Skinner with a Skinner box used to study operant conditioning.

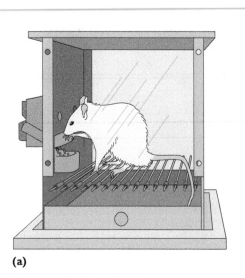

(a)

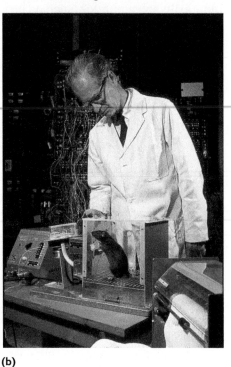

(b)

Photo Source: © Nina Leen/Time and Life Pictures/Getty Images.

probability that a preceding behaviour will be repeated. In other words, pressing the lever is more likely to occur again because of the stimulus of food.

In a situation such as this one, the food is called a reinforcer. A **reinforcer** is any stimulus that increases the probability that a preceding behaviour will occur again. Hence, food is a reinforcer because it increases the probability that the behaviour of pressing (formally referred to as the *response* of pressing) will take place. Again, many people use the term reward and reinforcer interchangeably. But behavioural psychologists prefer the term reinforcer because a reinforcer is anything that strengthens a behaviour, even if it is not a traditional reward. For someone who craves attention, any attention, even negative attention may work as a reinforcer. Conversely, someone who is painfully shy may not experience a speech in their honour as a reinforcer!

What kind of stimuli can act as reinforcers? Bonuses, toys, and good grades can serve as reinforcers—if they strengthen the probability of the response that occurred before their introduction. What makes something a reinforcer depends on individual preferences. Although a chocolate bar can act as a reinforcer for one person, an individual who dislikes chocolate may find $1 more desirable. The only way we can know if a stimulus is a reinforcer for a particular organism is to observe whether the frequency of a previously occurring behaviour increases after the presentation of the stimulus.

Of course, we are not born knowing that $1 can buy us a chocolate bar. Rather, through experience we learn that money is a valuable commodity because of its association with stimuli, such as food and drink, which are naturally

STUDY ALERT!

Remember that primary reinforcers satisfy a biological need; secondary reinforcers are effective due to previous association with a primary reinforcer.

Reinforcer
Any stimulus that increases the probability that a preceding behaviour will occur again.

reinforcing. This fact suggests a distinction between primary reinforcers and secondary reinforcers. A *primary reinforcer* satisfies some biological need and works naturally, regardless of a person's prior experience. Food for a hungry person, warmth for a cold person, and relief for a person in pain all would be classified as primary reinforcers. A *secondary reinforcer*, in contrast, is a stimulus that becomes reinforcing because of its association with a primary reinforcer. For instance, we know that money is valuable because we have learned that it allows us to obtain other desirable objects, including primary reinforcers such as food and shelter. Money thus becomes a secondary reinforcer.

Shaping: Reinforcing What Doesn't Come Naturally

Consider the difficulty of using operant conditioning to teach people to repair an automobile transmission. If you had to wait until they chanced to fix a transmission perfectly before you provided them with reinforcement, the Model T Ford might be back in style long before they mastered the repair process.

There are many complex behaviours, ranging from auto repair to zoo management, which we would not expect to occur naturally as part of anyone's spontaneous behaviour. For such behaviours, for which there might otherwise be no opportunity to provide reinforcement (because the behaviour would never occur in the first place), a procedure known as shaping is used. **Shaping** is the process of teaching a complex behaviour by rewarding closer and closer approximations of the desired behaviour. In shaping, you start by reinforcing any behaviour that is at all similar to the behaviour you want the person to learn. Later, you reinforce only responses that are closer to the behaviour you ultimately want to teach. Finally, you reinforce only the desired response. Each step in shaping, then, moves only slightly

APPLYING PSYCHOLOGY   in the Real World

A Nose for Danger: Saving Lives by Sniffing Out Land Mines

The Gambian giant pouched rat may be the best mine detector mankind or nature has yet devised. Just after sunup one dewy morning, on a football field-size patch of earth in the Mozambican countryside, Frank Weetjens and his squad of 16 giant pouched rats are proving it. Outfitted in tiny harnesses and hitched to 10-yard [9-metre] clotheslines, their footlong [30-cm-long] tails whipping to and fro, the rats lope up and down the lines, whiskers twitching, noses tasting the air. In places like Mozambique, these little animals are addressing a huge problem: a 17-year civil war left millions of buried mines throughout the countryside. The result is that each year thousands of people are killed and maimed by accidentally stepping on a mine.

Wanjiro, a sleek 2-year-old female in a bright red harness, pauses halfway down the line, sniffs, turns back, then sniffs again. She gives the red clay a decisive scratch with both forepaws. Her trainer, Kassim Mgaza, snaps a metal clicker twice, and Wanjiro waddles to him for her reward—a mouthful of banana and an affectionate pet (Wines, 2004, p. A1).

Score one for the Gambian giant pouched rat, who weighs in at just one to two kilograms, the size of a large gerbil (in fact, their size is part of what makes them ideal because, unlike dogs, these rats weigh so little they can stand right on top of a buried mine without detonating it). More precisely, score one for the principles of classical and operant conditioning, which are being harnessed in a process that has the potential to save a substantial number of lives.

To learn how to locate mines, trainers first teach pouched rats like Wanjiro to associate the sound of a clicker with food, in a process of classical conditioning. They then place the rats in a cage with a hole that is filled with explosive material. When the rats sniff the hole, the trainers sound the clicker and provide food. Through repeated presentations of food and explosive material, like in the classical conditioning training paradigm, rats learn to associate the smell of explosive with food, and they begin to eagerly seek out the smell of explosives.

From there, it is only a short leap to searching the ground for buried explosive. Before it can dig down to the mine, trainers give the rats a food reinforcement of a peanut and banana mixture. In short, sniffing the ground for explosive becomes a reinforced behaviour (Cookson, 2005; Corcoran, 2005).

The success of this project has led it to expanding beyond Mozambique to another war-ravaged African country, Sudan. Furthermore, the procedure has the potential to be used in other ways, such as finding buried victims in earthquakes. This is the power of the classical and operant conditioning.

Shaping
The process of teaching a complex behaviour by rewarding closer and closer approximations of the desired behaviour.

beyond the previously learned behaviour, permitting the person to link the new step to the behaviour learned earlier (Krueger & Dayan, 2009).

Shaping allows animals to learn complex responses that would never occur naturally, ranging from lions jumping through hoops, dolphins rescuing divers lost at sea, or—as we consider in nearby *Applying Psychology in the Real World* box—rodents finding hidden land mines. Shaping also underlies the learning of many complex human skills. For instance, the organization of most textbooks is based on the principles of shaping. Typically, information is presented so that new material builds on previously learned concepts or skills. Thus, the concept of shaping could not be presented until we had discussed the more basic principles of operant conditioning (Meyer & Ladewig, 2008). (Also see *PsychWork*.)

PsychWork

Seeing Eye Guide Dog Trainer

Name: Lea Johnson
Position: Seeing Eye Guide Dog Trainer
Education: BSc, Geography

For decades, guide dogs have provided a set of eyes to the visually impaired, expanding the opportunities open to them and increasing their independence. But it takes a great deal of training to make a dog an effective seeing eye guide dog, according to Lea Johnson, who works with The Seeing Eye agency in New Jersey. Johnson teaches apprentice instructors to carry out the demanding, but rewarding, process of training dogs.

"We hire college graduates, and while we don't require a specific major, a background in psychology or animal science allows employees to more easily connect with different aspects of the job," she said.

An apprentice instructor needs to have self-motivation in order to complete all aspects of the dog's training. In addition, they need to be able to work in a team setting, according to Johnson. But that's only part of it.

"The process of training the dogs is complex," says Johnson. "For example, the dog must be obedient and respond to their visually impaired owner. But they also get praised for sometimes refusing their owner's commands, if it would put their owner in danger."

Once a dog learns the skills it needs, the trainer must then teach a visually impaired person how to work with the dog.

"After training dogs for four months, the trainers must be able to teach blind people the skills to care for and travel with their seeing eye dog safely," Johnson said. Not only must trainers relate well to dogs, but they also must interact well with blind people. She adds, "The training of people is intense and emotionally challenging in a very different way from the dog training portion. Without a good heart to start with, trainers would never be successful."

Positive Reinforcers, Negative Reinforcers, and Punishment

In many respects, reinforcers can be thought of in terms of rewards; both a reinforcer and a reward increase the probability that a preceding response will occur again. But the term *reward* is limited to positive occurrences, and this is where it differs from a reinforcer—for it turns out that reinforcers can be positive or negative.

A **positive reinforcer** is a stimulus *added* to the environment that brings about an increase in a preceding response. If food, water, money, or praise is provided after a response, it is more likely that that response will occur again in the future. The paycheques that workers get at the end of the week, for example, increase the likelihood that they will return to their jobs the following week.

In contrast, a **negative reinforcer** refers to an unpleasant stimulus whose *removal* leads to an increase in the probability that a preceding response will be repeated in the future. For example, if you have an itchy rash (an unpleasant

Positive reinforcer
A stimulus added to the environment that brings about an increase in a preceding response.

Negative reinforcer
An unpleasant stimulus whose *removal* leads to an increase in the probability that a preceding response will be repeated in the future.

stimulus) that is relieved when you apply a certain brand of ointment, you are more likely to use that ointment the next time you have an itchy rash. Using the ointment, then, is negatively reinforcing, because it removes the unpleasant itch. Similarly, if your iPod volume is so loud that it hurts your ears when you first turn it on, you are likely to reduce the volume level. Lowering the volume is negatively reinforcing, and you are more apt to repeat the action in the future when you first turn it on. If you haven't eaten in a while and are experiencing hunger pangs, eating a snack will be negatively reinforcing as it will take away those unpleasant hunger pangs. Negative reinforcement, then, teaches the individual that taking an action removes an unpleasant condition that exists in the environment. Like positive reinforcement, negative reinforcement increases the likelihood that preceding behaviours will be repeated. Suppose you have a headache, so you decide to take a painkiller. If you feel better afterward, then the cessation of your headache will negatively reinforce the behaviour of taking a painkiller, meaning you will be more likely to take a painkiller in the future.

It is important to note that negative reinforcement is not the same as punishment. **Punishment** refers to a stimulus that *decreases* the probability that a prior behaviour will occur again. Unlike negative reinforcement, which produces an *increase* in behaviour, punishment reduces the likelihood of a prior response. If we receive a shock that is meant to decrease a certain behaviour, then we are receiving punishment, but if we are already receiving a shock and do something to stop that shock, the behaviour that stops the shock is considered to be negatively reinforced. In the first case, the specific behaviour is apt to decrease because of the punishment; in the second, it is likely to increase because of the negative reinforcement.

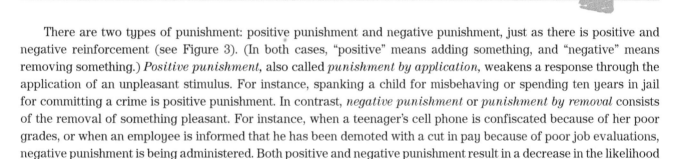

STUDY ALERT!

The differences between positive reinforcement, negative reinforcement, positive punishment, and negative punishment are tricky, so pay special attention to Figure 3 and the definitions in the text.

There are two types of punishment: positive punishment and negative punishment, just as there is positive and negative reinforcement (see Figure 3). (In both cases, "positive" means adding something, and "negative" means removing something.) *Positive punishment*, also called *punishment by application*, weakens a response through the application of an unpleasant stimulus. For instance, spanking a child for misbehaving or spending ten years in jail for committing a crime is positive punishment. In contrast, *negative punishment* or *punishment by removal* consists of the removal of something pleasant. For instance, when a teenager's cell phone is confiscated because of her poor grades, or when an employee is informed that he has been demoted with a cut in pay because of poor job evaluations, negative punishment is being administered. Both positive and negative punishment result in a decrease in the likelihood that a prior behaviour will be repeated.

The distinctions among positive reinforcement, negative reinforcement, positive punishment, and negative punishment may seem confusing initially, but the following rules (and the summary in Figure 3) can help you distinguish these concepts from one another:

- Reinforcement *increases* the frequency of the behaviour before it.
- Punishment *decreases* the frequency of the behaviour before it.
- *Removal of an unpleasant* stimulus will result in an increase in the frequency of behaviour. This is called negative reinforcement. An example would be getting out of jail for good behaviour.
- *Removal of a positive* stimulus will decrease the frequency of behaviour. This is called negative punishment (or punishment by removal). An example would be having your cell phone taken away if you come home late.
- *Application of a positive* stimulus brings about an increase in the frequency of behaviour. This is called positive reinforcement. An example would be getting an award for exceeding sales targets.
- *Application of a negative* stimulus decreases or reduces the frequency of behaviour. This is called positive punishment (or punishment by application). An example would be getting a ticket for speeding.

Punishment
A stimulus that decreases the probability that a previous behaviour will occur again.

FIGURE 3

Types of reinforcement and punishment.

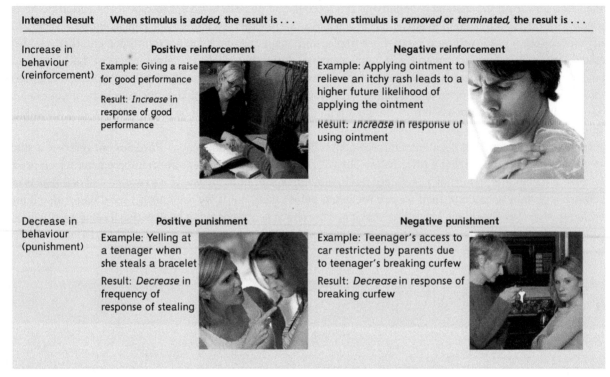

Intended Result	When stimulus is *added*, the result is . . .	When stimulus is *removed* or *terminated*, the result is . . .
Increase in behaviour (reinforcement)	**Positive reinforcement** Example: Giving a raise for good performance Result: *Increase* in response of good performance	**Negative reinforcement** Example: Applying ointment to relieve an itchy rash leads to a higher future likelihood of applying the ointment Result: *Increase* in response of using ointment
Decrease in behaviour (punishment)	**Positive punishment** Example: Yelling at a teenager when she steals a bracelet Result: *Decrease* in frequency of response of stealing	**Negative punishment** Example: Teenager's access to car restricted by parents due to teenager's breaking curfew Result: *Decrease* in response of breaking curfew

Sources: (top left): © Photo Disc/Getty Images RF; (top right): © Stockbyte/Corbis RF; (bottom left): © BananaStock/PunchStock RF; (bottom right): © Amy Etra/PhotoEdit.

The Pros and Cons of Punishment: Why Reinforcement Beats Punishment

Parking tickets, library fines, speeding tickets, jail sentences, time-outs, and detentions are all forms of punishment that we see in schools and the Canadian justice system. But is punishment an effective way to modify behaviour?

Punishment has several disadvantages that make its routine questionable. For one thing, punishment is frequently ineffective, particularly if it is not delivered shortly after the undesired behaviour or if the individual is able to leave the setting in which the punishment is being given. An employee who is reprimanded by the boss may quit; a teenager who loses the use of the family car may borrow a friend's car instead. In such instances, the initial behaviour that is being punished may be replaced by one that is even less desirable. Punishment may fail to produce long-lasting behavioural change. A child who receives a detention may learn not to get caught, rather than learn to modify his behaviour. A child who is reinforced for positive behaviour learns to modify his behaviour; in other words he learns what to do, rather than what not to do.

Even worse, physical punishment can convey to the recipient the idea that physical aggression is permissible and perhaps even desirable. A mother who yells at and hits her daughter for misbehaving teaches the daughter that aggression is an appropriate, adult response. The daughter soon may copy her mother's behaviour by acting aggressively toward others. In addition, physical punishment is often administered by people who are themselves angry or enraged. Ultimately, those who resort to physical punishment run the risk that they will grow to be feared. Punishment can also reduce the self-esteem of recipients unless they can understand the reasons for it (Leary et al., 2008; Zolotor et al., 2008; Miller-Perrin, Perrin, & Kocur, 2009).

In short, reinforcing desired behaviour is a more appropriate technique for modifying behaviour than using punishment. Both in and out of the scientific arena, then, reinforcement usually beats punishment (Pogarksy & Piquero, 2003; Hiby, Rooney, & Bradshaw, 2004; Sidman, 2006).

Schedules of Reinforcement: Timing Life's Rewards

The world would be a different place if poker players never played cards again after the first losing hand, fishermen returned to shore as soon as they missed a catch, or telemarketers never made another phone call after their first hang-up. The fact that such unreinforced behaviours continue, often with great frequency and persistence, illustrates that reinforcement need not be received continually for behaviour to be learned and maintained. In fact, behaviour that is reinforced only occasionally can ultimately be learned better than can behaviour that is always reinforced.

When we refer to the frequency and timing of reinforcement that follows desired behaviour, we are talking about **schedules of reinforcement.** Behaviour that is reinforced every time it occurs is said to be on a **continuous reinforcement schedule;** if it is reinforced some but not all of the time, it is on a **partial (intermittent) reinforcement schedule.** Although learning occurs more rapidly under a continuous reinforcement schedule, behaviour lasts longer after reinforcement stops when it is learned under a partial reinforcement schedule (Staddon & Cerutti, 2003; Gottlieb, 2004; Reed, 2007).

Why should intermittent reinforcement result in stronger, longer-lasting learning than continuous reinforcement? We can answer the question by examining how we might behave when using a candy vending machine compared with a Las Vegas slot machine. When we use a vending machine, prior experience has taught us that every time we put in the appropriate amount of money, the reinforcement, a candy bar, ought to be delivered. In other words, the schedule of reinforcement is continuous. In comparison, a slot machine offers intermittent reinforcement. We have learned that after putting in our cash, most of the time we will not receive anything in return. At the same time, though, we know that we will occasionally win something.

Now suppose that, unknown to us, both the candy vending machine and the slot machine are broken, and so neither one is able to dispense anything. It would not be very long before we stopped depositing coins into the broken candy machine. Probably at most we would try only two or three times before leaving the machine in disgust. But the story would be quite different with the broken slot machine. Here, we would drop in money for a considerably longer time, even though there would be no payoff.

In formal terms, we can see the difference between the two reinforcement schedules: Partial reinforcement schedules (such as those provided by slot machines) maintain performance longer than do continuous reinforcement schedules (such as those established in candy vending machines) before *extinction*—the disappearance of the conditioned response—occurs.

Certain kinds of partial reinforcement schedules produce stronger and lengthier responding before extinction than do others. Although many different partial reinforcement schedules have been examined, they can most readily be put into two categories: schedules that consider the *number of responses* made before reinforcement is given, called fixed-ratio and variable-ratio schedules, and those which consider the *amount of time* that elapses before reinforcement is provided, called fixed-interval and variable-interval schedules (Svartdal, 2003; Pellegrini et al., 2004; Reed & Morgan, 2008).

Schedules of reinforcement
Different patterns of frequency and timing of reinforcement following desired behaviour.

Continuous reinforcement schedule
Reinforcing of a behaviour every time it occurs.

Partial (intermittent) reinforcement schedule
Reinforcing of a behaviour some but not all of the time.

Fixed- and Variable-Ratio Schedules

In a **fixed-ratio schedule,** reinforcement is given only after a specific number of responses. For instance, a rat might receive a food pellet every tenth time it pressed a lever; here, the ratio would be 1:10. Similarly, garment workers are generally paid on fixed-ratio schedules: They receive a specific number of dollars for every blouse they sew. Because a greater rate of production means more reinforcement, people on fixed-ratio schedules are apt to work as quickly as possible (see Figure 4).

In a **variable-ratio schedule,** reinforcement occurs after a varying number of responses rather than after a fixed number. Although the specific number of responses necessary to receive reinforcement varies, the number of responses usually hovers around a specific average. A good example of a variable-ratio schedule is a telemarketer's job. She might make a sale during the third, eighth, ninth, and twentieth calls without being successful during any call in between.

FIGURE 4

Typical outcomes of different reinforcement schedules. (a) In a fixed-ratio schedule, short pauses occur after each response. Because the more responses, the more reinforcement, fixed-ratio schedules produce a high rate of responding. (b) In a variable-ratio schedule, responding also occurs at a high rate. (c) A fixed-interval schedule produces lower rates of responding, especially just after reinforcement has been presented, because the organism learns that a specified time period must elapse between reinforcements. (d) A variable-interval schedule produces a fairly steady stream of responses.

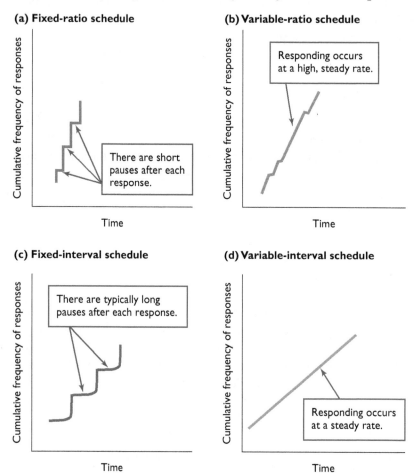

Source: Courtesy of Dr. Marian Bailey.

Fixed-ratio schedule
A schedule by which reinforcement is given only after a specific number of responses are made.

Variable-ratio schedule
A schedule by which reinforcement occurs after a varying number of responses rather than after a fixed number.

Although the number of responses that must be made before making a sale varies, it averages out to a 20-percent success rate. Under these circumstances, you might expect that the telemarketer would try to make as many calls as possible in as short a time as possible. This is the case with all variable-ratio schedules, which lead to a high rate of response and resistance to extinction. Slot machines work on a variable-ratio response schedule. Since variable-ratio schedules produce a high rate of response that is resistant to extinction, gambling can become a consuming addiction that is difficult to treat.

Fixed- and Variable-Interval Schedules: The Passage of Time

In contrast to fixed- and variable-ratio schedules, in which the crucial factor is the number of responses, fixed-*interval* and variable-*interval* schedules focus on the amount of time that has elapsed since a person or animal was rewarded. One example of a fixed-interval schedule is a weekly paycheque. For people who receive regular, weekly paycheques, it typically makes relatively little difference exactly how much they produce in a given week.

The variable-ratio schedule of a slot machine means that gamblers will develop a high-frequency, extinction-resistant behaviour. This is why gambling can become an addiction that is hard to treat.

Source: © Brand X Pictures RF.

Because a **fixed-interval schedule** provides reinforcement for a response only if a fixed time period has elapsed, overall rates of response are relatively low. This is especially true in the period just after reinforcement, when the time before another reinforcement is relatively great. Students' study habits often exemplify this reality. If the periods between exams are relatively long (meaning that the opportunity for reinforcement for good performance is given fairly infrequently), students often study minimally or not at all until the day of the exam draws near. Just before the exam, however, students begin to cram for it, signalling a rapid increase in the rate of their studying response. As you might expect, immediately after the exam there is a rapid decline in the rate of responding, with few people opening a book the day after a test. Fixed-interval schedules produce the kind of "scalloping effect" shown in Figure 4c (Saville, 2009).

One way to decrease the delay in responding that occurs just after reinforcement, and to maintain the desired behaviour more consistently throughout an interval, is to use a **variable-interval schedule.** In a variable-interval schedule, the time between reinforcements varies around some average rather than being fixed. For example, a professor who gives surprise quizzes that vary from one every three days to one every three weeks, averaging one every two weeks, is using a variable-interval schedule. Compared to the study habits we observed with a fixed-interval schedule, students' study habits under such a variable-interval schedule would most likely be very different. Students would be apt to study more regularly because they would never know when the next surprise quiz was coming. Variable-interval schedules, in general, are more likely to produce relatively steady rates of responding than are fixed-interval schedules, with responses that take longer to extinguish after reinforcement ends.

Discrimination and Generalization in Operant Conditioning

It does not take a child long to learn that a red light at an intersection means stop and a green light indicates that it is permissible to continue, in the same way that a pigeon can learn to peck a key when a green light goes on, but not when a red light appears. Just as in classical conditioning, then, operant learning involves the phenomena of discrimination and generalization.

Fixed-interval schedule
A schedule that provides reinforcement for a response only if a fixed time period has elapsed, making overall rates of response relatively low.

Variable-interval schedule
A schedule by which the time between reinforcements varies around some average rather than being fixed.

The process by which people learn to discriminate stimuli is known as *stimulus control training*. In stimulus control training, a behaviour is reinforced in the presence of a specific stimulus, but not in its absence. For example, one of the most difficult discriminations many people face is determining when someone's friendliness is not mere friendliness, but a signal of romantic interest. People learn to make the discrimination by observing the presence of certain nonverbal cues—such as increased eye contact and touching—that indicate romantic interest. When such cues are absent, people learn that no romantic interest is indicated. In this case, the nonverbal cue acts as a *discriminative stimulus*, one to which an organism learns to respond during stimulus control training. A discriminative stimulus signals the likelihood that reinforcement will follow a response. For example, if you wait until your roommate is in a good mood before you ask to borrow her favourite earrings, your behaviour can be said to be under stimulus control because you can discriminate between her moods.

Just as in classical conditioning, the phenomenon of stimulus generalization, in which an organism learns a response to one stimulus and then exhibits the same response to slightly different stimuli, occurs in operant conditioning. If you have learned that being polite helps you to get your way in a certain situation (reinforcing your politeness), you are likely to generalize your response to other situations. Sometimes, though, generalization can have unfortunate consequences, as when people behave negatively toward all members of a racial group because they have had an unpleasant experience with one member of that group.

Biological Constraints on Learning: You Can't Teach an Old Dog Just Any Trick

Psychologists Keller and Marian Breland were pleased with their idea: As professional animal trainers, they came up with the notion of having a pig pick up a wooden disk and place it in a piggy bank. With their experience in training animals through operant conditioning, they thought the task would be easy to teach, because it was certainly well within the range of the pig's physical capabilities. Yet almost every time they tried the procedure, it failed. Rather than picking up the disk, the pigs generally pushed it along the ground, something that they appeared to be biologically programmed to do.

To remedy the problem, the Brelands substituted a raccoon. Although the procedure worked fine with one disk, when two disks were used, the raccoon refused to deposit either of them and instead rubbed the two together, as if it were washing them. Once again, it appeared that the disks evoked biologically innate behaviours that were impossible to replace through even the most exhaustive training (Breland & Breland, 1961).

Biological constraints make it nearly impossible for animals to learn certain behaviours. Here, psychologist Marian Breland attempts to overcome the natural limitations that inhibit the success of conditioning this rooster.

Source: Courtesy of Dr. Marian Bailey.

The Brelands' difficulties illustrate an important point: Not all behaviours can be trained in all species equally well. Instead, there are *biological constraints*, built-in limitations in the ability of animals to learn particular behaviours. In some cases, an organism will have a special predisposition that will aid in its learning a behaviour (such as pecking behaviours in pigeons); in other cases, biological constraints will act to prevent or inhibit an organism from learning a behaviour.

The existence of biological constraints is consistent with evolutionary explanations of behaviour. Clearly, there are adaptive benefits that promote survival for organisms that quickly learn—or avoid—certain behaviours. For example, our ability to rapidly learn to avoid touching hot surfaces increases our chances of survival. Additional support for the evolutionary interpretation of biological constraints lies in the fact the associations that animals learn most readily involve stimuli that are most relevant to the specific environment in which they live (Terry, 2003; Cosmides & Tooby, 2004; Davis, 2007).

Comparing Classical and Operant Conditioning

We've considered classical conditioning and operant conditioning as two completely different processes. And, as summarized in Figure 5, there are a number of key distinctions between the two forms of learning. For example, the key concept in classical conditioning is the learning of an association between stimuli, whereas in operant conditioning it is learning through reinforcement and punishment. Furthermore, classical conditioning involves an involuntary, natural, innate behaviour, but operant conditioning is based on voluntary responses made by an organism. New behaviours can be learned through operant conditioning. In classical conditioning, a new behaviour is not learned; instead, a new trigger is learned for a behaviour that was already part of the organism's repertoire.

Some researchers are asking if, in fact, the two types of learning are so different after all. Learning psychologist John Donahoe and colleagues have suggested that classical and operant conditioning might share some underlying processes. Arguing from an evolutionary viewpoint, they contend that it is unlikely that two completely separate basic processes would evolve. Instead, one process—albeit with considerable complexity in the way it operates—might better explain behaviour (Donahoe, 2003; Donahoe & Vegas, 2004; Silva, Goncalves, & Garcia-Mijares, 2007).

Whether or not they are two distinct processes, it is clear that there are a number of processes that operate both in classical and operant conditioning, including extinction, stimulus generalization, and stimulus discrimination. Whether that means the distinctions between classical and operant conditioning will disappear remains to be seen.

FIGURE 5

Comparing key concepts in classical conditioning and operant conditioning.

Concept	Classical Conditioning	Operant Conditioning
Basic principle	Building associations between a conditioned stimulus and conditioned response.	Reinforcement *increases* the frequency of the behaviour preceding it; punishment *decreases* the frequency of the behaviour preceding it.
Nature of behaviour	Based on involuntary, natural, innate behaviour. Behaviour is elicited by the unconditioned or conditioned stimulus.	Organism voluntarily operates on its environment to produce a desirable result. After behaviour occurs, the likelihood of the behaviour occurring again is increased or decreased by the behaviour's consequences.
Order of events	Before conditioning, an unconditioned stimulus leads to an unconditioned response. After conditioning, a conditioned stimulus leads to a conditioned response.	Reinforcement leads to an increase in behaviour; punishment leads to a decrease in behaviour.
Example	After a physician gives a child a series of painful injections (an unconditioned stimulus) that produce an emotional reaction (an unconditioned response), the child develops an emotional reaction (a conditioned response) whenever she sees the physician (the conditioned stimulus).	A student who, after studying hard for a test, earns an A (the positive reinforcer), is more likely to study hard in the future. A student who, after going out drinking the night before a test, fails the test (punishment) is less likely to go out drinking the night before the next test.

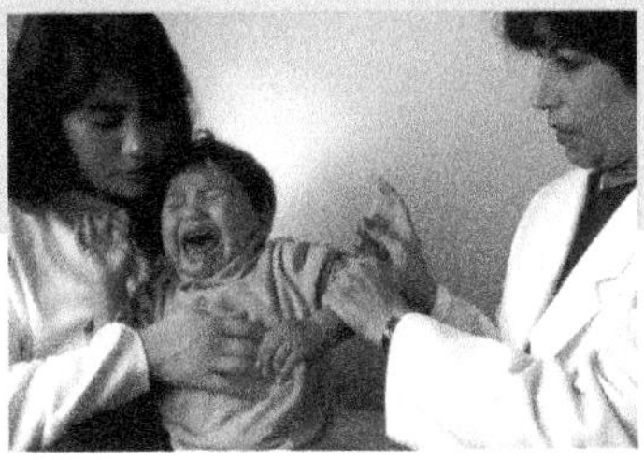

Source: (left): © McGraw Hill Education/Jill Braaten photographer; (right): © Robin Nelson/PhotoEdit.

Becoming an Informed Consumer of Psychology

Using Behaviour Analysis and Behaviour Modification

A couple who had been living together for three years began to fight more and more frequently. The issues of disagreement ranged from the seemingly petty, such as who was going to do the dishes, to the more profound, such as the quality of their love life. Disturbed about this increasingly unpleasant pattern of interaction, the couple went to a behaviour analyst, a psychologist who specialized in behaviour-modification techniques. He asked them to keep a detailed written record of their interactions over the next two weeks—focusing in particular on the events that preceded their arguments.

When they returned two weeks later, he carefully went over the records with them. In doing so, he noticed a pattern that the couple themselves had observed after they had started keeping their records: Each of their arguments had occurred just after one or the other had left a household chore undone. Using the data the couple had collected, the behaviour analyst devised a system for the couple to try out. He asked them to list all the chores that could possibly arise and assign each one a point value depending on how long it took to complete. Then he had them divide the chores equally and agree in a written contract to fulfill the ones assigned to them. If either failed to carry out one of the assigned chores, he or she would have to place $1 per point in a fund for the other to spend. They also agreed to a program of verbal praise, promising to reward each other verbally for completing a chore.

Although skeptical about the value of such a program, the couple agreed to try it for a month and to keep careful records of the number of arguments they had during that period. To their surprise, the number declined rapidly, and even the more basic issues in their relationship seemed on the way to being resolved.

This case provides an illustration of **behaviour modification,** a formalized technique for promoting the frequency of desirable behaviours and decreasing the incidence of unwanted ones. People with severe intellectual disabilities have learned the rudiments of language and have gained important skills for independent living. Behaviour modification has also helped people lose weight, give up smoking, and behave more safely (Wadden, Crerand, & Brock, 2005; Ntinas, 2007).

Participants in a behaviour-change program follow a series of similar steps that include the following:

- Identifying goals and target behaviours. The first step is to define *desired behaviour.* Is it an increase in time spent studying? A decrease in weight? An increase in the use of language? A reduction in the amount of aggression displayed by a child? The goals must be stated in observable terms and lead to specific targets. For instance, a goal might be "to increase study time," whereas the target behaviour would be "to study at least two hours per day on weekdays."

- Designing a data-recording system and recording preliminary data. To determine whether behaviour has changed, it is necessary to collect data before any changes are made in the situation. This information provides a baseline against which future changes can be measured.

- Selecting a behaviour-change strategy. The most crucial step is to select an appropriate strategy. Because all the principles of learning can be employed to bring about behaviour change, a "package" of treatments is normally used. This might include the systematic use of positive reinforcement for desired behaviour (verbal praise or something more tangible, such as food), as well as a program of extinction for undesirable behaviour (ignoring a child who throws a tantrum).

- Implementing the program. The most important aspect of program implementation is consistency. It is also important to make sure that one is reinforcing the behaviour he or she wants to reinforce. For example, suppose a mother wants her daughter to spend more time on her homework, but as soon as the child sits down to study, she asks for a snack. If the mother gets a snack for her, she is likely to be reinforcing her daughter's delaying tactic, not her studying. Instead, the mother might tell her child that she will provide her with a snack after a certain time interval has gone by during which she has studied—thereby using the snack as a reinforcement for studying.

- Keeping careful records after the program is implemented. If the target behaviours are not monitored, there is no way of knowing whether the program has actually been successful.

- Evaluating and altering the ongoing program. Finally, the results of the program should be compared with baseline, pre-implementation data to determine its effectiveness.

Behaviour-change techniques based on these general principles have enjoyed wide success and have proved to be one of the most powerful means of modifying behaviour (Greenwood et al., 1992). Clearly, it is possible to employ the basic notions of learning theory to improve our lives.

Behaviour modification

A formalized technique for promoting the frequency of desirable behaviours and decreasing the incidence of unwanted ones.

Evaluate

1. _____ conditioning describes learning that occurs as a result of reinforcement.

2. Match the type of operant learning with its definition:

   1. An unpleasant stimulus is presented to decrease behaviour.

   2. An unpleasant stimulus is removed to increase behaviour.

   3. A pleasant stimulus is presented to increase behaviour.

   4. A pleasant stimulus is removed to decrease behaviour.

   a. Positive reinforcement

   b. Negative reinforcement

   c. Positive punishment

   d. Negative punishment

3. Your parents promise you that if you get an A in Introduction to Psychology, they will give you $50. In operant conditioning terms, your parents are using _____ _____ to modify your behaviour.

4. In a _____ reinforcement schedule, behaviour is reinforced some of the time, whereas in a _____ reinforcement schedule, behaviour is reinforced all the time.

Answers to Evaluate Questions

1. operant 2. 1-c, 2-b, 3-a, 4-d; 3. positive reinforcement; 4. partial (or intermittent), continuous

Key Terms

behaviour modification	partial (intermittent) reinforcement	schedules of reinforcement
continuous reinforcement schedule	schedule	shaping
fixed-interval schedule	positive reinforcer	variable-interval schedule
fixed-ratio schedule	punishment	variable-ratio schedule
negative reinforcer	reinforcement	
operant conditioning	reinforcer	

Cognitive Approaches to Learning

MODULE

17

LEARNING OBJECTIVE

LO5 **What is** the role of cognition and thought in learning?

Consider what happens when people learn to drive a car. They don't just get behind the wheel and stumble around until they randomly put the key into the ignition, and later, after many false starts, accidentally manage to get the car to move forward, thereby receiving positive reinforcement. Instead, they already know the basic elements of driving from prior experience as passengers, when they more than likely noticed how the key was inserted into the ignition, the car was put in drive, and the gas pedal was pressed to make the car go forward.

Clearly, not all learning is due to operant and classical conditioning. In fact, activities like learning to drive a car imply that some kinds of learning must involve higher-order processes in which people's thoughts and memories and the way they process information account for their responses. Such situations argue against regarding learning as the unthinking, mechanical, and automatic acquisition of associations between stimuli and responses, as in classical conditioning, or the presentation of reinforcement, as in operant conditioning.

Some psychologists view learning in terms of the thought processes, or cognitions, that underlie it—an approach known as **cognitive learning theory.** Although psychologists working from the cognitive learning perspective do not deny the importance of classical and operant conditioning, they have developed approaches that focus on the unseen mental processes that occur during learning, rather than concentrating solely on external stimuli, responses, and reinforcements.

STUDY ALERT!

Remember that the cognitive learning approach focuses on the *internal* thoughts and expectations of learners, whereas classical and operant conditioning approaches focus on *external* stimuli, responses, and reinforcement.

In its most basic formulation, cognitive learning theory suggests that it is not enough to say that people make responses because there is an assumed link between a stimulus and a response as a result of a past history of reinforcement for a response. Instead, according to this point of view, people—and animals—develop an *expectation* that they will receive a reinforcer after making a response. Two types of learning in which no obvious prior reinforcement is present are latent learning and observational learning.

⬚ Latent Learning

Evidence for the importance of cognitive processes comes from a series of animal experiments that revealed a type of cognitive learning called latent learning. In **latent learning,** a new behaviour is learned but not demonstrated until some incentive is provided for displaying it (Tolman & Honzik, 1930). In short, latent learning occurs without reinforcement.

Cognitive learning theory
An approach to the study of learning that focuses on the thought processes that underlie learning.

Latent learning
Learning in which a new behaviour is acquired but is not demonstrated until some incentive is provided for displaying it.

In the studies demonstrating latent learning, psychologists examined the behaviour of rats in a maze such as the one shown in Figure 1a. In one experiment, a group of rats was allowed to wander around the maze once a day for seventeen days without ever receiving a reward. Understandably, those rats made many errors and spent a relatively long time reaching the end of the maze. A second group, however, was always given food at the end of the maze. Not surprisingly, those rats learned to run quickly and directly to the food box, making few errors.

A third group of rats started out in the same situation as the unrewarded rats, but only for the first ten days. On the eleventh day, a critical experimental manipulation was introduced: From that point on, the rats in this group were given food for completing the maze. The results of this manipulation were dramatic, as you can see from the graph in Figure 1b. The previously unrewarded rats, which had earlier seemed to wander about aimlessly, showed such reductions in running time and declines in error rates that their performance almost immediately matched that of the group that had received rewards from the start.

To cognitive theorists, it seemed clear that the unrewarded rats had learned the layout of the maze early in their explorations; they just never displayed their latent learning until the reinforcement was offered. Instead, those rats seemed to develop a *cognitive map* of the maze—a mental representation of spatial locations and directions.

People, too, develop cognitive maps of their surroundings. For example, latent learning may permit you to know the location of a kitchenware store at a local mall you've frequently visited, even though you've never entered the store and don't even like to cook.

FIGURE 1

(a) In an attempt to demonstrate latent learning, rats were allowed to roam through a maze of this sort once a day for seventeen days. (b) The rats that were never rewarded (the nonrewarded control condition) consistently made the most errors, whereas those which received food at the finish every day (the rewarded control condition) consistently made far fewer errors. But the results also showed latent learning: Rats that were initially unrewarded but began to be rewarded only after the tenth day (the experimental group) showed an immediate reduction in errors and soon became similar in error rate to the rats that had been rewarded consistently. According to cognitive learning theorists, the reduction in errors indicates that the rats had developed a cognitive map—a mental representation—of the maze. Can you think of other examples of latent learning?

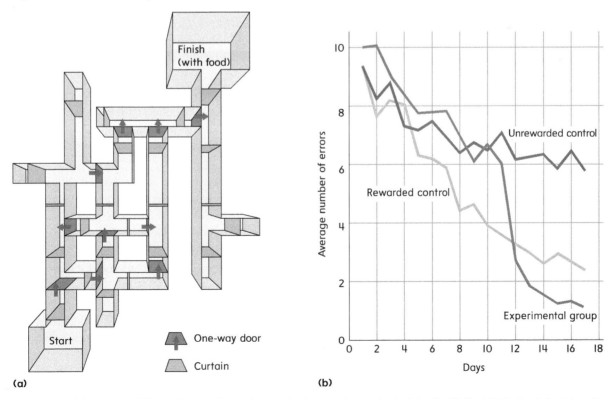

Source: E. C. Tolman, & C. H. Honzik, (1930). Introduction and removal of reward and maze performance in rats. *University of California Publications in Psychology, 4,* 257–275.

The possibility that we develop our cognitive maps through latent learning presents something of a problem for strict operant conditioning theorists. If we consider the results of the maze-learning experiment, for instance, it is unclear what reinforcement permitted the rats that initially received no reward to learn the layout of the maze, because there was no obvious reinforcer present. Instead, the results support a cognitive view of learning, in which changes occurred in unobservable mental processes (Beatty, 2002; Voicu & Schmajuk, 2002; Frensch & Rünger, 2003).

Observational Learning: Learning Through Imitation

Let's return for a moment to the case of a person learning to drive. How can we account for instances in which an individual with no direct experience in carrying out a particular behaviour learns the behaviour and then performs it? To answer this question, psychologists have focused on another aspect of cognitive learning: observational learning.

According to Canadian psychologist Albert Bandura and colleagues, a major part of human learning consists of **observational learning,** which is learning by watching the behaviour of another person, or *model*. Because of its reliance on observation of others—a social phenomenon—the perspective taken by Bandura is often referred to as a *social cognitive* approach to learning (Bandura, 1999, 2004).

Bandura dramatically demonstrated the ability of models to stimulate learning in a classic experiment. In the study, young children saw a film of an adult wildly hitting a 1.5-metre-tall inflatable punching toy called a Bobo doll (Bandura, Ross, & Ross, 1963a, 1963b). Later the children were given the opportunity to play with the Bobo doll themselves, and, sure enough, most displayed the same kind of behaviour, in some cases mimicking the aggressive behaviour almost identically.

Not only negative behaviours are acquired through observational learning. In one experiment, for example, children who were afraid of dogs were exposed to a model—dubbed the Fearless Peer—playing with a dog (Bandura, Grusec, & Menlove, 1967). After exposure, observers were considerably more likely to approach a strange dog than were children who had not viewed the Fearless Peer.

According to Bandura, observational learning takes place in four steps: (1) paying attention and perceiving the most critical features of another person's behaviour, (2) remembering the behaviour, (3) reproducing the action, and (4) being motivated to learn and carry out the behaviour in the future. Instead of learning occurring through trial and error, then, with successes being reinforced and failures being punished, many important skills are learned through observational processes (Bandura, 1986).

Observational learning is particularly important in acquiring skills in which the operant conditioning technique of shaping is inappropriate. Piloting an airplane and performing brain surgery, for example, are behaviours that could hardly be learned by using trial-and-error methods without grave cost—literally—to those involved in the learning process.

Observational learning may have a genetic basis. For example, we find observational learning at work with mother animals teaching their young such activities as hunting. In addition, the discovery of *mirror neurons* that fire when we observe another person carrying out a behaviour (discussed in Chapter 2 on neuroscience and behaviour) suggests that the capacity to imitate others may be innate (Thornton & McAuliffe, 2006; Lepage & Theoret, 2007; Schulte-Ruther et al., 2007).

Not all behaviour that we witness is learned or carried out, of course. One crucial factor that determines whether we later imitate a model is whether the model is rewarded for his or her behaviour. If we observe a friend being rewarded for putting more time into her studies by receiving higher grades, we are more likely to imitate her behaviour than we would be if her behaviour resulted only in being stressed and tired. Models who are rewarded for behaving in a particular way are more apt to be mimicked than are models who receive punishment. Interestingly, though, observing the punishment of a model does not necessarily stop observers from learning the behaviour. Observers can still describe the model's behaviour—they are just less apt to perform it (Bandura, 1977, 1986, 1994).

Observational learning is central to a number of important issues relating to the extent to which people learn simply by watching the behaviour of others. For instance, the degree to which observation of media aggression produces subsequent aggression on the part of viewers is a crucial—and controversial—question, as we discuss next.

Observational learning
Learning by observing the behaviour of another person, or model.

◯ Violence in Television and Video Games: Does the Media's Message Matter?

In an episode of *The Sopranos* television series, fictional mobster Tony Soprano murdered one of his associates. To make identification of the victim's body difficult, Soprano and one of his henchmen dismembered the body and dumped the body parts.

A few months later, two real-life half brothers in Riverside, California, strangled their mother and then cut her head and hands from her body. Victor Bautista, 20, and Matthew Montejo, 15, who were caught by police after a security guard noticed that the bundle they were attempting to throw in a dumpster had a foot sticking out of it, told police that the plan to dismember their mother was inspired by *The Sopranos* episode (Martelle, Hanley, & Yoshino, 2003).

Like other "media copycat" killings, the brothers' cold-blooded brutality raises a critical issue: Does observing violent and antisocial acts in the media lead viewers to behave in similar ways? Because research on modelling shows that people frequently learn and imitate the aggression that they observe, this question is among the most important being addressed by psychologists.

Certainly, the amount of violence in the mass media is enormous. By the time of elementary school graduation, the average child in the United States will have viewed more than 8,000 murders and more than 800,000 violent acts on network television (Huston et al., 1992; Mifflin, 1998).

Most experts agree that watching high levels of media violence makes viewers more susceptible to acting aggressively, and recent research supports this claim (Boxer et al., 2009). For example, one survey of serious and violent young male offenders incarcerated in Florida showed that one-fourth of them had attempted to commit a media-inspired copycat crime (Surette, 2002). A significant proportion of those teenage offenders noted that they paid close attention to the media.

Illustrating observational learning, this infant observes an adult on the television and then is able to imitate his behaviour. Learning has obviously occurred through the mere observation of the television model.

Violent video games have also been linked with actual aggression. In one of a series of studies by psychologist Craig Anderson and his colleagues, for example, college and university students who frequently played violent video games, such as *Postal* or *Doom*, were more likely to have been involved in delinquent behaviour and aggression. Frequent players also had lower academic achievement (Anderson et al., 2004; Anderson & Carnagey, 2009).

Several aspects of media violence may contribute to real-life aggressive behaviour (Bushman & Anderson, 2001; Johnson et al., 2002). For one thing, experiencing violent media content seems to lower inhibitions against carrying out aggression—watching television portrayals of violence or using violence to win a video game makes aggression seem a legitimate response to particular situations. Exposure to media violence also may distort our understanding of the meaning of others' behaviour, predisposing us to view even nonaggressive acts by others as aggressive. Finally, a continuous diet of aggression may leave us desensitized to violence, and what previously would have repelled us now produces little emotional response. Our sense of the pain and suffering brought about by aggression may be diminished (Bartholow, Bushman, & Sestir, 2006; Weber, Ritterfeld, & Kostygina, 2006; Carnagey, Anderson, & Bushman, 2007).

Source: From Meltzhoff, A. N. (1988). Imitation of televised models by infants. *Child Development, 59,* 1221–1229. Photo Courtesy of A.N. Meltzhoff & M. Hanak.

Exploring DIVERSITY

Does Culture Influence How We Learn?

When a member of the Chilcotin Indian tribe teaches her daughter to prepare salmon, at first she only allows the daughter to observe the entire process. A little later, she permits her child to try out some basic parts of the task. Her response to questions is noteworthy. For example, when the daughter asks about how to do "the backbone part," the mother's response is to repeat the entire process with another fish. The reason? The mother feels that one cannot learn the individual parts of the task apart from the context of preparing the whole fish (Tharp, 1989).

It should not be surprising that children raised in the Chilcotin tradition, which stresses instruction that starts by communicating the entire task, may have difficulty with traditional Western schooling. In the approach to teaching most characteristic of Western culture, tasks are broken down into their component parts. Only after each small step is learned is it thought possible to master the complete task.

Do the differences in teaching approaches between cultures affect how people learn? Some psychologists, taking a cognitive perspective on learning, suggest that people develop particular *learning styles,* characteristic ways of approaching material, based on their cultural background and unique pattern of abilities (Anderson & Adams, 1992; Barmeyer, 2004; Wilkinson & Olliver-Gray, 2006).

The Canadian Council on Learning (CCL) developed a task force on learning to explore the learning needs and educational priorities of First Nations students (Battiste & McLean, 2005). An important outcome of their findings was the development of the *"First Nations Holistic Lifelong Learning Model."* This unique model of learning, illustrated in Figure 2, used a graphic of a living tree to redefine how learning success is measured in Aboriginal communities.

Learning styles differ along several dimensions. For example, one central dimension is analytical versus relational approaches to learning. People with a *relational learning style* master material best through exposure to a full unit or phenomenon. Parts of the unit are comprehended only when their relationship to the whole is understood.

FIGURE 2

First Nations Holistic Lifelong Learning Model

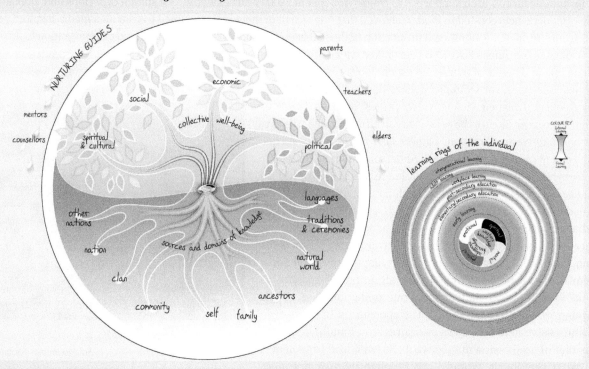

Source: Image Courtesy of The Canadian Council of Learning, www.ccl-cca.ca/CCL/Reports/RedefiningSuccessInAboriginalLearning/RedefiningSuccessModelsFirstNations.htm.

(*continued*)

In contrast, people with an *analytical learning style* do best when they can carry out an initial analysis of the principles and components underlying a phenomenon or situation. By developing an understanding of the parts, they are best able to understand the whole.

Although research findings are mixed, some evidence suggests that particular minority groups in Western societies display characteristic learning styles. For instance, James Anderson and Maurianne Adams (1992) argue that Caucasian females and African American, Native American, and Hispanic American males and females are more apt to use a relational style of learning than Caucasian and Asian American males, who are more likely to employ an analytical style.

The conclusion that members of particular ethnic and gender groups have similar learning styles is controversial. Because there is so much diversity within each particular racial and ethnic group, critics argue that generalizations about learning styles cannot be used to predict the style of any single individual, regardless of group membership. They suggest that it is more fruitful to concentrate on determining each individual's particular learning style and pattern of academic and social strengths. Still, it is clear that values about learning, which are communicated through a person's family and cultural background, have an impact on how successful students are in school.

Evaluate

1. In cognitive learning theory, it is assumed that people develop a(n) _____ about receiving a reinforcer when they behave a certain way.

2. In _____ learning, a new behaviour is learned but is not shown until appropriate reinforcement is presented.

3. Bandura's theory of _____ learning states that people learn through watching a(n) _____—another person displaying the behaviour of interest.

Answers to Evaluate Questions

1. expectation; 2. latent; 3. observational, model

Key Terms

cognitive learning theory	latent learning	observational learning

Epilogue

Here we have discussed several kinds of learning, ranging from classical conditioning, which depends on the existence of natural stimulus–response pairings, to operant conditioning, in which reinforcement is used to increase desired behaviour. These approaches to learning focus on outward, behavioural learning processes. Cognitive approaches to learning focus on mental processes that enable learning.

We have also noted that learning is affected by culture and individual differences, with individual learning styles potentially affecting the ways in which people learn most effectively. And we saw some ways in which our learning about learning can be put to practical use, through such means as behaviour-modification programs designed to decrease negative behaviours and increase positive ones.

Recap/Rethink

Module 15: Classical Conditioning

Recap

LO1 What is learning?

- Learning is a relatively permanent change in behaviour resulting from experience.

LO2 How do we learn to form associations between stimuli and responses?

- One major form of learning is classical conditioning, which occurs when a neutral stimulus—one that normally brings about no relevant response—is repeatedly paired with a stimulus (called an unconditioned stimulus) that brings about a natural, untrained response.
- Learning is not always permanent. Extinction occurs when a previously learned response decreases in frequency and eventually disappears.
- Stimulus generalization is the tendency for a conditioned response to follow a stimulus that is similar to, but not the same as, the original conditioned stimulus. The converse phenomenon, stimulus discrimination, occurs when an organism learns to distinguish between stimuli.
- Biological preparedness is the innate propensity to learn certain classically conditioned associations over others

Rethink

1. How likely is it that Little Albert, Watson's experimental subject, went through life afraid of Santa Claus? Describe what could have happened to prevent his continual dread of Santa.

2. *From the perspective of an advertising executive:* How might knowledge of classical conditioning be useful in creating an advertising campaign? What, if any, ethical issues arise from this use?

Module 16: Operant Conditioning

Recap

LO3 What is the role of reward and punishment in learning?

- Operant conditioning is a form of learning in which a voluntary behaviour is strengthened or weakened. According to B. F. Skinner, the major mechanism underlying learning is reinforcement, the process by which a stimulus increases the probability that a preceding behaviour will be repeated.
- Primary reinforcers are rewards that are naturally effective without prior experience because they satisfy a biological need. Secondary reinforcers begin to act as if they were primary reinforcers through association with a primary reinforcer.
- Positive reinforcers are stimuli that are added to the environment and lead to an increase in a preceding response. Negative reinforcers are stimuli that remove something unpleasant from the environment, also leading to an increase in the preceding response.
- Punishment decreases the probability that a prior behaviour will occur. Positive punishment weakens a response through the application of an unpleasant stimulus, whereas negative punishment weakens a response by the removal of something positive. In contrast to reinforcement, in which the goal is to increase the incidence of behaviour, punishment is meant to decrease or suppress behaviour.
- Schedules and patterns of reinforcement affect the strength and duration of learning. Generally, partial reinforcement schedules—in which reinforcers are not delivered on every trial—produce stronger and longer-lasting learning than do continuous reinforcement schedules.
- There are biological constraints, or built-in limitations, on the ability of an organism to learn: Certain behaviours will be relatively easy for individuals of a species to learn, whereas other behaviours will be either difficult or impossible for them to learn.

LO4 What are some practical methods for bringing about behaviour change, both in ourselves and in others?

- Behaviour modification is a method for formally using the principles of learning theory to promote the frequency of desired behaviours and to decrease or eliminate unwanted ones.

Rethink

1. *From the perspective of a teacher:* How would you utilize your knowledge of the effect of reinforcement schedules in the classroom to increase the likelihood children will complete their homework more reliably?

2. *Especially for Police Foundations students:* Given that research shows us that reinforcement is more powerful at producing behaviour change than punishment, what community policing programs could be used to prevent crime and teach positive behaviour? For example, currently, police officers give tickets to unsafe drivers to promote road safety. A ticket is a punishment; could reinforcement be used to promote safer driving instead?

3. *Especially for Behavioural Science students:* How would you apply the principles of operant conditioning, especially reinforcement and shaping, in a language acquisition program to teach a child with autism new words or signs?

4. Using the scientific literature as a guide, what would you tell parents who wish to know if the routine use of physical punishment is a necessary and acceptable form of discipline in child rearing?

Module 17: Cogntive Approaches to Learning

Recap

What is the role of cognition and thought in learning?

- Cognitive approaches to learning consider learning in terms of thought processes, or cognition. Phenomena such as latent learning—in which a new behaviour is learned but not performed until some incentive is provided for its performance—and the apparent development of cognitive maps support cognitive approaches.
- Learning also occurs from observing the behaviour of others. The major factor that determines whether an observed behaviour will actually be performed is the nature of the reinforcement or punishment a model receives.
- Observation of violence is linked to a greater likelihood of subsequently acting aggressively.
- Learning styles are characteristic ways of approaching learning, based on a person's cultural background and unique pattern of abilities. Whether an individual has an analytical or a relational style of learning, for example, may reflect family background or culture.

Rethink

1. The relational style of learning sometimes conflicts with the traditional school environment. Could a school be created that takes advantage of the characteristics of the relational style? How? Are there types of learning for which the analytical style is clearly superior?

2. *Especially for Social Service Worker students:* What advice would you give to families about children's exposure to violent media and video games?

CHAPTER 6
Memory

Source: © Ingram Publishing RF.

Prologue

Source: © Rich Legg/ Getty Images RF.

Mistaken Identity

David Milgaard and Thomas Sophonow share more than their Canadian citizenship. Both were wrongly convicted of a crime they did not commit and were falsely imprisoned by the provincial court system.

Each man had a robust defence case and an alibi placing him in a different place at the time of the murder and neither man could be connected to their so-called crimes by concrete, physical evidence. Despite the strength of their respective defence arguments, David Milgaard and Thomas Sophonow were eventually convicted and sentenced to life in prison—on the basis of faulty eyewitness testimony (combined with poor police procedures, including improper line-ups and improper police questioning).

Both men were ultimately exonerated on the basis of DNA evidence. Twenty-three years after being sentenced to life in prison, David Milgaard's conviction was overturned by the Supreme Court of Canada. Four years after being sentenced to life in prison, Thomas Sophonow was set free by the Manitoba Court of Appeal.

How could such a tragedy happen in the Canadian legal system? How could innocent people be convicted of crimes they did not commit? How could eyewitnesses falsely identify innocent people? Stories like Thomas Sophonow and David Milgaard's illustrate not only the important role memory plays in our lives, but also its inaccuracy.

Memory allows us to retrieve a vast amount of information. We are able to remember the name of a friend we haven't talked with for years and recall the details of a picture that hung in our bedroom as a child. At the same time, though, memory failures are common. We forget where we left the keys to the car and fail to answer an exam question about material we studied only a few hours earlier. Why does memory fail? Can we be influenced to remember something that did not happen? Why do some people have a greater memory capacity than others? The answers to these questions lie in the theories of memory and forgetting discussed at length in Chapter 6.

The Foundations of Memory

LEARNING OBJECTIVES

LO1 **What is** memory?

LO2 **Are there** different kinds of memory?

LO3 **What are** the biological bases of memory?

You are playing a game of Trivial Pursuit, and winning the game comes down to one question: On what body of water is Nunavut located? As you rack your brain for the answer, several fundamental processes relating to memory come into play. You may never, for instance, have been exposed to information regarding Nunavut's location. Or if you have been exposed to it, it may simply not have registered in a meaningful way. In other words, the information might not have been recorded properly in your memory. The initial process of recording information in a form usable to memory, a process called encoding, is the first stage in remembering something.

Even if you had been exposed to the information and originally knew the name of the body of water, you may still be unable to recall it during the game because of a failure to retain it. Memory specialists speak of *storage*, the maintenance of material saved in memory. If the material is not stored adequately, it cannot be recalled later.

Memory also depends on one last process—*retrieval:* Material in memory storage has to be located and brought into awareness to be useful. Your failure to recall Nunavut's location, then, may rest on your inability to retrieve information that you learned earlier.

In sum, psychologists consider **memory** to be the process by which we encode, store, and retrieve information (see Figure 1). Each of the three parts of this definition—encoding, storage, and retrieval—represents a different

FIGURE 1

Memory is built on three basic processes—encoding, storage, and retrieval—that are analogous to a computer's keyboard, hard drive, and software, which accesses the information for display on the screen. The analogy is not perfect, however, because human memory is less precise than a computer. How might you modify the analogy to make it more accurate?

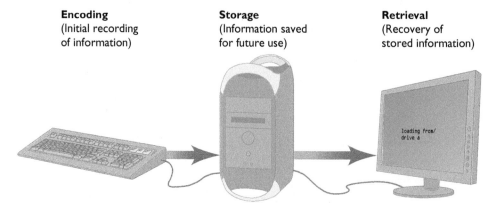

Encoding
(Initial recording
of information)

Storage
(Information saved
for future use)

Retrieval
(Recovery of
stored information)

loading from/
drive a

Source: Figure from "Human Memory: A Proposed System and Its Control Processes," by R. C. Atkinson and R. M. Shiffrin, from *The Psychology of Learning and Motivation: Advances in Research and Theory*, Volume 2, edited by K. W. Spence and J. T. Spence, copyright © 1968. Reprinted with permission from Elsevier.

Memory
The process by which we encode, store, and retrieve information.

process. You can think of these processes as being analogous to a computer's keyboard (encoding), hard drive (storage), and software that accesses the information for display on the screen (retrieval). Only if all three processes have operated will you experience success and be able to recall the body of water on which Nunavut is located: the Arctic Ocean.

Recognizing that memory involves encoding, storage, and retrieval gives us a start in understanding the concept. But how does memory actually function? How do we explain what information is initially encoded, what gets stored, and how it is retrieved?

According to the *three-system approach to memory* that dominated memory research for several decades, there are different memory storage systems or stages through which information must travel if it is to be remembered (Atkinson & Shiffrin, 1968, 1971). Historically, the approach has been extremely influential in the development of our understanding of memory, and—although new theories have augmented it—it still provides a useful framework for understanding how information is recalled.

The three-system memory theory proposes the existence of the three separate memory stores shown in Figure 2. **Sensory memory** refers to the initial, momentary storage of information that lasts only an instant. Here an exact replica of the stimulus recorded by a person's sensory system is stored very briefly. In a second stage, **short-term memory** holds information for fifteen to twenty-five seconds and stores it according to its meaning rather than as mere sensory stimulation. The third type of storage system is long-term memory. Information is stored in **long-term memory** on a relatively permanent basis, although it may be difficult to retrieve.

Although we'll be discussing the three types of memory as separate memory stores, keep in mind that these are not mini-warehouses located in specific areas of the brain. Instead, they represent three different types of memory systems with different characteristics.

FIGURE 2

In this three-stage model of memory, information initially recorded by the person's sensory system enters sensory memory, which momentarily holds the information. The information then moves to short-term memory, which stores it for fifteen to twenty-five seconds. Finally, the information can move into long-term memory, which is relatively permanent. Whether the information moves from short-term to long-term memory depends on the kind and amount of rehearsal of the material that is carried out.

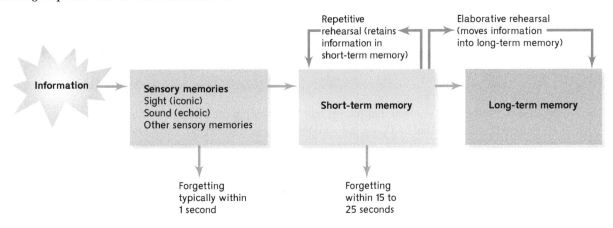

Sensory memory
The initial, momentary storage of information, lasting only an instant.

Short-term memory
Memory that holds information for fifteen to twenty-five seconds.

Long-term memory
Memory that stores information on a relatively permanent basis, although it may be difficult to retrieve.

Sensory Memory

A momentary flash of lightning, the sound of a twig snapping, and the sting of a pinprick all represent stimulation of exceedingly brief duration, but they may nonetheless provide important information that can require a response. Such stimuli are initially—and fleetingly—stored in sensory memory, the first repository of the information the world presents to us. Actually, there are several types of sensory memories, each related to a different source of sensory information. For instance, *iconic memory* reflects information from the visual system. *Echoic memory* stores auditory information coming from the ears. In addition, there are corresponding memories for each of the other senses.

Sensory memory can store information for only a very short time. If information does not pass into short-term memory, it is lost for good. For instance, iconic memory seems to last less than a second, and echoic memory typically fades within two or three seconds. However, despite the brief duration of sensory memory, its precision is high: Sensory memory can store an almost exact replica of each stimulus to which it is exposed (Darwin, Turvey, & Crowder, 1972; Long & Beaton, 1982; Sams et al., 1993; Deouell, Parnes, & Pickard, 2006).

Psychologist George Sperling (1960) demonstrated the existence of sensory memory in a series of clever and now-classic studies. He briefly exposed people to a series of twelve letters arranged in the following pattern:

```
F    T    Y    C
K    D    N    L
Y    W    B    M
```

When exposed to this pattern of letters for just one-twentieth of a second, most people could recall only four or five of the letters accurately. Although they knew that they had seen more, the memory of those letters had faded by the time they reported the first few letters. It was possible, then, that the information had initially been accurately stored in sensory memory, but during the time it took to verbalize the first four or five letters the memory of the other letters faded.

To test that possibility, Sperling conducted an experiment in which a high, medium, or low tone sounded just after a person had been exposed to the full pattern of letters. People were told to report the letters in the highest line if a high tone was sounded, the middle line if the medium tone occurred, or the lowest line at the sound of the low tone. Because the tone occurred after the exposure, people had to rely on their memories to report the correct row.

STUDY ALERT!

Although the three types of memory are discussed as separate memory stores, these are not mini-warehouses located in specific areas of the brain. Instead, they represent three different types of memory systems with different characteristics.

The results of the study clearly showed that people had been storing the complete pattern in memory. They accurately recalled the letters in the line that had been indicated by the tone regardless of whether it was the top, middle, or bottom line. Obviously, *all* the lines they had seen had been stored in sensory memory. Despite its rapid loss, then, the information in sensory memory was an accurate representation of what people had seen.

By gradually lengthening the time between the presentation of the visual pattern and the tone, Sperling was able to determine with some accuracy the length of time that information was stored in sensory memory. The ability to recall a particular row of the pattern when a tone was sounded declined progressively as the period between the visual exposure and the tone increased. This decline continued until the period reached about one second in duration, at which point the row could not be recalled accurately at all. Sperling concluded that the entire visual image was stored in sensory memory for less than a second.

In sum, sensory memory operates as a kind of snapshot that stores information—which may be of a visual, auditory, or other sensory nature—for a brief moment in time. But it is as if each snapshot, immediately after being taken, is destroyed and replaced with a new one. Unless the information in the snapshot is transferred to some other type of memory, it is lost.

Short-Term Memory

Because the information that is stored briefly in sensory memory consists of representations of raw sensory stimuli, it is not meaningful to us. If we are to make sense of it and possibly retain it, the information must be transferred to the next stage of memory: short-term memory. Short-term memory is the memory store in which information first has meaning, although the maximum length of retention there is relatively short (Hamilton & Martin, 2007).

The specific process by which sensory memories are transformed into short-term memories is not clear. Some theorists suggest that the information is first translated into graphical representations or images, and others hypothesize that the transfer occurs when the sensory stimuli are changed to words (Baddeley & Wilson, 1985). What is clear, however, is that unlike sensory memory, which holds a relatively full and detailed—if short-lived—representation of the world, short-term memory has incomplete representational capabilities.

In fact, the specific amount of information that can be held in short-term memory has been identified as seven items, or "chunks," of information, with variations up to plus or minus two chunks. A **chunk** is a meaningful grouping of stimuli that can be stored as a unit in short-term memory. According to George Miller (1956), a chunk can be individual letters or numbers, permitting us to hold a seven-digit phone number (like 226-4610) in short-term memory.

But a chunk also may consist of larger categories, such as words or other meaningful units. For example, consider the following list of twenty-one letters:

CTVBNNABCCBCMTVNBCYTV

Because the list exceeds seven chunks, it is difficult to recall the letters after one exposure. But suppose they were presented as follows:

CTV BNN ABC CBC MTV NBC YTV

In this case, even though there are still twenty-one letters, you'd be able to store them in short-term memory, since they represent only seven chunks.

Chunks can vary in size from single letters or numbers to categories that are far more complicated. The specific nature of what constitutes a chunk varies according to one's past experience. You can see this for yourself by trying an experiment that was first carried out as a comparison between expert and inexperienced chess players and is illustrated in Figure 3 (de Groot, 1966; Oberauer, 2007; Gilchrist, Cowan, & Naveh-Benjamin, 2009).

Although it is possible to remember seven or so relatively complicated sets of information entering short-term memory, the information cannot be held there very long. Just how brief is short-term memory? If you've ever looked up a telephone number in a phone directory, repeated the number to yourself, put away the directory, and then forgotten the number after you've tapped the first three numbers into your phone, you know that information does not remain in short-term memory very long. Most psychologists believe that information in short-term memory is lost after fifteen to twenty-five seconds—unless it is transferred to long-term memory.

Rehearsal

The transfer of material from short- to long-term memory proceeds largely on the basis of **rehearsal,** the repetition of information that has entered short-term memory. Rehearsal accomplishes two things. First, as long as the information is repeated, it is maintained in short-term memory. More important, however, rehearsal allows us to transfer the information into long-term memory (Kvavilashvili & Fisher, 2007).

Whether the transfer is made from short- to long-term memory seems to depend largely on the kind of rehearsal that is carried out. If the information is simply repeated over and over again—as we might do with a telephone number while we rush from the phone book to the phone—it is kept current in short-term memory, but it will not necessarily be placed in long-term memory. Instead, as soon as we stop punching in the phone numbers, the number is likely to be replaced by other information and will be completely forgotten.

In contrast, if the information in short-term memory is rehearsed using a process called elaborative rehearsal, it is much more likely to be transferred into long-term memory (Craik & Lockhart, 1972). *Elaborative rehearsal* occurs when the information is considered and organized in some fashion. The organization might include expanding the information to make it fit into a logical framework, linking it to another memory, turning it into an image, or transforming it

---

Chunk
A meaningful grouping of stimuli that can be stored as a unit in short-term memory.

Rehearsal
The repetition of information that has entered short-term memory.

FIGURE 3

Examine the chessboard containing the chess pieces for about five seconds, and then, after covering up the board, try to draw the position of the pieces on the blank chessboard. (You could also use a chessboard of your own and place the pieces in the same positions.) Unless you are an experienced chess player, you are likely to have great difficulty carrying out such a task. Yet chess masters—the kind who win tournaments—do this quite well (deGroot, 1966). They are able to reproduce correctly 90 percent of the pieces on the board. In comparison, inexperienced chess players are typically able to reproduce only 40 percent of the board properly. The chess masters do not have superior memories in other respects; they generally test normally on other measures of memory. What they can do better than others is see the board in terms of chunks or meaningful units and reproduce the position of the chess pieces by using those units.

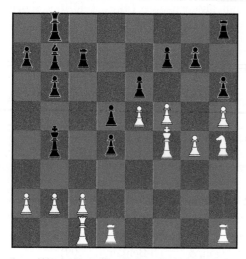 

Source: From "Perception and Memory Versus Thought: Some Old Ideas and Recent Findings," by A. D. deGroot in *Problem Solving: Research, Method & Theory,* by B. Kleinmuntz (ed.). Copyright © 1966 John Wiley & Sons, Inc. Reprinted by permission of John Wiley & Sons, Inc.

in some other way. For example, a list of vegetables to be purchased at a store could be woven together in memory as items being used to prepare an elaborate salad, could be linked to the items bought on an earlier shopping trip, or could be thought of in terms of the image of a farm with rows of each item.

By using organizational strategies such as these—called *mnemonics*—we can vastly improve our retention of information. Mnemonics (pronounced "neh MON ix") are formal techniques for organizing information in a way that makes it more likely to be remembered. For instance, when a beginning musician learns that the spaces on the music staff spell the word *FACE*, or when we learn the rhyme "Thirty days hath September, April, June, and November...," we are using mnemonics (Bellezza, 2000; Scruggs & Mastropieri, 2000; Carney & Levin, 2003; Sprenger, 2007).

Working Memory

Rather than seeing short-term memory as an independent way station into which memories arrive, either to fade or to be passed on to long-term memory, many contemporary memory theorists conceive of short-term memory as far more active. In this view, short-term memory is like an information processing system that manages both new material gathered from sensory memory and older material that has been pulled from long-term storage. In this increasingly influential view, short-term memory is referred to as **working memory** and defined as a set of active, temporary memory stores that actively manipulate and rehearse information (Bayliss et al., 2005a, 2005b; Unsworth & Engle, 2005).

Working memory is thought to contain a *central executive* processor that is involved in reasoning and decision making. The central executive coordinates three distinct storage-and-rehearsal systems: the *visual store*, the *verbal store*, and the *episodic buffer*. The visual store specializes in visual and spatial information, whereas the verbal store holds and manipulates material relating to speech, words, and numbers. The episodic buffer contains information that represents episodes or events (Baddeley, Chincotta, & Adlam, 2001; Bröder & Schiffer, 2006; Rudner & Rönnberg, 2008; see Figure 4).

Working memory
A set of active, temporary memory stores that actively manipulate and rehearse information.

FIGURE 4

Working memory is an active "workspace" in which information is retrieved and manipulated, and in which information is held through rehearsal (Gathercole & Baddeley, 1993). It consists of a "central executive" that coordinates the visual store (which concentrates on visual and spatial information), the verbal store (which concentrates on speech, words, and numbers), and the episodic buffer (which represents episodes or occurrences that are encountered).

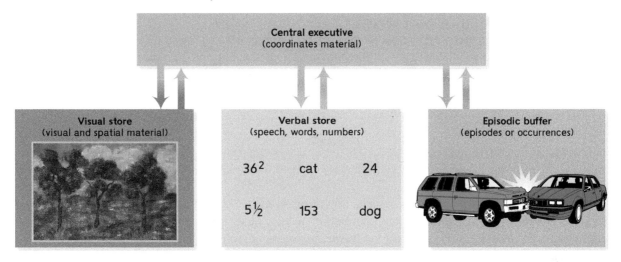

Working memory permits us to keep information in an active state briefly so that we can do something with the information. For instance, we use working memory when we're doing a multistep arithmetic problem in our heads, storing the result of one calculation while getting ready to move to the next stage. (For example, you make use of your working memory when you figure a 20-percent tip in a restaurant by first calculating 10 percent of the total bill and then doubling it.)

Although working memory aids in the recall of information, it uses a significant amount of cognitive resources during its operation. In turn, this can make us less aware of our surroundings—something that has implications for the debate about the use of cellular telephones in automobiles. In fact, the use of cellular telephones in automobiles has been outlawed in some Canadian provinces, including Ontario, Newfoundland, and Quebec, with other provinces tabling similar legislation. If a phone conversation requires thinking, it will burden working memory, leaving people less aware of their surroundings, an obviously dangerous state of affairs for the driver (de Fockert et al., 2001; Wickelgren, 2001; Verhaeghen, Cerella, & Basak, 2004; Sifrit, 2006; Strayer & Drews, 2007).

Furthermore, stress can reduce the effectiveness of working memory by reducing its capacity. In fact, one study found that students with the highest working memory capacity and greatest math ability were the ones who were most vulnerable to pressure to perform well. Those who should have performed best, then, were the ones most apt to choke on the test because their working memory capacities were reduced by the stress (Carey, 2004; Beilock & Carr, 2005).

Long-Term Memory

Material that makes its way from short-term memory to long-term memory enters a storehouse of almost unlimited capacity. Like a new file we save on a hard drive, the information in long-term memory is filed and coded so that we can retrieve it when we need it.

Evidence of the existence of long-term memory, as distinct from short-term memory, comes from a number of sources. For example, people with certain kinds of brain damage have no lasting recall of new information received after the damage occurred, although people and events stored in memory before the injury remain intact (Milner, 1966). Because information that was encoded and stored before the injury can be recalled and because short-term memory after the injury appears to be operational—new material can be recalled for a very brief period—we can infer that there are two distinct types of memory: one for short-term and one for long-term storage.

Results from laboratory experiments are also consistent with the notion of separate short-term and long-term memory. For example, in one set of studies people were asked to recall a relatively small amount of information (such as a set of three letters). Then, to prevent practise of the initial information, participants were required to recite some extraneous material aloud, such as counting backward by threes (Brown, 1958; Peterson & Peterson, 1959). By varying the amount of time between the presentation of the initial material and the need for its recall, investigators found that recall was quite good when the interval was very short but declined rapidly thereafter. After fifteen seconds had gone by, recall hovered at around 10 percent of the material initially presented.

Apparently, the distraction of counting backward prevented almost all the initial material from reaching long-term memory. Initial recall was good because it was coming from short-term memory, but those memories were lost at a rapid rate. Eventually, all that could be recalled was the small amount of material that had made its way into long-term storage despite the distraction of counting backward.

The distinction between short- and long-term memory is also supported by the *serial position effect,* in which the ability to recall information in a list depends on where in the list an item appears. For instance, often a *primacy effect* occurs, in which items presented early in a list are remembered better. There is also a *recency effect,* in which items presented late in a list are remembered best (Bonanni et al., 2007; Tan & Ward, 2008; Tydgat & Grainger, 2009).

Long-Term Memory Modules

Just as short-term memory is often conceptualized in terms of working memory, many contemporary researchers now regard long-term memory as having several different components, or *memory modules.* Each of these modules represents a separate memory system in the brain.

One major distinction within long-term memory is between declarative memory and procedural memory. **Declarative memory** is memory for factual information: names, faces, dates, and facts, such as "a bike has two wheels." In contrast, **procedural memory** (or *nondeclarative memory*) refers to memory for skills and habits, such as how to ride a bike or hit a baseball. Information about things is stored in declarative memory; information about *how to do things* is stored in procedural memory (Feldhusen, 2006; Brown & Robertson, 2007; Bauer, 2008).

Canadian researcher Carlyle Smith of Trent University studies the effect of sleep on both declarative and procedural memory. Smith found declarative memory (e.g., factual memory) to be most affected by length of NREM–REM sleep cycle while memory for motor procedural information was most influenced by quality of stage 2 sleep (Smith, 2001).

Declarative memory can be subdivided into semantic memory and episodic memory (Nyberg & Tulving, 1996; Tulving, 2002). **Semantic memory** is memory for general knowledge and facts about the world, as well as memory for the rules of logic that are used to deduce other facts. Because of semantic memory, we remember that the ZIP code for Beverly Hills is 90210, that Nunavut is on the Arctic Ocean, and that *memoree* is the incorrect spelling of *memory.* Thus, semantic memory is somewhat like a mental almanac of facts.

In contrast, **episodic memory** is memory for events that occur in a particular time, place, or context. For example, recall of learning to ride a bike, our first kiss, or arranging a surprise 21st birthday party for our brother is based on episodic memories. Episodic memories relate to particular contexts. For example, remembering *when* and *how* we learned that $2 \times 2 = 4$ would be an episodic memory; the fact itself (that $2 \times 2 = 4$) is a semantic memory. (To help your long-term memory keep the distinctions between the different types of long-term memory straight, study Figure 5.)

Episodic memories can be surprisingly detailed. Consider, for instance, how you'd respond if you were asked to identify what you were doing on a specific day two years ago. Impossible? You may think otherwise as you read the following exchange between a researcher and a participant in a study who was asked, in a memory experiment, what he was doing "on Monday afternoon in the third week of September two years ago."

Declarative memory
Memory for factual information: names, faces, dates, and the like.

Procedural memory
Memory for skills and habits, such as riding a bike or hitting a baseball, sometimes referred to as *nondeclarative memory.*

Semantic memory
Memory for general knowledge and facts about the world, as well as memory for the rules of logic that are used to deduce other facts.

Episodic memory
Memory for events that occur in a particular time, place, or context.

FIGURE 5

Long-term memory can be subdivided into several different types. What type of long-term memory is involved in your recollection of the moment you first arrived on your campus at the start of college or university? What type of long-term memory is involved in remembering the lyrics to a song, compared with the tune of a song?

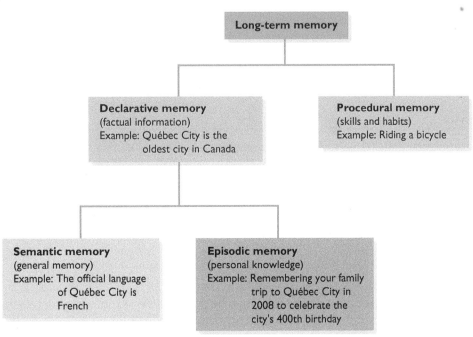

STUDY ALERT!

Use Figure 5 to help clarify the distinctions between the different types of long-term memory.

PARTICIPANT: Come on. How should I know?

EXPERIMENTER: Just try it anyhow.

PARTICIPANT: OK. Let's see: Two years ago . . . I would be in high school . . . That would be my senior year. Third week in September—that's just after summer—that would be the fall term. . . . Let me see. I think I had chemistry lab on Mondays. I don't know. I was probably in chemistry lab. Wait a minute—that would be the second week of school. I remember he started off with the atomic table—a big fancy chart. I thought he was crazy trying to make us memorize that thing. You know, I think I can remember sitting . . . (Lindsay & Norman, 1977).

Episodic memory, then, can provide information about events that happened long in the past (Reynolds & Takooshian, 1988). But semantic memory is no less impressive, permitting us to dredge up tens of thousands of facts ranging from the date of our birthday to the knowledge that $1 is less than $5.

Semantic Networks

Try to recall, for a moment, as many things as you can think of that are the colour red. Now pull from your memory the names of as many fruits as you can recall.

Did the same item appear on both tasks? For many people, an apple comes to mind in both cases, since it fits equally well in each category. And the fact that you might have thought of an apple on the first task makes it even more likely that you'll think of it when doing the second task.

It's actually quite amazing that we're able to retrieve specific material from the vast store of information in our long-term memories. According to some memory researchers, one key organizational tool that allows us to recall detailed information from long-term memory is the associations that we build between different pieces of information. In this view, knowledge is stored in **semantic networks,** mental representations of clusters of interconnected information (Collins & Quillian, 1969; Collins & Loftus, 1975; Cummings, Ceponiene, & Koyama, 2006).

Consider, for example, Figure 6, which shows some of the relationships in memory relating to fire engines, the colour red, and a variety of other semantic concepts. Thinking about a particular concept leads to recall of related concepts. For example, seeing a fire engine may activate our recollections of other kinds of emergency vehicles, such as an ambulance, which in turn may activate recall of the related concept of a vehicle. And thinking of a vehicle may lead us to think about a bus that we've seen in the past. Activating one memory triggers the activation of related memories in a process known as *spreading activation* (Foster et al., 2008; Kreher et al, 2008).

The Neuroscience of Memory

Can we pinpoint a location in the brain where long-term memories reside? Is there a single site that corresponds to a particular memory, or is memory distributed in different regions across the brain? Do memories leave an actual physical trace that scientists can view?

The search for the *engram*, the term for the physical memory trace that corresponds to a memory, has proved to be a major puzzle to psychologists and other neuroscientists interested in memory. Using advanced brain scanning procedures in their efforts to determine the neuroscientific basis of memory formation, investigators have learned that certain

---

FIGURE 6

Semantic networks in memory consist of relationships between pieces of information, such as those relating to the concept of a fire engine. The lines suggest the connections that indicate how the information is organized within memory. The closer two concepts are together, the greater the strength of the association.

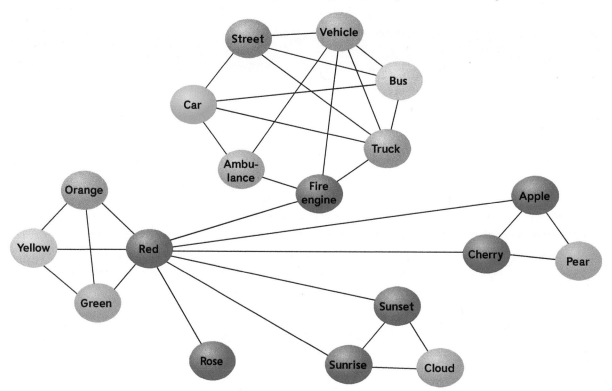

Source: Adapted from Collins, A. M., & Loftus, E. F. (1975). A spreading-activation theory of semantic processing. *Psychological Review, 82,* 407–428. Copyright © 1975 American Psychological Association. Adapted with permission.

Semantic networks
Mental representations of clusters of interconnected information.

areas and structures of the brain specialize in different types of memory-related activities. The *hippocampus*, a part of the brain's limbic system (see Figure 7), plays a central role in the consolidation of memories. Located within the brain's *medial temporal lobes*, just behind the eyes, the hippocampus aids in the initial encoding of information, acting as a kind of neurological e-mail system. That information is subsequently passed along to the cerebral cortex of the brain, where it is actually stored (Govindarajan, Kelleher, & Tonegawa, 2006; J. Peters et al., 2007; Lavenex & Lavenex, 2009).

The *amygdala*, another part of the limbic system, also plays a role in memory. The amygdala is especially involved with memories involving emotion For example, if you are frightened by a large Doberman, you're likely to remember the event vividly—an outcome related to the functioning of the amygdala. Encountering the Doberman, or any large dog, in the future is likely to reactivate the amygdala and bring back the unpleasant memory (Hamann, 2001; Buchanan & Adolphs, 2004; Talmi et al., 2008).

The Biochemistry of Memory

Although it is clear that the hippocampus and amygdala play a central role in memory formation, how is the transformation of information into a memory reflected at the level of neurons?

One answer comes from work on *long-term potentiation*, which shows that certain neural pathways become easily excited while a new response is being learned. At the same time, the number of synapses between neurons increases as the dendrites branch out to receive messages. These changes reflect a process called *consolidation*, in which memories become fixed and stable in long-term memory. Long-term memories take some time to stabilize; this explains why events and other stimuli are not suddenly fixed in memory. Instead, consolidation may continue for days and even years (McGaugh, 2003; Meeter & Murre, 2004; Kawashima, Izaki, & Grace, 2006).

Because a stimulus may contain different sensory aspects, visual, auditory, and other areas of the brain may be simultaneously processing information about that stimulus. Information storage appears to be linked to the sites where this processing occurs, and is therefore located in the particular areas that initially processed the information in terms of its visual, auditory, and other sensory stimuli. For this reason, memory traces are distributed throughout the brain. For example, when you recall a beautiful beach sunset, your recollection draws on memory stores located in visual areas of the brain (the view of the sunset), auditory areas (the sounds of the ocean), and tactile areas (the feel of the wind) (Desimone, 1992; Brewer et al., 1998; Squire, Clark, & Bayley, 2004).

Investigators using positron emission tomography (PET) scans, which measure biological activity in the brain, have found that neural memory traces are highly specialized. For instance, the participants in one experiment were given a list of nouns to read aloud. After reading each noun, they were asked to suggest a related verb. After reading the noun dog, for example, they might have proposed the verb *bark*.

Several distinct areas of the brain showed increased neural activity as the participants first did the task (see Figure 8). However, if they repeated the task with the same nouns several times, the activity in the brain shifted to another area. Most interestingly, if they were given a new list of nouns, the activity returned to the areas in the brain that were initially activated.

FIGURE 7

The hippocampus and amygdala, parts of the brain's limbic system, play a central role in the consolidation of memories.

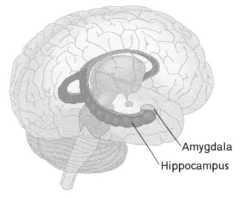

Amygdala

Hippocampus

FIGURE 8

PET scans of a participant in an experiment who was first asked to read a list of nouns and produce a related verb (left scan). When the participant was asked to carry out the task repeatedly with the same list of nouns, different areas of the brain became active (centre). However, when the participant was given a new list of nouns, the regions of the brain that were initially involved became reactivated (right).

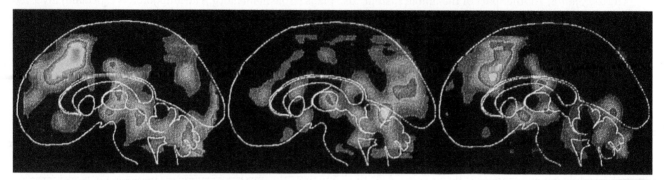

Source: From M. I. Posner, 10/29/93, "Seeing the Mind," *Science* 262: 673, Fig. 1, © AAAS/Photo, Marcus Raichle.

These results suggest that a particular part of the brain is involved in the production of words, but another part takes over when the process becomes routine—in other words, when memory comes into play. It also suggests that memory is distributed in the brain not just in terms of its content, but also in terms of its function (Corbetta, Kincade, & Shulman, 2002).

In short, the physical stuff of memory—the engram—is produced by a complex of biochemical and neural processes. Although memory researchers have made considerable strides in understanding the neuroscience behind memory, more remains to be learned—and remembered. (For more on the biological basis of memory, see the *Applying Psychology in the Real World* box.)

APPLYING PSYCHOLOGY in the Real World

Enhancing Memory: Are We on the Road to "Cosmetic Neurology"?

Would you take a drug to improve your cognitive abilities? Perhaps when studying for an exam or writing a paper? "Cosmetic neurology"—the use of drugs to improve our mental functioning can be seen as the equivalent to the use of Botox to improve physical appearance.

Bradley Cooper's character in the movie *Limitless* had access to a pill that increased his cognitive ability; however, it came with side-effects and exposed him to danger. There is growing evidence that although not approved for use in people without a sleep disorder, ADHD, or Alzheimer's, healthy people are gaining access to the following drugs on the black market and using them to enhance their cognitive ability. Modafinil (Provigil) is used to treat sleep disorders; however, it has also been known to increase alertness and the ability to concentrate. Methylphenidate (Ritalin) is used to treat ADHD, and has been linked to improving concentration. Donepezil (Aricept), prescribed for Alzheimer's disease, may also improve memory in healthy individuals (Big Picture on Drug Development, 2008).

Memory researchers are increasingly optimistic about the possibilities of developing drugs that affect how we remember; however, such drugs raise important moral issues. The Canadian Psychiatric Association questions the ethics of cognitive enhancement and the associated "gate-keeping" role of physicians. Is it ethical for doctors to prescribe neuropharmacological medications to enhance the perception, attention, memory, and reasoning of healthy patients? Is it moral for people to pop a pill to learn material with less effort than those who use only their unenhanced natural capabilities? Will those who can afford artificial enhancements have an unfair advantage over those who are unable to afford "cosmetic neurology?" Would the removal of unpleasant memories also rob people of their identity? The answers to these questions are likely to be nothing short of memorable (Miller, 2004; Begley, 2005; Forlini, Bouvier, & Racine, 2007).

Evaluate

1. Match the type of memory with its definition:

   1. Long-term memory

   2. Short-term memory

   3. Sensory memory

   a. Holds information for fifteen to twenty-five seconds.

   b. Stores information on a relatively permanent basis.

   c. Direct representation of a stimulus.

2. A(n) _____ is a meaningful group of stimuli that can be stored together in short-term memory.

3. There appear to be two types of declarative memory: _____ memory, for knowledge and facts, and _____ memory, for personal experiences.

4. Some memory researchers believe that long-term memory is stored as associations between pieces of information in _____ networks.

Answers to Evaluate Questions

1. 1-b, 2-a, 3-c; 2. chunk; 3. semantic, episodic; 4. semantic

Key Terms

chunk	memory	semantic networks
declarative memory	procedural memory	sensory memory
episodic memory	rehearsal	short-term memory
long-term memory	semantic memory	working memory

Recalling Long-Term Memories

LEARNING OBJECTIVE

LO4 **What causes** difficulties and failures in remembering?

An hour after his job interview, Ricardo was sitting in a coffee shop, telling his friend Laura how well it had gone, when the woman who had interviewed him walked in. "Well, hello, Ricardo. How are you doing?" Trying to make a good impression, Ricardo began to make introductions, but suddenly realized he could not remember the name of the interviewer. Stammering, he desperately searched his memory, but to no avail. "I *know* her name," he thought to himself, "but here I am, looking like a fool. I can kiss this job good-bye."

Have you ever tried to remember someone's name, convinced that you knew it, but unable to recall it no matter how hard you tried? This common occurrence—known as the **tip-of-the-tongue phenomenon**—exemplifies how difficult it can be to retrieve information stored in long-term memory (Schwartz, 2001, 2002, 2008).

Retrieval Cues

Perhaps recall of names and other memories is not perfect because there is so much information stored in long-term memory. Many psychologists have suggested that the material that makes its way to long-term memory is relatively permanent (Tulving & Psotka, 1971). If they are correct, given the broad range of people's experiences and educational backgrounds, the capacity of long-term memory is vast.

We sort through this vast array of material and retrieve specific information at the appropriate time through retrieval cues. A *retrieval cue* is a stimulus that allows us to recall more easily information that is in long-term memory (Tulving & Thompson, 1983; Ratcliff & McKoon, 1989). It may be a word, an emotion, or a sound; whatever the specific cue, a memory will suddenly come to mind when the retrieval cue is present. For example, the smell of roasting turkey may evoke memories of Thanksgiving or family gatherings.

Retrieval cues guide people through the information stored in long-term memory in much the same way that a search engine such as Google guides people through the World Wide Web. They are particularly important when we are making an effort to recall information, as opposed to being asked to *recognize* material stored in memory. In **recall,** a specific piece of information must be retrieved—such as that needed to answer a fill-in-the-blank question or write an essay on a test. In contrast, **recognition** occurs when people are presented with a stimulus and asked whether they have been exposed to it previously, or are asked to identify it from a list of alternatives.

Tip-of-the-tongue phenomenon
The inability to recall information that one realizes one knows—a result of the difficulty of retrieving information from long-term memory.

Recall
Memory task in which specific information must be retrieved.

Recognition
Memory task in which individuals are presented with a stimulus and asked whether they have been exposed to it in the past or to identify it from a list of alternatives.

Recognition is generally a much easier task than recall (see Figure 1). Recall is more difficult because it consists of a series of processes: a search through memory, retrieval of potentially relevant information, and then a decision regarding whether the information you have found is accurate. If the information appears to be correct, the search is over, but if it does not, the search must continue. In contrast, recognition is simpler because it involves fewer steps (Miserando, 1991; Leigh, Zinkhan, & Swaminathan, 2006).

STUDY ALERT!

Remember the distinction between recall (in which specific information must be retrieved) and recognition (in which information is presented and must be identified or distinguished from other material).

Levels of Processing

One determinant of how well memories are recalled is the way in which material is first perceived, processed, and understood. The **levels-of-processing theory** emphasizes the degree to which new material is mentally analyzed. It suggests that the amount of information processing that occurs when material is initially encountered is central in determining how much of the information is ultimately remembered. According to this approach, the depth of information processing during exposure to material—meaning the degree to which it is analyzed and considered—is critical; the greater the intensity of its initial processing is, the more likely we are to remember it (Craik, 1990; Troyer, Häfliger, & Cadieux, 2006; Craik & Lockhart, 2008).

Because we do not pay close attention to much of the information to which we are exposed, very little mental processing typically takes place, and we forget new material almost immediately. However, information to which we pay greater attention is processed more thoroughly. Therefore, it enters memory at a deeper level—and is less apt to be forgotten than is information processed at shallower levels.

The theory goes on to suggest that there are considerable differences in the ways in which information is processed at various levels of memory. At shallow levels, information is processed merely in terms of its physical and

FIGURE 1

Naming the seven dwarfs in *Snow White and the Seven Dwarfs* (a recall task) is more difficult than solving the recognition problem posed in this list.

Answer this recognition question:
Which of the following are the names of the seven dwarfs in the Disney movie *Snow White and the Seven Dwarfs***?**

Goofy	Bashful
Sleepy	Meanie
Smarty	Doc
Scaredy	Happy
Dopey	Angry
Grumpy	Sneezy
Wheezy	Crazy

(The correct answers are Bashful, Doc, Dopey, Grumpy, Happy, Sleepy, and Sneezy.)

Levels-of-processing theory
The theory of memory that emphasizes the degree to which new material is mentally analyzed.

sensory aspects. For example, we may pay attention only to the shapes that make up the letters in the word *dog*. At an intermediate level of processing, the shapes are translated into meaningful units—in this case, letters of the alphabet. Those letters are considered in the context of words, and specific phonetic sounds may be attached to the letters.

At the deepest level of processing, information is analyzed in terms of its meaning. We may see it in a wider context and draw associations between the meaning of the information and broader networks of knowledge. For instance, we may think of dogs not merely as animals with four legs and a tail, but also in terms of their relationship to cats and other mammals. We may form an image of our own dog, thereby relating the concept to our own lives. According to the levels-of-processing approach, the deeper the initial level of processing of specific information is, the longer the information will be retained.

Although the concept of depth of processing has proved difficult to test experimentally and the levels-of-processing theory has its critics (e.g., Baddeley, 1990), it is clear that there are considerable practical implications to the notion that recall depends on the degree to which information is initially processed. For example, the depth of information processing is critical when learning and studying course material. Rote memorization of a list of key terms for a test is unlikely to produce long-term recollection of information, because processing occurs at a shallow level. In contrast, thinking about the meaning of the terms and reflecting on how they relate to information that one currently knows is a far more effective route to long-term retention (Conway, 2002; Wenzel, Zetocha, & Ferraro, 2007).

Explicit and Implicit Memory

If you've ever had surgery, you probably hoped that the surgeons were focused completely on the surgery and gave you their undivided attention while slicing into your body. The reality in most operating rooms is quite different, though. Surgeons may be chatting with nurses about a new restaurant as soon as they sew you up.

If you are like most patients, you are left with no recollection of the conversation that occurred while you were under anesthesia. However, it is very possible that although you had no conscious memories of the discussions on the merits of the restaurant, on some level, you probably did recall at least some information. In fact, careful studies have found that people who are anesthetized during surgery can sometimes recall snippets of conversations they heard during surgery—even though they have no conscious recollection of the information (Kihlstrom et al., 1990; Sebel, Bonke, & Winograd, 1993).

The discovery that people have memories about which they are unaware has been an important one. It has led to speculation that two forms of memory, explicit and implicit, may exist side by side. **Explicit memory** refers to intentional or conscious recollection of information. When we try to remember a name or date we have encountered or learned about previously, we are searching our explicit memory.

In contrast, **implicit memory** refers to memories of which people are not consciously aware but that can affect subsequent performance and behaviour. Skills that operate automatically and without thinking, such as jumping out of the path of an automobile coming toward us as we walk down the side of a road, are stored in implicit memory. Similarly, a feeling of vague dislike for an acquaintance, without knowing why we have that feeling, may be a reflection of implicit memories. Perhaps the person reminds us of someone else in our past that we didn't like, even though we are not aware of the memory of that other individual (Tulving, 2000; Uttl, Graf, & Cosentino, 2003; Coates, Butler, & Berry, 2006; Voss & Paller, 2008).

Implicit memory is closely related to the prejudice and discrimination people exhibit toward members of minority groups. Even though people may say and even believe they harbour no prejudice, assessment of their implicit memories may reveal that they have negative associations about members of minority groups. Such associations can influence behaviour without people being aware of their underlying beliefs (Greenwald, Nosek, & Banaji, 2003; Greenwald, Nosek, & Sriram, 2006; Hofmann et al., 2008).

Explicit memory
Intentional or conscious recollection of information.

Implicit memory
Memories of which people are not consciously aware but that can affect subsequent performance and behaviour.

One way that memory specialists study implicit memory is through experiments that use priming. **Priming** is a phenomenon in which exposure to a word or concept (called a *prime*) later makes it easier to recall related information. Priming effects occur even when people have no conscious memory of the original word or concept (Schacter & Badgaiyan, 2001; Toth & Daniels, 2002; Schacter et al., 2004).

The typical experiment designed to illustrate priming helps clarify the phenomenon. In priming experiments, participants are rapidly exposed to a stimulus such as a word, an object, or perhaps a drawing of a face. The second phase of the experiment is done after an interval ranging from several seconds to several months. At that point, participants are exposed to incomplete perceptual information that is related to the first stimulus, and they are asked whether they recognize it. For example, the new material may consist of the first letter of a word that had been presented earlier, or a part of a face that had been shown earlier. If participants are able to identify the stimulus more readily than they identify stimuli that have not been presented earlier, priming has taken place. Clearly, the earlier stimulus has been remembered—although the material resides in implicit memory, not explicit memory.

The same thing happens to us in our everyday lives. Suppose several months ago you watched a documentary on the planets, and the narrator described the moons of Mars, focusing on its moon named Phobos. You promptly forget the name of the moon, at least consciously. Then, several months later, you're completing a crossword puzzle that is partially completed, and it includes the letters *obos*. As soon as you look at the set of letters, you think of Phobos, and suddenly recall for the first time since your initial exposure to the information that it is one of the moons of Mars. The sudden recollection occurred because your memory was primed by the letters *obos*.

In short, when information that we are unable to consciously recall affects our behaviour, implicit memory is at work. Our behaviour may be influenced by experiences of which we are unaware—an example of what has been called "retention without remembering" (Horton et al., 2005).

Flashbulb Memories

Where were you on January 12, 2010? You will most likely draw a blank until this piece of information is added: January 12, 2010, was the date of the catastrophic earthquake in Haiti.

You probably have little trouble recalling your exact location and a variety of other trivial details that occurred when you heard about the earthquake in Haiti, even though the incident happened several years ago. Your ability to remember details about this fatal event illustrates a phenomenon known as flashbulb memory. **Flashbulb memories** are memories related to a specific, important, or surprising event that are so vivid they represent a virtual snapshot of the event.

Several types of flashbulb memories are common among college and university students. For example, involvement in a car accident, meeting one's roommate for the first time, and the night of high school graduation are all typical flashbulb memories (Romeu, 2006; Bohn & Berntsen, 2007; Talarico, 2009; see Figure 2).

Of course, flashbulb memories do not contain every detail of an original scene. Furthermore, the details recalled in flashbulb memories are often inaccurate. For example, think back to the tragic day when the World Trade Center in New York was attacked by terrorists. Do you remember watching television that morning and seeing images of the first plane, and then the second plane, striking the towers?

If you do, you are among the 73 percent of North Americans who recall viewing the initial television images of both planes on September 11, 2001. However, that recollection is wrong. In fact, television broadcasts showed images only of the second plane on September 11. No video of the first plane was available until early the following morning, September 12, when it was shown on television (Begley, 2002).

Flashbulb memories illustrate a more general phenomenon about memory: Memories that are exceptional are more easily retrieved (although not necessarily accurately) than are those relating to events that are commonplace. The more distinctive a stimulus is, and the more personal relevance the event has, the more likely we are to recall it later (Berntsen & Thomsen, 2005; Shapiro, 2006; Talarico & Rubin, 2007).

Priming
A phenomenon in which exposure to a word or concept (called a *prime*) later makes it easier to recall related information, even when there is no conscious memory of the word or concept.

Flashbulb memories
Memories centred on a specific, important, or surprising event that are so vivid it is as if they represented a snapshot of the event.

FIGURE 2

These are the most common flashbulb memory events, based on a survey of college and university students (Rubin, 1985). What are some of your flashbulb memories?

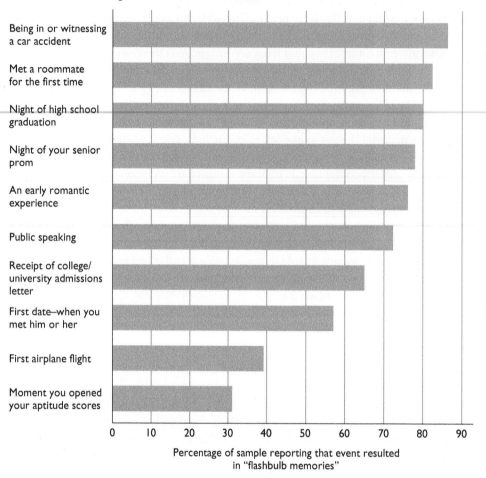

Percentage of sample reporting that event resulted in "flashbulb memories"

Source: From D. C. Rubin, "The Subtle Deceiver: Recalling Our Past," *Psychology Today,* September 1985, pp. 39–46. Reprinted with permission from *Psychology Today* Magazine. Copyright 1995 Sussex Publishers, Inc.

Even with a distinctive stimulus, however, we may not remember where the information came from. *Source amnesia* occurs when an individual has a memory for some material but cannot recall where he or she encountered it before. For example, you may have experienced source amnesia when you met someone you knew and you just couldn't remember where you'd met that person initially.

Similarly, our motivation to remember material when we are exposed to it initially affects how well we can later recall it. If we know we are going to need to recall material later, we are going to be more attentive to it. In contrast, if we don't expect to need to recall material later, then we are less likely to remember it (Naveh-Benjamin et al., 2000; Kassam et al., 2009).

Constructive Processes in Memory: Rebuilding the Past

As we have seen, although it is clear that we can have detailed recollections of significant and distinctive events, it is difficult to gauge the accuracy of such memories. In fact, it is apparent that our memories reflect, at least in part, **constructive processes,** processes in which memories are influenced by the meaning we give to events. When we

Constructive processes
Processes in which memories are influenced by the meaning we give to events.

retrieve information, then, the memory that is produced is affected not just by the direct prior experience we have had with the stimulus, but also by our guesses and inferences about its meaning.

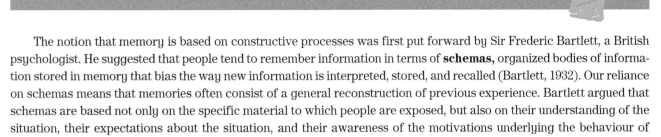

The notion that memory is based on constructive processes was first put forward by Sir Frederic Bartlett, a British psychologist. He suggested that people tend to remember information in terms of **schemas,** organized bodies of information stored in memory that bias the way new information is interpreted, stored, and recalled (Bartlett, 1932). Our reliance on schemas means that memories often consist of a general reconstruction of previous experience. Bartlett argued that schemas are based not only on the specific material to which people are exposed, but also on their understanding of the situation, their expectations about the situation, and their awareness of the motivations underlying the behaviour of others.

One of the earliest demonstrations of schemas came from a classic study that involved a procedure similar to the children's game of "telephone," in which information from memory is passed sequentially from one person to another. In the study, a participant viewed a drawing in which there were a variety of people of differing racial and ethnic backgrounds on a subway car, one of whom—a white person—was shown with a razor in his hand (Allport & Postman, 1958). The first participant was asked to describe the drawing to someone else without looking back at it. Then that person was asked to describe it to another person (without looking at the drawing), and then the process was repeated with still one more participant.

The report of the last person differed in significant, yet systematic, ways from the initial drawing. Specifically, many people described the drawing as depicting an African American with a knife—an incorrect recollection, given that the drawing showed a razor in the hand of a white person. The transformation of the white person's razor into an African American's knife clearly indicates that the participants held a schema that included the unwarranted prejudice that African Americans are more violent than white people and thus more apt to be holding a knife. In short, our expectations and knowledge—and prejudices—affect the reliability of our memories (McDonald & Hirt, 1997; Newby-Clark & Ross, 2003).

Memory in the Courtroom: The Eyewitness on Trial

For David Milgaard, inadequate memories of eyewitnesses cost him twenty-three years of his life. For Thomas Sophonow, inadequate memories of eyewitnesses cost him four years of his life. Both Milgaard and Sophonow were victims of mistaken identity when witnesses identified them as perpetrators of crimes they did not commit. On that basis, they were tried, convicted, and sentenced to life in prison.

Both were ultimately exonerated on the basis of DNA evidence. Twenty-three years after being sentenced to life in prison—David Milgaard's conviction was overturned by the Supreme Court of Canada. Four years after being sentenced to life in prison—Thomas Sophonow was set free by the Manitoba Court of Appeal.

For those wrongly convicted, though, it was too late (CBC.ca, 2008). In Sophonow's words, "I am still treated as a man who got away with murder" (CTV.ca, 2006).

Unfortunately, Milgaard and Sophonow are not the only victims to whom apologies have had to be made by the Canadian justice system; there have been many cases of mistaken identity that have led to unjustified legal actions (CBC.ca, 2008). Research on eyewitness identification of suspects, as well as on memory for other details of crimes, has shown that eyewitnesses are apt to make significant errors when they try to recall details of criminal activity— even if they are highly confident about their recollections (Miller, 2000; Thompson, 2000; Wells, Olson, & Charman, 2002; Loftus, 2003; Yarmey, 2003).

Schemas
Organized bodies of information stored in memory that bias the way new information is interpreted, stored, and recalled.

One reason is the impact of the weapons used in crimes. When a criminal perpetrator displays a gun or knife, it acts like a perceptual magnet, attracting the eyes of the witnesses. As a consequence, witnesses pay less attention to other details of the crime and are less able to recall what actually occurred (Belli & Loftus, 1996; Steblay et al., 2003).

Even when weapons are not involved, eyewitnesses are prone to errors relating to memory. For instance, viewers of a twelve-second film of a mugging that was shown on a New York City television news program were later given the opportunity to pick out the assailant from a six-person lineup (Buckout, 1974). Of some 2,000 viewers who called the station after the program, only 15 percent were able to pick out the right person—a percentage similar to random guessing.

One reason eyewitnesses are prone to memory-related errors is that the specific wording of questions posed to them by police officers or lawyers can affect the way they recall information, as a number of experiments illustrate. For example, in one experiment the participants were shown a film of two cars crashing into each other. Some were then asked the question, "About how fast were the cars going when they *smashed* into each other?" On average, they estimated the speed to be 40.8 miles (65 km) per hour. In contrast, when another group of participants was asked, "About how fast were the cars going when they *contacted* each other?" the average estimated speed was only 31.8 miles (50 km) per hour (Loftus & Palmer, 1974; see Figure 3).

CHILDREN'S RELIABILITY

The problem of memory reliability becomes even more acute when children are witnesses because increasing evidence suggests that children's memories are highly vulnerable to the influence of others (Loftus, 1993; Douglas-Brown, Goldstein, & Bjorklund, 2000). For instance, in one experiment, 5- to 7-year-old girls who had just had a routine physical examination were shown an anatomically explicit doll. The girls were shown the doll's genital area and asked, "Did the doctor touch you here?" Three of the girls who did not have a vaginal or anal exam said that the doctor had in fact touched them in the genital area, and one of those three made up the detail "The doctor did it with a stick" (Saywitz & Goodman, 1990).

FIGURE 3

After viewing an accident involving two cars, the participants in a study were asked to estimate the speed of the two cars involved in the collision. Estimates varied substantially, depending on the way the question was worded.

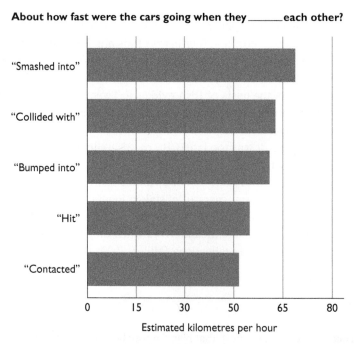

About how fast were the cars going when they _____ each other?

Estimated kilometres per hour

Source: Reprinted from *Journal of Verbal Learning and Verbal Behavior,* vol. 13, Loftus, E. F., & Palmer, J. C., "Reconstruction of automobile destruction: An example of the interface between language and memory," pp. 585–589, Copyright © 1974, with permission from Elsevier.

Children's memories are especially susceptible to influence when the situation is highly emotional or stressful. For example, in trials in which there is significant pretrial publicity or in which alleged victims are questioned repeatedly, often by untrained interviewers, the memories of the alleged victims may be influenced by the types of questions they are asked (Scullin, Kanaya, & Ceci, 2002; Lamb & Garretson, 2003; Quas, Malloy, & Melinder, 2007; Goodman & Quas, 2008).

REPRESSED AND FALSE MEMORIES: SEPARATING TRUTH FROM FICTION

Consider the case of George Franklin Sr., a man charged with murdering his daughter's playmate. The entire case was based on memories of Franklin's daughter, who claimed that she had repressed them until she began to have flashbacks of the event two decades later. Gradually, the memories became clearer until she recalled her father lifting a rock over his head and then seeing her friend covered with blood. On the basis of her memories, her father was convicted—but later was cleared of the crime after an appeal of the conviction.

Paul Shanley, a Catholic priest, was convicted of sexual abuse on the basis of memories of a man who claimed to have been abused for a six-year period during childhood, but only recalled the abuse years later when he was an adult.

Source: © Matt Stone/AFP/Getty Images.

There is good reason to question the validity of *repressed memories*, recollections of events that are initially so shocking that the mind responds by pushing them into the unconscious. Supporters of the notion of repressed memory (based on Freud's psychoanalytic theory) suggest that such memories may remain hidden, possibly throughout a person's lifetime, unless they are triggered by some current circumstance, such as the probing that occurs during psychological therapy.

However, memory researcher Elizabeth Loftus maintains that so-called repressed memories may well be inaccurate or even wholly false—representing *false memory*. For example, false memories develop when people are unable to recall the source of a memory of a particular event about which they have only vague recollections. When the source of the memory becomes unclear or ambiguous, people may become confused about whether they actually experienced the event or whether it was imagined. Ultimately, people come to believe that the event actually occurred (Loftus, 2004; Wade, Sharman, & Garry, 2007; Bernstein & Loftus, 2009a).

There is great controversy regarding the legitimacy of repressed memories. Many therapists give great weight to authenticity of repressed memories, and their views are supported by research showing that there are specific regions of the brain that help keep unwanted memories out of awareness. On the other side of the issue are researchers who maintain that there is insufficient scientific support for the existence of such memories. There is also a middle ground: memory researchers who suggest that false memories are a result of normal information processing. The challenge for those on all sides of the issue is to distinguish truth from fiction (Brown & Pope, 1996; Strange, Clifasefi, & Garry, 2007; Bernstein & Loftus, 2009b).

Autobiographical Memory: Where Past Meets Present

Your memory of experiences in your own past may well be a fiction—or at least a distortion of what actually occurred. The same constructive processes that make us inaccurately recall the behaviour of others also reduce the accuracy of autobiographical memories. **Autobiographical memories** are our recollections of circumstances and episodes from our own lives. Autobiographical memories encompass the episodic memories we hold about ourselves (Rubin et al., 2007; Sutin & Robins, 2007).

For example, we tend to forget information about our past that is incompatible with the way in which we currently see ourselves. One study found that adults who were well adjusted but who had been treated for emotional problems

Autobiographical memories
Our recollections of circumstances and episodes from our own lives.

FIGURE 4

We tend to distort memories of unpleasant events. For example, college and university students are much more likely to accurately recall their good grades, while inaccurately recalling their poor ones (Bahrick, Hall, & Berger, 1996). Now that you know this, how well do you think you can recall your high school grades?

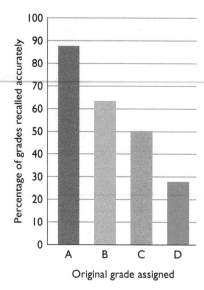

Original grade assigned

Source: Data from Table 2 (p. 266) from Bahrick, H. P., Hall, L. K., & Berger, S. A. (1996). Accuracy and distortion in memory for high school grades. *Psychological Science*, 7, 265–269. Copyright © 1996, Association for Psychological Science. Reprinted by permission of Sage Publications, Inc.

during the early years of their lives tended to forget important but troubling childhood events, such as being in foster care. College and university students misremember their bad grades—but remember their good ones (see Figure 4 above; Walker, Skowronski, & Thompson, 2003; Kemps & Tiggemann, 2007).

Similarly, when a group of 48-year-olds were asked to recall how they had responded on a questionnaire they had completed when they were first-year high school students, their accuracy was no better than chance. For example, although 61 percent of the questionnaire respondents said that playing sports and other physical activities was their favourite pastime, only 23 percent of the adults recalled it accurately (Offer et al., 2000).

It is not just certain kinds of events that are distorted; particular periods of life are remembered more easily than others are. For example, when people reach late adulthood, they remember periods of life in which they experienced major transitions, such as attending college or university and working at their first job, better than they remember their middle-age years. Similarly, although most adults' earliest memories of their own lives are of events that occurred when they were toddlers, toddlers show evidence of recall of events that occurred when they were as young as 6 months old (Simcock & Hayne, 2002; Wang, 2003; Cordnoldi, De Beni, & Helstrup, 2007).

Exploring DIVERSITY

Are There Cross-Cultural Differences in Memory?

Travellers who have visited areas of the world in which there is no written language often have returned with tales of people with phenomenal memories. For instance, storytellers in some preliterate cultures can recount long chronicles that recall the names and activities of people over many generations. Those feats led experts to argue initially that people in preliterate societies develop a different, and perhaps better, type of memory than do those in cultures that employ a written language. They suggested that in a society that lacks writing, people are motivated to recall information with accuracy, particularly information relating to tribal histories and traditions that would be lost if they were not passed down orally from one generation to another (Daftary & Meri, 2002; Berntsen & Rubin, 2004).

More recent approaches to cultural differences suggest a different conclusion. For one thing, preliterate peoples don't have an exclusive claim to amazing memory feats. Some Hebrew scholars memorize thousands of pages of text and can recall the locations of particular words on the page. Similarly, poetry singers in the Balkans can recall thousands of lines of poetry. Even in cultures in which written language exists, then, astounding feats of memory are possible (Strathern & Stewart, 2003; Rubin et al., 2007).

Memory researchers now suggest that there are both similarities and differences in memory across cultures. Basic memory processes such as short-term memory capacity and the structure of long-term memory—the "hardware" of memory—are universal and operate similarly in people in all cultures. In contrast, cultural differences can be seen in the way information is acquired and rehearsed—the "software" of memory. Culture determines how people frame information initially, how much they practise learning and recalling it, and the strategies they use to try to recall it (Mack, 2003; Wang & Conway, 2006; Rubin et al., 2007).

Evaluate

1. While with a group of friends at a dance, Eva bumps into a man she dated last month, but when she tries to introduce him to her friends, she cannot remember his name. What is the term for this occurrence?

2. _____ is the process of retrieving a specific item from memory.

3. A friend tells you, "I know exactly where I was and what I was doing when I heard that Michael Jackson died." What is this type of memory phenomenon called?

4. The same person could probably also accurately describe in detail what she was wearing when she heard about Michael Jackson's death, right down to the colour of her shoes. True or false?

5. _____ theory states that the more a person analyzes a statement, the more likely he or she is to remember it later.

Answers to Evaluate Questions

1. tip-of-the-tongue phenomenon; 2. recall; 3. flashbulb memory; 4. false, small details probably won't be remembered through flashbulb memory; 5. levels-of-processing

Key Terms

autobiographical memories	implicit memory	recognition
constructive processes	levels-of-processing theory	schemas
explicit memory	priming	tip-of-the-tongue phenomenon
flashbulb memories	recall	

Forgetting: When Memory Fails

LEARNING OBJECTIVES

LO5 **Why do** we forget information?

LO6 **What are** the major memory impairments?

LO7 **What are** the techniques for improving memory?

Known in the scientific literature by the pseudonym H. M., he could remember, quite literally, nothing—nothing, that is, that had happened since the loss of his brain's temporal lobes and hippocampus during experimental surgery to reduce epileptic seizures. Until that time, H. M.'s memory had been quite normal. But after the operation he was unable to recall anything for more than a few minutes, and then the memory was seemingly lost forever. He did not remember his address, or the name of the person to whom he was talking. H. M. would read the same magazine over and over again. According to his own description, his life was like waking from a dream and being unable to know where he was or how he got there (Milner, 1966, 2005).

As the case of H. M. illustrates, a person without a normal memory faces severe difficulties. All of us who have experienced even routine instances of forgetting—such as not remembering an acquaintance's name or a fact on a test—understand the very real consequences of memory failure.

Of course, memory failure is also essential to remembering important information. The ability to forget inconsequential details about experiences, people, and objects helps us avoid being burdened and distracted by trivial stores of meaningless data. Forgetting permits us to form general impressions and recollections. For example, the reason our friends consistently look familiar to us is because we're able to forget their clothing, facial blemishes, and other transient features that change from one occasion to the next. Instead, our memories are based on a summary of various critical features—a far more economical use of our memory capabilities.

Forgetting unnecessary information, then, is as essential to the proper functioning of memory as is remembering more important material. If you're uneasy about your own forgetfulness, try the quiz in Figure 1.

The first attempts to study forgetting were made by German psychologist Hermann Ebbinghaus about a hundred years ago. Using himself as the only participant in his study, Ebbinghaus memorized lists of three-letter nonsense syllables—meaningless sets of two consonants with a vowel in between, such as *FIW* and *BOZ*. By measuring how easy it was to relearn a given list of words after varying periods of time had passed since the initial learning, he found that forgetting occurred systematically, as shown in nearby Figure 2. As the figure indicates, the most rapid forgetting occurs in the first nine hours, particularly in the first hour. After nine hours, the rate of forgetting slows and declines little, even after the passage of many days.

Despite his primitive methods, Ebbinghaus's study had an important influence on subsequent research, and his basic conclusions have been upheld. There is almost always a strong initial decline in memory, followed by a more gradual drop over time. Furthermore, relearning of previously mastered material is almost always faster than starting from scratch, whether the material is academic information or a motor skill such as serving a tennis ball (Wixted & Carpenter, 2007).

Why We Forget

Why do we forget? One reason is that we may not have paid attention to the material in the first place—a failure of *encoding.* For example, if you live in Canada, you probably have been exposed to thousands of dimes during your life. Despite this experience, you probably don't have a clear sense of the details of the coin. Consequently, the reason for your memory failure is that you probably never encoded the information into long-term memory initially. Obviously, if information was not placed in memory to start with, there is no way the information can be recalled.

FIGURE 1

If you feel that your memory isn't what it used to be, try this quiz. Based on similar tests, it is used to determine serious loss of memory, from which you as a college or university student are quite unlikely to suffer.

Take a Measure of Your Memory

If you are concerned your memory is not what it should be (or used to be), try this quiz.

1. Remember these words: *orange, telephone, lamp*
2. Remember this address: *Mary Smith, 650 Park Street, Winnipeg MB*
3. Who were the past five Canadian prime ministers?
4. Who were the last three mayors of your city?
5. What were the names of the last two movies you saw?
6. What were the names of the last two restaurants in which you ate?
7. Have you had more difficulty than usual recalling events from the previous two weeks? _____ Yes _____ No
8. Have you noticed a decline in your ability to remember lists, such as shopping lists? _____ Yes _____ No
9. Have you noticed a decline in your ability to perform mental math, like calculating change? _____ Yes _____ No
10. Have you been more forgetful about paying bills? _____ Yes _____ No
11. Have you had more trouble remembering peoples' names? _____ Yes _____ No
12. Have you had more trouble recognizing faces? _____ Yes _____ No
13. Do you find it harder to find the right words you want to use? _____ Yes _____ No
14. Have you been having more trouble remembering how to perform simple physical tasks such as operating the microwave or the remote control? _____ Yes _____ No
15. Does your memory interfere with your ability to function:
    At work? _____ Yes _____ No
    At home? _____ Yes _____ No
    In social situations? _____ Yes _____ No
16. Do you recall the three words you were given earlier?
17. Do you recall the name and address you were given earlier?

SCORING

Questions 3–6: 1 point for each correct answer (total of 12 points); **Questions 7–15:** 1 point for each "No" answer (total of 11 points); **Questions 16–17:** 1 point for each correct answer (total of 9 points).

Interpretation

Note that poor scores may be due to factors such as anxiety and inattention and not just from memory difficulties. Doing well on this simple quiz also does not ensure that you have no memory or cognitive difficulties.

The best indicator of your memory is your own assessment of your abilities. A perceived consistent change in your mental capacity is a far more sensitive indicator of cognitive difficulties than most tests, including this one. You should seek further help if this is the case.

If you scored between **28–32 points,** Congratulations!

If you scored between **22–27 points,** you may have some memory difficulties that, if persistent and interfering with everyday functioning, may need to be evaluated.

If you scored **21 or below,** and you have noticed that you have difficulty with your memory or thinking abilities of sufficient severity to interfere with functioning, you probably would benefit from a good evaluation.

Source: Adapted from Devi, 2002.

But what about material that has been encoded into memory and that can't later be remembered? Several processes account for memory failures, including decay, interference, and cue-dependent forgetting.

Decay is the loss of information through nonuse. This explanation for forgetting assumes that **memory traces,** the physical changes that take place in the brain when new material is learned, simply fade away over time (Grann, 2007).

Decay
The loss of information in memory through its nonuse.

Memory traces
A physical change in the brain that occurs when new material is learned.

FIGURE 2

In his classic work, Ebbinghaus found that the most rapid forgetting occurs in the first nine hours after exposure to new material. However, the rate of forgetting then slows down and declines very little even after many days have passed (Ebbinghaus, 1885, 1913). Check your own memory: What were you doing exactly two hours ago? What were you doing last Tuesday at 5 P.M.? Which information is easier to retrieve?

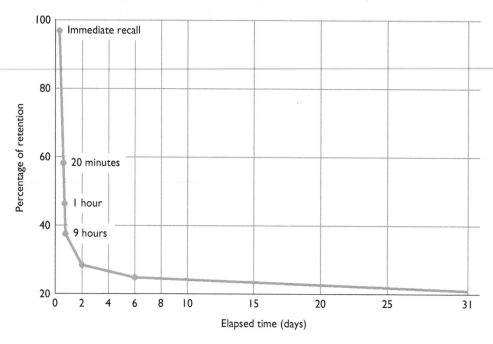

Although there is evidence that decay does occur, this does not seem to be the complete explanation for forgetting. Often there is no relationship between how long ago a person was exposed to information and how well that information is recalled. If decay explained all forgetting, we would expect that the more time that has elapsed between the initial learning of information and our attempt to recall it, the harder it would be to remember it, because there would be more time for the memory trace to decay. Yet people who take several consecutive tests on the same material often recall more of the initial information when taking later tests than they did on earlier tests. If decay were operating, we would expect the opposite to occur (Payne, 1986).

Because decay does not fully account for forgetting, memory specialists have proposed an additional mechanism: **interference.** In interference, information in memory disrupts the recall of other information (Naveh-Benjamin, Guez, & Sorek, 2007; Pilotti, Chodorow, & Shono, 2009).

To distinguish between decay and interference, think of the two processes in terms of a row of books on a library shelf. In decay, the old books are constantly crumbling and rotting away, leaving room for new arrivals. Interference processes suggest that new books knock the old ones off the shelf, where they become inaccessible.

Finally, forgetting may occur because of **cue-dependent forgetting,** forgetting that occurs when there are insufficient retrieval cues to rekindle information that is in memory (Tulving & Thompson, 1983). For example, you may not be able to remember where you lost a set of keys until you mentally walk through your day, thinking of each place you visited. When you think of the place where you lost the keys—say, the library—the retrieval cue of the library may be sufficient to help you recall that you left them on the desk in the library. Without that retrieval cue, you may be unable to recall the location of the keys.

Interference

The phenomenon by which information in memory disrupts the recall of other information.

Cue-dependent forgetting

Forgetting that occurs when there are insufficient retrieval cues to rekindle information that is in memory.

Most research suggests that interference and cue-dependent forgetting are key processes in forgetting (Mel'nikov, 1993; Bower, Thompson, & Tulving, 1994). We forget things mainly because new memories interfere with the retrieval of old ones or because appropriate retrieval cues are unavailable, not because the memory trace has decayed.

STUDY ALERT!

Memory loss through decay comes from nonuse of the memory; memory loss through interference is due to the presence of other information in memory.

Proactive and Retroactive Interference: The Before and After of Forgetting

There are actually two types of interference that influence forgetting: proactive and retroactive. In **proactive interference,** information learned earlier disrupts the recall of newer material. Suppose, as a student of foreign languages, you first learned French in grade 10, and then in grade 11 you took Spanish. When in grade 12 you take a scholastic achievement test in Spanish, you may find you have difficulty recalling the Spanish translation of a word because all you can think of is its French equivalent (Bunting, 2006).

In contrast, **retroactive interference** refers to difficulty in the recall of information because of later exposure to different material. If, for example, you have difficulty on a French achievement test because of your more recent exposure to Spanish, retroactive interference is the culprit (see Figure 3). One way to remember the difference between proactive and retroactive interference is to keep in mind that *pro*active interference progresses in time—the past

Proactive interference
Interference in which information learned earlier disrupts the recall of newer material.

Retroactive interference
Interference in which there is difficulty in the recall of information learned earlier because of later exposure to different material.

FIGURE 3

Proactive interference occurs when material learned earlier interferes with the recall of newer material. In this example, studying French before studying Spanish interferes with performance on a Spanish test. In contrast, retroactive interference exists when material learned after initial exposure to other material interferes with the recall of the earlier material. In this case, retroactive interference occurs when recall of French is impaired because of later exposure to Spanish.

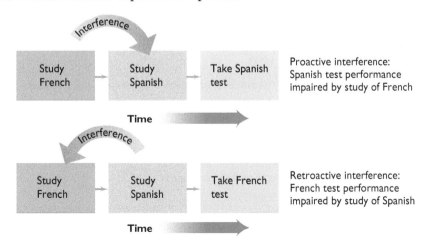

interferes with the present—whereas *retro*active interference retrogresses in time, working backward as the present interferes with the past (Jacoby et al., 2007).

Although the concepts of proactive and retroactive interference illustrate how material may be forgotten, they still do not explain whether forgetting is caused by the actual loss or modification of information or by problems in the retrieval of information. Most research suggests that material that has apparently been lost because of interference can eventually be recalled if appropriate stimuli are presented (Tulving & Psotka, 1971; Anderson, 1980), but the question has not been fully answered.

Memory Dysfunctions: Afflictions of Forgetting

Alzheimer's disease, is a progressive brain disorder that leads to a gradual and irreversible decline in cognitive abilities. Alzheimer's is the most common form of dementia among adults in Canada. Three in twenty Canadians ages of 65 and older have Alzheimer's disease and other dementias and it is estimated that this figure will continue to increase if nothing changes (Alzheimer Society Canada, 2011).

In the beginning, Alzheimer's symptoms appear as simple forgetfulness of things such as appointments and birthdays. As the disease progresses, memory loss becomes more profound, and even the simplest tasks—such as using a telephone or getting dressed correctly—are forgotten. Ultimately, victims may lose their ability to speak or comprehend language, and physical deterioration sets in, leading to death.

The causes of Alzheimer's disease are not fully understood; however. Increasing evidence suggests that Alzheimer's results from an inherited susceptibility to a defect in the production of the protein beta amyloid, which is necessary for the maintenance of nerve cell connections. When the synthesis of beta amyloid goes awry, large clumps of cells form, triggering inflammation and the deterioration of nerve cells in the brain (Selkoe, 2002; Detoledo-Morrell, Stoub, & Wang, 2007; Horínek, Varjassyová, & Hort, 2007; Selkoe, 2008).

Amnesia, another type of memory dysfunctions refers to memory loss that occurs without other mental difficulties. Amnesia has been immortalized in countless Hollywood films involving a victim who receives a blow to the head and is unable to remember anything from his or her past. In reality, amnesia of this type, known as retrograde amnesia, is quite rare. In **retrograde amnesia,** memory is lost for occurrences prior to a certain event. Usually, lost memories gradually reappear, although full restoration may take as long as several years. In certain cases, some memories are lost forever. But even in cases of severe memory loss, the loss is generally selective. For example, although people suffering from retrograde amnesia may be unable to recall friends and family members, they still may be able to play complicated card games or knit a sweater quite well (Verfaellie & Keane, 2002; Bright, Buckman, & Fradera, 2006).

A second type of amnesia is exemplified by people who remember nothing of their current activities. In **anterograde amnesia,** loss of memory occurs for events that follow an injury. Information cannot be transferred from short-term to long-term memory, resulting in the inability to remember anything other than what was in long-term storage before the accident (Gilboa, Winocur, & Rosenbaum, 2006).

Fortunately, most of us have intact memory, and the occasional failures we suffer may actually be preferable to having a perfect memory. Consider, for instance, the case of a man who had total recall. After reading passages of the *Divine Comedy* in Italian—a language he did not speak—he was able to repeat them from memory some fifteen years

---

Alzheimer's disease
A progressive brain disorder that leads to a gradual and irreversible decline in cognitive abilities.

Amnesia
Memory loss that occurs without other mental difficulties.

Retrograde amnesia
Amnesia in which memory is lost for occurrences prior to a certain event.

Anterograde amnesia
Amnesia in which memory is lost for events that follow an injury.

later. He could memorize lists of fifty unrelated words and recall them at will more than a decade later. He could even repeat the same list of words backward, if asked (Luria, 1968).

Such a skill at first may seem to be enviable, but it actually presented quite a problem. The man's memory became a jumble of lists of words, numbers, and names, and when he tried to relax, his mind was filled with images. Even reading was difficult, since every word evoked a flood of thoughts from the past that interfered with his ability to understand the meaning of what he was reading. Partially as a consequence of the man's unusual memory, psychologist A. R. Luria, who studied his case, found him to be a "disorganized and rather dull-witted person" (Luria, 1968, p. 65).

We might be grateful, then, that forgetfulness plays a role in our lives.

Becoming an Informed Consumer of Psychology

Improving Your Memory

Apart from the advantages of forgetting, say, a bad date, most of us would like to find ways to improve our memories. Is it possible to find practical ways to increase our recall of information? Most definitely. Research has revealed a number of strategies for developing a better memory (VanLehn, 1996; Hermann, Raybeck, & Gruneberg, 2002; West, Thorn, & Bagwell, 2003). Let's look at some of the best.

- *The keyword technique.* Suppose you are taking a foreign language class and need to learn vocabulary words. You can try the keyword technique of pairing a foreign word with a common English word that has a similar sound. This English word is known as the *keyword.* For example, to learn the Spanish word for duck (*pato,* pronounced *pat-o* as in *past*), you might choose the keyword *pot;* for the Spanish word for horse (*caballo,* pronounced *cab-eye-yo*), the keyword might be *eye.*

- *Once you have thought of a keyword, imagine the Spanish word "interacting" with the English keyword.* You might envision a duck taking a bath in a pot to remember the word pato, or a horse with a large, bulging eye in the centre of its head to recall *caballo.* This technique has produced considerably superior results in learning foreign language vocabulary compared with more traditional techniques involving memorization of the words themselves (Carney & Levin, 1998; Wyra, Lawson, & Hungi, 2007).

- *Encoding specificity.* Some research suggests that we remember information best in an environment that is the same as or similar to the one where we initially learned it—a phenomenon known as *encoding specificity.* You may do better on a test, then, if you study in the classroom where the test will be given. However, if you must take a test in a room different from the one in which you studied, don't despair: The features of the test itself, such as the wording of the test questions, are sometimes so powerful that they overwhelm the subtler cues relating to the original encoding of the material (Bjork & Richardson-Klarehn, 1989).

- *Organization cues.* Many of life's important recall tasks involve texts that you have read. One proven technique for improving recall of written material is to organize the material in memory as you read it for the first time. Organize your reading on the basis of any advance information you have about the content and about its organization. You will then be able to make connections and see relationships among the various facts and process the material at a deeper level, which in turn will later aid recall.

- *Effective note taking.* "Less is more" is perhaps the best advice for taking lecture notes that facilitate recall. Rather than trying to jot down every detail of a lecture, it is better to listen and think about the material, and take down the main points. In effective note taking, thinking about the material initially is more important than writing it down. This is one reason that borrowing someone else's notes is a bad idea; you will have no framework in memory that you can use to understand them (Feldman, 2010).

- *Practise and rehearse.* Although practise does not necessarily make perfect, it helps. By studying and rehearsing material past initial mastery—a process called overlearning—people are able to show better long-term recall than they show if they stop practising after their initial learning of the material. Keep in mind that as research clearly demonstrates, fatigue and other factors prevent long practise sessions from being as effective as distributed practise.

- *Don't believe claims about drugs that improve memory.* Advertisements for One-A-Day vitamins with ginkgo biloba would have you believe that taking a drug can improve your memory. Not so, according to the results of studies. No research has shown that commercial memory enhancers are effective (Gold, Cahill, & Wenk, 2002; McDaniel, Maier, & Einstein, 2002; Burns, Bryan, & Nettelbeck, 2006). So save your money!

Evaluate

1. If, after learning the history of the Middle East for a class two years ago, you now find yourself unable to recall what you learned, you are experiencing memory _____ caused by nonuse.

2. Difficulty in accessing a memory because of the presence of other information is known as _____.

3. _____ interference occurs when material is difficult to retrieve because of subsequent exposure to other material; _____ interference refers to difficulty in retrieving material as a result of the interference of previously learned material.

Answers to Evaluate Questions

1. decay; 2. interference; 3. retroactive, proactive

Key Terms

Alzheimer's disease	decay	retroactive interference
amnesia	interference	retrograde amnesia
anterograde amnesia	memory traces	
cue-dependent forgetting	proactive interference	

Epilogue

Source: © Ingram Publishing RF.

Our examination of memory has highlighted the processes of encoding, storage, and retrieval and theories about how these processes occur. We encountered the research of several Canadians including Fergus Craik, Endel Tulving, Robert Lockhart, and Daniel Schacter who all began their careers at the University of Toronto. Several phenomena related to memory, including the tip-of-the-tongue phenomenon and flashbulb memories were explored. Above all, we observed that memory is a constructive process by which interpretations, expectations, and guesses contribute to the nature of our memories.

Recap/Rethink

Module 18: The Foundations of Memory

Recap

What is memory?

- Memory is the process by which we encode, store, and retrieve information.

Are there different kinds of memory?

- Sensory memory, corresponding to each of the sensory systems, is the first place where information is saved. Sensory memories are very brief, but they are precise, storing a nearly exact replica of a stimulus.
- Roughly seven (plus or minus two) chunks of information can be transferred and held in short-term memory. Information in short-term memory is held from fifteen to twenty-five seconds and, if not transferred to long-term memory, is lost.
- Some theorists view short-term memory as a working memory, in which information is retrieved and manipulated, and held through rehearsal. In this view, it is a central executive processor involved in reasoning and decision making; it coordinates a visual store, a verbal store, and an episodic buffer.
- Memories are transferred into long-term storage through rehearsal. If memories are transferred into long-term memory, they become relatively permanent.
- Long-term memory can be viewed in terms of memory modules, each of which is related to separate memory systems in the brain. For instance, we can distinguish between declarative memory and procedural memory. Declarative memory is further divided into episodic memory and semantic memory.
- Semantic networks suggest that knowledge is stored in long-term memory as mental representations of clusters of interconnected information.

What are the biological bases of memory?

- The hippocampus and amygdala are particularly important in the establishment of memory.
- Memories are distributed across the brain, relating to the different sensory information-processing systems involved during the initial exposure to a stimulus.

Rethink

1. It is a truism that "you never forget how to ride a bicycle." Why might this be so? In what type of memory is information about bicycle riding stored?

2. *From a marketing specialist's perspective:* How might ways of enhancing memory be used by advertisers and others to promote their products? What ethical principles are involved? Can you think of a way to protect yourself from unethical advertising?

3. Should memory enhancement drugs be limited only to clear-cut cases of disease, or should they be available to enhance memory beyond normal limits? What kind of restrictions, if any, should be put on the distribution of such drugs, and why?

Module 19: Recalling Long-Term Memories

Recap

What causes difficulties and failures in remembering?

- The tip-of-the-tongue phenomenon is the temporary inability to remember information that one is certain one knows. Retrieval cues are a major strategy for recalling information successfully.
- The levels-of-processing approach to memory suggests that the way in which information is initially perceived and analyzed determines the success with which it is recalled. The deeper the initial processing, the greater the recall.
- Explicit memory refers to intentional or conscious recollection of information. In contrast, implicit memory refers to memories of which people are not consciously aware, but which can affect subsequent performance and behaviour.
- Flashbulb memories are memories centred on a specific, important event. The more distinctive a memory is, the more easily it can be retrieved.
- Memory is a constructive process: We relate memories to the meaning, guesses, and expectations we give to events. Specific information is recalled in terms of schemas, organized bodies of information stored in memory that bias the way new information is interpreted, stored, and recalled.
- Eyewitnesses are apt to make substantial errors when they try to recall the details of crimes. The problem of memory reliability becomes even more acute when the witnesses are children.
- Autobiographical memory is influenced by constructive processes.

Rethink

1. Research shows that an eyewitness's memory for details of crimes can contain significant errors. How might a lawyer use this information when evaluating an eyewitness's testimony? Should eyewitness accounts be permissible in a court of law?

2. *From a social worker's perspective:* Should a child victim of sexual abuse be allowed to testify in court, based on what you've learned about children's memories under stress?

Module 20: Forgetting: When Memory Fails

Recap

LO5   Why do we forget information?

- Several processes account for memory failure, including decay, interference (both proactive and retroactive), and cue-dependent forgetting.

LO6   What are the major memory impairments?

- Among the memory dysfunctions are Alzheimer's disease, which leads to a progressive loss of memory and amnesia, a memory loss that occurs without other mental difficulties and that can take two forms: retrograde amnesia and anterograde amnesia.

LO7   What are the techniques for improving memory?

- The keyword technique to memorize foreign language vocabulary; using the encoding specificity phenomenon; organizing text material and lecture notes; and practice and rehearsal, leading to overlearning.

Rethink

1. What are the implications of proactive and retroactive inhibition for learning multiple foreign languages? Would previous language training help or hinder learning a new language?

2. *From a healthcare provider's perspective:* Alzheimer's disease and amnesia are two of the most pervasive memory dysfunctions that threaten many individuals. What sorts of activities might healthcare providers offer their patients to help them combat their memory loss?

3. Before moving on to the next chapter, return to the prologue on David Milgaard and Thomas Sophonow and eyewitness testimony, and consider the following questions in light of what you now know about memory:

   1. Use the three-stage model of memory to explain false eyewitness identification of innocent people.

   2. Explain how retrieval cues influence eyewitness recall and recognition of accused in a photo line-up.

   3. Give two examples of how flashbulb memories alter eyewitness recall of crime.

   4. Can a police officer's or lawyer's wording of questions significantly alter eyewitness recall? Describe the research discussed in Module 19 that supports your answer.

   5. Use the levels-of-processing theory developed by Canadians Fergus Craik and Robert Lockhart to explain the degree to which new material is analyzed by witnesses to a crime.

CHAPTER 7
Thinking, Language, and Intelligence

Source: © Kim Gunkel/Getty Images RF.

Key Concepts for Chapter 7

Prologue

Source: © Alex Wong/Getty Images.

Wireless Freedom

You come to psychology class each week with the best intentions—pay close attention to your professor, take good lecture notes, and ultimately pass the course. But that was before you were given a BlackBerry for your birthday. These days, you are lucky if you can get through an entire lecture without texting friends, checking voicemail, and surfing the Internet. You ask yourself—what happened to my best intentions for passing psychology?

Canadian Mike Lazaridis, inventor of Research In Motion's BlackBerry technology, has a different perspective on handheld wireless communication. Lazaridis would encourage you to use your Blackberry in and out of the classroom. Rather being enslaved by the Internet, Lazaridis believes that handheld wireless technology liberates students like you—to learn wherever you want, whenever you want, and however you want (Znaimer, 2006).

As technology gets more and more complicated, BlackBerry-inventor Lazaridis has one objective for his invention: keep it simple. He wanted to invent a small, handheld device that "can do a lot without complicating the user's life" (Znaimer, 2006). Whether or not BlackBerry technology simplifies our lives, one thing is clear—Lazaridis has the elusive quality that marks successful inventors: creativity.

Where did Lazaridis's creativity come from? More generally, how do people use information to devise innovative solutions to problems? How do people think about, understand, and, through language, describe the world? And what is the nature of human intelligence, which permits people to learn about, understand, and adapt to their surroundings?

In this chapter, we focus on thinking, language, and intelligence. Each of these topics is central to the branch of psychology known as *cognitive psychology*. **Cognitive psychology** focuses on the study of higher mental processes, including thinking, language, memory, problem solving, knowing, reasoning, judging, and decision making. Clearly, the realm of cognitive psychology is broad.

Cognitive psychology
The branch of psychology that focuses on the study of higher mental processes, including thinking, language, memory, problem solving, knowing, reasoning, judging, and decision making.

Thinking and Reasoning

LEARNING OBJECTIVES

LO1 **What is** thinking?

LO2 **What processes** underlie reasoning and decision making?

LO3 **How do** people approach and solve problems?

LO4 **What are** the major obstacles to problem solving?

What are you thinking about at this moment?

The mere ability to pose such a question underscores the distinctive nature of the human ability to think. No other species contemplates, analyzes, recollects, or plans the way humans do. Understanding what thinking is, however, goes beyond knowing that we think. Philosophers, for example, have argued for generations about the meaning of thinking, with some placing it at the core of human beings' understanding of their own existence.

Thinking is the manipulation of mental representations of information. A representation may take the form of a word, a visual image, a sound, or data in any other sensory modality stored in memory. Thinking transforms a particular representation of information into new and different forms in order to answer questions, solve problems, or reach goals.

Although a clear sense of what specifically occurs when we think remains elusive, our understanding of the nature of the fundamental elements involved in thinking is growing. We begin by considering our use of mental images and concepts, the building blocks of thought.

Mental Images: Examining the Mind's Eye

Think of your best friend. Chances are that you "see" some kind of visual image when asked to think of her or him, or any other person or object, for that matter. To some cognitive psychologists, such mental images constitute a major part of thinking.

Mental images are representations in the mind of an object or event. They are not just visual representations; our ability to "hear" a tune in our heads also relies on a mental image. In fact, every sensory modality may produce corresponding mental images (Kosslyn, 2005; De Beni, Pazzaglia, & Gardini, 2007; Gardini et al., 2009).

Research has found that our mental images have many of the properties of the actual stimuli they represent. For example, it takes the mind longer to scan mental images of large objects than of small ones, just as the eye takes longer to scan an actual large object than an actual small one. Similarly, we are able to manipulate and rotate mental images of objects, just as we are able to manipulate and rotate them in the real world (Mast & Kosslyn, 2002; Iachini & Giusberti, 2004; Zacks, 2008; see Figure 1).

Some experts see the production of mental images as a way to improve various skills. For instance, many athletes use mental imagery in their training. Basketball players may try to produce vivid and detailed images of the court, the

---

Thinking
The manipulation of mental representations of information.

Mental images
Representations in the mind of an object or event.

FIGURE 1

Try to mentally rotate one of each pair of patterns to see if it is the same as the other member of that pair. It's likely that the farther you have to mentally rotate a pattern, the longer it will take to decide if the patterns match one another. Does this mean that it will take you longer to visualize a map of the world than a map of Canada? Why or why not?

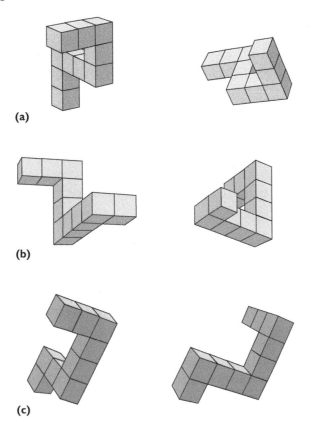

(a)

(b)

(c)

basket, the ball, and the noisy crowd. They may visualize themselves taking a foul shot, watching the ball, and hearing the swish as it goes through the net. And it works: The use of mental imagery can lead to improved performance in sports (Mamassis & Doganis, 2004; Moran, 2009).

Concepts: Categorizing the World

If someone asked you what was in your kitchen cabinets, you might answer with a detailed list of items ("a jar of peanut butter, three boxes of macaroni and cheese, six unmatched dinner plates," and so forth). More likely, though, you would respond by naming some broader categories, such as "food" and "dishes."

Using such categories reflects the operation of concepts. **Concepts** are mental groupings of similar objects, events, or people. Concepts enable us to organize complex phenomena into simpler, and therefore more easily usable, cognitive categories (Murphy, 2005; Connolly, 2007).

Concepts help us classify newly encountered objects on the basis of our past experience. For example, we can surmise that someone tapping a handheld screen is probably using some kind of computer or PDA, even if we have never encountered that specific model before. Ultimately, concepts influence behaviour; we would assume, for instance, that it might be appropriate to pet an animal after determining that it is a dog, whereas we would behave differently after classifying the animal as a wolf.

Concepts
A mental grouping of similar objects, events, or people.

When cognitive psychologists first studied concepts, they focused on those which were clearly defined by a unique set of properties or features. For example, an equilateral triangle is a closed shape that has three sides of equal length. If an object has these characteristics, it is an equilateral triangle; if it does not, it is not an equilateral triangle.

Other concepts—often those with the most relevance to our everyday lives—are more ambiguous and difficult to define. For instance, broader concepts such as "table" and "bird" have a set of general, relatively loose characteristic features, rather than unique, clearly defined properties that distinguish an example of the concept from a nonexample. When we consider these more ambiguous concepts, we usually think in terms of examples called **prototypes**. Prototypes are typical, highly representative examples of a concept that correspond to our mental image or best example of the concept. For instance, although a robin and an ostrich are both examples of birds, the robin is an example that comes to most people's minds far more readily. Consequently, robin is a prototype of the concept "bird." Similarly, when we think of the concept of a table, we're likely to think of a coffee table before we think of a drafting table, making a coffee table closer to our prototype of a table.

Concepts enable us to think about and understand more readily the complex world in which we live. For example, the suppositions we make about the reasons for other people's behaviour are based on the ways in which we classify behaviour. Hence, our conclusion that a person who washes her hands twenty times a day could vary, depending on whether we place her behaviour within the conceptual framework of a health-care worker or a mental patient. Similarly, physicians make diagnoses by drawing on concepts and prototypes of symptoms that they learned about in medical school.

Algorithms and Heuristics

When faced with making a decision, we often turn to various kinds of cognitive shortcuts, known as algorithms and heuristics, to help us. An **algorithm** is a rule that, if applied appropriately, guarantees a solution to a problem. We can use an algorithm even if we cannot understand why it works. For example, you may know that the length of the third side of a right triangle can be found by using the formula $a^2 + b^2 = c^2$, although you may not have the foggiest notion of the mathematical principles behind the formula.

For many problems and decisions, however, no algorithm is available. In those instances, we may be able to use heuristics to help us. A **heuristic** is a thinking strategy that may lead us to a solution to a problem or decision, but—unlike algorithms—may sometimes lead to errors. Heuristics enhance the likelihood of success in coming to a solution, but, unlike algorithms, they cannot ensure it. For example, when I play tic-tac-toe, I follow the heuristic of placing an X in the centre square when I start the game. This tactic doesn't guarantee that I will win, but experience has taught me that it will increase my chances of success. Similarly, some students follow the heuristic of preparing for a test by ignoring the assigned textbook reading and only studying the lecture notes—a strategy that may or may not pay off.

Although heuristics often help people solve problems and make decisions, certain kinds of heuristics may lead to inaccurate conclusions. For example, we sometimes use the *representativeness heuristic*, a rule we apply when we judge people by the degree to which they represent a certain category or group of people. Suppose, for instance, you are the owner of a fast-food store that has been robbed many times by teenagers. The representativeness heuristic

STUDY ALERT!

Remember that algorithms are rules that *always* provide a solution, while heuristics are shortcuts or strategies that *may* provide a solution.

Prototypes
Typical, highly representative examples of a concept.

Algorithm
A rule that, if applied appropriately, guarantees a solution to a problem.

Heuristic
A thinking strategy that may lead us to a solution to a problem or decision, but—unlike algorithms—may sometimes lead to errors.

would lead you to raise your guard each time someone of this age group enters your store (even though, statistically, it is unlikely that any given teenager will rob the store) (Fisk, Bury, & Holden, 2006; Nilsson, Juslin, & Olsson, 2008).

The *availability heuristic* involves judging the probability of an event on the basis of how easily the event can be recalled from memory. According to this heuristic, we assume that events we remember easily are likely to have occurred more frequently in the past—and are more likely to occur in the future—than events that are harder to remember.

For instance, people are usually more afraid of dying in a plane crash than in an auto accident, despite statistics clearly showing that airplane travel is much safer than auto travel. The reason is that plane crashes receive far more publicity than car crashes do, and they are therefore more easily remembered. The *availability heuristic* leads people to conclude that they are in greater jeopardy in an airplane than in a car (Oppenheimer, 2004; Fox, 2006; Kluger, 2006; Caruso, 2008).

Are algorithms and heuristics confined to human thinking, or can computers be programmed to use them to mimic human thinking and problem solving? As we discuss next, scientists are certainly trying.

Solving Problems

According to an old legend, a group of Vietnamese monks guard three towers on which sit sixty-four golden rings. The monks believe that if they succeed in moving the rings from the first tower to the third according to a series of rigid rules, the world as we know it will come to an end. (Should you prefer that the world remain in its present state, there's no need for immediate concern: The puzzle is so complex that it will take the monks about a trillion years to solve it.)

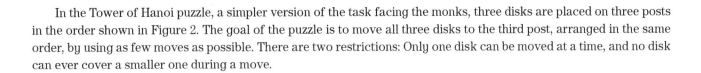

STUDY ALERT!

Use the three steps of problem solving to organize your studying: Preparation, Production, and Judgment (PPJ).

In the Tower of Hanoi puzzle, a simpler version of the task facing the monks, three disks are placed on three posts in the order shown in Figure 2. The goal of the puzzle is to move all three disks to the third post, arranged in the same order, by using as few moves as possible. There are two restrictions: Only one disk can be moved at a time, and no disk can ever cover a smaller one during a move.

FIGURE 2

The goal of the Tower of Hanoi puzzle is to move all three disks from the first post to the third and still preserve the original order of the disks, using the fewest number of moves possible while following the rules that only one disk at a time can be moved and no disk can cover a smaller one during a move. Try it yourself before you look at the solution, which is listed according to the sequence of moves. (Solution: Move C to 3, B to 2, C to 2, A to 3, C to 1, B to 3, and C to 3.)

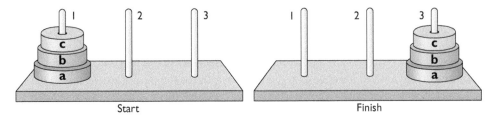

Start   Finish

Why are cognitive psychologists interested in the Tower of Hanoi problem? Because the way people go about solving such puzzles helps illuminate how people solve complex, real-life problems. Psychologists have found that problem solving typically involves the three steps illustrated in Figure 3: preparing to create solutions, producing solutions, and evaluating the solutions that have been generated.

FIGURE 3

Steps in problem solving.

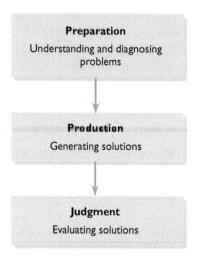

Preparation: Understanding and Diagnosing Problems

When approaching a problem like the Tower of Hanoi, most people begin by trying to understand the problem thoroughly. If the problem is a novel one, they probably will pay particular attention to any restrictions placed on coming up with a solution—such as the rule for moving only one disk at a time in the Tower of Hanoi problem. If, by contrast, the problem is a familiar one, they are apt to spend considerably less time in this preparation stage.

Problems vary from well defined to ill defined (Reitman, 1965; Arlin, 1989; Evans, 2004). In a *well-defined problem*—such as a mathematical equation or the solution to a jigsaw puzzle—both the nature of the problem itself and the information needed to solve it are available and clear. Thus, we can make straightforward judgments about whether a potential solution is appropriate. With an *ill-defined problem*, such as how to increase morale on an assembly line or bring peace to the Middle East, not only may the specific nature of the problem be unclear, the information required to solve the problem may be even less obvious (Evans, 2004; Vartanian, 2009).

KINDS OF PROBLEMS

Typically, a problem falls into one of the three categories shown in Figure 4: arrangement, inducing structure, and transformation. Solving each type requires somewhat different kinds of psychological skills and knowledge (Spitz, 1987; Chronicle, MacGregor, & Ormerod, 2004).

Arrangement problems require the problem solver to rearrange or recombine elements in a way that will satisfy a certain criterion. Usually, several different arrangements can be made, but only one or a few of the arrangements will produce a solution. Anagram problems and jigsaw puzzles are examples of arrangement problems (Coventry et al., 2003).

In *problems of inducing structure*, a person must identify the existing relationships among the elements presented and then construct a new relationship among them. In such a problem, the problem solver must determine not only the relationships among the elements but also the structure and size of the elements involved. In the example shown in Figure 4, a person must first determine that the solution requires the numbers to be considered in pairs (14-24-34-44-54-64). Only after identifying that part of the problem can a person determine the solution rule (the first number of each pair increases by one, while the second number remains the same).

The Tower of Hanoi puzzle represents the third kind of problem—*transformation problems*—which consist of an initial state, a goal state, and a method for changing the initial state into the goal state. In the Tower of Hanoi problem, the initial state is the original configuration, the goal state is to have the three disks on the third peg, and the method is the rules for moving the disks (Mataix-Cols & Bartres-Faz, 2002; Emick & Welsh, 2005; Majeres, 2007).

Whether the problem is one of arrangement, inducing structure, or transformation, the preparation stage of understanding and diagnosing is critical in problem solving because it allows us to develop our own cognitive representation of the problem and to place it within a personal framework. We may divide the problem into subparts or ignore some information as we try to simplify the task. Winnowing out nonessential information is often a critical step in the preparation stage of problem solving.

FIGURE 4

The three major categories of problems: (a) arrangement, (b) inducing structure, and (c) transformation. Solutions appear in Figure 5.

(a) Arrangement problems

1. Anagrams: Rearrange the letters in each set to make an English word:

2. Two strings hang from a ceiling but are too far apart to allow a person to hold one and walk to the other. On the floor are a book of matches, a screwdriver, and a few pieces of cotton. How could the strings be tied together?

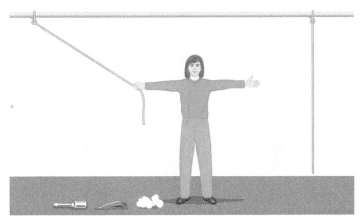

(b) Problems of inducing structure

1. What number comes next in the series?

   1 4 2 4 3 4 4 4 5 4 6 4

2. Complete these analogies:

   baseball is to bat as tennis is to _____

   merchant is to sell as customer is to _____

(c) Transformation problems

1. Water jars: A person has three jars with the following capacities:

   Jar A: 828 ml   Jar B: 207 ml   Jar C: 147 ml

   How can the person measure exactly 327 ml of water?

2. Ten coins are arranged in the following way. By moving only *two* of the coins, make two rows that each contains six coins.

FRAMING THE PROBLEM

Our ability to represent a problem—and the kind of solution we eventually come to—depends on the way a problem is phrased, or framed. Consider, for example, if you were a cancer patient having to choose between surgery and radiation and were given the two sets of treatment options shown in nearby Figure 6 (Tversky & Kahneman, 1987; Chandran & Menon, 2004). When the options are framed in terms of the likelihood of survival, only 18 percent of participants in a study chose radiation over surgery. However, when the choice was framed in terms of the likelihood of dying, 44 percent chose radiation over surgery—even though the outcomes are identical in both sets of framing conditions.

FIGURE 5

Solutions to the problems in Figure 4.

(a) Arrangement problems

1. FACET, DOUBT, THICK, NAIVE, ANVIL

2. The screwdriver is tied to one of the strings. This makes a pendulum that can be swung to reach the other string.

(b) Problems of inducing structure

1. 7

2. racquet; buy

(c) Transformation problems

1. Fill jar A; empty into jar B once and into jar C twice. What remains in jar A is 327 ml

2.

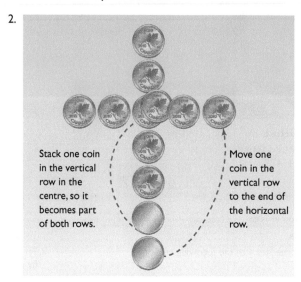

Stack one coin in the vertical row in the centre, so it becomes part of both rows.

Move one coin in the vertical row to the end of the horizontal row.

Production: Generating Solutions

After preparation, the next stage in problem solving is the production of possible solutions. If a problem is relatively simple, we may already have a direct solution stored in long-term memory, and all we need to do is retrieve the appropriate information. If we cannot retrieve or do not know the solution, we must generate possible solutions and compare them with information in long- and short-term memory.

At the most basic level, we can solve problems through trial and error. Thomas Edison invented the light bulb only because he tried thousands of different kinds of materials for a filament before he found one that worked (carbon). The difficulty with trial and error, of course, is that some problems are so complicated that it would take a lifetime to try out every possibility. For example, according to some estimates, there are some 10^{120} possible sequences of chess moves (Fine & Fine, 2003).

In place of trial and error, complex problem solving often involves the use of heuristics, cognitive shortcuts that can generate solutions. Probably the most frequently applied heuristic in problem solving is a **means-ends analysis**, which involves repeated tests for differences between the desired outcome and what currently exists. Consider this simple example (Newell & Simon, 1972; Huber, Beckmann, & Herrmann, 2004; Chrysikou, 2006):

Means-ends analysis
Involves repeated tests for differences between the desired outcome and what currently exists.

I want to get to campus for my morning classes. What's the difference between what I have and what I want? One of distance. What changes distance? My automobile. My automobile won't work. What is needed to make it work? A new battery. What has new batteries? An auto repair shop. . . .

In a means-end analysis, each step brings the problem solver closer to a resolution. Although this approach is often effective, if the problem requires indirect steps that temporarily *increase* the discrepancy between a current state and the solution, means-ends analysis can be counterproductive. For example, sometimes the fastest route to the summit of a mountain requires a mountain climber to backtrack temporarily; a means-end approach—which implies that the mountain climber should always forge ahead and upward—will be ineffective in such instances.

For other problems, the best approach is to work backward by focusing on the goal, rather than the starting point, of the problem. Consider, for example, the water lily problem:

> Water lilies are growing on Blue Lake. The water lilies grow rapidly, so that the amount of water surface covered by lilies doubles every 24 hours.

> On the first day of summer, there was just one water lily. On the 90th day of the summer, the lake was entirely covered. On what day was the lake half covered? (Reisberg, 1997).

If you start searching for a solution to the problem by thinking about the initial state on day 1 (one water lily) and move forward from there, you're facing a daunting task of trial-and-error estimation. But try taking a different approach: Start with day 90, when the entire lake was covered with lilies. Given that the lilies double their coverage daily, on the prior day only half the lake was covered. The answer, then, is day 89, a solution found by working backward (Bourne et al., 1986; Hunt, 1994).

FIGURE 6

A decision often is affected by the way a problem is framed. In this case, when mortality is the framework, most would choose radiation over surgery.

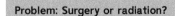

Problem: Surgery or radiation?

Survival Frame

Surgery: Of 100 people having surgery, 90 live through the post-operative period, 68 are alive at the end of the first year, and 34 are alive at the end of five years.

Radiation: Of 100 people having radiation therapy, all live through the treatment, 77 are alive at the end of one year, and 22 are alive at the end of five years.

Mortality Frame

Surgery: Of 100 people having surgery, 10 die during surgery, 32 die by the end of the first year, and 66 die by the end of five years.

Radiation: Of 100 people having radiation therapy, none die during the treatment, 23 die by the end of one year, and 78 die by the end of five years.

Far more patients choose surgery

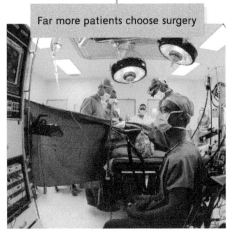

Far more patients choose radiation

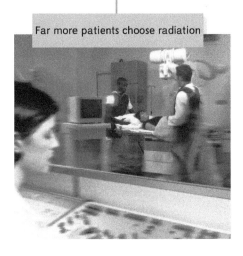

FORMING SUBGOALS: DIVIDING PROBLEMS INTO THEIR PARTS

Another heuristic commonly used to generate solutions is to divide a problem into intermediate steps, or *subgoals*, and solve each of those steps. For instance, in our modified Tower of Hanoi problem, we could choose several obvious subgoals, such as moving the largest disk to the third post.

If solving a subgoal is a step toward the ultimate solution to a problem, identifying subgoals is an appropriate strategy. In some cases, however, forming subgoals is not all that helpful and may actually increase the time needed to find a solution. For example, some problems cannot be subdivided. Others—like some complicated mathematical problems—are so complex that it takes longer to identify the appropriate subdivisions than to solve the problem by other means (Reed, 1996; Kaller et al., 2004; Fishbach, Dhar, & Zhang, 2006).

INSIGHT: SUDDEN AWARENESS

Some approaches to generating possible solutions focus less on step-by-step heuristics than on the sudden bursts of comprehension that one may experience during efforts to solve a problem. Just after World War I, the German psychologist Wolfgang Köhler examined learning and problem-solving processes in chimpanzees (Köhler, 1927). In his studies, Köhler exposed chimps to challenging situations in which the elements of the solution were all present; all the chimps needed to do was put them together.

In one of Köhler's studies, chimps were kept in a cage in which boxes and sticks were strewn about, and a bunch of tantalizing bananas hung from the ceiling, out of reach. Initially, the chimps made trial-and-error attempts to get to the bananas: They would throw the sticks at the bananas, jump from one of the boxes, or leap wildly from the ground. Frequently, they would seem to give up in frustration, leaving the bananas dangling temptingly overhead. But then, in what seemed like a sudden revelation, they would stop whatever they were doing and stand on a box to reach the bananas with a stick. Köhler called the cognitive process underlying the chimps' new behaviour **insight**, a sudden awareness of the relationships among various elements that had previously appeared to be unrelated.

In an impressive display of insight, Sultan, one of the chimpanzees in Köhler's experiments in problem solving, sees a bunch of bananas that is out of his reach (a). He then carries over several crates (b), stacks them, and stands on them to reach the bananas (c).

Source: © SuperStock.

Insight
A sudden awareness of the relationships among various elements that had previously appeared to be independent of one another.

Although Köhler emphasized the apparent suddenness of insightful solutions, subsequent research has shown that prior experience and trial-and-error practise in problem solving must precede "insight." Consequently, the chimps' behaviour may simply represent the chaining together of previously learned responses, which is no different from the way a pigeon learns by trial and error to peck a key (Epstein, 1996; Windholz & Lamal, 2002).

Judgment: Evaluating the Solutions

The final stage in problem solving is judging the adequacy of a solution. Often this is a simple matter: If the solution is clear—as in the Tower of Hanoi problem—we will know immediately whether we have been successful (Varma, 2007).

If the solution is less concrete or if there is no single correct solution, evaluating solutions becomes more difficult. In such instances, we must decide which alternative solution is best. Unfortunately, we often quite inaccurately estimate the quality of our own ideas (Eizenberg & Zaslavsky, 2004). For instance, a team of drug researchers working for a particular company may consider their remedy for an illness to be superior to all others, overestimating the likelihood of their success and downplaying the approaches of competing drug companies.

Theoretically, if we rely on appropriate heuristics and valid information to make decisions, we can make accurate choices among alternative solutions. However, as we see next, several kinds of obstacles to and biases in problem solving affect the quality of the decisions and judgments we make.

Impediments to Solutions: Why Is Problem Solving Such a Problem?

Consider the following problem-solving test (Duncker, 1945):

> You are given a set of tacks, candles, and matches, each in a small box, and told your goal is to place three candles at eye level on a nearby door, so that wax will not drip on the floor as the candles burn [see Figure 7]. How would you approach this challenge?

FIGURE 7

The problem here is to place three candles at eye level on a nearby door so that the wax will not drip on the floor as the candles burn—using only material in the figure. For a solution turn to Figure 9.

If you have difficulty solving the problem, you are not alone. Most people cannot solve it when it is presented in the manner illustrated in the figure, in which the objects are *inside* the boxes. However, if the objects were presented *beside* the boxes, just resting on the table, chances are that you would solve the problem much more readily—which, in case you are wondering, requires tacking the boxes to the door and then placing the candles inside them (see Figure 9).

The difficulty you probably encountered in solving this problem stems from its presentation, which misled you at the initial preparation stage. Actually, significant obstacles to problem solving can exist at each of the three major stages. Although cognitive approaches to problem solving suggest that thinking proceeds along fairly rational, logical lines as a person confronts a problem and considers various solutions, several factors can hinder the development of creative, appropriate, and accurate solutions.

- *Functional fixedness.* The difficulty most people experience with the candle problem is caused by **functional fixedness**, the tendency to think of an object only in terms of its typical use. For instance, functional fixedness probably leads you to think of this book as something to read, instead of its potential use as a doorstop or as kindling for a fire. In the candle problem, because the objects are first presented inside the boxes, functional fixedness leads most people to see the boxes simply as containers for the objects they hold rather than as a potential part of the solution. They cannot envision another function for the boxes.

Functional fixedness
The tendency to think of an object only in terms of its typical use.

- *Mental set.* Functional fixedness is an example of a broader phenomenon known as **mental set**, the tendency for old patterns of problem solving to persist. A classic experiment (Luchins, 1946) demonstrated this phenomenon. As you can see in Figure 8, the object of the task is to use the jars in each row to measure out the designated amount of liquid. (Try it yourself to get a sense of the power of mental set before moving on.)

FIGURE 8

Try this classic demonstration, which illustrates the importance of mental set in problem solving. The object is to use the jars in each row to measure out the designated amount of liquid. After you figure out the solution for the first five rows, you'll probably have trouble with the sixth row—even though the solution is actually easier. In fact, if you had tried to solve the problem in the sixth row first, you probably would have had no difficulty at all.

Given jars with these capacities (in ml):

	A	B	C	Obtain:
1.	21	127	3	100
2.	14	163	25	99
3.	18	43	10	5
4.	9	42	6	21
5.	20	59	4	31
6.	28	76	3	25

If you have tried to solve the problem, you know that the first five rows are all solved in the same way: First fill the largest jar (B) and then from it fill the middle-size jar (A) once and the smallest jar (C) two times. What is left in B is the designated amount. (Stated as a formula, the designated amount is $B - A - 2C$.) The demonstration of mental set comes in the sixth row of the problem, a point at which you probably encountered some difficulty. If you are like most people, you tried the formula and were perplexed when it failed. Chances are, in fact, that you missed the simple (but different) solution to the problem, which involves merely subtracting C from A. Interestingly, people who were given the problem in row 6 *first* had no difficulty with it at all.

- *Inaccurate evaluation of solutions.* When the American nuclear power plant at Three Mile Island in Pennsylvania suffered its initial malfunction in 1979, a disaster that almost led to a nuclear meltdown, the plant operators immediately had to solve a problem of the most serious kind. Several monitors gave contradictory information about the source of the problem: One suggested that the pressure was too high, leading to the danger of an explosion; others indicated that the pressure was too low, which could lead to a meltdown. Although the pressure was, in fact, too low, the supervisors on duty relied on the one monitor—which turned out to be faulty—that suggested that the pressure was too high. Once they had made their decision and acted on it, they ignored the contradictory evidence from the other monitors (Wickens, 1984).

The operators' mistake exemplifies **confirmation bias**, in which problem solvers seek out and weight more heavily initial hypotheses and ignore contradictory information that supports alternative hypotheses or solutions. Even when we find evidence that contradicts a solution we have chosen, we are apt to stick with our original hypothesis.

Mental set
The tendency for old patterns of problem solving to persist.

Confirmation bias
The tendency to seek out and weight more heavily information that supports one's initial hypotheses and to ignore contradictory information that supports alternative hypotheses or solutions.

FIGURE 9

A solution to the problem in Figure 7 involves tacking the boxes to the door and placing the candles in the boxes.

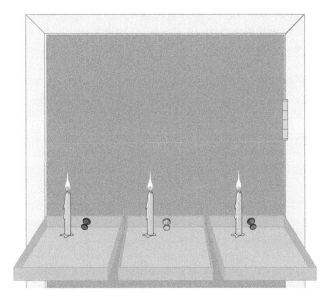

Confirmation bias occurs for several reasons. For one thing, rethinking a problem that appears to be solved already takes extra cognitive effort, and so we are apt to stick with our first solution. For another, we give greater weight to subsequent information that supports our initial position than to information that is not supportive of it (Gilovich, Griffin, & Kahneman, 2002; Evans & Feeney, 2004).

Creativity and Problem Solving

Despite obstacles to problem solving, many people adeptly discover creative solutions to problems. One enduring question that cognitive psychologists have sought to answer is what factors underlie **creativity**, the ability to generate original ideas or solve problems in novel ways.

Although identifying the stages of problem solving helps us understand how people approach and solve problems, it does little to explain why some people come up with better solutions than others do. For instance, even the possible solutions to a simple problem often show wide discrepancies. Consider, for example, how you might respond to the question "How many uses can you think of for a newspaper?"

Now compare your solution with this one proposed by a 10-year-old boy:

> You can read it, write on it, lay it down and paint a picture on it . . . You could put it in your door for decoration, put it in the garbage can, put it on a chair if the chair is messy. If you have a puppy, you put newspaper in its box or put it in your backyard for the dog to play with. When you build something and you don't want anyone to see it, put newspaper around it. Put newspaper on the floor if you have no mattress, use it to pick up something hot, use it to stop bleeding, or to catch the drips from drying clothes. You can use a newspaper for curtains, put it in your shoe to cover what is hurting your foot, make a kite out of it, shade a light that is too bright. You can wrap fish in it, wipe windows, or wrap money in it . . . You put washed shoes in newspaper, wipe eyeglasses with it, put it under a dripping sink, put a plant on it, make a paper bowl out of it, use it for a hat if it is raining, tie it on your feet for slippers. You can put it on the sand if you had no towel, use it for bases in baseball, make paper airplanes with it, use it as a dustpan when you sweep, ball it up for the cat to play with, wrap your hands in it if it is cold (Ward, Kogan, & Pankove, 1972).

This list shows extraordinary creativity. Unfortunately, it is much easier to identify *examples* of creativity than to determine its causes. For example, the invention of the BlackBerry by Mike Lazaridis discussed in the

Creativity
The ability to generate original ideas or solve problems in novel ways.

Prologue is an extraordinary illustration of creativity. Several factors, however, seem to be associated with creativity (Csikszentmihalyi, 1997; Niu & Sternberg, 2003; Kaufman & Baer, 2005; Simonton, 2003, 2009).

However, we do know that several characteristics are associated with creativity. For one thing, highly creative individuals show **divergent thinking**, the ability to generate unusual, yet appropriate, responses to problems or questions. This type of thinking contrasts with **convergent thinking**, which produces responses that are based primarily on knowledge and logic. For instance, someone relying on convergent thinking would answer "You can read it" to the query "What can you do with a newspaper?" In contrast, "You can use it as a dustpan" is a more divergent—and creative—response (Cropley, 2006; Runco, 2006; Schepers & van den Berg, 2007).

Another aspect of creativity is its *cognitive complexity,* or preference for elaborate, intricate, and complex stimuli and thinking patterns. For instance, creative people often have a wider range of interests and are more independent and more interested in philosophical or abstract problems than are less creative individuals (Barron, 1990, Richards, 2006). In addition, there may be differences in how the brain processes information in more creative people, as we discuss in the *Applying Psychology in the Real World* box.

The role of creativity in social settings is a more recent addition to the field of creativity. In his 2005 book *The Rise of Creative Cities: Cities and the Creative Class,* University of Toronto professor Richard Florida examines the role of creativity in social settings. Florida proposes that communities that accept diversity (e.g., sexual and cultural differences) are more open to creative and innovative concepts (Olive, 2007).

One factor that is *not* closely related to creativity is intelligence. Traditional intelligence tests, which ask focused questions that have only one acceptable answer, tap convergent thinking skills. Highly creative people may therefore find that such tests penalize their divergent thinking. This may explain why researchers consistently find that creativity is only slightly related to school grades and intelligence when intelligence is measured using traditional intelligence tests (Sternberg & O'Hara, 2000; Heilman, 2005).

STUDY ALERT!

Remember divergent thinking produces *different* and *diverse* kinds of responses, while convergent thinking produces more commonsense kinds of responses.

APPLYING PSYCHOLOGY in the Real World

Eureka! Understanding the Underpinnings of Creativity

The volunteers looked like electronic Medusas, with wires snaking from 30 electrodes glued to their scalps and recording their brain activity.

As they peered at a computer screen, a brainteaser flashed: Turn the incorrect Roman-numeral equation XI + I = X, made out of 10 sticks, into a correct one by moving as few sticks as possible. As soon as the volunteers figured it out, they hit a key, and another puzzle appeared. None could be solved by a plug-and-chug approach; all required insight and creativity (Begley, 2004, p. B1).

If you were one of the participants in this experiment, designed to examine the neuroscience of creativity, you might come to a quick answer. Many people arrive at a solution quite soon, saying that only one stick needs to be moved. They reason that by moving the "I" stick on the left-hand side of the equation to the right side, the equation becomes XI = XI.

Not bad—but not the most creative solution. The more creative response is that you need to move *no* sticks in order to make the equation correct. To make the equation correct, all you need to do is turn it upside down, making the equation X = I + IX.

(continued)

Divergent thinking
The ability to generate unusual, yet nonetheless appropriate, responses to problems or questions.

Convergent thinking
The ability to produce responses that are based primarily on knowledge and logic.

To the excitement of neuroscientists seeking to understand the biology underlying creativity, it turns out the more creative response also produces a different pattern of brain activity than more common responses. According to neuroscientist Bhavin Sheth and colleagues, problem-solvers who found the more creative solution tended to do so in a kind of "Eureka!" moment, in which the solution suddenly came to them. At that moment, a sudden decrease occurred in lower-frequency brain waves, waves that usually signify brain activity involving memory and other types of coordinated mental activity. However, the decrease in lower-frequency brain waves was followed by an increase in higher-frequency *theta brain waves* at the moment that the creative solution came to mind (Begley, 2004; Sheth, Bhattacharya, & Wu, 2004).

Because theta waves are associated with the encoding of novel information, their appearance at the "Eureka!" moment suggests that there may have been a shift in the way the problem was viewed. Specifically, problem-solvers may have suddenly seen the problem in spatial terms rather than viewing it as a numeric problem.

Psychologists at the University of Toronto and Harvard University discovered the brains of creative people to be more receptive to stimulation from the environment than average people. Researchers speculated that this openness to external stimuli combined with high IQ may explain the original thinking patterns of creative individuals (University of Toronto, 2003).

Other researchers, taking a different approach, have looked at the link between creativity and brain disorders. For example, some research has found a link between psychological problems and creativity, although the relationship is inconsistent. Despite some conspicuous examples of well-known and highly creative individuals who appear to have suffered from psychological disorders (such as writer Sylvia Plath and artist Vincent Van Gogh), there are also many creative people who appear quite psychologically healthy (Kaufman & Baer, 2005).

Still, according to psychologist James Kaufman, the incidence of mental illness is greater in certain types of creative artists. For example, poets are more likely to suffer from mental illness than are other kinds of writers (Kaufman, 2005).

Clearly, it's still too early for psychologists to claim they have unlocked the genius of highly creative people such as a musician like Bach or a painter like Picasso. However, they are beginning to understand the basis of creativity in more everyday sorts of people.

Evaluate

1. _____ are representations in the mind of an object or event.

2. _____ are categorizations of objects that share common properties.

3. Solving a problem by trying to reduce the difference between the current state and the goal state is known as a _____.

4. _____ is the term used to describe the sudden "flash" of revelation that often accompanies the solution to a problem.

5. Thinking of an object only in terms of its typical use is known as _____. A broader, related tendency for old problem-solving patterns to persist is known as a _____.

6. Generating unusual but appropriate approaches to a question is known as _____ _____.

Answers to Evaluate Questions

1. mental images; 2. concepts; 3. means-end analysis; 4. insight; 5. functional fixedness, mental set; 6. divergent thinking

Key Terms

algorithm	creativity	means-ends analysis
cognitive psychology	divergent thinking	mental images
concepts	functional fixedness	mental set
confirmation bias	heuristic	prototypes
convergent thinking	insight	thinking

Language

LEARNING OBJECTIVES

LO5 **How do** people use language?

LO6 **How does** language develop?

> 'Twas brillig, and the slithy toves
> Did gyre and gimble in the wabe:
> All mimsy were the borogoves,
> And the mome raths outgrabe.

Although few of us have ever come face to face with a tove, we have little difficulty in discerning that in Lewis Carroll's (1872) poem "Jabberwocky," the expression *slithy toves* contains an adjective, *slithy*, and the noun it modifies, *toves*.

Our ability to make sense out of nonsense, if the nonsense follows typical rules of **language**, illustrates the complexity of both human language and the cognitive processes that underlie its development and use. The use of language—the communication of information through symbols arranged according to systematic rules—is an important cognitive ability, one that is indispensable for communicating with others. Not only is language central to communication, it is also closely tied to the very way in which we think about and understand the world. No wonder psychologists have devoted considerable attention to studying language (Stapel & Semin, 2007; Hoff, 2008; Reisberg, 2009).

Grammar: Language's Language

To understand how language develops and relates to thought, we first need to review some of the formal elements of language. The basic structure of language rests on **grammar**, the system of rules that determine how our thoughts can be expressed.

Grammar deals with three major components of language: phonology, syntax, and semantics. **Phonology** is the study of the smallest basic units of speech, called **phonemes**, that affect meaning, and of the way we use those sounds to form words and produce meaning. For instance, the *a* sound in *fat* and the *a* sound in *fate* represent two different phonemes in English (Vihman, 1996; Baddeley, Gathercole, & Papagno, 1998).

Linguists have identified more than 800 different phonemes among all the world's languages. Although English speakers use just 52 phonemes to produce words, other languages use from as few as 15 to as many as 141. Differences

---

Language
The communication of information through symbols arranged according to systematic rules.

Grammar
The system of rules that determine how our thoughts can be expressed.

Phonology
The study of the smallest units of speech, called phonemes.

Phonemes
The smallest units of speech.

in phonemes are one reason people have difficulty learning other languages. For example, to a Japanese speaker, whose native language does not have an *r* phoneme, English words such as *roar* present some difficulty (Gibbs, 2002; Iverson et al., 2003).

Syntax refers to the rules that indicate how words and phrases can be combined to form sentences. Every language has intricate rules that guide the order in which words may be strung together to communicate meaning. English speakers have no difficulty recognizing that "Radio down the turn" is not a meaningful sequence, whereas "Turn down the radio" is. To understand the effect of syntax in English, consider the changes in meaning caused by the different word orders in the following three utterances: "John kidnapped the boy," "John, the kidnapped boy," and "The boy kidnapped John" (Lasnik, 1990; Eberhard, Cutting, & Bock, 2005; Robert, 2006).

The third major component of language is **semantics**, the meanings of words and sentences (Larson, 1990; Hipkiss, 1995; O'Grady & Dobrovolsky, 1996; Richgels, 2004). Semantic rules allow us to use words to convey the subtlest nuances. For instance, we are able to make the distinction between "The truck hit Laura" (which we would be likely to say if we had just seen the vehicle hitting Laura) and "Laura was hit by a truck" (which we would probably say if someone asked why Laura was missing class while she recuperated).

Despite the complexities of language, most of us acquire the basics of grammar without even being aware that we have learned its rules (Pinker, 1994; Plunkett & Wood, 2004). Moreover, even though we may have difficulty explicitly stating the rules of grammar, our linguistic abilities are so sophisticated that we can utter an infinite number of different statements. How do we acquire such abilities?

Language Development: Developing a Way with Words

To parents, the sounds of their infant babbling and cooing are music to their ears (except, perhaps, at three o'clock in the morning). These sounds also serve an important function. They mark the first step on the road to the development of language.

Babbling

Children **babble**—make speech-like but meaningless sounds—from around the age of 3 months through 1 year. While babbling, they may produce, at one time or another, any of the sounds found in all languages, not just the one to which they are exposed. Even deaf children display their own form of babbling, for infants who are unable to hear yet who are exposed to sign language from birth "babble" with their hands (Pettito, 1993; Locke, 2006).

An infant's babbling increasingly reflects the specific language being spoken in the infant's environment, initially in terms of pitch and tone and eventually in terms of specific sounds. Young infants can distinguish among all 869 phonemes that have been identified across the world's languages. However, after the age of 6 to 8 months, that ability begins to decline. Infants begin to "specialize" in the language to which they are exposed as neurons in their brains reorganize to respond to the particular phonemes infants routinely hear. Some theorists argue that a *critical period* exists for language development early in life, during which a child is particularly sensitive to language cues and most easily acquires language. In fact, if children are not exposed to language during this critical period, later they will have great difficulty overcoming this deficit (Bates, 2005; Shafer & Garrido-Nag, 2007). Cases in which abused children have been isolated from contact with others support the theory of such critical periods. In one case, for example, a girl named Genie was exposed to virtually no language from the age of 20 months until she was rescued at age 13. She was unable to speak at all. Despite intensive instruction, she learned only some words and was never able to master the complexities of language (Rymer, 1994; Veltman & Browne, 2001).

Syntax
Ways in which words and phrases can be combined to form sentences.

Semantics
The rules governing the meaning of words and sentences.

Babble
Meaningless speech-like sounds made by children from around the age of 3 months through 1 year.

Production of Language

By the time children are approximately 1 year old, they stop producing sounds that are not in the language to which they have been exposed. It is then a short step to the production of actual words. In English, these are typically short words that start with a consonant sound such as *b*, *d*, *m*, *p*, and *t*—this helps explain why *mama* and *dada* are so often among babies' first words. Of course, even before they produce their first words, children can understand a fair amount of the language they hear. Language comprehension precedes language production.

After the age of 1 year, children begin to learn more complicated forms of language. They produce two-word combinations, the building blocks of sentences, and sharply increase the number of different words they are able to use. By age 2, the average child has a vocabulary of more than fifty words. Just six months later, that vocabulary has grown to several hundred words. At that time, children can produce short sentences, although they use **telegraphic speech**—sentences that sound as if they were part of a telegram, in which words not critical to the message are left out. Rather than saying, "I showed you the book," a child using telegraphic speech may say, "I show book," and "I am drawing a dog" may become "Drawing dog." As children get older, of course, they use less telegraphic speech and produce increasingly complex sentences (Volterra et al., 2003).

By age 3, children learn to make plurals by adding *-s* to nouns and to form the past tense by adding *-ed* to verbs. This also leads to errors, since children tend to apply rules inflexibly. In such **overgeneralization**, children employ rules even when doing so results in an error. Thus, although it is correct to say "he walked" for the past tense of *walk*, the *-ed* rule doesn't work quite so well when children say "he runned" for the past tense of *run* (Marcus, 1996; Howe, 2002; Rice et al., 2004; Gershkoff-Stowe, Connell, & Smith, 2006; Kidd & Lum, 2008).

By age 5, children have acquired the basic rules of language. However, they do not attain a full vocabulary and the ability to comprehend and use subtle grammatical rules until later. For example, a 5-year-old boy who sees a blindfolded doll and is asked, "Is the doll easy or hard to see?" would have great trouble answering the question. In fact, if he were asked to make the doll easier to see, he would probably try to remove the doll's blindfold. By the time they are 8 years old, however, children have little difficulty understanding this question, because they realize that the doll's blindfold has nothing to do with an observer's ability to see the doll (Chomsky, 1969; Hoff, 2003).

The study of speech errors in language development provides important clues into how the language system works. Karin Humphreys, a cognitive psychologist at McMaster University, examines the psycholinguistics of language errors (see Chapter 2, Module 7 for additional work by Humphreys). A recent study examined the conditions under which individuals are more likely to make speech errors. Results indicated that the subjects who made speech errors on the first speech task were significantly more likely to make speech errors on subsequent tasks. Researchers concluded that subjects generalized their failure mentality to subsequent speech tasks (Warriner & Humphreys, 2008). This research emphasizes the importance of addressing an individual's mindset (e.g., learned helplessness vs. mastery) in speech and language therapy.

Understanding Language Acquisition: Identifying the Roots of Language

Anyone who spends even a little time with children will notice the enormous strides that they make in language development throughout childhood. However, the reasons for this rapid growth are far from obvious. Psychologists have offered two major explanations, one based on learning theory and the other based on innate processes.

The **learning-theory approach (to language development)** suggests that language acquisition follows the principles of reinforcement and conditioning discovered by psychologists who study learning. For example, a child

---

Telegraphic speech
Sentences in which words not critical to the message are left out.

Overgeneralization
The phenomenon by which children apply language rules even when the application results in an error.

Learning-theory approach (to language development)
The theory that language acquisition follows the principles of reinforcement and conditioning.

who says "mama" receives hugs and praise from her mother, which reinforces the behaviour of saying "mama" and makes its repetition more likely. This view suggests that children first learn to speak by being rewarded for making sounds that approximate speech. Ultimately, through a process of shaping, language becomes more and more like adult speech (Skinner, 1957; Ornat & Gallo, 2004).

To support the learning-theory approach to language acquisition, research shows that the more parents speak to their young children, the more proficient the children become in language use (see Figure 1). In addition, by the time they are 3 years old, children who hear higher levels of linguistic sophistication in their parents' speech show a greater rate of vocabulary growth, vocabulary use, and even general intellectual achievement than do children whose parents' speech is more simple (Hart & Risley, 1997).

Linda Phillips and her colleagues at the Canadian Centre for Research on Literacy (CCRL) at the University of Alberta found similar patterns with the literacy development of young children. Results of a longitudinal parent–child literacy intervention study revealed that children who are read to by parents with superior reading ability and advanced education show a greater rate of literacy growth and reading ability than children whose parents have less education and weaker reading skills (Phillips, Hayden, & Norris, 2006).

University of British Columbia professor Janet F. Werker studies the acquisition of language from birth to end of age 2 using both behavioural and neuroimaging techniques.

The learning-theory approach is less successful in explaining how children acquire language rules. Children are reinforced not only when they use language correctly, but also when they use it incorrectly. For example, parents answer a child's "Why the dog won't eat?" as readily as they do the correctly phrased question, "Why won't the dog eat?" Listeners understand both sentences equally well. Learning theory, then, has difficulty fully explaining language acquisition.

Pointing to such problems with learning-theory approaches to language acquisition, linguist Noam Chomsky (1968, 1978, 1991) provided a groundbreaking alternative. Chomsky argued that humans are born with an innate linguistic capability that emerges primarily as a function of maturation. According to his **nativist approach (to language development)**

FIGURE 1

The more words parents say to their children before the age of 3, the larger the children's vocabulary.

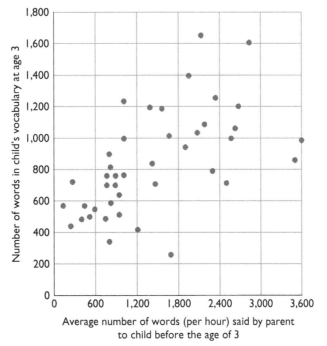

Source: Courtesy of Drs. Betty Hart and Todd Risley, 1997.

Nativist approach (to language development)
The theory that a genetically determined, innate mechanism directs language development.

to language, all the world's languages share a common underlying structure called a **universal grammar**. Chomsky suggested that the human brain has a neural system, the **language-acquisition device**, which not only lets us understand the structure language provides but also gives us strategies and techniques for learning the unique characteristics of our native language (Lidz & Gleitman, 2004; McGilvray, 2004).

Chomsky used the concept of the language-acquisition device as a metaphor, and he did not identify a specific area of the brain in which it resides. However, evidence collected by neuroscientists suggests that the ability to use language, which was a significant evolutionary advance in human beings, is tied to specific neurological developments.

For example, scientists have discovered a gene related to the development of language abilities that may have emerged as recently—in evolutionary terms—as 100,000 years ago. Furthermore, it is clear that there are specific sites within the brain that are closely tied to language, and the shape of the human mouth and throat are tailored to the production of speech (Hauser, Chomsky, & Fitch, 2002; Chandra, 2007; Dediu & Ladd, 2007; Gontier, 2008; Grigorenko, 2009).

Still, Chomsky's view has its critics. For instance, learning theorists contend that the apparent ability of certain animals, such as chimpanzees, to learn the fundamentals of human language (as we discuss later in this module) contradicts the innate linguistic capability view. To reconcile such data, some theorists, including Canadian-born Harvard professor Steven Pinker, suggest that the brain's hardwired language-acquisition device that Chomsky and geneticists posit provides the hardware for our acquisition of language, whereas the exposure to language in our environment that learning theorists observe allows us to develop the appropriate software. But the issue of how language is acquired remains hotly contested (Pinker, 1994, 2002; Fromkin, 2000; Lana, 2002).

Pinker theorizes that humans are not born with a "blank slate;" instead we are born with a predisposition to think, speak, and act in programmed ways. Pinker popularized his theory of the mind in five books, including: (1) *The Language Instinct* (1994), (2) *How the Mind Works* (1997), (3) *Words and Rules* (1999), (4) *The Blank Slate* (2002), and (5) *The Stuff of Thought: Language as a Window into Human Nature* (2007). Despite being chock full of scientific data, Pinker's books have twice been finalists for a Pulitzer Prize owing to Pinker's engaging, funny, and easy-to-read writing style (Long, 2007).

Interactionist Approaches

To reconcile the differing views, many theorists take an **interactionist approach (to language development)**. The interactionist approach suggests that language development is produced through a combination of genetically determined predispositions and environmental circumstances that help teach language.

STUDY ALERT!

It's important to be able to compare and contrast the major approaches to language development: learning theory, nativist, and interactionist approaches.

Universal grammar
Noam Chomsky's theory that all the world's languages share a common underlying structure.

Language-acquisition device
A neural system of the brain hypothesized by Noam Chomsky to permit understanding of language.

Interactionist approach (to language development)
The view that language development is produced through a combination of genetically determined predispositions and environmental circumstances that help teach language.

The Influence of Language on Thinking: Do the Inuit Have More Words for Snow than Texans Do?

Do the Inuit living in the frigid Arctic have a more expansive vocabulary for discussing snow than people living in warmer climates? How many words for snow exist in Inuktitut, the language of the Inuit?

It makes sense, and arguments that the Inuit language has many more words than English for snow have been made since the early 1900s. At that time, linguist Benjamin Lee Whorf contended that because snow is so relevant to the Inuit's lives, their language provides a particularly rich vocabulary to describe it—considerably larger than what we find in other languages, such as English (Martin & Pullum, 1991; Pinker, 1994).

The contention that the Inuit language is particularly abundant in snow-related terms led to the **linguistic-relativity hypothesis**, the notion that language shapes and, in fact, may determine the way people in a particular culture perceive and understand the world. According to this view, language provides us with categories that we use to construct our view of people and events in the world around us. Consequently, language shapes and produces thought (Whorf, 1956; Casasanto, 2008; Tan et al., 2008).

STUDY ALERT!

The linguistic-relativity hypothesis suggests language leads to thought.

Let's consider another possibility, however. Suppose that instead of language being the *cause* of certain ways of thinking, thought *produces* language. The only reason to expect that the Inuit language might have more words for snow than English does is that snow is considerably more relevant to the Inuit than it is to people in other cultures.

Which view is correct? Most recent research refutes the linguistic-relativity hypothesis and suggests, instead, that thinking produces language. In fact, new analyses of the Inuit language suggest that the Inuit have no more words for snow than English speakers, for if one examines the English language closely, one sees that it is hardly impoverished when it comes to describing snow (consider, for example, *sleet, slush, blizzard, dusting,* and *avalanche*).

Still, the linguistic relativity hypothesis has not been entirely discarded. A newer version of the hypothesis suggests that speech patterns may influence certain aspects of thinking. For example, in some languages, such as English, speakers distinguish between nouns that can be counted (such as "five chairs") and nouns that require a measurement unit to be quantified (such as "a litre of water"). In some other languages, such as the Mayan language called Yucatec, however, all nouns require a measurement unit. In such cultures, people appear to think more closely about what things are made of than do people in cultures in which languages such as English are spoken. In contrast, English speakers focus more on the shape of objects (Gentner, Goldin, & Goldin-Meadow, 2003; Tsukasaki & Ishii, 2004).

In short, although research does not support the linguistic-relativity hypothesis that language *causes* thought, it is clear that language influences how we think. And, of course, it certainly is the case that thought influences language, suggesting that language and thinking interact in complex ways (Ross, 2004; Thorkildsen, 2006; Proudfoot, 2009).

Do Animals Use Language?

One question that has long puzzled psychologists is whether language is uniquely human or if other animals are able to acquire it as well. Many animals communicate with one another in rudimentary forms. For instance, fiddler crabs wave their claws to signal, bees dance to indicate the direction in which food will be found, and certain birds call "zick, zick" during courtship and "kia" when they are about to fly away. However, researchers have yet to demonstrate conclusively that these animals use true language, which is characterized in part by the ability to produce and communicate new and unique meanings by following a formal grammar.

Linguistic-relativity hypothesis
The notion that language shapes and may determine the way people in a particular culture perceive and understand the world.

Sue Savage-Rumbaugh with a primate friend, Panbanisha. Does the use of sign language by primates indicate true mastery of language?

Source: © Anna Clopet/Corbis.

Psychologists have, however, been able to teach chimps to communicate at surprisingly high levels. For instance, after four years of training, a chimp named Washoe learned to make signs for 132 words and combine those signs into simple sentences. Even more impressively, Kanzi, a pygmy chimpanzee, has linguistic skills that some psychologists claim are close to those of a 2-year-old human being. Kanzi's trainers suggest that he can create grammatically sophisticated sentences and can even invent new rules of syntax (Raffaele, 2006; Savage-Rumbaugh, Toth, & Schick, 2007).

Despite the skills displayed by primates such as Kanzi, critics contend that the language such animals use still lacks the grammar and the complex and novel constructions of human language. Instead, they maintain that the chimps are displaying a skill no different from that of a dog that learns to lie down on command to get a reward. Furthermore, we lack firm evidence that animals can recognize and respond to the mental states of others of their species, an important aspect of human communication (Aboitiz et al., 2006; Hillix, 2007; Liszkowski et al., 2009).

Exploring DIVERSITY

Teaching with Linguistic Variety: Bilingual Education

In Canada, 57.8 percent of the population report English as their first language, 21.7 percent report French as their first language, and 20.6 percent report "other" as first language, which translates into almost 14 million Canadians with English as their second language (Statistic Canada, 2011).

How to appropriately and effectively teach the increasing number of children who do not speak English is not always clear. Many educators maintain that *bilingual education* is best. With a bilingual approach, students learn some subjects in their native language while simultaneously learning English. Proponents of bilingualism believe that students must develop a sound footing in basic subject areas and that, initially at least, teaching those subjects in their native language is the only way to provide them with that foundation. During the same period, they learn English, with the eventual goal of shifting all instruction into English.

In contrast, other educators insist that all instruction ought to be in English from the moment students, including those who speak no English at all, enroll in school. In *immersion programs,* students are immediately plunged into English instruction in all subjects. The reasoning is that teaching students in a language other than English simply hinders nonnative English speakers' integration into society and ultimately does them a disservice. As evidence for this point of view, proponents of English immersion programs cite improvements in standardized test scores that followed the end of bilingual education programs (Wildavsky, 2000).

Although the controversial issue of bilingual education versus immersion has strong political undercurrents, evidence shows that the ability to speak two languages provides significant cognitive benefits over speaking only one language. For example,

(continued)

bilingual speakers show more cognitive flexibility and may understand concepts more easily than those who speak only one language. They have more linguistic tools for thinking because of their multiple-language abilities. In turn, this makes them more creative and flexible in solving problems (Hong, 2000; Sanz, 2000; Heyman & Diesendruck, 2002; Bialystok & Martin, 2004).

Canadians may be especially interested in research on the bilingual brain given the country's two official languages. Research suggests that speaking several languages changes the organization of the brain, as does the timing of the acquisition of a second language. One study compared bilingual speakers on linguistic tasks in their native and second languages. For instance, do fMRI scans differ when a subject is speaking their native tongue versus a second language? The study found that those who had learned their second language as adults showed different areas of brain activation compared with those who had learned their second language in childhood (Kim et al., 1997).

Related to questions about bilingual education is the matter of *biculturalism,* that is, being a member of two cultures and its psychological impact. Some psychologists argue that society should promote an *alternation model* of bicultural competence. Such a model supports members of a culture in their efforts to maintain their original cultural identity, as well as in their integration into the adopted culture. In this view, a person can belong to two cultures and have two cultural identities without having to choose between them. Whether society will adopt the alternation model remains to be seen (LaFromboise, Coleman, & Gerton, 1995; Calderon & Minaya-Rowe, 2003; Carter, 2003).

Evaluate

1. Match the component of grammar with its definition:
   1. Syntax
   2. Phonology
   3. Semantics
   a. Rules showing how words can be combined into sentences
   b. Rules governing the meaning of words and sentences
   c. The study of the sound units that affect speech
2. Language production and language comprehension develop in infants at about the same time. True or false?
3. _____ refers to the phenomenon in which young children omit nonessential portions of sentences.
4. A child knows that adding -ed to certain words puts them in the past tense. As a result, instead of saying "He came," the child says "He comed." This is an example of _____.
5. _____ theory assumes that language acquisition is based on principles of operant conditioning and shaping.
6. In his theory of language acquisition, Chomsky argues that language acquisition is an innate ability tied to the structure of the brain. True or false?

Answers to Evaluate Questions

1. 1-a, 2-c, 3-b; 2. false, language comprehension precedes language production; 3. telegraphic speech; 4. overgeneralization; 5. learning; 6. true

Key Terms

babble	learning-theory approach (to language development)	phonemes
grammar		phonology
interactionist approach (to language development)	linguistic-relativity hypothesis	semantics
	nativist approach (to language development)	syntax
language		telegraphic speech
language-acquisition device	overgeneralization	universal grammar

231

Intelligence

LEARNING OBJECTIVES

LO7 **What are** the different definitions and conceptions of intelligence?

LO8 **What are** the major approaches to measuring intelligence, and what do intelligence tests measure?

LO9 **How are** the extremes of intelligence characterized?

LO10 **Are traditional** IQ tests culturally biased?

LO11 **To what** degree is intelligence influenced by the environment, and to what degree by heredity?

It is typical for the Trukese, people of a small tribe in the South Pacific, to sail a hundred miles in open ocean waters. Although their destination may be just a small dot of land less than a mile wide, the Trukese are able to sail unerringly toward it without the aid of a compass, chronometer, sextant, or any of the other sailing tools that are indispensable to modern Western navigation. They are able to sail accurately, even when prevailing winds do not allow a direct approach to the island and they must take a zigzag course (Gladwin, 1964; Mytinger, 2001).

How are the Trukese able to navigate so effectively? If you asked them, they could not explain it. They might tell you that they use a process that takes into account the rising and setting of the stars and the appearance, sound, and feel of the waves against the side of the boat. But at any given moment as they are sailing along, they could not identify their position or say why they are doing what they are doing. Nor could they explain the navigational theory underlying their sailing technique.

Some might say that the inability of the Trukese to explain in Western terms how their sailing technique works is a sign of primitive or even unintelligent behaviour. In fact, if we gave Trukese sailors a Western standardized test of navigational knowledge and theory or, for that matter, a traditional test of intelligence, they might do poorly on it. Yet, as a practical matter, it is not possible to accuse the Trukese of being unintelligent: Despite their inability to explain how they do it, they are able to navigate successfully through the open ocean waters.

Trukese navigation points out the difficulty in coming to grips with what is meant by intelligence. To a Westerner, travelling in a straight line along the most direct and quickest route by using a sextant and other navigational tools is likely to represent the most "intelligent" kind of behaviour; in contrast, a zigzag course, based on the "feel" of the waves, would not seem very reasonable. To the Trukese, who are used to their own system of navigation, however, the use of complicated navigational tools might seem so overly complex and unnecessary that they might think of Western navigators as lacking in intelligence.

It is clear from this example that the term *intelligence* can take on many different meanings. If, for instance, you lived in a remote part of the Australian outback, the way you would differentiate between more intelligent and less intelligent people might have to do with successfully mastering hunting skills, whereas to someone living in the heart of urban Montreal, intelligence might be exemplified by being streetwise or by business success.

Each of these conceptions of intelligence is reasonable. Each represents an instance in which more intelligent people are better able to use the resources of their environment than are less intelligent people, a distinction that is presumably basic to any definition of intelligence. Yet it is also clear that these conceptions represent very different views of intelligence.

That two such different sets of behaviour can exemplify the same psychological concept has long posed a challenge to psychologists. For years they have grappled with the issue of devising a general definition of intelligence. Interestingly, laypersons have fairly clear ideas of what intelligence is, although the nature of their ideas is related to their culture. Westerners view intelligence as the ability to form categories and debate rationally. In contrast, people in Eastern cultures view intelligence more in terms of understanding and relating to one another. And members of some African communities are more likely to view intelligence and social competence as similar (Nisbett, 2003; Brislin, Worthley, & MacNab, 2006; Sternberg, 2005, 2007).

The definition of intelligence that psychologists employ contains some of the same elements found in the layperson's conception. To psychologists, **intelligence** is the capacity to understand the world, think rationally, and use resources effectively when faced with challenges.

This definition does not lay to rest a key question asked by psychologists: Is intelligence a unitary attribute, or are there different kinds of intelligence? We turn now to various theories of intelligence that address the issue.

Theories of Intelligence: Are There Different Kinds of Intelligence?

Perhaps you see yourself as a good writer but as someone who lacks ability in math. Or maybe you view yourself as a "science" person who easily masters physics but has few strengths in literature. Perhaps you view yourself as generally fairly smart, with intelligence that permits you to excel across domains.

The different ways in which people view their own talents mirrors a question that psychologists have grappled with: Is intelligence a single, general ability, or is it multifaceted and related to specific abilities? Early psychologists interested in intelligence assumed that there was a single, general factor for mental ability, which they called **g or g-factor**. This general intelligence factor was thought to underlie performance in every aspect of intelligence, and it was the g-factor that was presumably being measured on tests of intelligence (Spearman, 1927; Colom, Jung, & Haier, 2006; Haier et al., 2009).

More recent theories see intelligence in a different light. Rather than viewing intelligence as a unitary entity, they consider it to be a multidimensional concept that includes different types of intelligence (Tenopyr, 2002; Stankov, 2003; Sternberg & Pretz, 2005).

Gardner's Multiple Intelligences: The Many Ways of Showing Intelligence

In his consideration of intelligence, psychologist Howard Gardner has taken an approach very different from traditional thinking about the topic. Gardner argues that rather than asking "How smart are you?" we should be asking a different question: "How are you smart?" In answering the latter question, Gardner has developed a **theory of multiple intelligences** that has become quite influential (Gardner, 2000).

Gardner argues that we have at a minimum eight different forms of intelligence, each relatively independent of the others: musical, bodily kinesthetic, logical-mathematical, linguistic, spatial, interpersonal, intrapersonal, and naturalist. (Figure 1 describes the eight types of intelligence, with some of Gardner's examples of people who excel in each type.)

STUDY ALERT!

Remember that Gardner's theory suggests that each individual has every kind of intelligence, but in different degrees.

Intelligence
The capacity to understand the world, think rationally, and use resources effectively when faced with challenges.

g or g-factor
The single, general factor for mental ability assumed to underlie intelligence in some early theories of intelligence.

Theory of multiple intelligences
Gardner's intelligence theory that proposes that there are eight distinct spheres of intelligence.

In Gardner's view, each of the multiple intelligences is linked to an independent system in the brain. Furthermore, he suggests that there may be even more types of intelligence, such as *existential intelligence*, which involves identifying and thinking about the fundamental questions of human existence. For example, the Dalai Lama might possess this type of intelligence (Gardner, 1999, 2000).

FIGURE 1

According to Howard Gardner, there are eight major kinds of intelligences, corresponding to abilities in different domains. In what area does your greatest intelligence reside, and why do you think you have particular strengths in that area?

1. Musical intelligence (skills in tasks involving music). Case example:

When he was 3, Yehudi Menuhin was smuggled into San Francisco Orchestra concerts by his parents. By the time he was 10 years old, Menuhin was an international performer.

2. Bodily kinesthetic intelligence (skills in using the whole body or various portions of it in the solution of problems or in the construction of products or displays, exemplified by dancers, athletes, actors, and surgeons). Case example:

Fifteen-year-old Babe Ruth played third base. During one game, his team's pitcher was doing very poorly and Babe loudly criticized him from third base. Brother Matthias, the coach, called out, "Ruth, if you know so much about it, *you* pitch!" Ruth said later that at the very moment he took the pitcher's mound, he *knew* he was supposed to be a pitcher.

3. Logical-mathematical intelligence (skills in problem solving and scientific thinking). Case example:

Barbara McClintock, who won the Nobel Prize in Medicine, describes one of her breakthroughs, which came after thinking about a problem for half an hour . . . : "Suddenly I jumped and ran back to the (corn) field. At the top of the field (the others were still at the bottom) I shouted, 'Eureka, I have it!'"

4. Linguistic intelligence (skills involved in the production and use of language). Case example:

At the age of 10, T. S. Eliot created a magazine called *Fireside*, to which he was the sole contributor.

5. Spatial intelligence (skills involving spatial configurations, such as those used by artists and architects). Case example:

Natives of the Truk Islands navigate at sea without instruments. During the actual trip, the navigator must envision mentally a reference island as it passes under a particular star and from that he computes the number of segments completed, the proportion of the trip remaining, and any corrections in heading.

6. Interpersonal intelligence (skills in interacting with others, such as sensitivity to the moods, temperaments, motivations, and intentions of others). Case example:

When Anne Sullivan began instructing the deaf and blind Helen Keller, her task was one that had eluded others for years. Yet, just two weeks after beginning her work with Keller, Sullivan achieved great success.

7. Intrapersonal intelligence (knowledge of the internal aspects of oneself; access to one's own feelings and emotions). Case example:

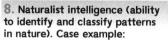

In her essay "A Sketch of the Past," Virginia Woolf displays deep insight into her own inner life through these lines, describing her reaction to several specific memories from her childhood that still, in adulthood, shock her: "Though I still have the peculiarity that I receive these sudden shocks, they are now always welcome; after the first surprise, I always feel instantly that they are particularly valuable. And so I go on to suppose that the shock-receiving capacity is what makes me a writer."

8. Naturalist intelligence (ability to identify and classify patterns in nature). Case example:

During prehistoric times, hunter/gatherers would rely on naturalist intelligence to identify what flora and fauna were edible. People who are adept at distinguishing nuances between large numbers of similar objects may be expressing naturalist intelligence abilities.

Although Gardner illustrates his conception of the specific types of intelligence with descriptions of well-known people, each person has the same eight kinds of intelligence, although in different degrees. Moreover, although the eight basic types of intelligence are presented individually, Gardner suggests that these separate intelligences do not operate in isolation. Normally, any activity encompasses several kinds of intelligence working together.

The concept of multiple intelligences has led to the development of intelligence tests that include questions in which more than one answer can be correct, providing an opportunity for test takers to demonstrate creative thinking. In addition, many educators have embraced the concept of multiple intelligences, designing classroom curricula that are meant to draw on different aspects of intelligence (Kelly & Tangney, 2006; Douglas, Burton, & Reese-Durham, 2008; Tirri & Nokelainen, 2008).

Emotional Intelligence: Toward a More Intelligent View of Intelligence

According to psychologist Daniel Goleman (1995), emotional intelligence underlies the ability to get along well with others. **Emotional intelligence** is the set of skills that underlie the accurate assessment, evaluation, expression, and regulation of emotions (Mayer, Salovey, Caruso, 2004; Humphrey et al., 2007; Mayer, Salovey, & Caruso, 2008). It provides us with an understanding of what other people are feeling and experiencing and permits us to respond appropriately to others' needs. Emotional intelligence is the basis of empathy for others, self-awareness, and social skills.

Abilities in emotional intelligence may help explain why people with only modest scores on traditional intelligence tests can be quite successful, despite their lack of traditional intelligence. High emotional intelligence may enable an individual to tune into others' feelings, permitting a high degree of responsiveness to others.

Although the notion of emotional intelligence makes sense, it has yet to be quantified in a rigorous manner. Furthermore, the view that emotional intelligence is so important that skills related to it should be taught in school has raised concerns among some educators. They suggest that the nurturance of emotional intelligence is best left to students' families, especially because there is no well-specified set of criteria for what constitutes emotional intelligence (Sleek, 1997; Becker, 2003). The *Applying Psychology in the Real World* box illustrates how our own views of intelligence affect our test performance.

APPLYING PSYCHOLOGY in the Real World

How You Think About Intelligence Helps Determine Your Success

What is your thinking on intelligence? Is it your view that what you're born with is what you've got and that your intelligence is largely fixed for life? Or do you believe intelligence is flexible and malleable, and through effort and practise, it can increase?

Think hard before you answer, because your response might well have an effect on your intellectual performance and on how your brain works. According to the research findings of cognitive neuroscientist Jennifer Mangels, people who believe that intelligence is fixed show specific brain-wave patterns after finding out they answered a question wrong. Furthermore, they are less likely to show that they learned from their errors on subsequent questions, performing less well than do people who consider intelligence a flexible trait (Mangels, 2004; Mangels, Dweck, & Good, 2005).

Mangels' research expands the findings of educational psychologist Carol Dweck, who discovered that people's beliefs about intelligence basically fall into two categories. *Entity theorists* believe that intelligence is primarily fixed at birth. In their view, no amount of life experience or hard work can change the intelligence we have at birth. In contrast, *incremental theorists* see intelligence as flexible, potentially changing over the course of life. In contrast to entity theorists, incremental theorists are more

(continued)

Emotional intelligence
The set of skills that underlie the accurate assessment, evaluation, expression, and regulation of emotions.

resilient when they fail at a task, because they believe that future academic success on a task is possible (Dweck, Mangels, & Good, 2004).

Entity theorists are sometimes victimized by their view of intelligence as largely fixed. Often they don't work hard in academic domains they assume they are not good at—"I'm not that smart at math, so why bother"—and when they don't perform well on a task, they tend to give up relatively quickly. They don't readily learn from their mistakes.

In contrast, incremental theorists often work harder, seeking to learn from their mistakes. When they do not succeed at a task, they put more effort into learning new material that will make success likelier in the future.

To learn whether entity theorists have distinct brain-wave patterns, researchers assessed college and university students' beliefs about intelligence. In the sample of Columbia University students who participated in the study, about 40 percent were entity theorists, half were incremental, and the rest were unclear. The students in the study were asked questions on a computer and provided with feedback about whether they were right or wrong. They also indicated their degree of confidence in their answers.

The study found that participants showed a *metamemory mismatch P3 wave* pattern each time they received feedback. The strength of the wave was particularly pronounced when the feedback was unexpected, as indicated by participants' confidence levels. Most interesting was the difference between entity and incremental theorists: When participants learned that their response was wrong, the P3 waves of entity theorists appeared about 50 milliseconds earlier than incremental theorists. The difference suggests that the entity theorists were particularly disappointed by their erroneous response, taking it as a signal of their inherent lack of ability. In fact, rather than using the information to improve their performance later, the participants in the entity group were less likely to do better on questions in which they had low confidence than were incremental theorists.

These findings help lead us to a better understanding of the nature of people's views of intelligence. Even more important, they show that the beliefs people hold about their own intelligence effects their performance and the processing of information that goes on in their brain (Glenn, 2004).

Assessing Intelligence

Given the variety of approaches to the components of intelligence, it is not surprising that measuring intelligence has proved challenging. Psychologists who study intelligence have focused much of their attention on the development of **intelligence tests** and have relied on such tests to quantify a person's level of intelligence. These tests have proved to be of great benefit in identifying students in need of special attention in school, diagnosing cognitive difficulties, and helping people make optimal educational and vocational choices. At the same time, their use has proved quite controversial, raising important social and educational issues.

Historically, the first effort at intelligence testing was based on an uncomplicated, but completely wrong, assumption: that the size and shape of a person's head could be used as an objective measure of intelligence. The idea was put forward by Sir Francis Galton (1822–1911), an eminent English scientist whose ideas in other domains proved to be considerably better than his notions about intelligence.

Galton's motivation to identify people of high intelligence stemmed from personal prejudices. He sought to demonstrate the natural superiority of people of high social class (including himself) by showing that intelligence is inherited. He hypothesized that head configuration, being genetically determined, is related to brain size, and therefore is related to intelligence.

Galton's theories proved wrong on virtually every count. Head size and shape are not related to intellectual performance, and subsequent research has found little relationship between brain size and intelligence. However, Galton's work did have at least one desirable result: He was the first person to suggest that intelligence could be quantified and measured in an objective manner (Jensen, 2002).

Binet and the Development of IQ Tests

The first real intelligence tests were developed by the French psychologist Alfred Binet (1857–1911). His tests followed from a simple premise: If performance on certain tasks or test items improved with *chronological*, or physical, age, performance could be used to distinguish more intelligent people from less intelligent ones within a particular age

---

Intelligence tests
Tests devised to quantify a person's level of intelligence.

group. On the basis of this principle, Binet devised the first formal intelligence test, which was designed to identify the "dullest" students in the Paris school system in order to provide them with remedial aid.

Binet began by presenting tasks to same-age students who had been labelled "bright" or "dull" by their teachers. If a task could be completed by the bright students but not by the dull ones, he retained that task as a proper test item; otherwise it was discarded. In the end he came up with a test that distinguished between the bright and dull groups, and—with further work—one that distinguished among children in different age groups (Binet & Simon, 1916; Sternberg & Jarvin, 2003).

On the basis of the Binet test, children were assigned a score relating to their **mental age**, the age for which a given level of performance is average or typical. For example, if the average 8-year-old answered, say, 45 items correctly on a test, anyone who answered 45 items correctly would be assigned a mental age of 8 years. Consequently, whether the person taking the test was 20 years old or 5 years old, he or she would have the same mental age of 8 years.

Assigning a mental age to students provided an indication of their general level of performance. However, it did not allow for adequate comparisons among people of different chronological ages. By using mental age alone, for instance, we might assume that a 20-year-old responding at an 18-year-old's level would be as bright as a 5-year-old answering at a 3-year-old's level, when actually the 5-year-old would be displaying a much greater *relative* degree of slowness.

A solution to the problem came in the form of the **intelligence quotient (IQ)**, a score that takes into account an individual's mental *and* chronological ages. Historically, the first IQ scores employed the following formula, in which *MA* stands for mental age and *CA* for chronological age:

$$\text{IQ score} = \frac{\text{MA}}{\text{CA}} \times 100$$

STUDY ALERT!

It's important to know the traditional formula for IQ scores in which IQ is the ratio of mental age divided by chronological age, then multiplied by 100. Remember, though, that the actual calculation of IQ scores today is done in a more sophisticated manner.

Using this formula, we can return to the earlier example of a 20-year-old performing at a mental age of 18 and calculate an IQ score of $(18/20) \times 100 = 90$. In contrast, the 5-year-old performing at a mental age of 3 comes out with a considerably lower IQ score: $(3/5) \times 100 = 60$.

As a bit of trial and error with the formula will show you, anyone who has a mental age equal to his or her chronological age will have an IQ equal to 100. Moreover, people with a mental age that is greater than their chronological age will have IQs that exceed 100.

Although the basic principles behind the calculation of an IQ score still hold, today IQ scores are figured in a different manner and are known as *deviation IQ scores*. First, the average test score for everyone of the same age who takes the test is determined, and that average score is assigned an IQ of 100. Then, with the aid of statistical techniques that calculate the differences (or "deviations") between each score and the average, IQ scores are assigned.

As you can see in Figure 2, when IQ scores from large numbers of people are plotted on a graph, they form a *bell-shaped distribution* (called "bell-shaped" because it looks like a bell when plotted). Approximately two-thirds of all individuals fall within 15 IQ points of the average score of 100. As scores increase or fall beyond that range, the percentage of people in a category falls considerably.

Mental age
The age for which a given level of performance is average or typical.

Intelligence quotient (IQ)
A score that takes into account an individual's mental and chronological ages.

FIGURE 2

The average and most common IQ score is 100, and 68 percent of all people are within a 30-point range centred on 100. Some 95 percent of the population have scores that are within 30 points above or below 100, and 99.8 percent have scores that are between 55 and 145.

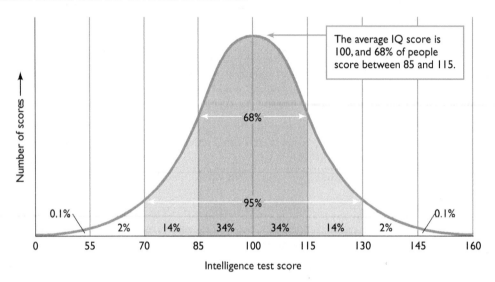

Contemporary IQ Tests: Gauging Intelligence

Remnants of Binet's original intelligence test are still with us, although the test has been revised in significant ways. Now in its fifth edition and called the *Stanford-Binet Intelligence Scale*, the test consists of a series of items that vary in nature according to the age of the person being tested (Roid et al., 2003). For example, young children are asked to copy figures or answer questions about everyday activities. Older people are asked to solve analogies, explain proverbs, and describe similarities that underlie sets of words.

The test is administered orally. An examiner begins by finding a mental age level at which a person is able to answer all the questions correctly, and then moves on to successively more difficult problems. When a mental age level is reached at which no items can be answered, the test is over. By examining the pattern of correct and incorrect responses, the examiner is able to compute an IQ score for the person being tested. In addition, the Stanford-Binet test yields separate subscores that provide clues to a test-taker's particular strengths and weaknesses.

The IQ test most frequently used in North America was devised by psychologist David Wechsler and is known as the *Wechsler Adult Intelligence Scale–IV*, or, more commonly, the *WAIS–IV*. There is also a children's version, the *Wechsler Intelligence Scale for Children–V*, or *WISC–V*. The WAIS–IV measures verbal comprehension, perceptual reasoning, working memory, and processing speed (see Figure 3). The primary index scales of the WISC-V include verbal comprehension, visual spatial, working memory, fluid reasoning, and processing speed. Both test yield full scale IQ scores (FSIQ).

Test items for Wechsler Intelligence Scales are consistent across North America. The only difference in assessment technique between Canada and United States are the standardized norms used to determine individual IQ scores. In particular, IQ scores of Canadians are determined by Canadian standardized norms and IQ scores of Americans are determined by American standardized norms (Redden, Whippler, & Reddon, 2007).

Because the Stanford-Binet, WAIS–IV, and WISC–V all require individualized, one-on-one administration, it is relatively difficult and time-consuming to administer and score them on a large-scale basis. Consequently, there are now a number of IQ tests that allow group administration. Rather than having one examiner ask one person at a time to respond to individual items, group IQ tests are strictly paper-and-pencil tests. The primary advantage of group tests is their ease of administration (Anastasi & Urbina, 1997).

However, sacrifices are made in group testing that in some cases may outweigh the benefits. For instance, group tests generally offer fewer kinds of questions than do tests administered individually. Furthermore, people may be more motivated to perform at their highest ability level when working on a one-to-one basis with a test administrator

FIGURE 3

Typical kinds of items found on the Wechsler Adult Intelligence Scales (WAIS-IV). (Simulated items similar to those in the *Wechsler Adult Intelligence Scale, Fourth Edition (WAIS-IV)*.

Types of Items on WAIS-IV		
Name	**Goal of Item**	**Example**
Information	Assess general information	Who wrote *Tom Sawyer?*
Comprehension	Assess understanding and evaluation of social norms and past experience	Why is copper often used for electrical wires?
Arithmetic	Assess math reasoning through verbal problems	Three women divided 18 golf balls equally among themselves. How many golf balls did each person receive?
Similarities	Test understanding of how objects or concepts are alike, tapping abstract reasoning	In what way are a circle and a triangle alike?
Figure weights	Test perceptual reasoning	Problems require test-taker to determine which possibility balances the final scale. 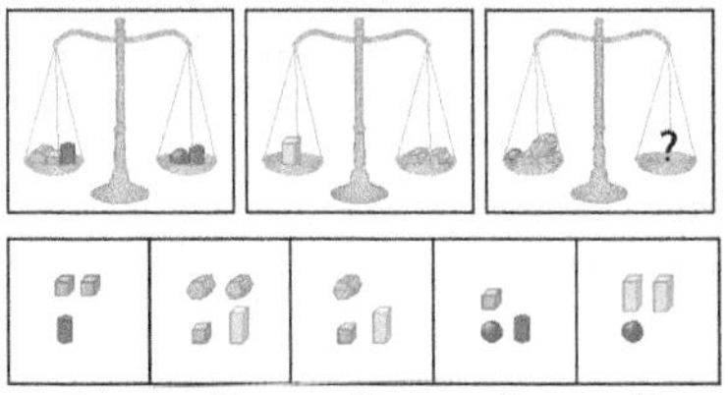
Matrix reasoning	Test spatial reasoning	Test-taker must decide which of the five possibilities replaces the question mark and completes the sequence. 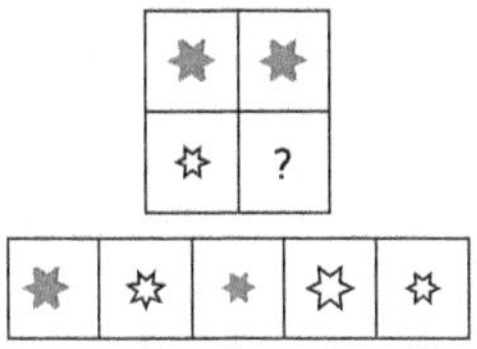
Block design item	Test understanding of relationship of parts to whole	Problems require test-takers to reproduce a design in fixed amount of time. 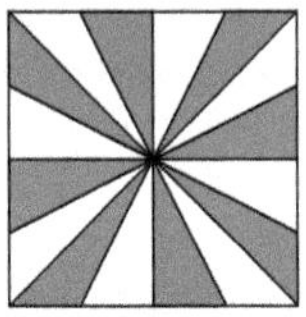

than they are in a group. Finally, in some cases, it is simply impossible to employ group tests, particularly with young children or people with unusually low IQs (Aiken, 1996).

Achievement and Aptitude Tests

IQ tests are not the only kind of tests that you might have taken during the course of your schooling. Two other kinds of tests, related to intelligence but intended to measure somewhat different phenomena, are achievement tests and aptitude tests. An **achievement test** is a test designed to determine a person's level of knowledge in a specific subject

> **Achievement test**
> A test designed to determine a person's level of knowledge in a given subject area.

Now in its fifth edition, the Stanford-Binet test consists of a series of items that vary in nature according to the age of the person being tested. What can we learn about a person from a test of this type?

Source: © Lewis J. Merrim/Science Source.

area. Rather than measuring general ability, as an intelligence test does, an achievement test concentrates on the specific material a person has learned. High school students sometimes take specialized achievement tests in particular areas such as world history and chemistry as a university entrance requirement; lawyers must pass an achievement test (in the form of the bar exam) in order to practise law.

An **aptitude test** is designed to predict a person's ability in a particular area or line of work. Canadian students applying to graduate school (e.g., Master's in Psychology) and professional schools (e.g., medical school) take aptitude tests in the process of pursuing admission: the Graduate Record Examination (GRE) for graduate school and the Medical College Admissions Test (MCAT) for medical school. The GRE and the MCAT are meant to predict how well people will do in graduate programs.

Although in theory the distinction between aptitude tests and achievement tests is precise, it is difficult to develop an aptitude test that does not rely at least in part on past achievement.

Reliability and Validity: Taking the Measure of Tests

When we use a ruler, we expect to find that it measures a millimetre in the same way it did the last time we used it. When we weigh ourselves on the bathroom scale, we hope that the variations we see on the scale are due to changes in our weight and not to errors on the part of the scale (unless the change in weight is in an unwanted direction!).

In the same way, we hope that psychological tests have **reliability**—that they measure consistently what they are trying to measure. We need to be sure that each time we administer the test, a test-taker will achieve the same results—assuming that nothing about the person has changed relevant to what is being measured.

Suppose, for instance, that when you first took the SAT, you scored 400 on the verbal section of the test. Then, after taking the test again a few months later, you scored 700. Upon receiving your new score, you might well stop celebrating for a moment to question whether the test is reliable, for it is unlikely that your abilities could have changed enough to raise your score by 300 points (Coyle, 2006).

Aptitude test
A test designed to predict a person's ability in a particular area or line of work.

Reliability
The property by which tests measure consistently what they are trying to measure.

But suppose your score changed hardly at all, and both times you received a score of about 400. You couldn't complain about a lack of reliability. However, if you knew your verbal skills were above average, you might be concerned that the test did not adequately measure what it was supposed to measure. In sum, the question has now become one of validity rather than reliability. A test has **validity** when it actually measures what it is supposed to measure.

Knowing that a test is reliable is no guarantee that it is also valid. For instance, Sir Francis Galton assumed that skull size is related to intelligence, and he was able to measure skull size with great reliability. However, the measure of skull size was not valid—it had nothing to do with intelligence. In this case, then, we have reliability without validity.

However, if a test is unreliable, it cannot be valid. Assuming that all other factors—motivation to score well, knowledge of the material, health, and so forth—are similar, if a person scores high the first time he or she takes a specific test and low the second time, the test cannot be measuring what it is supposed to measure. Therefore, the test is both unreliable and not valid.

Test validity and reliability are prerequisites for accurate assessment of intelligence—as well as for any other measurement task carried out by psychologists. Consequently, the measures of personality carried out by personality psychologists, clinical psychologists' assessments of psychological disorders, and social psychologists' measures of attitudes must meet the tests of validity and reliability for the results to be meaningful (Thompson, 2002; Feldt, 2005; Phelps, 2005).

Assuming that a test is both valid and reliable, one further step is necessary in order to interpret the meaning of a particular test-taker's score: the establishment of norms. **Norms** are standards of test performance that permit the comparison of one person's score on a test to the scores of others who have taken the same test. For example, a norm permits test-takers to know that they have scored, say, in the top 15 percent of those who have taken the test previously. Tests for which norms have been developed are known as *standardized tests*.

Test designers develop norms by calculating the average score achieved by a particular group of people for whom the test has been designed. Then the test designers can determine the extent to which each person's score differs from the scores of the other individuals who have taken the test in the past and provide future test-takers with a qualitative sense of their performance.

Obviously, the samples of test-takers who are employed in the establishment of norms are critical to the norming process. The people used to determine norms must be representative of the individuals to whom the test is directed.

Adaptive Testing: Using Computers to Assess Performance

Ensuring that tests are reliable and valid, and are based on appropriate norms, has become more critical with the introduction of computers to administer standardized tests. The Educational Testing Service (ETS)—the company that devises the SAT and the Graduate Record Examination (GRE), used for university and graduate school admission—is moving to computer administration of all its standardized tests.

In computerized versions, not only are test questions viewed and answered on a computer, the test itself is individualized. Under *adaptive testing*, students do not necessarily receive identical sets of test questions. Instead, the computer first presents a randomly selected question of moderate difficulty. If the test-taker answers it correctly, the computer will then present a randomly chosen item of slightly greater difficulty. If the answer is wrong, the computer will present a slightly easier item. Each question becomes slightly harder or easier than the question preceding it, depending on whether the previous response is correct. Ultimately, the greater the number of difficult questions answered correctly, the higher the score (Chang & Ansley, 2003; Marszalek, 2007; Belov & Armstrong, 2009).

Variations in Intellectual Ability

Individuals with low IQs—people with intellectual disabilities—as well as those with unusually high IQs, or the intellectually gifted, require special attention if they are to reach their full potential.

Validity
The property by which tests actually measure what they are supposed to measure.

Norms
Standards of test performance that permit the comparison of one person's score on a test with the scores of other individuals who have taken the same test.

Intellectual Disabilities

Although sometimes thought of a rare phenomenon, intellectual disabilities occur in about 2 to 3 percent of the population (Daily, Ardinger, & Holmes, 2000). The diagnosis of *intellectual disability* has been revised in the DSM-5 and replaces the term *mental retardation.*

Intellectual disabilities include both intellectual and adaptive functioning deficits in conceptual, social, and practical domains. The conceptual domain consists of skills in academics, knowledge, abstract thinking, and memory. The social domain includes social judgment, empathy, interpersonal communication skills, the ability to interpret social cues, and the ability to make and keep friends. The practical domain encompasses personal daily care, job responsibilities, management if money, and recreation. By assessing the individual across three domains it will ensure that the diagnosis is based on the individual's mental abilities and the impact it has on performance needed for daily life, as well as provide a more accurate portrayal of the individual (American Psychiatric Association, 2013).

An intellectual disability diagnosis is based on clinical assessment, as well as standardized testing of intellectual (IQ) and adaptive functioning. Adaptive functioning is measured using standardized tests and can help determine the level of support an individual needs. For example, identify who can be taught to work and function with little special attention to those who virtually cannot be trained and must receive institutional treatment throughout their lives (Accardo & Capute, 1998; Detterman, Gabriel, & Ruthsatz, 2000; Greenspan, 2006). They both may have the same IQ, but may require different levels of support. The levels of severity are determined by the level of adaptive functioning, rather than IQ and are categorized as mild, moderate, or severe.

STUDY ALERT!

Remember that in most cases of intellectual disabilities, there is no apparent biological deficiency but a history of intellectual disabilities in the family.

IDENTIFYING THE ROOTS OF INTELLECTUAL DISABILITIES

What are the causes of intellectual disabilities? In nearly one-third of the cases there is an identifiable biological reason. The most common biological cause is **fetal alcohol syndrome**, caused by a mother's use of alcohol while pregnant (West & Blake, 2005; Manning & Hoyme, 2007; Murthy et al., 2009).

Down syndrome represents another major biological cause of intellectual disabilities. *Down syndrome* results from the presence of an extra chromosome. In other cases of intellectual disabilities, an abnormality occurs in the structure of a chromosome (Sherman et al., 2007). Birth complications, such as a temporary lack of oxygen, may also cause intellectual disabilities. In some cases, intellectual disabilities occur after birth, following a head injury, a stroke, or infections such as meningitis (Plomin, 2005; Bittles et al., 2007).

However, the majority of cases of intellectual disabilities are classified as **familial intellectual disabilities**, in which no apparent biological defect exists but there is a history of intellectual disabilities in the family. Whether the family background of intellectual disabilities is caused by environmental factors, such as extreme continuous poverty leading to malnutrition, or by some underlying genetic factor is usually impossible to determine (Zigler et al., 2002).

Intellectual disabilities
A condition characterized by significant limitations in intellectual and adaptive functioning.

Fetal alcohol syndrome
The most common cause of intellectual disabilities in newborns, occurring when the mother consumes alcohol during pregnancy.

Familial intellectual disabilities
Intellectual disabilities in which no apparent biological defect exists but there is a history of intellectual disabilities in the family.

The Intellectually Gifted

Another group of people—the intellectually gifted—differ from those with average intelligence as much as do individuals with intellectual disabilities, although in a different manner. Accounting for 2 to 4 percent of the population, the **intellectually gifted** have IQ scores greater than 130.

Although the stereotype associated with the gifted suggests that they are awkward, shy social misfits who are unable to get along well with peers, most research indicates that just the opposite is true. The intellectually gifted are most often outgoing, well-adjusted, healthy, popular people who are able to do most things better than the average person can (Lubinski et al., 2006; Guldemond et al., 2007; Mueller, 2009).

PsychWork

Director of Special Education

Name: Shannon Lynch
Position: Director of Special Education
Education: BA, Psychology, Saint Mary's University, Halifax, Nova Scotia; MA, Special Education, Acadia University, Wolfville, Nova Scotia; Teacher Certification in Elementary and Special Education, Province of Nova Scotia

---

For Shannon Lynch, Director of Special Education at The Willow Creek School, being a special education teacher means providing ways for every student to achieve success. Each child presents different needs, and Lynch approaches her teaching accordingly.

"For children with specific learning disabilities, I have found it is helpful to utilize repetition, hands-on activities, music, movements with information, and rhymes to get the information to stick," she explained.

"Children on the autism spectrum have challenges with social skills. Great programs exist that provide models and scripts of appropriate social interactions," Lynch said. "Emotional disabilities require a very different approach and involve providing counselling to cope with the difficult emotions students face.

"The biggest factor for students with special needs is providing ways for them to achieve success. They have spent much of their academic career feeling incapable and inadequate, so just giving them small opportunities for success can make a huge difference in their confidence," Lynch noted.

Group Differences in Intelligence: Genetic and Environmental Determinants

Kwang is usually washed with a pleck tied to a:

(a) rundel

(b) flink

(c) pove

(d) quirj

If you found this kind of item on an intelligence test, you would probably complain that the test was totally absurd and had nothing to do with your intelligence or anyone else's—and rightly so. How could anyone be expected to respond to items presented in a language that was so unfamiliar?

Yet to some people, even more reasonable questions may appear just as nonsensical. Consider the example of a child raised in a city who is asked about procedures for milking cows, or someone raised in a rural area who is asked about subway ticketing procedures. Obviously, the previous experience of the test-takers would affect their ability to answer correctly. And if such types of questions were included on an IQ test, a critic could rightly contend that the test had more to do with prior experience than with intelligence.

Although IQ tests do not include questions that are so clearly dependent on prior knowledge as questions about cows and subways, the background and experiences of test-takers do have the potential to affect results. In fact,

---

Intellectually gifted
The 2 to 4 percent of the population who have IQ scores greater than 130.

the issue of devising fair intelligence tests that measure knowledge unrelated to culture and family background and experience is central to explaining an important and persistent finding: Members of certain racial and cultural groups consistently score lower on traditional intelligence tests than do members of other groups. For example, as a group, blacks tend to average 10 to 15 IQ points lower than whites. Does this reflect a true difference in intelligence, or are the questions biased in regard to the kinds of knowledge they test? Clearly, if whites perform better because of their greater familiarity with the kind of information that is being tested, their higher IQ scores are not necessarily an indication that they are more intelligent than members of other groups (Templer & Arikawa, 2006; Fagan & Holland, 2007; Morgan, Marsiske, & Whitfield, 2008).

STUDY ALERT!

Remember that the differences in IQ scores are much greater when comparing individuals than when comparing groups.

Exploring DIVERSITY

The Relative Influence of Genetics and Environment: Nature, Nurture, and IQ

In an attempt to produce a **culture-fair IQ test**, one that does not discriminate against the members of any minority group, psychologists have tried to devise test items that assess experiences common to all cultures or emphasize questions that do not require language usage. However, test makers have found this difficult to do, because past experiences, attitudes, and values almost always have an impact on respondents' answers (Fagan & Holland, 2009).

For example, children in North America asked to memorize the position of objects on a chess board perform better than do African children living in remote villages if household objects familiar to the North American children are used. But if rocks are used instead of household objects, the African children do better. In short, it is difficult to produce a test that is truly culture-fair (Sandoval et al., 1998; Serpell, 2000; Valencia & Suzuki, 2003).

The efforts of psychologists to produce culture-fair measures of intelligence relate to a lingering controversy over differences in intelligence between members of minority and majority groups. In attempting to identify whether there are differences between such groups, psychologists have had to confront the broader issue of determining the relative contribution to intelligence of genetic factors (heredity) and experience (environment)—the nature-nurture issue that is one of the basic issues of psychology.

Richard Herrnstein, a psychologist, and Charles Murray, a sociologist, fanned the flames of the debate with the publication of their book *The Bell Curve* in the mid-1990s (Herrnstein & Murray, 1994). They argued that an analysis of IQ differences between whites and blacks demonstrated that although environmental factors played a role, there were also basic genetic differences between the two races. They based their argument on a number of findings. For instance, on average, whites score 15 points higher than do blacks on traditional IQ tests even when socioeconomic status (SES) is taken into account.

Moreover, intelligence in general shows a high degree of **heritability**, a measure of the degree to which a characteristic can be attributed to genetic, inherited factors (e.g., Grigorenko, 2000; Plomin, 2003; Petrill, 2005). As can be seen in Figure 4, the closer the genetic link between two related people, the greater the correspondence of IQ scores. Using data such as these, Herrnstein and Murray argued that differences between races in IQ scores were largely caused by genetically based differences in intelligence.

However, many psychologists reacted strongly to the arguments laid out in *The Bell Curve*, refuting several of the book's basic arguments (e.g., Nisbett, 1994; American Psychological Association Task Force on Intelligence, 1996; Fish, 2002; Hall,

Culture-fair IQ test
A test that does not discriminate against the members of any minority group.

Heritability
A measure of the degree to which a characteristic is related to genetic, inherited factors.

2002; Horn, 2002). One criticism is that even when attempts are made to hold socioeconomic conditions constant, wide variations remain among individual households. Furthermore, no one can convincingly assert that the living conditions of blacks and whites are identical even when their socioeconomic status is similar.

Moreover, blacks who are raised in economically enriched environments have similar IQ scores to whites in comparable environments. For example, a study by Sandra Scarr and Richard Weinberg (1976) examined black children who had been adopted at an early age by white middle-class families of above-average intelligence. The IQ scores of those children averaged 106—about 15 points above the average IQ scores of unadopted black children in the study. Other research shows that the racial gap in IQ narrows considerably after a college or university education, and cross-cultural data demonstrate that when racial gaps exist in other cultures, it is the economically disadvantaged groups that typically have lower scores. In short, the evidence that genetic factors play the major role in determining racial differences in IQ is not compelling, although the question still evokes considerable controversy (Neisser et al., 1996; Fish, 2002; Winston, 2004).

FIGURE 4

The relationship between IQ and closeness of genetic relationship. In general, the more similar the genetic and environmental background of two people, the greater the correlation. Note, for example, that the correlation for spouses, who are genetically unrelated and have been reared apart, is relatively low, whereas the correlation for identical twins reared together is substantial.

Relationship	Genetic overlap	Rearing	Correlation	
Monozygotic (identical) twins	100%	Together	.86	
Dizygotic (fraternal) twins	50%	Together	.62	
Siblings	50%	Together	.41	The difference between these two correlations shows the impact of the environment
Siblings	50%	Apart	.24	
Parent-child	50%	Together	.35	
Parent-child	50%	Apart	.31	
Adoptive parent-child	0%	Together	.16	The relatively low correlation for unrelated children raised together shows the importance of genetic factors
Unrelated children	0%	Together	.25	
Spouses	0%	Apart	.29	

Source: Adapted from Henderson, 1982.

There is good reason to believe that some standardized IQ tests contain elements that discriminate against minority-group members whose experiences differ from those of the white majority. Consider the question "What should you do if another child grabbed your hat and ran off with it?" Most white middle-class children answer that they would tell an adult, and this response is scored as correct. However, a reasonable response might be to chase the person and fight to get the hat back, the answer that is chosen by many urban black children—but one that is scored as incorrect (Miller-Jones, 1991; Aiken, 1997; Reynolds & Ramsay, 2003).

It is also crucial to remember that IQ scores and intelligence have the greatest relevance in terms of individuals, not groups. In fact, considering group *racial* differences presents some conceptually troublesome distinctions. *Race* was originally meant to be a biological concept, referring to classifications based on the physical and structural characteristics of a species. Despite its biological origins, however, the term *race* has taken on additional meanings and is used in a variety of ways, ranging from skin colour to culture. In short, race is an extraordinarily inexact concept (Betancourt & Lopez, 1993; Yee et al., 1993; Beutler et al., 1996).

Consequently, drawing comparisons between different races on any dimension, including IQ scores, is an imprecise, potentially misleading, and often fruitless venture. By far, the greatest discrepancies in IQ scores occur when comparing *individuals*, not when comparing mean IQ scores of different *groups*. There are blacks who score high on IQ tests and whites who score low, just as there are whites who score high and blacks who score low. For the concept of intelligence to aid in the betterment of society, we must examine how *individuals* perform, not the groups to which they belong. We need to focus on the degree to which intelligence can be enhanced in an individual person, not in members of a particular group (Angoff, 1988; Fagan & Holland, 2002).

The more critical question to ask, then, is not whether hereditary or environmental factors primarily underlie intelligence, but whether there is anything we can do to maximize the intellectual development of each individual. If we can find ways to do this, we will be able to make changes in the environment—which may take the form of enriched home and school environments—that can lead each person to reach his or her potential.

Evaluate

1. _____ is a measure of intelligence that takes into account a person's chronological and mental ages.
2. _____ _____ _____ is the most common biological cause of intellectual disabilities.
3. People with high intelligence are generally shy and socially withdrawn. True or false?
4. A(n) _____ - _____ test tries to use only questions appropriate to all the people taking the test.

Answers to Evaluate Questions

1. IQ; 2. fetal alcohol syndrome; 3. false; the gifted are generally more socially adept than those with a lower IQ; 4. culture-fair

Key Terms

achievement test	g or g-factor	intelligence tests
aptitude test	heritability	mental age
culture-fair IQ test	intellectual disabilities	norms
emotional intelligence	intellectually gifted	reliability
familial intellectual disabilities	intelligence	theory of multiple intelligences
fetal alcohol syndrome	intelligence quotient (IQ)	validity

Epilogue

Source: © Kim Gunkel/Getty Images RF.

The topics in this chapter occupy a central place in the field of psychology, encompassing a variety of areas—including thinking, problem solving, decision making, creativity, language, memory, and intelligence. We first examined thinking and problem solving, focusing on the importance of mental images and concepts and identifying the steps commonly involved in solving problems. We discussed language, describing the components of grammar and tracing language development in children. Finally, we considered intelligence. Some of the most heated discussions in all of psychology focus on this topic, engaging educators, policymakers, politicians, and psychologists alike. The issues include the very meaning of intelligence, its measurement, individual extremes of intelligence, and finally, the heredity/environment question.

Recap/Rethink

Module 21: Thinking and Reasoning

Recap

What is thinking?

- Cognitive psychology encompasses the higher mental processes, including the way people know and understand the world, process information, make decisions and judgments, and describe their knowledge and understanding to others.
- Thinking is the manipulation of mental representations of information. Thinking transforms such representations into novel and different forms, permitting people to answer questions, solve problems, and reach goals.
- Mental images are representations in the mind of an object or event.
- Concepts are categorizations of objects, events, or people that share common properties. Prototypes are representative examples of concepts.

What processes underlie reasoning and decision making?

- Decisions sometimes (but not always) may be improved through the use of algorithms and heuristics. An algorithm is a rule that, if applied appropriately, guarantees a solution; a heuristic is a cognitive shortcut that may lead to a solution but is not guaranteed to do so.

How do people approach and solve problems?

- Problem solving typically involves three major stages: preparation, production of solutions, and evaluation of solutions that have been generated.
- In the preparation stage, how the problem is framed determines the kind of solution we choose.
- In arrangement problems, a group of elements must be arranged or recombined in a way that will satisfy a certain criterion. In problems of inducing structure, a person must first identity the existing relationships among the elements presented and then construct a new relationship among them. Finally, transformation problems consist of an initial state, a goal state, and a method for changing the initial state into the goal state
- In the production stage, people try to generate solutions. They may find solutions to some problems in long-term memory. Alternatively, they may solve some problems through simple trial and error and use algorithms and heuristics to solve more complex problems.
- Using the heuristic of a means-ends analysis, a person will repeatedly test for differences between the desired outcome and what currently exists, trying each time to come closer to the goal.
- Wolfgang Köhler's research with chimpanzees illustrates insight, a sudden awareness of the relationships among elements that had previously seemed unrelated.

What are the major obstacles to problem solving?

- Several factors hinder effective problem solving. Mental set, of which functional fixedness is an example, is the tendency for old patterns of problem solving to persist. Inappropriate use of algorithms and heuristics can also act as an obstacle to the production of solutions. Confirmation bias, in which initial hypotheses are favoured, can hinder the accurate evaluation of solutions to problems.
- Creativity is the ability to combine responses or ideas in novel ways. Creativity is related to divergent thinking (the ability to generate unusual, but still appropriate, responses to problems or questions) and cognitive complexity.

Rethink

1. How might the availability heuristic contribute to prejudices based on race, age, and gender? Can awareness of this heuristic prevent this from happening?

2. *From the perspective of a manufacturer:* How might you encourage your employees to develop creative ways to improve the products that you produce?

3. What are the difficulties that psychologists face in defining creativity in an objective way? What are some of the strategies you use to devise creative solutions to problems?

Module 22: Language

Recap

How do people use language?

- Language is the communication of information through symbols arranged according to systematic rules. All languages have a grammar—a system of rules that determines how thoughts can be expressed—that encompasses the three major components of language: phonology, syntax, and semantics.

LO6 How does language develop?

- Language production, which follows language comprehension, develops out of babbling, which then leads to the production of actual words. After 1 year of age, children use two-word combinations, increase their vocabulary, and use telegraphic speech, which drops words not critical to the message. By age 5, acquisition of language rules is relatively complete.
- Learning theorists suggest that language is acquired through reinforcement and conditioning. In contrast, Noam Chomsky and other linguists suggest that an innate language-acquisition device guides the development of language.
- The linguistic-relativity hypothesis suggests that language shapes and may determine the way people think about the world. Most evidence suggests that although language does not determine thought, it does affect the way people store information in memory and how well they can retrieve it.
- The degree to which language is a uniquely human skill remains an open question. Some psychologists contend that even though certain primates communicate at a high level, those animals do not use language; other psychologists suggest that those primates truly understand and produce language in much the same way humans do
- People who speak more than one language may have a cognitive advantage over those who speak only one.

Rethink

1. Do people who use two languages, one at home and one at school, automatically have two cultures? Why might people who speak two languages have cognitive advantages over those who speak only one?
2. *From the perspective of a childcare provider:* How would you encourage children's language abilities at the different stages of development?

Module 23: Intelligence

Recap

LO7 What are the different definitions and conceptions of intelligence?

- Because intelligence can take many forms, defining it is challenging. One commonly accepted view is that intelligence is the capacity to understand the world, think rationally, and use resources effectively when faced with challenges.
- The earliest psychologists assumed that there is a general factor for mental ability called g. However, later psychologists disputed the view that intelligence is unidimensional.
- Howard Gardner's theory of multiple intelligences proposes that there are at least eight spheres of intelligence.

LO8 What are the major approaches to measuring intelligence, and what do intelligence tests measure?

- Intelligence tests have traditionally compared a person's mental age and chronological age to yield an IQ, or intelligence quotient, score.
- Specific tests of intelligence include the Stanford-Binet test, the Wechsler Adult Intelligence Scale–IV (WAIS–IV), and the Wechsler Intelligence Scale for Children–V (WISC–V). Achievement tests and aptitude tests are other types of standardized tests.
- Tests are expected to be both reliable and valid. Reliability refers to the consistency with which a test measures what it is trying to measure. A test has validity when it actually measures what it is supposed to measure.

LO9 How are extremes of intelligence characterized?

- The levels of intellectual disabilities include mild, moderate, severe, and profound.
- The intellectually gifted are people with IQ scores greater than 130. Intellectually gifted people tend to be healthier and more successful than are the nongifted.

LO10 Are traditional IQ tests culturally biased?

- Traditional intelligence tests have frequently been criticized for being biased in favour of the white middle-class population. This controversy has led to attempts to devise culture-fair IQ tests, which avoid questions that depend on a particular cultural background.

LO11 To what degree is intelligence influenced by the environment, and to what degree by heredity?

- Attempting to distinguish environmental from hereditary factors in intelligence is probably futile and certainly misguided. Because individual IQ scores vary far more than do group IQ scores, it is more critical to ask what can be done to maximize the intellectual development of each individual.

Rethink

1. What is the role of emotional intelligence in the classroom? How might emotional intelligence be tested? Should emotional intelligence be a factor in determining academic promotion to the next grade?
2. *From the human resource specialist's perspective:* Job interviews are really a kind of test. In what ways does a job interview resemble an aptitude test? An achievement test? Do you think job interviews can be made to have validity and reliability?
3. Do you think of yourself as primarily an entity or incremental theorist in terms of intelligence? How do you think your view might have affected your performance on academic tasks? Do you think we should train students to think more incrementally about intelligence in order to improve their test performance?

CHAPTER 8
Motivation and Emotion

Source: © Carlos Gonzalez/MCT/Newscom.

Prologue

Olympic Hero

Joannie Rochette left home at the age of 13 to pursue a career in professional figure skating. She dedicated her young life to a rigorous training schedule of painstaking workouts and continual sacrifice. Her dedication, persistence, and sacrifice paid off when Rochette won her first Silver Medal at the age of 16 at the 2002 Canadian Figure Skating Championships.

Three years later, Rochette placed fifth at the 2006 Winter Olympics in Turin, Italy and in 2009, she earned a Silver Medal at the World Championships. Twenty-four year old Rochette ranked second in the world as she entered the 2010 Winter Olympics. Accordingly, medal expectations were high and hopeful for the young Canadian figure skater (DiManno, 2010).

Courage on Ice

In a shocking twist of fate, Rochette's mother died suddenly of a heart attack merely one day after arriving in Vancouver to support her daughter at the Olympic Games (Byers, 2010).

Only three short days after her mother's tragic death, Rochette made the courageous decision to compete in the Olympics. A determined young woman, Rochette refused to give up on her dreams of an Olympic Medal, and perhaps could think of no better way to honour her mother than to take to the ice at the Pacific Coliseum in front of 11,000 cheering spectators (Starkman, 2010).

On February 25, 2010, Rochette won the Bronze Medal in figure skating. In doing so, she inspired people around the world to face heartbreak head on, persist through challenge, and go after their dreams, no matter what!

What motivation lay behind Joannie Rochette's determination to compete in the Olympic Games, win a medal, and do so under the most tragic of family circumstances? Was it anticipation of the emotional thrill of winning the world's most prestigious competition in figure skating? The potential rewards that would follow if she succeeded? The excitement of participating? The satisfaction of achieving a long-sought goal? Perhaps all of the above, but most likely, Rochette's determination to compete was based on her intrinsic desire to achieve a lifelong dream while honouring her mother's memory.

In this chapter, we consider the issues that can help to answer such questions, as we address the topic of motivation and the related area of emotion. The topics of motivation and emotion are central in attempting to explain Rochette's extraordinary courage and determination. Psychologists who study motivation seek to discover the particular desired goals or motives that underlie behaviour—behaviours as basic as drinking to satisfy thirst and as inconsequential as taking a stroll to get exercise exemplify motives. Psychologists specializing in the study of motivation assume that such underlying motives steer our choices of activities.

Explaining Motivation

LEARNING OBJECTIVE

How does motivation direct and energize behaviour?

In just a moment, 27-year-old Aron Ralston's life changed. An 800-pound [362-kg] boulder dislodged in a narrow canyon where Ralston was hiking in an isolated Utah canyon, pinning his lower arm to the ground.

For the next five days, Ralston lay in the dense, lonely forest, unable to escape. An experienced climber who had search-and-rescue training, he had ample time to consider his options. He tried unsuccessfully to chip away at the rock, and he rigged up ropes and pulleys around the boulder in a vain effort to move it.

Finally, out of water and nearly dehydrated, Ralston reasoned there was only one option left short of dying. In acts of incredible bravery, Ralston broke two bones in his wrist, applied a tourniquet, and used a dull pen knife to amputate his arm beneath the elbow.

Freed from his entrapment, Ralston climbed down from where he had been pinned, and then hiked five miles [eight km] to safety (Cox, 2003; Lofholm, 2003).

Ralston, who now has a prosthetic arm, recovered from his ordeal. He remains an active outdoorsman and hiker.

What lies behind Ralston's incredible determination and will to live? To answer such questions, psychologists employ the concept of **motivation** the factors that direct and energize the behaviour of humans and other organisms. Motivation has biological, cognitive, and social aspects, and the complexity of the concept has led psychologists to develop a variety of approaches. All seek to explain the energy that guides people's behaviour in particular directions.

Instinct Approaches: Born to Be Motivated

When psychologists first tried to explain motivation, they turned to **instincts**, inborn patterns of behaviour that are biologically determined rather than learned. According to instinct approaches to motivation, people and animals are born preprogrammed with sets of behaviours essential to their survival. Those instincts provide the energy that channels behaviour in appropriate directions. Hence, sexual behaviour may be a response to an instinct to reproduce, and exploratory behaviour may be motivated by an instinct to examine one's territory.

This conception presents several difficulties, however. For one thing, psychologists do not agree on what, or even how many, primary instincts exist. One early psychologist, William McDougall (1908), suggested that there are eighteen instincts. Other theorists came up with even more—with one sociologist (Bernard, 1924) claiming that there are exactly 5,759 distinct instincts!

Motivation
The factors that direct and energize the behaviour of humans and other organisms.

Instincts
Inborn patterns of behaviour that are biologically determined rather than learned.

Furthermore, explanations based on the concept of instincts do not go very far toward explaining why one specific pattern of behaviour, and not others, has appeared in a given species. In addition, although it is clear that much animal behaviour is based on instincts, because much of the variety and complexity of human behaviour is learned, that behaviour cannot be seen as instinctual.

As a result of these shortcomings, newer explanations have replaced conceptions of motivation based on instincts. However, instinct approaches still play a role in certain theories, particularly those based on evolutionary approaches that focus on our genetic inheritance. Furthermore, Freud's work suggests that instinctual drives of sex and aggression motivate behaviour (Katz, 2001).

Drive-Reduction Approaches: Satisfying Our Basic Needs

After rejecting instinct theory, psychologists first proposed simple drive-reduction theories of motivation to take its place (Hull, 1943). **Drive-reduction approaches to motivation** suggest that a lack of some basic biological requirement such as water produces a drive to obtain that requirement (in this case, the thirst drive).

To understand this approach, we begin with the concept of drive. A **drive** is motivational tension, or arousal, that energizes behaviour to fulfill a need. Many basic drives, such as hunger, thirst, sleep, and sex, are related to biological needs of the body or of the species as a whole. These are called *primary drives*. Primary drives contrast with secondary drives, in which behaviour fulfills no obvious biological need. In *secondary drives*, prior experience and learning bring about needs. For instance, some people have strong needs to achieve academically and professionally. We can say that their achievement need is reflected in a secondary drive that motivates their behaviour (McKinley et al., 2004; Seli, 2007). For an in-depth discussion of "Need for Achievement," see Module 25.

We usually try to satisfy a primary drive by reducing the need underlying it. For example, we become hungry after not eating for a few hours and may raid the refrigerator, especially if the next scheduled meal is not imminent. If the weather turns cold, we put on extra clothing or raise the setting on the thermostat to keep warm. If our bodies need liquids to function properly, we experience thirst and seek out water.

Maslow's Hierarchy: Basic Needs Before Higher-Order Needs

What do Joannie Rochette, Albert Einstein, and Terry Fox have in common? According to a model of motivation devised by psychologist Abraham Maslow, the common thread, is that each of them fulfilled the highest levels of motivational needs underlying human behaviour.

Maslow's model places motivational needs in a hierarchy and suggests that before more sophisticated, higher-order needs can be met, certain primary needs must be satisfied (Maslow, 1970, 1987). A pyramid can represent the model, with the more basic needs at the bottom (e.g., food, sleep) and the higher-level needs (e.g., love, fulfillment) at the top (see Figure 1). To activate a particular higher-order need, thereby guiding behaviour, a person must first fulfill the more basic needs in the hierarchy.

The basic needs are primary drives: needs for water, food, sleep, sex, and the like. To move up the hierarchy, a person must first meet these basic physiological needs. Safety needs come next in the hierarchy; Maslow suggests that people need a safe, secure environment in order to function effectively. Physiological and safety needs compose the lower-order needs.

Only after meeting the basic lower-order needs can a person consider fulfilling higher-order needs, such as the needs for love and a sense of belonging, esteem, and self-actualization. Love and belongingness needs include the need to obtain and give affection and to be a contributing member of some group or society. After fulfilling these needs, a person strives for esteem. In Maslow's thinking, esteem relates to the need to develop a sense of self-worth by knowing that others know and value one's competence.

Drive-reduction approaches to motivation
Theories suggesting that a lack of a basic biological requirement such as water produces a drive to obtain that requirement (in this case, the thirst drive).

Drive
Motivational tension, or arousal, which energizes behaviour to fulfill a need.

Maslow's hierarchy shows how our motivation progresses up the pyramid from the broadest, most fundamental biological needs to higher-order ones. (Maslow, 1970.) Do you agree that lower-order needs must be satisfied before higher-order needs? Do hermits and monks who attempt to fulfill spiritual needs while denying basic physical needs contradict Maslow's hierarchy?

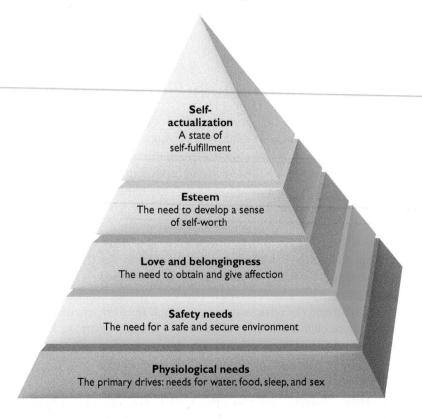

Once these four sets of needs are fulfilled—no easy task—a person is able to strive for the highest-level need, self-actualization. **Self-actualization** is a state of self-fulfillment in which people realize their highest potential in their own unique way. Although Maslow first suggested that self-actualization occurred in only a few, famous individuals, he later expanded the concept to encompass everyday people. For example, a student who reaches his academic potential and graduates with honours while working midnights at an automotive plant to support his family, a teacher who year after year creates an environment that maximizes students' opportunities for success, and an athlete such as Joannie Rochette who realizes her Olympic dream all may be self-actualized.

Homeostasis: Steady State

Homeostasis, the body's tendency to maintain a steady internal state, underlies primary drives. Using feedback loops, homeostasis brings deviations in body functioning back to an optimal state, similar to the way a thermostat and a furnace work in a home heating system to maintain a steady temperature. Receptor cells throughout the body constantly monitor factors such as temperature and nutrient levels, and when deviations from the ideal state occur, the body adjusts in an effort to return to an optimal state. Many fundamental needs, including the needs for food, water, stable body temperature, and sleep, operate via homeostasis (Canteras, 2002; Machado, Suchecki, & Tufik, 2005).

Self-actualization
A state of self-fulfillment in which people realize their highest potential in their own unique way.

Homeostasis
The body's tendency to maintain a steady internal state.

STUDY ALERT!

To remember the concept of homeostasis, keep in mind the analogy of a thermostat that regulates the temperature in a house.

Although drive-reduction theories provide a good explanation of how primary drives motivate behaviour, they cannot fully explain a behaviour in which the goal is not to reduce a drive, but rather to maintain or even increase the level of excitement or arousal. For instance, some behaviours seem to be motivated by nothing more than curiosity, such as rushing to check e-mail messages. Similarly, many people pursue thrilling activities such as riding a roller coaster and steering a raft down the rapids of a river. Such behaviours certainly don't suggest that people seek to reduce all drives, as drive-reduction approaches would indicate (Loewenstein, 1994; Begg & Langley, 2001; Rosenbloom & Wolf, 2002).

Both curiosity and thrill-seeking behaviour, then, shed doubt on drive-reduction approaches as a complete explanation for motivation. In both cases, rather than seeking to reduce an underlying drive, people and animals appear to be motivated to increase their overall level of stimulation and activity. To explain this phenomenon, psychologists have devised an alternative: arousal approaches to motivation.

Arousal Approaches: Beyond Drive Reduction

Arousal approaches seek to explain behaviour in which the goal is to maintain or increase excitement. According to **arousal approaches to motivation**, each person tries to maintain a certain level of stimulation and activity. As with the drive-reduction model, this model suggests that if our stimulation and activity levels become too high, we try to reduce them. But in contrast to the drive-reduction model, the arousal model also suggests that if levels of stimulation and activity are too low, we will try to increase them by seeking stimulation.

The arousal approach may explain why some people are motivated to risk their lives in pursuit of extreme sports. Reaching the top of Mount Everest used to be the ultimate climbing experience, but these days, climbers are pushing themselves harder and higher, with fewer resources. In fact, several elite climbers have died attempting to summit Mount Everest without oxygen! Case in point, on May, 21, 2009, a Calgary man died from hypothermia shortly after reaching the peak of Mount Everest without the assistance of bottled oxygen (The Canadian Press, 2009).

What motivates individuals to take such risks? People vary widely in the optimal level of arousal they seek out, with some people looking for especially high levels of arousal. For example, people who participate in extreme sports, high-stakes gamblers, and criminals who pull off high-risk robberies may be exhibiting a particularly high need for arousal (Zuckerman & Kuhlman, 2000; Zuckerman, 2002; Cavenett & Nixon, 2006; see Figure 2).

Incentive Approaches: Motivated by Temptation

When a luscious dessert appears on the table after a filling meal, its appeal has little or nothing to do with internal drives or the maintenance of arousal. Rather, if we choose to eat the dessert, such behaviour is motivated by the external stimulus of the dessert itself, which acts as an anticipated reward. This reward, in motivational terms, is an *incentive*.

Incentive approaches to motivation suggest that motivation stems from the desire to obtain valued external goals, or incentives. In this view, the desirable properties of external stimuli—whether grades, money, affection, food, or sex—account for a person's motivation (Festinger et al., 2009).

Arousal approaches to motivation
The belief that we try to maintain certain levels of stimulation and activity, increasing or reducing them as necessary.

Incentive approaches to motivation
Theories suggesting that motivation stems from the desire to obtain valued external goals, or incentives.

FIGURE 2

Some people seek high levels of arousal, while others are more easygoing. You can get a sense of your own preferred level of stimulation by completing this questionnaire.

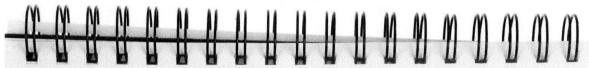

Do You Seek Out Sensation?

How much stimulation do you crave in your everyday life? You will have an idea after you complete the following questionnaire, which lists some items from a scale designed to assess your sensation-seeking tendencies. Circle either A or B in each pair or statements.

1. A I would like a job that requires a lot of travelling.
   B I would prefer a job in one location.
2. A I am invigorated by a brisk, cold day.
   B I can't wait to get indoors on a cold day.
3. A I get bored seeing the same old faces.
   B I like the comfortable familiarity of everyday friends.
4. A I would prefer living in an ideal society in which everyone was safe, secure, and happy.
   B I would have preferred living in the unsettled days of our history.
5. A I sometimes like to do things that are a little frightening.
   B A sensible person avoids activities that are dangerous.
6. A I would not like to be hypnotized.
   B I would like to have the experience of being hypnotized.
7. A The most important goal of life is to live it to the fullest and to experience as much as possible.
   B The most important goal of life is to find peace and happiness.
8. A I would like to try parachute jumping.
   B I would never want to try jumping out of a plane, with or without a parachute.
9. A I enter cold water gradually, giving myself time to get used to it.
   B I like to dive or jump right into the ocean or a cold pool.
10. A When I go on a vacation, I prefer the comfort of a good room and bed.
    B When I go on a vacation, I prefer the change of camping out.
11. A I prefer people who are emotionally expressive, even if they are a bit unstable.
    B I prefer people who are calm and even-tempered.
12. A A good painting should shock or jolt the senses.
    B A good painting should give one a feeling of peace and security.
13. A People who ride motorcycles must have some kind of unconscious need to hurt themselves.
    B I would like to drive or ride a motorcycle.

SCORING

Give yourself one point for each of the following responses: 1A, 2A, 3A, 4B, 5A, 6B, 7A, 8A, 9B, 10B, 11A, 12A, 13B. Find your total score by adding up the number of points and then use the following scoring key.

0–3 very low sensation seeking
4–5 low
6–9 average
10–11 high
12–13 very high

Keep in mind, of course, that this short questionnaire, for which the scoring is based on the results of college and university students who have taken it, provides only a rough estimate of your sensation-seeking tendencies. Moreover, as people get older, their sensation-seeking scores tend to decrease. Still, the questionnaire will at least give you an indication of how your sensation-seeking tendencies compare with those of others.

Source: "Do You Seek Out Sensation?" questionnaire from Marvin Zuckerman, "The Search for High Sensation?" *Psychology Today*, February 1978, pp. 30–46. Reprinted with permission from *Psychology Today* magazine. (Copyright © 1978 Sussex Publishers, LLC.)

Although the theory explains why we may succumb to an incentive (such as a mouthwatering dessert) even though we lack internal cues (such as hunger), it does not provide a complete explanation of motivation, because organisms sometimes seek to fulfill needs even when incentives are not apparent. Consequently, many psychologists believe that the internal drives proposed by drive-reduction theory work in tandem with the external incentives of incentive theory to "push" and "pull" behaviour, respectively. Thus, at the same time that we seek to satisfy our underlying hunger needs (the push of drive-reduction theory), we are drawn to food that appears particularly appetizing (the pull of incentive theory). Rather than contradicting each other, then, drives and incentives may work together in motivating behaviour (Pinel, Assanand, & Lehman, 2000; Lowery, Fillingim, & Wright, 2003; Berridge, 2004).

Cognitive Approaches: Thoughts Behind Motivation

We live in a world that rewards frivolous behaviour with fame and fortune, so it is no wonder that some students expect their motivation to come from the outside, in the same way that reality show contestants expect to win a million dollars, simply by "*showing up.*" In contrast to students who expect an A+ simply for coming to class, some students are motivated to attend class by the feeling of satisfaction they get from learning something new. These students have learned over time that motivation that comes from the outside (e.g., grades, money) is not enough to sustain their hard work over time. The only source of motivation that fuels their passion for learning is the motivation that begins on the inside (e.g., enjoyment, interest). What explains the difference between these two groups of students?

Cognitive approaches to motivation suggest that motivation is a product of people's thoughts, expectations, and goals—their cognitions. For instance, the degree to which people are motivated to study for a test is based on their expectation of how well studying will pay off in terms of a good grade (Wigfield & Eccles, 2000).

Cognitive theories of motivation draw a key distinction between intrinsic and extrinsic motivation. *Intrinsic motivation* causes us to participate in an activity for our own enjoyment rather than for any concrete, tangible reward that it will bring us. In contrast, *extrinsic motivation* causes us to do something for money, a grade, or some other concrete, tangible reward. For example, when a nursing student studies long hours because she loves medicine, intrinsic motivation is prompting her; if she studies hard hoping to one day make a lot of money, extrinsic motivation underlies her efforts (Lepper, Corpus, & Iyengar, 2005; Shaikholeslami & Khayyer, 2006; Finkelstein, 2009).

We are more apt to persevere, work harder, and produce work of higher quality when motivation for a task is intrinsic rather than extrinsic. In fact, in some cases providing rewards for desirable behaviour (thereby increasing extrinsic motivation) actually may decrease intrinsic motivation (Henderlong & Lepper, 2002; James, 2005; Grant, 2008).

STUDY ALERT!

Review distinctions between the different explanations for motivation (instinct, drive reduction, arousal, incentive, cognitive, and Maslow's hierarchy of needs).

Evaluate

1. _____ are forces that guide a person's behaviour in a certain direction.

2. Biologically determined, inborn patterns of behaviour are known as _____.

3. Your psychology professor tells you, "Explaining behaviour is easy! When we lack something, we are motivated to get it." Which approach to motivation does your professor subscribe to?

4. By drinking water after running a marathon, a runner tries to keep his or her body at an optimal level of functioning. This process is called _____.

Cognitive approaches to motivation
Theories suggesting that motivation is a product of people's thoughts, expectations, and goals—their cognitions.

5. I help an elderly person cross the street because doing a good deed makes me feel good. What type of motivation is at work here? What type of motivation would be at work if I were to help an elderly man across the street because he paid me $20?

6. According to Maslow, a person with no job, no home, and no friends can become self-actualized. True or false?

Answers to Evaluate Questions

1. motives; 2. instincts; 3. drive reduction; 4. homeostasis; 5. intrinsic, extrinsic; 6. false; lower-order needs must be fulfilled before self-actualization can occur.

Key Terms

arousal approaches to motivation

cognitive approaches to motivation

drive

drive-reduction approaches to motivation

homeostasis

incentive approaches to motivation

instincts

motivation

self-actualization

Human Needs and Motivation: Eat, Drink, and Be Daring

LEARNING OBJECTIVES

What biological and social factors underlie hunger?

What are the varieties of sexual behaviour?

How are needs relating to affiliation, power, and achievement motivation exhibited?

"I have been struggling with binge eating disorder for the past year of my life, and I have only come to recognize it as an eating disorder in the last two months or so. At this point I feel hopeless, and I feel so alone in this struggle" admits Karen, a second year college student. Karen suffers from binge eating disorder (BED), the largest growing eating disorder on college and university campuses in Canada—three times more prevalent than anorexia nervosa. For Karen, food is a means to forget about the strain and pressures of student life. Karen confesses to feeling out of control when she binges. Binge eaters like Karen wait until no one is around and then stuff themselves until painfully full. The secrecy and concealment of binge eating heightens the feelings of depression and lack of control afterwards (Li, 2008, p. 1).

Karen is one of the estimated 3 percent of Canadians who suffer from an eating disorder (Public Health Agency of Canada, 2002a). These disorders, which usually appear during adolescence, can bring about extraordinary health problems.

Why are Karen and others like her subject to such disordered eating, which revolves around the motivation to binge eat? What motivates others to avoid weight gain at all costs? And why do so many people engage in overeating, which leads to obesity?

To answer these questions, we must consider some of the specific needs that underlie behaviour. In this module, we examine several of the most important human needs. We begin with hunger and sex, the primary drives that have received the most attention from researchers. We then turn to secondary drives—those uniquely human endeavours, based on learned needs and past experience, that help explain why people affiliate with others, seek power over others, and strive to achieve.

The Motivation Behind Hunger and Eating

Six in ten Canadians are overweight, and almost a quarter are so heavy that they have **obesity**, body weight that is more than 20 percent above the average weight for a person of a particular height. And the rest of the world is not far behind: Americans have higher rates of obesity than their Canadian neighbours. This difference is most notable in females. One in three American women is classified as obese whereas one in five Canadian women fit this category (Statistics Canada, 2005; Lau, Douketis, Morrison, Hramiak, Sharma, & Ehud, 2007; Public Health Agency of Canada, 2007).

A billion people around the globe are overweight or obese. The World Health Organization has said that worldwide obesity has reached epidemic proportions, producing increases in heart disease, diabetes, cancer, and premature deaths (Grady, 2002; Calle & Kaaks, 2004; Hill, Catenacci, & Wyatt, 2005; McNeil, 2005).

Obesity

Body weight that is more than 20 percent above the average weight for a person of a particular height.

The most widely used measure of obesity is *body mass index (BMI)*, which is based on a ratio of weight to height. People with a BMI greater than 30 are considered obese, whereas those with a BMI between 25 and 30 are overweight. (Use the formulas in Figure 1 to determine your own BMI.)

Although the definition of obesity is clear from a scientific point of view, people's perceptions of what an ideal body looks like vary significantly across different cultures and, within Western cultures, from one time period to another. For instance, many contemporary Western cultures admire slimness in women—a relatively recent view. In nineteenth-century Hawaii, the most attractive women were those who were the heaviest. Furthermore, for most of the twentieth century—except for periods in the 1920s and the most recent decades—the ideal female figure was relatively full. Even today, weight standards differ among different cultural groups. For instance, African Americans generally judge heavier women more positively than whites do. In some traditional Arab cultures, obese women are so prized as wives that parents force-feed their female children to make them more desirable (Naik, 2004; Blixen et al., 2006; Marsh et al., 2007).

Regardless of cultural standards for appearance and weight, no one doubts that being overweight represents a major health risk. However, controlling weight is complicated, because eating behaviour involves a variety of mechanisms. In our discussion of what motivates people to eat, we'll start with the biological aspects of eating.

Biological Factors in the Regulation of Hunger

In contrast to human beings, other species are unlikely to become obese. Internal mechanisms regulate not only the quantity of food they take in but also the kind of food they desire. For example, rats that have been deprived of particular foods seek out alternatives that contain the specific nutrients their diet is lacking, and many species, given the choice of a wide variety of foods, select a well-balanced diet (Bouchard & Bray, 1996; Woods et al., 2000; Jones & Corp, 2003).

Complex mechanisms tell organisms whether they require food or should stop eating. It's not just a matter of an empty stomach causing hunger pangs and a full one alleviating those pangs. (Even individuals who have had their stomachs removed still experience the sensation of hunger.) One important factor is changes in the chemical composition of the blood. In particular, changes in levels of glucose, a kind of sugar, regulate feelings of hunger (Teff et al., 2007; Wren & Bloom, 2007; Kojima & Kangawa, 2008).

The brain's *hypothalamus* monitors glucose levels. Increasing evidence suggests that the hypothalamus carries the primary responsibility for monitoring food intake. Injury to the hypothalamus has radical consequences for eating

---

FIGURE 1

Use this procedure to find your body mass index (BMI).

To calculate your body mass index, follow these steps:

1. Indicate your weight in pounds: _____ pounds
2. Indicate your height in inches: _____ inches
3. Divide your weight (item 1) by your height (item 2), and write the outcome here: _____
4. Divide the result above (item 3) by your height (item 2), and write the outcome here: _____
5. Multiply the number above by 703, and write the product here: _____. This is your body mass index.

Example:

For a person who weighs 210 pounds and who is 6 feet tall, divide 210 pounds by 72 inches, which equals 2.917. Then divide 2.917 by 72 inches (item 3), which yields .041. Multiplying .041 (from item 4) by 703 yields a BMI of 28.5.

Interpretation:

- Underweight = less than 18.5
- Normal weight = 18.5–24.9
- Overweight = 25–29.9
- Obesity = BMI of 30 or greater

Keep in mind that a BMI greater than 25 may or may not be due to excess body fat. For example, professional athletes may have little fat but weigh more than the average person because they have greater muscle mass.

behaviour, depending on the site of the injury. For example, rats whose *lateral hypothalamus* is damaged may literally starve to death. They refuse food when it is offered, and unless they are force-fed, they eventually die. Rats with an injury to the *ventromedial hypothalamus* display the opposite problem: extreme overeating. Rats with this injury can increase in weight by as much as 400 percent. Similar phenomena occur in humans who have tumours of the hypothalamus (Woods & Seeley, 2002; Seymour, 2006; Fedeli et al., 2009).

Although the important role the hypothalamus plays in regulating food intake is clear, the exact way this organ operates is still unclear. One hypothesis suggests that injury to the hypothalamus affects the **weight set point**, or the particular level of weight that the body strives to maintain, which in turn regulates food intake. Acting as a kind of internal weight thermostat, the hypothalamus calls for either greater or less food intake (Capaldi, 1996; Woods et al., 2000; Berthoud, 2002).

In most cases, the hypothalamus does a good job. Even people who are not deliberately monitoring their weight show only minor weight fluctuations in spite of substantial day-to-day variations in how much they eat and exercise. However, injury to the hypothalamus can alter the weight set point, and a person then struggles to meet the internal goal by increasing or decreasing food consumption. Even temporary exposure to certain drugs can alter the weight set point (Cabanac & Frankham, 2002; Hallschmid et al., 2004; Khazaal et al., 2008).

Genetic factors determine the weight set point, at least in part. People seem destined, through heredity, to have a particular **metabolism**, the rate at which food is converted to energy and expended by the body. People with a high metabolic rate can eat virtually as much as they want without gaining weight, whereas others, with low metabolism, may eat literally half as much yet gain weight readily (Jequier, 2002; Westerterp, 2006).

Social Factors in Eating

You've just finished a full meal and feel completely stuffed. Suddenly your host announces with great fanfare that he will be serving his "house specialty" dessert, bananas flambé, and that he has spent the better part of the afternoon preparing it. Even though you are full and don't even like bananas, you accept a serving of his dessert and eat it all.

STUDY ALERT!

A key point: Eating and hunger are influenced by both biological and social factors.

Clearly, internal biological factors do not fully explain our eating behaviour. External social factors, based on societal rules and on what we have learned about appropriate eating behaviour, also play an important role. Take, for example, the simple fact that people customarily eat breakfast, lunch, and dinner at approximately the same times every day. Because we tend to eat on schedule every day, we feel hungry as the usual hour approaches, sometimes quite independently of what our internal cues are telling us.

Similarly, we put roughly the same amount of food on our plates every day, even though the amount of exercise we may have had, and consequently our need for energy replenishment, varies from day to day. We also tend to prefer particular foods over others. Rats and dogs may be a delicacy in certain Asian cultures, but few people in Western cultures find them appealing despite their potentially high nutritional value. Even the amount of food we eat varies according to cultural norms. For instance, people in the United States eat bigger portions than people in France. In sum, cultural influences and our individual habits play important roles in determining when, what, and how much we eat (Miller & Pumariega, 2001; Rozin et al., 2003).

Other social factors relate to our eating behaviour as well. Some of us head toward the refrigerator after a difficult day, seeking solace in a litre of Chapman's mocha almond fudge ice cream. Why? Perhaps when we were children, our parents gave us food when we were upset. Eventually, we may have learned, through the basic mechanisms of classical

Weight set point
The particular level of weight that the body strives to maintain.

Metabolism
The rate at which food is converted to energy and expended by the body.

and operant conditioning, to associate food with comfort and consolation. Similarly, we may learn that eating, which focuses our attention on immediate pleasures, provides an escape from unpleasant thoughts. Consequently, we may eat when we feel distressed (Bulik et al., 2003; O'Connor & O'Connor, 2004; Elfhag, Tynelius, & Rasmussen, 2007; also see *PsychWork*).

PsychWork

Nutritionist

Name: Gail K. Rupert
Position: Nutritionist
Education: Bachelor of Science in Foods and Nutrition, School of Nutrition–Ryerson University, Toronto, Ontario

Obesity has become a serious health issue for many Americans, who struggle to maintain a healthy diet and weight. For Gail Rupert, a nutritionist with The Weight Loss Clinic, motivation is a key ingredient in losing weight.

In her approach to getting people motivated, Rupert says, "It's important to empathize with the patient so they don't feel like they're on their own with no support. I tell them I understand that the weight loss process can be frustrating and emotional, and it may take a lot of persistence and consistency before seeing any reduction in weight.

"Each client is different. Some patients have absolutely no knowledge of nutrition, while others have at least some familiarity," she explained. "For those with little knowledge, I have to break down more difficult concepts to help them better understand the procedure.

"For all patients, I make sure to give a reason why I'm suggesting a change. Most patients wouldn't change eating or exercise habits if I didn't explain the positive consequences of their actions. For example, exercising three times per week will improve their metabolism and increase their weight loss," she added.

The Roots of Obesity

Given that both biological and social factors influence eating behaviour, determining the causes of obesity has proved to be a challenging task. Researchers have followed several paths.

Some psychologists suggest that oversensitivity to external eating cues based on social factors, coupled with insensitivity to internal hunger cues, produces obesity. Others argue that overweight people have higher weight set points than other people do. Because their set points are unusually high, their attempts to lose weight by eating less may make them especially sensitive to external, food-related cues and therefore more apt to overeat, perpetuating their obesity (Tremblay, 2004; West, Harvey-Berino, & Raczynski, 2004).

But why may some people's weight set points be higher than those of others? One biological explanation is that obese individuals have a higher level of the hormone *leptin*, which appears to be designed, from an evolutionary standpoint, to "protect" the body against weight loss. The body's weight-regulation system thus appears to be designed more to protect against losing weight than to protect against gaining it, meaning that it's easier to gain weight than to lose it (Ahiima & Osei, 2004; Zhang et al., 2005; Levin, 2006).

Another biologically based explanation for obesity relates to fat cells in the body. Starting at birth, the body stores fat either by increasing the number of fat cells or by increasing the size of existing fat cells. Furthermore, any loss of weight past infancy does not decrease the number of fat cells; it only affects their size. Consequently, people are stuck with the number of fat cells they inherit from an early age, and the rate of weight gain during the first four months of life is related to being overweight during later childhood (Stettler et al., 2005).

According to the weight-set-point hypothesis, the presence of too many fat cells from earlier weight gain may result in the set point becoming "stuck" at a higher level than is desirable. In such circumstances, losing weight becomes a difficult proposition, because one is constantly at odds with one's own internal set point when dieting (Freedman, 1995; Leibel, Rosenbaum & Hirsch, 1995).

Not everyone agrees with the set-point explanation for obesity. But one point everyone agrees on is the dramatic rise in obesity rates in Canada and other countries in recent years (Millar & Stephens, 1987; Statistics Canada, 2005; Lau et al., 2007). Because of this rapid rise in obesity over the last several decades, some researchers suggest that the body does not try to maintain a fixed weight set point. Instead, they suggest, the body has a *settling point*, determined by a combination of our genetic heritage and the nature of the environment in which we live. If high-fat foods are prevalent in our environment and we are genetically predisposed to obesity, we settle into an equilibrium that maintains relatively high weight. In contrast, if our environment is nutritionally healthier, a genetic predisposition to obesity will not be triggered, and we will settle into an equilibrium in which our weight is lower (Comuzzie & Allison, 1998; Pi-Sunyer, 2003).

Eating Disorders

One devastating weight-related disorder is **anorexia nervosa**. In this severe eating disorder, people may refuse to eat while denying that their behaviour and appearance, which can become skeleton like, is unusual. Some 10 percent of people with anorexia literally starve themselves to death (Striegel-Moore & Bulik, 2007).

Anorexia nervosa mainly afflicts females between the ages of 12 and 40, although both men and women of any age may develop it. People with the disorder typically come from stable homes, and they are often successful, attractive, and relatively affluent. The disorder often occurs after serious dieting, which somehow gets out of control. Life begins to revolve around food: Although people with the disorder eat little, they may cook for others, go shopping for food frequently, or collect cookbooks (Polivy, Herman, & Boivin, 2005; Myers, 2007; Jacobs et al., 2009).

A related problem, **bulimia**, is a disorder in which people binge on large quantities of food. For instance, they may consume an entire litre of ice cream and a whole pie in a single sitting. After such a binge, sufferers feel guilt and depression and often induce vomiting or take laxatives to rid themselves of the food—behaviour known as purging. Constant bingeing and purging cycles and the use of drugs to induce vomiting or diarrhea can lead to heart failure. Often, though, the weight of a person with bulimia remains normal (Mora-Giral et al., 2004; Couturier & Lock, 2006).

As explained at the beginning of this module, eating disorders represent a growing problem on college and university campuses in Canada. Estimates show that 2.1 percent of women have anorexia nervosa or bulimia. Furthermore, an increasing number of men are diagnosed with eating disorders; an estimated 10 percent of all cases occur in males. Binge eating disorder (BED) is the largest growing eating disorder on campus—three times more prevalent than anorexia nervosa (Public Health Agency of Canada, 2002a; Li, 2008). The complete explanations for anorexia nervosa and bulimia remain elusive. These disorders probably stem from both biological and social causes, and successful treatment probably encompasses several strategies, including therapy and dietary changes (O'Brien & LeBow, 2007; Wilson, Grilo, & Vitousek, 2007; Cooper & Shafran, 2008).

Sexual Motivation

Anyone who has seen two dogs mating knows that sexual behaviour has a biological basis. Their sexual behaviour appears to occur naturally, without much prompting on the part of others. A number of genetically controlled factors influence the sexual behaviour of nonhuman animals. For instance, animal behaviour is affected by the presence of certain hormones in the blood. Moreover, female animals are receptive to sexual advances only during certain relatively limited periods of the year.

Human sexual behaviour, by comparison, is more complicated, although the underlying biology is not all that different from that of related species. In males, for example, the *testes* begin to secrete **androgens**, male sex hormones,

---

Anorexia nervosa
A weight-related disorder where people may refuse to eat while denying that their behaviour and appearance, which can become skeleton like, is unusual.

Bulimia
A weight-related disorder in which people binge eat on large quantities of food. After such a binge, sufferers often purge by taking laxatives or vomiting to rid themselves of the food.

Androgens
Male sex hormones secreted by the testes.

Becoming an Informed Consumer of Psychology

Dieting and Losing Weight Successfully

Although most Canadians would admit to dieting at one time or another, unfortunately it's a losing battle for most of us. Television shows like *The Biggest Loser* where contestants are rewarded for losing a significant amount of weight in a short period of time further reinforce our desire for a "quick fix" to longstanding weight problems.

Most people who diet eventually regain the weight they have lost, and so they try again and get caught in a seemingly endless cycle of weight loss and gain. Given what we know about the causes of obesity, this is not entirely surprising, because so many factors affect eating behaviour and weight (Lowe, 1993; Newport & Carroll, 2002; Parker-Pope, 2003).

According to diet experts, you should keep several things in mind when trying to lose weight (Consumer Reports, 1993; Gatchel & Oordt, 2003; Heshka et al., 2003):

- *There is no easy route to weight control.* You will have to make permanent changes in your life to lose weight without gaining it back. The most obvious strategy—cutting down on the amount of food you eat—is just the first step toward a lifetime commitment to changing your eating habits. You must consider the nutrient content, as well as the overall quantity, of the food you consume.

- *Keep track of what you eat and what you weigh.* Unless you keep careful records, you won't really know how much you are eating and whether any diet is working.

- *Eat "big" foods.* Eat foods that are bulky and heavy but low in calories, such as grapes and soup. Such foods trick your body into thinking you've eaten more, decreasing hunger.

- *Cut out television.* One reason for the epidemic of obesity is the number of hours spent viewing television by people in North America. Not only does watching television preclude other activities that burn calories (even walking around the house is helpful), people often gorge on junk food while watching. One study found that after researchers took into account the effects of exercise, smoking, age, and diet, each two-hour increase in daily TV-viewing led to a 23-percent increase in obesity (Hu et al., 2003).

- *Exercise.* When you exercise, you use up fat stored in your body as fuel for muscles, which is measured in calories. As you use up this fat, you will probably lose weight. Almost any activity helps burn calories. The weight-set-point hypothesis suggests another advantage to moderate exercise: It may lower your set point. Although just how much exercise is sufficient to lower weight is disputed, most experts recommend at least thirty consecutive minutes of moderate exercise at least three times a week. (If nothing else, the release of endorphins, neurotransmitters involved in pain reduction, after exercise will make you feel better even if you don't lose weight.)

- *Decrease the influence of external, social stimuli on your eating behaviour.* For instance, serve yourself smaller portions of food, and leave the table before you see what is being served for dessert. Don't even buy snack foods such as nachos and potato chips; if they're not readily available in the kitchen cupboard, you're not apt to eat them. Wrap refrigerated foods in aluminum foil so that you cannot see the contents and be tempted every time you open the refrigerator.

- *Avoid fad diets.* No matter how popular they are at a particular time, extreme diets, including liquid diets, usually don't work in the long run and can be dangerous to your health.

- *Maintain good eating habits.* When you have reached your desired weight, maintain the new habits you learned while dieting to avoid gaining back the weight you have lost.

- *Set reasonable goals.* Know how much weight you want to lose before you start to diet. Don't try to lose too much weight too quickly or you may doom yourself to failure. Even small changes in behaviour—such as walking fifteen minutes a day or eating a few less bites at each meal—can prevent weight gain (Hill et al., 2003).

- *Don't feel guilty!* Above all, don't blame yourself if you don't succeed in losing weight. Given the evidence that obesity may be genetically determined, the inability to lose weight should not be seen as a moral failing. Indeed, you are in good company, for some 90 to 95 percent of dieters regain the weight they have lost (Fritsch, 1999; Friedman, 2003).

In light of the difficulty of losing weight, psychologists Janet Polivy and C. Peter Herman suggest—paradoxically—that the best approach may be to avoid dieting in the first place. They recommend that people eat what they really want to eat, even if this means indulging in candy or ice cream every so often. This freedom to eat anything may reduce binge eating, which is more likely to occur when dieters feel that bingeing represents their only opportunity to eat what they really wish to eat. Although such an approach may not produce major weight loss, even a relatively small weight loss is better than none: Just a ten- to fifteen-pound (or five to seven kg) drop in body weight may lower the major health risks that are associated with obesity (Bruce & Wilfley, 1996; *HealthNews,* 1999; Polivy & Herman, 2002; Avenell et al., 2004).

at puberty. (See Figure 2 for the basic anatomy of the male and female **genitals**, or sex organs.) Not only do androgens produce secondary sex characteristics, such as the growth of body hair and a deepening of the voice, they also increase the sex drive. Because the level of androgen production by the testes is fairly constant, men are capable of (and interested in) sexual activities without any regard to biological cycles. Given the proper stimuli leading to arousal, male sexual behaviour can occur at any time (Goldstein, 2000).

Women show a different pattern. When they reach maturity at puberty, the two *ovaries* begin to produce **estrogens** and **progesterone**, the female sex hormones. However, those hormones aren't produced consistently; instead, their

---

FIGURE 2

Cutaway side views of the female and male sex organs.

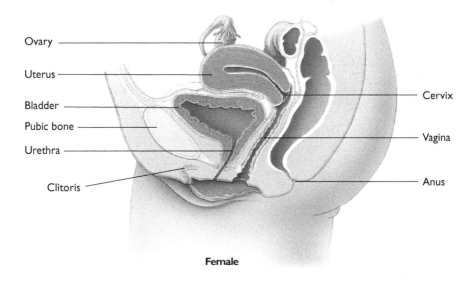

Female

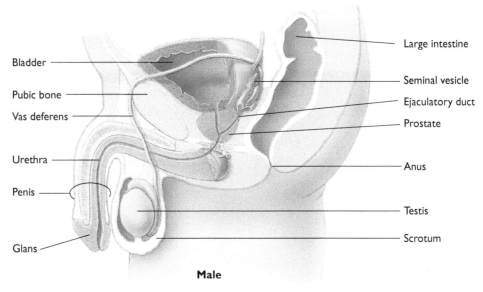

Male

Genitals
The male and female sex organs.

Estrogens
Class of female sex hormones.

Progesterone
A female sex hormone secreted by the ovaries.

production follows a cyclical pattern. The greatest output occurs during **ovulation**, when an egg is released from the ovaries to increase the chances of fertilization by a sperm cell. Whereas in nonhumans the period around ovulation is the only time the female is receptive to sex, humans are different; although there are reported variations in sex drive, women are receptive to sex throughout their cycles (Leiblum & Chivers, 2007).

In addition, some evidence suggests that males have a stronger sex drive than females do, although the difference may be the result of society's discouragement of overt displays of female sexuality rather than of inborn differences between men and women. It is clear that men think about sex more than women: while 54 percent of men report thinking about sex every day, only 19 percent of women report thinking about it on a daily basis (Mendelsohn, 2003; Gangestad et al., 2004; Baumeister & Stillman, 2006; Carvalho & Nobre, 2011).

Though biological factors prime people for sex, it takes more than hormones to motivate and produce sexual behavior. In animals the presence of a partner who provides arousing stimuli leads to sexual activity. Humans are considerably more versatile; not only other people but nearly any object, sight, smell, sound, or other stimulus can lead to sexual excitement. Due to prior associations, then, people may be turned on sexually by the smell of perfume or the sound of a favourite song hummed softly in their ears. The reaction to a specific potentially arousing stimulus, as we shall see, is highly individual—what turns one person on may do just the opposite for another (Benson, 2003).

Masturbation: Solitary Sex

If you listened to physicians seventy-five years ago, you would have been told that **masturbation**, sexual self-stimulation, often using the hand to rub the genitals, would lead to a wide variety of physical and mental disorders, ranging from hairy palms to insanity. If those physicians had been correct, however, most of us would be wearing gloves to hide the sight of our hair-covered palms—for masturbation is one of the most frequently practised sexual activities. Some 94 percent of all males and 63 percent of all females have masturbated at least once, and among both college and university students, the frequency ranges from "never" to "several times a day" (Hunt, 1974; Michael et al., 1994; Laqueur, 2003; Polonsky, 2006).

Men and women typically begin to masturbate for the first time at different ages, and men masturbate considerably more often than women, although there are differences in frequency according to age. Male masturbation is most common in the early teens and then declines, whereas females both begin and reach a maximum frequency later. There are also some racial differences: African American men and women masturbate less than whites do (Oliver & Hyde, 1993; Pinkerton et al., 2002; Das, Parish, & Laumann, 2009).

Although masturbation is often considered an activity to engage in only if no other sexual outlets are available, this view bears little relationship to reality. Close to three-quarters of married men (age 20 to 40) report masturbating an average of twenty-four times a year, and 68 percent of the married women in the same age group masturbate an average of ten times a year (Hunt, 1974; Michael et al., 1994; Das, 2007).

Despite the high incidence of masturbation, attitudes toward it still reflect some of the negative views of yesteryear. For instance, one survey found that around 10 percent of people who masturbated experienced feelings of guilt, and 5 percent of the males and 1 percent of the females considered their behaviour perverted (Arafat & Cotton, 1974). Despite these negative attitudes, however, most experts on sex view masturbation as a healthy and legitimate—and harmless—sexual activity. In addition, masturbation is seen as providing a means of learning about one's own sexuality and a way of discovering changes in one's body such as the emergence of precancerous lumps (Coleman, 2002; Levin, 2007; Herbenick et al., 2009).

Heterosexuality

Many people believe that the first time they have sexual intercourse they have achieved one of life's major milestones. However, **heterosexuality**—sexual attraction and behaviour directed to the other sex—consists of far more than

---

Ovulation
The point at which an egg is released from the ovaries.

Masturbation
Sexual self-stimulation.

Heterosexuality
Sexual attraction and behaviour directed to the other sex.

male–female intercourse. Kissing, petting, caressing, massaging, and other forms of sex play are all components of heterosexual behaviour. Still, the focus of sex researchers has been on the act of intercourse, particularly in terms of its first occurrence and its frequency.

Premarital Sex

Until fairly recently, premarital sexual intercourse, at least for women, was considered one of the major taboos in our society. Traditionally, women have been warned by society that "nice girls don't do it"; men have been told that premarital sex is okay for them, but they should marry virgins. This view that premarital sex is permissible for males but not for females is called the **double standard** (Liang, 2007).

Although as recently as the 1960s the majority of adult North Americans believed that premarital sex was always wrong, since that time there has been a dramatic change in public opinion. For example, the percentage of middle-aged people who say sex before marriage is "not wrong at all" has increased considerably, and overall 60 percent of Americans say premarital sex is okay. More than half say that living together before marriage is morally acceptable (Thornton & Young-DeMarco, 2001; Focus on the Family National Survey, 2002).

Changes in attitudes toward premarital sex were matched by changes in actual rates of premarital sexual activity. For instance, the most recent figures show that 43 percent of Canadian women and just over one-half of American women between the ages of 15 and 19 have had premarital sexual intercourse. These figures are close to double the number of women in the same age range who reported having intercourse in 1970. Clearly, the trend over the last several decades has been toward more women engaging in premarital sexual activity (Jones, Darroch, & Singh, 2005; Statistics Canada, 2008).

Males, too, have shown an increase in the incidence of premarital sexual intercourse, although the increase has not been as dramatic as it has been for females—probably because the rates for males were higher to begin with. For instance, the first surveys of premarital intercourse carried out in the 1940s in the United States showed an incidence of 84 percent across males of all ages; recent data put the figure at closer to 95 percent. The rate of premarital sex for males is slightly lower in Canada with 80 percent of males reporting sexual activity before marriage (Statistics Canada, 2005). Moreover, the average age of males' first sexual experience has been declining steadily. Almost half of males have had sexual intercourse by the age of 18; by the time they reach age 20, 88 percent have had intercourse. For both men and women, 70 percent of teens have had intercourse by their 19th birthday (Arena, 1984; Hyde, Mezulis, & Abramson, 2008).

Marital Sex

To judge by the number of articles about sex in heterosexual marriages, one would think that sexual behavior was the number one standard by which marital bliss is measured. Married couples are often concerned that they are having too little sex, too much sex, or the wrong kind of sex (Harvey, Wenzel, & Sprecher, 2005).

Although there are many different dimensions along which sex in marriage is measured, one is certainly the frequency of sexual intercourse. What is typical? As with most other types of sexual activities, there is no easy answer to the question because there are such wide variations in patterns between individuals. We know that 43 percent of married couples have sexual intercourse a few times a month and 36 percent of couples have it two or three times a week. With increasing age and length of marriage, the frequency of intercourse declines. Still, sex continues into late adulthood with almost half of people reporting that they engage in high-quality sexual activity at least once a month (Michael et al., 1994; Powell, 2006).

Although early research found **extramarital sex** to be widespread, the current reality appears to be otherwise. According to surveys, 85 percent of married women and more than 75 percent of married men are faithful to their spouses. Furthermore, the median number of sex partners inside and outside of marriage since the age of 18 was six for men and two for women. Accompanying these numbers is a high, consistent degree of disapproval of extramarital sex, with nine of ten people saying that it is "always" or "almost always" wrong (Daines, 2006; Whisman & Snyder, 2007; DeMaris, 2013).

Double standard
The view that premarital sex is permissible for males but not for females.

Extramarital sex
Sexual activity between a married person and someone who is not his or her spouse.

Sexual Orientation

What determines a person's sexual orientation? Although there are a number of theories, none has proved completely satisfactory.

Some explanations for sexual orientation are biological in nature, suggesting that there are genetic causes. Studies find that when one twin identified himself or herself as homosexual, the occurrence of homosexuality in the other twin was higher than it was in the general population. Such results occur even for twins who have been separated early in life and who therefore are not necessarily raised in similar social environments (Kirk, Bailey, & Martin, 2000; Gooren, 2006; LeVay, 2011).

> ## STUDY ALERT!
>
> The determinants of sexual orientation have proven difficult to pinpoint. It is important to know the variety of explanations that have been put forward.

Hormones also may play a role in determining sexual orientation. For example, research shows that women exposed to DES, or diethylstilbestrol, before birth (their mothers took the drug to avoid miscarriage) were more likely to be homosexual or bisexual (Meyer-Bahlburg, 1997).

Some evidence suggests that differences in brain structure may be related to sexual orientation. For instance, the structure of the anterior hypothalamus, an area of the brain that governs sexual behaviour, differs in male homosexuals and heterosexuals. Similarly, other research shows that, compared with heterosexual men or women, gay men have a larger anterior commissure, which is a bundle of neurons connecting the right and left hemispheres of the brain (LeVay, 1993; Byne, 1996; Witelson et al., 2008).

However, research suggesting that biological causes are at the root of homosexuality is not conclusive because most findings are based on only small samples of individuals. Still, the possibility is real that some inherited or biological factor exists that predisposes people toward homosexuality if certain environmental conditions are met (Veniegas, 2000; Teodorov et al., 2002; Rahman, Kumari, & Wilson, 2003).

Little evidence suggests that sexual orientation is brought about by child-rearing practices or family dynamics. Although classic psychoanalytic theories argued that the nature of the parent-child relationship can produce homosexuality (e.g., Freud, 1922/1959), research evidence does not support such explanations (Isay, 1994; Roughton, 2002).

Canadian Ray Blanchard's environmental theory of sexual orientation *fraternal birth order effect* correlates homosexuality with birth order. Often referred to as the *older brother effect*, Blanchard found a positive correlation between the number of older brothers a man has and the probability of his homosexual orientation (Blanchard & Lippa, 2007). Despite the significance of Blanchard's findings, we must remain cautious in its interpretation. Correlational studies simply explain the relationship between two variables (e.g., birth order and sexual orientation). They do not tell us which variable "caused" the other. A third variable (e.g., mother's hormones) may better explain the *fraternal birth order effect*.

Another explanation for sexual orientation rests on learning theory (Masters & Johnson, 1979). According to this view, sexual orientation is learned through rewards and punishments in much the same way that we may learn to prefer swimming over tennis. For example, a young adolescent who had an unpleasant heterosexual experience might develop disagreeable associations with the other sex. If the same person had a rewarding, pleasant gay or lesbian experience, homosexuality might be incorporated into his or her sexual fantasies. If such fantasies are used during later sexual activities—such as masturbation—they may be positively reinforced through orgasm, and the association of homosexual behaviour and sexual pleasure eventually may cause homosexuality to become the preferred form of sexual behaviour.

Although the learning-theory explanation is plausible, several difficulties rule it out as a definitive explanation. Because our society has traditionally held homosexuality in low esteem, one ought to expect that the negative treatment of homosexual behaviour would outweigh the rewards attached to it. Furthermore, children growing up with a gay or lesbian parent are statistically unlikely to become homosexual, which thus contradicts the notion that homosexual behaviour may be learned from others (Golombok et al., 1995; Victor & Fish, 1995; Tasker, 2005).

Because of the difficulty in finding a consistent explanation for sexual orientation, we can't definitively answer the question of what determines it. It seems unlikely that any single factor orients a person toward homosexuality or heterosexuality. Instead, it seems reasonable to assume that a combination of biological and environmental factors is involved (Bem, 1996; Hyde, Mezulis, & Abramson, 2008).

Although we don't know exactly why people develop a certain sexual orientation, one thing is clear: Despite increasingly positive attitudes toward homosexuality, many gays and lesbians face antigay attitudes and discrimination, and it can take a toll. Lesbians and gays have higher rates of depression and suicide than their straight counterparts. There are even physical health disparities due to prejudice that gays and lesbians may experience. Because of this, the American Psychological Association and other major mental health organizations have endorsed efforts to eliminate discrimination against gays and lesbians (Chakraborty et al., 2011; Ashley, 2013; Lick, Durso, & Johnson, 2013).

Homosexuality and Bisexuality

Homosexuals are sexually attracted to members of their own sex, whereas **bisexuals** are sexually attracted to people of the same sex and the other sex. Many male homosexuals prefer the term *gay* and female homosexuals the label *lesbian*, because they refer to a broader array of attitudes and lifestyles than the term *homosexual*, which focuses on the sexual act.

The number of people who choose same-sex sexual partners at one time or another is considerable. Estimates suggest that around 20 to 25 percent of males and about 15 percent of females have had at least one gay or lesbian experience during adulthood. The exact number of people who identify themselves as exclusively lesbian or gay has proved difficult to gauge, with some estimates as low as 1.1 percent and some as high as 10 percent. Most experts suggest that between 5 and 10 percent of both men and women are exclusively gay or lesbian during extended periods of their lives (Hunt, 1974; Sells, 1994; Firestein, 1996).

Although people often view homosexuality and heterosexuality as completely distinct sexual orientations, the issue is not that simple. Pioneering sex researcher Alfred Kinsey acknowledged this when he considered sexual orientation along a scale or continuum, with "exclusively homosexual" at one end and "exclusively heterosexual" at the other. In the middle were people who showed both homosexual and heterosexual behaviour. Kinsey's approach suggests that sexual orientation is dependent on a person's sexual feelings and behaviours and romantic feelings (Weinberg, Williams, & Pryor, 1991).

Extensive research has found that bisexuals and homosexuals enjoy the same overall degree of mental and physical health as heterosexuals.

Source: © Racheal Epstein/The Image Works.

Transsexualism

From the first day of kindergarten, Alyn Libman felt different. The other girls played with Barbies and dress-up games; Alyn wanted to climb trees. The big problem came at potty break, when Alyn headed for the boys' room—and the teacher stepped in the way. "I just said, 'Why?'" recalls Libman. "I didn't understand" (Fields-Meyer & Wihlborg, 2003, p. 109).

Although born a female, Libman never felt like one. Now considering reconstructive surgery, Libman represents a category of sexuality not encompassed by heterosexuality, homosexuality, or bisexuality: transsexualism.

Transsexuals are people whose sexual identification is with the opposite gender from that they were born with. Transsexuals feel that they are trapped in the body of the other gender. In fundamental ways, transsexualism represents less of a sexual difficulty than a gender issue involving one's sexual identity (Meyerowitz, 2004; Heath, 2006).

Transsexuals sometimes seek sex-change operations in which their existing genitals are surgically removed and the genitals of the desired sex are fashioned. Several steps, including intensive counseling, hormone injections, and living as a member of the desired sex for several years, precede surgery, which is, not surprisingly, highly complicated. The outcome, though, can be quite positive (O'Keefe & Fox, 2003; Stegerwald & Janson, 2003; Lobato, Koff, & Manenti, 2006; Richards, 2011).

Homosexuals
Persons who are sexually attracted to members of their own sex.

Bisexuals
Persons who are sexually attracted to people of the same sex and the other sex.

Transsexuals
People whose sexual identification is with the opposite gender from that they were born with; they feel they are trapped in the body of the other gender.

Transsexualism is part of a broader category known as transgenderism. The term *transgenderism* encompasses not only transsexuals, but also people who view themselves as a third gender (neither male nor female), transvestites (who dress in the clothes of the other gender), or others who believe that traditional male-female gender classifications inadequately characterize them (Prince, 2005; Hyde, Mezulis, & Abramson, 2008).

Transsexuals are distinct from individuals who are known as *intersex* or by the older term *hermaphrodite*. An intersex person is born with an atypical combination of sexual organs or chromosomal or gene patterns. In some cases, they are born with both male and female sexual organs, or the organs are ambiguous. It is an extremely rare condition found in one in 4,500 births. Intersexism involves a complex mix of physiological and psychological issues (Lehrman, 2007; Diamond, 2009).

The Needs for Affiliation, Power, and Achievement

Although primary drives such as hunger motivate us in our day-to-day lives, powerful secondary drives that have no clear biological basis also motivate us. Among the more prominent of these are the needs for affiliation, power, and achievement.

Need for Affiliation: Striving for Friendship

Few of us choose to lead our lives as hermits. Why?

One main reason is that most people have a **need for affiliation**, an interest in establishing and maintaining relationships with other people. Individuals with a high need for affiliation write Thematic Apperception Test (TAT) stories (see Figure 3) that emphasize the desire to maintain or reinstate friendships and show concern over being rejected by friends.

People who have higher affiliation needs are particularly sensitive to relationships with others. They desire to be with their friends more of the time, and alone less often, compared with people who are lower in the need for affiliation. However, gender is a greater determinant of how much time is actually spent with friends: Regardless of their affiliative orientation, female students spend significantly more time with their friends and less time alone than male students do (Cantwell & Andrews, 2002; Johnson, 2004; Semykina & Linz, 2007).

Technology has significantly influenced how we relate to each other in recent years. For many Canadians, social networking technology fulfills our need for affiliation. Today, face-to-face interactions are just one of many ways that

---

FIGURE 3

This ambiguous picture is similar to those used in the Thematic Apperception Test (TAT) to determine people's underlying motivation. What do you see? Do you think your response is related to your motivation?

Sources: © 1943 by the President and Fellows of Harvard College; 1971 by Henry A. Murray.

Need for affiliation
An interest in establishing and maintaining relationships with other people.

Canadians date and socialize. Online dating sites such as Lavalife and Match.com make finding international (and next door) companions possible. Social networking sites such as Facebook and MySpace allow friends to keep in touch no matter how close or how far away they live.

Need for Power: Striving for Impact on Others

If your fantasies include becoming prime minister of Canada or running Microsoft Canada, your dreams may reflect a high **need for power**. The need for power, a tendency to seek impact, control, or influence over others and to be seen as a powerful individual, is an additional type of motivation (Lee-Chai & Bargh, 2001; Winter, 2007; Zians, 2007).

As you might expect, people with strong needs for power are more apt to belong to organizations and seek office than are those low in the need for power. They also tend to work in professions in which their power needs may be fulfilled, such as business management and—you may or may not be surprised—teaching (Jenkins, 1994). In addition, they seek to display the trappings of power. Even in college or university, they are more likely to collect prestigious possessions, such as electronic equipment and sports cars.

Some significant gender differences exist in the display of need for power. Men with high power needs tend to show unusually high levels of aggression, drink heavily, act in a sexually exploitative manner, and participate more frequently in competitive sports—behaviours that collectively represent somewhat extravagant, flamboyant behaviour. In contrast, women display their power needs with more restraint; this is congruent with traditional societal constraints on women's behaviour. Women with high power needs are more apt than men are to channel those needs in a socially responsible manner, such as by showing concern for others or displaying highly nurturing behaviour (Winter, 1988, 1995, 2007; Maroda, 2004; Schubert & Koole, 2009).

Need for Achievement: Striving for Excellence

The **need for achievement** is a stable, learned characteristic in which a person obtains satisfaction by striving for and attaining a level of excellence (McClelland et al., 1953). People with a high need for achievement seek out situations in which they can compete against some standard—be it grades, money, or winning at a game—and prove themselves successful. But they are not indiscriminate when it comes to picking their challenges: They tend to avoid situations in which success will come too easily (which would be unchallenging) and situations in which success is unlikely. Instead, people high in achievement motivation generally choose tasks that are of intermediate difficulty.

In contrast, people with low achievement motivation tend to be motivated primarily by a desire to avoid failure. As a result, they seek out easy tasks, being sure to avoid failure, or seek out very difficult tasks for which failure has no negative implications, because almost anyone would fail at them. People with a high fear of failure will stay away from tasks of intermediate difficulty, because they may fail where others have been successful (Martin & Marsh, 2002; Puca, 2005; Morrone & Pintrich, 2006).

A high need for achievement generally produces positive outcomes, at least in a success-oriented society such as ours. For instance, people motivated by a high need for achievement are more likely to attend college or university than are their low-achievement counterparts, and once they are in college or university, they tend to receive higher grades in classes that are related to their future careers. Furthermore, high achievement motivation indicates future economic and occupational success (McClelland, 1985; Thrash & Elliot, 2002).

MEASURING ACHIEVEMENT MOTIVATION

How can we measure a person's need for achievement? The measuring instrument used most frequently is the *Thematic Apperception Test (TAT)* (Spangler, 1992). In the TAT, an examiner shows a series of ambiguous pictures, such as the one in Figure 3. The examiner tells participants to write a story that describes what is happening, who the people are, what led to the situation, what the people are thinking or wanting, and what will happen next. Researchers then use a standard scoring system to determine the amount of achievement imagery in people's stories. For example, someone who writes a story in which the main character strives to beat an opponent, studies in order to do well at some task, or works hard in order to get a promotion shows clear signs of an achievement orientation. The inclusion of such

Need for power
A tendency to seek impact, control, or influence over others, and to be seen as a powerful individual.

Need for achievement
A stable, learned characteristic in which a person obtains satisfaction by striving for and attaining a level of excellence.

achievement-related imagery in the participants' stories is assumed to indicate an unusually high degree of concern with—and therefore a relatively strong need for—achievement (Tuerlinckx, DeBoeck, & Lens, 2002).

STUDY ALERT!

A key feature of people with a high need for achievement is that they prefer tasks of *moderate* difficulty.

Evaluate

1. Match the following terms with their definitions:
   1. Hypothalamus
   2. Lateral hypothalamic damage
   3. Ventromedial hypothalamic damage
   a. Leads to refusal of food and starvation
   b. Responsible for monitoring food intake
   c. Causes extreme overeating
2. The _____ is the particular level of weight the body strives to maintain.
3. _____ is the rate at which energy is produced and expended by the body.
4. Although the incidence of masturbation among young adults is high, once men and women become involved in intimate relationships, they typically cease masturbating. True or false?
5. The increase in premarital sex in recent years has been greater for women than for men. True or false?
6. Julio is the type of person who constantly strives for excellence. He feels intense satisfaction when he is able to master a new task. Julio most likely has a high need for _____.
7. Debbie's Thematic Apperception Test (TAT) story depicts a young girl who is rejected by one of her peers and seeks to regain her friendship. What major type of motivation is Debbie displaying in her story?
   a. Need for achievement
   b. Need for motivation
   c. Need for affiliation
   d. Need for power

Answers to Evaluate Questions

1. 1-b, 2-a, 3-c; 2. weight set point; 3. Metabolism; 4. False; 5. True; 6. achievement; 7. c

Key Terms

androgens	genitals	need for power
anorexia nervosa	heterosexuality	obesity
bisexuals	homosexuals	ovulation
bulimia	masturbation	progesterone
double standard	metabolism	transsexuals
estrogens	need for achievement	weight set point
extramarital sex	need for affiliation	

Understanding Emotional Experiences

LEARNING OBJECTIVES

What are emotions, and how do we experience them?

What are the functions of emotions?

What are the explanations for emotions?

How does nonverbal behaviour relate to the expression of emotions?

Karl Andrews held in his hands the envelope he had been waiting for. It could be the ticket to his future: an offer of admission to his first-choice college. But what was it going to say? He knew it could go either way; his grades were pretty good and he had been involved in some extracurricular activities, but there were no guarantees. He felt so nervous that his hands shook as he opened the thin envelope (not a good sign, he thought). Here it comes. "Dear Mr. Andrews," it read. "The board of directors at Fanshawe College are pleased to admit you . . . ." That was all he needed to see. With a whoop of excitement, Karl found himself jumping up and down gleefully. A rush of emotion overcame him as it sank in that he had, in fact, been accepted. He was on his way.

At one time or another, all of us have experienced the strong feelings that accompany both very pleasant and very negative experiences. Perhaps we have felt the thrill of getting a sought-after job, the joy of being in love, sorrow over someone's death, or the anguish of inadvertently hurting someone. Moreover, we experience such reactions on a less intense level throughout our daily lives: the pleasure of a friendship, the enjoyment of a movie, and the embarrassment of breaking a borrowed item.

Despite the varied nature of these feelings, they all represent emotions. Although everyone has an idea of what an emotion is, formally defining the concept has proved to be an elusive task. We'll use a general definition: **Emotions** are feelings that generally have both physiological and cognitive elements and that influence behaviour.

Think, for example, about how it feels to be happy. First, we obviously experience a feeling that we can differentiate from other emotions. It is likely that we also experience some identifiable physical changes in our bodies: Perhaps the heart rate increases, or—as in the example of Karl Andrews—we find ourselves "jumping for joy." Finally, the emotion probably encompasses cognitive elements: Our understanding and evaluation of the meaning of what is happening prompts our feelings of happiness.

It is also possible, however, to experience an emotion without the presence of cognitive elements. For instance, we may react with fear to an unusual or novel situation (such as coming into contact with an erratic, unpredictable individual), or we may experience pleasure over sexual excitation without having cognitive awareness or understanding of just what it is about the situation that is exciting.

Some psychologists argue that entirely separate systems govern cognitive and emotional responses. A current controversy focuses on whether the emotional response predominates over the cognitive one or vice versa. Some theorists suggest that we first respond to a situation with an emotional reaction and later try to understand it. For example, we may enjoy a symphony without at first understanding it or knowing why we like it. In contrast, other theorists propose that people first develop cognitions about a situation and *then* react emotionally. This school of thought suggests that we must think about and understand a stimulus or situation by relating it to what we already know before we can react on an emotional level (Murphy & Zajonc, 1993; Lazarus, 1995; Oatley, Keltner, & Jenkins, 2006).

Emotions
Feelings that generally have both physiological and cognitive elements and that influence behaviour.

Because proponents of both sides of this debate can cite research to support their viewpoints, the question is far from resolved. Perhaps the sequence varies from situation to situation, with emotions predominating in some instances and cognitive processes occurring first in others. Both sides agree that we can experience emotions that involve little or no conscious thought. We may not know why we're afraid of mice, understanding objectively that they represent no danger, but we may still be frightened when we see them. Neuroimaging studies of the brain may help resolve this debate as well as others about the nature of emotions (Barrett & Wager, 2006; Niedenthal, 2007; Karaszewski, 2008).

The Functions of Emotions

Imagine what it would be like if we didn't experience emotion—no depths of despair, no depression, no remorse, but at the same time no happiness, joy, or love. Obviously, life would be considerably less satisfying, and even dull, if we lacked the capacity to sense and express emotion.

But do emotions serve any purpose beyond making life interesting? Indeed they do. Psychologists have identified several important functions that emotions play in our daily lives (Fredrickson & Branigan, 2005; Frijda, 2005; Gross, 2006; Siemer, Mauss, & Gross, 2007). Among the most important of those functions are the following:

- *Preparing us for action.* Emotions act as a link between events in our environment and our responses. For example, if we saw an angry dog charging toward us, the emotional reaction (fear) would be associated with physiological arousal of the sympathetic division of the autonomic nervous system, the activation of the fight-or-flight response. The role of the sympathetic division is to prepare us for emergency action, which presumably would get us moving out of the dog's way—quickly.

- *Shaping our future behaviour.* Emotions promote learning that will help us make appropriate responses in the future. For example, the emotional response that occurs when we experience something unpleasant—such as a threatening dog—teaches us to avoid similar circumstances in the future. In the same way, pleasant emotions act as positive reinforcement for prior behaviour and therefore may lead an individual to seek out similar situations in the future.

- *Helping us interact more effectively with others.* We often communicate the emotions we experience through our verbal and nonverbal behaviours, making our emotions obvious to observers. These behaviours can act as a signal to observers, allowing them to understand better what we are experiencing and to predict our future behaviour. In turn, this promotes more effective and appropriate social interaction.

Determining the Range of Emotions: Labelling Our Feelings

If we were to list the words in the English language that have been used to describe emotions, we would end up with at least 500 examples (Averill, 1975). The list would range from such obvious emotions as *happiness* and *fear* to less common ones, such as *adventurousness* and *pensiveness*.

One challenge for psychologists has been to sort through this list to identify the most important, fundamental emotions. Theorists have hotly contested the issue of cataloguing emotions and have come up with different lists, depending on how they define the concept of emotion. In fact, some reject the question entirely, saying that *no* set of emotions should be singled out as most basic, and that emotions are best understood by breaking them down into their component parts. Other researchers argue for looking at emotions in terms of a hierarchy, dividing them into positive and negative categories, and then organizing them into increasingly narrower subcategories (Manstead, Frijda, & Fischer, 2003; Dillard & Shen, 2007; see Figure 1).

Still, most researchers suggest that a list of basic emotions would include, at a minimum, happiness, anger, fear, sadness, and disgust. Other lists are broader, including emotions such as surprise, contempt, guilt, and joy (Ekman, 1994a; Shweder, 1994; Tracy & Robins, 2004).

One difficulty in defining a basic set of emotions is that substantial differences exist in descriptions of emotions among various cultures. For instance, Germans report experiencing *schadenfreude*, a feeling of pleasure over

FIGURE 1

One approach to organizing emotions is to use a hierarchy, which divides emotions into increasingly narrow subcategories.

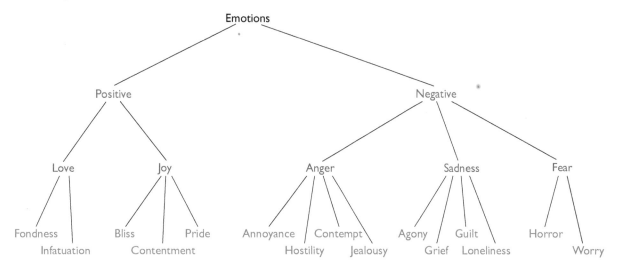

Source: Adapted from Figure 1 (p. 1067) from Shaver, P., Schwartz, J., Kirson, D., & O'Connor, C. (1987). Emotion knowledge: Further exploration of a prototype approach. *Journal of Personality and Social Psychology*, 52, 1061–1086. Published by The American Psychological Association, adapted with permission.

another person's difficulties, and the Japanese experience *hagaii*, a mood of vulnerable heartache coloured by frustration. In Tahiti, people experience *musu*, a feeling of reluctance to yield to unreasonable demands made by one's parents.

Finding *schadenfreude*, *hagaii*, or *musu* in a particular culture doesn't mean that the members of other cultures are incapable of experiencing such emotions, of course. It does suggest, though, that fitting a particular emotion into a linguistic category to describe that emotion may make it easier to discuss, contemplate, and perhaps experience (Russell & Sato, 1995; Li, Wang, & Fischer, 2004; Kuppens et al., 2006).

The Roots of Emotions

I've never been so angry before; I feel my heart pounding, and I'm trembling all over . . . I don't know how I'll get through the performance. I feel like my stomach is filled with butterflies . . . That was quite a mistake I made! My face must be incredibly red . . . When I heard the footsteps in the night, I was so frightened that I couldn't catch my breath.

If you examine our language, you will find that there are literally dozens of ways to describe how we feel when we experience an emotion, and that the language we use to describe emotions is, for the most part, based on the physical symptoms that are associated with a particular emotional experience (Kobayashi, Schallert, & Ogren, 2003; Manstead & Wagner, 2004; Spackman, Fujiki, & Brinton, 2006).

Consider, for instance, the experience of fear. Pretend that it is late on New Year's Eve. You are walking down a dark road, and you hear a stranger approaching behind you. It is clear that he is not trying to hurry by but is coming directly toward you. You think about what you will do if the stranger attempts to rob you or, worse, hurt you in some way.

While these thoughts are running through your head, something rather dramatic will be happening to your body. The most likely reactions, which are associated with activation of the autonomic nervous system, include an increase in your rate of breathing, an acceleration of your heart rate, a widening of your pupils (to increase visual sensitivity), and a dryness in your mouth as the functioning of your salivary glands, and in fact of your entire digestive system, ceases. At the same time, though, your sweat glands probably will increase their activity, because increased sweating will help you rid yourself of the excess heat developed by any emergency activity in which you engage.

Of course, all these physiological changes are likely to occur without your awareness. At the same time, though, the emotional experience accompanying them will be obvious to you: You most surely would report being fearful.

Although it is easy to describe the general physical reactions that accompany emotions, defining the specific role that those physiological responses play in the experience of emotions has proved to be a major puzzle for psychologists. As we shall see, some theorists suggest that specific bodily reactions *cause* us to experience a particular emotion—we experience fear, for instance, *because* the heart is pounding and we are breathing deeply. In contrast, other theorists suggest that the physiological reaction *results* from the experience of an emotion. In this view, we experience fear, and as a result the heart pounds and our breathing deepens.

The James-Lange Theory: Do Gut Reactions Equal Emotions?

To William James and Carl Lange, who were among the first researchers to explore the nature of emotions, emotional experience is, very simply, a reaction to instinctive bodily events that occur as a response to some situation or event in the environment. This view is summarized in James's statement, "we feel sorry because we cry, angry because we strike, afraid because we tremble" (James, 1890).

James and Lange took the view that the instinctive response of crying at a loss leads us to feel sorrow, that striking out at someone who frustrates us results in our feeling anger, that trembling at a menacing threat causes us to feel fear. They suggested that for every major emotion there is an accompanying physiological or "gut" reaction of internal organs—called a *visceral experience*. It is this specific pattern of visceral response that leads us to label the emotional experience.

In sum, James and Lange proposed that we experience emotions as a result of physiological changes that produce specific sensations. The brain interprets these sensations as particular kinds of emotional experiences (see Figure 2). This view has come to be called the **James-Lange theory of emotion** (Laird & Bressler, 1990; Cobos et al., 2002).

FIGURE 2

A comparison of three models of emotion.

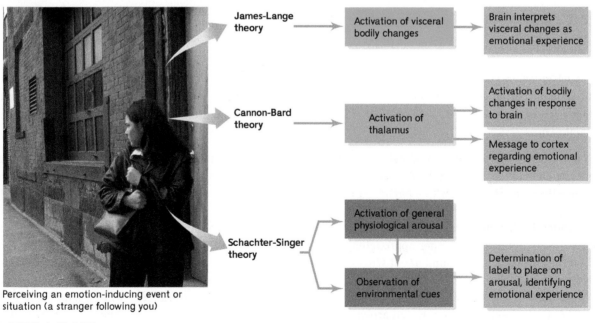

Perceiving an emotion-inducing event or situation (a stranger following you)

Source: © Erik Fowke/PhotoEdit.

James-Lange theory of emotion
The belief that emotional experience is a reaction to bodily events occurring as a result of an external situation ("I feel sad because I am crying").

The James-Lange theory has some serious drawbacks, however. For the theory to be valid, visceral changes would have to occur relatively quickly, because we experience some emotions—such as fear upon hearing a stranger rapidly approaching on a dark night—almost instantaneously. Yet emotional experiences frequently occur even before there is time for certain physiological changes to be set into motion. Because of the slowness with which some visceral changes take place, it is hard to see how they could be the source of immediate emotional experience.

The James-Lange theory poses another difficulty: Physiological arousal does not invariably produce emotional experience. For example, a person who is jogging has an increased heartbeat and respiration rate, as well as many of the other physiological changes associated with certain emotions. Yet joggers typically do not think of such changes in terms of emotions. There cannot be a one-to-one correspondence, then, between visceral changes and emotional experience. Visceral changes by themselves may not be sufficient to produce emotion.

Finally, our internal organs produce a relatively limited range of sensations. Although some types of physiological changes are associated with specific emotional experiences, it is difficult to imagine how each of the myriad emotions that people are capable of experiencing could be the result of a unique visceral change. Many emotions actually are associated with relatively similar sorts of visceral changes, a fact that contradicts the James-Lange theory (Davidson et al., 1994; Cameron, 2002).

The Cannon-Bard Theory: Physiological Reactions as the Result of Emotions

In response to the difficulties inherent in the James-Lange theory, Walter Cannon, and later Philip Bard, suggested an alternative view. In what has come to be known as the **Cannon-Bard theory of emotion**, they proposed the model illustrated in the second part of Figure 2 (Cannon, 1929). This theory rejects the view that physiological arousal alone leads to the perception of emotion. Instead, the theory assumes that both physiological arousal *and* the emotional experience are produced simultaneously by the same nerve stimulus, which Cannon and Bard suggested emanates from the thalamus in the brain.

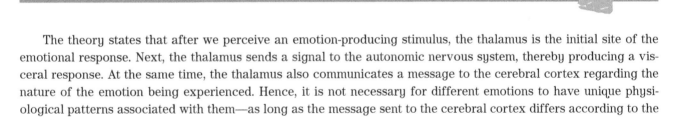

STUDY ALERT!

Use Figure 2 to distinguish the three classic theories of emotion (James-Lange, Cannon-Bard, and Schachter-Singer).

The theory states that after we perceive an emotion-producing stimulus, the thalamus is the initial site of the emotional response. Next, the thalamus sends a signal to the autonomic nervous system, thereby producing a visceral response. At the same time, the thalamus also communicates a message to the cerebral cortex regarding the nature of the emotion being experienced. Hence, it is not necessary for different emotions to have unique physiological patterns associated with them—as long as the message sent to the cerebral cortex differs according to the specific emotion.

The Cannon-Bard theory seems to have been accurate in rejecting the view that physiological arousal alone accounts for emotions. However, more recent research has led to some important modifications of the theory. For one thing, we now understand that the hypothalamus and the limbic system, not the thalamus, play a major role in emotional experience. In addition, the simultaneous occurrence of the physiological and emotional responses, which is a fundamental assumption of the Cannon-Bard theory, has yet to be demonstrated conclusively. This ambiguity has allowed room for yet another theory of emotions: the Schachter-Singer theory.

The Schachter-Singer Theory: Emotions as Labels

Suppose that, as you are being followed down a dark street on New Year's Eve, you notice a man being followed by another shady figure on the other side of the street. Now assume that instead of reacting with fear, the man begins to

Cannon-Bard theory of emotion
The belief that both physiological arousal and emotional experience are produced simultaneously by the same nerve stimulus.

laugh and act gleeful. Would the reactions of this other individual be sufficient to lay your fears to rest? Might you, in fact, decide there is nothing to fear, and get into the spirit of the evening by beginning to feel happiness and glee yourself?

According to an explanation that focuses on the role of cognition, the **Schachter-Singer theory of emotion**, this might very well happen. This approach to explaining emotions emphasizes that we identify the emotion we are experiencing by observing our environment and comparing ourselves with others (Schachter & Singer, 1962).

Schachter and Singer's classic experiment found evidence for this hypothesis. In the study, participants were told that they would receive an injection of a vitamin. In reality, they were given epinephrine, a drug that causes an increase in physiological arousal, including higher heart and respiration rates and a reddening of the face, responses that typically occur during strong emotional reactions. The members of both groups were then placed individually in a situation where a confederate of the experimenter acted in one of two ways. In one condition he acted angry and hostile, and in the other condition he behaved as if he were exuberantly happy.

The purpose of the experiment was to determine how the participants would react emotionally to the confederate's behaviour. When they were asked to describe their own emotional state at the end of the experiment, the participants exposed to the angry confederate reported that they felt angry, while those exposed to the happy confederate reported feeling happy. In sum, the results suggest that participants turned to the environment and the behaviour of others for an explanation of the physiological arousal they were experiencing.

The results of the Schachter-Singer experiment, then, supported a cognitive view of emotions, in which emotions are determined jointly by a relatively nonspecific kind of physiological arousal *and* the labelling of that arousal on the basis of cues from the environment (refer to the third part of Figure 2).

Although later research has found that arousal is not as nonspecific as Schachter and Singer assumed, it is clear that arousal can magnify, and be mistaken for, many emotions. For example, in one experiment, men who crossed a swaying 137-metre suspension bridge spanning a deep canyon in British Columbia were more attracted to a woman they encountered at the other end than were those who crossed a stable bridge spanning a shallow stream. Apparently, the men who crossed the frightening bridge attributed their subsequent high arousal to the woman, rather than to the swaying bridge (Dutton & Aron, 1974; Schorr, 2001).

In short, the Schachter-Singer theory of emotions is important because it suggests that, at least under some circumstances, emotional experiences are a joint function of physiological arousal and the labelling of that arousal. When the source of physiological arousal is unclear, we may look to our surroundings to determine just what we are experiencing.

Contemporary Perspectives on the Neuroscience of Emotions

When Schachter and Singer carried out their groundbreaking experiment in the early 1960s, the ways in which they could evaluate the physiology that accompanies emotion were relatively limited. However, advances in the measurement of the nervous system and other parts of the body have allowed researchers to examine more closely the biological responses involved in emotion. As a result, contemporary research on emotion points to a revision of earlier views that physiological responses associated with emotions are undifferentiated. Instead, evidence is growing that specific patterns of biological arousal are associated with individual emotions (Franks & Smith, 1999; Vaitl, Schienle, & Stark, 2005; Woodson, 2006).

For instance, researchers have found that specific emotions produce activation of very different portions of the brain. In one study, participants undergoing positron emission tomography (PET) brain scans were asked to recall events, such as deaths and funerals, that made them feel sad, or events that made them feel happy, such as weddings and births. They also looked at photos of faces that appeared to be happy or sad. The results of the PET scans were clear: Happiness was related to a decrease in activity in certain areas of the cerebral cortex, whereas sadness was associated with increases in activity in particular portions of the cortex (see Figure 3). Ultimately, it may be possible to map each particular emotion to a specific site in the brain (George et al., 1995; Hamann et al., 2002; Prohovnik et al., 2004).

Schachter-Singer theory of emotion
The belief that emotions are determined jointly by a nonspecific kind of physiological arousal and its interpretation, based on environmental cues.

Experiencing different emotions activates particular areas of the brain, as these scans illustrate.

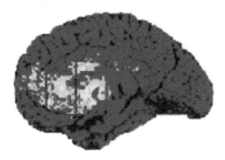

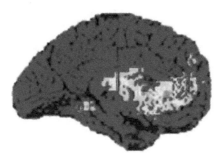

Source: © Mark George, NIMH.

The *amygdala*, in the brain's temporal lobe, also is important in the experience of emotions, for it provides a link between the perception of an emotion-producing stimulus and the recall of that stimulus later. For example, if we've once been attacked by a vicious pit bull, the amygdala processes that information and leads us to react with fear when we see a pit bull later—an example of a classically conditioned fear response (Miller et al., 2005; Berntson et al., 2007; Kensinger, 2007; LaBar, 2007).

Because neural pathways connect the amygdala, the visual cortex, and the *hippocampus* (which plays an important role in the consolidation of memories), some scientists speculate that emotion-related stimuli can be processed

Exploring DIVERSITY

Do People in All Cultures Express Emotion Similarly?

Consider, for a moment, the six photos displayed in Figure 4. Can you identify the emotions being expressed by the person in each of the photos?

If you're a good judge of facial expressions, you'll conclude that these expressions display six of the basic emotions: happiness, anger, sadness, surprise, disgust, and fear. Hundreds of studies of nonverbal behaviour show that these emotions are consistently distinct and identifiable, even by untrained observers (Ekman & O'Sullivan, 1991).

Interestingly, these six emotions are not unique to members of Western cultures; rather, they constitute the basic emotions expressed universally by members of the human race, regardless of where individuals have been raised and what learning experiences they have had. Psychologist Paul Ekman convincingly demonstrated this when he studied the members of an isolated New Guinea jungle tribe who had had almost no contact with Westerners (Ekman, 1972). The people of the tribe didn't speak or understand English, had never seen a movie, and had had very limited experience with Caucasians before Ekman's arrival. Yet their nonverbal responses to emotion-evoking stories, as well as their ability to identify basic emotions, were quite similar to those of Westerners.

(continued)

FIGURE 4

These photos demonstrate six of the primary emotions: happiness, anger, sadness, surprise, disgust, and fear.

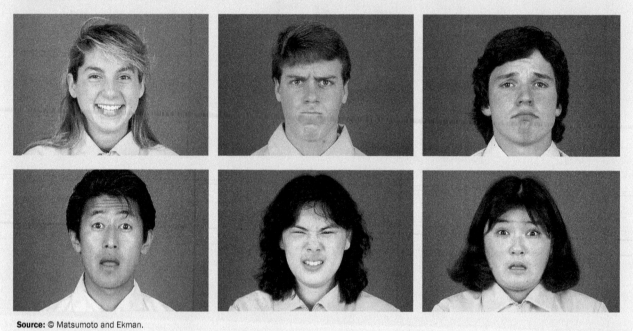

Source: © Matsumoto and Ekman.

STUDY ALERT!

It's important to understand the basic neuroscience of emotional experience.

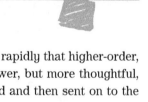

and responded to almost instantaneously (see Figure 5). This immediate response occurs so rapidly that higher-order, more rational thinking, which takes more time, seems not to be involved initially. In a slower, but more thoughtful, response to emotion-evoking stimuli, emotion-related sensory information is first evaluated and then sent on to the amygdala. It appears that the quicker system offers an immediate response to emotion-evoking stimuli, whereas the slower system helps confirm a threat and prepare a more thoughtful response (Dolan, 2002).

Making Sense of the Multiple Perspectives on Emotion

Paul Ekman, a pioneer in the research of emotion, continues to be a driving force in the field of psychology, having published more than 100 articles on the subject. Two of his books, *Emotions Revealed* and *Emotional Awareness* (co-written by the Dalai Lama), apply cutting-edge research to everyday emotional encounters (Ekman, 2007; Dalai Lama & Ekman, 2008). As new approaches to emotion continue to develop, it is reasonable to ask why so many theories of emotion exist and, perhaps more important, which one provides the most complete explanation. Actually, we have only scratched the surface. There are almost as many explanatory theories of emotion as there are individual emotions (e.g., Manstead, Frijda, & Fischer, 2003; Frijda, 2005; Prinz, 2007; Herzberg, 2009).

Why are theories of emotion so plentiful? For one thing, emotions are not a simple phenomenon but are intertwined closely with motivation, cognition, neuroscience, and a host of related branches of psychology. For example, evidence from brain imaging studies shows that even when people come to supposedly rational, nonemotional decisions—such as making moral, philosophical judgments—emotions come into play (Greene et al., 2001).

In short, emotions are such complex phenomena, encompassing both biological and cognitive aspects, that no single theory has been able to explain fully all the facets of emotional experience. Furthermore, contradictory

FIGURE 5

Connections from the amygdala, seen here in red, allow it to mediate many of the autonomic expressions of emotional states through the hippocampus (blue) and visual cortex (orange).

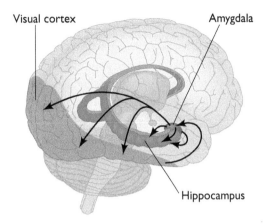

Visual cortex   Amygdala

Hippocampus

Source: Dolan, 2002.

evidence of one sort or another challenges each approach, and therefore no theory has proved invariably accurate in its predictions.

This abundance of perspectives on emotion is not a cause for despair—or unhappiness, fear, or any other negative emotion. It simply reflects the fact that psychology is an evolving, developing science. As we gather more evidence, the specific answers to questions about the nature of emotions will become clearer. Furthermore, even as our understanding of emotions continues to grow, ongoing efforts are applying our knowledge of emotions to practical problems.

Evaluate

1. Emotions are always accompanied by a cognitive response. True or false?
2. The _____-_____ theory of emotion states that emotions are a response to instinctive bodily events.
3. According to the _____-_____ theory of emotion, both an emotional response and physiological arousal are produced simultaneously by the same nerve stimulus.
4. Your friend—a psychology major—tells you, "I was at a party last night. During the course of the evening, my general level of arousal increased. Since I was at a party where people were enjoying themselves, I assume I must have felt happy." What theory of emotion does your friend subscribe to?
5. What are the six primary emotions that can be identified from facial expressions?

Answers to Evaluate Questions

5. surprise, sadness, happiness, anger, disgust, fear.

1. false; emotions may occur without a cognitive response; 2. James-Lange 3. Cannon-Bard; 4. Schachter-Singer;

Key Terms

Cannon-Bard theory of emotion	James-Lange theory	Schachter-Singer theory
emotions	of emotion	of emotion

Epilogue

Motivation and emotions are two interrelated aspects of psychology. In these modules, we first considered the topic of motivation, which has spawned a great deal of theory and research examining primary and secondary drives ranging from hunger to the need for achievement and affiliation. We then turned to a discussion of emotions, beginning with their functions and proceeding to a review of three major theories that seek to explain what emotions are and how they emerge in the individual.

Source: © Carlos Gonzalez/MCT/Newscom.

Recap/Rethink

Module 24: Explaining Motivation

Recap

How does motivation direct and energize behaviour?

- Motivation relates to the factors that direct and energize behaviour.
- Drive is the motivational tension that energizes behaviour to fulfill a need.
- Abraham Maslow's hierarchy suggests that there are five basic needs: physiological, safety, love and belonging-ness, esteem, and self-actualization. Only after the more basic needs are fulfilled can a person move toward meeting higher-order needs.
- Homeostasis, the maintenance of a steady internal state, often underlies motivational drives.
- Arousal approaches suggest that we try to maintain a particular level of stimulation and activity.
- Incentive approaches focus on the positive aspects of the environment that direct and energize behaviour.
- Cognitive approaches focus on the role of thoughts, expectations, and understanding of the world in producing motivation.

Rethink

1. Which approaches to motivation are more commonly used in the workplace? How might each approach be used to design employment policies that can sustain or increase motivation?

2. *From the perspective of an educator:* Do you think that giving students grades serves as an external reward that would decrease intrinsic motivation for the subject matter? Why or why not?

3. Which approach or approaches to motivation—instinctual, drive reduction, arousal, incentive, or cognitive—most effectively explain why an athlete like Rochette will work exceptionally hard over many years to become a competitive athlete?

Module 25: Human Needs and Motivation: Eat, Drink, and Be Daring

Recap

What biological and social factors underlie hunger?

- Eating behaviour is subject to homeostasis, as most people's weight stays within a relatively stable range. The hypothalamus in the brain is central to the regulation of food intake.
- Social factors, such as mealtimes, cultural food preferences, and other learned habits, also play a role in the regulation of eating, determining when, what, and how much one eats. An oversensitivity to social cues and an insensitivity to internal cues may also be related to obesity. In addition, obesity may be caused by an unusually high weight set point—the weight the body attempts to maintain—and genetic factors.

What are the varieties of sexual behaviour?

- Although biological factors, such as the presence of androgens (male sex hormones) and estrogens and progesterone (female sex hormones), prime people for sex, almost any kind of stimulus can produce sexual arousal, depending on a person's prior experience.
- The frequency of masturbation is high, particularly for males. Although increasingly liberal, attitudes toward masturbation have traditionally been negative even though no negative consequences have been detected.
- Heterosexuality, or sexual attraction to members of the other sex, is the most common sexual orientation. In terms of premarital sex, the double standard in which premarital sex is thought to be more permissible for men than for women has declined, particularly among young people.
- The frequency of marital sex varies widely. However, younger couples tend to have sexual intercourse more frequently than older ones. In addition, most men and women do not engage in extramarital sex.
- Homosexuals are sexually attracted to members of their own sex; bisexuals are sexually attracted to people of the same sex and the other sex. No explanation for why people become homosexual has been confirmed; among the possibilities are genetic or biological factors, childhood and family influences, and prior learning experiences and conditioning. However, no relationship exists between sexual orientation and psychological adjustment.

How are needs relating to affiliation, power, and achievement motivation exhibited?

- The need for affiliation is a concern with establishing and maintaining relationships with others, whereas the need for power is a tendency to seek to exert an impact on others.
- Need for achievement refers to the stable, learned characteristic in which a person strives to attain a level of excellence. Need for achievement is usually measured through the Thematic Apperception Test (TAT), a series of pictures about which a person writes a story.

Rethink

1. In what ways do societal expectations, expressed by television shows and commercials, contribute to both obesity and excessive concern about weight loss? How could television contribute to better eating habits and attitudes toward weight? Should it be required to do so?

2. *From the perspective of a human resources specialist:* How might you use characteristics such as need for affiliation, need for power, and need for achievement to select workers for jobs? What additional criteria would you have to consider?

Module 26: Understanding Emotional Experiences

Recap

LO5 What are emotions, and how do we experience them?

- Emotions are broadly defined as feelings that may affect behaviour and generally have both a physiological component and a cognitive component. Debate continues over whether separate systems govern cognitive and emotional responses and whether one has primacy over the other.

LO6 What are the functions of emotions?

- Emotions prepare us for action, shape future behaviour through learning, and help us interact more effectively with others.

LO7 What are the explanations for emotions?

- Several theories explain emotions. The James-Lange theory suggests that emotional experience is a reaction to bodily, or visceral, changes that occur as a response to an environmental event and are interpreted as an emotional response.
- In contrast, the Cannon-Bard theory contends that both physiological arousal and an emotional experience are produced simultaneously by the same nerve stimulus and that the visceral experience does not necessarily differ among differing emotions.
- The Schachter-Singer theory suggests that emotions are determined jointly by a relatively nonspecific physiological arousal and the subsequent labelling of that arousal, using cues from the environment to determine how others are behaving in the same situation.
- The most recent approaches to emotions focus on their biological origins. For instance, it now seems that specific patterns of biological arousal are associated with individual emotions. Furthermore, new scanning techniques have identified the specific parts of the brain that are activated during the experience of particular emotions.

LO8 How does nonverbal behaviour relate to the expression of emotions?

- A person's facial expressions can reveal emotions. In fact, members of different cultures understand the emotional expressions of others in similar ways.

Rethink

1. If researchers learned how to control emotional responses so that targeted emotions could be caused or prevented, what ethical concerns might arise? Under what circumstances, if any, should such techniques be used?

2. *From the perspective of an advertising executive:* How might you use the findings by Schachter and Singer on the labelling of arousal to create interest in a product? Can you think of other examples whereby people's arousal could be manipulated, which would lead to different emotional responses?

3. What function might Rochette's emotions have served in helping her to overcome her grief and continue her quest for an Olympic Medal?

4. Before competing in the Olympic Games, Rochette said, "My mom wanted me to have a better life than she did" (Starkman, 2010). How can this statement be interpreted in terms of your understanding of motivation and emotion?

CHAPTER 9
Development

Source: © Blend Images/Getty Images RF.

Key Concepts for Chapter 9

MODULE 27 Nature, Nurture, and Prenatal Development

- **LO1** How do psychologists study the degree to which development is an interaction of hereditary and environmental factors?
- **LO2** What is the nature of development before birth?
- **LO3** What factors affect a child during the mother's pregnancy?

Determining the Relative Influence of Nature and Nurture

Developmental Research Techniques

Prenatal Development: Conception to Birth

MODULE 28 Infancy and Childhood

- **LO4** What are the major competencies of newborns?
- **LO5** What are the milestones of physical and social development during childhood?
- **LO6** How does cognitive development proceed during childhood?

The Extraordinary Newborn

The Growing Child: Infancy Through Middle Childhood

PsychWork: **PsychWork:** *Child Protection Caseworker*

MODULE 29 Adolescence: Becoming an Adult

- **LO7** What major physical, social, and cognitive transitions characterize adolescence?

Physical Development: The Changing Adolescent

Moral and Cognitive Development: Distinguishing Right from Wrong

Social Development: Finding Oneself in a Social World

Exploring Diversity: *Rites of Passage: Coming of Age Around the World*

MODULE 30 Adulthood

- **LO8** What are the principal kinds of physical, social, and intellectual changes that occur in early and middle adulthood, and what are their causes?
- **LO9** How does the reality of late adulthood differ from the stereotypes about that period?
- **LO10** How can we adjust to death?

Physical Development: The Peak of Health

Prologue

Source: © AP Photo/ Alastair Grant.

Test-Tube Baby Birthday

A thousand guests are milling about the manicured lawns of this Jacobean estate in the English countryside, and families have travelled from Iceland, Norway, the Middle East, and the United States. There are clowns on stilts, a falcon demonstration, artists applying henna tattoos, and an inflatable castle for the young partygoers to bounce in.

Amid the din, everyone gathers and sings "Happy Birthday" to 25 year old Louise Brown, the world's first test tube baby. Her guests include hundreds also conceived by *in vitro* fertilization, a tiny fraction of the 1.5 million IVF babies born since 1978 (Rohm, 2003, p. 157).

If Louise Brown's conception was unconventional, her life has unfolded in more traditional ways. In fact, even her conception in a laboratory used a procedure that has now become nearly routine, nevertheless only accessible to Canadians that can afford to pay the high cost of *in vitro* fertilization.

Welcome to the brave new world of childhood—or rather one of the brave new worlds. From new ways of conceiving children to learning how to raise children most sensibly to dealing with the milestones of life that we all face, the issues involved in human development touch each of us.

Developmental psychology, the branch of psychology that studies the patterns of growth and change that occur throughout life, addresses these issues, along with many others. In large part, developmental psychologists study the interaction between the unfolding of biologically predetermined patterns of behaviour and a constantly changing, dynamic environment. They ask how our genetic background affects our behaviour throughout our lives and whether our potential is limited by heredity. Similarly, they seek to understand the way in which the environment works with—or against—our genetic capabilities, how the world we live in affects our development, and how we can be encouraged to reach our full potential.

We begin by examining the approaches developmental psychologists use to study the environmental and genetic factors: the nature–nurture issue. Then we consider the very start of development, beginning with conception and the nine months of life before birth. We describe both genetic and environmental influences on the unborn individual and the way they can affect behaviour throughout the remainder of the life cycle.

Nature, Nurture, and Prenatal Development

LEARNING OBJECTIVES

LO1   **How do** psychologists study the degree to which development is an interaction of hereditary and environmental factors?

LO2   **What is** the nature of development before birth?

LO3   **What factors** affect a child during the mother's pregnancy?

How many bald, six-foot-six, 250-pound (1.98-m, 114-kg) volunteer firefighters in New Jersey wear droopy mustaches, aviator-style eyeglasses, and a key ring on the right side of the belt?

The answer is two: Gerald Levey and Mark Newman. They are twins who were separated at birth. Each twin did not even know the other existed until they were reunited—in a fire station—by a fellow firefighter who knew Newman and was startled to see his double, Levey, at a firefighters' convention.

The lives of the twins, although separate, took remarkably similar paths. Levey went to college, studying forestry; Newman planned to study forestry in college but instead took a job trimming trees. Both had jobs in supermarkets. One had a job installing sprinkler systems; the other installed fire alarms.

Both men are unmarried and find the same kind of woman attractive: "tall, slender, long hair." They share similar hobbies, enjoying hunting, fishing, going to the beach, and watching old John Wayne movies and professional wrestling. Both like Chinese food and drink the same brand of beer. Their mannerisms are also similar—for example, each one throws his head back when he laughs. And, of course, there is one more thing: They share a passion for fighting fires.

The similarities we see in twins Gerald Levey and Mark Newman vividly raise one of the fundamental questions posed by **developmental psychology,** the study of the patterns of growth and change that occur throughout life. The question is this: How can we distinguish between the *environmental* causes of behaviour (the influence of parents, siblings, family, friends, schooling, nutrition, and all the other experiences to which a child is exposed) and *hereditary* causes (those based on the genetic makeup of an individual that influence growth and development throughout life)? This question embodies the **nature–nurture issue.** In this context, nature refers to hereditary factors, and nurture to environmental influences.

Although the question was first posed as a nature-*versus*-nurture issue, developmental psychologists today agree that *both* nature and nurture interact to produce specific developmental patterns and outcomes. Consequently, the question has evolved into *how and to what degree* do environment and heredity both produce their effects? No one grows up free of environmental influences, nor does anyone develop without being affected by his or her inherited *genetic makeup.* However, the debate over the comparative influence of the two factors remains active, with different approaches and theories of development emphasizing the environment or heredity to a greater or lesser degree (Gottesman & Hanson, 2005; Rutter, 2006; Belsky & Pluess, 2009).

For example, some developmental theories rely on basic psychological principles of learning and stress the role learning plays in producing changes in behaviour in a developing child. Such theories emphasize the role of the environment in development. In contrast, other developmental theories emphasize the influence of one's physiological makeup

---

Developmental psychology
The branch of psychology that studies the patterns of growth and change that occur throughout life.

Nature–nurture issue
The issue of the degree to which environment and heredity influence behaviour.

and functioning on development. Such theories stress the role of heredity and *maturation*—the unfolding of biologically predetermined patterns of behaviour—in producing developmental change. Maturation can be seen, for instance, in the development of sex characteristics (such as breasts and body hair) that occurs at the start of adolescence. Furthermore, the work of behavioural geneticists, who study the effects of heredity on behaviour, and the theories of evolutionary psychologists, who identify behaviour patterns that result from our genetic inheritance, have influenced developmental psychologists. Both behavioural geneticists and evolutionary psychologists have highlighted the importance of heredity in influencing human behaviour (Buss, 2003; Reif & Lesch, 2003; Ilies, Arvey, & Bouchard, 2006).

Despite their differences over theory, developmental psychologists concur on some points. They agree that genetic factors not only provide the potential for particular behaviours or traits to emerge, but also place limitations on the emergence of such behaviour or traits. For instance, heredity defines people's general level of intelligence, setting an upper limit that—regardless of the quality of the environment—people cannot exceed. Heredity also places limits on physical abilities; humans simply cannot run at a speed of 96 kilometres an hour, nor will they grow as tall as ten feet (3.04 m), no matter what the quality of their environment (Pinker, 2004; Dodge, 2004).

Figure 1 lists some of the characteristics most affected by heredity. As you consider these items, it is important to keep in mind that these characteristics are not *entirely* determined by heredity, but that environmental factors also play a role.

Developmental psychologists also agree that in most instances environmental factors play a critical role in enabling people to reach the potential capabilities that their genetic background makes possible. If Albert Einstein had received no intellectual stimulation as a child and had not been sent to school, it is unlikely that he would have reached his genetic potential. Similarly, a great athlete such as NHL hockey star Wayne Gretzky would have been unlikely to display much physical skill if he had not been raised in an environment that nurtured his innate talent and gave him the opportunity to train and perfect his natural abilities.

Clearly, the relationship between heredity and environment is far from simple. As a consequence, developmental psychologists typically take an *interactionist* position on the nature–nurture issue, suggesting that a combination of hereditary and environmental factors influences development. Developmental psychologists face the challenge of identifying the relative strength of each of these influences on the individual, as well as that of identifying the specific changes that occur over the course of development (McGregor & Capone, 2004; Moffitt, Caspi, & Rutter, 2006).

STUDY ALERT!

The nature–nurture issue is a key question that is pervasive throughout the field of psychology, asking how and to what degree do environment and heredity produce their joint effects.

FIGURE 1

Characteristics influenced significantly by genetic factors. Although these characteristics have strong genetic components, they are also affected by environmental factors.

Physical Characteristics	Intellectual Characteristics	Emotional Characteristics and Disorders
Height	Memory	Shyness
Weight	Intelligence	Extraversion
Obesity	Age of language acquisition	Emotionality
Tone of voice	Reading disability	Neuroticism
Blood pressure	Intellectual disabilities	Schizophrenia
Tooth decay		Anxiety
Athletic ability		Alcoholism
Firmness of handshake		
Age of death		
Activity level		

Determining the Relative Influence of Nature and Nurture

Human twins serve as an important source of information about the relative influence of genetic and environmental factors on behaviour. If **identical twins** (those who are genetically identical) display different patterns of development, those differences have to be attributed to variations in the environment in which the twins were raised. The most useful data come from identical twins (such as Gerald Levey and Mark Newman) who are adopted at birth by different sets of adoptive parents and raised apart in differing environments. Studies of nontwin siblings who are raised in totally different environments also shed some light on the issue. Because they have relatively similar genetic backgrounds, siblings who show similarities as adults provide strong evidence for the importance of heredity (Sternberg, 2002; Vitaro, Brendgen, & Arsenault, 2009).

Researchers can also take the opposite tack. Instead of concentrating on people with similar genetic backgrounds who are raised in different environments, they may consider people raised in similar environments who have totally dissimilar genetic backgrounds. If they find, for example, similar courses of development in two adopted children who have different genetic backgrounds and have been raised in the same family, they have evidence for the importance of environmental influences on development. Moreover, psychologists can carry out research involving animals with dissimilar genetic backgrounds; by experimentally varying the environment in which they are raised, we can determine the influence of environmental factors (independent of heredity) on development (Petrill & Deater-Deckard, 2004).

STUDY ALERT!

Be sure you can distinguish the three different types of developmental research: cross-sectional (comparing people of different ages at the same time); longitudinal (studying participants as they age); and sequential (a combination of cross-sectional and longitudinal).

Developmental Research Techniques

Because of the demands of measuring behavioural change across different ages, developmental researchers use several unique methods. The most frequently used, **cross-sectional research,** compares people of different ages at the same point in time. Cross-sectional studies provide information about differences in development between different age groups (Creasey, 2005; Huijie, 2006).

Suppose, for instance, we were interested in the development of intellectual ability in adulthood. To carry out a cross-sectional study, we might compare a sample of 25-, 45-, and 65-year-olds who all take the same IQ test. We then can determine whether average IQ test scores differ in each age group.

Cross-sectional research has limitations, however. For instance, we cannot be sure that the differences in IQ scores we might find in our example are due to age differences alone. Instead, the scores may reflect differences in the educational attainment of the cohorts represented. A *cohort* is a group of people who grow up at similar times, in similar places, and in similar conditions. In the case of IQ differences, any age differences we find in a cross-sectional study may reflect educational differences among the cohorts studied: People in the older age group may belong to a cohort that was less likely to attend college or university than were the people in the younger groups.

A longitudinal study, the second major research strategy used by developmental psychologists, provides one way around this problem. **Longitudinal research** traces the behaviour of one or more participants as the participants age.

Identical twins
Twins who are genetically identical.

Cross-sectional research
A research method that compares people of different ages at the same point in time.

Longitudinal research
A research method that investigates behaviour as participants age.

Longitudinal studies assess *change* in behaviour over time, unlike cross-sectional studies, which assess *differences* among groups of people.

For instance, consider how we might investigate intellectual development during adulthood by using a longitudinal research strategy. First, we might give an IQ test to a group of 25-year-olds. We'd then come back to the same people twenty years later and retest them at age 45. Finally, we'd return to them once more when they were 65 years old and test them again.

By examining changes at several points in time, we can clearly see how individuals develop. Unfortunately, longitudinal research requires an enormous expenditure of time (as the researcher waits for the participants to get older), and participants who begin a study at an early age may drop out, move away, or even die as the research continues. Moreover, participants who take the same test at several points in time may become "test-wise" and perform better each time they take it, having become more familiar with the test.

To make up for the limitations in both cross-sectional and longitudinal research, investigators have devised an alternative strategy. Known as **sequential research,** it combines cross-sectional and longitudinal approaches by taking a number of different age groups and examining them at several points in time. For example, investigators might use a group of 3-, 5-, and 7-year-olds, examining them every six months for a period of several years. This technique allows a developmental psychologist to tease out the specific effects of age changes from other possibly influential factors.

STUDY ALERT!

It's important to understand the basic building blocks of genetics: chromosomes that contain genes, which in turn are composed of sequences of DNA.

Prenatal Development: Conception to Birth

A routine prenatal test brought Jennifer and Brian Buchkovich horrifying news: Their unborn baby, Ethan, was afflicted with spina bifida, a failure of the spine to close over the spinal cord. The birth defect, which affects 2,000 children a year, usually leads to paralysis and cognitive delays. But doctors offered the couple a glimmer of hope—an experimental operation designed to reduce the damage and to eliminate or delay the need for a surgically implanted shunt to drain excess fluid from the brain. The hitch: The surgery would have to be performed while Ethan was still inside Jennifer's womb (People Weekly, 2000, p. 117).

The Buchkovichs took the risk, and it appears to have paid off: Although Ethan has shown some developmental delays, he's just a bit behind schedule.

Our increasing understanding of the first stirrings of life spent inside a mother's womb has permitted significant medical advances like those that helped Ethan Buchkovich. Yet our knowledge of the biology of *conception*—when a male's sperm cell penetrates a female's egg cell—and its aftermath makes the start of life no less of a miracle. Let's consider how an individual is created by looking first at the genetic endowment that a child receives at the moment of conception.

The Basics of Genetics

The one-cell entity established at conception contains twenty-three pairs of **chromosomes,** rod-shaped structures that contain all basic hereditary information. One member of each pair is from the mother, and the other is from the father.

Sequential research
A research method that combines cross-sectional and longitudinal research by considering a number of different age groups and examining them at several points in time.

Chromosomes
Rod-shaped structures that contain all basic hereditary information.

FIGURE 2

Every individual's characteristics are determined by the individual's specific genetic information. At the moment of conception (a), humans receive twenty-three pairs of chromosomes (b), half from the mother and half from the father. These chromosomes are made up of coils of DNA (c). Each chromosome contains thousands of genes (d) that "program" the future development of the body.

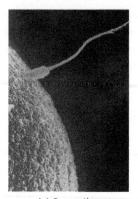 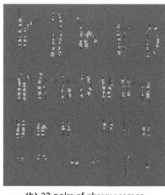 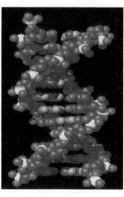 

(a) Conception   (b) 23 pairs of chromosomes   (c) DNA sequence   (d) Genes

Sources: (a) © Don W. Fawcett/Science Source; (b) © L. Willatt, East Anglian Regional Genetics Service/SPL/Science Source; (c) © Kenneth Eward/Science Source; (d) © Biophoto Associates/Science Source.

Each chromosome contains thousands of **genes**—smaller units through which genetic information is transmitted. Either individually or in combination, genes produce the particular characteristics of each person. Composed of sequences of *DNA (deoxyribonucleic acid)* molecules, genes are the biological equivalent of "software" that programs the future development of all parts of the body's hardware. Humans have some 25,000 different genes (see Figure 2 above).

Some genes control the development of systems common to all members of the human species—the heart, circulatory system, brain, lungs, and so forth; others shape the characteristics that make each human unique, such as facial configuration, height, and eye colour. The child's sex is also determined by a particular combination of genes. Specifically, a child inherits an X chromosome from its mother and either an X or a Y chromosome from its father. When it receives an XX combination, it is a female; with an XY combination, it develops as a male. Male development is triggered by a single gene on the Y chromosome, and without the presence of that specific gene, the individual will develop as a female.

As behavioural geneticists have discovered, genes are also at least partially responsible for a wide variety of personal characteristics, including cognitive abilities, personality traits, and psychological disorders. Of course, few of these characteristics are determined by a single gene. Instead, most traits result from a combination of multiple genes, which operate together with environmental influences (Plomin & McGuffin, 2003; Haberstick et al., 2005; Ramus, 2006).

Earliest Development

When an egg becomes fertilized by the sperm, the resulting one-celled entity, called a **zygote**, immediately begins to develop. The zygote starts out as a microscopic speck. Three days after fertilization, though, the zygote increases to around 32 cells, and within a week it has grown to 100–150 cells. These first two weeks are known as the *germinal period*.

Two weeks after conception, the developing individual enters the *embryonic period*, which lasts from week 2 through week 8, and he or she is now called an **embryo.** As an embryo develops through an intricate, preprogrammed process of cell division, it grows 10,000 times larger by week 4, attaining a length of about one-fifth of an inch

Genes
The parts of the chromosomes through which genetic information is transmitted.

Zygote
The new cell formed by the union of an egg and sperm.

Embryo
A developed zygote that has a heart, a brain, and other organs.

(five mm). At this point it has developed a rudimentary beating heart, a brain, an intestinal tract, and a number of other organs. Although all these organs are at a primitive stage of development, they are clearly recognizable. Moreover, by week 8, the embryo is about an inch (twenty-five mm) long, and has discernible arms and legs and a face.

From week 8 and continuing until birth, the developing individual enters the *fetal period* and is called a **fetus.** At the start of this period, it begins to be responsive to touch; it bends its fingers when touched on the hand. At 16 to 18 weeks, its movements become strong enough for the mother to sense them. At the same time, hair may begin to grow on the fetus's head, and the facial features become similar to those the child will display at birth. The major organs begin functioning, although the fetus could not be kept alive outside the mother. In addition, a lifetime's worth of brain neurons are produced—although it is unclear whether the brain is capable of thinking at this early stage.

By week 24, a fetus has many of the characteristics it will display as a newborn. In fact, when an infant is born prematurely at this age, it can open and close its eyes; suck; cry; look up, down, and around; and even grasp objects placed in its hands.

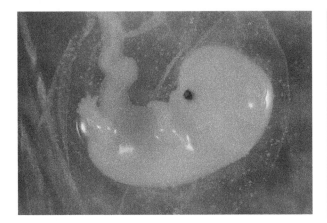 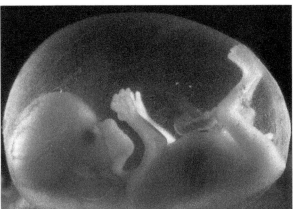

These remarkable photos of live fetuses display the degree of physical development at prenatal ages 4 and 15 weeks.

Sources: (left): © SPL/Science Source; (right): © Petit Format/Science Source.

The fetus continues to develop before birth. It begins to grow fatty deposits under the skin, and it gains weight. The fetus reaches the **age of viability**, the point at which it can survive if born prematurely, at about prenatal age 22 weeks, although through advances in medical technology this crucial age is getting earlier. At prenatal age 28 weeks, the fetus weighs less than three pounds (1.36 kg) and is about sixteen inches (forty cm) long. It may be capable of learning: One study found that the infants of mothers who had repeatedly read aloud the Dr. Seuss story *The Cat in the Hat* before the infants' birth preferred the sound of that particular story to other stories after they were born (Spence & DeCasper, 1982; Schenone et al., 2010).

Before birth, a fetus passes through several s*ensitive periods* (also referred to as *critical periods*). A sensitive period is the time when organisms are particularly susceptible to certain kinds of stimuli. However, the central nervous system can be compromised from the beginning of pregnancy and can even occur after birth. Teratogens such as illicit drugs, alcohol, radiation, and some prescription drugs to name a few, can alter or harm the development of the baby's body or brain (Lawryk, 2011).

During the final weeks of pregnancy, the fetus continues to gain weight and grow. At the end of the normal thirty-eight weeks of pregnancy the fetus typically weighs around seven pounds (three kg) and is about twenty inches (fifty cm) in length. However, the story is different for *preterm infants*, who are born before week 38. Because they have not been able to develop fully, they are at higher risk for illness, future problems, and even death. For infants who have been in the womb for more than thirty weeks, the prospects are relatively good. However, for those born before week 30, the story is often less positive. Such newborns, who may weigh as little as two pounds (0.9 kg) at birth, are in grave

Fetus
A developing individual from eight weeks after conception until birth.

Age of viability
The point at which a fetus can survive if born prematurely.

danger because they have immature organs; they have less than a 50–50 chance of survival. If they do survive—and it takes extraordinarily heroic (and expensive) medical intervention to assure this—they may later experience significant developmental delays.

GENETIC INFLUENCES ON THE FETUS

The process of fetal growth that we have just described reflects normal development, which occurs in 95 to 98 percent of all pregnancies. Some individuals are less fortunate, for in the remaining 2 to 5 percent of cases, children are born with serious birth defects. A major cause of such defects is faulty genes or chromosomes. Here are some of the more common genetic and chromosomal difficulties:

- *Phenylketonuria (PKU).* A child born with the inherited disease phenylketonuria cannot produce an enzyme that is required for normal development. This results in an accumulation of poisons that eventually cause profound intellectual disabilities. The disease is treatable, however, if it is caught early. Most infants today are routinely tested for PKU, and children with the disorder can be placed on a special diet that allows them to develop normally (Ievers-Landis et al., 2005; Christ et al., 2006: Widaman, 2009).

- *Sickle-cell anemia.* About 10 percent of the African American population has the possibility of passing on sickle-cell anemia, a disease that gets its name from the abnormally shaped red blood cells it causes. Children with the disease may have poor appetites, swollen stomachs, yellowish eyes, and cognitive difficulties; they frequently die during childhood (Taras & Potts-Datema, 2005; Selove, 2007).

- *Tay-Sachs disease.* Children born with Tay-Sachs disease, a disorder most often found in Jews of eastern European ancestry, usually die by age 3 or 4 because of the body's inability to break down fat. If both parents carry the genetic defect that produces the fatal illness, their child has a one in four chance of being born with the disease (Leib et al., 2005; Weinstein, 2007).

- *Down syndrome.* Down syndrome, one of the causes of intellectual disabilities, occurs when the zygote receives an extra chromosome at the moment of conception. Down syndrome is often related to the mother's age; mothers over 35 and younger than 18, in particular, stand a higher risk than other women of having a child with the syndrome (Roizen & Patterson, 2003; Sherman et al., 2007).

PRENATAL ENVIRONMENTAL INFLUENCES

Genetic factors are not the only causes of difficulties in fetal development. Environmental influences—the nurture part of the nature–nurture equation—also affect the fetus. Some of the more profound consequences are brought about by **teratogens**, environmental agents such as a drug, chemical, virus, or other factor that produce a birth defect. Among the major prenatal environmental influences on the fetus are the following:

- *Mother's nutrition and emotional state.* What a mother eats during her pregnancy can have important implications for the health of her baby. Seriously undernourished mothers cannot provide adequate nutrition to a growing fetus, and they are likely to give birth to underweight babies. Poorly nourished babies are also more susceptible to disease, and a lack of nourishment may have an adverse impact on their mental development (Zigler, Finn-Stevenson, & Hall, 2002; Najman et al., 2004; Everette, 2008). Moreover, the mother's emotional state affects her baby. Mothers who are anxious and tense during the last months of their pregnancies are more apt to have irritable infants who sleep and eat poorly. The reason? The autonomic nervous system of the fetus becomes especially sensitive as a result of chemical changes produced by the mother's emotional state (Relier, 2001; Hollins, 2007).

- *Mother's illness.* Several diseases that have a relatively minor effect on the health of a mother can have devastating consequences for a developing fetus if they are contracted during the early part of a pregnancy. For example, rubella (German measles), syphilis, diabetes, and high blood pressure may each produce a permanent effect on the fetus. The virus that causes AIDS can also be passed from mother to child before birth, as well as through breast-feeding after birth (Nesheim et al., 2004; Magoni et al., 2005).

Teratogens
Environmental agents such as a drug, chemical, virus, or other factor that produce a birth defect.

- *Mother's use of drugs.* Mothers who take illegal, physically addictive drugs such as cocaine, heroin or prescription pain killers run the risk of giving birth to babies who are similarly addicted. Their newborns suffer painful withdrawal symptoms and sometimes show permanent physical and cognitive impairments. Studies have shown that the effect of methadone when used as a treatment with drug addicted pregnant mothers is far less damaging to the fetus than opiates such as heroin or prescription pain killers. These babies have far better outcomes; however, can suffer from neonatal abstinence syndrome (NAS) opioid withdrawal (National Institute of Health, 2010). Mothers should also be aware that there are prescription and other over the counter medications that can also impact the development of the fetus. For example, drugs such as the acne medicine Accutane can produce abnormalities (Ikonomidou et al., 2000; Schecter, Finkelstein, & Koren, 2005). Mothers should avoid exposure to X-rays, lead, and radiation when pregnant.

- *Alcohol use.* Fetal Alcohol Spectrum Disorder (FASD) is an umbrella term used to describe the effects that can occur in an individual whose mother drank while she was pregnant. The medical diagnosis within the spectrum may include Fetal Alcohol Syndrome (FAS), Partial Fetal Alcohol Syndrome (pFAS), Alcohol Related Neurodevelopmental Disorder (ARND), and Alcohol Related Birth Defects (ARBD).

  FASD has lifelong impacts on individuals, their families, and society and it cannot be cured. The effects may range from mild to severe and can include physical abnormalities, sensory integration variables, learning disabilities, and/or behavioural issues (Lawryk, 2011).

  FASD is under-recognized and under-reported, which makes it difficult to establish the exact number of Canadian infants born with FASD. The incidence of FAS/FAE in high-risk Canadian populations (e.g., First Nations and Inuit communities) may be as high as one in five births (Health Canada, 2008a; Public Health Agency of Canada, 2008). It is estimated that 1 in 100 are born with FASD in Canada (Health Canada, 2006). Sadly, the prevalence of FASD, the primary preventable cause of intellectual disabilities, is higher than the prevalence of both spina bifida and Down syndrome in Canada (Niccols, 2007; Health Canada, 2008; Murthy et al., 2009).

  Even mothers who consume small amounts of alcohol during pregnancy place their child at risk. There is no safe level of alcohol intake during pregnancy and no safe time. Consuming alcohol while pregnant at any time and in any amount may be potentially harmful to the developing baby and their brain.

  What are the characteristics of women who drink alcohol during pregnancy? Liz Lawryk BSW, MSc., RSW, Chief Clinical Examiner, of the OBD (Organic Brain Dysfunction Triage) Institute in Alberta reported that women do not intentionally set out to drink while they are pregnant. Women may not know they are pregnant when they are drinking and reported that many women who confirmed drinking while they are pregnant also disclosed being sexually, physically and/or emotionally abused as a child, which may have resulted in an addiction to alcohol and/or drugs (Lawryk, 2011).

- *Nicotine use.* Pregnant mothers who smoke put their children at considerable risk. Smoking during pregnancy exposes unborn babies to over 4,000 harmful chemicals found in tobacco smoke including fifty toxins linked to cancer. Cigarette smoking also deprives unborn babies of oxygen and essential nutrients resulting in higher rates of miscarriage and complications before, during, and after birth (Government of Canada, 2008). Prenatal tobacco exposure has also been linked to poor growth of the fetus, low birth weight, and preterm delivery, as well as higher rates of respiratory problems and sudden infant death syndrome (SIDS) (Lawryk, 2011). Some research also indicates that prenatal tobacco exposure is also linked to physical, motor, sensory, and cognitive deficits (Wickstrom, 2007).

Evaluate

1. Developmental psychologists are interested in the effects of both _____ and _____ on development.

2. Environment and heredity both influence development, with genetic potentials generally establishing limits on environmental influences. True or false?

3. By observing genetically similar animals in differing environments, we can increase our understanding of the influences of hereditary and environmental factors in humans. True or false?

4. _____ research studies the same individuals over a period of time, whereas _____ research studies people of different ages at the same time.

5. Match each of the following terms with its definition:

   1. Zygote

   2. Gene

   3. Chromosome

   a. Smallest unit through which genetic information is passed

   b. Fertilized egg

   c. Rod-shaped structure containing genetic information

Answers to Evaluate Questions

1. heredity (or nature), environment (or nurture); 2. true; 3. true; 4. longitudinal, cross-sectional; 5. 1-b, 2-a, 3-c

Key Terms

age of viability	fetus	sequential research
chromosomes	genes	teratogens
cross-sectional research	identical twins	zygote
developmental psychology	longitudinal research	
embryo	nature–nurture issue	

Infancy and Childhood

LEARNING OBJECTIVES

LO4 **What are** the major competencies of newborns?
LO5 **What are** the milestones of physical and social development during childhood?
LO6 **How does** cognitive development proceed during childhood?

His head was moulded into a long melon shape and came to a point at the back . . . He was covered with a thick greasy white material known as "vernix," which made him slippery to hold, and also allowed him to slip easily through the birth canal. In addition to a shock of black hair on his head, his body was covered with dark, fine hair known as "lanugo." His ears, his back, his shoulders, and even his cheeks were furry . . . His skin was wrinkled and quite loose, ready to scale increased places such as his feet and hands . . . His ears were pressed to his head in unusual positions—one ear was matted firmly forward on his cheek. His nose was flattened and pushed to one side by the squeeze as he came through the pelvis (Brazelton, 1969, p. 3).

What kind of creature is this? Although the description hardly fits that of the adorable babies seen in advertisements for baby food, we are in fact talking about a normal, completely developed child just after the moment of birth. Called a **neonate**, a newborn arrives in the world in a form that hardly meets the standards of beauty against which we typically measure babies. Yet ask any parent: Nothing is more beautiful or exciting than the first glimpse of their newborn.

The Extraordinary Newborn

Several factors cause a neonate's strange appearance. The trip through the mother's birth canal may have squeezed the incompletely formed bones of the skull together and squashed the nose into the head. The skin secretes *vernix*, a white, greasy covering, for protection before birth, and the baby may have *lanugo*, a soft fuzz, over the entire body for a similar purpose. The infant's eyelids may be puffy with an accumulation of fluids because of the upside-down position during birth.

All this changes during the first two weeks of life as the neonate takes on a more familiar appearance. Even more impressive are the capabilities a neonate begins to display from the moment of birth—capabilities that grow at an astounding rate over the ensuing months.

Reflexes

A neonate is born with a number of **reflexes**—unlearned, involuntary responses that occur automatically in the presence of certain stimuli. Critical for survival, many of those reflexes unfold naturally as part of an infant's ongoing maturation. The *rooting reflex,* for instance, causes neonates to turn their heads toward things that touch their cheeks—such as the mother's nipple or a bottle. Similarly, a *sucking reflex* prompts infants to suck at things that touch

Neonate
A newborn child.

Reflexes
Unlearned, involuntary responses that occur automatically in the presence of certain stimuli.

their lips. Among other reflexes are a *gag reflex* (to clear the throat), the *startle reflex* (a series of movements in which an infant flings out the arms, fans the fingers, and arches the back in response to a sudden noise), and the *Babinski reflex* (a baby's toes fan out when the outer edge of the sole of the foot is stroked).

Infants lose these primitive reflexes after the first few months of life, replacing them with more complex and organized behaviours. Although at birth a neonate is capable of only jerky, limited voluntary movements, during the first year of life the ability to move independently grows enormously. The typical baby rolls over by the age of 3 months, sits without support at 6 months, stands alone at about 11 months, and walks at just over a year old. Not only does the ability to make large-scale movements improve during this time, fine-muscle movements become increasingly sophisticated (see Figure 1).

STUDY ALERT!

The basic neonatal reflexes—unlearned, involuntary responses—include the rooting reflex, the sucking reflex, the gag reflex, the startle reflex, and the Babinski reflex.

Development of the Senses: Taking in the World

When proud parents peer into the eyes of their neonate, is the child able to return their gaze? Although it was thought for some time that newborns can see only a hazy blur, most current findings indicate that the capabilities of neonates are far more impressive. Although their eyes have a limited capacity to focus on objects that are not within a seventeen to twenty-centimetre distance from the face, neonates can follow objects moving within their field of vision. They also show the rudiments of depth perception, as they react by raising their hands when an object appears to be moving rapidly toward the face (Gelman & Kit-Fong Au, 1996; Maurer et al., 1999).

You might think that it would be hard to figure out just how well neonates can see, because their lack of both language and reading ability clearly prevents them from saying what direction the *E* on a vision chart is facing. However, researchers have devised a number of ingenious methods, relying on the newborn's biological responses and innate reflexes, to test perceptual skills.

FIGURE 1

Although at birth a neonate can make only jerky, limited voluntary movements, during the first year of life the ability to move independently grows enormously. The ages indicate the time when 50 percent of children are able to perform each skill. Remember, however, that the time when each skill appears can vary considerably. For example, 25 percent of children are able to walk well at age 11 months, and by 15 months 90 percent of children are walking well.

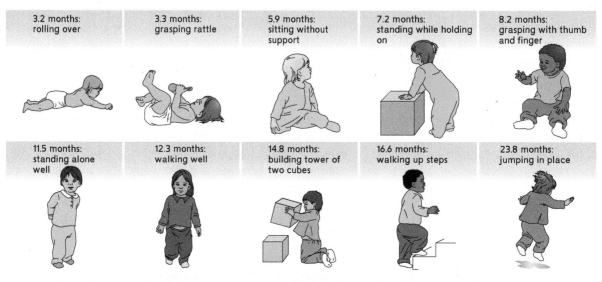

Source: Frankenberg et al., 1992.

For instance, infants who see a novel stimulus typically pay close attention to it, and, as a consequence, their heart rates increase. But if they repeatedly see the same stimulus, their attention to it decreases, as indicated by a return to a slower heart rate. This phenomenon is known as **habituation,** the decrease in the response to a stimulus that occurs after repeated presentations of the same stimulus. By studying habituation, developmental psychologists can tell when a stimulus can be detected and discriminated by a child who is too young to speak (Grunwald et al., 2003; Hannon & Johnson, 2005; del Rosal et al., 2006).

Researchers have developed many other methods for measuring neonate and infant perception. One technique, for instance, involves babies sucking on a nipple attached to a computer. A change in the rate and vigour with which the babies suck helps researchers infer that babies can perceive variations in stimuli. Other approaches include examining babies' eye movements and observing which way babies move their heads in response to a visual stimulus (George, 1999; Franklin, Pilling, & Davies, 2005).

Through the use of such research techniques, we now know that infants' visual perception is remarkably sophisticated from the start of life. At birth, babies prefer patterns with contours and edges over less distinct patterns, indicating that they can respond to the configuration of stimuli. Furthermore, even newborns are aware of size constancy, because they are apparently sensitive to the phenomenon by which objects stay the same size even though the image on the retina may change size as the distance between the object and the retina varies (Norcia et al., 2005; Moore et al., 2007).

In fact, neonates can discriminate facial expressions—and even imitate them. As you can see in Figure 2, newborns who see an adult with a happy, sad, or surprised facial expression can produce a good imitation of the adult's

FIGURE 2

This newborn infant is clearly imitating the expressions of the adult model in these amazing photos. How does this ability contribute to social development? (Courtesy of Dr. Tiffany Field.)

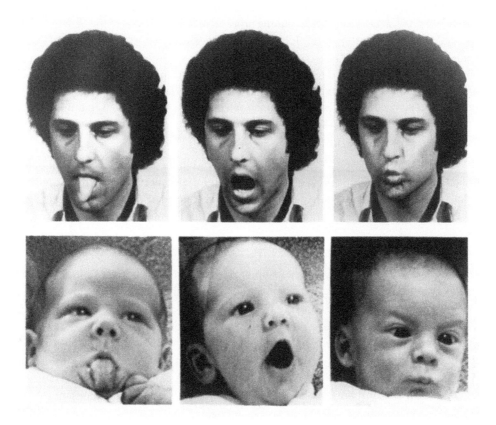

Source: From A. M. Meltzoff and M. K. Moore. 1977. "Imitation of facial and manual gestures by human neonates." *Science*, 198: 75–78. © 1977 American Association for the Advancement of Science.

Habituation
The decrease in the response to a stimulus that occurs after repeated presentations of the same stimulus.

expression. Even very young infants, then, can respond to the emotions and moods that their caregivers' facial expressions reveal. This capability provides the foundation for social interaction skills in children (Meltzoff, 1996; Lavelli & Fogel, 2005; Grossman, Striano, & Friederici, 2007).

Other visual abilities grow rapidly after birth. By the end of their first month, babies can distinguish some colours from others, and after four months they can focus on near or far objects. By age 4 or 5 months they are able to recognize two- and three-dimensional objects, and they can perceive the gestalt organizing principles discovered by psychologists who study perception. Furthermore, their perceptual abilities rapidly improve: Sensitivity to visual stimuli, for instance, becomes three to four times greater at 1 year of age than it was at birth (Johnson, 2004; Striano & Vaish, 2006; Leppanen et al., 2007).

In addition to vision, infants display other impressive sensory capabilities. Newborns can distinguish different sounds to the point of being able to recognize their own mothers' voices at the age of 3 days. They can also make the subtle perceptual distinctions that underlie language abilities. For example, at 2 days of age, infants can distinguish between their native tongue and foreign languages, and they can discriminate between such closely related sounds as ba and pa when they are 4 days old. By 6 months of age, they can discriminate virtually any difference in sound that is relevant to the production of language. Moreover, they can recognize different tastes and smells at a very early age. There even seems to be something of a built-in sweet tooth: Neonates prefer liquids that have been sweetened with sugar over their unsweetened counterparts (Cohen & Cashon, 2003; Rivera-Gaxiola et al., 2005).

The Growing Child: Infancy Through Middle Childhood

It was during the windy days of March that the problem in the day-care centre first arose. Its source: 10-month-old Russell Ruud. Otherwise a model of decorum, Russell had somehow learned how to unzip the Velcro chin strap to his winter hat. He would remove the hat whenever he got the urge, seemingly oblivious to the potential health problems that might follow.

But that was just the start of the real difficulty. To the chagrin of the teachers in the day-care centre, not to speak of the children's parents, soon other children were following his lead, removing their own caps at will. Russell's mother, made aware of the anarchy at the day-care centre—and the other parents' distress over Russell's behaviour—pleaded innocent. "I never showed Russell how to unzip the Velcro," claimed his mother, Judith Ruud. "He learned by trial and error, and the other kids saw him do it one day when they were getting dressed for an outing" (Goleman, 1993, p. C10).

At the age of 10 months, Russell asserted his personality, illustrating the tremendous growth that occurs in a variety of domains during the first year of life. Throughout the remainder of childhood, moving from infancy into middle childhood and the start of adolescence around age 11 or 12, children develop physically, socially, and cognitively in extraordinary ways. In the remainder of this module, we'll consider this development.

Physical Development

Children's physical growth provides the most obvious sign of development. During the first year of life, children typically triple their birthweight, and their height increases by about half. This rapid growth slows down as the child gets older—think how gigantic adults would be if that rate of growth were constant—and from age 3 to the beginning of adolescence at around age 13, growth averages a gain of about five pounds (2.2 kg) and three inches (seven cm) a year (see Figure 3).

The physical changes that occur as children develop are not just a matter of increasing growth; the relationship of the size of the various body parts to one another changes dramatically as children age. As you can see in Figure 4, the head of a fetus (and a newborn) is disproportionately large. However, the head soon becomes more proportional in size to the rest of the body as growth occurs mainly in the trunk and legs.

Development of Social Behaviour: Taking on the World

As anyone who has seen an infant smiling at the sight of his or her mother can guess, at the same time that infants grow physically and hone their perceptual abilities, they also develop socially. The nature of a child's early social development provides the foundation for social relationships that will last a lifetime.

The average heights and weights of males and females in the United States from birth through age 20. At what ages are girls typically heavier and taller than boys?

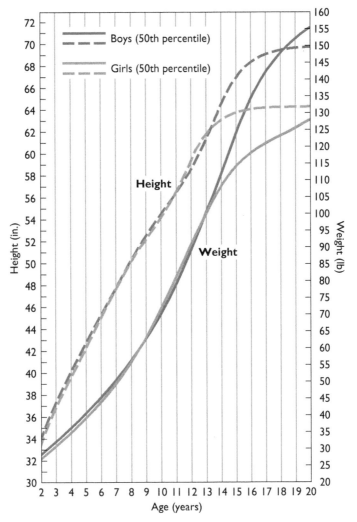

Source: National Center for Health Statistics, 2000.

Attachment, the positive emotional bond that develops between a child and a particular individual, is the most important form of social development that occurs during infancy. The earliest studies of attachment were carried out by animal ethologist Konrad Lorenz (1966). Lorenz focused on newborn goslings, which under normal circumstances instinctively follow their mother, the first moving object they perceive after birth. Lorenz found that goslings whose eggs were raised in an incubator and which viewed him immediately after hatching would follow his every movement, as if he were their mother. He labelled this process imprinting, behaviour that takes place during a critical period and involves attachment to the first moving object that is observed.

Our understanding of attachment progressed when psychologist Harry Harlow, in a classic study, gave infant monkeys the choice of cuddling a wire "monkey" that provided milk or a soft, terry-cloth "monkey" that was warm but did not provide milk. Their choice was clear: They spent most of their time clinging to the warm cloth "monkey," although they made occasional forays to the wire monkey to nurse. Obviously, the cloth monkey provided greater comfort to the infants; milk alone was insufficient to create attachment (Harlow & Zimmerman, 1959; Blum, 2002; see Figure 5).

Attachment
The positive emotional bond that develops between a child and a particular individual.

FIGURE 4

As development progresses, the size of the head relative to the rest of the body decreases until the individual reaches adulthood. Why do you think the head starts out so large?

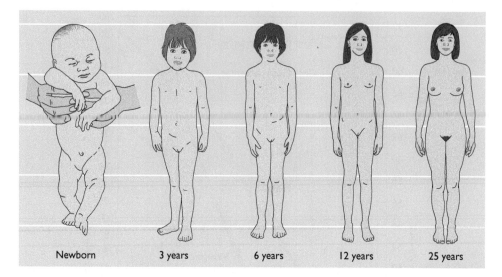

Newborn   3 years   6 years   12 years   25 years

Building on this pioneering work with nonhumans, developmental psychologists have suggested that human attachment grows through the responsiveness of infants' caregivers to the signals the babies provide, such as crying, smiling, reaching, and clinging. The greater the responsiveness of the caregiver to the child's signals, the more likely it is that the child will become securely attached. Full attachment eventually develops as a result of the complex series of interactions between caregiver and child illustrated in Figure 6. In the course of these interactions, the infant plays

FIGURE 5

Although the wire "mother" dispensed milk to the hungry infant monkey, the infant preferred the soft, terry-cloth "mother." Do you think human babies would react the same way? What does this tell us about attachment?

Source: © Nina Leen/Time Life Pictures/Getty Images.

FIGURE 6

The Attachment Behavioural System shows the sequence of activities that infants employ to keep their primary caregivers physically close and bring about attachment. Early in life, crying is the most effective behaviour. Later, though, infants keep the caregiver near through other, more socially appropriate behaviours such as smiling, looking, and reaching. After they are able to walk, children play a more active role in staying close to the caregiver. At the same time, the caregiver's behaviour interacts with the baby's activities to promote attachment.

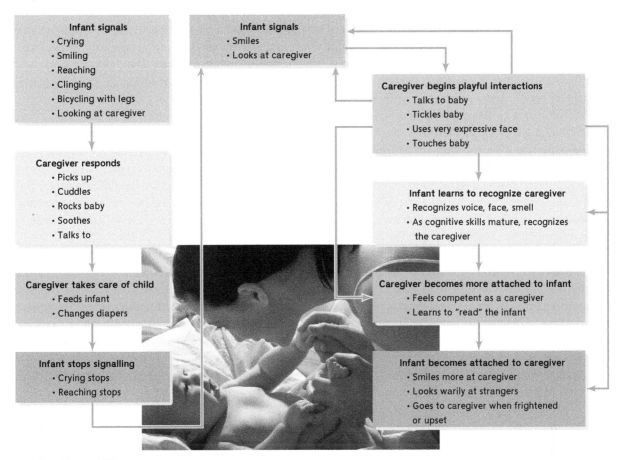

Source: Tomlinson-Keasey, 1985.

Photo Source: © Florian Franke/Purestock/SuperStock RF.

as critical and active a role as the caregiver in the formation of the bond. Infants who respond positively to a caregiver produce more positive behaviour on the part of the caregiver, which in turn produces an even stronger degree of attachment in the child.

THE FATHER'S ROLE

Although early developmental research focused largely on the mother-child relationship, more recent research has highlighted the father's role in parenting, and with good reason: The number of fathers who are primary caregivers for their children has grown significantly, and fathers play an increasingly important role in their children's lives. For example, in almost 20 percent of families with children, the father is the parent who stays at home to care for preschoolers (Day & Lamb, 2004; Parke, 2004; Halford, 2006). Source: ©

STUDY ALERT!

Attachment—the positive emotional bond that develops between a child and a particular individual—is a key concept in understanding the social development of children.

When fathers interact with their children, their play often differs from that of mothers. Fathers engage in more physical, rough-and-tumble sorts of activities, whereas mothers play more verbal and traditional games, such as peek-aboo. Despite such behavioural differences, the nature of attachment between fathers and children compared with that between mothers and children can be similar. In fact, children can form multiple attachments simultaneously (Borisenko, 2007; Pellis & Pellis, 2007; Diener et al., 2008).

ASSESSING ATTACHMENT

Developmental psychologists have devised a quick and direct way to measure attachment. Developed by Mary Ainsworth, the *Ainsworth strange situation* consists of a sequence of events involving a child and (typically) his or her mother. Initially, the mother and baby enter an unfamiliar room, and the mother permits the baby to explore while she sits down. An adult stranger then enters the room, after which the mother leaves. The mother returns, and the stranger leaves. The mother once again leaves the baby alone, and the stranger returns. Finally, the stranger leaves, and the mother returns (Ainsworth et al., 1978; Waters & Beauchaine, 2003; Izard & Abe, 2004).

Babies' reactions to the experimental situation vary drastically, depending, according to Ainsworth, on their degree of attachment to the mother. One-year-old children who are *securely attached* employ the mother as a kind of home base, exploring independently but returning to her occasionally. When she leaves, they exhibit distress, and they go to her when she returns. *Avoidant* children do not cry when the mother leaves, and they seem to avoid her when she returns, as if they were indifferent to her. *Ambivalent* children display anxiety before they are separated and are upset when the mother leaves, but they may show ambivalent reactions to her return, such as seeking close contact but simultaneously hitting and kicking her. A fourth reaction is *disorganized-disoriented;* these children show inconsistent, often contradictory behaviour.

The nature of attachment between children and their mothers has far-reaching consequences for later development. For example, children who are securely attached to their mothers tend to be more socially and emotionally competent than are their less securely attached peers, and others find them more cooperative, capable, and playful. Furthermore, children who are securely attached at age 1 show fewer psychological difficulties when they grow older compared with avoidant and ambivalent youngsters. As adults, children who are securely attached tend to have more successful romantic relationships. On the other hand, being securely attached at an early age does not guarantee good adjustment later, and, conversely, children who lack secure attachment do not always have difficulties later in life (Hamilton, 2000; Waters, Hamilton, & Wienfield, 2000; Bakermans-Kranenburg, van Ijzendoorn, & Juffer, 2003; Fraley & Spieker, 2003; Mikulincer & Shaver, 2005; Roisman et al., 2005).

SOCIAL RELATIONSHIPS WITH PEERS

By the time they are 2 years old, children become less dependent on their parents and more self-reliant, increasingly preferring to play with friends. Initially, play is relatively independent: Even though they may be sitting side by side, 2-year-olds pay more attention to toys than to one another when playing. Later, however, children actively interact, modifying one another's behaviour and later exchanging roles during play (Lindsey & Colwell, 2003; Colwell & Lindsey, 2005).

Cultural factors also affect children's styles of play. For example, Korean American children engage in a higher proportion of parallel play than their Anglo-American counterparts, while Anglo-American preschoolers are involved in more pretend play (Bai, 2005; Drewes, 2005; Suizzo & Bornstein, 2006).

In short, social interaction helps children interpret the meaning of others' behaviour and develop the capacity to respond appropriately. Furthermore, children learn physical and emotional self-control: They learn to avoid hitting a playmate who beats them at a game, be polite, and control their emotional displays and facial expressions (e.g., smiling even when receiving a disappointing gift). Situations that provide children with opportunities for social interaction, then, may enhance their social development (Feldman, 1993; Talukdar & Shastri, 2006; Whitebread et al., 2009).

THE CONSEQUENCES OF CHILDCARE OUTSIDE THE HOME

Research on the importance of social interaction is corroborated by work that examines the benefits of childcare outside the home, which is an important part of an increasing number of children's lives. For instance, almost 30 percent of preschool children whose mothers work outside the home spend their days in childcare centres. More than 80 percent of infants are cared for by people other than their mothers for part of the day during the first year of life (National Research Council, 2001; NICHD Early Child Care Research Network, 2006; see Figure 7).

FIGURE 7

According to a study by the U.S. National Institute of Child Health and Human Development, children were more likely to spend time in some kind of child care outside the home or family as they got older.

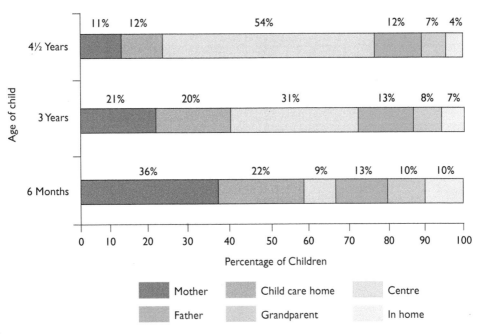

Source: NICHD, 2006.

Do out-of-the-home childcare arrangements benefit children's development? If the programs are of high quality, they can. According to the results of a large study supported by the U.S. National Institute of Child Health and Development, children who attend high-quality childcare centres may not only do as well as children who stay at home with their parents, but in some respects may actually do better. Children in childcare are generally more considerate and sociable than other children are, and they interact more positively with teachers. They may also be more compliant and regulate their own behaviour more effectively, and their mothers show increased sensitivity to their children (Lamb, 1996; NICHD Early Child Care Research Network, 1999, 2001).

In addition, especially for children from poor or disadvantaged homes, childcare in specially enriched environments— those with many toys, books, a variety of children, and high-quality care providers—often proves to be more intellectually stimulating than the home environment. Such childcare can lead to increased intellectual achievement, demonstrated in higher IQ scores and better language development. In fact, children in care centres sometimes are found to score higher on tests of cognitive abilities than those who are cared for by their mothers or by sitters or home day-care providers— effects lasting into adulthood (Wilgoren, 1999; Burchinal et al., 2000; Dearing, McCartney, & Taylor, 2009).

However, outside-the-home childcare does not have universally positive outcomes. Children may feel insecure after placement in low-quality childcare or in multiple childcare settings. Furthermore, some research suggests that infants who are involved in outside care more than twenty hours a week in the first year show less secure attachment to their mothers than do those who have not been in outside-the-home childcare. Finally, children who spent long hours in childcare as infants and preschoolers may have a reduced ability to work independently and to manage their time effectively when they reach elementary school (NICHD Early Child Care Research Network, 2001; Vandell et al., 2005; Pluess & Belsky, 2009).

The key to the success of nonparental childcare is its quality. High-quality childcare produces benefits; low-quality childcare provides little or no gain, and may even hinder children's development. In short, significant benefits result from the social interaction and intellectual stimulation provided by high-quality childcare centres—particularly for children from impoverished environments (NICHD Early Child Care Research Network, 2000, 2002; Ghazvini & Mullis, 2002; Friedman, 2004; National Association for the Education of Young Children, 2005; Zaslow et al., 2006).

PARENTING STYLES AND SOCIAL DEVELOPMENT

Parents' child-rearing practices are critical in shaping their children's social competence, and—according to classic research by developmental psychologist Diana Baumrind—four main categories describe different parenting styles

FIGURE 8

According to developmental psychologist Diana Baumrind (1971), four main parenting styles characterize child rearing.

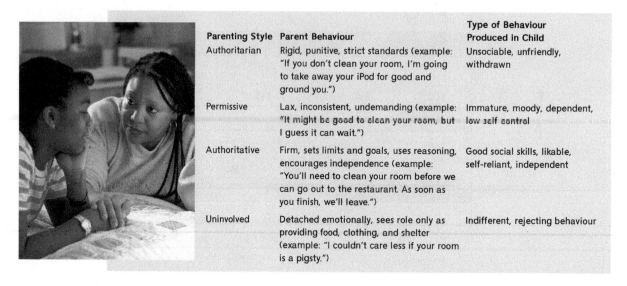

Parenting Style	Parent Behaviour	Type of Behaviour Produced in Child
Authoritarian	Rigid, punitive, strict standards (example: "If you don't clean your room, I'm going to take away your iPod for good and ground you.")	Unsociable, unfriendly, withdrawn
Permissive	Lax, inconsistent, undemanding (example: "It might be good to clean your room, but I guess it can wait.")	Immature, moody, dependent, low self control
Authoritative	Firm, sets limits and goals, uses reasoning, encourages independence (example: "You'll need to clean your room before we can go out to the restaurant. As soon as you finish, we'll leave.")	Good social skills, likable, self-reliant, independent
Uninvolved	Detached emotionally, sees role only as providing food, clothing, and shelter (example: "I couldn't care less if your room is a pigsty.")	Indifferent, rejecting behaviour

Photo Source: © S. W. Productions/Getty Images RF.

(Figure 8 above). Rigid and punitive, **authoritarian parents** value unquestioning obedience from their children. They have strict standards and discourage expressions of disagreement. **Permissive parents** give their children relaxed or inconsistent direction and, although warm, require little of them. In contrast, **authoritative parents** are firm, setting limits for their children. As the children get older, these parents try to reason and explain things to them. They also set clear goals and encourage their children's independence. Finally, **uninvolved parents** show little interest in their children. Emotionally detached, they view parenting as nothing more than providing food, clothing, and shelter for children. At their most extreme, uninvolved parents are guilty of neglect, a form of child abuse (Baumrind, 2005; Winsler, Madigan, & Aquilino, 2005; Lagacé-Seguin & d'Entremont, 2006).

STUDY ALERT!

Know the four major types of child-rearing practices—authoritarian, permissive, authoritative, and uninvolved—and their effects.

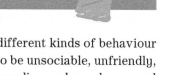

As you might expect, the four kinds of child-rearing styles seem to produce very different kinds of behaviour in children (with many exceptions, of course). Children of authoritarian parents tend to be unsociable, unfriendly, and relatively withdrawn. In contrast, permissive parents' children show immaturity, moodiness, dependence, and

Authoritarian parents
Parents who are rigid and punitive and value unquestioning obedience from their children.

Permissive parents
Parents who give their children relaxed or inconsistent direction and, although they are warm, require little of them.

Authoritative parents
Parents who are firm, set clear limits, reason with their children, and explain things to them.

Uninvolved parents
Parents who show little interest in their children and are emotionally detached.

low self-control. The children of authoritative parents fare best: With high social skills, they are likable, self-reliant, independent, and cooperative. Worst off are the children of uninvolved parents; they feel unloved and emotionally detached, and their physical and cognitive development is impeded (Saarni, 1999; Berk, 2005; Snyder et al., 2005).

Before we rush to congratulate authoritative parents and condemn authoritarian, permissive, and uninvolved ones, it is important to note that in many cases nonauthoritative parents also produce perfectly well-adjusted children. Moreover, children are born with a particular **temperament**—an innate disposition that emerges early in life. Some children are naturally easygoing and cheerful, whereas others are irritable and fussy. The kind of temperament a baby is born with may in part bring about particular kinds of parental child-rearing styles (Majdandzic & van den Boom, 2007; Miner & Clarke-Stewart, 2008; Coplan, Reichel, & Rowan, 2009).

In addition, children vary considerably in their degree of *resilience*, the ability to overcome circumstances that place them at high risk for psychological or even physical harm. Highly resilient children have temperaments that evoke positive responses from caregivers. Such children display unusual social skills: outgoingness, intelligence, and a feeling that they have control over their lives. In a sense, resilient children try to shape their own environment, rather than being victimized by it (Deater-Deckard, Ivy, & Smith, 2005; Vellacott, 2007). (Also see *PsychWork.*)

We also need to keep in mind that these findings regarding child-rearing styles apply primarily to North American society, which highly values children's growing independence and diminishing reliance on their parents. In contrast, Japanese parents encourage dependence to promote the values of cooperation and community life. These differences in cultural values result in very different philosophies of child rearing. For example, Japanese mothers believe it is a punishment to make a young child sleep alone, and so many children sleep next to their mothers throughout infancy and toddlerhood (Kawasaki et al., 1994; Dennis et al., 2002; Jones, 2007).

In sum, a child's upbringing results from the child-rearing philosophy parents hold, the specific practices they use, and the nature of their own and their child's personalities. As is the case with other aspects of development, then, behaviour is a function of a complex interaction of environmental and genetic factors.

ERIKSON'S THEORY OF PSYCHOSOCIAL DEVELOPMENT

In tracing the course of social development, some theorists have considered how the challenges of society and culture change as an individual matures. Following this path, psychoanalyst Erik Erikson developed one of the more comprehensive theories of social development. Erikson (1963) viewed the developmental changes occurring throughout life as a series of eight stages of psychosocial development, of which four occur during childhood. **Psychosocial development** involves changes in our interactions and understanding of one another as well as in our knowledge and understanding of ourselves as members of society.

Erikson suggests that passage through each of the stages necessitates the resolution of a crisis or conflict. Although each crisis is never resolved entirely—life becomes increasingly complicated as we grow older—it has to be resolved sufficiently to equip us to deal with demands made during the following stage of development.

In the first stage of psychosocial development, the **trust-versus-mistrust stage** (ages birth to 1½ years), infants develop feelings of trust if their physical requirements and psychological needs for attachment are consistently met and their interactions with the world are generally positive. In contrast, inconsistent care and unpleasant interactions with others can lead to mistrust and leave an infant unable to meet the challenges required in the next stage of development.

Temperament
The innate disposition that emerges early in life.

Psychosocial development
Development of individuals' interactions and understanding of each other and of their knowledge and understanding of themselves as members of society.

Trust-versus-mistrust stage
According to Erikson, the first stage of psychosocial development, occurring from birth to age 1½ years, during which time infants develop feelings of trust or lack of trust.

PsychWork

Child Protection Caseworker

Name: Jason Larson
Position: Child Protection Caseworker
Education: Bachelor of Social Work (BSW), Wilfrid Laurier University

Children are among the most vulnerable members of society. When they face abuse or neglect, a child protective services agency intervenes and a caseworker is assigned to advocate for the child.

Jason Larson, a child protection caseworker with the Child and Family Services Division of the Department of Public Health and Human Services, notes that every case is unique.

"The age of the children, the physical condition of the parents or caretakers, the physical condition of the home, whether the alleged perpetrator is living in the home or has access to the child are all factors to be considered," he said. "In addition, whether or not I can corroborate the information quickly enough to gauge whether or not a child can stay in the home or needs to be removed is important as well," he added.

Larson, who's been a caseworker for 15 years, works in a remote area, which adds its own challenges.

"Living and serving a rural area, I have to be very creative with the services we have, as we are very limited in a lot of small towns," Larson noted. "As a result, we use many different approaches to protect children."

One of those approaches, according to Larson, is a process called Family Group Decision Making, meetings in which the parents and all the service providers are at one table discussing the children and the family's situation.

"Everyone goes around the room and explains their concerns and positives the family has at the time and, once this is complete, a plan is made for them to follow," he notes. "These meetings are very effective in assisting the family as a whole so that we can apply all the resources available."

In the second stage, the **autonomy-versus-shame-and-doubt stage** (ages 1½ to 3 years), toddlers develop independence and autonomy if exploration and freedom are encouraged, or they experience shame, self-doubt, and unhappiness if they are overly restricted and protected. According to Erikson, the key to the development of autonomy during this period is for the child's caregivers to provide the appropriate amount of control. If parents provide too much control, children cannot assert themselves and develop their own sense of control over their environment; if parents provide too little control, the children become overly demanding and controlling.

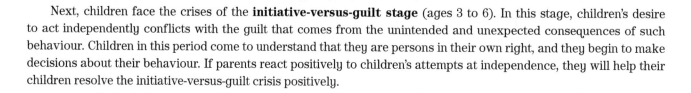

STUDY ALERT!

Four of Erikson's stages of psychosocial development occur during childhood: trust-versus-mistrust, autonomy-versus-shame-and-doubt, initiative-versus-guilt, and industry-versus-inferiority.

Next, children face the crises of the **initiative-versus-guilt stage** (ages 3 to 6). In this stage, children's desire to act independently conflicts with the guilt that comes from the unintended and unexpected consequences of such behaviour. Children in this period come to understand that they are persons in their own right, and they begin to make decisions about their behaviour. If parents react positively to children's attempts at independence, they will help their children resolve the initiative-versus-guilt crisis positively.

Autonomy-versus-shame-and-doubt stage
The period during which, according to Erikson, toddlers (ages 1½ to 3 years) develop independence and autonomy if exploration and freedom are encouraged, or shame and self-doubt if they are restricted and overprotected.

Initiative-versus-guilt stage
According to Erikson, the period during which children ages 3 to 6 years experience conflict between independence of action and the sometimes negative results of that action.

The fourth and last stage of childhood is the **industry-versus-inferiority stage** (ages 6 to 12). During this period, increasing competency in all areas, whether social interactions or academic skills, characterizes successful psychosocial development. In contrast, difficulties in this stage lead to feelings of failure and inadequacy.

Although his theory has been criticized on several grounds—such as the imprecision of the concepts he employs and his greater emphasis on male development than female development—it remains influential and is one of the few theories that encompass the entire life span.

This module addressed the four conflicts faced during childhood. The remaining four conflicts will be expanded upon in Module 29, Adolescence (e.g., identity-versus-role-confusion and intimacy-versus-isolation) and Module 30, Adulthood (e.g., generativity-versus-stagnation and ego-integrity-versus-despair).

Cognitive Development: Children's Thinking About the World

Suppose you had two drinking glasses of different shapes—one short and broad and one tall and thin. Now imagine that you filled the short, broad one with pop about halfway and then poured the liquid from that glass into the tall one. The pop would appear to fill about three-quarters of the second glass. If someone asked you whether there was more pop in the second glass than there had been in the first, what would you say?

You might think that such a simple question hardly deserves an answer; of course there is no difference in the amount of pop in the two glasses. However, most 4-year-olds would be likely to say that there is more pop in the second glass. If you then poured the pop back into the short glass, they would say there is now less pop than there was in the taller glass.

Why are young children confused by this problem? The reason is not immediately obvious. Anyone who has observed preschoolers must be impressed by how far they have progressed from the early stages of development. They speak with ease, know the alphabet, count, play complex games, use tape players, tell stories, and communicate ably. Yet despite this seeming sophistication, there are deep gaps in children's understanding of the world. Some theorists have suggested that children cannot understand certain ideas and concepts until they reach a particular stage of **cognitive development**— the process by which a child's understanding of the world changes as a function of age and experience. In contrast to the theories of physical and social development discussed earlier (such as those of Erikson), theories of cognitive development seek to explain the quantitative and qualitative intellectual advances that occur during development.

STUDY ALERT!

Use Figure 9 to help remember Piaget's stages of cognitive development.

PIAGET'S THEORY OF COGNITIVE DEVELOPMENT

No theory of cognitive development has had more impact than that of Swiss psychologist Jean Piaget. Piaget (1970) suggested that children around the world proceed through a series of four stages in a fixed order: sensorimotor, preoperational, concrete operational, and formal operational (see Figure 9). Let's examine each of them and the approximate ages that they span.

Sensorimotor Stage: Birth to 2 Years. During the **sensorimotor stage,** children base their understanding of the world primarily on touching, sucking, chewing, shaking, and manipulating objects. In the initial part of the stage, children have relatively little competence in representing the environment by using images, language, or other kinds of

Industry-versus-inferiority stage
According to Erikson, the last stage of childhood, during which children age 6 to 12 years may develop positive social interactions with others or may feel inadequate and become less sociable.

Cognitive development
The process by which a child's understanding of the world changes as a function of age and experience.

Sensorimotor stage
According to Piaget, the stage from birth to 2 years, during which a child has little competence in representing the environment by using images, language, or other symbols.

FIGURE 9

According to Jean Piaget, all children pass through four stages of cognitive development.

Cognitive Stage	Approximate Age Range	Major Characteristics
Sensorimotor	Birth–2 years	Development of object permanence, development of motor skills, little or no capacity for symbolic representation
Preoperational	2–7 years	Development of language and symbolic thinking, egocentric thinking
Concrete operational	7–12 years	Development of conservation, mastery of concept of reversibility
Formal operational	12 years–adulthood	Development of logical and abstract thinking

Photo Source: © Farrell Grehen/Corbis.

symbols. Consequently, infants lack what Piaget calls **object permanence,** the awareness that objects—and people—continue to exist even if they are out of sight. Object permanence is critical development during the sensorimotor stage.

Preoperational Stage: 2 to 7 Years. The most important development during the **preoperational stage** is the use of language. Children develop internal representational systems that allow them to describe people, events, and feelings. They even use symbols in play, pretending, for example, that a book pushed across the floor is a car.

Although children use more advanced thinking in this stage than they did in the earlier sensorimotor stage, their thinking is still qualitatively inferior to that of adults. We see this when we observe a preoperational child using **egocentric thought,** a way of thinking in which the child views the world entirely from his or her own perspective.

Children who have not mastered the principle of conservation assume that the volume of a liquid increases when it is poured from a short, wide container to a tall, thin one. What other tasks might a child under age 7 have difficulty comprehending?

Source: © Tony Freeman/PhotoEdit.

Preoperational children think that everyone shares their perspective and knowledge. Thus, children's stories and explanations to adults can be maddeningly uninformative, as they are delivered without any context. For example, a preoperational child may start a story with "He wouldn't let me go," neglecting to mention who "he" is or where the storyteller wanted to go. We also see egocentric thinking when children at the preoperational stage play hiding games. For instance, 3-year-olds frequently hide with their faces against a wall, covering their eyes—although they are still in plain view. It seems to them that if they cannot see, then no one else will be able to see them, because they assume that others share their view.

In addition, preoperational children have not yet developed the ability to understand the **principle of conservation,** which is the knowledge that quantity is unrelated to the arrangement and physical appearance of objects. Children who have not mastered this concept do not know that the amount, volume, or length of an object does not change when its shape or configuration changes. The question about the two glasses—one short and broad and the other tall and thin—with which we began our discussion of cognitive

Object permanence
The awareness that objects—and people—continue to exist even if they are out of sight.

Preoperational stage
According to Piaget, the period from 2 to 7 years of age that is characterized by language development.

Egocentric thought
A way of thinking in which a child views the world entirely from his or her own perspective.

Principle of conservation
The knowledge that quantity is unrelated to the arrangement and physical appearance of objects.

development illustrates this point clearly. Children who do not understand the principle of conservation invariably state that the amount of liquid changes as it is poured back and forth. (See Figure 10.)

Concrete Operational Stage: 7 to 12 Years. Mastery of the principle of conservation marks the beginning of the **concrete operational stage**. However, children do not fully understand some aspects of conservation—such as conservation of weight and volume—for a number of years.

During the concrete operational stage, children develop the ability to think in a more logical manner, and begin to overcome some of the egocentrism characteristic of the preoperational period. One of the major principles children learn during this stage is reversibility, the idea that some changes can be undone by reversing an earlier action. For example, they can understand that when someone rolls a ball of clay into a long sausage shape, that person can

---

FIGURE 10

These tests are frequently used to assess whether children have learned the principle of conservation across a variety of dimensions. Do you think children in the preoperational stage can be taught to avoid conservation mistakes before the typical age of mastery?

Conservation of ...	Modality	Change in physical appearance	Average age at full mastery
Number	Number of elements in a collection	Rearranging or dislocating elements	6–7 years
Substance (mass)	Amount of a malleable substance (e.g., clay or liquid)	Altering shape	7–8 years
Length	Length of a line or object	Altering shape or configuration	7–8 years
Area	Amount of surface covered by a set of plane figures	Rearranging the figures	8–9 years
Weight	Weight of an object	Altering shape	9–10 years
Volume	Volume of an object (in terms of water displacement)	Altering shape	14–15 years

Concrete operational stage
According to Piaget, the period from 7 to 12 years of age that is characterized by logical thought and a loss of egocentrism.

re-create the original ball by reversing the action. Children can even conceptualize this principle in their heads, without having to see the action performed before them.

Although children make important advances in their logical capabilities during the concrete operational stage, their thinking still displays one major limitation: They are largely bound to the concrete, physical reality of the world. For the most part, they have difficulty understanding questions of an abstract or hypothetical nature.

Formal Operational Stage: 12 Years to Adulthood. The **formal operational stage** produces a new kind of thinking that is abstract, formal, and logical and makes use of logical techniques to resolve problems.

The way in which children approach the "pendulum problem" devised by Piaget (Piaget & Inhelder, 1958) illustrates the emergence of formal operational thinking. The problem solver is asked to figure out what determines how fast a pendulum swings. Is it the length of the string, the weight of the pendulum, or the force with which the pendulum is pushed? (For the record, the answer is the length of the string.)

Children in the concrete operational stage approach the problem haphazardly, without a logical or rational plan of action. For example, they may simultaneously change the length of the string and the weight on the string and the force with which they push the pendulum. Because they are varying all the factors at once, they cannot tell which factor is the critical one. In contrast, people in the formal operational stage approach the problem systematically. Acting as if they were scientists conducting an experiment, they examine the effects of changes in one variable at a time. This ability to rule out competing possibilities characterizes formal operational thought.

Although formal operational thought emerges during the teenage years, some individuals use this type of thinking only infrequently. Moreover, it appears that many individuals never reach this stage at all; most studies show that only 40 to 60 percent of college and university students and adults fully reach it, with some estimates running as low as 25 percent of the general population. In addition, in certain cultures—particularly those which are less technologically sophisticated than most Western societies—almost no one reaches the formal operational stage (Keating & Clark, 1980; Super, 1980; Genovese, 2006). Piaget has also been criticized for underestimating the age at which infants and children can understand specific concepts and principles, as they seem to be more sophisticated in their cognitive abilities than Piaget believed.

Despite such criticisms, most developmental psychologists agree that although the processes that underlie changes in cognitive abilities may not unfold in the manner suggested by his theory, Piaget has generally provided us with an accurate account of age-related changes in cognitive development. Moreover, he has had an enormous influence in education by inspiring the nature and structure of educational curricula and teaching methods (Hauser, 2000; Egan, 2005; Cunningham, 2006).

INFORMATION-PROCESSING APPROACHES

If cognitive development does not proceed as a series of stages, as Piaget suggested, what does underlie the enormous growth in children's cognitive abilities that even the most untutored eye can observe? To many developmental psychologists, changes in **information processing,** the way in which people take in, use, and store information, account for cognitive development (Lacerda, von Hofsten, & Heimann, 2001; Cashon & Cohen, 2004; Munakata, 2006).

According to this approach, quantitative changes occur in children's ability to organize and manipulate information as they age. As some abilities become more automatic, their speed of processing increases, as well as the speed at which they can scan, recognize, and compare stimuli. As children grow older, they can pay attention to stimuli longer and discriminate between different stimuli more readily, and they are less easily distracted (Myerson et al., 2003; Van den Wildenberg & Van der Molen, 2004).

Improvement in information processing relates to advances in **metacognition,** an awareness and understanding of one's own cognitive processes. Metacognition involves the planning, monitoring, and revising of cognitive strategies. Younger children, who lack an awareness of their own cognitive processes, often do not realize their incapabilities.

Formal operational stage
According to Piaget, the period from age 12 to adulthood that is characterized by abstract thought.

Information processing
The way in which people take in, use, and store information.

Metacognition
An awareness and understanding of one's own cognitive processes.

Thus, when they misunderstand others, they may fail to recognize their own errors. It is only later, when metacognitive abilities become more sophisticated, that children are able to know when they *don't* understand. Such increasing sophistication reflects a change in children's *theory of mind*, their knowledge and beliefs about the way the mind operates (Bernstein, Loftus, & Meltzoff, 2005; Matthews & Funke, 2006; Lockl & Schneider, 2007)

VYGOTSKY'S VIEW OF COGNITIVE DEVELOPMENT: CONSIDERING CULTURE

According to Russian developmental psychologist Lev Vygotsky, the culture in which we are raised significantly affects our cognitive development. In an increasingly influential view, Vygotsky suggests that the focus on individual performance of both Piagetian and information-processing approaches is misplaced. Instead, he holds that we cannot understand cognitive development without taking into account the social aspects of learning (Vygotsky, 1926/1997; Maynard & Martini, 2005; Rieber & Robinson, 2006).

Vygotsky argues that cognitive development occurs as a consequence of social interactions in which children work with others to jointly solve problems. Through such interactions, children's cognitive skills increase, and they gain the ability to function intellectually on their own. More specifically, he suggests that children's cognitive abilities increase when they encounter information that falls within their zone of proximal development. The **zone of proximal development (ZPD)** is the level at which a child can almost, but not fully, comprehend or perform a task on his or her own. When children receive information that falls within the ZPD, they can increase their understanding or master a new task. In contrast, if the information lies outside children's ZPD, they will not be able to master it (see Figure 11).

In short, cognitive development occurs when parents, teachers, or skilled peers assist a child by presenting information that is both new and within the ZPD. This type of assistance, called *scaffolding*, provides support for learning and problem solving that encourages independence and growth. Vygotsky claims that scaffolding not only promotes the solution of specific problems, but also aids in the development of overall cognitive abilities (Schaller & Crandall, 2004).

More than other approaches to cognitive development, Vygotsky's theory considers how an individual's specific cultural and social context affects intellectual growth. The way in which children understand the world grows out of interactions with parents, peers, and other members of a specific culture (John-Steiner & Mahn, 2003; Kozulin et al., 2003).

FIGURE 11

Although the performances of the two children working at a task without aid are similar, Child B benefits more from aid and thus has a larger zone of proximal development (ZPD).

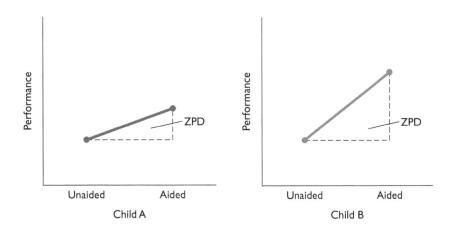

Zone of proximal development (ZPD)
According to Vygotsky, the level at which a child can almost, but not fully, comprehend or perform a task on his or her own.

Evaluate

1. Researchers studying newborns use _____, or the decrease in the response to a stimulus that occurs after repeated presentations of the same stimulus, as an indicator of a baby's interest.

2. The emotional bond that develops between a child and its caregiver is known as _____.

3. Match the parenting style with its definition:

   1. Permissive

   2. Authoritative

   3. Authoritarian

   4. Uninvolved

   a. Rigid; highly punitive; demanding obedience

   b. Gives little direction; lax on obedience

   c. Firm but fair; tries to explain parental decisions

   d. Emotionally detached and unloving

4. Erikson's theory of _____ development involves a series of eight stages, each of which must be resolved for a person to develop optimally.

5. Match the stage of development with the thinking style characteristic of that stage:

   1. Egocentric thought

   2. Object permanence

   3. Abstract reasoning

   4. Conservation; reversibility

   a. Sensorimotor

   b. Formal operational

   c. Preoperational

   d. Concrete operational

6. According to Vygotsky, information that is within a child's _____ _____ _____ _____ is most likely to result in cognitive development.

Answers to Evaluate Questions

1. habituation; 2. attachment 3. 1-b, 2-c, 3-a, 4-d; 4. psychosocial; 5. 1-c, 2- a, 3-b, 4-d; 6. zone of proximal development

Key Terms

attachment	habituation	principle of conservation
authoritarian parents	industry-versus-inferiority stage	psychosocial development
authoritative parents	information processing	reflexes
autonomy-versus-shame-and-doubt stage	metacognition	sensorimotor stage
cognitive development	neonate	temperament
concrete operational stage	object permanence	trust-versus-mistrust stage
egocentric thought	permissive parents	uninvolved parents
formal operational stage	preoperational stage	zone of proximal development (ZPD)

Adolescence: Becoming an Adult

LEARNING OBJECTIVE

What major physical, social, and cognitive transitions characterize adolescence?

Joseph Charles, Age 13: "Being 13 is very hard at school. I have to be bad in order to be considered cool. I sometimes do things that aren't good. I have talked back to my teachers and been disrespectful to them. I do want to be good, but it's just too hard" (Gibbs, 2005, p. 51).

Trevor Kelson, Age 15: "Keep the Hell Out of My Room!" says a sign on Trevor's bedroom wall, just above an unmade bed, a desk littered with dirty T-shirts and candy wrappers, and a floor covered with clothes. Is there a carpet? "Somewhere," he says with a grin. "I think it's gold" (Fields-Meyer, 1995, p. 53).

Lauren Barry, Age 18: "I went to an Honour Society induction. The parents were just staring at me. I think they couldn't believe someone with pink hair could be smart. I want to be a high-school teacher, but I'm afraid that, based on my appearance, they won't hire me" (Gordon et al., 1999, p. 47).

Although Joseph, Trevor, and Lauren have never met, they share anxieties that are common to adolescence—concerns about friends, parents, appearance, independence, and their futures. **Adolescence,** the developmental stage between childhood and adulthood, is a crucial period. It is a time of profound changes and, occasionally, turmoil. Considerable biological change occurs as adolescents attain sexual and physical maturity. At the same time, and rivalling these physiological changes, important social, emotional, and cognitive changes occur as adolescents strive for independence and move toward adulthood.

Because many years of schooling precede most people's entry into the workforce in Western societies, the stage of adolescence is fairly long, beginning just before the teenage years and ending just after them. No longer children but considered by society to be not quite adults, adolescents face a period of rapid physical, cognitive, and social change that affects them for the rest of their lives.

Dramatic changes in society also affect adolescents' development. More than half of all children in Canada and the United States will spend all or some of their childhood and adolescence in single-parent families. Furthermore, adolescents spend considerably less time with their parents, and more with their peers, than they did several decades ago. Finally, the ethnic and cultural diversity of adolescents as a group is increasing dramatically. A third of all adolescents today are of non-European descent, and by the year 2050 the number of adolescents of Hispanic, African American, Native American, and Asian origin will collectively pass that of whites (National Adolescent Health Information Center, 2003).

Physical Development: The Changing Adolescent

If you think back to the start of your own adolescence, the most dramatic changes you probably remember are physical ones. A spurt in height, the growth of breasts in girls, deepening voices in boys, the development of body hair, and intense sexual feelings cause curiosity, interest, and sometimes embarrassment for individuals entering adolescence.

Adolescence
The developmental stage between childhood and adulthood.

315

FIGURE 1

The range of ages during which major sexual changes occur during adolescence is shown by the coloured bars.

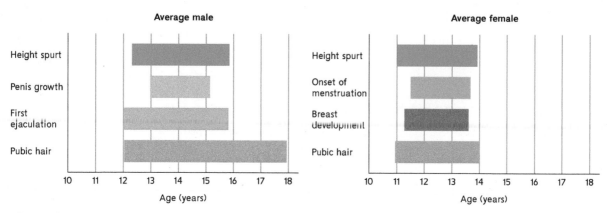

Source: Based on Tanner, 1978.

The physical changes that occur at the start of adolescence result largely from the secretion of various hormones, and they affect virtually every aspect of an adolescent's life. Not since infancy has development been so dramatic. Weight and height increase rapidly because of a growth spurt that typically begins around age 10 for girls and age 12 for boys. Adolescents may grow as much as five inches (twelve cm) in one year.

Puberty, the period at which maturation of the sexual organs occurs, begins at about age 11 or 12 for girls, when menstruation starts. However, there are wide variations (see Figure 1 above). For example, some girls begin to menstruate as early as age 8 or 9 or as late as age 16. Furthermore, in Western cultures, the average age at which adolescents reach sexual maturity has been steadily decreasing over the last century, most likely as a result of improved nutrition and medical care. Sexual attraction to others begins even before the maturation of the sexual organs, at around age 10 (Tanner, 1990; Finlay, Jones, & Coleman, 2002).

For boys, the onset of puberty is marked by their first ejaculation, known as *spermarche*. Spermarche usually occurs around the age of 13 (see Figure 1). At first, relatively few sperm are produced during an ejaculation, but the amount increases significantly within a few years.

The age at which puberty begins has implications for the way adolescents feel about themselves—as well as the way others treat them. Early-maturing boys have a distinct advantage over later-maturing boys. They do better in athletics, are generally more popular with peers, and have more positive self-concepts (Ge et al., 2003; Becker & Luthar, 2007).

The picture differs for girls. Although early-maturing girls are more sought after as dates and have better self-esteem than do later-maturing girls, some consequences of early physical maturation may be less positive. For example, early breast development may set them apart from their peers and be a source of ridicule (Franko & Striegel-Moore, 2002; Olivardia & Pope, 2002; Nadeem & Graham, 2005).

Late physical maturation may produce certain psychological difficulties for both boys and girls. Boys who are smaller and less coordinated than their more mature peers tend to feel ridiculed and less attractive. Similarly, late-maturing girls are at a disadvantage in middle school and early high school. They hold relatively low social status and may be overlooked in dating (Lanza & Collins, 2002).

Clearly, the rate at which physical changes occur during adolescence can affect the way in which people are viewed by others and the way they view themselves. Just as important as physical changes, however, are the psychological and social changes that unfold during adolescence.

Puberty
The period at which maturation of the sexual organs occurs, beginning at about age 11 or 12 for girls and 13 or 14 for boys.

Moral and Cognitive Development: Distinguishing Right from Wrong

In a European country, a woman is near death from a special kind of cancer. The one drug that the doctors think might save her is a medicine that a medical researcher has recently discovered. The drug is expensive to make, and the researcher is charging ten times the cost, or $5,000, for a small dose. The sick woman's husband, Henry, approaches everyone he knows in hopes of borrowing money, but he can get together only about $2,500. He tells the researcher that his wife is dying and asks him to lower the price of the drug or let him pay later. The researcher says, "No, I discovered the drug, and I'm going to make money from it." Henry is desperate and considers stealing the drug for his wife.

What would you tell Henry to do?

Kohlberg's Theory of Moral Development

In the view of psychologist Lawrence Kohlberg, the advice you give Henry reflects your level of moral development. According to Kohlberg, people pass through a series of stages in the evolution of their sense of justice and in the kind of reasoning they use to make moral judgments (Kohlberg, 1984). Largely because of the various cognitive limitations that Piaget described, preadolescent children tend to think either in terms of concrete, unvarying rules ("It is always wrong to steal" or "I'll be punished if I steal") or in terms of the rules of society ("Good people don't steal" or "What if everyone stole?").

Adolescents, however, can reason on a higher plane, having typically reached Piaget's formal operational stage of cognitive development. Because they are able to comprehend broad moral principles, they can understand that morality is not always black and white and that conflict can exist between two sets of socially accepted standards.

Kohlberg (1984) suggests that the changes in moral reasoning can be understood best as a three-level sequence (see Figure 2). His theory assumes that people move through the levels in a fixed order, and that they cannot reach the highest level until about age 13—primarily because of limitations in cognitive development before that age. However,

| FIGURE 2 |

Developmental psychologist Lawrence Kohlberg theorized that people move through a three-level sequence of moral reasoning in a fixed order. However, he contended that few people ever reach the highest level of moral reasoning.

Sample Moral Reasoning of Subjects

In Favour of Stealing the Drug	Against Stealing the Drug
"If you let your wife die, you will get in trouble. You'll be blamed for not spending the money to save her, and there'll be an investigation of you and the druggist for your wife's death."	"You shouldn't steal the drug because you'll be caught and sent to jail if you do. If you do get away, your conscience will bother you thinking how the police will catch up with you at any minute."
"If you let your wife die, you'll never be able to look anybody in the face again."	"After you steal the drug, you'll feel bad thinking how you've brought dishonour on your family and yourself; you won't be able to face anyone again."

Level

Level 1 Preconventional morality: At this level, the concrete interests of the individual are considered in terms of rewards and punishments.

Level 2 Conventional morality: At this level, people approach moral problems as members of society. They are interested in pleasing others by acting as good members of society.

Level 3 Postconventional morality: At this level, people use moral principles which are seen as broader than those of any particular society.

"If you don't steal the drug, and if you let your wife die, you'll always condemn yourself for it afterward. You won't be blamed and you'll have lived up to the outside rule of the law, but you won't have lived up to your own conscience and standards of honesty."	"If you steal the drug, you won't be blamed by other people, but you'll condemn yourself because you won't have lived up to your own conscience and standards of honesty."

many people never reach the highest level of moral reasoning. In fact, Kohlberg found that only a relatively small percentage of adults rise above the second level of his model (Kohlberg & Ryncarz, 1990; Hedgepeth, 2005; Powers, 2006).

Although Kohlberg's theory has had a substantial influence on our understanding of moral development, the research support is mixed. One difficulty with the theory is that it pertains to moral *judgments,* not moral *behaviour.* Knowing right from wrong does not mean that we will always act in accordance with our judgments. In addition, the theory applies primarily to Western society and its moral code; cross-cultural research conducted in cultures with different moral systems suggests that Kohlberg's theory is not necessarily applicable (Coles, 1997; Damon, 1999; Nucci, 2002; Barandiaran, Pascual, & Samaniego, 2006).

STUDY ALERT!

The difference between the Kohlberg and Gilligan approaches to moral development is significant, with Kohlberg's theory focusing on stages and Gilligan's highlighting gender differences.

Moral Development in Women

One glaring shortcoming of Kohlberg's research is that he primarily used male participants. Furthermore, psychologist Carol Gilligan (1996) argues that because of men's and women's distinctive socialization experiences, a fundamental difference exists in the way each gender views moral behaviour. According to Gilligan, men view morality primarily in terms of broad principles, such as justice and fairness. In contrast, women see it in terms of responsibility toward individuals and willingness to make sacrifices to help a specific individual within the context of a particular relationship. Compassion for individuals is a more salient factor in moral behaviour for women than it is for men.

Because Kohlberg's model defines moral behaviour largely in terms of abstract principles such as justice, Gilligan finds it inadequately describes the moral development of females. She suggests that women's morality centres on individual well-being and social relationships—a morality of *caring.* In her view, compassionate concern for the welfare of others represents the highest level of morality.

The fact that Gilligan's conception of morality differs greatly from Kohlberg's suggests that gender plays an important role in determining what a person sees as moral. Although the research evidence is not definitive, it seems plausible that their differing conceptions of what constitutes moral behaviour may lead men and women to regard the morality of a particular behaviour in different ways (Jorgensen, 2006; Sherblom, 2008; Walker & Frimer, 2009).

Social Development: Finding Oneself in a Social World

"Who am I?" "How do I fit into the world?" "What is life all about?"

Questions such as these assume particular significance during the teenage years, as adolescents seek to find their place in the broader social world. As we will see, this quest takes adolescents along several routes.

Erikson's Theory of Psychosocial Development: The Search for Identity

Erik Erikson's theory of psychosocial development emphasizes the search for identity during the adolescent years. As was noted earlier, psychosocial development encompasses the way people's understanding of themselves, one another, and the world around them changes during the course of development (Erikson, 1963).

The fifth stage of Erikson's theory (summarized, with the other stages, in Figure 3), the **identity-versus-role-confusion stage,** encompasses adolescence. During this stage, a time of major testing, people try to determine what is unique about themselves. They attempt to discover who they are, what their strengths are, and what kinds of roles

Identity-versus-role-confusion stage
According to Erikson, a time in adolescence of major testing to determine one's unique qualities.

FIGURE 3

Erikson's stages of psychosocial development. According to Erikson, shown in this photo, people proceed through eight stages of psychosocial development across their lives. He suggested that each stage requires the resolution of a crisis or conflict and may produce both positive and negative outcomes.

Stage	Approximate Age	Positive Outcomes	Negative Outcomes
1. Trust-vs.-mistrust	Birth–1½ years	Feelings of trust from environmental support	Fear and concern regarding others
2. Autonomy-vs.-shame-and-doubt	1½–3 years	Self-sufficiency if exploration is encouraged	Doubts about self, lack of independence
3. Initiative-vs.-guilt	3–6 years	Discovery of ways to initiate	Guilt from actions and actions thoughts
4. Industry-vs.-inferiority	6–12 years	Development of sense of competence	Feelings of inferiority, no sense of mastery
5. Identity-vs.-role-confusion	Adolescence	Awareness of uniqueness of self, knowledge of role to be followed	Inability to identify appropriate roles in life
6. Intimacy-vs.-isolation	Early adulthood	Development of loving, sexual relationships and close friendships	Fear of relationships with others
7. Generativity-vs.-stagnation	Middle adulthood	Sense of contribution to continuity of life	Trivialization of one's activities
8. Ego-integrity-vs.-despair	Late adulthood	Sense of unity in life's accomplishments	Regret over lost opportunities of life

Photo Source: © Joe Erikson/Science Source.

they are best suited to play for the rest of their lives—in short, their **identity.** A person confused about the most appropriate role to play in life may lack a stable identity, adopt an unacceptable role such as that of a social deviant, or have difficulty maintaining close personal relationships later in life (Updegraff et al., 2004; Vleioras & Bosma, 2005; Goldstein, 2006).

During the identity-versus-role-confusion period, an adolescent feels pressure to identify what to do with his or her life. Because these pressures come at a time of major physical changes as well as important changes in what society expects of them, adolescents can find the period a particularly difficult one. The identity-versus-role-confusion stage has another important characteristic: declining reliance on adults for information, with a shift toward using the peer group as a source of social judgments. The peer group becomes increasingly important, enabling adolescents to form close, adult-like relationships and helping them clarify their personal identities. According to Erikson, the identity-versus-role-confusion stage marks a pivotal point in psychosocial development, paving the way for continued growth and the future development of personal relationships.

During early adulthood, people enter the **intimacy-versus-isolation stage.** Spanning the period of early adulthood (from post-adolescence to the early thirties), this stage focuses on developing close relationships with others. Difficulties during this stage result in feelings of loneliness and a fear of such relationships, whereas successful resolution of the crises of the stage results in the possibility of forming relationships that are intimate on a physical, intellectual, and emotional level.

Development continues during middle adulthood as people enter the **generativity-versus-stagnation stage.** Generativity is the ability to contribute to one's family, community, work, and society, and assist the development of

Identity
The distinguishing character of the individual: who each of us is, what our roles are, and what we are capable of.

Intimacy-versus-isolation stage
According to Erikson, a period during early adulthood that focuses on developing close relationships.

Generativity-versus-stagnation stage
According to Erikson, a period in middle adulthood during which we take stock of our contributions to family and society.

the younger generation. Success in this stage results in a person feeling positive about the continuity of life, whereas difficulties lead a person to feel that his or her activities are trivial or stagnant and have done nothing for upcoming generations. In fact, if a person has not successfully resolved the identity crisis of adolescence, he or she may still be foundering as far as identifying an appropriate career is concerned.

Finally, the last stage of psychosocial development, the **ego-integrity-versus-despair stage,** spans later adulthood and continues until death. Now a sense of accomplishment signifies success in resolving the difficulties presented by this stage of life; failure to resolve the difficulties results in regret over what might have been achieved but was not.

Notably, Erikson's theory suggests that development does not stop at adolescence but continues throughout adulthood, a view that a substantial amount of research now confirms. For instance, a 22-year study by psychologist Susan Whitbourne found considerable support for the fundamentals of Erikson's theory, determining that psychosocial development continues through adolescence and adulthood. In sum, adolescence is not an end point but rather a way station on the path of psychosocial development (Whitbourne et al., 1992; McAdams et al., 1997).

Although Erikson's theory provides a broad outline of identity development, critics have pointed out that his approach is anchored in male-oriented concepts of individuality and competitiveness. In an alternative conception, psychologist Carol Gilligan suggests that women may develop identity through the establishment of relationships. In her view, a primary component of women's identity is the construction of caring networks among themselves and others (Gilligan, 2004).

Exploring DIVERSITY

Rites of Passage: Coming of Age Around the World

It is not easy for male members of the Awa tribe in New Guinea to make the transition from childhood to adulthood. First come whippings with sticks and prickly branches, both for the boys' own past misdeeds and in honour of those tribesmen who were killed in warfare. In the next phase of the ritual, adults jab sharpened sticks into the boys' nostrils. Then they force a 1.5-metre length of vine into the boys' throats, until they gag and vomit. Finally, tribesmen cut the boys' genitals, causing severe bleeding.

Although the rites that mark the coming of age of boys in the Awa tribe sound horrifying to Westerners, they are comparable to those in other cultures. In some, youths must kneel on hot coals without displaying pain. In others, girls must toss wads of burning cotton from hand to hand and allow themselves to be bitten by hundreds of ants (Selsky, 1997).

Other cultures have less fearsome, although no less important, ceremonies that mark the passage from childhood to adulthood. For instance, when a girl first menstruates in traditional Apache tribes, the event is marked by dawn-to-dusk chanting. Western religions, too, have several types of celebrations, including bar and bat mitzvahs at age 13 for Jewish boys and girls and confirmation ceremonies for children in many Christian denominations (Magida, 2006).

In most societies, males, but not females, are the focus of coming-of-age ceremonies. The renowned anthropologist Margaret Mead remarked, only partly in jest, that the preponderance of male ceremonies might reflect the fact that "the worry that boys will not grow up to be men is much more widespread than that girls will not grow up to be women" (1949, p. 195). Said another way, it may be that in most cultures men traditionally have higher status than women, and therefore those cultures regard boys' transition into adulthood as more important.

However, another fact may explain why most cultures place greater emphasis on male rites than on female ones. For females, the transition from childhood is marked by a definite, biological event: menstruation. For males, in contrast, no single event can be used to pinpoint entry into adulthood. Thus, men are forced to rely on culturally determined rituals to acknowledge their arrival into adulthood.

Ego-integrity-versus-despair stage
According to Erikson, a period from late adulthood until death during which we review life's accomplishments and failures.

Evaluate

1. _____ is the period during which the sexual organs begin to mature.

2. Delayed maturation typically provides both males and females with a social advantage. True or false?

3. _____ proposed a set of three levels of moral development ranging from reasoning based on rewards and punishments to abstract thinking involving concepts of justice.

4. Erikson believed that during adolescence, people must search for _____, whereas during the early adulthood, the major task is _____.

Answers to Evaluate Questions

1. puberty; 2. false; both male and female adolescents suffer if they mature late; 3. Kohlberg; 4. identity, intimacy

Key Terms

adolescence	generativity-versus-stagnation stage	intimacy-versus-isolation stage
ego-integrity-versus-despair stage	identity	puberty
	identity-versus-role-confusion stage	

Adulthood

MODULE

30

LEARNING OBJECTIVES

LO8 **What are** the principal kinds of physical, social, and intellectual changes that occur in early and middle adulthood, and what are their causes?

LO9 **How does** the reality of late adulthood differ from the stereotypes about that period?

LO10 **How can** we adjust to death?

I thought I got better as I got older. I found out that wasn't the case in a real hurry last year. After going twelve years in professional football and twelve years before that in amateur football without ever having surgery performed on me, the last two seasons of my career I went under the knife three times. It happened very quickly and without warning, and I began to ask myself, "Is this age? Is this what's happening?" Because up until that moment, I'd never realized that I was getting older (Kotre & Hall, 1990, pp. 257, 259–260).

As a former professional football player, Brian Sipes intensely felt the changes in his body brought about by aging. But the challenges he experienced are part of a normal process that affects all people as they move through adulthood.

Psychologists generally agree that early adulthood begins around age 20 and lasts until about age 40 to 45, with middle adulthood beginning then and continuing until around age 65. Despite the enormous importance of these periods of life in terms of both the accomplishments that occur in them and their overall length (together they span some forty-five years), they have been studied less than has any other stage. For one reason, the physical changes that occur during these periods are less apparent and more gradual than are those at other times during the life span. In addition, the diverse social changes that arise during this period defy simple categorization. However, developmental psychologists have recently begun to focus on the period, particularly on the social changes in the family and women's careers.

The self-exploration that occurs in early adulthood has led many developmental psychologists to view the start of the period as a transitional phase called emerging adulthood. **Emerging adulthood** is the period beginning in the late teenage years and extending into the mid-20s. During emerging adulthood, people are no longer adolescents, but they haven't fully taken on the responsibilities of adulthood either. Instead, they're still engaged in determining who they are and what their life and career paths should be (Schwartz, Côté, & Arnett, 2005; Bukobza, 2009; Lamborn & Groh, 2009).

The view that adulthood is preceded by an extended period of emerging adulthood is a response to the fact that the economies of industrialized countries have shifted away from manufacturing to technology and information, which require more time for education and training. Furthermore, the age at which most people marry and have children has risen significantly (Arnett, 2007).

There's also an increasing ambivalence about reaching adulthood. When people in their late teens and early twenties are asked if they feel they've reached adulthood, most say "yes and no" (see Figure 1). In short, emerging adulthood is an age of identity exploration during which individuals are more self-focused and uncertain than they will be at a later stage in early adulthood (Arnett, 2000, 2006).

As we discuss the changes that occur during emerging adulthood, early adulthood, middle adulthood, and ultimately late adulthood, keep in mind that demarcations between the periods are fuzzy. However, the changes are certainly no less profound than they were in earlier periods of development.

> **Emerging adulthood**
> The period beginning in the late teenage years and extending into the mid-20s.

FIGURE 1

Evidence of a period of emerging adulthood is provided by the responses to a questionnaire asking "Do you feel that you have reached adulthood?" Most people between the ages of 18–25 were ambivalent, responding "yes and no." Later, this ambivalence disappeared, with most people 26–35 saying "yes."

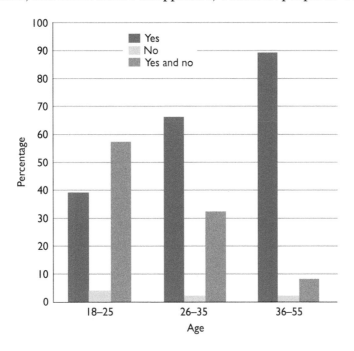

Source: Arnett, 2000.

Physical Development: The Peak of Health

For most people, early adulthood marks the peak of physical health. From about 18 to 25 years of age, people's strength is greatest, their reflexes are quickest, and their chances of dying from disease are quite slim. Moreover, reproductive capabilities are at their highest level.

Around age 25, the body becomes slightly less efficient and more susceptible to disease. Overall, however, ill health remains the exception; most people stay remarkably healthy during early adulthood. (Can you think of any machine other than the body that can operate without pause for so long a period?)

During middle adulthood people gradually become aware of changes in their bodies. People often begin to put on weight (although this can be avoided through diet and exercise). Furthermore, the sense organs gradually become less sensitive, and reactions to stimuli are slower. But generally, the physical declines that occur during middle adulthood are minor and often unnoticeable (DiGiovanna, 1994).

The major biological change that does occur pertains to reproductive capabilities during middle adulthood. On average, during their late forties or early fifties, women begin **menopause,** during which they stop menstruating and are no longer fertile. Because menopause is accompanied by a significant reduction in the production of estrogen, a female hormone, women sometimes experience symptoms such as hot flashes, sudden sensations of heat.

Menopause was once blamed for a variety of psychological symptoms, including depression and memory loss. However, such difficulties, if they do occur, may be caused by women's expectations about reaching an "old" age in a society that highly values youth.

Furthermore, women's reactions to menopause vary significantly across cultures. According to anthropologist Yewoubdar Beyene, the more a society values old age, the less difficulty its women have during menopause. In a study of women in Mayan villages, she found that women looked forward to menopause, because they then stopped having children. In addition, they didn't experience some of the classic symptoms of menopause; hot flashes, for example, were unheard of (Elliot, Berman, & Kim, 2002; Beyene, Gilliss, & Lee, 2007).

Menopause
The period during which women stop menstruating and are no longer fertile.

For men, the aging process during middle adulthood is somewhat subtler. There are no physiological signals of increasing age equivalent to the end of menstruation in women, and so no male menopause exists. In fact, men remain fertile and are capable of fathering children until well into late adulthood. However, some gradual physical decline occurs: Sperm production decreases, and the frequency of orgasm tends to decline. Once again, though, any psychological difficulties associated with these changes are usually brought about not so much by physical deterioration as by the inability of an aging individual to meet the exaggerated standards of youthfulness.

Social Development: Working at Life

Whereas physical changes during adulthood reflect development of a quantitative nature, social developmental transitions are qualitative and more profound. During this period, people typically launch themselves into careers, marriage, and families.

The entry into early adulthood is usually marked by leaving one's childhood home and entering the world of work. People envision life goals and make career choices. Their lives often centre on their careers, which form an important part of their identity (Levinson, 1990, 1992; Vaillant & Vaillant, 1990).

In their early forties, however, people may begin to question their lives as they enter a period called the *midlife transition*. The idea that life will end at some point becomes increasingly influential in their thinking, and they may question their past accomplishments (Gould, 1978). Facing signs of physical aging and feeling dissatisfaction with their lives, some individuals experience what has been popularly labelled a *midlife crisis*.

In most cases, though, the passage into middle age is relatively calm. Most 40-year-olds view their lives and accomplishments positively enough to proceed relatively smoothly through midlife, and the forties and fifties are often a particularly rewarding period. Rather than looking to the future, people concentrate on the present, and their involvement with their families, friends, and other social groups takes on new importance. A major developmental thrust of this period is coming to terms with one's circumstances (Whitbourne, 2000, 2010).

Finally, during the last stages of adulthood people become more accepting of others and of their own lives and are less concerned about issues or problems that once bothered them. People come to accept the fact that death is inevitable, and they try to understand their accomplishments in terms of the broader meaning of life. Although people may begin, for the first time, to label themselves as "old," many also develop a sense of wisdom and feel freer to enjoy life (Baltes & Kunzmann, 2003; Miner-Rubino, Winter, & Stewart, 2004; Ward-Baker, 2007).

The Later Years of Life: Growing Old

I've always enjoyed doing things in the mountains—hiking or, more recently, active cliff-climbing. The more difficult the climb, the more absorbing it is. The climbs I really remember are the ones I had to work on. Maybe a particular section where it took two or three tries before I found the right combination of moves that got me up easily—and, preferably, elegantly. It's a wonderful exhilaration to get to the top and sit down and perhaps have lunch and look out over the landscape and be so grateful that it's still possible for me to do that sort of thing (Lyman Spitzer, age 74, quoted in Kotre & Hall, 1990, pp. 358–359).

If you can't quite picture a 74-year-old rock-climbing, some rethinking of your view of late adulthood may be in order. In spite of the societal stereotype of "old age" as a time of inactivity and physical and mental decline, gerontologists, specialists who study aging, are beginning to paint a very different portrait of late adulthood.

By focusing on the period of life that starts at around age 65, gerontologists are making important contributions to clarifying the capabilities of older adults. Their work is demonstrating that significant developmental processes continue even during old age. And as life expectancy increases, the number of people who reach older adulthood will continue to grow substantially. Consequently, developing an understanding of late adulthood has become a critical priority for psychologists (Birren, 1996; Moody, 2000; Schaie, 2005).

Physical Changes in Late Adulthood: The Aging Body

Napping, eating, walking, conversing. It probably doesn't surprise you that these relatively nonstrenuous activities represent the typical pastimes of late adulthood. But it is striking that these activities are identical to the most common leisure activities reported in a survey of college and university students (Harper, 1978). Although the students cited more active pursuits—such as sailing and playing basketball—as their favourite activities, in actuality they engaged in such sports relatively infrequently, spending most of their free time napping, eating, walking, and conversing.

Although the leisure activities in which older adults engage may not differ all that much from the ones younger people pursue, many physical changes are, of course, brought about by the aging process. The most obvious are those of appearance—hair thinning and turning grey, skin wrinkling and folding, and sometimes a slight loss of height as the thickness of the disks between vertebrae in the spine decreases—but subtler changes also occur in the body's biological functioning. For example, sensory capabilities decrease as a result of aging: Vision, hearing, smell, and taste become less sensitive. Reaction time slows, and physical stamina changes (Stenklev & Laukli, 2004; Schieber, 2006; Madden, 2007).

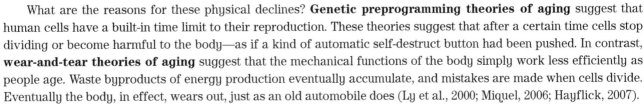

STUDY ALERT!

Two major theories of aging—the genetic preprogramming and the wear-and-tear views—explain some of the physical changes that happen in older adults.

What are the reasons for these physical declines? **Genetic preprogramming theories of aging** suggest that human cells have a built-in time limit to their reproduction. These theories suggest that after a certain time cells stop dividing or become harmful to the body—as if a kind of automatic self-destruct button had been pushed. In contrast, **wear-and-tear theories of aging** suggest that the mechanical functions of the body simply work less efficiently as people age. Waste byproducts of energy production eventually accumulate, and mistakes are made when cells divide. Eventually the body, in effect, wears out, just as an old automobile does (Ly et al., 2000; Miquel, 2006; Hayflick, 2007).

Evidence supports both the genetic preprogramming and the wear-and-tear views, and it may be that both processes contribute to natural aging. It is clear, however, that physical aging is not a disease, but a natural biological process. Many physical functions do not decline with age. For example, sex remains pleasurable well into old age (although the frequency of sexual activity decreases), and some people report that the pleasure they derive from sex increases during late adulthood (Gelfand, 2000; DeLamater & Sill, 2005).

Cognitive Changes: Thinking About—and During—Late Adulthood

At one time, many gerontologists would have agreed with the popular view that older adults are forgetful and confused. Today, however, most research indicates that this is far from an accurate assessment of older people's capabilities.

One reason for the change in view is that more sophisticated research techniques exist for studying the cognitive changes that occur in late adulthood. For example, if we were to give a group of older adults an IQ test, we might find that the average score was lower than the score achieved by a group of younger people. We might conclude that this signifies a decline in intelligence. Yet if we looked a little more closely at the specific test, we might find that that conclusion was unwarranted. For instance, many IQ tests include portions based on physical performance (such as arranging a group of blocks) or on speed. In such cases, poorer performance on the IQ test may be due to gradual decreases in reaction time—a physical decline that accompanies late adulthood and has little or nothing to do with the intellectual capabilities of older adults.

Other difficulties hamper research into cognitive functioning during late adulthood. For example, older people are often less healthy than younger ones; when only healthy older adults are compared to healthy younger adults, intellectual differences are far less evident. Furthermore, the average number of years in school is often lower in older adults (for historical reasons) than in younger ones, and older adults may be less motivated to perform well on intelligence

Genetic preprogramming theories of aging
Human cells have a built-in time limit to their reproduction and after a certain time, cells stop dividing or become harmful to the body

Wear-and-tear theories of aging
The mechanical functions of the body simply work less efficiently as people age.

tests than younger people. Finally, traditional IQ tests may be inappropriate measures of intelligence in late adulthood. Older adults sometimes perform better on tests of practical intelligence than do younger individuals (Willis & Schaie, 1994; Dixon & Cohen, 2003).

Still, some declines in intellectual functioning during late adulthood do occur, although the pattern of age differences is not uniform for different types of cognitive abilities (see Figure 2). In general, skills relating to *fluid intelligence* (which involves information-processing skills such as memory, calculations, and solving analogies) show declines in late adulthood. In contrast, skills relating to *crystallized intelligence* (intelligence based on the accumulation of information, skills, and strategies learned through experience) remain steady and in some cases actually improve (Rozencwajg et al., 2005; van Hooren et al., 2007; Kaufman, Johnson, & Liu, 2008).

Even when changes in intellectual functioning occur during late adulthood, people often are able to compensate for any decline. They can still learn what they want to; it may just take more time. Furthermore, teaching older adults strategies for dealing with new problems can prevent declines in performance (Saczynski, Willis, & Schaie, 2002; Cavallini, Pagnin, & Vecchi, 2003; Peters et al., 2007; also see the *Applying Psychology in the Real World* box).

Memory Changes in Late Adulthood: Are Older Adults Forgetful?

One of the characteristics most frequently attributed to late adulthood is forgetfulness. How accurate is this assumption?

Most evidence suggests that memory change is not an inevitable part of the aging process. For instance, research shows that older people in cultures in which older adults are held in high esteem, such as mainland China, are less likely to show memory losses than are those living in cultures in which the expectation is that memory will decline. Similarly, when older people in Western societies are reminded of the advantages of age (for example, "age brings wisdom"), they tend to do better on tests of memory (Levy, 1996; Hess, Hinson, & Statham, 2004; Dixon et al., 2007).

Even when people show memory declines during late adulthood, their deficits tend to be limited to particular types of memory. For instance, losses tend to be limited to episodic memories, which relate to specific experiences in people's lives. Other types of memories, such as semantic memories (which refer to general knowledge and facts) and implicit memories (memories of which we are not consciously aware), are largely unaffected by age (Fleischman et al., 2004; Mitchell & Schmitt, 2006; St. Jacques & Levine, 2007).

Declines in episodic memories can often be traced to changes in the lives of older adults. For instance, it is not surprising that a retired person, who may no longer face the same kind of consistent intellectual challenges encountered

---

FIGURE 2

Age-related changes in intellectual skills vary according to the specific cognitive ability in question.

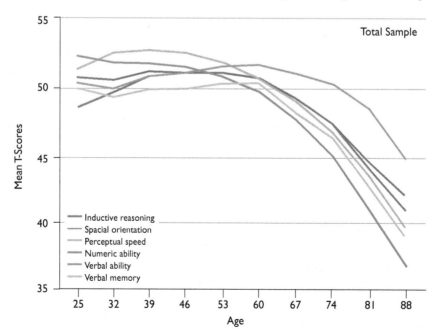

Source: Schaie, K. W. (2005). Longitudinal studies. In *Developmental influences on adult intelligence: The Seattle Longitudinal Study*, Figure 5.7a (p. 127). Copyright © 2005 by Oxford University Press, Inc. By permission of Oxford University Press, Inc. www.oup.co.uk.

on the job, may be less practised in using memory or even be less motivated to remember things, leading to an apparent decline in memory. Even in cases in which long-term memory declines, older adults can usually profit from compensatory efforts (Fritsch et al., 2007; West, Bagwell, & Dark-Freudeman, 2007).

In the past, older adults with severe cases of memory decline, accompanied by other cognitive difficulties, were said to suffer from senility. *Senility* is a broad, imprecise term typically applied to older adults who experience progressive deterioration of mental abilities, including memory loss, disorientation to time and place, and general confusion. Once thought to be an inevitable state that accompanies aging, senility is now viewed by most gerontologists as a label that has outlived its usefulness. Rather than senility being the cause of certain symptoms, the symptoms are deemed to be caused by some other factor.

ALZHEIMER'S DISEASE

Some cases of memory loss are produced by disease. For instance, **Alzheimer's disease** is a progressive brain disorder that leads to a gradual and irreversible decline in cognitive abilities. Nineteen percent of people age 75 to 84 have Alzheimer's, and almost 50 percent of people over age 85 are affected by the disease. Unless a cure is found, some 14 million people will experience Alzheimer's by 2050—more than three times the current number (Cowley, 2000; Feinberg, 2002; Rogers, 2007).

In other cases, cognitive declines may be caused by temporary anxiety and depression, which can be treated successfully, or may even be due to overmedication. The danger is that people with such symptoms may be labelled senile

APPLYING PSYCHOLOGY   in the Real World

Gaming in Late Adulthood: How Video Games May Improve Cognitive Functioning in Older Adults

Have you ever frittered away an afternoon—or maybe even an entire day—playing a video game like *World of Warcraft* or *Grand Theft Auto*? A lot of people do. Perhaps you've told yourself that you're doing something to improve yourself, such as increasing your eye-hand coordination or honing your mental skills beyond just whiling away the time.

Turns out you may have been right, according to recent research that looked at the benefits of playing video games. And that may be especially true if you're an older adult playing video games.

Claims that playing video games can enhance skills and even improve cognitive ability are not new. There are even games marketed specifically as "mental workouts" that supposedly sharpen brain skills. But it's only recently that researchers have become interested in the possible use of video games to help slow the normal declines of cognitive functioning in late adulthood. Although research has found that activities that involve cognitive stimulation are generally helpful, up to now it hasn't been clear if video games provide the right kind of stimulation in the right amounts to do the trick (Tsai et al., 2008; Nunes & Kramer, 2009).

Recent studies are encouraging, however. In one study, older adults played a real-time strategic video game called *Rise of Nations* that had them managing and defending an empire of cities for almost 24 hours over several sessions. Not only did their skill at playing the game improve over time, but they also improved at real-world skills such as task switching, short-term memory, and reasoning (Basak et al., 2008).

In another study, groups of older and younger adults received five weeks of computerized cognitive skills training that became progressively more challenging. After the training, both groups showed noticeable increases in cognitive functioning, both in tests and in their daily lives. What's more, the effects tended to last and could be measured several months after the training had concluded (Westerberg et al., 2008).

The potential cognitive-improvement benefits of video games to those in late adulthood are so promising that the U.S. National Science Foundation recently awarded a team of researchers at North Carolina State University and Georgia Tech a four-year, million-dollar grant to study the effects of playing selected Nintendo Wii games on older adults. Researchers will investigate not only what cognitive improvements can be realized from gaming, but also what aspects of game playing (such as the novelty of the games or the social interaction they require) are responsible for cognitive improvements. Ultimately they hope to create new games based on the research that maximizes the cognitive benefit to those in late adulthood (Hamilton, 2009).

Alzheimer's disease
A progressive brain disorder that leads to a gradual and irreversible decline in cognitive abilities.

and left untreated, thereby continuing their decline—even though treatment would have been beneficial (Selkoe, 1997; Sachs-Ericsson et al., 2005).

In sum, declines in cognitive functioning in late adulthood are, for the most part, not inevitable. The key to maintaining cognitive skills may lie in intellectual stimulation. Like the rest of us, older adults need a stimulating environment in order to hone and maintain their skills (Bosma et al., 2003; Glisky, 2007; Hertzog et al., 2008).

The Social World of Late Adulthood: Old But Not Alone

Just as the view that old age predictably means mental decline has proved to be wrong, so has the view that late adulthood inevitably brings loneliness. People in late adulthood most often see themselves as functioning members of society, with only a small number of them reporting that loneliness is a serious problem (Binstock & George, 1996; Jylha, 2004).

There is no single way to age successfully. According to the **disengagement theory of aging,** aging produces a gradual withdrawal from the world on physical, psychological, and social levels (Adams, 2004; Wrosch, Bauer, & Scheier, 2005). However, such disengagement serves an important purpose, providing an opportunity for increased reflectiveness and decreased emotional investment in others at a time of life when social relationships will inevitably be ended by death.

STUDY ALERT!

It's important to be able to describe the nature of intellectual changes during late adulthood.

The **activity theory of aging** presents an alternative view of aging, holding that the people who age most successfully are those who maintain the interests, activities, and level of social interaction they experienced during middle adulthood. According to activity theory, late adulthood should reflect a continuation, as much as possible, of the activities in which people participated during the earlier part of their lives (Crosnoe & Elder, 2002; Nimrod & Kleiber, 2007).

Although most research is supportive of activity theory, not all people in late adulthood need a life filled with activities and social interaction to be happy; as in every stage of life, some older adults are just as satisfied leading a relatively inactive, solitary existence.

What may be more important is how people view the aging process: Evidence shows that positive self-perceptions of aging are associated with increased longevity (Levy et al., 2002; Levy & Myers, 2004).

Regardless of whether people become disengaged or maintain their activities from earlier stages of life, most engage in a process of **life review,** in which they examine and evaluate their lives. Remembering and reconsidering what has occurred in the past, people in late adulthood often come to a better understanding of themselves, sometimes resolving lingering problems and conflicts, and facing their lives with greater wisdom and serenity.

Clearly, people in late adulthood are not just marking time until death. Rather, old age is a time of continued growth and development, as important as any other period of life.

Disengagement theory of aging
A theory that suggests that aging produces a gradual withdrawal from the world on physical, psychological, and social levels.

Activity theory of aging
A theory that suggests that the elderly who are most successful while aging are those who maintain the interests and activities they had during middle age.

Life review
The process by which people examine and evaluate their lives.

Becoming an Informed Consumer of Psychology

Adjusting to Death

At some time in our lives, we all face death—certainly our own, as well as the deaths of friends, loved ones, and even strangers. Although there is nothing more inevitable in life, death remains a frightening, emotion-laden topic. Certainly, little is more stressful than the death of a loved one or the contemplation of our own imminent death, and preparing for death is one of our most crucial developmental tasks (Aiken, 2000).

A generation ago, talk of death was taboo. The topic was never mentioned to dying people, and gerontologists had little to say about it. That changed, however, with the pioneering work of Elisabeth Kübler-Ross (1969), who brought the subject of death into the open with her observation that those facing impending death tend to move through five broad stages:

- *Denial.* In this stage, people resist the idea that they are dying. Even if told that their chances for survival are small, they refuse to admit that they are facing death.
- *Anger.* After moving beyond the denial stage, dying people become angry—angry at people around them who are in good health, angry at medical professionals for being ineffective, angry at their god.
- *Bargaining.* Anger leads to bargaining, in which the dying try to think of ways to postpone death. They may decide to dedicate their lives to religion if their god saves them; they may say, "If only I can live to see my son married, I will accept death then."
- *Depression.* When dying people come to feel that bargaining is of no use, they move to the next stage: depression. They realize that their lives really are coming to an end, leading to what Kübler-Ross calls "preparatory grief" for their own deaths.
- *Acceptance.* In this stage, people accept impending death. Usually they are unemotional and uncommunicative; it is as if they have made peace with themselves and are expecting death with no bitterness.

It is important to keep in mind that not everyone experiences each of these stages in the same way. In fact, Kübler-Ross's stages pertain only to people who are fully aware that they are dying and have the time to evaluate their impending death. Furthermore, vast differences occur in the way individuals react to impending death. Movement from stage one to stage five in the grieving process is not always linear. For example, some individuals may progress from denial to acceptance and then back again—numerous times. The specific cause and duration of dying, as well as the person's sex, age, personality, and the type of support received from family and friends, all have an impact on how people respond to death (Carver & Scheier, 2002; Coyle, 2006).

Few of us enjoy the contemplation of death. Yet awareness of its psychological aspects and consequences can make its inevitable arrival less anxiety-producing and perhaps more understandable.

Evaluate

1. Rob recently turned 40 and surveyed his goals and accomplishments to date. Although he has accomplished a lot, he realized that many of his goals will not be met in his lifetime. This stage is called a _____ _____.

2. _____ _____ theories suggest that there is a maximum time span in which cells are able to reproduce. This time limit explains the eventual breakdown of the body during old age.

3. Lower IQ test scores during late adulthood do not necessarily mean a decrease in intelligence. True or false?

4. During old age, a person's _____ intelligence continues to increase, whereas _____ intelligence may decline.

5. In Kübler-Ross's _____ stage, people resist the idea of death. In the _____ stage, they attempt to make deals to avoid death, and in the _____ stage, they passively await death.

Answers to Evaluate Questions

1. midlife transition; 2. genetic preprogramming; 3. true; 4. crystallized, fluid; 5. denial, bargaining, acceptance

Key Terms

activity theory of aging	emerging adulthood	life review
Alzheimer's disease	genetic preprogramming theories of	menopause
disengagement theory of aging	aging	wear-and-tear theories of aging

Epilogue

Source: © Blend Images/Getty Images RF.

We have traced major events in the development of physical, social, and cognitive growth throughout the life span. Clearly, people change throughout their lives.

As we explored each area of development, we encountered anew the nature–nurture issue, concluding in every significant instance that both nature and nurture contribute to a person's development of skills, personality, and interactions.

Specifically, our genetic inheritance—nature—lays down general boundaries within which we can advance and grow, and our environment—nurture—helps determine the extent to which we take advantage of our potential.

Recap/Rethink

Module 27: Nature, Nuture, and Prenatal Development

Recap

How do psychologists study the degree to which development is an interaction of hereditary and environmental factors?

- Developmental psychology studies growth and change throughout life. One fundamental question is how much developmental change is due to heredity and how much is due to environment—the nature–nurture issue. Heredity seems to define the upper limits of our growth and change, whereas the environment affects the degree to which the upper limits are reached.
- Cross-sectional research compares people of different ages with one another at the same point in time. In contrast, longitudinal research traces the behaviour of one or more participants as the participants become older. Finally, sequential research combines the two methods by taking several different age groups and examining them at several points in time.

What is the nature of development before birth?

- Genes affect not only physical attributes but also a wide array of personal characteristics such as cognitive abilities, personality traits, and psychological disorders.
- Each chromosome contains genes, through which genetic information is transmitted. Genes, which are composed of DNA sequences, are the "software" that programs the future development of the body's hardware.
- At the moment of conception, a male's sperm cell and a female's egg cell unite, with each contributing to the new individual's genetic makeup. The union of sperm and egg produces a zygote, which contains 23 pairs of chromosomes—with one member of each pair coming from the father and the other coming from the mother.
- After two weeks the zygote becomes an embryo. By week 8, the embryo is called a fetus and is responsive to touch and other stimulation. At about week 22 it reaches the age of viability, which means it may survive if born prematurely. A fetus is normally born after thirty-eight weeks of pregnancy, weighing around seven pounds (three kg) and measuring about twenty inches (fifty cm).

What factors affect a child during the mother's pregnancy?

- Genetic abnormalities produce birth defects such as phenylketonuria (PKU), sickle-cell anemia, Tay-Sachs disease, and Down syndrome.
- Among the environmental influences on fetal growth are the mother's nutrition, illnesses, and drug and alcohol intake.

Rethink

1. When researchers find similarities in development between very different cultures, what implications might such findings have for the nature–nurture issue?

2. *From the perspective of childcare provider:* Consider what factors might determine why a child is not learning to walk at the same pace as his peers. What kinds of environmental influences might be involved? What kinds of genetic influences might be involved? What recommendations might you make to the child's parents about the situation?

3. Do you think there is any way in which Louise Brown's birth, infancy, and development differ from those of her friends who were not conceived through *in vitro* fertilization? Why or why not?

4. If a future Louise Brown were cloned from one of her parents, do you think she would turn out to be exactly like that parent, or different in some ways? Why?

Module 28: Infancy and Childhood

Recap

What are the major competencies of newborns?

- Newborns, or neonates, have reflexes that include a rooting reflex, the startle reflex, and the Babinski reflex. After birth, physical development is rapid; children typically triple their birthweight in a year.
- Sensory abilities also develop rapidly; infants can distinguish colour, depth, sound, tastes, and smells relatively soon after birth.

LO5 What are the milestones of physical and social development during childhood?

- Attachment—the positive emotional bond between a child and a particular individual—marks social development in infancy. Measured in the laboratory by means of the Ainsworth strange situation, attachment relates to later social and emotional adjustment.
- As children become older, the nature of their social interactions with peers changes. Initially play occurs relatively independently, but it becomes increasingly cooperative.
- The different child-rearing styles include authoritarian, permissive, authoritative, and uninvolved.
- According to Erik Erikson, eight stages of psychosocial development involve people's changing interactions and understanding of themselves and others. During childhood, the four stages are trust-versus-mistrust (birth to 1½ years), autonomy-versus-shame-and-doubt (1½ to 3 years), initiative-versus-guilt (3 to 6 years), and industry-versus-inferiority (6 to 12 years).

LO6 How does cognitive development proceed during childhood?

- Piaget's theory suggests that cognitive development proceeds through four stages in which qualitative changes occur in thinking: the sensorimotor stage (birth to 2 years), the preoperational stage (2 to 7 years), the concrete operational stage (7 to 12 years), and the formal operational stage (12 years to adulthood).
- Information-processing approaches suggest that quantitative changes occur in children's ability to organize and manipulate information about the world, such as significant increases in speed of processing, attention span, and memory. In addition, children advance in metacognition, the awareness and understanding of one's own cognitive processes.
- Vygotsky argued that children's cognitive development occurs as a consequence of social interactions in which children and others work together to solve problems.

Rethink

1. Do you think the widespread use of IQ testing in North America contributes to parents' views that their children's academic success is due largely to the children's innate intelligence? Why? Would it be possible (or desirable) to change this view?

2. *From the perspective of a childcare provider:* If a parent wasn't sure whether to enroll his or her child in your program, what advice would you give about the possible positive and negative consequences about day care?

Module 29: Adolescence: Becoming an Adult

Recap

LO7 What major physical, social, and cognitive transitions characterize adolescence?

- Adolescence, the developmental stage between childhood and adulthood, is marked by the onset of puberty, the point at which sexual maturity occurs. The age at which puberty begins has implications for the way people view themselves and the way others see them.
- Moral judgments during adolescence increase in sophistication, according to Lawrence Kohlberg's three-level model. Although Kohlberg's levels provide an adequate description of males' moral judgments, Carol Gilligan suggests that women view morality in terms of caring for individuals rather than in terms of broad, general principles of justice.
- According to Erik Erikson's model of psychosocial development, adolescence may be accompanied by an identity crisis. Adolescence is followed by three more stages of psychosocial development that cover the remainder of the life span.

Rethink

1. In what ways do school cultures help or hurt teenage students who are going through adolescence? What school policies might benefit early-maturing girls and late-maturing boys? Explain how same-sex schools could help, as some have argued.

Module 30: Adulthood

Recap

LO8 What are the principal kinds of physical, social, and intellectual changes that occur in early and middle adulthood, and what are their causes?

- Early adulthood marks the peak of physical health. Physical changes occur relatively gradually in men and women during adulthood.

- One major physical change occurs at the end of middle adulthood for women: They begin menopause, after which they are no longer fertile.
- During middle adulthood, people typically experience a midlife transition in which the notion that life is not unending becomes more important. In some cases, this realization may lead to a midlife crisis, although the passage into middle age is typically relatively calm.
- As aging continues during middle adulthood, people realize in their fifties that their lives and accomplishments are fairly well set, and they try to come to terms with them.

How does the reality of late adulthood differ from the stereotypes about that period?

- Old age may bring marked physical declines caused by genetic preprogramming or physical wear and tear. Although the activities of people in late adulthood are not all that different from those of younger people, older adults experience declines in reaction time, sensory abilities, and physical stamina.
- Intellectual declines are not an inevitable part of aging. Even when people show memory declines during late adulthood, their deficits tends to be limited to particular types of memory. Declines in episodic memory can often be traced to life changes.
- Disengagement theory sees successful aging as a process of gradual withdrawal from the physical, psychological, and social worlds. In contrast, activity theory suggests that the maintenance of interests and activities from earlier years leads to successful aging.

How can we adjust to death?

- According to Elizabeth Kübler-Ross, dying people move through five stages as they face death: denial, anger, bargaining, depression, and acceptance.

Rethink

1. Is the possibility that life may be extended for several decades a mixed blessing? What societal consequences might an extended life span bring about?

2. *From the perspective of a healthcare provider:* What sorts of recommendations would you make to your older patients about how to deal with aging? How would you handle someone who believed that getting older had only negative consequences?

3. What aspects of video games do you think would most help prevent cognitive decline in late adulthood? What other activities do you think would be helpful to avert cognitive deterioration?

CHAPTER 10
Personality

Source: © Greg Hindsdale/Corbis.

Prologue

Who Is the Real Madoff?

To some, Bernard L. Madoff was an affable, charismatic man who moved comfortably among power brokers on Wall Street and in Washington. He secured a long-standing role as an elder statesman on Wall Street, allowing him to land on important boards and commissions where his opinions helped shape securities regulations. And his employees say he treated them like family. There was, of course, another side to Mr. Madoff. Reclusive, at times standoffish and aloof, this Bernard rarely rubbed elbows in Manhattan's cocktail circuit or at Palm Beach balls. This Bernard was quiet, controlled, and closely attuned to his image down to the minutest details (Creswell & Landon, 2009, p. 1).

Which was the real Bernard Madoff? Was he the powerful, charismatic Wall Street businessman? Or was he the self-conscious, detail-oriented recluse? And perhaps most important, were there any signs that Madoff was secretly operating a fraudulent investment scheme that ultimately cheated thousands of people out of billions of dollars? Many people, like Madoff, have different sides to their personalities, appearing one way to some and quite differently to others.

Determining who a person truly is falls to a branch of psychology that seeks to understand the characteristic ways people behave—personality psychology. **Personality** is the pattern of enduring characteristics that produce consistency and individuality in a given person. Personality encompasses the behaviours that make us unique and that differentiate us from others. It is also personality that leads us to act consistently in different situations and over extended periods of time.

We will consider a number of approaches to personality. For historical reasons, we begin with psychodynamic theories of personality, which emphasize the importance of the unconscious. Next, we consider approaches that concentrate on identifying the most fundamental personality traits, theories that view personality as a set of learned behaviours, biological and evolutionary perspectives on personality, and approaches, known as humanistic theories, which highlight the uniquely human aspects of personality. We end our discussion by focusing on how personality is measured and how personality tests can be used.

Personality
The pattern of enduring characteristics that produce consistency and individuality in a given person.

Psychodynamic Approaches to Personality

LEARNING OBJECTIVES

LO1 **How do** psychologists define and use the concept of personality?

LO2 **What do** the theories of Freud and his successors tell us about the structure and development of personality?

The university student was intent on making a good first impression on an attractive woman he had spotted across a crowded room at a party. As he walked toward her, he mulled over a line he had heard in an old movie the night before: "I don't believe we've been properly introduced yet." To his horror, what came out was a bit different. After threading his way through the crowded room, he finally reached the woman and blurted out, "I don't believe we've been properly seduced yet."

Although this student's error may seem to be merely an embarrassing slip of the tongue, according to some personality theorists, such a mistake is not an error at all (Motley, 1987). Instead, psychodynamic personality theorists might argue that the error illustrates one way in which behaviour is triggered by inner forces that are beyond our awareness. These hidden drives, shaped by childhood experiences, play an important role in energizing and directing everyday behaviour.

Psychodynamic approaches to personality are based on the idea that personality is motivated by inner forces and conflicts about which people have little awareness and over which they have no control. The most important pioneer of the psychodynamic approach was Sigmund Freud. A number of Freud's followers, including Carl Jung, Karen Horney, and Alfred Adler, refined Freud's theory and developed their own psychodynamic approaches.

Freud's Psychoanalytic Theory: Mapping the Unconscious Mind

Sigmund Freud, an Austrian physician, developed **psychoanalytic theory** in the early 1900s. According to Freud's theory, conscious experience is a small part of our psychological makeup and experience. He argued that much of our behaviour is motivated by the **unconscious**, a part of the personality that contains the memories, knowledge, beliefs, feelings, urges, drives, and instincts of which the individual is not aware.

Like the unseen mass of a floating iceberg, the contents of the unconscious far surpass in quantity the information in our conscious awareness. Freud maintained that to understand personality, it is necessary to expose what is

---

Psychodynamic approaches to personality
Approaches that assume that personality is motivated by inner forces and conflicts about which people have little awareness and over which they have no control.

Psychoanalytic theory
Freud's theory that unconscious forces act as determinants of personality.

Unconscious
A part of the personality that contains the memories, knowledge, beliefs, feelings, urges, drives, and instincts of which the individual is not aware.

in the unconscious. But because the unconscious disguises the meaning of the material it holds, the content of the unconscious cannot be observed directly. It is therefore necessary to interpret clues to the unconscious—slips of the tongue, fantasies, and dreams—to understand the unconscious processes that direct behaviour. A slip of the tongue such as the one quoted earlier (sometimes termed a *Freudian slip*) may be interpreted as revealing the speaker's unconscious sexual desires.

To Freud, much of our personality is determined by our unconscious. Some of the unconscious is made up of the *preconscious*, which contains material that is not threatening and is easily brought to mind, such as the knowledge that $2 + 2 = 4$. But deeper in the unconscious are instinctual drives, the wishes, desires, demands, and needs that are hidden from conscious awareness because of the conflicts and pain they would cause if they were part of our everyday lives. The unconscious provides a "safe haven" for our recollections of threatening events.

Structuring Personality: Id, Ego, and Superego

To describe the structure of personality, Freud developed a comprehensive theory that held that personality consists of three separate but interacting components: the id, the ego, and the superego. Freud suggested that the three structures can be diagrammed to show how they relate to the conscious and the unconscious (see Figure 1).

Although the three components of personality described by Freud may appear to be actual physical structures in the nervous system, they are not. Instead, they represent abstract conceptions of a general *model* of personality that describes the interaction of forces that motivate behaviour.

If personality consisted only of primitive, instinctual cravings and longings, it would have just one component: the id. The **id** is the raw, unorganized, inborn part of personality. From the time of birth, the id attempts to reduce tension created by primitive drives related to hunger, sex, aggression, and irrational impulses. Those drives are fueled by "psychic energy," which can be thought of as a limitless energy source constantly putting pressure on the various parts of the personality.

The id operates according to the *pleasure principle*, in which the goal is the immediate reduction of tension and the maximization of satisfaction. However, reality prevents the fulfillment of the demands of the pleasure principle in most cases: We cannot always eat when we are hungry, and we can discharge our sexual drives only when the time and place are appropriate. To account for this fact of life, Freud suggested a second component of personality, which he called the ego.

FIGURE 1

In Freud's model of personality, there are three major components: the id, the ego, and the superego. As the iceberg analogy shows, only a small portion of personality is conscious. Why do you think that only the ego and superego have conscious components?

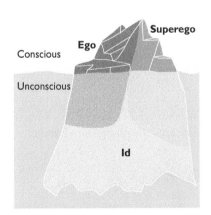

Id
The raw, unorganized, inborn part of personality whose sole purpose is to reduce tension created by primitive drives related to hunger, sex, aggression, and irrational impulses.

STUDY ALERT!

Remember that the three parts of personality in Freud's theory—the id, the ego, and the superego—are abstract conceptions that don't exist as physical structures in the brain.

The **ego**, which begins to develop soon after birth, strives to balance the desires of the id and the realities of the objective, outside world. In contrast to the pleasure-seeking id, the ego operates according to the *reality principle*, in which instinctual energy is restrained to maintain the safety of the individual and help integrate the person into society. In a sense, then, the ego is the "executive" of personality: It makes decisions, controls actions, and allows thinking and problem solving of a higher order than the id's capabilities permit.

The **superego**, the final personality structure to develop in childhood, represents the rights and wrongs of society as taught and modelled by a person's parents, teachers, and other significant individuals. The superego includes the *conscience*, which prevents us from behaving in a morally improper way by making us feel guilty if we do wrong. The superego helps us control impulses coming from the id, making our behaviour less selfish and more virtuous.

According to Freud's theory, both the superego and the id are unrealistic in that they do not consider the practical realities imposed by society. The superego, if left to operate without restraint, would create perfectionists unable to make the compromises that life requires. An unrestrained id would create a primitive, pleasure-seeking, thoughtless individual seeking to fulfill every desire without delay. As a result, the ego must mediate between the demands of the superego and the demands of the id. For example, a child in a candy store may be guided by their id to "steal as much candy as they can carry"; then mediated by their ego, the child's conscience takes over, as expressed by their superego, and as a result, the child realizes that "stealing is against the law" and puts the candy back.

Developing Personality: Psychosexual Stages

Freud also provided us with a view of how personality develops through a series of five **psychosexual stages**, during which individuals encounter conflicts between the demands of society and their own sexual urges (in which sexuality is more about experiencing pleasure and less about lust). According to Freud, failure to resolve the conflicts at a particular stage can result in **fixations**, conflicts or concerns that persist beyond the developmental period in which they first occur. Such conflicts may be due to having needs ignored or (conversely) being overindulged during the earlier period.

The sequence Freud proposed is noteworthy because it explains how experiences and difficulties during a particular childhood stage may predict specific characteristics in the adult personality. This theory is also unique in associating each stage with a major biological function, which Freud assumed to be the focus of pleasure in a given period.

In the first psychosexual stage of development, called the **oral stage**, the baby's mouth is the focal point of pleasure (see Figure 2 for a summary of the stages). During the first 12 to 18 months of life, children suck, mouth, and bite

Ego
The part of the personality that provides a buffer between the id and the outside world.

Superego
According to Freud, the final personality structure to develop; it represents the rights and wrongs of society as handed down by a person's parents, teachers, and other important figures.

Psychosexual stages
Developmental periods that children pass through during which they encounter conflicts between the demands of society and their own sexual urges.

Fixations
Conflicts or concerns that persist beyond the developmental period in which they first occur.

Oral stage
According to Freud, a stage from birth to age 12 to 18 months, in which an infant's centre of pleasure is the mouth.

FIGURE 2

Freud's theory of personality development suggests that there are several distinct stages.

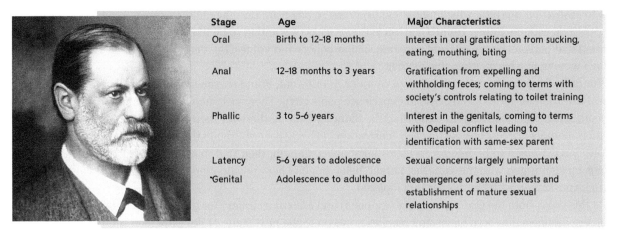

Stage	Age	Major Characteristics
Oral	Birth to 12–18 months	Interest in oral gratification from sucking, eating, mouthing, biting
Anal	12–18 months to 3 years	Gratification from expelling and withholding feces; coming to terms with society's controls relating to toilet training
Phallic	3 to 5–6 years	Interest in the genitals, coming to terms with Oedipal conflict leading to identification with same-sex parent
Latency	5–6 years to adolescence	Sexual concerns largely unimportant
Genital	Adolescence to adulthood	Reemergence of sexual interests and establishment of mature sexual relationships

Source: © Bettmann/Corbis.

anything that can be put into their mouths. If infants are either overindulged (perhaps by being fed every time they cry) or frustrated in their search for oral gratification, they may become fixated at this stage. For example, fixation might occur if an infant's oral needs were constantly gratified immediately at the first sign of hunger. Fixation at the oral stage might produce an adult who was unusually interested in oral activities—eating, talking, smoking—or who showed symbolic sorts of oral interests: being either "bitingly" sarcastic or very gullible ("swallowing" anything).

STUDY ALERT!

The five psychosexual stages of personality development in Freud's theory—oral, anal, phallic, latency, and genital—indicate how personality develops as people age.

From around age 12 to 18 months until 3 years of age—a period when the emphasis in Western cultures is on toilet training—a child enters the **anal stage**. At this point, the major source of pleasure changes from the mouth to the anal region, and children obtain considerable pleasure from both retention and expulsion of feces. If toilet training is particularly demanding, fixation might occur. Fixation during the anal stage might result in unusual rigidity, orderliness, punctuality—or extreme disorderliness or sloppiness—in adulthood.

At about age 3, the **phallic stage** begins. At this point there is another major shift in the primary source of pleasure for the child. Now interest focuses on the genitals and the pleasures derived from fondling them. During this stage the child must also negotiate one of the most important hurdles of personality development: the **Oedipal conflict**, which is experienced by young boys and the **Electra complex**, which is experienced by young girls.

According to Freudian theory, as children focus attention on their genitals, the differences between male and female anatomy become more salient. Furthermore, according to Freud, at this time the male unconsciously begins

Anal stage
According to Freud, a stage from age 12 to 18 months to 3 years of age, in which a child's pleasure is centred on the anus.

Phallic stage
According to Freud, a period beginning around age 3 during which a child's pleasure focuses on the genitals.

Oedipal conflict
A child's sexual interest in his or her opposite-sex parent, typically resolved through identification with the same-sex parent.

Electra complex
A daughter's unresolved, unconscious sexual desire for her father.

to develop a sexual interest in his mother, starts to see his father as a rival, and harbours a wish to kill his father—as Oedipus did in the ancient Greek tragedy. But because he views his father as too powerful, he develops a fear that his father may retaliate drastically by removing the source of the threat: the son's penis. The fear of losing one's penis leads to *castration anxiety*, which ultimately becomes so powerful that the child represses his desires for his mother and identifies with his father. **Identification** is the process of wanting to be like another person as much as possible, imitating that person's behaviour and adopting similar beliefs and values. By identifying with his father, a son seeks to obtain a woman like his unattainable mother.

For girls, the process, called the *Electra complex*, is different. Freud reasoned that girls begin to experience sexual arousal toward their fathers and begin to experience penis envy. They wish they had the anatomical part that, at least to Freud, seemed most clearly "missing" in girls. Blaming their mothers for their lack of a penis, girls come to believe that their mothers are responsible for their "castration." (This aspect of Freud's theory later provoked accusations that he considered women to be inferior to men.) Like males, though, they find that they can resolve such unacceptable feelings by identifying with the same-sex parent, behaving like her and adopting her attitudes and values. In this way, a girl's identification with her mother is completed.

At this point, both the *Oedipal conflict* (for boys) and *Electra complex* (for girls) is said to be resolved, and Freudian theory assumes that both males and females move on to the next stage of development. If difficulties arise during this period, however, all sorts of problems are thought to occur, including improper sex-role behaviour and the failure to develop a conscience.

After the resolution of the Oedipal conflict and the Electra complex, typically at around age 5 or 6, children move into the **latency period**, which lasts until puberty. During this period, sexual interests become dormant, even in the unconscious. Then, during adolescence, sexual feelings reemerge, marking the start of the final period, the **genital stage,** which extends until death. The focus during the genital stage is on mature, adult sexuality, which Freud defined as sexual intercourse.

Defence Mechanisms

Freud's efforts to describe and theorize about the underlying dynamics of personality and its development were motivated by very practical problems that his patients faced in dealing with *anxiety*, an intense, negative emotional experience. According to Freud, anxiety is a danger signal to the ego. Although anxiety can arise from realistic fears—such as seeing a poisonous snake about to strike—it can also occur in the form of *neurotic anxiety*, in which irrational impulses emanating from the id threaten to burst through and become uncontrollable.

Because anxiety, obviously, is unpleasant, Freud believed that people develop a range of defence mechanisms to deal with it. **Defence mechanisms** are unconscious strategies that people use to reduce anxiety by concealing the source from themselves and others.

The primary defence mechanism is **repression**, in which unacceptable or unpleasant id impulses are pushed back into the unconscious. Repression is the most direct method of dealing with anxiety; instead of handling an anxiety-producing

---

Identification
The process of wanting to be like another person as much as possible, imitating that person's behaviour and adopting similar beliefs and values.

Latency period
According to Freud, the period between the phallic stage and puberty during which children's sexual concerns are temporarily put aside.

Genital stage
According to Freud, the period from puberty until death, marked by mature sexual behaviour (that is, sexual intercourse).

Defence mechanisms
In Freudian theory, unconscious strategies that people use to reduce anxiety by concealing the source of it from themselves and others.

Repression
The primary defence mechanism in which unacceptable or unpleasant id impulses are pushed back into the unconscious.

impulse on a conscious level, one simply ignores it. For example, a university student who feels hatred for her mother may repress those personally and socially unacceptable feelings. The feelings remain lodged within the unconscious, because acknowledging them would provoke anxiety. Similarly, memories of childhood abuse may be repressed. Although such memories may not be consciously recalled, according to Freud, they can affect later behaviour, and they may be revealed through dreams or slips of the tongue or symbolically in some other fashion.

If repression is ineffective in keeping anxiety at bay, other defence mechanisms may be used. Freud, and later his daughter Anna Freud (who became a well-known psychoanalyst), formulated an extensive list of potential defence mechanisms. The major defence mechanisms are summarized in Figure 3 (Conte, Plutchik, & Draguns, 2004; Hentschel et al., 2004; Cramer, 2007).

All of us employ defence mechanisms to some degree, according to Freudian theory, and they can serve a useful purpose by protecting us from unpleasant information. Yet some people fall prey to them to such an extent that a large amount of psychic energy must constantly be directed toward hiding and rechannelling unacceptable impulses. When this occurs, everyday living becomes difficult. In such cases, the result is a mental disorder produced by anxiety—what Freud called "neurosis" (a term rarely used by psychologists today, although it endures in everyday conversation).

FIGURE 3

According to Freud, people are able to use a wide range of defence mechanisms to cope with anxieties.

Freud's Defence Mechanisms		
Defence Mechanism	**Explanation**	**Example**
Repression	Unacceptable or unpleasant impulses are pushed back into the unconscious.	A woman is unable to recall that she was abused as a child
Regression	People behave as if they were at an earlier stage of development.	A boss has a temper tantrum when an employee makes a mistake.
Displacement	The expression of an unwanted feeling or thought is redirected from a more threatening powerful person to a weaker one.	A brother yells at his younger sister after a teacher gives him a bad grade.
Rationalization	People provide self-justifying explanations in place of the actual, but threatening, reason for their behaviour.	A student who goes out drinking the night before a big test rationalizes his behaviour by saying the test isn't all that important.
Denial	People refuse to accept or acknowledge an anxiety-producing piece of information.	A student refuses to believe that he has flunked a course.
Projection	People attribute unwanted impulses and feelings to someone else.	A man who is unfaithful to his wife and feels guilty suspects that his wife is unfaithful.
Sublimation	People divert unwanted impulses into socially approved thoughts, feelings, or behaviours.	A person with strong feelings of aggression becomes a soldier.
Reaction formation	Unconscious impulses are expressed as their opposite in consciousness.	A mother who unconsciously resents her child acts in an overly loving way toward the child.

STUDY ALERT!

Use Figure 3 to remember the most common defence mechanisms (unconscious strategies used to reduce anxiety by concealing its source from ourselves and others).

The Neo-Freudian Psychoanalysts: Building on Freud

Freud laid the foundation for important work done by a series of successors who were trained in traditional Freudian theory but later rejected some of its major points. These theorists are known as **neo-Freudian psychoanalysts**.

The neo-Freudians placed greater emphasis than Freud had on the functions of the ego, suggesting that it has more control than does the id over day-to-day activities. They also minimized the importance of sex as a driving force in people's lives. Furthermore, they paid greater attention to social factors and the effects of society and culture on personality development.

Jung's Collective Unconscious

One of the most influential neo-Freudians, Carl Jung (pronounced "yoong"), rejected Freud's view of the primary importance of unconscious sexual urges. Instead, he looked at the primitive urges of the unconscious more positively, arguing that they represented a more general, and positive, life force that encompasses an inborn drive motivating creativity and more positive resolution of conflict (Lothane, 2005; Cassells, 2007).

Jung suggested that we have a universal **collective unconscious**, a common set of ideas, feelings, images, and symbols that we inherit from our relatives, the whole human race, and even animal ancestors from the distant past. This collective unconscious is shared by everyone and is displayed in behaviour that is common across diverse cultures—such as love of mother, belief in a supreme being, and even behaviour as specific as fear of snakes (Oehman & Mineka, 2003; Drob, 2005; Hauke, 2006).

Jung went on to propose that the collective unconscious contains **archetypes**, universal symbolic representations of a particular person, object, or experience. For instance, a mother archetype, which contains reflections of our ancestors' relationships with mother figures, is suggested by the prevalence of mothers in art, religion, literature, and mythology. (Think of the Virgin Mary, Earth Mother, wicked stepmothers in fairy tales, Mother's Day, and so forth!) Jung also suggested that men possess an unconscious feminine archetype affecting how they behave, whereas women have a male archetype that colours their behaviour (Jung, 1961; Bair, 2003; Smetana, 2007).

To Jung, archetypes play an important role in determining our day-to-day reactions, attitudes, and values. For example, Jung might explain the popularity of the *Harry Potter* movies as being due to their use of broad archetypes of good (Harry) and evil (Voldemort).

Although there is no reliable research evidence confirming the existence of the collective unconscious—and even Jung acknowledged that such evidence would be difficult to produce—Jung's theory has had significant influence in areas beyond psychology. For example, personality types derived from Jung's personality approach form the basis for the Myers-Briggs personality test, which is widely used in business and industry (Gladwell, 2004; Bayne, 2005; Furnham & Crump, 2005).

Horney's Neo-Freudian Perspective

Karen Horney (pronounced "HORN-eye") was one of the earliest psychologists to champion women's issues and is sometimes called the first feminist psychologist. Horney suggested that personality develops in the context of social relationships and depends particularly on the relationship between parents and child and how well the child's needs are met. She rejected Freud's suggestion that women have penis envy, asserting that what women envy most in men is not their anatomy but the independence, success, and freedom that women often are denied (Horney, 1937; Miletic, 2002, Smith, 2007).

Horney was also one of the first to stress the importance of cultural factors in the determination of personality. For example, she suggested that society's rigid gender roles for women lead them to experience ambivalence about success, fearing that they will lose their friends. Her conceptualizations, developed in the 1930s and 1940s, laid the groundwork for many of the central ideas of feminism that emerged decades later (Eckardt, 2005; Jones, 2006).

Neo-Freudian psychoanalysts
Psychoanalysts who were trained in traditional Freudian theory but who later rejected some of its major points.

Collective unconscious
According to Jung, a common set of ideas, feelings, images, and symbols that we inherit from our ancestors, the whole human race, and even animal ancestors from the distant past.

Archetypes
According to Jung, universal symbolic representations of a particular person, object, or experience (such as good and evil).

Adler and the Other Neo-Freudians

Alfred Adler, another important neo-Freudian psychoanalyst, also considered Freudian theory's emphasis on sexual needs misplaced. Instead, Adler proposed that the primary human motivation is a striving for superiority, not in terms of superiority over others but in a quest for self-improvement and perfection.

Adler used the term **inferiority complex** to describe situations in which adults have not been able to overcome the feelings of inferiority they developed as children, when they were small and limited in their knowledge about the world. Early social relationships with parents have an important effect on children's ability to outgrow feelings of personal inferiority and instead orient themselves toward attaining more socially useful goals, such as improving society.

Other neo-Freudians included such figures as Erik Erikson, whose theory of psychosocial development we discussed in earlier modules, and Freud's daughter, Anna Freud. Like Adler and Horney, they focused less than Freud on inborn sexual and aggressive drives and more on the social and cultural factors behind personality.

Inferiority complex
According to Adler, a problem affecting adults who have not been able to overcome the feelings of inferiority that they developed as children, when they were small and limited in their knowledge about the world.

Evaluate

1. _____ approaches state that behaviour is motivated primarily by unconscious forces.

2. Match each section of the personality (according to Freud) with its description:

   1. Ego

   2. Id

   3. Superego

   a. Determines right from wrong on the basis of cultural standards.

   b. Operates according to the "reality principle"; energy is redirected to integrate the person into society.

   c. Seeks to reduce tension brought on by primitive drives.

3. Which of the following represents the proper order of personality development, according to Freud?

   a. Oral, phallic, latency, anal, genital

   b. Anal, oral, phallic, genital, latency

   c. Oral, anal, phallic, latency, genital

   d. Latency, phallic, anal, genital, oral

4. _____ is the term Freud used to describe unconscious strategies used to reduce anxiety.

Answers to Evaluate Questions

1. psychodynamic; 2. 1-b, 2-c, 3-a; 3. c; 4. defence mechanisms

Key Terms

anal stage	id	phallic stage
archetypes	identification	psychoanalytic theory
collective unconscious	inferiority complex	psychodynamic approaches to
defence mechanisms	latency period	personality
ego	neo-Freudian psychoanalysts	psychosexual stages
Electra complex	Oedipal conflict	repression
fixations	oral stage	superego
genital stage	personality	unconscious

Trait, Learning, Biological and Evolutionary, and Humanistic Approaches to Personality

MODULE
32

LEARNING OBJECTIVE

LO3 **What are** the major aspects of trait, learning, biological and evolutionary, and humanistic approaches to personality?

"Tell me about Nelson," said Johnetta.

"Oh, he's just terrific. He's the friendliest guy I know—goes out of his way to be nice to everyone. He hardly ever gets mad. He's just so even-tempered, no matter what's happening. And he's really smart, too. About the only thing I don't like is that he's always in such a hurry to get things done. He seems to have boundless energy, much more than I have."

"He sounds great to me, especially in comparison to Rico," replied Johnetta. "He is so self-centred and arrogant that it drives me crazy. I sometimes wonder why I ever started going out with him."

Friendly. Even-tempered. Smart. Energetic. Self-centred. Arrogant.

The above exchange is made up of a series of trait characterizations of speakers' friends. In fact, much of our own understanding of others' behaviour is based on the premise that people possess certain traits that are consistent across different situations. For example, we generally assume that if someone is outgoing and sociable in one situation, he or she is outgoing and sociable in other situations (Gilbert et al., 1992; Gilbert, Miller, & Ross, 1998; Mischel, 2004).

Dissatisfaction with the emphasis in psychoanalytic theory on unconscious—and difficult to demonstrate—processes in explaining a person's behaviour led to the development of alternative approaches to personality, including a number of trait-based approaches. Other theories reflect established psychological perspectives, such as learning theory, biological and evolutionary approaches, and the humanistic approach.

Trait Approaches: Placing Labels on Personality

If someone asked you to characterize another person, it is probable that—like Johnetta and her friend—you would come up with a list of that individual's personal qualities, as you see them. But how would you know which of those qualities are most important to an understanding of that person's behaviour?

Personality psychologists have asked similar questions. To answer them, they have developed a model of personality known as trait theory. **Trait theory** seeks to explain, in a straightforward way, the consistencies in individuals' behaviour. **Traits** are consistent personality characteristics and behaviours displayed in different situations.

Trait theorists do not assume that some people have a trait and others do not; rather, they propose that all people possess certain traits, but that the degree to which a particular trait applies to a specific person varies and can be

---

Trait theory
A model of personality that seeks to identify the basic traits necessary to describe personality.

Traits
Consistent personality characteristics and behaviours displayed in different situations.

quantified. For instance, you may be relatively friendly, whereas I may be relatively unfriendly. But we both have a "friendliness" trait, although your degree of "friendliness" is higher than mine. The major challenge for trait theorists taking this approach has been to identify the specific primary traits necessary to describe personality. As we shall see, different theorists have come up with surprisingly different sets of traits.

STUDY ALERT!

All trait theories explain personality in terms of traits (consistent personality characteristics and behaviours), but they differ in terms of which and how many traits are seen as fundamental.

Allport's Trait Theory: Identifying Basic Characteristics

When personality psychologist Gordon Allport systematically pored over an unabridged dictionary in the 1930s he came up with some 18,000 separate terms that could be used to describe personality. Although he was able to pare down the list to a mere 4,500 descriptors after eliminating words with the same meaning, he was left with a problem crucial to all trait approaches: Which of those traits were the most basic?

Allport eventually answered this question by suggesting that there are three fundamental categories of traits: cardinal, central, and secondary (Allport, 1961, 1966). A *cardinal trait* is a single characteristic that directs most of a person's activities. For example, a totally selfless woman may direct all her energy toward humanitarian activities; an intensely power-hungry person may be driven by an all-consuming need for control.

Most people, however, do not develop a single, comprehensive cardinal trait. Instead, they possess a handful of central traits that make up the core of personality. *Central traits*, such as honesty and sociability, are the major characteristics of an individual; they usually number from five to ten in any one person. Finally, *secondary traits* are characteristics that affect behaviour in fewer situations and are less influential than central or cardinal traits. For instance, a reluctance to eat meat and a love of modern art would be considered secondary traits (Nicholson, 2003; Glicksohn & Nahari, 2007).

Cattell and Eysenck: Factoring Out Personality

Later attempts to identify primary personality traits have centred on a statistical technique known as factor analysis. *Factor analysis* is a statistical method of identifying associations among a large number of variables to reveal more general patterns. For example, a personality researcher might administer a questionnaire to many participants, asking them to describe themselves by referring to an extensive list of traits. By statistically combining responses and computing which traits are associated with one another in the same person, a researcher can identify the most fundamental patterns or combinations of traits—called *factors*—that underlie participants' responses.

Using factor analysis, personality psychologist Raymond Cattell (1965) suggested that sixteen pairs of *source traits* represent the basic dimensions of personality. Using those source traits, he developed the Sixteen Personality Factor Questionnaire, or 16 PF, a measure that provides scores for each of the source traits. Figure 1 shows the pattern of average scores on each of the source traits for two different groups of participants—airplane pilots, and writers (Cattell, Cattell, & Cattell, 2000).

Another trait theorist, psychologist Hans Eysenck (Eysenck et al., 1992; Eysenck 1994, 1995), also used factor analysis to identify patterns of traits, but he came to a very different conclusion about the nature of personality. He found that personality could best be described in terms of just three major dimensions: *extroversion, neuroticism,* and *psychoticism.* The extroversion dimension relates to the degree of sociability, whereas the neurotic dimension encompasses emotional stability. Finally, psychoticism refers to the degree to which reality is distorted. By evaluating people along these three dimensions, Eysenck was able to predict behaviour accurately in a variety of situations.

The Big Five Personality Traits

For the last two decades, the most influential trait approach contends that five traits or factors—called the "Big Five"— lie at the core of personality. Using modern factor analytic statistical techniques, a host of researchers have identified a

Personality profiles for source traits developed by Cattell for two groups of subjects: writers and airline pilots. The average score for the general population is between 4.5 and 6.5 on each scale. On what traits do airline pilots and writers differ most? How do these differences contribute to their chosen work?

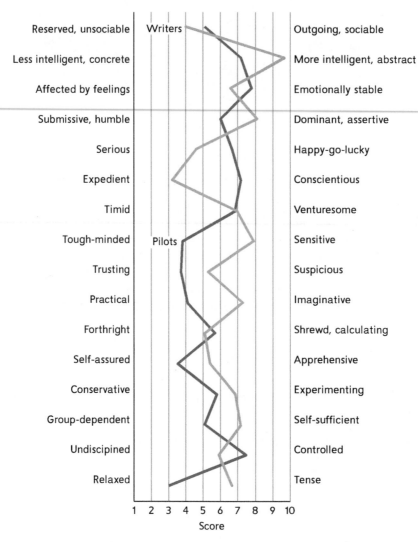

Reserved, unsociable	Outgoing, sociable
Less intelligent, concrete	More intelligent, abstract
Affected by feelings	Emotionally stable
Submissive, humble	Dominant, assertive
Serious	Happy-go-lucky
Expedient	Conscientious
Timid	Venturesome
Tough-minded	Sensitive
Trusting	Suspicious
Practical	Imaginative
Forthright	Shrewd, calculating
Self-assured	Apprehensive
Conservative	Experimenting
Group-dependent	Self-sufficient
Undisciplined	Controlled
Relaxed	Tense

1 2 3 4 5 6 7 8 9 10
Score

Source: Figure derived from Cattell, Eber, and Tatsuoka: *Handbook for the Sixteenth Personality Factor Questionnaire (16PF®)*. Copyright © 1970, 1988, 1992 by the Institute for Personality and Ability Testing Inc. (IPAT), Champaign, Illinois, USA. 16PF® is a registered trademark of IPAT. Reproduced with the permission of the Institute for Personality and Ability Testing, Inc.

similar set of five factors that underlie personality. The five factors, described in Figure 2, are *openness to experience, conscientiousness, extroversion, agreeableness,* and *neuroticism* (emotional stability).

STUDY ALERT!

You can remember the "Big Five" set of personality traits by using the acronym OCEAN (openness to experience, conscientiousness, extroversion, agreeableness, and neuroticism).

The Big Five emerge quite consistently across a number of domains. For example, factor analyses of major personality inventories, self-report measures made by observers of others' personality traits, and checklists of self-descriptions yield similar factors quite consistently. In addition, the Big Five emerge consistently in different populations of individuals, including children, college and university students, older adults, and speakers of different

FIGURE 2

Five broad trait factors, referred to as the "Big Five," are considered to be the core of personality. You can memorize these traits by using the mnemonic OCEAN, representing the first letter of each trait.

The Big Five Personality Factors and Dimensions of Sample Traits	
Openness to experience	**Agreeableness**
Independent—Conforming	Sympathetic—Fault-finding
Imaginative—Practical	Kind—Cold
Preference for variety—Preference for routine	Appreciative—Unfriendly
Conscientiousness	**Neuroticism (Emotional Stability)**
Careful—Careless	Stable—Tense
Disciplined—Impulsive	Calm—Anxious
Organized—Disorganized	Secure—Insecure
Extroversion	
Talkative—Quiet	
Fun-loving—Sober	
Sociable—Retiring	

Source: Adapted from Pervin, 1990, Chapter 3, and McCrae & Costa, 1986, p. 1002.

languages. Finally, cross-cultural research conducted in areas ranging from Europe to the Middle East to Africa also has been supportive. Finally, studies of brain functioning show that Big Five personality traits are related to the way the brain processes information (McCrae et al., 2005; Schmitt, Allik, & McCrae, 2007; Schmitt et al., 2008).

In short, a growing consensus exists that the "Big Five" represent the best description of personality traits we have today. Still, the debate over the specific number and kinds of traits—and even the usefulness of trait approaches in general—remains a lively one. See the *Applying Psychology in the Real World* box.

APPLYING PSYCHOLOGY in the Real World

Judged at First Sight

Imagine that you've just showed up to an important job interview dressed in your best business attire, and the personnel director greets you and ushers you into her office. Or perhaps you've arrived at a party where there are many other students from your campus that you'd like to get to know. In either case, you might be focused on how well you're coming across and thinking that you have only a few minutes to make a good first impression—and that's where you're wrong. Whatever impression you were going to make, you did so already.

At least that's the surprising finding of recent research on how people make judgments of others' personality. For instance, in one study, participants were shown photographs of faces of unfamiliar people and asked to rate those people on a number of characteristics, such as attractiveness, trustworthiness, and competence. These participants showed high agreement in their judgments of these characteristics. Then another group of participants were shown the same photographs, but they were asked to make the same judgments under time constraints. In some cases the judgment had to be made in 1 second, in others in 1/2 of a second, and in still others in just 1/10 of a second (Willis & Todorov, 2006; Oosterhof & Todorov, 2008).

When the time-constrained judgments were compared to the judgments made with no time constraints, the researchers found that the judgments were extremely similar. Moreover, the length of the time constraint made no difference—the judgments made in 1/10 of a second were just as accurate as those made in a 1/2 or 1 second.

(continued)

What these findings suggest is that people make virtually instantaneous judgments about others essentially the moment that they lay eyes on them. This may be particularly true of judgments about attractiveness and trustworthiness, which the participants were able to assess most quickly. But even other types of judgments—such as a person's sexual orientation—are made extremely quickly; sometimes such quick judgments are more accurate than those made more thoughtfully and deliberately (Rule, Ambady, & Hallett, 2009).

Researchers have theorized that the ability to judge characteristics quickly and accurately may have evolved in humans because it once had survival value. Today it means, for better or for worse, that we accurately size each other up at just a glance (Todorov & Duchaine, 2008; Oveis et al., 2009).

Learning Approaches: We Are What We've Learned

The psychodynamic and trait approaches we've discussed concentrate on the "inner" person—the fury of an unobservable but powerful id or a hypothetical but fundamental set of traits. In contrast, learning approaches to personality focus on the "outer" person. To a strict learning theorist, personality is simply the sum of learned responses to the external environment. Internal events such as thoughts, feelings, and motivations are ignored. Although the existence of personality is not denied, learning theorists say that it is best understood by looking at features of a person's environment.

Skinner's Behaviourist Approach

According to the most influential learning theorist, B. F. Skinner (who carried out pioneering work on operant conditioning), personality is a collection of learned behaviour patterns (Skinner, 1975). Similarities in responses across different situations are caused by similar patterns of reinforcement that have been received in such situations in the past. If I am sociable both at parties and at meetings, it is because I have been reinforced for displaying social behaviours—not because I am fulfilling an unconscious wish based on experiences during my childhood or because I have an internal trait of sociability.

Strict learning theorists such as Skinner are less interested in the consistencies in behaviour across situations than in ways of modifying behaviour. Their view is that humans are infinitely changeable through the process of learning new behaviour patterns. If one is able to control and modify the patterns of reinforcers in a situation, behaviour that other theorists would view as stable and unyielding can be changed and ultimately improved. Learning theorists are optimistic in their attitudes about the potential for resolving personal and societal problems through treatment strategies based on learning theory.

Social Cognitive Approaches to Personality

Not all learning theories of personality take such a strict view in rejecting the importance of what is "inside" a person by focusing solely on the "outside." Unlike other learning approaches to personality, **social cognitive approaches to personality** emphasize the influence of cognition—thoughts, feelings, expectations, and values—as well as observation of other's behaviour, on personality. According to Albert Bandura, one of the main proponents of this point of view, people can foresee the possible outcomes of certain behaviours in a particular setting without actually having to carry them out. This takes place mainly through the mechanism of *observational learning*—viewing the actions of others and observing the consequences (Bandura, 1986, 1999).

For instance, children who view a model behaving in, say, an aggressive manner tend to copy the behaviour if the consequences of the model's behaviour are seen to be positive. If, in contrast, the model's aggressive behaviour has resulted in no consequences or negative consequences, children are considerably less likely to act aggressively. According to social cognitive approaches, then, personality develops through repeated observation of the behaviour of others.

Social cognitive approaches to personality
Theories that emphasize the influence of a person's cognitions—thoughts, feelings, expectations, and values—as well as observation of others' behaviour, in determining personality.

SELF-EFFICACY

Bandura places particular emphasis on the role played by **self-efficacy**, belief in one's personal capabilities. Self-efficacy underlies people's faith in their ability to carry out a particular behaviour or produce a desired outcome. People with high self-efficacy have higher aspirations and greater persistence in working to attain goals and ultimately achieve greater success than do those with lower self-efficacy (Bandura & Locke, 2003; Glickler, 2006; Betz, 2007).

It is interesting to note cultural differences in self-efficacy. Robert Klassen, a psychology teacher at the University of Alberta, researches self-efficacy and motivation beliefs in a variety of cultural contexts. In 2004, Klassen compared the self-efficacy beliefs of South Asian (Indo Canadian) immigrant students with the self-efficacy beliefs of Anglo Canadian nonimmigrant students. Results indicated that self-efficacy of immigrant students were more "other-oriented" than self-efficacy of nonimmigrant students. More specifically, Indo Canadian students were more influenced by others' performance on academic tasks, while Anglo Canadian students remained focused on their own performance.

How do we develop self-efficacy? One way is by paying close attention to our prior successes and failures. If we try snowboarding and experience little success, we'll be less likely to try it again. However, if our initial efforts appear promising, we'll be more likely to attempt it again. Direct reinforcement and encouragement from others also play a role in developing self-efficacy (Devonport & Lane, 2006; Buchanan & Selmon, 2008).

Self-efficacy, the belief in one's own capabilities, leads to higher aspirations and greater persistence.

Source: © CP PICTURE ARCHIVE/Paul Chiasson.

Compared with other learning theories of personality, social cognitive approaches are distinctive in their emphasis on the reciprocity between individuals and their environment. Not only is the environment assumed to affect personality, but people's behaviour and personalities are also assumed to "feed back" and modify the environment (Bandura, 1999, 2000).

Biological and Evolutionary Approaches: Are We Born with Personality?

Coming at the question of what determines personality from a different direction, **biological and evolutionary approaches to personality** suggest that important components of personality are inherited. Building on the work of behavioural geneticists, researchers using biological and evolutionary approaches argue that personality is determined at least in part by our genes, in much the same way that our height is largely a result of genetic contributions from our ancestors. The evolutionary perspective assumes that personality traits that led to survival and reproductive success of our ancestors are more likely to be preserved and passed on to subsequent generations (Buss, 2001, 2009).

The importance of genetic factors in personality is illustrated by studies of twins. For instance, personality psychologists Auke Tellegen and colleagues examined the personality traits of pairs of twins who were genetically identical but were raised apart from each other (Tellegen et al., 1988, Bouchard et al., 2004). In the study, each twin was given a battery of personality tests, including one that measured eleven key personality characteristics.

Self-efficacy
Belief in one's personal capabilities. Self-efficacy underlies people's faith in their ability to carry out a particular behaviour or produce a desired outcome.

Biological and evolutionary approaches to personality
Theories that suggest that important components of personality are inherited.

STUDY ALERT!

Remember that biological and evolutionary approaches focus on the way in which people's genetic heritage affects personality.

The results of the personality tests indicated that in major respects the twins were quite similar in personality, despite being separated at an early age. Moreover, certain traits were more heavily influenced by heredity than were others. For example, social potency (the degree to which a person assumes mastery and leadership roles in social situations) and traditionalism (the tendency to follow authority) had particularly strong genetic components, whereas achievement and social closeness had relatively weak genetic components (see Figure 3).

Some researchers contend that specific genes are related to personality. For example, people with a longer dopamine-4 receptor gene are more likely to be thrill seekers than are those without such a gene. These thrill seekers tend to be extroverted, impulsive, quick-tempered, and always in search of excitement and novel situations (Hamer et al., 1993; Zuckerman & Kuhlman, 2000).

Does the identification of specific genes linked to personality, coupled with the existence of temperaments from the time of birth, mean that we are destined to have certain types of personalities? Hardly. First, it is unlikely that any single gene is linked to a specific trait. For instance, the dopamine-4 receptor accounts for only around 10 percent of the variation in novelty seeking between different individuals. The rest of the variation is attributable to other genes and environmental factors (Keltikangas-Järvinen et al., 2004; Lahti et al., 2005).

FIGURE 3

The roots of personality. The percentages indicate the degree to which eleven personality characteristics reflect the influence of heredity.

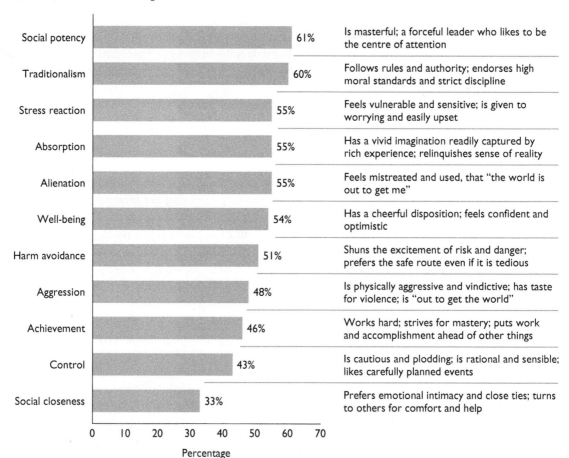

Social potency	61%	Is masterful; a forceful leader who likes to be the centre of attention
Traditionalism	60%	Follows rules and authority; endorses high moral standards and strict discipline
Stress reaction	55%	Feels vulnerable and sensitive; is given to worrying and easily upset
Absorption	55%	Has a vivid imagination readily captured by rich experience; relinquishes sense of reality
Alienation	55%	Feels mistreated and used, that "the world is out to get me"
Well-being	54%	Has a cheerful disposition; feels confident and optimistic
Harm avoidance	51%	Shuns the excitement of risk and danger; prefers the safe route even if it is tedious
Aggression	48%	Is physically aggressive and vindictive; has taste for violence; is "out to get the world"
Achievement	46%	Works hard; strives for mastery; puts work and accomplishment ahead of other things
Control	43%	Is cautious and plodding; is rational and sensible; likes carefully planned events
Social closeness	33%	Prefers emotional intimacy and close ties; turns to others for comfort and help

Percentage (0 10 20 30 40 50 60 70)

Source: Tellegen et al., 1988.

More importantly, genes interact with the environment. As we see in discussions of the heritability of intelligence and the nature-nurture issue, it is impossible to completely separate genetic factors from environmental factors. Although studies of identical twins raised in different environments are helpful, they are not definitive, because it is impossible to assess and control environmental factors fully. Furthermore, estimates of the influence of genetics are just that—estimates—and apply to groups, not individuals. Consequently, findings such as those shown in Figure 3 must be regarded as approximations.

Although an increasing number of personality theorists are taking biological and evolutionary factors into account, no comprehensive, unified theory that considers biological and evolutionary factors is widely accepted. Still, it is clear that certain personality traits have substantial genetic components, and that heredity and environment interact to determine personality (Ebstein, Benjamin, & Belmaker, 2003; Plomin et al., 2003; Bouchard, 2004).

Humanistic Approaches: The Uniqueness of You

Where, in all the approaches to personality that we have discussed, is an explanation for the saintliness of a Mother Teresa, the creativity of a Michelangelo, and the brilliance and perseverance of an Einstein? An understanding of such unique individuals—as well as more ordinary sorts of people who have some of the same attributes—comes from humanistic theory.

According to humanistic theorists, all the approaches to personality we have discussed share a fundamental misperception in their views of human nature. Instead of seeing people as controlled by unconscious, unseen forces (as do psychodynamic approaches), a set of stable traits (trait approaches), situational reinforcements and punishments (learning theory), or inherited factors (biological and evolutionary approaches), **humanistic approaches to personality** emphasize people's inherent goodness and their tendency to grow to higher levels of functioning. It is this conscious, self-motivated ability to change and improve, along with people's unique creative impulses, that humanistic theorists argue make up the core of personality.

Rogers and the Need for Self-Actualization

The major proponent of the humanistic point of view is Carl Rogers (1971). Along with other humanistic theorists, such as Abraham Maslow, Rogers maintains that all people have a fundamental need for *self-actualization,* a state of self-fulfillment in which people realize their highest potential in their own unique way. He further suggests that people develop a need for positive regard that reflects the desire to be loved and respected. Because others provide this positive regard, we grow dependent on them. We begin to see and judge ourselves through the eyes of other people, relying on their values and being preoccupied with what they think of us.

Have you ever wondered what your highest potential is? Have you ever asked yourself in what unique way will you fulfill your ultimate dreams and desires? Will it be as an NHL hockey player or as a pediatric nurse or as a happily married parent of three or all of the above? The beauty of self-actualization is that it encourages us to follow our own dreams, in our own unique way, ultimately achieving our highest potential.

According to Rogers, one outgrowth of placing importance on the opinions of others is that a conflict may grow between people's experiences and their *self-concepts*, the set of beliefs they hold about what they are like as individuals. If the discrepancies are minor, so are the consequences. But if the discrepancies are great, they will lead to psychological disturbances in daily functioning, such as the experience of frequent anxiety. For example, when the "ideal self," the person we would like to be, is significantly different from the "true self," who we are in reality, we experience anxiety and dissatisfaction.

Rogers suggests that one way of overcoming the discrepancy between experience and self-concept is through the receipt of unconditional positive regard from another person—a friend, a spouse, or a therapist. **Unconditional positive regard** refers to an attitude of acceptance and respect on the part of an observer, no matter what a person

Humanistic approaches to personality
Theories that emphasize people's innate goodness and desire to achieve higher levels of functioning.

Unconditional positive regard
An attitude of acceptance and respect on the part of an observer, no matter what a person says or does.

says or does. This acceptance, says Rogers, gives people the opportunity to evolve and grow both cognitively and emotionally and to develop more realistic self-concepts. You may have experienced the power of unconditional positive regard when you confided in someone, revealing embarrassing secrets because you knew the listener would still love and respect you, even after hearing the worst about you (Snyder, 2002; Marshall, 2007).

In contrast, *conditional positive regard* depends on your behaviour. In such cases, others withdraw their love and acceptance if you do something of which they don't approve. The result is a discrepancy between your true self and what others wish you would be, leading to anxiety and frustration (see Figure 4).

FIGURE 4

According to the humanistic view of Carl Rogers, people have a basic need to be loved and respected. If you receive unconditional positive regard from others, you will develop a more realistic self-concept; but if the response is conditional, it may lead to anxiety and frustration.

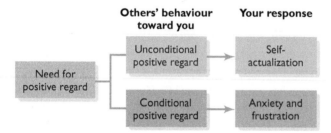

Comparing Approaches to Personality

In light of the multiple approaches we have discussed, you may be wondering which of the theories provides the most accurate description of personality. That is a question that cannot be answered precisely. Each theory is built on different assumptions and focuses on somewhat different aspects of personality (see Figure 5). Furthermore, there is no clear way to scientifically test the various approaches and their assumptions against one another. Given the complexity of every individual, it seems reasonable that personality can be viewed from a number of perspectives simultaneously (Pervin, 2003).

FIGURE 5

The multiple perspectives of personality.

Theoretical Approach and Major Theorists	Conscious versus Unconscious Determinants of Personality	Nature (Hereditary Factors) versus Nurture (Environmental Factors)	Free Will versus Determinism	Stability versus Modifiability
Psychodynamic (Freud, Jung, Horney, Adler)	Emphasizes the unconscious	Stresses innate, inherited structure of personality while emphasizing importance of childhood experience	Stresses determinism, the view that behaviour is directed and caused by factors outside one's control	Emphasizes the stability of characteristics throughout a person's life
Trait (Allport, Cattell, Eysenck)	Disregards both conscious and unconscious	Approaches vary	Stresses determinism, the view that behaviour is directed and caused by factors outside one's control	Emphasizes the stability of characteristics throughout a person's life
Learning (Skinner, Bandura)	Disregards both conscious and unconscious	Focuses on the environment	Stresses determinism, the view that behaviour is directed and caused by factors outside one's control	Stresses that personality remains flexible and resilient throughout one's life
Biological and Evolutionary (Tellegen)	Disregards both conscious and unconscious	Stresses the innate, inherited determinants of personality	Stresses determinism, the view that behaviour is directed and caused by factors outside one's control	Emphasizes the stability of characteristics throughout a person's life
Humanistic (Rogers, Maslow)	Stresses the conscious more than unconscious	Stresses the interaction between both nature and nurture	Stresses the freedom of individuals to make their own choices	Stresses that personality remains flexible and resilient throughout one's life

Evaluate

1. Carl's determination to succeed is the dominant force in all his activities and relationships. According to Gordon Allport's theory, this is an example of a _____ trait. In contrast, Cindy's fondness for old western movies is an example of a _____ trait.

2. Eysenck might describe a person who enjoys activities such as parties and hang-gliding as high on what trait?

3. Proponents of which approach to personality would be most likely to agree with the statement "Personality can be thought of as learned responses to a person's upbringing and environment"?

   a. Humanistic

   b. Biological and evolutionary

   c. Learning

   d. Trait

4. Bandura would rate a person who would make the statement, "I know I can't do it" as low on _____.

5. Which approach to personality emphasizes the innate goodness of people and their desire to grow?

   a. Humanistic

   b. Psychodynamic

   c. Learning

   d. Biological and evolutionary

Answers to Evaluate Questions

1. cardinal, secondary; 2. extroversion; 3. c; 4. self-efficacy; 5. a

Key Terms

biological and evolutionary approaches to personality	self-actualization	trait theory
humanistic approaches to personality	self-efficacy	traits
	social cognitive approaches to personality	unconditional positive regard

Assessing Personality: Determining What Makes Us Distinctive

LEARNING OBJECTIVES

LO4 **How can** we most accurately assess personality?
LO5 **What are** the major types of personality measures?

You have a need for other people to like and admire you.

You have a tendency to be critical of yourself.

You have a great deal of unused potential that you have not turned to your advantage.

Although you have some personality weaknesses, you generally are able to compensate for them.

Relating to members of the opposite sex has presented problems to you.

Although you appear to be disciplined and self-controlled to others, you tend to be anxious and insecure inside.

At times you have serious doubts about whether you have made the right decision or done the right thing.

You prefer a certain amount of change and variety and become dissatisfied when hemmed in by restrictions and limitations.

You do not accept others' statements without satisfactory proof.

You have found it unwise to be too frank in revealing yourself to others.

If you think these statements provide a surprisingly accurate account of your personality, you are not alone: Most college and university students think that these descriptions are tailored just to them. In fact, the statements were designed intentionally to be so vague that they apply to just about anyone (Forer, 1949; Russo, 1981).

The ease with which we can agree with such imprecise statements underscores the difficulty in coming up with accurate and meaningful assessments of people's personalities. Psychologists interested in assessing personality must be able to define the most meaningful ways of discriminating between one person's personality and another's. To do this, they use **psychological tests**, standard measures devised to assess behaviour objectively. With the results of such tests, psychologists can help people understand themselves better and make decisions about their lives. Psychological tests are also employed by researchers interested in the causes and consequences of personality (Aiken, 2000; Kaplan & Saccuzzo, 2001; Hambleton, 2006).

Like the assessments that seek to measure intelligence, all psychological tests must have reliability and validity. *Reliability* refers to the measurement consistency test. If a test is reliable, it yields the same result each time it is administered to a particular person or group. In contrast, unreliable tests give different results each time they are administered.

For meaningful conclusions to be drawn, tests also must be valid. Tests have *validity* when they actually measure what they are designed to measure. If a test is constructed to measure sociability, for instance, we need to know that it actually measures sociability, not some other trait.

Psychological tests
Standard measures devised to assess behaviour objectively; used by psychologists to help people make decisions about their lives and understand more about themselves.

Finally, psychological tests are based on *norms*, standards of test performance that permit the comparison of one person's score on a test with the scores of others who have taken the same test. For example, a norm permits test-takers who have received a particular score on a test to know that they have scored in the top 10 percent of all those who have taken the test.

Norms are established by administering a particular test to a large number of people and determining the typical scores. It is then possible to compare a single person's score with the scores of the group, providing a comparative measure of test performance against the performance of others who have taken the test.

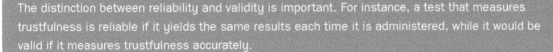

Exploring DIVERSITY

Should Race and Ethnicity Be Used to Establish Norms?

The passions of politics may confront the objectivity of science when test norms are established, at least in the realm of standardized tests that are meant to predict future job performance. In fact, controversy has developed around the question of whether different norms should be established for members of various racial and ethnic groups (Manly, 2005, 2006).

In Canada, workers are protected by the Human Rights Code. The code governs equal rights and treatment of Canadian workers—without discrimination. There are fifteen grounds for discrimination under the code, including: race, ancestry, place of origin, colour, ethnic origin, and citizenship (Ontario Human Rights Commission, 2008).

Despite the progressive intent of the Human Rights Code, standardized testing lags behind anti-discriminatory laws in Canada. Separate norms for minority groups on most standardized tests have yet to be developed as evidenced by a report prepared by the Public Service Commission (Gruber, 2000).

This report examined the use of standardized assessment tests for designated minorities (i.e., Aboriginal peoples, persons with disabilities, visible minorities, and women). The applicability of six standardized assessment tests for minority groups was examined. Tests included: (1) Values Scale, a measure of work-related values, (2) Jackson Vocational Interest Survey, a measure of occupational interest, (3) Myers-Briggs Type Indicator, a measure of personality, (4) NEO Personality Inventory-Revised, a measure of personality, (5) Multidimensional Aptitude Battery-II, a measure of aptitude, and (6) Test d'aptitudes informatisé, a measure of aptitude. Results indicated that all six standardized assessments had limited applicability to minority groups in Canada at this time. For example, none of the tests had a separate set of norms for Aboriginal peoples, persons with disabilities, visible minorities, or women (Gruber, 2000).

Our American neighbours have experienced similar issues with the U.S. government's fifty-year-old General Aptitude Test Battery, a test that measures a broad range of abilities from eye-hand coordination to reading proficiency. The problem that sparked the controversy is that African Americans and Hispanics tend to score lower on the test, on average, than do members of other groups. The lower scores often are due to a lack of prior relevant experience and job opportunities, which in turn has been due to prejudice and discrimination.

To promote the employment of minority racial groups, the U.S. government developed a separate set of norms for African Americans and Hispanics. Rather than using the pool of all people who took the test, the scores of African American and Hispanic applicants were compared only with the scores of other African Americans and Hispanics. Consequently, a Hispanic who scored in the top 20 percent of the Hispanics taking the test was considered to have performed equivalently to a white job applicant who scored in the top 20 percent of the whites who took the test, even though the absolute score of the Hispanic might be lower than that of the white applicant.

Critics of the adjusted norming system suggest that such a procedure discriminates in favour of certain racial and ethnic groups at the expense of others, thereby fanning the flames of racial bigotry. The practice was challenged legally, and with the passage of the Civil Rights Act in 1991, race norming on the General Aptitude Test Battery was discontinued (Galef, 2001).

(continued)

However, proponents of race norming continue to argue that norming procedures that take race into account are an affirmative action tool that simply permits minority job seekers to be placed on an equal footing with white job seekers. Furthermore, a panel of the U.S. National Academy of Sciences concurred with the practice of adjusting test norms. It suggested that the unadjusted test norms are not terribly useful in predicting job performance, and that they would tend to screen out otherwise qualified minority-group members. And a U.S. federal court opinion ruled in 2001 that using "bands" of score ranges was not necessarily discriminatory, unless the bands were designed on the basis of race (Fleming, 2000; Seventh U.S. Circuit Court of Appeals, 2001).

Job testing is not the only area in which issues arise regarding norms and the meaning of test scores. The issue of how to treat racial differences in IQ scores is also controversial and divisive. Clearly, race norming raises profound and intense feelings that may come into conflict with scientific objectivity (Leiter & Leiter, 2003; Ontario Human Rights Commission, 2008; Davis, 2009).

The issue of establishing norms for tests is further complicated by the existence of a wide array of personality measures and approaches to assessment. We consider some of these measures, which have a variety of characteristics and purposes, next.

The establishment of appropriate norms is not a simple endeavour. For instance, the specific group that is employed to determine norms for a test has a profound effect on the way an individual's performance is evaluated. In fact, as we discuss next, the process of establishing norms can take on political overtones.

Self-Report Measures of Personality

If someone wanted to assess your personality, one possible approach would be to carry out an extensive interview with you to determine the most important events in your childhood, your social relationships, and your successes and failures. Obviously, though, such a technique would take extraordinary time and effort.

It is also unnecessary. Just as physicians draw only a small sample of your blood to test it, psychologists can use **self-report measures** that ask people about a relatively small sample of their behaviour. This sampling of self-report data is then used to infer the presence of particular personality characteristics. For example, a researcher who was interested in assessing a person's orientation to life might administer the questionnaire shown in Figure 1. Although the questionnaire consists of only a few questions, the answers can be used to generalize about personality characteristics. (Try it yourself!)

Colleges and universities often use self-report personality tests to help students discover areas of strength. For example, the Myers-Briggs Type Indicator (MBTI) helps students determine if they are better suited to studying alone (e.g., introvert) or in groups (e.g., extrovert). True Colors International is another self-report personality measure for students. An added benefit of this measure is the online resources (e.g., online assessment, webcasts, and research articles) available for students on the True Colors International website (True Colors International, 2010). A downside of using self-administered questionnaires, such as MBTI and True Colors is limited reliability and validity.

One of the best examples of a self-report measure, and one of the most frequently used personality tests, is the **Minnesota Multiphasic Personality Inventory-2 (MMPI-2)**. Although the original purpose of this measure was to identify people with specific sorts of psychological difficulties, it has been found to predict a variety of other behaviours. For instance, MMPI-2 scores have been shown to be good predictors of whether college and university students will marry within ten years and will get an advanced degree. Police departments use the test to measure whether police officers are likely to use their weapons. Psychologists in Russia administer a modified form of the MMPI to their astronauts and Olympic athletes (Butcher, 1995, 2005; Craig, 1999; Friedman et al., 2000; Weis, Crockett, & Vieth, 2004).

Self-report measures
A method of gathering data about people by asking them questions about a sample of their behaviour.

Minnesota Multiphasic Personality Inventory-2 (MMPI-2)
A widely used self-report test that identifies people with psychological difficulties and is employed to predict some everyday behaviours.

FIGURE 1

The Life Orientation Test. Try this scale by indicating the degree to which you agree with each of the ten statements, using the scale from 0 to 4 for each item. Try to be as accurate as possible. There are no right or wrong answers.

The Life Orientation Test

Use the following scale to answer the items below:

0	1	2	3	4
Strongly disagree	Disagree	Neutral	Agree	Strongly agree

1. In uncertain times, I usually expect the best.
2. It's easy for me to relax.
3. If something can go wrong for me, it will.
4. I'm always optimistic about my future.
5. I enjoy my friends a lot.
6. It's important for me to keep busy.
7. I hardly ever expect things to go my way.
8. I don't get upset too easily.
9. I rarely count on good things happening to me.
10. Overall, I expect more good things to happen to me than bad.

SCORING.

First, reverse your answers to questions 3, 7, and 9. Do this by changing a 0 to a 4, a 1 to a 3, a 3 to a 1, and a 4 to a 0 (answers of 2 stay as 2). Then sum the reversed scores, and add them to the scores you gave to questions 1, 4, and 10. (Ignore questions 2, 5, 6, and 8, which are filler items.)

The total score you get is a measure of a particular orientation to life: your degree of optimism. The higher your scores, the more positive and hopeful you generally are about life. For comparison purposes the average score for college and university students is 14.3, according to the results of a study by Scheier, Carver, and Bridges (1994). People with a higher degree of optimism generally deal with stress better than do those with lower scores.

Source: Adapted from Scheier, Carver and Bridges, 1994.

The test consists of a series of 567 items to which a person responds "true," "false," or "cannot say." The questions cover a variety of issues, ranging from mood ("I feel useless at times") to opinions ("People should try to understand their dreams") to physical and psychological health ("I am bothered by an upset stomach several times a week" and "I have strange and peculiar thoughts").

There are no right or wrong answers. Instead, interpretation of the results rests on the pattern of responses. The test yields scores on ten separate scales, plus three scales meant to measure the validity of the respondent's answers. For example, there is a "lie scale" that indicates when people are falsifying their responses in order to present themselves more favourably (through items such as "I can't remember ever having a bad night's sleep") (Butcher, 2005; Stein & Graham, 2005; Sellborn, Fischler, & Ben-Porath, 2007).

How did the authors of the MMPI-2 determine what specific patterns of responses indicate? The procedure they used is typical of personality test construction—a process known as **test standardization**. To create the test, the test authors asked groups of psychiatric patients with a specific diagnosis, such as depression or schizophrenia, to complete a large number of items. They then determined which items best differentiated members of those groups from a comparison group of normal participants, and included those specific items in the final version of the test. By systematically carrying out this procedure on groups with different diagnoses, the test authors were able to devise a number of subscales that identified different forms of abnormal behaviour (see Figure 2).

Test standardization

A technique used to validate questions in personality tests by studying the responses of people with known diagnoses.

FIGURE 2

A profile on the MMPI-2 of a person who suffers from obsessional anxiety, social withdrawal, and delusional thinking.

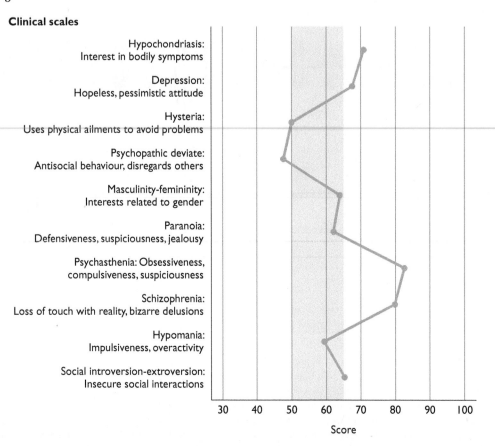

Clinical scales

Source: Based on data from Halgin & Whitbourne, 1994, p. 72, and Minnesota Multiphasic Personality Inventory-2. Copyright © by the Regents of the University of Minnesota, 1942, 1943 (renewed 1970, 1989).

When the MMPI-2 is used for the purpose for which it was devised—identification of personality disorders—it does a reasonably good job. However, like other personality tests, it presents an opportunity for abuse. For instance, employers who use it as a screening tool for job applicants may interpret the results improperly, relying too heavily on the results of individual scales instead of taking into account the overall patterns of results, which require skilled interpretation. Furthermore, critics point out that the individual scales overlap, making their interpretation difficult. In sum, although the MMPI-2 remains the most widely used personality test and has been translated into more than 100 different languages, it must be used with caution (Valsiner, Diriwächter, & Sauck, 2005; Ben-Porath & Archer, 2008).

STUDY ALERT!

In projective tests such as the Rorschach, researchers present an ambiguous stimulus and ask a person to describe or tell a story about it. They then use the responses to make inferences about personality.

☐ Projective Methods

If you were shown the shape presented in Figure 3 and asked what it represented to you, you might not think that your impressions would mean very much. But to a psychodynamic theoretician, your responses to such an ambiguous figure would provide valuable clues to the state of your unconscious, and ultimately to your general personality characteristics.

This inkblot is similar to the type used in the Rorschach personality test. What do you see in it?

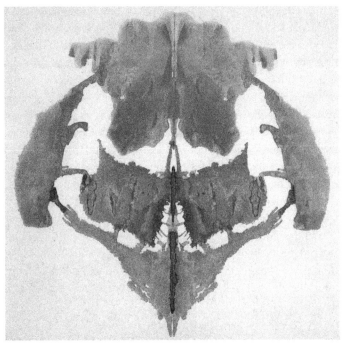

The shape in the figure is representative of inkblots used in **projective personality tests**, in which a person is shown an ambiguous stimulus and asked to describe it or tell a story about it. The responses are considered to be "projections" of the individual's personality.

The best-known projective test is the **Rorschach test**. Devised by Swiss psychiatrist Hermann Rorschach (1924), the test involves showing a series of symmetrical stimuli, similar to the one in Figure 3, to people who are then asked what the figures represent to them. Their responses are recorded, and through a complex set of clinical judgments on the part of the examiner, people are classified by their personality type. For instance, respondents who see a bear in one inkblot are thought to have a strong degree of emotional control, according to the scoring guidelines developed by Rorschach (Weiner, 2004b; Silverstein, 2007).

The **Thematic Apperception Test (TAT)** is another well-known projective test. The TAT consists of a series of pictures about which a person is asked to write a story. The stories are then used to draw inferences about the writer's personality characteristics (Weiner, 2004a; Langan-Fox & Grant, 2006).

Tests with stimuli as ambiguous as those used in the Rorschach and TAT require particular skill and care in their interpretation—too much, in many critics' estimation. The Rorschach in particular has been criticized for requiring too much inference on the part of the examiner, and attempts to standardize scoring have frequently failed. Furthermore, many critics complain that the Rorschach does not provide much valid information about underlying personality traits. Despite such problems, both the Rorschach and the TAT are widely used, particularly in clinical settings, and their proponents suggest that their reliability and validity are great enough to provide useful inferences about personality (Wood et al., 2003; Garb et al., 2005; Society for Personality Assessment, 2005).

Projective personality tests
A test in which a person is shown an ambiguous stimulus and asked to describe it or tell a story about it.

Rorschach test
A test that involves showing a series of symmetrical visual stimuli to people who then are asked what the figures represent to them.

Thematic Apperception Test (TAT)
A test consisting of a series of pictures about which a person is asked to write a story.

Behavioural Assessment

If you were a psychologist subscribing to a learning approach to personality, you would be likely to object to the indirect nature of projective tests. Instead, you would be more apt to use **behavioural assessment**—direct measures of an individual's behaviour designed to describe characteristics indicative of personality. As with observational research, behavioural assessment may be carried out naturalistically by observing people in their own settings: in the workplace, at home, or in school. In other cases, behavioural assessment occurs in the laboratory, under controlled conditions in which a psychologist sets up a situation and observes an individual's behaviour (Ramsay, Reynolds, & Kamphaus, 2002; Gladwell, 2004; Miller & Leffard, 2007).

Regardless of the setting in which behaviour is observed, an effort is made to ensure that behavioural assessment is carried out objectively, quantifying behaviour as much as possible. For example, an observer may record the number of social contacts a person initiates, the number of questions asked, or the number of aggressive acts. Another method is to measure the duration of events: the duration of a temper tantrum in a child, the length of a conversation, the amount of time spent working, or the time spent in cooperative behaviour.

Behavioural assessment is particularly appropriate for observing—and eventually remedying —specific behavioural difficulties, such as shyness in children. It provides a means of assessing the specific nature and incidence of a problem and subsequently allows psychologists to determine whether intervention techniques have been successful.

Behavioural assessment techniques based on learning theories of personality have also made important contributions to the treatment of certain kinds of psychological difficulties. Indeed, the knowledge of normal personality provided by the various personality theories has led to significant advances in our understanding and treatment of both physical and psychological disorders.

Behavioural assessment
Direct measures of an individual's behaviour used to describe personality characteristics.

Becoming an Informed Consumer of Psychology

Assessing Personality Assessments

Wanted: People with "kinetic energy," "emotional maturity," and the ability to "deal with large numbers of people in a fairly chaotic situation."

Although this job description may seem most appropriate for the job of cohost of *Wheel of Fortune,* in actuality it is part of an advertisement for managers for American MultiCinema's (AMC) theatres. To find people with such qualities, AMC has developed a battery of personality measures for job applicants. In developing its own tests, AMC joined scores of companies, ranging from General Motors to Microsoft, that employ personality tests to help with hiring decisions (Dentzer, 1986; Hogan, Hogan, & Roberts, 1996; Poundstone, 2003; Varela et al., 2004).

For example, potential Microsoft employees in the U.S. have been asked brain-teasers like "If you had to remove one of the 50 U.S. states, which would it be?" (Hint: First define "remove." If you mean the death of everyone in the state, suggest a low-population state. If you mean quitting the country, then go for an outlying-state like Alaska or Hawaii.) Other employers ask questions that are even more vague ("Describe November"). With such questions, it's not always clear that the tests are formally reliable or valid (McGinn, 2003).

Before relying too heavily on the results of personality testing as a potential employee, employer, or consumer of testing services, you should keep several points in mind:

- *Find out what aspects of personality best predict job success.* Standard personality measures can only be used in employment testing if they can be shown to predict job performance. Consult the literature and/or an industrial organizational psychologist to help determine which personality characteristics will best predict performance in the specific job you are applying for. For example, personality characteristics, such as conscientiousness, have been shown to predict job performance in a variety of occupations. In contrast, other personality characteristics, such as extroversion only determine job success in vocations requiring social interactions (e.g., salesperson, manager) (Barrick & Mount, 1991; Hurtz, 2000).

- *Understand what the test claims to measure.* Standard personality measures are accompanied by information that discusses how the test was developed, to whom it is most applicable, and how the results should be interpreted. Read any explanations of the test; they will help you understand the results.

- *Base no decision only on the results of any one test.* Test results should be interpreted in the context of other information—academic records, social interests, and home and community activities.

- *Remember that test results are not always accurate.* The results may be in error; the test may be unreliable or invalid. You may, for example, have had a "bad day" when you took the test, or the person scoring and interpreting the test may have made a mistake. You should not place too much significance on the results of a single administration of any test.

In sum, it is important to keep in mind the complexity of human behaviour—particularly your own. No single test can provide an understanding of the intricacies of someone's personality without considering a good deal more information than can be provided in a single testing session (Gladwell, 2004; Paul, 2004; Hogan, Davies, & Hogan, 2007).

Evaluate

1. _____ is the consistency of a personality test; _____ is the ability of a test to actually measure what it is designed to measure.

2. _____ are standards used to compare scores of different people taking the same test.

3. Tests such as the MMPI-2, in which a small sample of behaviour is assessed to determine larger patterns, are examples of

   a. Cross-sectional tests

   b. Projective tests

   c. Achievement tests

   d. Self-report tests

4. A person shown a picture and asked to make up a story about it would be taking a _____ personality test.

Answers to Evaluate Questions

1. reliability, validity; 2. norms; 3. d; 4. projective

Key Terms

behavioural assessment	projective personality tests	self-report measures
Minnesota Multiphasic Personality Inventory-2 (MMPI-2)	psychological tests	test standardization
	Rorschach test	Thematic Apperception Test (TAT)

Epilogue

Source: © Greg Hindsdale/Corbis.

We have discussed the different ways in which psychologists have interpreted the development and structure of personality. The perspectives we examined ranged from Freud's analysis of personality based primarily on internal, unconscious factors to the externally based view championed by learning theorists of personality as a learned set of traits and actions. We also noted that there are many ways to interpret personality; by no means does a consensus exist on what the key traits are that are central to personality.

Recap/Rethink

Module 31: Psychodynamic Approaches to Personality

Recap

LO1   How do psychologists define and use the concept of personality?

- Personality is the pattern of enduring characteristics that produce consistency and individuality in a given person.

LO2   What do the theories of Freud and his successors tell us about the structure and development of personality?

- According to psychodynamic explanations of personality, much behaviour is caused by parts of personality that are found in the unconscious and of which we are unaware.
- Freud's psychoanalytic theory, one of the psychodynamic approaches, suggests that personality is composed of the id, the ego, and the superego. The id is the unorganized, inborn part of personality whose purpose is to immediately reduce tensions relating to hunger, sex, aggression, and other primitive impulses. The ego restrains instinctual energy to maintain the safety of the individual and help the person be a member of society. The superego represents the rights and wrongs of society and includes the conscience.
- Freud's psychoanalytic theory suggests that personality develops through a series of psychosexual stages, each of which is associated with a primary biological function.
- Defence mechanisms, according to Freudian theory, are unconscious strategies with which people reduce anxieties relating to impulses from the id.
- Neo-Freudian psychoanalytic theorists built on Freud's work, although they placed greater emphasis on the role of the ego and paid more attention to the role of social factors in determining behaviour.

Rethink

1. Can you think of ways in which Freud's theories of unconscious motivations are commonly used in popular culture? How accurately do you think such popular uses of Freudian theories reflect Freud's ideas?

2. *From the perspective of an advertising executive:* How might you use Jung's concept of archetypes in designing your advertisements? Which of the archetypes would you use?

Module 32: Trait, Learning, Biological and Evolutionary, and Humanistic Approaches to Personailty

Recap

LO3   What are the major aspects of trait, learning, biological and evolutionary, and humanistic approaches to personality?

- Trait approaches have been used to identify relatively enduring dimensions along which people differ from one another—dimensions known as traits.
- Learning approaches to personality concentrate on observable behaviour. To a strict learning theorist, personality is the sum of learned responses to the external environment.
- Biological and evolutionary approaches to personality focus on the way in which personality characteristics are inherited.
- Humanistic approaches emphasize the inherent goodness of people. They consider the core of personality in terms of a person's ability to change and improve.
- The major personality approaches differ substantially from one another; that may reflect both their focus on different aspects of personality and the overall complexity of personality

Rethink

1. If personality traits are merely descriptive and not explanatory, of what use are they? Can assigning a trait to a person be harmful—or helpful? Why or why not?

2. *From the perspective of a substance abuse counsellor:* Many alcohol and substance abuse programs attempt to raise their clients' sense of self-worth by communicating "feel-good messages." Do you expect these messages to be beneficial or detrimental to a client? Why or why not? Can you think of alternative ways to assist and support individuals who have a drug or alcohol addiction?

3. Do you think people should attempt to override their first judgments about others' personalities and make more thoughtful judgments? Why and why not? Why would the ability to judge personality characteristics quickly be more valuable from an evolutionary perspective?

Module 33: Assessing Personality: Determining What Makes Us Distinctive

Recap

LO4 How can we most accurately assess personality?

- Psychological tests such as the MMPI-2 are standard assessment tools that measure behaviour objectively. They must be reliable (measuring what they are trying to measure consistently) and valid (measuring what they are supposed to measure).

LO5 What are the major types of personality measures?

- Self-report measures ask people about a sample range of their behaviours. These reports are used to infer the presence of particular personality characteristics.
- Projective personality tests (such as the Rorschach and the Thematic Apperception Test) present an ambiguous stimulus; the test administrator infers information about the test-taker from his or her responses.
- Behavioural assessment is based on the principles of learning theory. It employs direct measurement of an individual's behaviour to determine characteristics related to personality.

Rethink

1. Should personality tests be used for personnel decisions? Should they be used for other social purposes, such as identifying individuals at risk for certain types of personality disorders?

2. *From the perspective of a politician:* Imagine that you had to vote on a law that would require institutions and organizations to perform race norming procedures on standardized performance tests. Would you support such a law? Why or why not? In addition to race, should norming procedures take other factors into account? Which ones and why?

3. Might a personality test have indicated Madoff's criminal intentions? Why or why not?

CHAPTER 11
Health Psychology: Stress, Coping, and Well-Being

Source: © JGI/Jamie Grill LLC RF.

Key Concepts for Chapter 11

MODULE 34 Stress and Coping

LO1 How is health psychology a union between medicine and psychology?

LO2 What is stress, how does it affect us, and how can we best cope with it?

Stress: Reacting to Threat and Challenge

Coping with Stress

MODULE 35 Psychological Aspects of Illness and Well-Being

LO3 How do psychological factors affect health-related problems such as coronary heart disease, cancer, and smoking?

The A's, B's, and D's of Coronary Heart Disease

Psychological Aspects of Cancer

Smoking

MODULE 36 Health and Wellness

LO4 How do our interactions with physicians affect our health and compliance with medical treatment?

LO5 How does a sense of well-being develop?

Following Medical Advice

Well-Being and Happiness

Applying Psychology in the Real World: *Does Money Buy Happiness?*

Prologue

Never a Moment's Rest

Source: © JGI/Jamie Grill LLC RF.

Louis Denby's day began badly: He slept through his alarm and had to skip breakfast to catch the bus to campus. Then, when he went to the library to catch up on the reading he had to do before taking a test the next day, the one article he needed was missing. The librarian told him that replacing it would take 24 hours. Feeling frustrated, he walked to the computer lab to print out the paper he had completed at home the night before. The computer wouldn't read his USB flash drive. Louis searched for someone to help him, but he was unable to find anyone who knew any more about computers than he did. It was only 9:42 a.m., and Louis had a wracking headache. Apart from that pain, he was conscious of only one feeling: stress (Feldman, 2010).

It's not hard to understand why Louis Denby was experiencing stress. For people like him—and that probably includes most of us—the intensity of juggling multiple roles leads to feelings of never having sufficient time and, in some cases, takes a toll on both physical and psychological well-being.

Stress and how we cope with it have long been central topics of interest for psychologists. However, in recent years the focus has broadened as psychology has come to view stress in the broader context of one of psychology's newer subfields: health psychology. **Health psychology** investigates the psychological factors related to wellness and illness, including the prevention, diagnosis, and treatment of medical problems. Health psychologists investigate the effects of psychological factors such as stress on illness. They examine the psychological principles underlying treatments for disease and illness. They also study prevention: how healthier behaviour can help people avoid and reduce health problems such as stress and heart disease.

Health psychologists are among the primary investigators in a growing field called **psychoneuroimmunology (PNI)**, the study of the relationship among psychological factors, the immune system, and the brain. PNI has led to discoveries such as the existence of an association between a person's emotional state and the success of the immune system in fighting disease (Dickerson et al., 2004; Kemeny, 2007; Byrne-Davis & Vedhara, 2008).

Health psychologists view the mind and the body as two parts of a whole human being that cannot be considered independently. Previously, disease was seen as a purely biological phenomenon, and psychological factors were of little interest to most healthcare workers. In the early twentieth century, the primary causes of death were short-term infections from which one either rapidly recovered—or died. Now, however, the major causes of death, such as heart disease, cancer, and diabetes, are chronic illnesses that pose significant psychological issues because they often cannot be cured and may linger for years (Bishop, 2005; Rotan & Ospina-Kammerer, 2007).

Advances in health psychology have had an impact across a variety of disciplines and professions. For instance, healthcare professionals such as physicians and nurses, social workers, dieticians, pharmacists, occupational therapists, and even clergy are increasingly likely to receive training in health psychology.

In the three modules that follow, we discuss the ways in which psychological factors affect health. We first focus on the causes and consequences of stress as well as on the means of coping with it. Next, we explore the psychological aspects of several major health problems, including heart disease, cancer, and ailments resulting from smoking. Finally, we examine the ways in which patient-physician interactions influence our health and offer suggestions for increasing people's compliance with recommendations about behaviour that will improve their well-being.

Health psychology
The branch of psychology that investigates the psychological factors related to wellness and illness, including the prevention, diagnosis, and treatment of medical problems.

Psychoneuroimmunology (PNI)
The study of the relationship among psychological factors, the immune system, and the brain.

Stress and Coping

LEARNING OBJECTIVES

LO1   **How is** health psychology a union between medicine and psychology?

LO2   **What is** stress, how does it affect us, and how can we best cope with it?

Anthony Lepre started feeling awful almost as soon as the country was put on high alert for a terrorist attack. . . . He awoke in the middle of the night short of breath, his heart pounding. And the sound of his telephone seemed a sure sign of bad news. By midweek, he was rushing off to Costco to stock up on fruit juice, bottled water, peanut butter, canned tuna, "and extra food for my cats Monster, Monkey and Spike." He also picked up a first-aid kit, six rolls of duct tape, and a bulk package of plastic wrap to seal his windows. "The biggest problem was that I felt helpless," he says, "completely powerless over the situation" (Cowley, 2003, pp. 43–44).

Stress: Reacting to Threat and Challenge

Most of us need little introduction to the phenomenon of **stress**, people's response to events that threaten or challenge them. Whether it is a paper or an exam deadline, a family problem, or even the ongoing threat of a terrorist attack, life is full of circumstances and events, known as stressors, which produce threats to our well-being. Even pleasant events—such as planning a party or beginning a sought-after job—can produce stress, although negative events result in greater detrimental consequences than do positive ones.

All of us face stress in our lives. Some health psychologists believe that daily life actually involves a series of repeated sequences of perceiving a threat, considering ways to cope with it, and ultimately adapting to the threat, with greater or lesser success. Although adaptation is often minor and occurs without our awareness, adaptation requires a major effort when stress is more severe or longer lasting. Ultimately, our attempts to overcome stress may produce biological and psychological responses that result in health problems (Boyce & Ellis, 2005; Dolbier, Smith, & Steinhardt, 2007).

> ### STUDY ALERT!
> Remember the distinction between stressors and stress, which can be tricky: stressors (like an exam) cause stress (the physiological and psychological reaction that comes from the exam).

The Nature of Stressors: My Stress Is Your Pleasure

Stress is a very personal thing. Although certain kinds of events, such as the death of a loved one or participation in military combat, are universally stressful, other situations may or may not be stressful to a particular person (Affleck et al., 1994; Krohne, 1996; Robert-McComb, 2001).

Consider, for instance, bungee jumping. Some people would find jumping off a bridge while attached to a slender rubber tether extremely stressful. However, there are individuals who see such an activity as challenging and fun-filled. Whether bungee jumping is stressful depends in part, then, on a person's perception of the activity.

Stress

A person's response to events that are threatening or challenging.

For people to consider an event stressful, they must perceive it as threatening and must lack the resources to deal with it effectively. Consequently, the same event may at some times be stressful and at other times provoke no stressful reaction at all. A young man may experience stress when he is turned down for a date—if he attributes the refusal to his unattractiveness or unworthiness. But if he attributes it to some factor unrelated to his self-esteem, such as a previous commitment by the woman he asked, the experience of being refused may create no stress at all. Hence, a person's interpretation of events plays an important role in the determination of what is stressful (Folkman & Moskowitz, 2000; Giacobbi, Jr., et al., 2004; Friborg et al., 2006).

Categorizing Stressors

What kinds of events tend to be seen as stressful? There are three general types of stressors: cataclysmic events, personal stressors, and background stressors.

Cataclysmic events are strong stressors that occur suddenly and typically affect many people simultaneously. Disasters such as tornadoes and plane crashes, as well as terrorist attacks, are examples of cataclysmic events that can affect hundreds or thousands of people simultaneously.

Although it might seem that cataclysmic events would produce potent, lingering stress, in many cases they do not. In fact, cataclysmic events involving natural disasters may produce less stress in the long run than do events that initially are not as devastating. One reason is that natural disasters have a clear resolution. Once they are over, people can look to the future knowing that the worst is behind them. Moreover, the stress induced by cataclysmic events is shared by others who also experienced the disaster. This permits people to offer one another social support and a firsthand understanding of the difficulties others are going through (Hobfoll et al., 1996; Benight, 2004; Yesilyaprak, Kisac, & Sanlier, 2007).

In contrast, terrorist attacks like the one on the World Trade Center in New York City in 2001 are cataclysmic events that produce considerable stress. Terrorist attacks are deliberate, and victims (and observers) know that future attacks are likely. Government warnings in the form of heightened terror alerts may further increase an individual's stress levels as described in this Module's opener about Anthony Lepre (Murphy, Wismar, & Freeman, 2003; Laugharne, Janca, & Widiger, 2007).

The second major category of stressor is the personal stressor. **Personal stressors** include major life events such as the death of a parent or spouse, the loss of one's job, a major personal failure, or even something positive such as getting married. Typically, personal stressors produce an immediate major reaction that soon tapers off. For example, stress arising from the death of a loved one tends to be greatest just after the time of death, but people begin to feel less stress and are better able to cope with the loss after the passage of time.

Some victims of major catastrophes and severe personal stressors experience **posttraumatic stress disorder (PTSD)** in which a person has experienced a significantly stressful event that has long-lasting effects that may include re-experiencing the event in vivid flashbacks or dreams. An episode of PTSD may be triggered by an otherwise

Canadians returning from military service in Afghanistan are at considerable risk for posttraumatic stress disorder (PTSD), as well as other mental health problems.

Source: Corporal Shilo Adamson, Canadian Armed Forces Combat Camera. © 2010 DND-MDN Canada.

Cataclysmic events
Strong stressors that occur suddenly and typically affect many people at once (e.g., natural disasters).

Personal stressors
Major life events, such as the death of a family member, which have immediate consequences that generally fade with time.

Posttraumatic stress disorder (PTSD)
A phenomenon in which victims of major catastrophes or strong personal stressors feel long-lasting effects that may include re-experiencing the event in vivid flashbacks or dreams.

innocent stimulus, such as the sound of a honking horn, which leads someone to re-experience a past event that produced considerable stress.

Canadians returning from military service in Afghanistan are at considerable risk for posttraumatic stress disorder (PTSD) as well as other mental health problems. So much so that Canada's military surgeon general has recruited 450 mental health experts to treat traumatized soldiers battling addiction, depression, and PTSD (McLauchlin, 2006; CTV.ca, 2008).

Terrorist attacks produce high incidences of PTSD. For example, 11 percent of people in New York City had some form of PTSD in the months after the September 11 terrorist attacks. But the responses varied significantly with a resident's proximity to the attacks, as illustrated in Figure 1; the closer someone lived to ground zero, the greater the likelihood of PTSD (Susser, Herman, & Aaron, 2002). Furthermore, those who have experienced child abuse or rape, rescue workers facing overwhelming situations, and victims of sudden natural disaster or accidents that produce feelings of helplessness and shock may also suffer from PTSD (Hoge et al., 2004; Ozer & Weiss, 2004; Schnurr & Cozza, 2004; Marshall et al., 2007).

Symptoms of posttraumatic stress disorder include re-experiencing the event in flashbacks or dreams, emotional numbing, sleep difficulties, problems relating to other people, alcohol and drug abuse, and—in some cases—suicide. In the last 12 years that Canadians have fought in Afghanistan, there have been more military suicides than Armed Forces members killed in Afghanistan (Edmonton Sun, 2015).

FIGURE 1

The closer people lived to the site of the World Trade Center terrorist attack in New York City, the greater the rate of posttraumatic stress disorder.

Source: Map by Cleo Vilett, from Susser, E. S., Herman, D. B., & Aaron, B. (2002, August). Combating the terror of terrorism. *Scientific American*, p. 74. Reprinted by permission of Cleo Vilett.

Background stressors ("daily hassles") are the third major category of stressors. Exemplified by standing in a long line at a bank and getting stuck in a traffic jam, daily hassles are the minor irritations of life that we all face time and time again. Another type of background stressor is a long-term, chronic problem, such as experiencing dissatisfaction with school or a job, being in an unhappy relationship, or living in crowded quarters without privacy (Weinstein et al., 2004; McIntyre, Korn, & Matsuo, 2008).

By themselves, daily hassles do not require much coping or even a response on the part of the individual, although they certainly produce unpleasant emotions and moods. Yet daily hassles add up—and ultimately they may take as great a toll as a single, more stressful incident does. In fact, the *number* of daily hassles people face is associated with psychological symptoms and health problems such as flu, sore throat, and backaches.

The flip side of hassles is *uplifts*, the minor positive events that make us feel good—even if only temporarily. As indicated in Figure 2, uplifts range from relating well to a companion to finding one's surroundings pleasing. What is especially intriguing about uplifts is that they are associated with people's psychological health in just the opposite way that hassles are: The greater the number of uplifts people experienced, the fewer negative psychological symptoms people later report (Chamberlain & Zika, 1990; Ravindran et al., 2002; Jain, Mills, & Von Känel, 2007).

The High Cost of Stress

Stress can produce both biological and psychological consequences. Often the most immediate reaction to stress is a biological one. Exposure to stressors generates a rise in hormone secretions by the adrenal glands, an increase in heart rate and blood pressure, and changes in how well the skin conducts electrical impulses. On a short-term basis, these responses may be adaptive because they produce an "emergency reaction" in which the body prepares to defend itself through activation of the sympathetic nervous system. Those responses may allow more effective coping with the stressful situation (Akil & Morano, 1996; McEwen, 1998).

However, continued exposure to stress results in a decline in the body's overall level of biological functioning because of the constant secretion of stress-related hormones. Over time, stressful reactions can promote deterioration of body tissues such as blood vessels and the heart. Ultimately, we become more susceptible to disease as our ability to fight off infection is lowered (Brydon et al., 2004; Dean-Borenstein, 2007; Ellins et al, 2008).

Furthermore, an entire class of physical problems known as **psychophysiological disorders** often result from or are worsened by stress. Once referred to as psychosomatic disorders (a term dropped because people assumed that the disorders were somehow unreal), *psychophysiological disorders* are actual medical problems that are influenced by an interaction of psychological, emotional, and physical difficulties. The more common psychophysiological disorders range from major problems such as high blood pressure to usually less serious conditions, such as headaches, backaches, skin rashes, indigestion, fatigue, and constipation. Stress has even been linked to the common cold (Cohen et al., 2003; Andrasik, 2006).

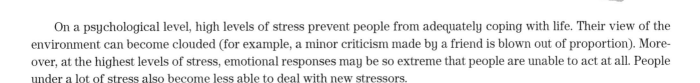

STUDY ALERT!

Remember the three categories of stressors—cataclysmic events, personal stressors, and background stressors—and that they produce different levels of stress.

On a psychological level, high levels of stress prevent people from adequately coping with life. Their view of the environment can become clouded (for example, a minor criticism made by a friend is blown out of proportion). Moreover, at the highest levels of stress, emotional responses may be so extreme that people are unable to act at all. People under a lot of stress also become less able to deal with new stressors.

Background stressors ("daily hassles")
Everyday annoyances, such as being stuck in traffic, that cause minor irritations and may have long-term ill effects if they continue or are compounded by other stressful events.

Psychophysiological disorders
Medical problems influenced by an interaction of psychological, emotional, and physical difficulties.

FIGURE 2

The most common everyday hassles and uplifts. How many of these are part of your life, and how do you cope with them?

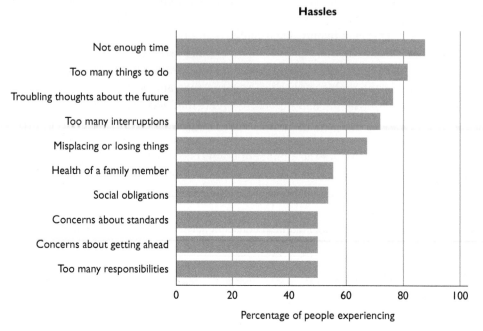

Hassles

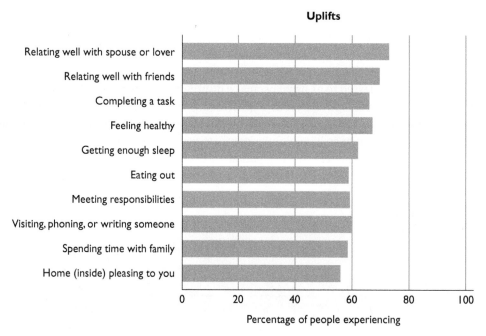

Uplifts

Sources: Figure 2 top: Adapted from Table 2 (p. 475) from Chamberlain, K., & Zika, S. (1990). The minor events approach to stress: Support for the use of daily hassles. Reproduced with permission from the *British Journal of Psychology*, 81, 469–481, © The British Psychological Society. Figure 2 bottom: Adapted from Table III (p. 14) from Kanner, A. D., Coyne, J. C., Schaefer, C., & Lazarus, R. S. (1981). Comparison of two modes of stress measurement: Daily hassles and uplifts versus major life events. *Journal of Behavioral Medicine*, 4, 1–39. © 1981 Plenum Publishing Corporation. With kind permission of Springer Science and Business Media.

In short, stress affects us in multiple ways. It may increase the risk that we will become ill, it may directly cause illness, it may make us less able to recover from a disease, and it may reduce our ability to cope with future stress. (See Figure 3 to get a measure of your own level of stress.)

The General Adaptation Syndrome Model: The Course of Stress

The effects of long-term stress are illustrated in a series of stages proposed by Hans Selye (pronounced "sell-yay"), a pioneering stress theorist born in Vienna, Austria in 1907 (Selye, 1976, 1993). Selye served as a professor and director

FIGURE 3

To get a sense of the level of stress in your life, complete this questionnaire.

How Stressful Is Your Life?

Test your level of stress by answering these questions, and adding the score from each box. Questions apply to the last month only. A key below will help you determine the extent of your stress.

1. How often have you been upset because of something that happened unexpectedly?

    ☐ 0=never, 1=almost never, 2=sometimes, 3=fairly often, 4=very often

2. How often have you felt that you were unable to control the important things in your life?

    ☐ 0=never, 1=almost never, 2=sometimes, 3= fairly often, 4 = very often

3. How often have you felt nervous and "stressed"?

    ☐ 0=never, 1=almost never, 2=sometimes, 3=fairly often, 4=very often

4. How often have you felt confident about your ability to handle your personal problems?

    ☐ 4=never, 3=almost never, 2=sometimes, 1 = fairly often, 0=very often

5. How often have you felt that things were going your way?

    ☐ 4=never, 3=almost never, 2=sometimes, 1=fairly often, 0=very often

6. How often have you been able to control irritations in your life?

    ☐ 4=never, 3=almost never, 2=sometimes, 1 =fairly often, 0=very often

7. How often have you found that you could not cope with all the things that you had to do?

    ☐ 0=never, 1=almost never, 2=sometimes, 3=fairly often, 4=very often

8. How often have you felt that you were on top of things?

    ☐ 4=never, 3=almost never, 2=sometimes, 1=fairly often, 0=very often

9. How often have you been angered because of things that were outside your control?

    ☐ 0=never, 1=almost never, 2=sometimes, 3=fairly often, 4=very often

10. How often have you felt difficulties were piling up so high that you could not overcome them?

    ☐ 0=never, 1=almost never, 2=sometimes, 3=fairly often, 4=very often

How You Measure Up

Stress levels vary among individuals—compare your total score to the averages below:

AGE		GENDER	
18–29	14.2	Man	12.1
30–44	13.0	Woman	13.7
45–54	12.6		
55–64	11.9		
65 & over	12.0		

MARITAL STATUS	
Widowed	12.6
Married or living with a partner	12.4
Single or never wed	14.1
Divorced	14.7
Separated	16.6

SCORING

If your score is significantly higher than the average score for your age group, and/or gender, help from a professional is strongly recommended.

Source: Cohen, Kamarck, & Mermelstein, 1983.

of the Institute of Experimental Medicine and Surgery at the University of Montreal. He died in 1982 in Montreal, where he had spent 50 years studying the causes and consequences of stress. Selye's renowned model of stress, the **general adaptation syndrome (GAS)**, suggests that the physiological response to stress follows the same set pattern regardless of the cause of stress.

As shown in Figure 4, the GAS has three phases. The first stage—*alarm and mobilization*—occurs when people become aware of the presence of a stressor. On a biological level, the sympathetic nervous system becomes energized, helping a person cope initially with the stressor.

However, if the stressor persists, people move into the second response stage: *resistance*. During this stage, the body fights the stressor. During resistance, people use a variety of means to cope with the stressor—sometimes successfully but at a cost of some degree of physical or psychological well-being. For example, a student who faces the stress of failing several courses might spend long hours studying, seeking to cope with the stress.

> **General adaptation syndrome (GAS)**
> A theory developed by Selye that suggests that a person's response to a stressor consists of three stages: alarm and mobilization, resistance, and exhaustion.

FIGURE 4

According to the general adaptation syndrome (GAS) model there are three major stages to stress responses: alarm and mobilization; resistance; and exhaustion. The graph below the illustration shows the degree of effort expended to cope with stressors at each of the three stages.

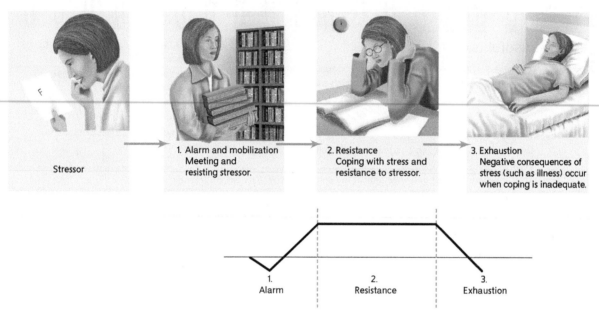

Source: Selye, 1976.

If resistance is inadequate, people enter the last stage of the GAS: *exhaustion*. During the exhaustion stage, a person's ability to adapt to the stressor declines to the point where negative consequences of stress appear: physical illness and psychological symptoms in the form of an inability to concentrate, heightened irritability, or, in severe cases, disorientation and a loss of touch with reality. In a sense, people wear out, and their physical reserves are used up.

How do people move out of the third stage after they have entered it? In some cases, exhaustion allows people to avoid a stressor. For example, people who become ill from overwork may be excused from their duties for a time, giving them a temporary respite from their responsibilities. At least for a time, then, the immediate stress is reduced.

The GAS has had a substantial impact on our understanding of stress. By suggesting that the exhaustion of resources in the third stage produces biological damage, it provides a specific explanation of how stress can lead to illness. Furthermore, the GAS can be applied to both people and nonhuman species.

Selye's theory has not gone unchallenged. For example, whereas the theory suggests that regardless of the stressor, the biological reaction is similar, some health psychologists disagree. They believe that people's biological responses are specific to the way they appraise a stressful event. If a stressor is seen as unpleasant but not unusual, then the biological response may be different than if the stressor is seen as unpleasant, out of the ordinary, and unanticipated. This perspective has led to an increased focus on psychoneuroimmunology (Taylor et al., 2000; Gaab et al., 2005; Irwin, 2008).

Psychoneuroimmunology and Stress

Contemporary health psychologists specializing in psychoneuroimmunology (PNI) have taken a broader approach to stress. Focusing on the outcomes of stress, they have identified three main consequences (see Figure 5).

First, stress has direct physiological results, including an increase in blood pressure, an increase in hormonal activity, and an overall decline in the functioning of the immune system. Second, stress leads people to engage in behaviour that is harmful to their health, including increased nicotine, drug, and alcohol use; poor eating habits; and decreased sleep. Finally, stress produces indirect consequences that result in declines in health: a reduction in the likelihood of obtaining health care and decreased compliance with medical advice when it is sought (Sapolsky, 2003; Broman, 2005; Lindblad, Lindahl, & Theorell, 2006).

Why is stress so damaging to the immune system? One reason is that stress may overstimulate the immune system. Rather than fighting invading bacteria, viruses, and other foreign invaders, it may begin to attack the body itself, damaging healthy tissue. When that happens, it can lead to disorders such as arthritis and an allergic reaction.

FIGURE 5

Three major types of consequences result from stress: direct physiological effects, harmful behaviours, and indirect health-related behaviours.

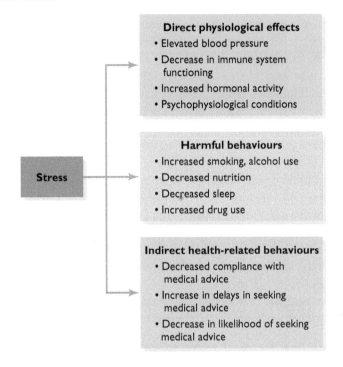

Source: Adapted from Baum, 1994.

Stress can also decrease the immune system response, permitting germs that produce colds to reproduce more easily or allowing cancer cells to spread more rapidly. In normal circumstances, our bodies produce *lymphocytes*, specialized white blood cells that fight disease, at an extraordinary rate—some 10 million every few seconds—and it is possible that stress can alter this level of production (Cohen, Hamrick, & Rodriguez, 2002; Dougall & Baum, 2004; Segerstrom & Miller, 2004).

Coping with Stress

Stress is a normal part of life—and not necessarily a completely bad part. For example, without stress, we might not be sufficiently motivated to complete the activities we need to accomplish. However, it is also clear that too much stress can take a toll on physical and psychological health. How do people deal with stress? Is there a way to reduce its negative effects?

Efforts to control, reduce, or learn to tolerate the threats that lead to stress are known as **coping.** We habitually use certain coping responses to deal with stress. Most of the time, we're not aware of these responses—just as we may be unaware of the minor stressors of life until they build up to aversive levels (Wrzeniewski & Chylinska, 2007).

We also have other, more direct, and potentially more positive ways of coping with stress, which fall into two main categories (Folkman & Moskowitz, 2000, 2004):

- *Emotion-focused coping.* In emotion-focused coping, people try to manage their emotions in the face of stress, seeking to change the way they feel about or perceive a problem. Examples of emotion-focused coping include managing stress around exam time by looking at the bright side of being in school (e.g., enhanced work opportunities; better income; interesting job). In addition to positive thinking, relaxing activities such as meditation, yoga, and breathing exercises are additional types of emotion-focused coping.

- *Problem-focused coping.* Problem-focused coping attempts to modify the stressful problem or source of stress. This "head on" approach to confronting the source of stress is often the most effective. Problem-focused strategies

Coping
The efforts to control, reduce, or learn to tolerate the threats that lead to stress.

lead to changes in behaviour or to the development of a plan of action to deal with stress. Starting a study group to improve poor classroom performance is an example of problem-focused coping. In addition, one might take a time-out from stress by creating positive events. For example, taking a day off from caring for a relative with a serious, chronic illness to go to a spa can bring significant relief from stress.

People often employ several types of coping strategies simultaneously. However, they use emotion-focused strategies more frequently when they perceive circumstances as being unchangeable and problem-focused approaches more often in situations they see as relatively modifiable (Stanton et al., 2000; Penley, Tomaka, & Wiebe, 2002).

Some forms of coping are less successful. One of the least effective forms of coping is *avoidant coping*. In avoidant coping, a person may use wishful thinking to reduce stress or use more direct escape routes, such as drug use, alcohol use, and overeating. An example of wishful thinking to avoid a test would be to say to oneself, "Maybe it will snow so hard tomorrow that the test will be cancelled." Alternatively, a person might get drunk to avoid a problem. Either way, avoidant coping usually results in a postponement of dealing with a stressful situation, and often makes it even worse (Roesch et al., 2005; Glass et al., 2009).

Another way of dealing with stress occurs unconsciously through the use of defence mechanisms. As we discussed when we considered the topic of personality, *defence mechanisms* are unconscious strategies that people use to reduce anxiety by concealing the source from themselves and others. Defence mechanisms permit people to avoid stress by acting as if the stress were not even there. For example, one U.S. study examined California college students who lived in dormitories close to a geological fault. Those who lived in dorms that were known to be unlikely to withstand an earthquake were significantly *more* likely to doubt experts' predictions of an impending earthquake than were those who lived in safer structures (Lehman & Taylor, 1988).

Another defence mechanism used to cope with stress is *emotional insulation*, in which a person stops experiencing any emotions at all, thereby remaining unaffected and unmoved by both positive and negative experiences. The problem with defence mechanisms, of course, is that they do not deal with reality but merely hide the problem.

Coping Styles: The Hardy Personality

Most of us cope with stress in a characteristic manner, employing a coping style that represents our general tendency to deal with stress in a specific way. For example, you may know people who habitually react to even the smallest amount of stress with hysteria, and others who calmly confront even the greatest stress in an unflappable manner. These kinds of people clearly have quite different coping styles (Gallagher, 1996; Taylor & Aspinwall, 1996; Taylor, 2003; Kato & Pedersen, 2005).

Among those who cope with stress most successfully are people who are equipped with **hardiness**, a personality characteristic associated with a lower rate of stress-related illness. Hardiness consists of three components (Baumgartner, 2002; Maddi, 2007):

- *Commitment.* Commitment is a tendency to throw ourselves into whatever we are doing with a sense that our activities are important and meaningful.
- *Challenge.* Hardy people believe that change, rather than stability, is the standard condition of life. To them, the anticipation of change serves as an incentive rather than a threat to their security.
- *Control.* Hardiness is marked by a sense of control—the perception that people can influence the events in their lives.

Hardy individuals approach stress in an optimistic manner and take direct action to learn about and deal with stressors, thereby changing stressful events into less threatening ones. As a consequence, hardiness acts as a defence against stress-related illness.

For those who confront the most profound difficulties, such as the death of a loved one and a permanent injury such as paralysis after an accident, a key ingredient in their psychological recovery is their degree of resilience. *Resilience* is the ability to withstand, overcome, and actually thrive after profound adversity (Bonanno, 2004; Norlander, Von Schedvin, & Archer, 2005; Jackson, 2006).

Resilient people are generally easygoing and good-natured and have good social skills. They are usually independent, and they have a sense of control over their own destiny—even if fate has dealt them a devastating blow. In short,

---

Hardiness

A personality characteristic that is associated with a lower rate of stress-related illness and consists of three components: commitment, challenge, and control.

they work with what they have and make the best of whatever situation they find themselves in (Spencer et al., 2003; Friborg et al., 2005; Deshields et al., 2006).

Social Support: Turning to Others

Our relationships with others also help us cope with stress. Researchers have found that **social support**, the knowledge that we are part of a mutual network of caring, interested others, enables us to experience lower levels of stress and be better able to cope with the stress we do undergo (Cohen, 2004; Martin & Brantley, 2004; Bolger & Amarel, 2007).

The social and emotional support people provide each other helps in dealing with stress in several ways. For instance, such support demonstrates that a person is an important and valued member of a social network. Similarly, other people can provide information and advice about appropriate ways of dealing with stress (Day & Livingstone, 2003; Lindorff, 2005).

Finally, people who are part of a social support network can provide actual goods and services to help others in stressful situations. For instance, they can supply a person whose house has burned down with temporary living quarters, or they can help a student who is experiencing stress because of poor academic performance study for a test (Natvig, Albrektsen, & Ovamstrom, 2003; Takizawa, Kondo, & Sakihara, 2007).

Social support
A mutual network of caring, interested others.

Evaluate

1. _____ is defined as a response to challenging or threatening events.

2. Match each portion of the GAS with its definition.

   1. Alarm and mobilization

   2. Exhaustion

   3. Resistance

   a. Ability to adapt to stress diminishes; symptoms appear.

   b. Activation of sympathetic nervous system.

   c. Various strategies are used to cope with a stressor.

3. Stressors that affect a single person and produce an immediate major reaction are known as

   a. Personal stressors

   b. Psychic stressors

   c. Cataclysmic stressors

   d. Daily stressors

4. People with the personality characteristic of _____ seem to be better able to successfully combat stressors.

Answers to Evaluate Questions

1. stress; 2. 1-b; 2-a; 3-c; 3. a; 4. hardiness.

Key Terms

background stressors ("daily hassles")	hardiness	psychoneuroimmunology (PNI)
cataclysmic events	health psychology	psychophysiological disorders
coping	personal stressors	social support
general adaptation syndrome (GAS)	posttraumatic stress disorder (PTSD)	stress

Psychological Aspects of Illness and Well-Being

LEARNING OBJECTIVE

LO3 **How do** psychological factors affect health-related problems such as coronary heart disease, cancer, and smoking?

I feel that it is absolutely necessary to be my own best advocate, and the best place to learn how to do that is in a group of other well-educated patients and their caregivers. We know what life post-diagnosis is like, and we help each other in ways that no docs, nurses, clergy, well-meaning friends and family possibly can. We laugh, we cry, we bitch, and we push and pull each other! We mourn the losses, celebrate small and large victories, and we educate ourselves and others. But most importantly—we embrace each other and our lives (Anonymous blogpost, 2010).

As recently as two decades ago, most psychologists and healthcare providers would have scoffed at the notion that a discussion group could improve a cancer patient's chances of survival. Today, however, such methods have gained increasing acceptance.

Growing evidence suggests that psychological factors have a substantial impact both on major health problems that were once seen in purely physiological terms and on our everyday sense of health, well-being, and happiness. We'll consider the psychological components of three major health problems—heart disease, cancer, and smoking—and then consider the nature of people's well-being and happiness.

The A's, B's, and D's of Coronary Heart Disease

Tim knew it wasn't going to be his day when he got stuck in traffic behind a slow-moving farm truck. How could the driver dawdle like that? Didn't he have anything of any importance to do? Things didn't get any better when Tim arrived on campus and discovered the library didn't have the books he needed. He could almost feel the tension rising. "I need that material to finish my paper," he thought to himself. He knew that meant he wouldn't be able to get his paper done early, and that meant he wouldn't have the time he wanted to revise the paper. He wanted it to be a first-class paper. This time Tim wanted to get a better grade than his roommate, Luis; although Luis didn't know it, Tim felt they were in direct competition and was always trying to better him, whether it was academically or just playing cards. "In fact," Tim mused to himself, "I feel like I'm in competition with everyone, no matter what I'm doing."

Have you, like Tim, ever seethed impatiently at being caught behind a slow-moving vehicle, felt anger and frustration at not finding material you needed at the library, or experienced a sense of competitiveness with your classmates?

Many of us experience these sorts of feelings at one time or another, but for some people they represent a pervasive, characteristic set of personality traits known as the **Type A behaviour pattern.** The Type A behaviour pattern is a cluster of behaviours involving hostility, competitiveness, time urgency, and feeling driven. In contrast, the **Type B behaviour pattern** is characterized by a patient, cooperative, noncompetitive, and nonaggressive manner. It's important to keep in mind that Type A and Type B represent the ends of a continuum, and most people fall somewhere in

---

Type A behaviour pattern
A cluster of behaviours involving hostility, competitiveness, time urgency, and feeling driven.

Type B behaviour pattern
A cluster of behaviours characterized by a patient, cooperative, noncompetitive, and nonaggressive manner.

between the two endpoints. Few people are purely a Type A or a Type B. (See Figure 1 to learn more about Type A and B tendencies.)

Type A's lead fast-paced, driven lives. They put in longer hours at work than do Type B's and are impatient with other people's performance, which they typically perceive as too slow. They also engage in "multitasking," doing several activities simultaneously, such as running on a treadmill, watching television, and reading a magazine.

The importance of the Type A behaviour pattern lies in its links to coronary heart disease. Men who display the Type A pattern develop coronary heart disease twice as often and suffer significantly more fatal heart attacks than do those classified as having the Type B pattern. Moreover, the Type A pattern predicts who is going to develop heart disease at least as well as—and independently of—any other single factor, including age, blood pressure, smoking habits, and cholesterol levels in the body (Rosenman et al., 1994; Wielgosz & Nolan, 2000, Beresnevaité, Taylor, & Bagby, 2007).

However, it turns out that not every component of the Type A behaviour pattern is bad. The key component linking the Type A behaviour pattern and heart disease is hostility. Although competition, time urgency, and feeling driven may produce stress and potentially other health and emotional problems, they aren't linked to coronary heart disease in the way that hostility is. In short, hostility seems to be the lethal component of the Type A behaviour pattern (Williams et al., 2000; Boyle et al., 2005; Ohira et al., 2007).

Why is hostility so toxic? The most convincing theory is that hostility produces excessive physiological arousal in stressful situations. That arousal, in turn, results in increased production of the hormones epinephrine and norepinephrine, as well as increases in heart rate and blood pressure. Such an exaggerated physiological response ultimately produces an increased incidence of coronary heart disease (Demaree & Everhart, 2004; Eaker et al., 2004; Myrtek, 2007).

FIGURE 1

No one is totally a Type A or Type B personality; rather, everyone is a combination of the two types. Take this quick test to determine which type is strongest in you.

Type Yourself

To get an idea of whether you have the characteristics of a Type A or Type B personality, answer the following questions

1. When you listen to someone talking and this person takes too long to come to the point how often do you feel like hurrying the person along?
   _____ Frequently
   _____ Occasionally
   _____ Never

2. Do you ever set deadlines of quotas for yourself at work or at home?
   _____ No
   _____ Yes, but only occasionally
   _____ Yes, once a week or more

3. Would people you know well agree that you tend to get irritated easily?
   _____ Definitely yes
   _____ Probably yes
   _____ Probably no
   _____ Definitely no

4. Would people who know you well agree that you tend to do most things in a hurry?
   _____ Definitely yes
   _____ Probably yes
   _____ Probably no
   _____ Definitely no

Photo Source: © Juice Images/Getty Images RF.

SCORING

The more frequently your answers reflect affirmative responses the more Type A characteristics you hold.

Source: Adapted from Jenkins, Zyzanski, & Rosenman, 1978.

STUDY ALERT!

It's important to distinguish among Type A (hostility, competitiveness), Type B (patience, cooperativeness), and Type D (distressed) behaviours.

It's important to keep in mind that not everyone who displays Type A behaviours is destined to have coronary heart disease. For one thing, a firm association between Type A behaviours and coronary heart disease has not been established for women; most findings pertain to males, not to females. In addition, other types of negative emotions, besides the hostility found in Type A behaviour, appear to be related to heart attacks. For example, psychologist Johan Denollet has found evidence that what he calls *Type D*—for "distressed"—behaviour is linked to coronary heart disease. In his view, insecurity, anxiety, and the negative outlook displayed by Type D's puts them at risk for repeated heart attacks (Denollet, 2005; Schiffer et al., 2005; Spindler et al., 2009).

Psychological Aspects of Cancer

Hardly any disease is feared more than cancer. Most people think of cancer in terms of lingering pain, and being diagnosed with the disease is typically viewed as receiving a death sentence.

Although a diagnosis of cancer is not as grim as one might at first suspect—several kinds of cancer have a high cure rate if detected early enough—cancer remains the second leading cause of death after coronary heart disease. The precise trigger for the disease is not well understood, but the process by which cancer spreads is straightforward. Certain cells in the body become altered and multiply rapidly and in an uncontrolled fashion. As those cells grow, they form tumours, which, if left unchecked, suck nutrients from healthy cells and body tissue, ultimately destroying the body's ability to function properly.

Although the processes involved in the spread of cancer are basically physiological, accumulating evidence suggests that the emotional responses of cancer patients to their disease may have a critical effect on its course. For example, one experiment found that people who adopt a fighting spirit are more likely to recover than are those who pessimistically suffer and resign themselves to death (Pettingale et al., 1985). The study analyzed the survival rates of women who had undergone the removal of a breast because of cancer.

The results suggested that the survival rates were related to the psychological response of the women three months after surgery. Women who stoically accepted their fate, trying not to complain, and those who felt the situation was hopeless and that nothing could be done showed the lowest survival rates; most of those women were dead after ten years. In comparison, the survival rates of women who showed a fighting spirit (predicting that they would overcome the disease and planning to take steps to prevent its recurrence) and the survival rates of women who (erroneously) denied that they had ever had cancer (saying that the breast removal was merely a preventive step) were significantly higher. In sum, according to this study, cancer patients with a positive attitude were more likely to survive than were those with a more negative one.

On the other hand, other research contradicts the notion that the course of cancer is affected by patients' attitudes and emotions. For example, some findings show that although a "fighting spirit" leads to better coping, the long-term survival rate is no better than it is for patients with a less positive attitude (Watson et al., 1999; Rom, Miller, & Peluso, 2009).

Despite the conflicting evidence, health psychologists believe that patients' emotions may at least partially determine the course of their disease. Specifically, psychologists specializing in psychoneuroimmunology (PNI) have found that a person's emotional state affects the immune system in the same way that stress affects it. For instance, in one brain imaging study, people who showed the greatest right prefrontal activation during a task involving negative emotions showed a weaker immune system response to a flu shot six months later (Rosenkranz et al., 2003).

Is a particular personality type linked to cancer? Some findings suggest that cancer patients are less emotionally reactive, suppress anger, and lack outlets for emotional release. However, the data are too tentative and inconsistent to suggest firm conclusions about a link between personality characteristics and cancer. Certainly no conclusive evidence suggests that people who develop cancer would not have done so if their personality had been of a different sort or if their attitudes had been more positive (Smith, 1988; Zevon & Corn, 1990; Holland & Lewis, 2001).

What is increasingly clear, however, is that certain types of psychological therapy have the potential for extending the lives of cancer patients. For example, the results of one study showed that women with breast cancer who received psychological treatment lived at least a year and a half longer, and experienced less anxiety and pain, than did women who did not participate in therapy. Research on patients with other health problems, such as heart disease, also has found that therapy can be beneficial, both psychologically and medically (Spiegel, 1996; Frasure-Smith, Lesperance, & Talajic, 2000; Butler et al., 2009).

The critical link between psychological functioning and cancer survival rates is recognized at Princess Margaret Hospital, a world leader in cancer treatment. Oncologists, neuropsychologists, health psychologists, and clinical psychologists work together as members of a multi-disciplinary team to care for cancer patients and their families (University Health Network, 2010). Treatment areas addressed by the Department of Psychosocial Oncology and Palliative Care at Princess Margaret Hospital include:

- Psychosocial assessment
- Neurocognitive assessment
- Individual and group psychotherapy
- Couples and family therapy
- Psycho-educational work
- Relaxation and stress management
- Grief and bereavement counselling

Smoking

Would you walk into a convenience store and buy an item with a label warning you that its use could kill you? Despite clear, well-publicized evidence that smoking is linked to cancer, heart attacks, strokes, bronchitis, emphysema, and a host of other serious illnesses, people continue to smoke. Although the prevalence has decreased, one in four Canadians smoke (Health Canada, 2012). Smoking is the greatest preventable cause of death in Canada; 100 Canadians die every day as a result of a smoking-related illness. Worldwide, 5 million people die per year from the effects of smoking (Rehm et al., 2006; World Health Organization, 2008).

Why People Smoke

Why do people smoke despite all the evidence showing that it is bad for their health? Researchers have suggests that environmental factors are the primary cause of the habit. Smoking at first may be seen as "cool" or sophisticated, as a rebellious act, or as facilitating calm performance in stressful situations. In addition, smoking a cigarette is sometimes viewed as a "rite of passage" for adolescents, undertaken at the urging of friends and viewed as a sign of growing up. But this appears to be changing: Since 1981, the percentage of Canadian teenagers aged 15–19 years who smoke has declined from 44 percent to 11 percent (CBC.ca, 2007; Sargent et al., 2007; Wills et al., 2008; Heatherton & Sargent, 2009; Heart and Stroke Foundation, 2012).

Although smoking is prohibited in an increasing number of places, it remains a substantial social problem.

Source: © Design Pics/Kristy-Anne Glubish RF.

Ultimately, smoking becomes a habit. People begin to label themselves smokers, and smoking becomes part of their self-concept. They become dependent physiologically as a result of smoking, because nicotine, a primary ingredient of tobacco, is highly addictive. A complex relationship develops among smoking, nicotine levels, and a smoker's emotional state, in which a certain nicotine level becomes associated with a positive emotional state. As a result, people smoke in an effort to regulate *both* emotional states and nicotine levels in the blood (Amos, Wiltshire, & Haw, 2006; Kassel et al., 2007; Ursprung, Sanouri, & DiFranza, 2009).

Quitting Smoking

Because smoking has both psychological and biological components, few habits are as difficult to break. Once smoking becomes a habit, it is as hard to stop as an addiction to cocaine or heroin. In fact, some of the biochemical reactions to nicotine are similar to those to cocaine, amphetamines, and morphine (Vanasse, Niyonsenga, & Courteau, 2004; Foulds et al., 2006; Dani & Montague, 2007).

Among the most effective tools for ending the smoking habit are drugs that replace the nicotine found in cigarettes. Whether in the form of gum, patches, nasal sprays, or inhalers, these products provide a dose of nicotine that reduces dependence on cigarettes. Another approach is exemplified by the drug Zyban, which, rather than replacing nicotine, raises dopamine levels in the brain, thereby reducing the desire to smoke (Garwood & Potts, 2007; Shiffman, 2007; Brody, 2008).

Behavioural strategies, which view smoking as a learned habit and concentrate on changing the smoking response, can also be effective. The best treatment seems to be a combination of nicotine replacement and counselling. What doesn't work? Going it alone: Only 5 percent of smokers who quit cold-turkey on their own are successful (Noble, 1999; Rock, 1999; Woodruff, Conway, & Edwards, 2007).

In the long term, the most effective means of reducing smoking may be changes in societal norms and attitudes toward the habit. For instance, many cities and towns have made smoking in public places illegal, and legislation banning smoking in places such as college and university classrooms and buildings—based on strong popular sentiment—is being passed with increasing frequency (Gibson, 1997; Jacobson, Wasserman, & Anderson, 1997).

Evaluate

1. Type _____ behaviour is characterized by cooperativeness and by being easy going; Type _____ behaviour is characterized by hostility and competitiveness.
2. The Type A behaviour pattern is known to directly cause heart attacks. True or false?
3. A cancer patient's attitude and emotions may affect that person's _____ system, helping or hindering the patient's fight against the disease.
4. Smoking is used to regulate both nicotine levels and emotional states in smokers. True or false?

Answers to Evaluate Questions

1. B, A; 2. false; Type A behaviour is related to a higher incidence of coronary heart disease but does not necessarily cause it directly; 3. immune; 4. true

Key Terms

Type A behaviour pattern
Type B behaviour pattern

Health and Wellness

LEARNING OBJECTIVES

How do our interactions with physicians affect our health and compliance with medical treatment?
How does a sense of well-being develop?

When Stuart Grinspoon first noticed the small lump in his arm, he assumed it was just a bruise from the touch football game he had played the previous week. But as he thought about it more, he considered more serious possibilities and decided that he'd better get it checked out at the university health service. But the visit was less than satisfactory. A shy person, Stuart felt embarrassed talking about his medical condition. Even worse, after answering a string of questions, he couldn't even understand the physician's diagnosis and was too embarrassed to ask for clarification.

Stuart Grinspoon's attitudes toward health care are shared by many of us. We approach physicians the same way we approach auto mechanics. When something goes wrong with the car, we want the mechanic to figure out the problem and then fix it. In the same way, when something isn't working right with our bodies, we want a diagnosis of the problem and then a (hopefully quick) repair.

Yet such an approach ignores the fact that—unlike auto repair—good health care requires taking psychological factors into account. Health psychologists have sought to determine the factors involved in the promotion of good health and, more broadly, a sense of well-being and happiness. Let's take a closer look at two areas they have tackled: producing compliance with health-related advice and identifying the determinants of well-being and happiness.

Following Medical Advice

We're not very good at taking medical advice. Consider these figures:

- As many as 85 percent of patients do not fully comply with a physician's recommendations.
- Between 14 and 21 percent of patients don't fill their drug prescriptions.
- Some 10 percent of adolescent pregnancies result from noncompliance with birth control medication.
- Sixty percent of all patients cannot identify their own medicines.
- From 30 percent to 50 percent of all patients ignore instructions or make errors in taking medication (Christensen & Johnson, 2002; Health Pages, 2003; Colland et al., 2004).

Noncompliance with medical advice can take many forms. For example, patients may fail to show up for scheduled appointments, not follow diets or not give up smoking, or discontinue medication during treatment. In some cases, they fail to take prescribed medicine at all.

Patients also may practise *creative nonadherence*, in which they adjust a treatment prescribed by a physician, relying on their own medical judgment and experience. In many cases patients' lack of medical knowledge may be harmful (Taylor, 1995; Hamani et al., 2007).

Noncompliance is sometimes a result of psychological reactance. **Reactance** is a negative emotional and cognitive reaction that results from the restriction of one's freedom. People who experience reactance feel hostility and anger.

Reactance
A negative emotional and cognitive reaction that results from the restriction of one's freedom.

Because of such emotions, they may seek to restore their sense of freedom, but in a self-destructive manner by refusing to accept medical advice and perhaps acting in a way that worsens their medical condition. For instance, a man who is placed on a strict diet may experience reactance and tend to eat even more than he did before his diet was restricted (Fogarty & Young, 2000; Dillard & Shen, 2004; Woller, Buboltz, & Loveland, 2007).

Failure to Communicate

I was lying on a gurney, trying to prepare myself for a six-hour breast-reconstruction surgery. A few months earlier, I'd had a mastectomy for breast cancer. Because I'm smallboned, my doctor told me I needed to have a muscle sliced from my back and moved to my chest to create a proper foundation for an implant. I knew the operation would slow me down—bad news for someone who swims, runs, and chases three young kids. But as the surgeon diagramed incision points on my chest with a felt-tip pen, my husband asked a question: "Is it really necessary to transfer this back muscle?" (Halpert, 2003, p. 63).

The surgeon's answer shocked the patient: No, it wasn't necessary. And if she didn't have the procedure, her recovery time would be cut in half. The surgeon had simply assumed, without asking the patient, that she would prefer the more complicated procedure, because cosmetically it would be preferable. But after a hurried consultation with her husband, the patient opted for the less invasive procedure.

Lack of communication between medical care providers and patients can be a major obstacle to good medical care. Such communication failures occur for several reasons. One is that physicians make assumptions about what patients prefer, or they push a particular treatment that they prefer without consulting patients. Furthermore, the relatively high prestige of physicians may intimidate patients. Patients may also be reluctant to volunteer information that might cast them in a bad light, and physicians may have difficulties encouraging their patients to provide information. In many cases, physicians dominate an interview with questions of a technical nature, whereas patients attempt to communicate a personal sense of their illness and the impact it is having on their lives (Ihler, 2003; Schillinger et al., 2004; Wain, Grammer, & Stasinos, 2006).

Furthermore, the view held by many patients that physicians are "all-knowing" can result in serious communication problems. Many patients do not understand their treatments yet fail to ask their physicians for clearer explanations of a prescribed course of action. About half of all patients are unable to report accurately how long they are to continue taking a medication prescribed for them, and about a quarter do not even know the purpose of the drug. In fact, some patients are not even sure, as they are about to be rolled into the operating room, why they are having surgery (Svarstad, 1976; Atkinson, 1997; Halpert, 2003)!

The amount of physician-patient communication also is related to the sex of a physician. Overall, female primary care physicians provide more patient-centred communications than do male primary care physicians (Roter, Hall, & Aoki, 2002; Kiss, 2004; Bertakis, 2009).

What are medical schools doing to improve communication between healthcare providers and their patients? Medical school training has traditionally lacked attention to issues of good doctor–patient communication—often referred to as "bedside manner." Innovative programs like McGill University's "Integrated Whole Person Care" address these gaps in physician training as well as bring awareness to the "whole person" in the healing process. Areas of training, research, and practice include: psychological, emotional, and spiritual factors in illness and death (McGill Medicine, 2010).

Here are some sample seminars offered by McGill's whole person care:

- Clinical listening: Two taxonomies
- Naturopathic medicine as a whole system of care: Evidence and application in real-world practice
- Optimizing wellness before, during, and after cancer treatment
- Disruptive physician behaviour and students' learning environment—a novel approach to healing through simulation

What can patients do to improve communication with healthcare providers? Here are some tips provided by physician Holly Atkinson (Atkinson, 2003):

- Make a list of health-related concerns before you visit a healthcare provider.
- Before a visit, write down the names and dosages of every drug you are currently taking.
- Determine if your provider will communicate with you via e-mail and the correct e-mail address.

- If you find yourself intimidated, take along an advocate—a friend or relative—who can help you communicate more effectively.

- Take notes during the visit.

Increasing Compliance with Advice

Although compliance with medical advice does not guarantee that a patient's medical problems will go away, it does optimize the possibility that the patient's condition will improve. What, then, can healthcare providers do to produce greater compliance on the part of their patients? One strategy is to provide clear instructions to patients regarding drug regimens. Maintaining good, warm relations between physicians and patients also leads to increased compliance (Cheney, 1996; Arbuthnott & Sharpe, 2009).

In addition, honesty helps. Patients generally prefer to be well informed—even if the news is bad—and their degree of satisfaction with their medical care is linked to how well and how accurately physicians are able to convey the nature of their medical problems and treatments (Haley, Clair, & Saulsberry, 1992; Zuger, 2005).

The way in which a message is framed also can result in more positive responses to health-related information. *Positively framed messages* suggest that a change in behaviour will lead to a gain, emphasizing the benefits of carrying out a health-related behaviour. For instance, suggesting that skin cancer is curable if it is detected early, and that you can reduce your chances of getting the disease by using a sunscreen, places information in a positive frame. In contrast, *negatively framed messages* highlight what you can lose by not performing a behaviour. For instance, one might say that if you don't use sunscreen, you're more likely to get skin cancer, which can kill you if it's not detected early—an example of a negative frame.

What type of message is more effective? According to psychologists Alex Rothman and Peter Salovey, it depends on the type of health behaviour one is trying to bring about. Negatively framed messages are best for motivating *preventive* behaviour. However, positively framed messages are most effective in producing behaviour that will lead to the detection of a disease (McCaul, Johnson, & Rothman, 2002; Lee & Aaker, 2004).

Well-Being and Happiness

What makes for a good life?

It's a question that philosophers and theologians have pondered for centuries, and now health psychologists are turning their spotlight on the question. They are doing that by investigating **subjective well-being**, people's evaluations of their lives in terms of both their thoughts and their emotions. Considered another way, subjective well-being is the measure of how happy people are (Diener, Lucas, & Oishi, 2002; Kesebir & Diener, 2008).

What Are the Characteristics of Happy People?

Research on the subject of well-being shows that happy people share several characteristics (Myers, 2000; Diener & Seligman, 2002; Otake, Shimai, & Tanaka-Matsumi, 2006):

- *Happy people have high self-esteem.* Particularly in Western cultures, which emphasize the importance of individuality, people who are happy like themselves. They see themselves as more intelligent and better able to get along with others than is the average person. In fact, they often hold *positive illusions* or moderately inflated views of themselves as good, competent, and desirable (Taylor et al., 2000; Boyd-Wilson, McClure, & Walkey, 2004).

- *Happy people have a firm sense of control.* They feel more in control of events in their lives.

- *Happy individuals are optimistic.* Their optimism permits them to persevere at tasks and ultimately to achieve more. In addition, their health is better (Peterson, 2000). Canadian Michael J. Fox is living proof of the potent link between optimism and well-being. Despite being diagnosed with Parkinson's disease at the young age of 30 (see Chapter 2's prologue for full details), Michael J. Fox refuses to be defined by his disease. Instead, he repeatedly describes himself as "lucky" in his memoir *Lucky Man*, and subsequently as an "incurable optimist" in his book *Always Looking Up: The Adventures of an Incurable Optimist.* Michael J. Fox models the defining characteristics

Subjective well-being
People's own evaluation of their lives in terms of both their thoughts and their emotions.

of optimists by focusing his attention on what is right in his world—his wife, children, career—rather than what is wrong—Parkinson's disease (Fox, 2002, 2009).

- *Men and women generally are made happy by the same sorts of activities—but not always.* Most of the time, adult men and women achieve the same level of happiness from the same things, such as hanging out with friends. But there are some differences: For example, women get less pleasure from being with their parents than men. The explanation? For women, time spent with their parents more closely resembles work, such as helping them cook or pay the bills. For men, it's more likely to involve recreational activities, such as watching a football game with their fathers. The result is that men report being slightly happier than women (Kreuger, 2007).

- *Happy people like to be around other people.* They tend to be extroverted and have a supportive network of close relationships.

Research shows that Canadians are happy and becoming increasingly happier! Nine out of ten Canadians reported they are satisfied or very satisfied with their lives. Next to Denmark, Canada is the second happiest county in the world, which has increased from fifth place in 2008 (Torontosun.com, 2012).

Does Money Buy Happiness?

If you won the lottery, would you be happier?

Probably not. At least that's the implication of health psychologists' research on subjective well-being. That research shows that although winning the lottery brings an initial surge in happiness, a year later winners' level of happiness seems to return to what it was before. The converse phenomenon occurs for people who have had serious injuries in accidents: Despite an initial decline in happiness, in most cases victims return to their prior levels of happiness after the passage of time (Diener & Biswas-Diener, 2002; Nissle & Bschor, 2002; Spinella & Lester, 2006).

Why is the level of subjective well-being so stable? One explanation is that people have a general *set point* for happiness, a marker that establishes the tone for one's life. Although particular events may temporarily elevate or depress one's mood (a surprise promotion or a job loss, for example), ultimately people return to their general level of happiness.

Happy people enjoy the company of others and have a supportive network of close relationships.

Source: © Steve Catney.

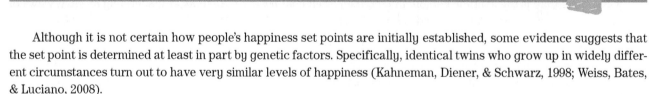

STUDY ALERT!

Remember the concept that individuals have a set point (a general, consistent level) relating to subjective well-being.

Although it is not certain how people's happiness set points are initially established, some evidence suggests that the set point is determined at least in part by genetic factors. Specifically, identical twins who grow up in widely different circumstances turn out to have very similar levels of happiness (Kahneman, Diener, & Schwarz, 1998; Weiss, Bates, & Luciano, 2008).

Most people's well-being set point is relatively high. For example, some 30 percent of people in the United States rate themselves as "very happy," and only one in ten rates himself or herself as "not too happy." Most people declare themselves to be "pretty happy." Such feelings are graphically confirmed by people who are asked to place themselves on the measure of happiness illustrated in Figure 1. The scale clearly illustrates that most people view their lives quite positively.

FIGURE 1

Most people rate themselves as happy, while only a small minority indicate they are "not too happy."

Faces Scale: "Which face comes closest to expressing how you feel about your life as a whole?"

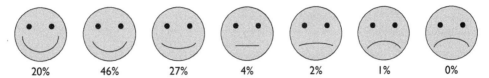

20%   46%   27%   4%   2%   1%   0%

Source: Myers, 2000, p. 57, drawn from *Social Indicators of Well-Being: Americans' Perceptions of Life Quality* (pp. 207 and 306), by F. M. Andrews and S. B. Withey, 1976. New York, Plenum. Copyright 1976 by Plenum.

Few differences exist between members of different demographic groups. Men and women report being equally happy, and African Americans are only slightly less likely than European Americans to rate themselves as "very happy." Furthermore, happiness is hardly unique to North American culture. Even countries that are far from economically prosperous have, on the whole, happy residents (Myers & Diener, 1996; Diener & Clifton, 2002; Suh, 2002; Suhail & Chaudhry, 2004).

The bottom line: Money does *not* seem to buy happiness. Despite the ups and downs of life, most people tend to be reasonably happy, and they adapt to the trials and tribulations—and joys and delights—of life by returning to a steady-state level of happiness. That habitual level of happiness can have profound—perhaps life-prolonging—implications (Diener & Seligman, 2004; Hecht, 2007; also see *Applying Psychology in the Real World*).

APPLYING PSYCHOLOGY in the Real World

Does Money Buy Happiness?

What would you do if you won a million-dollar lottery? Would you buy all the things you've always wanted but couldn't afford? Or would you perhaps take a long trip around the world? Or maybe you're more practical and would save it for a rainy day—or perhaps more generous, and would give most of it away to people and charities that really needed it. Which decision would make you the happiest?

It turns out that the option most of us would choose—buying lots of stuff—is the one that is least likely to make us happy. If we're going to blow the money on ourselves, we're more likely to enjoy it if we buy experiences, such as that trip around the world, rather than things. And recent research suggests that we'd be happier still if we gave the money away or did nothing with it at all.

In one study that looked at these issues, participants were given a chocolate candy to enjoy. Then some were told not to eat any chocolate for the next week, while others were given a huge bag of chocolate candy and told to eat it as much as they like.

The two groups of participants returned at the end of the week and were given another chocolate candy. Those who had not eaten candy all week enjoyed it as much as they had when they ate one piece the week before. Those who were able to eat candy all week did not enjoy it as much.

What this study tells us is that we enjoy things more when they are a rare treat than when we can have all we want. Overindulgence makes us feel bad; underindulgence, on the other hand, enhances our enjoyment (Quoidbach et al., 2010; Dunn & Norton, 2012).

In another study, people on the street were handed an envelope that contained $20 and some instructions. Some people were instructed to spend the money on themselves by the end of the day. Others were told to spend the money on someone else. Researchers then followed up to see which people were happier, and the results were clear: those who spent the money on someone else were much happier. Furthermore, this result held up in different countries and even with very young children. Apparently, then, the best way to buy happiness with money is to give it away (Aknin, Hamlin, & Dunn, 2012; Aknin et al., 2013).

Obviously, these studies aren't precisely analogous to what it's like to win the lottery or inherit a large amount of money. Still, they are instructive in adding to the consistent findings that money can't buy happiness—it depends what you do with it that determines whether, and for how long, you'll be happy.

Evaluate

1. Health psychologists are most likely to focus on which of the following problems with health care?
   a. Incompetent healthcare providers
   b. Rising healthcare costs
   c. Ineffective communication between physician and patient
   d. Scarcity of medical research funding
2. If you want people to floss more to prevent gum disease, the best approach is to
   a. Use a negatively framed message
   b. Use a positively framed message
   c. Have a dentist deliver an encouraging message on the pleasures of flossing
   d. Provide people with free dental floss
3. Winning the lottery is likely to
   a. Produce an immediate and long-term increase in the level of well-being
   b. Produce an immediate, but not lingering, increase in the level of well-being
   c. Produce a decline in well-being over the long run
   d. Lead to an increase in greed over the long run

Answers to Evaluate Questions

1. c; 2. a; 3. b

Key Terms

reactance
subjective well-being

Epilogue

Source: © JGI/Jamie Grill LLC RF.

In this set of modules, we have explored the intersection of psychology and biology. We have seen how the emotional and psychological experience of stress can lead to physical symptoms of illness, how personality factors may be related to major health problems, and how psychological factors can interfere with effective communication between physician and patient. We have also looked at the other side of the coin noting that some relatively simple strategies can help us control stress, affect illness, and improve our interactions with physicians.

Recap/Rethink

Module 34: Stress and Coping

Recap

How is health psychology a union between medicine and psychology?

- The field of health psychology considers how psychology can be applied to the prevention, diagnosis, and treatment of medical problems.

What is stress, how does it affect us, and how can we best cope with it?

- Stress is a response to threatening or challenging environmental conditions. People encounter stressors—the circumstances that produce stress—of both a positive and a negative nature.
- The way an environmental circumstance is interpreted affects whether it will be considered stressful. Still, there are general classes of events that provoke stress: cataclysmic events, personal stressors, and background stressors (daily hassles).
- Stress produces immediate physiological reactions. In the short term those reactions may be adaptive, but in the long term they may have negative consequences, including the development of psychophysiological disorders.
- The consequences of stress can be explained in part by Selye's general adaptation syndrome (GAS), which suggests that there are three stages in stress responses: alarm and mobilization, resistance, and exhaustion.
- Coping with stress can take a number of forms, including the unconscious use of defence mechanisms and the use of emotion-focused or problem-focused coping strategies.

Rethink

1. Why are cataclysmic stressors less stressful in the long run than are other types of stressors? Does the reason relate to the coping phenomenon known as social support? How?

2. *From the perspective of a social worker*: How would you help people deal with and avoid stress in their everyday lives? How might you encourage people to create social support networks?

3. Based on the description of Denby's day, which are personal stressors and which are background stressors? What might happen to "elevate" the stress level of a background stressor to a more serious level?

4. How does the GAS apply to Denby's situation? How might events in her life move her along the three stages of the model?

Module 35: Psychological Aspects of Illness and Well-Being

Recap

How do psychological factors affect health-related problems such as coronary heart disease, cancer, and smoking?

- Hostility, a key component of the Type A behaviour pattern, is linked to coronary heart disease. The Type A behaviour pattern is a cluster of behaviours involving hostility, competitiveness, time urgency, and feeling driven.
- Increasing evidence suggests that people's attitudes and emotional responses affect the course of cancer through links to the immune system.
- Smoking, the leading preventable cause of health problems, has proved to be difficult for many smokers to quit, even though most smokers are aware of the dangerous consequences of the behaviour.

Rethink

1. Is there a danger of "blaming the victim" when we argue that the course of cancer can be improved if a person with the disease holds positive attitudes or beliefs, particularly when we consider people with cancer who are not recovering? Why?

2. *From the perspective of a healthcare provider*: What type of advice would you give to your patients about the connections between personality and disease? For example, would you encourage Type A people to become "less Type A" in order to decrease their risk of heart disease?

Module 36: Health and Wellness

Recap

LO4 How do our interactions with physicians affect our health and compliance with medical treatment?

- Although patients would often like physicians to base a diagnosis only on a physical examination, communicating one's problem to the physician is equally important.
- Patients may find it difficult to communicate openly with their physicians because of the high social prestige of physicians and the technical nature of medical information.

LO5 How does a sense of well-being develop?

- Subjective well-being, the measure of how happy people are, is highest in people with high self-esteem, a sense of control, optimism, and a supportive network of close relationships.

Rethink

1. Do you think stress plays a role in making communication between physicians and patients difficult? Why?

2. *From the perspective of a healthcare provider*: How would you try to better communicate with your patients? How might your techniques vary depending upon the patient's background, gender, age, and culture?

3. If money doesn't buy happiness, what can you do to make yourself happier? As you answer, consider the research findings on stress and coping, as well as on emotions.

4. What steps would you advise Denby to take to keep her level of stress under control? How might others in her life be involved in such an effort?

CHAPTER 12
Psychological Disorders

Source: © Rubberball/Getty Images RF.

Key Concepts for Chapter 12

MODULE 37   Normal versus Abnormal: Making the Distinction

LO1   How can we distinguish normal from abnormal behaviour?

LO2   What are the major perspectives on psychological disorders used by mental health professionals?

LO3   What are the major categories of psychological disorders?

Defining Abnormality

Perspectives on Abnormality: From Superstition to Science

Classifying Abnormal Behaviour: The ABCs of *DSM*

MODULE 38   The Major Psychological Disorders

LO4   What are the major psychological disorders?

Anxiety Disorders

Obsessive-Compulsive Disorder

Mood Disorders

Schizophrenia

Personality Disorders

Childhood Disorders

Somatoform Disorders

Other Disorders

   Applying Psychology in the Real World: *Internet Addiction*

MODULE 39   Psychological Disorders in Perspective

LO5   How prevalent are psychological disorders?

Prevalence of Psychological Disorders: The Mental State of North America

The Social and Cultural Context of Psychological Disorders

   Becoming an Informed Consumer of Psychology: *Deciding When You Need Help*

Prologue

Appearances Can Be Deceiving: NHL Hockey Player Shayne Corson

On the outside, NHL hockey player Shayne Corson appears strong, powerful, and in control. On the inside, however, lies an entirely different story. To hockey fans, Corson is a fifteen-season NHL veteran, Stanley Cup champion, and member of Canada's 1998 Olympic team. Fellow NHL player Mark Recchi described Corson as "the bravest player I know" (Kennedy, 2001). But it is not Corson's public profile as NHL All-Star hockey player that deserves the heroic label; rather, it is his private battle with debilitating panic attacks that deserves our greatest respect.

His was a secret battle he has begun to openly share with others beginning with an interview with *Sports Illustrated* where "Corson was happy to discuss any aspect of his career, but mainly he wanted to talk about last season and the times he cried" (Kennedy, 2001).

Shayne Corson's panic disorder, a specific type of anxiety disorder, is one of many psychological disorders discussed in this chapter. Psychological disorders afflict as many as 10 percent of the Canadian population each year (Public Health Agency of Canada, 2002b).

Corson's story raises several questions. What caused his disorder? Were genetic factors involved, or were stressors in his life primarily responsible? Were there signs that others should have noticed earlier? Could his panic attacks have been prevented? What were the specific symptoms of his psychological disorder? And, more generally, how do we distinguish normal from abnormal behaviour, and how can Corson's behaviour be categorized and classified in such a way as to pinpoint the specific nature of his problem?

We address some of the issues raised by Shayne Corson's case in the following set of modules. We begin by discussing the difference between normal and abnormal behaviour, which can be surprisingly fuzzy. We then discuss the most significant categories of psychological disorders. Finally, we consider ways of evaluating behaviour—one's own and that of others—to determine whether seeking help from a mental health professional is warranted.

Normal versus Abnormal: Making the Distinction

LEARNING OBJECTIVES

LO1 **How can** we distinguish normal from abnormal behaviour?

LO2 **What are** the major perspectives on psychological disorders used by mental health professionals?

LO3 **What are** the major categories of psychological disorders?

Universally that person's acumen is esteemed very little perceptive concerning whatsoever matters are being held as most profitable by mortals with sapience endowed to be studied who is ignorant of that which the most in doctrine erudite and certainly by reason of that in them high mind's ornament deserving of veneration constantly maintain when by general consent they affirm that other circumstances being equal by no exterior splendour is the prosperity of a nation. . . .

It would be easy to conclude that these words are the musings of a madman. To most people, the passage does not seem to make any sense at all. But literary scholars would disagree. Actually, this passage is from James Joyce's classic *Ulysses,* hailed as one of the major works of twentieth-century literature (Joyce, 1934, p. 377).

As this example illustrates, casually examining a person's writing is insufficient to determine the degree to which that person is "normal." But even when we consider more extensive samples of a person's behaviour, we find that there may be only a fine line between behaviour that is considered normal and that which is considered abnormal. Furthermore, mental health can also be seen on a continuum with healthy mental functioning at one end (with or without a diagnosable mental disorder) and unhealthy functioning at the other end of the spectrum (with or without a diagnosable mental disorder).

Defining Abnormality

Because of the difficulty in distinguishing normal from abnormal behaviour, psychologists have struggled to devise a precise, scientific definition of "abnormal behaviour." For instance, consider the following definitions, each of which has advantages and disadvantages:

- *Abnormality as deviation from the average.* To employ this statistically based approach, we simply observe what behaviours are rare or occur infrequently in a particular society or culture and label those deviations from the norm "abnormal."

  The difficulty with this definition is that some statistically rare behaviours clearly do not lend themselves to classification as abnormal. If most people prefer to have corn flakes for breakfast but you prefer raisin bran, this hardly makes your behaviour abnormal. Similarly, such a concept of abnormality unreasonably labels a person who has an unusually high IQ as abnormal, simply because a high IQ is statistically rare. In short, a definition of abnormality that rests on deviation from the average is insufficient.

- *Abnormality as deviation from the ideal.* An alternative approach considers abnormality in relation to the standard toward which most people are striving—the ideal. This sort of definition considers behaviour abnormal if it deviates enough from some kind of ideal or cultural standard. However, society has few standards on which people universally agree. (For example, we would be hard-pressed to find agreement on whether the New Testament, the Koran, the Talmud, or the Book of Mormon provided the most reasonable standards.) Furthermore, standards that do arise tend to change over time and vary across cultures, the deviation-from-the-ideal approach is inadequate.

- *Abnormality as a sense of personal discomfort.* A more useful definition concentrates on the psychological consequences of the behaviour for the individual. In this approach, behaviour is considered abnormal if it produces a sense of personal distress, anxiety, or guilt in an individual—or if it is harmful to others in some way.

  Even a definition that relies on personal discomfort has drawbacks, though, because in some particularly severe forms of mental disturbance, people report feeling wonderful, even though their behaviour seems bizarre to others. In such cases, a personal state of well-being exists, yet most people would consider the behaviour abnormal. For example, most of us would think that a woman who says she is hearing uplifting messages from Martians would be considered to be displaying abnormal behaviour, even though she may say the messages make her feel happy.

- *Abnormality as the inability to function effectively.* Most people are able to feed themselves, hold a job, get along with others, and in general live as productive members of society. Yet there are those who are unable to adjust to the demands of society or function effectively.

  According to this view of abnormality, people who are unable to function effectively and adapt to the demands of society are considered abnormal. For example, an unemployed, homeless woman living on the street may be considered unable to function effectively. Therefore, her behaviour can be viewed as abnormal, even if she has chosen to live this way. Her inability to adapt to the requirements of society is what makes her "abnormal," according to this approach.

- *Abnormality as a legal concept.* In 1992, the Supreme Court of Canada acquitted Kenneth Parks of murder on the grounds that sleep-walking rendered him incapable of acting rationally. Consequently, Parks was not held responsible for stabbing his mother-in-law to death and was set free on all charges (Zdeb, 2006).

  Although you might question this view, it reflects the way in which the law defines abnormal behaviour. To the judicial system, the distinction between normal and abnormal behaviour rests on the definition of insanity, which is a legal, but not a psychological, term. The definition of insanity varies from one country to another. It also changes over time.

  According to the Supreme Court of Canada, in order to be deemed legally sane "the accused must possess the intellectual ability to know right from wrong in an abstract sense. But he or she most also possess the ability to apply the knowledge in a rational way to the alleged criminal act" (Pilon, 2002).

STUDY ALERT!

Remember the different definitions of abnormality (deviation from the average, deviation from the ideal, a sense of personal discomfort, inability to function effectively, and abnormality as a legal concept).

Clearly, none of the previous definitions is broad enough to cover all instances of abnormal behaviour. Consequently, the distinction between normal and abnormal behaviour often remains ambiguous even to trained professionals. Furthermore, to a large extent, cultural expectations for "normal" behaviour in a particular society influence the understanding of "abnormal behaviour" (Scheff, 1999).

Given the difficulties in precisely defining the construct, psychologists typically define **abnormal behaviour** broadly, considering it to be behaviour that causes people to experience distress and prevents them from functioning in their daily lives (Nolen-Hoeksema, 2007). Because of the imprecision of this definition, it's best to view abnormal behaviour and normal behaviour as marking two ends of a continuum rather than as absolute states. Behaviour should be evaluated in terms of gradations, ranging from fully normal functioning to extremely abnormal behaviour. Behaviour typically falls somewhere between those extremes.

Abnormal behaviour
Behaviour that causes people to experience distress and prevents them from functioning in their daily lives.

☐ Perspectives on Abnormality: From Superstition to Science

Throughout much of human history, people linked abnormal behaviour to superstition and witchcraft. Individuals who displayed abnormal behaviour were accused of being possessed by the devil or some sort of demonic god. Authorities felt justified in "treating" abnormal behaviour by attempting to drive out the source of the problem. This typically involved whipping, immersion in hot water, starvation, or other forms of torture in which the cure was often worse than the affliction (Berrios, 1996).

STUDY ALERT!

Use Figure 1 to review the six major perspectives on abnormality and consider how they relate to the major perspectives on the field of psychology that we discussed in Chapter 1.

Contemporary approaches take a more enlightened view. Today, six major perspectives are used to understand psychological disorders. These perspectives suggest not only different causes of abnormal behaviour but different treatment approaches as well. Furthermore, some perspectives are more applicable to particular disorders than are others. Figure 1 summarizes the perspectives and the way in which they can be applied to the experience of Shayne Corson, described in the prologue.

FIGURE 1

In considering Corson's case discussed in the prologue, we can employ each of the different perspectives on abnormal behaviour. Note, however, that because of the nature of his psychological disorder, some of the perspectives are more applicable than others.

Perspectives on Psychological Disorders		
Perspective	Description	Possible Application of Perspective to Shayne Corson's Case
Medical	Assumes that physiological causes are at the root of psychological disorders	Examine Corson for medical problems, such as brain tumour, chemical imbalance in the brain, or disease
Psychoanalytic	Argues that psychological disorders stem from childhood conflicts	Seek out information about Corson's past, considering possible childhood conflicts
Behavioural	Assumes that abnormal behaviours are learned responses	Concentrate on rewards and punishments for Corson's behaviour, and identify environmental stimuli that reinforce his behaviour
Cognitive	Assumes that cognitions (people's thoughts and beliefs) are central to psychological disorders	Focus on Corson's perceptions of self and his environment
Humanistic	Emphasizes people's responsibility for their own behaviour and the need to self-actualize	Consider Corson's behaviour in terms of his choices and efforts to reach his potential
Sociocultural	Assumes that behaviour is shaped by family, society, and culture	Focus on how societal demands contributed to Corson's disorder

Medical Perspective

When people display the symptoms of tuberculosis, medical professionals can generally find tubercular bacteria in their body tissue. Similarly, the **medical perspective (on psychological disorders)** suggests that when an individual

> **Medical perspective (on psychological disorders)**
> The perspective that suggests that when an individual displays symptoms of abnormal behaviour, the root cause will be found in a physical examination of the individual, which may reveal a hormonal imbalance, a chemical deficiency, or a brain injury.

displays symptoms of abnormal behaviour, the fundamental cause will be found through a physical examination of the individual, which may reveal a hormonal imbalance, a chemical deficiency, or a brain injury. Indeed, when we speak of mental "illness," "symptoms" of abnormal behaviour, and mental "hospitals," we are using terminology associated with the medical perspective.

Because many abnormal behaviours have been linked to biological causes, the medical perspective is a reasonable approach, yet serious criticisms have been levelled against it. For one thing, no biological cause has been identified for many forms of abnormal behaviour. In addition, some critics have argued that the use of the term *illness* implies that people who display abnormal behaviour have no responsibility for their actions (Szasz, 1994, 2004; Laing & Szasz, 2004).

Still, recent advances in our understanding of the biological bases of behaviour underscore the importance of considering physiological factors in abnormal behaviour. For instance, some of the more severe forms of psychological disturbance, such as major depression and schizophrenia, are influenced by genetic factors and malfunctions in neurotransmitter signals (Plomin & McGuffin, 2003; Iversen & Iversen, 2007; Howes & Kapur, 2009).

Psychoanalytic Perspective

Whereas the medical perspective suggests that biological causes are at the root of abnormal behaviour, the **psychoanalytic perspective (on psychological disorders)** holds that abnormal behaviour stems from childhood conflicts over opposing wishes regarding sex and aggression. According to Freud, children pass through a series of stages in which sexual and aggressive impulses take different forms and produce conflicts that require resolution. If these childhood conflicts are not dealt with successfully, they remain unresolved in the unconscious and eventually bring about abnormal behaviour during adulthood.

To uncover the roots of people's disordered behaviour, the psychoanalytic perspective scrutinizes their early life history. However, because there is no conclusive way to link people's childhood experiences with the abnormal behaviours they display as adults, we can never be sure that the causes suggested by psychoanalytic theory are accurate. Moreover, psychoanalytic theory paints a picture of people as having relatively little control over their behaviour, because much of it is guided by unconscious impulses. In the eyes of some critics, this suggests that people have little responsibility for their own behaviour.

On the other hand, the contributions of psychoanalytic theory have been significant. More than any other approach to abnormal behaviour, this perspective highlights the fact that people can have a rich, involved inner life and that prior experiences can have a profound effect on current psychological functioning (Elliott, 2002; Bornstein, 2003; Rangell, 2007).

Behavioural Perspective

Both the medical and psychoanalytic perspectives look at abnormal behaviours as symptoms of an underlying problem. In contrast, the **behavioural perspective (on psychological disorders)** views the behaviour itself as the problem. Using the basic principles of learning, behavioural theorists see both normal and abnormal behaviours as responses to various stimuli, responses that have been learned through past experience and that are guided in the present by stimuli in the individual's environment. To explain why abnormal behaviour occurs, we must analyze how an individual has learned abnormal behaviour and observe the circumstances in which it is displayed.

The emphasis on observable behaviour represents both the greatest strength and the greatest weakness of the behavioural approach to abnormal behaviour. This perspective provides the most precise and objective approach for examining behavioural symptoms of particular disorders, such as attention-deficit hyperactivity disorder (ADHD). At the same time, though, critics charge that the perspective ignores the rich inner world of thoughts, attitudes, and emotions that may contribute to abnormal behaviour.

Cognitive Perspective

The medical, psychoanalytic, and behavioural perspectives view people's behaviour as the result of factors largely beyond their control. To many critics of these views, however, people's thoughts cannot be ignored.

Psychoanalytic perspective (on psychological disorders)
The perspective that suggests that abnormal behaviour stems from childhood conflicts over opposing wishes regarding sex and aggression.

Behavioural perspective (on psychological disorders)
The perspective that looks at the behaviour itself as the problem.

In response to such concerns, some psychologists employ a **cognitive perspective (on psychological disorders)**. Rather than considering only external behaviour, as in traditional behavioural approaches, the cognitive approach assumes that cognitions (people's thoughts and beliefs) are central to a person's abnormal behaviour. A primary goal of treatment using the cognitive perspective is to explicitly teach new, more adaptive ways of thinking.

For instance, suppose a student forms the erroneous belief that "doing well on this exam is crucial to my entire future" whenever he or she takes an exam. Through therapy, that person might learn to hold the more realistic, and less anxiety-producing, thought, "my entire future is not dependent on this one exam." By changing cognitions in this way, psychologists working within a cognitive framework help people free themselves from thoughts and behaviours that are potentially maladaptive (Clark, 2004; Everly & Lating, 2007).

The cognitive perspective is not without critics. For example, it is possible that maladaptive cognitions are the symptoms or consequences of disorders, rather than their cause. Furthermore, there are circumstances in which negative beliefs may not be irrational at all, but simply reflect the unpleasant environments in which people live—after all, there are times when a single exam may be extremely important. Still, cognitive theorists would argue that one can find a more adaptive way of framing beliefs even in the most negative circumstances.

Humanistic Perspective

Psychologists who subscribe to the **humanistic perspective (on psychological disorders)** emphasize the responsibility people have for their own behaviour, even when their behaviour is seen as abnormal. The humanistic perspective—growing out of the work of Carl Rogers and Abraham Maslow—concentrates on what is uniquely human, viewing people as basically rational, oriented toward a social world, and motivated to seek self-actualization (Rogers, 1995).

Humanistic approaches focus on the relationship of the individual to society, considering the ways in which people view themselves in relation to others and see their place in the world. The humanistic perspective views people as having an awareness of life and of themselves that leads them to search for meaning and self-worth. Rather than assuming that individuals require a "cure," the humanistic perspective suggests that they can, by and large, set their own limits of what is acceptable behaviour. As long as they are not hurting others and do not feel personal distress, people should be free to choose the behaviours in which they engage.

Although the humanistic perspective has been criticized for its reliance on unscientific, unverifiable information and its vague, almost philosophical formulations, it offers a distinctive view of abnormal behaviour. It stresses the unique aspects of being human and provides a number of important suggestions for helping those with psychological problems.

Sociocultural Perspective

The **sociocultural perspective (on psychological disorders)** assumes that people's behaviour—both normal and abnormal—is shaped by the kind of family group, society, and culture in which they live. According to this view, the nature of one's relationships with others may support abnormal behaviours and even cause them. Consequently, the kinds of stresses and conflicts people experience in their daily interactions with others can promote and maintain abnormal behaviour.

This perspective finds statistical support for the position that sociocultural factors shape abnormal behaviour in the fact that some kinds of abnormal behaviour are far more prevalent among certain social classes than they are in others. For instance, diagnoses of schizophrenia tend to be higher among members of lower socioeconomic

---

Cognitive perspective (on psychological disorders)
The perspective that suggests that people's thoughts and beliefs are a central component of abnormal behaviour.

Humanistic perspective (on psychological disorders)
The perspective that emphasizes the responsibility people have for their own behaviour, even when such behaviour is abnormal.

Sociocultural perspective (on psychological disorders)
The perspective that assumes that people's behaviour—both normal and abnormal—is shaped by the kind of family group, society, and culture in which they live.

groups than among members of more affluent groups. Furthermore, poor economic times seem to be linked to general declines in psychological functioning, and social problems such as homelessness are associated with psychological disorders (López & Guarnaccia, 2005; Nasir & Hand, 2006; Greenberg & Rosenheck, 2008).

On the other hand, alternative explanations abound for the association between abnormal behaviour and social factors. For example, people from lower socioeconomic levels may be less likely than those from higher levels to seek help, gradually reaching a point where their symptoms become severe and warrant a more serious diagnosis. Furthermore, sociocultural explanations provide relatively little specific guidance for the treatment of individuals showing mental disturbance, because the focus is on broader societal factors (Paniagua, 2000).

Classifying Abnormal Behaviour: The ABCs of *DSM*

Crazy. Whacked. Mental. Loony. Insane. Neurotic. Psycho. Strange. Demented. Odd. Possessed.

Society has long placed labels on people who display abnormal behaviour. Unfortunately, most of the time these labels have reflected intolerance and have been used with little thought to what each label signifies.

Providing appropriate and specific names and classifications for abnormal behaviour has presented a major challenge to psychologists. It is not hard to understand why, given the difficulties discussed earlier in simply distinguishing normal from abnormal behaviour. Yet we need to classify abnormal behaviour in order to diagnose it and, ultimately, to treat it.

DSM-5: Determining Diagnostic Distinctions

Over the years, mental health professionals have developed many classification systems that vary in terms of their utility and the degree to which they have been accepted. However, one standard system, devised by the American Psychiatric Association, has emerged in the United States. Most professionals today use this classification system, known as the ***Diagnostic and Statistical Manual of Mental Disorders, Fifth Edition (DSM-5)***, to diagnose and classify abnormal behaviour (American Psychiatric Association, 2013).

The *DSM-5*, most recently revised in 2013, attempts to provide comprehensive and relatively precise definitions for more than 200 disorders. By following the criteria presented in the *DSM-5* classification system, diagnosticians use clients' reported symptoms to identify the specific problem an individual is experiencing. (Figure 2 provides a brief outline of the major diagnostic categories; American Psychiatric Association, 2013.)

The manual takes an *atheoretical* approach to identifying psychological disorders, though some practitioners have argued that this diagnostic approach is too heavily based on a medical model. The authors of the newest update of *DSM* suggest that the manual should be viewed as the "DSM-5.0." The "5.0" name emphasizes that the *DSM-5* is a work in progress, subject to revision based on users' feedback. (The next revision will be called DSM-5.1.)

Among the major changes to *DSM-5* are the following (Kupfer, Kuhl, & Regier, 2013; Wakefield, 2013):

- *A lifespan development focus.* Disorders have been arranged in terms of what age they are likely to first appear. In addition, the *DSM-5* is more specific about how the same disorder may change over the course of a person's lifetime.

- *Childhood and late-life conditions have been renamed.* Along with removing the outdated term "mental retardation" in favour of *intellectual disability*, the *DSM-5* renames childhood conditions as *neurodevelopmental disorders*, and "dementia and amnestic disorders" as *neurocognitive disorders*.

- *Autism disorder has been reclassified.* Different forms of autism are now grouped together and called *Autism Spectrum Disorder (ASD)*, which focuses on the degree of severity of autism.

- *Sexually based disorders have been reconceptualized and renamed.* "Gender identity disorder" has been reclassified as *gender dysphoria*. This distinction makes it clear that having a gender identity that is in conflict with one's biological sex does not imply a psychological disorder. Additionally, "paraphilia" has been renamed *paraphilic disorders*, emphasizing the presence of some atypical sexual interests that do not necessarily indicate a psychological disorder.

Diagnostic and Statistical Manual of Mental Disorders, Fifth Edition (DSM-5)
A system, devised by the American Psychiatric Association, used by most professionals to diagnose and classify abnormal behaviour.

FIGURE 2

This list of disorders represents the major categories from the *DSM-5*. It is only a partial list of the scores of disorders included in the diagnostic manual.

Categories of Disorders	Examples
Anxiety (problems in which anxiety impedes daily functioning)	Generalized anxiety disorder, panic disorder, phobic disorder
Somatic symptom and related disorders (psychological difficulties displayed through physical problems)	Illness anxiety disorder, conversion disorder
Dissociative (the splitting apart of crucial parts of personality that are usually integrated)	Dissociative identity disorder (multiple personality), dissociative amnesia, dissociative fugue
Mood (emotions of depression or euphoria that are so strong they intrude on everyday living)	Major depressive disorders, bipolar disorder
Schizophrenia spectrum and other psychotic disorders (declines in functioning, thought and language disturbances, perception disorders, emotional disturbances, and withdrawal from others)	Delusional disorder
Personality (problems that create little personal distress but that lead to an inability to function as a normal member of society)	Antisocial (sociopathic) personality disorder, narcissistic personality disorder
Sexual (problems related to sexual arousal from unusual objects or problems related to functioning)	Paraphilic disorders, sexual dysfunction
Substance-related (problems related to drug dependence and abuse)	Alcohol, cocaine, hallucinogens, marijuana
Neurocognitive disorders	Alzheimer's

Source: Adapted from *DSM-5*, 2013.
Photo Source: © Editorial Image, LLC/Alamy.

- *Criteria for some disorders have been made less restrictive.* In particular, the conditions that need to be met for an adult attention-deficit hyperactivity disorder (ADHD) diagnosis are broader—meaning that more people are likely to be classified with adult ADHD. Additionally, bereaved clients are no longer diagnosed with depression if symptoms arose within a few months of the death of a loved one.

- *The "five axes model" is eliminated.* In the previous version of DSM, disorders were categorized along one of five axes (Axis I, Clinical Disorders; Axis II, Personality Disorders and Mental Retardation; Axis III, General Medical Conditions; Axis IV, Psychosocial and Environmental Problems; and Axis V, Global Assessment of Functioning). These axes have been eliminated from the new version, *DSM-5*.

In many other respects, the *DSM* remains unchanged in the newest revision. Like its predecessors, *DSM-5* is primarily descriptive and avoids suggesting an underlying cause for an individual's behaviour and problems. For instance, the term neurotic—a label that is commonly used by people in their everyday descriptions of abnormal behaviour—is not listed as a *DSM-5* category. Because the term *neurosis* refers to problems associated with a specific cause based in Freud's theory of personality, it is not included in *DSM-5*.

DSM-5 has the advantage, then, of providing a descriptive system that does not specify the cause of or reason for a problem. Rather, it paints a picture of the behaviour that is being displayed. Why should this approach be important? For one thing, it allows communication between mental health professionals of diverse backgrounds and theoretical approaches. In addition, precise classification enables researchers to explore the causes of a problem. Without reliable descriptions of abnormal behaviour, researchers would be hard pressed to find ways to investigate the disorder. Finally, *DSM-5* provides a kind of conceptual shorthand through which professionals can describe the behaviours that tend to occur together in an individual (First, Frances, & Pincus, 2002; Gordon & Heimberg, 2011).

Conning the Classifiers: The Shortcomings of *DSM*

When clinical psychologist David Rosenhan and eight colleagues sought admission to separate mental hospitals in the 1970s, each stated that he or she was hearing voices—"unclear voices" that said "empty," "hollow," and "thud"—and each was immediately admitted to the hospital. However, the truth was that they actually were conducting a study, and none of them was really hearing voices. Aside from these misrepresentations, *everything* else they did and said represented their true behaviour, including the responses they gave during extensive admission interviews and their answers to the battery of tests they were asked to complete. In fact, as soon as they were admitted, they said they no longer heard any voices. In short, each of the pseudo-patients acted in a "normal" way (Rosenhan, 1973).

We might assume that Rosenhan and his colleagues would have been quickly discovered as the impostors they were, but this was not the case. Instead, each of them was diagnosed as severely abnormal on the basis of observed behaviour. Mental health professionals labelled most as suffering from schizophrenia and kept them in the hospital for three to fifty-two days, with the average stay being nineteen days. Even when they were discharged, most of the "patients" left with the label *schizophrenia—in remission*, implying that the abnormal behaviour had only temporarily subsided and could recur at any time. Most disturbing, no one on the hospital staff identified any of the pseudo-patients as impostors—although some of the actual patients figured out the ruse.

The Stigma of Labelling

The results of Rosenhan's classic study illustrate that placing labels on individuals powerfully influences the way mental health workers perceive and interpret their actions. It also points out that determining who is psychologically disordered is not always a clear-cut or accurate process.

Gender dysphoria (in which one's gender identity is in conflict with one's biological sex) provides a modern illustration of the dilemma between the pros of a formal diagnosis and the cons of patient labelling. For example, most medical insurance providers require a formal, specific diagnosis in order to provide healthcare coverage for procedures such as a sex change operation. Many individuals who experience a conflict between their gender identity and their biological sex object theoretically to the idea that their desire to be the other sex should be labelled a "disorder." Yet without a formal diagnosis, those same individuals may be forced to pay out-of-pocket for what is an expensive medical procedure.

This diagnosis-based system of insurance coverage often creates a Catch-22 for mental healthcare professionals: They must decide between potentially stigmatizing their clients by providing a formal diagnosis, implying some type of disorder, or leaving patients undiagnosed and potentially without the financial support necessary to receive important procedures that will significantly improve a client's quality of life (Kamens, 2011; Kleinplatz, Moser, & Lev, 2013).

Critics of the *DSM* argue that labelling an individual as abnormal provides a dehumanizing, lifelong stigma. (Think, for example, of political contenders whose candidacies have been terminated by the disclosure that they received treatment for severe psychological disorders.) Furthermore, after an initial diagnosis has been made, mental health professionals, who may concentrate on the initial diagnostic category, could overlook other diagnostic possibilities (McNally, 2011; Szasz, 2011; Frances, 2013).

Although the *DSM-5* was developed to provide more accurate and consistent diagnoses of psychological disorders, it isn't always successful. For instance, critics charge that it relies too much on the medical perspective. Because it was drawn up by psychiatrists—who are physicians—some condemn it for viewing psychological disorders primarily in terms of the symptoms of an underlying physiological disorder. Moreover, critics suggest that *DSM-5* compartmentalizes people into inflexible, all-or-none categories rather than considering the degree to which a person displays psychologically disordered behaviour (Samuel & Widiger, 2006; Francis, 2013).

STUDY ALERT!

It is important to understand the advantages and weaknesses of the *DSM* classification system.

Still, despite the drawbacks inherent in any labelling system, the *DSM-5* has had an important influence on the way in which mental health professionals view psychological disorders. It has increased both the reliability and the validity of diagnostic categorization. In addition, it offers a logical way to organize examination of the major types of mental disturbance.

Evaluate

1. One problem in defining abnormal behaviour is that
   a. Statistically rare behaviour may not be abnormal.
   b. Not all abnormalities are accompanied by feelings of discomfort.
   c. Cultural standards are too general to use as a measuring tool.
   d. All of the above.

2. If abnormality is defined as behaviour that causes personal discomfort or harms others, which of the following people is most likely to need treatment?
   a. An executive is afraid to accept a promotion because it would require moving from her ground floor office to the top floor of a tall office building.
   b. A man decides to quit his job and chooses to live on the street in order to live a "simpler life."
   c. A woman believes that friendly spacemen visit her house every Thursday.
   d. A photographer lives with nineteen cats in a small apartment, lovingly caring for them.

3. Virginia's mother thinks that her daughter's behaviour is clearly abnormal because, despite being offered admission to medical school, Virginia decides to become a waitress. What approach is Virginia's mother using to define abnormal behaviour?

4. Which of the following is a strong argument against the medical perspective on abnormality?
   a. Physiological abnormalities are almost always impossible to identify.
   b. There is no conclusive way to link past experience and behaviour.
   c. The medical perspective rests too heavily on the effects of nutrition.
   d. Assigning behaviour to a physical problem takes responsibility away from the individual for changing his or her behaviour.

5. Cheryl is painfully shy. According to the behavioural perspective, the best way to deal with her "abnormal" behaviour is to
   a. Treat the underlying physical problem
   b. Use the principles of learning theory to modify her shy behaviour
   c. Express a great deal of caring
   d. Uncover her negative past experiences through hypnosis

Answers to Evaluate Questions

1. d; 2. a; 3. deviation from the ideal; 4. d; 5. b

Key Terms

abnormal behaviour

behavioural perspective (on psychological disorders)

cognitive perspective (on psychological disorders)

Diagnostic and Statistical Manual of Mental Disorders, Fifth Edition (DSM-5)

humanistic perspective (on psychological disorders)

medical perspective (on psychological disorders)

psychoanalytic perspective (on psychological disorders)

sociocultural perspective (on psychological disorders)

The Major Psychological Disorders

LEARNING OBJECTIVE

What are the major psychological disorders?

Sally experienced her first panic attack out of the blue, 3 weeks after completing her final year in college. She had just finished a job interview and was meeting some friends for dinner. In the restaurant, she began to feel dizzy. Within a few seconds, her heart was pounding, and she was feeling breathless, as though she might pass out. Her friends noticed that she did not look well and offered to drive her home. Sally suggested they stop at the hospital emergency room instead. Although she felt better by the time they arrived at the hospital, and tests indicated nothing wrong, Sally experienced a similar episode a week later while at a movie. . . .

Her attacks became more and more frequent. Before long, she was having several attacks per week. In addition, she constantly worried about having attacks. She began to avoid exercise and other activities that produced physical sensations. She also noticed the attacks were worse when she was alone. She began to avoid driving, shopping in large stores, and eating in all restaurants. Some weeks she avoided leaving the house completely (Antony, Brown, & Barlow, 1992, p. 79).

Sally suffered from panic disorder, the same psychological disorder endured by NHL hockey player Shayne Corson (discussed in detail at the beginning of this chapter). Keep in mind that although we'll be discussing these disorders in a dispassionate manner, each represents a very human set of difficulties that influence, and in some cases considerably disrupt, people's lives.

Anxiety Disorders

Howie Mandel, Donny Osmond, Howard Stern. The common link among these famous performers? Each one of them has struggled with a psychological disorder known as **anxiety disorder**. Anxiety disorder is different from the experience *anxiety*, a feeling of apprehension or tension that we all feel at one time or another in reaction to stressful situations. There is nothing "wrong" with such anxiety. It is a normal reaction to stress that often helps, rather than hinders, our daily functioning. Without some anxiety, for instance, most of us probably would not have much motivation to study hard, undergo physical exams, or spend long hours at our jobs.

But some people experience anxiety in situations in which there is no external reason or cause for such distress. When anxiety occurs without external justification and begins to affect people's daily functioning, mental health professionals consider it a psychological problem known as anxiety disorder. We'll discuss three major types of anxiety disorders: phobic disorder, panic disorder, and generalized anxiety disorder.

Anxiety disorder
The occurrence of anxiety without an obvious external cause that affects daily functioning.

Generalized Anxiety Disorder

People with **generalized anxiety disorder** experience long-term, persistent anxiety and worry. Sometimes their concerns are about identifiable issues involving family, money, work, or health. In other cases, though, people with the disorder feel that something dreadful is about to happen but can't identify the reason, experiencing "free-floating" anxiety.

Because of persistent anxiety, people with generalized anxiety disorder cannot concentrate, cannot set their worry and fears aside; their lives become centred on their worry. Their anxiety may eventually cause medical problems. Because of heightened muscle tension and arousal, individuals with generalized anxiety disorder may develop headaches, dizziness, heart palpitations, or insomnia. Figure 1 shows the most common symptoms of generalized anxiety disorder.

FIGURE 1

Frequency of symptoms in cases of generalized anxiety disorder.

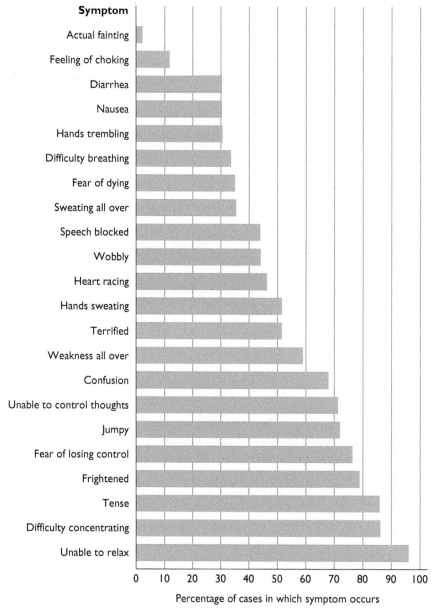

Source: Adapted from Beck & Emery, 1985, pp. 87–88.

Generalized anxiety disorder
The occurrence of long-term, persistent anxiety and worry.

Phobic Disorder

It's not easy moving through the world when you're terrified of electricity. "Donna," 45, a writer, knows that better than most. Get her in the vicinity of an appliance or a light switch or—all but unthinkable—a thunderstorm, and she is overcome by a terror so blinding she can think of nothing but fleeing. That, of course, is not always possible, so over time, Donna has come up with other answers. When she opens the refrigerator door, rubber-sole shoes are a must. If a light bulb blows, she will tolerate the dark until someone else changes it for her. Clothes shopping is done only when necessary, lest static on garments send her running from the store. And swimming at night is absolutely out of the question, lest underwater lights electrocute her (Kluger, 2001, p. 51).

Donna suffers from a **specific phobia**, an intense, irrational fear of a specific object or situation. For example, claustrophobia is a fear of enclosed places, acrophobia is a fear of high places, xenophobia is a fear of strangers, and—as in Donna's case—electrophobia is a fear of electricity. Although the objective danger posed by an anxiety-producing stimulus (which can be just about anything, as you can see from the list in Figure 2) is typically small or nonexistent, to the individual suffering from the phobia the danger is great, and a full-blown panic attack may follow exposure to the stimulus. Phobic disorders differ from generalized anxiety disorders and panic disorders in that there is a specific, identifiable stimulus that sets off the anxiety reaction.

Phobias may have only a minor impact on people's lives if those who suffer from them can avoid the stimuli that trigger fear. Unless one is a professional firefighter or tightrope walker, for example, a fear of heights will have little impact on one's daily life. On the other hand, a fear of strangers presents a more serious problem. In one extreme case, a Washington woman left her home just three times in 30 years—once to visit her family, once for an operation, and once to purchase ice cream for a dying companion (Kimbrel, 2007; Wong, Sarver, & Beidel, 2011; Stopa et al., 2013).

Panic Disorder

In another type of anxiety disorder, **panic disorder**, *panic attacks* occur that last from a few seconds to several hours. NHL hockey player Shayne Corson has bravely shared his private battle with panic disorder in a series of interviews

FIGURE 2

Phobic disorders differ from generalized anxiety and panic disorders because a specific stimulus can be identified. Listed here are a number of phobias and their triggers.

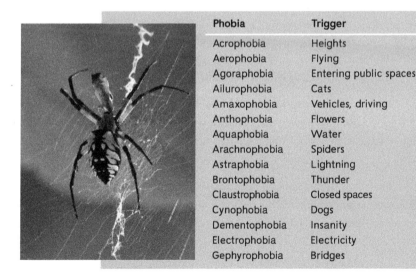

Phobia	Trigger	Phobia	Trigger
Acrophobia	Heights	Herpetophobia	Reptiles
Aerophobia	Flying	Hydrophobia	Water
Agoraphobia	Entering public spaces	Mikrophobia	Germs
Ailurophobia	Cats	Murophobia	Mice
Amaxophobia	Vehicles, driving	Mysophobia	Dirt or germs
Anthophobia	Flowers	Numerophobia	Numbers
Aquaphobia	Water	Nyctophobia	Darkness
Arachnophobia	Spiders	Ochlophobia	Crowds
Astraphobia	Lightning	Ophidiophobia	Snakes
Brontophobia	Thunder	Ornithophobia	Birds
Claustrophobia	Closed spaces	Phonophobia	Speaking out loud
Cynophobia	Dogs	Pyrophobia	Fire
Dementophobia	Insanity	Thanatophobia	Death
Electrophobia	Electricity	Trichophobia	Hair
Gephyrophobia	Bridges	Xenophobia	Strangers

Source: © GeoStock/Getty Images RF.

Specific phobia
Intense, irrational fears of specific objects or situations.

Panic disorder
The occurrence of panic attacks that last from a few seconds to a few hours.

(discussed in detail at the beginning of this chapter). Unlike phobias, which are stimulated by specific objects or situations, panic disorders do not have any identifiable stimuli. Instead, during an attack, such as the ones experienced by Sally in the case described earlier, anxiety suddenly—and often without warning—rises to a peak, and an individual feels a sense of impending, unavoidable doom. Although the physical symptoms differ from person to person, they may include heart palpitations, shortness of breath, unusual amounts of sweating, faintness and dizziness, an urge to urinate, gastric sensations, and—in extreme cases—a sense of imminent death. After such an attack, it is no wonder that people tend to feel exhausted (Rachman & deSilva, 2004; Laederach-Hofmann & Messerli-Buergy, 2007; Montgomery, 2011).

Panic attacks seemingly come out of nowhere and are unconnected to any specific stimulus. Because they don't know what triggers their feelings of panic, victims of panic attacks may become fearful of going places. In fact, some people with panic disorder develop a complication called *agoraphobia*, the fear of being in a situation in which escape is difficult and in which help for a possible panic attack would not be available. In extreme cases, people with agoraphobia never leave their homes (Marcaurelle, Belanger, & Marchand, 2005; Herran, Carrera, & Sierra-Biddle, 2006; Wittchen et al., 2008).

In addition to the physical symptoms, panic disorder affects how the brain processes information. For instance, people with panic disorder have reduced reactions in the anterior cingulate cortex to stimuli (such as viewing a fearful face) that normally produce a strong reaction in those without the disorder. It may be that recurring high levels of emotional arousal that patients with panic disorder experience desensitizes them to emotional stimuli (Pillay et al., 2006, 2007).

Obsessive-Compulsive Disorder

In **obsessive-compulsive disorder**, people are plagued by unwanted thoughts, called obsessions, or feel that they must carry out actions, termed compulsions, against their will.

An **obsession** is a persistent, unwanted thought or idea that keeps recurring. For example, a student may be unable to stop thinking that she has neglected to put her name on a test and may think about it constantly for the two weeks it takes to get the paper back. A man may go on vacation and wonder the whole time whether he locked his house. A woman may hear the same tune running through her head over and over. In each case, the thought or idea is unwanted and difficult to put out of mind. Of course, many people suffer from mild obsessions from time to time, but usually such thoughts persist only for a short period. For people with serious obsessions, however, the thoughts persist for days or months and may consist of bizarre, troubling images (Lee & Kwon, 2003; Lee et al., 2005; Rassin & Muris, 2007).

As part of an obsessive-compulsive disorder, people may also experience **compulsions**, irresistible urges to repeatedly carry out some act that seems strange and unreasonable, even to them. Whatever the compulsive behaviour is, people experience extreme anxiety if they cannot carry it out, and even if it is something they want to stop. The acts may be relatively trivial, such as repeatedly checking the stove to make sure all the burners are turned off, or more unusual, such as continuously washing oneself (Frost & Steketee, 2002; Clark, 2007; Moretz & McKay, 2009).

For example, consider this passage from the autobiography of a person with obsessive-compulsive disorder:

> I thought my parents would die if I didn't do everything in exactly the right way. When I took my glasses off at night I'd have to place them on the dresser at a particular angle. Sometimes I'd turn on the light and get out of bed seven times until I felt comfortable with the angle. If the angle wasn't right, I felt that my parents would die. The feeling ate up my insides.

> If I didn't grab the molding on the wall just the right way as I entered or exited my room; if I didn't hang a shirt in the closet perfectly; if I didn't read a paragraph a certain way; if my hands and nails weren't perfectly clean, I thought my incorrect behaviour would kill my parents (Summers, 2000, p. 42).

Obsessive-compulsive disorder
A disorder in which a person is plagued by unwanted thoughts, called obsessions, or feel that they must carry out actions, termed compulsions, against their will.

Obsession
Persistent, unwanted thoughts or ideas that keep recurring.

Compulsions
An irresistible urge to repeatedly carry out some act that seems strange and unreasonable.

Although carrying out compulsive rituals may lead to some immediate reduction of anxiety, in the long term the anxiety returns. In fact, people with severe cases lead lives filled with unrelenting tension (Goodman, Rudorfer, & Maser, 2000; Penzel, 2000).

The Causes of Anxiety Disorders and Obsessive-Compulsive Disorder

We've considered several of the major types of anxiety disorders and obsessive-compulsive disorder, but there are many other related disorders. The variety of anxiety disorders means that no single explanation fits all cases. Genetic factors clearly are part of the picture. For example, if one member of a pair of identical twins has panic disorder, there is a 30 percent chance that the other twin will have it also. Furthermore, a person's characteristic level of anxiety is related to a specific gene involved in the production of the neurotransmitter serotonin. This is consistent with findings indicating that certain chemical deficiencies in the brain appear to produce some kinds of anxiety disorder (Holmes et al., 2003; Beidel & Turner, 2007; Chamberlain et al., 2008).

Some researchers believe that an overactive autonomic nervous system may be at the root of panic attacks. Specifically, they suggest that poor regulation of the brain's locus ceruleus may lead to panic attacks, which cause the limbic system to become overstimulated. In turn, the overstimulated limbic system produces chronic anxiety, which ultimately leads the locus ceruleus to generate still more panic attacks (Balaban, 2002; Davies et al., 2008).

There are also biological causes at work in OCD. For example, researchers have found differences in the brains of those with the disorder compared to those without it (Christian et al., 2008).

Psychologists who employ the behavioural perspective have taken a different approach that emphasizes environmental factors. They consider anxiety to be a learned response to stress. For instance, suppose a dog bites a young girl. When the girl next sees a dog, she is frightened and runs away—a behaviour that relieves her anxiety and thereby reinforces her avoidance behaviour. After repeated encounters with dogs in which she is reinforced for her avoidance behaviour, she may develop a full-fledged phobia regarding dogs.

Finally, the cognitive perspective suggests that anxiety disorders grow out of inappropriate and inaccurate thoughts and beliefs about circumstances in a person's world. For example, people with anxiety disorders may view a friendly puppy as a ferocious and savage pit bull, or they may see an air disaster looming every moment they are in the vicinity of an airplane. According to the cognitive perspective, people's maladaptive thoughts about the world are at the root of an anxiety disorder (Frost & Steketee, 2002; Wang & Clark, 2002; Ouimet, Gawronski, & Dozois, 2009).

Mood Disorders

From the time I woke up in the morning until the time I went to bed at night, I was unbearably miserable and seemingly incapable of any kind of joy or enthusiasm. Everything—every thought, word, movement—was an effort. Everything that once was sparkling now was flat. I seemed to myself to be dull, boring, inadequate, thick brained, unlit, unresponsive, chill skinned, bloodless, and sparrow drab. I doubted, completely, my ability to do anything well. It seemed as though my mind had slowed down and burned out to the point of being virtually useless (Jamison, 1995a, p. 110).

We all experience mood swings. Sometimes we are happy, perhaps even euphoric; at other times we feel upset, saddened, or depressed. Such changes in mood are a normal part of everyday life. In some people, however, moods are so pronounced and lingering—like the feelings described above by writer (and psychiatrist) Kay Jamison—that they interfere with the ability to function effectively. In extreme cases, a mood may become life-threatening, and in others it may cause the person to lose touch with reality. Situations such as these represent **mood disorders**, disturbances in emotional experiences that are strong enough to intrude on everyday living.

Major Depression

Alanis Morissette, Margot Kidder, Jim Carrey. The common link among these Canadians? Each suffered from periodic attacks of **major depression**, a severe form of depression that interferes with concentration, decision making, and

Mood disorders
A disturbance in emotional experiences that is strong enough to intrude on everyday living.

Major depression
A severe form of depression that interferes with concentration, decision making, and sociability.

sociability. Major depression is one of the more common forms of mood disorders. Approximately one in ten Canadians will experience major depression during their lifetime (Public Health Agency of Canada, 2002b; Dryden, 2003; Ghaemi, 2003; Hoover, 2004).

Depression should be seen as an illness, not a weakness. So much so that, on average, depressed Canadians stay home sick thirty-two days per year because of debilitating symptoms that render them incapable of doing normal work activities. Furthermore, the economic costs of clinical depression are so high that the World Health Organization (WHO) identified depression as the number one cause of short-term disability in the world (CBC.ca, 2007).

Women are twice as likely to experience major depression as men, with one-fourth of all females apt to encounter it at some point during their lives. Furthermore, although no one is sure why, the rate of depression is going up throughout the world. Results of in-depth interviews conducted in the United States, Puerto Rico, Taiwan, Lebanon, Canada, Italy, Germany, and France indicate that the incidence of depression has increased significantly over previous rates in every area. In fact, in some countries, the likelihood that individuals will have major depression at some point in their lives is three times higher than it was for earlier generations. In addition, people are developing major depression at increasingly younger ages (Kendler et al., 2006; Staley, Sanacora, & Tagman, 2006; Sado et al., 2011).

Some types of depression follow a seasonal pattern, such as Seasonal Affect Disorder (SAD), which tends to be more common in northern countries that receive very little sunlight during winter months. In fact, the Canadian Mental Health Association (CMHA) predicts that 1 to 3 percent of Canadians experience SAD so severely that it interferes with their ability to function in their daily lives (CBC.ca, 2008).

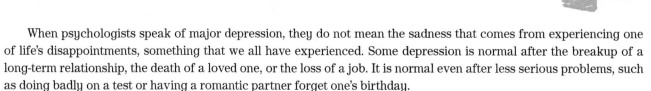

STUDY ALERT!

Major depression differs from the normal depression that occasionally occurs during most people's lives; major depression is more intense, lasts longer, and may have no clear trigger.

When psychologists speak of major depression, they do not mean the sadness that comes from experiencing one of life's disappointments, something that we all have experienced. Some depression is normal after the breakup of a long-term relationship, the death of a loved one, or the loss of a job. It is normal even after less serious problems, such as doing badly on a test or having a romantic partner forget one's birthday.

People who suffer from major depression experience similar sorts of feelings, but the severity tends to be considerably greater. They may feel useless, worthless, and lonely and may despair over the future. Moreover, they may experience such feelings for months or even years. They may cry uncontrollably, have sleep disturbances, and be at risk for suicide. The depth of such behaviour and the length of time it lasts are the hallmarks of major depression. (Figure 3 provides a self-assessment of depression.)

Mania and Bipolar Disorder

While depression leads to the depths of despair, mania leads to emotional heights. **Mania** is an extended state of intense, wild elation. People experiencing mania feel intense happiness, power, invulnerability, and energy. They may become involved in wild schemes, believing they will succeed at anything they attempt. Consider, for example, the following description of an individual who experienced a manic episode:

> Mr. O'Reilly took a leave of absence from his government job. He purchased a large number of cuckoo clocks and then an expensive car, which he planned to use as a mobile showroom for his wares, anticipating that he would make a great deal of money. He proceeded to "tear around town" buying and selling clocks and other merchandise, and when he was not out, he was continuously on the phone making "deals." He rarely slept and, uncharacteristically, spent every evening in neighbourhood bars drinking heavily and, according to him, "wheeling and dealing." . . . He was $3,000 in debt and had driven his family to exhaustion with his excessive activity and talkativeness. He said, however, that he felt "on top of the world" (Spitzer et al., 1983, p. 115).

Mania
An extended state of intense, wild elation.

FIGURE 3

This is a version of a test distributed by mental health organizations in the U.S. during the annual National Depression Screening Day, a nationwide event that seeks to identify people who are suffering from depression that is severe enough to warrant psychological intervention.

A Test for Depression

To complete the questionnaire, count the number of statements with which you agree:

1. I feel downhearted, blue, and sad.
2. I don't enjoy the things that I used to.
3. I feel that others would be better off if I were dead.
4. I feel that I am not useful or needed.
5. I notice that I am losing weight.
6. I have trouble sleeping through the night.
7. I am restless and can't keep still.
8. My mind isn't as clear as it used to be.
9. I get tired for no reason.
10. I feel hopeless about the future.

SCORING

If you agree with at least five of the statements, including either item 1 or 2, and if you have had these symptoms for at least two weeks, help from a professional is strongly recommended. If you answer yes to number 3, you should get help immediately.

Source: National Institute of Mental Health website at www.nimh.nih.gov/health/publications/depression/what-are-the-signs-and-symptoms-of-depression.shtml.

In many cases, people sequentially experience periods of mania and depression. This alternation of mania and depression is called **bipolar disorder** (a condition previously known as manic-depressive disorder). The swings between highs and lows may occur a few days apart or may alternate over a period of years. In addition, in bipolar disorder, periods of depression are usually longer than periods of mania.

Ironically, some of society's most creative individuals may have suffered from bipolar disorder. The imagination, drive, excitement, and energy that they display during manic stages allow them to make unusually creative contributions. For instance, historical analysis of the composer Robert Schumann's music shows that he was most prolific during periods of mania. In contrast, his output dropped off drastically during periods of depression (see Figure 4). On the other hand, the high output associated with mania does not necessarily lead to higher quality: On the other hand, the high output associated with mania does not necessarily lead to higher quality: Some of Schumann's greatest works were created outside his periods of mania (Szegedy Maszak, 2003; Kyaga et al., 2013).

Despite the creative fires that may be lit by mania, persons who experience this disorder often show a recklessness that produces self-injury—emotionally and sometimes physically. They may alienate others with their talkativeness, inflated self-esteem, and indifference to the needs of others.

Causes of Mood Disorders

Because they represent a major mental health problem, mood disorders—and, in particular, depression—have received a good deal of study. Several approaches have been used to explain the disorders.

Genetic and biological factors. Some mood disorders clearly have genetic and biological roots. In fact, most evidence suggests that bipolar disorders are caused primarily by biological factors. For instance, bipolar disorder (and some forms of major depression) clearly runs in some families, pointing to a genetic cause. Furthermore, researchers

Bipolar disorder
A disorder in which a person alternates between periods of euphoric feelings of mania and periods of depression.

FIGURE 4

The number of musical compositions written by composer Robert Schumann in a given year is related to his periods of depression and mania (Slater & Meyer, 1959; reprinted in Jamison, 1993). Why do you think mania might be associated with creative productivity in some people?

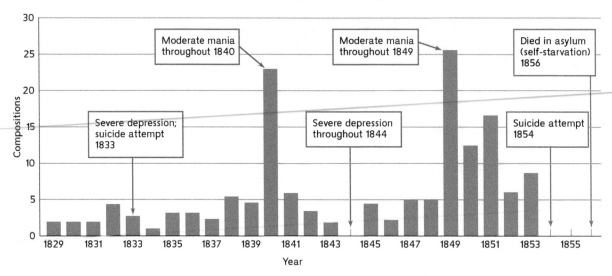

Source: Slater & Meyer, 1959; reprinted in Jamison, 1993.

have found that several neurotransmitters play a role in depression. For example, alterations in the functioning of serotonin and norepinephrine in the brain are related to the disorder.

Finally, research on neuroimaging suggests that a brain structure called area 25 is related to depression: When area 25 is smaller than normal, it is associated with a higher risk of depression. Furthermore, the right anterior insula, a region of the brain related to self-awareness and interpersonal experience, also appears to be related to depression (Popa et al., 2008; Insel, 2010; Cisler et al., 2013).

Psychological causes. Other explanations for depression have also included a focus on psychological causes. For instance, proponents of psychoanalytic approaches see depression as the result of feelings of loss (real or potential) or of anger directed at oneself. One psychoanalytic approach, for instance, suggests that depression is produced by the loss or threatened loss of a parent early in life (Vanheule et al., 2006).

Environmental factors. Behavioural theories of depression argue that the stresses of life produce a reduction in positive reinforcers. As a result, people begin to withdraw, which only reduces positive reinforcers further. In addition, people receive attention for their depressive behaviour, which further reinforces the depression (Lewinsohn & Essau, 2002; Lewinsohn et al., 2003; Domschke, 2013).

Cognitive and emotional factors. Some explanations for mood disorders attribute them to cognitive factors. For example, psychologist Martin Seligman suggests that depression is largely a response to learned helplessness. *Learned helplessness* is a learned expectation that events in one's life are uncontrollable and that one cannot escape from the situation. As a consequence, people simply give up fighting aversive events and submit to them, which thereby produces depression. Other theorists go a step further and suggest that depression results from hopelessness, a combination of learned helplessness and an expectation that negative outcomes in one's life are inevitable (Kwon & Laurenceau, 2002; Bjornstad, 2006; Li et al., 2011).

Clinical psychologist Aaron Beck has proposed that faulty cognitions underlie people's depressed feelings. Specifically, his cognitive theory of depression suggests that depressed individuals typically view themselves as life's losers, blaming themselves whenever anything goes wrong. By focusing on the negative side of situations, they feel inept and unable to act constructively to change their environment. In sum, their negative cognitions lead to feelings of depression (Newman et al., 2002).

Brain imaging studies suggest that people with depression experience a general blunting of emotional reactions. For example, one study found that the brains of people with depression showed significantly less activation when they viewed photos of human faces displaying strong emotions than those without the disorder (Gotlib et al., 2004; see Figure 5).

FIGURE 5

The brains of those with depression (*left*) show significantly less activation in response to photos of sad, angry, and fearful faces than those of people without the disorder (*right*).

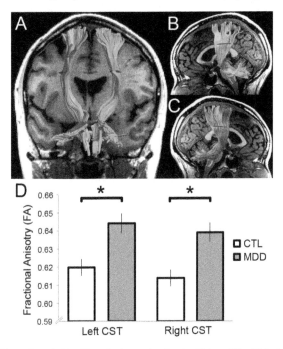

Source: Sacchet et al., Structural abnormality of the corticospinal tract in major depressive disorder. *Biology of Mood & Anxiety Disorders* 2014, 4: 8, Fig 1. Figure provided by Ian H. Gotlib.

Depression in Women

The various theories of depression have not provided a complete answer to an elusive question that has dogged researchers: Why does depression occur in approximately twice as many women as men—a pattern that is similar across a variety of cultures?

One explanation suggests that the stress women experience may be greater than the stress men experience at certain points in their lives—such as when a woman must simultaneously earn a living and be the primary caregiver for her children. In addition, women have a higher risk for physical and sexual abuse, typically earn lower wages than men, report greater unhappiness with their marriages, and generally experience chronic negative circumstances. Furthermore, women and men may respond to stress with different coping mechanisms. For instance, men may abuse drugs, while women respond with depression (Nolen-Hoeksema, 2007; Hyde, Mezulis, & Abramson, 2008; Komarovskaya et al., 2011).

Biological factors may also explain some women's depression. For example, the rate of female depression begins to rise during puberty, so some psychologists believe that hormones make women more vulnerable to the disorder. In addition, 25–50 percent of women who take oral contraceptives report symptoms of depression, and depression that occurs after the birth of a child is linked to hormonal changes. Finally, structural differences in men's and women's brains may be related to gender differences in depression (Holden, 2005; Graham, Bancroft, & Doll, 2007; Solomon & Herman, 2009; Silverstein et al., 2013). Ultimately, it is clear that researchers have discovered no definitive solutions to the puzzle of depression, and there are many alternative explanations. Most likely, a complex interaction of several factors causes mood disorders.

Schizophrenia

I'm a doctor, you know . . . I don't have a diploma, but I'm a doctor. I'm glad to be a mental patient, because it taught me how to be humble. I use Cover Girl creamy natural makeup. Oral Roberts has been here to visit me . . . This place is where *Mad* magazine is published. The Nixons make Noxon metal polish. When I was a little girl, I used to sit and tell stories to myself. When I was older, I turned off the sound on the TV set and made up dialogue to go with the shows I watched . . . I'm a week pregnant. I have schizophrenia—cancer of the nerves. My body is overcrowded with nerves. This is going to win me the Nobel Prize for medicine. I don't consider myself schizophrenic anymore. There's no such thing as schizophrenia, there's only mental telepathy. I once had a friend named Camilla Costello (Sheehan, 1982, pp. 72–73).

This excerpt illustrates the efforts of a woman with schizophrenia, one of the more severe forms of mental disturbance, to hold a conversation with a clinician. People with schizophrenia account for by far the largest percentage of those hospitalized for mental disorders. They are also in many respects the least likely to recover from their psychological difficulties.

Schizophrenia refers to a class of disorders in which severe distortion of reality occurs. Thinking, perception, and emotion may deteriorate; the individual may withdraw from social interaction; and the person may display bizarre behaviour. The symptoms displayed by persons with schizophrenia may vary considerably over time. Nonetheless, a number of characteristics reliably distinguish schizophrenia from other disorders. They include the following:

- *Decline from a previous level of functioning.* An individual can no longer carry out activities he or she was once able to do.

- *Disturbances of thought and language.* People with schizophrenia use logic and language in a peculiar way. Their thinking often does not make sense, and their information processing is frequently faulty. They also do not follow conventional linguistic rules (Penn et al., 1997). Consider, for example, the following response to the question "Why do you think people believe in God?"

Uh, let's, I don't know why, let's see, balloon travel. He holds it up for you, the balloon. He don't let you fall out, your little legs sticking down through the clouds. He's down to the smokestack, looking through the smoke trying to get the balloon gassed up you know. Way they're flying on top that way, legs sticking out. I don't know, looking down on the ground, heck, that'd make you so dizzy you just stay and sleep you know, hold down and sleep there. I used to be sleep outdoors, you know, sleep outdoors instead of going home (Chapman & Chapman, 1973, p. 3).

As this selection illustrates, although the basic grammatical structure may be intact, the substance of thinking characteristic of schizophrenia is often illogical, garbled, and lacking in meaningful content (Holden, 2003; Heinrichs, 2005).

- *Delusions.* People with schizophrenia often have delusions, firmly held, unshakable beliefs with no basis in reality. Among the common delusions experienced by people with schizophrenia are the beliefs that they are being controlled by someone else, they are being persecuted by others, and their thoughts are being broadcast so that others know what they are thinking (Coltheart, Langdon, & McKay, 2007; Startup, Bucci, & Langdon, 2009).

- *Hallucinations and perceptual disorders.* People with schizophrenia do not perceive the world as most other people do. They also may have hallucinations, the experience of perceiving things that do not actually exist. Furthermore, they may see, hear, or smell things differently from others (see Figure 6) and do not even have a sense of their bodies in the way that others do, having difficulty determining where their bodies stop and the rest of the world begins (Copolov et al., 2003; Botvinick, 2004; Thomas et al., 2007).

- *Emotional disturbances.* People with schizophrenia sometimes show a bland lack of emotion in which even the most dramatic events produce little or no emotional response. Conversely, they may display emotion that is inappropriate to a situation. For example, a person with schizophrenia may laugh uproariously at a funeral or react with anger when being helped by someone.

- *Withdrawal.* People with schizophrenia tend to have little interest in others. They tend not to socialize or hold real conversations with others, although they may talk at another person. In the most extreme cases they do not even acknowledge the presence of other people, appearing to be in their own isolated world.

Usually, the onset of schizophrenia occurs in early adulthood, and the symptoms follow one of two primary courses. In *process schizophrenia*, the symptoms develop slowly and subtly. There may be a gradual withdrawal from the world, excessive daydreaming, and a blunting of emotion, until eventually the disorder reaches the point where

Schizophrenia
A class of disorders in which severe distortion of reality occurs.

FIGURE 6

This unusual art was created by an individual with schizophrenia.

Source: © Victoria and Albert Museum, London.

others cannot overlook it. In other cases, known as *reactive schizophrenia*, the onset of symptoms is sudden and conspicuous. The treatment outlook for reactive schizophrenia is relatively favourable, but process schizophrenia has proved more difficult to treat.

DSM-5 classifies the symptoms of schizophrenia into two types. Positive-symptom schizophrenia is indicated by the presence of disordered behaviour such as hallucinations, delusions, and emotional extremes. In contrast, negative-symptom schizophrenia shows an absence or loss of normal functioning, such as social withdrawal or blunted emotions (Levine & Rabinowitz, 2007; Tandon et al., 2013).

The distinction between positive and negative symptoms of schizophrenia is important because it suggests that two different kinds of causes might trigger schizophrenia. Furthermore, it has implications for predicting treatment outcomes.

STUDY ALERT!

In positive-symptom schizophrenia disordered behaviour such as hallucinations, delusions, and emotional extremes are present; in negative-symptom schizophrenia absence or loss of normal functioning, such as social withdrawal or blunted emotions are dominant.

Solving the Puzzle of Schizophrenia: Biological Causes

Although schizophrenic behaviour clearly departs radically from normal behaviour, its causes are less apparent. It does appear, however, that schizophrenia has both biological and environmental origins (Sawa & Snyder, 2002).

Let's first consider the evidence pointing to a biological cause. Because schizophrenia is more common in some families than in others, genetic factors seem to be involved in producing at least a susceptibility to or readiness for developing schizophrenia. For example, the closer the genetic link between a person with schizophrenia and another individual, the greater the likelihood that the other person will experience the disorder (Brzustowicz et al., 2000; Plomin & McGuffin, 2003; Gottesman & Hanson, 2005; see Figure 7).

However, if genetics alone were responsible for schizophrenia, the chance of both of two identical twins having schizophrenia would be 100 percent instead of just under 50 percent, because identical twins have the same genetic makeup. Moreover, attempts to find a link between schizophrenia and a particular gene have been only partly successful. Apparently, genetic factors alone do not produce schizophrenia (Franzek & Beckmann, 1996; Lenzenweger & Dworkin, 1998).

One intriguing biological hypothesis to explain schizophrenia is that the brains of people with the disorder may harbour either a biochemical imbalance or a structural abnormality. For example, the *dopamine hypothesis* suggests that schizophrenia occurs when there is excess activity in the areas of the brain that use dopamine as a neurotransmitter. This hypothesis came to light after the discovery that drugs that block dopamine action in brain pathways can be highly effective in reducing the symptoms of schizophrenia. Other research suggests that glutamate, another

FIGURE 7

The closer the genetic links between two people, the greater the likelihood that if one experiences schizophrenia, so will the other sometime during his or her life. However, genetics is not the full story, because if it were, the risk of identical twins having schizophrenia would be 100 percent, not the 48 percent shown in this figure.

Risk of Developing Schizophrenia, Based on Genetic Relatedness to a Person with Schizophrenia		
Relationship	**Genetic Relatedness, %**	**Risk of Developing Schizophrenia, %**
Identical twin	100	48
Child of two schizophrenic parents	100	46
Fraternal twin	50	17
Offspring of one schizophrenic parent	50	17
Sibling	50	9
Nephew or niece	25	4
Spouse	0	2
Unrelated person	0	1

Source: Gottesman, 1991.

neurotransmitter, may be a major contributor to the disorder (Stone, Morrison, & Pilowsky, 2007; Howes & Kapur, 2009; Kendler & Schaffner, 2011).

Some biological explanations propose that structural abnormalities exist in the brains of people with schizophrenia, perhaps as a result of exposure to a virus during prenatal development. For example, some research shows abnormalities in the neural circuits of the cortex and limbic systems of individuals with schizophrenia. Consistent with such research, people with schizophrenia and those without the disorder show different brain functioning (Bartzokis et al., 2003; Reichenberg & Harvey, 2007; Reichenberg et al., 2009; see Figures 8).

FIGURE 8

These MRI scans compare deterioration in the grey matter of the cortex of adolescent patients with childhood onset schizophrenia.

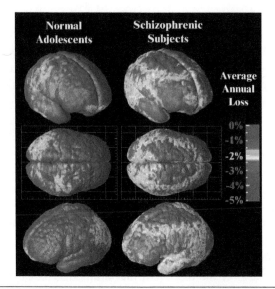

Sources: Paul Thompson and Arthur Toga, UCLA Laboratory of Neuro Imaging, and Judith Rapoport, National Institute of Mental Health.

Further evidence for the importance of biological factors shows that when people with schizophrenia hear voices during hallucinations, the parts of the brain responsible for hearing and language processing become active. When they have visual hallucinations, the parts of the brain involved in movement and colour are active. At the same time, people with schizophrenia often have unusually low activity in the brain's frontal lobes—the parts of the brain involved with emotional regulation, insight, and the evaluation of sensory stimuli (Stern & Silbersweig, 2001).

Environmental Perspectives on Schizophrenia

Although biological factors provide important pieces of the puzzle of schizophrenia, we still need to consider past and current experiences in the environments of people who develop the disturbance. For instance, psychoanalytic approaches suggest that schizophrenia is a form of regression to earlier experiences and stages of life. Freud believed, for instance, that people with schizophrenia lack strong enough egos to cope with their unacceptable impulses. They regress to the oral stage—a time when the id and ego are not yet separated. Therefore, individuals with schizophrenia essentially lack an ego and act out impulses without concern for reality.

Although this reasoning is theoretically plausible, little evidence supports psychoanalytic explanations. Somewhat more convincing theories look toward the emotional and communication patterns of the families of people with schizophrenia. For instance, some researchers suggest that schizophrenia results from high levels of expressed emotion. *Expressed emotion* is an interaction style characterized by criticism, hostility, and emotional intrusiveness by family members. Other researchers suggest that faulty communication patterns lie at the heart of schizophrenia (Lobban, Barrowclough, & Jones, 2006; Nader et al., 2013).

Psychologists who take a cognitive perspective on schizophrenia suggest that the problems in thinking experienced by people with the disorder point to a cognitive cause. Some suggest that schizophrenia results from *overattention* to stimuli in the environment. Rather than being able to screen out unimportant or inconsequential stimuli and focus on the most important things in the environment, people with schizophrenia may be excessively receptive to virtually everything in their environment. As a consequence, their information-processing capabilities become overloaded and eventually break down. Other cognitive experts argue that schizophrenia results from *underattention* to certain stimuli. According to this explanation, people with schizophrenia fail to focus sufficiently on important stimuli, and pay attention to other, less important information in their surroundings (Cadenhead & Braff, 1995).

Although it is plausible that overattention and underattention are related to different forms of schizophrenia, these phenomena do not explain the origins of such information-processing disorders. Consequently, cognitive approaches—like other environmental explanations—do not provide a full explanation of the disorder.

The Multiple Causes of Schizophrenia

The predominant approach used to explain the onset of schizophrenia today, the *predisposition model of schizophrenia,* incorporates a number of biological and environmental factors. This model suggests that individuals may inherit a predisposition or an inborn sensitivity to schizophrenia that makes them particularly vulnerable to stressful factors in the environment, such as social rejection or dysfunctional family communication patterns. The stressors may vary, but if they are strong enough and are coupled with a genetic predisposition, the result will be the onset of schizophrenia. Similarly, a strong genetic predisposition may lead to the onset of schizophrenia even when the environmental stressors are relatively weak.

STUDY ALERT!

Remember that the multiple causes of schizophrenia includes biological and environmental factors.

In short, the models used today associate schizophrenia with several kinds of biological and environmental factors. It is increasingly clear, then, that no single factor, but a combination of interrelated variables, produces schizophrenia (Meltzer, 2000; McDonald & Murray, 2004; Opler et al., 2008).

Personality Disorders

I had always wanted lots of things; as a child I can remember wanting a bullet that a friend of mine had brought in to show the class. I took it and put it into my school bag and when my friend noticed it was missing, I was the one who stayed after school with him and searched the room, and I was the one who sat with him and bitched about the other kids and how one of them took his bullet. I even went home with him to help him break the news to his uncle, who had brought it home from the war for him. But that was petty compared with the stuff I did later. I wanted a Ph.D. very badly, but I didn't want to work very hard—just enough to get by. I never did the experiments I reported; hell, I was smart enough to make up the results. I knew enough about statistics to make anything look plausible. I got my master's degree without even spending one hour in a laboratory. I mean, the professors believed anything. I'd stay out all night drinking and being with my friends, and the next day I'd get in just before them and tell 'em I'd been in the lab all night. They'd actually feel sorry for me (Duke & Nowicki, 1979, pp. 309–310).

STUDY ALERT!

Unlike most psychological disorders, personality disorders produce little or no personal distress.

This excerpt provides a graphic first-person account of a person with a **personality disorder**. A personality disorder is characterized by a set of inflexible, maladaptive behaviour patterns that keep a person from functioning appropriately in society. Personality disorders differ from the other problems we have discussed because those affected by them often have little sense of personal distress associated with the psychological maladjustment. In fact, people with personality disorders frequently lead seemingly normal lives. However, just below the surface lies a set of inflexible, maladaptive personality traits that do not permit these individuals to function as members of society (Clarkin & Lenzenweger, 2004; Friedman, Oltmanns, & Turkheimer, 2007).

The best-known type of personality disorder, illustrated by the case above, is the **antisocial personality disorder** (sometimes referred to as a sociopathic personality). Individuals with this disturbance show no regard for the moral and ethical rules of society or the rights of others. Although they can appear quite intelligent and likable (at least at first), upon closer examination they turn out to be manipulative and deceptive. Moreover, they lack any guilt or anxiety about their wrongdoing. When those with antisocial personality disorder behave in a way that injures someone else, they understand intellectually that they have caused harm but feel no remorse (Lykken, 1995; Goodwin & Hamilton, 2003; Hilarski, 2007).

What are the traits of individuals with antisocial personality disorder? People with antisocial personality disorder are often impulsive and lack the ability to withstand frustration. They can be extremely manipulative. They also may have excellent social skills; they can be charming, engaging, and highly persuasive. Some of the best con artists have antisocial personalities. Canadian Paul Bernardo, a convicted killer and serial rapist, displays several features of antisocial personality disorder. However, to the Canadian public's knowledge, a formal diagnosis of Bernardo's antisocial personality has yet to be made.

What causes such an unusual constellation of problem behaviours? A variety of factors have been suggested, ranging from an inability to experience emotions appropriately to problems in family relationships. For example, in many cases of antisocial behaviour, the individual has come from a home in which a parent has died or left, or one in which there is a lack of affection, a lack of consistency in discipline, or outright rejection. Other explanations

Personality disorder
A disorder characterized by a set of inflexible, maladaptive behaviour patterns that keep a person from functioning appropriately in society.

Antisocial personality disorder
A disorder in which individuals show no regard for the moral and ethical rules of society or the rights of others.

concentrate on sociocultural factors, because an unusually high proportion of people with antisocial personalities come from lower socioeconomic groups. Still, no one has been able to pinpoint the specific causes of antisocial personalities, and it is likely that some combination of factors is responsible (Rosenstein & Horowitz, 1996; Costa & Widiger, 2002; Chen et al., 2011).

People with **borderline personality disorder** have difficulty developing a secure sense of who they are. As a consequence, they tend to rely on relationships with others to define their identity. The problem with this strategy is that rejections are devastating. Individuals with borderline personality disorder are unable to cope with the "grey" in life so that most of their interactions are polarized into either good or bad. Furthermore, people with this disorder distrust others and have difficulty controlling their anger. Their emotional volatility leads to impulsive and self-destructive behaviour. Individuals with borderline personality disorder often feel empty and alone. They may form intense, sudden, one-sided relationships, demanding the attention of another person and then feeling angry when they don't receive it. One reason for this behaviour is that they may have a background in which others discounted or criticized their emotional reactions, and they may not have learned to regulate their emotions effectively (King-Casas et al., 2008; Hopwood et al., 2009; Samuel et al., 2013).

Another example of a personality disturbance is the **narcissistic personality disorder**, which is characterized by an exaggerated sense of self-importance. Those with the disorder expect special treatment from others, while at the same time disregarding others' feelings. In some ways, in fact, the main attribute of the narcissistic personality is an inability to experience empathy for other people.

There are several other categories of personality disorder, ranging in severity from individuals who may simply be regarded by others as eccentric, obnoxious, or difficult to people who act in a manner that is criminal and dangerous to others. Although they are not out of touch with reality in the way that people with schizophrenia are, people with personality disorders lead lives that put them on the fringes of society (Millon, Davis, & Millon, 2000; Trull & Widiger, 2003).

Childhood Disorders

We typically view childhood as a time of innocence and relative freedom from stress. In reality, though, almost 20 percent of children and 40 percent of adolescents experience significant emotional or behavioural disorders (Romano et al., 2001; Broidy, Nagin, & Tremblay, 2003; Nolen-Hoeksema, 2007).

For example, although major depression is more prevalent in adults, around 2.5 percent of children and more than 8 percent of adolescents suffer from the disorder. In fact, by the time they reach age 20, between 15–20 percent of children and adolescents will experience an episode of major depression (Garber & Horowitz, 2002).

Children do not always display depression the same way adults do. Rather than showing profound sadness or hopelessness, childhood depression may produce the expression of exaggerated fears, clinginess, or avoidance of everyday activities. In older children, the symptoms may be sulking, school problems, and even acts of delinquency (Wenar, 1994; Koplewicz, 2002; Seroczynski, Jacquez, & Cole, 2003).

A considerably more common childhood disorder is **attention-deficit hyperactivity disorder (ADHD)**, a disorder marked by inattention, impulsiveness, a low tolerance for frustration, and generally a great deal of inappropriate activity. Although all children show such behaviour some of the time, it is so common in children diagnosed with ADHD that it interferes with their everyday functioning (Swanson, Harris, & Graham, 2003; Barkley, 2005; Smith, Barkley, & Shapiro, 2006).

Borderline personality disorder
A disorder in which individuals have difficulty developing a secure sense of who they are.

Narcissistic personality disorder
A personality disturbance characterized by an exaggerated sense of self-importance.

Attention-deficit hyperactivity disorder (ADHD)
A disorder marked by inattention, impulsiveness, a low tolerance for frustration, and a great deal of inappropriate activity.

ADHD is surprisingly widespread with estimates ranging between 3–5 percent of the school-age population—or some 3.5 million children under the age of 18 in the United States. Children diagnosed with the disorder are often exhausting to parents and teachers, and even their peers find them difficult to deal with.

The cause of ADHD is not known, although most experts feel that it is produced by dysfunctions in the nervous system. For example, one theory suggests that unusually low levels of arousal in the central nervous system cause ADHD. To compensate, children with ADHD seek out stimulation to increase arousal. Still, such theories are speculative. Furthermore, because many children occasionally show behaviours characteristic of ADHD, it often is misdiagnosed or in some cases overdiagnosed. Only the frequency and persistence of the symptoms of ADHD allow for a correct diagnosis, which only a trained professional can do (Barkley, 2000; Sciutto & Eisenberg, 2007; Ketisch & Jones, 2013).

Autism spectrum disorder, a severe developmental disability that impairs children's ability to communicate and relate to others, is another childhood disorder that usually appears in the first three years and typically continues throughout life. Children with autism spectrum disorder have difficulties in both verbal and nonverbal communication, and they may avoid social contact. About 1 in 88 children are now thought to have the disorder, and its prevalence has risen significantly in the last decade. Whether the increase is the result of an actual rise in the incidence of autism or is due to better reporting is a question of intense debate among researchers (Rice, 2009; Neal, Matson, & Belva, 2013).

Somatoform Disorders

Somatoform disorders are psychological difficulties that take on a physical (somatic) form, but for which there is no medical cause. Even though an individual with a somatoform disorder reports physical symptoms, no biological cause exists, or if there is a medical problem, the person's reaction is greatly exaggerated.

One type of somatoform disorder is **illness anxiety disorder**, in which people have a constant fear of illness and a preoccupation with their health. These individuals believe everyday aches and pains are symptoms of a dreaded disease. The "symptoms" are not faked; rather, they are misinterpreted as evidence of some serious illness—often in the face of inarguable medical evidence to the contrary (Abramowitz, Olatunji, & Deacon, 2007; Olatunji, 2008; Weck et al., 2011).

Another somatoform disorder is conversion disorder. Unlike illness anxiety disorder, in which there is no physical problem, **conversion disorders** involve an actual physical disturbance, such as the inability to see or hear or to move an arm or leg. The *cause* of such a physical disturbance is purely psychological; there is no biological reason for the problem. Some of Freud's classic cases involved conversion disorders. For instance, one of Freud's patients suddenly became unable to use her arm, without any apparent physiological cause. Later, just as abruptly, the problem disappeared.

Conversion disorders often begin suddenly. People wake up one morning blind or deaf, or they experience numbness that is restricted to a certain part of the body. A hand, for example, may become entirely numb, while an area above the wrist, controlled by the same nerves, remains sensitive to touch—something that is physiologically implausible. Mental health professionals refer to such a condition as "glove anesthesia," because the numb area is the part of the hand covered by a glove, not a region related to pathways of the nervous system.

Autism spectrum disorder
A severe developmental disability that impairs children's ability to communicate and relate to others.

Somatoform disorders
Psychological difficulties that take on a physical (somatic) form, but for which there is no medical cause.

Illness anxiety disorder
A disorder in which people have a constant fear of illness and a preoccupation with their health.

Conversion disorders
A major somatoform disorder that involves an actual physical disturbance, such as the inability to use a sensory organ or the complete or partial inability to move an arm or leg.

Surprisingly, people who experience conversion disorders frequently remain unconcerned about symptoms that most of us would expect to be highly anxiety-producing. For instance, a person in good health who wakes up blind may react in a bland, matter-of-fact way. Considering how most of us would feel if we woke up unable to see, this unemotional reaction (called "*la belle indifference*," a French phrase meaning "a beautiful indifference") hardly seems appropriate (Brasic, 2002).

Other Disorders

It's important to keep in mind that the various forms of psychological disorders described in *DSM-5* cover much more ground than we have been able to discuss in this module. Some relate to topics previously considered in other chapters. For example, *psychoactive substance use disorder* relates to problems that arise from the use and abuse of drugs. Furthermore, *alcohol use disorders* are among the most serious and widespread problems. Both psychoactive substance use disorder and alcohol use disorder co-occur with many other psychological disorders such as mood disorders, posttraumatic stress disorder, and schizophrenia, which complicates treatment considerably (Salgado, Quinlan, & Zlotnick, 2007).

Another widespread problem is *eating disorders*. They include such disorders as *anorexia nervosa* and *bulimia*, which we considered in Chapter 8 on motivation and emotion, as well as binge-eating disorder, characterized by binge eating without behaviours designed to prevent weight gain. Finally, *sexual disorders*, in which one's sexual activity is unsatisfactory, are another important class of problems. They include *sexual desire disorders*, *sexual arousal disorders*, and *paraphilias*, atypical sexual activities that may include nonhuman objects or nonconsenting partners.

Another important class of disorders is *neurocognitive disorders, some of which we touched on previously*. These are problems that have a purely biological basis, such as Alzheimer's disease and some types of intellectual disabilities. Remember, there are other disorders that we have not mentioned at all, and each of the classes we have discussed can be divided into several subcategories (Kopelman & Fleminger, 2002; Pratt et al., 2003; Reijonen et al., 2003; also see *Applying Psychology in the Real World*).

APPLYING PSYCHOLOGY in the Real World

Internet Addiction

If someone challenged you to go for a week without plugging into the Internet, how easy would it be?

Many people feel an almost constant need to check their Twitter or Instagram accounts, e-mail, or Facebook feeds. For some people, though, the behaviour borders on an addictive behaviour, in which real-world tasks and activities get pushed aside by the need to compulsively check what's going on in their virtual world. In fact, some psychologists believe that such behaviour represents a new disorder: Internet addiction disorder.

The disorder has been given many names by different researchers studying it: iPhone addiction, Facebook addiction, and Facebook depression, among others. Researchers considered including what has been called *Internet addiction disorder* in DSM-5, but they ultimately decided to omit it, believing that the phenomenon has yet to be sufficiently delineated. But new research is beginning to suggest that the problem is real (Dokoupil, 2012).

The picture that is emerging of Internet addiction is one of depression and anxiety, obsessive and compulsive behaviours, attention deficits, and in some cases, occasional breaks with reality. One of the common signs of Internet addiction is a compulsion to check messages or social networks—checking them first thing in the morning, while driving, at work, during social events, and even taking a device to bed. Some people who appear to be addicted commonly spend more time online than they expect to or even realize, to the detriment of other activities and obligations. Many report feeling a sense of guilt and anxiety about the costs of their Internet compulsion, but they also feel anxious if they don't check in online—a fear that they might be missing something. And while they might cultivate a large network of social media friends, the obligation they feel to maintain an active online presence often leaves them feeling drained and disconnected from life (Carr, 2011; Rosen, 2012).

Moreover, some researchers are finding that online life creates a sort of alternative reality for people, one filled with opportunities for attention and validation. The technology also enables people to develop alternate personalities, whereby they can express radically different traits and behaviours online than they do in real life (Aboujaoude, 2008).

While the scope of the disorder and its specific symptoms and complications are still unresolved, the reality and seriousness of Internet addiction disorder are no longer easy to dismiss.

Evaluate

1. Kathy is terrified of elevators. She could be suffering from a(n)

   a. Obsessive-compulsive disorder

   b. Phobic disorder

   c. Panic disorder

   d. Generalized anxiety disorder

2. Carmen described an incident in which her anxiety suddenly rose to a peak and she felt a sense of impending doom. Carmen experienced a(n) _____.

3. Troubling thoughts that persist for days or months are known as

   a. Obsessions

   b. Compulsions

   c. Rituals

   d. Panic attacks

4. An overpowering urge to carry out a strange ritual is called a(n) _____.

5. States of extreme euphoria and energy paired with severe depression characterize _____ disorder.

6. _____ schizophrenia is characterized by symptoms that are sudden and of easily identifiable onset; _____ schizophrenia develops gradually over a person's life span.

7. The _____ states that schizophrenia may be caused by an excess of certain neurotransmitters in the brain.

Answers to Evaluate Questions

1. b; 2. panic attack; 3. a; 4. compulsion; 5. bipolar; 6. reactive, process; 7. dopamine hypothesis

Key Terms

antisocial personality disorder	compulsions	obsession
anxiety disorder	conversion disorders	obsessive-compulsive
attention-deficit hyperactivity	generalized anxiety disorder	disorder
disorder (ADHD)	illness anxiety disorder	panic disorder
autism spectrum disorder	major depression	personality disorder
bipolar disorder	mania	specific phobia
borderline personality	mood disorders	schizophrenia
disorder	narcissistic personality disorder	somatoform disorders

Psychological Disorders in Perspective

LEARNING OBJECTIVE

How prevalent are psychological disorders?

Prevalence of Psychological Disorders: The Mental State of North America

How common are the kinds of psychological disorders we've been discussing? Here's one answer: Every second person you meet is likely to suffer, at some point during his or her life, from a psychological disorder.

That's the conclusion drawn from a massive study on the prevalence of psychological disorders. In that study, researchers conducted face-to-face interviews with more than 8,000 men and women between the ages of 15 and 54 years. According to results of the study, 48 percent of those interviewed had experienced a disorder at some point in their lives. In addition, 30 percent experienced a disorder in any particular year, and the number of people who experienced simultaneous multiple disorders (known as *comorbidity*) was significant (Welkowitz et al., 2000; Kessler & Wang, 2008).

The most common disorder reported in the study was depression, with 17 percent of those surveyed reporting at least one major episode. Ten percent had suffered from depression during the current year. The next most common disorder was alcohol dependence, which occurred at a lifetime incidence rate of 14 percent. In addition, 7 percent of those interviewed had experienced alcohol dependence in the last year. Other frequently occurring psychological disorders were drug dependence, disorders involving panic (such as an overwhelming fear of talking to strangers and terror of heights), and posttraumatic stress disorder.

Although some researchers think the estimates of severe disorders may be too high (Narrow et al., 2002), the findings are consistent with studies of college and university students and their psychological difficulties. For example, in one study of the problems of students who visited a college counselling centre, more than 40 percent of students reported being depressed (see Figure 1). These figures include only students who sought help from the counselling centre, not those who did not seek treatment. Consequently, the figures are not representative of the entire college and university population (Benton et al., 2003).

The significant level of psychological disorders and mental difficulties is a global concern, according to the World Health Organization (WHO). Throughout the world, psychological disorders are widespread. Furthermore, there are economic disparities in treatment, such that more affluent people with mild disorders receive more and better treatment than poor people who have more severe disorders (The WHO World Mental Health Survey Consortium, 2004; Wang et al., 2007; see nearby Figure 2).

STUDY ALERT!

Remember that the incidence of various types of psychological disorders in the general population is surprisingly high.

FIGURE 1

The problems reported by students visiting a college counselling centre. Would you have predicted this pattern of psychological difficulties?

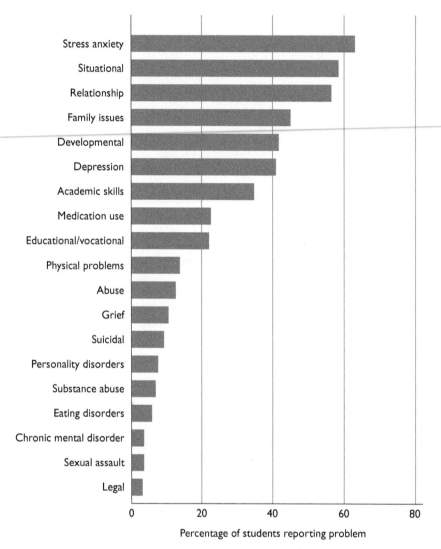

Source: Benton et al., 2003.

Also, keep in mind that the incidence of specific disorders varies significantly in other cultures. For instance, cross-cultural surveys show that the incidence of major depression varies significantly from one culture to another. The probability of having at least one episode of depression is only 1.5 percent in Taiwan and 2.9 percent in Korea, compared with 11.6 percent in New Zealand and 16.4 percent in France. Such notable differences underscore the importance of considering the cultural context of psychological disorders (Weissman et al., 1997; Tseng, 2003).

The Social and Cultural Context of Psychological Disorders

In considering the nature of the psychological disorders described in *DSM-5*, it's important to keep in mind that the specific disorders reflect turn-of-the-twenty-first-century Western cultures. The classification system provides a snapshot of how its authors viewed mental disorders when it was published in 1994. In fact, the development of the most recent version of *DSM* was a source of great debate, in part reflecting issues that divide society.

One specific, newly classified disorder that has been added to *DSM-5* that has caused controversy is known as disruptive mood dysregulation disorder. This particular diagnosis is characterized by temperamental outbursts

FIGURE 2

According to a global survey conducted by the World Health Organization, the prevalence of psychological disorders is widespread. These figures show the prevalence of any psychological disorder within a 12-month period.

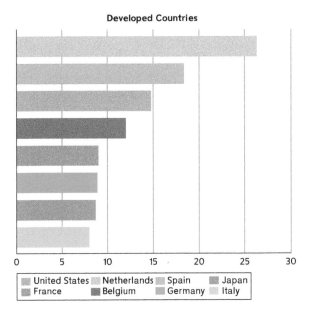

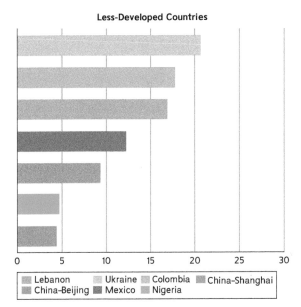

Source: The WHO World Mental Health Survey Consortium, 2004, Table 3.

STUDY ALERT!

It is important to understand that the *DSM* is a living document that presents a view of disorders that reflects the culture and historical context of its authors.

grossly out of proportion to the situation, both verbally and physically, in children between the ages of 6 and 18. Some practitioners argue these symptoms simply define a child having a temper tantrum rather than a disorder (Dobbs, 2012; Marchand & Phillips, 2012; Frances, 2013).

Similarly, someone who overeats 12 times in three months can be considered to be suffering from the new classification of binge eating disorder, which seems to some critics to be overly inclusive. Finally, hoarding behaviour is now placed in its own category of psychological disorder. Some critics suggest this change is more a reflection of the rise of reality shows focusing on hoarding rather than reflecting a distinct category of psychological disturbance (Hudson et al., 2012).

Such controversies underline the fact that our understanding of abnormal behaviour reflects the society and culture in which we live. Future revisions of *DSM* may include a different catalogue of disorders. Even now, other cultures might include a list of disorders that look very different from the list that appears in the current *DSM*.

Becoming an Informed Consumer of Psychology

Deciding When You Need Help

After you've considered the range and variety of psychological disturbances that can afflict people, you may begin to feel that you suffer from one (or more) of the problems we have discussed. In fact, this perception has a name: *medical student's disease*. Although in this case it might more aptly be labelled "psychology student's disease," the basic symptoms are the same: feeling that you suffer from the same sorts of problems you are studying.

(continued)

Most often, of course, your concerns will be unwarranted. As we have discussed, the differences between normal and abnormal behaviour are often so fuzzy that it is easy to jump to the conclusion that one has the same symptoms that are involved in serious forms of mental disturbance.

Before coming to such a conclusion, though, keep in mind that from time to time we all experience a wide range of emotions, and it is not unusual to feel deeply unhappy, fantasize about bizarre situations, or feel anxiety about life's circumstances. It is the persistence, depth, and consistency of such behaviour that set normal reactions apart from abnormal ones. If you have not previously had serious doubts about the normality of your behaviour, it is unlikely that reading about others' psychological disorders will prompt you to reevaluate your earlier conclusion.

On the other hand, many people do have problems that merit concern, and in such cases, it is important to consider the possibility that professional help is warranted. The following list of symptoms can serve as a guideline to help you determine whether outside intervention might be useful (Engler & Goleman, 1992):

- Long-term feelings of distress that interfere with your sense of well-being, competence, and ability to function effectively in daily activities
- Occasions in which you experience overwhelmingly high stress, accompanied by feelings of inability to cope with the situation
- Prolonged depression or feelings of hopelessness, particularly when they do not have any clear cause (such as the death of someone close)
- Withdrawal from other people
- A chronic physical problem for which no physical cause can be determined
- A fear or phobia that prevents you from engaging in everyday activities
- Feelings that other people are out to get you or are talking about and plotting against you
- Inability to interact effectively with others, preventing the development of friendships and loving relationships

This list offers a rough set of guidelines for determining when the normal problems of everyday living have escalated beyond your ability to deal with them by yourself. In such situations, the *least* reasonable approach would be to pore over the psychological disorders we have discussed in an attempt at self-diagnosis. A more reasonable strategy is to consider seeking professional help.

Evaluate

1. The latest version of *DSM* is considered to be the conclusive guideline on defining psychological disorders. True or false?

2. _____, characterized by severe, incapacitating mood changes or depression related to a woman's menstrual cycle, was eventually added to the appendix of *DSM-5* despite controversy surrounding its inclusion.

3. Match the disorder with the culture in which it is most common:

   1. amok
   2. anorexia nervosa
   3. brain fag
   4. catatonic schizophrenia

   a. India
   b. Malaysia
   c. North America
   d. West Africa

Answers to Evaluate Questions

1. false; the development of the latest version of *DSM* was a source of great controversy, in part reflecting issues that divide society; 2. premenstrual dysphoric disorder; 3. 1-b, 2-c, 3-d, 4-a

Epilogue

Source: © Rubberball/Getty Images RF.

We've discussed some of the many types of psychological disorders to which people are prone, noting the difficulty psychologists and physicians have in clearly differentiating normal from abnormal behaviour and looking at some of the approaches mental health professionals have taken to explain and treat psychological disorders. We considered today's most commonly used classification scheme, categorized in *DSM-5,* and examined some of the more prevalent forms of psychological disorders. To gain a perspective on the topic of psychological disorders, we discussed the surprisingly broad incidence of psychological disorders in Canada and the cultural nature of such disorders.

Recap/Rethink

Module 37: Normal versus Abnormal: Making the Distinction

Recap

LO1 How can we distinguish normal from abnormal behaviour?

- Definitions of abnormality include deviation from the average, deviation from the ideal, a sense of personal discomfort, the inability to function effectively, and legal conceptions.
- Although no single definition is adequate, abnormal behaviour can be considered to be behaviour that causes people to experience distress and prevents them from functioning in their daily lives. Most psychologists believe that abnormal and normal behaviour should be considered in terms of a continuum.

LO2 What are the major perspectives on psychological disorders used by mental health professionals?

- The medical perspective views abnormality as a symptom of an underlying disease.
- Psychoanalytic perspectives suggest that abnormal behaviour stems from childhood conflicts in the unconscious.
- Behavioural approaches view abnormal behaviour not as a symptom of an underlying problem, but as the problem itself.
- The cognitive approach suggests that abnormal behaviour is the result of faulty cognitions (thoughts and beliefs). In this view, abnormal behaviour can be remedied by changing one's flawed thoughts and beliefs.
- Humanistic approaches emphasize the responsibility people have for their own behaviour, even when such behaviour is seen as abnormal.
- Sociocultural approaches view abnormal behaviour in terms of difficulties arising from family and other social relationships.

LO3 What are the major categories of psychological disorders?

- The most widely used system for classifying psychological disorders is *DSM-5—Diagnostic and Statistical Manual of Mental Disorders, Fifth Edition.*

Rethink

1. Do you agree or disagree that the *DSM* should be updated every several years? Why? What makes abnormal behaviour so variable?

2. *From the perspective of an employer:* Imagine that a well-paid employee was arrested for shoplifting a $15 sweater. What sort of explanation for this behaviour would be provided by the proponents of each perspective on abnormality: the medical perspective, the psychoanalytic perspective, the behavioural perspective, the cognitive perspective, the humanistic perspective, and the sociocultural perspective? Based on the potential causes of the shoplifting, would you fire the employee? Why or why not?

Module 38: The Major Psychological Disorders

Recap

LO4 What are the major psychological disorders?

- Anxiety disorders are present when a person experiences so much anxiety that it affects daily functioning. Specific types of anxiety disorders include phobic disorder, panic disorder, and generalized anxiety disorder.
- Mood disorders are characterized by emotional states of depression or euphoria so strong that they intrude on everyday living. They include major depression and bipolar disorder.
- Schizophrenia is one of the more severe forms of mental illness. Symptoms of schizophrenia include declines in functioning, thought and language disturbances, perceptual disorders, emotional disturbance, and withdrawal from others.
- Strong evidence links schizophrenia to genetic, biochemical, and environmental factors. According to the predisposition model, an interaction among various factors produces the disorder.
- People with personality disorders experience little or no personal distress, but they do suffer from an inability to function as normal members of society. These disorders include antisocial personality disorder, borderline personality disorder, and narcissistic personality disorder.
- Childhood disorders include autism spectrum disorder, major depression and attention deficit hyperactivity disorder (ADHD), which is marked by inattention, impulsiveness, a low tolerance for frustration, and inappropriate activity.
- Somatoform disorders are psychological difficulties that take on a physical (somatic) form, but for which there is no medical cause. Examples are illness anxiety disorder and conversion disorders.

Rethink

1. *From the perspective of a social worker:* Personality disorders are often not apparent to others, and many people with these problems seem to live basically normal lives and are not a threat to others. Because these people often appear from the outside to function well in society, why should they be considered psychologically disordered?

2. What are some features of online activity that might make it particularly addictive? If heavy Internet use leaves people feeling anxious, guilty, and empty, why would they keep coming back to it?

3. Corson was suffering from a panic disorder. What elements of his behaviour seem to fit the description of a panic disorder?

Module 39: Psychological Disorders in Perspective

Recap

How prevalent are psychological disorders?

- About half the people in North America are likely to experience a psychological disorder at some point in their lives; 30 percent experience a disorder in any specific year.

Rethink

1. *From the perspective of a college or university counsellor:* What indicators might be most important in determining whether a college or university student is experiencing a psychological disorder? Do you believe that all students who show signs of a psychological disorder should seek professional help? How might your responses change if the student was from a different culture (e.g., an African society)?

2. Why is inclusion in the *DSM-5* of disorders such as hoarding behaviour so controversial and political? What disadvantages does inclusion bring? Does inclusion bring any benefits?

3. Initially, Corson hid his disorder from his NHL teammates because he felt embarrassment and shame. Why do you think this happened? What societal changes need to occur in order to make psychological disorders be perceived less negatively?

4. Do you think a person who has been treated for a psychological disorder could become prime minister of Canada? Should such a person become prime minister?

CHAPTER 13
Treatment of Psychological Disorders

Source: © Andrea Morini/Getty Images RF.

Key Concepts for Chapter 13

MODULE 40 Psychotherapy: Psychodynamic, Behavioural, and Cognitive Approaches to Treatment

LO1 What are the goals of psychologically and biologically based treatment approaches?

LO2 What are the psychodynamic, behaviourial, and cognitive approaches to treatment?

Psychodynamic Approaches to Therapy

Behavioural Approaches to Therapy

Cognitive Approaches to Therapy

MODULE 41 Psychotherapy: Humanistic, Interpersonal, and Group Approaches to Treatment

LO3 What are the humanistic approaches to treatment?

LO4 What is interpersonal therapy?

LO5 How does group therapy differ from individual types of therapy?

LO6 How effective is psychotherapy, and which kind of psychotherapy works best in a given situation?

Humanistic Therapy

Interpersonal Therapy

Group Therapy, Self-Help Groups, and Family Therapy

Evaluating Psychotherapy: Does Therapy Work?

   Exploring Diversity: *Racial and Ethnic Factors in Treatment*

MODULE 42 Biomedical Therapy: Biological Approaches to Treatment

LO7 How are drug, electroconvulsive, and psychosurgical techniques used today in the treatment of psychological disorders?

Drug Therapy

Electroconvulsive Therapy (ECT)

Psychosurgery

Biomedical Therapies in Perspective

Community Psychology: Focus on Prevention

   Applying Psychology in the Real World: *Beating the Odds: Preventing Psychological Disorders Before They Start*

Prologue

Laughter Is The Best Medicine: Stand Up For Mental Health!

They say laughter is the best medicine. So what better cure than stand-up comedy? Counsellor and comedian David Granirer leads a cutting-edge program called "Stand Up for Mental Health," with support from the Canadian Mental Health Association (CMHA). The Vancouver-based agency empowers Canadians with a mental illness to challenge the stigma and humiliation of their disorders using comedy routines. During a twelve-week course, participants are taught how to write, edit, and perform 3 to 10 minute comedy skits drawing from their own trials and tribulations with mental illness. Throughout the process, feelings of shame and isolation about their diagnosis begin to diminish. At the end of three months, students perform comedy routines in front of a live audience (Mason, 2008; Stand Up for Mental Health, 2008).

Award-winning counselor and comedian David Granirer leads a cutting-edge program called "Stand Up For Mental Health" that he runs in partnership with mental health organizations across Canada, the U.S., and Australia.

Source: Courtesy of David Granirer.

"Stand Up for Mental Health" is an innovative approach to helping individuals with psychological disorders boost their confidence and self-esteem. Belief in oneself is an important first step in the treatment of psychological disorders. Research by Dr. Rod Martin at the University of Western Ontario confirms the impact of humour on psychological functioning (Martin, 2007). Consistent with participants in "Stand Up for Mental Health," Martin's body of research demonstrates the positive influences of humour on coping, social bonding, and self-image (Kazarian & Martin, 2004; Yip & Martin, 2006). Enhancing self-esteem and belief in oneself are important first steps in the treatment of psychological disorders.

Despite their diversity, approaches to treating psychological disorders fall into two main categories: psychologically based and biologically based therapies. Psychologically based therapy, or **psychotherapy**, is treatment in which a trained professional—a therapist—uses psychological techniques to help someone overcome psychological difficulties and disorders, resolve problems in living, or bring about personal growth. In psychotherapy, the goal is to produce psychological change in a person (called a "client" or "patient") through discussions and interactions with the therapist. In contrast, **biomedical therapy** relies on drugs and medical procedures to improve psychological functioning.

As we describe the various approaches to therapy, keep in mind that although the distinctions may seem clear cut, the classifications and procedures overlap a good deal. In fact, many therapists today take an *eclectic approach* to therapy and use a variety of methods with an individual patient. Assuming that both psychological and biological processes often produce psychological disorders, eclectic therapists may draw from several perspectives simultaneously to address both the psychological and the biological aspects of a person's problems (Goin, 2005; Berman, Jobes, & Silverman, 2006).

Psychotherapy
Treatment in which a trained professional—a therapist—uses psychological techniques to help a person overcome psychological difficulties and disorders, resolve problems in living, or bring about personal growth.

Biomedical therapy
Therapy that relies on drugs and other medical procedures to improve psychological functioning.

Psychotherapy: Psychodynamic, Behavioural, and Cognitive Approaches to Treatment

LEARNING OBJECTIVES

LO1 **What are** the goals of psychologically and biologically based treatment approaches?

LO2 **What are** the psychodynamic, behaviourial, and cognitive approaches to treatment?

Therapists use some 400 different varieties of psychotherapy—approaches to therapy that focus on psychological factors. Although diverse in many respects, all psychological approaches see treatment as a way of solving psychological problems by modifying people's behaviour and helping them gain a better understanding of themselves and their past, present, and future. For instance, the mental health program "Stand Up for Mental Health" discussed in the prologue empowers mentally ill Canadians to challenge the stigma of their own psychological disorders.

In light of the variety of psychological approaches, it is not surprising that the people who provide therapy vary considerably in educational background and training (see Figure 1). Many have doctoral degrees in psychology (meaning that they have attended graduate school, learned clinical and research techniques, and held an internship). But therapy is also provided by people in fields allied with psychology, such as psychiatry and social work.

Regardless of their specific training, almost all psychotherapists employ one of four major approaches to therapy: psychodynamic, behavioural, cognitive, or humanistic treatments. These approaches are based on the models of personality and psychological disorders developed by psychologists. Here we'll consider the psychodynamic, behavioural, and cognitive approaches in turn. In the next module, we'll explore the humanistic approach, as well as interpersonal psychotherapy and group therapy, and evaluate the effectiveness of psychotherapy.

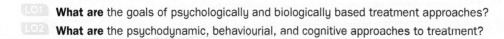 Psychodynamic Approaches to Therapy

Psychodynamic therapy seeks to bring unresolved past conflicts and unacceptable impulses from the unconscious into the conscious, where patients may deal with the problems more effectively. Psychodynamic approaches are based on Freud's psychoanalytic approach to personality, which holds that individuals employ *defence mechanisms*, psychological strategies to protect themselves from unacceptable unconscious impulses.

The most common defence mechanism is repression, which pushes threatening conflicts and impulses back into the unconscious. However, since unacceptable conflicts and impulses can never be completely buried, some of the anxiety associated with them can produce abnormal behaviour in the form of what Freud called *neurotic symptoms*.

How does one rid oneself of the anxiety produced by unconscious, unwanted impulses and drives? To Freud, the answer was to confront the conflicts and impulses by bringing them out of the unconscious part of the mind and into

---

Psychodynamic therapy
Therapy that seeks to bring unresolved past conflicts and unacceptable impulses from the unconscious into the conscious, where patients may deal with the problems more effectively.

FIGURE 1

A variety of professionals provide therapy and counselling. Each could be expected to give helpful advice and direction. However, the nature of the problem a person is experiencing may make one or another therapy more appropriate. For example, a person who is suffering from a severe disturbance and who has lost touch with reality will typically require some sort of biologically based drug therapy. In that case, a psychiatrist—who is a physician—would be the professional of choice. In contrast, those suffering from milder disorders, such as difficulty adjusting to the death of a family member, have a broader choice that might include any of the professionals listed below. The decision can be made easier by initial consultations with professionals in mental health facilities in communities, colleges, universities, and health organizations, who can provide guidance in selecting an appropriate therapist.

Getting Help from the Right Person

Clinical Psychologists
Registered Psychologists with a Ph.D. or Psy.D. or master's degree (in certain provinces) who specialize in assessment and treatment of psychological difficulties.

Counselling Psychologists
Registered Psychologists with a Ph.D. or Ed.D. or master's degree (in certain provinces) typically treat day-to-day adjustment problems.

Psychiatrists
M.D.s with postgraduate training in abnormal behaviour. They can prescribe medication and often treat the most severe disorders.

Psychoanalysts
Either M.D.s or Psychologists who specialize in psychoanalysis, the treatment technique first developed by Freud.

Licensed Professional Counsellors or Clinical Mental Health Counsellors
Professionals with a master's degree, as well as hold a federal or provincial certification. They provide therapy to individuals, couples, and families.

Clinical or Psychiatric Social Workers
Professionals with a master's degree and specialized training who provide therapy, usually regarding common family and personal problems.

the conscious part. Freud assumed that this technique would reduce anxiety stemming from past conflicts and that the patient could then participate in his or her daily life more effectively.

A psychodynamic therapist, then, faces the challenge of finding a way to assist patients' attempts to explore and understand the unconscious. The technique that has evolved has a number of components, but basically it consists of guiding patients to consider and discuss their past experiences, in explicit detail, from the time of their first memories. This process assumes that patients will eventually stumble upon long-hidden crises, traumas, and conflicts that are producing anxiety in their adult lives. They will then be able to "work through"—understand and rectify—those difficulties.

Psychoanalysis: Freud's Therapy

Classic Freudian psychodynamic therapy, called psychoanalysis, tends to be a lengthy and expensive affair. **Psychoanalysis** is Freudian psychotherapy in which the goal is to release hidden unconscious thoughts and feelings in order to reduce their power in controlling behaviour.

In psychoanalysis, patients typically meet with the therapist an hour a day, four to six days a week, for several years. While some may see their therapist that often, others may only see the therapist once or twice a week. In their sessions, they often use a technique developed by Freud called *free association*. Psychoanalysts using this technique

Psychoanalysis
Freudian psychotherapy in which the goal is to release hidden unconscious thoughts and feelings in order to reduce their power in controlling behaviour.

Freud's psychoanalytic therapy is an intensive, lengthy process that includes techniques such as free association and dream interpretation. What are some advantages and disadvantages of psychoanalysis compared with other approaches?

Source: © Patrick Heagney/iStockphoto.com.

tell patients to say aloud whatever comes to mind, regardless of its apparent irrelevance or senselessness, and the analysts attempt to recognize and label the connections between what a patient says and the patient's unconscious. Therapists also use *dream interpretation*, examining dreams to find clues to unconscious conflicts and problems. Moving beyond the surface description of a dream (called the *manifest content*), therapists seek its underlying meaning (the *latent content*), thereby revealing the true unconscious meaning of the dream (Galatzer-Levy & Cohler, 1997; Auld, Hyman, & Rudzinski, 2005; Bodin, 2006).

The processes of free association and dream interpretation do not always move forward easily. The same unconscious forces that initially produced repression may keep past difficulties out of the conscious mind, producing resistance. *Resistance* is an inability or unwillingness to discuss or reveal particular memories, thoughts, or motivations. Patients can express resistance in many ways. For instance, patients may be discussing a childhood memory and suddenly forget what they were saying, or they may change the subject completely. It is the therapist's job to pick up instances of resistance and interpret their meaning, as well as to ensure that patients return to the subject—which is likely to hold difficult or painful memories for the patients.

Because of the close, almost intimate interaction between patient and psychoanalyst, the relationship between the two often becomes emotionally charged and takes on a complexity unlike most other relationships. Patients may eventually think of the analyst as a symbol of a significant other in their past, perhaps a parent or a lover, and apply some of their feelings for that person to the analyst—a phenomenon known as transference. **Transference** is the transfer of feelings to a psychoanalyst of love or anger that had been originally directed to a patient's parents or other authority figures (Van Beekum, 2005; Evans, 2007; Steiner, 2008).

STUDY ALERT!

To better understand how psychodynamic therapy works, review Freud's psychoanalytic theory discussed in Chapter 10, Personality.

Contemporary Psychodynamic Approaches

Few people have the time, money, or patience to participate in years of traditional psychoanalysis. Moreover, no conclusive evidence shows that psychoanalysis, as originally conceived by Freud in the nineteenth century, works better than other, more recent forms of psychodynamic therapy.

Today, psychodynamic therapy tends to be of shorter duration, usually lasting no longer than three months or twenty sessions. The therapist takes a more active role than Freud would have liked, controlling the course of therapy and prodding and advising the patient with considerable directness. Finally, the therapist puts less emphasis on a patient's past history and childhood, concentrating instead on an individual's current relationships and specific complaints (Goode, 2003; Charman, 2004; Wolitzky, 2006).

Evaluation of Psychodynamic Therapy

Even with its current modifications, psychodynamic therapy has its critics. In its longer versions, it can be time-consuming and expensive, especially in comparison with other forms of psychotherapy, such as behavioural and cognitive approaches. Furthermore, less articulate patients may not do as well as more verbal ones do.

> **Transference**
> The transfer of feelings to a psychoanalyst of love or anger that had been originally directed to a patient's parents or other authority figures.

Ultimately, the most important concern about psychodynamic treatment is whether it actually works, and there is no simple answer to this question. Psychodynamic treatment techniques have been controversial since Freud introduced them. Part of the problem is the difficulty in establishing whether patients have improved after psychodynamic therapy. Determining effectiveness depends on reports from the therapist or the patients themselves, reports that are obviously open to bias and subjective interpretation.

Critics have questioned the entire theoretical basis of psychodynamic theory, maintaining that constructs such as the unconscious have not been proved to exist. Despite the criticism, though, the psychodynamic treatment approach has remained viable. To proponents, it not only provides effective treatment in many cases of psychological disturbance but also permits the potential development of an unusual degree of insight into one's life (Clay, 2000; Ablon & Jones, 2005; Bond, 2006).

Behavioural Approaches to Therapy

Perhaps, when you were a child, your parents rewarded you with an ice cream cone when you were especially good . . . or sent you to your room if you misbehaved. Sound principles back up such a child-rearing strategy: Good behaviour is maintained by reinforcement, and unwanted behaviour can be eliminated by punishment.

These principles represent the basic underpinnings of behavioural treatment approaches. Building on the basic processes of learning, **behavioural treatment approaches** make this fundamental assumption: Both abnormal behaviour and normal behaviour are *learned*. People who act abnormally either have failed to learn the skills they need to cope with the problems of everyday living or have acquired faulty skills and patterns that are being maintained through some form of reinforcement. To modify abnormal behaviour, then, behavioural approaches propose that people must learn new behaviour to replace the faulty skills they have developed and unlearn their maladaptive behaviour patterns (Krijn et al., 2004; Norton & Price, 2007).

Behavioural psychologists do not need to delve into people's pasts or their psyches. Rather than viewing abnormal behaviour as a symptom of an underlying problem, they consider the abnormal behaviour as the problem in need of modification. Changing people's behaviour to allow them to function more effectively solves the problem—with no need for concern about the underlying cause. In this view, then, if you can change abnormal behaviour, you've cured the problem.

Aversive Conditioning

Suppose you bite into your favourite candy bar and find that not only is it infested with ants but you've also swallowed a bunch of them. You immediately become sick to your stomach and throw up. Your long-term reaction? You never eat that kind of candy bar again, and it may be months before you eat any type of candy. You have learned to avoid candy so that you will not get sick and throw up.

This simple example illustrates how a person can be classically conditioned to modify behaviour. Behaviour therapists use this principle when they employ **aversive conditioning**, a form of therapy that reduces the frequency of undesired behaviour by pairing an aversive, unpleasant stimulus with undesired behaviour. For example, behaviour therapists might use aversive conditioning by pairing alcohol with a drug that causes severe nausea and vomiting. After the two have been paired a few times, the person associates the alcohol alone with vomiting and finds alcohol less appealing.

Although aversion therapy works reasonably well in inhibiting substance-abuse problems such as alcoholism and certain kinds of sexual disorders, critics question its long-term effectiveness. Also, important ethical concerns surround aversion techniques that employ such potent stimuli as electric shock, which therapists use only in the most extreme cases, such as patient self-mutilation. Clearly, though, aversion therapy offers an important procedure for eliminating maladaptive responses for some period of time—a respite that provides, even if only temporarily, an opportunity to encourage more adaptive behaviour patterns (Bordnick et al., 2004; Delgado, Labouliere, & Phelps, 2006).

Behavioural treatment approaches
Treatment approaches that build on the basic processes of learning, such as reinforcement and extinction, and assume that normal and abnormal behaviour are both learned.

Aversive conditioning
A form of therapy that reduces the frequency of undesired behaviour by pairing an aversive, unpleasant stimulus with undesired behaviour.

Systematic Desensitization

The most successful behavioural treatment based on classical conditioning is systematic desensitization. In **systematic desensitization**, gradual exposure to an anxiety-producing stimulus is paired with relaxation to extinguish the response of anxiety (Dowling, Jackson, & Thomas, 2008).

Suppose, for instance, you were extremely afraid of flying. The very thought of being in an airplane would make you begin to sweat and shake, and you couldn't get yourself near enough to an airport to know how you'd react if you actually had to fly somewhere. Using systematic desensitization to treat your problem, you would first be trained in relaxation techniques by a behaviour therapist, learning to relax your body fully—a highly pleasant state, as you might imagine (see Figure 2).

The next step would involve constructing a *hierarchy of fears*—a list, in order of increasing severity, of the things you associate with your fears. For instance, your hierarchy might resemble this one:

1. Watching a plane fly overhead.
2. Going to an airport.
3. Buying a ticket.
4. Stepping into the plane.
5. Seeing the plane door close.
6. Having the plane taxi down the runway.
7. Taking off.
8. Being in the air.

Once you had developed this hierarchy and had learned relaxation techniques, you would learn to associate the two sets of responses. To do this, your therapist might ask you to put yourself into a relaxed state and then imagine yourself in the first situation identified in your hierarchy. Once you could consider that first step while remaining relaxed, you would move on to the next situation, eventually moving up the hierarchy in gradual stages until you could imagine yourself being in the air without experiencing anxiety. Ultimately, you would be asked to make a visit to an airport and later to take a flight.

Flooding is another method utilized for reducing fears and anxiety that involves exposing the person to the anxiety-provoking stimulus at the beginning. Exposure is rapid, as opposed to gradual in systematic desensitization as described above. For example a person who is fearful of dogs, may be placed in a room with dogs. At first that

---

FIGURE 2

Following these basic steps will help you achieve a sense of calmness by employing the relaxation response.

Step I.	Pick a focus word or short phrase that's firmly rooted in your personal belief system. For example, a nonreligious individual might choose a neutral word like *one* or *peace* or *love*. A Christian person desiring to use a prayer could pick the opening words of Psalm 23. *The Lord is my shepherd;* a Jewish person could choose *Shalom.*
Step 2.	Sit quietly in a comfortable position.
Step 3.	Close your eyes.
Step 4.	Relax your muscles.
Step 5.	Breathe slowly and naturally, repeating your focus word or phrase silently as you exhale.
Step 6.	Throughout, assume a passive attitude. Don't worry about how well you're doing. When other thoughts come to mind, simply say to yourself, "Oh, well," and gently return to the repetition.
Step 7.	Continue for 10 to 20 minutes. You may open your eyes to check the time, but do not use an alarm. When you finish, sit quietly for a minute or so, at first with your eyes closed and later with your eyes open. Then do not stand for one or two minutes.
Step 8.	Practise the technique once or twice a day.

Photo Source: © Bill Aaron/PhotoEdit.

> **Systematic desensitization**
> A behavioural technique in which gradual exposure to an anxiety-producing stimulus is paired with relaxation to extinguish the response of anxiety.

person may be anxious, but eventually calms down and realizes that they are safe and unharmed, thus associating their fear with a positive experience. A considerable amount of debate exists as to whether or not this treatment is ethical and if directly exposing someone to their fear can increase their anxiety or result in trauma.

STUDY ALERT!

To help remember the concept of hierarchy of fears, think of something that you are afraid of and construct your own hierarchy of fears.

Systematic desensitization has proved to be an effective treatment for a number of problems, including phobias, anxiety disorders, and even impotence and fear of sexual contact. Through this technique, we can learn to enjoy the things we once feared (Tryon, 2005; Dowling, Jackson, & Thomas, 2008).

Operant Conditioning Techniques

Some behavioural approaches make use of the operant conditioning principles that we discussed earlier in the book when considering learning. These approaches are based on the notion that we should reward people for carrying out desirable behaviour and extinguish undesirable behaviour by either ignoring it or punishing it.

One example of the systematic application of operant conditioning principles is the token system, which rewards a person for desired behaviour with a token such as a poker chip or some kind of play money. Although it is most frequently employed in institutional settings for individuals with relatively serious problems, and sometimes with children as a classroom management technique, the system resembles what parents do when they give children money for being well behaved—money that the children can later exchange for something they want. The desired behaviour may range from simple things such as keeping one's room neat to personal grooming and interacting with other people. In institutions, patients can exchange tokens for some object or activity, such as snacks, new clothes, or, in extreme cases, being able to sleep in one's own bed rather than in a sleeping bag on the floor.

Contingency contracting, a variant of the token system, has proved quite effective in producing behaviour modification. In *contingency contracting*, the therapist and client (or teacher and student, or parent and child) draw up a written agreement. The contract states a series of behavioural goals the client hopes to achieve. It also specifies the positive consequences for the client if the client reaches goals—usually an explicit reward such as money or additional privileges. Contracts frequently state negative consequences if the client does not meet the goals. For example, clients who are trying to quit smoking might write out a cheque to a cause they have no interest in supporting. If the client smokes on a given day, the therapist will mail the cheque.

Behaviour therapists also use *observational learning*, the process in which the behaviour of other people is modelled, to systematically teach people new skills and ways of handling their fears and anxieties. For example, modelling helps when therapists are teaching basic social skills such as maintaining eye contact during conversation and acting assertively. Similarly, children with dog phobias have been able to overcome their fears by watching another child—called the "Fearless Peer"—repeatedly walk up to a dog, touch it, pet it, and finally play with it. Modelling, then, can play an effective role in resolving some kinds of behaviour difficulties, especially if the model receives a reward for his or her behaviour (Bandura, Grusec, & Menlove, 1967; Egliston & Rapee, 2007).

Dialectical Behaviour Therapy

In **dialectical behaviour therapy**, the focus is on getting people to accept who they are, regardless of whether it matches their ideal. Even if their childhood has been dysfunctional or they have ruined relationships with others, that's in the past. What matters is who they wish to become (Manning, 2005; Linehan et al., 2007; Wagner, Rizvi, & Hamed, 2007).

Therapists using dialectical behaviour therapy seek to have patients realize that they basically have two choices: Either they remain unhappy, or they change. Once patients agree that they wish to change, it is up to them to modify their behaviour. Patients are taught that even if they experience unhappiness, or anger, or any other negative emotion, it

Dialectical behaviour therapy
A form of treatment in which the focus is on getting people to accept who they are, regardless of whether it matches their ideal.

A "Fearless Peer" who models appropriate and effective behaviour can help children overcome their fears.

Source: © Royalty-Free/Corbis.

doesn't need to rule their behaviour. It's their behaviour that counts—not their inner life.

Dialectical behaviour therapy teaches behavioural skills that help people behave more effectively and keep their emotions in check. Although it is a relatively new form of therapy, increasing evidence supports its effectiveness, particularly with certain personality disorders (Swales & Heard, 2007; Katz, Fotti, & Postl, 2009; Soler et al., 2009).

How Does Behaviour Therapy Stack Up?

Behaviour therapy works particularly well for treating phobias and compulsions, establishing control over impulses, and learning complex social skills to replace maladaptive behaviour. More than any of the other therapeutic techniques, it provides methods that nonprofessionals can use to change their own behaviour. Moreover, it is efficient, because it focuses on solving carefully defined problems (Barlow, 2007).

Behaviour therapy does have some disadvantages. For instance, it does not treat deep depression or other severe disorders particularly successfully. In addition, because it emphasizes changing external behaviour, people receiving behaviour therapy do not necessarily gain insight into thoughts and expectations that may be fostering their maladaptive behaviour. For these reasons, some psychologists have turned to cognitive approaches.

Cognitive Approaches to Therapy

If you assumed that illogical thoughts and beliefs lie at the heart of psychological disorders, wouldn't the most direct treatment route be to teach people new, more adaptive modes of thinking? The answer is yes, according to psychologists who take a cognitive approach to treatment.

Cognitive treatment approaches teach people to think in more adaptive ways by changing their dysfunctional cognitions about the world and themselves. Unlike behaviour therapists, who focus on modifying external behaviour, cognitive therapists attempt to change the way people think as well as their behaviour. Because they often use basic principles of learning, the methods they employ are sometimes referred to as the **cognitive-behavioural approach** (Beck & Rector, 2005; Butler et al., 2006; Friedberg, 2006).

Although cognitive treatment approaches take many forms, they all share the assumption that anxiety, depression, and negative emotions develop from maladaptive thinking. Accordingly, cognitive treatments seek to change the thought patterns that lead to getting "stuck" in dysfunctional ways of thinking. Therapists systematically teach clients to challenge their assumptions and adopt new approaches to old problems.

Cognitive therapy is relatively short-term, usually lasting a maximum of twenty sessions. Therapy tends to be highly structured and focused on concrete problems. Therapists often begin by teaching the theory behind the approach and then continue to take an active role throughout the course of therapy, acting as a combination of teacher, coach, and partner.

One good example of cognitive treatment, **rational-emotive behaviour therapy**, attempts to restructure a person's belief system into a more realistic, rational, and logical set of views. According to psychologist Albert Ellis

---

Cognitive treatment approaches
An approach that teaches people to think in more adaptive ways by changing their dysfunctional cognitions about the world and themselves.

Cognitive-behavioural approach
Cognitive therapists attempt to change the way people think as well as their behaviour by utilizing basic principles of learning.

Rational-emotive behaviour therapy
A form of therapy that attempts to restructure a person's belief system into a more realistic, rational, and logical set of views by challenging dysfunctional beliefs that maintain irrational behaviour.

(2002, 2004), many people lead unhappy lives and suffer from psychological disorders because they harbour irrational, unrealistic ideas such as these:

- We need the love or approval of virtually every significant other person for everything we do.
- We should be thoroughly competent, adequate, and successful in all possible respects in order to consider ourselves worthwhile.
- It is horrible when things don't turn out the way we want them to.

Such irrational beliefs trigger negative emotions, which in turn support the irrational beliefs, leading to a self-defeating cycle. Ellis calls it the A-B-C model, in which negative activating conditions (A) lead to the activation of an irrational belief system (B), which in turn leads to emotional consequences (C). For example, if a person experiences the breakup of a close relationship (A) and holds the irrational belief (B) that "I'll never be loved again," this triggers negative emotions (C) that in turn feed back into support of the irrational belief (see Figure 3).

Rational-emotive behaviour therapy aims to help clients eliminate maladaptive thoughts and beliefs and adopt more effective thinking. To accomplish this goal, therapists take an active, directive role during therapy, openly challenging patterns of thought that appear to be dysfunctional. Consider this example:

Martha: The basic problem is that I'm worried about my family. I'm worried about money. And I never seem to be able to relax.

Therapist: Why are you worried about your family? . . . What's to be concerned about? They have certain demands which you don't want to adhere to.

Martha: I was brought up to think that I mustn't be selfish.

Therapist: Oh, we'll have to knock that out of your head!

Martha: My mother feels that I shouldn't have left home—that my place is with them. There are nagging doubts about what I should—

Therapist: Why are there doubts? Why should you?

Martha: I think it's a feeling I was brought up with that you always have to give of yourself. If you think of yourself, you're wrong.

Therapist: That's a belief. Why do you have to keep believing that—at your age? You believed a lot of superstitions when you were younger. Why do you have to retain them? Your parents indoctrinated you with this nonsense, because that's their belief. . . . Who needs that philosophy? All it's gotten you, so far, is guilt (Ellis, 1974, pp. 223–286).

By poking holes in Martha's reasoning, the therapist is attempting to help her adopt a more realistic view of herself and her circumstances (Ellis, 2002; Dryden & David, 2008).

An approach to therapy that is gaining in popularity is **mindfulness-based cognitive therapy (MBCT)**. MBCT builds on a cognitive perspective and teaches people to focus on maintaining a non-judgmental, moment by moment

FIGURE 3

In the A-B-C model of rational-emotive behaviour therapy, negative activating conditions (A) lead to the activation of an irrational belief system (B), which leads to emotional consequences (C). Those emotional consequences then feedback and support the belief system. At what steps in the model could change occur as a result of rational-emotive behaviour therapy?

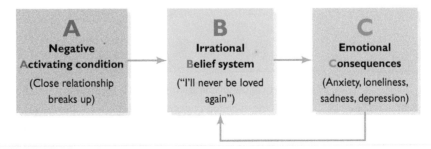

Mindfulness-based cognitive therapy (MBCT)
An approach that teaches people to focus on maintaining a non-judgmental, moment by moment awareness of their environment, physical sensations, thoughts, and feelings.

awareness of their environment, physical sensations, thoughts, and feelings. Therapy typically consists of eight weekly group sessions with a trained therapist, as well as homework and at-home practice. Research has shown that mindful-based therapies can have significant physical, psychological, and social benefits such as improving the immune system, as well as reducing negative emotions, anxiety, stress, and reducing the risk of depression relapse. In 1979, Jon Kabat-Zinn et al. adapted the teachings of mindfulness meditation and yoga to create mindfulness-based stress reduction (MBSR) to assist people with chronic medical problems and decrease pain. (Segal, 2008; Mental Health Foundation, 2010; GlobeandMail.com, 2012; University of Toronto, 2014).

Another form of therapy that builds on a cognitive perspective is that of Aaron Beck (1995, 2004). Like rational-emotive behaviour therapy, Beck's *cognitive therapy* aims to change people's illogical thoughts about themselves and the world. However, cognitive therapy is considerably less confrontational and challenging than rational-emotive behaviour therapy. Instead of the therapist actively arguing with clients about their dysfunctional cognitions, cognitive therapists more often play the role of teacher. Therapists urge clients to obtain information on their own that will lead them to discard their inaccurate thinking. During the course of treatment, therapists help clients discover ways of thinking more appropriately about themselves and others (Rosen, 2000; Beck, Freeman, & Davis, 2004; Moorey, 2007).

Cognitive approaches to therapy have proved successful in dealing with a broad range of disorders, including anxiety disorders, depression, substance abuse, and eating disorders. Furthermore, the willingness of cognitive therapists to incorporate additional treatment approaches (e.g., combining cognitive and behavioural techniques in cognitive behavioural therapy) has made this approach a particularly effective form of treatment (Mitte, 2005; Ishikawa et al., 2007; Bhar et al., 2008).

At the same time, critics have pointed out that the focus on helping people to think more rationally ignores the fact that life is in reality sometimes irrational. Changing one's assumptions to make them more reasonable and logical thus may not always be helpful—even assuming it is possible to bring about true cognitive change. Still, the success of cognitive approaches has made it one of the most frequently employed therapies (Leahy, 2003; Beck & Rector, 2005).

Evaluate

1. According to Freud, people use _____ as a means of preventing unwanted impulses from intruding on conscious thought.

2. In dream interpretation, a psychoanalyst must learn to distinguish between the _____ content of a dream, which is what appears on the surface, and the _____ content, its underlying meaning.

3. Which of the following treatments deals with phobias by gradual exposure to the item producing the fear?

   a. Systematic desensitization

   b. Partial reinforcement

   c. Behavioural self-management

   d. Aversion therapy

Answers to Evaluate Questions

1. defence mechanisms; 2. manifest, latent; 3. a

Key Terms

aversive conditioning	dialectical behaviour therapy	psychotherapy
behavioural treatment approaches	mindfulness-based cognitive therapy	rational-emotive behaviour
biomedical therapy	(MBCT)	therapy
cognitive-behavioural approach	psychoanalysis	systematic desensitization
cognitive treatment approaches	psychodynamic therapy	transference

Psychotherapy: Humanistic, Interpersonal, and Group Approaches to Treatment

MODULE

41

LEARNING OBJECTIVES

What are the humanistic approaches to treatment?

What is interpersonal therapy?

How does group therapy differ from individual types of therapy?

How effective is psychotherapy, and which kind of psychotherapy works best in a given situation?

Humanistic Therapy

As you know from your own experience, a student cannot master the material covered in a course without some hard work, no matter how good the teacher and the textbook are. You must take the time to study, memorize the vocabulary, and learn the concepts. Nobody else can do it for you. If you choose to put in the effort, you'll succeed; if you don't, you'll fail. The responsibility is primarily yours.

Humanistic therapy draws on this philosophical perspective of self-responsibility in developing treatment techniques. The many different types of therapy that fit into this category have a similar rationale: We have control of our own behaviour, we can make choices about the kinds of lives we want to live, and it is up to us to solve the difficulties we encounter in our daily lives.

Humanistic therapists view themselves as guides or facilitators and by using humanistic techniques, seek to help people understand themselves and find ways to come closer to the ideal they hold for themselves. In this view, psychological disorders result from the inability to find meaning in life and feeling lonely and unconnected to others (Cain, 2002).

Humanistic approaches have produced many therapeutic techniques. Among the most important is person-centred therapy.

Person-Centred Therapy

Consider the following therapy session excerpt:

Alice: I was thinking about this business of standards. I somehow developed a sort of a knack, I guess, of—well—habit—of trying to make people feel at ease around me, or to make things go along smoothly . . .

Therapist: In other words, what you did was always in the direction of trying to keep things smooth and to make other people feel better and to smooth the situation.

Alice: Yes. I think that's what it was. Now the reason why I did it probably was—I mean, not that I was a good little Samaritan going around making other people happy, but that was probably the role that felt easiest for me to play . . .

Therapist: You feel that for a long time you've been playing the role of kind of smoothing out the frictions or differences or what not . . .

Alice: M-hm.

Therapist: Rather than having any opinion or reaction of your own in the situation. Is that it? (Rogers, 1951, pp. 152–153).

Humanistic therapy
Therapy in which the underlying rationale is that people have control of their behaviour, can make choices about their lives, and are essentially responsible for solving their own problems.

437

The therapist does not interpret or answer the questions the client has raised. Instead, the therapist clarifies or reflects back what the client has said (e.g., "In other words, what you did . . ."; "You feel that . . ."; "Is that it?"). This therapeutic technique, known as *nondirective counselling*, is at the heart of person-centred therapy, which was first practised by Carl Rogers in the mid-twentieth century (Rogers, 1951, 1995; Raskin & Rogers, 1989).

Person-centred therapy (also called *client-centred therapy*) aims to enable people to reach their potential for self-actualization. By providing a warm and accepting environment, therapists hope to motivate clients to air their problems and feelings. In turn, this enables clients to make realistic and constructive choices and decisions about the things that bother them in their current lives (Bozarth, Zimring, & Tausch, 2002; Kirschenbaum, 2004; Bohart, 2006).

STUDY ALERT!

To better remember the concept of unconditional positive regard, try offering it to a friend during a conversation by showing your support, acceptance, and understanding no matter what thought or attitude is being offered.

Instead of directing the choices clients make, therapists provide what Rogers calls *unconditional positive regard*— expressing acceptance and understanding, regardless of the feelings and attitudes the client expresses. By doing this, therapists hope to create an atmosphere that enables clients to come to decisions that can improve their lives (Kirschenbaum & Jourdan, 2005; Vieira & Freire, 2006).

Furnishing unconditional positive regard does not mean that therapists must approve of everything their clients say or do. Rather, therapists need to communicate that they are caring, nonjudgmental, and empathetic—understanding of a client's emotional experiences (Fearing & Clark, 2000).

Person-centred therapy is rarely used today in its purest form. Contemporary approaches tend to be somewhat more directive, with therapists nudging clients toward insights rather than merely reflecting back their statements. However, therapists still view clients' insights as central to the therapeutic process.

Humanistic Approaches in Perspective

The notion that psychological disorders result from restricted growth potential appeals philosophically to many people. Furthermore, when humanistic therapists acknowledge that the freedom we possess can lead to psychological difficulties, clients find an unusually supportive environment for therapy. In turn, this atmosphere can help clients discover solutions to difficult psychological problems (Cooper, 2007).

However, humanistic treatments lack specificity, a problem that has troubled their critics. Humanistic approaches are not very precise and are probably the least scientifically and theoretically developed type of treatment. Moreover, this form of treatment works best for the same type of highly verbal client who profits most from psychoanalytic treatment.

Interpersonal Therapy

Interpersonal therapy (IPT) considers therapy in the context of social relationships. Although its roots stem from psychodynamic approaches, interpersonal therapy concentrates more on the here and now with the goal of improving a client's current relationships. It typically focuses on interpersonal issues such as conflicts with others, social skills issues, role transitions (such as divorce), or grief (Weissman, Markowitz, & Klerman, 2007).

Person-centred therapy
Therapy in which the goal is to reach one's potential for self-actualization.

Interpersonal therapy (IPT)
Short-term therapy that focuses on the context of current social relationships.

Interpersonal therapy is more active and directive than traditional psychodynamic approaches. Sessions are more structured and shorter in duration than traditional psychodynamic approaches and typically last only twelve–sixteen weeks. During sessions, therapists make concrete suggestions on improving relations with others and offer recommendations and advice. The approach makes no assumptions about the underlying causes of psychological disorders, but focuses on the interpersonal context in which a disorder is developed and maintained. Evaluations of the approach have shown that interpersonal therapy is especially effective in dealing with depression, anxiety, addictions, and eating disorders (Salsman, 2006; Grigoriadis & Ravitz, 2007; Miller et al., 2008).

Group Therapy, Self-Help Groups, and Family Therapy

Although most treatment takes place between a single individual and a therapist, some forms of therapy involve groups of people seeking treatment together. In **group therapy**, people typically discuss with the group their psychological difficulties or problems, which often centre on a common difficulty, such as alcoholism or a lack of social skills. The other members of the group provide emotional support and dispense advice on ways they have coped effectively with similar problems (Alonso, Alonso, & Piper, 2003; Scaturo, 2004; Rigby & Waite, 2007). In some groups, the therapist is quite directive; in others, the members of the group set their own agenda and determine how the group will proceed (Beck & Lewis, 2000; Stockton, Morran, & Krieger, 2004).

Because several people are treated simultaneously in group therapy, it is a much more economical means of treatment than individual psychotherapy. On the other hand, critics argue that group settings lack the individual attention inherent in one-to-one therapy and that especially shy and withdrawn individuals may not receive the attention they need in a group setting.

Self-Help Groups

In many cases, group therapy does not involve a professional therapist. In **self-help groups** people with similar problems get together to discuss their shared feelings and experiences without a professional therapist. For example, people who have recently experienced the death of a spouse might meet in a *bereavement support group*, or students may get together to discuss their adjustment to college or university.

One of the best-known self-help groups is Alcoholics Anonymous (AA), designed to help members deal with alcohol-related problems. AA prescribes twelve steps that alcoholics must pass through on their road to recovery; they begin with an admission that they are alcoholics and powerless over alcohol. AA provides more treatment for alcoholics than any other therapy; AA and other twelve-step programs (such as Narcotics Anonymous) can be as successful in treating alcohol and other substance-abuse problems as traditional types of therapy (Bogenschutz, Geppert, & George, 2006; Galanter, 2007; Gossop, Stewart, & Marsden, 2008).

Family Therapy

One specialized form of group therapy is family therapy. As the name implies, **family therapy** involves two or more family members, one (or more) of whose problems led to treatment. But rather than focusing simply on the members of the family who present the initial problem, family therapists consider the family as a unit, to which each member contributes. By meeting with the entire family simultaneously they expect each member to contribute to the resolution of the problem as they try to understand how the family members interact with one another (Cooklin, 2000; Strong & Tomm, 2007).

Group therapy
Therapy in which people meet in a group with a therapist to discuss their problems and receive support and advice from group members.

Self-help groups
People who have experienced similar problems get together to discuss their shared feelings and experiences without a professional therapist.

Family therapy
An approach that focuses on the family and its dynamics.

Family therapists view the family as a "system" and assume that individuals in the family cannot improve without understanding the conflicts found in interactions among family members. Many family therapists believe that family members fall into rigid roles or set patterns of behaviour, with one person acting as the scapegoat, another as a bully, and so forth. In their view, that system of roles perpetuates family disturbances. One goal of this type of therapy, then, is to get the family members to adopt new, more constructive roles and patterns of behaviour (Sprenkle & Moon, 1996; Sori, 2006).

STUDY ALERT!

Pay special attention to the discussion of (1) whether therapy is effective in general and (2) what specific types of therapy are effective because it is a key issue for therapists.

Evaluating Psychotherapy: Does Therapy Work?

Is therapy effective? This question requires a complex response. In fact, identifying the single most appropriate form of treatment is a controversial, and still unresolved, task for psychologists specializing in psychological disorders. In fact, even before considering whether one form of therapy works better than another, we need to determine whether therapy in any form effectively alleviates psychological disturbances.

Until the 1950s, most people simply assumed that therapy was effective. But in 1952 psychologist Hans Eysenck published what has become a classic article challenging that assumption. He claimed that people who received psycho-dynamic treatment and related therapies were no better off at the end of treatment than were people who were placed on a waiting list for treatment but never received it. According to his analysis, about two-thirds of the people who reported suffering from "neurotic" symptoms believed that those symptoms had disappeared after two years, regardless of whether they had been in therapy. Eysenck concluded that people would go into **spontaneous remission**, recovery without treatment, if they were simply left alone—certainly a cheaper and simpler process.

Although others quickly challenged Eysenck's conclusions, his review stimulated a continuing stream of better controlled, more carefully crafted studies on the effectiveness of psychotherapy, and today most psychologists agree: Therapy does work. Several comprehensive reviews indicate that therapy brings about greater improvement than does no treatment at all, with the rate of spontaneous remission being fairly low. In most cases, then, the symptoms of abnormal behaviour do not go away by themselves if left untreated—although the issue continues to be hotly debated (Seligman, 1996; Westen, Novotny, & Thompson-Brenner, 2004; Lutz et al., 2006).

Which Kind of Therapy Works Best?

Although most psychologists feel confident that psychotherapeutic treatment *in general* is more effective than no treatment at all, the question of whether any specific form of treatment is superior to any other has not been answered definitively (Nathan, Stuart, & Dolan, 2000; Westen, Novotny, & Thompson-Brenner, 2004; Abboud, 2005).

For instance, one classic study comparing the effectiveness of various approaches found that although success rates vary somewhat by treatment form, most treatments show fairly equal success rates. As Figure 1 indicates, the rates ranged from about 70 to 85 percent greater success for treated compared with untreated individuals. Behavioural and cognitive approaches tended to be slightly more successful, but that result may have been due to differences in the severity of the cases treated (Smith, Glass, & Miller, 1980; Orwin & Condray, 1984).

Other research, relying on *meta-analysis*, in which data from a large number of studies are statistically combined, yields similar general conclusions. Furthermore, a large-scale survey of 186,000 individuals found that although survey respondents felt they had benefited substantially from psychotherapy, there was little difference in "consumer satisfaction" on the basis of the specific type of treatment they had received (Consumer Reports (CR), 1995; Seligman, 1995; Strupp, 1996; Nielsen et al., 2004).

Spontaneous remission
Recovery without treatment.

FIGURE 1

Estimates of the effectiveness of different types of treatment, in comparison to control groups of untreated people. The percentile score shows how much more effective a particular type of treatment is for the average patient than is no treatment. For example, people given psychodynamic treatment score, on average, more positively on outcome measures than about three-quarters of untreated people.

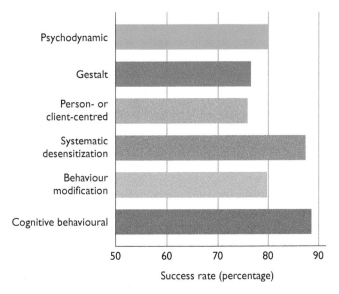

Success rate (percentage)

Source: Smith, Glass, & Miller, 1980.

Consequently, there is no single, definitive answer to the broad question, "Which therapy works best?" because of the complexity in sorting out the various factors that enter into successful therapy. Recently, however, clinicians and researchers have reframed the question by focusing on evidence-based psychotherapy practice. *Evidence-based psychotherapy practice* seeks to use research findings to determine the best practices for treating a specific disorder. To determine best practices, researchers use clinical interviews, client self-reports of improvement in quality of life, reductions in symptoms, observations of behaviour, and other outcomes to compare different therapies. By using objective research findings, clinicians are increasingly able to determine the most effective treatment for a specific disorder (APA Presidential Task Force, 2006; Brownlee, 2007; Kazdin, 2008).

Because no single type of psychotherapy is invariably effective for every individual, some therapists use an **eclectic approach to therapy**. In an eclectic approach to therapy, therapists use a variety of techniques, thus integrating several perspectives, to treat a person's problems. By employing more than one approach, therapists can choose the appropriate mix of evidence-based treatments to match the individual's specific needs. Furthermore, therapists with certain personal characteristics may work better with particular individuals and types of treatments, and—as we consider next—even racial and ethnic factors may be related to the success of treatment (Cheston, 2000; Chambless et al., 2006; Hayes, 2008).

Therapists cannot take a "one size fits all approach" to psychological treatment in culturally diverse Canada. Immigrant populations have their own unique perspective on therapy that must be recognized, assessed, and respected for treatment to be successful. Elez (2008) identified several factors to consider when doing therapy with immigrants in Canada, including, but not limited to: clients' language skills (e.g., interpreter required), appropriate meeting place (e.g., client's home vs. therapists' office), culturally appropriate ways of relating (e.g., eye contact, touch), war-related trauma (e.g., PTSD), cultural ways of healing (e.g., Tree of Life), and cultural stigma of mental health services (e.g., shame). The *Exploring Diversity* box explores the critical role of racial and ethnic factors in the treatment of psychological disorders in more detail.

Eclectic approach to therapy
An approach that uses techniques taken from a variety of treatment methods, rather than just one.

Exploring DIVERSITY

Racial and Ethnic Factors in Treatment

Consider the following case report, written by a school counsellor about Jimmy Jones, a 12-year-old student who was referred to a counsellor because of his lack of interest in schoolwork:

> Jimmy does not pay attention, daydreams often, and frequently falls asleep during class. There is a strong possibility that Jimmy is harbouring repressed rage that needs to be ventilated and dealt with. His inability to directly express his anger had led him to adopt passive aggressive means of expressing hostility, i.e., inattentiveness, daydreaming, falling asleep. It is recommended that Jimmy be seen for intensive counselling to discover the basis of the anger (Sue & Sue, 1990, p. 44).

The counsellor was wrong, however. Rather than suffering from "repressed rage," Jimmy lived in a poverty-stricken and disorganized home. Because of overcrowding at his house, he did not get enough sleep and consequently was tired the next day. Frequently, he was also hungry. In short, the stresses arising from his environment caused his problems, not any deep-seated psychological disturbances.

This incident underscores the importance of taking people's environmental and cultural backgrounds into account during treatment for psychological disorders. In particular, members of racial and ethnic minority groups, especially those who are also poor, may behave in ways that help them deal with a society that discriminates against them. As a consequence, behaviour that may signal psychological disorder in middle- and upper-class whites may simply be adaptive in people from other racial and socioeconomic groups. For instance, characteristically suspicious and distrustful people may be displaying a survival strategy to protect themselves from psychological and physical injury, rather than suffering from a psychological disturbance (Aponte & Wohl, 2000; Paniagua, 2000; Tseng, 2003; Pottick et al., 2007).

In fact, therapists must question some basic assumptions of psychotherapy when dealing with racial, ethnic, and cultural minority-group members. For example, compared with the dominant culture, Asian and Latino cultures typically place much greater emphasis on the group, family, and society. When an Asian or Latino faces a critical decision, the family helps make it—suggesting that family members should also play a role in psychological treatment. Similarly, the traditional Chinese recommendation for dealing with depression or anxiety is to urge people who experience such problems to avoid thinking about whatever is upsetting them. Consider how this advice contrasts with treatment approaches that emphasize the value of insight (Ponterotto, Gretchen, & Chauhan, 2001; McCarthy, 2005; Leitner, 2007).

Therapists must take into account the racial, ethnic, cultural, and social class backgrounds of their clients in determining the nature of a psychological disorder and the course of treatment (Aponte & Wohl, 2000; Pedersen et al., 2002).

Evaluate

1. Match each of the following treatment strategies with the statement you might expect to hear from a therapist using that strategy.

   1. Group therapy

   2. Unconditional positive regard

   3. Behavioural therapy

   4. Nondirective counselling

   a. "In other words, you don't get along with your mother because she hates your girlfriend, is that right?"

   b. "I want you all to take turns talking about why you decided to come and what you hope to gain from therapy."

   c. "I can understand why you wanted to wreck your friend's car after she hurt your feelings. Now tell me more about the accident."

   d. "That's not appropriate behaviour. Let's work on replacing it with something else."

2. _____ therapies assume that people should take responsibility for their lives and the decisions they make.

3. One of the major criticisms of humanistic therapies is that

   a. They are too imprecise and unstructured.

   b. They treat only the symptom of the problem.

   c. The therapist dominates the patient-therapist interaction.

   d. They work well only on clients of lower socioeconomic status.

4. In a controversial study, Eysenck found that some people go into _____, or recovery without treatment, if they are simply left alone instead of treated.

Answers to Evaluate Questions

1. 1-b, 2-c, 3-d, 4-a; 2. humanistic; 3. a; 4. spontaneous remission

Key Terms

eclectic approach to therapy	humanistic therapy	self-help groups
family therapy	interpersonal therapy (IPT)	spontaneous remission
group therapy	person-centred therapy	

Biomedical Therapy: Biological Approaches to Treatment

LEARNING OBJECTIVE

LO7 **How are** drug, electroconvulsive, and psychosurgical techniques used today in the treatment of psychological disorders?

If you get a kidney infection, your doctor gives you an antibiotic, and with luck, about a week later your kidney should be as good as new. If your appendix becomes inflamed, a surgeon removes it and your body functions normally once more. Could a comparable approach, focusing on the body's physiology, be effective for psychological disturbances?

According to biological approaches to treatment, the answer is yes. Therapists routinely use biomedical therapies. This approach suggests that rather than focusing on a patient's psychological conflicts or past traumas, or on environmental factors that may produce abnormal behaviour, focusing treatment directly on brain chemistry and other neurological factors may be more appropriate. To do this, therapists can use drugs, electric shock, or surgery to provide treatment.

Drug Therapy

Drug therapy, the control of psychological disorders through drugs, works by altering the operation of neurotransmitters and neurons in the brain. Some drugs operate by inhibiting neurotransmitters or receptor neurons, reducing activity at particular synapses, the sites where nerve impulses travel from one neuron to another. Other drugs do just the opposite: They increase the activity of certain neurotransmitters or neurons, allowing particular neurons to fire more frequently (see Figure 1).

Antipsychotic Drugs

Probably no greater change has occurred in mental hospitals than the successful introduction in the mid-1950s of **antipsychotic drugs**—drugs used to reduce severe symptoms of disturbance, such as loss of touch with reality and agitation. Previously, the typical mental hospital wasn't very different from the stereotypical nineteenth-century insane asylum, giving mainly custodial care to screaming, moaning, clawing patients who displayed bizarre behaviours. Suddenly, in just a matter of days after hospital staff members administered antipsychotic drugs, the wards became considerably calmer environments in which professionals could do more than just try to get patients through the day without causing serious harm to themselves or others.

This dramatic change came about through the introduction of a drug called *chlorpromazine*. Along with other, similar drugs, chlorpromazine rapidly became the most popular and successful treatment for schizophrenia. Today

> **Drug therapy**
> Control of psychological disorders through the use of drugs.
>
> **Antipsychotic drugs**
> Drugs that temporarily reduce psychotic symptoms such as agitation, hallucinations, and delusions.

FIGURE 1

The major classes of drugs used to treat psychological disorders have different effects on the brain and nervous system.

Drug Treatments			
Class of Drug	**Effects of Drug**	**Primary Action of Drug**	**Examples**
Antipsychotic Drugs, Atypical Antipsychotic Drugs	Reduction in loss of touch with reality, agitation	Block dopamine receptors	Antipsychotic: Chlorpromazine (Thorazine), clozapine (Clozaril), haloperidol (Haldol) Atypical Antipsychotic: rizperadone, olanzapine
Antidepressant Drugs			
Tricyclic antidepressants	Reduction in depression	Permit rise in neurotransmitters such as norepinepherine	Trazodone (Desyrel), amitriptyline (Elavil), desipramine (Norpamin)
MAO inhibitors	Reduction in depression	Prevent MAO from breaking down neurotransmitters	Phenelzine (Nardil), tranylcypromine (Parnate)
Selective serotonin reuptake inhibitors (SSRIs)	Reduction in depression	Inhibit reuptake of serotonin	Fluoxetine (Prozac), Luvox, Paxil, Celexa, Zoloft, nefazodone (Serzone)
Mood Stabilizers			
Lithium	Mood stabilization	Can alter transmission of impulses within neurons	Lithium (Lithonate), Depakote, Tegretol
Antianxiety Drugs	Reduction in anxiety	Increase activity of neurotransmitter GABA	Benzodiazepines (Valium, Xanax)

drug therapy is the preferred treatment for most cases of severely abnormal behaviour and, as such, is used for most patients hospitalized with psychological disorders. The newest generation of antipsychotics, referred to as *atypical antipsychotics*, have fewer side effects; they include *rizperidone, olanzapine,* and *paliperidone* (Lublin, Eberhard, & Levander, 2005; Savas, Yumru, & Kaya, 2007; Nasrallah et al., 2008).

How do antipsychotic drugs work? Most block dopamine receptors at the brain's synapses. Some newer drugs, such as clozapine, increase dopamine levels in certain parts of the brain, such as those related to planning and goal-directed activity (Moghaddam & Adams, 1998; Sawa & Snyder, 2002; Advokat, 2005).

Despite the effectiveness of antipsychotic drugs, they do not produce a "cure" in the same way that, say, penicillin cures an infection. Most of the time, when the drug is withdrawn, the symptoms reappear. Furthermore, such drugs can have long-term side effects, such as dryness of the mouth and throat, dizziness, and sometimes tremors and loss of muscle control, which may continue after drug treatments are stopped (Voruganti et al., 2007).

Antidepressant Drugs

As you might guess from the name, **antidepressant drugs** are a class of medications used in cases of severe depression to improve the moods of patients. They were discovered by accident: Medical doctors found that patients with tuberculosis who received the drug iproniazid suddenly became happier and more optimistic. When researchers tested that drug on people with depression, a similar result occurred, and these drugs became an accepted form of treatment for depression (Hedges et al., 2007). Originally only intended to treat depression, antidepressants are also being prescribed and shown effective in the treatment of a range of anxiety disorders (Zohar & Westenburg, 2000).

Antidepressant drugs
Medications that improve a severely depressed patient's mood and feeling of well-being.

STUDY ALERT!

To help organize your study of different drugs used in therapy, review Figure 1, which classifies them according to the categories of antipsychotic, atypical antipsychotic, antidepressant, mood-stabilizing, and antianxiety drugs.

Most antidepressant drugs work by changing the concentration of particular neurotransmitters in the brain. For example, *tricyclic drugs* increase the availability of norepinepherine at the synapses of neurons, whereas *MAO inhibitors* prevent the enzyme monoamine oxidase (MAO) from breaking down neurotransmitters. Newer antidepressants—such as Lexapro—are *selective serotonin reuptake inhibitors (SSRIs)*. SSRIs target the neurotransmitter serotonin, permitting it to linger at the synapse. One of the latest antidepressants, nefazodone (Serzone), blocks serotonin at some receptor sites but not others (Lucki & O'Leary, 2004; Dhillon, Yang, & Curran, 2008; see Figure 2).

Although antidepressant drugs may produce side effects such as drowsiness and faintness, their overall success rate is quite good. Unlike antipsychotic drugs, antidepressants can produce lasting, long-term recovery from depression. In many cases, even after patients stop taking the drugs, their depression does not return (Gibbons et al., 2007; Olfson & Markus, 2008).

Consumers spend billions of dollars each year on antidepressant drugs, and sales are increasing more than 20 percent a year. In particular, the antidepressant *fluoxetine*, sold under the trade name Prozac, has been highlighted on magazine covers and has been the topic of best-sellers.

Does Prozac deserve its acclaim? In some respects, yes. Despite its high expense—each daily dose costs around $2—it has significantly improved the lives of thousands of depressed individuals. Compared with other antidepressants, Prozac (along with its cousins Luvox, Paxil, Celexa, and Zoloft) has relatively few side effects. Furthermore, many people who do not respond to other types of antidepressants do well on Prozac. However, like all drugs, Prozac does not agree with everyone. For example, 20 to 30 percent of users report experiencing nausea and diarrhea, and a smaller number report sexual dysfunctions (Kramer, 1993; Brambilla et al., 2005; Fenter, 2006).

FIGURE 2

In (a), selective serotonin reuptake inhibitors (SSRIs) reduce depression by permitting the neurotransmitter serotonin to remain in the synapse. In (b), a newer antidepressant, nefazodone (Serzone), operates more selectively to block serotonin at some sites but not others, helping to reduce the side effects of the drug.

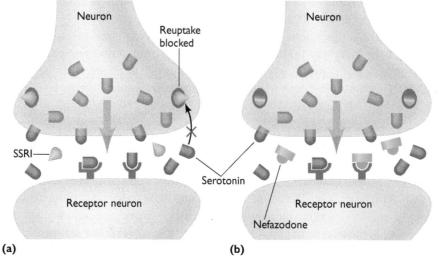

Source: Based on Mischoulon, 2000.

Lithium

The drug **lithium,** a form of mineral salts, has been used very successfully in patients with bipolar disorders. Although no one knows definitely why, lithium and drugs such as *Depakote* and *Tegretol* effectively reduce manic episodes. However, they do not effectively treat depressive phases of bipolar disorder, so antidepressants are usually prescribed during those phases (Abraham & Calabrese, 2007; Salvi et al., 2008).

Lithium and similar drugs have a quality that sets them apart from other drug treatments: They can be a *preventive* treatment, blocking future episodes of manic depression. Often, people who have had episodes of bipolar disorder can take a daily dose of lithium to prevent a recurrence of their symptoms. Most other drugs are useful only when symptoms of psychological disturbance occur.

Antianxiety Drugs

As the name implies, **antianxiety drugs** reduce the level of anxiety a person experiences and increase feelings of well-being. They are prescribed not only to reduce general tension in people who are experiencing temporary difficulties but also to aid in the treatment of more serious anxiety disorders (Zito, 1993).

Antianxiety drugs such as Xanax and Valium are among the medications most frequently prescribed by physicians. In fact, more than half of all North American families have someone who has taken such a drug at one time or another.

Although the popularity of antianxiety drugs suggests that they hold few risks, they can produce a number of potentially serious side effects. For instance, they can cause fatigue, and long-term use can lead to dependence. Moreover, when taken in combination with alcohol, some antianxiety drugs can be lethal. But a more important issue concerns their use to suppress anxiety. Almost every therapeutic approach to psychological disturbance views continuing anxiety as a signal of some other sort of problem. Thus, drugs that mask anxiety may simply be hiding other difficulties. Consequently, rather than confronting their underlying problems, people may be hiding from them through the use of antianxiety drugs.

Electroconvulsive Therapy (ECT)

Martha Manning had contemplated all kinds of suicide—by pills, hanging, even guns. Her depression was so deep that she lived each minute "afraid I [wouldn't] make it to the next hour." But she balked when her therapist recommended electroconvulsive therapy, commonly known as "shock treatment." Despite her training and practice as a clinical psychologist, Manning immediately flashed to scenes from *One Flew Over the Cuckoo's Nest,* "with McMurphy and the Chief jolted with electroshock, their bodies flailing with each jolt" (Guttman, 1995, p. 16).

The reality, it turned out, was quite different. Although it did produce some memory loss and temporary headaches, the procedure also brought Manning back from the brink of suicide.

First introduced in the 1930s, **electroconvulsive therapy (ECT)** is a procedure used in the treatment of severe depression in which an electric current of 70 to 150 volts is briefly administered to a patient's head, causing a loss of consciousness and often causing seizures. Usually health professionals sedate patients and give them muscle relaxants before administering the current, and this helps reduce the intensity of muscle contractions produced during ECT. The typical patient receives about ten such treatments in the course of a month, but some patients continue with maintenance treatments for months afterward (Greenberg & Kellner, 2005; Stevens & Harper, 2007).

Lithium
A drug made up of mineral salts, which is used to treat and prevent manic episodes of bipolar disorder.

Antianxiety drugs
Drugs that reduce the level of anxiety a person experiences, essentially by reducing excitability and increasing feelings of well-being.

Electroconvulsive therapy (ECT)
A procedure used in the treatment of severe depression in which an electric current of 70 to 150 volts is briefly administered to a patient's head.

ECT is a controversial technique. Apart from the obvious distastefulness of a treatment that evokes images of electrocution, side effects occur frequently. For instance, after treatment patients often experience disorientation, confusion, and sometimes memory loss that may remain for months. Furthermore, ECT often does not produce long-term improvement; one study found that without follow-up medication, depression returned in most patients who had undergone ECT treatments. Finally, even when ECT does work, we do not know why, and some critics believe it may cause permanent brain damage (Sackeim et al., 2001; Kato, 2009).

In light of the drawbacks to ECT, why do therapists use it at all? Basically, they use it because, in many severe cases of depression, it offers the only quickly effective treatment. For instance, it may prevent depressed, suicidal individuals from committing suicide, and it can act more quickly than antidepressive medications.

The use of ECT has risen in the last decade, with more than 100,000 people undergoing it each year. Still, ECT tends to be used only when other treatments have proved ineffective, and researchers continue to search for alternative treatments (Fink, 2000; Eranti & McLoughlin, 2003; Pandya, Pozuelo, & Malone, 2007).

One new and promising alternative to ECT is **transcranial magnetic stimulation (TMS).** TMS creates a precise magnetic pulse in a specific area of the brain. By activating particular neuorns, TMS has been found to be effective in relieving the symptoms of depression in a number of controlled experiments; however, the therapy can produce side effects, such as seizures and convulsions (Kim, Persiridou, & O'Reardon, 2009).

Psychosurgery

If ECT strikes you as a questionable procedure, the use of **psychosurgery**—brain surgery in which the object is to reduce symptoms of mental disorder—probably appears even more dubious. A technique used only rarely today, psychosurgery was introduced as a "treatment of last resort" in the 1930s.

The initial form of psychosurgery, a *prefrontal lobotomy*, consisted of surgically destroying or removing parts of a patient's frontal lobes, which, surgeons thought, controlled emotionality. In the 1930s and 1940s, surgeons performed the procedure on thousands of patients, often with little precision. For example, in one common technique, a surgeon would jab an ice pick under a patient's eyeball and swivel it back and forth (Miller, 1994; El-Hai, 2005).

Psychosurgery often did improve a patient's behaviour—but not without drastic side effects. Along with remission of the symptoms of the mental disorder, patients sometimes experienced personality changes, becoming bland, colourless, and unemotional. In other cases, patients became aggressive and unable to control their impulses. In the worst cases, treatment resulted in the death of the patient.

With the introduction of effective drug treatments—and the obvious ethical questions regarding the appropriateness of forever altering someone's personality—psychosurgery became nearly obsolete. However, it is still used in very rare cases when all other procedures have failed and the patient's behaviour presents a high risk to the patient and others. For example, surgeons sometimes use a more precise form of psychosurgery called a *cingulotomy* in rare cases of obsessive-compulsive disorder in which they destroy tissue in the *anterior cignulate* area of the brain. In another technique, *gamma knife surgery*, beams of radiation are used to destroy areas of the brain related to obsessive-compulsive disorder (Shah et al., 2008; Carey, 2009; Lopes et al, 2009; Wilkinson, 2009).

Occasionally, dying patients with severe, uncontrollable pain also receive psychosurgery. Still, even these cases raise important ethical issues, and psychosurgery remains a highly controversial treatment (Mashour, Walker, & Martuza, 2005; Steele et al., 2007).

Biomedical Therapies in Perspective

In some respects, no greater revolution has occurred in the field of mental health than biological approaches to treatment. As previously violent, uncontrollable patients have been calmed by the use of drugs, mental hospitals have been

---

Transcranial magnetic stimulation (TMS)
A depression treatment in which a precise magnetic pulse is directed to a specific area of the brain.

Psychosurgery
Brain surgery once used to reduce the symptoms of mental disorder but rarely used today.

able to concentrate more on actually helping patients and less on custodial functions. Similarly, patients whose lives have been disrupted by depression or bipolar episodes have been able to function normally, and other forms of drug therapy have also shown remarkable results.

The use of biomedical therapy for everyday problems is rising. For example, one survey of users of a college counselling service found that from 1989 to 2001, the proportion of students receiving treatment who were taking medication for psychological disorders increased from 10 percent to 25 percent (Benton et al., 2003).

Furthermore, new forms of biomedical therapy are promising. For example, the newest treatment possibility—which remains experimental at this point—is gene therapy. As we discussed when considering behavioural genetics, specific genes may be introduced to particular regions of the brain. These genes then have the potential to reverse or even prevent biochemical events that give rise to psychological disorders (Grady & Kolata, 2003; Sapolsky, 2003; Tuszynski, 2007).

Despite their current usefulness and future promise, biomedical therapies do not represent a cure-all for psychological disorders. For one thing, critics charge that such therapies merely provide relief of the symptoms of mental disorder; as soon as the drugs are withdrawn, the symptoms return. Many argue that people using biomedical therapies, should use them in conjunction with psychotherapy. Although it is considered a major step in the right direction, biomedical treatment may not solve the underlying problems that led a patient to therapy in the first place. Moreover, biomedical therapies can produce side effects, ranging from physical reactions to the development of *new* symptoms of abnormal behaviour.

STUDY ALERT!

Remember that biomedical treatments have both benefits and drawbacks.

Still, biomedical therapies—sometimes alone and more often in conjunction with psychotherapy—have permitted millions of people to function more effectively. Furthermore, although biomedical therapy and psychotherapy appear distinct, research shows that biomedical therapies ultimately may not be as different from talk therapies as one might imagine, at least in terms of their consequences.

Specifically, measures of brain functioning as a result of drug therapy compared with psychotherapy show little difference in outcomes. For example, one study compared the reactions of patients with major depression who received either an antidepressant drug or psychotherapy. After six weeks of either therapy, activity in the portion of the brain related to the disorder—the basal ganglia—had changed in similar ways, and that area appeared to function more normally. Although such research is not definitive, it does suggest that at least for some disorders, psychotherapy may be just as effective as biomedical interventions—and vice versa. Research also makes it clear that no single treatment is effective universally, and that each type of treatment has both advantages and disadvantages (Hollon, Thase, & Markowitz, 2002; DeRubeis, Hollon, & Shelton, 2003; Pinquart, Duberstein, & Lyness, 2006; Greenberg & Goldman, 2009).

Community Psychology: Focus on Prevention

Each of the treatments we have reviewed has a common element: It is a "restorative" treatment, aimed at alleviating psychological difficulties that already exist. However, an approach known as community psychology has a different aim. **Community psychology** focuses on prevention to optimize the welfare of communities and individuals, as well as minimize the incidence of psychological disorders. It aims to prevent problems before they start through seeking to understand how social issues and environmental conditions affect and interact with individuals and their well-being. Collaboration with community members on interventions, as well as empowerment while respecting diversity is also a key part of community psychology.

Community psychology came of age in the 1960s in both Canada and the United States, when mental health professionals developed plans for a nationwide network of community mental health centres. The hope was that those

Community psychology

A branch of psychology that focuses on the prevention and minimization of psychological disorders in the community.

centres would provide low-cost mental health services, including short-term therapy and community educational programs. In another development, the population of mental hospitals has plunged as drug treatments made physical restraint of patients unnecessary. This transfer of former mental patients out of institutions and into the community—a process known as **deinstitutionalization**—was encouraged by the growth of the community psychology movement (see Figure 3). Proponents of deinstitutionalization wanted to ensure not only that deinstitutionalized patients received proper treatment but also that their individual rights were maintained (Wolff, 2002; St. Dennis et al., 2006).

Unfortunately, the promise of deinstitutionalization has not been met, largely because insufficient resources are provided to deinstitutionalized patients. What started as a worthy attempt to move people out of mental institutions and into the community ended, in many cases, with former patients being dumped into the community without any real support. Many became homeless—between a third and a half of all homeless adults are thought to have a major psychological disorder—and some became involved in illegal acts caused by their disorders. In short, many people who need treatment do not get it, and in some cases care for people with psychological disorders has simply shifted from one type of treatment site to another (Price, 2000; Shinn et al., 2007; Dumont & Dumont, 2008).

On the other hand, the community psychology movement has had some positive outcomes. Its emphasis on prevention has led to new approaches to psychological disorders as we discuss in the *Applying Psychology in the Real World* box. Furthermore, telephone hot lines are now common. At any time of the day or night, people experiencing acute stress can call a trained, sympathetic listener who can provide immediate—although obviously limited—treatment (Blewett, 2000; Reese, Conoley, & Brossart, 2002; Paukert, Stagner, & Hope, 2004).

College, university, and high school crisis centres are another innovation that grew out of the community psychology movement. Modelled after suicide prevention hot-line centres (services that enable potential suicide victims to call and speak to someone about their difficulties), crisis centres give callers an opportunity to discuss life crises with a sympathetic listener, who is often a volunteer.

Deinstitutionalization

The transfer of former mental patients from institutions to the community.

FIGURE 3

As deinstitutionalization has become more prevalent over the last fifty years, the number of patients being treated in U.S. state mental hospitals has declined significantly, while the number of outpatient facilities has increased.

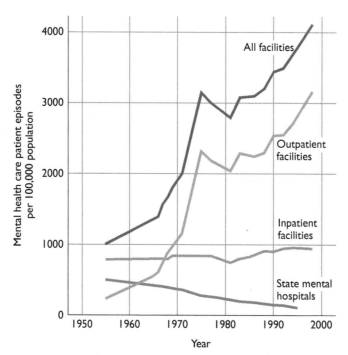

Source: National Mental Health Information Center, U.S. Department of Health and Human Services, reprinted in *Scientific American*, December 2002, p. 38.

Beating the Odds: Preventing Psychological Disorders Before They Start

When we think about the possibility of contracting physical diseases such as cancer, diabetes, or heart disease, we often think of preventive measures we can take: lose weight, eat nutritious foods, exercise regularly, don't smoke. But when we think of psychological disorders such as depression, anxiety disorders, or schizophrenia, we tend to assume that we are just passive victims and can do nothing to prevent them. But is that assumption really true?

Rather than treating psychological disorders after the symptoms fully appear, some researchers now suggest that an alternative might be to provide appropriate intervention as soon as the initial signs of an impending problem emerge before a disorder fully develops. Taking advantage of opportunities to potentially stop or reduce the progression of psychological disorders would reduce the cost of mental health care as well as lessen the suffering of individual patients. Essentially, these researchers argue, it is cheaper and less painful to prevent a problem from occurring than it is to fix it after the fact (Cloud, 2009; National Research Council and Institute of Medicine of the National Academies, 2009).

But can psychological disorders be prevented, particularly when they have a genetic component? The answer, according to a growing body of research, is yes. The expression of a genetic disposition toward mental illness often depends on environmental factors. Research is finding that young people who are at risk of developing a disorder (because one of their parents suffers from the disorder themselves, for example) benefit from school- and home-based interventions that reduce the environmental stress factors that might trigger the disorder.

Consider, for example, depression. Children of depressed parents are at increased risk of developing depression themselves. But when these children are active and engaged with others, and when they understand what depression is and that it can be treated, their increased risk of becoming depressed appears to diminish. Specifically, family-based interventions to help children of depressed parents develop resilience have been shown to be effective in reducing the onset of depression. In such programs, parents are taught communication skills, and the children are taught coping skills. In addition, the entire family is educated about depression and how it affects their relationships with one another. Interventions such as this can reduce children's predepressive symptoms and provide better long-term outcomes (Beardslee et al., 2007; Riley et al. 2008; Garber et al., 2009).

Other research suggests that early interventions can reduce the onset of additional psychological disorders and related problems, such as substance abuse, conduct disorders, antisocial behaviour, aggression, and even schizophrenia. The key is to catch and stop these problems early in life among at-risk children.

The potential benefits in terms of improved quality of life for those individuals as well as potential benefits to society of reducing the cost of care are great, generating increasing interest in approaches to prevention of psychological disorders (National Research Council and Institute of Medicine of the National Academies, 2009).

Evaluate

1. Antipsychotic drugs have provided effective, long-term, and complete cures for schizophrenia. True or false?

2. One highly effective biomedical treatment for a psychological disorder, used mainly to arrest and prevent manic-depressive episodes, is

   a. Chlorpromazine

   b. Lithium

   c. Librium

   d. Valium

3. Psychosurgery has grown in popularity as a method of treatment as surgical techniques have become more precise. True or false?

4. The trend toward releasing more patients from mental hospitals and into the community is known as _____.

Answers to Evaluate Questions

1. false; schizophrenia can be controlled, but not cured, by medication; 2. b; 3. false; psychosurgery is now used only as a treatment of last resort; 4. deinstitutionalization

Key Terms

antianxiety drugs	deinstitutionalization	psychosurgery
antidepressant drugs	drug therapy	transcranial magnetic stimulation
antipsychotic drugs	electroconvulsive therapy (ECT)	(TMS)
community psychology	lithium	

Epilogue

We have examined how psychological professionals treat people with psychological disorders. We considered a range of approaches, including both psychologically based and biologically based therapies. Clearly, the field has made substantial progress in recent years both in treating the symptoms of mental disorders and in understanding their underlying causes.

Source: © Andrea Morini/Getty Images RF.

Recap/Rethink

Module 40: Psychotherapy: Psychodynamic, Behavioural, and Cognitive Approaches to Treatment

Recap

LO1   What are the goals of psychologically and biologically based treatment approaches?

- Psychotherapy (psychologically based therapy) and biomedical therapy (biologically based therapy) share the goal of resolving psychological problems by modifying people's thoughts, feelings, expectations, evaluations, and ultimately behaviour.

LO2   What are the psychodynamic, behavioural, and cognitive approaches to treatment?

- Psychoanalytic approaches seek to bring unresolved past conflicts and unacceptable impulses from the unconscious into the conscious, where patients may deal with the problems more effectively. To do this, therapists use techniques such as free association and dream interpretation.
- Behavioural approaches to treatment view abnormal behaviour as the problem, rather than viewing that behaviour as a symptom of some underlying cause. To bring about a "cure," this view suggests that the outward behaviour must be changed by using methods such as aversive conditioning, systematic desensitization, observational learning, token systems, contingency contracting, and dialectical behaviour therapy.
- Cognitive approaches to treatment consider the goal of therapy to be to help a person restructure his or her faulty belief system into a more realistic, rational, and logical view of the world. Two examples of cognitive treatments are the rational-emotive behaviour therapy and cognitive therapy.

Rethink

1.   In what ways are psychoanalysis and cognitive therapy similar, and how do they differ?

2.   *From the perspective of a childcare provider:* How might you use systematic desensitization to help children overcome their fears?

Module 41: Psychotherapy: Humanistic, Interpersonal, and Group Approaches to Treatment

Recap

LO3 What are the humanistic approaches to treatment?

- Humanistic therapy is based on the premise that people have control of their behaviour, that they can make choices about their lives, and that it is up to them to solve their own problems. Humanistic therapies, which take a nondirective approach, include person-centred therapy.

LO4 What is interpersonal therapy?

- Interpersonal therapy focuses on interpersonal relationships and strives for immediate improvement during short-term therapy.

LO5 How does group therapy differ from individual types of therapy?

- In group therapy, several unrelated people meet with a therapist to discuss some aspect of their psychological functioning, often centring on a common problem.

LO6 How effective is psychotherapy, and which kind of psychotherapy works best in a given situation?

- Most research suggests that, in general, therapy is more effective than no therapy, although how much more effective is not known.
- Because no single type of psychotherapy is invariably effective, eclectic approaches in which a therapist uses a variety of techniques, and thus integrates several perspectives are sometimes used.

Rethink

1. How can people be successfully treated in group therapy when individuals with the "same" problem are so different? What advantages might group therapy offer over individual therapy?

2. *From the perspective of a social worker:* How might the types of therapies you employ vary depending on a client's cultural and socio-economic background?

Module 42: Biomedical Therapy: Biological Approaches to Treatment

Recap

LO7 How are drug, electroconvulsive, and psychosurgical techniques used today in the treatment of psychological disorders?

- Biomedical treatment approaches suggest that therapy should focus on the physiological causes of abnormal behaviour, rather than considering psychological factors. Drug therapy, the best example of biomedical treatments, has brought about dramatic reductions in the symptoms of mental disturbance.
- Antipsychotic drugs such as chlorpromazine very effectively reduce psychotic symptoms. Antidepressant drugs such as Prozac reduce depression so successfully that they are used very widely. Antianxiety drugs, or minor tranquilizers, are among the most frequently prescribed medications of any sort.
- In electroconvulsive therapy (ECT), used only in severe cases of depression, a patient receives a brief electric current of 70 to 150 volts.
- Psychosurgery typically consists of surgically destroying or removing certain parts of a patient's brain.
- The community psychology approach encouraged deinstitutionalization, in which previously hospitalized mental patients were released into the community.

Rethink

1. One of the main criticisms of biological therapies is that they treat the symptoms of mental disorder without uncovering and treating the underlying problems from which people are suffering. Do you agree with this criticism? Why?

2. *From the perspective of a politician:* How would you go about regulating the use of electroconvulsive therapy and psychosurgery? Would you restrict their use or make either one completely illegal? Why?

3. Do you think children of individuals with moderate or severe psychological disorders should receive genetic screening to determine if they carry genes related to the disorder? Why or why not?

4. Because it's important to catch the symptoms of psychological disorders early on, would you favour routine in-school behavioural screening of children for symptoms of disorders? Why or why not?

CHAPTER 14
Social Psychology

Source: © simplequiet/iStockphoto.com.

Key Concepts for Chapter 14

Prologue

A Heroic Escape

On May 6, 2013, Charles Ramsey was enjoying a Big Mac on his front porch when he heard screams for help coming from his neighbour's house. There he found a woman, later identified as kidnap victim Amanda Berry, who had disappeared more than 10 years ago, trying to escape the house with her 6-year old daughter. Ramsey helped to break down the door, called 911, and assisted Berry, her daughter, and two other women held captive in the house to escape. All three women had been kidnapped between 2002 and 2004. Their kidnapper, Ariel Castro, was convicted of kidnapping, rape, and aggravated murder. He later killed himself in his prison cell.

Called a hero by the press and the public, Ramsey remained modest about his part in the drama, saying he just did what he was supposed to do. When asked about potential reward money, Ramsey told CNN: "I tell you what you do: give it to them" [the kidnapped women] (Levs, Gast, & Almasy, 2013).

What led Charles Ramsey to behave so heroically? Was it simply the circumstances, or was it something about the kind of person he is? Ramsey said he was just doing what he was supposed to do "as a Christian [and] an American," and his advice to others was "just do the right thing." But research shows that doing the right thing is not so easy for many, and in similar situations many people will do nothing, ignoring others' pleas for help. What, in general, drives some people to help others—and conversely, why do other people show no concern for the welfare of others? More broadly, how can we improve social conditions so that people can live together in harmony?

We can fully answer these questions only by taking into account findings from the field of social psychology, the branch of psychology that focuses on the aspects of human behaviour that unite—and separate—us from one another. **Social psychology** is the scientific study of how people's thoughts, feelings, and actions are affected by others. Social psychologists consider the kinds and causes of the individual's behaviour in social situations. They examine how the nature of situations in which we find ourselves influences our behaviour in important ways.

Social psychology
The scientific study of how people's thoughts, feelings, and actions are affected by others.

Attitudes and Social Cognition

LEARNING OBJECTIVES

LO1 **What are** attitudes, and how are they formed, maintained, and changed?

LO2 **How do** people form impressions of what others are like and the causes of their behaviour?

LO3 **What are** the biases that influence the ways in which people view others' behaviour?

What do Sidney Crosby, Justin Bieber, and Pamela Anderson have in common? Each has appeared frequently in advertisements designed to mould or change our attitudes. Such commercials are part of the barrage of messages we receive each day from sources as varied as politicians, sales staff in stores, and celebrities, all of which are meant to influence us.

Persuasion: Changing Attitudes

Persuasion is the process of changing attitudes, one of the central concepts of social psychology. **Attitudes** are evaluations of a particular person, behaviour, belief, or concept. For example, you probably hold attitudes toward the prime minister or local mayor (a person), abortion (a behaviour), affirmative action (a belief), or architecture (a concept) (Brock & Green, 2005; Simon & Hoyt, 2008).

The ease with which attitudes can be changed depends on a number of factors, including:

- *Message source.* The characteristics of a person who delivers a persuasive message, known as an *attitude communicator*, have a major impact on the effectiveness of that message. Communicators who are physically and socially attractive—think athletes and celebrities—produce greater attitude change than those who are less attractive. Moreover, the expertise and trustworthiness of a communicator are related to the impact of a message—except in situations in which the audience believes the communicator has an ulterior motive (Ariyanto, Hornsey, & Gallois, 2006; McClure, Sutton, & Sibley, 2007; Messner, Reinhard, & Sporer, 2008).

- *Characteristics of the message.* It is not just *who* delivers a message but what the message is like that affects attitudes. Generally, two-sided messages—which include both the communicator's position and the one he or she is arguing against—are more effective than one-sided messages, assuming the arguments for the other side can be effectively refuted and the audience is knowledgeable about the topic. In addition, fear-producing messages ("Smoking cigarettes will kill you") are generally effective when they provide the audience with a means for reducing the fear ("the nicotine patch can help you quit"). However, if the fear aroused is too strong, messages may evoke people's defence mechanisms and be ignored (Perloff, 2003).

- *Characteristics of the target.* Once a communicator has delivered a message, characteristics of the *target* of the message may determine whether the message will be accepted. For example, intelligent people are more resistant to persuasion than are those who are less intelligent. Gender differences in persuasibility also seem to exist. In public settings, women are somewhat more easily persuaded than men, particularly when they have less knowledge about the message's topic. However, they are as likely as men to change their private attitudes. In fact, the magnitude of the differences in resistance to persuasion between men and women is not large (Wood & Stagner, 1994; Wood, 2000; Guadagno & Cialdini, 2002).

Attitudes
Evaluations of a particular person, behaviour, belief, or concept.

The Link Between Attitudes and Behaviour

Not surprisingly, attitudes influence behaviour. The strength of the link between particular attitudes and behaviour varies, of course, but generally people strive for consistency between their attitudes and their behaviour. Furthermore, people hold fairly consistent attitudes. For instance, you would probably not hold the attitude that eating meat is immoral and still have a positive attitude toward hamburgers (Ajzen, 2002; Conner et al., 2003; Levi, Chan, & Pence, 2006).

Ironically, the consistency that leads attitudes to influence behaviour sometimes works the other way around, for in some cases it is our behaviour that shapes our attitudes. Consider, for instance, the following incident:

> You've just spent what you feel is the most boring hour of your life, turning pegs for a psychology experiment. Just as you finally finish and are about to leave, the experimenter asks you to do him a favour. He tells you that he needs a helper for future experimental sessions to introduce subsequent participants to the peg-turning task. Your specific job will be to tell them that turning the pegs is an interesting, fascinating experience. Each time you tell this tale to another participant, you'll be paid $1.

If you agree to help the experimenter, you may be setting yourself up for a state of psychological tension called cognitive dissonance. According to a prominent social psychologist, Leon Festinger (1957), **cognitive dissonance** occurs when a person holds two contradictory attitudes or thoughts (referred to as *cognitions*).

If you participate in the situation just described, you are left with two contradictory thoughts: (1) I believe the task is boring, but (2) I said it was interesting with little justification ($1). These two thoughts should arouse dissonance. How can you reduce cognitive dissonance? You cannot deny having said that the task is interesting without breaking with reality. Relatively speaking, it is easier to change your attitude toward the task—and thus the theory predicts that participants will reduce dissonance by adopting more positive attitudes toward the task (Cooper, Mirabile, & Scher, 2005; Cooper, 2007; Rydell, McConnell, & Mackie, 2008).

A classic experiment (Festinger & Carlsmith, 1959) confirmed this prediction. The experiment followed essentially the same procedure outlined earlier, in which a participant was offered $1 to describe a boring task as interesting. In addition, in a comparison condition, some participants were offered $20 to say that the task was interesting. The reasoning behind this condition was that $20 was so much money that participants in this condition had a good reason to be conveying incorrect information; dissonance would not be aroused, and less attitude change would be expected. The results supported this notion. More of the participants who were paid $1 changed their attitudes (becoming more positive toward the peg-turning task) than did participants who were paid $20.

We now know that dissonance explains many everyday events involving attitudes and behaviour. For example, smokers who know that smoking leads to lung cancer hold contradictory cognitions: (1) I smoke, and (2) smoking leads to lung cancer. The theory predicts that these two thoughts will lead to a state of cognitive dissonance. More important, it predicts that—assuming that they don't change their behaviour by quitting smoking—smokers will be motivated to reduce their dissonance by one of the following methods: (1) modifying one or both of the cognitions, (2) changing the perceived importance of one cognition, (3) adding cognitions, or (4) denying that the two cognitions are related to each other. Hence, a smoker may decide that he really doesn't smoke all that much or that he'll quit soon (modifying the cognition), that the evidence linking smoking to cancer is weak (changing the importance of a cognition), that the amount of exercise he gets compensates for the smoking (adding cognitions), or that there is no evidence linking smoking and cancer (denial). Whichever technique the smoker uses results in reduced dissonance (see Figure 1).

What helped the Beliebers form their impression of their idol, Justin Bieber? What would it take to change it?

Source: © WP#RSP/ZOJ/WENN/Newscom.

Social Cognition: Understanding Others

Despite his arrests for drunk driving and other misdemeanours, and his general objectionable behaviour that ranges from taunting paparazzo and defence attorneys to egging his neighbour's home, Justin Bieber's popularity remains, at

Cognitive dissonance
The conflict that occurs when a person holds two contradictory attitudes or thoughts (referred to as cognitions).

FIGURE 1

Cognitive dissonance. The simultaneous presence of two contradictory cognitions ("I smoke" and "Smoking leads to cancer") produces dissonance, which may be reduced through several methods. What are additional ways in which dissonance can be reduced?

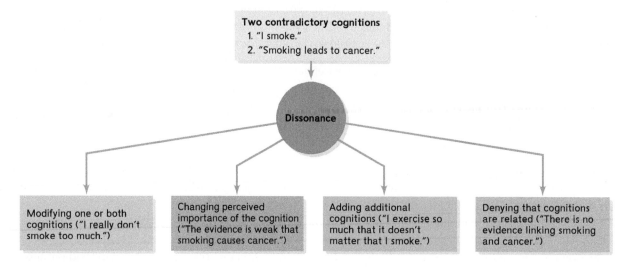

least among his legion of fans, the Beliebers, soaring and untarnished (Grigoriadis, 2014). What would it take to change a Belieber's impression of their idol? Cases like this illustrate the lasting power of our impressions and attest to the importance of determining how people develop an understanding of others. One of the dominant areas in social psychology during the last few years has focused on learning how we come to understand what others are like and how we explain the reasons underlying others' behaviour.

Understanding What Others Are Like

Consider for a moment the enormous amount of information about other people to which we are exposed. How can we decide what is important and what is not and make judgments about the characteristics of others? Social psychologists interested in this question study **social cognition**—the way people understand and make sense of others and themselves. Those psychologists have learned that individuals have highly developed *schemas,* which are sets of cognitions about people and social experiences. These schemas are mental shortcuts that allow us to categorize people or events into broad types based on our previous experiences and general understanding of the world. Those schemas organize information stored in memory, represent in our minds the way the social world operates, and give us a framework to recognize, categorize, and recall information relating to social stimuli such as people and groups (Brewer & Hewstone, 2003; Moskowitz, 2004; Smith & Semin, 2007).

We typically hold schemas for particular types of people. Our schema for "teacher," for instance, generally consists of a number of characteristics: knowledge of the subject matter he or she is teaching, a desire to impart that knowledge, and an awareness of the student's need to understand what is being said. Or we may hold a schema for "mother" that includes the characteristics of warmth, nurturance, and caring. Regardless of their accuracy, schemas are important because they organize the way in which we recall, recognize, and categorize information about others. Moreover, they help us predict what others are like on the basis of relatively little information, because we tend to fit people into schemas even when we do not have much concrete evidence to go on (Bargh & Chartrand, 2000; Ruscher, Fiske, & Schnake, 2000).

Impression Formation

How do we decide that Sayreeta is ambitious, Jason is obnoxious, or Jean-Pierre is a really nice guy? The earliest work on social cognition examined *impression formation,* the process by which an individual organizes information about

Social cognition
The cognitive processes by which people understand and make sense of others and themselves.

another person to form an overall impression of that person. In a classic study, for instance, students learned that they were about to hear a guest lecturer (Kelley, 1950). Researchers told one group of students that the lecturer was "a rather warm person, industrious, critical, practical, and determined," and told a second group that he was "a rather cold person, industrious, critical, practical, and determined."

The simple substitution of "cold" for "warm" caused drastic differences in the way the students in each group perceived the lecturer, even though he gave the same talk in the same style in each condition. Students who had been told he was "warm" rated him considerably more positively than students who had been told he was "cold."

The findings from this experiment led to additional research on impression formation that focused on the way in which people pay particular attention to certain unusually important traits—known as **central traits**—to help them form an overall impression of others. According to this work, the presence of a central trait alters the meaning of other traits. Hence, the description of the lecturer as "industrious" presumably meant something different when it was associated with the central trait "warm" than it meant when it was associated with "cold" (Asch, 1946; Widmeyer & Loy, 1988; Glicksohn & Nahari, 2007).

We make impressions remarkably quickly. In just a few seconds, using what have been called "thin slices of behaviour," we are able to make judgments of people that are accurate and that match those of people who make judgments based on longer snippets of behaviour (Carney, Colvin, & Hall, 2007; Pavitt, 2007; Holleran, Mehl, & Levitt, 2009).

Of course, as we gain more experience with people and see them exhibiting behaviour in a variety of situations, our impressions of them become more complex. However, because our knowledge of others usually has gaps, we still tend to fit individuals into personality schemas that represent particular "types" of people. For instance, we may hold an "extroverted person" schema, made up of the traits of friendliness, aggressiveness, and openness. The presence of just one or two of those traits may be sufficient to make us assign a person to a particular schema.

However, our schemas are susceptible to error. For example, mood affects how we perceive others. Happy people form more favourable impressions and make more positive judgments than people who are in a bad mood (Forgas & Laham, 2005).

Even when schemas are not entirely accurate, they serve an important function: They allow us to develop expectations about how others will behave. Those expectations permit us to predict others' behaviour and plan our interactions with others to operate more effectively in the social world.

Attribution Processes: Understanding the Causes of Behaviour

When Barbara Taylor, a new employee at the Ablex Computer Company, completed a major staffing project two weeks early, her boss, Yolanda, was delighted. "What a dedicated worker", she thought. At the next staff meeting, Yolanda announced how pleased she was with Barbara and explained that *this* was an example of the kind of performance she was looking for in her staff. The other staff members looked on resentfully, trying to figure out why Barbara had worked night and day to finish the project not just on time but two weeks early. She must be an awfully compulsive person, they decided. She must have no life.

At one time or another, most of us have puzzled over the reasons behind someone's behaviour. Perhaps it was in a situation similar to the one above, or it may have been in more formal circumstances, such as being a judge on a student judiciary board in a cheating case. In contrast to theories of social cognition, which describe how people develop an overall impression of others' personality traits, **attribution theory** seeks to explain how we decide, on the basis of samples of an individual's behaviour, what the specific causes of that person's behaviour are.

The general process we use to determine the causes of behaviour and other social occurrences proceeds in several steps, as illustrated in Figure 2. After first noticing that something unusual has happened—for example, NHL star Sidney Crosby has played a terrible shift during a hockey game—we try to interpret the meaning of the event. This

Central traits
The major traits considered in forming impressions of others.

Attribution theory
The theory of personality that seeks to explain how we decide, on the basis of samples of an individual's behaviour, what the specific causes of that person's behaviour are.

FIGURE 2

Determining why people behave the way they do. The general process we use to determine the causes of others' behaviour proceeds in several steps. The kind of explanation we come up with depends on the time available to us, our cognitive resources, and our degree of motivation to come up with an accurate explanation. If time, cognitive resources, and motivation are limited, we'll make use of our first impression, which may be inaccurate.

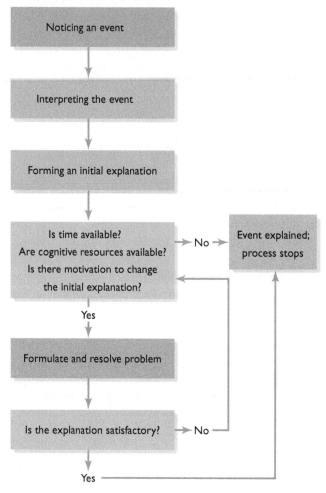

Source: Adapted from Krull & Anderson, 1997, p. 2.

leads us to formulate an initial explanation (maybe Crosby stayed up late the night before the game). Depending on the time available, the cognitive resources on hand (such as the attention we can give to the matter), and our motivation (determined in part by how important the event is to us—are we Crosby's coach or just another hockey fan?), we may choose to accept our initial explanation or seek to modify it (Crosby was sick, perhaps). If we have the time, cognitive resources, and motivation, the event triggers deliberate problem solving as we seek a fuller explanation. During the problem formulation and resolution stage, we may try out several possibilities before we reach a final explanation that seems satisfactory to us (Malle, 2004; Brown, 2006).

In seeking an explanation for behaviour, we must answer one central question: Is the cause situational or dispositional (Heider, 1958)? **Situational causes (of behaviour)** are those brought about by something in the environment. For instance, someone who knocks over a litre of milk and then cleans it up probably does it not because he or she is necessarily a neat person but because the *situation* requires it. In contrast, a person who spends hours shining the

Situational causes (of behaviour)
Perceived causes of behaviour that are based on environmental factors.

kitchen floor probably does so because he or she is a neat person—hence, the behaviour has a **dispositional cause (of behaviour)**, prompted by the person's disposition (his or her internal traits or personality characteristics).

In our example involving Barbara, her fellow employees attributed her behaviour to her disposition rather than to the situation. But from a logical standpoint, it is equally plausible that something about the situation caused the behaviour. If asked, Barbara might attribute her accomplishment to situational factors, explaining that she had so much other work to do that she just had to get the project out of the way, or that the project was not all that difficult and so it was easy to complete ahead of schedule. To her, then, the reason for her behaviour might not be dispositional at all; it could be situational.

STUDY ALERT!

The central question in making an attribution is whether the cause of behaviour is due to situational or dispositional factors.

Attribution Biases: To Err Is Human

If we always processed information in the rational manner that attribution theory suggests, the world might run a lot more smoothly. Unfortunately, although attribution theory generally makes accurate predictions, people do not always process information about others in as logical a fashion as the theory seems to suggest. In fact, research reveals consistent biases in the ways people make attributions. Typical ones include the following:

- *The halo effect.* Harry is intelligent, kind, and loving. Is he also conscientious? If you were to guess, your most likely response probably would be yes. Your guess reflects the **halo effect**, a phenomenon in which an initial understanding that a person has positive traits is used to infer other uniformly positive characteristics. The opposite would also hold true. Learning that Harry was unsociable and argumentative would probably lead you to assume that he was lazy as well. However, because few people have either uniformly positive or uniformly negative traits, the halo effect leads to misperceptions of others (Goffin, Jelley, & Wagner, 2003; Dennis, 2007).

- *Assumed-similarity bias.* The **assumed-similarity bias** is the tendency to think of people as being similar to oneself, even when meeting them for the first time. Given the range of people in the world, this assumption often reduces the accuracy of our judgments (Lemay, Clark, & Feeney, 2007; Lemay & Clark, 2008). It is why we are shocked when people behave in ways that are different from us. An honest person is particularly shocked to be lied to; a trusting person is particularly shocked by a betrayal.

- *The self-serving bias.* When the team wins, coaches usually feel that the team's success is due to their coaching. But when they coach a losing team, coaches may think it's due to the poor skills of their players. Similarly, if you get an A on a test, you may think it's due to your hard work, but if you get a poor grade, it's due to the professor's inadequacies. The reason is the **self-serving bias**, the tendency to attribute success to personal factors (skill, ability, or effort) and attribute failure to factors outside of oneself (Krusemark, Campbell, & Clementz, 2008; Shepperd, Malone, & Sweeny, 2008).

Dispositional cause (of behaviour)
Perceived cause of behaviour that is based on internal traits or personality factors.

Halo effect
A phenomenon in which an initial understanding that a person has positive traits is used to infer other uniformly positive characteristics.

Assumed-similarity bias
The tendency to think of people as being similar to oneself, even when meeting them for the first time.

Self-serving bias
The tendency to attribute personal success to personal factors (skill, ability, or effort) and to attribute failure to factors outside oneself.

- *The fundamental attribution error.* One of the more common attribution biases, known as the **fundamental attribution error**, is the tendency to overattribute others' behaviour to dispositional causes and the corresponding failure to recognize the importance of situational causes. We tend to exaggerate the importance of personality characteristics (dispositional causes) in producing others' behaviour, minimizing the influence of the environment (situational factors). For example, we are more likely to jump to the conclusion that someone who is late to class is disorganized or unmotivated (a dispositional cause) rather than to assume that the lateness is due to situational factors, such as the bus running behind schedule. These conclusions are not necessarily wrong, but just indicate an over-reliance on dispositional cues when evaluating others' behaviour. As such, some psychologists prefer the term **correspondence bias** over fundamental attribution error, since our attributions may, at times at least, be correct (Vonk, 1999).

Why is the fundamental attribution error so common? One reason pertains to the nature of information available to the people making an attribution. When we view the behaviour of another person in a particular setting, the most conspicuous information is the person's behaviour. Because the individual's immediate surroundings remain relatively unchanged and less attention-grabbing, we centre our attention on the person whose behaviour we're considering. Consequently, we are more likely to make attributions based on personal, dispositional factors and less likely to make attributions relating to the situation (Follett & Hess, 2002; Langdridge & Butt, 2004; Tal-Or & Papirman, 2007).

Despite the importance of the fundamental attribution error in shaping the perceptions of members of Western cultures, it turns out that it's not so fundamental when one looks at non-Western cultures, as we discuss next.

Fundamental attribution error

A tendency to overattribute others' behaviour to dispositional causes and minimize the importance of situational causes.

Correspondence bias

A tendency to draw inferences about a person's unique and enduring dispositions from behaviours that can be entirely explained by the situations in which they occur.

Exploring DIVERSITY

Attributions in a Cultural Context: How Fundamental Is the Fundamental Attribution Error?

The culture in which we are raised clearly plays a role in the way we attribute others' behaviour. Take, for example, the fundamental attribution error, the tendency to overestimate the importance of personal, dispositional factors and underattribute situational factors in determining the causes of others' behaviour. The error is pervasive in Western cultures and not in Asian societies.

Specifically, social psychologist Joan Miller (1984) found that adults in India were more likely to use situational attributions than dispositional ones in explaining events. These findings are the opposite of those for Western cultures, and they contradict the fundamental attribution error. Miller suggested that we can discover the reason for these results by examining the norms and values of Indian society, which emphasize social responsibility and societal obligations to a greater extent than in Western societies. Furthermore, parents in Asia tend to attribute good academic performance to effort and hard work (situational factors). In contrast, parents in Western cultures tend to deemphasize the role of effort and attribute school success to innate ability (a dispositional factor). As a result, Asian students may strive harder to achieve and ultimately outperform North American students in school (Stevenson, Lee, & Mu, 2000; Lien et al., 2006).

The difference in thinking between people in Asian and Western cultures is a reflection of a broader difference in the way the world is perceived. Asian societies generally have a *collectivistic orientation,* a worldview that promotes the notion of interdependence. People with a collectivistic orientation generally see themselves as part of a larger, interconnected social network and as responsible to others. In contrast, people in Western cultures are more likely to hold an *individualist orientation* that emphasizes personal identity and the uniqueness of the individual. They focus more on what sets them apart from others and what makes them special (Markus & Kitayama, 2003; Wang, 2004; Markus, 2007).

Evaluate

1. An evaluation of a particular person, behaviour, belief, or concept is called a(n) _____.

2. Cognitive dissonance theory suggests that we commonly change our behaviour to keep it consistent with our attitudes. True or false?

3. Sopan was happy to lend his textbook to a fellow student who seemed bright and friendly. He was surprised when his classmate did not return it. His assumption that the bright and friendly student would also be responsible reflects the _____ effect.

Answers to Evaluate Questions

1. attitude; 2. false; we typically change our attitudes, not our behaviour, to reduce cognitive dissonance; 3. halo

Key Terms

assumed-similarity bias	correspondence bias	self-serving bias
attitudes	dispositional cause	situational causes (of behaviour)
attribution theory	(of behaviour)	social cognition
central traits	fundamental attribution error	social psychology
cognitive dissonance	halo effect	

Social Influence and Groups

LEARNING OBJECTIVE

LO1 **What are** the major sources and tactics of social influence?

You have just transferred to a new college or university and are attending your first class. When the professor enters, your fellow classmates instantly rise, bow to the professor, and then stand quietly, with their hands behind their backs. You've never encountered such behaviour, and it makes no sense to you. Is it more likely that you will (1) jump up to join the rest of the class or (2) remain seated?

On the basis of what research has told us about **social influence**, the process by which the actions of an individual or group affect the behaviour of others, a person would almost always choose the first option. As you undoubtedly know from your own experience, pressures to conform can be painfully strong and can bring about changes in behaviour that otherwise never would have occurred.

> ## STUDY ALERT!
>
> The distinction between the three types of social pressure—conformity, compliance, and obedience—depends on the nature and strength of the social pressure brought to bear on a person.

☐ Conformity: Following What Others Do

Conformity is a change in behaviour or attitudes brought about by a desire to follow the beliefs or standards of other people. Subtle or even unspoken social pressure often results in conformity.

The classic demonstration of pressure to conform comes from a series of studies carried out in the 1950s by Solomon Asch (1951). In the experiments, the participants thought they were taking part in a test of perceptual skills with six other people. The experimenter showed the participants one card with three lines of varying length and a second card that had a fourth line that matched one of the first three (see Figure 1). The task was seemingly straightforward: Each of the participants had to announce aloud which of the first three lines was identical in length to the "standard" line on the second card. Because the correct answer was always obvious, the task seemed easy to the participants.

Indeed, because the participants all agreed on the first few trials, the procedure appeared to be quite simple. But then something odd began to happen. From the perspective of the participant in the group who answered last on each trial, all the answers of the first six participants seemed to be wrong—in fact, unanimously wrong. And this pattern persisted. Over and over again, the first six participants provided answers that contradicted what the last participant believed to be correct. The last participant faced the dilemma of whether to follow his or her own perceptions or follow the group by repeating the answer everyone else was giving.

Social influence
The process by which the actions of an individual or group affect the behaviour of others.

Conformity
A change in behaviour or attitudes brought about by a desire to follow the beliefs or standards of other people.

FIGURE 1

Which of the three comparison lines is the same length as the "standard" line?
If everyone said 3, would you still give the correct answer, 2?

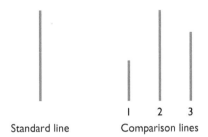

Standard line   Comparison lines

As you might have guessed, this experiment was more contrived than it appeared. The first six participants were actually confederates (paid employees of the experimenter) who had been instructed to give unanimously erroneous answers in many of the trials. And the study had nothing to do with perceptual skills. Instead, the issue under investigation was conformity. Specifically, Asch wanted to know if people would give an answer that they knew was informationally incorrect, just to conform to the group.

Asch found that in about one-third of the trials, the participants conformed to the unanimous but erroneous group answer, with about 75 percent of all participants conforming at least once. However, he found strong individual differences. Some participants conformed nearly all the time, whereas others never did.

Conformity Conclusions

Since Asch (1951)'s pioneering work on conformity, literally hundreds of studies have examined conformity, and we now know a great deal about the phenomenon. Significant findings focus on:

- *The characteristics of the group.* The more attractive a group appears to its members, the greater is its ability to produce conformity (Hogg & Hains, 2001). Furthermore, a person's relative **status**, the social rank held within a group, is critical: The lower a person's status in the group, the greater the power of the group over that person's behaviour.

- *The situation in which the individual is responding.* Conformity is considerably higher when people must respond publicly than it is when they can do so privately, as the Fathers of Confederation noted when they authorized secret ballots in voting.

- *Unanimity of the group.* Groups that unanimously support a position show the most pronounced conformity pressures. But what of the case in which people with dissenting views have an ally in the group, known as a **social supporter**, who agrees with them? Having just one person present who shares the minority point of view is sufficient to dramatically reduce conformity pressures (Prislin, Brewer, & Wilson, 2002; Levine & Moreland, 2006).

Groupthink: Caving in to Conformity

Although we usually think of conformity in terms of our individual relations with others, in some instances conformity pressures in organizations can lead to disastrous effects with long-term consequences. In the 2000 movie *The Perfect Storm*, George Clooney portrayed swordfishing boat captain Billy Tyne who sailed his boat, the *Andrea Gail*, and its crew into a hurricane in 1991. Despite Tyne and his crew's considerable experience at sea, the decision was made to try to ride through the storm rather than wait it out. The *Andrea Gail*, its captain, and its entire crew went to a watery grave. Neither the boat nor the bodies were ever recovered.

How could such an experienced group of sailors make such a poor decision?

Status
The social rank held within a group.

Social supporter
A group member whose dissenting views make nonconformity to the group easier.

Groupthink is a type of thinking in which group members share such a strong motivation to achieve consensus that they lose the ability to critically evaluate alternative points of view. Groupthink is most likely to occur when a popular or powerful leader is surrounded by people of lower status—obviously the case with any prime minister or U.S. president and his or her advisers, but also true in a variety of other organizations (Janis, 1989; Kowert, 2002; Baron, 2005; Henningsen, Henningsen, & Eden, 2006). In fact, groupthink often occurs in groups that are particularly cohesive, like the crew of the *Andrea Gail* (Janis, 1982).

Groupthink almost always produces negative consequences. Groups tend to limit the list of possible solutions to just a few and spend relatively little time considering any alternatives once the leader seems to be leaning toward a particular solution. In fact, group members may completely ignore information that challenges a developing consensus. Because historical research shows that many disastrous decisions reflect groupthink, it is important for groups to be on guard (Kowert, 2002; Chapman, 2006; Packer, 2009). When working in a group, consider having group members put their thoughts on paper before coming together as a group. This serves as a reference point for each group member and helps to foster the sharing of alternate views and to avoid the tendency to uncritically go along with the group,

Compliance: Submitting to Direct Social Pressure

When we refer to conformity, we usually mean a phenomenon in which the social pressure is subtle or indirect. But in some situations social pressure is much more obvious, with direct, explicit pressure to endorse a particular point of view or behave in a certain way. Social psychologists call the type of behaviour that occurs in response to direct social pressure **compliance**.

Several specific techniques represent attempts to gain compliance. Those frequently employed include:

- *Foot-in-the-door technique.* A friend asks you to drive her home, and you agree, thinking it's no trouble. A little later comes a larger request: now she wants you to drive half an hour out of your way to pick up her boyfriend and drop the two of them off at her place. Because you have already agreed to the first request, you will have a hard time now turning her down.

    Your friend in this case is using a tried-and-true strategy that social psychologists call the *foot-in-the-door technique.* In the foot-in-the-door technique, you ask a person to agree to a small request and later ask that person to comply with a more important one. It turns out that compliance with the more important request increases significantly when the person first agrees to the smaller favour.

    Researchers first demonstrated the foot-in-the-door phenomenon in a study in which a number of experimenters went door to door asking residents to sign a petition in favour of safe driving (Freedman & Fraser, 1966). Almost everyone complied with that small, benign request. A few weeks later, different experimenters contacted the residents and made a much larger request: that the residents erect a huge sign reading "Drive Carefully" on their front lawns. The results were clear: 55 percent of those who had signed the petition agreed to the request to put up a sign, whereas only 17 percent of the people in a control group who had not been asked to sign the petition agreed to put up a sign.

    Why does the foot-in-the-door technique work? For one reason, involvement with the small request leads to an interest in an issue, and taking an action—any action—makes the individual more committed to the issue, thereby increasing the likelihood of future compliance. Another explanation revolves around people's self-perceptions. By complying with the initial request, individuals may come to see themselves as people who provide help when asked. Then, when confronted with the larger request, they agree in order to maintain the kind of consistency in attitudes and behaviour that we described earlier. Although we don't know which of these two explanations is more accurate, it is clear that the foot-in-the-door strategy is effective (Burger & Caldwell, 2003; Bloom, McBride, & Pollak, 2006; Guéguen et al., 2008).

- *Door-in-the-face technique.* A fund-raiser asks for a $500 contribution. You laughingly refuse, telling her that the amount is way out of your league. She then asks for a $10 contribution. What do you do? If you are like most

---

Groupthink

A type of thinking in which group members share such a strong motivation to achieve consensus that they lose the ability to critically evaluate alternative points of view.

Compliance

Behaviour that occurs in response to direct social pressure.

people, you'll probably be a lot more compliant than you would be if she hadn't asked for the huge contribution first. In this tactic, called the *door-in-the-face technique,* someone makes a large request, expecting it to be refused, and follows it with a smaller one. This strategy, which is the opposite of the foot-in-the-door approach, has also proved to be effective (Pascual & Guéguen, 2005, 2006; Turner et al., 2007; Ebster & Neumayr, 2008).

In a field experiment that demonstrates the success of this approach, experimenters stopped university students on the street and asked them to agree to a substantial favour—acting as unpaid counsellors for young offenders two hours a week for two years (Cialdini et al., 1975). Not surprisingly, no one agreed to make such an enormous commitment. But when they were later asked the considerably smaller favour of taking a group of young offenders on a two-hour trip to the zoo, half the people complied. In comparison, only 17 percent of a control group of participants who had not first received the larger request agreed.

- *That's-not-all technique.* In this technique, a salesperson offers you a deal at an inflated price. But immediately after the initial offer, the salesperson offers an incentive, discount, or bonus to clinch the deal.

  Although it sounds transparent, this practice can be quite effective. In one study, the experimenters set up a booth and sold cupcakes for 75 cents each. In one condition, the experimenters directly told customers that the price was 75 cents. But in another condition, they told customers that the price was originally $1 but had been reduced to 75 cents. As we might predict, more people bought cupcakes at the "reduced" price—even though it was identical to the price in the other experimental condition (Burger, Reed, & DeCesare, 1999; Pratkanis, 2007).

- *Not-so-free sample.* If you ever receive a free sample, keep in mind that it comes with a psychological cost. Although they may not couch it in these terms, salespeople who provide samples to potential customers do so to instigate the norm of reciprocity. The *norm of reciprocity* is the well-accepted societal standard dictating that we should treat other people as they treat us. Receiving a *not-so-free sample,* then, suggests the need for reciprocation—in the form of a purchase, of course (Burger et al., 1999; Cialdini, 2006).

Companies seeking to sell their products to consumers often use the techniques identified by social psychologists for promoting compliance. But employers also use them to bring about compliance and raise the productivity of employees in the workplace. We all use them every day to help meet our social goals, whether that is to obtain a ride home, to get an extension on a deadline, or to convince mom and dad to raise our allowance.

Obedience: Following Direct Orders

Compliance techniques are used to gently lead people toward agreement with a request. In some cases, however, requests aim to produce **obedience**, a change in behaviour in response to the commands of others. Although obedience is considerably less common than conformity and compliance, it does occur in several specific kinds of relationships. For example, we may show obedience to our bosses, teachers, or parents merely because of the power they hold to reward or punish us.

To acquire an understanding of obedience, consider for a moment how you might respond if a stranger said to you:

I've devised a new way of improving memory. All I need is for you to teach people a list of words and then give them a test. The test procedure requires only that you give learners a shock each time they make a mistake on the test. To administer the shocks you will use a "shock generator" that gives shocks ranging from 30 to 450 volts. You can see that the switches are labelled from "slight shock" through "danger: severe shock" at the top level, where there are three red *X*'s. But don't worry; although the shocks may be painful, they will cause no permanent damage.

Presented with this situation, you would be likely to think that neither you nor anyone else would go along with the stranger's unusual request. Clearly, it lies outside the bounds of what we consider acceptable behaviour.

Or does it? Suppose the stranger asking for your help were a psychologist conducting an experiment. Or suppose the request came from your teacher, your employer, or your military commander—all people in authority with a seemingly legitimate reason for the request.

If you still believe it unlikely that you would comply—think again. The situation presented above describes a classic experiment conducted by social psychologist Stanley Milgram (1974). In the study, an experimenter told participants to give increasingly stronger shocks to another person as part of a study on learning (see Figure 2). In reality, the

Obedience
A change in behaviour in response to the commands of others.

FIGURE 2

This impressive-looking "shock generator" in Stanley Milgram's experiment on obedience led participants to believe they were administering electric shocks to another person, who was connected to the generator by "electrodes" that were attached to the skin.

Photos Source: Copyright 1965 by Stanley Milgram. From the film *Obedience*, distributed by the New York University Film Library and Pennsylvania State University, PCR.

experiment had nothing to do with learning; the real issue under consideration was the degree to which participants would comply with the experimenter's requests. In fact, the "learner" supposedly receiving the shocks was a confederate who never really received any punishment (Milgram, 1974).

Most people who hear a description of Milgram's experiment feel that it is unlikely that *any* participant would give the maximum level of shock—or, for that matter, any shock at all. Even a group of psychiatrists to whom the situation was described predicted that fewer than 2 percent of the participants would fully comply and administer the strongest shocks.

However, the actual results contradicted both experts' and nonexperts' predictions. Some 65 percent of the participants eventually used the highest setting on the shock generator—450 volts—to shock the learner. This obedience occurred even though the learner, who had mentioned at the start of the experiment that he had a heart condition, demanded to be released, screaming, "Let me out of here! Let me out of here! My heart's bothering me. Let me out of here!" Despite the learner's pleas, most participants continued to administer the shocks.

Why did so many individuals comply with the experimenter's demands? The participants, who were extensively interviewed after the experiment, said they obeyed primarily because they believed that the experimenter would be responsible for any potential ill effects that befell the learner. The participants accepted the experimenter's orders, then, because they thought that they personally could not be held accountable for their actions—they could always blame the experimenter (Darley, 1995; Blass, 1996).

Although most participants in the Milgram experiment said later that they felt the knowledge gained from the study outweighed the discomfort they may have felt, the experiment has been criticized for creating an extremely trying set of circumstances for the participants, thereby raising serious ethical concerns. (Undoubtedly, the experiment could not be conducted today because of ethical considerations.)

Despite these concerns, Milgram's research remains the strongest laboratory demonstration of obedience. We need only consider actual instances of obedience to authority to witness some frightening real-life parallels. For instance, after World War II, the major defence that Nazi officers gave to excuse their participation in atrocities during the war was that they were "only following orders." Milgram's experiment, which was motivated in part by his desire to explain the behaviour of everyday Germans during World War II, forces us to ask ourselves this question: Would we be able to withstand the intense power of authority? Milgram's results teach us why history repeats itself with acts of genocide and wartime atrocities: because good people will go along with terrible acts when commanded to by an authority figure. But there is hope, even in Milgram's findings. Just like in Asch's conformity study, participants were far more likely to resist authority and refuse to comply with the experimenter's commands when they saw another person (a confederate) doing so. If one person resists authority, others are likely to follow.

STUDY ALERT!

Because of its graphic demonstration of obedience, to authority, the Milgram experiment is one of the most famous and influential studies in social psychology. The only other experiment that rivals it in notoriety is the one we will discuss next: the Stanford Prison Experiment.

The Prison Study: The Power of the Situation

Stanford University psychologist Philip Zimbardo also wondered why good people sometimes did evil things. He wondered whether direct orders, as in the Milgram experiment, were even necessary, or whether indirect pressure, derived from social roles and the power of the situation, would be enough to make ordinary people act in ways that most would consider immoral. In his famous Prison Experiment, Zimbardo set up a fake prison in the basement of the psychology building at Stanford University. Participants, who had been screened for mental health issues, were randomly assigned to be either prisoners or guards. Although Zimbardo suspected the setup might lead to out-of-character behaviour, even he was surprised by how quickly the situation become out of control. After two days, the guards began showing cruel and abusive behaviour towards the prisoners, refusing to let them use the bathroom, making them clean the messes with their bare hands, forcing them to strip and simulate sex acts, and more. This was despite that fact that the guards were not instructed to behave in a forceful or threatening way, and they knew they were being videotaped at all times. Alarmingly, the prisoners became servile, depressed, and accepting of this inhumane treatment. The experiment was supposed to run for two weeks but had to be stopped after just six days as the situation became so frightening that Zimbardo was concerned it could induce permanent psychological damage in the participants (Zimbardo, 1972). In his analysis of the situation and in later writings Zimbardo wrote about the power of the situation and of social roles to elicit what he called the Lucifer Effect (Zimbardo, 2008), the tendency for ordinarily good people to do extraordinarily bad things. Zimbardo (2004) has argued for a situationalist, rather than dispositional, perspective on evil. This means that we all have the capacity for both good and evil within us, and the behaviour we engage in will depend on the situation we find ourselves in—and of course, on whether or not we choose to act. Hopefully conscious awareness of the capacity for evil acts that lies within us will help us to choose wisely.

The Stanford Prison Experiment (left) can help explain real-world atrocities, like prisoner abuse in Abu Ghraib (right).

Sources: (left) © Philip G. Zimbardo; (right) © EdStock/iStockphoto.com.

Evaluate

1. A _____, or person who agrees with the dissenting viewpoint, is likely to reduce conformity.

2. Who pioneered the study of conformity?

   a. Skinner

   b. Asch

   c. Milgram

   d. Zimbardo

3. The _____ technique begins with an outrageous request that makes a subsequent, smaller request seem reasonable.

4. _____ is a change in behaviour that is due to another person's orders.

Answers to Evaluate Questions

1. social supporter; 2. b; 3. Door-in-the-face; 4. obedience

Key Terms

compliance	obedience	social supporter
conformity	social influence	status
groupthink		

Prejudice and Discrimination

LEARNING OBJECTIVES

How do stereotypes, prejudice, and discrimination differ?
How can we reduce prejudice and discrimination?

What do you think when someone says, "He's a senior citizen," "She's Asian," or "That's a female driver"?

If you're like most people, you'll probably automatically form some sort of impression of what each person is like. Most likely your impression is based on a **stereotype**, a set of generalized beliefs and expectations about a particular group and its members.

Stereotypes, which may be negative or positive, grow out of our tendency to categorize and organize the vast amount of information we encounter in our everyday lives. All stereotypes share the common feature of oversimplifying the world: We view individuals not in terms of their unique, personal characteristics, but in terms of characteristics we attribute to all the members of a particular group.

Stereotypes can lead to **prejudice**, a negative (or positive) evaluation of a group and its members. For instance, racial prejudice occurs when a member of a racial group is evaluated in terms of race and not because of his or her own characteristics or abilities. Although prejudice can be positive ("I love the Irish"), social psychologists have focused on understanding the roots of negative prejudice ("I hate immigrants").

Common stereotypes and forms of prejudice involve racial, religious, and ethnic groups. Over the years, various groups have been called "lazy" or "shrewd" or "cruel" with varying degrees of regularity by those who are not members of that group. Even today, despite major progress toward reducing legally sanctioned forms of prejudice, such as school segregation in the U.S., stereotypes and prejudice remain (Eberhardt et al., 2004; Pettigrew, 2004; Hunt, Seifert, & Armenta, 2006).

The events of Tuesday, November 4, 2008 have altered North America's long history of prejudice and discrimination and dramatically shifted societal perceptions of African Americans. That was the day that Barack Obama was elected as the first African American President of the United States. In North America some forms of blatant prejudice (sometimes referred to as classic prejudice) may be less socially acceptable—at least when it comes to race—but prejudice against the elderly, those with disabilities, and other forms of prejudice continue to be tolerated. However, even people who on the surface appear to be unprejudiced may harbour what psychologists call modern prejudice. Dr. Victoria Esses at the University of Western Ontario has done extensive research on prejudice and discrimination. Dr. Esses and her research team examine factors associated with prejudice and discrimination in Canada and around the world (Esses & Vernon, 2008; Esses Lab for the Study of Intergroup Relations, 2010). Esses described modern prejudice as the denial of continued prejudice, the resentment of "special favours" accorded to minority groups, and antagonism towards the demands of minority groups (Miglietta, Gattino, & Esses, 2014). Research shows that this type of prejudice is widespread.

Although usually backed by little or no evidence, stereotypes can have harmful consequences. Acting on negative stereotypes results in **discrimination**—behaviour directed toward individuals on the basis of their membership

Stereotype
A set of generalized beliefs and expectations about a particular group and its members.

Prejudice
A (usually) negative evaluation of a particular group and its members.

Discrimination
Behaviour directed toward individuals on the basis of their membership in a particular group.

in a particular group. Discrimination can lead to exclusion from jobs, neighbourhoods, and educational opportunities and may result in members of particular groups receiving lower salaries and benefits. Discrimination can also result in more favourable treatment to favoured groups, as when an employer hires a job applicant of his or her own racial group because of the applicant's race (Avery, McKay, & Wilson, 2008; Pager & Shepherd, 2008).

STUDY ALERT!

Remember that *prejudice* relates to *attitudes* about a group and its members, while *discrimination* relates to behaviour directed to a group and its members.

Foundations of Prejudice

No one has ever been born disliking a particular racial, religious, or ethnic group. People learn to hate, in much the same way that they learn the alphabet.

According to *observational learning approaches* to stereotyping and prejudice, the behaviour of parents, other adults, and peers shapes children's feelings about members of various groups. For instance, bigoted parents may commend their children for expressing prejudiced attitudes. Likewise, young children learn prejudice by imitating the behaviour of adult models. Such learning starts at an early age: children as young as 3 years of age begin to show preferences for members of their own race (Dovidio & Gaertner, 2006; Ponterotto, Utsey, & Pedersen, 2006; Bronson & Merryman, 2009). The mass media also provide information about stereotypes, not just for children but for adults as well. Even today, some television shows and movies portray Italians as Mafia-like mobsters, Jewish characters as greedy bankers, and First Nations Canadians as lazy. When such inaccurate portrayals are the primary source of information about minority groups, they can lead to the development and maintenance of unfavourable stereotypes (Coltraine & Messineo, 2000; Ward, 2004; Do, 2006).

Other explanations of prejudice and discrimination focus on how being a member of a particular group helps to magnify one's sense of self-esteem. According to *social identity theory*, we use group membership as a source of pride and self-worth. Slogans such as "gay pride" and "Black is beautiful" illustrate that the groups to which we belong furnish us with a sense of self-respect (Tajfel & Turner, 2004; Hogg, 2006).

However, the use of group membership to provide social respect produces an unfortunate outcome. In an effort to maximize our sense of self-esteem, we may come to think that our own group (our *ingroup*) is better than groups to which we don't belong (our *outgroups*). Consequently, we inflate the positive aspects of our ingroup—and, at the same time, devalue outgroups. Ultimately, we come to view members of outgroups as inferior to members of our ingroup (Tajfel & Turner, 2004). The end result is prejudice toward members of groups of which we are not a part.

Neither the observational learning approach nor the social identity approach provides a full explanation for stereotyping and prejudice. For instance, some psychologists argue that prejudice results when there is perceived competition for scarce societal resources. Thus, when competition exists for jobs or housing, members of majority groups may believe (however unjustly or inaccurately) that minority group members are hindering their efforts to attain their goals, and this can lead to prejudice. In addition, other explanations for prejudice emphasize human cognitive limitations that lead us to categorize people on the basis of visually conspicuous physical features such as race, sex, and ethnic group. Such categorization can lead to the development of stereotypes and, ultimately, to discriminatory behaviour (Mullen & Rice, 2003; Weeks & Lupfer, 2004; Hugenberg & Sacco, 2008).

The most recent approach to understanding prejudice comes from an increasingly important area in social psychology: social neuroscience. **Social neuroscience** seeks to identify the neural basis of social behaviour. It looks at how we can illuminate our understanding of groups, interpersonal relations, and emotions by understanding their neuroscientific underpinnings (Cacioppo, Visser, & Pickett, 2005; Harmon-Jones & Winkielman, 2007).

In one example of the value of social neuroscience approaches, researchers examined activation of the *amygdala*, the structure in the brain that relates to emotion-evoking stimuli and situations, while viewing white and black faces.

Social neuroscience
The subfield of social psychology that seeks to identify the neural basis of social behaviour.

Because the amygdala is especially responsive to threatening, unusual, or highly arousing stimuli, the researchers hypothesized greater activation of the amygdala during exposure to black faces due to negative cultural associations with racial minorities (Lieberman et al., 2005; Lieberman, 2007).

The hypothesis was confirmed: The amygdala showed more activation when participants saw a black face than when they saw a white one. The study included both black and white participants, so it is unlikely that the amygdala activation was simply the result of the novelty of viewing members of a racial minority. Instead, the researchers theorized that culturally learned societal messages about race led to the brain activation.

Ziva Kunda and colleagues (2002) from the University of Waterloo published a paper on techniques for reducing stereotypes. Researchers discovered that stereotypes dis-

Flawed information about minority groups is one of the main sources of prejudice and unfavourable stereotypes.

Source: © Ron Bailey/iStockphoto.com.

appeared as subjects' exposure to the "stereotyped individual" continued. Additional techniques for reducing negative consequences of prejudice and discrimination are discussed next.

Reducing the Consequences of Prejudice and Discrimination

How can we diminish the effects of prejudice and discrimination? Psychologists have developed several strategies that have proved effective, including these:

- *Increasing contact between the target of stereotyping and the holder of the stereotype.* Research has shown that increasing the amount of interaction between people can reduce negative stereotyping. But only certain kinds of contact are likely to reduce prejudice and discrimination. Situations in which contact is relatively intimate, the individuals are of equal status, or participants must cooperate with one another or are dependent on one another are more likely to reduce stereotyping (Dovidio, Gaertner, & Kawakami, 2003; Tropp & Pettigrew, 2005; Pettigrew & Tropp, 2006).

- *Making values and norms against prejudice more conspicuous.* Sometimes just reminding people about the values they already hold regarding equality and fair treatment of others is enough to reduce discrimination. Similarly, people who hear others making strong, vehement antiracist statements are subsequently more likely to strongly condemn racism (Czopp & Monteith, 2006; Ponterotto, Utsey, & Pedersen, 2006; Tropp & Bianchi, 2006).

- *Providing information about the objects of stereotyping.* Probably the most direct means of changing stereotypical and discriminatory attitudes is education: teaching people to be more aware of the positive characteristics of targets of stereotyping. For instance, when the meaning of puzzling behaviour is explained to people who hold stereotypes, they may come to appreciate the true significance of the behaviour—even though it may still appear foreign and perhaps even threatening (Isbell & Tyler, 2003; Banks, 2006; Nagda, Tropp, & Paluck, 2006).

Evaluate

1. Any expectation—positive or negative—about an individual solely on the basis of that person's membership in a group can be a stereotype. True or false?

2. The negative (or positive) evaluation of a group and its members is called

   a. Stereotyping

   b. Prejudice

   c. Self-fulfilling prophecy

   d. Discrimination

Answers to Evaluate Questions

1. true; 2. b

Key Terms

discrimination	social neuroscience
prejudice	stereotype

Positive and Negative Social Behaviour

LEARNING OBJECTIVES

LO7 **Why are** we attracted to certain people, and what progression do social relationships follow?

LO8 **What factors** underlie aggression and prosocial behaviour?

Are people basically good or bad?

Like philosophers and theologians, social psychologists have pondered the basic nature of humanity. Is it represented mainly by the violence and cruelty we see throughout the world, or does something special about human nature permit loving, considerate, unselfish, and even noble behaviour as well?

We turn to two routes that social psychologists have followed in seeking answers to these questions. We first consider what they have learned about the sources of our attraction to others, and we end with a look at two opposite sides of human behaviour: aggression and helping.

Liking and Loving: Interpersonal Attraction and the Development of Relationships

Nothing is more important in most people's lives than their feelings for others. Consequently, it is not surprising that liking and loving have become a major focus of interest for social psychologists. Known more formally as the study of **interpersonal attraction (or close relationship)**, this area addresses the factors that lead to positive feelings for others.

How Do I Like Thee? Let Me Count the Ways

By far the greatest amount of research has focused on liking, probably because it is easier for investigators conducting short-term experiments to produce states of liking in strangers who have just met than to instigate and observe loving relationships over long periods. Consequently, research has given us a good deal of knowledge about the factors that initially attract two people to each other (Harvey & Weber, 2002). The important factors considered by social psychologists are the following:

- *Proximity.* If you live in a dormitory or an apartment, consider the friends you made when you first moved in. Chances are, you became friendliest with those who lived geographically closest to you. In fact, this is one of the more firmly established findings in the literature on interpersonal attraction: *Proximity* leads to liking (Burgoon et al., 2002; Smith & Weber, 2005).

- *Mere exposure.* Repeated exposure to a person is often sufficient to produce attraction. Interestingly, repeated exposure to *any* stimulus—a person, picture, song, or virtually anything—usually makes us like the stimulus more (Zajonc, 2001; Butler & Berry, 2004).

- *Similarity.* Folk wisdom tells us that birds of a feather flock together. However, it also maintains that opposites attract. Social psychologists have come up with a clear verdict regarding which of the two statements is correct: We

---

Interpersonal attraction (or close relationship)
Positive feelings for others; liking and loving.

tend to like those who are similar to us. Discovering that others have similar attitudes, values, or traits promotes our liking for them. Furthermore, the more similar others are, the more we like them. One reason similarity increases the likelihood of interpersonal attraction is that we assume that people with similar attitudes will evaluate us positively. Because we experience a strong **reciprocity-of-liking effect** (a tendency to like those who like us), knowing that someone evaluates us positively promotes our attraction to that person (Bates, 2002; Umphress, Smith-Crowe, & Brief, 2007; Montoya & Insko, 2008).

- *Physical attractiveness.* For most people, the equation *beautiful = good* is quite true. As a result, physically attractive people are more popular than are physically unattractive ones, if all other factors are equal. Physical attractiveness may be the single most important element promoting initial liking in college or university dating situations, although its influence eventually decreases when people get to know each other better (Zebrowitz & Montepare, 2005; Little, Burt, & Perrett, 2006; Luo & Zhang, 2009). The importance of physical attractiveness may be deeply rooted in our evolutionary heritage: across cultures, features that are judged as being attractive just so happen to be reliable indicators of fertility and genetic health (Neuberg, Kenrick, & Schaller, 2010).

These factors alone, of course, do not account for liking. For example, in one experiment that examined the desired qualities in a friendship, the top-rated qualities in a same-sex friend included sense of humour, warmth and kindness, expressiveness and openness, an exciting personality, and similarity of interests and leisure activities (Sprecher & Regan, 2002). The results are summarized in Figure 1. (For more on friendship, see the nearby *Applying Psychology in the Real World* box for a discussion of online social networking.)

How Do I Love Thee? Let Me Count the Ways

Whereas our knowledge of what makes people like one another is extensive, our understanding of love is more limited in scope and recently acquired. For some time, many social psychologists believed that love is too difficult to observe and study in a controlled, scientific way. However, love is such a central issue in most people's lives that eventually social psychologists could not resist its allure.

As a first step, researchers tried to identify the characteristics that distinguish between mere liking and full-blown love. They discovered that love is not simply a greater quantity of liking, but a qualitatively different psychological

FIGURE 1

These are the key friendship qualities according to some 40,000 questionnaire respondents.

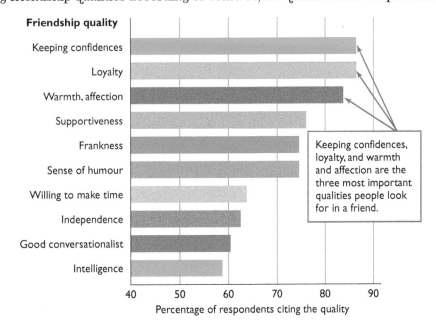

Source: Parlee, 1979.

Reciprocity-of-liking effect

A tendency to like those who like us.

state. For instance, at least in its early stages, love includes relatively intense physiological arousal, an all-encompassing interest in another individual, fantasizing about the other, and relatively rapid swings of emotion. Similarly, love, unlike liking, includes elements of passion, closeness, fascination, exclusiveness, sexual desire, and intense caring. We idealize partners by exaggerating their good qualities and minimizing their imperfections (Garza-Guerrero, 2000; Murray, Holmes, & Griffin, 2004).

Other researchers have theorized that there are two main types of love: passionate love and companionate love. **Passionate (or romantic) love** represents a state of intense absorption in someone. It includes intense physiological arousal, psychological interest, and caring for the needs of another. In contrast, **companionate love** is the strong affection we have for those with whom our lives are deeply entwined. The love we feel for our parents, other family members, and close friends falls into the category of companionate love (Masuda, 2003; Regan, 2006; Loving, Crockett, & Paxson, 2009).

Psychologist Robert Sternberg makes an even finer differentiation between types of love. He proposes that love consists of three parts: a *decision/commitment component*, encompassing the initial cognition that one loves someone and the longer-term feelings of commitment to maintain love; *an intimacy component*, encompassing feelings of closeness and connectedness; and a *passion component*, made up of the motivational drives relating to sex, physical closeness, and romance. These three components combine to produce the different types of love (Sternberg, Hojjat, & Barnes, 2001; Sternberg, 2004; see Figure 2).

Is love a necessary ingredient in a good marriage? Yes, if you live in North America. In contrast, it's considerably less important in other cultures. Although mutual attraction and love are the two most important characteristics desired in a mate by men and women in North America, men in China rated good health as most important, and women there rated emotional stability and maturity as most important. Among the Zulu in South Africa, men rated emotional stability first and women rated dependable character first (Buss et al., 1990; see Figure 3).

Liking and loving clearly show a positive side of human social behaviour. Now we turn to behaviours that are just as much a part of social behaviour: aggression and helping behaviour.

FIGURE 2

According to Sternberg, love has three main components: intimacy, passion, and decision/commitment. Different combinations of these components can create other types of love. Nonlove contains none of the three components.

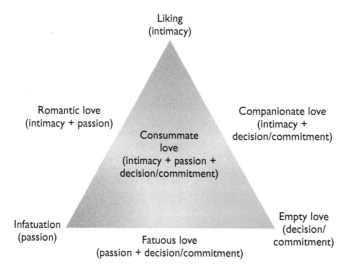

Passionate (or romantic) love
A state of intense absorption in someone that includes intense physiological arousal, psychological interest, and caring for the needs of another.

Companionate love
The strong affection we have for those with whom our lives are deeply involved.

FIGURE 3

Although love may be an important factor in choosing a marriage partner if you live in the United States, other cultures place less importance on it.

Rank Ordering of Desired Characteristics in a Mate						
	United States		China		South Africa Zulu	
	Females	Males	Females	Males	Females	Males
Mutual attraction—love	1	1	8	4	5	10
Emotional stability and maturity	2	2	1	5	2	1
Dependable character	3	3	7	6	1	3
Pleasing disposition	4	4	16	13	3	4
Education and intelligence	5	5	4	8	6	6
Good health	9	6	3	1	4	5
Good looks	13	7	15	11	16	14
Sociability	8	8	9	12	8	11
Desire for home and children	7	9	2	2	9	9
Refinement, neatness	12	10	10	7	10	7
Ambition and industriousness	6	11	5	10	7	8
Similar education	10	12	12	15	12	12
Good cook and housekeeper	16	13	11	9	15	2
Favourable social status or rating	14	14	13	14	14	17
Similar religious background	15	15	18	18	11	16
Good financial prospect	11	16	14	16	13	18
Chastity (no prior sexual intercourse)	18	17	6	3	18	13
Similar political background	17	18	17	17	17	15

Source: Buss et al., 1990.

APPLYING PSYCHOLOGY   in the Real World

Friends Online: Is Facebook the New Student Union?

If you're a typical college or university student, you probably use Facebook, Twitter, or some other social networking website. In fact, estimates of usage rates of social networking sites on school campuses run as high as 90 percent, compared to 33 percent of older Internet users. When that many people are using a new technology for interpersonal communication, social psychologists take note, and they have begun to examine how college and university students use social network sites (Lenhart, 2009).

One finding is clear: Students use Facebook primarily to keep in touch with their friends. Few use it to keep in touch with their parents or to meet new people. What seems to interest college and university students most is the ability to maintain social connections across geographic boundaries efficiently. Specifically, social networking sites allow them to easily keep tabs on old

(continued)

friends from home while at the same time interacting with new friends made at school (Wiley & Sisson, 2006; Subrahmanyam et al., 2008; Pempek, Yermolayeva, & Calvert, 2009).

Another way college and university students use social network sites is to explore their developing identities. Because users can control how they present themselves to the world on a social network profile, it is easy for students to "try on" an identity by posting selected photos of themselves, revealing specific tastes and interests, or otherwise presenting themselves in new and different ways. The feedback they get from others may help them decide which identities and forms of self-expression suit them best.

College and university students report that religion, political ideology, work, and tastes in media such as music and movies are their most important identity expressions (Pempek, Yermolayeva, & Calvert, 2009).

But how do social network sites affect users' nonvirtual social lives? Maintaining social connections that might otherwise have withered and died seems like a good thing, but it may be detrimental if students spend so much time maintaining online distant or superficial friendships that they sacrifice time spent on intimate, face-to-face interactions with close friends.

New research suggests that social networking sites provide a less intimidating social outlet for students who otherwise have trouble making and keeping friendships, such as those who are introverted or have low self-esteem. One study that tracked college and university students' Facebook use over time found that those with low self-esteem benefitted the most in terms of building greater social networks through Facebook. Students reported that they found it less awkward to initiate contact with people through Facebook than through other means. They were also better able to learn about social events and other opportunities for face-to-face interaction through Facebook postings than by direct word of mouth, which thereby improved their offline social lives (Steinfeld, Ellison, & Lampe, 2008).

In addition, intensity of Facebook use is positively related to students' life satisfaction, social trust, and civic engagement. In short, research suggests that users of social network sites are not disengaged from the real world and that the benefits of social networking outweigh the costs to students' social lives (Valenzuela, Park, & Kee, 2009).

Aggression and Prosocial Behaviour: Hurting and Helping Others

Drive-by shootings, carjackings, and abductions are just a few examples of the violence that seems all too common today. Yet we also find examples of generous, unselfish, thoughtful behaviour that suggest a more optimistic view of humankind. Consider, for instance, people such as Mother Teresa, who ministered to the poor in India. Or contemplate the simple kindnesses of life: lending a valuable car, stopping to help a child who has fallen off her bicycle, or merely sharing a candy bar with a friend. Such instances of helping are no less characteristic of human behaviour than are the distasteful examples of aggression (Miller, 1999).

Hurting Others: Aggression

We need look no further than the daily paper or the nightly news to be bombarded with examples of aggression, both on a societal level (war, invasion, assassination) and on an individual level (crime, child abuse, and the many petty cruelties humans are capable of inflicting on one another). Is such aggression an inevitable part of the human condition? Or is aggression primarily a product of particular circumstances that, if changed, could lead to its reduction?

The difficulty of answering such knotty questions becomes apparent as soon as we consider how best to define the term *aggression*. Depending on the way we define the word, many examples of inflicted pain or injury may or may not qualify as aggression. For instance, a rapist is clearly acting with aggression toward his victim. On the other hand, it is less certain that a physician carrying out an emergency medical procedure without an available anesthetic, thereby causing incredible pain to the patient, should be considered aggressive.

Most social psychologists define aggression in terms of the intent and the purpose behind the behaviour. **Aggression** is intentional injury of or harm to another person (Berkowitz, 2001). By this definition, the rapist is clearly acting aggressively, whereas the physician causing pain during a medical procedure is not.

We now turn to two main approaches to aggressive behaviour developed by social psychologists.

Aggression
The intentional injury of, or harm to, another person.

FRUSTRATION-AGGRESSION APPROACHES: AGGRESSION AS A REACTION TO FRUSTRATION

Suppose you've been working on a paper that is due for a class early the next morning, and your computer printer runs out of ink just before you can print out the paper. You rush to the store to buy more ink, only to find the sales clerk locking the door for the day. Even though the clerk can see you gesturing and begging him to open the door, he refuses, shrugging his shoulders and pointing to a sign that indicates when the store will open the next day. At that moment, the feelings you experience toward the sales clerk probably place you on the verge of real aggression, and you are undoubtedly seething inside.

Frustration-aggression theory tries to explain aggression in terms of events like this one. When first put forward, the theory said flatly that frustration *always* leads to aggression of some sort, and that aggression is *always* the result of some frustration, where **frustration** is defined as the thwarting or blocking of some ongoing, goal-directed behaviour (Dollard et al., 1939). More recent explanations have modified the original theory, suggesting instead that frustration produces anger, leading to a *readiness* to act aggressively. Whether actual aggression occurs depends on the presence of *aggressive cues*, stimuli that have been associated in the past with actual aggression or violence and that will trigger aggression again. In addition, frustration produces aggression to the degree to which it produces negative feelings (Berkowitz, 2001).

What kinds of stimuli act as aggressive cues? They can range from the most overt, such as the presence of weapons, to the subtlest, such as the mere mention of the name of an individual who behaved violently in the past. For example, in one experiment, angered participants behaved significantly more aggressively when in the presence of a rifle and a revolver than they did in a comparable situation in which no guns were present (Berkowitz & LePage, 1967). Similarly, frustrated participants in an experiment who had viewed a violent movie were more physically aggressive toward a confederate with the same name as the star of the movie than they were toward a confederate with a different name (Berkowitz & Geen, 1966). It appears, then, that frustration does lead to aggression, at least when aggressive cues are present (Marcus-Newhall, Pederson, & Carlson, 2000; Berkowitz, 2001).

OBSERVATIONAL LEARNING APPROACHES: LEARNING TO HURT OTHERS

Do we learn to be aggressive? The *observational learning* (sometimes called *social learning*) approach to aggression says that we do. Taking an almost opposite view from instinct theories, which focus on innate explanations of aggression, observational learning theory emphasizes that social and environmental conditions can teach individuals to be aggressive. Is road rage a result of frustration? According to frustration-aggression approaches, frustration is a likely cause. The theory sees aggression not as inevitable, but rather as a learned response that can be understood in terms of rewards and punishments.

Observational learning theory pays particular attention not only to direct rewards and punishments that individuals themselves receive, but also to the rewards and punishments that models—individuals who provide a guide to appropriate behaviour—receive for their aggressive behaviour. According to observational learning theory, people observe the behaviour of models and the subsequent consequences of that behaviour. If the consequences are positive, the behaviour is likely to be imitated when observers find themselves in a similar situation.

Suppose, for instance, a girl hits her younger brother when he damages one of her new toys Frustration-aggression theory would examine the girl's frustration at no longer being able to use her new toy; observational learning theory would look to previous situations in which the girl had viewed others being rewarded for their aggression. For example, perhaps she had watched a friend get to play with a toy after he painfully twisted it out of the hand of another child.

Observational learning theory has received wide research support. For example, nursery-school-age children who have watched an adult model behave aggressively and then receive reinforcement for it later display similar behaviour

STUDY ALERT!

Understand the distinction between the frustration-aggression and observational learning approaches to aggression.

Frustration
The thwarting or blocking of some ongoing, goal-directed behaviour.

themselves if they have been angered, insulted, or frustrated after exposure. Furthermore, a significant amount of research links watching television shows containing violence with subsequent viewer aggression (Winerman, 2005; Greer, Dudek-Singer, & Gautreaux, 2006; Carnagey, Anderson, & Bartholow, 2007). Individuals raised in violent homes are themselves more likely to be in abusive relationships—either as victim or abuser—as adults (Glasser et al., 2001).

Helping Others: The Brighter Side of Human Nature

Turning away from aggression, we move now to the opposite—and brighter—side of human nature: helping behaviour. Helping behaviour, or **prosocial behaviour** as it is more formally known, has been considered under many different conditions. However, the question that psychologists have looked at most closely relates to bystander intervention in emergency situations. What are the factors that lead someone to help a person in need?

One critical factor is the number of others present. When more than one person witnesses an emergency situation, a sense of **diffusion of responsibility** can arise among the bystanders witnessing the crisis, causing **bystander apathy** (as we discussed earlier in the book when we considered research methods in Chapter 1). Diffusion of responsibility is the tendency for people to feel that responsibility for acting is shared, or diffused, among those present. The more people who are present in an emergency, the less personally responsible each individual feels, the more *bystander apathy* they experience—and therefore the less help he or she provides (Barron & Yechiam, 2002; Blair, Thompson, & Wuensch, 2005; Gray, 2006).

The concept of *diffusion of responsibility* was first identified after the 1964 murder of Kitty Genovese, which was witnessed by 38 bystanders, none of whom called for help (see Chapter 1 for a more thorough discussion of the Kitty Genovese case and the subsequent research that it sparked). Sadly, other real-life examples of this phenomenon have followed since. For example, in 2012, Ahmad Nehme killed his wife on a Thursday morning in his busy condo building. Despite many of his neighbours being at home, the first call to the police was not made until an hour after Nehme began his attack—and it was placed by Nehme's teenage daughter who witnessed the murder. Another example of *diffusion of responsibility* took place in Canada on April 26, 2010, when a 79-year-old man was mugged in a Toronto subway station while several bystanders looked on and did nothing to stop the assault. The public outcry was heard across the country, with Canadians asking: "Why did nobody help?" in a letter writing campaign to local newspapers and news channels (White, 2010). As discussed above, *diffusion of responsibility* is one of many possible answers to this heartfelt question. Newspaper accounts indicated that over two dozen subway passengers witnessed the mugging of the 79-year-old man. Perhaps each passenger thought someone else would intervene? Or perhaps the other passengers were unsure of what to do and/or fearful for their own safety?

Although most research on helping behaviour supports the diffusion-of-responsibility explanation, other factors are clearly involved in helping behaviour. According to a model developed by Latané and Darley (1970), and explored in detail in Modules 1 and 2, the process of helping involves four basic steps (see Figure 4):

- *Noticing a person, event, or situation that may require help.*

- *Interpreting the event as one that requires help.* Even if we notice an event, it may be sufficiently ambiguous for us to interpret it as a nonemergency situation (Shotland, 1985; Harrison & Wells, 1991). It is here that the presence of others first affects helping behaviour. If others are ignoring a person lying on the sidewalk, we are likely to do so as well.

- *Assuming responsibility for helping.* It is at this point that diffusion of responsibility is likely to occur if others are present. Moreover, a bystander's particular expertise is likely to play a role in determining whether he or she helps. For instance, if people with training in medical aid or lifesaving techniques are present, untrained bystanders are less likely to intervene because they feel they have less expertise. This point was well illustrated in a study by Jane and Irving Piliavin (1972), who conducted a field experiment in which an individual seemed to collapse

---

Prosocial behaviour
Helping behaviour.

Diffusion of responsibility
The tendency for people to feel that responsibility for acting is shared, or diffused, among those present.

Bystander apathy
When witnesses to an emergency fail to help the victim in distress.

FIGURE 4

The basic steps of helping.

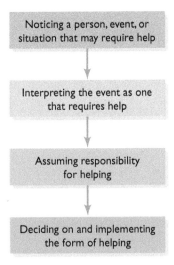

Source: Based on Latané & Darley, 1970.

in a subway car with blood trickling out of the corner of his mouth. The results of the experiment showed that bystanders were less likely to help when a person (actually a confederate) who appeared to be a medical intern was present than when the "intern" was not present.

- *Deciding on and implementing the form of helping.* After we assume responsibility for helping, we must decide how to provide assistance. Helping can range from very indirect forms of intervention, such as calling the police, to more direct forms, such as giving first aid or taking the victim to a hospital. Most social psychologists use a *rewards-costs approach* for helping to predict the nature of the assistance a bystander will choose to provide. The general notion is that the rewards for helping, as perceived by the bystander, must outweigh the costs if helping is to occur, and most research tends to support this notion (Koper & Jaasma, 2001; Bartlett & DeSteno, 2006; Lin & Lin, 2007).

STUDY ALERT!

The distinction between *prosocial behaviour* and *altruism* is important. Prosocial behaviour need not have a self-sacrificing component; altruism, by definition, contains an element of self-sacrifice.

After we determine the nature of the assistance needed, one step remains: the implementation of the assistance. A rewards-costs analysis suggests that we are most likely to use the least costly form of implementation. However, this is not always the case: In some situations, people behave altruistically. **Altruism** is helping behaviour that is beneficial to others but clearly requires self-sacrifice. For example, following Hurricane Katrina's catastrophe in 2005, many Canadians brought relief and medical aid to their American neighbours without expecting anything in return. People who helped strangers escape from the burning World Trade Center towers during the September 11, 2001, terrorist attack in New York City, putting themselves at mortal risk, would also be considered altruistic (Krueger, Hicks, & McGue, 2001; Batson & Powell, 2003; Manor & Gailliot, 2007).

People who intervene in emergency situations tend to possess certain personality characteristics that differentiate them from nonhelpers. For example, helpers are more self-assured, sympathetic, emotionally understanding, and have greater *empathy* (a personality trait in which someone observing another person experiences the emotions of that person) than nonhelpers (Graziano et al., 2007; Walker & Frimer, 2007; Stocks, Lishner, & Decker, 2009).

Altruism
Helping behaviour that is beneficial to others but clearly requires self-sacrifice.

Still, most social psychologists agree that no single set of attributes differentiates helpers from nonhelpers. For the most part, temporary situational factors (such as the mood we're in or what we see others doing) determine whether we will intervene in a situation requiring aid (Eisenberg, Guthrie, & Cumberland, 2002; Dovidio et al., 2006; Sallquist et al., 2009).

More generally, what leads people to make moral decisions? Clearly, situational factors make a difference. Research has shown that one reliable indicator of whether or not a person helps others is whether or not they see others helping. Even seeing someone perform unrelated acts of kindness makes people more likely to engage in altruistic behaviours (Schnall et al., 2010). Never underestimate the power of the actions of one individual. The Milgram experiment showed us that if one person resisted authority, others would follow. If one person helps, others are likely to follow their lead. Be the one to, as Charles Ramsey said in the opening of this chapter "just do the right thing": research shows that if you do, others will follow.

Altruism is helping behaviour that is beneficial to others but clearly requires self-sacrifice. For example, Red cross workers, Bombadier Joseph Hawkins (left), from Chetwynd, B.C., and Able Seaman Jeff Larivierre, from Ottawa, with Canada's Disaster Assistance Response Team, help an earthquke survivor into the medical clinic in Garidopata, Pakistan Monday, October 24, 2005.

Source: © CP PHOTO/Ryan Remiorz.

Becoming an Informed Consumer of Psychology

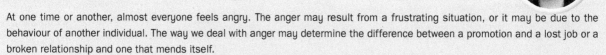

Dealing Effectively with Anger

At one time or another, almost everyone feels angry. The anger may result from a frustrating situation, or it may be due to the behaviour of another individual. The way we deal with anger may determine the difference between a promotion and a lost job or a broken relationship and one that mends itself.

Social psychologists who have studied the topic suggest several good ways to deal with anger, strategies that maximize the potential for positive consequences (Ellis, 2000; Nelson & Finch, 2000). Among the most useful strategies are the following:

- *Look again at the anger-provoking situation from the perspective of others.* By taking others' point of view, you may be able to understand the situation better, and with increased understanding you may become more tolerant of the apparent shortcomings of others.

- *Minimize the importance of the situation.* Does it really matter that someone is driving too slowly and that you'll be late to an appointment as a result? Reinterpret the situation in a way that is less bothersome.

- *Fantasize about getting even—but don't act on it.* Fantasy provides a safety valve. In your fantasies, you can yell at that unfair professor all you want and suffer no consequences at all. However, don't spend too much time brooding: Fantasize, but then move on.

- *Relax.* By teaching yourself the kinds of relaxation techniques used in systematic desensitization (see Chapter 13), you can help reduce your reactions to anger. In turn, your anger may dissipate.

No matter which of these strategies you try, above all, don't ignore your anger. People who always try to suppress their anger may experience a variety of consequences, such as self-condemnation, frustration, and even physical illness (Burns, Quartana, & Bruehl, 2007; Quartana & Burns, 2007; Gardner & Moore, 2008).

Evaluate

1. We tend to like people who are similar to us. True or false?

2. Which of the following sets are the three components of love proposed by Sternberg?

    a. Passion, closeness, sexuality

    b. Attraction, desire, complementarity

    c. Passion, intimacy, decision/commitment

    d. Commitment, caring, sexuality

3. If a person in a crowd does not help in an apparent emergency situation because many other people are present, that person is falling victim to the phenomenon of _____.

Answers to Evaluate Questions

1. true; 2. c; 3 diffusion of responsibility

Key Terms

aggression

altruism

bystander apathy

companionate love

diffusion of responsibility

frustration

interpersonal attraction (or close
  relationship)

passionate (or romantic) love

prosocial behaviour

reciprocity-of-liking effect

Epilogue

Source: © simplequiet/iStockphoto.com.

We have touched on some of the major ideas, research topics, and experimental findings of social psychology. We examined how people form, maintain, and change attitudes and how they form impressions of others and assign attributions to them. We also saw how groups, through conformity, tactics of compliance, and the power of the situation, can influence individuals' actions and attitudes. Finally, we discussed interpersonal relationships, including both liking and loving, and looked at aggression and prosocial behaviour, the two sides of a coin that represent the extremes of social behaviour.

Recap/Rethink

Module 43: Attitudes and Social Cognition

Recap

LO1 What are attitudes and how are they formed, maintained and changed?

- Social psychology is the scientific study of the ways in which people's thoughts, feelings, and actions are affected by others and the nature and causes of individual behaviour in social situations.
- Attitudes are evaluations of a particular person, behaviour, belief, or concept.
- Cognitive dissonance occurs when an individual simultaneously holds two cognitions—attitudes or thoughts—that contradict each other. To resolve the contradiction, the person may modify one cognition, change its importance, add a cognition, or deny a link between the two cognitions, thereby bringing about a reduction in dissonance.

LO2 How do people form impressions of what others are like and the causes of their behaviour?

- Social cognition involves the way people understand and make sense of others and themselves. People develop schemas that organize information about people and social experiences in memory and allow them to interpret and categorize information about others.
- People form impressions of others in part through the use of central traits, personality characteristics that receive unusually heavy emphasis when we form an impression.
- Attribution theory tries to explain how we understand the causes of behaviour, particularly with respect to situational or dispositional factors.

LO3 What are the biases that influence the ways in which we view others' behaviour?

- Even though logical processes are involved, attribution is prone to error. For instance, people are susceptible to the halo effect, assumed-similarity bias, self-serving bias, and fundamental attribution error.

Rethink

1. Joan sees Annette, a new coworker, act in a way that seems abrupt and curt. Joan concludes that Annette is unkind and unsociable. The next day Joan sees Annette acting kindly toward another worker. Is Joan likely to change her impression of Annette? Why or why not? Finally, Joan sees several friends of hers laughing and joking with Annette, treating her in a very friendly fashion. Is Joan likely to change her impression of Annette? Why or why not?

2. *From the perspective of a marketing student:* Suppose you were assigned to develop a full advertising campaign for a product, including television, radio, and print ads. How might theories of persuasion guide your strategy to suit the different media?

Module 44: Social Influence and Groups

Recap

LO4 What are the major sources and tactics of social influence?

- Social influence is the area of social psychology concerned with situations in which the actions of an individual or group affect the behaviour of others.
- Conformity refers to changes in behaviour or attitudes that result from a desire to follow the beliefs or standards of others.
- Compliance is behaviour that results from direct social pressure. Among the ways of eliciting compliance are the foot-in-the-door, door-in-the-face, that's-not-all, and not-so-free-sample techniques.
- Obedience is a change in behaviour in response to the commands of others.
- The Stanford Prison Experiment demonstrates the power of the situation in shaping our behaviour.

Rethink

1. *From the perspective of a sales representative:* Imagine that you have been trained to use the various compliance techniques described in this section. Because these compliance techniques are so powerful, should the use of certain such techniques be forbidden? Should consumers be taught defences against such techniques? Is the use of such techniques ethically and morally defensible? Why?

2. *From the perspective of an ECE student:* Student obedience in the kindergarten classroom is a major issue for many teachers coping with ever larger class sizes. How might you promote student obedience in the classroom? What are some of the potentially harmful ways that teachers could use their social influence to elicit student obedience?

3. Why do you think the Milgram experiment is so controversial? What sorts of effects might the experiment have had on participants? Do you think the experiment would have had similar results if it had been conducted not in a laboratory setting, but among members of a social group (such as a fraternity or sorority) with strong pressures to conform?

Module 45: Prejudice and Discrimination

Recap

How do stereotypes, prejudice, and discrimination differ?

- Stereotypes are generalized beliefs and expectations about a particular group and its members. Stereotyping can lead to prejudice.
- Prejudice is the negative (or, more rarely, positive) evaluation of a particular group and its members.
- Stereotyping and prejudice can lead to discrimination, behaviour directed toward individuals on the basis of their membership in a particular group.
- According to observational learning approaches, children learn stereotyping and prejudice by observing the behaviour of parents, other adults, and peers. Social identity theory suggests that group membership is used as a source of pride and self-worth, and this may lead people to think of their own group as better than others.

How can we reduce prejudice and discrimination?

- Among the ways of reducing prejudice and discrimination are increasing contact particularly in tasks that require cooperation, demonstrating positive values against prejudice, and education.

Rethink

1. *Especially for Police Foundations students*: How might overt forms of prejudice and discrimination toward disadvantaged groups (such as First Nations Canadians) be reduced in a provincial or federal penitentiary?

Module 46: Positive and Negative Social Behaviour

Recap

Why are we attracted to certain people, and what progression do social relationships follow?

- The primary determinants of liking include proximity, exposure, similarity, and physical attractiveness.
- Loving is distinguished from liking by the presence of intense physiological arousal, an all-encompassing interest in another, fantasies about the other, rapid swings of emotion, fascination, sexual desire, exclusiveness, and strong feelings of caring.

What factors underlie aggression and prosocial behaviour?

- Aggression is intentional injury of or harm to another person.
- Explanations of aggression include frustration-aggression theory and observational learning.
- Helping behaviour in emergencies is determined in part by the phenomenon of diffusion of responsibility, which results in a lower likelihood of helping when more people are present.

Rethink

1. Can love be studied scientifically? Is there an elusive quality to love that makes it at least partially unknowable? How would you define "falling in love"? How would you study it?
2. How would the assault of the 79-year-old man who was mugged in a Toronto subway station, while several bystanders looked on and did nothing to stop the assault (discussed in more detail earlier in this Module), be interpreted by proponents of the two main approaches to the study of aggression (frustration-aggression and observational learning approaches)? Do you think either of these approaches fits the Toronto subway case more closely than the other? What factors would have changed the outcome? What would have made it more likely that people would help?

Glossary

abnormal behaviour Behaviour that causes people to experience distress and prevents them from functioning in their daily lives (Module 37, p. 393)

absolute threshold The smallest intensity of a stimulus that must be present for the stimulus to be detected (Module 8, p. 77)

achievement test A test designed to determine a person's level of knowledge in a given subject area (Module 23, p. 239)

action potential An electric nerve impulse that travels through a neuron's axon when it is set off by a "trigger," changing the neuron's charge from negative to positive (Module 5, p. 47)

activation-synthesis theory Hobson's theory that the brain produces random electrical energy during REM sleep that stimulates memories stored in the brain (Module 12, p. 120)

activity theory of aging A theory that suggests that the elderly who are more successful while aging are those who maintain the interests and activities they had during middle age (Module 30, p. 328)

addictive drugs Drugs that produce a biological or psychological dependence (or both) in the user so that withdrawal from them leads to a craving for the drug that, in some cases, may be nearly irresistible (Module 14, p. 129)

adolescence The developmental stage between childhood and adulthood (Module 29, p. 315)

age of viability The point at which a fetus can survive if born prematurely (Module 27, p. 293)

aggression The intentional injury of, or harm to, another person (Module 46, p. 478)

algorithm A rule that, if applied appropriately, guarantees a solution to a problem (Module 21, p. 212)

all-or-none law The rule that neurons are either on or off (Module 5, p. 46)

altruism Helping behaviour that is beneficial to others but clearly requires self-sacrifice (Module 46, p. 481)

Alzheimer's disease A progressive brain disorder that leads to a gradual and irreversible decline in cognitive abilities (Module 20, p. 202; Module 30, p. 327)

amnesia Memory loss that occurs without other mental difficulties (Module 20, p. 202)

anal stage According to Freud, a stage from age 12 to 18 months to 3 years of age, in which a child's pleasure is centred on the anus (Module 31, p. 339)

androgens Male sex hormones secreted by the testes (Module 25, p. 263)

anorexia nervosa A weight-related disorder where people may refuse to eat while denying that their behaviour and appearance, which can become skeleton like, is unusual (Module 25, p. 263)

anterograde amnesia Amnesia in which memory is lost for events that follow an injury (Module 20, p. 202)

antianxiety drugs Drugs that reduce the level of anxiety a person experiences, essentially by reducing excitability and increasing feelings of well-being (Module 42, p. 447)

antidepressant drugs Medications that improve a severely depressed patient's mood and feeling of well-being (Module 42, p. 445)

antipsychotic drugs Drugs that temporarily reduce psychotic symptoms such as agitation, hallucinations, and delusions (Module 42, p. 444)

antisocial personality disorder A disorder in which individuals show no regard for the moral and ethical rules of society or the rights of others (Module 38, p. 414)

anxiety disorder The occurrence of anxiety without an obvious external cause that affects daily functioning (Module 38, p. 401)

aptitude test A test designed to predict a person's ability in a particular area or line of work (Module 23, p. 240)

archetypes According to Jung, universal symbolic representations of a particular person, object, or experience (such as good and evil) (Module 31, p. 342)

arousal approaches to motivation The belief that we try to maintain certain levels of stimulation and activity, increasing or reducing them as necessary (Module 24, p. 255)

association areas One of the major regions of the cerebral cortex; the site of the higher mental processes, such as thought, language, memory, and speech (Module 6, p. 59)

assumed-similarity bias The tendency to think of people as being similar to oneself, even when meeting them for the first time (Module 43, p. 461)

attachment The positive emotional bond that develops between a child and a particular individual (Module 28, p. 301)

attention-deficit hyperactivity disorder (ADHD) A disorder marked by inattention, impulsiveness, a low tolerance for frustration, and a great deal of inappropriate activity (Module 38, p. 415)

attitudes Evaluations of a particular person, behaviour, belief, or concept (Module 43, p. 456)

attribution theory The theory of personality that seeks to explain how we decide, on the basis of samples of an individual's behaviour, what the specific causes of that person's behaviour are (Module 43, p. 459)

authoritarian parents Parents who are rigid and punitive and value unquestioning obedience from their children (Module 28, p. 306)

authoritative parents Parents who are firm, set clear limits, reason with their children, and explain things to them (Module 28, p. 306)

autism spectrum disorder A severe developmental disability that impairs children's ability to communicate and relate to others (Module 38, p. 416)

autobiographical memories Our recollections of circumstances and episodes from our own lives (Module 19, p. 195)

autonomic division The part of the peripheral nervous system that controls involuntary movement of the heart, glands, lungs, and other organs (Module 7, p. 66)

autonomy-versus-shame-and-doubt stage The period which, according to Erik Erikson, toddlers (ages 1½ to 3 years) develop independence and autonomy if exploration and freedom are encouraged, or shame and self-doubt if they are restricted and overprotected (Module 28, p. 308)

aversive conditioning A form of therapy that reduces the frequency of undesired behaviour by pairing an aversive, unpleasant stimulus with undesired behaviour (Module 40, p. 431)

axon The part of the neuron that carries messages destined for other neurons (Module 5, p. 45)

babble Meaningless speech-like sounds made by children from around the age of 3 months through 1 year (Module 22, p. 225)

background stressors ("daily hassles") Everyday annoyances, such as being stuck in traffic, that cause minor irritations and may have long-term ill effects if they continue or are compounded by other stressful events (Module 34, p. 369)

basilar membrane A vibrating structure that runs through the centre of the cochlea, dividing it into an upper chamber and a lower chamber and containing sense receptors for sound (Module 10, p. 90)

behaviour modification A formalized technique for promoting the frequency of desirable behaviours and decreasing the incidence of unwanted ones (Module 16, p. 164)

behavioural assessment Direct measures of an individual's behaviour used to describe personality characteristics (Module 33, p. 360)

behavioural genetics The study of the effects of heredity on behaviour (Module 7, p. 68)

behavioural neuroscientists (or biopsychologists) Psychologists who specialize in considering the ways in which the biological structures and functions of the body affect behaviour (Module 5, p. 43)

behavioural perspective (on psychological disorders) The perspective that looks at the behaviour itself as the problem (Module 37, p. 395)

behavioural perspective The approach that suggests that observable, measurable behaviour should be the focus of study (Module 2, p. 14)

behavioural treatment approaches Treatment approaches that build on the basic processes of learning, such as reinforcement and extinction, and assume that normal and abnormal behaviour are both learned (Module 40, p. 431)

biological and evolutionary approaches to personality Theories that suggest that important components of personality are inherited (Module 32, p. 349)

biological preparedness A theory that explains our propensity to learn certain classically conditioned associations over others that is linked to our evolutionary history (Module 15, p. 150)

biomedical therapy Therapy that relies on drugs and other medical procedures to improve psychological functioning (Module 40, p. 427)

bipolar disorder A disorder in which a person alternates between periods of euphoric feelings of mania and periods of depression (Module 38, p. 407)

bisexuals Persons who are sexually attracted to people of the same sex and the other sex (Module 25, p. 269)

borderline personality disorder A disorder in which individuals have difficulty developing a secure sense of who they are (Module 38, p. 415)

bottom-up processing Perception that consists of the progression of recognizing and processing information from individual components of a stimuli and moving to the perception of the whole (Module 11, p. 101)

bulimia A weight-related disorder in which people binge eat on large quantities of food. After such a binge, sufferers often purge by taking laxatives or vomiting to rid themselves of the food (Module 25, p. 263)

bystander apathy When witnesses to an emergency fail to help the victim in distress (Module 46, p. 480)

Cannon-Bard theory of emotion The belief that both physiological arousal and emotional experience are produced simultaneously by the same nerve stimulus (Module 26, p. 277)

case study An in-depth, intensive investigation of an individual or small group of people (Module 3, p. 25)

cataclysmic events Strong stressors that occur suddenly and typically affect many people at once (e.g., natural disasters) (Module 34, p. 367)

central nervous system (CNS) The part of the nervous system that includes the brain and spinal cord (Module 7, p. 64)

central traits The major traits considered in forming impressions of others (Module 43, p. 459)

cerebellum (ser uh BELL um) The part of the brain that controls bodily balance (Module 6, p. 54)

cerebral cortex The "new brain," responsible for the most sophisticated information processing in the brain; contains four lobes (Module 6, p. 56)

chromosomes Rod-shaped structures that contain all basic hereditary information (Module 27, p. 291)

chunk A meaningful grouping of stimuli that can be stored as a unit in short-term memory (Module 18, p. 179)

circadian rhythms Biological processes that occur regularly on approximately a twenty-four-hour cycle (Module 12, p. 123)

classical conditioning A type of learning in which a neutral stimulus comes to bring about a response after it is paired with a stimulus that naturally brings about that response (Module 15, p. 145)

cochlea (KOKE lee uh) A coiled tube in the ear filled with fluid that vibrates in response to sound (Module 10, p. 90)

cognitive approaches to motivation Theories suggesting that motivation is a product of people's thoughts, expectations, and goals—their cognitions (Module 24, p. 257)

cognitive-behavioural approach Cognitive therapists attempt to change the way people think as well as their behaviour by utilizing basic principles of learning (Module 40, p. 434)

cognitive development The process by which a child's understanding of the world changes as a function of age and experience (Module 28, p. 309)

cognitive dissonance The conflict that occurs when a person holds two contradictory attitudes or thoughts (referred to as *cognitions*) (Module 43, p. 457)

cognitive learning theory An approach to the study of learning that focuses on the thought processes that underlie learning (Module 17, p. 166)

cognitive perspective (on psychological disorders) The perspective that suggests that people's thoughts and beliefs are a central component of abnormal behaviour (Module 37, p. 396)

cognitive perspective The approach that focuses on how people think, understand, and know about the world (Module 2, p. 14)

cognitive psychology The branch of psychology that focuses on the study of higher mental processes, including thinking, language, memory, problem solving, knowing, reasoning, judging, and decision making (Module 21, p. 209)

cognitive treatment approaches An approach that teaches people to think in more adaptive ways by changing their dysfunctional cognitions about the world and themselves (Module 40, p. 434)

collective unconscious According to Jung, a common set of ideas, feelings, images, and symbols that we inherit from our ancestors, the whole human race, and even animal ancestors from the distant past (Module 31, p. 342)

community psychology A branch of psychology that focuses on the prevention and minimization of psychological disorders in the community (Module 42, p. 449)

companionate love The strong affection we have for those with whom our lives are deeply involved (Module 46, p. 476)

compliance Behaviour that occurs in response to direct social pressure (Module 44, p. 466)

compulsions An irresistible urge to carry out some act that seems strange or unreasonable (Module 38, p. 404)

concepts A mental grouping of similar objects, events, or people (Module 21, p. 211)

concrete operational stage According to Piaget, the period from 7 to 12 years of age that is characterized by logical thought and a loss of egocentrism (Module 28, p. 311)

conditioned response (CR) A response that, after conditioning, follows a previously neutral stimulus (e.g., salivation at the ringing of a bell) (Module 15, p. 147)

conditioned stimulus (CS) A once-neutral stimulus that has been paired with an unconditioned stimulus to bring about a response formerly caused only by the unconditioned stimulus (Module 15, p. 146)

cones Cone-shaped, light-sensitive receptor cells in the retina that are responsible for sharp focus and colour perception, particularly in bright light (Module 9, p. 83)

confirmation bias The tendency to seek out and weight more heavily information that supports one's initial hypotheses and to ignore contradictory information that supports alternative hypotheses or solutions (Module 21, p. 220)

conformity A change in behaviour or attitudes brought about by a desire to follow the beliefs or standards of other people (Module 44, p. 464)

confound Any extraneous variable that could affect the dependent variable and therefore the validity of the experiment (Module 3, p. 29)

consciousness The awareness of the sensations, thoughts, and feelings being experienced at a given moment (Module 12, p. 113)

constructive processes Processes in which memories are influenced by the meaning we give to events (Module 19, p. 192)

continuous reinforcement schedule Reinforcing of a behaviour every time it occurs (Module 16, p. 159)

control group A group participating in an experiment that receives no treatment (Module 3, p. 28)

convergent thinking The ability to produce responses that are based primarily on knowledge and logic (Module 21, p. 222)

conversion disorders A major somatoform disorder that involves an actual physical disturbance, such as the inability to use a sensory organ or the complete or partial inability to move an arm or leg (Module 38, p. 416)

coping The efforts to control, reduce, or learn to tolerate the threats that lead to stress (Module 34, p. 373)

correlational research Research in which the relationship between two sets of variables is examined to determine whether they are associated, or "correlated" (Module 3, p. 25)

correspondence bias A tendency to draw inferences about a person's unique and enduring dispositions from behaviours that can be entirely explained by the situations in which they occur (Module 43, p. 462)

creativity The ability to generate original ideas or solve problems in novel ways (Module 21, p. 221)

cross-sectional research A research method that compares people of different ages at the same point in time (Module 27, p. 290)

cue-dependent forgetting Forgetting that occurs when there are insufficient retrieval cues to rekindle information that is in memory (Module 20, p. 200)

culture-fair IQ test A test that does not discriminate against the members of any minority group (Module 23, p. 244)

decay The loss of information in memory through its non-use (Module 20, p. 199)

declarative memory Memory for factual information: names, faces, dates, and the like (Module 18, p. 182)

defence mechanisms In Freudian theory, unconscious strategies that people use to reduce anxiety by concealing the source of it from themselves and others (Module 31, p. 340)

deinstitutionalization The transfer of former mental patients from institutions to the community (Module 42, p. 450)

dendrites A cluster of fibres at one end of a neuron that receives messages from other neurons (Module 5, p. 45)

dependent variable The variable that is measured and is expected to change as a result of changes caused by the experimenter's manipulation of the independent variable (Module 3, p. 29)

depressants Drugs that slow down the nervous system (Module 14, p. 135)

depth perception The ability to view the world in three dimensions and to perceive distance (Module 11, p. 103)

descriptive research An approach to research designed to systematically investigate a person, group, or patterns of behaviour (Module 3, p. 24)

developmental psychology The branch of psychology that studies the patterns of growth and change that occur throughout life (Module 27, p. 288)

Diagnostic and Statistical Manual of Mental Disorders, Fifth Edition (DSM-5) A system, devised by the American Psychiatric Association, used by most professionals to diagnose and classify abnormal behaviour (Module 37, p. 397)

dialectical behaviour therapy A form of treatment in which the focus is on getting people to accept who they are, regardless of whether it matches their ideal (Module 40, p. 433)

difference threshold (just noticeable difference) The smallest level of added or reduced stimulation required to sense that a change in stimulation has occurred (Module 8, p. 79)

diffusion of responsibility The tendency for people to feel that responsibility for acting is shared, or diffused, among those present (Module 46, p. 480)

discrimination Behaviour directed toward individuals on the basis of their membership in a particular group (Module 45, p. 470)

disengagement theory of aging A theory that suggests that aging produces a gradual withdrawal from the world on physical, psychological, and social levels (Module 30, p. 328)

dispositional cause (of behaviour) Perceived cause of behaviour that is based on internal traits or personality factors (Module 43, p. 461)

divergent thinking The ability to generate unusual, yet nonetheless appropriate, responses to problems or questions (Module 21, p. 222)

double standard The view that premarital sex is permissible for males but not for females (Module 25, p. 267)

dreams-for-survival theory The theory suggesting that dreams permit information that is critical for our daily survival to be reconsidered and reprocessed during sleep (Module 12, p. 119)

drive Motivational tension, or arousal, which energizes behaviour to fulfill a need (Module 24, p. 253)

drive-reduction approaches to motivation Theories suggesting that a lack of a basic biological requirement such as water produces a drive to obtain that requirement (in this case, the thirst drive) (Module 24, p. 253)

drug therapy Control of psychological disorders through the use of drugs (Module 42, p. 444)

eardrum The part of the ear that vibrates when sound waves hit it (Module 10, p. 89)

eclectic approach to therapy An approach that uses techniques taken from a variety of treatment methods, rather than just one (Module 41, p. 441)

ego The part of the personality that provides a buffer between the id and the outside world (Module 31, p. 338)

egocentric thought A way of thinking in which a child views the world entirely from his or her own perspective (Module 28, p. 310)

ego-integrity-versus-despair stage According to Erikson, a period from late adulthood until death during which we review life's accomplishments and failures (Module 29, p. 320)

Electra complex A daughter's unresolved, unconscious sexual desire for her father (Module 31, p. 339)

electroconvulsive therapy (ECT) A procedure used in the treatment of severe depression in which an electric current of 70 to 150 volts is briefly administered to a patient's head (Module 42, p. 447)

embryo A developed zygote that has a heart, a brain, and other organs (Module 27, p. 292)

emerging adulthood The period beginning in the late teenage years and extending into the mid-20s (Module 30, p. 322)

emotional intelligence The set of skills that underlie the accurate assessment, evaluation, expression, and regulation of emotions (Module 23, p. 235)

emotions Feelings that generally have both physiological and cognitive elements and that influence behaviour (Module 26, p. 273)

endocrine system A chemical communication network that sends messages throughout the body via the bloodstream (Module 7, p. 69)

episodic memory Memory for events that occur in a particular time, place, or context (Module 18, p. 182)

estrogens Class of female sex hormones (Module 25, p. 265)

evolutionary psychology The branch of psychology that seeks to identify behaviour patterns that are a result of our genetic inheritance from our ancestors (Module 7, p. 67)

excitatory messages A chemical message that makes it more likely that a receiving neuron will fire and an action potential will travel down its axon (Module 5, p. 49)

experiment The investigation of the relationship between two (or more) variables by deliberately producing a change in one variable in a situation and observing the effects of that change on other aspects of the situation (Module 3, p. 27)

experimental bias Factors that distort how the independent variable affects the dependent variable in an experiment (Module 4, p. 36)

experimental group Any group participating in an experiment that receives a treatment (Module 3, p. 28)

experimental manipulation The change that an experimenter deliberately produces in a situation (Module 3, p. 28)

explicit memory Intentional or conscious recollection of information (Module 19, p. 190)

extinction A basic phenomenon of learning that occurs when a previously conditioned response decreases in frequency and eventually disappears (Module 15, p. 148)

extramarital sex Sexual activity between a married person and someone who is not his or her spouse (Module 25, p. 267)

familial intellectual disabilities Intellectual disabilities in which no apparent biological defect exists but there is a history of intellectual disabilities in the family (Module 23, p. 242)

family therapy An approach that focuses on the family and its dynamics (Module 41, p. 439)

feature detection The activation of neurons in the cortex by visual stimuli of specific shapes or patterns (Module 9, p. 86)

fetal alcohol syndrome The most common cause of intellectual disabilities in newborns, occurring when the mother consumes alcohol during pregnancy (Module 23, p. 242)

fetus A developing individual from eight weeks after conception until birth (Module 27, p. 293)

fixations Conflicts or concerns that persist beyond the developmental period in which they first occur (Module 31, p. 338)

fixed-interval schedule A schedule that provides reinforcement for a response only if a fixed time period has elapsed, making overall rates of response relatively low (Module 16, p. 161)

fixed-ratio schedule A schedule by which reinforcement is given only after a specific number of responses are made (Module 16, p. 160)

flashbulb memories Memories centred on a specific, important, or surprising event that are so vivid it is as if they represented a snapshot of the event (Module 19, p. 191)

formal operational stage According to Piaget, the period from age 12 to adulthood that is characterized by abstract thought (Module 28, p. 312)

frequency theory of hearing The theory that the entire basilar membrane acts like a microphone, vibrating as a whole in response to a sound (Module 10, p. 92)

frustration The thwarting or blocking of some ongoing, goal-directed behaviour (Module 46, p. 479)

functional fixedness The tendency to think of an object only in terms of its typical use (Module 21, p. 219)

functionalism An early approach to psychology that concentrated on what the mind does—the functions of mental activity—and the role of behaviour in allowing people to adapt to their environments (Module 2, p. 11)

fundamental attribution error A tendency to overattribute others' behaviour to dispositional causes and minimize the importance of situational causes (Module 43, p. 462)

g or g-factor The single, general factor for mental ability assumed to underlie intelligence in some early theories of intelligence (Module 23, p. 233)

gate-control theory of pain When particular nerve receptors are activated because of an injury or problem with part of the body, a "gate" to the brain is opened allowing us to experience the sensation of pain. When stimulated, another set of neural receptors can close the "gate" and reduce the experience of pain (Module 10, p. 97)

general adaptation syndrome (GAS) A theory developed by Selye that suggests that a person's response to a stressor consists of three stages: alarm and mobilization, resistance, and exhaustion (Module 34, p. 371)

generalized anxiety disorder The occurrence of long-term, persistent anxiety and worry (Module 38, p. 402)

generativity-versus-stagnation stage According to Erikson, a period in middle adulthood during which we take stock of our contributions to family and society (Module 29, p. 319)

genes The parts of the chromosomes through which genetic information is transmitted (Module 27, p. 292)

genetic preprogramming theories of aging Human cells have a built-in time limit to their reproduction and after a certain time, cells stop dividing or become harmful to the body (Module 30, p. 325)

genital stage According to Freud, the period from puberty until death, marked by mature sexual behaviour (that is, sexual intercourse) (Module 31, p. 340)

genitals The male and female sex organs (Module 25, p. 265)

gestalt laws of organization A series of principles that describe how we organize bits and pieces of information into meaningful wholes (Module 11, p. 100)

grammar The system of rules that determine how our thoughts can be expressed (Module 22, p. 224)

group therapy Therapy in which people meet in a group with a therapist to discuss their problems and receive support and advice from group members (Module 41, p. 439)

groupthink A type of thinking in which group members share such a strong motivation to achieve consensus that they lose the ability to critically evaluate alternative points of view (Module 44, p. 466)

habituation The decrease in response to a stimulus that occurs after repeated presentations of the same stimulus (Module 28, p. 299)

hair cells Tiny cells covering the basilar membrane that, when bent by vibrations entering the cochlea, transmit neural messages to the brain (Module 10, p. 90)

hallucinogen A class of drug that is capable of producing hallucinations, or changes in the perceptual process (Module 14, p. 138)

halo effect A phenomenon in which an initial understanding that a person has positive traits is used to infer other uniformly positive characteristics (Module 43, p. 461)

hardiness A personality characteristic that is associated with a lower rate of stress-related illness and consists of three components: commitment, challenge, and control (Module 34, p. 374)

health psychology The branch of psychology that investigates the psychological factors related to wellness and illness, including the prevention, diagnosis, and treatment of medical problems (Module 34, p. 365)

hemispheres Symmetrical left and right halves of the brain that each control the *opposite* side of the body (Module 6, p. 61)

heritability A measure of the degree to which a characteristic is related to genetic, inherited factors (Module 23, p. 244)

heterosexuality Sexual attraction and behaviour directed to the other sex (Module 25, p. 266)

heuristic A thinking strategy that may lead us to a solution to a problem or decision, but—unlike algorithms—may sometimes lead to errors (Module 21, p. 212)

hindbrain The part of the brain that controls basic functions such as eating and sleeping and is common to all vertebrates (Module 6, p. 54)

homeostasis The body's tendency to maintain a steady internal state (Module 24, p. 254)

homosexuals Persons who are sexually attracted to members of their own sex (Module 25, p. 269)

hormones Chemicals that circulate through the blood and regulate the functioning or growth of the body (Module 7, p. 69)

humanistic approaches to personality Theories that emphasize people's innate goodness and desire to achieve higher levels of functioning (Module 32, p. 351)

humanistic perspective (on psychological disorders) The perspective that emphasizes the responsibility people have for their own behaviour, even when such behaviour is abnormal (Module 37, p. 396)

humanistic perspective The approach that suggests that all individuals naturally strive to grow, develop, and be in control of their lives and behaviour (Module 2, p. 15)

humanistic therapy Therapy in which the underlying rationale is that people have control of their behaviour, can make choices about their lives, and are essentially responsible for solving their own problems (Module 41, p. 437)

hypnosis A trance-like state of heightened susceptibility to the suggestions of others (Module 13, p. 125)

hypothalamus A tiny part of the brain, located below the thalamus, that maintains homeostasis and produces and regulates vital behaviour, such as eating, drinking, and sexual behaviour (Module 6, p. 55)

hypothesis A prediction, stemming from a theory, stated in a way that allows it to be tested (Module 3, p. 23)

id The raw, unorganized, inborn part of personality whose sole purpose is to reduce tension created by primitive drives related to hunger, sex, aggression, and irrational impulses (Module 31, p. 337)

identical twins Twins who are genetically identical (Module 27, p. 290)

identification The process of wanting to be like another person as much as possible, imitating that person's behaviour and adopting similar beliefs and values (Module 31, p. 340)

identity The distinguishing character of the individual: who each of us is, what our roles are, and what we are capable of (Module 29, p. 319)

identity-versus-role-confusion stage According to Erikson, a time in adolescence of major testing to determine one's unique qualities (Module 29, p. 318)

illness anxiety disorder A disorder in which people have a constant fear of illness and a preoccupation with their health (Module 38, p. 416)

implicit memory Memories of which people are not consciously aware but that can affect subsequent performance and behaviour (Module 19, p. 190)

incentive approaches to motivation Theories suggesting that motivation stems from the desire to obtain valued external goals, or incentives (Module 24, p. 255)

independent variable The variable that is manipulated by an experimenter (Module 3, p. 29)

industry-versus-inferiority stage According to Erikson, the last stage of childhood, during which children age 6 to 12 years may develop positive social interactions with others or may feel inadequate and become less sociable (Module 28, p. 309)

inferiority complex According to Adler, a problem affecting adults who have not been able to overcome the feelings of inferiority that they developed as children, when they were small and limited in their knowledge about the world (Module 31, p. 343)

information processing The way in which people take in, use, and store information (Module 28, p. 312)

informed consent A document signed by participants affirming that they have been told the basic outlines of the study and are aware of what their participation will involve (Module 4, p. 35)

inhibitory messages A chemical message that prevents or decreases the likelihood that a receiving neuron will fire (Module 5, p. 50)

initiative-versus-guilt stage According to Erik Erikson, the period during which children ages 3 to 6 years experience conflict between independence of action and the sometimes negative results of that action (Module 28, p. 308)

insight A sudden awareness of the relationships among various elements that had previously appeared to be independent of one another (Module 21, p. 218)

instincts Inborn patterns of behaviour that are biologically determined rather than learned (Module 24, p. 252)

intellectual disabilities A condition characterized by significant limitations in intellectual and adaptive functioning (Module 23, p. 242)

intellectually gifted The 2 to 4 percent of the population who have IQ scores greater than 130 (Module 23, p. 243)

intelligence The capacity to understand the world, think rationally, and use resources effectively when faced with challenges (Module 23, p. 233)

intelligence quotient (IQ) A score that takes into account an individual's mental and chronological ages (Module 23, p. 237)

intelligence tests Tests devised to quantify a person's level of intelligence (Module 23, p. 236)

interactionist approach (to language development) The view that language development is produced through a combination of genetically determined predispositions and environmental circumstances that help teach language (Module 22, p. 228)

interference The phenomenon by which information in memory disrupts the recall of other information (Module 20, p. 200)

interneurons Neurons that connect sensory and motor neurons, carrying messages between the two (Module 7, p. 65)

interpersonal attraction (or close relationship) Positive feelings for others; liking and loving (Module 46, p. 474)

interpersonal therapy (IPT) Short-term therapy that focuses on the context of current social relationships (Module 41, p. 438)

intimacy-versus-isolation stage According to Erikson, a period during early adulthood that focuses on developing close relationships (Module 29, p. 319)

introspection A procedure used to study the structure of the mind in which subjects are asked to describe in detail what they are experiencing when they are exposed to a stimulus (Module 2, p. 10)

James-Lange theory of emotion The belief that emotional experience is a reaction to bodily events occurring as a result of an external situation ("I feel sad because I am crying") (Module 26, p. 276)

language The communication of information through symbols arranged according to systematic rules (Module 22, p. 224)

language-acquisition device A neural system of the brain hypothesized by Noam Chomsky to permit understanding of language (Module 22, p. 228)

latency period According to Freud, the period between the phallic stage and puberty during which children's sexual concerns are temporarily put aside (Module 31, p. 340)

latent content of dreams According to Freud, the "disguised" meaning of dreams, hidden by more obvious subjects (Module 12, p. 119)

latent learning Learning in which a new behaviour is acquired but is not demonstrated until some incentive is provided for displaying it (Module 17, p. 166)

lateralization The dominance of one hemisphere of the brain in specific functions, such as language (Module 6, p. 61)

learning A relatively permanent change in behaviour brought about by experience (Module 15, p. 144)

learning-theory approach (to language development) The theory that language acquisition follows the principles of reinforcement and conditioning (Module 22, p. 226)

levels-of-processing theory The theory of memory that emphasizes the degree to which new material is mentally analyzed (Module 19, p. 189)

life review The process by which people examine and evaluate their lives (Module 30, p. 328)

limbic system The part of the brain that controls eating, aggression, and reproduction (Module 6, p. 55)

linguistic-relativity hypothesis The notion that language shapes and may determine the way people in a particular culture perceive and understand the world (Module 22, p. 229)

lithium A drug made up of mineral salts, which is used to treat and prevent manic episodes of bipolar disorder (Module 42, p. 447)

lobes The four major sections of the cerebral cortex: frontal, parietal, temporal, and occipital (Module 6, p. 56)

longitudinal research A research method that investigates behaviour as participants age (Module 27, p. 290)

long-term memory Memory that stores information on a relatively permanent basis, although it may be difficult to retrieve (Module 18, p. 177)

major depression A severe form of depression that interferes with concentration, decision making, and sociability (Module 38, p. 405)

mania An extended state of intense, wild elation (Module 38, p. 406)

manifest content of dreams According to Freud, the apparent story line of dreams (Module 12, p. 119)

masturbation Sexual self-stimulation (Module 25, p. 266)

means-ends analysis Involves repeated tests for differences between the desired outcome and what currently exists (Module 21, p. 216)

medical perspective (on psychological disorders) The perspective that suggests that when an individual displays symptoms of abnormal behaviour, the root cause will be found in a physical examination of the individual, which may reveal a hormonal imbalance, a chemical deficiency, or a brain injury (Module 37, p. 394)

meditation A learned technique for refocusing attention that brings about an altered state of consciousness (Module 13, p. 127)

memory traces A physical change in the brain that occurs when new material is learned (Module 20, p. 199)

memory The process by which we encode, store, and retrieve information (Module 18, p. 176)

menopause The period during which women stop menstruating and are no longer fertile (Module 30, p. 323)

mental age The age for which a given level of performance is average or typical (Module 23, p. 237)

mental images Representations in the mind of an object or event (Module 21, p. 210)

mental set The tendency for old patterns of problem solving to persist (Module 21, p. 220)

metabolism The rate at which food is converted to energy and expended by the body (Module 25, p. 261)

metacognition An awareness and understanding of one's own cognitive processes (Module 28, p. 312)

mindfulness-based cognitive therapy (MBCT) An approach that teaches people to focus on maintaining a non-judgmental, moment by moment awareness of their environment, physical sensations, thoughts, and feelings (Module 40, p. 435)

Minnesota Multiphasic Personality Inventory-2 (MMPI-2) A widely used self-report test that identifies people with psychological difficulties and is employed to predict some everyday behaviours (Module 33, p. 356)

mirror neurons Neurons that fire when a person enacts a particular behaviour and when a person observes *another* individual carrying out the same behaviour (Module 5, p. 48)

mood disorders A disturbance in emotional experience that is strong enough to intrude on everyday living (Module 38, p. 405)

motivation The factors that direct and energize the behaviour of humans and other organisms (Module 24, p. 252)

motor (efferent) neurons Neurons that communicate information from the nervous system to muscles and glands (Module 7, p. 65)

motor area The part of the cortex that is largely responsible for the body's voluntary movement (Module 6, p. 57)

myelin sheath A protective coat of fat and protein that wraps around the neuron (Module 5, p. 45)

narcissistic personality disorder A personality disturbance characterized by an exaggerated sense of self-importance (Module 38, p. 415)

narcotics Drugs that increase relaxation and relieve pain and anxiety (Module 14, p. 137)

nativist approach (to language development) The theory that a genetically determined, innate mechanism directs language development (Module 22, p. 227)

naturalistic observation Research in which an investigator simply observes some naturally occurring behaviour and does not make a change in the situation (Module 3, p. 24)

nature–nurture issue The issue of the degree to which environment and heredity influence behaviour (Module 27, p. 288)

need for achievement A stable, learned characteristic in which a person obtains satisfaction by striving for and attaining a level of excellence (Module 25, p. 271)

need for affiliation An interest in establishing and maintaining relationships with other people (Module 25, p. 270)

need for power A tendency to seek impact, control, or influence over others, and to be seen as a powerful individual (Module 25, p. 271)

negative reinforcer An unpleasant stimulus whose *removal* leads to an increase in the probability that a preceding response will be repeated in the future (Module 16, p. 156)

neo-Freudian psychoanalysts Psychoanalysts who were trained in traditional Freudian theory but who later rejected some of its major points (Module 31, p. 342)

neonate A newborn child (Module 28, p. 297)

neurogenesis The creation of new neurons (Module 6, p. 60)

neurons Nerve cells, the basic elements of the nervous system (Module 5, p. 44)

neuroplasticity Changes in the brain that occur throughout the life span relating to the addition of new neurons, new interconnections between neurons, and the reorganization of information-processing areas (Module 6, p. 60)

neuroscience perspective The approach that views behaviour from the perspective of the brain, the nervous system, and other biological functions (Module 2, p. 13)

neurotransmitters Chemicals that carry messages across the synapse to the dendrite (and sometimes the cell body) of a receiver neuron (Module 5, p. 49)

neutral stimulus A stimulus that, before conditioning, does not naturally bring about the response of interest (Module 15, p. 145)

norms Standards of test performance that permit the comparison of one person's score on a test with the scores of other individuals who have taken the same test (Module 23, p. 241)

obedience A change in behaviour in response to the commands of others (Module 44, p. 467)

obesity Body weight that is more than 20 percent above the average weight for a person of a particular height (Module 25, p. 259)

object permanence The awareness that objects—and people—continue to exist even if they are out of sight (Module 28, p. 310)

observational learning Learning by observing the behaviour of another person, or model (Module 17, p. 168)

obsession Persistent, unwanted thoughts or ideas that keep recurring (Module 38, p. 404)

obsessive-compulsive disorder A disorder in which a person is plagued by unwanted thoughts, called obsessions, or feel that they must carry out actions, termed compulsions, against their will (Module 38, p. 404).

Oedipal conflict A child's sexual interest in his or her opposite-sex parent, typically resolved through identification with the same-sex parent (Module 31, p. 339)

operant conditioning Learning in which a voluntary response is strengthened or weakened, depending on its favourable or unfavourable consequences (Module 16, p. 152)

operational definition The translation of a hypothesis into specific, testable procedures that can be measured and observed (Module 3, p. 24)

opponent-process theory of colour vision The theory that receptor cells for colour are linked in pairs, working in opposition to each other (Module 9, p. 87)

optic nerve A bundle of ganglion axons that carry visual information to the brain (Module 9, p. 84)

oral stage According to Freud, a stage from birth to age 12 to 18 months, in which an infant's centre of pleasure is the mouth (Module 31, p. 338)

otoliths Tiny, motion-sensitive crystals within the semicircular canals that sense body acceleration (Module 10, p. 93)

overgeneralization The phenomenon by which children apply language rules even when the application results in an error (Module 22, p. 226)

ovulation The point at which an egg is released from the ovaries (Module 25, p. 266)

panic disorder The occurrence of panic attacks that last from a few seconds to a few hours (Module 38, p. 403)

parasympathetic division The part of the autonomic division of the nervous system that acts to calm the body after an emergency has ended (Module 7, p. 67)

partial (intermittent) reinforcement schedule Reinforcing of a behaviour some but not all of the time (Module 16, p. 159)

passionate (or romantic) love A state of intense absorption in someone that includes intense physiological arousal, psychological interest, and caring for the needs of another (Module 46, p. 476)

perception The sorting out, interpretation, analysis, and integration of stimuli by the sense organs and brain (Module 8, p. 76)

perceptual constancy The phenomenon in which physical objects are perceived as unvarying and consistent despite changes in their appearance or in the physical environment (Module 11, p. 102)

peripheral nervous system The part of the nervous system that includes the autonomic and somatic subdivisions; made up of neurons with long axons and dendrites, it branches out from the spinal cord and brain and reaches the extremities of the body (Module 7, p. 66)

permissive parents Parents who give their children relaxed or inconsistent direction and, although warm, require little of them (Module 28, p. 306)

personal stressors Major life events, such as the death of a family member, that have immediate consequences that generally fade with time (Module 34, p. 367)

personality disorder A disorder characterized by a set of inflexible, maladaptive behaviour patterns that keep a person from functioning appropriately in society (Module 38, p. 414)

personality The pattern of enduring characteristics that produce consistency and individuality in a given person (Module 31, p. 335)

person-centred therapy Therapy in which the goal is to reach one's potential for self-actualization (Module 41, p. 438)

phallic stage According to Freud, a period beginning around age 3 during which a child's pleasure focuses on the genitals (Module 31, p. 339)

phonemes The smallest units of speech (Module 22, p. 224)

phonology The study of the smallest units of speech, called phonemes (Module 22, p. 224)

pituitary gland The major component of the endocrine system, or "master gland," which secretes hormones that control growth and other parts of the endocrine system (Module 7, p. 70)

place theory of hearing The theory that different areas of the basilar membrane respond to different frequencies (Module 10, p. 92)

placebo A false treatment, such as a pill, "drug," or other substance, without any significant chemical properties or active ingredient (Module 4, p. 37)

positive reinforcer A stimulus added to the environment that brings about an increase in a preceding response (Module 16, p. 156)

posttraumatic stress disorder (PTSD) A phenomenon in which victims of major catastrophes or strong personal stressors feel long-lasting effects that may include re-experiencing the event in vivid flashbacks or dreams (Module 34, p. 367)

prejudice A (usually) negative evaluation of a particular group and its members (Module 45, p. 470)

preoperational stage According to Piaget, the period from 2 to 7 years of age that is characterized by language development (Module 28, p. 310)

priming A phenomenon in which exposure to a word or concept (called a *prime*) later makes it easier to recall related information, even when there is no conscious memory of the word or concept (Module 19, p. 191)

principle of conservation The knowledge that quantity is unrelated to the arrangement and physical appearance of objects (Module 28, p. 310)

proactive interference Interference in which information learned earlier disrupts the recall of newer material (Module 20, p. 201)

procedural memory Memory for skills and habits, such as riding a bike or hitting a baseball, sometimes referred to as *nondeclarative memory* (Module 18, p. 182)

progesterone A female sex hormone secreted by the ovaries (Module 25, p. 265)

projective personality tests A test in which a person is shown an ambiguous stimulus and asked to describe it or tell a story about it (Module 33, p. 359)

prosocial behaviour Helping behaviour (Module 46, p. 480)

prototypes Typical, highly representative samples of a concept (Module 21, p. 212)

psychoactive drugs Legal or illegal drugs that influence a person's emotions, perceptions, and behaviour (Module 14, p. 129)

psychoanalysis Freudian psychotherapy in which the goal is to release hidden unconscious thoughts and feelings in order to reduce their power in controlling behaviour (Module 40, p. 429)

psychoanalytic perspective (on psychological disorders) The perspective that suggests that abnormal behaviour stems from childhood conflicts over opposing wishes regarding sex and aggression (Module 37, p. 395)

psychoanalytic theory Freud's theory that unconscious forces act as determinants of personality (Module 31, p. 336)

psychodynamic approaches to personality Approaches that assume that personality is motivated by inner forces and conflicts about which people have little awareness and over which they have no control (Module 31, p. 336)

psychodynamic perspective The approach based on the view that behaviour is motivated by unconscious inner forces over which the individual has little control (Module 2, p. 13)

psychodynamic therapy Therapy that seeks to bring unresolved past conflicts and unacceptable impulses from the unconscious into the conscious, where patients may deal with the problems more effectively (Module 40, p. 428)

psychological tests Standard measures devised to assess behaviour objectively; used by psychologists to help people make decisions about their lives and understand more about themselves (Module 33, p. 354)

psychology The scientific study of behaviour and mental processes (Module 1, p. 4)

psychoneuroimmunology (PNI) The study of the relationship among psychological factors, the immune system, and the brain (Module 34, p. 365)

psychophysics The study of the relationship between the physical aspects of stimuli and our psychological experience of them (Module 8, p. 77)

psychophysiological disorders Medical problems influenced by an interaction of psychological, emotional, and physical difficulties (Module 34, p. 369)

psychosexual stages Developmental periods that children pass through during which they encounter conflicts between the demands of society and their own sexual urges (Module 31, p. 338)

psychosocial development Development of individuals' interactions and understanding of each other and of their knowledge and understanding of themselves as members of society (Module 28, p. 307)

psychosurgery Brain surgery once used to reduce the symptoms of mental disorder but rarely used today (Module 42, p. 448)

psychotherapy Treatment in which a trained professional—a therapist—uses psychological techniques to help a person overcome psychological difficulties and disorders, resolve problems in living, or bring about personal growth (Module 40, p. 427)

puberty The period at which maturation of the sexual organs occurs, beginning at about age 11 or 12 for girls and 13 or 14 for boys (Module 29, p. 316)

punishment A stimulus that decreases the probability that a previous behaviour will occur again (Module 16, p. 157)

random assignment to condition A procedure in which participants are assigned to different experimental groups or "conditions" on the basis of chance and chance alone (Module 3, p. 29)

rapid eye movement (REM) sleep Sleep occupying 20 percent of an adult's sleeping time, characterized by increased heart rate, blood pressure, and breathing rate; erections; eye movements; and the experience of dreaming (Module 12, p. 117)

rational-emotive behaviour therapy A form of therapy that attempts to restructure a person's belief system into a more realistic, rational, and logical set of views by challenging dysfunctional beliefs that maintain irrational behaviour (Module 40, p. 434)

reactance A negative emotional and cognitive reaction that results from the restriction of one's freedom (Module 36, p. 381)

recall Memory task in which specific information must be retrieved (Module 19, p. 188)

reciprocity-of-liking effect A tendency to like those who like us (Module 46, p. 475)

recognition Memory task in which individuals are presented with a stimulus and asked whether they have been exposed to it in the past or to identify it from a list of alternatives (Module 19, p. 188)

reflex An automatic, involuntary response to an incoming stimulus (Module 7, p. 65)

reflexes Unlearned, involuntary responses that occur automatically in the presence of certain stimuli (Module 28, p. 297)

rehearsal The repetition of information that has entered short-term memory (Module 18, p. 179)

reinforcement The process by which a stimulus increases the probability that a preceding behaviour will be repeated (Module 16, p. 153)

reinforcer Any stimulus that increases the probability that a preceding behaviour will occur again (Module 16, p. 154)

reliability The property by which tests measure consistently what they are trying to measure (Module 23, p. 240)

replicated research Research that is repeated, sometimes using other procedures, settings, and groups of participants, to increase confidence in prior findings (Module 3, p. 32)

repression The primary defence mechanism in which unacceptable or unpleasant id impulses are pushed back into the unconscious (Module 31, p. 340)

resting state The state in which there is a negative electrical charge of about –70 millivolts within a neuron (Module 5, p. 46)

reticular formation The part of the brain extending from the medulla through the pons and made up of groups of nerve cells that can immediately activate other parts of the brain to produce general bodily arousal (Module 6, p. 54)

retina The part of the eye that converts the electromagnetic energy of light to electrical impulses for transmission to the brain (Module 9, p. 82)

retroactive interference Interference in which there is difficulty in the recall of information learned earlier because of later exposure to different material (Module 20, p. 201)

retrograde amnesia Amnesia in which memory is lost for occurrences prior to a certain event (Module 20, p. 202)

reuptake The reabsorption of neurotransmitters by a terminal button (Module 5, p. 50)

rods Thin, cylindrical receptor cells in the retina that are highly sensitive to light (Module 9, p. 83)

Rorschach test A test that involves showing a series of symmetrical visual stimuli to people who then are asked what the figures represent to them (Module 33, p. 359)

Schachter-Singer theory of emotion The belief that emotions are determined jointly by a nonspecific kind of physiological arousal and its interpretation, based on environmental cues (Module 26, p. 278)

schedules of reinforcement Different patterns of frequency and timing of reinforcement following desired behaviour (Module 16, p. 159)

schemas Organized bodies of information stored in memory that bias the way new information is interpreted, stored, and recalled (Module 19, p. 193)

schizophrenia A class of disorders in which severe distortion of reality occurs (Module 38, p. 410)

scientific method The approach through which psychologists systematically acquire knowledge and understanding about behaviour and other phenomena of interest (Module 3, p. 21)

self-actualization A state of self-fulfillment in which people realize their highest potential in their own unique way (Module 24, p. 254)

self-efficacy Belief in one's personal capabilities. Self-efficacy underlies people's faith in their ability to carry out a particular behaviour or produce a desired outcome (Module 32, p. 349)

self-help groups People who have experienced similar problems get together to discuss their shared feelings and experiences without a professional therapist (Module 41, p. 439)

self-report measures A method of gathering data about people by asking them questions about a sample of their behaviour (Module 33, p. 356)

self-serving bias The tendency to attribute personal success to personal factors (skill, ability, or effort) and to attribute failure to factors outside oneself (Module 43, p. 461)

semantic memory Memory for general knowledge and facts about the world, as well as memory for the rules of logic that are used to deduce other facts (Module 18, p. 182)

semantic networks Mental representations of clusters of interconnected information (Module 18, p. 184)

semantics The rules governing the meaning of words and sentences (Module 22, p. 225)

semicircular canals Three tube-like structures of the inner ear containing fluid that sloshes through them when the head moves, signalling rotational or angular movement to the brain (Module 10, p. 93)

sensation The activation of the sense organs by a source of physical energy (Module 8, p. 76)

sensorimotor stage According to Piaget, the stage from birth to 2 years, during which a child has little competence in representing the environment by using images, language, or other symbols (Module 28, p. 309)

sensory (afferent) neurons Neurons that transmit information from the perimeter of the body to the central nervous system (Module 7, p. 65)

sensory adaptation An adjustment in sensory capacity after prolonged exposure to unchanging stimuli (Module 8, p. 79)

sensory area The site in the brain of the tissue that corresponds to each of the senses, with the degree of sensitivity related to the amount of the tissue (Module 6, p. 57)

sensory memory The initial, momentary storage of information, lasting only an instant (Module 18, p. 177)

sequential research A research method that combines cross-sectional and longitudinal research by considering a number of different age groups and examining them at several points in time (Module 27, p. 291)

shaping The process of teaching a complex behaviour by rewarding closer and closer approximations of the desired behaviour (Module 16, p. 155)

short-term memory Memory that holds information for fifteen to twenty-five seconds (Module 18, p. 177)

significant outcome Meaningful results that make it possible for researchers to feel confident that they have confirmed their hypotheses (Module 3, p. 32)

situational causes (of behaviour) Perceived causes of behaviour that are based on environmental factors (Module 43, p. 460)

skin senses The senses of touch, pressure, temperature, and pain (Module 10, p. 96)

social cognition The cognitive processes by which people understand and make sense of others and themselves (Module 43, p. 458)

social cognitive approaches to personality Theories that emphasize the influence of a person's cognitions—thoughts, feelings, expectations, and values—as well as observation of others' behaviour, in determining personality (Module 32, p. 348)

social influence The process by which the actions of an individual or group affect the behaviour of others (Module 44, p. 464)

social neuroscience The subfield of social psychology that seeks to identify the neural basis of social behaviour (Module 45, p. 471)

social psychology The scientific study of how people's thoughts, feelings, and actions are affected by others (Module 43, p. 455)

social support A mutual network of caring, interested others (Module 34, p. 375)

social supporter A group member whose dissenting views make nonconformity to the group easier (Module 44, p. 465)

sociocultural perspective (on psychological disorders) The perspective that assumes that people's behaviour—both normal and abnormal—is shaped by the kind of family group, society, and culture in which they live (Module 37, p. 396)

somatic division The part of the peripheral nervous system that specializes in the control of voluntary movements and the communication of information to and from the sense organs (Module 7, p. 66)

somatoform disorders Psychological difficulties that take on a physical (somatic) form, but for which there is no medical cause (Module 38, p. 416)

sound The movement of air molecules brought about by a source of vibration (Module 10, p. 89)

specific phobia Intense, irrational fears of specific objects or situations (Module 38, p. 403)

spinal cord A bundle of neurons that leaves the brain and runs down the length of the back and is the main means for transmitting messages between the brain and the body (Module 7, p. 64)

spontaneous recovery The re-emergence of an extinguished conditioned response after a period of rest and with no further conditioning (Module 15, p. 148)

spontaneous remission Recovery without treatment (Module 41, p. 440)

stage 1 sleep The state of transition between wakefulness and sleep, characterized by relatively rapid, low-amplitude brain waves (Module 12, p. 116)

stage 2 sleep A sleep deeper than that of stage 1, characterized by a slower, more regular wave pattern, along with momentary interruptions of "sleep spindles" (Module 12, p. 116)

stage 3 sleep A sleep characterized by slow brain waves, with greater peaks and valleys in the wave pattern than in stage 2 sleep (Module 12, p. 116)

stage 4 sleep The deepest stage of sleep, during which we are least responsive to outside stimulation (Module 12, p. 116)

status The social rank held within a group (Module 44, p. 465)

stereotype A set of generalized beliefs and expectations about a particular group and its members (Module 45, p. 470)

stimulants Drugs that have an arousal effect on the central nervous system, causing a rise in heart rate, blood pressure, and muscular tension (Module 14, p. 131)

stimulus Energy that produces a response in a sense organ (Module 8, p. 76)

stimulus discrimination The process that occurs if two stimuli are sufficiently distinct from one another that one evokes a conditioned response but the other does not; the ability to differentiate between stimuli (Module 15, p. 150)

stimulus generalization A process in which, after a stimulus has been conditioned to produce a particular response, stimuli that are similar to the original stimulus produce the same response (Module 15, p. 149)

stress A person's response to events that are threatening or challenging (Module 34, p. 366)

structuralism Wilhelm Wundt's approach, which focuses on uncovering the fundamental mental components of consciousness, thinking, and other kinds of mental states and activities (Module 2, p. 9)

subjective well-being People's own evaluation of their lives in terms of both their thoughts and their emotions (Module 36, p. 383)

superego According to Freud, the final personality structure to develop; it represents the rights and wrongs of society as handed down by a person's parents, teachers, and other important figures (Module 31, p. 338)

survey research Research in which people chosen to represent a larger population are asked a series of questions about their behaviour, thoughts, or attitudes (Module 3, p. 24)

sympathetic division The part of the autonomic division of the nervous system that acts to prepare the body for action in stressful situations, engaging all the organism's resources to respond to a threat (Module 7, p. 67)

synapse The space between two neurons where the axon of a sending neuron communicates with the dendrites of a receiving neuron by using chemical messages (Module 5, p. 48)

synaptogenesis The process by which the web of connections between neurons becomes more complex throughout life (Module 6, p. 60)

syntax Ways in which words and phrases can be combined to form sentences (Module 22, p. 225)

systematic desensitization A behavioural technique in which gradual exposure to an anxiety-producing stimulus is paired with relaxation to extinguish the response of anxiety (Module 40, p. 432)

telegraphic speech   Sentences in which words not critical to the message are left out (Module 22, p. 226)

temperament   The innate disposition that emerges early in life (Module 28, p. 307)

teratogens   Environmental agents such as a drug, chemical, virus, or other factor that produce a birth defect (Module 27, p. 294)

terminal buttons   Small bulges at the end of axons that send messages to other neurons (Module 5, p. 45)

test standardization   A technique used to validate questions in personality tests by studying the responses of people with known diagnoses (Module 33, p. 357)

thalamus   The part of the brain located in the middle of the central core that acts primarily to relay information about the senses (Module 6, p. 55)

Thematic Apperception Test (TAT)   A test consisting of a series of pictures about which a person is asked to write a story (Module 33, p. 359)

theories   Plausible explanations for existing and true facts (Module 3, p. 21)

theory of multiple intelligences   Gardner's intelligence theory that proposes that there are eight distinct spheres of intelligence (Module 23, p. 233)

thinking   The manipulation of mental representations of information (Module 21, p. 210)

tip-of-the-tongue phenomenon   The inability to recall information that one realizes one knows—a result of the difficulty of retrieving information from long-term memory (Module 19, p. 188)

tolerance   An insensitivity to the effects of a drug caused by repeated use of the drug, such that larger amounts of the drug are needed to produce the same effect (Module 14, p. 138)

top-down processing   Perception that is guided by higher-level knowledge, experience, expectations, and motivations (Module 11, p. 101)

trait theory   A model of personality that seeks to identify the basic traits necessary to describe personality (Module 32, p. 344)

traits   Consistent personality characteristics and behaviours displayed in different situations (Module 32, p. 344)

transcranial magnetic stimulation (TMS)   A depression treatment in which a precise magnetic pulse is directed to a specific area of the brain (Module 42, p. 448)

transference   The transfer of feelings to a psychoanalyst of love or anger that had been originally directed to a patient's parents or other authority figures (Module 40, p. 430)

transsexuals   People whose sexual identification is with the opposite gender from that they were born with; they feel they are trapped in the body of the other gender (Module 25, p. 269)

treatment   The manipulation implemented by the experimenter (Module 3, p. 28)

trichromatic theory of colour vision   The theory that there are three kinds of cones in the retina, each of which responds primarily to a specific range of wavelengths (Module 9, p. 86)

trust-versus-mistrust stage   According to Erikson, the first stage of psychosocial development, occurring from birth to age 1½ years, during which time infants develop feelings of trust or lack of trust (Module 28, p. 307)

Type A behaviour pattern   A cluster of behaviours involving hostility, competitiveness, time urgency, and feeling driven (Module 35, p. 376)

Type B behaviour pattern   A cluster of behaviours characterized by a patient, cooperative, noncompetitive, and non-aggressive manner (Module 35, p. 376)

unconditional positive regard   An attitude of acceptance and respect on the part of an observer, no matter what a person says or does (Module 32, p. 351)

unconditioned response (UOR)   A response that is natural and needs no training (e.g., salivation at the smell of food) (Module 15, p. 145)

unconditioned stimulus (UCS)   A stimulus that naturally brings about a particular response without having been learned (Module 15, p. 145)

unconscious wish fulfillment theory   Sigmund Freud's theory that dreams represent unconscious wishes that dreamers desire to see fulfilled (Module 12, p. 119)

unconscious   A part of the personality that contains the memories, knowledge, beliefs, feelings, urges, drives, and instincts of which the individual is not aware (Module 31, p. 336)

uninvolved parents   Parents who show little interest in their children and are emotionally detached (Module 28, p. 306)

universal grammar   Noam Chomsky's theory that all the world's languages share a common underlying structure (Module 22, p. 228)

validity   The property by which tests actually measure what they are supposed to measure (Module 23, p. 241)

variable-interval schedule   A schedule by which the time between reinforcements varies around some average rather than being fixed (Module 16, p. 161)

variable-ratio schedule   A schedule by which reinforcement occurs after a varying number of responses rather than a fixed number (Module 16, p. 160)

variables   Behaviours, events, or other characteristics that can change, or vary, in some way (Module 3, p. 25)

visual illusions   Physical stimuli that consistently produce errors in perception (Module 11, p. 104)

wear-and-tear theories of aging   The mechanical functions of the body simply work less efficiently as people age (Module 30, p. 325)

Weber's law   A basic law of psychophysics stating that a just noticeable difference is a constant proportion to the intensity of an initial stimulus (rather than a constant amount) (Module 8, p. 79)

weight set point   The particular level of weight that the body strives to maintain (Module 25, p. 261)

working memory   A set of active, temporary memory stores that actively manipulate and rehearse information (Module 18, p. 180)

zone of proximal development (ZPD)   According to Lev Vygotsky, the level at which a child can almost, but not fully, comprehend or perform a task on his or her own (Module 28, p. 313)

zygote   The new cell formed by the union of an egg and sperm (Module 27, p. 292)

References

AAA Foundation for Traffic Safety. (2008). Cell phones and driving: Research update. Retrieved from www.aaafoundation.org/pdf/CellPhonesandDrivingReport.pdf

AAA Foundation for Traffic Safety. (2009). Distracted Driving the Top Reason that 35 Percent of Drivers Feel Less Safe Than Five Years Ago, According to the AAA Foundation. Retrieved from www.aaafoundation.org/pdf/2009TSCIndexPR.pdf

Aazh, H., & Moore, B. C. J. (2007). Dead regions in the cochlea at 4 kHz in elderly adults: Relation to absolute threshold, steepness of audiogram, and pure-tone average. *Journal of the American Academy of Audiology, 18,* 97–106.

Abboud, L. (2005, July 27). The next phase in psychiatry. *The Wall Street Journal,* pp. D1, D5.

Ablon, J. S., & Jones, E. E. (2005). On analytic process. *Journal of the American Psychoanalytic Association, 53,* 541–568.

Aboitiz, F., Garcia, R., & Brunetti, E. (2006). The origin of Broca's area and its connections from an ancestral working memory network. In Y. Grodzinsky & K. Amunts, *Broca's region.* New York: Oxford University Press.

Abraham, P. F., & Calabrese, J. R. (2007). Review of: Lithium treatment of mood disorders: A practical guide (6th rev. ed.). *Bipolar Disorders, 9,* 548.

Abramowitz, J. S., Olatunji, B. O., & Deacon, B. J. (2007). Health anxiety, hypochondriasis, and the anxiety disorders. *Behavior Therapy, 38,* 86–94.

Abrams, R. L., Klinger, M. R., & Greenwald, A. G. (2002). Subliminal words activate semantic categories (not automated responses). *Psychonomic Bulletin & Review, 9,* 100–106.

Accardi, M., & Milling, L. (2009, August). The effectiveness of hypnosis for reducing procedure-related pain in children and adolescents: A comprehensive methodological review. *Journal of Behavioral Medicine, 32,* 328–339.

Accardo, P. J., & Capute, A. J. (1998). Mental retardations. *Mental Retardation & Developmental Disabilities Research Reviews, 4,* 2–5.

Adams, K. B. (2004). Changing investment in activities and interests in elders' lives: Theory and measurement. *International Journal of Aging and Human Development, 58,* 87–108.

Adler, J. (1984, April 23). The fight to conquer fear. *Newsweek,* pp. 66–72.

Advokat, C. (2005). Differential effects of clozapine versus other antipsychotics on clinical outcome and dopamine release in the brain. *Essential Psychopharmacology, 6,* 73–90.

Affleck, G., Tennen, H., Urrows, S., & Higgins, P. (1994). Person and contextual features of daily stress reactivity: Individual differences in relations of undesirable daily events with mood disturbance and chronic pain intensity. *Journal of Personality and Social Psychology, 66,* 329–340.

Aftanas, L., & Golosheykin, S. (2005). Impact of regular meditation practice on EEG activity at rest and during evoked negative emotions. *International Journal of Neuroscience, 115,* 893–909.

Ahiima, R. S., & Osei, S. Y. (2004). Leptin signaling. *Physiology and Behavior, 81,* 223–241.

Aiken, L. (2000). *Dying, death, and bereavement* (4th ed.). Mahwah, NJ: Erlbaum.

Aiken, L. R. (1996). *Assessment of intellectual functioning* (2nd ed.). New York: Plenum.

Aiken, L. R. (1997). *Psychological testing and assessment* (9th ed.). Needham Heights, MA: Allyn & Bacon.

Ainsworth, M. D. S., Blehar, M. C., Waters, E., & Wall, S. (1978). *Patterns of attachment: A psychological study of the strange situation.* Hillsdale, NJ: Erlbaum.

Ajzen, I. (2002). Residual effects of past on later behavior: Habituation and reasoned action perspectives. *Personality and Social Psychology Review, 6,* 107–122.

Akil, H., & Morano, M. I. (1996). The biology of stress: From periphery to brain. In S. J. Watson (Ed.), *Biology of schizophrenia and affective disease.* Washington, DC: American Psychiatric Press.

Aknin, L. B., Barrington-Leigh, C. P., Dunn, E. W., Helliwell, J. F., Burns, J., Biswas-Diener, R., & Norton, M. I. (2013). Prosocial spending and well-being: Cross-cultural evidence for a psychological universal. *Journal of Personality and Social Psychology.* Retrieved from www.hbs.edu/faculty/Publication%20Files/11-038.pdf

Aknin, L. B., Hamlin, J., & Dunn, E. W. (2012). Giving leads to happiness in young children. *Plos ONE, 7,* 88–93.

Alberts, A., Elkind, D., & Ginsberg, S. (2007). The personal fable and risk-taking in early adolescence. *Journal of Youth and Adolescence, 36,* 71–76.

Alho, K., Vorobyev, V. A., Medvedev, S. V., Pakhomov, S. V., Starchenko, M. G., Terganiemi, M., & Näätänen, R. (2006). Selective attention to human voice enhances brain activity bilaterally in the superior temporal sulcus. *Brain Research, 1075,* 142–150.

Alloy, L. B., Jacobson, N. S., & Acocella, J. (1999). *Abnormal psychology* (8th ed.). New York: McGraw-Hill.

Allport, G. W. (1961). *Pattern and growth in personality.* New York: Holt, Rinehart and Winston.

Allport, G. W. (1966). Traits revisited. *American Psychologist, 21,* 1–10.

Allport, G. W., & Postman, L. J. (1958). The basic psychology of rumor. In E. D. Maccoby, T. M. Newcomb, & E. L. Hartley (Eds.), *Readings in social psychology* (3rd ed.). New York: Holt, Rinehart and Winston.

Aloia, M. S., Smith, K., & Arnedt, J. T. (2007). Brief behavioral therapies reduce early positive airway pressure discontinuation rates in sleep apnea syndrome: Preliminary findings *Behavioral Sleep Medicine, 5,* 89–104.

Alonso, A., Alonso, S., & Piper, W. (2003). Group psychotherapy. In G. Stricker, T. A. Widiger, et al. (Eds.), *Handbook of psychology: Clinical psychology* (Vol. 8). New York: Wiley.

American Psychiatric Association. (2013). Intellectual disability. Retrieved from www.dsm5.org/Documents/Intellectual%20Disability%20Fact%20Sheet.pdf.

American Psychological Association (APA). (2000). Psychology careers for the twenty-first century. Washington, DC: American Psychological Association.

American Psychological Association (APA). (2002, August 21). *APA ethics code, 2002.* Washington, DC: American Psychological Association.

American Psychological Association (APA). (2007). *Where psychologists work.* Washington, DC: American Psychological Association.

American Psychological Association Presidential Task Force on Evidence-Based Practice. (2006). *Evidence-based practice in psychology, 61,* 271–285.

American Psychological Association Task Force on Intelligence. (1996). *Intelligence: Knowns and unknowns.* Washington, DC: American Psychological Association.

American Psychological Association. (APA). (1993, January/February). Subgroup norming and the Civil Rights Act. *Psychological Science Agenda, 5,* 6.

American Speech-Language-Hearing Association. (2006). Poll commissioned by American Speech-Language-Hearing Association, survey suggests multi-pronged prevention needed to head off risk to nation's hearing health: Hearing loss symptoms reported in high school students and adults. Retrieved from www.asha.org/about/news/2006/release-hearing-loss.htm.

American Speech-Language-Hearing Association. (2006). Survey of teens and adults about the use of personal electronic devices and head phones: Summary. Retrieved from www.asha.org/about/news/atitbtot/zogby.htm.

References

American Speech-Language-Hearing Association (2015). Retrieved from www.asha.org/public/hearing/disorders/hearing_protect.htm.

Amos, A., Wiltshire, S., & Haw, S. (2006). Ambivalence and uncertainty: Experiences of and attitudes towards addiction and smoking cessation in the mid-to-late teens. *Health Education Research, 21,* 181–191.

Anagnostou, E., Latha, S., Chaplin, W., Bartz, J., Halpern, D., & Wasserman, S. (2012). Intranasal oxytocin versus placebo in the treatment of adults with autism spectrum disorders: A randomized controlled trial. Molecular Autism, 3, 16-25.

Anastasi, A., & Urbina, S. (1997). *Psychological testing* (7th ed.). Englewood Cliffs, NJ: Prentice Hall.

Anderson, B. F. (1980). *The complete thinker: A handbook of techniques for creative and critical problem solving.* Englewood Cliffs, NJ: Prentice Hall.

Anderson, C., & Carnagey, N. (2009). Causal effects of violent sports video games on aggression: Is it competitiveness or violent content? *Journal of Experimental Social Psychology, 45,* 731–739.

Anderson, C., & Home, J. A. (2006). Sleepiness enhances distraction during monotonous task. *Sleep: Journal of Sleep and Sleep Disorders Research, 29,* 573–576.

Anderson, C., Carnagey, N. L., Flanagan, M., Benjamin, A. J., Jr., Eubanks, J., & Valentine, J. C. (2004). Violent video games: Specific effects of violent content on aggressive thoughts and behavior. In M. P. Zanna (Ed.), *Advances in experimental social psychology* (Vol. 36). San Diego, CA: Elsevier Academic Press.

Anderson, J. A., & Adams, M. (1992). Acknowledging the learning styles of diverse student populations: Implications for instructional design. *New Directions for Teaching and Learning, 49,* 19–33.

Anderson, J. R. (1981). Interference: The relationship between response latency and response accuracy. *Journal of Experimental Psychology: Human Learning and Memory, 7,* 311–325.

Andrasik, F. (2006). Psychophysiological disorders: Headache as a case in point. In F. Andrasik, *Comprehensive handbook of personality and psychopathology, Vol. 2: Adult psychopathology.* Hoboken, NJ: John Wiley & Sons.

Angier, N. (1991, January 22). A potent peptide prompts an urge to cuddle. *The New York Times,* p. C1.

Angier, N. (2007, October 23). In the dreamscape of nightmares, clues to why we dream at all. *The New York Times: NYTimes Online.* Retrieved from www.nytimes.com/2007/10/23/science/23angi.html?pagewanted=print.

Angoff, W. H. (1988). The nature-nurture debate, aptitudes, and group differences. *American Psychologist, 43,* 713–720.

Ansaldo, A. I., Arguin, M., & Roch Locours, L. A. (2002). The contribution of the right cerebral hemisphere to the recovery from aphasia: A single longitudinal case study. *Brain Languages, 82,* 206–222.

Antonini, A., & Barone, P. (2008, December). Dopamine agonist-based strategies in the treatment of Parkinson's disease. *Neurological Sciences, 29,* S371–SS374.

Antony, M. M., Brown, T. A., & Barlow, D. H. (1992). Current perspectives on panic and panic disorder. *Current Directions in Psychological Science, 1,* 79–82.

Aponte, J. F., & Wohl, J. (2000). *Psychological intervention and cultural diversity.* Needham Heights, MA: Allyn & Bacon.

Arafat, I., & Cotton, W. L. (1974). Masturbation practices of males and females. *Journal of Sex Research, 10,* 293–307.

Arbuthnott, A., & Sharpe, D. (2009). The effect of physician–patient collaboration on patient adherence in non-psychiatric medicine. *Patient Education and Counseling, 77,* 60–67.

Arena, J. M. (1984, April). A look at the opposite sex. *Newsweek on Campus,* p. 21.

Ariyanto, A., Hornsey, M. J., & Gallois, C. (2006). Group-directed criticism in Indonesia: Role of message source and audience. *Asian Journal of Social Psychology, 9,* 96–102.

Arlin, P. K. (1989). The problem of the problem. In J. D. Sinnott (Ed.), *Everyday problem solving: Theory and applications.* New York: Praeger.

Arnett, J. J. (2000). Emerging adulthood. *American Psychologist, 55,* 469–480.

Arnett, J. J. (2006). *Emerging adulthood: The winding road from the late teens through the twenties* New York: Oxford University Press.

Arnett, J. J. (2007), Afterword: Aging out of care—Toward realizing the possibilities of emerging adulthood. *New Directions for Youth Development, 113,* 151–161,

Asch, S. E. (1946). Forming impressions of personality. *Journal of Abnormal and Social Psychology, 41,* 258–290.

Asch, S. E. (1951). Effects of group pressure upon the modification and distortion of judgments. In H. Guetzkow (Ed.), *Groups, leadership, and men.* Pittsburgh: Carnegie Press.

Aschcraft, M. H. (1994). *Human memory and cognition* (2nd ed.). New York: Harper-Collins.

Ashley, K. B. (2013). The science on sexual orientation: A review of the recent literature. *Journal of Gay & Lesbian Mental Health, 17,* 175–182.

Atkinson, H. (Ed.). (1997, January 21). Understanding your diagnosis. *Health-News,* p. 3.

Atkinson, H. G. (2003, August). Are you a "good" patient? *Health-News,* p. 5.

Atkinson, R. C., & Shiffrin, R. M. (1968). Human memory: A proposed system and its control processes. In K. W. Spence & J. T. Spence (Eds.), *The psychology of learning and motivation: Advances in research and theory* (Vol. 2). New York: Academic Press.

Atkinson, R. C., & Shiffrin, R. M. (1971). The control of short-term memory. *Scientific American, 225,* pp. 82–90.

Auer, J. A., Goodship, A., Arnoczky, S., Pearce, S., Price, J., Claes, L., von Rechenberg, B., Hofmann-Amtenbrinck, M., Schneider, E., Muller-Terpitz, R., Thiele, F., Rippe, K. P., & Grainger, D. W. (2007). Refining animal models in fracture research: seeking consensus for changing the agenda in optimising both animal welfare and scientific validity for appropriate biomedical use. *BMC Musculoskeletal Disorders, 8,* 72.

Auld, F., Hyman, M., & Rudzinski, D. (2005). Theory and strategy of dream interpretation. In F. Auld & M. Hyman (Eds.), *Resolution of inner conflict: An introduction to psychoanalytic therapy* (2nd ed.). Washington, DC: American Psychological Association.

Avenell, A. Brown, T. J., McGee, M. A., Campbell, M. K., Grant, A. M., Broom, J., Jung, R. T., & Smith, W. C. S. (2004). What are the long-term benefits of weight reducing diets in adults? A systematic review of randomized controlled trials. *Journal of Human Nutrition and Dietetics, 17,* 317–335.

Averill, J. R. (1975). A semantic atlas of emotional concepts. *Catalog of Selected Documents in Psychology, 5,* 330.

Avery, D., McKay, P., & Wilson, D. (2008). What are the odds? How demographic similarity affects the prevalence of perceived employment discrimination. *Journal of Applied Psychology, 93,* 235–249.

Babson, K., Feldner, M., Trainor, C., & Smith, R. (2009, September). An experimental investigation of the effects of acute sleep deprivation on panic-relevant biological challenge responding. *Behavior Therapy, 40,* 239–250.

Baddeley, A. D. (1990). *Human memory: Theory and practice.* Boston: Allyn & Bacon.

Baddeley, A., & Wilson, B. (1985). Phonological coding and short-term memory in patients without speech. *Journal of Memory and Language, 24,* 490–502.

Baddeley, A., Chincotta, D., & Adlam, A. (2001). Working memory and the control of action: Evidence from task switching. *Journal of Experimental Psychology: General, 130,* 641–657.

Baddeley, A., Gathercole, S., & Papagno, C. (1998). The phonological loop as a language learning device. *Psychological Review, 105,* 158–173.

Baer, J. S., Sampson, P. D., Barr, H. M., Connor, P. D., & Streissguth, A. P. (2003). A 21-year longitudinal analysis of the effects of prenatal alcohol exposure on young adult drinking. *Obstetrical and Gynecological Survey, 58,* 638–639.

Bahrick, H. P., Hall, L. K., & Berger, S. A. (1996). Accuracy and distortion in memory for high school grades. *Psychological Science, 7,* 265–269.

Bai, L. (2005). Children at play: A childhood beyond the Confucian shadow. *Childhood: A Global Journal of Child Research, 12,* 9–32.

Bains, O. S. (2006). Insomnia: Difficulty falling and staying asleep. In N. F. Watson, & B. V. Bradley, *Clinician's guide to sleep disorders*. Philadelphia: Taylor & Francis.

Bair, D. (2003). *Jung: A biography*. New York: Little, Brown, and Company.

Bakermans-Kranenburg, M. J., van Ijzendoorn, M. H., & Juffer, F. (2003). Less is more: Meta-analyses of sensitivity and attachment interventions in early childhood. *Psychological Bulletin, 129*, 195–215.

Balaban, C. D. (2002). Neural substrates linking balance control and anxiety [Special issue: The Pittsburgh special issue]. *Physiology and Behavior, 77*, 469–475.

Ball, D. (2004). Genetic approaches to alcohol dependence. *British Journal of Psychiatry, 185*, 449–451.

Ball, H., Arseneault, L., Taylor, A., Maughan, B., Caspi, A., & Moffitt, T. (2008, January). Genetic and environmental influences on victims, bullies and bully-victims in childhood. *Journal of Child Psychology and Psychiatry, 49*, 104–112.

Baltes, P. B., & Kunzmann, U. (2003). Wisdom. *Psychologist, 16*, 131–133.

Bandura, A. (1977). *Social learning theory*. Englewood Cliffs, NJ: Prentice Hall.

Bandura, A. (1986). *Social foundations of thought and action: A social cognitive theory*. Englewood Cliffs, NJ: Prentice Hall.

Bandura, A. (1994). Social cognitive theory of mass communication. In J. Bryant, & D. Zillmann (Eds.), *Media effects: Advances in theory and research: LEA's communication series*. Hillsdale, NJ: Erlbaum.

Bandura, A. (1999). Social cognitive theory of personality. In D. Cervone & Y. Shod (Eds.), *The coherence of personality*. New York: Guilford.

Bandura, A. (2000). Self-efficacy: The foundation of agency. In W. J. Perrig & A. Grob (Eds.), *Control of human behavior, mental processes, and consciousness: Essays in honor of the 60th birthday of August Flammer*. Mahwah, NJ: Erlbaum.

Bandura, A. (2002). Social cognitive theory in cultural context. *Applied Psychology: An International Review, 151*, 269–290.

Bandura, A. (2004). Swimming against the mainstream: The early years from chilly tributary to transformative mainstream. *Behaviour Research and Therapy, 42*, 613–630.

Bandura, A., & Locke, E. A. (2003). Negative self-efficacy and goal effects revisited. *Journal of Applied Psychology, 88*, 87–99.

Bandura, A., Grusec, J. E., & Menlove, F. L. (1967). Vicarious extinction of avoidance behavior. *Journal of Personality and Social Psychology, 5*, 16–23.

Bandura, A., Ross, D., & Ross, S. (1963a). Imitation of film-mediated aggressive models. *Journal of Abnormal and Social Psychology, 66*, 3–11.

Bandura, A., Ross, D., & Ross, S. (1963b). Vicarious reinforcement and imitative learning. *Journal of Abnormal and Social Psychology, 67*, 601–607.

Banich, T., & Heller, W. (1998). Evolving perspectives on lateralization of function. *Current Directions in Psychological Science, 7*, 1–2.

Banks, J. A. (2006). Improving race relations in schools: From theory and research to practice. *Journal of Social Issues, 62*, 607–614.

Baraas, R. C., Foster, D. H., & Amano, K. (2006). Anomalous trichromats' judgments of surface color in natural scenes under different daylights. *Neuroscience, 23*, 629–635.

Barandiaran, A. A., Pascual, A. C., & Samaniego, C. M. (2006). A criticism of the Kohlberg theory: The moral development in adults and educative implications. *Revista de Psicología General y Aplicada, 59*, 165–182.

Bargh, J. A., & Chartrand, T. L. (2000). The mind in the middle: A practical guide to priming and automaticity research. In H. T. Reis & C. M. Judd (Eds.), *Handbook of research methods in social and personality psychology*. New York: Cambridge University Press.

Barker, J., & Jones, M. (2008, June). The effects of hypnosis on self-efficacy, affect, and soccer performance: A case study. *Journal of Clinical Sport Psychology, 2*, 127–147.

Barkley, R. (2000). *Taking charge of ADHD* (rev. ed.). New York: Guilford Press.

Barkley, R. (2005). *ADHD and the nature of self-control*. New York: Guildford.

Barlow, D. H. (2007). *Clinical handbook of psychological disorders: A step-by-step treatment manual* (4th ed.). New York: Guilford Press.

Barmeyer, C. I. (2004). Learning styles and their impact on cross-cultural training: An international comparison in France, Germany and Quebec. *International Journal of Intercultural Relations, 28*, 577–594.

Barnes, V. A., Davis, H. C., Murzynowski, J., & Treiber, F. A. (2004). Impact of meditation on resting and ambulatory blood pressure and heart rate in youth. *Medicine, 66*, 909–914.

Barnett, J. E., Wise, E. H., & Johnson-Greene, D. (2007). Informed consent: Too much of a good thing or not enough? *Professional Psychology: Research and Practice, 38*, 179–186.

Baron, R. S. (2005). So right it's wrong: Groupthink and the ubiquitous nature of polarized group decision making. In M. P. Zanna (Ed.), *Advances in experimental social psychology* (Vol. 37). San Diego, CA: Elsevier Academic Press.

Barrett, L. F., & Wager, T. D. (2006). The structure of emotion: Evidence from neuroimaging studies. *Current Directions in Psychological Science, 15*, 79–83.

Barrick, M. R., & Mount, M.K. (1991). The big five dimensions and job performance: A meta-analysis. *Personnel Psychology, 44*, 1–26.

Barron, F. (1990). *Creativity and psychological health: Origins of personal vitality and creative freedom*. Buffalo, NY: Creative Education Foundation.

Barron, G., & Yechiam, E. (2002). Private e-mail requests and the diffusion of responsibility. *Computers in Human Behavior, 18*, 507–520.

Bartholow, B. D., Bushman, B. J., & Sestir, M. A. (2005). Chronic violent video game exposure and desensitization to violence: Behavioral and event-related brain potential data. *Journal of Experimental Social Psychology, 42*, 532–539.

Bartlett, F. (1932). *Remembering: A study in experimental and social psychology*. Cambridge, England: Cambridge University Press.

Bartlett, M. Y., & DeSteno, D. (2006). Gratitude and prosocial behavior: Helping when it costs you. *Psychological Science, 17*, 319–325.

Bartocci, G. (2004). Transcendence techniques and psychobiological mechanisms underlying religious experience. *Mental Health, Religion and Culture, 7*, 171–181.

Bartoshuk, L. (2000, July/August). The bitter with the sweet. *APS Observer, 11*, 33.

Bartoshuk, L., & Lucchina, L. (1997, January 13). Are you a supertaster? *U.S. News & World Report*, pp. 58–59.

Bartzokis, G., Nuechterlein, K. H., Lu, P. H., Gitlin, M., Rogers, S., & Mintz, J. (2003). Dysregulated brain development in adult men with schizophrenia: A magnetic resonance imaging study. *Biological Psychiatry, 53*, 412–421.

Baruss, I. (2003). *Alterations of consciousness: An empirical analysis for social scientists*. Washington, DC: American Psychological Association.

Basak, C., Boot, W., Voss, M., & Kramer, A. (2008). Can training in a real-time strategy video game attenuate cognitive decline in older adults? *Psychology and Aging, 23*, 765–777.

Bassottdi, G., Villanacci, V., Fisogni, S., Rossi, E., Baronio, P., Clerici, C., et al. (2007). Enteric glial cells and their role in gastrointestinal motor abnormalities: Introducing the neurogliopathies. *World Journal of Gastroenterology, 14*, 4035–4041.

Bates, E. (2005). Plasticity, localization, and language development. In S. T. Parker & J. Langer (Eds.), *Biology and knowledge revisited: From neurogenesis to psychogenesis*. Mahwah, NJ: Lawrence Erlbaum Associates.

Bates, R. (2002). Liking and similarity as predictors of multi-source ratings. *Personnel Review, 31*, 540–552.

Batson, C. D., & Powell, A. A. (2003). Altruism and prosocial behavior. In T. Millon & M. J. Lerner (Eds.), *Handbook of psychology: Personality and social psychology* (Vol. 5). New York: Wiley.

Battiste, M., & McLean, S. (2005). State of First Nations learning: Prepared for Canadian Council on Learning (CCL). Retrieved from www.ccl-cca.ca/NR/rdonlyres/4F9A3F29-7170-4812-ADA7-43CA468 F00ED/0/StateOfFirstNationsLearning.pdf.

Bauer, P. (2008). Toward a neuro-developmental account of the development of declarative memory. *Developmental Psychobiology, 50*, 19–31.

Baum, A. (1994). Behavioral, biological, and environmental interactions in disease processes. In S. Blumenthal, K. Matthews, & S. Weiss (Eds.), *New research frontiers in behavioral medicine: Proceedings of the National Conference.* Washington, DC: NIH Publications.

Baumeister, R. F., & Stillman, T. (2006). Erotic plasticity: Nature, culture, gender, and sexuality. In R. D. McAnulty, & M. M. Burnette, *Sex and sexuality, Vol 1: Sexuality today: Trends and controversies.* Westport, CT: Praeger Publishers/Greenwood Publishing.

Baumgartner, F. (2002). The effect of hardiness in the choice of coping strategies in stressful situations. *Studia Psychologica, 44,* 69–75.

Baumrind, D. (1971). Current patterns of parental authority. *Developmental Psychology Monographs, 4* (1, pt. 2).

Baumrind, D. (2005). Patterns of parental authority and adolescent autonomy. *New Directions for Child and Adolescent Development, 108,* 61–69.

Bayliss, D. M., Jarrold, C., Baddeley, A. D., & Gunn, D. M. (2005a). The relationship between short-term memory and working memory: Complex span made simple? *Memory, 13,* 414–421.

Bayliss, D. M., Jarrold, C., Baddeley, A. D., Gunn, D. M., & Leigh, E. (2005b). Mapping the developmental constraints on working memory span performance. *Developmental Psychology, 41,* 579–597.

Bayne, R. (2005). *Ideas and evidence: Critical reflections on MBTI® theory and practice.* Gainesville, FL: Center for Applications of Psychological Type, CAPT.

Baynes, K., Eliassenk J. C., Lutsep, H. L., & Gazzaniga, M. S. (1998, May 8). Modular organization of cognitive systems marked by interhemispheric integration. *Science, 280,* 902–905.

Bazalakova, M. H., Wright, J., Schneble, E. J., McDonald, M. P., Heilman, C. J., Levey, A. I., & Blakely, R. D. (2007). Deficits in acetylcholine homeostasis, receptors and behaviors in choline transporter heterozygous mice. *Genes, Brain & Behavior, 6,* 411–424.

Beardslee, W., Wright, E., Gladstone, T., & Forbes, P. (2007). Long-term effects from a randomized trial of two public health preventive interventions for parental depression. *Journal of Family Psychology, 21,* 703–713.

Beatty, J. (2000). *The human brain: Essentials of behavioral neuroscience.* Thousand Oaks, CA: Sage.

Beatty, W. W. (2002). Sex difference in geographical knowledge: Driving experience is not essential. *Journal of the International Neuropsychological Society, 8,* 804–810.

Beck, A. P., & Lewis, C. M. (Eds.). (2000). *The process of group psychotherapy: Systems for analyzing change.* Washington, DC: American Psychological Association.

Beck, A. T. (1995). Cognitive therapy: Past, present, and future. In M. J. Mahoney (Ed.), *Cognitive and constructive psychotherapies: Theory, research, and practice.* New York: Springer.

Beck, A. T. (2004). Cognitive therapy, behavior therapy, psychoanalysis, and pharmacotherapy: A cognitive continuum. In A. Freeman, M. J. Mahoney, P. Devito, & D. Martin (Eds.), *Cognition and Psychotherapy* (2nd ed.). New York: Springer Publishing Co.

Beck, A. T., & Emery, G., with Greenberg, R. L. (1985). *Anxiety disorders and phobias: A cognitive perspective.* New York: Basic Books.

Beck, A. T., & Rector, N. A. (2005). Cognitive approaches to schizophrenia: Theory and therapy. *Annual Review of Clinical Psychology, 1,* 577–606.

Beck, A. T., Freeman, A., & Davis, D. D. (2004). *Cognitive therapy of personality disorders* (2nd ed.). New York: Guilford Press.

Beck, H. P., Levinson, S., & Irons, G. (2009). Finding little Albert: A journey to John B. Watson's infant laboratory. *American Psychologist, 64,* 605–614.

Becker, B. E., & Luthar, S. S. (2007). Peer-perceived admiration and social preference: Contextual correlates of positive peer regard among suburban and urban adolescents. *Journal of Research on Adolescence, 17,* 117–144.

Becker, T. (2003). Is emotional intelligence a viable concept? *Academy of Management Review, 28,* 192–195.

Bedard, W. W., & Parsinger, M. A. (1995). Prednisolone blocks extreme intermale social aggression in seizure-induced, brain-damaged rats: Implications for the amygdaloid central nucleus, corticotrophin-releasing factor, and electrical seizures. *Psychological Reports, 77,* 3–9.

Begg, D., & Langley, J. (2001). Changes in risky driving behavior from age 21 to 26 years. *Journal of Safety Research, 32,* 491–499.

Begley, S. (2002, September 13). The memory of September 11 is seared in your mind; but is it really true? *The Wall Street Journal,* p. B1.

Begley, S. (2005, April 29). Evolution psychology may not help explain our behavior after all. *The Wall Street Journal,* p. D1.

Begley, S. (2005, August 19). A spotless mind may ease suffering but erase identity. *The Wall Street Journal,* p. B1.

Beidel, D. C., & Turner, S. M. (2007). Etiology of social anxiety disorder. In D. C. Beidel, & S. M. Turner, *Shy children, phobic adults: Nature and treatment of social anxiety disorders* (2nd ed.). Washington, DC: American Psychological Association.

Beilock, S. L., & Carr, T. H. (2005). When high-powered people fail: Working memory and "choking under pressure" in math. *Psychological Science, 16,* 101–105.

Belar, C. (2008, April). Clinical health psychology: A health care specialty in professional psychology. *Professional Psychology: Research and Practice, 39,* 229–233.

Bellezza, F. S. (2000). Mnemonic devices. In A. E. Kazdin (Ed.), *Encyclopedia of psychology* (Vol. 5). Washington, DC: American Psychological Association.

Belli, R. F., & Loftus, E. F. (1996). The pliability of autobiographical memory: Misinformation and the false memory problem. In D. C. Rubin (Ed.), *Remembering our past: Studies in autobiographical memory* (pp. 157–179). New York: Cambridge University Press.

Belov, D. I., & Armstrong, R. D. (2009). Direct and inverse problems of item pool design for computerized adaptive testing. *Educational and Psychological Measurement, 69,* 533–547.

Belsky, J., & Pluess, M. (2009). The nature (and nurture?) of plasticity in early human development. *Perspectives on Psychological Science, 4,* 345–351.

Bem, D. J. (1996). Exotic becomes erotic: A developmental theory of sexual orientation. *Psychological Review, 103,* 320–335.

Benca, R. M. (2005). Diagnosis and treatment of chronic insomnia: A review. *Psychiatric Services, 56,* 332–343.

Benderly, B. L. (2004). Looking beyond the SAT. *American Psychological Society, 17,* 12–18.

Benham, G., Woody, E. Z., & Wilson, K. S. (2006). Expect the unexpected: Ability, attitude, and responsiveness to hypnosis. *Journal of Personality and Social Psychology, 91,* 342–350.

Benight, C. C. (2004). Collective efficacy following a series of natural disasters. *Stress and Coping: An International Journal, 17,* 401–420.

Benjamin, L. T., Jr. (1985, February). Defining aggression: An exercise for classroom discussion. *Teaching of Psychology, 12*(1), 40–42.

Ben-Porath, Y., & Archer, R. (2008). The MMPI-2 and MMPI-A. *Personality assessment.* New York: Routledge/Taylor & Francis Group.

Benson, E. (2003, April). The science of sexual arousal. *Monitor on Psychology,* pp. 50–56.

Benson, H., Kornhaber, A., Kornhaber, C., LeChanu, M. N., et al. (1994). Increases in positive psychological characteristics with a new relaxation-response curriculum in high school students. *Journal of Research and Development in Education, 27,* 226–231.

Benton, S. A., Robertson, J. M., Tseng, W. C., Newton, F. B., & Benton, S. L. (2003). Changes in counseling center client problems across 13 years. *Professional Psychology: Research and Practice, 34,* 66–72.

Beresnevaité, M., Taylor, G. J., & Bagby, R. M. (2007). Assessing alexithymia and type A behavior in coronary heart disease patients: A multimethod approach. *Psychotherapy and Psychosomatics, 76,* 186–192.

Berk, L. E. (2005). Why parenting matters. In S. Olfman (Ed.), *Childhood lost: How American culture is failing our kids.* Westport, CT: Praeger Publishers/Greenwood Publishing Group.

Berkowitz, L. (2001). On the formation and regulation of anger and aggression: A cognitive-neoassociationistic analysis. In W. G. Parrott (Ed.), *Emotions in social psychology: Essential readings.* New York: Psychology Press.

Berkowitz, L., & Geen, R. G. (1966). Film violence and the cue properties of available targets. *Journal of Personality and Social Psychology, 3*, 525–530.

Berkowitz, L., & LePage, A. (1967). Weapons as aggression-eliciting stimuli. *Journal of Personality and Social Psychology, 7*, 202–207.

Berman, A. L., Jobes, D. A., & Silverman, M. M. (2006). An integrative-eclectic approach to treatment. In A. L. Berman, D. A. Jobes, & M. M. Silverman, *Adolescent suicide: Assessment and intervention* (2nd ed.). Washington, DC: American Psychological Association.

Bernard, L. L. (1924). *Instinct: A study in social psychology.* New York: Holt.

Bernstein, D. M., Loftus, G. R., & Meltzoff, A. N. (2005). Object identification in preschool children and adults. *Developmental Science, 8*, 151–161.

Bernstein, D., & Loftus, E. (2009a). How to tell if a particular memory is true or false. *Perspectives on Psychological Science, 4*, 370–374.

Bernstein, D., & Loftus, E. (2009b). The consequences of false memories for food preferences and choices. *Perspectives on Psychological Science, 4*, 135–139.

Berntsen, D., & Rubin, D. C. (2004). Cultural life scripts structure recall from autobiographical memory. *Memory and Cognition, 32*, 427–442.

Berntsen, D., & Thomsen, D. K. (2005). Personal memories for remote historical events: Accuracy and clarity of flashbulb memories related to World War II. *Journal of Experimental Psychology: General, 134*, 242–257.

Berntson, G. G., Bechara, A., Damasio, H., Tranel, D., & Cacioppo, J. T. (2007). Amygdala contribution to selective dimensions of emotion. *Social Cognitive and Affective Neuroscience, 2*, 123–129.

Berrettini, W. H. (2000). Are schizophrenic and bipolar disorders related? A review of family and molecular studies [Special issue: A special issue on bipolar disorder]. *Biological Psychiatry, 48*, 531–538.

Berridge, K. C. (2004). Motivation concepts in behavioral neuroscience. *Physiology and Behavior, 81*, 179–209.

Berrios, G. E. (1996). *The history of mental symptoms: Descriptive psychopathology since the 19th century.* Cambridge: Cambridge University Press.

Bertakis, K. (2009). The influence of gender on the doctor–patient interaction. *Patient Education and Counseling, 76*, 356–360.

Berthoud, H. R. (2002). Multiple neural systems controlling food intake and body weight. *Neuroscience and Biobehavioral Reviews, 26*, 393–428.

Betancourt, H., & Lopez, S. R. (1993). The study of culture, ethnicity, and race in American Psychology. *American Psychologist, 48*, 1586–1596.

Betz, N. (2007). Career self-efficacy: Exemplary recent research and emerging directions. *Journal of Career Assessment, 15*, 403–422.

Beutler, L. E., Brown, M. T., Crothers, L., Booker, K., et al. (1996). The dilemma of factitious demographic distinctions in psychological research. *Journal of Consulting and Clinical Psychology, 64*, 892–902.

Beyene, Y., Gilliss, C., & Lee, K. (2007). "I take the good with the bad, and I moisturize": Defying middle age in the new millennium. *Menopause, 14*, 734–741.

Bhar, S., Gelfand, L., Schmid, S., Gallop, R., DeRubeis, R., Hollon, S., et al. (2008). Sequence of improvement in depressive symptoms across cognitive therapy and pharmacotherapy. *Journal of Affective Disorders, 110*, 161–166.

Bialystok, E., & Martin, M. M. (2004). Attention and inhibition in bilingual children: Evidence from the dimensional change card sort task. *Developmental Science, 7*, 325–339.

Bianchi, S. M., & Casper, L. M. (2000). American families. *Population Bulletin, 55*(4).

Big Picture on Drug Development. Issue 7, January 2008. Retrieved from www.bigpictureeducation.com

Bindemann, M., Burton, A., Leuthold, H., & Schweinberger, S. (2008, July). Brain potential correlates of face recognition: Geometric distortions and the N250r brain response to stimulus repetitions. *Psychophysiology, 45*, 535–544.

Binet, A., & Simon, T. (1916). *The development of intelligence in children (The Binet-Simon Scale).* Baltimore: Williams & Wilkins.

Binstock, R., & George, L. K. (Eds.). (1996). *Handbook of aging and the social sciences* (4th ed.). San Diego, CA: Academic Press.

Birren, J. E. (Ed.). (1996). *Encyclopedia of gerontology: Age, aging and the aged.* San Diego, CA: Academic Press.

Bishop, M. (2005). Quality of life and psychosocial adaptation to chronic illness and disability: Preliminary analysis of a conceptual and theoretical synthesis. *Rehabilitation Counseling Bulletin, 48*, 219–231.

Bitterman, M. E. (2006). Classical conditioning since Pavlov. *Review of General Psychology, 10*, 365–376.

Bittles, A. H., Bower, C., & Hussain, R. (2007). The four ages of Down syndrome. *European Journal of Public Health, 17*, 121–225.

Bizley, J., Walker, K., Silverman, B., King, A., & Schnupp, J. (2009, February). Interdependent encoding of pitch, timbre, and spatial location in auditory cortex. *Journal of Neuroscience, 29*, 2064–2075.

Bjork, R. A., & Richardson-Klarehn, A. (1989). On the puzzling relationship between environmental context and human memory. In C. Izawa (Ed.), *Current issues in cognitive processes: The Tulane-Floweree symposium on cognition.* Hillsdale, NJ: Erlbaum.

Bjorklund, D. F., & Ellis, B. J. (2005). *Evolutionary psychology and child development: An emerging synthesis.* New York: Guilford Press.

Bjornstad, R. (2006). Learned helplessness, discouraged workers, and multiple unemployment equilibria. *The Journal of Socio-Economics, 35*, 458–475.

Blair, C. A., Thompson, L. F., & Wuensch, K. L. (2005). Electronic helping behavior: The virtual presence of others makes a difference. *Basic and Applied Social Psychology, 27*, 171–178.

Blakeslee, S. (1992, August 11). Finding a new messenger for the brain's signals to the body. *The New York Times*, p. C3.

Blanchard, R., & Lippa, R. A. (2007). Birth order, sibling sex ratio, handedness, and sexual orientation of male and female participants in a BBC Internet research project. *Archives of Sexual Behavior, 36*, 163–176.

Blass, T. (1996). Attribution of responsibility and trust in the Milgram obedience experiment. *Journal of Applied Social Psychology, 26*, 1529–1535.

Blass, T. (2004). *The man who shocked the world: The life and legacy of Stanley Milgram.* New York: Basic Books.

Blewett, A. E. (2000). Help cards for patients. *Psychiatric Bulletin, 24*, 276.

Blixen, C. E., Singh, A., & Xu, M. (2006). What women want: Understanding obesity and preferences for primary care weight reduction interventions among African-American and Caucasian women. *Journal of the National Medical Association, 98*, 1160–1170.

Bloom, P. N., McBride, C. M., & Pollak, K. I. (2006). Recruiting teen smokers in shopping malls to a smoking-cessation program using the foot-in-the-door technique. *Journal of Applied Social Psychology, 36*, 1129–1144.

Blum, D. (2002). *Love at goon park: Harry Harlow and the science of affection.* Cambridge, MA: Perseus.

Boahen, K. (2005, May). Neuromorphic micro-chips. *Scientific American*, pp. 56–64.

Bodin, G. (2006). Review of harvesting free association. *Psychoanalytic Quarterly, 75*, 629–632.

Boehm, K. E., & Campbell, N. B. (1995). Suicide: A re-view of calls to an adolescent peer listening phone service. *Child Psychiatry and Human Development, 26*, 61–66.

Bogenschutz, M. P., Geppert, C. M., & George, J. (2006). The role of twelve-step approaches in dual diagnosis treatment and recovery. *American Journal of Addiction, 15*, 50–60.

Bohart, A. C. (2006). Understanding person-centered therapy: A review of Paul Wilkins' person-centered therapy in focus. *Person-Centered and Experiential Psychotherapies, 5*, 138–143.

Bohn, A., & Berntsen, D. (2007). Pleasantness bias in flashbulb memories: Positive and negative flashbulb memories of the fall of the Berlin Wall among East and West Germans. *Memory and Cognition, 35*, 565–577.

References

Boles, D. B. (2005). A large-sample study of sex differences in functional cerebral lateralization. *Journal of Clinical and Experimental Neuropsychology, 27,* 759–768.

Bolger, N., & Amarel, D. (2007). Effects of social support visibility on adjustment to stress: Experimental evidence. *Journal of Personality and Social Psychology, 92,* 458–475.

Boller, F. (2004). Rational basis of rehabilitation following cerebral lesions: A review of the concept of cerebral plasticity. *Functional Neurology: New Trends in Adaptive and Behavioral Disorders, 19,* 65–72.

Bonanni, R., Pasqualetti, P., Caltagirone, C., & Carlesimo, G. (2007). Primacy and recency effects in immediate free recall of sequences of spatial positions. *Perceptual and Motor Skills, 105,* 483–500.

Bonanno, G.A. (2004). Loss, trauma, and human resilience: Have we underestimated the human capacity to thrive after extremely aversive events? *American Psychologist, 59,* 20–28.

Bond, M. (2006).Psychodynamic psychotherapy in the treatment of mood disorders. *Current Opinion in Psychiatry, 19,* 40–43.

Bonnardel, V. (2006). Color naming and categorization in inherited color vision deficiencies. *Visual Neuroscience, 23,* 637–643.

Borbely, A. (1988). *Secrets of sleep* (p. 43, graph). New York: Basic Books.

Bordnick, P. S., Elkins, R. L., Orr, T. E., Walters, P., & Thyer, B. A. (2004). Evaluating the relative effectiveness of three aversion therapies designed to reduce craving among cocaine abusers. *Behavioral Interventions, 19,* 1–24.

Borisenko, J. (2007). Fatherhood as a personality development factor in men. *The Spanish Journal of Psychology, 10,* 82–90.

Bornstein, R. F. (2003). Psychodynamic models of personality. In T. Millon & M. J. Lerner (Eds.), *Handbook of psychology: Personality and social psychology* (Vol. 5). New York: Wiley.

Bosma, H., van Boxtel, M. P. J., Ponds, R. W. H. M., Houx, P. J. H., & Jolles, J. (2003). Education and age-related cognitive decline: The contribution of mental workload. *Educational Gerontology, 29,* 165–173.

Botvinick, M. (2004, August 6). Probing the neural basis of body ownership. *Science, 305,* 782–783.

Bouchard, C., & Bray, G. A. (Eds.). (1996). *Regulation of body weight: Biological and behavioral mechanisms.* New York: Wiley.

Bouchard, T. J., Jr. (2004). Genetic influence on human psychological traits: A survey. *Current Directions in Psychological Science, 13,* 148–151.

Bouchard, T. J., Jr., Segal, N. L., Tellegen, A., McGue, M., Keyes, M. & Krueger, R. (2004). Genetic influence on social attitudes: Another challenge to psychology from behavior genetics. In L. F. DiLalla (Ed.), *Behavior genetics principles: Perspectives in development, personality, and psychopathology.* Washington, DC: American Psychological Association.

Bourne, L. E., Dominowski, R. L., Loftus, E. F., & Healy, A. F. (1986). *Cognitive processes* (2nd ed.). Englewood Cliffs, NJ: Prentice Hall.

Bower, G. H., Thompson, S. S., & Tulving, E. (1994). Reducing retroactive interference: An interference analysis. *Journal of Experimental Psychology Learning, Memory, and Cognition, 20,* 51–66.

Bower, J. M., & Parsons, L. M. (2003, August). Rethinking the "lesser brain." *Scientific American,* pp. 51–57.

Boxer, P., Huesmann, L., Bushman, B., O'Brien, M., & Moceri, D. (2009). The role of violent media preference in cumulative developmental risk for violence and general aggression. *Journal of Youth and Adolescence, 38,* 417–428.

Boyce, W. T., & Ellis, B. J. (2005). Biological sensitivity to context: An evolutionary-developmental theory of the origins and functions of stress reactivity. *Development and Psychopathology, 17,* 271–301.

Boyd-Wilson, B. M., McClure, J., & Walkey, F. H. (2004). Are well-being and illusory perceptions linked? The answer may be yes, but. . . . *Australian Journal of Psychology, 56,* 1–9.

Boyle, S. H., Williams, R. B., Mark, D. B., Brummett, B. H., Siegler, I. C., & Barefoot, J. C. (2005). Hostility, age, and mortality in a sample of cardiac patients. *American Journal of Cardiology, 96,* 64–72.

Bozarth, J. D., Zimring, F. M., & Tausch, R. (2002). Client-centered therapy: The evolution of a revolution. In D. J. Cain (Ed.), *Humanistic psychotherapies: Handbook of research and practice.* Washington, DC: American Psychological Association.

Brambilla, P., Cipriani, A., Hotopf, M., & Barbui, C. (2005). Side-effect profile of fluoxetine in comparison with other SSRIs, tricyclic and newer antidepressants: A meta-analysis of clinical trial data. *Pharmacopsychiatry, 38,* 69–77.

Brasic, J. R. (2002). Conversion disorder in childhood. *German Journal of Psychiatry, 5,* 54–61.

Brazelton, T. B. (1969). *Infants and mothers: Differences in development.* New York: Dell.

Breland, K., & Breland, M. (1961). Misbehavior of organisms. *American Psychologist, 16,* 681–684.

Brewer, J. B., Zhao, Z., Desmond, J. E., Glover, G. H., & Gabrieli, J. D. E. (1998, August 21). Making memories: Brain activity that predicts how well visual experience will be remembered. *Science, 281,* 1185–1187.

Brewer, M. B., & Hewstone, M. (Eds.). (2003). *Social cognition.* Malden, MA: Blackwell Publishers.

Bright, P., Buckman, J., & Fradera, A. (2006). Retrograde amnesia in patients with hippo-campal, medial temporal, temporal lobe, or frontal pathology. *Learning & Memory, 13,* 545–557.

Brislin, R., Worthley, R., & MacNab, B. (2006). Cultural intelligence: Understanding behaviors that serve people's goals. *Group & Organization Management, 31,* 40–55.

Brock, T. C., & Green, M. C. (Eds.). (2005). *Persuasion: Psychological insights and perspectives* (2nd ed.). Thousand Oaks, CA: Sage Publications.

Bröder, A., & Schiffer, S. (2006). Stimulus format and working memory in fast and frugal strategy selection. *Journal of Behavioral Decision Making, 19,* 361–380.

Brody, J. (2008, May 20). Trying to break nicotine's grip. *The New York Times,* p. E9.

Broidy, L. M., Nagin, D. S., & Tremblay, R. E. (2003). Developmental trajectories of childhood disruptive behaviors and adolescent delinquency: A six-site, cross-national study. *Developmental Psychology, 39,* 222–245.

Broman, C. L. (2005). Stress, race and substance use in college. *College Student Journal, 39,* 340–352.

Bronson, P., & Merryman, A. (2009). *NurtureShock.* New York: Twelve.

Brooker, R. J., Widmaier, E. P., Graham, L., & Stiling, P. (2008). *Biology.* New York: McGraw-Hill.

Brooks, P.L., & Peever, J.H. (2008). Glycinergic and GABAA mediated inhibition of somatic motoneurons does not mediate rapid eye movement sleep motor atonia. *The Journal of Neuroscience, 28(14),* 3535–3545.

Brown, L. S., & Pope, K. S. (1996). *Recovered memories of abuse: Assessment, therapy, forensics.* Washington, DC: American Psychological Association.

Brown, P. K., & Wald, G. (1964). Visual pigments in single rod and cones of the human retina. *Science, 144,* 45–52.

Brown, R. (1958). How shall a thing be called? *Psychological Review, 65,* 14–21.

Brown, R. J. (2006). Different types of "dissociation" have different psychological mechanisms. *Journal of Trauma Dissociation, 6,* 7–28.

Brown, R., & Robertson, E. (2007). Off-line processing: Reciprocal interactions between declarative and procedural memories. *The Journal of Neuroscience, 27(39),* 10468–10475.

Brown, S., & Martinez, M. J. (2007). Activation of premotor vocal areas during musical discrimination. *Brain and Cognition, 63,* 9–69.

Brown, S., Martinez, M. J., & Parson, L. M. (2006). Music and language side by side in the brain: A PET study of the generation of melodies and sentences. *European Journal of Neuroscience, 23,* 2791–2803.

Brownlee, K. (2007). What works for whom? A critical review of psychotherapy research. *Psychiatric Rehabilitation Journal, 30,* 239–240.

Bruce, B., & Wilfley, D. (1996). Binge eating among the overweight population: A serious and prevalent problem. *Journal of the American Dietetic Association, 96,* 58–61.

Bruce, V., Green, P. R., & Georgeson, M. (1997). *Visual perception: Physiology, psychology and ecology* (3rd ed.). Mahwah, NJ: Erlbaum.

Bruggeman, H., Yonas, A., & Konczak, J. (2007). The processing of linear perspective and binocular information for action and perception. *Neuropsychologia, 45,* 1420–1426.

Brydon, L., Edwards, S., Mohamed-Ali, V., & Steptoe, A. (2004). Socio-economicstatus and stress-induced increases in interleukin-6. *Brain, Behavior, and Immunity, 18*, 281–290.

Brzustowicz, L. M., Hodgkinson, K. A., Chow, E. W. C., Honer, W. G., & Bassett, A. S. (2000, April 28). Location of major susceptibility locus for familial schizophrenia on chromosome 1q21–q22. *Science, 288*, 678–682.

Buchanan, T. W., & Adolphs, R. (2004). The neuroanatomy of emotional memory in humans. In D. Reisberg & P. Hertel (Eds.), *Memory and emotion*. London: Oxford University Press.

Buchanan, T., & Selmon, N. (2008). Race and gender differences in self-efficacy: Assessing the role of gender role attitudes and family background. *Sex Roles, 58*, 822–836.

Buchert, R., Thomasius, R., Wilke, F., Petersen, K., Nebeling, B., Obrocki, J., Schulze, O., Schmidt, U., & Clausen, M. (2004). A voxel-based PET investigation of the long-term effects of "ecstasy" consumption on brain serotonin transporters. *American Journal of Psychiatry, 161*, 1181–1189.

Buckout, R. (1974). Eyewitness testimony. *Scientific American, 231*, pp. 23–31.

Bukobza, G. (2009). Relations between rebelliousness, risk-taking behavior, and identity status during emerging adulthood. *Identity, 9*, 159–177.

Bulik, C. M., Tozzi, F., Anderson, C., Mazzeo, S. E., Aggen, S., & Sullivan, P. F. (2003). The relation between eating disorders and components of perfectionism. *American Journal of Psychiatry, 160*, 366–368.

Bunting, M. (2006). Proactive interference and item similarity in working memory. *Journal of Experimental Psychology: Learning, Memory, and Cognition, 32*, 183–196.

Burchinal, M. R., Roberts, J. E., & Riggins, R., Jr. (2000). Relating quality of center-based child care to early cognitive and language development longitudinally. *Child Development, 71*, 338–357.

Burger, J. M. (2009). Replicating Milgram: Would people still obey today? *American Psychologist, 64*, 1–11.

Burger, J. M., & Caldwell, D. F. (2003). The effects of monetary incentives and labeling on the foot-in-the-door effect: Evidence for a self-perception process. *Basic and Applied Social Psychology, 25*, 235–241.

Burger, J. M., Reed, M., & DeCesare, K. (1999). The effects of initial request size on compliance: More about the that's-not-all technique. *Basic and Applied Social Psychology, 21*, 243–249.

Burgoon, J. K., Bonito, J. A., Ramirez, A. J. R., Dunbar, N. E., Kam, K., & Fischer, J. (2002). Testing the interactivity principle: Effects of mediation, propinquity, and verbal and nonverbal modalities in interpersonal interaction [Special Issue: Research on the relationship between verbal and nonverbal communication: Emerging integrations]. *Journal of Communication, 52*, 657–677.

Burns, J. W., Quartana, P. J., & Bruehl, S. (2007). Anger management style moderates effects of emotion suppression during initial stress on pain and cardiovascular responses during subsequent pain-induction. *Annals of Behavioral Medicine, 34*, 154–165.

Burns, N. R., Bryan, J., & Nettelbeck, T. (2006). Ginkgo biloba: No robust effect on cognitive abilities or mood in healthy young or older adults. *Human Psychopharmacology: Clinical and Experimental, 21*, 27–37.

Bushman, B. J., & Anderson, C. (2001). Media violence and the American public: Scientific facts versus media misinformation. *American Psychologist, 56*, 477–489.

Bushman, B. J., & Anderson, C. A. (2002). Violent video games and hostile expectations: A test of the general aggression model. *Personality and Social Psychology Bulletin, 28*, 1679–1686.

Buss, D. (2003). *Evolutionary psychology*. Boston: Allyn & Bacon.

Buss, D. (2009). How can evolutionary psychology successfully explain personality and individual differences? *Perspectives on Psychological Science, 4*, 359–366.

Buss, D. M. (2001). Human nature and culture: An evolutionary psychological perspective. *Journal of Personality, 69*, 955–978.

Buss, D. M. (2003a). *The evolution of desire: Strategies of human mating*. New York: Basic Books.

Buss, D. M. (2004). Sex differences in human mate preferences: Evolutionary hypotheses tested in 37 cultures. In H. T. Reis & C. E. Rusbult (Eds.), *Close relationships: Key readings*. Philadelphia: Taylor & Francis.

Buss, D. M., Abbott, M., & Angleitner, A. (1990). International preferences in selecting mates: A study of 37 cultures. *Journal of Cross-Cultural Psychology, 21*, 5–47.

Butcher, J. N. (1995). Interpretation of the MMPI-2. In L. E. Beutler, & M. R. Berren (Eds.), *Integrative assessment of adult personality*. New York: Guilford Press.

Butcher, J. N. (2005). *A beginner's guide to the MMPI-2* (2nd ed.). Washington, DC: American Psychological Association.

Butler, A. C., Chapman, J. E., Forman, E. M., & Beck, A. T. (2006). The empirical status of cognitive-behavioral therapy: A review of meta-analyses. *Clinical Psychology Review, 26*, 17–31.

Butler, L. D., Koopman, C., Neri, E., Giese-Davis, J., Palesh, O., Thorne-Yocam, K. A., et al. (2009). Effects of supportive-expressive group therapy on pain in women with metastatic breast cancer. *Health Psychology, 28*, 579–587.

Butler, L. T., & Berry, D. C. (2004). Understanding the relationship between repetition priming and mere exposure. *British Journal of Psychology, 95*, 467–487.

Byers, J. (2010, February 21). Joannie Rochette's mother dies after arriving at Games. *The Star.com*. Retrieved from olympics.thestar.com/2010/article/769119—joannie-rochette-s-mother-dies-after-arriving-at-games.

Byne, W. (1996). Biology and homosexuality: Implications of neuroendocrinological and neuroanatomical studies. In R. P. Cabaj & T. S. Stein (Eds.), *Textbook of homosexuality and mental health*. Washington, DC: American Psychiatric Press.

Byrne-Davis, L., & Vedhara, K. (2008). Psychoneuroimmunology. *Social and Personality Psychology Compass, 2*, 751–764.

Cabanac, M., & Frankham, P. (2002). Evidence that transient nicotine lowers the body weight set point. *Physiology & Behavior, 76*, 539–542.

Cacioppo, J. T., Visser, P. S., & Pickett, C. L. (2005). *Social neuroscience: People thinking about thinking people*. Cambridge, MA: MIT Press.

Cadenhead, K. & Braff, D. L. (1995). Neurophysiology of schizophrenia: Attention, information processing, and inhibitory processes in schizophrenia. In J. A. Den Boer., H. G. M. Westenberg & H. M. van Praag (Eds.), *Advances in the neurobiology of schizophrenia*. Oxford, England: John Wiley & Sons.

Cahill, L. (2005, May). His brain, her brain. *Scientific American*, pp. 40–47.

Cain, D. J. (Ed.). (2002). *Humanistic psychotherapies: Handbook of research and practice*. Washington, DC: American Psychological Association.

Calderon, M. E., & Minaya-Rowe, L. (2003). *Designing and implementing two-way bilingual programs: A step-by-step guide for administrators, teachers, and parents*. Thousand Oaks, CA: Corwin Press.

Calle, E. E., & Kaaks, R. (2004). Overweight, obesity and cancer: Epidemiological evidence and proposed mechanisms. *Nature Reviews Cancer 4*, 579–591.

Cameron, O. G. (2002). *Visceral sensory neuroscience: Interoception*. London: Oxford University Press.

Canadian Addiction Survey (CAS). (2004). Substance abuse by Canadian youth. Retrieved from www.hc-sc.gc.ca/hl-vs/pubs/adp-apd/cas-etc/youth-jeunes/chap5_page3_e.html.

Canadian Association of the Deaf (CAD). (2008a). Statistics on deaf Canadians. Retrieved from www.cad.ca/en/issues/statistics_on_deaf_canadians.asp.

Canadian Association of the Deaf (CAD). (2008b). Official languages. Retrieved from www.cad.ca/en/issues/official_languages.asp.

Canadian Council on Learning (CCL). (2008). Redefining how success is measured in aboriginal learning: First Nations holistic lifelong learning model. Retrieved from www.ccl-cca.ca/CCL/Reports/RedefiningSuccessInAboriginalLearning/RedefiningSuccessModels-FirstNations.htm.

Canadian Lung Association. (2008). Sleep apnea: What is sleep apnea? Retrieved from www.lung.ca/diseases-maladies/apnea-apnee/what-quoi/index_e.php.

Canadian Psychological Association (CPA). (1999). Geographic locations survey of clinical psychologists in Canada. Monograph Series. Retrieved from www.cpa.ca/documents/geographic_survey.html.

Canadian Psychological Association (CPA). (2000). *Canadian code of ethics for psychologists* (3rd ed.). Ottawa: Author. Retrieved from www.cpa.ca/cpasite/userfiles/Documents/Canadian%20Code%20of%20Ethics%20for%20Psycho.pdf.

Canadian Psychological Association (CPA). (2007). Annual report. *Annual General Meeting, 11.* Retrieved from www.cpa.ca/cpasite/userfiles/Documents/Annual%20Report07%20FINAL.pdf.

Canadian Psychological Association (CPA). (2007). *Guidelines for ethical psychological practice with women.* Ottawa: Section on Women and Psychology. Retrieved from www.cpa.ca/cpasite/userfiles/Documents/publications/guidelines%20for%20psychological%20practice%20women.pdf.

Canadian Psychological Association (CPA). (2007). Special feature. Terrorism: difficulty to define. *Crime Scene: Psychology behind bars and in front of the bench, 14(1),* 9–11. Retrieved from www.cpa.ca/cpasite/userfiles/Documents/Criminal%20Justice/Crime%20Scene%202007-04.pdf.

Canadian Psychological Association (CPA). (2008). Health psychology. Retrieved from www.cpa.ca/sections/healthpsychology/.

Canadian Psychological Association (CPA). (2008). What is psychology? *Your Health: Psychology Works Quick Facts.* Retrieved from www.cpa.ca/cpasite/userfiles/Documents/QFacts.pdf.

Canadian Psychological Association (CPA). (2008). Your psychology works fact sheet: Chronic pain. Retrieved from www.cpa.ca/publications/yourhealthpsychologyworksfactsheets/chronicpain/.

Cannon, W. B. (1929). Organization for physiological homeostatics. *Physiological Review, 9,* 280–289.

Canteras, N. S. (2002). The medial hypothalamic defensive system: Hodological organization and functional implications [Special issue: Functional role of specific systems within the extended amygdala and hypothalamus]. *Pharmacology, Biochemistry and Behavior, 71,* 481–491.

Cantwell, R. H., & Andrews, B. (2002). Cognitive and psychological factors underlying secondary school students' feelings towards group work. *Educational Psychology, 22,* 75–91.

Capaldi, E. D. (Ed.). (1996). *Why we eat what we eat: The psychology of eating.* Washington, DC: American Psychological Association.

Carey, B. (2004, December 21). When pressure is on, good students suffer. *The New York Times,* p. D7.

Carey, B. (2009, November 27). Surgery for mental ills offers hope and risk. *The New York Times,* p. A1

Carhart-Harris, R., (2007). Speed > Ecstasy > Ritalin: The science of amphetamines. *Journal of Psychopharmacology, 21,* 225.

Carnagey, N., Anderson, C. A., & Bushman, B. J. (2007). The effect of video game violence on physiological desensitization to real-life violence. *Journal of Experimental Social Psychology, 43,* 489–496.

Carnagey, N., Anderson, C., & Bartholow, B. (2007). Media violence and social neuroscience: New questions and new opportunities. *Current Directions in Psychological Science, 16,* 178–182.

Carney, D., Colvin, C., & Hall, J. (2007). A thin slice perspective on the accuracy of first impressions. *Journal of Research in Personality, 41,* 1054–1072.

Carney, R. N., & Levin, J. R. (1998). Coming to terms with the keyword method in introductory psychology: A "neuromnemonic" example. *Teaching of Psychology, 25,* 132–135.

Carney, R. N., & Levin, J. R. (2003). Promoting higher-order learning benefits by building lower-order mnemonic connections. *Applied Cognitive Psychology, 17,* 563–575.

Carr, N. (2011). *The shallows: What the Internet is doing to our brains.* New York: W. W. Norton & Co.

Carrillo, M., Ricci, L., Coppersmith, G., & Melloni, R. (2009, August). The effect of increased serotonergic neurotransmission on aggression: A critical meta-analytical review of preclinical studies. *Psychopharmacology, 205,* 349–368.

Carter, R. T. (2003). Becoming racially and culturally competent: The racial-cultural counseling laboratory. *Journal of Multicultural Counseling and Development, 31,* 20–30.

Cartwright, R., Agargum, M. Y., & Kirkby, J. (2006). Relation of dreams to waking concerns. *Psychiatry Research, 141,* 261–270.

Caruso, E. (2008). Use of experienced retrieval ease in self and social judgments. *Journal of Experimental Social Psychology, 44,* 148–155.

Carvalho, F. M., Pereira, S. R. C., Pires, R. G. W., Ferraz, V. P., Romano-Silva, M. A., Oliveira-Silva, I. F., & Ribeiro, A. M. (2006). Thiamine deficiency decreases glutamate uptake in the prefrontal cortex and impairs spatial memory performance in a water maze test. *Pharmacology, Biochemistry and Behavior, 83,* 481–489.

Carvalho, J., & Nobre, P. (2011). Gender differences in sexual desire: How do emotional and relationship factors determine sexual desire according to gender? *Sexologies, 20,* 207–211.

Carver, C., & Scheier, M. (2002). Coping processes and adjustment to chronic illness. In A. Christensen & M. Antoni (Eds.), *Chronic physical disorders: Behavioral medicine's perspective.* Malden: Blackwell Publishers.

Casasanto, D. (2008). Who's afraid of the big bad whorf? Crosslinguistic differences in temporal language and thought. *Language Learning, 58,* 63–79.

Cashon, C. H., & Cohen, L. B. (2004). Beyond U-shaped development in infants' processing of faces: An information-processing account. *Journal of Cognition and Development, 5,* 59–80.

Cassells, J. V. S. (2007). The virtuous roles of truth and justice in integral dialogue: Research, theory, and model practice of the evolution of collective consciousness. *Dissertation Abstracts International Section A: Humanities and Social Sciences, 67*(10-A), 4005.

Cattell, Eber, & Tatsuoka. (1970, 1988, 1992). *Handbook for the 16P.* Institute for Personality and Ability Testing, Inc. Champaign, IL.

Cattell, R. B. (1965). *The scientific analysis of personality.* Chicago: Aldine.

Cattell, R. B., Cattell, A. K., & Cattell, H. E. P. (2000). *The sixteen personality factor™ (16PF®) questionnaire.* Champaign, IL: Institute for Personality and Ability Testing.

Cavallini, E., Pagnin, A., & Vecchi, T. (2003). Aging and everyday memory: The beneficial effect of memory training. *Archives of Gerontology & Geriatrics, 37,* 241–257.

Cavenett, T., & Nixon, R. D. V. (2006). The effect of arousal on memory for emotionally-relevant information: A study of skydivers. *Behaviour Research and Therapy, 44,* 1461–1469.

CBC.ca. (2006, December). David Milgaard: Timeline. Retrieved from www.cbc.ca/news/background/milgaard/.

CBC.ca. (2007, February 15). Smoking in Canada being snuffed out. Retrieved from www.cbc.ca/news/background/smoking/stats.html.

CBC.ca. (2007, January 12). Depression: An illness, not a weakness. Retrieved from www.cbc.ca/news/background/mental-health/index.html.

CBC.ca. (2008, January 22). Winter's SAD times. Retrieved from www.cbc.ca/news/background/mental-health/sad.html.

CBC.ca (2008, February 7). Risk of obesity greater for sleep-deprived children: Study. *CBC News.* Retrieved from www.cbc.ca/health/story/2008/02/07/child-sleep.html.

CBC.ca. (2008, March 14). Wrongly convicted. Retrieved from www.cbc.ca/news/background/wrongfullyconvicted/.

Centre for Addiction and Mental Health (CAMH). (2004). College campus survey. Retrieved from www.camh.net/Research/Areas_of_research/Population_Life_Course_Studies/CCS_2004_report.pdf.

Centre for Addiction and Mental Health (CAMH). (2006). Transforming lives. 2006 award winner Jessica Weihrich. Retrieved from www.supportcamh.ca/2006courage_jessica.asp.

Chakraborty, A., McManus, S., Brugha, T. S., Bebbington, P., & King, M. (2011). Mental health of the nonheterosexual population of England. *The British Journal of Psychiatry, 198,* 143–148.

Chamberlain, K., & Zika, S. (1990). The minor events approach to stress: Support for the use of daily hassles. *British Journal of Psychology, 81,* 469–481.

Chamberlain, S. R., Menzies, L., Hampshire, A., Suckling, J., Fineberg, N. A., del Campo, N., et al. (2008, July 18). Orbitofrontal dysfunction in patients with obsessive-compulsive disorder and their unaffected relatives. *Science, 321,* 421–422.

Chambless, D. L., Crits-Christoph, P., Wampold, B. E., Norcross, J. C., Lambert, M. J., Bohart, A. C., et al. (2006). What should be validated? In J. C. Norcross, L. E. Beutler, & R. F. Levant, (Eds.). *Evidence-based practices in mental health: Debate and dialogue on the fundamental questions.* Washington, DC: American Psychological Association.

Chandra, P. (2007). Review of Language, mind, and brain: Some psychological and neurological constraints on theories of grammar. *Cognitive Systems Research, 8,* 53–56.

Chandran, S., & Menon, G. (2004). When a day means more than a year: Effects of temporal framing on judgments of health risk. *Journal of Consumer Research, 31,* 375–389.

Chang, S. W., & Ansley, T. N. (2003). A comparative study of item exposure control methods in computerized adaptive testing. *Journal of Educational Measurement, 40,* 71–103.

Chapkis, W., & Webb, R. (2008). *Dying to get high: Marijuana as medicine.* New York: New York University Press.

Chapman, J. (2006). Anxiety and defective decision making: An elaboration of the group-think model. *Management Decision, 44,* 1391–1404.

Chapman, L. J., & Chapman, J. P. (1973). *Disordered thought in schizophrenia.* New York: Appleton-Century-Crofts.

Charman, D. P. (2004). *Core processes in brief psychodynamic psychotherapy: Advancing effective practice.* Mahwah, NJ: Lawrence Erlbaum Associates.

Chechile, R. A. (2003). Review of 'Elements of Psychophysical Theory.' *Journal of Mathematical Psychology, 47,* 385.

Chen, A., Zhou, Y., & Gong, H. (2004). Firing rates and dynamic correlated activities of ganglion cells both contribute to retinal information processing. *Brain Research, 1017,* 13–20.

Chen, Z., Fu, L., Peng, Y., Cai, R., & Zhou, S. (2011). The relationship among childhood abuse, parenting styles, and antisocial personality disorder tendency. *Chinese Journal of Clinical Psychology, 19,* 212–214.

Cheney, C. D. (1996). Medical non adherence: A behavior analysis. In J. R. Cautela & W. Ishaq (Eds.), *Contemporary issues in behavior therapy: Improving the human condition: Applied Clinical Psychology.* New York: Plenum Press.

Cheston, S. E. (2000). A new paradigm for teaching counseling theory and practice. *Counselor Education & Supervision, 39,* 254–269.

Cho, A. (2000, June 16). What's shakin' in the ear? *Science, 288,* 1954–1955.

Chomsky, N. (1968). *Language and mind.* New York: Harcourt Brace Jovanovich.

Chomsky, N. (1969). *Aspects of the theory of syntax.* Cambridge, MA: MIT Press.

Chomsky, N. (1978). On the biological basis of language capacities. In G. A. Miller & E. Lennenberg (Eds.), *Psychology and biology of language and thought.* New York: Academic Press.

Chomsky, N. (1991). Linguistics and cognitive science: Problems and mysteries. In A. Kasher (Ed.), *The Chomskyan turn.* Cambridge, MA: Blackwell.

Choudhary, M. I., Nawaz, S. A., Zaheer-ul-Haq, A., Azim, M. K., Ghayur, M. N., Lodhi, M. A., Jalil, S., Khalid, A., Ahmed, A., Rode, B. M., Attaur-Rahman, R., Gilani, A. U., & Ahmad, V. U. (2005, July 15). Juliflorine: A potent natural peripheral anionic-site-binding inhibitor of acetylcholinesterase with calcium-channel blocking potential, a leading candidate for Alzheimer's disease therapy. *Biochemical and Biophysical Research Communications, 15,* 1171–1177.

Christ, S. E., Steiner, R. D., & Grange, D. K. (2006). Inhibitory control in children with phenylketonuria. *Developmental Neuropsychology, 30,* 845–864.

Christensen, A. J., & Johnson, J. A. (2002). Patient adherence with medical treatment regimens: An interactive approach. *Current Directions in Psychological Science, 11,* 94–101.

Chronicle, E. P., MacGregor, J. N., & Ormerod, T. C. (2004). What makes an insight problem? The roles of heuristics, goal conception, and solution recoding in knowledge-lean problems. *Journal of Experimental Psychology: Learning, Memory, and Cognition, 30,* 14–27.

Chrysikou, E. G. (2006). When a shoe becomes a hammer: Problem solving as goal-derived, ad hoc categorization. *Dissertation Abstracts International: Section B: The Sciences and Engineering, 67*(1-B), 569.

Cialdini, R. B. (2006). *Influence: The psychology of persuasion.* New York: Collins.

Cialdini, R. B., Schaller, M., Houlihan, D., Arps, K., Fultz, J., & Beaman, A. L. (1975). Reciprocal concessions procedure for inducing compliance: The door-in-the-face technique. *Journal of Personality and Social Psychology, 31,* 206–215.

Cisler, J. M., James, G. A., Tripathi, S., Mletzko, T., Heim, C., Hu, X. P., Mayberg, H. S., Nemeroff, C. B., & Kilts, C. D. (2013). Differential functional connectivity within an emotion regulation neural network among individuals resilient and susceptible to the depressogenic effects of early life stress. *Psychological Medicine, 43,* 507–518.

Clark, D. A. (2004). *Cognitive-behavioral therapy for OCD.* New York: Guilford.

Clark, D. A. (2007). Obsessions and compulsions. In N. Kazantzis & L. L'Abate, *Handbook of homework assignments in psychotherapy: Research, practice, prevention.* New York: Springer Science + Business Media.

Clarkin, J. F., & Lenzenweger, M. F. (Eds.) (2004). *Major theories of personality disorders* (2nd ed.). New York: Guilford.

Clay D. L. (2000). Commentary: Rethinking our interventions in pediatric chronic pain and treatment research. *Journal of Pediatric Psychology, 25,* 53–55.

Clay, R. (2002, April). Overcoming barriers to pain relief. *Monitor on Psychology, 33*(4), 58.

Clayton, K., & Lundberg-Love, P. (2009). Caffeine: Pharmacology and effects of the world's most popular drug. *The Praeger international collection on addictions, Vol 2: Psychobiological profiles.* Santa Barbara, CA: Praeger/ABC-CLIO.

Clements, A. M., Rimrodt, S. L., & Abel, J. R. (2006). Sex differences in cerebral laterality of language and visuospatial processing. *Brain and Language, 98,* 150–158.

Cloud, J. (2000, June 5). The lure of ecstasy. *Time,* pp. 60–68.

Cloud, J. (2009, January 19). Minds on the edge. *Time,* pp. 40–46.

CNN.com (August 25, 2009). Coroner's preliminary finding: Michael Jackson overdosed on propofol. Retrieved from: http://www.cnn.com/2009/SHOWBIZ/Music/08/24/michael.jackson.propofol/index.html?iref=nextin

Coates, S. L., Butler, L. T., & Berry, D. C. (2006). Implicit memory and consumer choice: The mediating role of brand familiarity. *Applied Cognitive Psychology, 20,* 1101–1116.

Cobos, P., Sanchez, M., Garcia, C., Vera, M. N., & Vila, J. (2002). Revisiting the James versus Cannon debate on emotion: Startle and autonomic modulation in patients with spinal cord injuries. *Biological Psychology, 61,* 251–269.

Cohen, B. H. (2002). *Explaining psychological statistics* (2nd ed.). New York: Wiley.

Cohen, J. (2003). Things I have learned (so far). In A. E. Kazdin (Ed.), *Methodological issues and strategies in clinical research* (3rd ed.). Washington, DC: American Psychological Association.

Cohen, L., & Cashon, C. (2003). Infant perception and cognition. In R. Lerner & M. Easterbrooks (Eds.), *Handbook of psychology: Developmental psychology* (Vol. 6). New York: Wiley.

Cohen, P. (2009). Medical marijuana: The conflict between scientific evidence and political ideology. Part one of two. *Journal of Pain & Palliative Care Pharmacotherapy, 23,* 4–25.

Cohen, S. (2004, November). Social relationships and health. *American Psychologist,* 676–684.

Cohen, S., Doyle, W. J., Turner, R., Alper, C. M., & Skoner, D. P. (2003). Sociability and susceptibility to the common cold. *Psychological Science, 14,* 389–395.

Cohen, S., Hamrick, N., & Rodriguez, M. (2002). Reactivity and vulnerability to stress-associated risk for upper respiratory illness. *Psychosomatic Medicine, 64,* 302–310.

Cohen, S., Kamarck, T., & Mermelstein, R. (1983). A global measure of perceived stress. *Journal of Health and Social Behavior, 24,* 385–396.

Coleman, E. (2002). Masturbation as a means of achieving sexual health. *Journal of Psychology and Human Sexuality, 14,* 5–16.

Coles, R. (1997). *The moral intelligence of children.* New York: Random House.

Colland, V. T., Van Essen-Zandvliet, L. E. M., Lans, C., Denteneer, A., Westers, P., & Brackel, H. J. L. (2004). Poor adherence to self-medication instructions in children with asthma and their parents. *Patient Education and Counseling, 55,* 416–421.

Collins, A. M., & Loftus, E. F. (1975). A spreading-activation theory of semantic processing. *Psychological Review, 82,* 407–428.

Collins, A. M., & Quillian, M. R. (1969). Retrieval times from semantic memory. *Journal of Verbal Learning and Verbal Behavior, 8,* 240–247.

Colom, R., Jung, R. E., & Haier, R. J. (2006). Finding the g-factor in brain structure using the method of correlated vectors. *Intelligence, 34,* 561–570.

Coltheart, M., Langdon, R., & McKay, R. (2007). Schizophrenia and monothematic delusions. *Schizophrenia Bulletin, 33,* 642–647.

Coltraine, S., & Messineo, M. (2000). The perpetuation of subtle prejudice: Race and gender imagery in 1990s television advertising. *Sex Roles, 42,* 363–389.

Colwell, M. J., & Lindsey, E. W. (2005). Preschool children's pretend and physical play and sex of play partner: Connections to peer competence. *Sex Roles, 52,* 497–509.

Compagni, A., & Manderscheid, R. W. (2006). A neuroscientist-consumer alliance to transform mental health care, *Journal of Behavioral Health Services & Research, 33,* 265–274.

Comuzzie, A. G., & Allison, D. B. (1998, May 29). The search for human obesity genes. *Science, 280,* 1374–1377.

Conduit, R., Crewther, S. G., & Coleman, G. (2004). Spontaneous eyelid movements (ELMS) during sleep are related to dream recall on awakening. *Journal of Sleep Research, 13,* 137–144.

Conner, M., Povey, R., Sparks, P., James, R., & Shepherd, R. (2003). Moderating role of attitudinal ambivalence within the theory of planned behaviour. *British Journal of Social Psychology, 42,* 75–94.

Connolly, A. C. (2007). Concepts and their features: Can cognitive science make good on the promises of concept empiricism? *Dissertation Abstracts International: Section B: The Sciences and Engineering, 67*(7-B), 4125.

Consumer Reports (CR). (1993, June). Dieting and weight loss, p. 347.

Consumer Reports (CR). (1995, November). Mental health: Does therapy help? pp. 734–739.

Conte, H. R., Plutchik, R., & Draguns, J. G. (2004). The measurement of ego defenses in clinical research. In U. Hentschel, G. Smith, J. G. Draguns, & W. Ehlers (Eds.), *Defense mechanisms: Theoretical, research and clinical perspectives.* Oxford, England: Elsevier Science Ltd.

Conway, M. A. (Ed.) (2002). *Levels of processing 30 years on special issue of memory.* Hove, UK: Psychology Press.

Cooke, J. R., & Ancoli-Israel, S. (2006). Sleep and its disorders in older adults. *Psychiatric Clinics of North America, 29,* 1077–1093.

Cooklin, A. (2000). Therapy, the family and others. In H. Maxwell, *Clinical psychotherapy for health professionals.* Philadelphia: Whurr Publishers.

Cookson, R. (2005, March 10). A noise for danger: Ten years ago, a Belgian rodentlover decided that rats were smart. *The Independent* (London), p. F7.

Cooper, H., & Patall, E. (2009, June). The relative benefits of meta-analysis conducted with individual participant data versus aggregated data. *Psychological Methods, 14,* 165–176.

Cooper, J. (2007). *Cognitive dissonance: Fifty years of a classic theory.* Thousand Oaks, CA: Sage Publications.

Cooper, J., & Strayer, D. (2008). Effects of simulator practice and real world experience on cell-phone-related driver distraction. *Human Factors, 50,* 893–902.

Cooper, J., Mirabile, R., & Scher, S. J. (2005). Actions and attitudes: The theory of cognitive dissonance. In T. C. Brock &M. C. Green (Eds.), *Persuasion: Psychological insights and perspectives* (2nd ed.). Thousand Oaks, CA: Sage Publications.

Cooper, Z., & Shafran, R. (2008). Cognitive behaviour therapy for eating disorders. *Behavioural and Cognitive Psychotherapy, 36,* 713–722.

Coplan, R., Reichel, M., & Rowan, K. (2009). Exploring the associations between maternal personality, child temperament, and parenting: A focus on emotions. *Personality and Individual Differences, 46,* 241–246.

Copolov, D. L., Seal, M. L., Maruff, P., Ulusoy, R., Wong, M. T. H., Tochon-Danguy, et al. (2003). Cortical activation associated with the human experience of auditory hallucinations and perception of human speech in schizophrenia: A PET correlation study. *Psychiatry Research: Neuroimaging, 123,* 139–152.

Corbetta, M., Kincade, J. M., & Shulman, G. L. (2002). Neural systems for visual orienting and their relationships to spatial working memory. *Journal of Cognitive Neuroscience, 14,* 508–523.

Corcoran, B. (2005, July 5). Large African rats being used to find landmines in Mozambique. *The Irish Times,* p. 10.

Cordnoldi, C., De Beni, R., & Helstrup, T. (2007). Memory sensitivity in autobiographical memory. In S. Magnussen, & T. Helstrup, *Everyday memory.* New York: Psychology Press.

Coren, S. (1992). The moon illusion: A different view through the legs. *Perceptual and Motor Skills, 75,* 827–831.

Coren, S. (2004). Sensation and perception. In I. B. Weiner. *Handbook of Psychology* (Vol. 1). Hoboken, NJ: John Wiley & Sons.

Coren, S., & Ward, L. M. (1989). *Sensation and perception* (3rd ed.). San Diego, CA: Harcourt Brace Jovanovich.

Coren, S., Porac, C., & Ward, L. M. (1984). *Sensation and perception* (2nd ed.). New York: Academic Press.

Cosmides, L., & Tooby, J. (2004). Social exchange: The evolutionary design of a neurocognitive system. In M. S. Gazzaniga (Ed.), *Cognitive neurosciences* (3rd ed.). Cambridge, MA: MIT.

Costa, P. T., Jr., & Widiger, T. A. (Eds.). (2002). *Personality disorders and the Five-Factor Model of personality* (2nd ed.). Washington, DC: American Psychological Association.

Couturier, J., & Lock, J. (2006). Eating disorders: Anorexia nervosa, bulimia nervosa, and binge eating disorder. In T. G. Plante, *Mental disorders of the new millennium: Biology and function* (Vol 3.). Westport, CT: Praeger Publishers/Greenwood Publishing.

Coventry, K. R., Venn, S. F., Smith, G. D., & Morley, A. M. (2003). Spatial problem solving and functional relations. *European Journal of Cognitive Psychology, 15,* 71–99.

Cowan, N., Towse, J. N., Hamilton, Z., Saults, J. S., Elliott, E. M., Lacey, J. F., et al. (2003). Children's working-memory processes: A response-timing analysis. *Journal of Experimental Psychology: General, 132,* 113–132.

Cowley, G. (2003, February 24). Our bodies, our fears. *Newsweek,* pp. 43–44.

Cox, J. (2003, May 6). How far would you go to save your life? *Denver Post,* p. F1.

Coyle, N. (2006). The hard work of living in the face of death. *Journal of Pain and Symptom Management, 32,* 266–274.

Craig, R. J. (1999). *Interpreting personality tests: A clinical manual for the MMPI-2, MCMI-III, CPI-R, and 16PF.* New York: Wiley.

Craig, W. M., & Pepler, D. J. (2007). Understanding bullying: From research to policy. *Canadian Psychology, 48,* 86–93.

Craig, W.M., Pepler, D. J., & Blais, J. (2007). Responding to bullying: What works? *International Journal of School Psychology, 28,* 15–24.

Craik, F. I. M. (1990). Levels of processing. In M. E. Eysenck (Ed.), *The Blackwell dictionary of cognitive psychology.* London: Blackwell.

Craik, F. I., & Lockhart, R. S. (1972). Levels of processing: A framework for memory research. *Journal of Verbal Behavior, 11,* 671–684.

Craik, F., & Lockhart, R. (2008). Levels of processing and Zinchenko's approach to memory research. *Journal of Russian & East European Psychology, 46,* 52–60.

Cramer, P. (2007). Longitudinal study of defense mechanisms: Late childhood to late adolescence. *Journal of Personality, 75,* 1–23.

Crawford, N. (2002). Science-based program curbs violence in kids. *APA Monitor, 33,* 38–39.

Creasey, G. L. (2005). *Research methods in lifespan development* (6th ed.). Boston: Allyn & Bacon.

Creswell, J., & Landon, T. (2009, January 25). The talented Mr. Madoff. *The New York Times*, p. 1.

Criswell, H., Ming, Z., Kelm, M., & Breese, G. (2008, August). Brain regional differences in the effect of ethanol on GABA release from presynaptic terminals. *Journal of Pharmacology and Experimental Therapeutics, 326*, 596–603.

Crombag, H. S., & Robinson, R. E. (2004). Drugs, environment, brain, and behavior. *Current Directions in Psychological Science, 13*, 107–111.

Cropley, A. (2006). In praise of convergent thinking. *Creativity Research Journal, 18*, 391–404.

Crosnoe, R., & Elder, G. H., Jr. (2002). Successful adaptation in the later years: A life course approach to aging. *Social Psychology Quarterly, 65*, 309–328.

Csikszentmihalyi, M. (1997). *Creativity: Flow and the psychology of discovery and invention.* New York: BasicBooks/Mastermind Series.

CTV.ca. (2006, February 4). Victims of justice. Retrieved from www.ctv.ca/servlet/ArticleNews/story/CTVNews/20060203/wfive_Victimsof Justice_060204/20060204?hub=WFive.

CTV.ca/Canadian Press. (2005, November 17). One in seven suffers insomnia, StatsCan reports. Retrieved from www.ctv.ca/servlet/ArticleNews/story/CTVNews/20051116/insomnia_statscan_051116?s_name=&no_ads=.

CTV.ca/Canadian Press. (2006, September 6). Disabled Alberta boy can bring service dog to school. Retrieved from www.ctv.ca/servlet/ArticleNews/story/CTVNews/20060901/service_dog_update_060907/2006090/.

CTV.ca/Canadian Press. (2008, March 6). Military recruiting hundreds to combat PTSD. Retrieved from www.ctv.ca/servlet/ArticleNews/story/CTVNews/20080306/PTSD_military_080306?s_name=&no_ads=.

Cummings, A., Ceponiene, R., & Koyama, A. (2006). Auditory semantic networks for words and natural sounds. *Brain Research, 1115*, 92–107.

Cunningham, P. (2006). Early years teachers and the influence of Piaget: Evidence from oral history. *Early Years An International Journal of Research and Development, 26*, 5–16.

Cwikel, J., Behar, L., & Rabson-Hare, J. (2000). A comparison of a vote count and a meta-analysis review of intervention research with adult cancer patients. *Research on Social Work Practice, 10*, 139–158.

Cynkar, A. (2007), The changing gender composition of psychology. *Monitor on Psychology, 38*, 46–48.

Czeisler, C. A., Duffy, J. F., Shanahan, T. L., Brown, E. N., Mitchell, J. F., Rimmer, D. W., Ronda, J. M., Silva, E. J., Allan, J. S., Emens, J. S., Dijk, D. J., & Kronauer, R. E. (1999, June 25). Stability, precision, and near-24-hour period of the human circadian pacemaker. *Science, 284*, 2177–2181.

Czopp, A. M., & Monteith, M. J. (2006). Thinking well of African Americans: Measuring complimentary stereotypes and negative prejudice. *Basic and Applied Social Psychology, 28*, 233–250.

Daftary, F., & Meri, J. W. (2002). *Culture and memory in medieval Islam.* London: I. B. Tauris.

Daily, D., Ardinger H., & Holmes G. (February 2000). Identification and evaluation of mental retardation. American Family Physician. 61 (4); 1059–67

Daines, B. (2006). Violations of agreed and implicit sexual and emotional boundaries in couple relationships—some thoughts arising from Levine's 'A clinical perspective on couple infidelity'. *Sexual and Relationship Therapy, 21*, 45–53.

Dalai Lama, & Ekman, P. (2008). *Emotional awareness: Overcoming the obstacles to psychological balance and compassion.* New York: Time Books.

Dale, A. (2006). Quality issues with survey research. *International Journal of Social Research Methodology: Theory & Practice, 9, Special issue: Quality in Social Research*, 143–158.

Daley, E. M., McDermott, R. J., Brown, K. R. M., & Kittleson, M. J. (2003). Conducting Web-based survey research: A lesson in Internet designs. *American Journal of Health Behavior, 27*, 116–124.

Damasio, A. (1999). *The feeling of what happens: Body and emotion in the making of consciousness.* New York: Harcourt Brace.

Damon, W. (1999, August). The moral development of children. *Scientific American*, pp. 72–78.

Dani, J. A., & Montague, P. (2007). Disrupting addiction through the loss of drug-associated internal states. *Nature Neuroscience, 10*, 403–404.

Darley, J. M. (1995). Constructive and destructive obedience: A taxonomy of principal-agent relationships. *Journal of Social Issues, 51*, 125–154.

Darwin, C. J., Turvey, M. T., & Crowder, R. G. (1972). An auditory analogue of the Sperling partial-report procedure: Evidence for brief auditory storage. *Cognitive Psychology, 3*, 255–267.

Das, A. (2007). Masturbation in the United States. *Journal of Sex & Marital Therapy, 33*, 301–317.

Das, A., Parish, W., & Laumann, E. (2009). Masturbation in urban China. *Archives of Sexual Behavior, 38*, 108–120.

Davidson, R. J., Gray, J. A., LeDoux, J. E., Levenson, R. W., Pankseep, J., & Ekman, P. (1994). Is there emotion-specific physiology? In P. Ekman & R. J. Davidson (Eds.), *The nature of emotion.* New York: Oxford University Press.

Davies, S., Jackson, P., Lewis, G., Hood, S., Nutt, D., & Potokar, J. (2008). Is the association of hypertension and panic disorder explained by clustering of autonomic panic symptoms in hypertensive patients? *Journal of Affective Disorders, 111*, 344–350.

Davis, L. J. (2009, June 15). Sotomayor and the New Haven firefighters case: More myths than facts. *The Washington Times*, p. A04.

Davis, O., Haworth, C., & Plomin, R. (2009, January). Learning abilities and disabilities: Generalist genes in early adolescence. *Cognitive Neuropsychiatry, 14*, 312–331.

Davis, P. (2007). The time 100: The people who shape our world. *Time Magazine: U.S. Special Edition, 169(20)*, 54. Retrieved from www.time.com/time/specials/2007/time100.

Day, A. L., & Livingstone, H. A. (2003). Gender differences in perceptions of stressors and utilization of social support among university students. *Canadian Journal of Behavioural Science, 35*, 73–83.

Day, R. D., & Lamb, M. E. (2004). *Conceptualizing and measuring father involvement.* Mahwah, NJ: Lawrence Erlbaum Associates.

De Beni, R., Pazzaglia, F., & Gardini, S. (2007). The generation and maintenance of visual mental images: Evidence from image type and aging. *Brain and Cognition, 63*, 271–278.

de Fockert, J. W., Rees, G., Frith, C. D., & Lavie, N. (2001, March 2). The role of working memory in visual selective attention. *Science, 291*, 1803–1806.

de Gelder, B. (2000). More to seeing than meets the eye. *Science, 289*, 1148–1149.

de Groot, A. D. (1966). Perception and memory versus thought: Some old ideas and recent findings. In B. Kleinmuntz (Ed.), *Problem solving: Research, method, and theory.* New York: Wiley.

DeMaris, A. (2013). Burning the candle at both ends: Extramarital sex as a precursor of marital disruption. *Journal of Family Issues, 34*, 1474–1499.

De Oliveira-Souza, R., Hare, R. D., Bramati, I. E., Garrido, G. J., Ignácio, F. A., Tovar-Moll, F., & Moll, J. (2008). Psychopathy as a disorder of the moral brain: Fronto-temporo-limic grey matter reductions demonstrated by voxel-based morphometry. *NeuroImage, 40(3)*, 1202–1213.

Dean, C., & Dresbach, T. (2006). Neuroligins and neurexins: Linking cell adhesion, synapse formation and cognitive function. *International Journal of Psychiatry in Clinical Practice, 10 (Suppl.)*, 5–11.

Dean-Borenstein, M. T. (2007). The long-term psychosocial effects of trauma on survivors of human-caused extreme stress situations. *Dissertation Abstracts International: Section B: The Sciences and Engineering, 67(11-B)*, 6733.

Dearing, E., McCartney, K., & Taylor, B. (2009). Does higher quality early child care promote low-income children's math and reading achievement in middle childhood? *Child Development, 80*, 1329–1349.

Deater-Deckard, K., Ivy, L., & Smith, J. (2005). Resilience in gene-environment transactions. In S. Goldstein & R. B. Brooks (Eds.), *Handbook of resilience in children.* New York: Kluwer Academic/Plenum Publishers.

Deci, E. L., Koestner, R., & Ryan, R. M. (2001). Extrinsic rewards and intrinsic motivation in education: Reconsidered once again. *Review of Educational Research, 71,* 1–27.

Dediu, D., & Ladd, D. R. (2007). From the Cover: Linguistic tone is related to the population frequency of the adaptive haplogroups of two brain size genes, ASPM and microcephalin. *Proceedings of the National Academy of Sciences, 104,* 10944–10949.

del Rosal, E., Alonso, L., & Moreno, R. (2006). Simulation of habituation to simple and multiple stimuli. *Behavioural Processes, 73,* 272–277.

DeLamater, J. D., & Sill, M. (2005). Sexual desire in later life. *Journal of Sex Research, 42,* 138–149.

Delgado, M. R., Labouliere, C. D., & Phelps, E. A. (2006). Fear of losing money? Aversive conditioning with secondary reinforcers [Special issue: Genetic, comparative and cognitive studies of social behavior] *Social Cognitive and Affective Neuroscience, 1,* 250–259.

Demaree, H. A., & Everhart, D. E. (2004). Healthy high-hostiles: Reduced para-sympathetic activity and decreased sympathovagal flexibility during negative emotional processing. *Personality and Individual Differences, 36,* 457–469.

Dempster, F. N. (1981). Memory span: Sources for individual and developmental differences. *Psychological Bulletin, 89,* 63–100.

Denmark, G. L., & Fernandez, L. C. (1993). Historical development of the psychology of women. In F. L. Denmark & M. A. Paludi (Eds.), *A handbook of issues and theories.* Westport, CT: Greenwood Press.

Dennis, I. (2007). Halo effects in grading student projects. *Journal of Applied Psychology, 92,* 1169–1176.

Dennis, T. A., Cole, P. M., Zahn-Waxler, C., & Mizuta, I. (2002). Self in context: Autonomy and relatedness in Japanese and U.S. mother-preschooler dyads. *Child Development, 73,* 1803–1817.

Denollet, J. (2005). DS14: Standard assessment of negative affectivity, social inhibition, and Type D personality. *Psychosomatic Medicine, 67,* 89–97.

Dentzer, S. (1986, May 5). Can you pass the job test? *Newsweek,* pp. 46–53.

Deouell, L. Y., Parnes, A., & Pickard, N. (2006). Spatial location is accurately tracked by human auditory sensory memory: Evidence from the mismatch negativity. *European Journal of Neuroscience, 24,* 1488–1494.

Department of Justice. (2008). Canadian charter of right and freedoms. Retrieved from laws.justice.gc.ca/en/charter/#garantie.

Deregowski, J. B. (1973). Illusion and culture. In R. L. Gregory & G. H. Combrich (Eds.), *Illusion in nature and art.* New York: Scribner.

DeRubeis, R., Hollon, S., & Shelton, R. (2003, May 23). Presentation, American Psychiatric Association meeting, Philadelphia.

Deshields, T., Tibbs, T., Fan, M. Y., & Taylor, M. (2006). Differences in patterns of depression after treatment for breast cancer [Electronic article published August 12, 2005]. *Psycho-Oncology, 15*(5), 398–406.

Desimone, R. (1992, October 9). The physiology of memory: Recordings of things past. *Science, 258,* 245–255.

Detoledo-Morrell, L., Stoub, T. R., & Wang, C. (2007). Hippocampal atrophy and disconnection in incipient and mild Alzheimer's disease. *Progressive Brain Research, 163C,* 741–823.

Detterman, D. K., Gabriel, L. T., & Ruthsatz, J. M. (2000). Intelligence and mental retardation. In R. J. Sternberg et al. (Eds.), *Handbook of intelligence.* New York: Cambridge University Press.

Devi, G. (2002). *Take a measure of your memory.* Dr. Gayatri Devi.

Devonport, J. J., & Lane, A. M. (2006). Relationships between self-efficacy, coping and student retention. *Social Behavior and Personality, 34,* 127–138.

Dhillon, S., Yang, L., & Curran, M. (2008). Spotlight on bupropion in major depressive disorder. *CNS Drugs, 22,* 613–617.

Di Forti, M., Lappin, J., & Murray, R. (2007, March). Risk factors for schizophrenia—All roads lead to dopamine. *European Neuropsychopharmacology, 17,* S101–SS107.

Diamond, M. (2009). Human intersexuality: Difference or disorder? *Archives of Sexual Behavior, 38,* 172.

DiCano, P., & Everitt, B. J. (2002). Reinstatement and spontaneous recovery of cocaine-seeking following extinction and different durations of withdrawal. *Behavioural Pharmacology, 13,* 397–406.

Dickerson, S. S., Kemeny, M. E., Aziz, N., Kim, K. H., & Fahey, J. L. (2004). Immunological effects of induced shame and guilt. *Psychosomatic Medicine, 66,* 124–131.

Diener, E., & Biswas-Diener, R. (2002). Will money increase subjective well-being? *Social Indicators Research, 57,* 119–169.

Diener, E., & Clifton, D. (2002). Life satisfaction and religiosity in broad probability samples. *Psychological Inquiry, 13,* 206–209.

Diener, E., & Seligman, M. E. P. (2002). Very happy people. *Psychological Science, 18,* 81–84.

Diener, E., & Seligman, M. E. P. (2004). Beyond money: Toward an economy of well-being. *Psychological Science in the Public Interest, 5,* 1–31.

Diener, E., Lucas, R. E., & Oishi, S. (2002). Subjective well being. The science of happiness and life satisfaction. In C. R. Snyder & S. J. Lopez (Eds.), *Handbook of positive psychology.* London: Oxford University Press.

Diener, M., Isabella, R., Behunin, M., & Wong, M. (2008). Attachment to mothers and fathers during middle childhood: Associations with child gender, grade, and competence. *Social Development, 17,* 84–101.

DiGiovanna, A. G. (1994). *Human aging: Biological perspectives.* New York: McGraw-Hill.

Digital Journal. Retrieved from http://www.digitaljournal.com/article /328128.

Dijksterhuis, A., Chartrand, T. L., & Aarts, H. (2007). Effects of Priming and Perception on Social Behavior and Goal Pursuit. *Frontiers of Social Psychology, 17,* 33–40.

Dillard, J. P., & Shen, L. (2004). On the nature of reactance and its role in persuasive health communication. *Communication Monographs, 72,* 144–168.

Dillard, J. P., & Shen, L. (2007). Self-report measures of discrete emotions. In R. A. Reynolds, R. Woods, & J. D. Baker, *Handbook of research on electronic surveys and measurements.* Hershey, PA: Idea Group Reference/IGI Global, 2007.

DiLorenzo, P. M., & Yougentob, S. L. (2003). Olfaction and taste. In M. Gallagher & R. J. Nelson, *Handbook of psychology: Biological psychology* (Vol 3). New York: Wiley.

DiManno, R. (2010, February 24). Triumph and tears for heartbroken Joannie Rochette. *The Star.com.* Retrieved from olympics.thestar.com/2010/article/771171—rochette-mom-wanted-me-to-have-a-better-life-than-she-had.

Dixon, R. A., & Cohen, A. L. (2003). Cognitive development in adulthood. In R. M. Lerner, M. A. Easterbrooks, et al. (Eds.), *Handbook of psychology: Developmental psychology* (Vol. 6). New York: Wiley.

Dixon, R. A., Rust, T. B., & Feltmate, S. E. (2007). Memory and aging: Selected research directions and application issues. *Canadian Psychology Psychologie Canadienne, 48,* 67–76.

Do, V. T. (2006). Asian American men and the media: The relationship between ethnic identity, self-esteem, and the endorsement of stereotypes. *Dissertation Abstracts International: Section B: The Sciences and Engineering, 67*(6-B), 3446.

Dobbins, A. C., Jeo, R. M., Fiser, J., & Allman, J. M. (1998, July 24). Distance modulation of neural activity in the visual cortex. *Science, 281,* 552–555.

Dobbs, D. (2012). The new temper tantrum disorder. Posted Friday, Dec. 7, 2012 in *Slate.* Retrieved from http://www.slate.com/.

Dodge, K. A. (2004). The nature-nurture debate and public policy [Special issue: 50th anniversary issue, part 2: The maturing of the human development sciences—Appraising past, present, and prospective agendas]. *Merrill-Palmer Quarterly: Journal of Developmental Psychology, 50,* 418–427.

Doidge, N. (2015). The brain's way of healing: Remarkable discoveries and recoveries from the frontiers of neuroplasticity. Toronto: Viking Press.

Dokoupil, T. (2012, July 16). Is the onslaught making us crazy? *Newsweek,* 24–30.

Dolan, R. J. (2002, November 8). Emotion, cognition, and behavior. *Science, 298,* 1191–1194.

Dolbier, C. L., Smith, S. E., & Steinhardt, M. A. (2007). Relationships of protective factors to stress and symptoms of illness. *American Journal of Health Behavior, 31*, 423–433.

Dollard, J., Doob, L., Miller, N., Mower, O. H., & Sears, R. R. (1939). *Frustration and aggression.* New Haven, CT: Yale University Press.

Domhoff, G. W. (1996). *Finding meaning in dreams: A quantitative approach.* New York: Plenum Press.

Domhoff, G. W. (2001). A new neurocognitive theory of dreams. *Dreaming, 11*, 13–33.

Domhoff, G. W. (2003). *The scientific study of dreams: Neural networks, cognitive development, and content analysis.* Washington, DC: American Psychological Association.

Domschke, K. (2013). Clinical and molecular genetics of psychotic depression. *Schizophrenia Bulletin, 39*, 766–775.

Donahoe, J. W. (2003). Selectionism. In K. A. Lattal, & P. N. Chase (Eds.), *Behavior theory and philosophy.* New York: Kluwer Academic/Plenum Publishers.

Donahoe, J. W., & Vegas, R. (2004). Pavlovian Conditioning: The CSUR Relation. *Journal of Experimental Psychology: Animal Behavior Processes, 30*, 17–33.

Dortch, S. (1996, October). Our aching heads. *American Demographics*, pp. 4–8.

Doty, R. L., Green, P. A., Ram, C., & Yankell, S. L. (1982). Communication of gender from human breath odors: Relationship to perceived intensity and pleasantness. *Hormones and Behavior, 16*, 13–22.

Dougall, A. L., & Baum, A. (2004). Psychoneuroimmunology and trauma. In P. P. Schnurr & B. L. Green (Eds.), *Trauma and health: Physical health consequences of exposure to extreme stress.* Washington, DC: American Psychological Association.

Douglas, O., Burton, K. S., & Reese-Durham, N. (2008). The effects of the multiple intelligence teaching strategy on the academic achievement of eighth grade math students. *Journal of Instructional Psychology, 35*, 182–187.

Douglas–Brown, R., Goldstein, E., & Bjorklund, D. F. (2000). The history and zeitgeist of the repressed-false-memory debate: Scientific and sociological perspectives on suggestibility and childhood memory. In D. F. Bjorklund (Ed.), *False-memory creation in children and adults: Theory, research, and implications.* Mahwah, NJ: Lawrence Erlbaum.

Dovidio, J. F., & Gaertner, S. L. (2006). A multilevel perspective on prejudice: Crossing disciplinary boundaries. In P. A. M. Van Lange, *Bridging social psychology: Benefits of transdisciplinary approaches.* Mahwah, NJ: Lawrence Erlbaum Associates.

Dovidio, J. F., Gaertner, S. L., & Kawakami, K. (2003). Intergroup contact: The past, present, and the future. *Group Processes and Intergroup Relations, 6*, 5–20.

Dovidio, J. F., Piliavin, J. A., Schroeder, D. A., & Penner, L. A. (2006). *The social psychology of prosocial behavior.* Mahwah, NJ: Lawrence Erlbaum Associates.

Dowling, N., Jackson, A., & Thomas, S. (2008). Behavioral interventions in the treatment of pathological gambling: A review of activity scheduling and desensitization. *International Journal of Behavioral Consultation and Therapy, 4*, 172–187.

Drewes, A. A. (2005). Play in selected cultures: Diversity and universality. In E. Gil & A. A. Drewes, *Cultural issues in play therapy.* New York: Guilford Press.

Drob, S. (2005). The mystical symbol: Some comments on Ankor, Giegerich, Scholem, and Jung. *Journal of Jungian Theory & Practice, 7*, 25–29.

Drogin, E. (2005). Civil and criminal trial matters. In E. Drogin, *Law & mental health professionals: Kentucky.* Washington, DC: American Psychological Association.

Dryden, W. (2003). *Overcoming depression.* London: Sheldon Press.

Dryden, W., & David, D. (2008). Rational emotive behavior therapy: Current status. *Journal of Cognitive Psychotherapy, 22*, 195–209.

Duffy, M., Gillig, S. E., Tureen, R. M., & Ybarra, M. A. (2002). A critical look at the DSM-IV. *Journal of Individual Psychology, 58*, 363–373.

Duke, M., & Nowicki, S., Jr. (1979). *Abnormal psychology: Perspectives on being different.* Monterey, CA: Brooks/Cole.

Dumont, M., & Dumont, D. (2008). Deinstitutionalization in the United States and Italy: A historical survey. *International Journal of Mental Health, 37*, 61–70.

Duncker, K. (1945). On problem solving. *Psychological Monographs, 58* (5, whole no. 270).

Dunn, E., & Norton, M. (2012, July 8). Don't indulge. Be happy. *The New York Times Sunday Review*, p. 1.

Durik, A. M., Hyde, J. S., & Marks, A. C. (2006). Ethnicity and gender stereotypes of emotion. *Sex Roles, 54*, 429–445.

Dutton, D. G., & Aron, A. P. (1974). Some evidence for heightened sexual attraction under conditions of high anxiety. *Journal of Personality and Social Psychology, 30*, 510–517.

Dweck, C. S., Mangels, J., & Good, C. (2004). Motivational effects on attention, cognition, and performance. In D.Y. Dai & R.J. Sternberg (Eds.), *Motivation, emotion, and cognition: Integrated perspectives on intellectual functioning.* Mahwah, NJ: Erlbaum. Annual Meeting of the American Psychological Society, May, 2004, Chicago.

Eaker, E. D., Sullivan, L. M., Kelly-Hayes, M., D'Agostino, R. B., Sr., & Benjamin, E. J. (2004). Anger and hostility predict the development of atrial fibrillation in men in the Framingham Offspring Study. *Circulation, 109*, 1267–1271.

Ebbinghaus, H. (1885/1913). *Memory: A contribution to experimental psychology* (H. A. Roger & C. E. Bussenius, Trans.). New York: Columbia University Press.

Eberhard, K. M., Cutting, J. C., & Bock, K. (2005). Making syntax of sense: Number agreement in sentence production. *Psychological Review, 112*, 531–559.

Eberhardt, J. L., Goff, P. A., Purdie, V. J., & Davies, P. G. (2004). Seeming black: Race, crime, and visual processing. *Journal of Personality and Social Psychology, 87*, 876–893.

Ebstein, R. P., Benjamin, J., & Belmaker, R. H. (2003). Behavioral genetics, genomics, and personality. In R. Plomin & J. C. DeFries (Eds.), *Behavioral genetics in the postgenomic era.* Washington, DC: American Psychological Association.

Ebster, C., & Neumayr, B. (2008). Applying the door-in-the-face compliance technique to retailing. *The International Review of Retail, Distribution and Consumer Research, 18*, 121–128.

Eckardt, M. H. (2005). Karen Horney: A portrait: The 120th anniversary, Karen Horney, September 16, 1885. *American Journal of Psychoanalysis, 65*, 95–101.

Edinger, J. D., Wohlgemuth, W. K., Radtke, R. A., Marsh, G. R., & Quillian, R. E. (2001). Cognitive behavioral therapy for treatment of chronic primary insomnia A randomized controlled trial. *Journal of the American Medical Association, 285*, 1856–1864.

Edmonton Sun 2015). Military suicides outnumbered deaths in Afghanistan, new stats show. Retrieved from www.edmontonsun.com/2014/09/16/military-suicides-outnumbered-deaths-in-afghanistan-new-stats-show.

Edwards, R. R., & Fillingim, R. B. (2007). Self-reported pain sensitivity: Lack of correlation with pain threshold and tolerance. *European Journal of Pain, 11*, 594–598.

Egan, K. (2005). Students' development in theory and practice: The doubtful role of research. *Harvard Educational Review, 75*, 25–41.

Eggertson, L. (2009). Canada lags U.S. in adoption of e-prescribing. *Canadian Medical Association Journal, 180*, E25–E26.

Egliston, K., & Rapee, R. (2007). Inhibition of fear acquisition in toddlers following positive modelling by their mothers. *Behaviour Research and Therapy, 45*, 1871–1882.

Eisch, A., Cameron, H., Encinas, J., Meltzer, L., Ming, G., & Overstreet-Wadiche, L. (2008, November). Adult neurogenesis, mental health, and mental illness: Hope or hype? *Journal of Neuroscience, 28*(46), 1785–1791.

Eisenberg, N., Guthrie, I. K., & Cumberland, A. (2002). Prosocial development in early adulthood: A longitudinal study. *Journal of Personality and Social Psychology, 82*, 993–1006.

Eizenberg, M. M., & Zaslavsky, O. (2004). Students' verification strategies for combinatorial problems. *Mathematical Thinking and Learning, 6*, 15–36.

References

Ekman, P. (1972). Universals and cultural differences in facial expressions of emotion. In J. Cole (Ed.), *Darwin and facial expression: A century of research in review.* New York: Academic Press.

Ekman, P. (1994a). All emotions are basic. In P. Ekman & R. J. Davidson (Eds.), *The nature of emotion: Fundamental questions.* New York: Oxford University Press.

Ekman, P. (2007). *Emotions revealed: Recognizing faces and feelings to improve communication and emotional life* (2nd ed.). New York: Holt Paperbacks.

Ekman, P., & O'Sullivan, M. (1991). Facial expression: Methods, means, and moues. In R. S. Feldman & B. Rimé (Eds.), *Fundamentals of nonverbal behavior.* Cambridge, England: Cambridge University Press.

Ekroll, V., & Scherzer, T. R. (2009). Apparent visual motion of the observer's own limbs. *Perception, 38,* 778–780.

Elez, T. (2008). Therapy with immigrants in Canada. *Family Therapy Magazine,* January–February, 28–30.

Elfhag, K., Tynelius, P., & Rasmussen, F. (2007). Sugar-sweetened and artificially sweetened soft drinks in association to restrained, external and emotional eating. *Physiology & Behavior, 91,* 191–195.

El-Hai, J. (2005). *The lobotomist: A maverick medical genius and his tragic quest to rid the world of mental illness.* New York: Wiley.

Elkins, G., Marcus, J., Bates, J., Hasan, R. M., & Cook, T. (2006). Intensive hypnotherapy for smoking cessation: a prospective study. *International Journal of Clinical Experimental Hypnosis, 54,* 303–315.

Ellins, E., Halcox, J., Donald, A., Field, B., Brydon, L., Deanfield, J., et al. (2008). Arterial stiffness and inflammatory response to psychophysiological stress. *Brain, Behavior, and Immunity, 22,* 941–948.

Elliott, A. (2002). *Psychoanalytic theory: An introduction* (2nd ed.). Durham, NC: Duke University Press.

Elliott, J., Berman, H., & Kim, S. (2002). Critical ethnography of Korean Canadian women's menopause experience. *Health Care for Women International, 23,* 377–388.

Ellis, A. (1974). *Growth through reason.* Hollywood, CA: Wilshire Books.

Ellis, A. (2000). *How to control your anger before it controls you.* New York: Citadel.

Ellis, A. (2002). *Overcoming resistance: A rational emotive behavior therapy integrated approach* (2nd ed.). New York: Springer.

Ellis, A. (2004). Expanding the ABCs of rational emotive behavior therapy. In A. Freeman, M. J. Mahoney, P. Devito, & D. Martin (Eds.), *Cognition and psychotherapy* (2nd ed.). New York: Springer Publishing Co.

El-Mallakh, R. S., & Abraham, H. D. (2007). MDMA (Ecstasy). *Annals of Clinical Psychiatry, 19,* 45–52.

Emick, J., & Welsh, M. (2005). Association between formal operational thought and executive function as measured by the Tower of Hanoi-Revised. *Learning and Individual Differences, 15,* 177–188.

Engen, T. (1987). Remembering odors and their names. *American Scientist, 75,* 497–503.

Engler, J., & Goleman, D. (1992). *The consumer's guide to psychotherapy.* New York: Simon & Schuster.

Epstein, R. (1996). *Cognition, creativity, and behavior: Selected essays.* Westport, CT: Praeger/Greenwood.

Eranti, S. V., & McLoughlin, D. M. (2003). Electroconvulsive therapy: State of the art. *British Journal of Psychiatry, 182,* 8–9.

Erickson, R. (2008, February). A study of the science of taste: On the origins and influence of the core ideas. *Behavioral and Brain Sciences, 31,* 59–75.

Erikson, E. H. (1963). *Childhood and society.* New York: Norton.

Esses Lab for the Study of Intergroup Relations. (2010). ELSIR research. Retrieved from www.psychology.uwo.ca/faculty/esseslab/research.htm.

Esses, V. M., & Vernon, R. A. (Eds.). (2008). *Explaining the breakdown of ethnic relations: Why neighbors kill.* Malden, MA: Blackwell.

Etchegary, H. (2004). Psychological aspects of predictive genetic-test decision: What do we know so far? *Analyses of Social Issues and Public Policy, 4,* 13–31.

Evans, A. M. (2007). Transference in the nurse-patient relationship. *Journal of Psychiatric and Mental Health Nursing, 14,* 189–195.

Evans, J. B. T. (2004). Informal reasoning: Theory and method. *Canadian Journal of Experimental Psychology, 58,* 69–74.

Evans, J. B. T., & Feeney, A. (2004). The role of prior belief in reasoning. In J. P. Leighton (Ed.), *Nature of reasoning.* New York: Cambridge University Press.

Everette, M. (2008). Gestational weight and dietary intake during pregnancy: Perspectives of African American women. *Maternal & Child Health Journal, 12,* 718–724.

Everly, G. S., Jr., & Lating, J. M. (2007). Psychotherapy: A cognitive perspective. In A. Monat, R. S. Lazarus, & G. Reevy, *The Praeger handbook on stress and coping* (Vol. 2). Westport, CT: Praeger Publishers/Greenwood Publishing.

Everson, C. A., Bergmann, B. M., & Rechtschaffen, A. (1989). Sleep deprivation in the rat III: Total sleep deprivation. *Sleep,* 12 (1) 13–21.

Eysenck, H. J. (1994). The big five or giant three: Criteria for a paradigm. In C. F. Halverson, Jr., G. A. Kohnstamm, & R. P. Martin (Eds.), *The developing structure of temperament and personality from infancy to adulthood.* Hillsdale, NJ: Erlbaum.

Eysenck, H. J. (1995). *Eysenck on extraversion.* New York: Wiley.

Eysenck, H. J., Barrett, P., Wilson, G., & Jackson, C. (1992). Primary trait measurement of the 21 components of the P-E-N system. *European Journal of Psychological Assessment, 8,* 109–117.

Fagan, J. F., & Holland, C. R. (2002). Equal opportunity and racial differences in IQ. *Intelligence, 30,* 361–387.

Fagan, J. F., & Holland, C. R. (2007). Racial equality in intelligence: Predictions from a theory of intelligence as processing. *Intelligence, 35,* 319–334.

Fagan, J. F., & Holland, C. R. (2009). Culture-fair prediction of academic achievement. *Intelligence, 37,* 62–67.

Falck-Ytter, T., & Gredebäck, G. (2006). Infants predict other people's action goals. *Nature Neuroscience, 9,* 878–879.

Falk, D., Forese, N., Sade, D. S., & Dudek, B. C. (1999). Sex differences in brain/body relationships of Rhesus monkeys and humans. *Journal of Human Evolution, 36,* 233–238.

Fallon, A. (2006). Informed consent in the practice of group psychotherapy. *International Journal of Group Psychotherapy, 56,* 431–453.

Fanselow, M. S., & Poulos, A. M. (2005). The neuroscience of mammalian associative learning. *Annual Review of Psychology, 56,* 207–234.

Farkas, R. (2004, February 24). Ray Farkas stayed awake during brain surgery for Parkinson's—and filmed it. *People,* pp. 99–100.

Fearing, V. G., & Clark, J. (Eds.). (2000). *Individuals in context: A practical guide to client-centered practice.* Chicago: Slack Publishing.

Fedeli, A., Braconi, S., Economidou, D., Cannella, N., Kallupi, M., Guerrini, R., et al. (2009). The paraventricularnucleus of the hypothalamus is a neuroanatomical substrate for the inhibition of palatable food intake by neuropeptide S. *European Journal of Neuroscience, 30,* 1594–1602.

Fee, E., Brown, T. M., Lazarus, J., & Theerman, P. (2002). Exploring acupuncture: Ancient ideas, modern techniques. *American Journal of Public Health, 92,* 1592.

Feinberg, A. W. (2002, April). Homo-cysteine may raise Alzheimer's risk: A physician's perspective. *HealthNews,* p. 4.

Feldhusen, J. F., (2006). The role of the knowledge base in creative thinking. In J. C. Kaufman, & J. Baer, *Creativity and reason in cognitive development.* New York: Cambridge University Press.

Feldman, R. S. (2010). *P.O.W.E.R. Learning: Strategies for Success in College and Life* (5th ed.). NY: McGraw-Hill.

Feldman, R. S. (Ed.). (1993). *Applications of non-verbal behavioral theories and research.* Hillsdale, NJ: Erlbaum.

Feldt, L. S. (2005). Estimating the reliability of cichotomous or trichotomous scores. *Educational and Psychological Measurement, 65,* 28–41.

Fenter, V. L. (2006). Concerns about Prozac and direct-to-consumer advertising of prescription drugs. *International Journal of Risk & Safety in Medicine, 18,* 1–7.

Festinger, D., Marlowe, D., Croft, J., Dugosh, K., Arabia, P., & Benasutti, K. (2009). Monetary incentives improve recall of research consent information: It pays to remember. *Experimental and Clinical Psychopharmacology, 17,* 99–104.

Festinger, L. (1957). *A theory of cognitive dissonance*. Stanford, CA: Stanford University Press.

Festinger, L., & Carlsmith, J. M. (1959). Cognitive consequences of forced compliance. *Journal of Abnormal and Social Psychology, 58,* 203–210.

Fields, R. D. (2004, April). The other half of the brain. *Scientific American*, pp. 55–61.

Fields-Meyer, T. (1995, September 25). Having their say. *People*, pp. 50–60.

Fields-Meyer, T., & Wihlborg, U. (2003, March 17). Gender jump. *People Magazine*, 109–111.

Fine, R., & Fine, L. (2003). *Basic chess endings*. New York: Random House.

Fingelkurts, A., Fingelkurts, A. A., & Kallio, S. (2007). Hypnosis induces a changed composition of brain oscillations in EEG: A case study. *Contemporary Hypnosis, 24,* 3–18.

Fink, G. (Ed.). (2000). *Encyclopedia of stress*. New York: Academic Press.

Finkelstein, M. (2009). Intrinsic vs. extrinsic motivational orientations and the volunteer process. *Personality and Individual Differences, 46,* 653–658.

Finkler, K. (2004). Traditional healers in Mexico: The effectiveness of spiritual practices. In U. P. Gielen, J. M. Fish, & J. G. Draguns (Eds.), *Handbook of culture, therapy, and healing*. Mahwah, NJ: Lawrence Erlbaum Associates.

Finlay, F. O., Jones, R., & Coleman, J. (2002). Is puberty getting earlier? The views of doctors and teachers. *Child: Care, Health and Development, 28,* 205–209.

Finley, C. L., & Cowley, B. J. (2005). The effects of a consistent sleep schedule on time taken to achieve sleep. *Clinical Case Studies, 4,* 304–311.

Firestein, B. A. (Ed.). (1996). *Bisexuality: The psychology and politics of an invisible minority*. Thousand Oaks, CA: Sage.

First, M. B., Frances, A., & Pincus, H. A. (2002). *DSM-IV guidebook*. Washington, DC: American Psychiatric Press.

Fischer, K. W., Shaver, P. R., & Carnochan, P. (1990). How emotions develop and how they organize development. *Cognition and Emotion, 4,* 81–127.

Fish, J. M. (Ed.) (2002). *Race and intelligence: Separating science from myth*. Mahwah, NJ: Erlbaum.

Fishbach, A., Dhar, R., & Zhang, Y. (2006). Subgoals as substitutes or complements: The role of goal accessibility. *Journal of Personality and Social Psychology, 91,* 232–242.

Fisher, C. B. (2003). *Decoding the ethics code: A practical guide for psychologists*. Thousand Oaks, CA: Sage.

Fisher, C. B., Hoagwood, K., Boyce, C., Duster, T., Frank, D. A., Grisso, T., et al. (2002). Research ethics for mental health science involving ethnic minority children and youths. *American Psychologist, 57,* 1024–1040.

Fisk, J. E., Bury, A. S., & Holden, R. (2006). Reasoning about complex probabilistic concepts in childhood. *Scandinavian Journal of Psychology, 47,* 497–504.

Fitzgerald, P., & Daskalakis, Z. (2008, January). The use of repetitive transcranial magnetic stimulation and vagal nerve stimulation in the treatment of depression. *Current Opinion in Psychiatry, 21,* 25–29.

Flam, F. (1991, June 14). Queasy riders. *Science, 252,* 1488.

Flavell, S. W., Cowan, C. W., Kim, T., Greer, P. L., Lin, Y., Paradis, S., et al. (2006, February 17). Activity-dependent regulation of MEF2 transcription factors suppresses excitatory synapse number. *Science, 311,* 1008–1010.

Fleischman, D. A., Wilson, R. S., Gabrieli, J. D. E., Bienias, J. L., & Bennett, D. A. (2004). A longitudinal study of implicit and explicit memory in old persons. *Psychology and Aging, 19,* 617–625.

Fleming, J. (2000). Affirmative action and standardized test scores. *Journal of Negro Education, 69,* 27–37.

Fletcher, J. M., Page, J. B., Francis, D. J., Copeland, K., Naus, M. J., Davis, C. M., Morris, R., Kroskopf, D., & Satz, P. (1996). Cognitive correlates of long-term cannabis use in Costa Rican men. *Archives of General Psychiatry, 53* (11), 1051–1057.

Florida, R. L. (2005). *The rise of creative cities: Cities and the creative class*. New York, NY: Routledge.

Focus on the Family National Survey. (2002). Canadian attitudes on the family: A complete report. Retrieved from www.imfcanada.org/article_files/Canadian%20Attitudes%20on%20the%20Family.pdf.

Fogarty, J. S., & Young, G. A., Jr. (2000). Patient-physician communication. *Journal of the American Medical Association, 289,* 92.

Folk, C., & Remington, R. (2008, January). Bottom-up priming of top-down attentional control settings. *Visual Cognition, 16,* 215–231.

Folkman, S., & Moskowitz, J. T. (2004). Coping: Pitfalls and promise. *Annual Review of Psychology, 55,* 745–774.

Follett, K., & Hess, T. M. (2002). Aging, cognitive complexity, and the fundamental attribution error. *Journal of Gerontology: Series B: Psychological Sciences and Social Sciences, 57B,* P312–P323.

Fombonne, E., Zakarian, R., Bennett, A. & McLean-Heywood, D. (2006). Pervasive developmental disorders in Montreal, Quebec, Canada: Prevalence and links with immunizations. Pediatrics, 118 (1), 139–150. doi: 10.1542/peds.2005-2993

Forer, B. (1949). The fallacy of personal validation: A classroom demonstration of gullibility. *Journal of Abnormal and Social Psychology, 44,* 118–123.

Forgas, J. P., & Laham, S. M. (2005). The interaction between affect and motivation in social judgments and behavior. In J. P. Forgas, K. P. Williams, & S. M. Laham (Eds.), *Social motivation: Conscious and unconscious processes*. New York: Cambridge University Press.

Forlenza, M. J., & Baum, M. J. (2004). Psychoneuroimmunology. In T. J. Boll, R. G. Frank, A. Baum, & J. L. Wallander (Eds.) *Handbook of clinical health psychology, Vol. 3: Models and perspectives in health psychology*. Washington, DC: American Psychological Association 81–114.

Foster, P., Drago, V., FitzGerald, D., Skoblar, B., Crucian, G., & Heilman, K. (2008). Spreading activation of lexical-semantic networks in Parkinson's disease. *Neuropsychologia, 46,* 1908–1914.

Foulds, J., Gandhi, K. K., Steinberg, M. B., Richardson, D. L., Williams, J. M., Burke, M. V., et al. (2006). Factors associated with quitting smoking at a tobacco dependence treatment clinic. *American Journal of Health Behavior, 30,* 400–412.

Fowler, C. A., & Galantucci, B. (2008). The relation of speech perception and speech production. In Pisoni, D. B. & Remez, R. E. (Eds)., *The handbook of speech perception*. Malden, MA: Blackwell Publishing.

Fox, C. R. (2006). The availability heuristic in the classroom: How soliciting more criticism can boost your course ratings. *Judgment and Decision Making, 1,* 86–90.

Fox, Michael J. (2002). *Lucky man: A memoir*. New York: Hyperion.

Fox, Michael J. (2009). *Always looking up: The adventures of an incurable optimist*. New York: Hyperion.

Fraley, R. C., & Spieker, S. J. (2003). Are infant attachment patterns continuously or categorically distributed? A taxometric analysis of strange situation behavior. *Developmental Psychology, 39,* 387–404.

Frances, A. (2013). *Saving normal: An insider's revolt against out-of-control psychiatric diagnosis, DSM-5, Big Pharma, and the medicalization of ordinary life*. New York: Morrow.

Frankenberg, W. K., et al. (1992). *Denver II training manual*. Denver, CO: Denver Developmental Materials.

Frankl, V. E. (1963). *Man's search for meaning: An introduction to logotherapy*. New York: Pocket Books.

Franklin, A., Pilling, M., & Davies, I. (2005). The nature of infant color categorization: Evidence from eye movements on a target decision task. *Journal of Experimental Child Psychology, 91,* 227–248.

Franko, D., & Striegel-Moore, R. (2002). The role of body dissatisfaction as a risk factor for depression in adolescent girls: Are the differences black and white? *Journal of Psychosomatic Research, 53,* 975–983.

Franks, D. D., & Smith, T. S. (1999) (Eds.). *Mind, brain, and society: Toward a neuro-sociology of emotion*. Stamford, CT: JAI Press.

Franzek, E., & Beckmann, H. (1996). Gene-environment interaction in schizophrenia: Season-of-birth effect reveals etiologically different subgroups. *Psychopathology, 29,* 14–26.

Frasure-Smith, N., Lesperance, F., & Talajic, M. (2000). The prognostic importance of depression, anxiety, anger, and social support following myocardial infarction: Opportunities for improving survival. In P. M. McCabe, N. Schneiderman, T. M. Field, & A. R. Wellens (Eds.), *Stress, coping, and cardiovascular disease.* Mahwah, NJ: Erlbaum.

Fredrickson, B. L., & Branigan, C. (2005). Positive emotions broaden the scope of attention and thought-action repertoires. *Cognition and Emotion, 19*, 313–332.

Freedman, D. S. (1995). The importance of body fat distribution in early life. *American Journal of the Medical Sciences, 310*, S72–S76.

Freedman, J. L., & Fraser, S. C. (1966). Compliance without pressure: The foot-in-the-door technique. *Journal of Personality and Social Psychology, 4*, 195–202.

Frensch, P. A., & Rünger, D. (2003). Implicit learning. *Current Directions in Psychological Science, 12*, 13–10.

Freud, S. (1900). *The interpretation of dreams.* New York: Basic Books.

Freud, S. (1922/1959). *Group psychology and the analysis of the ego.* London: Hogarth.

Friborg, O., Barlaug, D., Martinussen, M., Rosenvinge, J. H., & Hjemdal, O. (2005). Resilience in relation to personality and intelligence. *International Journal of Methods in Psychiatric Research, 14*, 29–42.

Friborg, O., Hjemdal, O., & Rosenvinge, J. H. (2006). Resilience as a moderator of pain and stress. *Journal of Psychosomatic Research, 61*, 213–219.

Friedberg, R. D. (2006). A cognitive-behavioral approach to family therapy. *Journal of Contemporary Psychotherapy, 36*, 159–165.

Friedman, A. F., Lewak, R., Nichols, D. S., & Webb, J. T. (2000). *Psychological assessment with the MMPI-2.* Mahwah, NJ: Erlbaum.

Friedman, D. E. (2004). *The new economics of preschool.* Washington, DC: Early Childhood Funders' Collaborative/NAEYC.

Friedman, J. M. (2003, February 7). A war on obesity, not the obese. *Science, 299*, 856–858.

Friedman, J. N. W., Oltmanns, T. F., & Turkheimer, E. (2007). Interpersonal perception and personality disorders: Utilization of a thin slice approach. *Journal of Research in Personality, 41*, 667–688.

Friedman, M. J. (2006). Posttraumatic stress disorder among military returnees from Afghanistan and Iraq. *American Journal of Psychiatry, 163*, 586–593.

Frijda, N. H. (2005). Emotion experience. *Cognition and Emotion, 19*, 473–497.

Fritsch, J. (1999, October 5). Scientists unmask diet myth: Willpower. *The New York Times*, pp. D1, D9.

Fritsch, T., McClendon, M. J., Smyth, K. A., Lerner, A. J., Friedland, R. P., & Larsen, J. D. (2007). Cognitive functioning in healthy aging: The role of reserve and lifestyle factors early in life. *Gerontologist, 47*, 307–322.

Fromkin, V. A. (2000). On the uniquenessof language. In K. Emmorey, H. Lane, et al. (Eds.), *The signs of language revisited: An anthology to honor Ursula Bellugi and Edward Klima.* Mahwah, NJ: Erlbaum.

Frost, R. O., & Steketee, G. (Eds.). (2002). *Cognitive approaches to obsessions and compulsions: Theory, assessment, and treatment.* New York: Pergamon Press.

Fuller, A. (2006). Hypnosis and ideomotor compliance in the treatment of smoking tobacco and cannabis. *Australian Journal of Clinical Hypnotherapy and Hypnosis, 27*, 14–18.

Furnham, A., & Crump, J. (2005). Personality traits, types, and disorders: An examination of the relationship between three self-report measures. *European Journal of Personality, 19*, 167–184.

Furumoto, L., & Scarborough, E. (2002). Placing women in the history of psychology: The first American women psychologists. In W. E. Pickren (Ed.), *Evolving perspectives on the history of psychology.* Washington, DC: American Psychological Association.

Fusari, A., & Ballesteros, S. (2008, August). Identification of odors of edible and nonedible stimuli as affected by age and gender. *Behavior Research Methods, 40*, 752–759.

Gaab, J., Rohleder, N., Nater, U. M., & Ehlert, U. (2005). Psychological determinants of the cortisol stress response: The role of anticipatory cognitive appraisal. *Psychoneuroendocrinology, 30*, 599–610.

Galanter, E. (1962). Contemporary psychophysics. In R. Brown, E. Galanter, E. Hess, & G. Maroler (Eds.), *New directions in psychology.* New York: Holt.

Galanter, M. (2007). Spirituality and recovery in 12-step programs: An empirical model. *Journal of Substance Abuse Treatment, 33*, 265–272.

Galanter, M., & Kleber, H. D. (Eds.). (1999). *The American Psychiatric Press textbook of substance abuse: Abuse treatment* (2nd ed.), Washington, DC: American Psychiatric Press.

Galatzer-Levy, R. M., & Cohler, B. J. (1997). *Essential psychoanalysis: A contemporary introduction.* New York: Basic Books.

Galef, D. (2001, April 27). The information you provide is anonymous, but what was your name again? *The Chronicle of Higher Education, 47*, p. B5.

Gallagher, D. J. (1996). Personality, coping, and objective outcomes: Extraversion, neuroticism, coping styles, and academic performance. *Personality & Individual Differences, 21*, 421–429.

Gami, A. S., Howard, D. E., Olson, E. J., & Somers, V. K. (2005). Day-night pattern of sudden death in obstructive sleep apnea. *New England Journal of Medicine, 353*, 1206–1214.

Gangestad, S. W., Simpson, J. A., Cousins, A. J., Garver-Apgar, C. E., & Christensen, P. N. (2004). Women's preferences for male behavioral displays change across the menstrual cycle. *Psychological Science, 15*, 203–207.

Gannon, P. J., Holloway, R. L., Broadfield, D.C., & Braun, A. R. (1998). Asymmetry of chimpanzee planum temporale: humanlike pattern of Wernicke's brain language area homolog. *Science, 279*, 220–222.

Garb, H. N., Wood, J. M., Lilenfeld, S. O., & Nezworski, M. T. (2005). Roots of the Rorschach controversy. *Clinical Psychology Review, 25*, 97–118.

Garber, J., & Horowitz, J. L. (2002). Depression in children. In I. H. Gotlib & C. L. Hammen (Eds.), *Handbook of depression.* New York: Guilford Press.

Garber, J., Clarke, G., Weersing, V., Beardslee, W., Brent, D., Gladstone, T., et al. (2009). Prevention of depression in at-risk adolescents: A randomized controlled trial. *Journal of the American Medical Association, 301*, 2215–2224.

Garcia, J. (1990). Learning without memory. *Journal of Cognitive Neuroscience, 2*, 287–305.

Garcia, J. (2003). Psychology is not an enclave. In R. J. Sternberg (Ed.), *Psychologists defying the crowd: Stories of those who battled the establishment and won.* Washington, DC: American Psychological Association.

Gardner, E. P., & Kandel, E. R. (2000). Touch. In E. R. Kandel, J. H. Schwartz, & T. M. Jessell (Eds.), *Principles of neural science* (4th ed.). New York: McGraw-Hill.

Gardner, F., & Moore, Z. (2008). Understanding clinical anger and violence: The anger avoidance model. *Behavior Modification, 32*, 897–912.

Gardner, H. (1975). *The shattered mind: The person after brain damage.* New York: Knopf.

Gardner, H. (1999). *Intelligence reframed: Multiple intelligences for the 21st century.* New York, NY: Basic Books.

Gardner, H. (2000). The giftedness matrix: A developmental perspective. In R. C. Friedman & B. M. Shore (Eds.). *Talents unfolding: Cognition and development.* Washington, DC: American Psychological Association.

Gardner, H. (2005). Scientific psychology: Should we bury it or praise it? In R. J. Sternberg (Ed.), *Unity in psychology: Possibility or pipe dream?* Washington, DC: American Psychological Association.

Gardner, H. (2006). *Multiple intelligences: New horizons in theory and practice* by New York: Basic Books.

Garwood, C. L., & Potts, L. A. (2007). Emerging pharmacotherapies for smoking cessation. *American Journal of Health Systems Pharmacology, 64*, 1693–1698.

Garza-Guerrero, C. (2000). Idealization and mourning in love relationships: Normal and pathological spectra. *Psychoanalytic Quarterly, 69*, 121–150.

Gatchel, R. J. & Weisberg, J. N. (2000). *Personality characteristics of patients with pain.* Washington, DC: APA Books.

Gatchel, R. J., & Oordt. M. S. (2003). Obesity. In R. J. Gatchel & M. S. Oordt, *Clinical health psychology and primary care: Practical advice and clinical guidance for successful collaboration.* Washington, DC: American Psychological Association.

Gathercole, S. E., & Baddeley, A.D. (1993). *Working memory and language processing.* Hillsdale, NJ: Erlbaum.

Gazzaniga, M. S. (1998, July). The split brain revisited. *Scientific American,* pp. 50–55.

Gazzaniga, M. S., Ivry, R. B., & Mangun, G. R. (2002). *Cognitive neuroscience: The biology of the mind* (2nd ed.). New York: W. W. Norton.

Ge, X., Kim, I. J., Brody, G. H., Conger, R. D., Simons, R. L., Gibbons, F. X., et al. (2003). It's about timing and change: Pubertal transition effects on symptoms of major depression among African American youths. *Developmental Psychology, 39,* 430–439.

Gegenfurtner, K. R. (2003). Color vision. *Annual Review of Neuroscience, 26,* 181–206.

Gelfand, M. M. (2000). Sexuality among older women. *Journal of Women's Health and Gender Based Medicine, 9*(Suppl. 1), S15–S20.

Gelman, R., & Kit-Fong Au, T. (Eds.). (1996). *Perceptual and cognitive development.* New York: Academic Press.

Genovese, J. E. C. (2006). Piaget, pedagogy, and evolutionary psychology. *Evolutionary Psychology, 4,* 2127–2137.

Gentner, D., Goldin, S., & Goldin-Meadow, S. (Eds.). (2003). *Language in mind: Advances in the study of language and cognition.* Cambridge, MA: MIT.

George, M. S., Wassermann, E. M., Williams, W. A., Callahan, A., Ketter, T. A., Baser, P., et al. (1995). Daily repetitive transcranial magnetic stimulations (rTMS) improves mood in depression. *Neuroreport: An International Journal for the Rapid Communication of Research in Neuroscience, 6,* 1853–1856.

George, S., & Moselhy, H. (2005). Cocaine-induced trichotillomania. *Addiction, 100,* 255–256.

George, T. P. (1999). Design, measurement, and analysis in developmental research. In M. Bornstein & M. Lamb, *Developmental psychology.* Mahwah, NJ: Erlbaum.

Gershkoff-Stowe, L., Connell, B., & Smith, L. (2006). Priming overgeneralizations in two- and four-year-old children. *Journal of Child Language, 33,* 461–486.

Ghaemi, S. N. (2003). *Mood disorders: A practical guide. Practical Guides in Psychiatry.* New York: Lippincott Williams & Wilkins.

Ghazvini, A., & Mullis, R. L. (2002). Center-based care for young children: Examining predictors of quality. *Journal of Genetic Psychology, 163,* 112–125.

Giacobbi, P. R., Jr., Lynn, T. K., Wetherington, J. M., Jenkins, J., Bodendorf, M., & Langley, B. (2004). Stress and coping during the transition to university for first-year female athletes. *Sports Psychologist, 18,* 1–20.

Gibbons, R. D., Brown, C. H., Hur, K., Marcus, S. M., Bhamik, D. K., Erkens, J. A., et al. (2007). Early evidence on the effects of regulators' suicidal warnings on SSRI prescriptions and suicide in children and adolescents. *American Journal of Psychiatry, 164,* 1356–1363.

Gibbs, N. (2005, August 8). Being 13. *Time,* pp. 41–55.

Gibbs, W. W. (2002, August.) From mouth to mind. *Scientific American,* p. 26.

Gibson, B. (1997). Smoker-nonsmoker conflict: Using a social psychological framework to understand a current social controversy. *Journal of Social Issues, 53,* 97–112.

Gilbert, D. T., McNulty, S. E., Guiliano, T. A., & Benson, J. E. (1992). Blurry words and fuzzy deeds: The attribution of obscure behavior. *Journal of Personality and Social Psychology, 62,* 18–25.

Gilbert, D. T., Miller, A. G., & Ross, L. (1998). Speeding with Ned: A personal view of the correspondence bias. In J. M. Darley & J. Cooper (Eds.), *Attribution and social interaction: The legacy of Edward E. Jones.* Washington, DC: American Psychological Association.

Gilboa, A., Winocur, G., & Rosenbaum, R. S. (2006). Hippocampal contributions to recollection in retrograde and anterograde amnesia. *Hippocampus, 16,* 966–980.

Gilchrist, A., Cowan, N., & Naveh-Benjamin, M. (2009). Investigating the childhood development of working memory using sentences: New evidence for the growth of chunk capacity. *Journal of Experimental Child Psychology, 104,* 252–265.

Gilligan, C. (1996). The centrality of relationships in psychological development: A puzzle, some evidence, and a theory. In G. G. Noam & K. W. Fischer (Eds.), *Development and vulnerability in close relationships.* Hillsdale, NJ: Erlbaum.

Gilligan, C. (2004). Recovering psyche: Reflections on life-history and history. *Annual of Psychoanalysis, 32,* 131–147.

Gilovich, T., Griffin, D., & Kahneman, D. (Eds.). (2002). *Heuristics and biases: The psychology of intuitive judgment.* Cambridge, England: Cambridge University Press.

Gladwell, M. (2004, September 20). Annals of psychology: Personality, plus how corporations figure out who you are. *The New Yorker,* 42–45.

Gladwin, T. (1964). Culture and logical process. In N. Goodenough (Ed.), *Explorations in cultural anthropology: Essays in honor of George Peter Murdoch.* New York: McGraw-Hill.

Glass, K., Flory, K., Hankin, B., Kloos, B., & Turecki, G. (2009). Are coping strategies, social support, and hope associated with psychological distress among Hurricane Katrina survivors? *Journal of Social and Clinical Psychology, 28,* 779–795.

Glasser, M. & Campbell, D. & Glasser, A., Leitch I. & Farrelly S. (2001). Cycle of child sexual abuse: links between being a victim and becoming a perpetrator. *The British Journal of Psychiatry, 179:* 482-494

Glenn, D. (2004, June 1). Students' performance on tests is tied to their views of their innate intelligence, researchers say. *The Chronicle of Higher Education,* p. 28.

Glickler, J. (2006). Advancing in advancement: A self-efficacy study of development practitioners in higher education. *Dissertation Abstracts International: Section B: The Sciences and Engineering, 67*(2-B), 1190.

Glicksohn, J., & Nahari, G. (2007). Interacting personality traits? Smoking as a test case. *European Journal of Personality, 21,* 225–234.

Glisky, E. L. (2007). Changes in cognitive function in human aging. In D. R. Riddle, *Brain aging: Models, methods, and mechanisms.* Boca Raton, FL: CRC Press.

Globeandmail.com. (2012, August 24). Stressed out? Try mindfulness medication. Retrieved from www.theglobeandmail.com/life /health-and-fitness/stressed-out-try-mindfulness-meditation/article 561130/.

Goffin, R. D., Jelley, R. B., & Wagner, S. H. (2003). Is halo helpful? Effects of inducing halo on performance rating accuracy. *Social Behavior and Personality, 31,* 625–636.

Goin, M. K. (2005). A current perspective on the psychotherapies. *Psychiatric Services, 56,* 255–257.

Gold, P. E., Cahill, L., & Wenk, G. L. (2002). Ginkgo biloba: A cognitive enhancer? *Psychological Science in the Public Interest, 3,* 2–7.

Golden, R. N., Gaynes, B. N., Ekstsrom, R. D., Hamer, R. M., Jacobsen, F. M., Suppes, T., et al. (2005). The efficacy of light therapy in the treatment of mood disorders: A review and meta-analysis of the evidence. *The American Journal of Psychiatry, 162,* 656–662.

Golden, W. L. (2006). Hypnotherapy for anxiety, phobias and psychophysiological disorders. In R. A. Chapman, *The clinical use of hypnosis in cognitive behavior therapy: A practitioner's casebook.* New York: Springer Publishing.

Goldstein, I. (2000). Female sexual arousal disorder: new insights. *International Journal of Impotence Research, 12*(Suppl. 4), S152–S157.

Goldstein, S. N. (2006). The exploration of spirituality and identity status in adolescence. *Dissertation Abstracts International: Section B: The Sciences and Engineering, 67*(6-B), 3481.

Goleman, D. (1993, July 21). "Expert" babies found to teach others. *The New York Times,* p. C10.

Goleman, D. (1995). *Emotional intelligence.* New York: Bantam.

Golombok, S., Cook, R., Bish, A., & Murray, C. (1995). Families created by the new reproductive technologies: Quality of parenting and social and emotional development of the children. *Child Development, 66,* 285–298.

Gontier, N. (2008). Genes, brains, and language: An epistemological examination of how genes can underlie human cognitive behavior. *Review of General Psychology, 12,* 170–180.

Gontkovsky, S. T. (2005). Neurobiological bases and neuropsychological correlates of aggression and violence. In J. P. Morgan (Ed.), *Psychology of aggression.* Hauppauge, NY: Nova Science Publishers.

Goode, E. (1999, April 13). If things taste bad, "phantoms" may be at work. *The New York Times,* pp. D1–D2.

Goode, E. (2003, January 28). Even in the age of Prozac, some still prefer the couch. *The New York Times,* Section F, p. 1.

Goodman, G., & Quas, J. (2008). Repeated interviews and children's memory: It's more than just how many. *Current Directions in Psychological Science, 17,* 386–390.

Goodman, W., K., Rudorfer, M. V., & Maser, J. D. (2000). *Obsessive-compulsive disorder: Contemporary issues in treatment.* Mahwah, NJ: Lawrence Erlbaum Associates.

Goodwin, R. D., & Hamilton, S. P. (2003). Lifetime comorbidity of antisocial personality disorder and anxiety disorders among adults in the community. *Psychiatry Research, 117,* 159–166.

Gooren, L. (2006). The biology of human psychosexual differentiation. *Hormones and Behavior, 50,* 589–601.

Gordon, D., & Heimberg, R. G. (2011). Reliability and validity of DSM-IV generalized anxiety disorder features. *Journal of Anxiety Disorders, 25,* 813–821.

Gossop, M., Stewart, D., & Marsden, J. (2008). Attendance at Narcotics Anonymous and Alcoholics Anonymous meetings, frequency of attendance and substance use outcomes after residential treatment for drug dependence: A 5-year follow-up study. *Addiction, 103,* 119–125.

Gotlib, I. H., Krasnoperova, E., Yue, D. N., & Joorman, J. (2004). Attentional biases for negative interpersonal stimuli in clinical depression. *Journal of Abnormal Psychology, 113,* 127–135.

Gottesman, I. I. (1991). *Schizophrenia genesis: The origins of madness.* New York: Freeman.

Gottesman, I. I., & Hanson, D. R. (2005). Human development: Biological and genetic processes. *Annual Review of Psychology, 56,* 263–286.

Gottlieb, D. A. (2004). Acquisition with partial and continuous reinforcement in pigeon autoshaping. *Learning and Behavior, 32,* 321–334.

Gould, R. L. (1978). *Transformations.* New York: Simon & Schuster.

Government of Canada. (2002). Rural Canada: Access to health care. *Depository Service Program.* Retrieved from http://dsp-psd.pwgsc.gc.ca/Collection-R/LoPBdP/BP/prb0245-e.htm.

Government of Canada. (2008). Smoking and pregnancy. Retrieved from www.phac-aspc.gc.ca/hp-gs/know-savoir/smoke_fumer_e.html.

Govindarajan, A., Kelleher, R. J., & Tonegawa, S. (2006). A clustered plasticity model of long-term memory engrams. *Nature Reviews Neuroscience, 7,* 575–583.

Grady, D. (2002, November 26). Why we eat (and eat and eat). *The New York Times,* pp. D1, D4.

Grady, D., & Kolata, G. (2003, August, 29). Gene therapy used to treat patient with Parkinson's. *The New York Times,* pp. A1, A18.

Graham, C. A., Bancroft, J., & Doll, H. A. (2007). Does oral contraceptive-induced reduction in free testosterone adversely affect the sexuality or mood of women? *Psychoneuroendocrinology, 32,* 246–255.

Graham, S. (1992). Most of the subjects were white and middle class. *American Psychologist 47*(5), 629–639.

Grahek, N. (2007). *Feeling pain and being in pain* (2nd ed.). Cambridge, MA: MIT Press.

Granic, I., Hollenstein, T., & Dishion, T. (2003). Longitudinal analysis of flexibility and reorganization in early adolescence: A dynamic systems study of family interactions. *Developmental Psychology, 39,* 606–617.

Grann, J. D. (2007). Confidence in knowledge past: An empirical basis for a differential decay theory of very long-term memory monitoring. *Dissertation Abstracts International Section A: Humanities and Social Sciences, 67,* 2462.

Grant, A. (2008). Does intrinsic motivation fuel the prosocial fire? Motivational synergy in predicting persistence, performance, and productivity. *Journal of Applied Psychology, 93,* 48–58.

Gray, G. C. (2006). The regulation of corporate violations: Punishment, compliance, and the blurring of responsibility. *British Journal of Criminology, 46,* 875–892.

Graziano, W. G., Habashi, M. M., Sheese, B. E., & Tobin, R. M. (2007). Agreeableness, empathy, and helping: A person situation perspective. *Journal of Personality and Social Psychology, 93,* 583–599.

Great Canadian Psychology website. (2008). Brenda Milner. Retrieved from www.psych.ualberta.ca/GCPWS/Milner.

Green, J., Lynn, S., & Montgomery, G. (2008, January). Gender-related differences in hypnosis-based treatments for smoking: A follow-up meta-analysis. *American Journal of Clinical Hypnosis, 50,* 259–271.

Greenberg, G., & Rosenheck, R. (2008).Jail incarceration, homelessness, and mental health: A national study. *Psychiatric Services, 59,* 170–177.

Greenberg, R. M., & Kellner, C. H. (2005). Electroconvulsive therapy: A selected review. *The American Journal of Geriatric Psychiatry, 13,* 268–281.

Greenberg, R., & Goldman, E. (2009). Antidepressants, psychotherapy or their combination: Weighing options for depression treatments. *Journal of Contemporary Psychotherapy, 39,* 83–91.

Greene, J. D., Sommerville, R. B., Nystrom, L. E., Darley, J. M., & Cohen, J. D. (2001, September 14). An fMRI investigation of emotional engagement in moral judgment. *Science, 293,* 2105–2108.

Greenspan, S. (2006). Functional concepts in mental retardation: Finding the natural essence of an artificial category. *Exceptionality, 14,* 205–224.

Greenwald, A. G., Draine S. C., & Abrams, R. L. (1996, September 20). Three cognitive markers of unconscious semantic activation. *Science, 272,* 1699–1702.

Greenwald, A. G., Nosek, B. A., & Banaji, M. R. (2003). Understanding and using the Implicit Association Test: 1. An improved scoring algorithm. *Journal of Personality and Social Psychology 85,* 197–216.

Greenwald, A. G., Nosek, B. A., & Sriram, N. (2006). Consequential validity of the implicit association test: Comment on Blanton and Jaccard. *American Psychologist, 61,* 56–61.

Greenwood, C. R., Carta, J. J., Hart, B., Kamps, D., Terry, B., Arreaga-Mayer, C., Atwater, J., Walker, D., Risley, T., & Delquadri, J. C. (1992). Out of the laboratory and into the community: 26 years of applied behavior analysis at the Juniper Gardens children's project. *American Psychologist, 47,* 1464–1474.

Greer, R. D., Dudek-Singer, J., & Gautreaux, G. (2006). Observational learning. *International Journal of Psychology, 41,* 486–499.

Gregory, R. L. (1978). *The psychology of seeing* (3rd ed.). New York: McGraw-Hill.

Gregory, R. L. (2008). Emmert's Law and the moon illusion. *Spatial Vision, 21,* 407–720.

Gregory, S. (1856). *Facts for young women.* Boston.

Greist-Bousquet, S., & Schiffman, H. R. (1986). The basis of the Poggendorff effect: An additional clue for Day and Kasperczyk. *Perception and Psychophysics, 39,* 447–448.

Grigorenko, E. (2009). Speaking genes or genes for speaking? Deciphering the genetics of speech and language. *Journal of Child Psychology and Psychiatry, 50,* 116–125.

Grigorenko, E. L. (2000). Heritability and intelligence. In R. J. Sternberg, et al. (Eds.), *Handbook of intelligence.* New York: Cambridge University Press.

Grigoriadis, S., & Ravitz, P. (2007). An approach to interpersonal psychotherapy for postpartum depression: Focusing on interpersonal changes. *Canadian Family Physician, 53,* 1469–1475.

Grigoriadis, V. (July 2, 2014). Justin Bieber: A case study in growing up cossetted and feral. NY Mag/Vulture. Retrieved from http://www.vulture.com/2014/06/justin-bieber-experiment.html.

Gronholm, P., Rinne, J. O., Vorobyev, V., & Laine, M. (2005). Naming of newly learned objects: A PET activation study. *Brain Research and Cognitive Brain Research, 14,* 22–28.

Gross, D. M. (2006). *The secret history of emotion: From Aristotle's rhetoric to modern brain science.* Chicago: University of Chicago Press.

Grossi, G., Semenza, C., Corazza, S., & Volterra, V. (1996). Hemispheric specialization for sign language. *Neuropsychologia, 34,* 737–740.

Grossmann, T., Striano, T., & Friederici, A. D. (2007). Developmental changes in infants' processing of happy and angry facial expressions: A neurobehavioral study. *Brain and Cognition, 64*, 30–41.

Groves, R. M., Singer, E., Lepkowski, J. M., Heeringa, S. G., & Alwin, D. F. In S. J. House, F. T. Juster, R. L. Kahn, H. Schuman, & E. Singer. (2004). *A telescope on society: Survey research and social science at the University of Michigan and beyond.* Ann Arbor, MI: University of Michgan Press.

Gruber, P. J. (2000). Standardized testing and employment equity career counselling: A literature review of six tests. Prepared for the Employment Equity Career Development Office of the Public Service Commission of Canada. Retrieved from www.psc-cfp.gc.ca/ee/eecco/standardized_e.htm.

Grunwald, T., Boutros, N. N., Pezer, N., von Oertzen, J., Fernandez, G., Schaller, C., & Elger, C. E. (2003). Neuronal substrates of sensory gating within the human brain. *Biological Psychiatry, 15*, 511–519.

Guadagno, R. E., & Cialdini, R. B. (2002). Online persuasion: An examination of gender differences in computer-mediated interpersonal influence [Special issue: Groups and Internet]. *Group Dynamics, 6*, 38–51.

Guastella, A., Mitchell, P., & Dadds, M. (2008, January). Oxytocin increases gaze to the eye region of human faces. *Biological Psychiatry, 63*, 3–5.

Guéguen, N., Marchand, M., Pascual, A., & Lourel, M. (2008). Foot-in-the-door technique using a courtship request: A field experiment. *Psychological Reports, 103*, 529–534.

Guerrero, L., La Valley, A., & Farinelli, L. (2008, October). The experience and expression of anger, guilt, and sadness in marriage: An equity theory explanation. *Journal of Social and Personal Relationships, 25*, 699–724.

Guilleminault, C., Kirisoglu, C., Bao, G., Arias, V., Chan, A., & Li, K. K. (2005). Adult chronic sleepwalking and its treatment based on polysomnography. *Brain, 128* (Pt. 5), 1062–1069.

Guldemond, H., Bosker, R., Kuyper, H., & van der Werf, G. (2007). Do highly gifted students really have problems? [Special issue: Current research on giftedness: International perspectives]. *Educational Research and Evaluation, 13*, 555–568.

Gur, R. C., Gur, R. E., Obrist, W. D., Hungerbuhler, J. P., Younkin, D., Rosen, A. D., Skilnick, B. E., & Reivich, M. (1982). Sex and handedness differences in cerebral blood flow during rest and cognitive activity. *Science, 217*, 659–661.

Gur, R. C., Turetsky, B. I., Matsui, M., Yan, M., Bilker, W., Hughett, P., & Gur, R. E. (1999). Sex differences in brain gray and white matter in healthy young adults: correlations with cognitive performance. *Journal of Neuroscience, 19*, 4065–4072.

Gurin, P. (2006). Informing theory from practice and applied research. *Journal of Social Issues, 62*, 621–628.

Guttman, M. (1995, March 3–5). She had electroshock therapy. *USA Weekend*, p. 16.

Gwynn, M. I., & Spanos, N. P. (1996). Hypnotic responsiveness, nonhypnotic suggestibility, and responsiveness to social influence. In R. G. Kunzendorf, N. P. Spahos, & B. Wallace (Eds.), *Hypnosis and imagination*. Amityville, NY: Baywood.

Haberstick, B. C., Schmitz, S., Young, S. E., & Hewitt, J. K. (2005). Contributions of genes and environments to stability and change in externalizing and internalizing problems during elementary and middle school. *Behavior Genetics, 35*, 381–396.

Haberstick, B. C., Timberlake, D., Smolen, A., Sakai, J.T., Hopfer, C.J., Corley, R.P., Young, S.E., Stallings, M.C., Huizinga, D., Menard, S., Hartman, C., Grotpeter, J., & Hewitt, J.K. (2007). Between- and within-family association test of the dopamine receptor D2 TaqIA polymorphism and alcohol abuse and dependence in a general population sample of adults. *Journal of Studies on Alcohol and Drugs, 68*, 362–370.

Hackam, D. G. (2007). Translating animal research into clinical benefit. *British Medical Journal, 334*, 163–1644.

Hadjistavropoulos, T., Craig, K. D., & Fuchs-Lacelle, S. (2004). *Social influences and the communication of pain.* Mahwah, NJ: Lawrence Erlbaum Associates.

Haier, R. J., Colom, R., Schroeder, D. H., Condon, C. A., Tang, C., Eaves, E., et al. (2009). Gray matter and intelligence factors: Is there a neuro-g? *Intelligence, 37*, 136–144.

Haley, W. E., Clair, J. M., & Saulsberry, K. (1992). Family caregiver satisfaction with medical care of their demented relatives. *Gerontologist, 32*, 219–226.

Halford, S. (2006). Collapsing the boundaries? Fatherhood, organization and home-working. *Gender, Work & Organization, 13*, 383–402.

Halgin, R. P., & Whitbourne, S.K. (1994). *Abnormal psychology.* Fort Worth, TX: Harcourt Brace.

Hall, R. E. (2002). *The Bell Curve:* Implications for the performance of black/white athletes. *Social Science Journal, 39*, 113–118.

Hallschmid, M., Benedict, C., Born, J., Fehm, H., & Kern, W. (2004). Manipulating central nervous mechanisms of food intake and body weight regulation by intranasal administration of neuropeptides in man. *Physiology and Behavior, 83*, 55–64.

Halpert, J. (2003, April 28). What do patients want? *Newsweek*, pp. 63–64.

Hamani, Y., Sciaki-Tamir, Y., Deri-Hasid, R., Miller-Pogrund, T., Milwidsky, A., & Haimov-Kochman, R. (2007). Misconceptions about oral contraception pills among adolescents and physicians. *Human Reproduction, 22*, 3078–3083.

Hamann, S. (2001). Cognitive and neural mechanisms of emotional memory. *Trends in Cognitive Sciences, 5*, 394–400.

Hamann, S. B., Ely, T. D., Hoffman, J. M., & Kilts, C. D. (2002). Ecstasy and agony: Activation of human amygdala in positive and negative emotion. *Psychological Science, 13*, 135–141.

Hambleton, R. K. (2006). Psychometric models, test designs and item types for the next generation of educational and psychological tests. In D. Bartram, & R. K. Hambleton, *Computer-based testing and the Internet: Issues and advances.* New York: John Wiley & Sons.

Hamer, D. H., Hu, S., Magnuson, V. L., Hu, N., & Pattatucci, A. M. L. (1993, July 16). A linkage between DNA markers on the X chromo-some and male sexual orientation. *Science, 261*, 321–327.

Hamilton, A. (2009, July 11). Can gaming slow mental decline in the elderly? *Time.* Retrieved from http://www.time.com/time/health/article/0,8599,1909852,00.html.

Hamilton, A. C., & Martin, R. C. (2007). Semantic short-term memory deficits and resolution of interference: A case for inhibition? In D. S. Gorfein & C. M. Macleod, *Inhibition in cognition.* Washington, DC: American Psychological Association.

Hamilton, C. E. (2000). Continuity and discontinuity of attachment from infancy through adolescence. *Child Development, 71*, 690–694.

Hammond, C., & Gold, M. (2008). Caffeine dependence, withdrawal, overdose and treatment. A review. *Directions in Psychiatry, 28*, 177–190.

Hammond, D. C. (2007, April). Review of the efficacy of clinical hypnosis with headaches and migraines [Special issue: Evidence-based practice clinical hypnosis—part 1]. *International Journal of Clinical and Experimental Hypnosis 55*, 207–219.

Hannon, E. E., & Johnson, S. P. (2005). Infants use meter to categorize rhythms and melodies: Implications for musical structure learning. *Cognitive Psychology, 50*, 354–377.

Harding, D.J., & Jencks, C. (2003). Changing Attitudes toward premarital sex: Cohort, period, and aging effects. *The Public Opinion Quarterly, 67*, 211–226

Harlaar, N., Spinath, F. M., Dale, P. S., & Plomin, R. (2005). Genetic influences on early word recognition abilities and disabilities: A study of 7-year-old twins. *Journal of Child Psychology and Psychiatry, 46*, 373–384.

Harlow, H. F., & Zimmerman, R. R. (1959). Affectional responses in the infant monkey. *Science, 130*, 421–432.

Harlow, J. M. (1869). Recovery from the passage of an iron bar through the head. *Massachusetts Medical Society Publication, 2*, 329–347.

Harmon-Jones, E., & Winkielman, P. (2007). *Social neuroscience: Integrating biological and psychological explanations of social behavior.* New York, NY: Guilford Press.

Harper, T. (1978, November 15). It's not true about people 65 or over. *Green Bay Press-Gazette* (Wisconsin), p. D-1.

Harris, M. (2007, October 30). One quarter of Canadians sleep deprived. *Canwest News Service*. Retrieved from www.canada.com/topics /bodyandhealth/story.html?id=62a9052b-02ec-4852-b9a4 -67aa0edc03ee&k=15490.

Harrison, J. A., & Wells, R. B. (1991). Bystander effects on male helping behavior: Social comparison and diffusion of responsibility. *Representative Research in Social Psychology, 19*, 53–63.

Hart, B., & Risley, T. R. (1997). Use of language by three-year-old children. Courtesy of Drs.Betty Hart and Todd Risley, University of Kansas.

Hartmann, E. (1967). *The biology of dreaming*. Springfield, IL: Charles C. Thomas Publisher.

Harvey, J. H., & Weber, A. L. (2002). *Odyssey of the heart: Close relationships in the 21st century* (2nd ed.). Mahwah, NJ: Erlbaum.

Harvey, J. H., Wenzel, A., & Sprecher, S. (Eds.). (2005). *The handbook of sexuality in close relationships*. Mahwah, NJ: Lawrence Erlbaum Associates.

Hauke, C. (2006). The unconscious: Personal and collective. In R. K. Papadopoulos, *The handbook of Jungian psychology: Theory, practice and applications*. New York: Routledge.

Hauser, M. D. (2000). The sound and the fury: Primate vocalizations as reflections of emotion and thought. In N. L. Wallin & B. Merker (Eds.), *The origins of music*. Cambridge, MA: MIT.

Hauser, M. D., Chomsky, N., & Fitch, W. T. (2002, November, 22). The faculty for language: What is it, who has it, and how did it evolve? *Science, 298*, 1569–1579.

Haviland-Jones, J. M., & Wilson, P. J. (2008). A 'nose' for emotion: Emotional information and challenges in odors and semiochemicals. In M. Lewis, J. M. Haviland-Jones, & L. G. Barrett (Eds.), *Handbook of emotions* (3rd ed.). New York: Guilford Press.

Haviland-Jones, J., & Chen, D. (1999, April 17). *Human olfactory perception*. Paper presented at the Association for Chemoreception Sciences, Sarasota, Florida.

Hawkes, Christopher H., & Doty, R. L. (2009). *The neurology of olfaction*. Cambridge, UK: Cambridge University Press.

Hayflick, L. (2007). Biological aging is no longer an unsolved problem. *Annals of the New York Academy of Sciences, 1100*, 1–13.

Haynes, P., Nixon, J. C., & West, J. F. (2007). Time perception and consumer behaviour: Some cross-cultural implications. *International Journal of Consumer Studies, 14*, 14–27.

Hays, P. A. (2008). *Addressing cultural complexities in practice: Assessment, diagnosis, and therapy* (2nd ed.). Washington, DC: American Psychological Association.

Health Canada (2006). *It's your health: Fetal alcohol spectrum disorder, Minister of Health*. Retrieved from Health Canada website: http:// www.hc-sc.gc.ca/hl-vs/iyh-vsv/diseases-maladies/fasd-etcaf-eng.php.

Health Canada (2012). Canadian alcohol and drug Use monitoring survey: Summary of results for 2012. Retrieved March 19, 2015 from: http://www.hc-sc.gc.ca/hc-ps/drugs-drogues/stat/_2012/summary -sommaire-eng.php#s5.

Health Canada. (1999, January). Deaths in Canada due to smoking. Retrieved from www.hc-sc.gc.ca/ahc-asc/media/nr-cp/1999/1999 _07bk6_e.html.

Health Canada. (2004, November 23). Results of major alcohol and drug use survey fills gaps in knowledge. Retrieved from www.hc-sc.gc.ca /ahc-asc/media/nr-cp/2004/2004_alc-dr_e.html.

Health Canada. (2008). Fetal alcohol syndrome/fetal alcohol effects. Retrieved from www.hc-sc.gc.ca/fnih-spni/famil/preg-gros/intro_ e.html.

Health Canada. (2008). It's your health: Caffeine. Retrieved from www .hc-sc.gc.ca/iyh-vsv/food-aliment/caffeine_e.html.

Health Canada. (2008). Straight facts about drugs and drinking: When does drug use become a problem? Retrieved from www.hc-sc.gc.ca /hl-vs/pubs/adp-apd/straight_facts-faits_mefaits/become_problem -quand_problems_e.html.

Health Canada. (2009). Aromatic amines: Contribution to the mutagenic activity of tobacco smoke. *Health Canada: Health Concerns*. Retrieved from www.hc-sc.gc.ca/hc-ps/pubs/tobac-tabac/arom-amines-arom /index-eng.php.

Health Canada. (2012). Canadian Tobacco Use Monitoring Use Survey (CTUMS). Retrieved from http://www.hc-sc.gc.ca/hc-ps/tobac-tabac /research-recherche/stat/ctums-esutc_2012-eng.php.

Health Pages. (2003, March 13). Just what the doctor ordered. Retrieved from http://www.thehealthpages.com/articles/ar-drord.html.

HealthNews. (1999, November 20). Losing weight: A little goes a long way. *HealthNews*, p. 1.

Heart and Stroke Foundation of Canada. (2012). Smoking statistics. Retrieved from www.heartandstroke.com/site/c.ikIQLcMWJtE /b.3483991/k.34A8/Statistics.htm#smoking.

Heath, R. A. (2006). *The Praeger handbook of transsexuality: Changing gender to match mindset*. Westport, CT: Praeger Publishers/Greenwood Publishing.

Heatherton, T., & Sargent, J. (2009). Does watching smoking in movies promote teenage smoking? *Current Directions in Psychological Science, 18*, 63–67.

Hebb, D. O. (1949). *The organization of behavior*. New York: Wiley.

Hecht, J. M. (2007). *The happiness myth: Why what we think is right is wrong. A history of what really makes us happy*. New York: HarperSanFrancisco/HarperCollins.

Hedgepeth, E. (2005). Different lenses, different vision. *School Administrator, 62*, 36–39.

Hedges, D. W., Brown, B. L., Shwalk, D. A., Godfrey, K., & Larcher, A. M. (2007). The efficacy of selective serotonin reuptake inhibitors in adult social anxiety disorder: A meta-analysis of double-blind, placebo-controlled trials. *Journal of Psychopharmacology, 21*, 102–111.

Heider, F. (1958). *The psychology of interpersonal relations*. New York: Wiley.

Heilman, K. M. (2005). *Creativity and the brain*. New York: Psychology Press.

Heinrichs, R. W. (2005). The primacy of cognition in schizophrenia. *American Psychologist, 60*, 229–242.

Heller, S. (2005). *Freud A to Z*. New York: Wiley.

Helmuth, L. (2000, August 25). Synapses shout to overcome distance. *Science, 289*, 1273.

Henderlong, J., & Lepper, M. R. (2002). The effects of praise on children's intrinsic motivation: A review and synthesis. *Psychological Bulletin, 128*, 774–795.

Henderson, N. D. (1982). Correlations in IQ for pairs of people with varying degrees of genetic relatedness and shared environment. *Annual Review of Psychology, 33*, 219–243.

Henningsen, D. D., Henningsen, M. L., & Eden, J. (2006). Examining the symptoms of group-think and retrospective sensemaking. *Small Group Research, 37*, 36–64.

Henry, D., McClellen, D., Rosenthal, L., Dedrick, D., & Gosdin, M. (2008, February). Is sleep really for sissies? Understanding the role of work in insomnia in the US. *Social Science & Medicine, 66*, 715–726.

Hentschel, U., Smith, G., Draguns, J. G., & Elhers, W. (2004). *Defense mechanisms: Theoretical, research and clinical perspectives*. Oxford, England: Elsevier Science.

Herbenick, D., Reece, M., Sanders, S., Dodge, B., Ghassemi, A., & Fortenberry, J. (2009). Prevalence and characteristics of vibrator use by women in the United States: Results from a nationally representative study. *Journal of Sexual Medicine, 6*, 1857–1866.

Hermann, D., Raybeck, D., & Gruneberg, M. M. (2002). *Improving memory and study skills: Advances in theory and practice*. Cambridge, MA: Hogrefe & Huber.

Herrán, A., Carrera, M., & Sierra-Biddle, D. (2006). Panic disorder and the onset of agoraphobia. *Psychiatry and Clinical Neurosciences, 60*, 395–396.

Herrnstein, R. J., & Murray, D. (1994). *The bell curve*. New York: Free Press.

Hertzog, C., Kramer, A., Wilson, R., & Lindenberger, U. (2008). Enrichment effects on adult cognitive development: Can the functional capacity of older adults be preserved and enhanced? *Psychological Science in the Public Interest, 9*, 1–65.

Herzberg, L. (2009). Direction, causation, and appraisal theories of emotion. *Philosophical Psychology, 22*, 167–186.

Heshka, S., Anderson, J. W., Atkinson, R. L., Greenway, F. L., Hill, J. O., Phinney, S. D., et al. (2003). Weight loss with self-help compared with a structured commercial program: A randomized trial. *Journal of the American Medical Association, 289,* 1792–1798.

Hess, T. M., Hinson, J. T., & Statham, J. A. (2004). Explicit and implicit stereotype activation effects on memory: Do age and awareness moderate the impact of priming? *Psychology and Aging, 19,* 495–505.

Hewitt, B., & Egan, H. W. (2009, February 23). Flight 1549: The right stuff. *People, 71,* pp. 10–14.

Heyman, G. D., & Diesendruck, G. (2002). The Spanish *ser/estar* distinction in bilingual children's reasoning about human psychological characteristics. *Developmental Psychology, 38,* 407–417.

Hibbard, P. (2007, February). A statistical model of binocular disparity. *Visual Cognition, 15,* 149–165.

Hiby, E. F., Rooney, N. J., & Bradshaw, J. W. S. (2004). Dog training methods: Their use, effectiveness and interaction with behaviour and welfare. *Animal Welfare, 13,* 63–69.

Hilarski, C. (2007). Antisocial personality disorder. In B. A. Thyer & J. S. Wodarski, *Social work in mental health: An evidence-based approach.* Hoboken, NJ: John Wiley & Sons.

Hildebrant, A. (2009, June 22). Oddly legal defences: A look at peculiar arguments in the Canadian courtrooms and beyond. *CBC News.* Retrieved from www.cbc.ca/canada/story/2009/06/18/f-legal-defence.html.

Hilgard, E. (1992). Disassociation and theories of hypnosis. In E. Fromm & M. E. Nash (Eds.), *Contemporary hypnosis research.* New York: Guilford.

Hill, J. O., Catenacci, V., & Wyatt, H. R. (2005). Obesity: Overview of an epidemic. *Psychiatric Clinics of North America, 28,* 1–23.

Hill, J. O., Wyatt, H. R., Reed, G. W., & Peters, J. C. (2003, February 7). Obesity and the environment: Where do we go from here? *Science, 299,* 853–855.

Hillix, W. A. (2007). The past, present, and possible futures of animal language research. In D. A. Washburn, *Primate perspectives on behavior and cognition.* Washington, DC: American Psychological Association.

Hillman, C. H., Erickson, K. I., & Kramer, A. F. (2008). Be smart, exercise your heart: Exercise effects on brain and cognition. Nature Reviews Neuroscience, 9, 58-65.

Hincks-Dellcrest Treatment Centre. (2010). Evaluation and research. Retrieved from www.hincksdellcrest.org/Home/Evaluation-and-Research/Research.aspx.

Hines, M. (2004). *Brain gender.* New York: Oxford University Press.

Hipkiss, R. A. (1995). *Semantics: Defining the discipline.* Mahwah, NJ: Erlbaum.

Hirsh, I. J., & Watson, C. S. (1996). Auditory psychophysics and perception. *Annual Review of Psychology, 47,* 461–484.

Hobfoll, S. E., Freedy, J. R., Green B. L., & Solomon, S. D. (1996). Coping in reaction to extreme stress: The roles of resource loss and resource availability. In M. Zeidner & N. S. Endler (Eds.), *Handbook of coping: Theory, research, applications.* New York: Wiley.

Hobson, J. A. (2005). In bed with Mark Solms? What a nightmare! A reply to Domhoff (2005). *Dreaming, 15,* 21–29.

Hobson, J. A. *Sleep.* (1989) New York: W. H. Freeman.

Hobson, J. A., & Silvestri, L. (1999, February). Parasomnias. *The Harvard Mental Health Letter, 15*(8), 3–5.

Hock, H. S., & Ploeger, A. (2006). Linking dynamical perceptual decisions at different levels of description in motion pattern formation: Psychophysics. *Perception & Psychophysics, 68,* 505–514.

Hodnett, E. (2002). Pain and women's satisfaction with the experience of childbirth: A systematic review. *American Journal of Obstetrics and Gynecology, 186:* 160–72.

Hoff, E. (2003). Language development in childhood. In R. M. Lerner et al. (Eds.), *Handbook of psychology: Developmental psychology* (Vol. 6). New York: Wiley.

Hoff, E. (2008). *Language development.* New York: Wadsworth.

Hofmann, W., Gschwendner, T., Castelli, L., & Schmitt, M. (2008). Implicit and explicit attitudes and interracial interaction: The moderating role of situationally available control resources. *Group Processes & Intergroup Relations, 11,* 69–87.

Hogan, J., Davies, S., & Hogan, R. (2007). Generalizing personality-based validity evidence. In S. M. McPhail, *Alternative validation strategies: Developing new and leveraging existing validity evidence.* Hoboken, NJ: John Wiley & Sons.

Hogan, R., Hogan, J., & Roberts, B. W. (1996). Personality measurement and employment decisions: Questions and answers. *American Psychologist, 51,* 469–477.

Hoge, C. W., Castro, C. A., Messer, S. C., McGurk, D., Cotting, D. I., & Koffman, R. L. (2004). Combat duty in Iraq and Afghanistan, mental health problems and barriers to care. *New England Journal of Medicine, 351,* 13–22.

Hogg, M. A. (2006). Social identity theory. In P. J. Burke, *Contemporary social psychological theories.* Palo Alto, CA: Stanford University Press.

Hogg, M. A., & Hains, S. C. (2001). Intergroup relations and group solidarity: Effects of group identification and social beliefs on depersonalized attraction. In M. A. Hogg & D. Abrams (Eds.), *Intergroup relations: Essential readings.* New York: Psychology Press.

Holden, C. (2003, January 17). Deconstructing schizophrenia. *Science, 299,* 333–335.

Holden, L. M. (2005). Complex adaptive systems: Concept analysis. *Journal of Advanced Nursing, 52,* 651–657.

Holland, J. C., & Lewis, S. (2001). *The human side of cancer: Living with hope, coping with uncertainty.* New York: Quill.

Holleran, S., Mehl, M., & Levitt, S. (2009). Eavesdropping on social life: The accuracy of stranger ratings of daily behavior from thin slices of natural conversations. *Journal of Research in Personality, 43,* 660–672.

Hollingworth, H. L. (1943/1990). *Leta Stetter Hollingworth: A biography.* Boston: Anker.

Hollins, K. (2007). Consequences of antenatal mental health problems for child health and development. *Current Opinions on Obstetric Gynecology, 19,* 568–573.

Hollis, K. L. (1997, September). Contemporary research on Pavlovian conditioning: A "new" functional analysis. *American Psychologist, 52,* 956–965.

Hollon, S. D., Thase, M. E., & Markowitz, J. C. (2002). Treatment and prevention of depression. *Psychological Science in the Public Interest, 3,* 39–77.

Holmes, A., Yang, R. J., Lesch, K. P., Crawley, J. N., & Murphy, D. L. (2003). Mice lacking the Serotonin Transporter Exhibit 5-HT-sub(1A) receptor-mediated abnormalities in tests for anxiety-like behavior. *Neuropsychopharmacology, 28,* 2077–2088.

Holowka, S., & Pettito, L. A. (2002, August 30). Left hemisphere cerebral specialization for babies while babbling. *Science, 297,* 1515.

Holt, M., & Jahn, R. (2004, March, 26). Synaptic vesicles in the fast lane. *Science, 303,* 1986–1987.

Holy, T. E., Dulac, C., & Meister, M. (2000, September 1). Responses of vomeronasal neurons to natural stimuli. *Science, 289,* 1569–1572.

Hong, S. (2000). Exercise and psychoneuroimmunology [Special issue: Exercise psychology]. *International Journal of Sport Psychology, 31,* 204–227.

Hongchun, W., & Ming, L. (2006). About the research on suggestibility and false memory. *Psychological Science (China), 29,* 905–908.

Hoover, E. (2004). More college students report diagnoses of depression, survey finds. *The Chronicle of Higher Education.* Retrieved from http://chronicle.com/daily/2004/11/2004113004n.htm.

Hopkins, W., & Cantalupo, C. (2008, June). Theoretical speculations on the evolutionary origins of hemispheric specialization. *Current Directions in Psychological Science, 17,* 233–237.

Hopwood, C., Newman, D., Donnellan, M., Markowitz, J., Grilo, C., Sanislow, C., et al. (2009). The stability of personality traits in individuals with borderline personality disorder. *Journal of Abnormal Psychology, 118,* 806–815.

Horgan, J. (1993, December). Fractured functions: Does the brain have a supreme integrator? *Scientific American,* pp. 36–37.

References

Horinek, D., Varjassyová, A., & Hort, J. (2007). Magnetic resonance analysis of amygdalar volume in Alzheimer's disease. *Current Opinion in Psychiatry, 20,* 273–277.

Horn, J. L. (2002). Selections of evidence, misleading assumptions, and over-simplifications: The political message of *The Bell Curve.* In J. M. Fish (Ed.), *Race and intelligence: Separating science from myth.* Mahwah, NJ: Erlbaum.

Horney, K. (1937). *Neurotic personality of our times.* New York: Norton.

Horton, K. D., Wilson, D. E., Vonk, J., Kirby, S. L., & Nielsen, T. (2005). Measuring automatic retrieval: A comparison of implicit memory, process dissociation, and speeded response procedures. *Acta Psychologica, 119,* 235–263.

Howard, A., Pion, G. M., Gottfredson, G. D., Flattau, P. E., Oskamp, S., Pfafflin, S. M., Bray, D. W., & Burstein, A. D. (1986). The changing face of American psychology. A report from the committee on employment and human resources. *American Psychologist, 41,* 1311–1327.

Howe, C. J. (2002). The countering of overgeneralization. *Journal of Child Language, 29,* 875–895.

Howes, O., & Kapur, S. (2009). The dopamine hypothesis of schizophrenia: Version III—The final common pathway. *Schizophrenia Bulletin, 35,* 549–562.

Howitt, D., & Cramer, D. (2000). *First steps in research and statistics: A practical workbook for psychology students.* Philadelphia: Psychology Press.

Hu, F. B., Li, T. Y., Colditz, G. A., Willett, W. C., & Manson, J. E. (2003). Television watching and other sedentary behaviors in relation to risk of obesity and type 2 diabetes mellitus in women. *Journal of the American Medical Association, 289,* 1785–1791.

Hubel, D. H., & Wiesel, T. N. (2004). *Brain and visual perception: The story of a 25-year collaboration.* New York: Oxford University Press.

Huber, F., Beckmann, S. C., & Herrmann, A. (2004). Means-end analysis: Does the affective state influence information processing style? *Psychology and Marketing, 21,* 715–737.

Hudson, J. I., Coit, C. E., Lalonde, J. K., & Pope, H. G. (2012). By how much will the proposed new DSM-5 criteria increase the prevalence of binge eating disorder? *International Journal of Easting Disorders, 45,* 139–141.

Hudson, W. (1960). Pictorial depth perception in subcultural groups in Africa. *Journal of Social Psychology, 52,* 183–208.

Hudspeth, A. J. (2000). Hearing. In E. R. Kandel, J. H. Schwartz, & T. M. Jessell (Eds.), *Principles of neural science* (4th ed.). New York: McGraw-Hill.

Hugdahl, K., & Davidson, R. J. (2002). *The asymmetrical brain.* Cambridge, MA: The MIT Press.

Hugenberg, K., & Sacco, D. (2008). Social categorization and stereotyping: How social categorization biases person perception and face memory. *Social and Personality Psychology Compass, 2,* 1052–1072.

Huijie, T. (2006). The measurement and assessment of mental health: A longitudinal and cross-sectional research on undergraduates, adults and patients. *Psychological Science (China), 29,* 419–422.

Hull, C. L. (1943). *Principles of behavior.* New York: Appleton-Century-Crofts.

Hummer, T. A., & McClintock, M. K. (2009). Putative human pheromone and rostadienone attunes the mind specifically to emotional information. *Hormones and Behavior, 55,* 548–559.

Humphrey, N., Curran, A., & Morris, E. (2007). Emotional intelligence and education: A critical review. *Educational Psychology, 27,* 235–254.

Humphreys, G. W., & Müller, H. (2000). A search asymmetry reversed by figure-ground assignment. *Psychological Science, 11,* 196–200.

Hunt, E. (1994). Problem solving. In R. J. Sternberg (Ed.), *Thinking and problem solving: Handbook of perception and cognition* (2nd ed.). San Diego, CA: Academic Press.

Hunt, J. S., Seifert, A. L., & Armenta, B. E. (2006). Stereotypes and prejudice as dynamic constructs: Reminders about the nature of intergroup bias from the hurricane Katrina relief efforts. *Analyses of Social Issues and Public Policy (ASAP), 6,* 237–253.

Hunt, M. (1974). *Sexual behaviors in the 1970s.* New York: Dell.

Hurtz, G. M. (2000). Personality and job performance: The big five revisited. *Journal of Applied Psychology, 85 (6),* 869–879.

Huston, A. C., Donnerstein, E., Fairchild, H. H., Feshback, N. D., Katz, P., Murray, J. P., et al. (1992). *Big world, small screen: The role of television in American society.* Omaha, NE: University of Nebraska Press.

Hyde, J. S., Mezulis, A. H., & Abramson, L. Y. (2008). The ABCs of depression: Integrating affective, biological and cognitive models to explain the emergence of the gender difference in depression. *Psychological Review, 115,* 291–313.

Hyde, K.L., Peretz, I. & Zatorre, R.J. (2008). Evidence for the role of the right auditory cortex in fine pitch resolution. *Neuropsychologia, 46*(2), 632–639.

Iachini, T., & Giuoberti, F. (2004). Metric properties of spatial images generated from locomotion: The effect of absolute size on mental scanning. *European Journal of Cognitive Psychology, 16,* 573–596.

Iacoboni, M. (2009, January). Imitation, empathy, and mirror neurons. *Annual Review of Psychology, 60,* 653–670.

Iaria, G., Palermo, L., Committeri, G., & Barton, J. (2009). Age differences in the formation and use of cognitive maps. *Behavioural Brain Research, 196,* 187–191.

Ievers-Landis, C. E., Hoff, A. L., Brez, C., Cancilliere, M. K., McConnell, J., & Kerr, D. (2005). Situational analysis of dietary challenges of the treatment regimen for children and adolescents with phenylketonuria and their primary caregivers. *Journal of Developmental and Behavioral Pediatrics, 26,* 186–193.

Iglesias, A. (2005). Awake-alert hypnosis in the treatment of panic disorder: A case report. *American Journal of Clinical Hypnosis, 47,* 249–257.

Igo, S. E. (2006). Review of A telescope on society: Survey research and social science at the University of Michigan and beyond. *Journal of the History of the Behavioral Sciences, 42,* 95–96.

Ihler, E. (2003). Patient-physician communication. *Journal of the American Medical Association, 289,* 92.

Ikonomidou, C., Bittigau, P., Ishimaru, M. J., Wozniak, D. F., Koch, C., Genz, K., et al. (2000, February 11). Ethanol-induced apoptotic neurodegeneration and fetal alcohol syndrome. *Science, 287,* 1056–1060.

Ilies, R., Arvey, R. D., & Bouchard, T. J., Jr. (2006). Darwinism, behavioral genetics, and organizational behavior: A review and agenda for future research [Special issue: Darwinian perspectives on behavior in organizations]. *Journal of Organizational Behavior, 27,* 96–141.

Insel, T. R. (2010, April). Faulty circuits. *Science,* pp. 44–51.

Interlandi, J. (2008, March 3). What addicts need. *Newsweek,* p. 31–16.

Irwin, M. (2008). Human psychoneuroimmunology: 20 years of discovery. *Brain, Behavior, and Immunity, 22,* 129–139.

Irwin, R. R. (2006). Spiritual development in adulthood: Key concepts and models. In C. Hoare, *Handbook of adult development and learning.* New York: Oxford University Press.

Isay, R. A. (1994). *Being homosexual: Gay men and their development.* Lanham, MD: Jason Aronson.

Isbell, L. M., & Tyler, J. M. (2003). Teaching students about in-group favoritism and the minimal groups paradigm. *Teaching of Psychology, 30,* 127–130.

Ishikawa, S., Okajima, I., Matsuoka, H., & Sakano, Y. (2007). Cognitive behavioural therapy for anxiety disorders in children and adolescents: A meta-analysis. *Child and Adolescent Mental Health, 12,* 164–172.

Iversen, S., & Iversen, L. (2007). Dopamine: 50 years in perspective. *Trends in Neurosciences, 30,* 188–193.

Iverson, L. (2000). *The science of marijuana.* Oxford, England: Oxford University Press.

Iverson, P., Kuhl, P. K., Reiko, A. Y., Diesch, E., Tohkura, Y., Ketterman, A., et al. (2003). A perceptual interference account of acquisition difficulties for non-native phonemes. *Cognition, 87,* B47–B57.

Izard, C. E., & Abe, J. A. (2004). Developmental changes in facial expressions of emotions in the strange situation during the second year of life. *Emotion, 4,* 251–265.

Jackson, J. D. (2006). Trauma, attachment, and coping: Pathways to resilience. *Dissertation Abstracts International: Section B: The Sciences and Engineering, 67*(1-B), 547.

Jacobs, M., Roesch, S., Wonderlich, S., Crosby, R., Thornton, L., Wilfley, D., et al. (2009). Anorexia nervosa trios: Behavioral profiles of individuals with anorexia nervosa and their parents. *Psychological Medicine, 39*, 451–461.

Jacobson, P. D., Wasserman, J., & Anderson, J. R. (1997). Historical overview of tobacco legislation and regulation. *Journal of Social Issues, 53*, 75–95.

Jacoby, L. L., Bishara, A. J., Hessels, S., & Hughes, A. (2007). Probabilistic retroactive interference: The role of accessibility bias in interference effects. *Journal of Experimental Psychology: General, 136*, 200–216.

Jain, S., Mills, P. J., & Von Känel, R. (2007). Effects of perceived stress and uplifts on inflammation and coagulability. *Psychophysiology, 44*, 154–160.

James, H. S., Jr. (2005). Why did you do that? An economic examination of the effect of extrinsic compensation on intrinsic motivation and performance. *Journal of Economic Psychology, 26*, 549–566.

James, W. (1890). *The principles of psychology*. New York: Holt.

Jamieson, G. A. (2007). *Hypnosis and conscious states: The cognitive neuroscience perspective*. New York: Oxford University Press.

Jamison, K. R. (1993). *Touched with fire: Manic depressive illness and the artistic temperament*. New York: Free Press.

Jamison, K. R. (1995a). *An unquiet mind: A memoir of moods and madness*. New York: Knopf.

Jang, S. J., You, S. H., & Ahn, S. H. (2007). Neurorehabilitation-induced cortical reorganization in brain injury: A 14-month longitudinal follow-up study. *NeuroRehabilitation, 22*, 117–122.

Janis, I. L. (1989). *Crucial decisions: Leadership in policy-making management*. New York: Free Press.

Janis, I.L. (1982). Groupthink: Psychological studies of policy decisions and fiascoes (2nd ed.). Boston: Houghton Mifflin.

Jarlais, D. C. D., Arasteh, K., & Perlis, T. (2007). The transition from injection to non-injection drug use: Long-term outcomes among heroin and cocaine users in New York City. *Addiction, 102*, 778–785.

Jefferson, D. J. (2005, August 8). American's most dangerous drug. *Newsweek*, pp. 41–47.

Jenkins, C. D., Zyzanski, S. J., & Rosenman, R. H. (1978). Coronary-prone behavior: One pattern or several? *Psychosomatic Medicine, 40*, 25–43.

Jenkins, S. R. (1994). Need for power and women's careers over 14 years: Structural power, job satisfaction, and motive change. *Journal of Personality and Social Psychology, 66*, 155–165.

Jensen, A. R. (2002). Galton's legacy to research on intelligence. *Journal of Biosocial Science, 34*, 145–172.

Jequier, E. (2002). Pathways to obesity. *International Journal of Obesity and Related Metabolic Disorders, 26*, S12–S17.

Johnson, G. B. (2000). *The living world* (p. 600), Boston: McGraw-Hill.

Johnson, H. D. (2004). Gender, grade and relationship differences in emotional closeness within adolescent friendships. *Adolescence, 39*, 243–255.

Johnson, J. G., Cohen, P., Smailes, E. M., Kasen, S., & Brook, J. S. (2002, March 29). Television viewing and aggressive behavior during adolescence and adulthood. *Science, 295*, 2468–2471.

Johnson, S. P. (2004). Development of perceptual completion in infancy. *Psychological Science, 15*, 769–775.

John-Steiner, V., & Mahn, H. (2003). Sociocultural contexts for teaching and learning. In W. M. Reynolds & G. E. Miller (Eds.), *Handbook of psychology: Educational psychology* (Vol. 7). New York: Wiley.

Johnston, L. D., O'Malley, P. M., Bachman, J. G., & Schulenberg, J. E. (2009). *Monitoring the future national results on adolescent drug use; overview of key findings, 2008* (NIH Publication No. 09-7401). Bethesda, MD: National Institute on Drug Abuse.

Johnston, L. D., O'Malley, P. M., Bachman, J. G., & Schulenberg, J. E. (2009). *Monitoring the future national survey results on drug use: 1975–2008. Volume I: Secondary school students* (NIH Publication No. 09-7402). Bethesda, MD: National Institute on Drug Abuse.

Johnston, L. D., O'Malley, P. M., Bachman, J. G., & Schulenberg, J. E. (2004, December 21). *Overall teen drug use continues gradual decline; but use of inhalants rises*. University of Michigan News and Information Services: Ann Arbor, MI. Retrieved August 23, 2005, from http://www.monitoringthefuture.org.

Johnston, M. V. (2004). Clinical disorders of brain plasticity. *Brain and Development, 26*, 73–80.

Jones, A. L. (2006). The contemporary psychoanalyst: Karen Horney's theory applied in today's culture. *PsycCRITIQUES, 51*, 127–134.

Jones, J. E., & Corp, E. S. (2003). Effect of naltrexone on food intake and body weight in Syrian hamsters depends on metabolic status. *Physiology and Behavior, 78*, 67–72.

Jones, J. M. (2007). Exposure to chronic community violence: Resilience in African American children. *Journal of Black Psychology, 33*, 125–149.

Jones, K., Callen, F., Blagrove, M., & Parrott, A. (2008). Sleep, energy and self rated cognition across 7 nights following recreational ecstasy/MDMA use. *Sleep and Hypnosis, 10*, 2–38.

Jones, R. K., Darroch, J. E., & Singh, S. (2005). Religious differentials in the sexual and reproductive behaviors of young women in the United States. *Journal of Adolescent Health, 36*, 279–288.

Jorgensen, G. (2006). Kohlberg and Gilligan: Duet or duel? *Journal of Moral Education, 35*, 179–196.

Joyce, J. (1934). *Ulysses*. New York: Random House.

Jung, C. G. (1961). *Freud and psychoanalysis*. New York: Pantheon.

Jung, J. (2002). *Psychology of alcohol and other drugs: A research perspective*. Thousand Oaks, CA: Sage.

Jung, S. K. (2004). A young onset Parkinson's patient: A case study. *Journal of Neuroscience Nursing*. Retrieved from http://goliath.ecnext.com/coms2/summary_0199-2782962.

Jylha, M. (2004). Old age and loneliness: Cross-sectional and longitudinal analyses in the Tampere longitudinal study on aging. *Canadian Journal on Aging/La Revue Canadienne du Vieillissement, 23*, 157–168.

Kahneman, D., Diener, E., & Schwarz, N. (1998). *Well-being: The foundations of hedonic psychology*. New York: Russell Sage Foundation.

Kahng, S. W., Iwata, B. A., & Lewin, A. B. (2002). Behavioral treatment of self-injury, 1964 to 2000. *American Journal on Mental Retardation, 107*, 212–221.

Kaller, C. P., Unterrainer, J. M., Rahm, B., & Halsband, U. (2004). The impact of problem structure on planning: Insights from the Tower of London task. *Cognitive Brain Research, 20*, 462–472.

Kallio, S., & Revonsuo, A. (2003). Hypnotic phenomena and altered states of consciousness: A multilevel framework of description and explanation. *Contemporary Hypnosis, 20*, 111–164.

Kamens, S. R. (2011). On the proposed sexual and gender identity diagnoses for DSM-5: History and controversies. *The Humanistic Psychologist, 39*, 37–59.

Kandel, E. R., Schwartz, J. H., & Jessell, T. M. (Eds.) (2000). *Principles of neural science* (4th ed.). New York: McGraw-Hill.

Kanner, A. D., Coyne, J. C., Schaefer, C., & Lazarus, R. S. (1981). Comparison of two modes of stress measurement: Daily hassles and uplifts versus major life events. *Journal of Behavioral Medicine, 4*, 14.

Kaplan, J. R., & Manuck, S. B. (1989). The effect of propranolol on behavioral interactions among adult male cynomolgus monkeys (*Macaca fascicularis*) housed in disrupted social groupings. *Psychosomatic Medicine, 51*, 449–462.

Kaplan, R. M., & Saccuzzo, D. P. (2001). *Psychological testing: Principles, applications, and issues* (5th ed.). Belmont, CA: Wadsworth/Thomson Learning.

Kara, P., & Boyd, J. (2009, April). A micro-architecture for binocular disparity and ocular dominance in visual cortex. *Nature, 458*(7238), 627-631.

Karaszewski, B. (2008). Sub-neocortical brain: A mechanical tool for creative generation? *Trends in Cognitive Sciences, 12*, 171–172.

Karni, A., Tanne, D., Rubenstein, B. S., Askenasy, J. J. M., & Sagi, D. (1994, July 29). Dependence on REM sleep of overnight improvement of a perceptual skill. *Science, 265*, 679–682.

Kasof, J. (2009, May). Cultural variation in seasonal depression: Cross-national differences in winter versus summer patterns of seasonal affective disorder. *Journal of Affective Disorders, 115,* 79–86.

Kassam, K. S., Gilbert, D. T., Swencionis, J. K., & Wilson, T. D. (2009). Misconceptions of memory: The Scooter Libby effect. *Psychological Science, 20,* 551–552.

Kassel, J. D., Evatt, D. P., Greenstein, J. E., Wardle, M. C., Yates, M. C., & Veilleux, J. C. (2007). The acute effects of nicotine on positive and negative affect in adolescent smokers. *Journal of Abnormal Psychology, 116,* 543–553.

Kassin, S. M. (2005). On the psychology of confessions: Does innocence put innocents at risk? *American Psychologist, 60,* 215–228.

Kato, K., & Pedersen, N. L. (2005). Personality and coping: A study of twins reared apart and twins reared together. *Behavior Genetics, 35,* 147–158.

Katz, L., Fotti, S., & Postl, L. (2009). Cognitive-behavioral therapy and dialectical behavior therapy: Adaptations required to treat adolescents. *Psychiatric Clinics of North America, 32,* 95–109.

Katz, M. (2001). The implications of revising Freud's empiricism for drive theory. *Psychoanalysis and Contemporary Thought, 24,* 253–272.

Kaufman, A., Johnson, C., & Liu, X. (2008). A CHC theory-based analysis of age differences on cognitive abilities and academic skills at ages 22 to 90 years. *Journal of Psychoeducational Assessment, 26,* 350–381.

Kaufman, G. (2009). MTV News: Chris Brown Haunted by Family History of Domestic Violence. Retrieved from: http://www.mtv.com/news/1604730/chris-brown-haunted-by-familys-history-of-domestic-violence/.

Kaufman, J. C. (2005). The door that leads into madness: Eastern European poets and mental illness. *Creativity Research Journal, 17,* 99–103.

Kaufman, J. C., & Baer, J. (2005). *Creativity across domains: Faces of the muse.* Mahwah, NJ: Lawrence Erlbaum Associates.

Kawasaki, C., Nugent, J. K., Miyashita, H., Miyahara, H., & Brazelton, T. B. (1994). The cultural organization of infants' sleep [Special issue: Environments of birth and infancy]. *Children's Environment, 11,* 135–141.

Kawashima, H., Izaki, Y., & Grace, A. A. (2006). Cooperativity between hippocampal-pre-frontal short-term plasticity through associative long-term potentiation. *Brain Research, 1109,* 37–44.

Kazarian, S. S., & Martin, R. A. (2004). Humor styles, personality, and well-being among Lebanese university students. *European Journal of Personality, 18,* 209–219.

Kazdin, A. (2008). Evidence-based treatment and practice: New opportunities to bridge clinical research and practice, enhance the knowledge base, and improve patient care. *American Psychologist, 63,* 146–159.

Kearns, K. P. (2005). Broca's aphasia. In L. L. LaPointe (Ed.), *Aphasia and related neurogenic language disorders* (3rd ed.). New York: Thieme New York.

Keating, D. P., & Clark, L. V. (1980). Development of physical and social reasoning in adolescence. *Developmental Psychology, 16,* 23–30.

Keehn, J. D. (1996). *Master builders of modern psychology: From Freud to Skinner.* New York: New York University Press.

Kelley, H. (1950). The warm-cold variable in first impressions of persons. *Journal of Personality and Social Psychology, 18,* 431–439.

Kelly, D., & Tangney, B. (2006). Adapting to intelligence profile in an adaptive educational system. *Interacting with Computers, 18,* pp. 385–409.

Keltikangas-Järvinen, L., Räikkönen, K., Ekelund, J., & Peltonen, L. (2004). Nature and nurture in novelty seeking. *Molecular Psychiatry, 9,* 308–311.

Kemeny, M. E. (2007). Psychoneuroimmunology. In H. S. Friedman & R. C. Silver, *Foundations of health psychology.* New York: Oxford University Press.

Kemps, E., & Tiggemann, M. (2007). Reducing the vividness and emotional impact of distressing autobiographical memories: The importance of modality-specific interference. *Memory, 15,* 412–422.

Kendler, K. S., Gatz, M., & Gardner, C. O. (2006). Personality and major depression. *Archives of General Psychiatry, 63,* 1113–1120.

Kendler, K. S., & Schaffner, K. F. (2011). The dopamine hypothesis of schizophrenia: An historical and philosophical analysis. *Philosophy, Psychiatry, & Psychology, 18,* 41–63.

Kennedy, K. (2001, October 22). Brotherly love: Beset by panic attacks, Toronto's Shayne Corson turned to linemate and in-law Darcy Tucker for help. *Sports Illustrated.* Retrieved from vault.sportsillustrated.cnn.com/vault/article/magazine/MAG1024020/index.htm.

Kenshalo, D. R. (1968). *The skin senses.* Springfield, IL: Charles C. Thomas.

Kensinger, E. (2007). Negative emotion enhances memory accuracy: Behavioral and neuroimaging evidence. *Current Directions in Psychological Science, 16,* 213–218.

Kenway, L., & Wilson, M. A. (2001). Temporally structured replay of awake hippocampal ensemble activity during rapid eye movement sleep. *Neuron, 29,* 145–156.

Kesebir, P., & Diener, E. (2008). In pursuit of happiness: Empirical answers to philosophical questions. *Perspectives on Psychological Science, 3,* 117–125.

Kessler, R. C., & Wang, P. S. (2008). The descriptive epidemiology of commonly occurring mental disorders in the United States. *Annual Review of Public Health, 29,* 115–129.

Ketisch, T., & Jones, R. A. (2013). Review of 'ADHD diagnosis & management'. *American Journal of Family Therapy, 41,* 272–274.

Kettenmann, H., & Ransom, B. R. (2005). *Neuroglia* (2nd ed.). New York: Oxford University Press.

Key, W. B. (2003). Subliminal sexuality: The fountainhead for America's obsession. In T. Reichert & J. Lambaiase (Eds.), *Sex in advertising: Perspectives on the erotic appeal. LEA's communication series.* Mahwah, NJ: Lawrence Erlbaum.

Khazaal, Y., Chatton, A., Claeys, F., Ribordy, F., Zullino, D., & Cabanac, M. (2008). Antipsychotic drug and body weight set-point. *Physiology & Behavior, 95,* 157–160.

Kidd, E., & Lum, J. (2008). Sex differences in past tense overregularization. *Developmental Science, 11,* 882–889.

Kihlstrom, J. F. (2005b). Is hypnosis an altered state of consciousness or what? Comment. *Contemporary Hypnosis, 22,* 34–38.

Kihlstrom, J. F., Schacter, D. L., Cork, R. C., Hurt, C. A., & Behr, S. E. (1990). Implicit and explicit memory following surgical anesthesia. *Psychological Science, 1,* 303–306.

Kim, D. R., Pesiridou, A., & O'Reardon, J. P. (2009). Transcranial magnetic stimulation in the treatment of psychiatric disorders. *Current Psychiatry Reports, 11,* 447–52.

Kim, H., Clark, D., & Dionne, R. (2009, July). Genetic contributions to clinical pain and analgesia: Avoiding pitfalls in genetic research. *The Journal of Pain, 10,* 663–693.

Kim, N. (2008). The moon illusion and the size-distance paradox. In Cummins-Sebree, S., Riley, M. A., & Shockley, K. (Eds). *Studies in perception and action IX: Fourteenth International Conference on Perception and Action.* Mahwah, NJ: Lawrence Erlbaum Associates.

Kimbrel, N. A. (2007). A model of the development and maintenance of generalized social phobia. *Clinical Psychological Review, 8,* 69–75.

Kimura, D. (1992, September). Sex differences in the brain. *Scientific American,* pp. 119–125.

King-Casas, B., Sharp, C., Lomax-Bream, L., Lohrenz, T., Fonagy, P., & Montague, P. R. (2008, August, 8). The rupture and repair of cooperation in borderline personality disorder. *Science, 321,* 806–810.

Kirk, K. M., Bailey, J. M., & Martin, N. G. (2000). Etiology of male sexual orientation in an Australian twin sample. *Psychology, Evolution & Gender, 2,* 301–311.

Kirsch, I., Lynn, S. J., Vigorito, M., & Miller, R. R. (2004). The role of cognition in classical and operant conditioning. *Journal of Clinical Psychology, 60,* 369–392.

Kirschenbaum, H. (2004). Carl Rogers's life and work: An assessment on the 100th anniversary of his birth. *Journal of Counseling and Development, 82,* 116–124.

Kirschenbaum, H., & Jourdan, A. (2005). The current status of Carl Rogers and the person-centered approach. *Psychotherapy: Theory, Research, Practice, Training, 42,* 37–51.

Kiss, A. (2004). Does gender have an influence on the patient-physician communication? *Journal of Men's Health and Gender, 1,* 77–82.

Kitterle, F. L. (Ed.). (1991). *Cerebral laterality: Theory and research.* Hillsdale, NJ: Erlbaum.

Kleinplatz, P. J., Moser, C., & Lev, A. (2013). Sex and gender identity disorders. In G. Stricker, T. A. Widiger, & I. B. Weiner (Eds.), *Handbook of psychology, Vol. 8: Clinical psychology* (2nd ed.). Hoboken, NJ: John Wiley & Sons Inc.

Klötz, F., Garle, M., & Granath, F. (2006). Criminality among individuals testing positive for the presence of anabolic androgenic steroids. *Archives of General Psychiatry, 63,* 1274–1279.

Kluger, J. (2001, April 2). Fear not! *Time,* pp. 51–62.

Kluger, J. (2006, December 4). Why we worry about the things we shouldn't and ignore the things we should. *Time,* pp. 64–71.

Knight, S. C., & Meyer, R. G. (2007). Forensic hypnosis. In A. M. Goldstein, *Forensic psychology: Emerging topics and expanding roles.* Hoboken, NJ: John Wiley & Sons.

Knoblich, G., & Sebanz, N. (2006). The social nature of perception and action. *Current Directions in Psychological Science, 15,* 99–111.

Knops, A., Nuerk, H. C., Fimm, B., Vohn, R., & Willmes, K. (2005). A special role for numbers in working memory? An fMRI study. *Neuroimage, 22,* 125–132.

Kobayashi, F., Schallert, D. L., & Ogren, H. A. (2003). Japanese and American folk vocabularies for emotions. *Journal of Social Psychology, 143,* 451–478.

Koch, C., & Greenfield, S. (2007, October.) How does consciousness happen? *Scientific American,* pp. 76–83.

Kohlberg, L. (1984). *The psychology of moral development: Essays on moral development* (Vol. 2). San Francisco: Harper & Row.

Kohlberg, L., & Ryncarz, R. A. (1990). Beyond justice reasoning: Moral development and consideration of a seventh stage. In C. N. Alexander & E. J. Langer (Eds.), *Higher stages of human development: Perspectives on adult growth.* New York: Oxford University Press.

Köhler, W. (1927). *The mentality of apes.* London: Routledge & Kegan Paul.

Kojima, M., & Kangawa, K. (2008). Structure and function of ghrelin. *Results & Problems in Cell Differentiation, 46,* 89–115.

Kolb, B., Gibb, R., & Robinson, T. E. (2003). Brain plasticity and behavior. *Current Directions in Psychological Science, 12,* 1–5.

Komarovskaya, I., Loper, A., Warren, J., & Jackson, S. (2011). Exploring gender differences in trauma exposure and the emergence of symptoms of PTSD among incarcerated men and women. *Journal of Forensic Psychiatry & Psychology, 22,* 395–410.

Koocher, G. P., Norcross, J. C., & Hill, S. S. (2005). *Psychologists' desk reference* (2nd ed.). New York: Oxford University Press.

Kopelman, M. D., & Fleminger, S. (2002). Experience and perspectives on the classification of organic mental disorders. *Psychopathology, 35,* 76–81.

Koper, R. J., & Jaasma, M. A. (2001). Interpersonal style: Are human social orientations guided by generalized interpersonal needs? *Communications Reports, 14,* 117–129.

Koplewicz, H. (2002). *More than moody: Recognizing and treating adolescent depression.* New York: Putnam.

Kosambi, D. D. (1967). The Vedic "Five Tribes." *American Oriental Society, 14,* 5–12.

Kosfeld, M., Heinrich, M., Zak, P. J., Fischbacher, U., & Fehr, E. (2005, June 2). Oxytocin increases trust in humans. *Nature, 435,* 673–676.

Kosslyn, S. M. (2005). Mental images and the brain. *Cognitive Neuropsychology, 22,* 333–347.

Kosslyn, S. M., Cacioppo, J. T., Davidson, R. J., Hugdahl, K., Lovallo, W. R., Spiegel, D., et al. (2002). Bridging psychology and biology. *American Psychologist, 57,* 341–351.

Kotre, J., & Hall, E. (1990). *Seasons of life.* Boston: Little, Brown.

Kovelman, I., Shalinsky, M.H., Berens, M.S., &, Petitto, L.A. (2008). Shining new light on the brain's "bilingual signature": A functional Near Infrared Spectroscopy investigation of semantic processing. *Neuroimage, 39,* 1457–1471.

Kowert, P. A. (2002). *Groupthink or deadlock: When do leaders learn from their advisors? SUNY Series on the presidency.* Albany: State University of New York Press.

Kozaric-Kovacic, D., & Borovecki, A. (2005). Prevalence of psychotic comorbidity in combat-related post- traumatic stress disorder. *Military Medicine, 170,* 223–226.

Kozulin, A., Gindis, B., Ageyev, V. S., & Miller, S. M. (2003). *Vygotsky's educational theory in cultural context.* New York: Cambridge University Press.

Kramer, P. (1993). *Listening to Prozac.* New York: Viking.

Krause, S. S. (2003). *Aircraft safety: Accident investigations, analyses, and applications* (2nd ed.). New York: McGraw-Hill.

Kreher, D., Holcomb, P., Goff, D., & Kuper-berg, G. (2008). Neural evidence for faster and further automatic spreading activation in schizophrenic thought disorder. *Schizophrenia Bulletin, 34,* 473–482.

Kreuger, A. (2007). Are we having fun yet? Categorizing and evaluating changes in time allocation. *Brookings Papers on Economic Activity* (Vol. 2), *38,* 193–218.

Krijn, M., Emmelkamp, P. M. G., Olafsson, R. P., & Biemond, R. (2004). Virtual reality exposure therapy of anxiety disorders: A review. *Clinical Psychology Review, 24,* 259–281.

Krohne, H. W. (1996). Individual differences in coping. In M. Zeidner & N. S. Endler (Eds.), *Handbook of coping: Theory, research, applications.* New York: Wiley.

Krueger, K., & Dayan, P. (2009). Flexible shaping: How learning in small steps helps. *Cognition, 110,* 380–394.

Krueger, R. G., Hicks, B. M., & McGue, M. (2001). Altruism and antisocial behavior: Independent tendencies, unique personality correlates, distinct etiologies. *Psychological Science, 12,* 397–402.

Krull, D. S., & Anderson, C. A. (1997). The process of explanation. *Current Directions in Psychological Science, 6,* 1–5.

Krusemark, E., Campbell, W., & Clementz, B. (2008). Attributions, deception, and event related potentials: An investigation of the self-serving bias. *Psychophysiology, 45,* 511–515.

Kübler-Ross, E. (1969). *On death and dying.* New York: Macmillan.

Kubovy, M., Epstein, W., & Gepshtein, S. (2003). Foundations of visual perception. In A. F. Healy, & R. W. Proctor (Eds.). *Handbook of psychology: Experimental psychology* (Vol. 4). New York: Wiley.

Kulynych, J. J., Vladar, K., Jones, D. W., & Weinberger, D. R. (1994). Gender differences in the normal lateralization of the supratemporal cortex: MRI surface-rendering morphometry of Heschl's gyrus and the planum temporale. *Cerebral Cortex, 4,* 107–118.

Kunda, Z. (2000). The case for motivated reasoning. In D. T. Higgins & A. W. Kruglanski (Eds.), *Motivational science: Social and personality perspectives. Key readings in social psychology* (pp. 313–335). Philadelphia: Psychology Press.

Kunda, Z., Davies, P. G. Adams, B. D., & Spencer, S. J. (2002). The dynamic time course of stereotype activation: Activation, dissipation, and resurrection. *Journal of Personality and Social Psychology, 82 (3),* 283–299.

Kupfer, D. J., Kuhl, E. A., & Regier, D. A. (2013). DSM-5—The future arrived. *JAMA: Journal of the American Medical Association, 309,* 1691–1692.

Kuppens, P., Ceulemans, E., Timmerman, M. E., Diener, E., & Kim-Prieto, C. (2006). Universal intracultural and intercultural dimensions of the recalled frequency of emotional experience. *Journal of Cross Cultural Psychology, 37,* 491–515.

Kuriyama, K., Stickgold, R., & Walker, M. P. (2004). Sleep-dependent learning and motor-skill complexity. *Learning and Memory, 11,* 705–713.

Kuther, T. L. (2003). *Your career in psychology: Psychology and the law.* New York: Wadsworth.

Kvavilashvili, L., & Fisher, L. (2007). Is time-based prospective remembering mediated by self-initiated rehearsals? Role of incidental cues, ongoing activity, age, and motivation. *Journal of Experimental Psychology: General, 136,* 112–132.

Kwon, P., & Laurenceau, J. P. (2002). A longitudinal study of the hopelessness theory of depression: Testing the diathesis-stress model within a differential reactivity and exposure framework [Special issue: Reprioritizing the role of science in a realistic version of the scientist-practitioner model]. *Journal of Clinical Psychology, 50,* 1305–1321.

Kyaga, S., Landén, M., Boman, M., Hultman, C. M., Langström, N., & Lichtenstein, P. (2013). Mental illness, suicide and creativity: 40-year prospective total population study. *Journal of Psychiatric Research, 47,* 83–90.

LaBar, K. (2007). Beyond fear: Emotional memory mechanisms in the human brain. *Current Directions in Psychological Science, 16,* 173–177.

Lacerda, F., von Hofsten, C., & Heimann, M. (2001). *Emerging cognitive abilities in early infancy.* Mahwah, NJ: Lawrence Erlbaum Associates.

Laederach-Hofmann, K., & Messerli-Buergy, N. (2007). Chest pain, angina pectoris, panic disorder, and Syndrome X. In J. Jordan, B. Barde & A. M. Zeiher, *Contributions toward evidence-based psychocardiology: A systematic review of the literature.* Washington, DC: American Psychological Association.

LaFromboise, T., Coleman, H. L. K., & Gerton, J. (1995). Psychological impact of biculturalism: Evidence and theory. In N. R. Goldberger & J. B. Veroff (Eds.), *The culture and psychology reader.* New York: New York University Press.

Lagacé-Séguin, D. G., & d'Entremont, M. L. (2006). The role of child negative affect in the relations between parenting styles and play. *Early Child Development and Care, 176,* 461–477.

Lahti, J., Räikkönen, K., Ekelund, J., Peltonen, L., Raitakari, O. T., & Keltikangas-Järvinen, L. (2005). Novelty seeking: Interaction between parental alcohol use and dopamine D4 receptor gene exon III polymorphism over 17 years. *Psychiatric Genetics, 15,* 133–139.

Laing, R. D., & Szasz, T. (2004). "Knowing what ain't so." *Psychoanalytic Review, 91,* 331–346.

Laird, J. D., & Bressler, C. (1990). William James and the mechanisms of emotional experience. *Personality and Social Psychology Bulletin, 16,* 636–651.

Lakhan, S., & Vieira, K. (2009, May 15). Schizophrenia pathophysiology: Are we any closer to a complete model? *Annals of General Psychiatry, 8.*

Lal, S. (2002). Giving children security: Mamie Phipps Clark and the racialization of child psychology. *American Psychologist, 57,* 20–28.

Lamal, P. A. (1979). College students' common beliefs about psychology. *Teaching of Psychology, 6,* 155–158.

Lamb, M. E. (1996). Effects of nonparental child care on child development: An update. *Canadian Journal of Psychiatry, 41,* 330–342.

Lamb, M. E., & Garretson, M. E. (2003). The effects of interviewer gender and child gender on the informativeness of alleged child sexual abuse victims in forensic interviews. *Law and Human Behavior, 27,* 157–171.

Lamborn, S. D., & Groh, K. (2009). A four-part model of autonomy during emerging adulthood: Associations with adjustment. *International Journal of Behavioral Development, 33,* 393–401.

Lana, R. E. (2002). The cognitive approach to language and thought [Special issue: Choice and chance in the formation of society: Behavior and cognition in social theory]. *Journal of Mind and Behavior, 23,* 51–57.

Lane, S. D., Cherek, D. R., & Tcheremissine, O. V. (2007). Response perseveration and adaptation in heavy marijuana-smoking adolescents. *Addictive Behaviors, 32,* 977–990.

Lang, A. J., Sorrell, J. T., & Rodgers, C. S. (2006). Anxiety sensitivity as a predictor of labor pain. *European Journal of Pain, 10,* 263–270.

Langan-Fox, J., & Grant, S. (2006). The Thematic Apperception Test: Toward a standard measure of the big three motives. *Journal of Personality Assessment, 87,* 277–291.

Langdridge, D., & Butt, T. (2004). The fundamental attribution error: A phenomenological critique. *British Journal of Social Psychology, 43,* 357–369.

Lanza, S. T., & Collins, L. M. (2002). Pubertal timing and the onset of substance use in females during early adolescence. *Prevention Science, 3,* 69–82.

Laqueur, T. W. (2003). *Solitary sex: A cultural history of masturbation.* New York: Zone.

Larson, R. K. (1990). Semantics. In D. N. Osherson & H. Lasnik (Eds.), *Language.* Cambridge, MA: MIT.

Lascaratos, G., Ji, D., & Wood, J. P. (2007). Visible light affects mitochondrial function and induces neuronal death in retinal cell cultures. *Vision Research, 47,* 1191–1201.

Lasnik, H. (1990). Syntax. In D. N. Osherson & H. Lasnik (Eds.), *Language.* Cambridge, MA: MIT.

Latané, B., & Darley, J. M. (1970). *The unresponsive bystander: Why doesn't he help?* New York: Appleton-Century-Crofts.

Lau, D.C.W., Douketis, J. D., Morrison, K. M., Hramiak, I. M., Sharma, A. M., & Ehud, U. (2007). Canadian clinical practice guidelines on the management and prevention of obesity in adults and children. *Canadian Medical Association Journal, 176 (8),* 1356–1364.

Laugharne, J., Janca, A., & Widiger, T. (2007). Posttraumatic stress disorder and terrorism: 5 years after 9/11. *Current Opinion in Psychiatry, 20, 36* 41.

Lavelli, M., & Fogel, A. (2005). Developmental changes in the relationship between the infant's attention and emotion during early face-to-face communication. *Developmental Psychology, 41,* 265–280.

Lavenex, P., & Lavenex, P. (2009). Spatial memory and the monkey hippocampus: Not all space is created equal. *Hippocampus, 19,* 8–19.

Lawryk, L. (2011). Adopting a child living with fetal alcohol spectrum disorder. Calgary, Alberta: OBD Triage Institute Inc. pp. 1–21. ISBN 978-0-973 7739-1-0.

Lazarus, R. S. (1995). Emotions express a social relationship, but it is an individual mind that creates them. *Psychological Inquiry, 6,* 253–265.

Leahy, R. L. (2003). *Roadblocks in cognitive-behavioral therapy: Transforming challenges into opportunities for change.* New York: Guilford Press.

Leary, C., Kelley, M., Morrow, J., & Mikulka, P. (2008). Parental use of physical punishment as related to family environment, psychological well-being, and personality in undergraduates. *Journal of Family Violence, 23,* 1–7.

Lee, A. Y., & Aaker, J. L. (2004). Bringing the frame into focus: The influence of regulatory fit on processing fluency and persuasion. *Journal of Personality and Social Psychology, 86,* 205–218.

Lee, H. J., & Kwon, S. M. (2003). Two different types of obsession: Autogenous obsessions and reactive obsessions. *Behaviour Research & Therapy, 41,* 11–29.

Lee, H. J., Kwon, S. M., Kwon, J. S., & Telch, M. J. (2005). Testing the autogenous reactive model of obsessions. *Depress Anxiety, 21,* 118–129.

Lee-Chai, A. Y., & Bargh, J. A. (Eds.). (2001). *The use and abuse of power: Multiple perspectives on the causes of corruption.* Philadelphia, PA: Psychology Press.

Lehar, S. (2003). *The world in your head: A gestalt view of the mechanism of conscious experience.* Mahwah, NJ: Lawrence Erlbaum Associates.

Lehman, D. R., & Taylor, S. E. (1988). Date with an earthquake: Coping with a probable, unpredictable disaster. *Personality and Social Psychology Bulletin, 13,* 546–555.

Lehrman, S. (2007). Going beyond X and Y. *Scientific American,* pp. 40–41.

Leib, J. R., Gollust, S. E., Hull, S. C., & Wilfond, B. S. (2005). Carrier screening panels for Ashkenazi Jews: Is more better? *Genetic Medicine, 7,* 185–190.

Leibel, R. L., Rosenbaum, M., & Hirsch, J. (1995, March 9). Changes in energy expenditure resulting from altered body. *New England Journal of Medicine, 332,* 621–628.

Leiblum, S. R., & Chivers, M. L. (2007). Normal and persistent genital arousal in women: New perspectives. *Journal of Sex & Marital Therapy, 33,* 357–373.

Leigh, J. H., Zinkhan, G. M. & Swaminathan, V. (2006). Dimensional relationships of recall and recognition measures with selected cognitive and affective aspects of print ads. *Journal of Advertising, 35,* 105–122.

Leiter, S., & Leiter, W. M. (2003). *Affirmative action in antidiscrimination law and policy: An overview and synthesis.* SUNY series in American constitutionalism. Albany: State University of New York Press.

Leitner, L. M. (2007). Diversity issues, postmodernism, and psychodynamic therapy. *PsycCRITIQUES, 52,* no pagination specified.

Lemay, E. P., Jr., Clark, M. S., & Feeney, B. C. (2007). Projection of responsiveness to needs and the construction of satisfying communal relationships. *Journal of Personality and Social Psychology, 92,* 834–853.

Lemay, E., & Clark, M. (2008). How the head liberates the heart: Projection of communal responsiveness guides relationship promotion. *Journal of Personality and Social Psychology, 94,* 647–671.

Lemonick, M. D. (2000, December 11). Downey's downfall. *Time,* p. 97.

Lenhart, A. (2009, January 14). *Adults and social network websites.* Washington, DC: Pew Internet & American Life Project.

Lenzenweger, M. F., & Dworkin, R. H. (Eds.). (1998). *The origins and development of schizophrenia: Advances in experimental psychopathology.* Washington, DC: American Psychological Association.

Lepage, J. F., & Theoret, H. (2007). The mirror neuron system: grasping others' actions from birth? *Developmental Science, 10,* 513–523.

Leppänen, J. M., Moulson, M. C., Vogel-Farley, V. K. & Nelson, C.A. (2007). An ERP study of emotional face processing in the adult and infant brain. *Child Development, 78,* 232–245.

Lepper, M. R., Corpus, J. H., & Iyengar, S. S. (2005). Intrinsic and extrinsic motivational orientations in the classroom: Age differences and academic correlates. *Journal of Educational Psychology, 97,* 184–196.

LeVay, S. (1993). *The sexual brain.* Cambridge, MA: MIT.

LeVay, S. (2011). *Gay, straight, and the reason why: The science of sexual orientation.* New York: Oxford University Press.

Levi, A., Chan, K. K., & Pence, D. (2006). Real men do not read labels: The effects of masculinity and involvement on college students' food decisions. *Journal of American College Health, 55,* 91–98.

Levin, B. E., (2006). Metabolic sensing neurons and the control of energy homeostasis. *Physiology & Behavior, 89,* 486–489.

Levin, R. J. (2007). Sexual activity, health and well-being—the beneficial roles of coitus and masturbation. *Sexual and Relationship Therapy, 22,* 135–148.

Levin, R., & Nielsen, (2007) Disturbed dreaming, posttraumatic stress disorder, and affect distress: A review and neurocognitive model. *Psychological Bulletin.* 133(3): 482–528.

Levin, R., & Nielsen, T. (2009, April). Nightmares, bad dreams, and emotion dysregulation: A review and new neurocognitive model of dreaming. *Current Directions in Psychological Science, 18,* 84–88.

Levine, J. M., & Moreland, R. L. (2006). Small groups: An overview. In J. M. Levine & R. L. Moreland (Eds.), *Small groups.* New York: Psychology Press.

Levine, S. Z., & Rabinowitz, J. (2007). Revisiting the 5 dimensions of the Positive and Negative Syndrome Scale. *Journal of Clinical Psychopharmacology, 27,* 431–436.

Levinson, D. (1992). *The seasons of a woman's life.* New York: Knopf.

Levinson, D. J. (1990). A theory of life structure development in adulthood. In C. N. Alexander & E. J. Langer (Eds.), *Higher stages of human development: Perspectives on adult growth.* New York: Oxford University Press.

Levs, J., Gast, G., & Almasy, S. (May 9, 2013). Charles Ramsey: I'm no hero in freeing captive women. CNN Anderson Cooper 360 Exclusive. Retrieved from www.cnn.com/2013/05/07/us/ohio-cleveland-ramsey/.

Levy, B. (1996). Improving memory in old age through implicit self-stereotyping. *Journal of Personality and Social Psychology, 71,* 1092–1107.

Levy, B. R., & Myers, L. M. (2004). Preventive health behaviors influenced by self-perceptions of aging. *Preventive Medicine: An International Journal Devoted to Practice and Theory, 39,* 625–629.

Levy, B. R., Slade, M. D., Kunkel, S. R., & Kasl, S. V. (2002). Longevity increased by positive self-perceptions of aging. *Journal of Personality & Social Psychology, 83,* 261–270.

Lewin, T. (2003, December 22). For more people in their 20s and 30s, going home is easier because they never left. *The New York Times,* p. A27.

Lewinsohn, P. M., & Essau, C. A. (2002). Depression in adolescents. In I. H. Gotlib & C. L. Hammen (Eds.), *Handbook of depression.* New York: Guilford Press.

Lewinsohn, P. M., Petit, J. W., Joiner, T. E., Jr., & Seeley, J. R. (2003). The symptomatic expression of major depressive disorder in adolescents and young adults. *Journal of Abnormal Psychology, 112,* 244–252.

Li, B. (2008, May 5). Binge eating. *Campus life magazine.* Retrieved from www.campuslifemagazine.ca/article2.php?id=binge_eating.

Li, B., Piriz, J., Mirrione, M., Chung, C., Proulx, C. D., Schulz, D., Henn, F., Malinow, R. (2011). Synaptic potentiation onto habenula neurons in learned helplessness model of depression. *Nature, 470,* 535–539.

Li, J. (2005). Mind or virtue: Western and Chinese beliefs about learning. *Current Directions in Psychological Science,* 14, 190–194.

Li, J., Wang, L., & Fischer, K. W. (2004). The organization of Chinese shame concepts. *Cognition and Emotion, 18,* 767–797.

Liang, K. A. (2007). Acculturation, ambivalent sexism, and attitudes toward women who engage in premarital sex among Chinese American young adults. *Dissertation Abstracts International: Section B: The Sciences and Engineering, 67*(10-B), 6065.

Licata S. C. & Rowlett, J. K. (2008). Abuse and dependence liability of benzodiazepine-type drugs: GABA (A) receptor modulation and beyond. Pharmacology, Biochemistry and Behavior, 90 (1), 74-89.

Lick, D. J., Durso, L. E., & Johnson, K. L. (2013). Minority stress and physical health among sexual minorities. *Perspectives on Psychological Science, 8,* 521–548.

Lidz, J., & Gleitman, L. R. (2004). Argument structure and the child's contribution to language learning. *Trends in Cognitive Sciences, 8,* 157–161.

Lieberman, M. D. (2007). Social cognitive neuro-science: A review of core processes. *Annual Review of Psychology, 58,* 259–289.

Lien, Y-W., Chu, R-L., Jen, C-H., & Wu, C-H. (2006). Do Chinese commit neither fundamental attribution error nor ultimate attribution error? *Chinese Journal of Psychology, 48,* 163–181.

Lin, C-H., & Lin, H-M. (2007). What price do you ask for the 'extra one'? A social value orientation perspective. *Social Behavior and Personality, 35,* 9–18.

Lindblad, F., Lindahl, M., & Theorell, T. (2006). Physiological stress reactions in 6th and 9th graders during test performance. *Stress and Health: Journal of the International Society for the Investigation of Stress, 22,* 189–195.

Lindemann, O., & Bekkering, H. (2009). Object manipulation and motion perception: Evidence of an influence of action planning on visual processing. *Journal of Experimental Psychology: Human Perception and Performance, 35,* 1062–1071.

Lindorff, M. (2005). Determinants of received social support: Who gives what to managers? *Journal of Social and Personal Relationships, 22,* 323–337.

Lindsay, P. H., & Norman, D. A. (1977). *Human information processing* (2nd ed.). New York: Academic Press.

Lindsay, P., Maynard, I., & Thomas, O. (2005). Effects of hypnosis on flow states and cycling performance. *Sport Psychologist, 19,* 164–177.

Lindsey, E., & Colwell, M. (2003). Preschoolers' emotional competence: Links to pretend and physical play. *Child Study Journal, 33,* 39–52.

Linehan, M., Davison, G., Lynch, T., & Sanderson, C. (2007). Principles of therapeutic change in the treatment of personality disorders. In L. Beutler, & L. Castonguay (Eds.), *Identification of principles of therapeutic change.* New York: Oxford University Press.

Liszkowski, U., Schäfer, M., Carpenter, M., & Tomasello, M. (2009). Prelinguistic infants, but not chimpanzees, communicate about absent entities. *Psychological Science, 20,* 654–660.

Little, A., Burt, D. M., & Perrett, D. I. (2006). What is good is beautiful: Face preference reflects desired personality. *Personality and Individual Differences, 41,* 1107–1118.

Little, K., Ramssen, E., Welchko, R., Volberg, V., Roland, C., & Cassin, B. (2009). Decreased brain dopamine cell numbers in human cocaine users. *Psychiatry Research, 168,* 173–180.

Livesley, W., & Jang, K. (2008). The behavioral genetics of personality disorder. *Annual Review of Clinical Psychology, 4,* 247–274.

Living in Canada. (2010). Psychologists—Canada salary and wage guide. In *Living in Canada.* Retrieved from www.livingin-canada.com/salaries-for-psychologists.html.

References

Lobato, M. I., Koff, W. J., & Manenti, C. (2006). Follow-up of sex reassignment surgery in transsexuals: A Brazilian cohort. *Archives of Sexual Behavior, 35,* 711–715.

Lobban, F., Barrowclough, C., & Jones, S. (2006). Does expressed emotion need to be understood within a more systemic framework? An examination of discrepancies in appraisals between patients diagnosed with schizophrenia and their relatives. *Social Psychiatry and Psychiatric Epidemiology, 41,* 50–55.

Lobo, I., & Harris, R. (2008, July). GABAa receptors and alcohol. *Pharmacology, Biochemistry and Behavior, 90,* 90–94.

Locke, J. L. (2006). Parental selection of vocal behavior: Crying, cooking, babbling, and the evolution of language. *Human Nature, 17,* 155–168.

Lockl, K., & Schneider, W. (2007). Knowledge about the mind: Links between theory of mind and later metamemory. *Child Development, 78,* 148–167.

Lockrane, B., Bhatia, P., & Gore, R. (2005). Successful treatment of narcolepsy and cataplexy: a review. *Canadian Respiratory Journal, 12,* 225–227.

Loewenstein, G. (1994). The psychology of curiosity: A review and reinterpretation. *Psychological Bulletin, 116,* 75–98.

Lofholm, N. (2003, May 6). Climber's kin share relief: Ralston saw 4 options, they say; death wasn't one of them. *Denver Post,* p. A1.

Loftus, E. F. (1993). Psychologists in the eyewitness world. *American Psychologist, 48,* 550–552.

Loftus, E. F. (1997). Memory for a past that never was. *Current Directions in Psychological Science, 6,* 60–65.

Loftus, E. F. (1998, November). The memory police. *APA Observer, 3,* 14.

Loftus, E. F. (2003). Memory in Canadian courts. *Canadian Psychology, 44(3),* 207–211.

Loftus, E. F. (2003). The dangers of memory. In R. J. Sternberg (Ed.), *Psychologists defying the crowd: Stories of those who battled the establishment and won* (pp. 105–117). Washington, DC: American Psychological Association.

Loftus, E. F. (2004). Memories of things unseen. *Current Directions in Psychological Science, 13,* 145–147.

Loftus, E. F., & Bernstein, D. M. (2005). Rich false memories: The royal road to success. In A. F. Healy, *Experimental cognitive psychology and its applications.* Washington, DC: American Psychological Association.

Loftus, E. F., & Palmer, J. C. (1974). Reconstruction of automobile destruction: An example of the interface between language and memory. *Journal of Verbal Learning and Verbal Behavior, 13,* 585–589.

Loftus, E.F., & Wortmann, C. (1989). *Psychology* (4th ed.). New York: McGraw-Hill.

Long, G. M., & Beaton, R. J. (1982). The case for peripheral persistence: Effects of target and background luminance on a partial-report task. *Journal of Experimental Psychology: Human Perception and Performance, 8,* 383–391.

Long, M. (2007, September 17). Why has Steven Pinker studied verbs for 20 years? *Discover Magazine.* Retrieved from discovermagazine.com/2007/sep/the-discover-interview.

Lopes, A. C., Greenberg, B. D., Noren, G., Canteras, M. M., Busatto, G. F. de Mathis, et al. (2009). Treatment of resistant obsessive-compulsive disorder with ventral capsular/ventral striatal gamma capsulotomy: A pilot prospective study. *The Journal of Neuropsychiatry and Clinical Neurosciences, 21,* 381–392.

López, S. R., & Guarnaccia, P. J. J. (2000). Cultural psychopathology: Uncovering the social world of mental illness. *Annual Review of Psychology, 51,* 571–598.

Lorenz, K. (1966). *On aggression.* New York: Harcourt Brace Jovanovich.

Lorenz, K. (1974). *Civilized man's eight deadly sins.* New York: Harcourt Brace Jovanovich.

Lothane, Z. (2005). Jung, A biography. *Journal of the American Psychoanalytic Association, 53,* 317–324.

Loving, T., Crockett, E., & Paxson, A. (2009). Passionate love and relationship thinkers: Experimental evidence for acute cortisol elevations in women. *Psychoneuroendocrinology, 34,* 939–946.

Lowe, M. R. (1993). The effects of dieting on eating behavior: A three-factor model. *Psychological Bulletin, 114,* 100–121.

Lowery, D., Fillingim, R. B., & Wright, R. A. (2003). Sex differences and incentive effects on perceptual and cardiovascular responses to cold pressor pain. *Psychosomatic Medicine, 65,* 284–291.

Lu, J., Sherman, D., Devor, M., & Saper, C. B. (2006). A putative flip-flop switch for control of REM sleep. *Nature, 441,* 589–594.

Lubinski D., Benbow, C.P., Webb, R.M., & Bleske-Rechek, A. (2006). Tracking exceptional human capital over two decades. *Psychological Science 17,* 194–199.

Lublin, H., Eberhard, J., & Levander, S. (2005). Current therapy issues and unmet clinical needs in the treatment of schizophrenia: A review of the new generation antipsychotics. *International Clinical Psychopharmacology, 20,* 183–198.

Luchins, A. S. (1946). Classroom experiments on mental set. *American Journal of Psychology, 59,* 295–298.

Lucki, I., & O'Leary, O. F. (2004). Distinguishing roles for norepinephrine and serotonin in the behavioral effects of antidepressant drugs. *Journal of Clinical Psychiatry, 65,* 11–24.

Luders, E., Narr, K. L., Zaidel, E., Thompson, P. M., & Toga, A. W. (2006). Gender effects on callosal thickness in scaled and unscaled space. *Neuroreport, 17,* 1103–1106.

Lunn, J. S., Sakowski, S. A., Hur, J., & Feldman, E. L. (2011). Stem cell technology for neurodegenerative diseases. *Annals of Neurology, 70* (3) 353–361.

Luo, S., & Zhang, G. (2009). What leads to romantic attraction: Similarity, reciprocity, security, or beauty? Evidence from a speed-dating study. *Journal of Personality, 77,* 933–964.

Luria, A. R. (1968). *The mind of a mnemonist.* Cambridge, MA: Basic Books.

Lutz, C. K. & Novak, M. A. (2005) Environmental enrichment for nonhuman primates: theory and application. *ILAR Journal, 46,* 178–191.

Lutz, W., Lambert, M. J., Harmon, S. C., Tschitsaz, A., Schurch, E., & Stulz, N (2006). The probability of treatment success, failure and duration—What can be learned from empirical data to support decision making in clinical practice? *Clinical Psychology & Psychotherapy, 13,* 223–232.

Ly, D. H., Lockhart, D. J., Lerner, R. A., & Schultz, P. G. (2000, March 31). Mitotic misregulation and human aging. *Science, 287,* 2486–2492.

Lykken, D. T. (1995). *The antisocial personalities.* Mahwah, NJ: Erlbaum.

Lynch, T. R., Trost, W. T, Salsman, N., & Linehan, M. M. (2007). Dialectical behavior therapy for borderline personality disorder. *Annual Review of Clinical Psychology, 3,* 181–205.

Lynn, S. J., Fassler, O., & Knox, J. (2005). Hypnosis and the altered state debate: Something more or nothing more? Comment. *Contemporary Hypnosis, 22,* 39–45.

Lynn, S. J., Lock, T., Loftus, E. F., Krackow, E., & Lilienfeld, S. O. (2003). The remembrance of things past: Problematic memory recovery techniques in psychotherapy. In S. O. Lilienfeld, S. J. Lynn, & J. M. Lohr (Eds.), *Science and pseudoscience in clinical psychology.* New York: Guilford Press.

Macaluso, E., Frith, C. D., & Driver, J. (2000, August 18). Modulation of human visual cortex by crossmodal spatial attention. *Science, 289,* 1206–1208.

Macduff, I. (2006). Your pace or mine? Culture, time and negotiation. *Negotiation Journal, 22,* 31–45.

Machado, R. B., Suchecki, D., & Tufik, S. (2005). Sleep homeostasis in rats assessed by a long-term intermittent paradoxical sleep deprivation protocol. *Behavioural Brain Research, 160,* 356–364.

Mack, J. (2003). *The museum of the mind.* London: British Museum Publications.

Macmillan, M. (2000). *An odd kind of fame: Stories of Phineas Gage.* Cambridge, MA: MIT.

MacNeilage, P. F., Rogers, L. J., & Vallortigara, G. (2009, July). Origins of the left & right brain. *Scientific American,* pp. 60–67.

Madden, D. J. (2007). Aging and visual attention. *Current Directions in Psychological Science, 16,* 70–74.

Maddi, S. R. (2007). The story of hardiness: Twenty years of theorizing, research, and practice. In A. Monat, R. S. Lazarus, & G. Reevy, *The Praeger handbook on stress and coping* (Vol. 2). Westport, CT: Praeger Publishers/ Greenwood Publishing.

Mader, S. S. (2000). *Biology* (6th ed.). Boston: McGraw-Hill.

Madon, S., Willard, J., & Guyll, M. (2006). Self-fulfilling prophecy effects of mothers' beliefs on children's alcohol use: Accumulation, dissipation, and stability over time. *Journal of Personality and Social Psychology, 90,* 911–926.

Magida, A. J. (2006). *Opening the doors of wonder: Reflections on religious rites of passage.* Berkeley, CA: University of California Press.

Magoni, M., Bassani, L., Okong, P., Kituuka, P., Germinario, E. P., Giuliano, M., et al. (2005). Mode of infant feeding and HIV infection in children in a program for prevention of mother-to-child transmission in Uganda. *AIDS, 19,* 433–437.

Maguire, E. A., Kumaran, D., Hassabis, D., & Kopelman, M.D. (2010). Autobiographical memory in semantic dementia: A longitudinal fMRI study. *Neuropsychologia, 48,* 123–136.

Mahmood, M., & Black, J. (2005). Narcolepsycataplexy: How does recent understanding help in evaluation and treatment. *Current Treatment Options in Neurology, 7,* 363–371.

Majdandzic, M., & van den Boom, D. C. (2007). Multimethod longitudinal assessment of temperament in early childhood. *Journal of Personality, 75,* 121–167.

Majeres, R. L. (2007). Sex differences in phono-logical coding: Alphabet transformation speed. *Intelligence, 35,* 335–346.

Malle, B. F. (2004). *How the mind explains behavior: Folk explanations, meaning, and social interaction.* Cambridge, MA: MIT.

Malpas, P. (2008, April). Predictive genetic testing of children for adult-onset diseases and psychological harm. *Journal of Medical Ethics, 34,* 275–278.

Mamassis, G., & Doganis, G. (2004). The effects of a mental training program on juniors pre-competitive anxiety, self-confidence, and tennis performance. *Journal of Applied Sport Psychology, 16,* 118–137.

Mancinelli, R., Binetti, R., & Ceccanti, M. (2007). Woman, alcohol and environment: Emerging risks for health. *Neuroscience & Biobehavioral Reviews, 31,* 246–253.

Mangels, J. (2004). *The influence of intelligence beliefs on attention and learning a neurophysiological approach.* Presentation at the 16th Annual Convention of Social Cognitive Neuroscience. Washington, DC: American Psychological Society.

Mangels, J., Dweck, C., & Good, C. (2005, May). *Achievement motivation modulates the neural dynamics of error correction.* CASL Meeting, U.S. Department of Education.

Manly, J. J. (2005). Advantages and disadvantages of separate norms for African Americans. *Clinical Neuropsychologist, 19,* 270–275.

Manly, J. J. (2006). Deconstructing race and ethnicity: Implications for measurement of health outcomes [Special issue: Measurement in a multi-ethnic society]. *Medical Care, 44,* S10–S16.

Mann, K., Ackermann, K., Croissant, B., Mundle, G., Nakovics, H., & Diehl, A. (2005). Neuroimaging of gender differences in alcohol dependence: are women more vulnerable? *Alcoholism: Clinical & Experimental Research, 29,* 896–901.

Manning, M. A., & Hoyme, E. H. (2007). Fetal alcohol spectrum disorders: A practical clinical approach to diagnosis. *Neuroscience & Biobehavioral Reviews, 31,* 230–238.

Manning, S. Y. (2005). Dialectical behavior therapy of severe and chronic problems. In L. VandeCreek (Ed.), *Innovations in clinical practice: Focus on adults.* Sarasota, FL: Professional Resource Press/Professional Resource Exchange.

Manor, J. K., & Gailliot, M. T. (2007). Altruism and egoism: Prosocial motivations for helping depend on relationship context. *European Journal of Social Psychology, 37,* 347–358.

Manstead, A. S. R., & Wagner, H. L. (2004). *Experience emotion.* Cambridge, England: Cambridge University Press.

Manstead, A. S. R., Frijda, N., & Fischer, A. H. (Eds.). (2003). *Feelings and emotions: The Amsterdam Symposium.* Cambridge, England: Cambridge University Press.

Marcaurelle, R., Bélanger, C., & Marchand, A. (2005). Marital predictors of symptom severity in panic disorder with agoraphobia. *Journal of Anxiety Disorders, 19,* 211–232.

Marchand, S., & Phillips, G. E. (2012). Hoarding's place in the DSM-5: Another symptom, or a newly listed disorder? *Issues in Mental Health Nursing, 33,* 591–597.

Marcus, G. F. (1996). Why do children say "breaked"? *Current Directions in Psychological Science, 5,* 81–85.

Marcus-Newhall, A., Pedersen, W. C., & Carlson, M. (2000). Displaced aggression is alive and well: A meta-analytic review. *Journal of Personality and Social Psychology, 78,* 670–689.

Marks, I. M. (2004). The Nobel Prize award in Physiology to Ivan Petrovich Pavlov–1904. *Australian and New Zealand Journal of Psychiatry, 38,* 674–677.

Markus, H. R. (2007). Sociocultural psychology: The dynamic interdependence among self systems and social systems. In S. Kitayama, & D. Cohen, (Eds.), *Handbook of cultural psychology.* New York: Guilford Press.

Markus, H. R., & Kitayama, S. (2003). Models of agency: Sociocultural diversity in the construction of action. In V. Murphy-Berman & J. J. Berman (Eds.), *Cross-cultural differences in perspectives on the self.* Lincoln, NE: University of Nebraska Press.

Maroda, K. J. (2004). A relational perspective on women and power. *Psychoanalytic Psychology, 21,* 428–435.

Marsh, H. W., Hau, K. T., & Sung, R. Y. T. (2007). Childhood obesity, gender, actual-ideal body image discrepancies, and physical self-concept in Hong Kong children: Cultural differences in the value of moderation. *Developmental Psychology, 43,* 647–662.

Marshall, K., Laing, D. G., & Jinks, A. L. (2006). The capacity of humans to identify components in complex odor-taste mixtures. *Chemical Senses, 31,* 539–545.

Marshall, L., & Born, J. (2007, October). The contribution of sleep to hippocampus-dependent memory consolidation. *Trends in Cognitive Sciences, 11*(10), 442–450.

Marshall, M. K. (2007). The critical factors of coaching practice leading to successful coaching outcomes. *Dissertation Abstracts International: Section B: The Sciences and Engineering, 67*(7-B), 4092.

Marshall, R. D., Bryant, R. A, & Amsel, L. (2007). The psychology of ongoing threat: Relative risk appraisal, the September 11 attacks, and terrorism-related fears. *American Psychologist, 62,* 304–316.

Marszalek, J. (2007). Computerized adaptive testing and the experience of flow in examinees. *Dissertation Abstracts International Section A: Humanities and Social Sciences, 67*(7-A), 2465.

Martelle, S., Hanley, C., & Yoshino K. (2003, January 28) "Sopranos" scenario in slaying? *Los Angeles Times,* p. B1.

Martin, A. J., & Marsh, H. W. (2002). Fear of failure: Friend or foe? *Australian Psychologist, 38,* 31–38.

Martin, L., & Pullum, G. K. (1991). *The great Eskimo vocabulary hoax.* Chicago: University of Chicago Press.

Martin, P. D., & Brantley, P. J. (2004). Stress, coping, and social support in health and behavior. In J. M. Raczynski & L. C. Leviton (Eds.), *Handbook of clinical health psychology, Vol. 2: Disorders of behavior and health.* Washington, DC: American Psychological Association.

Martin, R. A. (2007). *The psychology of humor: An integrative approach.* Burlington, MA: Elsevier Academic Press.

Martindale, C. (1981). *Cognition and consciousness.* Homewood, IL: Dorsey.

Marx, J. (2004, July 16). Prolonging the agony. *Science, 305,* 326–328.

Mascia, K., & Servis, R. (2009, August 24). Mail carriers to the rescue. *People,* p. 108–110.

Mashour, G. A., Walker, E. E., & Martuza, R. L. (2005). Psychosurgery: Past, present, and future. *Brain Research Reviews, 48,* 409–419.

Maslow, A. H. (1970). *Motivation and personality.* New York: Harper & Row.

Maslow, A. H. (1987). *Motivation and personality* (3rd ed.). New York: Harper & Row.

Mason, G. (2008, March 29). Standing up for mental illness. *The Globe and Mail,* p. A14.

Massaro, D. W., & Chen, T. H. (2008). The motor theory of speech perception revisited. *Psychonomic Bulletin & Review, 15,* 453–457.

Mast, F. W., & Kosslyn, S. M. (2002). Visual mental images can be ambiguous: Insights from individual differences in spatial transformation abilities. *Cognition, 86,* 57–70.

Masters, W. H., & Johnson, V. E. (1979). *Homosexuality in perspective.* Boston: Little, Brown.

Masuda, M. (2003). Meta-analyses of love scales: Do various love scales measure the same psychological constructs? *Japanese Psychological Research, 45,* 25–37.

Mataix-Cols, D., & Bartres-Faz, D. (2002). Is the use of the wooden and computerized versions of the Tower of Hanoi Puzzle equivalent? *Applied Neuropsychology, 9,* 117–120.

Matthews, G., & Funke, G. J. (2006). Worry and information-processing. In G. C. L. Davey & A. Wells, *Worry and its psychological disorders: Theory, assessment and treatment.* Hoboken, NJ: Wiley Publishing.

Maurer, D., Lewis, T. L., Brent, H. P., & Levin, A. V. (1999, October 1). Rapid improvement in the acuity of infants after visual input. *Science, 286,* 108–110.

Mayer, J. D., Salovey, P., & Caruso, D. R. (2004). Emotional intelligence: Theory, findings, and implications. *Psychological Inquiry, 15,* 197–215.

Mayer, J. D., Salovey, P., & Caruso, D. R. (2008). Emotional intelligence: New ability or eclectic traits? *American Psychologist, 63,* 503–517.

Maynard, A. E., & Martini, M. I. (2005). *Learning in cultural context: Family, peers, and school.* New York: Kluwer Academic/Plenum Publishers.

Mazard, A., Laou, L., Joliot, M., & Mellet, E. (2005). Neural impact of the semantic content of visual mental images and visual percepts. *Brain Research and Cognitive Brain Research, 24,* 423–435.

McAdams, D. P., Diamond, A., de St. Aubin, E., & Mansfield, E. (1997). Stories of commitment: The psychosocial construction of generative lives. *Journal of Personality and Social Psychology, 72,* 678–694.

McCabe, C., & Rolls, E. T. (2007). Umami: A delicious flavor formed by convergence of taste and olfactory pathways in the human brain. *European Journal of Neuroscience, 25,* 1855–1864.

McCarthy, J. (2005). Individualism and collectivism: What do they have to do with counseling? *Journal of Multicultural Counseling and Development, 33,* 108–117.

McCarthy, J. (May 9, 2010). Huffpost Healthy Living: Whose afraid of the truth about autism? Retrieved from: http://www.huffingtonpost.com /jenny-mccarthy/whos-afraid-of-the-truth_b_490918.html.

McCarthy-Jones, S., Barnes, L. J., Hill, G. E., Marwood, L., Moseley, P., & Fernyhough, C. (2011). When words and pictures come alive: Relating the modality of intrusive thoughts to modalities of hypnagogic/hypnopompic hallucinations. Personality and Individual Differences, 51 (6), 787-790.

McCaul, K. D., Johnson, R. J., & Rothman, A. J. (2002). The effects of framing and action instructions on whether older adults obtain flu shots. *Health Psychology, 21,* 624–628.

McClelland, D. C. (1985). How motives, skills, and values determine what people do. *American Psychologist, 40,* 812–825.

McClelland, D. C., Atkinson, J. W., Clark, R. A., & Lowell, E. L. (1953). *The achievement motive.* New York: Appleton-Century-Crofts.

McClure, J., Sutton, R. M., & Sibley, C. G. (2007). Listening to reporters or engineers? How instance-based messages about building design affect earthquake fatalism. *Journal of Applied Social Sciences, 37,* 1956–1973.

McCrae, R. R., & Costa, P. T., Jr. (1986). A five-factor theory of personality. In L. A. Pervin & O. P. John (Eds.), *Handbook of personality: Theory and research* (2nd ed.). New York: Guilford.

McCrae, R. R., Terracciano A., & 78 Members of the Personality Profiles of Cultures Project. (2005). Universal features of personality traits from the observer's perspective: Data from 50 cultures. *Journal of Personality and Social Psychology, 88,* 547–561.

McDaniel, M. A., Maier, S. F., & Einstein, G. O. (2002). "Brain specific" nutrients: A memory cure? *Psychological Science in the Public Interest, 3,* 12–18.

McDonald, C., & Murray, R. M. (2004). Can structural magnetic resonance imaging provide an alternative phenotype for genetic studies of schizophrenia? In M. S. Keshavan, J. L. Kennedy, & R. M. Murray (Eds.), *Neurodevelopment and schizophrenia.* New York: Cambridge University Press.

McDonald, H. E., & Hirt, E. R. (1997). When expectancy meets desire: Motivational effects in reconstructive memory. *Journal of Personality and Social Psychology, 72,* 5–23.

McDougall, W. (1908). *Introduction to social psychology.* London: Methuen.

McDowell, D. M., & Spitz, H. I. (1999). *Substance abuse.* New York: Brunner/ Mazel.

McEwen, B. S. (1998, January 15). Protective and damaging effects of stress mediators [Review article]. *New England Journal of Medicine, 338,* 171–179.

McGaugh, J. L. (2003). *Memory and emotion: The making of lasting memories.* New York: Columbia University Press.

McGill Medicine. (2010). Integrated whole person care. Retrieved from www.mcgill.ca/wholepersoncare.

McGilvray, J. (Ed.). (2004). *The Cambridge companion to Chomsky.* Oxford, England: Cambridge University Press.

McGinn, D. (2003, June 9). Testing, testing: The new job search. *Time,* pp. 36–38.

McGregor, K. K., & Capone, N. C. (2004). Genetic and environmental interactions in determining the early lexicon: Evidence from a set of tri-zygotic quadruplets. *Journal of Child Language, 31,* 311–337.

McGuire, S. (2003). The heritability of parenting. Parenting: *Science & Practice, 3,* 73–94.

McGuire, W. J. (1997). Creative hypothesis generating in psychology: Some useful heuristics. *Annual Review of Psychology, 48,* 1–30.

McIntyre, K., Korn, J., & Matsuo, H. (2008). Sweating the small stuff: How different types of hassles result in the experience of stress. *Stress and Health: Journal of the International Society for the Investigation of Stress, 24,* 383–392.

McKinley, M. J., Cairns, M. J., Denton, D. A., Egan, G., Mathai, M. L., Uschakov, A., et al. (2004). Physiological and pathophysiological influences on thirst. *Physiology and Behavior, 81,* 795–803.

McLauchlin, P. (2006). Afghanistan war poses unique challenges for military MDs. *Canadian Medical Association Journal, 175 (11),* 1357–1359.

McMurtray, A. M., Licht, E., Yeo, T., Krisztal, E., Saul, R. E., & Mendez, M. F. (2007). Positron emission tomography facilitates diagnosis of early-onset Alzheimer's disease. *European Neurology, 59,* 31–37.

McNally, R. J. (2011). *What is mental illness?* Cambridge, MA: Harvard University Press.

McNamara, P. (2004). *An evolutionary psychology of sleep and dreams.* Westport, CT: Praeger Publishers/Greenwood Publishing Group.

McNeil, D. G., Jr. (2005, August 24). Obesity rate is nearly 25 percent, group says. *The New York Times,* p. A3.

Medley, M. (2009, February 26). Steven Page interview: 'Wow, I'm not a Barenaked Lady anymore'. *The Vancouver Sun.* Retrieved from www.vancouversun.com/entertainment/Barenaked+Ladies+founder+Steven+Page+splits+from+band/1328899/story.html.

Meeter, M., & Murre, J. M. J. (2004). Consolidation of long-term memory: Evidence and alternatives. *Psychological Bulletin, 130,* 843–857.

Mehl-Madrona, L. E. (2004). Hypnosis to facilitate uncomplicated birth. *American Journal of Clinical Hypnosis, 46,* 299–312.

Meinlschmidt, G., & Heim, C. (2007). Sensitivity to intranasal oxytocin in adult men with early parental separation. *Biological Psychiatry, 61,* 1109–1111.

Mel, B. W. (2002, March 8). What the synapse tells the neuron. *Science, 295,* 1845–1846.

Mel'nikov, K. S. (1993, October–December). On some aspects of the mechanistic approach to the study of processes of forgetting. *Vestnik Moskovskogo Universiteta Seriya 14 Psikhologiya,* pp. 64–67.

Meltzer, H. Y. (2000). Genetics and etiology of schizophrenia and bipolar disorder. *Biological Psychiatry, 47,* 171–173.

Meltzoff, A. N. (1996). The human infant as imitative generalist: A 20-year progress report on infant imitation with implications for comparative psychology. In C. M. Heyes & B. G. Galef, Jr. (Eds.), *Social learning in animals: The roots of culture.* San Diego, CA: Academic Press.

Melzack, R., & Katz, J. (2001). The McGill Pain Questionnaire: Appraisal and current status. In D. Turk & R. Melzack, (Eds.). *Handbook of pain assessment* (2nd ed.). New York: Guilford Press.

Melzack, R., & Katz, J. (2004). *The gate control theory: Reaching for the brain.* Mahwah, NJ: Lawrence Erlbaum Associates.

Mendelsohn, J. (2003, November 7–9). What we know about sex. *USA Weekend,* pp. 6–9.

Mendelsohn, M. E., & Rosano, G. M. C. (2003). Hormonal regulation of normal vascular tone in males. *Circulation Research.* 93, 1142.

Mental Health Foundation. (2010). Mindfulness report 2010. Retrieved from http://healthandwellness.utoronto.ca/Mindfulness-Meditation.htm.

Merlin, D. (1993). Origins of the modern mind: Three stages in the evolution of culture and cognition. *Behavioral and Brain Sciences, 16,* 737–791.

Messner, M., Reinhard, M., & Sporer, S. (2008). Compliance through direct persuasive appeals: The moderating role of communicator's attractiveness in interpersonal persuasion. *Social Influence, 3,* 67–83.

Meyer, I., & Ladewig, J. (2008). The relationship between number of training sessions per week and learning in dogs. *Applied Animal Behaviour Science, 111,* 311–320.

Meyer-Bahlburg, H. (1997). The role of prenatal estrogens in sexual orientation. In L. Ellis & L. Ebertz (Eds.), *Sexual orientation: Toward biological understanding.* Westport, CT: Praeger.

Meyerowitz, J. (2004). *How sex changed: A history of transsexuality in the United States.* Cambridge, MA: Harvard University Press.

Michael, R. T., Gagnon, J. H., Laumann, E. O., & Kolata, G. (1994). *Sex in America: A definitive survey.* Boston: Little, Brown.

Midanik, L. T., Tam, T. W., & Weisner, C. (2007). Concurrent and simultaneous drug and alcohol use: Results of the 2000 national alcohol survey. *Drug and Alcohol Dependence, 90,* 72–80.

Middlebrooks, J. C., Furukawa, S., Stecker, G. C., & Mickey, B. J. (2005). Distributed representation of sound-source location in the auditory cortex. In R. König, P. Heil, E. Budinger, & H. Scheich (Eds.), *Auditory cortex: A synthesis of human and animal research.* Mahwah, NJ: Lawrence Erlbaum Associates.

Mifflin, L. (1998, January 14). Study finds a decline in TV network violence. *The New York Times,* p. A14.

Miglietta, A., Gattino, S., & Esses, V. (2014, May). What causes prejudice? How may we solve it? Lay beliefs and their relations with classical and modern prejudice and social dominance orientation. *International Journal of Intercultural Relations, 40,* 11–21.

Miklowitz, D. J., & Thompson, M. C. (2003). Family variables and interventions in schizophrenia. In G. Sholevar & G. Pirooz (Eds.), *Textbook of family and couples therapy: Clinical applications.* Washington, DC: American Psychiatric Publishing.

Mikulincer, M., & Shaver, P. R. (2005). Attachment security, compassion, and altruism. *Current Directions in Psychological Science, 14,* 34–38.

Miletic, M. P. (2002). The introduction of a feminine psychology to psychoanalysis: Karen Horney's legacy [Special issue: Interpersonal psychoanalysis and feminism]. *Contemporary Psychoanalysis, 38,* 287–299.

Milgram, S. (1974). *Obedience to authority.* New York: Harper & Row.

Milgram, S. (2005). *Obedience to authority.* Pinter & Martin: New York.

Millar, W.J., & Stephens, T. (1987). The prevalence of overweight and obesity in Britain, Canada, and the United States. *American Journal of Public Health, 77 (1),* 38–41.

Miller, A. G. (1999). Harming other people: Perspectives on evil and violence. *Personality and Social Psychology Review, 3,* 176–178.

Miller, D. W. (2000, February 25). Looking askance at eyewitness testimony. *The Chronicle of Higher Education,* pp. A19–A20.

Miller, G. (2004, April 2). *Learning to forget. Science, 304,* 34–36.

Miller, G. A. (1956). The magical number seven, plus or minus two: Some limits on our capacity for processing information. *Psychology Review, 63,* 81–97.

Miller, J. A., & Leffard, S. A. (2007). Behavioral assessment. In S. R. Smith & L. Handler, *The clinical assessment of children and adolescents: A practitioner's handbook.* Mahwah, NJ: Lawrence Erlbaum Associates.

Miller, J. G. (1984). Culture and the development of everyday social explanation. *Journal of Personality and Social Psychology, 46,* 961–978.

Miller, L. A., Taber, K. H., Gabbard, G. O., & Hurley, R. A. (2005). Neural underpinnings of fear and its modulation: Implications for anxiety disorders. *The Journal of Neuropsychiatry and Clinical Neurosciences, 17,* 1–6.

Miller, M. N., & Pumariega, A. J. (2001). Culture and eating disorders: A historical and cross-cultural review. *Psychiatry: Interpersonal and Biological Processes, 64,* 93–110.

Miller, M. W. (1994, December 1). Brain surgery is back in a limited way to treat mental ills. *The Wall Street Journal,* pp. A1, A12.

Miller-Jones, D. (1991). Informal reasoning in inner-city children. In J. F. Voss & D. N. Perkins (Eds.), *Informal reasoning and education.* Hillsdale, NJ: Lawrence Erlbaum.

Miller-Perrin, C., Perrin, R., & Kocur, J. (2009). Parental physical and psychological aggression: Psychological symptoms in young adults. *Child Abuse & Neglect, 33,* 1–11.

Millon, T., Davis, R., & Millon, C. (2000). *Personality disorders in modern life.* New York: Wiley.

Milner, B. (1966). Amnesia following operation on temporal lobes. In C. W. M. Whitty & P. Zangwill (Eds.), *Amnesia.* London: Butterworth.

Milner, B. (2005). The medial temporal-lobe amnesic syndrome. *Psychiatric Clinics of North America, 28,* 599–611.

Miner, J., & Clarke-Stewart, K. (2008). Trajectories of externalizing behavior from age 2 to age 9: Relations with gender, temperament, ethnicity, parenting, and rater. *Developmental Psychology, 44,* 771–786.

Miner-Rubino, K., Winter, D. G., & Stewart, A. J. (2004). Gender, social class, and the subjective experience of aging: Self-perceived personality change from early adulthood to late midlife. *Personality and Social Psychology Bulletin, 30,* 1599–1610.

Miquel, J., (2006). Integración de teorías del envejecimiento (parte I). Integration of theories of ageing. *Revista Espanola de Geriatria y Gerontologia, 41,* 55–63.

Mischel, W. (2004). Toward an integrative science of the person. *Annual Review of Psychology, 55,* 1–22.

Mischel, W. (2009). From Personality and Assessment (1968) to Personality Science, 2009. *Journal of Research in Personality, 43,* 282–290.

Mischoulon, D. (2000, June). Anti-depressants: Choices and controversy. *HealthNews,* p. 4.

Miserando, M. (1991). Memory and the seven dwarfs. *Teaching of Psychology, 18,* 169–171.

Mitchell, D. B., & Schmitt, F. A. (2006). Short- and long-term implicit memory in aging and Alzheimer's disease. *Neuropsychological Development and Cognition, B, Aging and Neuropsychological Cognition, 13,* 611–635.

Mitte, K. (2005). Meta-analysis of cognitive-behavioral treatments for generalized anxiety disorder: A comparison with pharmacotherapy. *Psychological Bulletin, 131,* 785–795.

Moffitt, T. E., & Caspi, A. (2007). Evidence from behavioral genetics for environmental contributions to antisocial conduct. In J. E. Grusec & P. D. Hastings, *Handbook of socialization: Theory and research.* New York: Guilford Press.

Moffitt, T. E., Caspi, A., & Rutter, M. (2006). Measured gene-environment interactions in psychopathology: Concepts, research strategies, and implications for research, intervention, and public understanding of genetics. *Perspectives on Psychological Science, 1,* 5–27.

Moghaddam, B., & Adams, B. W. (1998, August 28). Reversal of phencyclidine effects by a group II metabotropic glutamate receptor agonist in rats. *Science, 281,* 1349–1352.

Mograss, M., Guillem, F., Brazzini-Poisson, V., & Godbout, R. (2009, May). The effects of total sleep deprivation on recognition memory processes: A study of event-related potential. *Neurobiology of Learning and Memory, 91,* 343–352.

Mohapel, P., Leanza, G., Kokaia, M., & Lindvall, O. (2005). Forebrain ace-tylcholine regulates adult hippo-campal neurogenesis and learning. *Neurobiology of Aging, 26*, 939–946.

Montgomery, K. L. (2011). Living with panic, worry, and fear: Anxiety disorders. In C. Franklin & R. Fong (Eds.), *The church leader's counseling resource book: A guide to mental health and social problems.* New York: Oxford University Press.

Montgomery, S. A., Nil, R., Dürr-Pal, N., Loft, H., & Boulenger, J. P. (2005). A 24-week randomized, double-blind, placebo-controlled study of escitalopram for the prevention of generalized social anxiety disorder. *Journal of Clinical Psychiatry, 66*, 1270–1278.

Montoya, R., & Insko, C. (2008). Toward a more complete understanding of the reciprocity of liking effect. *European Journal of Social Psychology, 38*, 477–498.

Moody, H. R. (2000). *Aging: Concepts and controversies.* Thousand Oaks, CA: Sage.

Moore, D. G., Goodwin, J. E., & George, R. (2007). Infants perceive human point-light displays as solid forms. *Cognition, 104*, 377–396.

Moore, M. M. (2002). Behavioral observation. In M. W. Wiederman & B. E. Whitley (Eds.), *Handbook for conducting research on human sexuality.* Mahwah, NJ: Lawrence Erlbaum.

Moorey, S. (2007). Cognitive therapy. In W. Dryden, *Dryden's handbook of individual therapy* (5th ed.). Thousand Oaks, CA: Sage Publications.

Morad, Y., Barkana, Y., Zadok, D., Hartstein, M., Pras, E., & Bar-Dayan, Y. (2009, July). Ocular parameters as an objective tool for the assessment of truck drivers fatigue. *Accident Analysis and Prevention, 41*, 856–860.

Mora-Giral, M., Raich-Escursell, R. M., Segues, C.V., Torras-Claras, A. J., & Huon, G. (2004). Bulimia symptoms and risk factors in university students. *Eating and Weight Disorders, 9*, 163–169.

Moran, A. (2009). Cognitive psychology in sport: Progress and prospects. *Psychology of Sport and Exercise, 10*, 420–426.

Moretz, M., & McKay, D. (2009). The role of perfectionism in obsessive-compulsive symptoms: 'Not just right' experiences and checking compulsions. *Journal of Anxiety Disorders, 23*, 640–644.

Morgan, A. A., Marsiske, M., & Whitfield, K. E. (2008). Characterizing and explaining differences in cognitive test performance between African American and European American older adults. *Experimental Aging Research, 34*, 80–100.

Morrone, A. S., & Pintrich, P. R. (2006). Achievement motivation. In G. G. Bear & K. M. Minke, *Children's needs III: Development, prevention, and intervention.* Washington, DC: National Association of School Psychologists.

Mosher, C. J., & Akins, S. (2007). *Drugs and drug policy: The control of consciousness alteration.* Thousand Oaks, CA: Sage Publications.

Moskowitz, G. B. (2004). *Social cognition: Understanding self and others.* New York: Guilford Press.

Motley, M. T. (1987, February). What I meant to say. *Psychology Today,* pp. 25–28.

Mueller, C. E. (2009). Protective factors as barriers to depression in gifted and nongifted adolescents. *Gifted Child Quarterly, 53*, 3–14.

Mullen, B., & Rice, D. R. (2003). Ethnophaulisms and exclusion: The behavioral consequences of cognitive representation of ethnic immigrant groups. *Personality and Social Psychology Bulletin, 29*, 1056–1067.

Munakata, Y. (2006). Information processing approaches to development. In D. Kuhn, R. S. Siegler, W. Damon, & R. M. Lerner, *Handbook of child psychology: Vol 2, Cognition, perception, and language* (6th ed.) Hoboken, NJ: John Wiley & Sons.

Munger, D. (2009, April 20). Super-recognizers: people with an amazing ability to recognize faces. Retrieved from http://scienceblogs.com/cognitivedaily/2009/04/super-recognizers_people_with.php.

Murphy, G.J., Glickfield, L. L., Balsen, Z., & Isaacson, J. S. (2004). Sensory neuron signaling to the brain: Properties of transmitter release from olfactory nerve terminals. *Journal of Neuroscience, 24*, 3023–3030.

Murphy, G. L. (2005). The study of concepts inside and outside the laboratory: Medin versus Medin. In W. Ahn, R. L. Goldstone, B. C. Love, A. B. Markman, & P. Wolff (Eds.), *Categorization inside and outside the laboratory: Essays in honor of Douglas L. Medin.* Washington, DC: American Psychological Association.

Murphy, R. T., Wismar, K., & Freeman, K. (2003). Stress symptoms among African-American college students after the September 11, 2001 terrorist attacks. *Journal of Nervous and Mental Disease, 191*, 108–114.

Murphy, S. T., & Zajonc, R. B. (1993). Affect, cognition, and awareness: Affective priming with optimal and suboptimal stimulus exposures. *Journal of Personality and Social Psychology, 64*, 723–739.

Murray, B. (June 2002). Good news for bachelor's grads. *Monitor on Psychology,* pp. 30–32.

Murray, R., Lappin, J., & Di Forti, M. (2008, August). Schizophrenia: From developmental deviance to dopamine dysregulation. *European Neuropsychopharmacology, 18*, S129–SS134.

Murray, S. L., Holmes, J. G., & Griffin, D. W. (2004). The benefits of positive illusions: Idealization and the construction of satisfaction in close relationships. In H. T. Reis & C. E. Rusbult (Eds.), *Close relationships: Key readings.* Philadelphia, PA: Taylor & Francis.

Murthy, P., Kudlur, S., George, S., & Mathew, G. (2009). A clinical overview of fetal alcohol syndrome. *Addictive Disorders & Their Treatment, 8*, 1–12.

Myers, D. G. (2000). The funds, friends, and faith of happy people. *American Psychologist, 55*, 56–67.

Myers, D. G., & Diener, E. (1996, May). The pursuit of happiness: New research uncovers some anti-intuitive insights into how many people are happy—and why. *Scientific American,* pp. 70–72.

Myers, L. L. (2007). Anorexia nervosa, bulimia nervosa, and binge eating disorder. In B. A. Thyer, & J. S. Wodarski. *Social work in mental health: An evidence-based approach.* Hoboken, NJ: John Wiley & Sons.

Myerson, J., Adams, D. R., Hale, S., & Jenkins, L. (2003). Analysis of group differences in processing speed: Brinley plots, Q-Q plots, and other conspiracies. *Psychonomic Bulletin and Review, 10*, 224–237.

Myrtek, M. (2007). Type a behavior and hostility as independent risk factors for coronary heart disease. In J. Jordan, B. Barde & A. M. Zeiher, *Contributions toward evidence-based psychocardiology: A systematic review of the literature.* Washington, DC: American Psychological Association.

Mytinger, C. (2001). *Headhunting in the Solomon Islands: Around the Coral Sea.* Santa Barbara, CA: Narrative Press.

Nadeem, E., & Graham, S. (2005). Early puberty, peer victimization, and internalizing symptoms in ethnic minority adolescents. *Journal of Early Adolescence, 25*, 197–222.

Nader, E. G., Kleinman, A., Gomes, B., Bruscagin, C., Santos, B., Nicoletti, M., & Caetano, S. C. (2013). Negative expressed emotion best discriminates families with bipolar disorder children. *Journal of Affective Disorders, 148*, 418–423.

Nagda, B. A., Tropp, L. R., & Paluck, E. L. (2006). Looking back as we look ahead: Integrating research, theory, and practice on intergroup relations. *Journal of Social Research, 62*, 439–451.

Naidoo, R., Warriner, E.M., Oczkowski, W.J., Sévigny, A., & Humphreys K.R. (2008). A case of foreign accent syndrome resulting in regional dialect. *Canadian Journal of Neurological Sciences, 35*, 360–365.

Naik, G. (2004, December 29). New obesity boom in Arab countries has old ancestry. *The Wall Street Journal,* p. A1.

Najman, J. M., Aird, R., Bor, W., O'Callaghan, M., Williams, G. M., & Shuttlewood, G. J. (2004). The generational transmission of socioeconomic inequalities in child cognitive development and emotional health. *Social Science and Medicine, 58*, 1147–1158.

Nakamura, M., Kyo, S., Kanaya, T., Yatabe, N., Maida, Y., Tanaka, M., Ishida, Y., Fujii, C., Kondo, T., Inoue, M., & Mukaida, N. (2004). hTERT-promoter-based tumor-specific expression of MCP-1 effectively sensitizes cervical cancer cells to a low dose of cisplatin. *Cancer Gene Therapy, 2*, 1–7.

Narrow, W. E., Rae, D. S., Robins, L. N., & Regier, D. A. (2002). Revised prevalence estimates of mental disorders in the United States: Using a clinical significance criterion to reconcile 2 surveys' estimates. *Archives of General Psychiatry, 59*, 115–123.

Nasir, N. S., & Hand, V. (2006). From the court to the classroom: Opportunities for engagement, learning, and identity in basketball and classroom mathematics. *Journal of the Learning Sciences, 17,* 143–179.

Nasrallah, H., Black, D., Goldberg, J., Muzina, D., & Pariser, S. (2008). Issues associated with the use of atypical antipsychotic medications. *Annals of Clinical Psychiatry, 20,* S24-S29.

Nathan, P. E., Stuart, S. P., & Dolan, S. L. (2000). Research on psychotherapy efficacy and effectiveness: Between Scylla and Charybdis? *Psychological Bulletin, 126,* 964–981.

Nathan, P. E., & Gorman, J. M. (Eds.). (1997). *A guide to treatments that work.* New York: Oxford University Press.

Nathans, J., Davenport, C. M., Maumenee, I. H., Lewis, R. A., Hejtmancik, J. F., Litt, M., Lovrien, E., Weleber, R., Bachynski, B., Zwas, F., Klingaman, R., & Fishman, G. (1989, August 25). Molecular genetics of human blue cone monochromacy. *Science, 245,* 831–838.

National Adolescent Health Information Center. (2003). *Fact Sheet on Demographics: Adolescents.* San Francisco: University of California, San Francisco.

National Association for the Education of Young Children. (2005). *Position statements of the NAEYC.* Retrieved from http://www.naeyc.org/about/positions.asp#where.

National Center for Health Statistics. (2000). *Health United States, 2000 with adolescent health chartbook.* National Center for Health Statistics, Hyattsville, MD.

National Depression Screening Day. (2003, March 26). Questionnaire on website. Retrieved from http://www.mentalhealthscreening.org/dep/depsample.htm#sampletest.

National Institute of Child Health and Human Development (NICHD) Early Child Care Research Network. (1999). Child care and mother–child interaction in the first 3 years of life. *Psychology, 35,* 1399–1413.

National Institute of Child Health and Human Development (NICHD) Early Child Care Research Network. (2000). The relation of child care to cognitive and language development. *Child Development, 71,* 960–980.

National Institute of Child Health and Human Development (NICHD) Early Child Care Research Network. (2001). Child-care and family predictors of preschool attachment and stability from infancy. *Development Psychology, 37,* 847–862.

National Institute of Child Health and Human Development (NICHD) Early Child Care Research Network. (2002). Child-care structure—process—outcome: Direct and indirect effects of child-care quality on young children's development. *Psychological Science, 13,* 199–206.

National Institute of Child Health and Human Development (NICHD) Early Child Care Research Network. (2006). Child-care effect sizes for the NICHD study of early child care and youth development. *American Psychologist, 61,* 99–116.

National Institute of Health (2010). Buprenorphine treatment in pregnancy: less distress to babies. Retrieved from http://www.nih.gov/news/health/dec2010/nida-09.htm.

National Institute on Drug Abuse. (2000). *Principles of drug addiction treatment: A research-based guide.* Washington, DC: National Institute on Drug Abuse.

National Research Council (2000). *Eager to learn: Educating our preschoolers.* Washington, DC: National Academy Press.

National Research Council and Institute of Medicine of the National Academies. (2009). *Preventing mental, emotional, and behavioral disorders among young people: Progress and possibilities.* Washington, DC: National Academies Press.

Natvig, G. K., Albrektsen, G., & Ovarnstrom, U. (2003). Methods of teaching and class participation in relation to perceived social support and stress: Modifiable factors for improving health and well-being among students. *Educational Psychology, 23,* 261–274.

Naveh-Benjamin, M., Craik, F. I. M., Gavrilescu, D., & Anderson, N. D. (2000). Asymmetry between encoding and retrieval processes: Evidence from divided attention and a calibration analysis. *Memory & Cognition, 28,* 965–967.

Naveh-Benjamin, M., Guez, J., & Sorek, S. (2007). The effects of divided attention on encoding processes in memory: Mapping the locus of interference. *Canadian Journal of Experimental Psychology, 61,* 1–12.

Neal, D., Matson, J. L., & Belva, B. C. (2013). An examination of the reliability of a new observation measure for Autism spectrum disorders: The autism spectrum disorder observation for children. *Research in Autism Spectrum Disorders, 7,* 29–34.

Neher, A. (2006). Evolutionary psychology: Its programs, prospects, and pitfalls. *American Journal of Psychology, 119,* 517–566.

Neisser, U., Boodoo, G., Bouchard, T. J., Jr., Boykin, A. W., Brody, N., Ceci, S. J., Halpern, D. F., Loehlin, J. C., Perloff, R., Sternberg, R. J., & Urbina, S. (1996). Intelligence: Knowns and unknowns. *American Psychologist, 51,* 77–101.

Neitz, J., Neitz, M., & Kainz, P. M. (1996, November 1). Visual pigment gene structure and the severity of color vision defects. *Science, 274,* 801–804.

Nelson, E., & Sherwood, R. (August 26, 2010). Chris Benoit's murder, suicide: Was brain damage to blame? (ABC News). Retrieved from: http://abcnews.go.com/Nightline/chris-benoits-dad-son-suffered-severe-brain-damage/story?id=11471875.

Nelson, P. D. (2007). The globalization of psychology: What does it mean? *The Educator, 5,* 1–4.

Nelson, W. M., III, & Finch, A. J., Jr. (2000). Managing anger in youth: A cognitive-behavioral intervention approach. In P. C. Kendall, *Child & adolescent therapy: Cognitive-behavioral procedures* (2nd ed.). New York: Guilford Press.

Neron, S., & Stephenson, R. (2007). Effectiveness of hypnotherapy with cancer patients' trajectory: Emesis, acute pain, and analgesia and anxiolysis in procedures. *International Journal of Clinical Experimental Hypnosis, 55,* 336–354.

Nesheim, S., Henderson, S., Lindsay, M., Zuberi, J., Grimes, V., Buehler, J., et al. (2004). *Prenatal HIV testing and antiretroviral prophylaxis at an urban hospital—Atlanta, Georgia, 1997–2000.* Atlanta, GA: Centers for Disease Control.

Nestler, E. J., & Malenka, R. C. (2004, March). The addicted brain. *Scientific American,* pp. 78–83.

Neuberg, S.L., Kenrick, D. T. & Schaller, M. (2010). Evolutionary social psychology. In S. T. Fiske, D. T. Gilbert, & G. Lindzey (Eds.), *The handbook of social psychology* (5th ed, Vol. 2), New York: Wiley.

Newby-Clark, I. R., & Ross, M. (2003). Conceiving the past and future. *Personality and Social Psychology Bulletin, 29,* 807–818.

Newell, A., & Simon, H. (1972). *Human problem solving.* Englewood Cliffs, NJ: Prentice Hall.

Newman, C. F., Leahy, R. L., Beck, A. T., Reilly-Harrington, N. A., & Gyulai, L. (2002). *Bipolar disorder: A cognitive therapy approach.* Washington, DC: American Psychological Association.

Newport, F., & Carroll, J. (2002, November 27). Battle of the bulge: Majority of Americans want to lose weight. *Gallup News Service,* pp. 1–9.

Niccols, A. (2007). Fetal alcohol syndrome and the developing socioemotional brain. *Brain Cognition, 65,* 135–142.

Nicholson, I. A. M. (2003). *Inventing personality: Gordon Allport and the science of selfhood.* Washington, DC: American Psychological Association.

Nickerson, R. S., & Adams, M. J. (1979). *Cognitive Psychology, 11,* 297.

Niedenthal, P. M. (2007, May 18). Embodying emotion. *Science, 316,* 1002–1005.

Nielsen, C., Staud, R., & Price, D. (2009, March). Individual differences in pain sensitivity: Measurement, causation, and consequences. *The Journal of Pain, 10,* 231–237.

Nielsen, C., Stubhaug, A., Price, D., Vassend, O., Czajkowski, N., & Harris, J. (2008, May). Individual differences in pain sensitivity: Genetic and environmental contributions. *Pain, 136,* 21–29.

Nielsen, S. L., Smart, D. W., Isakson, R. L., Worthen, V. E., Gregersen, A. T., & Lambert, M. J. (2004). The *Consumer Reports* effectiveness score: What did consumers report? *Journal of Counseling Psychology, 51,* 25–37.

Nielson, T. A., Stenstrom, P., & Levin, R. (2006). Nightmare frequency as a function of age, gender, and September 11, 2001: Findings from an internet questionnaire. *Dreaming, 16,* 145–158.

References

Nilsson, H., Juslin, P., & Olsson, H. (2008). Exemplars in the mist: The cognitive substrate of the representativeness heuristic. *Scandinavian Journal of Psychology, 49,* 201–212.

Nimrod, G., & Kleiber, D. A. (2007). Reconsidering change and continuity in later life: Toward an innovation theory of successful aging. *International Journal of Human Development, 65,* 1–22.

Nisbett, R. (1994, October 31). Blue genes. *New Republic, 211,* 15.

Nisbett, R. (2003). *The geography of thought.* New York: Free Press.

Nishida, M., Pearsall, J., Buckner, R., & Walker, M. (2009, May). REM sleep, prefrontal theta, and the consolidation of human emotional memory. *Cerebral Cortex, 19,* 1158–1166.

Nissle, S., & Bschor, T. (2002). Winning the jackpot and depression: Money cannot buy happiness. *International Journal of Psychiatry in Clinical Practice, 6,* 183–186.

Nittrouer, S., & Lowenstein, J. H. (2007). Children's weighting strategies for word-final stop voicing are not explained by auditory sensitivities. *Journal of Speech, Language, and Hearing Research, 50,* 58–73.

Niu, W., & Sternberg, R. J. (2003). Societal and school influences on student creativity: The case of China [Special issue: Psychoeducational and psychosocial functioning of Chinese children]. *Psychology in the Schools, 40,* 103–114.

Noble, H. B. (1999, March 12). New from the smoking wars: Success. *The New York Times,* pp. D1–D2.

Nolen-Hoeksema, S. (2007). *Abnormal psychology* (4th ed.). New York: McGraw-Hill.

Norcia, A. M., Pei, F., Bonneh, Y., Hou, C., Sampath, V., & Petter, M. W. (2005). Development of sensitivity to texture and contour information in the human infant. *Journal of Cognitive Neuroscience, 17,* 569–579.

Norlander, T., Von Schedvin, H., & Archer, T. (2005). Thriving as a function of affective personality: Relation to personality factors, coping strategies and stress. *Anxiety, Stress & Coping: An International Journal, 18,* 105–116.

Norton, P. J., & Price, E. C. (2007). A meta-analytic review of adult cognitive-behavioral treatment outcome across the anxiety disorders. *Journal of Nervous and Mental Disease, 195,* 521–531.

Novak, M. A., & Petto, A. J. (1991). *Through the looking glass: Issues of psychological well-being in captive nonhuman primates.* Washington, DC: American Psychological Association.

Ntinas, K. M. (2007). Behavior modification and the principle of normalization: Clash or synthesis? *Behavioral Interventions, 22,* 165–177.

Nucci, L. P. (2002). The development of moral reasoning. In U. Goswami (Ed.), *Blackwell handbook of childhood cognitive development. Blackwell Handbooks of developmental psychology.* Malden, MA: Blackwell.

Nunes, A., & Kramer, A. F. (2009). Experience-based mitigation of age-related performance declines: Evidence from air traffic control. *Journal of Experimental Psychology: Applied, 15,* 12–24.

Nussbaum, R. L., & Ellis, C. E. (2003). Alzheimer's disease and Parkinson's disease. *New England Journal of Medicine, 348*(14), 1356–1364.

Nyberg, L., & Tulving, E. (1996). Classifying human long-term memory: Evidence from converging dissociations. *European Journal of Cognitive Psychology, 8,* 163–183.

O'Brien, K. M., & LeBow, M. D. (2007). Reducing maladaptive weight management practices: Developing a psychoeducational intervention program. *Eating Behaviors, 8,* 195–210.

O'Connor, D. B., & O'Connor, R. C. (2004). Perceived changes in food intake in response to stress: The role of conscientiousness. *Stress and Health: Journal of the International Society for the Investigation of Stress, 20,* 279–291.

O'Grady, W. D., & Dobrovolsky, M. (Eds.). (1996). *Contemporary linguistic analysis: An introduction* (3rd ed.). Toronto: Copp Clark Pitman.

O'Keefe, T., & Fox, K. (Eds.). (2003). *Finding the real me: True tales of sex and gender diversity.* San Francisco: Jossey-Bass.

Oatley, K., Keltner, D., & Jenkins, J. M. (2006). *Understanding emotions.* Oxford, England: Blackwell.

Oberauer, K. (2007). In search of the magic number. *Experimental Psychology, 54,* 245–246.

Offer, D., Kaiz, M., Howard, K. I., & Bennett, E. S. (2000). The altering of reported experiences. *Journal of the American Academy of Child & Adolescent Psychiatry, 39,* 735–742.

Ohira, T., Hozawa, A., Iribarren, C., Daviglus, M. L., Matthews, K. A., Gross, M. D., et al. (2007). Longitudinal association of serum carotenoids and tocopherols with hostility: The CARDIA study. *American Journal of Epidemiology, 18,* 235–241.

Olfson, M., & Marcus, S. (2008). A case-control study of antidepressants and attempted suicide during early phase treatment of major depressive episodes. *Journal of Clinical Psychiatry, 69,* 425–432.

Olivardia, R., & Pope, H. (2002). Body image disturbance in childhood and adolescence. In D. Castle & K. Phillips (Eds.), *Disorders of body image.* Petersfield, England: Wrightson Biomedical Publishing.

Olive, D. (2007, September 20). Rotman's new man: Richard Florida. TheTorontoStar.com. Retrieved from www.thestar.com/article /257985.

Oliver, M. B., & Hyde, J. S. (1993). Gender differences in sexuality: A meta-analysis. *Psychological Bulletin, 114,* 29–51.

Ontario Human Rights Commission. (2008). The Ontario Human Rights Code. Retrieved from www.ohrc.on.ca/en/resources/.

Oosterhof, N. N., & Todorov, A. (2008). The functional basis of face evaluation. *Proceedings of the National Academy of Sciences of the United States of America, 105,* 11087–11092.

Opler, M., Perrin, M., Kleinhaus, K., & Malaspina, D. (2008). Factors in the etiology of schizophrenia: Genes, parental age, and environment. *Primary Psychiatry, 15,* 37–45.

Oppenheimer, D. M. (2004). Spontaneous discounting of availability in frequency judgment tasks. *Psychological Science, 15,* 100–105.

Oren, D. A., & Terman, M. (1998, January 16). Tweaking the human circadian clock with light. *Science, 279,* 333–334.

Ornat, S. L., & Gallo, P. (2004). Acquisition, learning, or development of language? Skinner's "Verbal behavior" revisited. *Spanish Journal of Psychology, 7,* 161–170.

Orwin, R. G., & Condray, D. S. (1984). Smith and Glass' psychotherapy conclusions need further probing: On Landman and Dawes' re-analysis. *American Psychologist, 39,* 71–72.

Oskamp, S. (Ed.). (2000). *Reducing prejudice and discrimination.* Mahwah, NJ: Erlbaum.

Oswald, I. (1959). Sudden bodily jerks on falling asleep. *Brain, 82* (1), 92-103.

Otake, K., Shimai, S., & Tanaka-Matsumi, J. (2006). Happy people become happier through kindness: A counting kindnesses intervention. *Journal of Happiness Studies, 7,* 361–375.

Ouimet, A., Gawronski, B., & Dozois, D. (2009). Cognitive vulnerability to anxiety: A review and an integrative model. *Clinical Psychology Review, 29,* 459–470.

Oveis, C., Gruber, J., Keltner, D., Stamper, J., & Boyce, W. (2009). Smile intensity and warm touch as thin slices of child and family affective style. *Emotion, 9,* 544–548.

Ozer, E. J., & Weiss, D. S. (2004). Who develops posttraumatic stress disorder? *Current Directions in Psychological Science, 13,* 169–172.

Packer, D. (2009). Avoiding groupthink: Whereas weakly identified members remain silent, strongly identified members dissent about collective problems. *Psychological Science, 20,* 546–548.

Pager, D., & Shepherd, H. (2008). The sociology of discrimination: Racial discrimination in employment, housing, credit, and consumer markets. *Annual Review of Sociology, 34,* 181–209.

Pagonis, T. A., Angelopoulos, N., & Koukoulis, G. N. (2006). Psychiatric side effects induced by supraphysiological doses of combinations of anabolic steroids correlate to the severity of abuse. *European Psychiatry, 21,* 551–562.

Pallanti, S., & Bernardi, S. (2009, July). Neurobiology of repeated transcranial magnetic stimulation in the treatment of anxiety: A critical review. *International Clinical Psychopharmacology, 24,* 163–173.

Pandya, M., Pozuelo, L., & Malone, D. (2007). Electroconvulsive therapy: What the internist needs to know. *Cleveland Clinic Journal of Medicine, 74,* 679–685.

Paniagua, F. A. (2000). *Diagnosis in a multicultural context: A casebook for mental health professionals.* Thousand Oaks, CA: Sage.

Paquier, P. F., & Mariën, P. (2005). A synthesis of the role of the cerebellum in cognition. *Aphasiology, 19,* 3–19.

Paraherakis, A., Charney, D., & Gill K. (2001). Neuropsychological functioning in substance-dependent patients. *Substance Use and Misuse, 36,* 257-271.

Parke, R. D. (2004). Development in the family. *Annual Review of Psychology, 55,* 365–399.

Parker-Pope, T. (2003, April 22). The diet that works. *The Wall Street Journal,* pp. R1, R5.

Parlee, M. B. (1979, October). The friendship bond. *Psychology Today,* pp. 43–45.

Pascual, A., & Guéguen, N. (2005). Foot-in-the-door and door-in-the-face: A comparative meta-analytic study. *Psychological Reports, 96,* 122–128.

Pascual, A., & Guéguen, N. (2006). Door-in-the-face technique and monetary solicitation: An evaluation in a field setting. *Perceptual and Motor Skills, 103,* 974–978.

Pascual, M. A., & Rodriguez, M. A. (2006). Learning by operant conditioning as a nonlinear self-organized process. *Nonlinear Dynamics, Psychology, and Life Sciences, 10,* 341–364.

Paukert, A., Stagner, B., & Hope, K. (2004). The assessment of active listening skills in helpline volunteers. *Stress, Trauma, and Crisis: An International Journal, 7,* 61–76.

Paul, A. M. (2004). *Cult of personality: How personality tests are leading us to miseducate our children, mismanage our companies and misunderstand ourselves.* New York: Free Press.

Pavitt, C. (2007). Impression formation. In B. B. Whaley & W. Samter, *Explaining communication: Contemporary theories and exemplars.* Mahwah, NJ: Lawrence Erlbaum Associates.

Pavlov, I. P. (1927). *Conditioned reflexes.* London: Oxford University Press.

Payne, D. G. (1986). Hyperamnesia for pictures and words: Testing the recall level hypothesis. *Journal of Experimental Psychology: Learning, Memory, and Cognition, 12,* 16–29.

Pearson, C.M., & Porath, C.L. (2005). On the nature, consequences and remedies of incivility: No time for 'nice'? Think again. *Academy of Management Executive, 19,* 7–18.

Pearson, J., & Clifford, C. W. G. (2005). When your brain decides what you see: Grouping across monocular, binocular, and stimulus rivalry. *Psychological Science, 16,* 516–519.

Pedersen, P. B., Draguns, J. G., Lonner, W. J., & Trimble, J. E. (Eds.). (2002). *Counseling across cultures* (5th ed.). Thousand Oaks, CA: Sage.

Pell, M. D., Monetta, L., Paulmann, S., & Kotz, S. A. (2009). Recognizing emotions in a foreign language. *Journal of Nonverbal Behavior, 33,* 107–120.

Pellegrini, S., Muzio, R. N., Mustaca, A. E., & Papini, M. R. (2004). Successive negative contrast after partial reinforcement in the consummatory behavior of rats. *Learning and Motivation, 35,* 303–321.

Pelli, D. G., Burns, C. W., & Farell, B. (2006). Feature detection and letter identification. *Vision Research, 46,* 4646–4674.

Pellis, S. M., & Pellis, V. C. (2007). Rough-and-tumble play and the development of the social brain. *Current Directions in Psychological Science, 16,* 95–97.

Pempek, T., Yermolayeva, Y., & Calvert, S. (2009). College students' social networking experiences on Facebook. *Journal of Applied Developmental Psychology, 30,* 227–238.

Penley, J. A., Tomaka, J., & Wiebe, J. S. (2002). The association of coping to physical and psychological health outcomes: A meta-analytic review. *Journal of Behavioral Medicine, 25,* 551–603.

Penn, D. L., Corrigan, P. W., Bentall, R. P., Racenstein, J. M., & Newman, L. (1997). Social cognition in schizophrenia. *Psychological Bulletin, 121,* 114–132.

Penney, J. B., Jr. (2000). Neurochemistry. In B. S. Fogel, et al. (Eds.), *Synopsis of neuropsychiatry.* New York: Lippincott Williams & Wilkins.

Pentland, W. (2009, January 8). The strangest sleep disorders. *CBC News.* Retrieved from www.cbc.ca/health/story/2009/01/07/f-forbes-sleep-disorders.html.

Penzel, F. (2000). *Obsessive-compulsive disorders: A complete guide to getting well and staying well.* New York: Oxford University Press.

People Weekly. (2000, May 8). Giant steps. p. 117.

Perkins, D. N. (1983). Why the human perceiver is a bad machine. In J. Beck, B. Hope, & A. Rosenfeld (Eds.), *Human and machine vision.* New York: Academic Press.

Perkins, T., Stokes, M., McGillivray, J., & Bittar, R. (2010). Mirror neuron dysfunction in autism spectrum disorders. *Journal of Clinical Neurosciences, 17* (10), 1239–1243.

Perloff, R. M. (2003). *The dynamics of persuasion: Communication and attitudes in the 21st century* (2nd ed.). Mahwah, NJ: Erlbaum.

Perry, B. (2008, May 19) 'I don't know how to forget.' *People,* p. 143.

Pert, C. B. (2002). The wisdom of the receptors: Neuropeptides, the emotions, and body-mind. *Advances in Mind-Body Medicine, 18,* 30–35.

Perusse, B. (2008, February 2). Old rockers pay the price. *The Gazette.* Retrieved from www.canada.com/topics/technology/story.html?id=c37008ef-4aab-49d8-be03-82431e499736&p=1.

Pervin, L. A. (1990). *Handbook of personality: Theory and research.* New York: Guilford Press.

Pervin, L. A. (2003). *The science of personality* (2nd ed.). London: Oxford University Press.

Peterfi, Z., McGinty, D., Sarai, E., & Szymusiak, R. (2010). Growth hormone-releasing hormone activates sleep regulatory neurons of the rat preoptic hypothalamus. *American Journal of Physiology: Regulatory, Integrative and Comparative Physiology, 298,* R147–R156.

Peters, E., Hess, T. M., Västfjäll, D., & Auman, C. (2007). Adult age differences in dual information processes. *Perspectives on Psychological Science, 2,* 1–23.

Peters, J., Suchan, B., Koster, O., & Daum, I. (2007). Domain-specific retrieval of source information in the medial temporal lobe. *European Journal of Neuroscience, 26,* 1333–1343.

Petersen, S. E., & Fiez, J. A. (1993). The processing of single words studied with positron emission tomography. *Annual Review of Neuroscience, 16,* 509–530.

Peterson, C. (2000). The future of optimism. *American Psychologist, 55,* 44–55.

Peterson, L. R., & Peterson, M. J. (1959). Short-term retention of individual items. *Journal of Experimental Psychology, 58,* 193–198.

Petrill, S. A. (2005). Introduction to this special issue: Genes, environment, and the development of reading skills. *Scientific Studies of Reading, 9,* 189–196.

Petrill, S. A., & Deater-Deckard, K. (2004). The heritability of general cognitive ability: A within-family adoption design. *Intelligence, 32,* 403–409.

Pettigrew, T. F. (2004). Justice deferred: A half century after *Brown v. Board of Education. American Psychologist, 59,* 521–529.

Pettigrew, T. F., & Tropp, L. R. (2006). A meta-analytic test of intergroup contact theory. *Journal of Personality and Social Psychology, 90,* 751–783.

Pettingale, K. W., Morris, T., Greer, S., & Haybittle, J. L. (1985). Mental attitudes to cancer: An additional prognostic factor. *Lancet,* p. 750.

Pettito, L. A. (1993). On the ontogenetic requirements for early language acquisition. In B. de Boysson-Bardies, S. de Schonen, P. W. Jusczyk, P. McNeilage, & J. Morton (Eds.), *Developmental neurocognition: Speech and face processing in the first year of life. NATO ASI series D: Behavioural and social sciences* (Vol. 69). Dordrecht, Netherlands: Kluwer Academic.

Phelps, R. P. (2005). *Defending standardized testing.* Mahwah, NJ: Lawrence Erlbaum Associates.

Philip, P., Sagaspe, P., Moore, N., Taillard, J., Charles, A., Guilleminault, C., et al. (2005). Fatigue, sleep restriction and driving performance. *Accident Analysis and Prevention, 37,* 473–478.

Phillips, L. M., Hayden, R., & Norris, S.P. (2006). *Family literacy matters: A longitudinal parent–child literacy intervention study.* Calgary, AB: Temeron.

Piaget, J. (1970). Piaget's theory. In P. H. Mussen (Ed.), *Carmichael's manual of child psychology* (3rd ed., Vol. I). New York: Wiley.

References

Piaget, J., & Inhelder, B. (1958). *The growth of logical thinking from childhood to adolescence* (A. Parsons & S. Seagrin, Trans.). New York: Basic Books.

Picchioni, D., Goeltzenleucher, B., Green, D. N., Convento, M. J., Crittenden, R., Hallgren, M., et al. (2002). Nightmares as a coping mechanism for stress. *Dreaming: Journal of the Association for the Study of Dreams, 12,* 155–169.

Pickering, G. J., & Gordon, R. (2006). Perception of mouthfeel sensations elicited by red wine are associated with sensitivity to 6-N-propylthiouracil. *Journal of Sensory Studies, 21,* 249–265.

Piliavin, J. A., & Piliavin, I. M. (1972). Effect of blood on reactions to a victim. *Journal of Personality and Social Psychology, 23,* 353–362.

Pillay, S. S., Gruber, S. A., Rogowska, J., Simpson, N., & Yurgelun-Todd, D. A. (2006). fMRI of fearful facial affect recognition in panic disorder: the cingulate gyrus-amygdala connection. *Journal of Affective Disorders, 94,* 173–181.

Pillay, S. S., Rogowska, J., Gruber, S. A., Simpson, N., & Yurgelun-Todd, D. A. (2007). Recognition of happy facial affect in panic disorder: an fMRI study. *Journal of Anxiety Disorders, 21,* 381–393.

Pilon, M. (2002, January 22). Mental disorder and Canadian criminal law. Government of Canada. Retrieved from dsp-psd.pwgsc.gc.ca/Collection-R/LoPBdP/BP/prb9922-e.htm.

Pilotti, M., Chodorow, M., & Shono, Y. (2009). The benefits and costs of prior exposure: A large-scale study of interference effects in stimulus identification. *American Journal of Psychology, 122,* 191–208.

Pincus, T., & Morley, S. (2001). Cognitive-processing bias in chronic pain: A review and integration. *Psychological Bulletin, 127,* 599–617.

Pinel, J. P. J., Assanand, S., & Lehman, D. R. (2000). Hunger, eating and ill health. *American Psychologist, 55,* 1105–1116.

Pinker, S. (1994). *The language instinct.* New York: William Morrow.

Pinker, S. (2002). *The blank slate: The modern denial of human nature.* New York: Viking.

Pinker, S. (2004). Clarifying the logical problem of language acquisition. *Journal of Child Language, 31,* 949–953.

Pinker, S., & Jackendoff, R. (2005). The faculty of language: What's special about it? *Cognition, 96,* 201–236.

Pinkerton, S. D., Bogart, L. M., Cecil, H., & Abramson, P. R. (2002). Factors associated with masturbation in a collegiate sample. *Journal of Psychology and Human Sexuality, 14,* 103–121.

Pinquart, M., Duberstein, P. R., & Lyness J. M. (2006). Treatments for later-life depressive conditions: A meta-analytic comparison of pharmacotherapy and psychotherapy. *American Journal of Psychiatry, 163,* 1493–1501.

Pi-Sunyer, X. (2003). A clinical view of the obesity problem. *Science, 299,* 859–860.

Pitman, R. K., & Delahanty, D. L. (2005). Conceptually driven pharmacologic approaches to acute trauma. *CNS Spectrums, 10,* 99–106.

Platek, S., & Kemp, S. (2009, February). Is family special to the brain? An event-related fMRI study of familiar, familial, and self-face recognition. *Neuropsychologia, 47,* 849–858.

Plomin, R. (2003). 50 years of DNA: What it has meant to psychological science. *American Psychological Society, 16,* 7–8.

Plomin, R. (2005). Finding genes in child psychology and psychiatry: When are we going to be there? *Journal of Child Psychology and Psychiatry, 46,* 1030–1038.

Plomin, R., DeFries, J. C., Craig, I. W., & McGuffin, P. (2003). *Behavioral genetics in the postgenomic era.* Washington, DC: American Psychological Association.

Plowright, C. M. S., Simonds, V. M., & Butler, M. A. (2006). How bumblebees first find flowers: Habituation of visual pattern preferences, spontaneous recovery, and dishabituation. *Learning and Motivation, 37,* 66–78.

Pluess, M., & Belsky, J. (2009). Differential susceptibility to rearing experience: The case of childcare. *Journal of Child Psychology and Psychiatry, 50,* 396–404.

Plunkett, K., & Wood, C. (2004). The development of children's understanding of grammar. In J. Oates and A. Grayson (Eds.), *Cognitive and language development in children* (pp. 163–204). Malden, MA: Blackwell Publishers Open University Press.

Pogarksy, G., & Piquero, A. R. (2003). Can punishment encourage offending? Investigating the 'resetting' effect. *Journal of Research in Crime and Delinquency, 40,* 95–120.

Polivy, J., & Herman, C. P. (2002). Causes of eating disorders. *Annual Review of Psychology, 53,* 187–213.

Polivy, J., Herman, C. P., & Boivin, M. (2005). Eating disorders. In J. E. Maddux and B. A. Winstead, *Psychopathology: Foundations for a contemporary understanding.* Mahwah, NJ: Lawrence Erlbaum Associates.

Polonsky, D. C. (2006). Review of the big book of masturbation: From angst to zeal. *Journal of Sex & Marital Therapy, 32,* 75–78.

Ponterotto, J. G., Gretchen, D., Chauhan, R. V. (2001). Cultural identity and multicultural assessment: Quantitative and qualitative tools for the clinician. In L. A. Suzuki, & J. G. Ponterotto (Eds.), *Handbook of multicultural assessment: Clinical, psychological, and educational applications* (2nd ed.). San Francisco: Jossey-Bass/Pfeiffer.

Ponterotto, J. G., Utsey, S. O., & Pedersen, P. B. (2006). *Preventing prejudice: A guide for counselors, educators, and parents.* Thousand Oaks, CA: Sage Publications.

Poo, C. & Isaacson, J. S. (2007). An early critical period for long-term plasticity and structural modification of sensory synapses in olfactory cortex. *Journal of Neuroscience, 27,* 7553–7558.

Popa, D., Léna, C., Alexandre, C., & Adrien, J. (2008). Lasting syndrome of depression produced by reduction in serotonin uptake during postnatal development: Evidence from sleep, stress, and behavior. *The Journal of Neuroscience, 28,* 88–97.

Porte, H. S., & Hobson, J. A. (1996). Physical motion in dreams: One measure of three theories. *Journal of Abnormal Psychology, 105,* 329–335.

Posner, M. I., & DiGiorlamo, G. J. (2000). Cognitive neuroscience: Origins and promise. *Psychological Bulletin, 126,* 873–889.

Potheraju, A., & Soper, B. (1995). A comparison of self-reported dream themes for high school and college students. *College Student Journal, 29,* 417–420.

Pottick, K. J., Kirk, S. A., Hsieh, D. K., & Tian, X. (2007). Judging mental disorder in youths: Effects of client, clinician, and contextual differences. *Journal of Consulting Clinical Psychology, 75,* 1–8.

Poundstone, W. (2003). *How would you move Mount Fuji?: Microsoft's cult of the puzzle.* Boston: Little, Brown.

Powell, L. H. (2006). Review of marital and sexual lifestyles in the United States: Attitudes, behaviors, and relationships in social context. *Family Relations, 55,* 149.

Powers, K. D. (2006). An analysis of Kohlbergian moral development in relationship to biblical factors of morality in seminary students (Lawrence Kohlberg). *Dissertation Abstracts International: Section B: The Sciences and Engineering, 67*(6-B), 3485.

Pratkanis, A. R. (2007). Social influence analysis: An index of tactics. In A. R. Pratkanis, *The science of social influence: Advances and future progress.* New York: Psychology Press.

Pratkanis, A. R., Epley, N., & Savitsky, K. (2007). Issue 12: Is subliminal persuasion a myth? In J. A. Nier, *Taking sides: Clashing views in social psychology* (2nd ed.) New York: McGraw-Hill.

Pratt, H. D., Phillips, E. L., Greydanus, D. E., & Patel, D. R. (2003). Eating disorders in the adolescent population: Future directions [Special issue: Eating disorders in adolescents]. *Journal of Adolescent Research, 18,* 297–317.

Price, D. D. (2000, June 9). Psychological and neural mechanisms of the affective dimension of pain. *Science, 288,* 1769–1772.

Prince, C. V. (2005). Homosexuality, transvestism and transsexuality: Reflections on their etymology and differentiation. *International Journal of Transgenderism, 8,* 15–18.

Prinz, J. J. (2007). Emotion: Competing theories and philosophical issues. In P. Thagard, *Philosophy of psychology and cognitive science.* Amsterdam, Netherlands: North Holland/ Elsevier.

Prislin, R., Brewer, M., & Wilson, D. J. (2002). Changing majority and minority positions within a group versus an aggregate. *Personality and Social Psychology Bulletin, 28,* 640–647.

Proffitt, D. R. (2006). Distance perception. *Current Directions in Psychological Science, 15,* 131–139.

Prohovnik, I., Skudlarski, P., Fulbright, R. K., Gore, J. C., & Wexler, B. E. (2004). Functional MRI changes before and after onset of reported emotions. *Psychiatry Research: Neuroimaging, 132*, 239–250.

Proudfoot, D. (2009). Meaning and mind: Wittgenstein's relevance for the 'does language shape thought?' debate. *New Ideas in Psychology, 27*, 163–183.

Province of Manitoba (2000). Inquiry regarding Thomas Sophonow. Retrieved from www.gov.mb.ca/justice/publications/sophonow/intro/index.html.

Public Health Agency of Canada. (2002). A report on mental illnesses in Canada. Retrieved from www.phac-aspc.gc.ca/publicat/miic-mmac/pref_e.html.

Public Health Agency of Canada. (2007). The burden of adult obesity in Canada. *Chronic diseases in Canada, 27 (4)*, 1–11. Retrieved from www.phac-aspc.gc.ca/publicat/cdic-mcc/27-4/pdf/cdic274-1_e.pdf.

Public Health Agency of Canada. (2008). Fetal alcohol spectrum disorder. Retrieved from www.phac-aspc.gc.ca/fasd-etcaf/index.html.

Puca, R. M. (2005). The influence of the achievement motive on probability estimates in pre- and post-decisional action phases. *Journal of Research in Personality, 39*, 245–262.

Quartana, P. J., & Burns, J. W. (2007). Painful consequences of anger suppression. *Emotion, 7*, 400–414.

Quas, J. A., Malloy, L. C., & Melinder, A. (2007). Developmental differences in the effects of repeated interviews and interviewer bias on young children's event memory and false reports. *Developmental Psychology, 43*, 823–837.

Quenot, J. P., Boichot, C., Petit, A., Falcon-Eicher, S., d'Athis, P., Bonnet, C., et al. (2005). Usefulness of MRI in the follow-up of patients with repaired aortic coarctation and bicuspid aortic valve. *International Journal of Cardiology, 103*, 312–316.

Quinn, D. M., Kahng, S. K., & Crocker, J. (2004). Discreditable: Stigma effects of revealing a mental illness history on test performance. *Personality and Social Psychology Bulletin, 30*, 803–815.

Quiroga, R. (2012). Concept cells: The building blocks of declarative memory functions. *Nature Reviews Neuroscience, 13*, 587–597.

Quiroga, R., Fried, I., & Koch, C. (2013, February). Brain cells for grandmother. *Scientific American*, 31–35.

Quoidbach, J., Dunn, E. W., Petrides, K. V., & Mikolajczak, M. (2010). Money giveth, money taketh away: The dual effect of wealth on happiness. *Psychological Science, 21*, 759–763.

Rabin, J. (2004). Quantification of color vision with cone contrast sensitivity. *Visual Neuroscience, 21*, 483–485.

Rachman, S., & deSilva, P. (2004). *Panic disorders: The facts*. Oxford, England: Oxford University Press.

Rado, J., Dowd, S., & Janicak, P. (2008). The emerging role of transcranial magnetic stimulation (TMS) for treatment of psychiatric disorders. *Directions in Psychiatry, 28*, 315–332.

Raffaele, P. (2006, November). Speaking Bonobo. *Smithsonian Magazine*.

Rahman, Q., Kumari, V., & Wilson, G. D. (2003). Sexual orientation-related differences in pre-pulse inhibition of the human startle response. *Behavioral Neuroscience, 117*, 1096–1102.

Ramachandran, V. (2009, February). On whether mirror neurons play a significant role in processing affective prosody. *Perceptual and Motor Skills, 108*, 30–36.

Ramachandran, V. S. (1995). Filling in gaps in logic: Reply to Durgin et al. *Perception, 24*, 841–845.

Ramachandran, V. S., & Hubbard, E. M. (2001). Synesthesia—a window into perception, thought and language. *Journal of Consciousness Studies, 8*, 3–34.

Ramsay, M. C., Reynolds, C. R., & Kamphaus, R. W. (2002). *Essentials of behavioral assessment*. New York: Wiley.

Ramus, F. (2006). Genes, brain, and cognition: A roadmap for the cognitive scientist. *Cognition, 101*, 247–269.

Randolph-Seng, B., & Nielsen, M. E. (2009). Opening the doors of perception: Priming altered states of consciousness outside of conscious awareness. *Archiv für Religionspsychologie/Archive for the Psychology of Religions, 31*, 237–260.

Rangell, L. (2007). *The road to unity in psychoanalytic theory*. Lanham, MD: Jason Aronson.

Rapport, R. L. (2005). *Nerve endings: The discovery of the synapse*. New York: W. W. Norton.

Rasch, B. & Born, J. (2008). Reactivation and consolidation of memory during sleep. *Current Directions in Psychological Science, 17* (3) 188–192.

Raskin, N. J., & Rogers, C. R. (1989). Person-centered therapy. In R. J. Corsini & D. Wedding (Eds.), *Current psychotherapies* (4th ed.). Itasca, IL: F. E. Peacock.

Rassin, E. (2008). Individual differences in the susceptibility to confirmation bias. *Netherlands Journal of Psychology, 64*, 87–93.

Rassin, E., & Muris, P. (2007). Abnormal and normal obsessions: A reconsideration. *Behaviour Research and Therapy, 45*, 1065–1070.

Ratcliff, R., & McKoon, G. (1989). Memory models, text processing, and cuedependent retrieval. In H. L. Roediger III & F. I. M. Craik (Eds.), *Varieties of memory and consciousness: Essays in honour of Endel Tulving*. Hillsdale, NJ: Erlbaum.

Rattazzi, M. C., LaFuci, G., & Brown, W. T. (2004). Prospects for gene therapy in the Fragile X Syndrome. *Mental Retardation and Developmental Disabilities Research Reviews, 10*, 75–81.

Ravindran, A. V., Matheson, K., Griffiths, J., Merali, Z., & Anisman, H. (2002). Stress, coping, uplifts, and quality of life in subtypes of depression: A conceptual framework and emerging data. *Journal of Affective Disorders, 71*, 121–130.

Ray, L. A., & Hutchison, K. E. (2007). Effects of naltrexone on alcohol sensitivity and genetic moderators of medication response: a double-blind placebo-controlled study. *Archives of General Psychiatry, 64*, 1069–1077.

Ray, R., et al. (2008). Neuroimaging, genetics and the treatment of nicotine addiction. *Behavioural Brain Research, 193*, 159–169.

Ray, W. J. (2000). *Methods: Toward a science of behavior and experience* (6th ed.). Belmont, CA: Wadsworth.

Raz, A. (2007). Suggestibility and hypnotizability: Mind the gap. *American Journal of Clinical Hypnosis, 49*, 205–210.

Redden, J. R., Whippler, S. M., & Reddon, J. E. (2007). Seemingly anomalous WISC-IVfull scale IQ scores in the American and Canadian standardization samples. *Current Psychology, 26* (1), 60–69.

Redding, G. M., & Hawley, E. (1993). Length illusion in fractional Müller-Lyer stimuli: An object-perception approach. *Perception, 22*, 819–828.

Redish, A. D. (2004). Addiction as a computational process gone awry. *Science, 306*, 1944–1947.

Reed, P. (2007). Response rate and sensitivity to the molar feedback function relating response and reinforcement rate on VI + schedules of reinforcement. *Journal of Experimental Psychology: Animal Behavior Processes, 33*, 428–439.

Reed, P., & Morgan, T. (2008). Effect on subsequent fixed-interval schedule performance of prior exposure to ratio and interval schedules of reinforcement. *Learning & Behavior, 36*, 82–91.

Reed, S. K. (1996). *Cognition: Theory and applications* (4th ed.). Pacific Grove, CA: Brooks/ Cole.

Reese, R. J., Conoley, C. W., & Brossart, D. F. (2002). Effectiveness of telephone counseling: A field-based investigation. *Journal of Counseling Psychology, 49*, 233–242.

Regan, P. C. (2006). Love. In R. D. McAnulty, & M. M. Burnette, *Sex and sexuality, Vol 2: Sexual function and dysfunction*. Westport, CT: Praeger Publishers/Greenwood Publishing.

Rehm J., Baliunas D., Brochu S., Fischer B., Gnam W., Patra J., et al. (2006). The costs of substance abuse in Canada 2002. Ottawa: Canadian Centre on Substance Abuse, p. 7.

Reichenberg, A., & Harvey, P. D. (2007). Neuropsychological impairments in schizophrenia: Integration of performance-based and brain imaging findings. *Psychological Bulletin, 133*, 212–223.

Reichenberg, A., Harvey, P., Bowie, C., Mojtabai, R., Rabinowitz, J., Heaton, R., et al. (2009). Neuropsychological function and dysfunction in schizophrenia and psychotic affective disorders. *Schizophrenia Bulletin, 35*, 1022–1029.

Reif, A., & Lesch, K. P. (2003). Toward a molecular architecture of personality. *Behavioural Brain Research, 139*, 1–20.

Reijonen, J. H., Pratt, H. D., Patel, D. R., & Greydanus, D. E. (2003). Eating disorders in the adolescent population: An overview

[Special issue: Eating disorders in adolescents]. *Journal of Adolescent Research, 18,* 209–222.

Reilly, T., & Waterhouse, J. (2007). Altered sleep-wake cycles and food intake: The Ramadan model. *Physiology & Behavior, 90,* 219–228.

Reisberg, D. (2009). *Cognition: Exploring the science of the mind.* New York: Norton.

Reitman, J. S. (1965). *Cognition and thought.* New York: Wiley.

Relier, J. P. (2001). Influence of maternal stress on fetal behavior and brain development. *Biology of the Neonate, 79,* 168–171.

Rende, R. (2007). Thinking inside and outside the (black) box: Behavioral genetics and human development. *Human Development, 49,* 343–346.

Reynolds, C. R., & Ramsay, M. C. (2003). Bias in psychological assessment: An empirical review and recommendations. In J. R. Graham & J. A. Naglieri (Eds.), *Handbook of psychology: Assessment psychology* (Vol. 10). New York: Wiley.

Reynolds, D. (2006, September 5). School board reverses position on teen's service dog. *Inclusion Daily Express.* Retrieved from www.mnddc.org/news/inclusion-daily/2006/09/090506abeductechdog.htm.

Reynolds, R. I., & Takooshian, H. (1988, January). Where were you August 8, 1985? *Bulletin of the Psychonomic Society, 26,* 23–25.

Rice, C. (2009, December 18). Prevalence of Autism Spectrum Disorders—Autism and Developmental Disabilities Monitoring Network, United States, 2006. *MMWR, 58*(SS10), 1–20.

Rice, M. L., Tomblin, J. B., Hoffman, L., Richman, W. A., & Marquis, J. (2004). Grammatical tense deficits in children with SLI and nonspecific language impairment: Relationships with non-verbal IQ over time. *Journal of Speech, Language, and Hearing Research, 47,* 816–834.

Rich, E. L., & Shapiro, M. L. (2007). Prelimbic/infralimbic inactivation impairs memory for multiple task switches, but not flexible selection of familiar tasks. *Journal of Neuroscience, 27,* 4747–4755.

Richards, R. (2006). Frank Barron and the study of creativity: A voice that lives on. *Journal of Humanistic Psychology, 46,* 352–370.

Richards, C. (2011). Transsexualism and existentialism. *Existential Analysis, 22* (2), 272–279.

Richardson, A. S., Bergen, H. A., Martin, G., Roeger, L., & Allison, S. (2005). Perceived academic performance as an indicator of risk of attempted suicide in young adolescents. *Archives of Suicide Research, 9,* 163–176.

Richgels, D. J. (2004). Paying attention to language. *Reading Research Quarterly, 39,* 470–477.

Rieber, R. W., & Robinson, D. K. (2006). Review of the essential Vygotsky. *Journal of the History of the Behavioral Sciences, 42,* 178–180.

Riedel, G., Platt, B., & Micheau, J. (2003). Glutamate receptor function in learning and memory. *Behavioural Brain Research, 140,* 1–47.

Rigby, L., & Waite, S. (2007). Group therapy for self-esteem: Using creative approaches and metaphor as clinical tools. *Behavioural and Cognitive Psychotherapy, 35,* 361–364.

Riley, A., Valdez, C, Barrueco, S., Mills, C., Beardslee, W., Sandler, I., et al. (2008). Development of a family-based program to reduce risk and promote resilience among families affected by maternal depression: Theoretical basis and program description. *Clinical Child and Family Psychology Review, 11,* 12–29.

Rivera-Gaxiola, M., Klarman, L., Garcia-Sierra, A., & Kuhl, P. K. (2005). Neural patterns to speech and vocabulary growth in American infants. *Neuroreport: For Rapid Communication of Neuroscience Research, 16,* 495–498.

Rizzolatti, G., Fabbri-Destro, M., & Cattaneo, L. (2009). Mirror neurons and their clinical relevance. *Nature Clinical Practice Neurology, 5* (1) 24–34.

Robbins, B. (2008). What is the good life? Positive psychology and the renaissance of humanistic psychology. *The Humanistic Psychologist, 36,* 96–112.

Robert, S. (2006). Deictic space in Wolof: Discourse, syntax and the importance of absence. In M. Hickman & S. Robert (Eds.), *Space in languages: Linguistic systems and cognitive categories.* Amsterdam, Netherlands: John Benjamins.

Robert-McComb, J. J. (2001). Physiology of stress. In J. J. Robert-McComb (Ed.), *Eating disorders in women and children: Prevention, stress management, and treatment,* pp. 119–146. Boca Raton, FL: CRC Press.

Roberts, M. E., Moore, S. D., & Beckham, J. C. (2007). Post-traumatic stress disorder and substance use disorders. In M. Al'bsi, *Stress and addiction: Biological and psychological mechanisms.* San Diego, CA: Elsevier Academic Press.

Rock, A. (1999, January). Quitting time for smokers. *Money,* pp. 139–141.

Roesch, S. C., Adams, L., Hines, A., Palmores, A., Vyas, P., Tran, C., et al. (2005). Coping with prostate cancer: A meta-analytic review. *Journal of Behavioral Medicine, 28,* 281–293.

Roffwarg, H., Muzio, J., & Dement W. (1966). Ontogenic development of the human sleepdream cycle. *Science, 152,* 604–619.

Rogers, C. R. (1951). *Client-centered therapy.* Boston: Houghton-Mifflin.

Rogers, C. R. (1971). A theory of personality. In S. Maddi (Ed.), *Perspectives on personality.* Boston: Little, Brown.

Rogers, C. R. (1995). *A way of being.* Boston: Houghton Mifflin.

Rogers, J. M. (2009). Tobacco and pregnancy: Overview of exposures and effects. *Birth Defects Res. C. Embryo Today, 84,* 152–160.

Rogers, S. (2007). The underlying mechanisms of semantic memory loss in Alzheimer's disease and semantic dementia. *Dissertation Abstracts International: Section B: The Sciences and Engineering, 67*(10-B), 5591.

Rohm, W. G. (2003). Test-tube family reunion: Louise Brown turns 25. Happy birthday, IVF. *Wired.*

Roid, G., Nellis, L. & McLellan, M. (2003). Assessment with the Leiter International Performance Scale—Revised and the S-BIT. In R. S. McCallum & R. Steve (Eds.), *Handbook of nonverbal assessment.* New York: Kluwer Academic/Plenum Publishers.

Roisman, G. I., Collins, W. A. Sroufe, L. A., & Egeland, B. (2005). Predictors of young adults' representations of and behavior in their current romantic relationship: Prospective tests of the prototypehypothesis. *Attachment and Human Development, 7,* 105–121.

Roizen, N. J., & Patterson, D. (2003). Down's syndrome. *Lancet, 361,* 1281–1289.

Rollman, G. B. (2004). *Ethnocultural variationsin the experience of pain.* Mahwah, NJ: Lawrence Erlbaum Associates.

Rom, S. A., Miller, L., & Peluso, J. (2009). Playing the game: Psychological factors in surviving cancer. *International Journal of Emergency Mental Health, 11,* 25–36.

Romano, E., Tremblay, R. E., Vitaro, E., Zoccolillo, M., & Pagani, L. (2001.) Prevalence of psychiatric diagnoses and the role of perceived impairment: Findings from an adolescent community sample. *Journal of Child Psychology and Psychiatry and Allied Disciplines, 42,* 451–461.

Romeu, P. F. (2006). Memories of the terrorist attacks of September 11, 2001: A study of the consistency and phenomenal characteristics of flashbulb memories. *The Spanish Journal of Psychology, 9,* 52–60.

Rorschach, H. (1924). *Psychodiagnosis: A diagnostic test based on perception.* New York: Grune & Stratton.

Rosen, H. (2000). The creative evolution of the theoretical foundations for cognitive therapy [Special issue: Creativity in the context of cognitive therapy]. *Journal of Cognitive Psychotherapy, 14,* 123–134.

Rosen, L. D. (2012). *iDisorder: Understanding our obsession with technology and overcoming its hold on us.* New York: Palgrave Macmillan.

Rosenbloom, T., & Wolf, Y. (2002). Sensation seeking and detection of risky road signals: A developmental perspective. *Accident Analysis and Prevention, 34,* 569–580.

Rosenhan, D. L. (1973). On being sane in insane places. *Science, 179,* 250–258.

Rosenkranz, M. A., Jackson, D. C., Dalton, K. M., Dokski, I., Ryff, C. D., Singer, B. H., Muller, D., Kalin, N. H., Davidson, R. J. (2003). Affective style and in vivo immune response: neurobehavioral mechanisms. *Proceedings of the National Academy of Sciences, 100,* 48–52.

Rosenkranz, M. A., Jackson, D. C., Dalton, K. M., Dolski, I., Ryff, C. D., Singer, B. H., Muller, D., Kalin, N. H., & Davidson, R. J. (2003,

September 16). Affective style and in vivo immune response: neurobehavioral mechanisms. *Proceedings of the National Academy of Sciences, USA, 100,* 11148–11152. Retrieved from http://www.pnas.org/cgi/reprint/100/19/11148?maxtoshow=&HITS=10&hits=10&RESULTFORMAT=&fulltext=davidson+2003&searchid=1125413201748_4140&stored_search=&FIRSTINDEX=0&journalcode=pnas.

Rosenman, R. H., Grand R. J., Jenkins, C. D., Friedman, M, Straus, R., & Wurm, M. (1994). Coronary heart disease in the Western Collaborative Group Study: Final follow-up experience of 8 years. In A. Steptoe & J. Wardle, (Eds). *Psychosocial processes and health: A reader.* New York: Cambridge University Press.

Rosenstein, D. S., & Horowitz, H. A. (1996). Adolescent attachment and psychopathology. *Journal of Consulting and Clinical Psychology, 64,* 244–253.

Rosenthal, A. M. (1964). Thirty-eight witnesses. New York: McGraw-Hill.

Rosenthal, R. (2002). Covert communication in classrooms, clinics, courtrooms and cubicles. *American Psychologist, 57,* 838–849.

Rosenthal, R. (2003). Covert communication in laboratories, classrooms, and the truly real world. *Current Directions in Psychological Science, 12,* 151–154.

Ross, H. E., & Plug, C. (2002). *The mystery of the moon illusion: Exploring size perception.* Oxford: University Press.

Ross, J. (2006). Sleep on a problem . . . It works like a dream. *The Psychologist, 19,* 738–740.

Ross, P. E. (2004, April). Draining the language out of color. *Scientific American,* pp. 46–51.

Rossato, M., Pagano, C., & Vettor, R. (2008). The cannabinoid system and male reproductive functions. *Journal of Neuroendocrinology, 20,* 90–93.

Rotan, L. W., & Ospina-Kammerer, V. (2007). *Mindbody medicine: Foundations and practical applications.* New York: Routledge/Taylor & Francis Group.

Roter, D. L., Hall, J. A., & Aoki, Y. (2002). Physician gender effects in medical communication: A meta-analytic review. *Journal of the American Medical Association, 288,* 756–764.

Rothblum, E. D. (1990). Women and weight: Fad and fiction. *Journal of Psychology, 124,* 5–24.

Roughton, R. E. (2002). Rethinking homosexuality: What it teaches us about psychoanalysis. *Journal of the American Psychoanalytic Association, 50,* 733–763.

Rowe, J. B., Toni, I., Josephs, O., Frackowiak, R. S. J., & Passingham, R. E. (2000, June 2). The prefrontal cortex: Response selection or maintenance within working memory? *Science, 288,* 1656–1660.

Rozencwajg, P., Cherfi, M., Ferrandez, A. M., Lautrey, J., Lemoine, C., & Loarer, E. (2005). Age-related differences in the strategies used by middle aged adults to solve a block design task. *International Journal of Aging and Human Development, 60,* 159–182.

Rozin, P., Kabnick, K., Pete, E., Fischler, C., & Shields, C. (2003). The ecology of eating: Smaller portion sizes in France than in the United States help explain the French paradox. *Psychological Science, 14,* 450–454.

Rubenstein, C. (1982, July). Psychology's fruit flies. *Psychology Today,* pp. 83–84.

Rubichi, S., Ricci, F., Padovani, R., & Scaglietti, L. (2005). Hypnotic susceptibility, baseline attentional functioning, and the Stroop task. *Consciousness and Cognition: An International Journal, 14,* 296–303.

Rubin, B. D., & Katz, L. C. (1999). Optical imaging of odorant representations in the mammalian olfactory bulb. *Neuron 23,* 499–511.

Rubin, D. C. (1985, September). The subtle deceiver: Recalling our past. *Psychology Today,* pp. 39–46.

Rubin, D. C., Schrauf, R. W., Gulgoz, S., & Naka, M. (2007). Cross-cultural variability of component processes in autobiographical remembering: Japan, Turkey, and the USA. *Memory, 15,* 536–547.

Rudner, M., & Rönnberg, J. (2008). The role of the episodic buffer in working memory for language processing. *Cognitive Processing, 9,* 19–28.

Rule, N. O., Ambady, N., & Hallett, K. C. (2009). Female sexual orientation is perceived accurately, rapidly, and automatically from the face and its features. *Journal of Experimental Social Psychology, 45,* 1245–1251.

Rumleski, K. (2007, April 25). Psychology pioneers. *London Free Press,* Retrieved from http://lfpress.ca/newsstand/Today/2007/04/25/4127796-sun.html.

Runco, M. A. (2006). Introduction to the special issue: Divergent thinking. *Creativity Research Journal, 18,* 249–250.

Ruocco, J. (October 18, 2010). National Post News Timeline: The case of Russell Williams. Retrieved from: http://news.nationalpost.com/2010/10/18/timeline-colonel-russell-williams/.

Rusche, B. (2003) The 3Rs and animal welfare—conflict or the way forward? *ALTEX, 20, (Suppl. 1),* 63–76.

Ruscher, J. B., Fiske, S. T., & Schnake, S. B. (2000). The motivated tactician's juggling act: Compatible vs. incompatible impression goals. *British Journal of Social Psychology, 39,* 241–256.

Russell, J. A., & Sato, K. (1995). Comparing emotion words between languages. *Journal of Cross Cultural Psychology, 26,* 384–391.

Russell, R., Duchaine, B., & Nakayama, K. (2009). Super-recognizers: People with extraordinary face recognition ability. *Psychonomic Bulletin & Review, 16,* 252–257.

Russo, N. (1981). Women in psychology. In L. T. Benjamin, Jr. & K. D. Lowman (Eds.), *Activities handbook for the teaching of psychology.* Washington, DC: American Psychological Association.

Rustin, M. (2006). Infant observation research: What have we learned so far? *Infant Observation, 9,* 35–52.

Rydell, R., McConnell, A., & Mackie, D. (2008). Consequences of discrepant explicit and implicit attitudes: Cognitive dissonance and increased information processing. *Journal of Experimental Social Psychology, 44,* 1526–1532.

Rymer, R. (1994). *Genie: A scientific tragedy.* New York: Penguin.

Saarni, C. (1999). *Developing emotional competence.* New York: Guilford.

Sachs-Ericsson, N., Joiner, T., Plant, E. A., & Blazer, D. G. (2005). The influence of depression on cognitive decline in community-dwelling elderly persons. *American Journal of Geriatric Psychiatry, 13,* 402–408.

Sackeim, H. A., Haskett, R. F., Mulsant, B. H., Thase, M. E., Mann, J. J., Pettinati, H. M., et al. (2001). Continuation pharmaco-therapy in the prevention of relapse following electroconvulsive therapy: A randomized controlled trial. *Journal of the American Medical Association, 285,* 1299–1307.

Sacks, O. (2003, July 28). The mind's eye. *The New Yorker,* pp. 48–59.

Saczynski, J., Willis, S., & Schaie, K. (2002). Strategy use in reasoning training with older adults. *Aging, Neuropsychology, & Cognition, 9,* 48–60.

Sadker, M., & Sadker, D. (1994). *Failing atfairness: How America's schools cheat girls.* New York: Scribners.

Sado, M., Yamauchi, K., Kawakami, N., Ono, Y., Furukawa, T. A., Tsuchiya, M., Tajima, M., & Kashima, H. (2011). Cost of depression among adults in Japan in 2005. *Psychiatry and Clinical Neurosciences, 65,* 442–450.

Salgado, D. M., Quinlan, K. J., & Zlotnick, C. (2007). The relationship of lifetime polysubstance dependence to trauma exposure, symptomatology, and psychosocial functioning in incarcerated women with comorbid PTSD and substance use disorder. *Journal of Trauma Dissociation, 8,* 9–26.

Sallquist, J., Eisenberg, N., Spinrad, T. L., Eggum, N. D., & Gaertner, B. (2009). Assessment of preschoolers' positive empathy: Concurrent and longitudinal relations with positive emotion, social competence, and sympathy. *The Journal of Positive Psychology, 4,* 223–233.

Salsman, N. L. (2006). Interpersonal change as an outcome of Time-Limited Interpersonal Therapy. *Dissertation Abstracts International: Section B: The Sciences and Engineering, 66*(9-B), 5103.

Salvi, V., Fagiolini, A., Swartz, H., Maina, G., & Frank, E. (2008). The use of antidepressants in bipolar disorder. *Journal of Clinical Psychiatry, 69,* 1307–1318.

Samoilov, V., & Zayas, V. (2007). Ivan Petrovich Pavlov (1849–1936). *Journal of the History of the Neurosciences, 16,* 74–89.

Sams, M., Hari, R., Rif, J., & Knuutila, J. (1993). The human auditory memory trace persists about 10 sec: Neuromagnetic evidence. *Journal of Cognitive Neuroscience, 5*, 363–370.

Samuel, D. B., Carroll, K. M., Rounsaville, B. J., & Ball, S. A. (2013). Personality disorders as maladaptive, exreme variants of normal personality: Borderline personality disorder and neuroticism in a substance using sample. *Journal of Personality Disorders, 27*, 625–635.

Samuel, D. B., & Widiger, T. A. (2006). Differentiating normal and abnormal personality from the perspective of the DSM. In S. Strack, *Differentiating normal and abnormal personality* (2nd ed.). New York: Springer Publishing.

Sanders, C., Field, T., & Diego, M.A. (2001). Adolescents' academic expectations and achievement. *Adolescence, 36* (144), 795-802.

Sandomir, R. (2007, July 17). W. W. E.'s testing is examined after Benoit murder-suicide. *The New York Times*, p. 33.

Sandoval, J., Frisby, C. L., Geisinger, K. F., Scheuneman, J. D., & Grenier, J. R. (Eds.). (1998). *Test interpretation and diversity: Achieving equity in assessment*. Washington, DC: American Psychological Association.

Sanz, C. (2000). Implementing LIBRA for the design of experimental research in SLA. *Language Learning and Technology* Millennial issue *13*, 27–31.

Saper, C. B., Lu, J., Chou, T. C., & Gooley, J. (2005). The hypothalamic integrator for circadian rhythms. *Trends in Neuroscience, 28*, 152–157.

Sapolsky, R. M. (2003). Gene therapy for psychiatric disorders. *American Journal of Psychiatry, 160*, 208–220.

Sargent, J. D., Stoolmiller, M., Worth, K. A., Cal, C. S., Wills, T. A., Gibbons, F. X., et al. (2007). Exposure to smoking depictions in movies: Its association with established adolescent smoking. *Archives of Pediatric Adolescent Medicine, 161*, 849–856.

Saucier, D. A., & Cain, M. E. (2006). The foundations of attitudes about animal research. *Ethics & Behavior, 16*, 117–133.

Savage-Rumbaugh, E. S., Toth, N., & Schick, K. (2007). Kanzi learns to knap stone tools. In D. A. Washburn, *Primate perspectives on behavior and cognition*. Washington, DC: American Psychological Association.

Savas, H. A., Yumru, M., & Kaya, M. C. (2007). Atypical antipsychotics as 'mood stabilizers': A retrospective chart review. *Progress in Neuro-Psychopharmacology & Biological Psychiatry, 31*, 1064–1067.

Saville, B. (2009). Performance under competitive and self-competitive fixed-interval schedules of reinforcement. *The Psychological Record, 59*, 21–38.

Sawa, A., & Snyder, S. H. (2002, April 26). Schizophrenia: Diverse approaches to a complex disease. *Science, 296*, 692–695.

Sayette, M. A. (1993). An appraisal disruption model of alcohol's effects on stress responses in social drinkers. *Psychological Bulletin, 114*, 459–476.

Saywitz, K., & Goodman, G. (1990). Unpublished study reported in Goleman, D. (1990, November 6). Doubts rise on children as witnesses. *The New York Times*, pp. C1, C6.

Scarr, S., & Weinberg, R. A. (1976). I.Q. test performance of black children adopted by white families. *American Psychologist, 31*, 726–739.

Scaturo, D. J. (2004). Fundamental clinical dilemmas in contemporary group psychotherapy. *Group Analysis, 37*, 201–217.

Scelfo, J. (2007, February 26). Men & depression: Facing darkness. *Newsweek*, p. 43–50.

Schachter, S., & Singer, J. E. (1962). Cognitive, social, and physiological determinants of emotional state. *Psychological Review, 69*, 379–399.

Schacter, D. L., & Badgaiyan, R. D. (2001). Neuroimaging of priming: New perspectives on implicit and explicit memory. *Current Directions in Psychological Science, 10*, 1–4.

Schacter, D. L., Dobbins, I. G., & Schnyer, D. M. (2004). Specificity of priming: A cognitive neuroscience perspective. *Nature Reviews Neuroscience, 5*, 853–862.

Schaie, K. W. (2005a). Longitudinal studies. In *Developmental influences on adult intelligence: The Seattle Longitudinal Study*. New York: Oxford University Press.

Schaie, K. W. (2005b). What can we learn from longitudinal studies of adult development? *Research in Human Development, 2*, 133–158.

Schaller, M., & Crandall, C. S. (Eds.) (2004). *The psychological foundations of culture*. Mahwah, NJ: Lawrence Erlbaum Associates.

Schechter, T., Finkelstein, Y., & Koren, G. (2005). Pregnant "DES daughters" and their offspring. *Canadian Family Physician, 51*, 493–494.

Scheff, T. J. (1999). *Being mentally ill: A sociological theory* (3rd ed.). Hawthrone, NY: Aldine de Gruyter.

Scheier, M. F., Carver, C. S., & Bridges, M. W. (1994). Distinguishing optimism from neuroticism (and trait anxiety, self-mastery, and self-esteem): A reevaluation of the Life Orientation Test. *Journal of Personality and Social Psychology, 67*, 1063–1078.

Schenone, M. H., Aquin, E., Li, Y., Lee, C., Kruger, M., & Bahado-Singh, R. O. (2010). Prenatal prediction of neonatal survival at the borderline viability. *Journal of Maternal-Fetal Neonatal Medicine, 12*, 31–38.

Schepers, P., & van den Berg, P. T. (2007). Social factors of work-environment creativity. *Journal of Business and Psychology, 21*, 407–428.

Schieber, F. (2006). Vision and aging. In J. E. Birren & K. W. Schaire, *Handbook of the psychology of aging* (6th ed.). Amsterdam, Netherlands: Elsevier.

Schiffer, A. A., Pedersen, S. S., Widdershoven, J. W., Hendriks, E. H., Winter, J. B., & Denollet, J. (2005). The distressed (type D) personality is independently associated with impaired health status and increased depressive symptoms in chronic heart failure. *European Journal of Cardiovascular Prevention and Rehabilitation, 12*, 341–346.

Schillinger, D., Bindman, A., Wang, F., Stewart, A., & Piette, J. (2004). Functional health literacy and the quality of physician-patient communication among diabetes patients. *Patient Education and Counseling, 52*, 315–323.

Schmidt, J. P. (2006). The Discovery of neuro– transmitters: A fascinating story and a scientific object lesson. *PsycCRITIQUES, 61*, 101–115.

Schmidt, N. B., Kotov, R., & Joiner, T. E., Jr. (2004). *Taxometrics: Toward a new diagnostic scheme for psychopathology*. Washington, DC: American Psychological Association.

Schmitt, D. P., Allik, J., & McCrae, R. R. (2007). The geographic distribution of Big Five personality traits: Patterns and profiles of human self-description across 56 nations. *Journal of Cross-Cultural Psychology, 38*, 173–212.

Schmitt, D., Realo, A., Voracek, M., & Allik, J. (2008). Why can't a man be more like a woman? Sex differences in Big Five personality traits across 55 cultures. *Journal of Personality and Social Psychology, 94*, 168–182.

Schnall, M., Roper, J., & Fessler, D. M. T. (2010). Elevation leads to altruistic behaviors. *Psychological Science, 21* (3), 315–320.

Schnall, S., Haidt, J., Clore, G. L., & Jordan, A. H. (2008). Disgust as embodied moral judgment. *Personality and Social Psychology Bulletin, 34*, 1096–1109.

Schneider, A. & Domhoff, G. W. (2002). *The quantitative study of dreams*. www.dreamresearch.net.

Schnurr, P. P., & Cozza, S. J. (Eds.). (2004). *Iraq war clinician guide* (2nd ed.). Washington, DC: National Center for Post-Traumatic Stress Disorder.

Schoenpflug, U. (2003). The handbook of culture and psychology. *Journal of Cross-Cultural Psychology, 34*, 481–483.

Schorr, A. (2001). Appraisal: The evolution of an idea. In K. R. Scherer, A. Schorr, et al. (Eds.), *Appraisal processes in emotion: Theory, methods, research. Series in affective science*, pp. 20–34. London: Oxford University Press.

Schredl, M., & Piel, E. (2005). Gender differences in dreaming: Are they stable over time? *Personality and Individual Differences, 39*, 309–316.

Schredl, M., Fricke-Oerkermann, L., Mitschke, A., Wiater, A., & Lehmkuhl, G. (2009, September). Longitudinal study of nightmares in children: Stability and effect of emotional symptoms. *Child Psychiatry and Human Development, 40*, 439–449.

Schroers, M., Prigot, J., & Fagen, J. (2007, December). The effect of a salient odor context on memory retrieval in young infants. *Infant Behavior & Development, 30*, 685–689.

Schubert, T., & Koole, S. (2009). The embodied self: Making a fist enhances men's power-related self-conceptions. *Journal of Experimental Social Psychology, 45,* 828–834.

Schulte-Ruther, M., Markowitsch, J. J., Fink, G. R., & Piefke, M. (2007). Mirror neuron and theory of mind mechanisms involved in face-to-face interactions: A functional magnetic resonance imaging approach to empathy. *Journal of Cognitive Neuroscience, 19,* 1354–1372.

Schutt, R. K. (2001). *Investigating the social world: The process and practice of research.* Thousand Oaks, CA: Sage.

Schwartz, B. (2008). Working memory load differentially affects tip-of-the-tongue states and feeling-of-knowing judgments. *Memory & Cognition, 36,* 9–19.

Schwartz, B. L. (2001). The relation of tip-of-the-tongue states and retrieval time. *Memory & Cognition, 29,* 117–126.

Schwartz, B. L. (2002). The phenomenology of naturally-occurring tip-of-the-tongue states: A diary study. In S. P. Shohov (Ed.), *Advances in psychology research* (Vol. 8). Huntington, NY: Nova.

Schwartz, J. M., & Begley, S. (2002). *The mind and the brain: Neuroplasticity and the power of mental force.* (2002). New York: Regan Books/Harper Collins.

Schwartz, P., Maynard, A., & Uzelac, S. (2008). Adolescent egocentrism: A contemporary view. *Adolescence, 43*(171), 441–448.

Schwartz, S. J., Côté, J. E., & Arnett, J. J. (2005). Identity and agency in emerging adulthood: Two developmental routes in the individualization process. *Youth & Society, 37,* 201–229.

Sciutto, M., & Eisenberg, M. (2007). Evaluating the evidence for and against the overdiagnosis of ADHD. *Journal of Attention Disorders, 11,* 106–113.

Scruggs, T. E., & Mastropieri, M. A. (2000). The effectiveness of mnemonic instruction for students with learning and behavior problems: An update and research synthesis. *Journal of Behavioral Education, 10,* 163–173.

Scullin, M. H., Kanaya, T., & Ceci, S. J. (2002). Measurement of individual differences in children's suggestibility across situations. *Journal of Experimental Psychology: Applied, 8,* 233–246.

Seamon, M. J., Fass, J. A., Maniscalco-Feichtl, M., & Abu-Shraie, N. A. (2007). Medical marijuana and the developing role of the pharmacist. *American Journal of Health System Pharmacy, 64,* 1037–1044.

Sears, D. O. (1986). College sophomores in the laboratory: Influences of a narrow data base on social psychology's view of human nature. *Journal of Personality and Social Psychology, 51,* 515–530.

Sebel, P. S., Bonke, B., & Winograd, E. (Eds.). (1993). *Memory and awareness in anesthesia.* Englewood Cliffs, NJ: Prentice-Hall.

Seeley, R., Stephens, T., & Tate, P. (2000). *Anatomy & Physiology* (5th ed.). Boston: McGraw-Hill.

Sefcek, J. A., Brumbach, B. H., & Vasquez, G. (2007). The evolutionary psychology of human mate choice: How ecology, genes, fertility, and fashion influence mating strategies. *Journal of Psychology & Human Sexuality, 18,* 125–182.

Segal, Z. (2008, January.) Finding Daylight. *Psychotherapy Networker Magazine.* Vol. 32 Issue 1 p44-59. 5p

Segal, Z. (2008). *Mindfulness-based cognitive therapy for depression* (2nd ed.). New York: The Guilford Press.

Segall, M. H., Campbell, D. T., & Herskovits, M. J. (1966). *The influence of culture on visual perception.* New York: Bobbs-Merrill.

Segerstrom, S. C., & Miller, G. E. (2004). Psychological stress and the human immune system: A meta-analytic study of 30 years of inquiry. *Psychological Bulletin, 130,* 601–630.

Seibt, B., & Förster, J. (2005). Stereotype threat and performance: How self-stereotypes influence processing by inducing regulatory foci. *Journal of Personality and Social Psychology, 87,* 38–56.

Seli, H. (2007). Self in self-worth protection: The relationship of possible selves to achievement motives and self-worth protective strategies. *Dissertation Abstracts International Section A: Humanities and Social Sciences, 67*(9-A), 3302.

Seligman, M. E. P. (1995, December). The effectiveness of psychotherapy: The *Consumer Reports* study. *American Psychologist, 50,* 965–974.

Seligman, M. E. P. (1971). Phobias and preparedness. *Behavior Therapy, 2,* 307-321.

Selkoe, D. (2008). Soluble oligomers of the amyloid b-protein impair synaptic plasticity and behavior. *Behavioural Brain Research, 192,* 106–113.

Selkoe, D. J. (1997, January 31). Alzheimer's disease: Genotypes, phenotype, and treatments. *Science, 275,* 630–631.

Selkoe, D. J. (2002). Alzheimer's disease is a synaptic failure. *Science, 298,* 789–791.

Sellbom, M., Fischler, G., & Ben-Porath, Y. (2007). Identifying MMPI-2 Predictors of police officer integrity and misconduct. *Criminal Justice and Behavior, 34,* 985-1004.

Sells, R. (1994, August). *Homosexuality study.* Paper presented at the annual meeting of the American Statistical Association, Toronto.

Selove, R. (2007). The glass is half full: Current knowledge about pediatric cancer and sickle cell anemia. *PsycCRITIQUES, 52,* 88–99.

Selsky, A. (1997, February 16). African males face circumcision rite. *The Boston Globe,* p. C7.

Selye, H. (1976). *The stress of life.* New York: McGraw-Hill.

Selye, H. (1993). History of the stress concept. In L. Goldberger & S. Breznitz (Eds.), *Handbook of stress: Theoretical and clinical aspects* (2nd ed.). New York: Free Press.

Semler, C. N., & Harvey, A. G. (2005). Misperception of sleep can adversely affect daytime functioning in insomnia. *Behaviour Research and Therapy, 43,* 843–856.

Semykina, A., & Linz, S. J. (2007). Gender differences in personality and earnings: Evidence from Russia. *Journal of Economic Psychology, 28,* 387–410.

Seroczynski, A. D., Jacquez, F. M., & Cole, D. A. (2003). Depression and suicide during adolescence. In G. R. Adams & M. D. Berzonsky (Eds.), *Blackwell handbook of adolescence.* Malden, MA: Blackwell Publishers.

Serpell, R. (2000). Intelligence and culture. In R. Sternberg (Ed.), *Handbook of intelligence.* Cambridge, England: Cambridge University Press.

Seventh U.S. Circuit Court of Appeals. (2001). *Chicago Firefighters Local 2, et al. v. City of Chicago, et al.* Nos. 00–1272, 00–1312, 00–1313, 00–1314, and 00–1330. Chicago, IL.

Seymour, B. (2006). Carry on eating: Neural pathways mediating conditioned potentiation of feeding. *Journal of Neuroscience, 26,* 1061–1062.

Shadish, W. R., Cook, T. D., & Campbell, D. T. (2002). *Experimental and quasi-experimental designs for generalized causal inference.* Boston: Houghton Mifflin.

Shafer, V. L. & Garrido-Nag, K. (2007). The neurodevelopmental bases of language. In E. Hoff & M. Shatz, *Blackwell handbook of language development.* Malden, MA: Blackwell Publishing.

Shah, D. B., Pesiridou, A., Baltuch, G. H., Malone, D. A. & O'Reardon, J. P. (2008). Functional neurosurgery in the treatment of severe obsessive compulsive disorder and major depression: Overview of disease circuits and therapeutic targeting for the clinician. *Psychiatry, 5,* 24–33.

Shaikholeslami, R., & Khayyer, M. (2006). Intrinsic motivation, extrinsic motivation, and learning English as a foreign language. *Psychological Reports, 99,* 813–818.

Shankar, G., & Simmons, A. (2009, January). Understanding ethics guidelines using an internet-based expert system. *Journal of Medical Ethics, 35,* 65–68.

Shapiro, L. R. (2006). Remembering September 11th: The role of retention interval and rehearsal on flashbulb and event memory. *Memory, 14,* 129–147.

Shappell, S., & Wiegmann, D. A. (2003). *A human error approach to aviation accident analysis: The human factors analysis and classification system.* Aldershot, England: Ashgate.

Shargorodsky, J., Curhan, S., Curhan, G., Eavey, R. (2010). Change in Prevalence of Hearing Loss in US Adolescents. *The Journal of the American Medical Association, 304,* No.7.

Shaughnessy, J. J., Zechmeister, E. B., & Zechmeister, J. S. (2000). *Research methods in psychology* (5th ed.). New York: McGraw-Hill.

References

Shaywitz, B. A., Shaywitz, S. E., Pugh, K. R., Constable, R. T., Skudlarski, P., Fulbright, R. K., Bronen, R. A., Fletcher, J. M., Shankweller, D. P., Katz, L., & Gore, J. C. (1995, February 16). Sex differences in the functional organization of the brain for language. *Nature, 373,* 607–609.

Sheehan, S. (1982). *Is there no place on earth for me?* Boston: Houghton Mifflin.

Shepard, R. N., & Metzler, J. (1971). Mental rotation of three-dimensional objects. *Science, 171*(3972), 701–703.

Shepperd, J., Malone, W., & Sweeny, K. (2008). Exploring causes of the self-serving bias. *Social and Personality Psychology Compass, 2,* 895–908.

Sherblom, S. (2008). The legacy of the 'care challenge': Re-envisioning the outcome of the justice-care debate. *Journal of Moral Education, 37,* 81–98.

Sherman, S. L., Allen, E. G., Bean, L. H., & Freeman, S. B. (2007). Epidemiology of Down syndrome [Special issue: Down syndrome]. *Mental Retardation and Developmental Disabilities Research Reviews, 13,* 221–227.

Sheth, B. R., & Bhattacharya, J., & Wu, D. J. (2004). On the neural track of eureka. *Program No. 138.4.* Washington, DC: Society for Neuroscience, 2004.

Shier, D., Butler, J., & Lewis, R. (2000). *Hole's essentials of human anatomy and physiology* (7th ed.). Boston: McGraw-Hill.

Shiffman, S. (2007). Use of more nicotine lozenges leads to better success in quitting smoking. *Addiction, 102,* 809–814.

Shimono, K., & Wade N. J. (2002). Monocular alignment in different depth planes. *Vision Research, 42,* 1127–1135.

Shinn, M., Gottlieb, J., Wett, J. L., Bahl, A., Cohen, A., & Baron, E. D. (2007). Predictors of homelessness among older adults in New York City: Disability, economic, human and social capital and stressful events. *Journal of Health Psychology, 12,* 696–708.

Shmuel, A., Chaimow, D., Raddatz, G., Ugurbil, K., & Yacoub, E. (2010). Mechanisms underlying decoding at 7 T: Ocular dominance columns, broad structures, and macroscopic blood vessels in V1 convey information on the stimulated eye. *NeuroImage, 49,* 1957–1964.

Shors, T. J. (2009, March). Saving new brain cells. *Scientific American,* pp. 47–54.

Shotland, R. L. (1985, June). When bystanders just stand by. *Psychology Today,* pp. 50–55.

Shweder, R. (2003). *Why do men barbecue? Recipes for cultural psychology.* Cambridge, MA: Harvard University Press.

Shweder, R. A. (1994). You're not sick, you're just in love: Emotion as an interpretive system. In P. Ekman & R. J. Davidson (Eds.), *The nature of emotion: Fundamental questions.* New York: Oxford.

Sidman, M. (2006). The distinction between positive and negative reinforcement: Some additional considerations. *Behavior Analyst, 29,* 135–139.

Siegel, J. M. (2003, November). Why we sleep. *Scientific American,* pp. 92–97.

Siegel, R. K., (1989). *Intoxication: Life in pursuit of artificial paradise.* New York: E. P. Dutton.

Siemer, M., Mauss I., & Gross, J. J. (2007). Same situation—different emotions: How appraisals shape our emotions. *Emotion, 7,* 592–600.

Sifrit, K. J. (2006). The effects of aging and cognitive decrements on simulated driving performance. *Dissertation abstracts international: Section B: The sciences and engineering, 67,* 2863.

Silva, M. T. A., Gonçalves, F. L., & Garcia-Mijares, M. (2007). Neural events in the reinforcement contingency. *Behavior Analyst, 30,* 17–30.

Silverman, K., Roll, J., & Higgins, S. (2008). Introduction to the special issue on the behavior analysis and treatment of drug addiction. *Journal of Applied Behavior Analysis, 41,* 471–480.

Silverstein, B. B., Edwards, T. T., Gamma, A. A., Ajdacic-Gross, V. V., Rossler, W. W., & Angst, J. J. (2013). The role played by depression associated with somatic symptomatology in accounting for the gender difference in the prevalence of depression. *Social Psychiatry and Psychiatric Epidemiology, 48,* 257–263.

Silverstein, M. L. (2007). Rorschach test findings at the beginning of treatment and 2 years later, with a 30-year follow-up. *Journal of Personality Assessment, 88,* 131–143.

Simcock, G., & Hayne, H. (2002). Breaking the barrier? Children fail to translate their pre-verbal memories into language. *Psychological Science, 13,* 225–231.

Simon, S., & Hoyt, C. (2008). Exploring the gender gap in support for a woman for president. *Analyses of Social Issues and Public Policy (ASAP), 8,* 157–181.

Simonton, D. K. (2003). Scientific creativity as constrained stochastic behavior: the integration of product, person, and process perspectives. *Psychological Bulletin, 129,* 475–494.

Simonton, D. K. (2009). Varieties of (scientific) creativity: A hierarchical model of domain-specific disposition, development, and achievement. *Perspectives on Psychological Science, 4,* 441–452.

Sinclair, C. (1998). Nine unique features of the Canadian code of ethics for psychologists. *Canadian Psychology, 39*(3), 167–176.

Sinoski, K. (2008, May 23). Michael J. Fox "deeply moved" by honorary degree from UBC. *The Vancouver Sun.* Retrieved from www.canada.com/vancouversun/news/story.html?id=411f8372-c535-49fc-bf38-2145f5e5cb7c.

Skelton, C. (2008, March 11). Brain health gets $25-million boost from BC government. *The Vancouver Sun.* Retrieved www.canada.com/vancouversun/news/westcoastnews/story.html?id=ebd3f643-df14-49d8-8850-25fcd67b7b64.

Skinner, B. F. (1957). *Verbal behavior.* New York: Appleton-Century-Crofts.

Skinner, B. F. (1975). The steep and thorny road to a science of behavior. *American Psychologist, 30,* 42–49.

Slater, E., & Meyer, A. (1959). Contributions to a pathography of the musicians: Robert Schumann. *Confinia Psychiatrica.* Reprinted in K. R. Jamison, *Touched with fire: Manic-depressive illness and the artistic temperament.* New York: Free Press.

Sleek, S. (1997 June). Can "emotional intelligence" be taught in today's schools? *APA Monitor,* p. 25.

Sloan, E. P., et al. (1993). The nuts and bolts of behavioral therapy for insomnia. *Journal of Psychosomatic Research, 37* (Suppl.), 19–37.

Smart, R. G. (2007). Review of introduction to addictive behaviours. *Addiction, 102,* 831.

Smetana, J. B. (2007). Strategies for understanding archetypes and the collective unconscious of an organization. *Dissertation Abstracts International Section A: Humanities and Social Sciences, 67*(12-A), 4714.

Smetana, J. G. (2005). Adolescent-parent conflict: Resistance and subversion as developmental process. In L. Nucci (Ed.), *Conflict, contradiction, and contrarian elements in moral development and education.* Mahwah, NJ: Lawrence Erlbaum Associates.

Smetana, J., Daddis, C., & Chuang, S. (2003). "Clean your room!" A longitudinal investigation of adolescent-parent conflict and conflict resolution in middle-class African American families. *Journal of Adolescent Research, 18,* 631–650.

Smith, B. H., Barkley, R. A., & Shapiro, C. J. (2006). Attention-Deficit/Hyperactivity Disorder. In E. J. Mash & R. A. Barkley, *Treatment of childhood disorders* (3rd. ed). New York: Guilford Press.

Smith, C. (2001). Sleep states and memory processes in humans: procedural versus declarative memory systems. *Sleep Medicine Review, 5*(6), 491–506.

Smith, D. (October 2001). Can't get your 40 winks? Here's what the sleep experts advise. *Monitor on Psychology, 37.*

Smith, E. (1988, May). Fighting cancerous feelings. *Psychology Today,* pp. 22–23.

Smith, E. R., & Semin, G. R. (2007). Situated social cognition. *Current Directions in Psychological Science, 16,* 132–135.

Smith, M. B. (2003). Moral foundations in research with human participants. In A. E. Kazdin (Ed.), *Methodological issues & strategies in clinical research* (3rd ed.). Washington, DC: American Psychological Association.

Smith, M. L., Glass, G. V., & Miller, T. I. (1980). *The benefits of psychotherapy.* Baltimore: the Johns Hopkins University Press.

Smith, R. A., & Weber, A. L. (2005). Applying social psychology in everyday life. In F. W. Schneider, J. A. Gruman, & L. M. Coutts, *Applied social psychology: Understanding and addressing social and practical.* Thousand Oaks, CA: Sage Publications.

Smith, W. B. (2007). Karen Horney and psychotherapy in the 21st century. *Clinical Social Work Journal, 35,* 57–66.

Smolowe, J. (2008, June 23). Medical miracle surgery for an unborn child. *People,* p. 96.

Snowdon, D. (2002). *Aging with grace: What the Nun Study teaches us about leading longer, healthier, and more meaningful lives.* New York: Bantam Books.

Snyder, D. J., Fast, K., & Bartoshuk, L. M. (2004). Valid comparisons of suprathreshold sensations. *Journal of Consciousness Studies, 11,* 96–112.

Snyder, J., Cramer, A., & Afrank, J. (2005). The contributions of ineffective discipline and parental hostile attributions of child misbehavior to the development of conduct problems at home and school. *Developmental Psychology, 41,* 30–41.

Snyder, M. (2002). Applications of Carl Rogers' theory and practice to couple and family therapy: A response to Harlene Anderson and David Bott. *Journal of Family Therapy, 24,* 317–325.

Sobel, K., Gerrie, M., Poole, B., & Kane, M. (2007, October). Individual differences in working memory capacity and visual search: The roles of top-down and bottom-up processing. *Psychonomic Bulletin & Review, 14,* 840–845.

Society for Personality Assessment. (2005). The status of Rorschach in clinical and forensic practice: An official statement by the board of trustees of the Society for Personality Assessment. *Journal of Personality Assessment, 85,* 219–237.

Soh, Y. (2007, April 26). The taint of post-hypnosis evidence and fallibility of memory. *The Court.* Retrieved from www.thecourt.ca/2007/04/26/the-taint-of-post-hypnosis-evidence-and-the-fallibility-of-memory.

Soler, J., Pascual, J., Tiana, T., Cebrià, A., Barrachina, J., Campins, M., et al. (2009). Dialectical behaviour therapy skills training compared to standard group therapy in borderline personality disorder: A 3-month randomised controlled clinical trial. *Behaviour Research and Therapy, 47,* 353–358.

Solomon, M., & Herman, J. (2009). Sex differences in psychopathology: Of gonads, adrenals and mental illness. *Physiology & Behavior, 97,* 250–258.

Solowji, N., Stephens, R.S., Roffman, R. A., Babor, T., Kadden, R., Miller, M., Christiansen, K., McRee, B., & Vendetti, J. (2002). Cognitive functioning of long-term heavy cannabis users seeking treatment. *Journal of the American Medical Association, 287* (9), 1123-1131.

Sommer, R., & Sommer, B. (2001). *A practical guide to behavioral research: Tools and techniques* (5th ed.). New York: Oxford University Press.

Sommerhof, G. (2000). *Understanding consciousness: Its function and brain processes.* Thousand Oaks, CA: Sage.

Sori, C. F. (Ed.). (2006). *Engaging children in family therapy: Creative approaches to integrating theory and research in clinical practice.* New York: Routledge/Taylor & Francis Group.

Spackman, M. P., Fujiki, M., & Brinton, B. (2006). Understanding emotions in context: The effects of language impairment on children's ability to infer emotional reactions. *International Journal of Language & Communication Disorders, 41,* 173–188.

Spangler, W. D. (1992). Validity of questionnaire and TAT measures of need for achievement: Two meta-analyses. *Psychological Bulletin, 112,* 140–154.

Spearman, C. (1927). *The abilities of man.* London: Macmillan.

Spence, M. J., & DeCasper, A. J. (1982, March). *Human fetuses perceive maternal speech.* Paper presented at the meeting of the International Conference on Infant Studies, Austin, TX.

Sperling, G. (1960). The information available in brief visual presentation. *Psychological Monographs, 74,* pp. 29.

Sperry, R. (1982). Some effects of disconnecting the cerebral hemispheres. *Science, 217,* 1223–1226.

Spiegel, D. (1996). Hypnosis. In R. E. Hales & S. C. Yudofsky (Eds.), *The American Psychiatric Press synopsis of psychiatry.* Washington, DC: American Psychiatric Press.

Spindler, H., Kruse, C., Zwisler, A., & Pedersen, S. (2009). Increased anxiety and depression in Danish cardiac patients with a type D personality: Cross-validation of the Type D Scale (DS14). *International Journal of Behavioral Medicine, 16,* 98–107.

Spinella, M., & Lester, D. (2006). Can money buy happiness? *Psychological Reports, 99,* 992.

Spitz, H. H. (1987). Problem-solving processes in special populations. In J. G. Borkowski & J. D. Day (Eds.), *Cognition in special children: Comparative approaches to retardation, learning disabilities, and giftedness.* Norwood, NJ: Ablex.

Spitzer, R. L., Skodol, A. E., Gibbon, M., & Williams, J. B. W. (1983). *Psychopathology: A case book.* New York: McGraw-Hill.

Sprecher, S., & Regan, P. C. (2002). Liking some things (in some people) more than others: Partner preferences in romantic relationships and friendships. *Journal of Social and Personal Relationships, 19,* 436–481.

Sprenger, M. (2007). *Memory 101 for educators.* Thousand Oaks, CA: Corwin Press.

Sprenkle, D. H., & Moon, S. M. (Eds.). (1996). *Research methods in family therapy.* New York: Guilford Press.

Springen, K. (2004, August 9). Anxiety: Sweet and elusive sleep. *Newsweek,* p. 21.

Squire, L. R., Clark, R. E., & Bayley, P. J. (2004). Medial temporal lobe function and memory. In M. S. Gazzaniga (Ed.), *Cognitive neurosciences* (3rd ed.). Cambridge, MA: MIT.

St. Dennis, C., Hendryx, M., Henriksen, A. L., Setter, S. M., & Singer, B. (2006). Postdischarge treatment costs following closure of a state geropsychiatric ward: Comparison of 2 levels of community care. *Primary Care Companion Journal of Clinical Psychiatry, 8,* 279–284.

St. Jacques, P. L., & Levine, B. (2007). Ageing and autobiographical memory for emotional and neutral events. *Memory, 15,* 129–144.

Staddon, J. E. R., & Cerutti, D. T. (2003). Operant conditioning. *Annual Review of Psychology, 54,* 115–144.

Staley, J. K., Sanacora, G., & Tamagnan, G. (2006). Sex differences in diencephalon serotonin transporter availability in major depression. *Biological Psychiatry, 59,* 40–47.

Stand Up for Mental Health. (2008). About stand up for mental health. Retrieved from standupformentalhealth.com/about.shtml.

Stankov, L. (2003). Complexity in human intelligence. In R. J. Sternberg, J. Lautrey, et al. (Eds.), *Models of intelligence: International perspectives.* Washington, DC: American Psychological Association.

Stanton, A. L., Danoff-Burg, S., Cameron, C. L., Bishop, M., Collins, C. A., Kirk, S. B., et al. (2000). Emotionally expressive coping predicts psychological and physical adjustment to breast cancer. *Journal of Consulting and Clinical Psychology, 68,* 875–882.

Stapel, D. A., & Semin, G. R. (2007). The magic spell of language: Linguistic categories and their perceptual consequences. *Journal of Personality and Social Psychology, 93,* 23–33.

Starkman, R. (2010, February 25). Rochette: "Mom wanted me to have a better life than she had." *The Star.com.* Retrieved from olympics.thestar.com/2010/article/771171—rochette-mom-wanted-me-to-have-a-better-life-than-she-had.

Startup, M., Bucci, S., & Langdon, R. (2009). Delusions of reference: A new theoretical model. *Cognitive Neuropsychiatry, 14,* 110–126.

Statistics Canada. (2001). Mother tongue, 2001 counts for both sexes, for Canada, provinces, and territories. Retrieved from www12.statcan.ca/english/census01/products/highlight/LanguageComposition/Page.cfm?Lang=E&Geo=PR&View=1a&Table=1a&StartRec=1&Sort=2&B1=Counts&B2=Both.

Statistics Canada. (2002). Study: Insomnia. Retrieved from www.statcan.ca/Daily/English/051116/d051116a.htm.

Statistics Canada. (2005). Early sexual intercourse, condom use and sexually transmitted diseases. Retrieved from www.statcan.gc.ca/daily-quotidien/050503/dq050503a-eng.htm.

Statistics Canada. (2005, July 6). Canadian community health survey: Obesity among children and adults. *The Daily.* Retrieved from www.statcan.ca/Daily/English/050706/d050706a.htm.

Statistics Canada. (2008). Study: Teen sexual behaviour and condom use. Retrieved from www.statcan.gc.ca/daily-quotidien/080820/dq080820c-eng.htm.

Statistics Canada. (2011). Population by mother tongue, by province and territory, excluding institutional residents (2011 Census). Retrieved from http://www12.statcan.gc.ca/census-recensement/2011/as-sa/98-314-x/98-314-x2011001-eng.pdf.

Statistics Canada (February 2013). Job futures Quebec: Psychologists. Retrieved from: http://www.servicecanada.gc.ca/eng/qc/job_futures/statistics/4151.shtml.

Steblay, N., Dysart, J., Fulero, S., & Lindsay, R. C. L. (2003). Eyewitness accuracy rates in police showup and lineup presentations: A meta-analytic comparison. *Law & Human Behavior, 27,* 523–540.

Steele, C. M., & Josephs, R. A. (1990). Alcohol myopia: Its prized and dangerous effects. *American Psychologist, 45,* 921–933.

Steele, J. D., Christmas, D., Eljamel, M. S., & Matthews, K. (2007). Anterior cingulotomy for major depression: clinical outcome and relationship to lesion characteristics. *Biological Psychiatry, 12,* 127–134.

Stegerwald, F., & Janson, G. R. (2003). Conversion therapy: Ethical considerations in family counseling. *Family Journal—Counseling and Therapy for Couples and Families, 11,* 55–59.

Steiger, A. (2007). Neurochemical regulation of sleep. *Journal of Psychiatric Research, 41,* 537–552.

Stein, L. A. R., & Graham, J. R. (2005). Ability of substance abusers to escape detection on the Minnesota Multiphasic Personality Inventory-Adolescent (MMPI-A) in a juvenile correctional facility. *Assessment, 12,* 28–39.

Steinberg, L. (2007). Risk taking in adolescence: New perspectives from brain and behavioral science. *Current Directions in Psychological Science, 16,* 55–59.

Steiner, J. (2008). Transference to the analyst as an excluded observer. *The International Journal of Psychoanalysis, 89,* 39–54.

Steinfeld, C., Ellison, N., & Lampe, C. (2008). Social capital, self-esteem, and use of online social network sites: A longitudinal analysis. *Journal of Applied Developmental Psychology, 29,* 434–445.

Steinmetz, J. E., Kim, J., & Thompson, R. F. (2003). Biological models of associative learning. In M. Gallagher & R. J. Nelson (Eds.), *Handbook of psychology: Biological psychology* (Vol. 3, pp. 499–541). New York: Wiley.

Stenbacka, L., & Vanni, S. (2007). fMRI of peripheral visual field representation. *Clinical Neurophysiology, 108,* 1303–1314.

Stenklev, N. C., & Laukli, E. (2004). Cortical cognitive potentials in elderly persons. *Journal of the American Academy of Audiology, 15,* 401–413.

Stern, E., & Silbersweig, D. A. (2001). Advances in functional neuroimaging methodology for the study of brain systems underlying human neuropsychological function and dysfunction. In D. A. Silbersweig & E. Stern (Eds.), *Neuropsychology and functional neuroimaging: Convergence, advances and new directions.* Amsterdam, Netherlands: Swets and Zeitlinger.

Stern, R. M., & Koch, K. L. (1996). Motion sickness and differential susceptibility. *Current Directions in Psychological Science, 5,* 115–120.

Sternberg, R. J. (2004). A triangular theory of love. In H. T. Reis & C. E. Rusbult (Eds.), *Close relationships: Key readings.* Philadelphia, PA: Taylor & Francis.

Sternberg, R. J. (2005). Culture and measurement. *Measurement: Interdisciplinary Research and Perspectives, 3,* 108–113.

Sternberg, R. J. (2007). Who are the bright children? The cultural context of being and acting intelligent. *Educational Researcher, 36,* 148–155.

Sternberg, R. J., & Beall, A. E. (1991). How can we know what love is? An epistemological analysis. In G. J. O. Fletcher & F. D. Fincham (Eds.), *Cognition in close relationships.* Hillsdale, NJ: Erlbaum.

Sternberg, R. J., & Jarvin, L. (2003). Alfred Binet's contributions as a paradigm for impact in psychology. In R. J. Sternberg (Ed.), *The anatomy of impact: What makes the great works of psychology great.* Washington, DC: American Psychological Association.

Sternberg, R. J., Hojjat, M., & Barnes, M. L. (2001). Empirical aspects of a theory of love as a story. *European Journal of Personality, 15,* 1–20.

Stettler, N., Stallings, V. A., Troxel, A. B., Zhao, J. Z., Schinnar, R., Nelson, S. E., et al. (2005). Weight gain in the first week of life and overweight in adulthood. *Circulation, 111,* 1897–1903.

Stevens, C. F. (1979, September). The neuron. *Scientific American,* p. 56.

Stevens, G., & Gardner, S. (1982). *The women of psychology: Pioneers and innovators* (Vol. 1). Cambridge, MA: Schenkman.

Stevens, M. C., Skudlarski, P., Pearlson, G. D., & Calhoun, V. D. (2009). Age-related cognitive gains are mediated by the effects of white matter development on brain network integration. *Neuroimage, 48,* 738–746.

Stevens, P., & Harper, D. J. (2007). Professional accounts of electroconvulsive therapy: A discourse analysis. *Social Science & Medicine, 64,* 1475–1486.

Stevenson, H. W., Lee, S., & Mu, X. (2000). Successful achievement in mathematics: China and the United States. In C. F. M. van Lieshout & P. G. Heymans (Eds.), *Developing talent across the life span.* New York: Psychology Press.

Stevenson, R. J., & Case, T. I. (2005). Olfactory imagery: A review. *Psychonomic Bulletin and Review, 12,* 244–264.

Stocks, E., Lishner, D., & Deckor, S. (2009). Altruism or psychological escape: Why does empathy promote prosocial behavior? *European Journal of Social Psychology, 39,* 649–665.

Stockton, R., Morran, D. K., & Krieger, K. (2004). An overview of current research and best practices for training beginning group leaders. In J. L. DeLucia-Waack, D. A. Gerrity, C. R. Kalodner, & M. T. Riva (Eds.), *Handbook of group counseling and psychotherapy.* Thousand Oaks, CA: Sage Publications.

Stone, J., Morrison, P., & Pilowsky, L. (2007). Glutamate and dopamine dysregulation in schizophrenia—A synthesis and selective review. *Journal of Psychopharmacology, 21,* 440–452.

Stopa, L., Denton, R., Wingfield, M., & Taylor, K. (2013). The fear of others: A qualitative analysis of interpersonal threat in social phobia and paranoia. *Behavioural and Cognitive Psychotherapy, 41,* 188–209.

Strange, D., Clifasefi, S., & Garry, M. (2007). False memories. In M. Garry & H. Hayne, *Do justice and let the sky fall: Elizabeth Loftus and her contributions to science, law, and academic freedom.* Mahwah, NJ: Lawrence Erlbaum Associates.

Strathern, A., & Stewart, P. J. (2003). *Landscape, memory and history: Anthropological perspectives.* London: Pluto Press.

Strauss, E. (1998, May 8). Writing, speech separated in split brain. *Science, 280,* 287.

Strayer, D. L., & Drews, F. A. (2007). Cell-phone-induced driver distraction. *Current Directions in Psychological Science, 16,* 128–131.

Streissguth, A. (1997). *Fetal alcohol spectrum disorder: A guide for families and communities.* Baltimore, MD: Brookes Publishing Co.

Striano, T., & Vaish, A. (2006). Seven- to 9-month-old infants use facial expressions to interpret others' actions. *British Journal of Developmental Psychology, 24,* 753–760.

Striegel-Moore, R., & Bulik, C. M. (2007). Risk factors for eating disorders. *American Psychologist, 62,* 181–198.

Strong, T., & Tomm, K. (2007). Family therapy as re-coordinating and moving on together. *Journal of Systemic Therapies, 26,* 42–54.

Strupp, H. H. (1996, October). The tripartite model and the *Consumer Reports* study. *American Psychologist, 51,* 1017–1024.

Subrahmanyam, K., Reich, S., Waechter, N., & Espinoza, G. (2008). Online and offline social networks: Use of social networking sites by emerging adults. *Journal of Applied Developmental Psychology, 29,* 420–433.

Sue, D. W., & Sue, D. (1990). *Counseling the culturally different: Theory and practice* (2nd ed.). Oxford, England: John Wiley & Sons.

Sue, D. W., Sue, D., & Sue, S. (1990). *Understanding abnormal behavior* (3rd ed.). Boston: Houghton-Mifflin.

Suh, E. M. (2002). Culture, identity consistency, and subjective well-being. *Journal of Personality & Social Psychology, 83,* 1378–1391.

Suhail, K., & Chaudhry, H. R. (2004). Predictors of subjective well-being in an Eastern Muslim culture. *Journal of Social and Clinical Psychology, 23,* 359–376.

Suizzo, M-A., & Bornstein, M. H. (2006). French and European American child-mother play: Culture and gender considerations. *International Journal of Behavioral Development, 30,* 498–508.

Summers, M. (2000) *Everything in its place.* New York: Putnam.

Super, C. M. (1980). Cognitive development: Looking across at growing up. In C. M. Super & S. Harakness (Eds.), *New directions for child development: Anthropological perspectives on child development.* San Francisco: Jossey-Bass.

Supreme Court of Canada. (2007, February 1). *R. v. Trochym*. Judgments of the Supreme Court of Canada. Retrieved from scc.lexum.umontreal.ca/en/2007/2007scc6/2007scc6.html.

Surette, R. (2002). Self-reported copycat crime among a population of serious and violent juvenile offenders. *Crime & Delinquency, 48*, 46–69.

Susser, E. S., Herman, D. B., & Aaron, B. (2002, August). Combating the terror of terrorism. *Scientific American*, pp. 70–77.

Sutin, A. R., & Robins, R. W. (2007). Phenomenology of autobiographical memories: The Memory Experiences Questionnaire. *Memory, 15*, 390–411.

Svarstad, B. (1976). Physician-patient communication and patient conformity with medical advice. In D. Mechanic (Ed.), *The growth of bureaucratic medicine*. New York: Wiley.

Svartdal, F. (2003). Extinction after partial reinforcement: Predicted vs. judged persistence. *Scandinavian Journal of Psychology, 44*, 55–64.

Swales, M. A., & Heard, H. L. (2007). The therapy relationship in dialectical behaviour therapy. In P. Gilbert & R. L. Leahy, *The therapeutic relationship in the cognitive behavioral psychotherapies*. New York: Routledge/Taylor & Francis.

Swanson, H. L., Harris, K. R., & Graham, S. (Eds.). (2003). *Handbook of learning disabilities*. New York: Guilford Press.

Szasz, T. (2004). "Knowing what ain't so": R. D. Laing and Thomas Szasz. *Psychoanalytic Review, 91*, 331–346.

Szasz, T. S. (1994). *Cruel compassion: Psychiatric control of society's unwanted*. New York: Wiley.

Szasz, T. S. (2011). *The myth of mental illness: Foundations of a theory of personal conduct*. New York: HarperCollins.

Szegedy–Maszak, M. (2003, January 13). The sound of unsound minds. *U.S. News & World Report*, pp. 45–46.

Tajfel, H., & Turner, J. C. (2004). The social identity theory of intergroup behavior. In J. T. Jost & J. Sidanius (Eds.), *Political psychology: Key readings*. New York: Psychology Press.

Takahashi, M., Nakata, A., Haratani, T., Ogawa, Y., & Arito, H. (2004). Post-lunch nap as a worksite intervention to promote alertness on the job. *Ergonomics, 47*, 1003–1013.

Takizawa, T., Kondo, T., & Sakihara, S. (2007). Stress buffering effects of social support on depressive symptoms in middle age: Reciprocity and community mental health: Corrigendum. *Psychiatry and Clinical Neurosciences, 61*, 336–337.

Talarico, J. (2009). Freshman flashbulbs: Memories of unique and first-time events in starting college. *Memory, 17*, 256–265.

Talarico, J., & Rubin, D. (2007). Flashbulb memories are special after all; in phenomenology, not accuracy. *Applied Cognitive Psychology, 21*, 557–578.

Talmi, D., Anderson, A., Riggs, L., Caplan, J., & Moscovitch, M. (2008). Immediate memory consequences of the effect of emotion on attention to pictures. *Learning & Memory, 15*, 172–182.

Tal-Or, N., & Papirman, Y. (2007). The fundamental attribution error in attributing fictional figures' characteristics to the actors. *Media Psychology, 9*, 331–345.

Talukdar, S., & Shastri, J. (2006). Contributory and adverse factors in social development of young children. *Psychological Studies, 51*, 294–303.

Tan, D. W., Schiefer, M. A., Keith, M. W., Anderson, J. R., Tyler, J., & Tyler, D. J. (2014). A neural interface provides long-term stable natural touch perception. *Science Translational Medicine, 6* (257), 138. doi: 10.1126/scitranslmed.3008669.

Tan, L., & Ward, G. (2008). Rehearsal in immediate serial recall. *Psychonomic Bulletin & Review, 15*, 535–542.

Tan, L., Chan, A., Kay, P., Khong, P., Yip, L., & Luke, K. (2008). Language affects patterns of brain activation associated with perceptual decision. *PNAS Proceedings of the National Academy of Sciences of the United States of America, 105*(10), 4004–4009.

Tandon, R., Gaebel, W., Barch, D. M., Bustillo, J., Gur, R. E., Heckers, S., Malaspina, D., Owen, M.J., Schultz, S., Tsuang, M., Van Os, J., Carpenter, W. (2013). Definition and description of schizophrenia in the dsm-5. *Schizophrenia Research*. Retrieved from http://ccpweb.wustl.edu/pdfs/2013_defdes.pdf

Tanner, J. M. (1978). *Education and physical growth* (2nd ed.). New York: International Universities Press.

Tanner, J. M. (1990). *Foetus into man: Physical growth from conception to maturity* (rev. ed.). Cambridge, MA: Harvard University Press.

Taras, H., & Potts-Datema, W. (2005). Chronic health conditions and student performance at school. *Journal of School Health, 75*, 255–266.

Tasker, F. (2005). Lesbian mothers, gay fathers, and their children: A review. *Journal of Developmental and Behavioral Pediatrics, 26*, 224–240.

Taylor, F., & Bryant, R. A. (2007). The tendency to suppress, inhibiting thoughts, and dream rebound. *Behaviour Research and Therapy, 45*, 163–168.

Taylor, S. (2003). Anxiety sensitivity and its implications for understanding and treating PTSD. *Journal of Cognitive Psychotherapy, 17*, 179–186.

Taylor, S. E. (1995). Quandary at the crossroads: Paternalism versus advocacy surrounding end-of-treatment decisions. *American Journal of Hospital Palliatory Care, 12*, 43–46.

Taylor, S. E., & Aspinwall, L. G. (1996). Mediating and moderating processes in psychosocial stress: Appraisal, coping, resistance, and vulnerability. In H. B. Kaplan (Ed.), *Psychosocial stress: Perspectives on structure, theory, life-course, and methods*. San Diego: Academic Press.

Taylor, S. E., Kemeny, M. E., Reed, G. M., Bower, J. E., & Gruenewald, T. L. (2000). Psychological resources, positive illusions, and health. *American Psychologist, 55*, 99–109.

Teff, K. L., Petrova, M., & Havel, P. J. (2007). 48-h Glucose infusion in humans: Effect on hormonal responses, hunger and food intake. *Physiology & Behavior, 90*, 733–743.

Tellegen, A., Lykken, D. T., Bouchard, T. J., Jr., Wilcox, K. J., Segal, N. L., & Rich, S. (1988). Personality similarity in twins reared apart and together. *Journal of Personality and Social Psychology, 54*, 1031–1039.

Templer, D. I., & Arikawa, H. (2006). Association of race and color with mean IQ across nations. *Psychological Reports, 99*, 191–196.

Tenenbaum, H. R., & Ruck, M. D. (2007). Do teachers hold different expectations for ethnic minority than for European-American children?: A meta-analysis. *Journal of Educational Psychology, 99*, 253–273.

Tenopyr, M. L. (2002). Theory versus reality: Evaluation of 'g' in the workplace. *Human Performance, 15*, 107–122.

Teodorov, E., Salzgerber, S. A., Felicio, L. F., Varolli, F. M. F., & Bernardi, M. M. (2002). Effects of perinatal picrotoxin and sexual experience on heterosexual and homosexual behavior in male rats. *Neurotoxicology and Teratology, 24*, 235–245.

Terry, W. S. (2003). *Learning and memory: Basic principles, processes, and procedures* (2nd ed.). Boston: Allyn & Bacon.

Tharp, R. G. (1989). Psychocultural variables and constants: Effects on teaching and learning in schools [Special issue: Children and their development: Knowledge base, research agenda, and social policy application]. *American Psychologist, 44*, 349–359.

Thatcher, D. L., & Clark, D. B. (2006). Adolescent alcohol abuse and dependence: Development, diagnosis, treatment and outcomes. *Current Psychiatry Reviews, 2*, 159–177.

The Canadian Press. (2009, May 27). Calgary climber dies after reaching top of Mount Everest. *CBC.ca*. Retrieved from www.cbc.ca/canada/calgary/story/2009/05/27/calgary-everest-climber-death.html.

The Globe and Mail (July 3, 2013). Timeline: Tim Bosma, who disappeared in early May, found dead. Retrieved from: www.theglobeandmail.com/news/national/timeline-tim-bosma-who-disappeared-in-early-may-found-dead/article11911126/.

The Michael J. Fox Foundation. (2008) *Parkinson's 101*. Retrieved from www.michaeljfox.org/living_aboutParkinsons_parkinsons101.cfm#q7.

Thomas, P., Mathur, P., Gottesman, I. I., Nagpal, R., Nimgaonkar, V. L., & Deshpande, S. N. (2007). Correlates of hallucinations in schizophrenia: A cross-cultural evaluation. *Schizophrenia Research, 92*, 41–49.

Thompson, B. (2002). *Score reliability: Contemporary thinking on reliability issues*. Thousand Oaks, CA: Sage.

Thompson, J. (2000, June 18). "I was certain, but I was wrong." *The New York Times*, p. E14.

Thompson, P. M., Hayaski, K. M., Simon, S. L., Geaga, J. A., Hong, M. S., Sui, Y., Lee, J. Y., Toga, A. W., Ling, W., & London, E. D. (2004, June 30). Structural abnormalities in the brains of human subjects who use methamphetamine. *The Journal of Neuroscience, 24*(26), 6028–6036.

Thorkildsen, T. A. (2006). An empirical exploration of language and thought. *PsycCRITIQUES, 51*, no pagination specified.

Thorndike, E. L. (1932). *The fundamentals of learning*. New York: Teachers College.

Thornton, A., & McAuliffe, K. (2006, July 14). Teaching in wild meerkats. *Science, 313*, 227–229.

Thornton, A., & Young-DeMarco, L. (2001). Four decades of trends in attitudes toward family issues in the United States: The 1960s through the 1990s. *Journal of Marriage and the Family, 63*, 1009–1017.

Thrash, T. M., & Elliot, A. J. (2002). Implicit and self-attributed achievement motives: Concordance and predictive validity. *Journal of Personality, 70*, 729–755.

Tippin, J., Sparks, J., & Rizzo, M. (2009, August). Visual vigilance in drivers with obstructive sleep apnea. *Journal of Psychosomatic Research, 67*, 143–151.

Tirri, K., & Nokelainen, P. (2008). Identification of multiple intelligences with the Multiple Intelligence Profiling Questionnaire III [Special issue: High-ability assessment]. *Psychology Science, 50*, 206–221.

Titone, D. A. (2002). Memories bound: The neuroscience of dreams. *Trends in Cognitive Science, 6*, 4–5.

Todorov, A., & Duchaine, B. (2008). Reading trustworthiness in faces without recognizing faces. *Cognitive Neuropsychology, 25*, 1–16.

Tolman, E. C., & Honzik, C. H. (1930). Introduction and removal of reward and maze performance in rats. *University of California Publications in Psychology, 4*, 257–275.

Tomlinson-Keasey, C. (1985). *Child development: Psychological, sociological, and biological factors*. Homewood, IL: Dorsey.

Tommasi, L. (2009). Mechanisms and functions of brain and behavioural asymmetries. *Philosophical Transactions of the Royal Society B, 364*, 855–859.

Toronto Sun. (2012). Ninety per cent of Canadians happy, Nova Scotians happiest: Report. Retrieved from http://m.torontosun.com/2012/09/25/ninety-per-cent-of-canadians-happy-nova-scotians-happiest-report.

Toth, J. P., & Daniels, K. A. (2002). Effects of prior experience on judgments of normative word frequency: Automatic bias and correction. *Journal of Memory and Language, 46*, 845–874.

Touhara, K. (2007). Molecular biology of peptide pheromone production and reception in mice. *Advanced Genetics, 59*, 147–171.

Tracy, J. L., & Robins, R. W. (2004). Show your pride: Evidence for a discrete emotion expression. *Psychological Science, 15*, 194–197.

Travis, F. (2006). From I to I: Concepts of self on a object-referral/self-referral continuum. In A. P. Prescott, *The concept of self in psychology*. Hauppauge, NY: Nova Science Publishers.

Travis, F., et al. (2009, February). Effects of transcendental meditation practice on brain functioning and stress reactivity in college students. *International Journal of Psychophysiology, 71*, 170–176.

Tremblay, A. (2004). Dietary fat and body weight set point. *Nutrition Review, 62*(7, Pt 2), S75–S77.

Triesch, J., Jasso, H., & Deák, G. O. (2007). Emergence of mirror neurons in a model of gaze following. *Adaptive Behavior, 15*, 149–165.

Tropp, L. R., & Bianchi, R. A. (2006). Valuing diversity and interest in intergroup contact. *Journal of Social Issues, 62*, 533–551.

Tropp, L. R., & Pettigrew, T. F. (2005). Differential relationships between intergroup contact and affective and cognitive dimensions of prejudice. *Personality and Social Psychology Bulletin, 31*, 1145–1158.

Troyer, A. K., Häfliger, A., & Cadieux, M. J. (2006). Name and face learning in older adults: Effects of level of processing, self-generation, and intention to learn. *Journals of Gerontology: Series B: Psychological Sciences and Social Sciences, 61*, P67–P74.

True Colors International. (2010). True colors online assessment. Retrieved from www.true-colors.com/onlineassessment.html.

Trull, T. J., & Widiger, T. A. (2003). Personality disorders. In G. Stricker, T. A. Widiger, et al. (Eds.), *Handbook of psychology: Clinical psychology* (Vol. 8). New York: Wiley.

Tryon, W. W. (2005). Possible mechanisms for why desensitization and exposure therapy work. *Clinical Psychology Review, 25*, 67–95.

Tryon, W. W., & Bernstein, D. (2003). Understanding measurement. In J. C. Thomas & M. Hersen (Eds.), *Understanding research in clinical and counseling psychology*. Mahwah, NJ: Erlbaum.

Tsai, A., Yang, M., Lan, C., & Chen, C. (2008). Evaluation of effect of cognitive intervention programs for the community-dwelling elderly with subjective memory complaints. *International Journal of Geriatric Psychiatry, 23*, 1172–1174.

Tsai, K. J., Tsai, Y. C., & Shen, C. K. (2007). GCSF rescues the memory impairment of animal models of Alzheimer's disease. *Journal of Experimental Medicine, 11*, 1273–1289.

Tseng, W. S. (2003). *Clinician's guide to cultural psychiatry*. San Diego, CA: Elsevier Publishing.

Tsukasaki, T., & Ishii, K. (2004). Linguistic-cultural relativity of cognition: Rethinking the Sapir-Whorf hypothesis. *Japanese Psychological Review, 47*, 173–186.

Tucker Blackwell, V.G. (2006). Factors which influence the academic motivation and disengagement of adolescent, African American males within a social-historical and psychological context. *Dissertation Abstracts International, 67*, 1654A.

Tuerlinckx, F., De Boeck, P., & Lens, W. (2002). Measuring needs with the Thematic Apperception Test: A psychometric study. *Journal of Personality and Social Psychology, 82*, 448–461.

Tulving, E. (2000). Concepts of memory. In E. Tulving, F. I. M. Craik, et al. (Eds.). *The Oxford handbook of memory*. New York: Oxford University Press.

Tulving, E. (2002). Episodic memory and common sense: How far apart? In A. Baddeley & J. P. Aggleton (Eds.), *Episodic memory: New directions in research*. London: Oxford University Press.

Tulving, E., & Psotka, J. (1971). Retroactive inhibition in free recall: Inaccessibility of information available in the memory store. *Journal of Experimental Psychology, 87*, 1–8.

Tulving, E., & Thompson, D. M. (1983). Encoding specificity and retrieval processes in episodic memory. *Psychological Review, 80*, 352–373.

Turk, D. C. (1994). Perspectives on chronic pain: The role of psychological factors. *Current Directions in Psychological Science, 3*, 45–49.

Turkewitz, G. (1993). The origins of differential hemispheric strategies for information processing in the relationships between voice and face perception. In B. de Boysson-Bardies, S. de Schonen, P. W. Jusczyk, P. McNeilage, & J. Morton (Eds.), *Developmental neurocognition: Speech and face processing in the first year of life. NATO ASI series D: Behavioural and social sciences* (Vol. 69). Dordrecht, Netherlands: Kluwer Academic.

Turner, M., Tamborini, R., Limon, M., & Zuckerman-Hyman, C. (2007). The moderators and mediators of door-in-the-face requests: Is it a negotiation or a helping experience? *Communication Monographs, 74*, 333–356.

Turner, W. J. (1995). Homosexuality, Type 1: An Xq28 phenomenon. *Archives of Sexual Behavior, 24*, 109–134.

Tuszynski, M. H. (2007). Nerve growth factor gene therapy in Alzheimer's disease. *Alzheimer's Disease and Associated Disorders, 21*, 179–189.

Tversky, A., & Kahneman, D. (1987). Rational choice and the framing of decisions. In R. Hogarth & M. Reder (Eds.), *Rational choice: The contrast between economics and psychology*. Chicago: University of Chicago Press.

Tydgat, I., & Grainger, J. (2009). Serial position effects in the identification of letters, digits, and symbols. *Journal of Experimental Psychology: Human Perception and Performance, 35*, 480–498.

Ubell, E. (1993, January 10). Could you use more sleep? *Parade*, pp. 16–18.

Umphress, E. E., Smith-Crowe, K., & Brief, A. P. (2007). When birds of a feather flock together and when they do not: Status composition, social dominance orientation, and organizational attractiveness. *Journal of Applied Psychology, 92*, 396–409.

University Health Network. (2010). Psychosocial oncology and palliative care. Retrieved from www.uhn.ca/About_UHN/programs/psychosocial_oncology/psychology.asp.

University of Toronto (2003, October 1). Biological basis for creativity linked to mental illness. *ScienceDaily*. Retrieved from www.sciencedaily.com/releases/2003/10/031001061055.htm.

University of Toronto. (2014). Mindfulness meditation. Retrieved from http://healthandwellness.utoronto.ca/Mindfulness-Meditation.htm.

Unsworth, N., & Engle, R. W. (2005). Individual differences in working memory capacity and learning: Evidence from the serial reaction time task. *Memory and Cognition, 33*, 213–220.

Updegraff, K. A., Helms, H. M., McHale, S. M., Crouter, A. C., Thayer, S. M., & Sales, L. H. (2004). Who's the boss? Patterns of perceived control in adolescents' friendships. *Journal of Youth & Adolescence, 33*, 403–420.

Ursprung, W. W., Sanouri, A., & DiFranza, J. R. (2009). The loss of autonomy over smoking in relation to lifetime cigarette consumption. *Addictive Behaviors, 22*, 12–19.

U.S. Bureau of Labor Statistics. (2003). *Women's weekly earnings as a percentage of men's earnings*. Washington, DC: U.S. Bureau of Labor Statistics.

Uttl, B., Graf, P., & Cosentino, S. (2003). Implicit memory for new associations: Types of conceptual representations. In J. S. Bowers & C. J. Marsolek (Eds.), *Rethinking implicit memory*. London: Oxford University Press.

Vaillant, G. E., & Vaillant, C. O. (1990). Natural history of male psychological health: XII. A 46-year study of predictors of successful aging at age 65. *American Journal of Psychiatry, 147*, 31–37.

Vaitl, D., Schienle, A., & Stark, R. (2005). Neurobiology of fear and disgust. *International Journal of Psychophysiology, 57*, 1–4.

Valencia, R. R., & Suzuki, L. A. (2003). *Intelligence testing and minority students: Foundations, performance factors, and assessment issues*. Thousand Oaks, CA: Sage.

Valenzuela, S., Park, N., & Kee, K. F. (2009). Is there social capital in a social network site? Facebook use and college students' life satisfaction, trust, and participation. *Journal of Computer-Mediated Communications, 14*, 875–901.

Valsiner, J., Diriwächter, R., & Sauck, C. (2005). Diversity in unity: Standard questions and nonstandard interpretations. In *Science and medicine in dialogue: Thinking through particulars and universals*. Westport, CT: Praeger Publishers/Greenwood Publishing Group.

Van Beekum, S. (2005). The therapist as a new object. *Transactional Analysis Journal, 35*, 187–191.

Van De Graaff, K. (2000). *Human anatomy* (5th ed.). Boston: McGraw-Hill.

Van den Wildenberg, W. P. M., & Van der Molen, M. W. (2004). Developmental trends in simple and selective inhibition of compatible and incompatible responses. *Journal of Experimental Child Psychology, 87*, 201–220.

van der Helm, P. A. (2006). Review of perceptual dynamics: Theoretical foundations and philosophical implications of gestalt psychology. *Philosophical Psychology, 19*, 274–279.

van Hooren, S. A. H., Valentijn, A. M., & Bosma, H. (2007). Cognitive functioning in healthy older adults aged 64–81: A cohort study into the effects of age, sex, and education. *Aging, Neuropsychology, and Cognition, 14*, 40–54.

van Wel, F., Linssen, H., & Abma, R. (2000). The parental bond and the well-being of adolescents and young adults. *Journal of Youth & Adolescence, 29*, 307–318.

Vanasse, A., Niyonsenga, T., & Courteau, J. (2004). Smoking cessation within the context of family medicine: Which smokers take action? *Preventive Medicine: An International Journal Devoted to Practice and Theory, 38*, 330–337.

Vandell, D. L., Burchinal, M. R., Belsky, J., Owen, M. T., Friedman, S. L., Clarke-Stewart, et al. (2005). *Early child care and children's development in the primary grades: Follow-up results from the NICHD Study of Early Child Care*. Paper presented at the biennial meeting of the Society for Research in Child Development, Atlanta, GA.

Vandervert, L. R., Schimpf, P. H., & Liu, H. (2007). How working memory and the cerebellum collaborate to produce creativity and innovation. *Creativity Research Journal, 19*, 1–18.

Vanheule, S., Desmet, M., Rosseel, Y., & Meganck, R. (2006). Core transference themes in depression. *Journal of Affective Disorders, 91*, 71–75.

VanLehn, K. (1996). Cognitive skill acquisition. *Annual Review of Psychology, 47*, 513–539.

Vansteenkiste, M., Simons, J., Lens, W., Soenens, B., & Matos, L. (2009). Examining the motivational impact of intrinsic versus extrinsic goal framing and autonomy-supportive versus internally controlling communication style on early adolescents' academic achievement. *Child Development, 76*, 483–501.

Varela, J. G., Boccaccini, M. T., Scogin, F., Stump, J., & Caputo, A. (2004). Personality testing in law enforcement employment settings: A meta-analytic review. *Criminal Justice and Behavior, 31*, 649–675.

Varma, S. (2007). A computational model of Tower of Hanoi problem solving. *Dissertation Abstracts International: Section B: The Sciences and Engineering, 67*(8-B), 4736.

Vartanian, O. (2009). Variable attention facilitates creative problem solving. *Psychology of Aesthetics, Creativity, and the Arts, 3*, 57–59.

Vellacott, J. (2007). Resilience: A psychoanalytic exploration. *British Journal of Psychotherapy, 23*, 163–170.

Veltman, M. W. M., & Browne, K. D. (2001). Three decades of child maltreatment research: Implications for the school years. *Trauma Violence and Abuse, 2*, 215–239.

Veniegas, R. C. (2000). Biological research on women's sexual orientations: Evaluating the scientific evidence. *Journal of Social Issues, 56*, 267–282.

Verfaellie, M., & Keane, M. M. (2002). Impaired and preserved memory processes in amnesia. In L. R. Squire & D. L. Schacter (Eds.), *Neuropsychology of memory* (3rd ed.). New York: Guilford Press.

Verhaeghen, P., Cerella, J., & Basak, C. (2004). A working memory workout: How to change to size of the focus of attention from one to four in ten hours or less. *Journal of Experimental Psychology: Learning, Memory, and Cognition, 30*, 1322–1337.

Vernon, P., Villani, V., Vickers, L., & Harris, J. (2008, January). A behavioral genetic investigation of the Dark Triad and the Big 5. *Personality and Individual Differences, 44*, 445–452.

Victor, S. B., & Fish, M. C. (1995). Lesbian mothers and the children: A review for school psychologists. *School Psychology Review, 24*, 456–479.

Viding, E., Blair, R. J., Moffitt, T. E., & Plomin, R. (2005). Evidence for substantial genetic risk for psychopathy in 7-year-olds. *Journal of Child Psychology and Psychiatry, 46*, 592–597.

Vieira, E. M., & Freire, J. C. (2006). Alteridade e psicologia humanista: Uma leitura ética da abordagem centrada na pessoa. Alterity and humanistic psychology: An ethical reading of the person-centered approach. *Estudos de Psicologia, 23*, 425–432.

Vihman, M. M. (1996). *Phonological development: The origins of language in the child*. London, England: Blackwell.

Villemure, C., Slotnick, B. M., & Bushnell, M. C. (2003). Effects of odors on pain perception: Deciphering the roles of emotion and attention. *Pain, 106*, 101–108.

Viskontas, I. V., Quiroga, R. Q., & Fried, I. (2009, December 1). Human medial temporal lobe neurons respond referentially to personally relevant images. *Proceedings of the National Academy of Science of the United States of America (PNAS), 106*, 21329–21334.

Vitaro, F., Brendgen, M., & Arseneault, L. (2009). Methods and measures: The discordant MZ-twin method: One step closer to the holy grail of causality. *International Journal of Behavioral Development, 33*, 376–382.

Vleioras, G., & Bosma, H. A. (2005). Are identity styles important for psychological well-being? *Journal of Adolescence, 28*, 397–409.

Voicu, H., & Schmajuk, N. (2002). Latent learning, shortcuts and detours: A computational model. *Behavioural Processes, 59*, 67–86.

Volterra, V., Caselli, M. C., Capirci, O., Tonucci, F., & Vicari, S. (2003). Early linguistic abilities of Italian children with Williams syndrome

[Special issue: Williams syndrome]. *Developmental Neuropsychology, 23*, 33–58.

Vonk, R. (1999). Effects of outcome dependency on correspondence bias. *Personality and Social Psychology Bulletin, 25* (3), 382-389.

Vonk, R. (2014). *You are what you do.* Holland: Maven Publishing.

Voruganti, L. P., Awad, A. G., Parker, B., Forrest, C., Usmani, Y., Fernando, M. L. D., et al. (2007). Cognition, functioning and quality of life in schizophrenia treatment: Results of a one-year randomized controlled trial of olanzapine and quetiapine. *Schizophrenia Research, 96*, 146–155.

Voss, J., & Paller, K. (2008). Brain substrates of implicit and explicit memory: The importance of concurrently acquired neural signals of both memory types. *Neuropsychologia, 46*(13), 3021–3029.

Vygotsky, L. S. (1926/1997). *Educational psychology.* Delray Beach, FL: St. Lucie Press.

Wachtel, P. L., & Messer, S. B. (Eds.). (1997). *Theories of psychotherapy: Origins and evolution.* Washington, DC: American Psychological Association.

Waddell, J., & Shors, T.J. (2008). Neurogenesis, learning and associative strength. *European Journal of Neurosciences, 27*, 3020–3028.

Wadden, T. A., Crerand, C. E., & Brock, J. (2005). Behavioral treatment of obesity. *Psychiatric Clinics of North America, 28*, 151–170.

Wade, K. A., Sharman, S. J., & Garry, M. (2007). False claims about false memory research. *Consciousness and Cognition: An International Journal, 16*, 18–28.

Wagner, A. W., Rizvi, S. L., & Hamed, M. S. (2007). Applications of dialectical behavior therapy to the treatment of complex trauma-related problems: When one case formulation does not fit all. *Journal of Trauma Stress, 20*, 391–400.

Wagner, R. K. (2002). Smart people doing dumb things: The case of managerial incompetence. In R. J. Sternberg (Ed.), *Why smart people can be so stupid.* New Haven, CT: Yale University Press.

Wagstaff, G. (2009, January). Is there a future for investigative hypnosis? *Journal of Investigative Psychology and Offender Profiling, 6*, 43–57.

Wain, H. J., Grammer, G. G., & Stasinos, J. (2006). Psychiatric intervention for medical and surgical patients following traumatic injuries. In E. C. Ritchie, P. J. Watson, & M. J. Friedman, *Interventions following mass violence and disasters: Strategies for mental health practice.* New York: Guilford Press.

Wakefield, J. C. (2013). DSM-5: An overview of changes and controversies. *Clinical Social Work Journal, 41*, 139–154.

Walker, L. J., & Frimer, J. A. (2007). Moral personality of brave and caring exemplars. *Journal of Personality and Social Psychology, 93*, 845–860.

Walker, L., & Frimer, J. (2009). The song remains the same: Rebuttal to Sherblom's re-envisioning of the legacy of the care challenge. *Journal of Moral Education, 38*, 53–68.

Walker, W. (2008, May). Introducing hypnosis for pain management to your practice. *Australian Journal of Clinical & Experimental Hypnosis, 36*, 23–29.

Walker, W. R., Skowronski, J. J., & Thompson, C. P. (2003). Consolidation of long-term memory: Evidence and alternatives. *Review of General Psychology, 7*, 203–210.

Waller, B., Cray, J., & Burrows, A. (2008, June). Selection for universal facial emotion. *Emotion, 8*, 435–439.

Wang, A., & Clark, D. A. (2002). Haunting thoughts: The problem of obsessive mental intrusions [Special issue: Intrusions in cognitive behavioraltherapy]. *Journal of Cognitive Psychotherapy, 16*, 193–208.

Wang, O. (2003). Infantile amnesia reconsidered: A cross-cultural analysis. *Memory, 11*, 65–80.

Wang, P. S., Aguilar-Gaxiola, S., Alonso, J., Angermeyer, M. C., Borges, G., Bromet, E. J., et al. (2007, September 8). Use of mental health services for anxiety, mood, and substance disorders in 17 countries in the WHO world mental health surveys. *Lancet, 370*, 841–850.

Wang, Q. (2004). The emergence of cultural self-constructs: Autobiographical memory and self-description in European American and Chinese children. *Developmental Psychology, 40*, 3–15.

Wang, Q., & Conway, M. A. (2006). Autobiographical memory, self, and culture. In L-G. Nilsson & N. Ohta, *Memory and society: Psychological perspectives.* New York: Psychology Press.

Wang, V. O., & Sue, S. (2005). In the eye of the storm: Race and genomics in research and practice. *American Psychologist, 60*, 37–45.

Wang, X., Lu, T., Snider, R. K., & Liang, L. (2005). Sustained firing in auditory cortex evoked by preferred stimuli. *Nature, 435*, 341–346.

Ward, L. M. (2004). Wading through the stereotypes: Positive and negative associations between media use and Black adolescents' conceptions of self. *Developmental Psychology, 40*, 284–294.

Ward, W. C., Kogan, N., & Pankove, E. (1972). Incentive effects in children's creativity. *Child Development, 43*, 669–677.

Ward-Baker, P. D. (2007). The remarkable oldest old: A new vision of aging. *Dissertation Abstracts International Section A: Humanities and Social Sciences, 67*(8-A), 3115.

Wark, B., Lundstrom, B., & Fairhall, A. (2007, August). Sensory adaptation. *Current Opinion in Neurobiology, 17*, 423–429.

Warriner, A. B., & Humphreys, K.R. (2008). Learning to fail: Reoccurring tip-of-the-tongue states. *Quarterly Journal of Experimental Psychology, 61*, 535–542.

Wasserman, E. A., & Miller, R. R. (1997). What's elementary about associative learning? *Annual Review of Psychology, 48*, 573–607.

Waters, E., & Beauchaine, T. P. (2003). Are there really patterns of attachment? Comment on Fraley and Spieker (2003). *Developmental Psychology, 39*, 417–422.

Waters, E., Hamilton, C. E., & Weinfield, N. S. (2000). The stability of attachment security from infancy to adolescence and early adulthood: General introduction. *Child Development, 71*, 678–683.

Watson, J. B. (1924). *Behaviorism.* New York: Norton.

Watson, J. B., & Rayner, R. (1920). Conditioned emotional reactions. *Journal of Experimental Psychology, 3*, 1–14.

Watson, M., Haviland, J. S., Greer, S., Davidson, J., & Bliss, J. M. (1999). Influence of psychological response on survival in breast cancer: A population-based cohort study. *Lancet, 354*, 1331–1336.

Waxman, S. (2009). Learning from infants' first verbs. *Monographs of the Society for Research in Child Development, 74*, 127–132.

We need to talk (about our drinking). (June 29, 2014). The Globe and Mail. Retrieved from: http://www.theglobeandmail.com/life/health-and-fitness/health/we-need-to-talk-about-our-drinking/article19377132/.

Webb, W. B. (1992). *Sleep: The gentle tyrant* (2nd ed.). Boston: Anker.

Wechsler, H., Davenport, A., Dowdall, G., Moeykens, B., & Castillo, S. (1994). Health and behavioral consequences of binge drinking in college. A national survey of students at 140 campuses. *Journal of the American Medical Association, 272*, 1672–1677.

Weber, R., Ritterfeld, U., & Kostygina, A. (2006). Aggression and violence as effects of playing violent video games? In P. Vorderer, & J. Bryant, (Eds.), *Playing video games: Motives, responses, and consequences.* Mahwah, NJ: Lawrence Erlbaum Associates.

Wechsler, H., Lee, J. E., Kuo, M., & Lee, H. (2000). College binge drinking in the 1990s: A continuing problem. Results of the Harvard School of Public Health 1999 College Alcohol Study. *Journal of American College Health, 48*, 199–210.

Weck, F., Bleichhardt, G., Witthöft, M., & Hiller, W. (2011). Explicit and implicit anxiety: Differences between patients with hypochondriasis, patients with anxiety disorders, and healthy controls. *Cognitive Therapy and Research, 35*, 317–325.

Weeks, M., & Lupfer, M. B. (2004). Complicating race: The relationship between prejudice, race, and social class categorizations. *Personality and Social Psychology Bulletin, 30*, 972–984.

Wegener, D. T., Petty, R. E., Smoak, N. D., & Fabrigar, L. R. (2004). Multiple routes to resisting attitude change. In E. S. Knowles & J. A. Linn (Eds.), *Resistance and persuasion.* Mahwah, NJ: Lawrence Erlbaum Associates.

Weinberg, M. S., Williams, C. J., & Pryor, D. W. (1991, February 27). Personal communication. Indiana University, Bloomington.

Weiner, I. B. (2004a). Monitoring psychotherapy with performance-based measures of personality functioning. *Journal of Personality Assessment, 83*, 323–331.

Weiner, I. B. (2004b). Rorschach Inkblot method. In M. E. Maruish (Ed.), *Use of psychological testing for treatment planning and outcomes assessment, Vol. 3: Instruments for adults* (3rd ed.). Mahwah, NJ: Lawrence Erlbaum Associates.

Weinreb, A. (July 8, 2012). Montreal mom stabbed to death while neighbours ignore her screams. *Digital Journal.*

Weinstein, L. (2007). Selected genetic disorders affecting Ashkenazi Jewish families. *Family & Community Health, 30,* 50–62.

Weinstein, M., Glei, D. A., Yamazaki, A., & Ming-Cheng, C. (2004). The role of intergenerational relations in the association between life stressors and depressive symptoms. *Research on Aging, 26,* 511–530.

Weis, R., Crockett, T. E., & Vieth, S. (2004). Using MMPI-A profiles to predict success in a military-style residential treatment program for adolescents with academic and conduct problems. *Psychology in the Schools, 41,* 563–574.

Weiss, A., Bates, T., & Luciano, M. (2008). Happiness is a personal(ity) thing: The genetics of personality and well-being in a representative sample. *Psychological Science, 19,* 205–210.

Weissman, M. M., Bland, R. C., Canino, G. J., Faravelli, C., Greenwald, S., Hwu, H. G., et al. (1997, July 24–31). Cross-national epidemiology of major depression and bipolar disorder. *Journal of the American Medical Association, 276,* 293–299.

Weissman, M., Markowitz, J., & Klerman, G. L. (2007). *Clinician's quick guide to interpersonal psychotherapy.* New York: Oxford University Press.

Welkowitz, L. A., Struening, E. L., Pittman, J., Guardino, M., & Welkowitz, J. (2000). Obsessive-compulsive disorder and comorbid anxiety problems in a national anxiety screening sample. *Journal of Anxiety Disorders, 14,* 471–482.

Wells, G. L., Olson, E. A., & Charman, S. D. (2002). The confidence of eyewitnesses in their identifications from lineups. *Current Directions in Psychological Science, 11,* 151–154.

Wenar, C. (1994). *Developmental psychopathology: From infancy through adolescence* (3rd ed.). New York: McGraw-Hill.

Wenzel, A., Zetocha, K., & Ferraro, R. F. (2007). Depth of processing and recall of threat material in fearful and nonfearful individuals. *Anxiety, Stress & Coping: An International Journal, 20,* 223–237.

Werblin, F., & Roska, B. (2007, April). The movies in our eyes. *Scientific American,* pp. 73–77.

Werker, J. F., & Tees, R. C. (2005). Speech perception as a window for understanding plasticity and commitment in language systems of the brain. *Developmental Psychobiology, 46,* 233–234.

Werner, J. S., Pinna, B., & Spillmann, L. (2007, March). Illusory color and the brain. *Scientific American,* 90–96.

Wertheimer, M. (1923). Untersuchungen zur Lehre von der Gestalt, II. *Psychol. Forsch., 5,* 301–350. In R. Beardsley & M. Wertheimer (Eds.). (1958), *Readings in perception.* New York: Van Nostrand.

West, D. S., Harvey-Berino, J., & Raczynski, J. M. (2004). Behavioral aspects of obesity, dietary intake, and chronic disease. In J. M. Raczynski and L. C. Leviton (Eds.), *Handbook of clinical health psychology: Vol. 2. Disorders of behavior and health.* Washington, DC: American Psychological Association.

West, J. R., & Blake, C. A. (2005). Fetal alcohol syndrome: An assessment of the field. *Experimental Biological Medicine, 6,* 354–356.

West, R. L., Bagwell, D. K., & Dark-Freudeman, A. (2007). Self-efficacy and memory aging: The impact of a memory intervention based on self-efficacy. *Neuropsychological Development and Cognition, B, Aging and Neuropsychological Cognition, 14,* 1–28.

West, R. L., Thorn, R. M., Bagwell, D. K. (2003). Memory performance and beliefs as a function of goal setting and aging. *Psychology & Aging, 18,* 111–125.

Westen, D., Novotny, C. M., & Thompson-Brenner, H. (2004). The empirical status of empirically supported psychotherapies: Assumptions, findings, and reporting in controlled clinical trials. *Psychological Bulletin, 130,* 631–663.

Westerberg, H., Brehmer, Y., D'Hondt, N., Söderman, D., & Bäckman, L. (2008, April). *Computerized training of working memory: A controlled, randomized trial.* Paper presented at the 2008 annual meeting of the Cognitive Neuroscience Society.

Westerhausen, R., Moosmann, M., Alho, K., Medvedev, S., Hämäläinen, H., & Hugdahl, K. (2009, January). Top-down and bottom-up interaction: Manipulating the dichotic listening ear advantage. *Brain Research, 1250,* 183–189.

Westerterp, K. R. (2006). Perception, passive overfeeding and energy metabolism. *Physiology & Behavior, 89,* 62–65.

Whitbourne, S. (2010). *The search for fulfillment.* New York: Ballantine.

Whitbourne, S. K. (2000). The normal aging process. In S. K. Whitbourne & S. Krauss (Eds.), *Psychopathology in later adulthood.* New York: Wiley.

Whitbourne, S. K., Zuschlag, M. K., Elliot, L. B., & Waterman, A. S. (1992). Psychosocial development in adulthood: A 22-year sequential study. *Journal of Personality and Social Psychology, 63,* 260–271.

White, M. (2010, April 26). Why did nobody help, asks mugged man, 79. TheStar.com. Retrieved from www.thestar.com/news/gra/crime/article/800974.

Whitebread, D., Coltman, P., Jameson, H., & Lander, R. (2009). Play, cognition and self-regulation: What exactly are children learning when they learn through play? *Educational and Child Psychology, 26,* 40–52.

Whitehouse, W. G., Orne, E. C., Dinges, D. F., Bates, B. L., Nadon, R., & Orne, M. T. (2005). The cognitive interview: Does it successfully avoid the dangers of forensic hypnosis? *American Journal of Psychology, 118,* 213–234.

Whitfield, J. B., Zhu, G., Madden, P. A., Neale, M. C., Heath, A. C., & Martin, N. G. (2004). The genetics of alcohol intake and of alcohol dependence. *Alcoholism: Clinical and Experimental Research, 28,* 1153–1160.

WHO World Mental Health Survey Consortium. (2004). Prevalence, severity, and unmet need for treatment of mental disorders in the World Health Organization World Mental Health Surveys. *Journal of the American Medical Association, 291,* 2581–2590.

Whorf, B. L. (1956). *Language, thought, and reality.* New York: Wiley.

Wickelgren, I. (2001, March, 2). Working memory helps the mind focus. *Science, 291,* 1684–1685.

Wickens, C. D. (1984). *Engineering psychology and human performance.* Columbus, OH: Merrill.

Wickstrom, R. (2007). Effects of Nicotine during pregnancy: Human and Experimental evidence. Retrieved from http://www.ncbi.nlm.nih.gov/pmc/articles/PMC2656811/.

Widaman, K. (2009). Phenylketonuria in children and mothers: Genes, environments, behavior. *Current Directions in Psychological Science, 18,* 48–52.

Widmeyer, W. N., & Loy, J. W. (1988). When you're hot, you're hot! Warm-cold effects in first impressions of persons and teaching effectiveness. *Journal of Educational Psychology, 80,* 118–121.

Wielgosz, A. T., & Nolan, R. P. (2000). Biobehavioral factors in the context of ischemic cardiovascular disease. *Journal of Psychosomatic Research, 48,* 339–345.

Wigfield, A., & Eccles, J. S. (2000). Expectancy-value theory of achievement motivation. *Contemporary Educational Psychology, 25,* 68–81.

Wildavsky, B. (2000, September 4). A blow to bilingual education. *U.S. News & World Report,* pp. 22–28.

Wiley, C., & Sisson, M. (2006, November). *Ethics, accuracy, and assumption: The use of Facebook by students and employers.* Paper presented at the Southwestern Ohio Council for Higher Education Special Topics Forum, Dayton, OH.

Wilgoren, J. (1999, October 22). Quality day care, early, is tied to achievements as an adult. *The New York Times,* p. A16.

Wilkinson, H. A. (2009). Cingulotomy. *Journal of Neurosurgery, 110,* 607–611.

Wilkinson, L., & Olliver-Gray, Y. (2006). The significance of silence: Differences in meaning, learning styles, and teaching strategies in cross-cultural settings [Special issue: Child language]. *Psychologia: An International Journal of Psychology in the Orient, 49,* 74–88.

Williams, J. E., Paton, C. C., Siegler, I. C., Eigenbrodt, M. L., Nieto, F. J., & Tyroler, H. A. (2000). Anger proneness predicts coronary heart disease risk: Prospective analysis from the Atherosclerosis Risk in Communities (ARIC) Study. *Circulation, 101,* 2034–2039.

Williams, J. W., Mulrow, C. D., Chiquette, E., Noel, P. H., Aguilar, C., & Cornell, J. (2000). A systematic review of newer pharmacotherapies for depression in adults: Evidence report summary. *Annals of Internal Medicine, 132,* 743–756.

Willis, G. L. (2005). The therapeutic effects of dopamine replacement therapy and its psychiatric side effects are mediated by pineal function. *Behavioural Brain Research, 160,* 148–160.

Willis, J., & Todorov, A. (2006). First impressions: Making up your mind after a 100-ms exposure to a face. *Psychological Science, 17,* 592–598.

Willis, S. L., & Schaie, K. W. (1994). In C. B. Fisher & R. M. Lerner (Eds.), *Applied developmental psychology.* New York: McGraw-Hill.

Willoughby, T., Chalmers, H., & Busseri, M. (2004). Where is the syndrome? Where is the risk? Co-occurrence among multiple "problem" behaviors in adolescence. *Journal of Consulting and Clinical Psychology, 72,* 1022–1037.

Willoughby, T., Chalmers, H., Busseri, M., Bosacki, S., Dupont, D., Marini, Z., Rose-Krasnor, L., Sadava, S., & Ward, T. (2007). Adolescent non-involvement in multiple risk behaviors: An indicator of successful development? *Applied Developmental Science, 11 (2),* 89–103.

Wills, T., Sargent, J., Stoolmiller, M., Gibbons, F., & Gerrard, M. (2008). Movie smoking exposure and smoking onset: A longitudinal study of mediation processes in a representative sample of U.S. adolescents. *Psychology of Addictive Behaviors, 22,* 269–277.

Wilson, T. G., Grilo, C. M., & Vitousek, K. M. (2007). Psychological treatment of eating disorders [Special issue: Eating disorders]. *American Psychologist, 62,* 199–216.

Windholz, G., & Lamal, P. A. (2002). Koehler's insight revisited. In R. A. Griggs (Ed.), *Handbook for teaching introductory psychology, Vol. 3: With an emphasis on assessment.* Mahwah, NJ: Erlbaum.

Winerman, L. (2005, June). ACTing up. *Monitor on Psychology,* pp. 44–45.

Wines, M. (2004, March 18). For sniffing out land mines, a platoon of twitching noses. *The New York Times,* pp. A1, A4.

Winsler, A., Madigan, A. L., & Aquilino, S. A. (2005). Correspondence between maternal and paternal parenting styles in early childhood. *Early Childhood Research Quarterly, 20,* 1–12.

Winson, J. (1990, November). The meaning of dreams. *Scientific American,* pp. 86–96.

Winston, A. S. (2004). *Defining difference: Race and racism in the history of psychology.* Washington, DC: American Psychological Association.

Winston, J. S., O'Doherty, J., & Kilner, J. M. (2006). Brain systems for assessing facial attractiveness. *Neuropsychologia, 45,* 195–206.

Winter, D. G. (1988). The power motive in women—and men. *Journal of Personality and Social Psychology, 54,* 510–519.

Winter, D. G. (1995). *Personality: Analysis and interpretation of lives.* New York: McGraw-Hill.

Winter, D. G. (2007). The role of motivation, responsibility, and integrative complexity in crisis escalation: Comparative studies of war and peace crises. *Journal of Personality and Social Psychology, 92,* 920–937.

Winters, B. D., & Bussey, T. J. (2005). Glutamate receptors in perirhinal cortex mediate encoding, retrieval, and consolidation of object recognition memory. *Journal of Neuroscience, 25,* 4243–4251.

Witelson, S., Kigar, D., Scamvougeras, A., Kideckel, D., Buck, B., Stanchev, P., et al. (2008). Corpus callosum anatomy in right-handed homosexual and heterosexual men. *Archives of Sexual Behavior, 37,* 857–863.

Witt, C. M., Jena, S., & Brinkhaus, B. (2006). Acupuncture for patients with chronic neck pain. *Pain, 125,* 98–106.

Wittchen, H., Nocon, A., Beesdo, K., Pine, D., Höfler, M., Lieb, R., et al. (2008). Agoraphobia and panic. *Psychotherapyand Psychosomatics, 77,* 147–157.

Wixted, J. T., & Carpenter, S. K. (2007). The Wickelgren Power Law and the Ebbinghaus Savings Function. *Psychological Science, 18,* 133–134.

Wolff, N. (2002). Risk, response, and mental health policy: Learning from the experience of the United Kingdom. *Journal of Health Politic and Policy Law, 27,* 801–802.

Wolitzky, D. L. (2006). Psychodynamic theories. In J. C. Thomas, D. L. Segal, & M. Hersen, *Comprehensive handbook of personality and psychopathology, Vol. 1: Personality and everyday functioning.* Hoboken, NJ: John Wiley & Sons.

Woller, K., Buboltz, W., & Loveland, J. (2007). Psychological reactance: Examination across age, ethnicity, and gender. *American Journal of Psychology, 120,* 15–24.

Wong, N., Sarver, D. E., & Beidel, D. C. (2011). Quality of life impairments among adults with social phobia: The impact of subtype. *Journal of Anxiety Disorders, 14,* 88–95.

Wood, J. M., Nezworski, M. T., Lilienfeld, S. O., & Garb, H. N. (2003). *What's wrong with the Rorschach? Science confronts the controversial inkblot test.* New York: Wiley.

Wood, W. (2000). Attitude change: Persuasion and social influence. *Annual Review of Psychology, 51,* 539–570.

Wood, W., & Stagner, B. (1994). Why are some people easier to influence than others? In S. Savitt & T. C. Brock (Eds.), *Persuasion: Psychological insights and perspectives.* Boston: Allyn & Bacon.

Woodruff, S. I., Conway, T. L., & Edwards, C. C. (2007). Sociodemographic and smoking- related psychosocial predictors of smoking behavior change among high school smokers. *Addictive Behaviors, 33,* 354–358.

Woods, S. C., & Seeley, R. J. (2002). Hunger and energy homeostasis. In H. Pashler & R. Gallistel (Eds.). *Steven's handbook of experimental psychology* (3rd ed.), *Vol. 3: Learning, motivation, and emotion.* New York: Wiley.

Woods, S. C., Schwartz, M. W., Baskin, D. G., & Seeley, R. J. (2000). Food intake and the regulation of body weight. *Annual Review of Psychology, 51,* 255–277.

Woodson, S. R. J. (2006). Relationships between sleepiness and emotion experience: An experimental investigation of the role of subjective sleepiness in the generation of positive and negative emotions. *Dissertation Abstracts International: Section B: The Sciences and Engineering, 67*(5–B), 2849.

World Health Organization. (2008). WHO Report on the Global Tobacco Epidemic, 2008: The MPOWER Package. Retrieved from http://www.who.int/tobacco/mpower/mpower_report_full_2008.pdf.

Wren, A. M., & Bloom, S. R. (2007). Gut hormones and appetite control. *Gastroenterology, 132,* 2116–2130.

Wright, K. (2002, September). Times of our lives. *Scientific American,* pp. 59–65.

Wright, M. J. (2002). Flashbacks in the history of psychology in Canada: Some early "headline makers." *Canadian Psychology, 43(1),* 21–34.

Wrosch, C., Bauer, I., & Scheier, M. (2005, December). Regret and quality of life across the adult life span: The influence of disengagement and available future goals. *Psychology and Aging, 20,* 657–670.

Wrzesniewski, K., & Chylinska, J. (2007). Assessment of coping styles and strategies with school-related stress. *School Psychology International, 28,* 179–194.

Wu, L-T., Schlenger, W. E., & Galvin, D. M. (2006). Concurrent use of methamphetamine, MDMA, LSD, ketamine, GHB, and flunitrazepam among American youths. *Drug and Alcohol Dependence, 84,* 102–113.

Wuethrich, B. (2001, March 16). Does alcohol damage female brains more? *Science, 291,* 2077–2079.

Wurtz, R. H., & Kandel, E. R. (2000). Central visual pathways. In E. R. Kandel, J. H. Schwartz, & T. M. Jessell (Eds.), *Principles of neural science* (4th ed.). New York: McGraw-Hill.

Wyra, M., Lawson, M. J., & Hungi, N. (2007). The mnemonic keyword method: The effects of bidirectional retrieval training and of ability to image on foreign language vocabulary recall. *Learning and Instruction, 17,* 360–371.

Yapko, M. D. (2006). Utilizing hypnosis in addressing ruminative depression-related insomnia. In M. D. Yapko, *Hypnosis and treating depression: Applications in clinical practice.* New York: Routledge/Taylor & Francis Group.

Yardley, L., & Moss-Morris, R. (2009, January). Current issues and new directions in psychology and health: Increasing the quantity and quality of health psychology research. *Psychology & Health, 24,* 1–4.

Yarmey, A. D. (2003). Eyewitness identification: Guidelines and recommendations for identification procedures in the United States and in Canada. *Canadian Psychology, 44(3),* 181–189.

Yee, A. H., Fairchild, H. H., Weizmann, F., & Wyatt, G. E. (1993). Addressing psychology's problem with race. *American Psychologist, 48,* 1132–1140.

Yeomans, M. R., Tepper, B. J., & Ritezschel, J. (2007). Human hedonic responses to sweetness: Role of taste genetics and anatomy. *Physiology & Behavior, 91,* 264–273.

Yesilyaprak, B., Kisac, I., & Sanlier, N. (2007). Stress symptoms and nutritional status among survivors of the Marmara region earthquakes in Turkey. *Journal of Loss & Trauma, 12,* 1–8.

Yip, J. A., & Martin, R. A. (2006). Sense of humor, emotional intelligence, and social competence. *Journal of Research in Personality, 40,* 1202–1208.

Yost, W. A. (2000). *Fundamentals of hearing* (4th ed.). New York: Academic Press.

Young, M. W. (2000, March). The ticktock of the biological clock. *Scientific American,* pp. 64–71.

Zacks, J. (2008). Neuroimaging studies of mental rotation: A meta-analysis and review. *Journal of Cognitive Neuroscience, 20,* 1–19.

Zajonc, R. B. (2001). Mere exposure: A gateway to the subliminal. *Current Directions in Psychological Science, 10,* 224–228.

Zarren, J. I., & Eimer, B. N. (2002). *Brief cognitive hypnosis: Facilitating the change of dysfunctional behavior.* New York: Springer.

Zaslow, M., Halle, T., & Martin, L. (2006). Child outcome measures in the study of child care quality. *Evaluation Review, 30,* 577–610.

Zdeb, C. (2006, June 22). Brain waves key to sleepwalking. *Windsor Star*/CanWest News Service. Retrieved from www.canada.com/topics/bodyandhealth/story.html?id=a7ca34fb-4ea2-49ba-bb2a-ac5f3147866c.

Zebrowitz, L. A., & Montepare, J. M. (2005, June 10). Appearance DOES matter. *Science, 308,* 1565–1566.

Zeigler, D. W., et al. (2005). The neurocognitive effects of alcohol on adolescents and college students. *Preventive Medicine: An International Journal Devoted to Practice and Theory, 40,* 23–32.

Zevon, M., & Corn, B. (1990). Paper presented at the annual meeting of the American Psychological Association, Boston, MA.

Zhang, F., Chen, Y., Heiman, M., & Dimarchi, R. (2005). Leptin: Structure, function and biology. *Vitamins and Hormones: Advances in Research and Applications, 71,* 345–372.

Zhou, Z., & Buck, L. B. (2006, March 10). Combinatorial effects of odorant mixes in olfactory cortex. *Science, 1477–1481.*

Zhou, Z., Liu, Q., & Davis, R. L. (2005). Complex regulation of spiral ganglion neuron firing patterns by neurotrophin-3. *Journal of Neuroscience, 25,* 7558–7566.

Zians, J. (2007). A comparison of trait anger and depression on several variables: Attribution style, dominance, submissiveness, need for power, efficacy and dependency. *Dissertation Abstracts International: Section B: The Sciences and Engineering, 67*(7-B), 4124.

Zigler, E. F., Finn-Stevenson, M., & Hall, N. W. (2002). The first three years and beyond: Brain development and social policy. In E. F. Zigler, M. Finn-Stevenson, & N. W. Hall, *Current perspectives in psychology.* New Haven, CT: Yale University Press.

Zigler, E., Bennett-Gates, D., Hodapp, R., & Henrich, C. (2002). Assessing personality traits of individuals with mental retardation. *American Journal on Mental Retardation, 107,* 181–193.

Zimbardo, P. (1972). Pathology of imprisonment. *Society, 9* (6), 4-8.

Zimbardo, P. (2004). A situationist perspective on the psychology of evil: Understanding how good people are transformed into perpetrators. In A. G. Miller (Ed.), *The Social Psychology of Good and Evil* (21–50). New York: Guilford Press.

Zimbardo, P. (2008). *The Lucifer Effect: Understanding how good people turn evil.* New York: Random House.

Zimmermann, U. S., Blomeyer, D., & Laucht, M. (2007). How gene-stress-behavior interactions can promote adolescent alcohol use: The roles of predrinking allostatic load and childhood behavior disorders [Special issue: Adolescents, drug abuse and mental disorders]. *Pharmacology, Biochemistry and Behavior, 86,* 246–262.

Zito, J. M. (1993). *Psychotherapeutic drug manual* (3rd ed., rev.). New York: Wiley.

Znaimer, L. (2006, July 8). BlackBerry inventor tries to keep it simple. *The National Post.* Retrieved from canada.com/topics/technology/story.html?id=0bb79c79-fa2a-4a8e-9552-3141ee27e5e9.

Zohar, J., & Westenburg, H.G.M. (2000, September). Anxiety disorders: a review of tricyclic antidepressants and selective serotonin reuptake inhibitors. *Acta Psychiatrica Scandinavica, 101*: 39-49. doi: 10.1111/j.1600-0447.2000.tb10947.x

Zolotor, A., Theodore, A., Chang, J., Berkoff, M., & Runyan, D. (2008). Speak softly—and forget the stick: Corporal punishment and child physical abuse. *American Journal of Preventive Medicine, 35,* 364–369.

Zuckerman, M. (1978, February). The search for high sensation. *Psychology Today,* pp. 30–46.

Zuckerman, M. (1994). *Behavioral expression and biosocial expression of sensation seeking.* Cambridge, England: Cambridge University Press.

Zuckerman, M. (2002). Genetics of sensation seeking. In J. Benjamin, R. P. Ebstein, et al. (Eds.), *Molecular genetics and the human personality.* Washington, DC: American Psychiatric Publishing.

Zuckerman, M., & Kuhlman, D. M. (2000). Personality and risk-taking: Common biosocial factors [Special issue: Personality processes and problem behavior]. *Journal of Personality, 68,* 999–1029.

Zuger, A. (2005, November 10). Doctors learn how to say what no one wants to hear. *The New York Times,* p. S1.

Name Index

Subject Index